Housing law caseboo

fourth edition

Nic Madge is a circuit judge. He was formerly a recorder and district judge and head of the housing department at Bindman and Partners, London. He is co-author of *Defending Possession Proceedings* (LAG, 6th edn, 2006) and author of *Annotated Housing Statutes* (Sweet & Maxwell, 2005) and a member of the senior editorial board of *Civil Procedure* ('the White Book') (Sweet & Maxwell). He writes regularly on housing law and procedure, including contributions to *Law Society Gazette* and *New Law Journal* and co-authors 'Recent developments in housing law' in *Legal Action*. He is a founder member of the Housing Law Practitioners' Association.

Claire Sephton is a solicitor specialising in housing law. She has worked in the voluntary sector for 17 years, initially at North Kensington Law Centre® and more recently at Shelter. She is an experienced trainer and lecturer.

The purpose of the Legal Action Group is to promote equal access to justice for all members of society who are socially, economically or otherwise disadvantaged. To this end, it seeks to improve law and practice, the administration of justice and legal services.

Housing law casebook

FOURTH EDITION

Nic Madge and Claire Sephton

Legal Action Group
2008

Fourth edition published in Great Britain 2008
by LAG Education and Service Trust Limited
242 Pentonville Road, London N1 9UN
www.lag.org.uk

© Nic Madge and Claire Sephton 2008

British Library Cataloguing in Publication Data
a CIP catalogue record for this book is available from the British Library.

Crown copyright material is produced with the permission of the Controller of
HMSO and the Queen's Printer for Scotland.

ISBN 978 1 903307 45 8

Typeset by Regent Typesetting, London
Printed in Great Britain by Hobbs the Printer, Totton, Hampshire

Contents

Table of cases

References in the right-hand column are to paragraph numbers. References in **bold** are to full case summaries

Table of local government ombudsman complaints

References in the right-hand column are to paragraph numbers. References in **bold** are to full case summaries

Table of statutes

References in the right-hand column are to paragraph numbers.

Access to Justice Act 1999	
	P16.19
s22	U12.1
Administration of Justice Act 1970	
	R2.17, R2.24
s36	R1.13, R2, R2.2,
	R2.3, R2.4, R2.6,
	R2.9, R2.10, R2.11,
	R2.12, R2.13, R2.14,
	R2.19, R2.20, R2.21,
	R2.23, R2.25, R2.27,
	R2.29, R2.30, R2.31,
	R4.5, R4.6, r5.2
s36(1)	R2.19
s36(2)	R2.13
s39	R5.12
Administration of Justice Act 1973	
	R2.17
s8	R2, R2.3, R2.9,
	R2.13, R2.27
s8(1)	R2.19
Adoption and Children Act 2002	
	U4.2, U4.12
Agricultural Holdings Act 1948	
	C5
Agricultural Holdings Act 1986	
	N4.1
Anti-Social Behaviour Act 2003	
	J2
Asylum and Immigration Act 1996	
	U5.4
s9	T41.3
Asylum and Immigration Appeals Act 1993	
s4	T41.3
Asylum and Immigration (Treatment of Claimants, etc) Act 2004	
s9	U8
s11	T31.1
Bail Act 1976	E2.7
Building Act 1984	
	P16.4
Caravan Sites Act 1968	
	L1.8, L3.1

Carers and Disabled Children Act 2000	
s2	U4.2
s6	U3.9
Child Support, Pensions and Social Security Act 2000	
	A2.8
Children Act 1989	
	F4.5, F4.5, L3.15,
	T19.1, T47.3, U3,
	U3.1, U3.2
Pt III	L3.16, U1, U6.6,
	U7.8
s8	S1.9
s15	L1.8
s17	S1.7, S3.6, T2.11,
	T19.1, T20.3, T20.5,
	U3.6, U3.9, U4.2,
	U4.7, U4.9, U4.11,
	U4.12, U4.13, U4.15,
	U4.16, U4.17, U6.1,
	U6.4, U6.5, U8,
	U8.2, U8.4, U8.7,
	U8.8, U10.1
s17(1)	U4, U4.2
s17(3)	U4
s17(6)	U4.2
s17(10)	U4, U4.2
s17(11)	U3.6
s19B(2)(b)	U4.12
s20	T15, T19.1, T19.2,
	T20.1, T20.2, T20.3,
	T20.5, U4, U4.2,
	U4.4, U4.5, U4.6,
	U4.7, U4.10, U4.12,
	U4.15, U8.6, U8.7
s20(1)	U4, U4.5
s20(1)(c)	U4.5, U4.6, U4.15
s22	U4.11
s23	T20.2, U4.5, U4.6,
	U8.6
s23(2)	U4.6
s23B	U4.5
s23C	U8
s23D	U4.14

Table of statutory instruments

References in the right-hand column are to paragraph numbers.

Table of European legislation

References in the right-hand column are to paragraph numbers.

CONVENTIONS AND TREATIES
Consolidated Treaty Establishing the
    European Community

Art 49	R1.6, T2.14
European Community Treaty (Nice)	U8.9
Art 39	U8.8
Art 48	R1.6
European Convention for the Protection	A1, A6.2, J1.3, L1, O5.3, R1.6, T57.5,
of Human Rights and	U6.4, U7.1, U7.6, U8, U8.1, U8.2, U8.3,
Fundamental Freedoms 1956	U8.6, U9.1, U10.2
Art 3	L4.4, T56.1, U2.1, U2.3, U7.1, U7.6,
	U8.6, U8.10, U9, U9.1, U9.2, U9.3, U9.4,
	U10.2, U10.5, U11.1, U11.2
Art 6	A2.1, A2.2, A2.4, A2.5, A2.6, A2.7, A2.8,
	A2.9, A3.13, A5.3, A5.5, A5.7, A5.11,
	A5.13, A5.20, A5.21, I6.15, J1.4, J1.10,
	J1.12, J2.1, L4.4, L4.6, Q3.8, R1.11, T60,
	T60.2, T60.3, U9.2, U10.6
Art 6(1)	A2, A2.9, A5.11, A5.13, A5.21, I6.15,
	L4.6, T60.3
Art 7	L4.6
Art 8	A3, A3.1, A3.2, A3.3, A3.4, A3.5, A3.6,
	A3.8, A3.9, A3.10, A3.11, A3.12, A3.13,
	A3.14, A3.15, A3.16, A3.17, A4.1, A4.2,
	A4.3, A5.22, A6.3, E11.23, E14.9, E14.14,
	E14.18, E16.3, F4.3, F4.5, F4.11, H4.7,
	H4.13, H4.15, I5.2, I5.6, I6.15, I6.15,
	J1.4, K2.1, L1.1, L1.2, L1.4, L1.9, L3.8,
	L3.19, L4.4, O3.3, O3.8, P1.7, P4.9,
	P11.58, P15.14, P15.16, R2.4, S1.1, T2.2,
	T2.6, T51.19, T53.3, T53.5, T53.25,
	T53.27, T55.7, T55.8, T56.1, U2.1, U2.3,
	U4.2, U6.1, U6.5, U6.6, U8.2, U8.3,
	U8.4, U8.6, U8.7, U8.10, U9.2, U10.2,
	U10.5, U10.6, U11.1, U11.2
Art 8(1)	A3.8, A3.11, E14.14, F4.3, J1.4, L1.1,
	L1.2, L4.4, P16.34, T16.3, T53.27, U10.6
Art 8(2)	A3.2, A3.4, A3.5, E14.9, E14.14, J1.4,
	L1.1, L1.2, L4.4, L4.6, T53.25, T53.27,
	T55.7, U6.5, U10.6
Art 13	A2.6, A5.17, A5.20
Art 14	A3.3, A4, A4.3, A4.4, A5.14, A5.20,
	E11.23, E14.9, E16.3, F4.11, I6.15, L1.9,
	P15.16, T2.2, T2.6, T53.3, U10.1

Introduction

Housing law is hard law. Twentieth and twenty-first century legislation, from the Rent and Mortgage Interest (Restrictions) Act 1915 to the Housing Act 2004 has grafted a complex statutory framework onto the existing body of English and Welsh land law dating back to feudal times. Many of the Acts of Parliament are long, complicated, and, particularly in recent years, poorly drafted. The increasing use of often complex and frequently amended statutory instruments to supplement provisions of the Acts makes ascertaining the law at times tortuous. To do so within the confines of public funding is becoming increasingly difficult. The failure to seek to implement the rationalisation of the law proposed by the Law Commission in their report *Renting Homes** is, in this context, lamentable. Housing law is also hard law because of the effect that housing cases can have on people. At worst they may result in homelessness for tenants or severe economic problems for landlords. At best they may result in the provision of good quality accommodation for tenants or the realisation of substantial economic assets for landlords. The conflict of interest between landlord and tenant is frequently great, with cases bitterly fought. There may be an equally stark conflict of interest between often destitute homeless people and local authorities, which frequently do not have the financial resources or organisation to comply with their statutory obligations. The complexity of the law and the benefits which can be lost or won have resulted in a plethora of cases before the courts. Some of these are reported in a range of different law reports. Others are not formally reported. The result is that a knowledge of housing case law is particularly important in understanding the legal rights of tenants and landlords, homeless people and local authorities but particularly difficult to achieve.

The aim of the *Housing Law Casebook*, like all the other housing books in LAG's law and practice series, is to make housing law easier and more accessible – for those who are advising about housing problems, for those who are representing clients in court and for those who are studying the subject. We hope that experienced housing law practitioners, with easy access to law reports, will find this book useful in helping to track down and read quickly cases which they know about, but the details of which they have forgotten. Similarly, we hope that it will be useful to less experienced

---

* Law Com No 284, November 2003.

advisers who do not have ready access to law libraries and who need short summaries of cases to help them understand particular areas of housing law. It is not, however, intended to be a replacement for the law reports – it is always wise for advisers who intend to rely upon a particular case to obtain a copy of the full law report.

Our aim – almost certainly impossible to achieve – has been to note all the cases that housing practitioners will ever need. The problem that we have faced in trying to achieve that aim is the sheer volume of cases. It is no longer possible to summarise all relevant cases in one volume. So, some cases have been culled. For example, many of the older county court cases on damages have been omitted. We have not been able to find space for the chapter on rent registration cases involving protected and statutory tenancies under Rent Act 1977. We have been forced to leave out cases on home loss and disturbance payments – although, where possible, we have included references to such cases in the third edition. In view of this, housing practitioners may find it helpful to retain their copies of the third edition.

As with previous versions, the fourth edition of the *Housing Law Casebook* is organised by subject, with subdivisions within each area of housing law. We have, however, altered the chapter headings so that cases decided under different provisions, but dealing with common themes (eg, reasonableness, anti-social behaviour) are brought together. Within the divisions, cases are listed alphabetically, but with those from the higher courts, which carry greater weight, appearing first. Many cases, such as those decided in the House of Lords and Court of Appeal, are included because they are precedents in the strict legal sense, cases which the lower courts are bound to follow. Others, such as High Court judgments, Scottish cases and some circuit judge decisions, are included because they may have persuasive authority in the sense that, although other judges are not bound to follow their conclusions, they may be influenced by them in arriving at their own decisions. The remaining cases, decided in county courts and by local government ombudsmen, are included because they are useful examples of the ways in which, in practice, the law is interpreted and housing cases are resolved.

Many of the cases decided over the last twenty-two years have been noted in 'Recent developments in housing law' which Jan Luba QC and Nic Madge write monthly for *Legal Action*. Indeed, it was Nic and Jan's original intention that they should write this book together, but the demands of Jan's busy and successful practice at the Bar have prevented this. We have drawn heavily on Jan's input into 'Recent developments in housing law' and the debt which we owe him in writing this book is immense. Likewise, we are very grateful to Beatrice Prevatt, Marina Segides and Derek McConnell, whose reports in *Legal Action*'s annual 'Housing repairs update' and 'Owner-occupiers law review' have also been relied on. We hope that the continuing monthly contributions to *Legal Action* will operate as an updating service for this book. We are very grateful to all the staff at LAG who over many years have worked on different parts of the text. We owe a special thanks to Lesley Exton at Regent Typesetting, who has worked on all four editions of the *Housing Law Casebook*. Finally this book and 'Recent developments in housing law' would be so much the poorer if it were not for all the practitioners and colleagues who, over the years, have engendered debate in this field and written to us with details of their cases. If readers do spot any errors or omissions, or disagree with the interpretation of a judgment, we would be pleased to hear from them so that changes can be made to future editions. Please write to us with any comments c/o Legal Action Group, 242 Pentonville Road, London N1 9UN or e-mail c/o epilger@lag.org.uk

The law in this book is up to date to 9 December 2007.

Nic Madge
Claire Sephton

CHAPTER A

Human rights and housing

A1   European Convention on Human Rights

Since the passing of the Human Rights Act 1998, housing lawyers have been far more conscious of the impact of the European Convention on Human Rights (ECHR) on housing law. Nevertheless, although most people consider that decent housing is a fundamental human right, it is generally accepted that the Convention has not yet made much difference to English and Welsh housing law. The ECHR does not contain any equivalent to article 25 of the Universal Declaration of Human Rights, which provides that everyone has a right to a standard of living adequate for the health and well-being of himself or herself and of his or her family. That article specifically refers to housing. Nor is there any equivalent to article 27 of the UN Convention on the Rights of the Child, which provides that States which are parties to the Convention shall, in case of need, provide material assistance and support programmes with regard to housing. Although Britain is a signatory to both these conventions, they are not enforceable in British courts.

This chapter includes summaries of cases decided in Strasbourg by the European Court of Human Rights (ECtHR) and the Commission, and a few cases decided in other jurisdictions involving human rights and housing. (All cases are decisions of the ECtHR or the Commission, unless otherwise stated.) This chapter does not include any decisions of the UK courts – they are included in the relevant chapters dealing with specific housing law subjects.

A2   Article 6: Right to a fair trial

Article 6(1) provides:

> 1. In the determination of his civil rights and obligations or of any criminal charge against him, everyone is entitled to a fair and public hearing within a reasonable time by an independent and impartial tribunal established by law. Judgment shall be pronounced publicly but the press and public may be excluded from all or part of the trial in the interest of morals, public order or national security in a democratic society, where the interests of juveniles or the protection of the private life of the parties so require, or to the extent strictly necessary in the opinion of the court in special circumstances where publicity would prejudice the interests of justice.

A2.1   *Gorlova v Russia*
Application no 29898/03; 15 February 2007 (see A5.5)

Delay in enforcement of right to flat breached art 6 and art 1 1st Protocol

A2.2   *Kletsova v Russia*
Application no 24842/04; 12 April 2007

Judgment against state should be satisfied without necessity of enforcement proceedings

Ms Kletsova, a tenant of a flat, took court proceedings against the Kamyshin municipal housing maintenance enterprise. She obtained orders that the enterprise carry out maintenance works (repairing and white-washing the ceiling and the floor) and payment of non-pecuniary damages of 200 roubles. The judgment became enforceable in September 2003, but the damages were only paid in April 2005, after insolvency proceedings had been initiated. In finding a breach of article 6 and article 1 of the First Protocol, the ECtHR stated that:

> A person who has obtained an enforceable judgment against the State as the result of successful litigation cannot be required to resort to enforcement proceedings in order to have it executed.

A2.3 **Kunic v Croatia**

Application no 22344/02; 11 January 2007 (see A5.11)

Length of proceedings to recover property excessive

A2.4 **Malinovskiy v Russia**

Application no 41302/02; 7 July 2005 (see A5.13)

Failure to enforce order requiring applicant to be granted tenancy breach of art 6

A2.5 **Palumbo v Italy**

Unreported, 9 November 2000

Excessive delay in enforcement of possession order breached art 6; art 6 applies to eviction procedure after court order

Mr Palumbo owned a flat in Rome, which he let to a tenant. The lease was extended by a temporary law until 31 December 1983. After the landlord served a notice to quit, the Rome Magistrate ordered that the premises be vacated by 31 December 1984. During 1986 the bailiff made seven attempts to evict the tenant without police assistance. A further law suspended enforcement proceedings until 31 March 1987. Mr Palumbo then made a statutory declaration that he urgently required the premises as accommodation for himself. This was followed by four further unsuccessful attempts to evict the tenant. A new law then suspended enforcement of the order for possession until 31 April 1989. In June 1992, after more unsuccessful attempts by the bailiff, Mr Palumbo recovered possession of his flat. He alleged violations of article 6 and article 1 of the First Protocol.

Following *Immobiliare Saffi v Italy* [1999] ECtHR 22774/93; 28 July 1999, the ECtHR confirmed that the Italian legislation had a legitimate aim in the general interest. It reiterated that any interference with property rights

> ... must strike a 'fair balance' between the demands of the general interest and the requirements of the protection of the individual's fundamental rights. There must be a reasonable relationship of proportionality between the means employed and the aim pursued. In determining whether this requirement is met, the Court recognises that the State enjoys a wide margin of appreciation with regard both to choosing the means of enforcement and to ascertaining whether the consequences of enforcement are justified in the general interest for the purpose of achieving the object of the law in question. In spheres such as housing, which plays a central role in the welfare and economic policies of modern societies, the Court will respect the legislature's judgment as to what is in the general interest unless that judgment is manifestly without reasonable foundation.

Although the Italian system of staggering the enforcement of court orders was not in itself open to criticism, it carried the risk of imposing on landlords an excessive burden in terms of their ability to dispose of their property. It ought accordingly to provide procedural safeguards to ensure that its operation was neither arbitrary nor unforeseeable. In this case, Mr Palumbo was left in a state of uncertainty for over seven years. The authorities did not take any action in response to his declaration of necessity. There was no justification for the lengthy restriction of his use of the apartment. The court found that, in the particular circumstances of the case, this placed an excessive burden on Mr Palumbo and upset the balance that should be struck between the protection of the right of property and the requirements of the general interest. The court found a violation of article 1 of the First Protocol. The court also found a breach of article 6. It confirmed that that article does apply to eviction proceedings after a court order. It stated:

> ... the execution of a judicial decision cannot be unduly delayed. While a stay of execution of a judicial decision for such period as is strictly necessary to enable a satisfactory solution to be found to public-order problems may be justified in exceptional circumstances (see *Immobiliare Saffi*), the present case does not concern ... an isolated refusal by the prefect to provide police assistance, owing to the risk of a serious disturbance of public order. The enforcement of the order issued in the applicant's favour was stayed as a result of the intervention of the legislature, which reopened the Magistrate's decision. ... The postponement of the date by which the premises had to be vacated rendered nugatory the Rome Magistrate's decision. ... In addition, the prefect's decisions refusing police assistance, which resulted in a de facto extension of the lease, were not subject to any effective review by the courts.
>
> Mr Palumbo was deprived of his right under article 6 to have his dispute with his tenant decided by a court. The Court awarded Mr Palumbo the difference between the rent he paid for alternative premises and the rent paid to him by his tenant (21,930,000 Italian lire), non-pecuniary damages of 30,000,000 lire and costs.

See too *Indelicato v Italy* [2003] ECtHR 34442/97; 6 November 2003 (delay of eight years – non-pecuniary damage of €3,000 and costs and expenses.); *Ciccariello v Italy* [2003] ECtHR 35088/97, 9 January 2003 (delay of ten years between date ordered for vacation and actual vacation; award of pecuniary damage of €13,000 and non-pecuniary damage of €6,000); *Di Mauro v Italy* [1999] ECtHR 34256/96, July 1999 (delay of 13 years for possession claim); *Rosati v Italy* Application no 55725/00; 17 July 2003 (award of non-pecuniary damage of €6,000 for delay of over six years) and *GL v Italy* Unreported, August 2000 (delay of over seven years; loss of rent was awarded in full with non-pecuniary damages).

A2.6   *Panteleeva v Ukraine*
Application no 31780/02; 5 July 2007

Delay in eviction of tenant after possession order a breach of art 6 and art 13

In 1994, Ms Panteleeva let a flat to Ms N. Ms N did not move into the flat, but instead allowed Ms T to move in. In December 1997 Ms T began proceedings against Ms Panteleeva, who counterclaimed, seeking Ms T's eviction. In October 2001 the court dismissed Ms T's claim and ordered her eviction. Ms T appealed. Ms Panteleeva complained that the judgment remained unenforced by the time of the ECtHR hearing.

The ECtHR found that the length of the proceedings was excessive and failed to meet the 'reasonable time' requirement. There was a breach of article 6. It also found a breach of article 13 (guarantee of an effective remedy). It awarded non-pecuniary damages of €2,800.

A2.7 *Teteriny v Russia*
Application no 11931/03; 30 June 2005 (see A5.21)

Unenforced judgment violated art 6

A2.8 *Tsfayo v UK*
Application no 60860/00; [2007] ECHR 656; [2007] LGR 1; (2006) *Times* 23 November; 14 November 2006

Housing Benefit Review Board did not provide independent determination of factual dispute ('good cause' for delay) and omission not made good by judicial review

Ms Tsfayo, a housing association tenant, applied to Hammersmith and Fulham LBC for backdating of her housing benefit claim. She said that she had 'good cause' why she had not claimed benefits earlier. The council refused the application and that decision was upheld by a housing benefit and council tax benefit review board (HBRB) which comprised elected councillors from the council, advised by a barrister from the council's legal department. (Since 2001 such boards have been replaced by tribunals set up under Child Support, Pensions and Social Security Act 2000.) Ms Tsfayo was refused permission to seek a judicial review of that decision. She complained to the ECtHR that there had been no 'independent' determination of her claim for backdating. The UK government's case was that the availability of judicial review met the requirements of article 6 of the European Convention on Human Rights.

The ECtHR unanimously held that article 6 had been infringed. The court distinguished *Bryan v United Kingdom* [1995] ECtHR 19178/91; 22 November 1995 (decision of planning inspector) and *Begum (Runa) v Tower Hamlets LBC* (T60.2) (homelessness review) because in those cases 'the issues to be determined required a measure of professional knowledge or experience and the exercise of administrative discretion pursuant to wider policy aims'. However, in this case, 'the HBRB was deciding a simple question of fact, namely whether there was 'good cause' for the applicant's delay in making a claim'. The ECtHR stated:

> No specialist expertise was required to determine this issue, which is, under the new system, determined by a non-specialist tribunal ... Nor, unlike the cases referred to, can the factual findings in the present case be said to be merely incidental to the reaching of broader judgments of policy or expediency which it was for the democratically accountable authority to take.

Furthermore, the HBRB was not merely lacking in independence from the executive, but was directly connected to one of the parties to the dispute, since it included five councillors from the local authority which would be required to pay the benefit if awarded. There had been no independent determination of the factual dispute and that omission could not be made good by judicial review because the Administrative Court 'did not have jurisdiction to rehear the evidence or substitute its own views as to the applicant's credibility'. The court awarded €2,000 for non-pecuniary loss and costs.

A2.9   *Vyrovyy v Ukraine*
Application no 28746/03; 12 July 2007

Delays in proceedings to assert applicant's right to accommodation in breach of art 6

In 1997, Mr Vyroyy requested the State Co-operative Association, his employer, to give him and his family priority in the allocation of housing. That request was granted as his father had fought and perished in World War II. The same year, he started proceedings against the Association, asserting rights to a particular apartment. Those proceedings lasted slightly over five and a half years, for two levels of jurisdiction.

The ECtHR found a breach of article 6 para 1. The reasonableness of the length of proceedings must be assessed in the light of the circumstances of the case and with reference to the complexity of the case, the conduct of the applicant and the authorities and what was at stake. The state authorities were responsible for a number of delays. The court awarded non-pecuniary damages of €1,600.

A3   ## Article 8: Right to respect for private and family life

Article 8 provides:

> 1. Everyone has the right to respect for his private and family life, his home and his correspondence.

> 2. There shall be no interference by a public authority with the exercise of this right except such as is in accordance with the law and is necessary in a democratic society in the interests of national security, public safety or the economic well-being of the country, for the prevention of disorder or crime, for the protection of health or morals, or for the protection of the rights and freedoms of others.

A3.1   *Blecic v Croatia*
Application no 59532/00; 29 July 2004

Possession based on tenant's absence (due to armed conflict) not manifestly disproportionate and within state's margin of appreciation

In 1953 Mrs Blecic, with her husband, obtained a specially protected tenancy in Zadar, Croatia. After her husband's death she became the sole holder of the tenancy. In July 1991 she went to stay with her daugher in Rome for the summer. She locked the flat and left all her belongings in it. She asked a neighbour to pay her bills. However, by August 1991 the armed conflict created severe travel difficulties in the area. The town was subject to constant shelling and the supply of water and electricity was disrupted. In November 1991 a family broke into the flat and lived there. In February 1992 the Zadar Municipality brought a civil action claiming possession, on the basis that Mrs Blecic had been absent from the flat for six months without justified reason. The court terminated the tenancy but there was a series of appeals. In 1996 the Supreme Court found that her reasons for being absent were not justified. The Constitutional Court dismissed a further appeal in 1999.

The ECtHR (First Section), sitting as a chamber, consdiered whether or not the Croatian courts' decisions to terminate Mrs Blecic's specially protected tenancy amounted to a violation of ECHR article 8. It was satisfied that she did not intend to abandon the flat, but had made appropriate arrangements for its maintenance, with a view to her return. The flat in question could therefore reasonably be regarded as her home for the purposes of article 8. It also found that the termination of the tenancy by the domestic courts constituted an interference with her right to respect for her home. The court therefore went on to consider whether the interference was justified. It was satisfied that the legislation pursued a legitimate aim, namely, the satisfaction of the housing needs of citizens, and that it was thus intended to promote the economic well-being of the country and the protection of the rights of others. The Croatian legislature was entitled to prescribe the termination of specially protected tenancies held by individuals who no longer lived in the publicly-owned flats allocated to them and the subsequent redistribution of such flats to those in need. The only issue was whether the Croatian courts infringed Mrs Blecic's right to respect for her home in a disproportionate manner. The court accepted that

> ... where State authorities reconcile the competing interests of different groups in society, they must inevitably draw a line marking where a particular interest prevails and another one yields, without knowing precisely its ideal location. Making a reasonable assessment as to where the line is most properly drawn, especially if that assessment involves balancing conflicting interests and allocating scarce resources on this basis, falls within the State's margin of appreciation. ... [States enjoy] an equally wide margin of appreciation as regards respect for the home in circumstances such as those prevailing in the present case, in the context of Article 8. Thus, the Court will accept the judgment of the domestic authorities as to what is necessary in a democratic society unless that judgment is manifestly without reasonable foundation, that is, unless the measure employed is manifestly disproportionate to the legitimate aim pursued.

In this case, it could not be argued that the Croatian courts' decisions were arbitrary or unreasonable or that the solution reached was manifestly disproportionate to the legitimate aim pursued. There was, accordingly, no violation of article 8. The court also concluded that there was no breach of article 1 of the First Protocol.

A3.2   *Chapman v UK*

Application no 27238/95; (2001) 10 BHRC 48

Eviction of gypsies whose caravans were stationed in contravention of planning laws and who had nowhere else to go not in breach of art 8; ECtHR jurisprudence does not acknowledge a right to a home

The applicants were Roma gypsies who stationed their caravans on land that they owned. They were prohibited from lawful occupation by planning laws and faced eviction pursuant to enforcement notices, without the prospect of alternative lawful sites for their homes being available.

They contended, among other things, that such action would amount to a breach of their right to respect for their homes (article 8).

The ECtHR rejected that contention. Although the court found that the enforcement action was an interference with the right to occupy a home by a public authority, it was satisfied that the conditions in article 8(2) for lawful interference were satisfied. The state's actions were in accordance with domestic law, pursued a legitimate aim (environmental protection) and, having regard to the margin of appreciation allowed to national governments, were both necessary and proportionate. The court held that, in considering whether a requirement that an individual leave his or her home is proportionate to the legitimate aim pursued, it is highly relevant whether the home was established unlawfully. As to the contention that, if evicted, the applicants would have no alternative lawful site available, the court stated:

> It is important to recall that article 8 does not in terms give a right to be provided with a home. Nor does any of the jurisprudence of the Court acknowledge such a right. While it is clearly desirable that every human being has a place where he or she can live in dignity and which he or she can call home, there are unfortunately in the Contracting States many persons who have no home. Whether the State provides funds to enable everyone to have a home is a matter for political not judicial decision.

In a powerful dissenting judgment, eight judges of the ECtHR took issue with that statement, drawing attention to the court's finding in *Mazari v Italy* (A3.9) that refusal of housing might in certain circumstances engage article 8.

A3.3   *Connors v UK*
Application no 66746/01; [2004] HLR 52; (2004) *Times* 10 June; 27 May 2004

Statutory scheme for summary eviction of gypsies from council site not justified under art 8; vulnerable position of gypsies such that they require special consideration

Mr Connors and his family were gypsies. For 14 or 15 years, they lived on a gypsy site run by Leeds City Council. Mr Connors had a contractual licence to occupy one plot where he lived with his wife and four children. Several members of the family suffered from health problems. An adult daughter lived on a neighbouring plot with a man who became her husband. After allegations of nuisance made against Mr Connors' adult sons, who were visitors to the site, and his daughter's husband, the council served notice requiring the family to vacate both plots. An application for judicial review of the council's decision to determine the licences was unsuccessful. The council then obtained a possession order in proceedings brought under CCR Ord 24 (the former summary procedure available to land owners who entered land without permission.). In proceedings before the ECtHR, Mr Connors complained that, among other things, the eviction of his family breached ECHR articles 8 and 14. The parties agreed that article 8 applied and that the eviction was an interference with his right to respect for his private life, family life and home. It was also agreed that the interference was 'in accordance with the law' and pursued a legitimate aim. Accordingly, the issue before the ECtHR was whether the interference was 'necessary in a democratic society'. Mr Connors stated that he had no control over the conduct of visitors to the site and that it was not reasonable or proportionate to evict him and his family for reasons relating to other adults.

Considering the margin of appreciation, the ECtHR stated that in spheres such as housing, which play a central role in the welfare and economic policies of modern societies, it will respect the legislature's judgment as to what is in the general interest unless that judgment is manifestly without reasonable foundation. However, the vulnerable position of gypsies as a minority group means that some special consideration should be given to their needs and their different lifestyle both in the relevant regulatory framework and in reaching decisions in particular cases. There is therefore a positive obligation for states to facilitate the gypsy way of life. The ECtHR referred to the seriousness of evicting Mr Connors and his family with consequent difficulties in finding a lawful alternative location for their caravans, in coping with health problems and young children and in ensuring the children's education. Such serious interference with article 8 rights required particularly weighty reasons of public interest by way of justification and the margin of appreciation to be afforded to the national authorities should be correspondingly narrowed. The mere fact that anti-social behaviour occurs on local authority gypsy sites cannot, in itself, justify a summary power of eviction, since such problems also occur on local authority housing estates and other mobile home sites. The ECtHR was not persuaded that there was any particular feature about local authority gypsy sites which would render their management unworkable if they were required to establish reasons for evicting long-standing occupants.

Even allowing for the margin of appreciation, the ECtHR was not persuaded that the necessity for a statutory scheme which permitted the summary eviction of Mr Connors and his family had been sufficiently demonstrated by the government. The power to evict without the burden of giving reasons which were liable to be examined on the merits by an independent tribunal had not been convincingly shown to respond to any specific goal or to provide any specific benefit to members of the gypsy community. The ECtHR found that the eviction Mr Connors and his family from the local authority site was not attended by the requisite procedural safeguards, namely the requirement to establish proper justification for the serious interference with his rights and consequently could not be regarded as justified by a 'pressing social need' or proportionate to the legitimate aim being pursued. There was, accordingly, a violation of article 8. The ECtHR awarded damages in respect of distress and suffering of €14,000 and costs.

A3.4   *Di Palma v UK*

(1988) 10 EHRR 149

Forfeiture of applicant's flat not in breach of art 8

The claimant was a long lessee of a flat. It was forfeited by her landlord for relatively low arrears of service charges. She alleged violation of article 8 and article 1 of the First Protocol. The Commission rejected both complaints as inadmissible, stating:

... the Commission finds that any interference with the applicant's right to respect for her home which the forfeiture of her lease engendered was in conformity with Article 8(2) as a measure which was in accordance with the law and necessary in a democratic society for the protection of the right of others.

and

It would not appear that the mere fact that an individual was the unsuccessful party to private litigation concerning his tenancy arrangements with a private landlord could be sufficient to make the State responsible for an alleged violation of Article 1 of the First Protocol. Hence the respondent Government was not required under this provision to take further measures to secure the applicant's peaceful enjoyment of her possessions.

A3.5   *Fadeyeva v Russia*
Application no 55723/00; 9 June 2005

Failure to resettle applicant not justified where dangerous levels of toxins from privately owned plant interfered with her art 8 rights

The applicant's home in the town of Cherepovets was situated 450 metres from the perimeter of a substantial steel-making plant. She moved in during 1982. In 1990 the national government adopted a resettlement scheme, having found that 'the concentration of toxic substances in the town's air exceeds the acceptable norms many times'. The applicant was not offered resettlement. After becoming concerned about the effect on her family's health, the applicant took proceedings in the domestic courts to compel the authorities to move her but no resettlement was offered. She complained to the ECtHR that the state's failure to protect her private life and home from severe environmental pollution amounted to a breach of ECHR article 8.

The ECtHR held that: (1) 'in order to raise an issue under Article 8 the interference must directly affect the applicant's home, family or private life' [para 68]; (2) 'the adverse effects of environmental pollution must attain a certain minimum level if they are to fall within the scope of Article 8' [para 69] and; (3) proof of that minimum level of interference may

... follow from the co-existence of sufficiently strong, clear and concordant inferences or of similar unrebutted presumptions of fact. It should be also noted that it has been the Court's practice to allow flexibility in this respect, taking into consideration the nature of the substantive right at stake and any evidentiary difficulties involved.

Although the applicant had no medical evidence directly linking her ill health to the toxins produced by the steel plant, the court accepted that the prolonged exposure 'inevitably made the applicant more vulnerable to various diseases' and 'adversely affected the quality of life at her home'. On that basis, 'the actual detriment to the applicant's health and well-being reached a level sufficient to bring it within the scope of Article 8' [para 88]. The fact that the steel plant was privately owned did *not* absolve the state of responsibility because it had the powers to prevent or reduce the plant's emissions. The positive obligation to protect the applicant's human rights was engaged. On the question of whether article 8(2) justification could be made out, the court was satisfied that continued operation of the plant was a 'legitimate aim' and in the economic interests of the state. The determinative issue was 'whether the authorities have struck a fair balance between the interests of the applicant and those of the community as a whole' [para 101]. The court concluded that

> although the situation around the plant called for a special treatment of those living within the zone, the State did not offer the applicant any effective solution to help her move from the dangerous area. Furthermore, although the polluting enterprise at issue operated in breach of domestic environmental standards, there is no information that the State designed or applied effective measures which would take into account the interests of the local population, affected by the pollution, and which would be capable of reducing the industrial pollution to acceptable levels. [para 133]

It awarded €6,000 non-pecuniary damages (plus costs).

A3.6   *Gomez v Spain*
Application no 4143/02; 16 November 2004

Noise from night clubs interfered with applicant's art 8 rights; failure to control the noise was unjustified

Mr Gomez lived in a residential flat in Valencia. Since 1974 the council had granted licences for pubs, bars and discotheques to operate in the city. By 1980 residents were complaining of excessive night-time noise and in 1983 the council resolved not to permit further nightclubs to open. That resolution was never implemented and more clubs opened. By 1993 a council-commissioned expert found that night-time noise levels were excessive and unacceptable, reaching over 100 decibels at 3.55 am on Saturday mornings. In 1995 local police reported that the bars and clubs were not closing on time and that residents' complaints were justified. By 1997 the council declared the applicant's neighbourhood an 'acoustically saturated zone' but three days later granted a licence for a new nightclub in Mr Gomez's building (later quashed on appeal).

The ECtHR set out the following statement of principle [para 53]:

> Article 8 of the Convention protects the individual's right to respect for his private and family life, his home and his correspondence. A home will usually be the place, the physically defined area, where private and family life develops. The individual has a right to respect for his home, meaning not just the right to the actual physical area, but also to the quiet enjoyment of that area. Breaches of the right to respect of the home are not confined to concrete or physical breaches, such as unauthorised entry into a person's home, but also include those that are not concrete or physical, such as noise, emissions, smells or other forms of interference. A serious breach may result in the breach of a person's right to respect for his home if it prevents him from enjoying the amenities of his home (see *Hatton and Others v United Kingdom* ECtHR Application no 36022/97; 8 July 2003).

Applying that approach (and the decision in *Surugiu v Romania* (A3.14)) the court held that the state authorities had failed to 'take action to put a stop to third-party breaches' of Mr Gomez's rights. The breaches were caused by the volume of noise at night, beyond permitted levels, extending over many years. The court awarded compensation for the cost of double glazing (€879) and a further €3,005 for non-pecuniary damage.

A3.7   **Karner v Austria**

Application no 40016/98; 24 July 2003 (see A4.3)

Interpretation of succession rules to deny rights to deceased tenant's gay part-ner discriminatory; case not struck out despite death of applicant

A3.8   **López Ostra v Spain**

(1994) 20 EHRR 277

Severe environmental pollution a breach of resident's art 8 rights

Mrs López Ostra lived in Lorca. The town had a heavy concentration of leather industries. A waste-treatment plant was built but, owing to a mal-function, it released gas fumes, pestilential smells and contamination, which immediately caused health problems and nuisance. The town council evacuated the local residents and rehoused them free of charge. Mrs López Ostra lodged a local court application alleging an unlawful interference with her home and her peaceful enjoyment of it, a violation of her right to choose freely her place of residence, attacks on her phys-ical and psychological integrity, and infringements of her liberty and her safety. The court found against her. Although the plant's operation could unquestionably cause nuisance because of the smells, fumes and noise, it did not constitute a serious risk to the health of the families living in its vicinity but, rather, impaired their quality of life, though not enough to infringe the fundamental rights claimed. She appealed to the Spanish Supreme Court, the Constitutional Court and then to the ECtHR, relying on article 8.

The ECtHR decided that the Spanish state did not succeed in striking a fair balance between the interest of the town's economic well-being – that of having a waste-treatment plant – and the applicant's effective enjoy-ment of her right to respect for her home and her private and family life. There was a violation of article 8. It stated:

> ... severe environmental pollution may affect individuals' well-being and prevent them from enjoying their homes in such a way as to affect their private and family life adversely, without, however, seriously endangering their health.
>
> Whether the question is analysed in terms of a positive duty on the State – to take reasonable and appropriate measures to secure the appli-cant's rights under paragraph 1 of Article 8 ... or in terms of an 'interfer-ence by a public authority' to be justified in accordance with paragraph 2, the applicable principles are broadly similar. In both contexts regard must be had to the fair balance that has to be struck between the competing in-terests of the individual and of the community as a whole, and in any case the State enjoys a certain margin of appreciation.

A3.9   **Mazari v Italy**

[1999] 28 EHRR CD 175

Refusal to provide housing can in some circumstances breach art 8

The applicant was a disabled man. He claimed that he was unable to leave hospital because the public authorities had not secured appropriate accom-modation for him.

The ECtHR dismissed his complaint, but stated:

> The court considers that although Article 8 does not guarantee the right to have one's housing problem resolved by the authorities, a refusal of the authorities to provide assistance in this respect to an individual suffering from a severe disease might in certain circumstances raise an issue under Article 8 of the Convention because of the impact of such refusal on the private life of the individual.

A3.10 *Novoseletskiy v Ukraine*
Application no 47148/99; 22 May 2005

Legal complexity of case not such as to warrant delay in proceedings; state-owned higher education establishment with power to allocate flats under the supervision of the authorities performed 'public duties' and was a 'governmental organisation'

In June 1995 Mr Novoseletskiy was granted indefinite authorisation to occupy and use a two-room flat by his employer, the Melitopol State Teacher Training Institute. In August 1995 he resigned from the Institute and went to live in Vladimir, Russia to prepare his doctoral thesis. In October 1995 the Institute annulled its June decision and granted authorisation to occupy and use the flat to T, another of its employees. In November 1995 T, accompanied by four witnesses, entered the flat. They noted that the flat was empty and made a statement to that effect. According to Mr Novoseletskiy, his possessions were removed or stolen from the flat. In February 1996, Mr Novoseletskiy filed a civil claim against the Institute with the Melitopol City Court, claiming compensation for pecuniary and non-pecuniary damage and seeking to assert his right to free use of the flat. The Institute in turn lodged an application to have that right withdrawn from him. In May 1996, the Institute annulled its October 1995 decision, finding that it had been unlawful, and restored Mr Novoseletskiy's rights to the flat. In 27 June 1996, the Melitopol City Court dismissed Mr Novoseletskiy's claim and granted the Institute's application. It found that, in accordance with the legislation in force and his employment contract, Mr Novoseletskiy had forfeited his right to use the flat after taking up permanent residence elsewhere. The court also noted that the flat had been empty when it was entered.

However, Mr Novoseletskiy's appeal was partially successful: it was held that he had the right to free use of the flat because his absence was only temporary, but his claim for damages was dismissed. There were delays in enforcement of the order. In March 2001, Mr Novoseletskiy and the court bailiff certified that the flat was empty and unfit for human habitation and needed substantial repairs before it could be used. Among many other things, the sanitary fittings and electrical wiring had been seriously damaged, the sink and surrounding pipes had been removed, making it impossible to use any running water, and the contents of the sewage pipes emptied into the flat, creating a powerful stench. Furthermore, T refused to hand over the keys to the flat to the court bailiff. In February 2004 Mr Novoseletskiy complained that since March 2001 he had been unable to live in the flat owing to its deplorable state and that there had been a breach of article 8.

The ECtHR noted that, although article 8 is primarily intended to protect the individual against arbitrary interference by public authorities, it may also entail the adoption of measures to secure article 8 rights by public authorities even in the sphere of relations between individuals (*López Ostra v Spain* (A3.8) and *Surugiu v Romania* (A3.14)). A fair balance has to be struck between the competing interests of the individual and of the community as a whole. The ECtHR did not consider that the legal complexity of the case was such as to warrant proceedings comprising three hearings and lasting three years, particularly in view of what was at stake in terms of the applicant's private and family life. Furthermore, it was particularly struck by the rejection of Mr Novoseletskiy's claim for damages, on the ground that the law made no provision for compensation in respect of non-pecuniary damage in landlord–tenant disputes. It held that that the Ukrainian courts had not acquitted themselves fully of the tasks incumbent on them as part of the positive duty of the state under article 8. The court also noted that the Institute was a state-owned higher education establishment which had power, subject to the Ukrainian Housing Code and state supervision, to allocate flats. It therefore performed 'public duties' assigned to it by law and under the supervision of the authorities, with the result that it could be considered a 'governmental organisation'. The ECtHR therefore rejected the government's arguments seeking to deny any state liability for the acts and omissions of the Institute. In view of the judicial decisions and the conduct of the relevant authorities, the ECtHR found that the state had not discharged itself of its positive obligation to restore and protect Mr Novoseletskiy's effective enjoyment of his right to respect for his home and his private and family life. Accordingly, there was a violation of article 8.

A3.11   *Office public d'habitation de la Ville de Paris v Yedei*
French Cour de Cassation, 6 March 1996 (note available at www.courdecassation.fr – No 534 (regles generales))

Anti-sharing clause in tenancy a breach of art 8

A public landlord brought possession proceedings for breach of a clause in a tenancy agreement prohibiting sharing with third parties. The tenant was sharing with her sister and the father of two of her children.

The Cour de Cassation held that the clause was ineffective because it breached ECHR article 8.1 in that it prevented her from living with her close relatives.

A3.12   *O'Rourke v UK*
Application no 39022/97; 26 June 2001 (see T56.1)

Eviction of homeless applicant from temporary accommodation and offers of alternative temporary accommodation did not breach any art 8 rights

A3.13   *Stanková v Slovakia*
Application no 7205/02; 9 October 2007

Possession claim not necessary in a democratic society and so breach of art 8

Mrs Stanková and her husband held a joint tenancy of a three-room flat owned by a cooperative in Poprad. After matrimonial differences, she and her two children left that flat and went to live in a two-room flat rented by her father from the Poprad Municipality. The father suffered from a long-term illness and died in 1994. After his death Mrs Stanková continued to live in his flat and paid the rent. She asked to be registered as permanently residing in the flat, but in 1995, the Poprad Municipal Office informed her that the right to use her father's flat had not passed to her after his death. In October 1996, the Poprad District Court ordered her to move out of the flat within 30 days. It held that she had not become a tenant of the flat originally used by her father since, at the time of his death, she had been registered as a user of the flat in which she had lived with her former husband. Enforcement action was taken and she was evicted. Mrs Stanková complained to the ECtHR of breaches of articles 6 and 8.

The ECtHR found that there had been a violation of article 8. It was not disputed that the obligation that Mrs Stanková leave the flat amounted to an interference with her right to respect for her home. It was 'in accordance with the law' and pursued the legitimate aim of protecting the rights of the Poprad Municipality, which owned the flat. However, the ECtHR decided that the interference was not 'necessary in a democratic society'. The notion of necessity implies a pressing social need and any measure employed must be proportionate to the legitimate aim pursued. After referring to the margin of appreciation enjoyed by the national authorities, the ECtHR accepted the conclusions of the Slovakian Constitutional Court that the effect of ordering Mrs Stanková to leave the flat without being provided with any alternative accommodation produced effects which were incompatible with her right to respect for her private and family life and for her home. The interference was not necessary in a democratic society as it had not been based on relevant and sufficient reasons. The ECtHR also noted that the Poprad Municipality was in charge of public housing and was under an obligation to assist the town's citizens in resolving their accommodation problems. It awarded non-pecuniary damage of €3,000.

Note: This decision raises interesting questions about whether the ECtHR would now approve the decisions in *Harrow LBC v Qazi* (L1.1); *Lambeth LBC v Kay; Leeds CC v Price* (L1.2) and *Michalak v Wandsworth LBC* (E14.9). It is arguable that there is, in principle, little difference between the nature of Mr Qazi's defence and that of Mrs Stanková. Furthermore, there is little difference between the facts of *Stanková* and those in *Michalak* where the Court of Appeal held that on a claim for possession against a non-successor, the county court was not required to investigate the individual circumstances of the defendant in order to find the conditions of article 8 made out. Notwithstanding *Stanková, Qazi, Kay* and *Michalak* remain binding on all English and Welsh Courts, up to and including the Court of Appeal. It remains to be seen what the House of Lords will decide when, as they inevitably will have to, they consider these issues for a third time.

A3.14   *Surugiu v Romania*

Application no 48995/99; 20 April 2004

Failure by state authorities to take steps to stop repeated interference with applicant's home a breach of art 8

Mr Surugiu owned the land next to his home but the local land commission failed to enforce his title to it and granted rights over part of it to a third party (M). M and his family then regularly went on to the land to cut and gather grass, dump manure, and threaten Mr Surugiu. Eventually he was barred from his own home by the actions of the M family who threatened to demolish it. He brought proceedings in trespass but obtained no relief despite four declarations that the land was his. Eventually, the national government revoked M's rights, imposed an administrative penalty on him (after an 18-month delay), and Mr Surugiu was able to return.

The ECtHR found a violation of Mr Surugiu's article 8 right to respect for his home. The state authorities had not taken the steps that they could reasonably have been expected to have taken to stop the repeated interference with Mr Surugiu's right to peaceful enjoyment of his home. He was awarded €4,000 in compensation.

A3.15   *Tuleshov v Russia*

Application no 32718/02; 24 May 2007 (see A5.22)

Compensation terms for loss of home did not strike fair balance required by art 1 First Protocol; delay in providing applicant alternative accommodation a breach of art 8

A3.16   *Velosa Barretto v Portugal*

[1996] EHRLR 212

Restriction on private landlord's right to possession pursued legitimate aim

Portuguese law gives tenants security of tenure, subject to various grounds for possession – eg, 'landlord needs property in order to live there or to build his home there'. A landlord was refused a possession order because he and his family could continue living with relatives. The landlord complained unsuccessfully that there was a breach of article 8.

The ECtHR stated

> ... although the object of Article 8 is essentially that of protecting the individual against arbitrary interference by the public authorities, it may also give rise to positive obligations ... effective protection of respect for private and family life cannot require the existence in national law of legal protection enabling each family to have a home for themselves alone. It does not go so far as to place the State under an obligation to give a landlord the right to recover possession of a rented house on request and in any circumstances.
>
> Like the Commission, the Court considers that the legislation applied in this case pursues a legitimate aim, namely the social protection of tenants, and that it thus tends to promote the economic well-being of the country and the protection of the rights of others.

The court also found that the restriction on the landlord's right to terminate his tenant's lease constituted control of the use of property within the meaning of the second paragraph of article 1 of the First Protocol. That restriction pursued a legitimate social policy aim. It struck a fair balance between the demands of the general interest of the community and the requirements of the protection of the individual's fundamental rights.

A3.17 *Wood v UK*

(1997) 24 EHRR CD 69

Possession order against mortgage borrower did not offend art 8

The complainant borrowed from a mortgage lender. The lender obtained a possession order due to arrears. She complained that there had been a violation of her rights under article 8 and article 1 of the First Protocol. The Commission rejected her complaint, stating:

> In so far as the repossession constituted an interference with the applicant's home, the Commission finds that this was in accordance with the terms of the loan and the domestic law and was necessary for the rights and freedoms of others, namely the lender. To the extent that the applicant is deprived of her possessions by the repossession, the Commission considers that this deprivation is in the public interest in ensuring payment of contractual debts, and also in accordance with the rules provided for by law.

A3.18 *X v FRG*

(1956) 1 YB 202

No right to a decent home under ECHR

In a case involving a refugee from East Germany, the ECtHR decided that the right to a satisfactory standard of living and to decent housing do not figure among the rights and liberties provided by the ECHR.

A4 Article 14: Prohibition of discrimination

ECHR article 14 provides:

> The enjoyment of the rights and freedoms set forth in this Convention shall be secured without discrimination on any ground such as sex, race, colour, language, religion, political or other opinion, national or social origin, association with a national minority, property, birth or other status.

A4.1 *Connors v UK*

Application no 66746/01; [2004] HLR 52; (2004) *Times* 10 June; 27 May 2004 (see A3.3)

Statutory scheme for summary eviction of gypsies from council site not justified under art 8; vulnerable position of gypsies means that the require special consideration

A4.2 *Di Palma v UK*

(1988) 10 EHRR 149 (see A3.4)

Forfeiture of applicant's flat not a breach of art 8

A4.3 *Karner v Austria*

Application no 40016/98; 24 July 2003

Interpretation of succession rules to deny rights to deceased tenant's gay partner discriminatory; case not struck out despite death of complainant

Mr W rented a flat in Vienna. From 1989 Mr Karner lived in the flat with Mr W, with whom he had a gay relationship. They shared the outgoings on the flat. In 1993 Mr W developed Aids. Mr W designated Mr Karner as his heir. Mr Karner nursed him until 1994 when Mr W died. In 1995 the landlord of the flat brought proceedings against Mr Karner for termination of the tenancy. Mr Karner relied on section 14 of the Austrian Rent Act which provides:

> On the death of the main tenant of a flat, ... the following shall be entitled to succeed to the tenancy ... a spouse, a life companion, relatives in the direct line including adopted children, and siblings of the former tenant, in so far as such persons have a pressing need for accommodation and have already lived in the accommodation with the tenant as members of the same household. For the purposes of this provision, 'life companion' shall mean a person who has lived in the flat with the former tenant until the latter's death for at least three years, sharing a household on an economic footing like that of a marriage ...

Although the District Court and the Regional Civil Court dismissed the landlord's claim for possession, the Austrian Supreme Court granted the landlord's appeal, quashed the lower courts' decisions and terminated the lease. It held that in 1974 the legislature could not have contemplated that a gay or lesbian partner would be a form of 'life companion'.

The ECtHR rejected the Austrian government's application to strike out the case following the death of Mr Karner. By a majority of six to one, it held that Mr Karner's complaint related to the manner in which a difference in treatment adversely affected the enjoyment of his right to respect for his home guaranteed under article 8. If it had not been for his sexual orientation, he could have been accepted as a life companion. Accordingly, ECHR article 14 (discrimination) applied. It stated that, for the purposes of article 14, a difference in treatment is discriminatory if it has no objective and reasonable justification, ie, if it does not pursue a legitimate aim or if there is not a reasonable relationship of proportionality between the means employed and the aim sought to be realised. As the Austrian government had not offered convincing and weighty reasons justifying a narrow interpretation of the Rent Act preventing a surviving partner of a couple of the same sex from relying on that provision, there had been a violation of article 14. In the absence of an injured party, the ECtHR decided that no award of compensation for pecuniary damage could be made, but awarded costs against the Austrian government.

A4.4   ## Larkos v Cyprus
(1999) 7 BHRC 244; [1998] EHRLR 653

Disapplication of security of tenure provisions to lettings by state discriminatory

In 1967 Mr Larkos, a civil servant, rented a house from the government of Cyprus. He lived there with his wife and four children. The agreement had many of the features of a typical contract for a lease. It provided that it would come to an end in the event that he was transferred to a district other than the one in which the property was situated. In 1987 the government served a notice to quit and took eviction proceedings. Mr Larkos claimed that he enjoyed protection under the Cyprus Rent Control Law 1983. The government claimed that he was outside the protection of that legislation because the premises had been allocated to him by an administrative order because of his position in the civil service. The District Court of Nicosia made a possession order, finding that the Rent Control Law only bound private owners of property and not the government.

The ECtHR stated that under article 14:

> ... a difference in treatment is discriminatory if 'it has no objective and reasonable justification', that is if it does not pursue a 'legitimate aim' or if there is not a 'reasonable relationship of proportionality between the means employed and the aim sought to be realised'.

It was significant that the government rented the property to Mr Larkos in a private law capacity. He was in a 'relevantly similar situation' to that of other private tenants. The government did not adduce any reasonable or objective justification for the distinction between them, even having regard to the margin of appreciation. The court concluded unanimously that there had been a violation of article 14 in conjunction with article 8. In view of this it was not necessary to give separate consideration to Mr Larkos's complaint that there had been a violation of article 14 in conjunction with article 1 of the First Protocol.

A4.5 *Mellacher v Austria*

(1989) 12 EHRR 391 (see A5.14)

Rent restrictions not disproportionate and were within state's margin of appreciation

A5 Article 1 of the First Protocol: Protection of property

Article 1 provides:

> Every natural or legal person is entitled to the peaceful enjoyment of his possessions. No one shall be deprived of his possessions except in the public interest and subject to the conditions provided for by law and by the general principles of international law.

> The preceding provisions shall not, however, in any way impair the right of a State to enforce such laws as it deems necessary to control the use of property in accordance with the general interest or to secure the payment of taxes or other contributions or penalties.

A5.1 *Akimova v Azerbaijan*

Application no 19853/03; 27 September 2007

Occupancy voucher constituted a 'possession' falling within the ambit of art 1 of 1st Protocol

Ms Akimova was granted an occupancy voucher to an apartment in a state-owned residential building. She did not move in because construction had not been completed, but, four years later, allowed an acquaintance to move in free of charge. Later, in breach of that agreement, the acquaintance allowed a relative and his family, who were internally displaced persons from Nagorno-Karabakh, to move into the apartment. Ms Akimova filed a law suit requesting their eviction. Eventually she obtained an eviction order, but execution was postponed until Nagorno-Karabakh was liberated from Armenian occupation. Ms Akimova complained that she had been deprived of her property rights in breach of article 1 of the First Protocol.

In finding such a breach, the ECtHR stated that (1) Ms Akimova's claims to the apartment were sufficiently established to constitute a 'possession' falling within the ambit of article 1 and (2), as the domestic judgment did not rely on any domestic legal provision which would serve as a basis for postponing execution, the interference complained of was in breach of Azerbaijani law and incompatible with her right to peaceful enjoyment of her possession.

A5.2   *Baygayev v Russia*
Application no 36398/04; 5 July 2007

Delay in proceedings and enforcement breached art 6 and art 1 First Protocol

In 1993 Mr Baygayev bought a two-room flat in Groznyy, the capital of the Chechen Republic. Some time later, as a result of a military operation, it was destroyed. In November 2003, the Tsentralnyy District Court allowed his claim against the Ministry of Finance of the Russian Federation and awarded him 300,000 Russian roubles for the loss of housing. That judgment was not enforced until December 2005.

After finding a breach of article 6 and article 1 of the First Protocol, the ECtHR awarded pecuniary damages of €2,400 and non-pecuniary damages of €1,600.

A5.3   *Bistrović v Croatia*
Application no 25774/05; 31 May 2007

Compensation terms did not ensure adequate protection of applicants' property rights when new motorway put through their land

Mr and Mrs Bistrović owned a house and a plot of land. A public company began expropriation proceedings for part of the plot of land with a view to building a motorway. Mr and Mrs Bistrović opposed this proposal, asking that the house and the surrounding land be expropriated in its entirety, saying that as farmers, they would have no further use for the house and the small area around it and that there would be no vehicle access to the courtyard. They also complained that the planned motorway would pass in close proximity to the house, causing significant noise pollution. The motorway and the exit road would pass less then 20 metres and five metres respectively from the house. In 2003, the Varaždin County Administration ruled that some of the land would be expropriated, but that Mr and Mrs Bistrović would retain ownership of the house and a surrounding courtyard. The Varaždin County Court dismissed their claim seeking expropriation of their entire estate and reconsideration of the amount of compensation awarded. Mr and Mrs Bistrović complained to the ECtHR that there had been a breach of article 1 of the First Protocol because they had not received the full market value of their expropriated property and no account had been taken in the expropriation proceedings of the significantly decreased value of their remaining property.

The ECtHR found that there had been a breach of article 1 of the First Protocol. A fair balance must be struck between the demands of the general interest of the community and the requirements of the protection of the individual's fundamental rights. Compensation terms under the relevant legislation are material to the assessment of whether the contested measure respects the requisite fair balance and, notably, whether it does not impose a disproportionate burden on the applicant. By failing to establish all the relevant factors for establishing the compensation for the expropriated property, and by failing to grant indemnity for the decrease in the value of the remaining estate, the national authorities failed to strike a fair balance between the interests involved and failed to make efforts to ensure adequate protection of Mr and Mrs Bistrović's property rights.

A5.4   *Edwards v Malta*
Application no 17647/04; [2006] ECHR 887; 24 October 2006

Compensation terms did not ensure adequate protection of applicants' property rights when new motorway put through their land

Mr Edwards was the trustee of four tenements and a neighbouring field. At various times between 1941 and 1976 the Maltese government made requisition orders or amended requisition orders relating to the tenements in order to house homeless people. In 1996 Mr Edwards instituted proceedings before the Civil Court (First Hall) against the Director of Social Accommodation. He alleged that the latest requisition order had been issued as a result of an abuse of power and was therefore null and void. He also claimed an infringement of his right to the enjoyment of his property as guaranteed by article 1 of the First Protocol because the requisition order had not been made in accordance with the public interest. He also maintained that he had not received adequate and appropriate compensation. His claim was dismissed by the Civil Court and his subsequent appeal rejected by the Constitutional Court. Mr Edwards complained about the requisition of the tenement and of the adjacent field to the ECtHR, invoking article 1 of the First Protocol.

The ECtHR held that the tenements and field were possessions within the meaning of article 1, even though Mr Edwards was only a trustee. He had been acting as the owner of the premises without disturbance and receiving rent for more than 30 years. It also held that, by requisitioning and assigning the use of his property to others, Mr Edwards had been prevented from enjoying his property. His right to receive a market rent and to terminate leases had been substantially affected. However, he never lost his right to sell his property, nor had the authorities applied any measures resulting in the transfer of his title. The measures taken by the authorities were aimed at subjecting his tenement and field to a continuing tenancy and not at taking it away from him permanently. Therefore, the interference complained of could not be considered a formal or even de facto expropriation, but constituted a means of state control of the use of property. It followed that the case should be examined under the second paragraph of article 1. It was not disputed that the requisition of the tenements was carried out in accordance with the provisions of the Housing Act. The measure was, therefore, 'lawful' within the meaning of article 1. The court accepted the government's argument that the requisition and

rent control were aimed at ensuring the just distribution and use of housing resources in a country where land available for construction could not
meet the demand. These measures, implemented with a view to securing
the social protection of tenants, were also aimed at preventing homelessness and protecting the dignity of impoverished tenants. The legislation
therefore had a legitimate aim in the general interest, as required by the
second paragraph of article 1. However, having regard to the extremely
low amount of rent, to the fact that the applicant's premises had been
requisitioned for more than 30 years, and to other restrictions of landlords' rights, the court found that a disproportionate and excessive burden
had been imposed on Mr Edwards. He had been requested to bear most
of the social and financial costs of supplying housing accommodation to
the family which was renting one of the tenements. It followed that the
Maltese state had failed to strike the requisite fair balance between the
general interests of the community and the protection of the applicant's
right of property. There was, accordingly, a violation of article 1 of the First
Protocol. The court reserved the question of compensation for pecuniary damage and/or non-pecuniary damage because it was not ready for
decision.

See too *Ghigo v Malta* Application no 31122/05; [2006] ECHR 808; 26
September 2006.

A5.5   *Gorlova v Russia*
Application no 29898/03; 15 February 2007

Delay in enforcement of right to flat breached art 6 and art 1 of First Protocol
Ms Gorlova was the tenant of a flat. In 1994 a housing maintenance company cut off the heating. She sued the company, seeking restoration of
the heating supply and compensation for damage. After a court hearing
in 1999, the maintenance company restored the heating. Ms Gorlova sued
the Yakutsk Town Council claiming compensation for damage caused to
her flat due to the absence of the heating. In August 2002, the Yakutsk
Town Court dismissed the action because the municipal authorities had
not been responsible for the damage. In October 2002 the Yakutsk Town
Court ordered that the Yakutsk Town Council should provide the applicant
with a well-equipped one-room flat. The order was not complied with and
in December 2004 the Yakutsk Town Court amended the judgment and
ordered that the Yakutsk mayor's office (which had taken over the functions of the council) should pay the applicant 700,000 Russian roubles in
lieu of the flat. That was done. Ms Gorlova complained to the ECtHR that
the October 2002 order was not timeously enforced and that there was a
breach of ECHR article 6 and article 1 of the First Protocol.

The ECtHR noted that it had frequently found violations of article 6
and article 1 of the First Protocol in cases raising similar issues. (See
Malinovskiy v Russia (A5.13); *Teteriny v Russia* (A5.21) and *Plotnikovy v
Russia* Application no 43883/02; 24 February 2005 (a case involving failure to enforce court judgments for arrears of welfare pensions). The government had not put forward any fact or argument capable of persuading
the court to reach a different conclusion in the present case. The ECtHR
reiterated that it is not open to a state authority to cite the lack of funds or

other resources, such as housing, as an excuse for not honouring a judgment debt. By failing for years to comply with the enforceable judgment, the domestic authorities impaired the essence of Ms Gorlova's 'right to a court' and prevented her from receiving a flat, or subsequently the sum of money that she could reasonably have expected to receive. There were, accordingly violations of article 6 and article 1 of the First Protocol. However, the ECtHR rejected Ms Gorlova's claim in respect of pecuniary damage (the cost of acquiring a flat in Yakutsk) because she had already received money in lieu of a flat. It did, though, award €3,100 in respect of non-pecuniary damage.

Note: See too *Nevolin v Russia* Application no 38103/05; 12 July 2007 (non-pecuniary damages of €1,200 for delay of approximately 16 months); *Telyatyeva v Russia* Application no 18762/06; 12 July 2007 (non-pecuniary damages of €1,600 for delay of almost two years); *Pridatchenko v Russia* Application no 2191/03; 21 June 2007 (delay of over two years in enforcement of the judgment for provision of free housing; pecuniary damages based on the rate of inflation and non-pecuniary damages of €1,600 to reflect 'mental distress ... which [could] not sufficiently be compensated by the finding of a violation'); *Ponomarenko v Russia* Application no 14656/03; 15 February 2007 (delay of almost four years in provision of accommodation; award of €3,100 in respect of non-pecuniary damage for the violations of article 6 and article 1 of the First Protocol) and *Lykov v Russia* Application no 18557/06; 12 July 2007 (non-pecuniary damages of €2,300 for delay of almost three years).

A5.6   *Hutten-Czapska v Poland*
Application no 35014/97; [2006] ECHR 628; 19 June 2006

Extent of state control of use of property impaired essence of right to property

Mrs Hutten-Czapska owned a house and a plot of land in Gdynia, Poland which had previously belonged to her parents. During World War II, it was appropriated by the Nazis and subsequently occupied by soldiers of the Red Army. Later, it was taken over by the Housing Department of the Gdynia City Council. In 1946 the house became subject to the so-called 'State management of housing matters' and rent control provisions which drastically restricted the amount of rent chargeable. In 1975, the Mayor of Gdynia issued a decision allowing the Head of the Housing Department to exchange the flat he was leasing in another building under the special lease scheme for the ground floor flat in the applicant's house. The same year, the Head of the Local Management and Environment Office of the Gdynia City Council ordered that the house should become subject to state management. In the 1990s, Mrs Hutten-Czapska tried to have that decision declared null and void but succeeded only in obtaining a decision declaring that it had been issued contrary to the law. In 1990 the Mayor of Gdynia issued a decision restoring the management of the house to Mrs Hutten-Czapska, although it was still occupied by tenants. In the 1990s claims for possession against the tenants were dismissed. The rent control provisions did not change significantly after the end of communist rule in 1989. Indeed, by the 1990s the state-controlled rent, which also applied to privately owned buildings, covered merely 30% of the actual cost of maintenance of buildings. In the ECtHR, Mrs Hutten-Czapska alleged that the implementation of laws imposing restrictions in rent increases and the termination of leases amounted to a violation of article 1 of the First Protocol.

The Grand Chamber of the ECtHR noted that, although Mrs Hutten-Czapska could not exercise her right of use in terms of physical possession as the house had been occupied by tenants and her rights in respect of letting the flats, including her right to receive rent and to terminate leases, had been subject to a number of statutory limitations, she had never lost her right to sell her property. Nor had the authorities applied any measures resulting in the transfer of her ownership. In the Chamber's judgment, those issues concerned the degree of the state's interference, and not its nature. The aim of all the measures taken was to subject the applicant's house to continued tenancies, and not to take it away from her permanently. They could not be considered a formal or even de facto expropriation but constituted a means of state control of the use of her property. Accordingly, the case should be examined under the second paragraph of article 1 of the First Protocol. It is for national authorities to make the initial assessment of the existence of a problem of public concern warranting measures to be applied in the sphere of the exercise of the right of property and, in doing so, they enjoy a wide margin of appreciation. The Grand Chamber accepted that the interference respected the principle of lawfulness. It also agreed that the rent control scheme in Poland originated in the continued shortage of dwellings, the low supply of flats for rent on the lease market and the high costs of acquiring a flat. It was implemented with a view to securing the social protection of tenants and ensuring the gradual transition from state-controlled rent to a fully negotiated contractual rent during the fundamental reform of the country following the collapse of the communist regime. The court accepted that, in the social and economic circumstances of the case, the impugned legislation had a legitimate aim in the general interest, as required by the second paragraph of article 1. However, after noting that the rent which Mrs Hutten-Czapska received was very low, the court held that the legislation 'impaired the very essence of her right of property' and individual landlords had been 'deprived even of the slightest substance of their property rights'. Their 'right to derive profit from property, ... an important element of the right of property ha[d] been destroyed and ... the[ir] right to dispose of one's property ha[d] been stripped of its substance.' The legislation 'unduly restricted [Mrs Hutten-Czapska's] property rights and placed a disproportionate burden on her, which [could] not be justified in terms of the legitimate aim pursued by the authorities in implementing the relevant remedial housing legislation.' The ECtHR accordingly found that there had been a violation of article 1 of the First Protocol. The court reserved the question of compensation for pecuniary damage because it was not ready for decision, but made an award for non-pecuniary damage of €30,000.

A5.7   *Ilić v Serbia*

Application no 30132/04; 9 October 2007

Violation of art 6 and art 1 of the First Protocol where delay in possession proceedings and order not enforced

Mr Ilić inherited the legal title to a flat owned by his father before his death. However, he could not effectively enjoy it because the flat was subjected to a 'protected tenancy regime' and was physically occupied by other persons whose rent was controlled by the public authorities. In January 1993 the Palilula Housing Department accepted Mr Ilić's eviction request and ordered the Municipality of Palilula to provide the 'protected tenant' with adequate alternative accommodation by December 1995. In August 2006, the municipality offered the original protected tenant's legal heir specific alternative accommodation, but the tenant's heir said that it was inadequate in terms of its overall size as well as the number of rooms available. Mr Ilić sought compensation for the pecuniary damage sustained due to his continuing inability to use or lease the flat. Mr Ilić complained that the non-enforcement of the final eviction order was a breach of article 1 of the First Protocol.

The ECtHR found that there had been a violation of article 1 of the First Protocol. Mr Ilić's repossession claim was 'sufficiently established' to amount to a 'possession' within the meaning of article 1 of the First Protocol. When the deadline set by the court expired, the State's interference was clearly in breach of the relevant domestic legislation and, as such, it was incompatible with Mr Ilić's right to the peaceful enjoyment of his possessions. With regards article 6, the ECtHR observed that by March 2004 the proceedings had already been pending for approximately eight years. By the time of the hearing in the ECtHR the proceedings had still not been concluded. Having regard to the criteria laid down in Serbian jurisprudence, the relevant facts of the case, including its complexity and the conduct of parties, the court held that the length of the proceedings failed to satisfy the reasonable time requirement. There was, accordingly, also a violation of article 6. The court awarded €3,700 for the distress suffered.

A5.8   *JA Pye (Oxford) Ltd v United Kingdom*
Application no 44302/02; 30 August 2007; (2007) *Times* 1 October

12-year limitation period for actions for recovery of land pursued a legitimate aim in the general interest; no requirement that landowner be compensated

In 1983 Pye permitted Mr Graham to occupy four fields for grazing. When the permission expired, the company required Mr Graham to vacate, but he remained in occupation, continuing to use the land for grazing and other agricultural purposes. The land, which adjoined his own land, was enclosed by hedges and was only accessible, except by foot, via a padlocked gate to which only Mr Graham had a key. Mr Graham died in 1998. Pye sought possession of the four fields against his executors. The defendants claimed that Mr Graham and members of his family who subsequently occupied the land had acquired possessory title as a result of 12 years' adverse possession. That defence succeeded at first instance. Neuberger J concluded that from 1984 onwards the Grahams had enjoyed factual possession and had the necessary intention, despite their willingness to renew the agreement. Pye's appeal succeeded before the Court of Appeal, but the executors' appeal was allowed by the House of Lords (*JA Pye (Oxford) Ltd v Graham* [2002] UKHL 30; [2003] 1 AC 419) which held that Mr Graham and his successors had obtained possessory title by adverse possession. Pye applied to the ECtHR, claiming that there was a breach of article 1 of the First Protocol.

A Chamber of the Fourth Section found by a narrow majority that there was a breach, but the Grand Chamber, also by a majority, found that there was no breach. The Grand Chamber noted that article 1 of the First Protocol 'protects 'possessions', which can be either 'existing possessions' or assets, including claims, in respect of which the applicant can argue that he or she has at least a 'legitimate expectation' of obtaining effective enjoyment of a property right. It does not, however, guarantee the right to acquire property.'

It stated that article 1

> ... contains three distinct rules: 'the first rule, set out in the first sentence of the first paragraph, is of a general nature and enunciates the principle of the peaceful enjoyment of property; the second rule, contained in the second sentence of the first paragraph, covers deprivation of possessions and subjects it to certain conditions; the third rule, stated in the second paragraph, recognises that the Contracting States are entitled, amongst other things, to control the use of property in accordance with the general interest ... The three rules are not, however, 'distinct' in the sense of being unconnected. The second and third rules are concerned with particular instances of interference with the right to peaceful enjoyment of property and should therefore be construed in the light of the general principle enunciated in the first rule'

The court continued:

> Any 'interference with the right to the peaceful enjoyment of possessions must strike a 'fair balance' between the demands of the general interest of the community and the requirements of the protection of the individual's fundamental rights ... A taking of property under the second sentence of the first paragraph of Article 1 without payment of an amount reasonably related to its value will normally constitute a disproportionate interference that cannot be justified under Article 1 ... [However,] States enjoy a wide margin of appreciation with regard both to choosing the means of enforcement and to ascertaining whether the consequences of enforcement are justified in the general interest for the purpose of achieving the object of the law in question.

In this case, Pye 'was affected, not by a 'deprivation of possessions' within the meaning of the second sentence of the first paragraph of article 1, but rather by a 'control of use' of land within the meaning of the second paragraph of the provision.' Furthermore, the existence of a 12-year limitation period for actions for recovery of land as such pursued a legitimate aim in the general interest. There is a general interest in both the limitation period itself and the extinguishment of title at the end of the period.

Turning to the lack of compensation, the court stated that case-law on compensation for deprivation of possessions was not directly applicable to a control of use case. It accepted the government's contention that a requirement of compensation for the situation brought about by a party failing to observe a limitation period would sit uneasily alongside the very concept of limitation periods.

The court concluded that the fair balance required by article 1 was not upset in the present case.

A5.9   *Kirilova v Bulgaria*

Applications nos 42908/98, 44038/98, 44816/98 and 7319/02; 14 June 2007

Damages for failure to compensate applicants for expropriated properties

The applicants' properties were expropriated by the state between 1983 and 1990. For many years after 1992, the date when the ECHR and the First Protocol came into force in Bulgaria, the authorities failed to deliver the flats which were due to the applicants in compensation for the expropriated properties. Indeed, they actively resisted endeavours to compel them to comply with their obligations. Although some of the applicants were settled in municipal housing, the ECtHR took the view that this was not sufficient to mitigate those facts.

The ECtHR concluded that there was a breach of article 1 of the First Protocol because the uncertainty facing the applicants for many years, coupled with the lack of effective domestic remedies, caused them to bear a special and excessive burden which upset the fair balance which has to be struck between the demands of the public interest and the protection of the right to peaceful enjoyment of possessions. The court held that the pecuniary damage sustained by the applicants comprised, first, the value of the flats which had still not been delivered. As regards the damage stemming from the continuing failure of the authorities to deliver the flats, the best way to wipe out the consequences of the breach of article 1 of the First Protocol was for the state to deliver the flats, or equivalent flats. However, as states are free to choose the means whereby they comply with its judgments, the ECtHR ruled that, if Bulgaria did not make such delivery within three months, it should pay the applicants a sum corresponding to the current value of the flats. Second, pecuniary damage included the impossibility of using and enjoying the flats before their delivery. The applicants proposed that this head of damage should be assessed by estimating, on the basis of experts' reports, the rent which they could have obtained if they had leased the flats out, plus compound interest. The court accepted that this approach was reasonable, but only on the assumption that the applicants would have indeed been able to lease out the flats due to them. In fact, most of the applicants would have lived in the flats themselves. Accordingly, in the absence of proof that the applicants could indeed have leased their flats out, the damage sustained by them was the expense incurred for finding alternative accommodation. However, the court found that the applicants had suffered a loss of opportunity because they were unable to use and enjoy the flats due to them for long periods of time. It awarded pecuniary damages ranging from €4,000 to €9,000. The court also awarded non-pecuniary damages of €2,000 to each applicant,

> arising from the feeling of helplessness and frustration in the face, firstly, of the prolonged failure of the authorities to deliver the flats to which they were entitled and, secondly, of the authorities' marked reluctance to solve their problem for such a long time. Some of the applicants were further distressed by the need to live in worse conditions, in the municipal housing where they were lodged. ... [Two applicants] must have been disgruntled by the years of fruitless judicial proceedings whereby they tried to remedy the situation they were in.

A5.10   *Kletsova v Russia*

Application no 24842/04; 12 April 2007 (see A2.2)

Judgment against state to be satisfied without necessity of enforcement proceedings

A5.11   *Kunic v Croatia*

Application no 22344/02; 11 January 2007

Length of proceedings to recover property excessive; Inordinate delay interfered with peaceful enjoyment of possessions

Mr Kunic and his family lived in a property in Krnjak, comprising a house and restaurant. The owner was his father, who died in 1992. In January 1999 Mr Kunic was declared his legal heir. In August 1995 the Kunic family left for Bosnia and Herzegovina. In September 1995 the Temporary Takeover and Managing of Certain Property Act ('the Takeover Act') became law. It provided that property situated in the previously occupied territories and belonging to persons who had left Croatia was to be taken into the care of and controlled by the state. It also authorised local authorities (takeover commissions) to entrust such property for temporary use by third persons. In 1996, the Takeover Commission entitled VP to use the property temporarily, with a view to running the restaurant. In 1997 and 1998 Mr Kunic requested repossession of the property. The Takeover Commission replied that it had made no decision and had no competence to decide the request. In August 1998 the Act on Termination of the Takeover Act became law. It provided that those persons whose property had, during their absence from Croatia, been given for accommodation of others had to apply for repossession of their property with the competent local authorities. Mr Kunic immediately made such an application. In October 1999 the Housing Commission set aside the Takeover Commission's 1996 decision. VP appealed. In February 2001 his appeal was dismissed and VP was ordered to vacate the house. He did not do so, and in March 2001 the Housing Commission brought an action in the Karlovac Municipal Court seeking his eviction. In February 2002 the court gave judgment accepting the Housing Commission's claim and ordering VP to vacate the premises. In March 2002 VP appealed. In March 2003 the Karlovac County Court dismissed the appeal and upheld the first-instance judgment, which thereby became final. In March 2003 VP lodged an appeal on points of law. It was declared inadmissible but in May 2003 VP brought the issue of the admissibility of his appeal on points of law to the Supreme Court. By the time of judgment in the ECtHR, it appeared that the Supreme Court had not given its decision. However, in December 2003 the bailiff evicted VP and Mr Kunic repossessed his property. Mr Kunic applied to the ECtHR alleging breaches of article 6.1 and article 1 of the First Protocol.

The ECtHR noted that the execution of a judgment must be regarded as an integral part of the 'hearing' for the purposes of article 6 (*Hornsby v Greece* 19 March 1997). It also reiterated that the reasonableness of the length of proceedings must be assessed with reference to the complexity of the case, the conduct of the applicant and the relevant authorities and what was at stake for the applicant in the dispute (*Cocchiarella v Italy* Application no 64886/01; and *Frydlender v France* Application no 30979/96). It noted that it took more than six years for the domestic authorities to give and enforce a final decision in a case of undeniable importance for Mr Kunic, which was of no particular complexity. It held that the length of the proceedings was excessive and failed to meet the 'reasonable time' requirement. There was accordingly a breach of article 6.1. With regards article 1 of the First Protocol, there was indisputably an interference with Mr Kunic's right to property as his house was allocated for use to another person and he was unable to use it for a prolonged period of time. However, he was not deprived of his title, and so the interference complained of constituted a control of use of property within the meaning of second paragraph of article 1 of the First Protocol. In the court's view, the inordinate length of proceedings also had a direct impact on Mr Kunic's right to peaceful enjoyment of his possessions for over six years. That delay imposed an excessive individual burden on Mr Kunic and therefore upset the fair balance that had to be struck between his right to peaceful enjoyment of his possessions and the general interest involved. There was accordingly a breach of article 1 of the First Protocol. The ECtHR awarded €16,000 on account of loss of rent and €2,500 for non-pecuniary damage.

A5.12 **Larkos v Cyprus**

(1999) 7 BHRC 244; [1998] EHRLR 653 (see A4.4)

Disapplication of security of tenure provisions to lettings by state discriminatory

A5.13 **Malinovskiy v Russia**

Application no 41302/02; 7 July 2005

Non-enforcement of order to be granted tenancy in breach of art 6; claim to a social tenancy sufficiently established to constitute a 'possession' under art 1 First Protocol

The Russian Law on Social Protection of Citizens Exposed to Radiation as a Result of the Chernobyl Nuclear Power Station Explosion provided that disabled victims of the Chernobyl explosion were to be granted social housing within three months of submitting an appropriate application. The RSFSR Housing Code provided that Russian citizens were entitled to possess flats owned by the state or municipal authorities or other public bodies, and that certain 'protected' categories of individuals (disabled persons, war veterans, Chernobyl victims, police officers, judges etc.) had a right to priority treatment in the allocation of flats. In 1986, Mr Malinovskiy was engaged in emergency operations at the site of the Chernobyl nuclear plant disaster. In 1999, he applied for free accommodation from the state. His entitlement was linked to the category of disability assigned to him due to deterioration of his health. Mr Malinovskiy's housing conditions were recognised as substandard and he was placed on a waiting list. In 2001, he brought proceedings against the Belgorod Regional Administration to challenge its failure to make accommodation available to him within three months after placing him on a waiting list. In December 2001, the Starooskolskiy Town Court ruled in his favour and ordered the Belgorod Regional Administration to provide him with a flat 'in accordance with the applicable standard conditions and in accordance with the order of precedence on the waiting list'. Enforcement proceedings were instituted in February 2002. In December 2002 the Oktyabrskiy District Court examined Mr Malinovskiy's complaint about the failure of the bailiffs' service to enforce the 2001 judgment. It found no fault on the part of the service because the judgment had not set a time limit for enforcement. In July 2003, the Presidium of the Belgorod Regional Court conducted supervisory review of the judgment. It held that the statutory time limit of three months was applicable and not amenable to further extensions. It removed the condition that the flat was to be provided in accordance with the order of precedence on the waiting list and upheld the remainder of the judgment. In March 2004 Mr Malinovskiy was still waiting for accommodation. He went on a hunger strike to protest against the poor social protection of the Chernobyl victims. In July 2004 he received an occupancy voucher from the mayor in respect of a satisfactory flat. Mr Malinovskiy complained that the prolonged non-enforcement of the December 2001 judgment violated his 'right to a court' under ECHR article 6 and his right to the peaceful enjoyment of possessions as guaranteed in article 1 of the First Protocol.

The ECtHR stated that it was clear that, at least after the decision in July 2003, the authorities had no legitimate ground to delay enforcement proceedings for more than three months. Nevertheless, between July 2003 and July 2004 no steps were taken to enforce the award. Article 6(1) rights

> ... would be illusory if a Contracting State's domestic legal system allowed a final, binding judicial decision to remain inoperative to the detriment of one party. It would be inconceivable that Article 6(1) should describe in detail the procedural guarantees afforded to litigants – proceedings that are fair, public and expeditious – without protecting the implementation of judicial decisions; to construe Article 6 as being concerned exclusively with access to a court and the conduct of proceedings would be likely to lead to situations incompatible with the principle of the rule of law which the Contracting States undertook to respect when they ratified the Convention. Execution of a judgment given by any court must therefore be regarded as an integral part of the 'trial' for the purposes of Article 6.

Furthermore,

> it is not open to a State authority to cite the lack of funds or other resources as an excuse for not honouring a court award. Admittedly, a delay in the execution of a judgment may be justified in particular circumstances, but the delay may not be such as to impair the essence of the right protected under Article 6(1). The applicant should not be prevented from benefiting from the success of the litigation on the ground of alleged financial difficulties experienced by the State.

In this case, the Russian government did not advance any justification for the failure to enforce the order, other than a generic reference to budgetary constraints. By failing, for a substantial period of time, to take the necessary measures to comply with the final judicial decisions, the state authorities deprived the provisions of article 6(1) of their useful effect.

With regards article 1 of the First Protocol, the ECtHR noted that:

the right to any social benefit is not included as such among the rights and freedoms guaranteed by the Convention [and] that a right to live in a particular property not owned by the applicant does not as such constitute a 'possession' within the meaning of Article 1 of Protocol 1 ... However, pecuniary assets, such as debts, by virtue of which the applicant can claim to have at least a 'legitimate expectation' of obtaining effective enjoyment of a particular pecuniary asset ... may also fall within the notion of 'possessions' contained in Article 1 of Protocol No 1. In particular, the Court has consistently held that a 'claim' — even concerning a particular social benefit — can constitute a 'possession' within the meaning of Article 1 of Protocol No 1 if it is sufficiently established to be enforceable.

In this case, from the time of the judgments in December 2001 and July 2003, Mr Malinovskiy had

established [a] 'legitimate expectation' to acquire a pecuniary asset ... [and therefore his] claim to a 'social tenancy agreement' was sufficiently established to constitute a 'possession' falling within the ambit of Article 1 of Protocol No 1.

The ECtHR awarded €3,000 in respect of non-pecuniary damage for the breaches of article 6 and article 1 of the First Protocol.

A5.14 *Mellacher v Austria*
(1989) 12 EHRR 391

Rent restrictions not disproportionate and within state's margin of appreciation

The applicants were property owners who complained about the reduction of rent under tenancy agreements imposed under the 1981 Austrian Rent Act (Mietrechtsgesetz). They let a two-room apartment in September 1978 at a freely negotiated rent of 1,870 Austrian schillings per month. The tenant applied to the Graz Arbitration Board which reduced the rent to 330 schillings per month because, under section 16(2) of the 1981 Austrian Rent Act, the monthly rent for the type of apartment could not exceed 5.50 schillings per square metre. The applicants appealed unsuccessfully, claiming that the rent restrictions were unconstitutional and then applied to the ECtHR claiming that the Act violated article 1 of the First Protocol (protection of property) and article 14 (discrimination).

The ECtHR found that there was no violation of the Convention.

1) It was not disputed that the reductions made pursuant to the 1981 Austrian Rent Act constituted an interference with the enjoyment of the applicants' rights as owners of the rented properties. However, the court found that the measures taken did not amount either to a formal or to a de facto expropriation within the meaning of the first paragraph of article 1 of the First Protocol. There was no transfer of the applicants' property nor were they deprived of their right to use, let or sell it. The measures which, admittedly, deprived them of part of their income from the property, amounted in the circumstances merely to a control of the use of property.

2) In relation to the second paragraph, the court stated:

The second paragraph [allows] States the right to enact such laws as they deem necessary to control the use of property in accordance with the general interest.

Such laws are especially called for and usual in the field of housing, which in our modern societies is a central concern of social and economic policies.

In order to implement such policies, the legislature must have a wide margin of appreciation both with regard to the existence of a problem of public concern warranting measures of control and as to the choice of the detailed rules for the implementation of such measures. The Court will respect the legislature's judgment as to what is in the general interest unless that judgment be manifestly without reasonable foundation.

The ECtHR therefore considered the aim of the interference. It found that the 1981 Austrian Rent Act was intended to reduce excessive and unjustified disparities between rents for equivalent apartments, to combat property speculation and to make accommodation more easily available at reasonable prices to less affluent members of the population, while at the same time providing incentives for the improvement of substandard properties. Those aims were 'not such as could be characterised as being manifestly unreasonable'. The court, accordingly, accepted that the 1981 Rent Act had a legitimate aim in the general interest.

3) There must be a reasonable relationship of proportionality between the means employed and the aim pursued. States must strike a 'fair balance' between the demands of the general interest of the community and the requirements of the protection of the individual's fundamental rights.' The ECtHR found that the 1981 Austrian Rent Act was not 'so inappropriate or disproportionate as to take them outside the state's margin of appreciation.'

4) There was no violation of ECHR article 14.

A5.15 *Palumbo v Italy*
Unreported, 9 November 2000 (see A2.5)

Excessive delay in enforcement of possession order such that wrong balance had been struck between competing interests of property owners and the public interest under art 1 First Protocol

A5.16 *R (Boyle) and Others v Northern Ireland Housing Executive*
[2005] NI QB 22; 16 March 2005, High Court of Justice in Northern Ireland, Queen's Bench Division

Requirement for private HMO landlords to prevent ASB breached art 1 of First Protocol

The claimants were private landlords. They sought judicial review of the scheme of registration of houses in multiple occupation introduced by the Housing (Northern Ireland) Order 2003. In particular they contended that clause 10.4 of the scheme, which imposed as a condition of registration that the person in control of the house should take 'reasonably practicable' steps to prevent anti-social behaviour by committed in the area by residents of the house infringed the owner's rights under article 1 of the First Protocol.

Girvan J allowed the application. He held that the scheme, and the Fees Order made pursuant to it, unlawfully infringed the owners' convention rights. Those responsible for formulating the scheme ought to have had, and had not had, regard to the owners' rights under article 1 of the First Protocol. In relation to the detail of the scheme, the control provision in clause 10.4 was 'so vague and lacking in defined scope that it would in any event fall foul of the principles of legal certainty required under Convention law'.

A5.17   *Radanovic v Croatia*
Application no 9056/02; 21 December 2006

Right balance not struck by state where applicant's home taken over and used by others for an excessive period

Mrs Radanovic was the owner of a flat in Karlovac. She lived there until October 1991, when she left to join her son in Germany. In September 1995, the Temporary Takeover and Managing of Certain Property Act became law. It provided that property belonging to persons who had left Croatia after October 1990 was to be taken into the care of, and controlled, by the state. It also authorised local authorities temporarily to accommodate other persons in such property. In September 1996, Mrs Radanovic brought a civil action in the Karlovac Municipal Court against people who were occupying her flat, seeking their eviction. In August 1998 the Act on Termination of the Takeover Act became law. It provided that those persons, whose property had during their absence from Croatia been given for accommodation of others, had to apply for repossession of their property with the competent local authorities – the housing commissions. In March 2000, the Municipal Court declared Mrs Radanovic's action inadmissible for lack of jurisdiction, finding that instead of bringing a civil action, she should have applied for repossession of her property to the competent housing commission, as provided by the Termination Act. In October 2000, the Housing Commission set aside the Takeover Commission's decision to allow other people the right to use the applicant's property and ordered them to vacate. In June 2001, the Housing Commission issued a warrant ordering the occupants to vacate the flat within 15 days, but then took no action against them. In December 2003 the occupants delivered the flat to the Ministry and Mrs Radanovic repossessed it in January 2004. However, she found that it had been looted and rendered uninhabitable.

The ECtHR found that there had indisputably been an interference with Mrs Radanovic's right to property as her flat was allocated for use to another person and she was unable to use it for a prolonged period of time. It further noted that she was not deprived of her title and so the interference complained of constituted a control of use of property within the meaning of article 1 of the First Protocol, para 2. Assuming that the interference complained of was lawful and in the general interest, the court had to consider whether it struck the requisite fair balance between the demands of the general interest of the public and the requirements of the protection of the individual's fundamental rights, and whether it imposed a disproportionate and excessive burden on the applicant. The court recognised that the Croatian authorities faced an exceptionally difficult task in having to balance the rights of owners against those of temporary occupants in the context of the return of refugees and displaced persons, as this involved dealing with socially sensitive issues. Those authorities had to secure the protection of property and social rights. The court therefore accepted that a wide margin of appreciation should be accorded to the state. However, in this case Mrs Radanovic was forced to bear the burden of providing the temporary occupant with a place to stay for more than six years. This burden should have been borne by the state. Notwithstanding the state's margin of appreciation, the court considered that the Croatian authorities failed to strike the requisite fair balance between the general interest of the community and the protection of Mrs Radanovic's right to property. As a result, she had to bear an excessive individual burden. The interference with her right to property could not be considered proportionate to the legitimate aim pursued. There was accordingly a breach of article 1 of the First Protocol. The court also concluded that Mrs Radanovic had no effective remedy for the protection of her ECHR right to property and that there had been a breach of article 13. The court awarded €6,000 on account of the loss of rent and €2,500 in respect of non-pecuniary damage.

A5.18   *Scollo v Italy*
[1996] 22 EHRR 514

Failure to evict applicant's tenant following court order a breach of art 1 of First Protocol

A magistrate confirmed a notice to quit and set a date for eviction – 30 June 1984. The bailiff made 27 unsuccessful visits to evict the tenant. Various temporary laws suspending evictions were passed. The prefectorial committee failed to give priority to the eviction despite the fact that the tenant stopped paying rent and the landlord was diabetic/71% disabled. Possession was eventually recovered on 15 January 1995.

The ECtHR held that the temporary laws suspending evictions were not a breach of article 1 of the First Protocol. They provided neither for a transfer of property nor a de facto appropriation. They amounted to a control of property, but that was in the general interest. However, the restriction on the owner's use of the flat resulting from the authorities' failure to apply the law (ie, to give priority) was a breach of article 1 of the First Protocol.

A5.19   *Spadea and Scalabino v Italy*
(1995) 21 EHRR 482

Italian laws controlling use of property (delaying possession orders) legitimate

Italian laws staggering or delaying the operation of possession orders do not breach article 1 of the First Protocol. The ECtHR said:

> The second paragraph reserves to States the right to enact such laws as they deem necessary to control the use of property in accordance with the general interest.
>
> Such laws are especially common in the field of housing, which in our modern societies is a central concern of social and economic policies.
>
> In order to implement such policies, the legislature must have a wide margin of appreciation ... The Court will respect the legislature's judgment as to what is in the general interest unless that judgment is manifestly without reasonable foundation. ... an interference must strike a fair balance between the demands of the general interest of the community and the requirements of the protection of the individual's fundamental rights.

... There must be a reasonable relationship of proportionality between the means employed and the aim pursued.'

A5.20   ## Spath Holme Ltd v UK
Application no 78031/01

Order restricting increase in fair rents not disproportionate

The applicants were freehold owners of a block of flats which included 12 Rent Act regulated tenancies. They sought judicial review of the Rent Acts (Maximum Fair Rent) Order 1999 SI No 6 ('the Order') which capped increases in fair rents to a level between 5% and 7.5% above inflation. The House of Lords (on appeal) dismissed the application (*R v Secretary of State for the Environment, Transport and Regions ex p Spath Holme Ltd* [2001] 2 WLR 15).

The ECtHR decided that Spath Holme's complaint that the Order breached their ECHR rights was inadmissible. There was no breach of article 1 of the First Protocol (peaceful enjoyment of possessions). The Order did not amount to a formal or de facto appropriation. Although it did deprive the applicant of part of its income from its property and so constituted a 'control of use' it was provided by law and represented 'a legitimate aim of social policy, the regulation of which cannot entirely be left to the play of market forces.' Bearing in mind the wide margin of appreciation afforded to states in determining the existence of social problems, and ways for remedying them, the effects of the Order were in no way disproportionate. (See *Mellacher v Austria* (A5.14) and *James v UK* [1988] ECtHR (Commission) Application no 10622/83; 15 December 1988.) There was no breach of articles 6 (right to a fair hearing), 13 (effective remedy) or 14 (discrimination).

A5.21   ## Teteriny v Russia
Application no 11931/03; 30 June 2005

Unenforced judgment violated art 6; claim to social tenancy agreement sufficiently established to constitute a 'possession' under art 1 of First Protocol

In Russia, judges are eligible for state housing. Mr and Mrs Teteriny, although born in 1954 and 1955, were both retired judges. In September 1994 the Ezhvinskiy District Court ordered the town council to '... grant or purchase for Mr Teterin, whose family comprises five members, a separate well-equipped flat or house taking account of the plaintiff's entitlement to one additional room or having a habitable surface of no less than 65 square metres, located near the Knyazhpogostskiy District Court in the town of Yemva'. In October 1994, enforcement proceedings were instituted. However, the judgment could not be enforced because the town authorities did not possess any available housing or the financial resources to purchase a flat. Mr and Mrs Teteriny complained to the Courts Administration Department at the Supreme Court of the Russian Federation, the Court Bailiffs' Department of the Ministry of Justice of the Russian Federation and the Court Bailiffs' Department of the Komi Republic Department of Justice. The responses received by the applicants in 2001 and 2002 indicated that the judgment could not be enforced as the town authorities had no available housing. Further attempts at enforcement were unsuccessful. In January

2004, the Yemva Town Council offered Mr Teterin a two-room flat of 25 square metres with central heating. He did not accept the offer. Mr and Mrs Teteriny complained that the continued failure to enforce the 1994 judgment violated their 'right to a court' under article 6 and their right to the peaceful enjoyment of possessions under article 1 of the First Protocol.

The ECtHR decided that the 1994 judgment did not determine Mrs Teterin's civil rights and obligations and did not confer any entitlement on her. Accordingly, her complaints were incompatible ratione personae with the provisions of the ECHR. With regards Mr Teterin's claim, the court repeated that article 6 rights would be illusory if a contracting state's domestic legal system allowed a final, binding judicial decision to remain inoperative to the detriment of one party and that it was not open to a state authority to cite the lack of funds or other resources (such as housing) as an excuse for not honouring a judgment debt. It noted that the judgment remained unenforced in its entirety. The offer made by the Yemva Town Council in 2004 did not meet the terms of that judgment. By failing for years to take the necessary measures to comply with a final judicial decision, the Russian authorities deprived the provisions of article 6(1) of all useful effect. There was, accordingly, a violation of article 6. With regards article 1 of the First Protocol, the ECtHR noted that pecuniary assets, such as debts, to which an applicant can claim to have at least a 'legitimate expectation' of obtaining effective enjoyment, may fall within the notion of 'possessions' contained in article 1 of the First Protocol. A 'claim' – even to a particular social benefit – can constitute a 'possession' within the meaning of article 1 of the First Protocol if it is sufficiently established to be enforceable. In this case, the judgment did not require the authorities to give Mr Teterin ownership of a particular flat, but rather obliged them to issue him with an occupancy voucher in respect of any flat satisfying the court-defined criteria. On the basis of the voucher, a 'social tenancy agreement' would have been signed between the competent authority and Mr Teterin. Under the terms of a 'social tenancy agreement', as established in the RSFSR Housing Code, he would have had a right to possess and make use of the flat and, under certain conditions, to privatise it in accordance with the Privatisation of State Housing Act. From the moment the September 1994 judgment was issued, he had an established 'legitimate expectation' to acquire a pecuniary asset. As a result, his claim to a 'social tenancy agreement' was sufficiently established to constitute a 'possession' falling within the ambit of article 1 of the First Protocol. The fact that it was impossible to obtain the execution of the judgment for more than ten years constituted an interference with his right to peaceful enjoyment of his possessions. Accordingly, there was a violation of article 1 of the First Protocol. The ECtHR held that the Government should secure, within three months, by appropriate means, the enforcement of the award made by the domestic courts. It also awarded Mr Teterin €3,000 in respect of non-pecuniary damage.

A5.22 *Tuleshov v Russia*

Application no 32718/02; 24 May 2007

Compensation terms for loss of home did not strike fair balance required by art 1 of First Protocol; delay in providing applicant alternative accommodation a breach of art 8

Following a commercial dispute between a company and a third party, the Marx Town Court ordered the sale of a house. In 1996, the sale was administered by the court bailiff. Mr Tuleshov offered to buy the house for the equivalent of approximately US$2,800. The court approved the sale. Mr Tuleshov and his family moved in and renovated the property. However, neither the court nor Mr Tuleshov was aware that the company had previously sold the property to Mr Kh. In 1999 the Marx Town Court found that the bailiff had sold the house to Mr Tuleshov unlawfully and declared the sale null and void. In 2003, Mr Tuleshov and his family were granted social housing in a municipal hostel. Mr Tuleshov brought claims for compensation against Mr Kh, the Ministry of Finance, the Ministry of Justice and the Judicial Administration Department, but was only awarded a small part of his losses because he 'had not made sufficient effort to recover the debt' from the company. Mr Tuleshov and his family complained that there had been a breach of article 1 of the First Protocol and article 8.

The ECtHR reiterated that an interference with the peaceful enjoyment of possessions must strike a 'fair balance' between the demands of the public, or general interest of the community, and the requirements of the protection of the individual's fundamental rights. Compensation terms under the relevant legislation are material to the assessment of whether the contested measure respects the requisite fair balance, and notably, whether it does not impose a disproportionate burden. The court concluded that the failure to pay adequate compensation imposed on the Tuleshovs an individual and excessive burden and upset the fair balance between the demands of the public interest on the one hand and their right to the peaceful enjoyment of their possessions on the other. Accordingly there had been a violation of article 1 of the First Protocol. Turning to article 8, the ECtHR accepted that the statutory provision which resulted in the family's eviction was lawful in domestic terms and in the pursuit of the 'public interest' – ie, protecting the rights of the lawful owner. However, the accommodation in the municipal hostel was offered more than two years after the eviction order and the possibility of private rental or purchase of accommodation was limited because the compensation awarded was insufficient. Accordingly, the interference with the Tuleshovs' right to respect for their home was disproportionate to the legitimate aim pursued and there had been a violation of article 8. The ECtHR awarded the Tuleshovs jointly €18,350 for any pecuniary damage they sustained as a result of the loss of their house and their eviction and €20,000 in respect of non-pecuniary damage.

A5.23 ## Velikovi v Bulgaria
Applications nos 43278/98, 45437/99, 48014/99, 48380/99, 51362/99, 53367/99, 60036/00, 73465/01 and 194/02; 15 March 2007

Law restoring property expropriated during communist regime in public interest; failure to compensate persons who thus lost their property after acquiring it in good faith not proportionate

In 1968 the Velikovi family jointly bought an apartment from the Sofia municipality. The apartment had been nationalised in 1949. In 1993, the heirs of the pre-nationalisation owner brought an action against the Velikovi family under the Restitution Law. In 1995 the Sofia District Court declared the 1968 contract null and void because it had not been signed by the relevant official – the mayor of the district. The family unsuccessfully requested the Sofia municipality to provide them with municipal apartments at fixed rental rates. Later, some of the sons were given compensation in the form of bonds under the Compensation Law. Complaints were brought by the Velikovi family and others in a similar situation, relying on article 1 of the First Protocol.

The ECtHR found that there was a deprivation of property within the meaning of the second sentence of article 1 of the First Protocol. It accepted that the interference with the applicants' property rights was provided for by Bulgarian law. On whether it pursued a legitimate aim, the court reiterated that, because of their direct knowledge of their society and its needs, the national authorities are in principle better placed than international judges to appreciate what is 'in the public interest'. There was no doubt that the Restitution Law, which provided that the state should restore property it had expropriated during the communist regime without compensation, pursued an important aim in the public interest. The approach of authorising persons whose property had been expropriated by the state in the 1940s without compensation to claim it back not only from the state but also from private individuals, whenever the latter's title had been tainted by abuse of power or breaches of the law, could not be considered illegitimate or not in the public interest. However, legislation should make it possible to take into account the particular circumstances of each case, so that persons who acquired their possessions in good faith are not made to bear the burden of responsibility which is rightfully that of the state which once confiscated those possessions. The issue of proportionality should be decided having regard to whether the factual and legal basis of the case falls clearly within the legitimate aims of the Restitution Law, and the hardship suffered and the adequacy of the compensation obtained. After examining individual cases, the court found violations of article 1 of the First Protocol in four cases and that there was no violation in five other cases.

A5.24   *Velosa Barretto v Portugal*
[1996] EHRLR 212 (see A3.16)

Restriction on private landlord's right to possession pursued legitimate aim

A5.25   *Veselinski v Former Yugoslav Republic of Macedonia*
Application no 45658/99; 24 February 2005

Applicant had legitimate expectation to purchase apartment at reduced price; denial of this violated art 1 First Protocol

Mr Veselinski was an officer in the Yugoslav Army until he retired in 1985. As a soldier, he paid monthly contributions from his salary to the Yugoslav Army for the construction of army apartments. In 1990, the Yugoslav Federal Assembly enacted a Law on Housing of the Army Servicemen which allowed army servicemen, current and retired, to purchase their apartments with a price adjustment for the amount of the monthly contributions which they had paid. In 1992, the Macedonian Ministry of Defence took over all the obligations of the Yugoslav Army for army apartments, including the obligation to sell those apartments with a price reduction. In 1993, a new Macedonian law provided that tenants were entitled to purchase socially owned apartments on credit and at a beneficial price but, unlike the earlier law, it did not provide for a price adjustment for the amount of the monthly contributions previously paid. In 1992, Mr Veselinski asked the Macedonian Ministry of Defence to allow him to purchase his current apartment at a reduced price or to give him another apartment which used to be owned by the former Yugoslav Army. A dispute arose about the terms of his purchase and in 1997 the Supreme Court held that Mr Veselinski had no right to buy at the reduced price. As a result of that decision, he became liable to pay further sums of money.

The ECtHR stated that the concept of 'possessions' in article 1 of the First Protocol has an autonomous meaning. In substance it guarantees the right of property. A 'possession' may be either an 'existing possession' or a claim, in respect of which the applicant can argue that he has at least a 'legitimate expectation' of obtaining effective enjoyment of a property right. The 'legitimate expectation' may also encompass the conditions attaching to the acquisition or enjoyment of property rights. Taking into account Mr Veselinski's previous contributions and the agreements in force at the time, he had a 'legitimate expectation' that the purchase of his apartment would be at a reduced price. The Supreme Court's decision was an unjustified interference with his peaceful enjoyment of his possessions and therefore a violation of article 1 of the First Protocol.

A5.26   *Wood v UK*
(1997) 24 EHRR CD 69 (see A3.17)
Possession order against mortgage borrower did not offend art 1 First Protocol

A6   **Other jurisdictions**

A6.1   *Department of Land Affairs v Goedgelegen Tropical Fruits (Pty) Ltd*
[2007] ZACC 12; 6 June 2007, South African Constitutional Court
Indigenous occupants had a right to land which was dispossessed under racist laws and accordingly had claim for restitution under the post-apartheid Restitution Act

The ancestors of the individual applicants originally settled on land in the 1800s. They enjoyed 'undisturbed indigenous rights to the land and exercised all the rights that came with it', including cultivating it, using it for livestock, enjoying family life, burying their dead and paying spiritual tribute to their ancestors. In 1889, the South African Republic granted the land to white settlers who required the original occupants to render services for a certain period every year in return for being allowed to stay on and use their farms. They were forced into a 'labour tenancy'. In 1969, for 'business purposes', the white owners of the land terminated the labour tenancies, without compensation. The indigenous community was dispossessed of its cropping and grazing rights. Within two years they had to dispose of all livestock.

After a detailed analysis of the social, historical, political and legal background, the Constitutional Court found that the individual claimants were part of a community that had a right to land which was dispossessed after 1913 as a result of past racially discriminatory laws or practices. They accordingly had a claim for restitution under Restitution Act s2. The court granted a declaration to that effect.

A6.2   *Dublin CC v Fennell*
[2005] IESC 33; 12 May 2005, Irish Supreme Court

Irish Human Rights Act did not operate retrospectively

Council tenants in Eire do not enjoy security of tenure. The (Irish) Housing Act 1966 s62 provides that if a local authority tenancy has been terminated and possession demanded, but the occupier fails to give up possession, the court has no discretion and must issue a warrant. On 12 December 2003, after a notice to quit had been served, a judge sitting in a district court made a possession order against Ms Fennell, a former tenant of Dublin City Council. She appealed. On 31 December 2003 the (Irish) European Convention on Human Rights Act 2003 came into operation. It imposed an obligation on courts, when interpreting or applying any statutory provision or rule of law, to do so in a manner compatible with the state's obligations under the European Convention. In her appeal, Ms Fennell argued that the Act operated retrospectively.

The Irish Supreme Court, after considering Irish and British authorities, held that the Act could not be seen as having retrospective effect or as affecting past events and so could not be taken into account when the appeal was heard.

A6.3   *Office public d'habitation de la Ville de Paris v Yedei*
French Cour de Cassation, 6 March 1996 (note available at www.courdecassation.fr – No 534 (regles generales)) (see A3.11)

Anti-sharing clause in tenancy a breach of art 8

A6.4   *Port Elizabeth Municipality v Various Occupiers*
[2004] ZACC 7; 1 October 2004, South African Constitutional Court (www.saflii.org/za/cases/ZACC/2004/7.html)

Competing interests of land owners and occupiers considered under post-apartheid legislation and Bill of Rights; court obliged to consider morality, fairness, social values etc; not just and equitable in circumstances to order eviction of unauthorised occupiers

Sixty-eight people, including 23 children, occupied 29 shacks which they had erected on privately owned land in Port Elizabeth. One thousand, six hundred people, including the owners of the property, petitioned the Port Elizabeth Municipality. As a result, the Municipality sought an eviction order in the South Eastern Cape Local Division of the High Court. The key issue was whether the occupiers could be evicted without the provision of satisfactory alternative accommodation. After various appeals the matter came before the Constitutional Court

In a fascinating judgment, Sachs J reviewed the legal position, initially from a historical perspective. In the pre-democratic era 'once it was determined that the occupiers had no permission to be on the land, they not only faced summary eviction, they were liable for criminal prosecution

... The process was deliberately made as swift as possible: conviction followed by eviction ... For all black people, and for Africans in particular, dispossession was nine-tenths of the law.'

However, the Prevention of Illegal Eviction from and Unlawful Occupation of Land Act 19 of 1998 not only repealed the earlier legislation, but inverted it. Squatting was decriminalised and the eviction process was made subject to a number of requirements. South African courts now 'have to hold the balance between illegal eviction and unlawful occupation'. The Bill of Rights section 25, provides:

> Property
> (1) No one may be deprived of property except in terms of law of general application, and no law may permit arbitrary deprivation of property.

However, section 26 states:

> Housing
> (1) Everyone has the right to have access to adequate housing.
> (2) The state must take reasonable legislative and other measures, within its available resources, to achieve the progressive realisation of this right.
> (3) No one may be evicted from their home, or have their home demolished, without an order of court made after considering all the relevant circumstances. No legislation may permit arbitrary evictions.

Sachs J stated that section 26(3)

> ... evinces special constitutional regard for a person's place of abode. It acknowledges that a home is more than just a shelter from the elements. It is a zone of personal intimacy and family security. Often it will be the only relatively secure space of privacy and tranquillity in what (for poor people in particular) is a turbulent and hostile world. Forced removal is a shock for any family, the more so for one that has established itself on a site that has become its familiar habitat.

He stated that sections 25 and 26 create a broad overlap between land rights and socio-economic rights, emphasising the duty on the state to seek to satisfy both. The courts must maintain a balance between land hunger, homelessness and respect for property rights. The constitution counterposes to the normal ownership rights of possession, use and occupation, a new and equally relevant right not arbitrarily to be deprived of a home:

> The judicial function in these circumstances is not to establish a hierarchical arrangement between the different interests involved, privileging in an abstract and mechanical way the rights of ownership over the right not to be dispossessed of a home, or vice versa. Rather it is to balance out and reconcile the opposed claims in as just a manner as possible taking account of all the interests involved and the specific factors relevant in each particular case.

Turning to the Prevention of Illegal Eviction from and Unlawful Occupation of Land Act, he noted that section 6 (eviction at instance of organ of state) provides that 'An organ of state may institute proceedings for the eviction of an unlawful occupier from land which falls within its area of jurisdiction.' In such cases, the 'court may grant such an order if it is just and equitable to do so ... [and] it is in the public interest to grant such an order.' In deciding whether it is just and equitable to grant an order for eviction,

> the court must have regard to –
> (a) the circumstances under which the unlawful occupier occupied the land and erected the building or structure;
> (b) the period the unlawful occupier and his or her family have resided on the land in question; and
> (c) the availability to the unlawful occupier of suitable alternative accommodation or land.

Considering this section, Sachs J stated that:

> The public interest requires that the legislative framework and general principles which govern the process of housing development should not be undermined and frustrated by the unlawful and arbitrary actions of a relatively small group of people. Thus the well-structured housing policies of a municipality could not be allowed to be endangered by the unlawful intrusion of people at the expense of those inhabitants who may have had equal claims to be housed on the land earmarked for development by the applicant. Municipalities represent all the people in their area and should not seek to curry favour with or bend to the demands of individuals or communities, whether rich or poor. They have to organise and administer their affairs in accordance with the broader interests of all the inhabitants.

He noted that section 6(3) states that the availability of a suitable alternative place to go to is something to which regard must be had, not an inflexible requirement. In general terms, however, a court should be reluctant to grant an eviction against relatively settled occupiers unless it is satisfied that a reasonable alternative is available. There is nothing in section 6 to suggest that the three specifically identified circumstances are intended to be the only ones to which the court may refer in deciding what is just and equitable. They are peremptory but not exhaustive. It is clear both from the open-ended way in which they are framed and from the width of decision-making involved in the concept of what is just and equitable, that the court has a very wide mandate and must give due consideration to all circumstances that might be relevant. This is precisely why, even though unlawfulness is established, the eviction process is not automatic and why the courts are called on to exercise a broad judicial discretion on a case by case basis.

Sachs J approved the analysis of section 6 by Horn J in *Port Elizabeth Municipality v Peoples Dialogue on Land and Shelter* (2002 (2)SA 1074 (SECLD)). He pointed out that, in matters brought under the Prevention of Illegal Eviction from and Unlawful Occupation of Land Act,

> one is dealing with two diametrically opposed fundamental interests. On the one hand there is the traditional real right inherent in ownership reserving exclusive use and protection of property by the landowner.

He held that the statute also implies that a court, when deciding on a matter of this nature, would be obliged to break away from a purely legalistic approach and have regard to extraneous factors such as morality, fairness, social values and implications and circumstances which would necessitate bringing out an equitably principled judgment.

Sachs J stated that 'the judiciary cannot of itself correct all the systemic unfairness to be found in ... society. Yet it can at least soften and minimise the degree of injustice and inequity which the eviction of the weaker parties in conditions of inequality of necessity entails.'

He noted that there had been no effective mediation in this case. Given the special nature of the competing interests involved in eviction proceedings launched under section 6, 'absent special circumstances it would not ordinarily be just and equitable to order eviction if proper discussions, and where appropriate, mediation, have not been attempted'.

He concluded that 'in the light of the lengthy period during which the occupiers have lived on the land in question, the fact that there is no evidence that either the Municipality or the owners of the land need to evict the occupiers in order to put the land to some other productive use, the absence of any significant attempts by the Municipality to listen to and consider the problems of this particular group of occupiers, and the fact that this is a relatively small group of people who appear to be genuinely homeless and in need, I am not persuaded that it is just and equitable to order the eviction of the occupiers'.

A6.5 ## R (Boyle) and Others v Northern Ireland Housing Executive

[2005] NI QB 22; 16 March 2005, High Court of Justice in Northern Ireland, Queen's Bench Division (see A5.16)

Requirement that private HMO landlords prevent ASB breached art 1 First Protocol

A6.6 ## South Africa v Grootboom

[2001] 10 BHRC 84, South African Constitutional Court

Constitutional right 'to have access to adequate housing' did not equate to an absolute right to housing

Residents in a squatter settlement applied for municipal housing but were simply put on waiting lists. Conditions in the settlement were appalling and 390 adults and 510 children moved on to private land that had been earmarked for low cost housing. The owner obtained a possession order. The occupiers were evicted 'prematurely and inhumanely' at the expense of the local authority and their possessions and temporary structures were destroyed. They moved on to a public sports field under such temporary structures as they could muster. When the winter rains set in, the local and state authorities failed to assist and the squatters applied for an urgent High Court order. They relied on Constitution of South Africa s26 which provides:

1) Everyone has the right to have access to adequate housing.
2) The State must take reasonable legislative and other measures, within its available resources, to achieve the progressive realisation of this right.

The High Court granted an order requiring provision of shelter to the children and their parents to include tents, water supplies and latrines. The state authorities, including the central government, appealed.

The Constitutional Court allowed the appeal in part and discharged the injunction. It held that on its true construction section 26 meant that:

1) the state must create the conditions for access to adequate housing for people at all economic levels
2) that obligation was not an absolute or unqualified one
3) if the state had adopted reasonable measures to meet its obligations the courts would not interfere
4) no citizen was entitled to shelter or housing immediately upon demand
5) both positive and negative obligations were cast on the state in terms of access to housing.

The injunction had, accordingly, been wrongly granted but the manner of the evictions had breached section 26(1) and the failure of the state's housing programme to provide temporary shelter for 'those desperately in need of access to housing' was a breach of section 26(2). In reaching these conclusions, the court considered the jurisprudence relating to article 11(1) of the International Covenant on Economic Social and Cultural Rights ('The state parties ... recognise the right of everyone to an adequate standard of living, ... including adequate ... housing').

CHAPTER B

Tenancies and licences at common law

B1   # Creation of tenancies

The three requirements for the creation of a tenancy are:

1   Exclusive possession. This is the right to exclude all other people from the premises.
2   An obligation to pay rent. Rent is most commonly a money payment, but may in some circumstances be payment of some other material thing (eg, a 'peppercorn rent') or even the provision of services.
3   A 'term'. Usually this means that a tenancy must be for either a fixed period (eg, six months) or that rent must be paid on a regular periodic basis (eg, weekly, monthly or quarterly).

Court of Appeal

B1.1   ## Battersea Churches Housing Trust v Hunte
(1997) 29 HLR 346, CA

Invitation to take tenancy merely an invitation to treat; actual tenancy was written agreement later entered into

A couple were invited to take a joint periodic tenancy of a flat. The woman contacted the trust and asked them to let her have instead a tenancy in her sole name with the man simply recorded as an additional occupier. The trust agreed and the written tenancy agreement was drawn up accordingly. The woman subsequently left and the trust claimed possession. The judge found that the trust's earlier offer of joint tenancy had merely been an 'invitation to treat' and rejected the defendant's contention that the trust had offered a joint tenancy which had been accepted by the woman on behalf of them both.

The Court of Appeal dismissed his appeal. The trust had been clear from the outset that the eventual agreement would be a formal written one, so the 'invitation' to take a tenancy was simply an invitation to treat and not an offer. Even if, in the alternative, it was an 'offer', the woman had plainly rejected it by refusing to enter into a joint tenancy agreement and the trust was under no further obligation to let the flat on a joint tenancy.

B1.2   ## Brent LBC v O'Bryan
(1992) 65 P&CR 258; [1993] 1 EGLR 59; [1993] 02 EG 113, CA

Agreement to let on terms to be laid down by valuers did not amount to a tenancy

A letter from a local education authority officer agreeing to the monthly letting of non-residential premises on terms to be laid down by valuers could not be construed as an agreement to grant the occupier a monthly tenancy. The letter was no more than a statement of willingness by the authority to let the premises when the valuer had decided what the rent should be.

B1.3   ## Levy v Vesely
[2007] EWCA Civ 367; 27 April 2007

Payments were to joint household expenses not 'rent'; no tenancy created

Ms Vesely's landlords were trustees of a protective trust set up for a Ms Miller who had mental health problems. Ms Vesely claimed to be an assured tenant. The trustees claimed that she was an assured shorthold tenant. The dispute centred on the date on which Ms Vesely became a tenant of premises owned by the same landlords prior to moving to her present flat, and whether it was before or after 28 February 1997 when the provisions of Housing Act 1996 s96 came into force. In early 1996, Ms Miller, who was in hospital, gave the keys to a flat to Ms Vesely. She moved in, but did not pay any rent. Towards the end of 1996, after being discharged from hospital, Ms Miller began to spend more time in the flat, sharing it with Ms Vesely. In December 1996 the trustees agreed with Ms Vesely that she would make a weekly contribution of £65 to the joint household expenses of the two women. The payments were not intended to be rent. Ms Vesely had exclusive occupation of two rooms and shared the kitchen and bathroom facilities with Ms Miller. In September 1997, the trustees made an agreement with Ms Vesely, regularising her position, whereby she paid a rent. HHJ Faber found that this agreement created an assured shorthold tenancy. Ms Vesely appealed.

The Court of Appeal dismissed her appeal. The evidence showed that during 1996, there was some continuing uncertainty about the future occupation of the flat. There was ample evidence from which HHJ Faber was entitled to conclude that Ms Vesely's exclusive occupation of two rooms at the rear of the flat prior to 28 February 1997 was not as a result of a tenancy granted to her by the trustees and that the arrangement for Ms Vesely to make a weekly contribution to the two women's joint expenditure was not intended by either party to be rent. A rent-free arrangement for the exclusive use and occupation of premises does not create a tenancy, if the correct inference from the purpose of the arrangement and the surrounding circumstances is that there is no intention to create the landlord and tenant relationship between the parties. The judge's finding that the arrangement was for the continued sharing of the expenses of a joint household by two friends made it very difficult, applying an objective test, to infer that there was an intention to grant a tenancy to one of them, the only other occupant neither having, nor being in need of, a tenancy, as she was a beneficiary under the trusts on which the entire flat was held.

B1.4   *Restormel BC v Buscombe*
(1982) 14 HLR 91, CA

Landlord had no subjective intention to create tenancy; no intention inferred from conduct

The local authority determined that Mr and Mrs Buscombe were intentionally homeless. However, in February 1981, pending a court challenge of that decision, it offered them temporary accommodation for a period of six weeks, in accordance with its duty under Housing (Homeless Persons) Act 1977 s4(3) (now Housing Act 1996 s190(2)(a)). In March 1981, the council wrote to Mr Buscombe, stating that the temporary accommodation would terminate on 6 April 1981. On 3 April, the council sent a 'Rent Record Card', specifying a higher rent, although shortly afterwards a housing officer said to Mr Buscombe that this had been sent in error. The council took no steps to evict the family pending the outcome of the court challenge to its decision. In September 1981, the contention that

Mrs Buscombe was not intentionally homeless was rejected in court and about two weeks later, on 28 September, the council wrote requiring the family to vacate the temporary accommodation. In new court proceedings, a possession order was made.

Dismissing the occupants' appeal, the Court of Appeal held that there was ample material on which the trial judge could conclude that there was no subjective intention on the council's part to create a tenancy and that no such intention could be inferred from its conduct. Furthermore, on the expiry of the initial six weeks, there was no grant of a fresh licence which could qualify as a secure tenancy. The licence granted under Housing (Homeless Persons) Act 1977 s4(3) was validly determined by the letter of 28 September, even though it did not expire on 'a rent day', and so the defendants then became trespassers. The fact that the family remained in occupation pending the outcome of the court proceedings did not mean that they acquired a 'secure' licence.

B1.5   *Tower Hamlets LBC v Ayinde*
(1994) 26 HLR 631, CA

Grant of tenancy inferred where council aware that previous tenants had left

In 1984, two joint secure tenants invited the defendant, who was then homeless, to move in and share their council home. Shortly afterwards, the joint tenants left and moved abroad. They wrote to the Greater London Council, which was then the landlord, to say that they would not be returning and that the tenancy should be transferred to the defendant. (The tenancy could not be assigned because none of the conditions of Housing Act 1985 s91(3) could be satisfied.) After ownership of the property had been transferred to Tower Hamlets LBC, a council officer visited the flat and told the defendant and her husband that they did not need other housing and could stay in the flat. Rent was paid. In 1990 the council served notice to quit and brought proceedings for possession.

On appeal against the dismissal of those proceedings, the Court of Appeal affirmed the judge's finding that the letter from the original joint tenants was an offer of surrender. The council had accepted that offer by the grant of a new tenancy to the defendant. Such a grant could be inferred (notwithstanding the absence of any written agreement or rent book in the defendant's name) from the facts that: (a) the council had known since 1986 that the tenants had gone and would not be returning; (b) it had accepted the rent knowing that it was being paid by the defendant; and (c) it had taken no action on the defendant's original application for housing made in 1985. The case was wholly distinguishable from *Westminster CC v Basson* (B1.6). The appeal was dismissed.

B1.6   *Westminster CC v Basson*
(1991) 23 HLR 225; (1990) 62 P&CR 57; [1991] 1 EGLR 277, CA

No tenancy despite rent book (sent in error) as council did not consent to tenancy

The defendant remained in possession of a council flat after the departure of the secure tenants and the termination of the tenancy. The council then wrote to her asking her to leave, describing her as being in 'unlawful occupation' and inviting her to pay 'damages by way of use and occupation charges', pending her departure which would be enforced by possession proceedings if necessary. Over a year later, no action had been taken and she had claimed housing benefit to help meet the weekly charge (permitted by the definition of 'rent' in Housing Benefit (General) Regulations 1987 SI No 1971). One section of the council issued her with a rent book. The occupier then argued that, as she enjoyed exclusive occupation for payment, she had become the secure tenant of the property.

The Court of Appeal held that the initial letter was not consistent with the proposition that the occupation was with the council's consent. Therefore, neither a tenancy nor a licence had been granted and the council was entitled to possession. The events after the initial letter 'merely showed that one department of the council was unaware of what was happening in other departments' ((1991) 23 HLR at 228).

High Court

B1.7 *Hammersmith and Fulham LBC v Jastrzebska*
May 2001 *Legal Action* 22; 20 October 2000, ChD

No tenancy inferred from acceptance of payments where unresolved issue of succession

The defendant lived with a secure tenant. Following the tenant's death on 29 January 1999 the defendant promptly informed the council and claimed to have succeeded to the tenancy. She began to pay the rent. On 24 February 1999 she was sent a standard form letter indicating that she was in occupation without any tenancy or licence and without the council's consent. The council then sought to determine the late tenant's tenancy by notice to quit. The defendant sought to persuade the council that she had succeeded under Housing Act 1985 s87. Her solicitors wrote to the council in August 1999 asserting that she 'is the great-grand-daughter of [the deceased's] mother's sister'. The council's housing department did not accept that she was a 'member of the family' within the meaning of Housing Act 1985 s113. In October 1999 the council's legal department wrote to confirm that it was not accepted that there had been a succession and possession would be sought. HHJ Cotran dismissed the council's possession claim. He held that from February 1999 the defendant had tendered payment for exclusive possession which the council had accepted. Accordingly the defendant enjoyed a tenancy or licence.

Sir Oliver Popplewell (sitting as an additional Chancery Division judge of the High Court) allowed the council's appeal. After reviewing the modern authorities on the implications to be drawn from tender and acceptance of rent in the absence of express grant of a tenancy (*Marcroft Wagons v Smith* (B3.2); *Longrigg, Borough and Trounson v Smith* [1979] 2 EG 42; *Westminster CC v Basson* (B1.6) and *Tower Hamlets LBC v Ayinde* (B1.5), he held that the council's correspondence made plain that in this case no tenancy, licence or consent was to be inferred from the tender and acceptance of payments whilst the issue of succession was resolved. On 21 March 2001 Chadwick LJ refused an application for permission to appeal.

B2   # The distinction between tenancies and licences –
generally

A licensee is someone who merely has permission to be in premises.
In the private sector the distinction between a tenancy and a licence is
crucially important. Licensees cannot have security of tenure under the
Rent Act 1977 or the Housing Act 1988, because those rights are dependent on the existence of a tenancy. Many repairing duties are also dependent on occupants being tenants, not licensees. Similarly, although courts
may intervene to prevent activities which interfere with licensees' use of
premises (see, eg, *Smith v Nottinghamshire CC* (O2.14)), in practice, since
they lack security of tenure, it may be difficult for licensees to prevent
harassment or unlawful eviction.

House of Lords

B2.1   ## Bruton v London and Quadrant Housing Trust
[2000] 1 AC 406; [1999] 3 WLR 150; [1999] 3 All ER 481; (1999) 31 HLR 902; [1999] 30
EG 91; (1999) *Times* 25 June, HL

*Exclusive occupation led to tenancy; character and lack of title of landlord
irrelevant*

Lambeth LBC compulsorily purchased a mansion block. Before the proposed
redevelopment began, the council granted a written licence to London and
Quadrant (L&Q) so that L&Q could give short-term occupancy agreements
to people on its waiting list. Mr Bruton entered into such an agreement with
L&Q, which recited the fact that L&Q 'has the property on licence from
[the council]' and offered it to him 'on a weekly licence'. He subsequently
brought proceedings under Landlord and Tenant Act 1985 s11 for breach of
repairing obligations. HHJ James found that he was a licensee.

The Court of Appeal (by a majority) dismissed Mr Bruton's appeal, but
it was allowed by the House of Lords. The facts that the Housing Trust
was itself only a licensee and that it performed an important social function in providing accommodation for the homeless were not special circumstances that made the grant of exclusive possession something other
than a tenancy. The character of the landlord was irrelevant. The Housing
Trust's lack of title was also irrelevant. The House of Lords upheld *Family
Housing Association v Jones* (B2.11).

B2.2   ## Eastleigh BC v Walsh
[1985] AC 809; [1985] 1 WLR 525; [1985] 2 All ER 112; (1985) 17 HLR 392; (1985) 83
LGR 525, HL)

Tenancy existed where label put on agreement was a tenancy

Mr Walsh and his family were offered temporary accommodation in a
three-bedroomed house while the council made enquiries about their
application for housing under the Housing (Homeless Persons) Act 1977
(now Housing Act 1996 Part VII). The letter offering them the accommodation referred to a 'tenancy ... pending a decision' and they received
the council's standard 'conditions of tenancy'. Mrs Walsh and the children later left the house and the council then notified Mr Walsh that he

had no priority need and required him to leave the house. The council did not serve a notice to quit complying with the Protection from Eviction Act 1977, but took possession proceedings, contending that he was a licensee and that the licence had been terminated. (If a proper notice to quit had been served, Mr Walsh would have had no defence, because his occupation would have been excluded from security by Housing Act 1985 Sch 3 para 5.) Mr Walsh defended, contending that he had a tenancy, not a licence, and that the tenancy had not been terminated by notice to quit.

The House of Lords held that Mr Walsh had a tenancy. He had signed the conditions of tenancy and the documents were unambiguous.

B2.3   *Elitestone Ltd v Morris*
[1997] 1 WLR 687; [1997] 2 All ER 513; (1998) 30 HLR 266; [1997] 2 EGLR 115, HL

Bungalow which could not be removed without being destroyed part of land

The defendants occupied a wooden bungalow which rested on concrete pillars, which were attached to the ground on the plaintiff's land. They occupied under a 'licence agreement', which provided for an annual payment and permitted them to enter on to the land and to 'keep thereon a bungalow and to reside'. The bungalow could not be moved without being demolished. In possession proceedings, the owner claimed that the occupants were merely licensees and not entitled to any statutory security of tenure. An assistant recorder dismissed the plaintiff's claim for possession. The landlord's appeal was allowed by the Court of Appeal but the House of Lords restored the order of the assistant recorder.

The House of Lords held that the question to be asked was whether the bungalow was a chattel or realty. After considering the 'particular facts and circumstances' and having regard to the purpose of the bungalow, the House of Lords held that, when a dwelling is built in such a way that it cannot be removed without being destroyed, it cannot be intended to remain a chattel and must be taken to form part of the realty. The integrity of the bungalow depended on it remaining where it was and that element of permanence pointed to its having acceded to the ground. The claim for possession was dismissed.

B2.4   *Street v Mountford*
[1985] AC 809; [1985] 2 WLR 877; [1985] 2 All ER 289; (1985) 17 HLR 402; (1985) 50 P&CR; [1985] 1 EGLR 128, HL

Agreement for exclusive possession at a rent for a term a tenancy, despite label

Mr Street was the owner of a house divided up into furnished rooms. Mrs Mountford signed a 'licence agreement' giving her the right to occupy two rooms. It was conceded by Mr Street that under the agreement Mrs Mountford was entitled to exclusive possession of those two rooms. The agreement contained ten 'rules' which were to be observed by Mrs Mountford. No one apart from her was to sleep in the rooms. The owner was entitled to enter the rooms to inspect their condition, to empty meters, to carry out repairs, etc. The owner reserved a right of re-entry and was entitled to terminate the agreement on giving 14 days' notice. The agreement also stated that the occupant understood that she did not have protection under the Rent Act 1977.

The House of Lords held that the agreement created a tenancy, not a licence. In the absence of special circumstances, if it is agreed that an occupant should have exclusive possession for a fixed or periodic term in return for paying rent, a tenancy is created, irrespective of how the parties may describe the arrangement. Lord Templeman stated that the key distinction is between tenants on the one hand and lodgers, who are merely licensees, on the other:

> An occupier of residential accommodation at a rent for a term is either a lodger or a tenant. The occupier is a lodger if the landlord provides attendance or services which require the landlord or his servants to exercise unrestricted access to and use of the premises. ([1985] 2 All ER 289 at 293f)

The fact that the parties describe an agreement as 'a licence' cannot turn a tenancy into a licence:

> If the agreement satisfied all the requirements of a tenancy, then the agreement produced a tenancy and the parties cannot alter the effect of the agreement by insisting that they only created a licence. The manufacture of a five-pronged implement for manual digging results in a fork even if the manufacturer, unfamiliar with the English language, insists that he intended to make and has made a spade. (Ibid at 294h)

Exceptions to the basic rule that the grant of exclusive possession for a term in return for the payment of rent creates a tenancy include:

1) Service occupants. 'Where the occupation is necessary for the performance of services, and the occupier is required to reside in the house in order to perform those services, the occupation being strictly ancillary to the performance of the duties which the occupier is to perform, the occupation is that of a servant.' (*Smith v Seghill Overseers* (1875) LR 10 QB 422 at 428);
2) Where there is no intention to create legal relations (eg, *Marcroft Wagons Ltd v Smith* (B3.2) and *Errington v Errington and Woods* (B3.1)); and
3) Other exceptional circumstances which negative the prima facie intention to create a tenancy.

Court of Appeal

B2.5   *Aslan v Murphy (No 1)*
[1990] 1 WLR 766; [1989] 3 All ER 130; (1989) 21 HLR 532; (1990) 59 P&CR 389; [1989] 2 EGLR 57; [1989] 38 EG 109, CA

Requirement for occupier to leave room for 90 minutes each day a sham; no requirement for exclusive possession of keys

Mr Murphy occupied a single room under an agreement which stated that he was a licensee with the right to use the room between midnight and 10.30 am, and noon and midnight. The Court of Appeal held that he was a tenant, not a licensee. The provisions requiring Mr Murphy to leave the room for 90 minutes a day 'were wholly unrealistic and were clearly pretences'. The fact that the landlord retained keys was not decisive:

> Provisions as to keys, if not a pretence, which they often are, do not have any magic in themselves. It is not a requirement of a tenancy that the occupier

shall have exclusive possession of the keys to the property. What matters is what underlies the provisions as to keys. ([1989] 3 All ER at 135)

B2.6   *Brennan v Lambeth LBC*
(1998) 30 HLR 481, CA

Provision enabling residents (homeless applicants) to be moved resulted in licence

The plaintiff applied to the council as a homeless person and was provided with accommodation in a converted house. The house (together with others in the same road) consisted of seven rooms occupied by homeless households and had a kitchen, bathroom and toilet for shared use by the residents. The occupiers were responsible for cleaning their own rooms and council staff cleaned the common parts. The agreement between the occupier and the council was described as a licence and contained the provision: 'We can change the rooms we give you at any time without giving you notice.' The council later refused an application for accommodation as homeless people, gave notice to end the licence, and proposed (without proceedings) to exclude the occupier. He sought an injunction to restrain his eviction. The judge refused that application on the grounds that (a) the occupier enjoyed only a licence rather than a tenancy and (b) no proceedings were necessary to recover possession because the licence of a 'hostel', as defined in Housing Act 1985 s622, was not covered by the Protection from Eviction Act 1977 (see s3A(8)(a)).

The Court of Appeal dismissed the plaintiff's application for leave to appeal. It held that, although the courts must be astute to detect shams, the provision enabling residents to be moved from room to room here served a practical and real purpose (applying *Westminster CC v Clarke* (C2.3)) and the agreement was for a licence, as it purported to be. Since the building did not provide self-contained premises (but merely rooms) and since facilities in a shared kitchen were available for food preparation, it was a 'hostel' within the statutory definition and so the Protection from Eviction Act 1977 did not apply.

B2.7   *Bretherton v Paton*
(1986) 18 HLR 257; [1986] 1 EGLR 172; (1986) 278 EG 615, CA

Prospective purchaser occupied under a tenancy where no binding contract of sale

Ms Paton wished to rent a house from Mr Bretherton. He said that he would not let it, but would sell it to her. They agreed that she would move into the house straight away, carry out repairs so that she could raise a mortgage, and, in the meantime, pay £1.20 per week for insurance and Mr Bretherton's expenses in collecting and paying insurance premiums. It was accepted that this oral agreement gave her exclusive possession. Subsequently, the parties failed to agree a sale price and possession proceedings were instituted.

The Court of Appeal held that Ms Paton had a tenancy. Although the parties intended that the house should be sold, there was no binding contract for its sale since no purchase price had been agreed. The only legally enforceable contract entered into by the parties had given Ms Paton exclusive possession in return for weekly payments of £1.20. The case clearly fell within the three criteria set out in *Street v Mountford* (B2.4).

B2.8   *Brillouet v Landless*

(1996) 28 HLR 836, CA

Hotel resident lacked exclusive occupation and was a licensee

The defendant lived in a room in a hotel. He applied for an injunction to prevent his eviction, arguing that he was a tenant protected by the Housing Act 1988 and the Protection from Eviction Act 1977.

His application was refused and his appeal to the Court of Appeal dismissed. It was held that his lack of exclusive possession and the fact that he had taken advantage of hotel services meant that he was a hotel guest booking accommodation at a daily rate. He was a licensee who did not enjoy statutory protection. His occupation was not in respect of a dwelling for the purposes of Protection from Eviction Act 1977 s3.

B2.9   **Chelsea Yacht and Boat Co Ltd v Pope**

[2000] 1 WLR 1941; [2001] 2 All ER 409; [2000] 22 EG 147; [2001] L&TR 401; (2001) 33 HLR 245; (2000) *Times* 7 June, CA

Houseboat a chattel and occupant a licensee rather than tenant

The claimant sought possession of a houseboat which had been let to the defendant as his home by the original owner since 1993. It was moored by ropes to pontoons on the Thames at Cheyne Walk and was also held by a chain and anchor. It ran aground at low tide for six hours. The claimant provided water, gas, electricity, telephone and vacuum sewage by means of plug-in or snap-on connections. In the county court it was held that the houseboat was a dwelling-house and was subject to an assured tenancy under Housing Act 1988.

The Court of Appeal allowed the claimant's appeal. The houseboat was a chattel and had not become part of the land. It was not capable of being the subject of an assured tenancy under Housing Act 1988. The correct considerations relating to the movability of the chattel, the degree of annexation and the degree of permanence were those set out in *Elitestone Ltd v Morris* (B2.3). The houseboat was not immobile. The fact that it could not move under its own power was not to the point. The tenancy itself had contemplated that the houseboat would be moved. The judge had been wrong to consider that the terms of the tenancy had any relevance when considering the purpose or degree of annexation. On the facts it was difficult to see how the houseboat could have become part of the land. All attachments could be undone without causing any damage to the houseboat or to the land. The defendant had had a contractual licence which had come to an end. Any residual rights which he might have had were effectively dealt with by the notice to quit.

B2.10   *Crancour Ltd v Da Silvaesa*

(1986) 18 HLR 265; [1986] 1 EGLR 80; (1986) 278 EG 618, CA

Terms of 'licence' agreement extreme; defence of 'sham' needed consideration

Summary possession proceedings were brought under RSC Ord 113 against Mr Da Silvaesa and Ms Santos, who had entered into a written agreement with a previous landlord. The agreement was described as a 'licence' and allowed them to use one particular room in a house 'on each day between the hours of midnight and 10.30 am and between noon and midnight but at no other times for a period of 26 weeks from 26 June 1985 for the purpose of temporary accommodation for the licensees' personal use only ...' Other clauses stated that the 'licensor' retained 'possession, management and control' of the room, had an absolute right of entry for the purposes of providing attendances and could remove furniture with no obligation to replace it. He was to provide a housekeeper, window cleaning, cleaning of the room, collection of rubbish and laundered bed linen. Hirst J refused an application for an adjournment by the occupants, concluded that the agreement created a 'lodger-type' licence and made a possession order.

The Court of Appeal, however, remitted the case to the county court for a full trial, stating that the landlord's claim was 'on the evidence not so clear and straightforward that an order for possession should be made in proceedings under Order 113'. Some of the clauses appeared never to have been enforced and 'were astonishingly extreme'. The clause limiting rights of occupation to 22½ hours per day provided a 'foundation for the defence of sham' and was prima facie 'an artificial contrivance intended to mislead'. However, in passing, both Ralph Gibson and Nicholls LJJ agreed that, if the document had represented the real agreement between the parties, on its true construction, the occupants would have been lodgers and not tenants. In distinguishing between tenants and lodgers,

> ... the question to be answered is whether in all the circumstances having regard to the landlord's obligations it is clear that the landlord requires un-restricted access and has reserved the right to exercise such access in order to look after the house and furniture. ((1986) 18 HLR 265 at 273).

(Although the case was remitted to the county court, before it was heard, the landlord made the defendant an offer of alternative accommodation on a protected tenancy.)

B2.11   *Family Housing Association v Jones*
[1990] 1 WLR 779; [1990] 1 All ER 385; (1990) 22 HLR 45; (1990) 60 P&CR 27; [1990] 1 EGLR 82; [1990] 24 EG 118, CA

Self-contained flat provided to homeless applicant resulted in tenancy despite label

A local authority 'licensed' properties to a housing association for the temporary accommodation of homeless persons. In 1985 the association and Mrs Jones entered into an agreement for her and her son to occupy a self-contained flat. The agreement described her as licensee without exclusive possession and the association retained a key.

The Court of Appeal held that, as it was clearly intended that Mrs Jones and her son were to be the only occupants and as she paid a weekly charge, she was a tenant. It 'felt bound to refuse to follow' the earlier Court of Appeal decision in *Ogwr BC v Dykes* [1989] 1 WLR 295, CA, where it had been held that a local authority providing temporary accommodation had granted only a licence.

Note: The decision in *Family Housing Association v Jones* was approved by the House of Lords in *Bruton v London and Quadrant Housing Trust* (B2.1).

B2.12 **Gray v Taylor**

[1998] 1 WLR 1093; [1998] 4 All ER 17, (1999) 31 HLR 262, CA

Occupation of almshouse; beneficiary under a trust was a licensee

The plaintiffs were trustees of the Peterborough Almshouses and Relief in Need charity. The almshouses were to be used for the residence of almspersons being 'poor persons of good character ... not less than 60 years of age'. Mrs Taylor was an almsperson entitled under the trust to occupy a flat in an almshouse. The trustees sought possession after allegations that her behaviour had been vexatious and had disturbed the quiet enjoyment of the almshouse. She defended, claiming that she was an assured tenant because she enjoyed exclusive possession in return for payment of a weekly sum which she paid towards the cost of maintaining the almshouse.

Following *Errington v Errington and Woods* (B3.1), the Court of Appeal held that, as a beneficiary under the trust, Mrs Taylor enjoyed the privilege of occupation of the rooms as a beneficiary only and had no interest in the property. Her occupation was referable to a legal relationship other than one of tenancy and could only be characterised as a licence. It fell outside the general category of cases identified in *Street v Mountford* (B2.4). The weekly sums were not rent and payment of them did not convert her occupation as a beneficiary into occupation as a tenant.

B2.13 **Huwyler v Ruddy**

(1996) 28 HLR 550, CA

Occupant contractually entitled to services a licensee despite services being run down

In 1985 the defendant signed an agreement to occupy a room which stated that the landlord intended to retain legal possession and did not intend to create a tenancy. The rent was £50 per week and included services, laundry and cleaning. The cleaning took about 20 minutes per week and rubbish was cleared. Clean bed linen was provided once a week. In 1988 the defendant moved into another room in the same flat, but this was not recorded by any change in the documentation. Although the landlord retained a key to each room, the 'services were gradually run down'. In the county court, a judge found that the initial arrangement and the services provided meant that the defendant was initially a lodger. He also found that, after moving rooms, the defendant was still entitled to the services and so remained a lodger. A possession order was made.

The Court of Appeal dismissed the defendant's appeal. The judge's approach had been correct. The defendant was initially a licensee. As a matter of construction, the defendant remained contractually entitled to the services and the landlord retained unrestricted access to the room to provide those services.

B2.14 **Nutt v Read**

(2000) 32 HLR 761; (1999) *Times* 3 December, CA

Agreement to buy chalet void for mistake; a tenancy existed

The claimants ran a caravan site which comprised defined plots or pitches which were each occupied by a chalet or caravan. The subject matter of the proceedings was 'The Rest', a chalet made up of large pre-formed parts resting on brick or concrete piers. It had been occupied as a residence since the last war. Mr and Mrs Read agreed to purchase The Rest from Mr and Mrs Nutt for £8,500. They paid £8,000 in part payment and went into occupation. They also signed a standing order form directing their bank to pay £70 per month. In addition Mr and Mrs Read spent about £6,000 in making improvements. Six months later Mr Nutt served a notice to quit. The claimants brought proceedings seeking injunctions to prevent trespass and for the removal of the chalet. HHJ Hull QC found that The Rest was annexed to the land and that accordingly the parties had entered into the common mistake that the chalet was distinct from the land and could be bought and sold separately from it. He also decided that the fee which was paid was for the right to occupy the pitch. He concluded that the sale was void for mistake. Instead Mr and Mrs Read had acquired an assured tenancy by their entry into possession. That tenancy was voidable because of the common mistake. The court had power to grant rescission. He decided that the 'just solution to the problem' was to order rescission.

The defendants appealed claiming that the judge had (1) given insufficient reasons for exercising his discretion in favour of rescission; (2) failed to take into account the facts that the defendants would be homeless and that the claimants would obtain the benefit of the defendants' improvements. The Court of Appeal dismissed the appeal. The judge had been right to find that there were two distinct but inter-linked agreements (one for the sale, the other for the right to station the chalet on the land). He had also been right to conclude that he had power in equity to set aside the second agreement. It was impossible to criticise the exercise of his discretion.

B2.15   ## Skipton Building Society v Clayton
(1993) 25 HLR 596; (1993) 66 P&CR 223, CA

Where reality was that occupiers had exclusive possession a tenancy existed

Mr Clayton and a partner, trading as the Mortgage Advice Centre, bought premises from Mr and Mrs Browne for a third of their value and in return granted the Brownes a rent-free 'licence' for the rest of their lives. The agreement provided that 'possession, management and control of the flat should remain vested' in Mr Clayton and his partner and that at no time were the Brownes to 'enjoy exclusive physical possession of the property as against the licensors'. Subsequently, Mr Clayton and his partner dishonestly obtained a mortgage advance from the building society and defaulted on the repayments. Possession proceedings were brought. The building society accepted that the Brownes had been in occupation on the date of the mortgage, but contended that they were merely licensees.

The Court of Appeal upheld the county court's finding that in reality the Brownes were to have exclusive possession. In view of Law of Property Act 1925 s149(6), the term granted for their joint lives took effect as a term of 90 years. The premium for that grant was the discount of two-thirds of the value of the flat paid by the purchasers. There was, accordingly, a tenancy which was binding on the building society.

B3   # The distinction between tenancies and licences – informal arrangements

Court of Appeal

B3.1   ## Errington v Errington and Woods
[1952] 1 KB 290; [1952] 1 All ER 149, CA

Family relationship negated any intention to create tenancy

There was an agreement between a father and his son whereby the son agreed to pay the instalments on the father's mortgage and in return would acquire ownership of the house. The son went to live in the house.

It was held that the circumstances, including the family relationship, negatived any intention to create a tenancy. (Decision approved in *Street v Mountford* (B2.4).)

B3.2   ## Marcroft Wagons Ltd v Smith
[1951] 2 KB 496; [1951] 2 All ER 271, CA

No intention to create a contact where deceased tenant's daughter stayed on

A landlord allowed a deceased tenant's daughter to stay on in a house for six months after the death of the tenant. The landlord accepted two weeks' rent, but expressly refused to add the daughter's name to the rent book.

The court deduced from the conduct of the parties that there was no intention to contract at all. (Decision approved in *Street v Mountford* (B2.4).)

B3.3   ## Meynell Family Properties Ltd v Meynell
June 1998 *Legal Action* 12, CA

Licence where 'strong family flavour' to arrangement

In 1911 the grandfather of the defendant's husband bought an estate of four houses with extensive grounds. In 1960 the defendant's mother-in-law formed the plaintiff company to ensure continuing family ownership and occupation of the property as a place where members of the family could carry on living and spend weekends. The defendant occupied a bungalow on the estate from 1989 when she married Wilfred Meynell. She continued to live there after his death in 1995. Witnesses gave evidence that there was never any intention to create legal relations and that Mr and Mrs Meynell had shared occupation of the bungalow with other family members. However, company documents referred to 'tenancies' and 'rents'.

The Court of Appeal held that there was a 'strong family flavour' to the arrangements. Hirst LJ said that '... the set up of the estate ... bears all the hallmarks of a loose family arrangement'. The labels in the documents were not conclusive and '... words such as 'tenant' and 'rent' when they appear, were not used as terms of art reflecting any particular legal status, but rather as convenient shorthand'. Mrs Meynell was, accordingly, a licensee.

B3.4   **Nunn v Dalrymple**
(1989) 21 HLR 569; (1990) 59 P&CR 231, CA

Exclusive possession and weekly rent resulted in tenancy despite family relationship

The defendants gave up their tenancy of a council home and moved into a farm cottage owned by a relative. There was no written agreement. They had exclusive possession and paid £12 per week.

     Stocker LJ held (at p587) that it was not open to the circuit judge to conclude that the prima facie result that exclusive possession and regular weekly payments gave rise to a tenancy had been displaced by reason of the family relationship of the parties. He concluded that a tenancy had been created.

B3.5   **Sharp v McArthur**
(1987) 19 HLR 364, CA

Exceptional circumstances rebutted presumption of a tenancy

The owner of a flat took pity on Mr McArthur and allowed him into premises as a favour pending sale. It was agreed that Mr McArthur would be given one month's notice of when he had to leave. He was given a rent book so that the DHSS would pay his 'weekly outgoings in respect of accommodation'. At trial the defendant occupant did not give evidence.

     It was held that, although he had exclusive possession and a rent book, there were exceptional circumstances which rebutted the presumption of a tenancy. There was no intention to create legal relations.

B3.6   **Vaughan-Armatrading v Sarsah**
(1995) 27 HLR 631, CA

No inference of a tenancy when subtenant stayed on after termination of head lease

Mr Vaughan-Armatrading had been an assured subtenant. After the termination of the head lease, he was allowed by the owner to stay in the premises in order to finish his exams. He was later evicted by the owner and claimed damages for unlawful eviction.

     The Court of Appeal held that there had been no intention on the owner's part to create a new tenancy. Although money was paid to and subsequently returned by the landlord, it was not rent in a technical sense and no inference of the creation of a new tenancy could be drawn.

B3.7   **Ward v Warmke**
(1990) 22 HLR 496, CA

Daughter had tenancy where exclusive possession at a rent

Mr Ward bought a cottage for his retirement, but allowed his daughter and her husband to live there in the meantime. They made weekly payments for their occupation. A circuit judge found that although Mr and Mrs Ward retained a key and although they came to stay from time to time, their daughter and her husband had exclusive possession. There was an agreement for occupation at a rent and, therefore, a tenancy.

     The Court of Appeal dismissed the landlord's appeal.

B4   **The distinction between tenancies and licences – 'non-exclusive occupation agreements'**

House of Lords

B4.1   *AG Securities v Vaughan*

[1990] 1 AC 417; [1988] 3 WLR 1205; [1988] 3 All ER 1058; (1989) 21 HLR 79; (1989) 57 P&CR 17; [1988] 47 EG 193, HL

Shared accommodation with individual agreements entered into at different times not a joint tenancy; no tenancy where no exclusive possession of individual rooms

The flat in question consisted of four bedrooms, two other living rooms and a kitchen and a bathroom. At different times AG Securities entered into four separate agreements with four different individual 'licensees'. The agreements were for six-month periods beginning on different dates and provided for payment of different monthly sums. Although they did not reserve a right for the owners to share the flat with the occupants, they did provide that the owners could grant further licences, up to a maximum of four in total. When occupants moved out, they were replaced with new occupants, by agreement between the owners and the remaining 'licensees'. The new occupants signed forms of agreement in the same terms, but with different dates and often a different monthly payment. It was never specified by the landlord that any occupant should have a particular bedroom, and, from time to time, people changed rooms.

The occupants claimed that in view of the provision in the agreements limiting the maximum number of occupants at any one time to four and in view of the fact that the owners did not retain keys and rarely visited the premises, the four occupants at any given time enjoyed exclusive possession and accordingly had a joint tenancy. They also submitted that the consensual replacement of existing occupants with new people amount to the surrender and implied re-grant of a new tenancy.

Although these contentions were accepted by a majority of the Court of Appeal, they were rejected by the House of Lords, which held that each individual had separate contractual rights and obligations, without exclusive possession of the flat or any part of it. Lord Bridge stated that there was nothing artificial about these contracts and that he did not understand 'by what legal alchemy they could ever become joint'. The position would have been different if it could have been shown that individuals had exclusive possession of particular rooms, in which case there would have been individual tenancies.

B4.2   *Antoniades v Villiers and Bridger*

[1990] 1 AC 417; [1988] 3 WLR 1205; [1988] 3 All ER 1058; (1989) 21 HLR 79; (1989) 57 P&CR 17; [1988] 47 EG 193, HL

Separate licence agreements where couple sharing flat artificial; joint tenancy existed

The premises in question were a small attic flat, comprising a bedroom, a bed-sitting room, a kitchen and a bathroom. The furniture in the bed-sitting room was a bed-settee, a table-bed, a sideboard and a chair. Mr Villiers and Ms Bridger, who were looking for a flat where they could live together, were shown round by the owner, Mr Antoniades. He agreed that he would put a double bed in the bedroom. Mr Villiers and Ms Bridger each signed separate 'licence agreements' which were very similar in form to those in *Somma v Hazelhurst* [1978] 1 WLR 1014, CA. The wording stated, among other things, that 'the licensee is anxious to secure the use of the rooms notwithstanding that such use be in common with the licensor and such other licensees or invitees as the licensor may permit from time to time to use the said rooms'. The wording of the agreements denied that 'the licensees' had exclusive possession. Each agreement provided for payment of £87 per month.

Although the Court of Appeal held that two licences had been created, the House of Lords found that the agreements signed by Mr Villiers and Ms Bridger were interdependent and that they together enjoyed joint and exclusive possession of the whole of the flat in consideration of periodical payments. Among other factors, the flat was too small to share with strangers. Accordingly, they had a joint tenancy. Lord Bridge referred to the 'artificiality' of the separate agreements and the provision which purported to allow the 'licensor' or other people to use the flat. Lord Templeman referred to them as 'a pretence only intended to deprive the [occupants] of the protection of the Rent Acts' and pointed out that the provisions allowing the owner to insert other occupants could 'not be lawfully exercised because they [were] inconsistent with the provisions of the Rent Acts'. Lords Ackner, Oliver and Jauncey contrasted the 'substance and reality' or 'true nature' of the arrangement with the written agreements which were a 'smoke screen' or 'window dressing'.

B5 Licences – occupation granted to employees

Employees who live in premises as a term of their contract of employment 'for the better performance of their duties' are likely to be licensees, not tenants. See too Housing Act 1985 Sch 1 para 2. However, if the occupation is a fringe benefit or if it is offered as an inducement to encourage an employee to perform a job better and the employee has exclusive possession and pays rent, that would almost inevitably establish a service tenancy. A service tenancy may be a secure tenancy under Housing Act 1985, an assured tenancy under the Housing Act 1988 or a protected tenancy under the Rent Act 1977, but may be subject to a discretionary ground for possession (Housing Act 1985 Sch 2, Ground 12, Housing Act 1988 Sch 2 Ground 16, Rent Act 1977 Sch 15 Case 8).

Court of Appeal

B5.1   *Burgoyne v Griffiths*
(1991) 23 HLR 303; [1991] 1 EGLR 14; [1991] 12 EG 164, CA (see H3.2)
Former agricultural worker's claim to rent free licence for life rejected

B5.2   *Norris v Checksfield*
[1991] 1 WLR 1241; [1991] 4 All ER 321; (1991) 23 HLR 425; (1991) 63 P&CR 38; [1992] 1 EGLR 159, CA

Licence where there was a factual nexus between occupation and employment; no notice to quit required when employment terminated

The defendant, who had started work as a semi-skilled mechanic, was allowed to live in a bungalow close to work on condition that he would apply for a public service vehicle licence and would drive coaches for his employer. In such circumstances it would have been necessary for him to live in the bungalow to be readily available in emergencies or for urgent work. However, his employer subsequently discovered that he was disqualified from driving and so dismissed him summarily and brought possession proceedings.

The Court of Appeal held that, although the employee was never able to perform the duties for which he was employed, he was a licensee since there was a factual nexus between occupation of the premises and employment. It was enough that he was required to occupy the premises for the work which it was anticipated that he would carry out. As the employee's contract provided that his rights of occupation would end on termination of his employment, no notice to terminate the licence was required in accordance with Protection from Eviction Act 1977 s5(1a). The employee's appeal against a possession order was dismissed.

B5.3   *Postcastle Properties v Perridge*
(1986) 18 HLR 100; [1985] EGLR 107, CA

Tenancy created after termination of employment and change of owner

The defendant occupied a cottage as a condition of his employment, under the terms of a 'licence agreement'. Subsequently, his employment was terminated and the cottage was sold to another company. The new company did not evict the defendant and he was asked 'to carry on as usual'. He did so, paying weekly rent as before.

The Court of Appeal held that by implication there was a grant of a new weekly tenancy.

B5.4   *Royal Philanthropic Society v County*
(1986) 18 HLR 83; [1985] 2 EGLR 109, CA

No exceptional circumstances where employee rented accommodation at low rent under informal arrangement – tenancy existed

Mr County was employed as a houseparent in a school owned by the plaintiff but run by the London Borough of Wandsworth. Initially he was provided with accommodation in a room within the school building, for which a relatively small sum, covering also board, linen, light, heat, laundry and cooking facilities, was deducted from his salary. It was accepted that he was a licensee. Subsequently, on his marriage, the plaintiff provided Mr County with a house about two miles from the school. A relatively low rent was again deducted from his salary, but it was accepted that he enjoyed exclusive possession. After Mr County stopped working at the school, possession proceedings were brought. The county court held that he occupied the house on the same terms as the room, and so was merely a licensee.

The Court of Appeal found that Mr County was a tenant. Fox LJ stated:

> The overall effect of *Street v Mountford* as we understand it is that an occupier of residential accommodation at a rent for a term is either a lodger or a tenant. He will be a lodger if the landlord provides attendance or services which require the landlord, or his servants, to have unrestricted access to the premises.

Mr County's employment was not relevant because there was not a 'true service occupancy', ie, he did not have to live in the school premises for the better performance of his job. The court rejected the plaintiff's argument that because: (a) it was not in the business of providing accommodation; (b) the rent was low; (c) Mr County had earlier occupied the room in the school as a licensee; and (d) the arrangements were informal, that took the case into the 'exceptional category' referred to by Lord Templeman in *Street* (B2.4). The court apparently had no hesitation in holding that none of these factors took the case outside the usual rule enumerated in *Street*.

B5.5 **Whitbread West Pennines Ltd v Reedy**
(1988) 20 HLR 642, CA (see L3.12)

Former employee could not defend possession claim by relying on claim for unfair dismissal and reinstatement

B6 Subtenancies

Court of Appeal

B6.1 *Islington LBC v Green*
[2005] EWCA Civ 56; [2005] HLR 35; [2006] L&TR 24

Where council gave licence of accommodation to housing association which granted tenancy, tenancy not binding on council

Islington granted a licence of a residential property to Patchwork Community Housing Association so that it could be used for temporary housing. The licence also provided that on its termination, the housing association had to ensure that the property was vacated. Islington served written notice of termination of the licence and then brought possession proceedings. The defendants were occupants of the premises who had been granted secure tenancies by Patchwork. They claimed that Patchwork had acted as agents for Islington and so the tenancy agreement bound the council. That contention was rejected and a possession order made. One defendant appealed unsuccessfully to a circuit judge and then to the Court of Appeal.

The Court of Appeal dismissed the appeal. Islington had granted the licence to Patchwork with the strict intention of bearing no responsibility towards its tenants. This was clearly reflected in the terms of the licence. The licence did not authorise Patchwork to create a tenancy binding on Islington. Alternatively, even if it had such authority, any tenancies granted to the individual occupiers were terminated by the termination of the licence under the principle that when a head lease ends, whether through expiry of time, forfeiture or notice, any subtenancy derived under it also ends. The only exception is where the head lease is ended by surrender.

B6.2   *Keepers and Governors of the Free Grammar School of John Lyon v James*
[1996] QB 163; [1995] 3 WLR 908; [1995] 4 All ER 740; (1995) 27 HLR 727; (1996) 72 P&CR 402, CA

Subtenant became protected tenant of head lessee when lease forfeited

The head lease of the premises was forfeited. The issue was whether the subtenant became the protected or the statutory tenant of the landlord.

The Court of Appeal held that the subtenant became the protected tenant of the landlord.

B6.3   *Monmouth BC v Marlog*
(1995) 27 HLR 30; [1994] 2 EGLR 68; [1994] 44 EG 240, CA

Occupant was mere licensee where she shared council flat with tenant

The council let a three-bedroomed house on a secure tenancy. The tenant occupied one bedroom and allowed the defendant and her children to occupy the other two rooms for payment of £20 per week. The other parts of the house were shared. Later, after the council had issued possession proceedings, the tenant gave up possession. The defendant claimed that she was a tenant and that, on the secure tenant's surrender, her tenancy was held directly from the council.

The Court of Appeal dismissed her appeal against an order for possession. Nourse LJ held that she was a lodger and, given the entirely informal nature of the arrangement for sharing the house, it would be 'ludicrous' to infer that the parties had intended to create a legal relationship of landlord and tenant.

Note: It is difficult to see how the occupier could have been a 'secure' tenant in any event, because her sharing with the 'landlord' would have indicated that what she occupied was not a 'separate' dwelling: Housing Act 1985 s79(1).

B6.4   *Shepherd's Bush Housing Association v HATS Co-operative of Hammersmith Ltd*
(1992) 24 HLR 176, CA

On termination of head licence any interests of occupants also ended

The plaintiff held properties for conversion and redevelopment. It granted a temporary 'licence' to the defendant co-operative, which, in turn, permitted a succession of its members to occupy the premises. The licence was terminated by notice to quit and possession was sought. The co-operative could not be a secure tenant or licensee because it was not an 'individual' (Housing Act 1985 s81).

The Court of Appeal held that, on termination of the licence, any interests of the occupiers granted to them by the co-operative also fell. The occupiers could not establish a tenancy or licence between themselves and the plaintiffs. Accordingly, no question of security could arise, nor could the exception in Housing Act 1985 Sch 1 para 3.

B6.5 *Wellcome Trust v Hamad*
[1998] QB 638; [1998] 2 WLR 156; (1998) 30 HLR 629; [1998] 1 EGLR 73, CA

Effect of Rent Act 1977 s137 was that lawful subtenants of flats above shops retained protection when head lease ended

In three appeals heard together, the Court of Appeal considered the construction of Rent Act 1977 s137(3) and the protection which it affords to subtenants. In each case, buildings which comprised business premises (such as shops) on the ground floor and flats upstairs were let on long leases. These leases came within the provisions of Landlord and Tenant Act 1954 Part II. Subsequently, Rent Act protected subtenancies of the residential parts of the buildings were granted. In all three cases, county court judges, relying on *Pittalis v Grant* [1989] QB 605; [1989] 3 WLR 139; [1989] 2 All ER 622; (1989) 21 HLR 368; [1989] 2 EGLR 90, CA, found that, after the termination of the head leases, the subtenants fell outside Rent Act protection. The subtenants appealed, contending that *Pittalis v Grant* had been decided per incuriam.

After giving detailed consideration to the Rent Acts from a historical perspective, the Court of Appeal granted the tenants' appeals and in two cases set aside possession orders made against them. The court stated:

> [Rent Act s137(3)] appears to contemplate that where there is a flat over a shop, and the flat is lawfully sublet for residential use, so as to afford the subtenant protection under the Rent Act as against the tenant, the subtenant should continue to enjoy the same protection against the head landlord when the superior letting comes to an end.

Pittalis v Grant had been decided per incuriam because:

1) The argument relied on, that if a tenancy is not regulated, the premises cannot be treated as a dwelling-house, was fallacious. Premises may amount to a dwelling-house without being let on a regulated tenancy.
2) The Court of Appeal had overlooked all the authorities in which the accepted principles referred to by Lord Wilberforce in *Maunsell v Olins* [1975] AC 373; [1974] 3 WLR 835; [1975] 1 All ER 16; (1974) 30 P&CR 1, HL were contained.

In each of the three cases the premises concerned constituted a dwelling-house and, accordingly, s137(3) did afford protection to the subtenants.

High Court

B6.6 *Camden LBC v Shortlife Community Housing Ltd and Others*
(1993) 25 HLR 330; (1992) 90 LGR 358, ChD

Co-op was licensee of council; council entitled to possession

The council owned three blocks of flats which had been emptied for modernisation. It arranged for Shortlife Community Housing (SCH) to use over 60 flats for temporary housing accommodation.

Millett J granted a declaration that the council was entitled to possession. SCH was not a tenant but a licensee of the blocks, because it did not have exclusive possession. The occupiers' rights were lost on termination of the licence between Camden and SCH.

Requirements for security of tenure

C1   Introduction

There are three main statutory regimes giving residential occupiers security of tenure: the Rent Act 1977, the Housing Act 1985 and the Housing Act 1988.

Rent Act 1977 s1 states that 'a tenancy under which a dwelling-house (which may be a house or part of a house) is let as a separate dwelling is a protected tenancy for the purposes of this Act'. Rent Act protected tenancies are *mainly* tenancies granted by private landlords before 15 January 1989, but see Housing Act 1988 s34.

Housing Act 1985 s79 states that 'A tenancy under which a dwelling-house is let as a separate dwelling is a secure tenancy at any time when the conditions described in sections 80 and 81 as the landlord condition and the tenant condition are satisfied.' Secure tenancies under Housing Act 1985 are *mainly* tenancies or licences granted by public sector landlords such as local authorities, although housing association tenants whose tenancies were granted before 15 January 1989 may remain secure tenants if all the other requirements of a secure tenancy exist (see Housing Act 1985 s80(1) prior to amendment by the Housing Act 1988 and the Housing Act 1988 s35).

Housing Act 1988 s1 states that:

A tenancy under which a dwelling-house is let as a separate dwelling is for the purposes of this Act an assured tenancy if and so long as
(a) the tenant or, as the case may be, each of the joint tenants is an individual; and
(b) the tenant or, as the case may be, at least one of the joint tenants occupies the dwelling-house as his only or principal home; and
(c) the tenancy is not one which, by virtue of subsection (2) or subsection (6) below, cannot be an assured tenancy.'

Assured tenancies are *mainly* tenancies granted by private sector or registered social landlords since 15 January 1989 (Housing Act 1988 ss34–36) but, if assured tenancies also satisfy the requirements in Housing Act 1988 ss19–20 (see chapter K), they are assured shorthold tenancies without long-term security of tenure.

Rent Act 1977, Housing Act 1985 and Housing Act 1988 all contain different requirements which have to be met before a protected, secure to assured tenancy can come into existence. However, there are some common themes: letting as a separate dwelling, conditions which apply to the landlord and the tenant, and residential occupation. Cases in which these requirements have been considered are set out in this chapter. Cases in which the various exceptions to security of tenure have been considered are set out in chapter D.

The transitional provisions, governing the introduction of the assured tenancy regime are also included in this chapter.

C2   Let as a separate dwelling

Rent Act 1977 s1, Housing Act 1985 s79 and Housing Act 1988 s1 all contain requirements that premises (whether they are a house, a flat or a single room such as a bed-sit) be let 'as a separate dwelling'. As a general rule, there can be no separate dwelling if any living accommodation is shared (whether with the landlord's representatives or with other tenants), although there is nothing to prevent one or more joint tenants from jointly renting premises together as a separate dwelling – the fact that they share obviously does not prevent premises being let as a separate dwelling. Note, however, that Housing Act 1988 s3 and Rent Act 1977 s22 provide that where premises are shared with persons other than a landlord they may be deemed to be let as a separate dwelling.

House of Lords

C2.1   *Goodrich v Paisner*

[1957] AC 15; [1956] 2 WLR 1053; [1956] 2 All ER 176, HL

Tenant's four rooms a separate dwelling despite sharing other rooms with landlord

A landlord let four unfurnished rooms on the first floor of a house 'together with the use in common with the landlord of the back bedroom on the first floor'. The tenant also had shared use, with the landlord and others, of the bathroom and lavatories. After the landlord's death, her successors in title served notice to quit and took possession proceedings.

    The House of Lords held that the four rooms were let as 'a separate dwelling' with full Rent Act protection.

C2.2   *Uratemp Ventures Ltd v Collins*

[2001] UKHL43; [2002] 1 AC 301; [2001] 3 WLR 806; [2002] 1 All ER 46; (2001) 33 HLR 972; [2002] L&TR 15; (2001) *Times* 18 October

'Dwelling' is the place where an occupier lives; no requirement for cooking facilities

The claimant sought possession of a hotel room occupied by the defendant. The room was basically furnished and did not include any cooking facilities, although there was a power point. Breakfast was initially available in the restaurant and included in the rent. Mr Collins brought in a pizza warmer, a toasted sandwich maker, a kettle and a warming plate. HHJ Cotran held that the defendant enjoyed a tenancy of a dwelling-house and that he had an assured tenancy within the meaning of Housing Act 1988. The claimant appealed successfully to the Court of Appeal, contending that he was a licensee as he did not enjoy exclusive possession and that, in any event, the room was not a dwelling-house (Housing Act 1988 s1).

    Mr Collins's appeal was allowed by the House of Lords. Lord Millett, with whom the other members of the House of Lords agreed, said that the word 'dwelling' is not a term of art with a specialised legal meaning. It is 'the place where [an occupier] lives and to which he returns and which forms the centre of his existence ... No doubt he will sleep there and usually eat there; he will often prepare at least some of his meals there.' However, there is no legislative requirement that cooking facilities must be available for premises to qualify as a dwelling. In deciding whether an occupant has security of tenure:

The first step is to identify the subject-matter of the tenancy agreement. If this is a house or part of a house of which the tenant has exclusive possession with no element of sharing, the only question is whether, at the date when proceedings were brought, it was the tenant's home. If so, it was his dwelling. ... The presence or absence of cooking facilities in the part of the premises of which the tenant has exclusive occupation is not relevant.

Note: In the light of this case, the decisions in *Central YMCA Housing Association v Saunders* (1991) 23 HLR 212, CA and *Central YMCA Housing Association v Goodman* (1992) 24 HLR 109, CA should no longer be regarded as good law.

C2.3   *Westminster CC v Clarke*
[1992] 2 AC 288; [1992] 2 WLR 229; [1992] 1 All ER 695; (1992) 24 HLR 360; (1992) 90 LGR 210, HL

Special nature of hostel meant occupant did not have exclusive possession of his room

The council provided a single man with a self-contained bed-sitting room with cooking facilities and its own lockable door in a hostel. The hostel was a council-run, single men's hostel with a resident warden employed to manage the building, assist residents and enter rooms as necessary with a duplicate key. The occupancy agreement was called a 'licence to occupy'. It provided that (a) the occupier could be required to share with others (although it was a single room) and (b) the occupier could be required to transfer to a different room on request.

The House of Lords held that, for a licence to be secure under Housing Act 1985, it must confer exclusive possession on the occupier. Here, the agreement and the special nature of the hostel indicated that the council kept such a degree of control over the room that this was not so. Possession was granted.

Court of Appeal

C2.4   *Andrews v Brewer*
(1998) 30 HLR 203, CA

House was let as a dwelling; tenancy was an AST not a business tenancy

Tenants claimed that a house which was purportedly subject to an assured shorthand tenancy had not been let as a dwelling and so was a business tenancy. They relied on the surrounding circumstances and, in particular, the fact that all the other houses in the street were used as guest houses.

The Court of Appeal rejected this contention, holding that the surrounding circumstances were only relevant if the purpose of the letting was not made clear in the lease. In this case, a user restriction in the lease meant that it was not permissible to infer an intention for business purposes. The Court of Appeal also dismissed a counterclaim for breach of repairing covenants because proper notice had not been given.

C2.5   *Gray v Brown*
(1993) 25 HLR 144; [1993] 1 EGLR 119; [1993] 07 EG 97, CA

Clear words reserving right for landlord to live on premises necessary to deprive tenant of protected tenancy

An oral tenancy agreement to rent a room included a term that the tenant would share the house with whoever the landlord might choose. The landlord did not live in the house but contended that the clause meant that, in accordance with Rent Act 1977 s21, the tenancy was a restricted contract (see Rent Act 1977 s19), not a protected tenancy.

However, the Court of Appeal held that the term used was not sufficiently specific to show that the landlord was reserving the right to live there himself in accordance with section 21 and so did not deprive the tenant of protection under section 22. To come within the terms of section 21, the tenancy agreement must include clear words reserving the right of the landlord to live on the premises.

C2.6   *Grosvenor Estates Belgravia v Cochran*
(1992) 24 HLR 98; [1991] 2 EGLR 83; [1991] 44 EG 169, CA

Basement let under head lease with rest of building not let as a separate dwelling

The lessee under a long lease sublet two basement flats to the defendant for a term in excess of the length of the remainder of the long lease. Legally that took effect as an assignment and not a subtenancy (*Milmo v Carreras* [1946] KB 306, CA). The defendant started to carry out major works to the flats. Before she moved in, the freeholders issued possession proceedings against the head lessee, claiming that some of the works were in breach of the terms of the lease, and obtained judgment in default against the head lessee. In the meantime, the defendant's assigned tenancy came to an end on the term date of the original head lease.

The Court of Appeal held that the defendant could not enjoy protection under Landlord and Tenant Act 1954 Part I (a long tenancy at a low rent) because there was no letting of a separate dwelling. The basement was let under the head lease with the rest of the building and so was not 'subject to a protected or statutory tenancy'. For the same reason, Rent Act 1977 s137 did not give her security of tenure after the head lease expired.

C2.7   *Horford Investments v Lambert*
[1976] Ch 39; [1973] 3 WLR 872; [1974] 1 All ER 131; (1973) 27 P&CR 88, CA

Premises let as several dwellings not let as 'a dwelling'

A 19th-century house was let for a term of 20 years. The ground and upper floors were to be sublet as single rooms. The basement was to be sublet as a self-contained flat. The tenant claimed the protection of the Rent Act.

The Court of Appeal held that such a letting for multiple occupation was outside the Rent Act. The premises were let as several dwellings, not as 'a dwelling'. The terms of the tenancy, not subsequent events, are the primary consideration when deciding whether premises are let as a separate dwelling.

C2.8   *Kavanagh v Lyroudias*
[1985] 1 All ER 560; (1983) 10 HLR 20; (1984) 269 EG 629, CA

Where occupant did not occupy premises separately from adjoining premises he was not a statutory tenant

The defendant occupied a house (no 21) from 1955, but it was too small for him. As a result, in 1973 the landlord granted him a tenancy of an adjoining house (no 23), which was almost identical. The tenant slept in no 23 and used the study there. However, he never cooked or ate there. The landlord served a notice to quit in respect of no 23 and brought possession proceedings. A county court judge dismissed the claim for possession, finding that the defendant was the statutory tenant of no 23.

The landlord appealed successfully. The Court of Appeal indicated that the judge should have considered whether no 23 'was occupied separately from the adjoining premises as a complete home in itself'. The defendant did not satisfy that test. Leave to appeal to the House of Lords was granted, but not pursued.

Note: See also comments on this decision by the House of Lords in *Hampstead Way Investments Ltd v Lewis-Weare* (C4.1).

C2.9   *Miller v Eyo*
(1999) 31 HLR 306, CA

Landlord had no right to enter premises and share with tenant in absence of clear term

The defendant landlord appealed against an award of £21,804 damages for illegal eviction, including an award of £18,000 under Housing Act 1988 ss27 and 28. She did not challenge the quantum, but claimed that the plaintiff did not have an assured tenancy at the time of her eviction. The terms of the plaintiff's tenancy were that she had exclusive use of her bedroom with shared use of a living room, kitchen and bathroom/lavatory. Initially the only other bedroom in the flat was occupied by another tenant, but when she moved out the landlord and her family moved into the other bedroom and started to share the other parts of the flat with the plaintiff. The plaintiff claimed that the landlord was not entitled to take up possession of the part of the property not let to her and that, in view of Housing Act 1988 s3, she was an assured tenant.

The Court of Appeal accepted this submission and dismissed the landlord's appeal. Following *Gray v Brown* (C2.5), the Court of Appeal held that the trial judge was correct in finding that, in the absence of an express term in the tenancy, the landlord had no right to re-enter and occupy. Accordingly, the tenancy came within s3 and was assured. For a landlord to avoid this situation, a landlord's right to re-enter and share must be 'clear and specific'.

C2.10   *Mortgage Corporation v Ubah*
(1997) 29 HLR 489; (1997) 73 P&CR 500, CA

Issue is whether sharing arrangement with landlord is exercisable, not whether it is actually shared

The tenancy of a maisonette included a right for the landlord to use the kitchen in common with the tenant. After the landlord had fallen into arrears with his mortgage, the mortgagee repossessed the property, subject to the tenancy, which had preceded the grant of the mortgage. The tenant argued that the mortgagee, as a corporation, 'being a mere creature of the law without appetite or culinary capability was incapable of submitting to a shared use of its kitchen because it could not itself make use of the kitchen at all'. The judge rejected this submission and found that the defendant merely had a restricted contract (see Rent Act 1977 s19). He appealed.

The Court of Appeal dismissed his appeal. Waite LJ found it unnecessary to decide whether a company was capable of sharing a kitchen. He held that the true issue was whether the sharing arrangements remained exercisable. As landlords 'came and went' the right to share the kitchen was 'merely in abeyance' and, if the landlord's interest passed to an individual, it would once again become possible and practicable for the rights of kitchen user to become common rights. The Court of Appeal also found that the tenant was not entitled to set off against rent due to the Mortgage Corporation sums which, with the agreement of the former owner, he had spent on repairs and which the former owner had accepted were due to be reimbursed to the tenant. This was not an agreement binding on successors in title and, accordingly, could not be an overriding interest in accordance with Land Registration Act 1925 s70(1)(g).

C2.11   *Parkins v Westminster CC*
[1998] 1 EGLR 22; [1998] 13 EG 145, CA

Where occupant of council flat shared with others he was a licensee

Mr Parkins was employed as a teacher. As part of a staff accommodation scheme he was offered a room in a flat consisting of three bedrooms, a kitchen, a living room, a bathroom and separate lavatory. He signed a licence agreement and was given the keys to the flat and the room. Another teacher was allocated another room in the flat and signed a similar agreement. Later, the plaintiff was dismissed and the council served a notice to quit. At first instance it was held that he was a secure tenant, and the council's claim for possession was dismissed.

The Court of Appeal allowed the council's appeal. Although the flat could be let 'as a separate dwelling' because there was a separate sitting room with facilities for cooking and a bathroom and lavatory, the individual room did not satisfy those requirements on its own. Mr Parkins only had exclusive possession of the room. He did not have exclusive possession of the flat as a separate dwelling and so he did not occupy under a secure tenancy.

C2.12   *St Catherine's College v Dorling*
[1980] 1 WLR 66; [1979] 3 All ER 250; (1979) 39 P&CR 110; (1979) 251 EG 265, CA

Where lease indicated house let as a number of units, it was not let as separate dwelling

The owner of a furnished house let it to the college for occupation by five separate subtenants. Each had a room to be used as a bedroom, study and sitting room. They shared a kitchen and bathroom. The college then applied to the rent officer to register a fair rent. A county court judge refused to grant the college a declaration that its tenancy enjoyed Rent Act protection because the house was not let as a separate dwelling. There were a number of individual subtenancies, not a joint subtenancy.

The college's appeal was dismissed. The clause in the college's lease whereby it covenanted to use the house 'as private residence only in occupation of one person per room' was to be interpreted as showing that it was intended that the house was to be let as a number of units and not 'as a separate dwelling'.

C2.13 *Tomkins v Basildon DC*
[2002] EWCA Civ 876; [2002] 43 EG 206; [2003] L&TR 7

Business lease not varied to 'housing tenancy' when business ended

In 1966 the claimant went to live with a Mrs Barker. She worked for her as a kennel hand and assisted her domestically. She was not paid wages, but was kept by Mrs Barker. In 1978 Basildon Development Corporation granted Mrs Barker and the claimant a lease of a bungalow and kennels for a term of twenty years. There was a covenant by the tenants 'to use the demised premises for carrying on the trade or business of the keeping and training of greyhounds and for residential accommodation incidental thereto'. It was, accordingly, a business tenancy within the meaning of Landlord and Tenant Act 1954 Part II. The freehold reversion was transferred to the defendant in 1994. By 1986 commercial activity at the property had ceased and the claimant devoted herself full time to the care of Mrs Barker, who eventually died in 1995. There was evidence from its files that the defendant knew about this and agreed to treat the lease as 'non-commercial' and to convert it to a 'housing tenancy'. In a claim for a declaration, a circuit judge found on the facts that there had been an agreed variation of the lease to treat the property as a house 'let as a separate dwelling' within the Housing Act 1985. However, since there was no surrender and re-grant, the tenant continued to hold under the 20-year lease as varied, and therefore did not have the benefit of Landlord and Tenant Act 1985 s11, since that section only applies to leases for seven years or less. The claimant appealed and the defendant cross-appealed.

The claimant's appeal was dismissed. There was no evidence to suggest that Mrs Barker and the claimant ever intended to give up their rights under the lease. Indeed, solicitors acting for the claimant wrote to the defendant in 1997 asserting that 'she has a lease of the above property which expires on 14 November 1998'. Furthermore, the defendant continued to operate rent reviews under the provisions of the lease. Hart J, with whom Latham LJ agreed, rejected the submission that the fact that rent was being paid and received via housing benefit meant that there must have been some agreement to convert the lease into a periodic purely residential tenancy (see Social Security Contributions and Benefits Act 1992 s130(1), s137(1) and Housing Benefit (General) Regulations 1987 reg 10). The council's cross-appeal was allowed. The Court of Appeal did not consider that, on an application of conventional principles of the law of contract, the judge's conclusion that there was a contractual variation of the lease could be justified. Most of the matters considered by him were purely of relevance to the landlord for its internal administration. The highest it could be put was that the landlord for the time being was content not to enforce the user covenant and to review the rent on the basis of the actual as opposed to the permitted or required user. The property did not become 'let as a separate dwelling' for the purposes of the Housing Act 1985.

C2.14 *Tyler v Kensington and Chelsea RLBC*
(1991) 23 HLR 380, CA

Licence to occupy flat contingent on tenancy of other flat and lost on buying other flat

The plaintiff was the secure tenant of a ground floor flat. Because of its poor condition, and so that building works could be undertaken on the ground floor, the council gave him permission also to occupy the first floor flat in the same building. Work was never started and the tenant simply occupied both flats. He then submitted an application to buy the two flats together as a single unit. In subsequent proceedings in 1987, HHJ Oddie found that there was not a single letting but two separate units and, therefore, they could not be purchased under a single right to buy (compare *Jenkins v Renfrew DC* (C2.17)). Accordingly, the tenant arranged his affairs so that the ground floor flat became his principal home and in 1988 he applied to buy that alone. His right to buy was accepted and the lease conveyed. On the day of completion he moved upstairs to take up occupation of the first floor flat as his 'principal' home and then claimed the right to buy that.

The Court of Appeal held that the licence to occupy the first floor flat had been contingent on a continuing tenancy of the ground floor. As the tenant had purchased the ground floor flat, the tenancy had ended and with it the contingent first floor licence. The occupier was an ex-licensee or trespasser in the first floor flat, could not be secure, and so did not have the right to buy.

C2.15 *Webb v Barnet LBC*
(1989) 21 HLR 228; [1989] 1 EGLR 49; [1989] 11 EG 80, CA

Premises let for business and residential use were not 'let as a separate dwelling'

Premises comprising a house, a yard and a workshop were let to the tenant 'to use the demised premises only for residential purposes and for the purposes of trade and business for which they are let, namely as a motor body repairs workshop'. The tenant and family lived in the house and carried on a business from the yard and workshop until 1979/80. When his business ended, the tenancy was no longer within Housing Act 1985 Sch 1 para 11, which excludes from protection tenancies to which Landlord and Tenant Act 1954 Part II applies. Accordingly, he sought a declaration that he was a secure tenant.

The Court of Appeal held that Housing Act 1985 s79(1) was not satisfied, because the premises had not originally been 'let as a separate dwelling', even though business use had now ceased. Mr Webb was a non-secure tenant without the protection of the Rent Act 1977, Housing Act 1985 or Landlord and Tenant Act 1954.

Note: See too *Tan v Sitkowski* (D5.7).

High Court

C2.16   *R v Rent Officer of Nottinghamshire Registration Area ex p Allen*
(1985) 17 HLR 481; (1985) 52 P&CR 41; [1985] 2 EGLR 153; (1985) 275 EG 251, QBD

Large caravan moved from time to time not a house

A large caravan was rented out at a high rent. The local authority made
an application to the rent officer for registration of a fair rent because the
occupant was receiving housing benefit. The owner sought an order of
certiorari to quash the registration.

Farquharson J held that a caravan could be a house within the meaning of Rent Act 1977 s1 if it had been made completely immobile by the
removal of its wheels, or because it was blocked up by some concrete or
brick structure. However, in this case, the caravan was moved from time
to time and the services were easily disconnected. Therefore, it was not a
'house'.

Scottish courts

C2.17   *Jenkins v Renfrew DC*
1989 SLT (Lands Tr) 41, Lands Tribunal

Two adjoining, connecting flats comprised one unit; let as a separate dwelling

The tenant rented a flat. About 13 years later, an adjoining flat in the same
building became vacant and, in view of the large size of his family, he was
granted a tenancy of that flat as well. He then constructed an opening
between the two flats. Later, while carrying out improvement works, the
council replaced this with a new connection.

The Lands Tribunal, applying the provisions of the Housing (Scotland)
Act 1987 (which are similar to those of the Housing Act 1985) held that:
(a) the units taken together constituted the tenant's home; (b) they combined to form a single unit 'let as a separate dwelling'; and (c) it followed
that the whole was occupied by the tenant as his 'only or principal home'
and he was the secure tenant of the whole.

C2.18   *Thompson v City of Glasgow DC*
1986 SLT (Lands Tr) 6, Lands Tribunal

Room in council run hostel not let as a separate dwelling

The applicant occupied a bedroom in a tower block run by the council as a
hostel for single men. The block comprised 253 separate single bedrooms
all inhabited by single men. His room did not have a wash-basin or any
cooking facilities. On the ground floor there was a common room, a communal reading room and a TV lounge, as well as toilets, showers and a
laundry room. Mr Thompson sought to exercise the right to buy his room.
The council defended the proceedings on the basis that the room he occupied was not 'let as a separate dwelling'.

Applying the English Rent Act case-law, Lord Elliott found that the
room was not let as a separate dwelling, since the essential living activities
of the occupier were not confined to the premises let. He took into account
the fact that Mr Thompson had no cooking facilities, used the communal
canteen and reading rooms and had no individual washing facilities.

C3 Occupation as only or principal home: Housing Act 1985 s81 and Housing Act 1988 s1(1)(b); Prohibition against subletting: Housing Act 1985 s93

Both Housing Act 1985 s81 (the 'tenant condition') and Housing Act 1988 s1(1)(b) provide that security of tenure can only be gained and retained if tenants occupy premises as their 'only or principal home'. The requirement in Housing Act 1985 s81 is that:

> the tenant is an individual and occupies the dwelling-house as his only or principal home; or, where the tenancy is a joint tenancy, that each of the joint tenants is an individual and at least one of them occupies the dwelling-house as his only or principal home.

Security of tenure is lost if secure tenants cease to occupy premises as their only or principal home or if they sublet or part with possession of the whole of them (Housing Act 1985 s93). (For assured tenants subletting may amount to a breach of tenancy but does not automatically result in loss of security (see Housing Act 1988, s15).) The requirement in Housing Act 1988 s1 is that:

> the tenant or, as the case may be, each of the joint tenants is an individual; and ... the tenant or, as the case may be, at least one of the joint tenants occupies the dwelling-house as his only or principal home.

It is possible for tenants to have two or more homes, but only the one which is the 'principal' home can be secure or assured.

The requirement for Rent Act protected tenants is different – see C4 below.

Court of Appeal

C3.1   *Brent LBC v Cronin*
(1998) 30 HLR 48, CA

Where tenant sublet premises and stayed with a relative temporarily, s93 applied

A disabled council tenant left his one-bedroomed home temporarily to stay with a relative. Through a friend, he found a young couple willing to occupy the flat in his absence. They paid a £20 deposit, agreed a rent of £40 per week, were given the keys, moved in and began redecorating. The council brought possession proceedings on the basis that security of tenure had been lost by subletting or parting with possession (Housing Act 1985 s93(2)) or that the tenant was in breach of the implied term not to sublet without consent (s93(1)(b)). The trial judge found that the tenant had got himself into a muddle and had never really intended to sublet at all.

The Court of Appeal allowed the council's appeal and granted possession. The judge had found that the oral agreement contained all the hallmarks of a (sub)tenancy. Neither the tenant's intention to return after a short while nor his uncertainty about his plans had ever been communicated to the subtenants and, even if they had been, they would have been unlikely to have turned the subletting into something else.

C3.2   **Camden LBC v Alexandrou**

(1998) 30 HLR 534, CA (see N4.7)

Possession ordered where tenant treated as having assigned his interest to joint tenant

C3.3   **Camden LBC v Goldenberg**

(1996) 28 HLR 727; (1997) 73 P&CR 376; (1997) 95 LGR 693, CA (see E3.3)

Residence test satisfied where occupant intended to return to grandmother's flat – intention not displaced by intention to set up home elsewhere if he could

C3.4   **Crawley BC v Sawyer**

(1988) 20 HLR 98; (1988) 86 LGR 629, CA

Intention to return after temporary absence coupled with physical sign of continued occupation satisfies residence requirement

In 1985 the defendant council tenant went to live with his girlfriend. During 1985 and 1986, the gas and electricity supplies to his premises were cut off. In July 1986 he told the council that he was 'living with his girlfriend' and that they intended to buy her home. In August 1986, the council served a notice to quit, expiring on 30 September. By that time the relationship between the defendant and his girlfriend had broken up and, shortly after the expiry of the notice to quit, the defendant returned to live in his own home. In possession proceedings, the defendant gave evidence that he had not abandoned the premises and that he had always intended returning to them.

The Court of Appeal confirmed that, in order to maintain a 'home', a tenant need not be physically resident, so long as there is an intention to return after a temporary absence and some physical sign of continued occupation (eg, furniture and possessions in the property). Two houses can be occupied as a home at the same time. On the evidence before the trial judge, he was entitled to form the view that the defendant was only occupying his girlfriend's home on a temporary basis and that his own home remained his principal home throughout the period.

C3.5   **Gay v Sheeran**

[2000] 1 WLR 673; [1999] 3 All ER 795; (1999) 31 HLR 1126; (1999) *Times* 30 June, CA

Tenancy cannot be transferred under FLA 1996 where residence requirement no longer satisfied or deemed satisfied; part interest in joint tenancy cannot be transferred

The council granted a joint secure tenancy to Mr Sheeran and his then partner, Ms Gunn. She left and Ms Gay moved in to live with him as his new partner. Mr Sheeran then left the property. Ms Gay applied for transfer of his interest in the joint tenancy into her name (Family Law Act 1996 s53 and Sch 7).

The Court of Appeal held that: (1) a tenancy can only be vested pursuant to s53 if it is a 'secure' tenancy at the date the order for transfer is sought or made; (2) the tenancy was not 'secure' in this case because neither joint tenant was occupying at either date (Housing Act 1985 s81) and Ms Gay had not before either date obtained an 'occupation order' capable of deeming her to be satisfying the occupation condition (Family Law Act

1996 s36(13)); and (3) there is in any event no power to order transfer of a part interest in a joint secure tenancy unless the only joint tenants are the applicant and respondent themselves. Here, there would have been no jurisdiction because the tenancy was held jointly with a third party (Ms Gunn).

C3.6 *Hammersmith and Fulham LBC v Clarke*
(2001) 33 HLR 881; (2001) 81 P&CR D41, CA

Date of expiry of NTQ is date for determining whether premises are tenant's only or principal home; 'enduring intention' rather than 'fleeting changes of mind' relevant

A frail elderly secure tenant occupied her council home from 1981. It was adapted for her needs. In 1997 her grandson and his wife moved in to look after her and she later submitted a right-to-buy application jointly with her grandson. In November 1998 she was admitted to a nursing home experiencing depression in addition to physical disabilities. Her furniture remained in her home and the grandson and his wife continued living there. Whilst in the nursing home in January 1999 she signed a social worker's note that she had decided to become a permanent resident of the nursing home and that it was 'not now my choice' to live in her former home. The council served notice to quit in February 1999 and, on its expiry in March, claimed possession. By the date of trial the tenant had returned to live in her home. The trial judge accepted her evidence that: (1) she had initially gone to the nursing home intending to move back; (2) the note had been made at a time when she was very depressed and had just had her medication sorted out; and (3) she 'had every intention of returning'. He dismissed the possession claim. The council appealed contending that the material date for determining whether an absent tenant had an intention to return was the date of the expiry of the notice to quit. Evidence as to earlier or subsequent intention was immaterial and the social worker's note was the best evidence of intention at date of expiry.

The Court of Appeal agreed that the position was to be considered as at the date of the expiry of the notice but dismissed the appeal. It held that, in determining whether an absent tenant was still 'occupying' premises, a court should focus on 'the enduring intention of that person' and not on 'fleeting changes of mind'. That was particularly true of an elderly tenant in poor health whose intentions 'may well have fluctuated from time to time and even from day to day'. The judge was entitled to find in this case that the note did not represent the tenant's more general and enduring intent which was borne out by her evidence, by the continuing presence of her family and furniture in her adapted home, and all the other circumstances.

C3.7 *Hussey v Camden LBC*
(1995) 27 HLR 5, CA

Tenant who has lost secure status can regain it by resuming occupation; parting with possession not to be inferred simply from temporary occupancy by others

Camden, as landlord, served a notice to quit and claimed possession. It contended that the tenant had lost security by failing to occupy and, in the

alternative, asserted that security had been lost by parting with possession. A county court judge found for the council on the first proposition.
He determined that the tenant had ceased to occupy as his only or principal home in 1986 and that security of tenure had thus been lost, despite
his return to the property before service of notice to quit (Housing Act
1985 s93).

The Court of Appeal allowed the tenant's appeal. It was perfectly possible for a tenant to have lost security of tenure through non-occupation
in the past and, thereafter, to regain it by reoccupying the property before
service of a notice to quit. Since the tenant was occupying the property as
his only or principal home at the time of service of the notice to quit, the
earlier loss of security was irrelevant. The Court of Appeal also held that
there was insufficient evidence before the judge to establish any parting
with possession. Parting with possession was not to be inferred simply
from the fact that another person had been allowed to use and occupy the
tenant's home during his temporary absence (*Lam Kee Ying v Lam Shes
Tong* [1975] AC 247, PC).

C3.8   **Jennings v Epping Forest DC**
(1993) 25 HLR 241, CA

Secure status and right to buy lost when tenants left

The joint tenants were an elderly couple. The man moved to a nursing
home and the woman took a flat close to the nursing home to be near to
him. Their daughter arranged for their council home to be sublet. In proceedings concerning the right to buy, the Court of Appeal held that secure
status had been lost and with it the right to buy.

C3.9   **Lambeth LBC v Vandra**
[2005] EWCA Civ 1801; [2006] HLR 19

*Judge entitled to find unlawful subletting in absence of credible explanation
by tenant*

The defendant was a secure tenant. A housing officer visited the premises
on two occasions and concluded that the tenant had unlawfully sublet and
was no longer occupying as her only or principal residence. As a result,
Lambeth served a notice to quit and took possession proceedings. A district judge found that: (1) the defendant had not been in occupation of the
premises at the time of either of the housing officer's two visits; (2) there
was no evidence or sign of any family occupation of the premises by the
defendant or her four children; (3) five or more people who were in occupation had been met during the two visits; (4) there were Yale locks on all
the doors and one had a padlock; (5) there was no sign of any room being
used as a living room and there were beds in all the rooms which the
housing officer saw; and (6) four of the occupants said that they paid rent
to a person whom the defendant claimed to have put into occupation of
the premises rent-free as a caretaker. In the light of those facts, the district
judge found that an explanation was called for by the defendant. The ex-
planations offered by the defendant were not accepted by the district judge
as credible. The district judge concluded that the whole of the premises
had been unlawfully sublet, and that the defendant had ceased to be a

secure tenant. She made an order for possession. The defendant appealed and a circuit judge found that the district judge had erred in reversing the burden of proof. He found that, on the evidence, it was possible that the defendant had only let part of the premises, allowed the appeal and set aside the order for possession. Lambeth appealed to the Court of Appeal.

The Court of Appeal allowed the appeal. The district judge had been entitled to come to her conclusions, and the circuit judge had been wrong to interfere with them. The fact that there was another possible explanation for the various people who appeared to be living in the property did not mean that there was no evidence or insufficient evidence for the inference made by the district judge from the primary facts found as to the subletting of the whole property. The claimant's evidence required the defendant to explain why she was not living at the flat and other occupants were. The district judge was entitled to make inferences of probability from established primary facts and was entitled to conclude there had been an unlawful subletting of the whole of the premises.

Note: This decision is in line with earlier Rent Act authorities that (1) the burden of proof initially lies on a landlord to show that a tenant is absent; but (2) once a landlord has established this, it is for the tenant to show a physical presence in the premises and an intention to return (see eg, *Roland House v Cravtitz* (1974) 29 P&CR 432, CA).

C3.10 *Luton LBC v Menni*
[2006] EWCA Civ 1850; 20 December 2006

Subletting of whole of flat found; evidence included tenant's advert for tenants

Mrs Menni was a secure tenant. She exercised the right to buy. The council contended that before completing that process she sublet the flat and thereby lost irrevocably her status as a secure tenant and, in consequence, her right to buy. She accepted that there was a subletting of the lounge and large bedroom to a Mr Howe and Miss Scott, but claimed that the smaller second bedroom was reserved out of the subletting and used for some months by her husband, from whom she was at the time estranged. The council claimed possession. HHJ Everall, after hearing a number of witnesses and considering Mrs Menni's advertisement to let a 'furnished, spacious & comfortable' two-bedroom flat in the local paper, found that the whole of the premises had been sublet. Mrs Menni sought permission to appeal on the basis that the judge's finding of fact as to the extent of the subletting, which was based on his assessment of the credibility of the respective witnesses, was flawed.

Lloyd LJ refused permission to appeal. Although there were discrepancies in the council's evidence, they did not 'go to the heart of the issue of the probability of Mrs Menni's story as against any subletting of the whole'. There was no reasonable prospect of a successful appeal.

C3.11 *Merton LBC v Salama*
June 1989 *Legal Action* 25, CA (CAT 89/169)

Consideration needed as to whether tenant had parted with possession of whole or part

A secure tenancy was granted in 1980. In 1986 the tenant bought other premises and moved out, allowing a third party into occupation. In 1987 the tenant moved back in, with the third party still present. Later the same year, the council purported to end the tenancy by notice to quit. The tenant responded by giving the third party notice to quit and counterclaimed (in an action for harassment brought by the third party) for possession. In those proceedings, the county court ruled that the third party was a subtenant. The council then brought proceedings for possession against the tenant, based on its earlier notice to quit and the findings of fact in the earlier action that the tenant had parted with possession (see Housing Act 1985 s93(2)).

Allowing the tenant's appeal against a 28-day possession order and remitting the case for retrial, the Court of Appeal held that the tenant should be given the opportunity of raising the defence that she had parted with possession of part rather than the whole of the property. If the landlord felt that that issue had already been settled in earlier proceedings, it could apply to strike out the defence as an abuse of process.

C3.12   *Muir Group Housing Association Ltd v Thornley*
(1993) 25 HLR 89; [1993] 1 EGLR 51; [1993] 10 EG 144; (1992) 91 LGR 1, CA

Secure status lost by subletting; tenant could not compel completion of right to buy

A secure tenant exercised the right to buy in May 1989, but in October 1989 (before the purchase was completed) moved out and sublet the whole house on an assured shorthold tenancy at a profit rent. The landlords alleged that, by operation of Housing Act 1985 s93, secure status had been lost by the subletting and that a subsequent notice to quit had determined the remaining contractual tenancy. The tenant alleged that the right to buy had already arisen and been admitted by the landlord, who was thus compelled to convey the house.

The Court of Appeal held that secure status had been lost by the subletting. Furthermore, applying *Sutton LBC v Swann* (C3.13), it held that a tenancy had to be secure for the tenant to have the right to compel completion of the right to buy. Possession was granted.

C3.13   *Sutton LBC v Swann*
(1986) 18 HLR 140, CA

Where security lost by subletting, tenant could not finalise exercise of right to buy

The secure tenant of a council flat made an application under the 'right to buy' scheme. He then bought a different house and moved out of his flat and into the house. He subsequently again applied to buy the flat. The council responded with a notice to quit and possession proceedings in respect of the flat.

The Court of Appeal held, granting possession, that the tenant had lost his secure status on ceasing to occupy the flat and that Housing Act 1980 s16(11) (now Housing Act 1985 s139(2)) required the tenancy to be secure in order to perfect acquisition under the right to buy scheme.

C3.14   *Ujima Housing Association v Ansah*
(1998) 30 HLR 831, CA

Viewed objectively a tenant who had sublet premises did not have intention to occupy

The defendant was an assured tenant. He sublet the entire flat on an assured shorthold tenancy on terms which were inconsistent with his remaining in occupation as his only or principal home. The rent under the subtenancy was a market rent which was £90 more than the rent that the defendant paid. He left furniture in the flat, but no personal possessions. Ujima served a notice to quit and brought possession proceedings. The trial judge held that the defendant had security since he continued to occupy the flat as his principal home.

Ujima's appeal was allowed by the Court of Appeal. The test introduced by the Housing Act 1988 was strict and, since the defendant was no longer in physical occupation, the onus was on him to establish that he was still occupying the flat as his principal home. He had granted the right to immediate occupation to others and was unable to return unless they voluntarily surrendered it to him. Viewed objectively, the defendant did not have the intention to preserve his occupation of the flat as his principal residence.

C3.15   *Zionmor v Islington LBC*
(1998) 30 HLR 822; March 1998 *Legal Action* 10, CA (see N4.21)

No inference that tenant had intended to give up tenancy where friend and possessions left in property

High Court

C3.16   *Amoah v Barking and Dagenham LBC*
(2001) 81 P&CR D12; March 2001 *Legal Action* 28, 23 January 2001, ChD

Prisoner serving long sentence had not ceased to reside

Mr Amoah was a secure tenant. On 18 April 1997, he was sentenced to 12 years' imprisonment. He left items of furniture in the property and appointed a relative to act as 'caretaker' in his absence. The council served a notice to quit and obtained a possession order on the basis that Mr Amoah had lost his status as a secure tenant.

Mr Amoah appealed successfully. Etherton J held that he had retained his secure status. Whilst there was some doubt as to the evidence of a resident caretaker, an intention to return could in any event be evinced by other factors. *Brickfield Properties v Hughes* (C4.4) made clear that the presence of furniture alone for a period of nine years could be sufficient to show an intention to return. Mr Amoah had already been transferred to open conditions and had visited the property when able to do so. Furthermore, it was clear that the property was the only accommodation in which the appellant could and would reside on his release. In those circumstances, the fact that the appellant had left furniture in the property was of itself sufficient to show an outward visible sign of an intention to return. Etherton J drew the following principles from the authorities:

(1) Absence by a tenant might be sufficiently prolonged to raise a presumption that the tenant was no longer a secure tenant. Whether or not that was the case was a matter of fact and degree; (2) Assuming an absence of this length (a) the onus was on the tenant to rebut the presumption; (b) the tenant had to establish a de facto intention to return; (c) whilst there was no set limit to the length of any absence, a tenant was required to show that there was a practical or real possibility of the fulfilment of his intention to return to the property within a reasonable time; and (d) the tenant had to show that his inward intent had some formal outward and visible sign, which was sufficiently substantial and permanent that, in all the circumstances, it was sufficiently adequate to rebut the presumption that he had ceased to be in possession.

C3.17 *Waltham Forest CBHA v Fanning*
July 2001 *Legal Action* 33; 12 March 2001, QBD

Tenant had not discharged burden of proving that she genuinely intended to return

The defendant was an assured tenant. Her tenancy agreement did not permit subletting. On 28 June 1999, she signed an agreement with a letting agency which authorised the agency to form a legally binding tenancy agreement with any tenants. In July 1999, the agency, on behalf of the defendant, granted an assured shorthold tenancy to tenants. The claimant brought possession proceedings. HHJ Bradbury held that:

(1) The defendant had, knowingly, authorised the letting agency to let the property.

(2) In considering matters objectively, the defendant did not occupy the property as her principal residence under Housing Act 1988 s1. The defendant's assured tenancy ended in July 1999 when she authorised the agency to allow tenants into occupation of the property. By leaving personal possessions and furniture in the property, the defendant had not maintained a sufficient presence to sustain any assured tenancy (*Ujima Housing Association v Ansah* (C3.14)).

(3) The notice to quit was correctly served and had expired. The claimant was entitled to a possession order.

Rougier J dismissed the defendant's appeal. Despite the subletting of assured premises, it was still open to the tenant to show a genuine intention to return and use those premises as her permanent residence. However, on the evidence the judge had not acted unreasonably in holding that the appellant had not discharged the burden of proving objectively that she genuinely intended to return.

County courts

C3.18 *Notting Hill Housing Trust v Etoria*
April 1989 *Legal Action* 22; [1989] CLY 1912, Bloomsbury County Court

Where real possibility of life prisoner returning within 8 years, residence satisfied

The defendant was the secure tenant of a small flat. He lived there until October 1986, when he was convicted of murder and sentenced to life imprisonment. No recommendation was given about the term that he should serve. The defendant's brother stayed in the flat, looking after it. The landlord served a notice to quit and brought possession proceedings, contending that it was no longer the tenant's only or principal home. The judge accepted the tenant's evidence that he continued to regard the flat as his home, that his brother lived there as a caretaker, that furniture and belongings remained and that the tenant's case would be reviewed for parole in 1995.

HHJ Dobry QC held that, although it was a 'borderline' case, there was a real and practicable possibility that the defendant's intention to return would be realised in 1995 and that a period of eight years from the date of service of the notice to quit, although a long time, was, in the circumstances, reasonable.

Scottish courts

C3.19 *Johnson v Dundee CC*
2006 Hous LR 68, Lands Tribunal

Where tenant married, presumption that he lived with wife and not in his property

Mr Johnson sought a finding that he was entitled to exercise the right to buy under the Housing (Scotland) Act 1987. He was a secure tenant who suffered from a psychotic illness. He was cared for by a friend who lived in the next street. In May 2004 he married her. In 2005 he applied to buy his property, but the council refused to entertain the application, contending that he had not been living in the property continuously for two years prior to the application.

The Scottish Lands Tribunal refused his application. The marriage was enough to give rise to a presumption that he and his wife were living together in her home. The onus was on Mr Johnson to show that this was not the case. He had failed to do this. He clearly found giving evidence very stressful and it was not possible to make an accurate assessment of his credibility. His wife was a hesitant and unforthcoming witness who appeared to choose answers which she felt would assist Mr Johnson's case and which were often inconsistent or contradictory. The housing officer was a reliable witness who said that Mr Johnson's property was largely unfurnished and appeared unoccupied when she had visited. The evidence of the neighbours, though largely circumstantial, pointed to the couple living together at Mr Johnson's wife's property.

Note: Although this is a decision under the Housing (Scotland) Act 1987, it is likely that an English or Welsh court which made the same findings of fact would have reached the same conclusion.

C3.20 *McLoughlin's Curator Bonis v Motherwell DC*
1994 SLT (Lands Tr) 31, Lands Tribunal

Where tenant ill and could not form intention to return, security lost

The tenant was taken seriously ill and was admitted to hospital for about five months. His illness was such that he could not immediately return to his own home nor, more importantly, form the intention to return to it (cf,

Tickner v Hearn (C4.14)). A 'curator bonis' was appointed to administer his affairs. The curator bonis paid the rent and maintained the tenant's tenancy. In order to improve the assets available to the estate of the tenant, he exercised the right to buy.

The Lands Tribunal held that security of tenure had been lost. The tenant was no longer occupying the property as his 'only or principal home' (Housing (Scotland) Act 1987 s44(1)(b); in England and Wales, Housing Act 1985 s81).

C3.21   *Roxburgh DC v Collins*
1991 SLT (Sh Ct) 49; 1991 1 SCLR 575; 1991 8 GWD 483, Sheriff Court (see E14.22)

Son succeeded to mother's tenancy despite living in lodgings elsewhere for six years

C4   Occupation as a residence

The Rent Acts provided that a tenant wishing to maintain a statutory tenancy must continue to occupy the premises in question as a residence (Rent Act 1977 s2(1)(a)). In many circumstances the courts treat tenants as occupying premises as a residence even though they are temporarily absent for surprisingly long periods of time, provided that they maintain an intention to return and a physical manifestation of that intention. If tenants cease to occupy as a residence, there can be no statutory tenancy and, if the contractual tenancy has been determined, the tenants lose security of tenure. Although the test of occupation 'as a residence' is different to that of occupation as an 'only or principal home' (see C3), the Rent Act cases concerning temporary absence may be relevant to cases involving secure and assured tenants who are temporarily absent.

A considerable body of case-law on this subject has built up over the years (see, eg, Madge, McConnell, Gallagher and Luba, *Defending Possession Proceedings*, 6th edn, LAG, chapter 14.) See too *Housing Law Casebook* 3rd edn for the following, which have been omitted from this edition:

C10.6 *DJ Crocker Securities (Portsmouth) Ltd v Johal* [1989] 2 EGLR 102; (1989) 42 EG 103, CA

C10.7 *Duke v Porter* (1987) 19 HLR 1; [1986] 2 EGLR 101; (1986) 280 EG 633, CA

C10.13 *Robert Thackray's Estate Ltd v Kaye* (1989) 21 HLR 160; [1989] 1 EGLR 127; [1989] 22 EG 95, CA

House of Lords

C4.1   *Hampstead Way Investments Ltd v Lewis-Weare*
[1985] 1 WLR 164; [1985] 1 All ER 564, (1985) 17 HLR 269; [1985] 1 EGLR 120; (1985) 274 EG 281, HL

Where tenant moved into another home and used flat merely to sleep on work nights, not a residence

The tenant rented a flat with two living rooms and two bedrooms. Later he and his wife bought a three-bedroomed house half a mile away. He and his family moved into the house. The tenant worked in a nightclub and, in order not to disturb his wife, slept in the flat five nights a week. He slept until early afternoon, when he went to the house and ate with his wife. He spent Sundays and Mondays, when he was not working, at the house. He had no meals in the flat and did not entertain any friends there.

The House of Lords held that the use made of the flat was very limited and insufficient for it to be a second home. Accordingly, it was not occupied as a residence. The flat was too far away to be treated as part of a combined unit. The tenant's appeal against the possession order made in the Court of Appeal was dismissed.

Court of Appeal

C4.2 *Bevington v Crawford*
(1974) 232 EG 191, CA

Flat remained residence despite tenant only staying in it ten days every year

The tenant rented a two-room flat in Harrow. Later he also took a three-room flat in the Grand Hotel in Cannes, France. On average he spent two to three months per year in England and the rest of the year in Cannes, where he had property interests and owned a golf course, which he ran. When he was in England he regarded the flat as his home, but spent much of the time visiting relations and friends in other parts of England. He actually stayed in the flat nine or ten days per year. His furniture and personal belongings remained in the flat in Harrow. At first instance, the landlord's claim for possession was dismissed.

The landlord's appeal was also dismissed. Lord Denning MR stated that the flat in Harrow had started off as the tenant's home and that he had not given it up. The judge's finding was justified on the evidence before him.

C4.3 *Blanway Investments Ltd v Lynch*
(1993) 25 HLR 378, CA

Residence where 2/3 nights in flat and rest of week spent in home outside London

The defendant had a statutory tenancy of a flat in Islington. The original tenancy agreement had contained a covenant not to part with possession of the premises or any part of them and an obligation that the tenant should use them 'as a private residence' only. The tenant stayed at the flat for two or three nights a week, spending the rest of the time with a Mrs Mountney who lived in Essex. Two of Mrs Mountney's daughters also stayed at the flat with their boyfriends. It was held that the tenant was 'a two-home man' who continued to enjoy Rent Act protection. However, at first instance a possession order was made on the ground that allowing Mrs Mountney's daughters to set up residence in the flat amounted to a breach of the user covenant.

On appeal, setting aside the possession order, the Court of Appeal held that, where tenancies are granted to individuals, they are entitled to occupy with their spouses and family. In the present age there could be no objection to the fact that Mr Lynch was not married to Mrs Mountney or to him sharing with her daughters, who could be regarded as part of his wider family.

C4.4   **Brickfield Properties Ltd v Hughes**
(1988) 20 HLR 108; [1988] 1 EGLR 106; [1988] 24 EG 95, CA

Tenant maintained intention to return to residence despite prolonged absence

Mr Hughes, aged 74, was a statutory tenant of a flat in London. His wife inherited a cottage in Lancashire in 1970 and from 1978 he and his wife remained there permanently. Between 1978 and 1987 he did not return to the flat in London at all and his wife only went there three times. However, their children lived in the flat and their furniture and books stayed there. The tenant said that he intended to return to the London flat if his wife predeceased him or if their health meant that they could not manage on their own in Lancashire. Their daughter gave evidence that she did not think that they would last another winter in the cottage.

The county court judge refused to make a possession order and the landlord's appeal was dismissed by the Court of Appeal. The court stated that, where a tenant's absence is prolonged, the burden of proof is on the tenant to establish an intention to return. That intention must be accompanied by some outward and visible sign. The continued occupation by a caretaker or relative or the presence of furniture may be sufficient. There must also be a 'practical possibility' or a 'real possibility' of fulfilment of the intention to return within a reasonable time. Although a statutory tenancy may be maintained even though the tenant has another home, courts should look at 'two-home' cases with particular care.

C4.5   **Brown v Brash**
[1948] 2 KB 247; [1948] 1 All ER 922, CA

Prisoner's residence not established where wife left house taking furniture with her

The tenant was sent to prison for two years for stealing six tons of tea. His partner and their two children continued living in the house, but then she left, taking the children and much of the furniture with her.

The Court of Appeal held that the tenant had ceased occupying the premises as a residence and that his statutory tenancy had come to an end. The question of whether a tenant's absence is sufficiently long to infer a cessation of occupation is one of fact and degree. Where the absence is sufficiently long to allow that inference, the onus is on the tenant to rebut the presumption that possession has ceased. In order to do so, the tenant must establish a de facto intention to return and some formal outward and visible sign of that intention – an 'animus possidendi' and a 'corpus possessionis'. If the physical sign of the intention (eg, the tenant's caretaker or furniture) is removed, then the statutory tenancy ends.

C4.6   **Carphone Warehouse UK Ltd v Malekout**
[2006] EWCA Civ 767; [2007] HLR 3; (2006) *Times* 28 June

Where prior claim for possession settled, landlord could not later assert not a residence

In 1985 Dr Malekout was granted a Rent Act protected tenancy of a flat. In 1997 or 1998 the landlord terminated the contractual tenancy, with the effect that Dr Malekout became a statutory tenant 'if and so long as he occupied the premises as his residence'. In 1998 or 1999, the flat became uninhabitable and no one occupied it. In 2002, as a result of rent arrears, the landlord sought possession, claiming that Dr Malekout had ceased to occupy the premises as his residence. Dr Malekout defended, asserting that the statutory tenancy continued and counterclaimed for breach of repairing obligations. The claim was settled in 2003 by a Tomlin order which provided for the carrying out of repairs and that 'both sets of proceedings are discontinued and all claims therein settled in full and final settlement'. The premises remained unoccupied and in 2004 Carphone sought possession, claiming rent arrears and that Dr Malekout was no longer a statutory tenant because he had ceased to occupy them as his residence. Dr Malekout resumed residence in the flat during the course of the trial. HHJ Walker rejected as untruthful Dr Malekout's evidence that he had remained in residence until 1998 but found that the only 'sensible inference' from the terms of the Tomlin order was that Dr Melkout was a statutory tenant in 2003. Carphone was estopped from contending that Dr Malekout had lost his statutory tenancy before 2003. The claim for possession failed. Carphone appealed.

The Court of Appeal dismissed the appeal. Carphone could have challenged Dr Malekout's status as statutory tenant in the 2002 proceedings. Indeed, it did so on the pleadings, but did not take the issue to trial. The agreement reached was predicated on the assumption that Dr Malekout had a statutory tenancy. The Tomlin order settled between the parties the issue of his intention to return to actual occupation once the premises were habitable.

C4.7   *Gofor Investments v Roberts*
(1975) 29 P&CR 366, CA

Ten years not too long a time to fulfil requirement to return within a reasonable period

On the expiry of a fixed-term Rent Act protected tenancy the landlord took possession proceedings, claiming that the tenant had ceased to occupy the flat in question as a residence. The tenant, her husband and their six children had lived in the flat until 1970. Then she, her husband and four children went to live abroad. The two eldest sons lived in the flat, but by the time of the court hearing the flat was occupied by a licensee of the tenant. One son and the husband had stayed in the flat at various times. Some of the tenant's furniture remained there. The tenant's evidence that she originally intended to return to the flat when her children's education was completed in 1978 or 1980, but that she now intended to return in 1976, was accepted. A county court judge dismissed the landlord's claim for possession.

The Court of Appeal dismissed the landlord's appeal. The judge had been entitled to find that the tenant intended to return within a reasonable period. Ten years was not too long a time to fulfil the requirement to return within a reasonable period. The presence of the tenant's furniture together with the visits by members of her family were enough to constitute a 'corpus possessionis'.

C4.8   *Hall v King*

(1987) 19 HLR 440; (1988) 55 P&CR 307; [1987] 2 EGLR 121; (1987) 283 EG 1400, CA

Wife occupying premises which were not the matrimonial home not a statutory tenant

After the breakdown of his marriage, Mr King took a protected tenancy of premises in his own name in which it was proposed that his wife should live. He lived elsewhere with a Miss Driver. When the tenancy came to an end, the landlord sought to evict Mrs King. She claimed a statutory tenancy.

The Court of Appeal held that the landlord was entitled to a possession order. Mrs King was not entitled to rely on the protection of Matrimonial Homes Act 1983 s1(6) (now Family Law Act 1996 s30(4)) nor on the line of Rent Act cases starting with *Brown v Draper* [1944] KB 309, CA, in which a wife's occupation of a matrimonial home has been deemed to be that of the husband, because the property had never been Mr and Mrs King's matrimonial home.

C4.9   *Moreland Properties (UK) Ltd v Dhokia*

[2003] EWCA Civ 1639; [2004] L&TR 20

Where tenant no longer in residence and did not contest possession, subtenants could not defend possession claim successfully

A flat was let to Mr Dhokia in 1974. He remained in occupation until 1987 when he moved to another property. He took all the furniture and carpets. The flat was empty until November 1991, when Mr Dhokia purported to sublet the flat to his nephew, who lived there with other members of his family. He did not charge a profit rent, merely the amount that he himself paid to the landlord. When the landlord discovered the position it brought possession proceedings. Mr Dhokia did not resist the claim and a possession order was made against him. However, his nephew and the other members of the family contended that Mr Dhokia had been a protected tenant and that their subtenancy survived the order for possession as a result of Rent Act 1977 s137(2). The trial judge accepted this argument and dismissed the possession claim.

The landlord's appeal was allowed by the Court of Appeal. After considering *Trustees of Henry Smith's Charity v Wilson* [1983] QB 316, CA, Sir Martin Nourse stated that it would be extraordinary if someone who had abandoned the right to occupy premises for four or five years could either return to possession or give anyone else the right to possession. In any event, even if Mr Dhokia had not lost his statutory tenancy by abandoning the premises, as a statutory tenant, he could not grant an effective subtenancy. The property had therefore not been lawfully sublet under s137. An order for possession was made.

C4.10   *Prince v Robinson*

(1999) 31 HLR 89, CA

Where tenant hardly stayed in premises and had few possessions there, not a residence

The plaintiff, Mr Prince, sought a declaration that he had a subsisting tenancy of a ground floor sitting room of premises which the defendants had recently bought, apparently with vacant possession, for £240,000. He had been granted a tenancy by the previous owner in the early 1970s. In 1989 he went to Devon, taking most of his personal belongings with him, but leaving a guitar and a few other items. Over the next two years he only stayed at the premises twice. The property was then squatted. On 6 February 1991 a serious fire occurred in which the squatter died and the interior of the house was badly damaged. Mr Prince tried to negotiate with the then landlord for payment of a capital sum in return for the surrender of his tenancy but no agreement was reached. However, the landlord proceeded to refurbish the house. He did so in such a way that the tenant's bed-sit ceased to exist as identifiable separate accommodation and became part of an open-plan kitchen. Mr Prince relied on Land Registration Act 1925 s70(1)(k), which provides that a lease (which includes a tenancy) granted for a term of less than 21 years is an overriding interest.

His claim and subsequent appeal were both dismissed. He was not occupying as a residence within the meaning of Rent Act 1977 s2 because he had not stayed in the flat, even as an occasional visitor, since 1990, had no possessions there since the fire and only minimal possessions before then. The Court of Appeal did not find it necessary to express a definite view on the landlord's contention that the tenancy had been frustrated but Robert Walker LJ doubted whether the doctrine of frustration could apply to a weekly or other periodic tenancy in circumstances where fire damage can be repaired in a matter of weeks or months.

C4.11 **Regalian Securities Ltd v Scheuer**
(1982) 5 HLR 48; (1982) 47 P&CR 362; (1982) 263 EG 973, CA

Where tenant lived with family elsewhere, use of flat not as a residence

The tenant rented a flat with one bedroom, a living room, kitchen and bathroom. Subsequently he formed a relationship with a woman who lived three or four miles away. He moved in with her and married her. Later, she had a baby. The tenant kept furniture and clothes in his flat. He used the flat during the daytime and worked there as a script-writer. For two months the family lived in the flat when their other home was rented out on a 'winter let'. A county court judge held that the tenant was not occupying the flat as a residence and made a possession order.

The tenant's appeal was dismissed. The question was primarily one of fact for the judge. There was plenty of material on which to conclude that it would be artificial to describe the tenant's user of the flat as a home when it was close to the home where he lived with his family.

C4.12 **Richards v Green**
(1983) 11 HLR 1; (1983) 268 EG 443, CA

Difficult for landlord to reverse on appeal decision that tenant only temporarily absent

The tenant left his rented flat in June 1980 to look after his parents who were seriously ill. His mother died shortly after that date. His father died in January 1981. The tenant continued living in his parents' house to carry out work to put it into good shape and to sell it. It was on the market in December 1982 when possession proceedings brought by the landlord of the flat were heard. The tenant gave evidence that he intended to return to the flat when the house was sold and that his furniture, books, records and some clothes had been left in the flat. The county court judge held that the flat was the tenant's home and dismissed the claim for possession.

The landlord's appeal was dismissed. It was a case where the tenant was temporarily absent. In cases such as this, where a county court judge has properly applied his or her mind, it is very difficult to persuade the Court of Appeal to reverse the decision.

C4.13   *Stephens v Kerr*
[2006] EWCA Civ 187; [2006] HLR 21

Where tenant driven out by neighbours, she remained a statutory tenant

Ms Stephens issued proceedings for breach of various covenants in her tenancy agreement and sought a declaration that she was a statutory tenant. Her landlord defended on the basis that Ms Stephens did not occupy the premises as a residence because she lived predominantly with a friend after she had been driven out by neighbours (Rent Act 1977 s2(1)(a)). On a trial of a preliminary issue, a judge found that, on the evidence, Ms Stephens was a statutory tenant because the connection she had with the property was sufficiently great that it could be taken that she occupied it as her residence. The landlord appealed.

The Court of Appeal dismissed the appeal. The judge had approached the issue carefully and conscientiously. The findings were plainly open to the judge on the evidence available and the fact that a different judge might have reached a different conclusion was irrelevant. The only error was the judge's granting of permission to appeal. The appeal was unsustainable.

C4.14   *Tickner v Hearn*
[1960] 1 WLR 1406; [1961] 1 All ER 65, CA

Fact that tenant 'mentally unsound' did not prevent intention to return

The tenant spent five and a half years in a mental hospital suffering from schizophrenia. The Court of Appeal held that the fact that she was 'mentally unsound' did not mean that she was incapable of forming an intention to return to the premises.

C4.15   *Wigley v Leigh*
[1950] 2 KB 305; [1950] 1 All ER 73, CA

Residence where prolonged absence due to war and TB

The tenant was absent from the home that she rented from 1940 to 1949. Initially she stayed with relatives because of the war. Later she was prevented from returning home because she had tuberculosis. It was held that she continued to occupy the property as a residence.

C5   **Company lets**

Lettings to companies cannot be secure or assured tenancies because companies are not 'individuals' – see Housing Act 1985 s81 (the 'tenant condition') and Housing Act 1988 s1(1)(b). Although a letting to a company can be a protected tenancy under Rent Act 1977, no statutory tenancy can arise because a company cannot 'occupy as a residence' in order to satisfy the provisions of Rent Act 1977 s2(1)(a). See *Hiller v United Dairies (London) Ltd* [1934] 1 KB 57, CA, where the Court of Appeal held that there was a genuine letting to a company.

There are dicta which indicate that the courts may not accept 'company let' agreements where the company is a mere nominee of the tenant. In *Firstcross Ltd v East West Export/Import Ltd* (1980) 7 HLR 98; (1980) 255 EG 255; (1980) 41 P&CR 145, CA, Stephenson LJ stated that if the individual occupant had said that

> ... the company were merely his agent or nominee, and if the Judge had believed him, he could and should have given effect to the real agreement and dismissed the claim for possession. ((1980) 7 HLR at 112)

In *Dando v Hitchcock* [1954] 2 QB 317; [1954] 3 WLR 76; [1954] 2 All ER 335, CA, Denning LJ said:

> I can well see that the court would not allow the landlord to avoid the Acts by taking someone as a nominal tenant, while knowing that the real tenant was to be somebody else. ([1954] 2 All ER at 336)

See also *Cove v Flick* [1954] 2 QB 326 at 328 and the approach of the Court of Appeal in *Gisborne v Burton* [1989] QB 390; [1988] 3 WLR 921, CA (involving the Agricultural Holdings Act 1948) and *Evans v Engelson* (G23.7) (involving Rent Act 1977 Sch 15 Case 9).

Court of Appeal

C5.1   *Eaton Square Properties Ltd v O'Higgins*
[2001] L&TR 165; (2001) 33 HLR 771, CA

Tenancy entered into in name of company for tax advantages not a sham

Initially Mr O'Higgins had a tenancy of residential premises. However, in 1979 Eaton Square granted a 20-year tenancy of the property to Greylane Ltd. Mr O'Higgins, who had a 75 per cent interest in Greylane, continued to occupy the property and guaranteed the company's obligations under the lease. On the expiry of the contractual term, he remained in occupation and claimed that he had a statutory tenancy under Rent Act 1977. The claimant sought possession contending that a company as tenant could not claim statutory protection. The judge at first instance found that Mr O'Higgins had replaced the previous statutory tenant and paid sums of money that were accepted by the claimant as rent. He dismissed the claim. He held that the common intention was that the defendant was the true tenant and so he was entitled to statutory protection. Jonathan Parker J allowed the company's appeal. Mr O'Higgins appealed against that decision contending that the tenancy agreement with the company was a sham since it had been entered into solely for tax purposes and that he remained the true tenant.

The Court of Appeal dismissed his appeal. Although at the time the first lease was entered into with Mr O'Higgins personally he might have become a statutory tenant, that lease ceased when the agreement with Greylane was entered into. Sham transactions had been considered by the courts in *Hilton v Plustitle Ltd* (C5.3) and *Antoniades v Villiers and Bridger*

(B4.2) where the definition given by Diplock LJ in *Snook v London and West Riding Investments Ltd* [1967] 2 QB 786; [1967] 1 All ER 518, CA was approved, namely:

> ... acts done or documents executed by the parties to the 'sham' which are intended by them to give to third parties or to the court the appearance of creating between the parties legal rights and obligations different from the actual legal rights and obligations (if any) which the parties intend to create.

There had been no allegation of dishonesty and Jonathan Parker J had been correct to say that the findings of fact led to the conclusion that the company was the true tenant. The agreement had not failed to create the legal relations that on its face it did create. Mr O'Higgins had said in evidence that he had asked for the tenancy to be put into the name of the company to enable the company to take a tax advantage. Such a purpose did not mean that the transaction was a sham. The dicta in *Snook* showed that there had to be a common intention to show to third parties rights which were different from those intended. The purpose of the agreement was to show the Revenue that a tenancy had been entered into with the company.

C5.2   *Estavest Investments Ltd v Commercial Express Travel Ltd*
(1989) 21 HLR 106; [1988] 2 EGLR 91; [1988] 49 EG 73, CA

Company let not sham where company paid the rent

Landlords let premises to a limited company with the intention of avoiding the provisions of the Rent Act. It was intended that the flat should be occupied by a director of the company and/or the daughter of the managing director of the company. Later, although the same person was to occupy the flat, a new tenancy was granted to a different company. Rent demands were sent to and paid by the companies.

The Court of Appeal held that there was no evidence of sham or artificiality, noting that the companies named as tenants in the tenancy agreements had performed all the obligations under the lease and that the individual director who lived in the premises performed none.

C5.3   *Hilton v Plustitle Ltd*
[1989] 1 WLR 149; [1988] 3 All ER 1051; (1989) 21 HLR 72; [1989] 1 EGLR 119; (1989) 58 P&CR 25, CA

Where prospective occupant required to set up company to obtain tenancy, no sham

Ms Rose was looking for accommodation to rent. She saw and answered a newspaper advertisement. It was made clear to her by the landlord that the letting was to be to a company. She was advised by solicitors and bought an 'off the shelf' company, Plustitle Ltd, for £150. She became a shareholder and a director. The tenancy was granted in the name of Plustitle Ltd. Before the agreement was signed, the landlord obtained a reference from Ms Rose's own bank. The agreement gave the company the right to nominate the occupiers of the property who were to pay no rent. The rent, which was to be paid by the company, was guaranteed by Ms Rose's brother. Ms Rose claimed that the letting was a sham and that she was the real tenant.

The Court of Appeal upheld the circuit judge's conclusion that the transaction was not a sham. Croom-Johnson LJ referred to the 'accepted definition' of sham in *Snook v London and West Riding Investments Ltd* [1967] 2 QB 786, CA, at 802 (see C5.1). Ms Rose unsuccessfully petitioned the House of Lords for leave to appeal.

C5.4   *Kaye v Massbetter Ltd and Kanter*

(1992) 24 HLR 28; [1991] 2 EGLR 97; [1991] 39 EG 129, CA

Tenancy not a sham where parties intended company to be the tenant

Mr Kanter responded to an advertisement in an evening newspaper, and, after viewing the flat in question and discussing rent, was informed that the landlord would only let to a company. He did not have a company and, as he was an undischarged bankrupt, he could not become a director of an 'off the shelf' company. Instead, two friends bought a company for him and a tenancy agreement was drawn up naming the company as the tenant. In the county court, it was held that this was a genuine letting to a company and a possession order was made.

    In the Court of Appeal, Lord Donaldson MR stated:

> The test is: Was the letting genuine? If you look at the facts and find that there are indicia that the company was never intended to be the tenant, then you may conclude that it was not genuine. But the issue is simply one of genuineness. ((1992) 24 HLR at 32)

However, the Court of Appeal decided that this was essentially a question of fact for the trial judge and saw no reason to disturb his decision that the parties intended the company to be the tenant. Mr Kanter unsuccessfully petitioned the House of Lords for leave to appeal.

C5.5   *Navinter SA v Pastoll*

(1990) 21 March, CA (CAT 90/308)

Where occupier neither director of shareholder of company, arguable tenancy was a sham

Landlords took proceedings under RSC Ord 113 following the expiry of a renewed, fixed-term 'company let'. The defendant had been the true occupier throughout, having bought an 'off the shelf' company to take the tenancy because the landlords were not willing to let to an individual. He argued that the arrangement was a sham, as the landlords had known from the outset that the flat was required for his personal use. At first instance Jowitt J granted possession, holding that *Hilton v Plustitle* Ltd (C5.3) could not be distinguished. However, the occupier's application for a stay of possession pending appeal was granted.

    In the Court of Appeal, Taylor LJ held that it was at least arguable that *Hilton* could be distinguished because (a) the occupier was neither a director nor shareholder of the company and (b) the tenant had personally signed the acceptance of the offer of renewal.

C6   **The landlord condition**

There was no restriction on the type of landlord that could grant a Rent Act protected tenancy. Similarly, any landlord (except a local authority) can grant an assured tenancy. However, it is an essential requirement for the creation of a secure tenancy under Housing Act 1985 that the 'landlord condition' is fulfilled, ie, that the interest of the landlord belongs to one of the prescribed authorities listed in Housing Act 1985 s80(1). These include local authorities, housing associations (where the tenancy was granted before 15 January 1989), new town corporations and urban development corporations.

Court of Appeal

C6.1   **Ali Bhai and Cabare v Black Roof CHA Ltd**
[2001] 2 All ER 865; (2001) 33 HLR 607; (2000) *Times* 14 November, CA
Fully mutual co-op tenants became secure when co-op ceased to be fully mutual

The claimants were tenants of a flat under a contractual periodic tenancy granted by the association in 1985. They maintained that they had a secure tenancy and so could exercise the right to buy under Housing Act 1985 Part V. HHJ Brian Knight QC decided that the tenancy was not a secure tenancy because the association was a fully mutual registered housing co-operative when the tenancy was granted, although it ceased to be fully mutual in December 1991.

The claimants' appeal was allowed. The tenancy was a secure 'housing association tenancy' within the meaning of Housing Act 1988 Sch 18 para 4(c). Although the expression was not there defined, it was to be inferred that the relevant definition was that found in Rent Act 1977 Part VI. This conclusion was reinforced by the fact that the expression was also to be found in Housing Act 1988 s35(5) (expressly referred to in Sch 18 para 4(a)) where it was expressed to have the same meaning as in Part VI of the 1977 Act. Therefore, while it was a housing association tenancy, the 'landlord condition' in relation to the tenancy was the 'landlord condition' as it was immediately before the repeals took effect, so the relevant list of prescribed landlords in Housing Act 1985 s80 was the unamended list, which included a non-mutual association. The effect was that, when the defendant became a non-mutual association, the 'landlord condition' was thereby satisfied in relation to it, and the tenancy thereupon became a secure tenancy.

C6.2   **Banjo v Brent LBC**
[2005] EWCA Civ 292; [2005] 1 WLR 2520; [2005] HLR 32; (2005) *Times* 29 March
Tenancy at will cannot be secure even when landlord and tenant condition satisfied

In the early 1970s Mr Banjo was a subtenant of a housing association. Brent LBC then became the freeholder. In 1974 Mr Banjo acquired a long leasehold interest from his immediate landlord and became a tenant of Brent for the remaining term of the lease. It was a 'long tenancy', which, by virtue of Housing Act 1985 Sch 1 para 1, could not be a secure tenancy. The contractual term of his lease expired in September 1980. He remained in occupation after that date, but paid no rent. In February 2002 Brent gave notice of its intention to take proceedings to recover possession. Mr Banjo sought a declaration that he was entitled to exercise the right to buy. Brent brought a Part 20 claim seeking possession. A judge dismissed his claim and held that his claim to exercise the right to buy was barred by limitation and, in so far as relevant, by equitable principles of laches. The judge also dismissed Brent's claim for possession, holding that, on the determination of the long lease, Mr Banjo had remained in occupation as a tenant at will and on that basis the tenancy was a secure tenancy. Brent appealed.

The Court of Appeal allowed the appeal. No periodic tenancy arose on the determination of the long lease in June 1982, either under Housing Act 1985 s86 (because the fixed-term tenancy which Mr Banjo had previously held was not itself a secure tenancy) or by implication from the demand, payment or acceptance of rent. Security of tenure is dependent on there being a tenancy that the landlord cannot bring to an end without obtaining an order for possession. The tenancy at will was determined in February 2002. Thereafter, Mr Banjo remained in possession as a trespasser. He was neither a tenant nor a licensee. It is doubtful whether parliament intended that a tenancy at will could be a secure tenancy, even where the conditions in ss80 and 81 are satisfied. Accordingly the judge was wrong to refuse to grant possession.

The House of Lords subsequently refused a petition for leave to appeal ([2005] 1 WLR 2818).

C6.3 *R v Plymouth CC and Cornwall CC ex p Freeman*
(1987) 19 HLR 328, CA

All joint landlords need to satisfy landlord condition

Mr Freeman was the tenant of a lodge in parkland. In 1970 the parkland was bought jointly by Plymouth City Council and Cornwall County Council. After the Housing Act 1980 came into force, Mr Freeman claimed the right to buy. The councils claimed that he was not entitled to do this because the property was owned jointly and, at that time, before the implementation of the Housing and Building Control Act 1984, only the city council satisfied the landlord condition under Housing Act 1980 s28(2) (now Housing Act 1985 s80).

The Court of Appeal held that the landlord condition was not satisfied if only one of the joint landlords was among the list of bodies specified in Housing Act 1980 s18(4) (now Housing Act 1985 s80(1)).

Scottish courts

C6.4 *Knowles Housing Association v Millar*
2001 SLT 1326, Court of Session

Secure status lost on change of landlord where new landlord did not satisfy landlord condition

In 1995 the defendant was granted a secure tenancy by Scottish Homes. In 1998 the claimant housing association took a transfer of tenanted housing stock from Scottish Homes, including the defendant's home. In 1999 the association claimed possession on the mandatory rent arrears ground (equivalent to Housing Act 1988 Sch 2 Ground 8). The defendant contended that she remained a secure tenant. A sheriff granted possession. The sheriff principal dismissed an appeal.

The Court of Session dismissed a further appeal. The court reviewed the statutory provisions governing secure and assured status (substantially equivalent to those contained in Housing Act 1985 and Housing Act 1988 in England and Wales). It held that once the interest of the landlord had passed to a body which was not in the list of bodies capable of granting secure tenancies (see Housing Act 1985 s80) the secure status 'simply flies off'. The defendant was accordingly an assured tenant from the moment the identity of her landlord changed.

C7 Assured tenancy transitional provisions

The intention behind the Housing Act 1988 was to create completely new types of tenancy (ie, assured and assured shorthand tenancies). However, some protection was provided for existing Rent Act and housing association tenants. Section 34(1) states that:

(1) A tenancy which is entered into on or after the commencement of this Act cannot be a protected tenancy, unless –

    (a) it is entered into in pursuance of a contract made before the commencement of this Act; or

    (b) it is granted to a person (alone or jointly with others) who, immediately before the tenancy was granted, was a protected or statutory tenant and is so granted by the person who at that time was the landlord (or one of the joint landlords) under the protected or statutory tenancy; or

    (c) it is granted to a person (alone or jointly with others) in the following circumstances –

        (i) prior to the grant of the tenancy, an order for possession of a dwelling-house was made against him (alone or jointly with others) on the court being satisfied as mentioned in section 98(1)(a) of, or Case 1 in Schedule 16 to, the Rent Act 1977 or Case 1 in Schedule 4 to the Rent (Agriculture) Act 1976 (suitable alternative accommodation available); and

        (ii) the tenancy is of the premises which constitute the suitable alternative accommodation as to which the court was so satisfied; and

        (iii) in the proceedings for possession the court considered that, in the circumstances, the grant of an assured tenancy would not afford the required security and, accordingly, directed that the tenancy would be a protected tenancy; or

    (d) it is a tenancy under which the interest of the landlord was at the time the tenancy was granted held by a new town corporation, within the meaning of section 80 of the Housing Act 1985, and, before the date which has effect by virtue of paragraph (a) or paragraph (b) of subsection (4) of section 38 below, ceased to be so held by virtue of a disposal by the Commission for the New Towns made pursuant to a direction under section 37 of the New Towns Act 1981.

Similarly, s35(4) provides that tenancies granted by housing associations on or after 15 January 1989 'cannot' be secure 'unless' one of the exceptions contained in the subsection is met. The most common exception is that which applies to a letting by the same landlord to a person who was immediately beforehand a secure tenant: s35(4)(d).

Court of Appeal

C7.1 *Laimond Properties Ltd v Al-Shakarchi*

(1998) 30 HLR 1099; (1998) *Times* 23 February; [1998] EGCS 21, CA

Where possession ordered against protected tenant on basis of suitable alternative accommodation, the new tenancy did not have to be protected; s34(1)(b) mandatory

The plaintiff company was the freeholder of a house in Oakley Street, London SW3. The defendant was the Rent Act protected tenant of a first floor flat. The plaintiff also owned a house in Cranley Place, London SW7 which it held under a lease expiring in 2013. In February 1997 the plaintiff sought and obtained an order for possession of the defendant's flat in the Oakley Street house on the ground that suitable alternative accommodation would be available. This was the first floor flat of the Cranley Place house, which the plaintiff proposed to let to the defendant on an assured tenancy within the meaning of the Housing Act 1988. It was accepted that this was suitable alternative accommodation. At first instance, HHJ Hallgarten QC, hearing the case before the Court of Appeal decision in *Wellcome Trust v Hamad* (B6.5), held that, although Rent Act 1977 s137 might afford sufficient protection on the expiry of the landlord's lease, there was sufficient doubt that the court could not be satisfied that a protected tenancy would be suitable. However, it was possible for the plaintiff to grant an assured tenancy and, in view of Housing Act 1988 s18, that tenancy would be binding on the freeholders when the lease ended (see [1997] CLY 3310, Central London County Court). The defendant appealed, contending that, because her tenancy in the Oakley Street house was a protected tenancy within the meaning of the Rent Act 1977, no valid assured tenancy could be granted to her on its termination because of Housing Act 1988 s34(1)(b).

Her appeal was dismissed. The Court of Appeal held that s34(1)(a), (b) and (c) deal with three separate situations. Section 34(1)(b) has no application in a case where the landlords have obtained an order for possession since the court 'will have considered whether the new tenancy affords 'the required security' and whether the court should direct that the new tenancy be a protected tenancy'. Roch LJ also (1) accepted submissions that s34(1)(b) was mandatory, not permissive, and (2), approving *Goringe v Twinsectra Ltd* (C7.6), held that s34(1)(b) protection applies both to new tenancies of the same premises and to tenancies of other premises granted by the same landlords.

Note too in Scotland *Queens Cross Housing Association Ltd v McAllister* 2003 SLT 971, a case involving a similar provision in Housing (Scotland) Act 1987 s43(3)(c) – no requirement that the earlier tenancy should be of the same premises.

C7.2 *Rajah v Arogol Co Ltd*

[2001] EWCA Civ 454; [2002] HLR 21; (2001) *Times* 13 April

Section 34(1)(b) not limited to tenancies of the same or substantially the same premises

From 1982 the defendant was the Rent Act protected tenant of the back room on the ground floor of a property. In 1990 he moved to the entire floor. In possession proceedings a circuit judge found that the move amounted to a surrender of the protected tenancy.

The Court of Appeal allowed the tenant's appeal and set aside the possession order made. Following *Laimond Properties Ltd v Al-Shakarchi* (C7.1), it held that the protection given by Housing Act 1988 s34(1)(b) was not limited to the same or substantially the same premises. It is the identity of the landlord and tenant that matters, not the identity of the premises. Furthermore, the fact that the landlord had changed between 1982 and 1990 did not affect the position. Section 34(1)(b) clearly refers to a grant at a later date by the person who was the landlord at the time of the later grant. The move did not constitute a surrender. The defendant retained the protection of the Rent Act.

C7.3   **Santos v Compatriot Holdings Limited**
[2007] EWCA Civ 863; 16 July 2007

No evidence of gap between end of protected tenancy and grant of new tenancy

The claimant was a Rent Act 1977 statutory tenant of a room in a building. The landlord's housekeeper granted her a new tenancy of a different room in the same building, saying that she was acting on behalf of the landlord. The claimant surrendered her existing tenancy and moved into the new room. The landlord later claimed that the new tenancy was an assured shorthold tenancy because it had been entered into after Housing Act 1988 came into force. The claimant, however, relied on s34(1)(b). At the close of the landlord's case, it sought for the first time to adduce evidence that there had been a gap between the surrender of the old tenancy and the start of the new tenancy, and that s34(1)(b) did not apply because the claimant had not been a protected tenant immediately before the grant of the new tenancy. The judge refused to allow the company to raise this argument and granted a declaration that the claimant was a Rent Act protected tenant. The landlord appealed.

The Court of Appeal dismissed the appeal. If the judge had permitted the gap point to be raised, he would have had to grant an adjournment to allow evidence to be obtained. There had been no error of law. In any event, the landlord had not pleaded the point and there was no evidence before the judge to show that there had been a gap between the tenancies.

C7.4   **Secretarial Nominee Co Ltd v Thomas**
[2005] EWCA Civ 1008; [2006] HLR 5; [2006] L&TR 6; (2005) *Times* 20 September

Section 34 does not apply to tenant who was not protected prior to Housing Act 1988

In 1988, before the Housing Act 1988 came into force, Secretarial let a flat for a term of one year on a Rent Act protected tenancy to three joint tenants including a Mr Marshall. In 1989 the flat was again let on a one-year tenancy to Mr Marshall and two others. The tenancy was described as an assured shorthold tenancy. In 1990 it was let to Mr Marshall, a Ms Sucdev and one other. Mr Marshall then moved out but in 1991 the flat was let to Ms

Sucdev, Mr Thomas (the defendant) and one other. There was then a series of one-year tenancies which included Mr Thomas as one of the joint tenants. It followed that by this time none of the joint tenants had been a party to a pre-Housing Act tenancy. The landlord served a Housing Act 1988 s21 notice and sought possession. District Judge Langley held that, in view of Housing Act 1988 s34(1)(b), Mr Thomas enjoyed Rent Act protection.

The Court of Appeal allowed the landlord's appeal. It may be that new (ie, after 15 January 1989) joint tenants of an existing Rent Act tenant enjoy Rent Act protection. However, s34 'begins with the concept of a person who, after the commencement of the 1988 Act, is both a Rent Act tenant and has entered into a new tenancy. Such a person, moreover, has to have been a Rent Act tenant already before the new tenancy'. The words 'and prior to the commencement of this Act' in s34 'have to be understood (in addition to the express requirement of 'immediately before the tenancy was granted') as inherently qualifying the words 'was a protected or statutory tenant'. It is for the sake of such a tenant, and no other that the transitional protection of a protected tenancy is extended.' The statutory language shows that the protection is for a particular person. The Court of Appeal concluded that Mr Thomas was not a Rent Act tenant within the protection of s34(1)(b).

High Court

C7.5   *Rowe v Matthews*
(2001) 33 HLR 921, QBD

On end of restricted contract in 1990, new tenancy was entered into; it was assured

The defendant rented a basement flat from about 1985. At that time the landlord was resident elsewhere in the building and so the tenancy was a restricted contract (Rent Act 1977 ss12 and 19). In April 1990 there was a variation of the rent within the meaning of Housing Act 1988 s36(2)(a) which prevented the creation of a new restricted contract after 15 January 1989. At some time between 1995 and 1997, the landlord and his wife ceased to use their flat as their residence and the landlord transferred the premises to his wife, the present landlord and claimant. The tenant fell into arrears of rent and HHJ Rose made a possession order on the basis that the defendant was an assured tenant. The tenant appealed, contending that the effect of the rent variation had been to create a common-law tenancy, so that when the landlord ceased to reside in the building the defendant became a Rent Act protected tenant.

McCombe J dismissed the tenant's appeal. The combined effect of Housing Act 1988 ss34(1) and 36(2)(a) was the creation of an assured tenancy. The scheme of the transitional provisions was to remove the tenancy from its status as a restricted contract with effect from the 1990 variation. Once the old contract had ended, the tenant had to be regarded as having entered into a 'new contract'. That tenancy had been entered into after the commencement of the Housing Act 1988 and, by virtue of s34(1), could not be a protected tenancy. Permission to appeal to the Court of Appeal was refused ([2001] EWCA Civ 1125).

County courts

C7.6   *Goringe v Twinsectra Ltd*
June 1994 *Legal Action* 11; [1994] CLY 2723, Staines County Court

Section 34(1)(b) not limited to tenancies of the same or substantially the same premises

The plaintiff was a statutory tenant by succession within the meaning of the Rent Act 1977. In April 1989 she agreed with her landlords to move to other accommodation owned by them. They then claimed that, since the new tenancy commenced after 15 January 1989, she was an assured tenant and served notice to increase her rent. The tenant sought a declaration that, in view of the provisions of Housing Act 1988 s34(1)(b), she remained a statutory tenant with Rent Act protection. The landlords claimed that s34(1)(b) did not apply where the accommodation was not 'the same or substantially the same premises'.

It was held that there was ambiguity in the wording of s34(1)(b) and that, therefore, in the light of *Pepper v Hart* [1993] AC 593, HL, the court was entitled to look at *Hansard* as an aid to construction. In parliament this issue was debated in full, and it was made clear that it was not necessary for the premises to be the same or substantially the same. The tenant was accordingly granted a declaration that she continued to enjoy Rent Act protection.

C7.7   *Kotecha v Rimington*
March 1991 *Legal Action* 15, Leicester County Court

New tenancy granted by new landlord to protected tenant remained protected

The tenant was initially granted a Rent Act protected tenancy in 1984. His landlord then granted what purported to be a protected shorthold tenancy, but was in reality a further protected tenancy (see Housing Act 1980 s52(2)). After the premises had been sold, the new landlord granted 'an assured shorthold tenancy'.

HHJ Appleby held that this new tenancy was in fact a further Rent Act protected tenancy, not an assured shorthold tenancy. He considered that the intention of parliament in passing the Housing Act 1988 'was not to release [on to the market] property which was already protected, but to encourage landlords to release property not already let'. He noted that this accorded with the views expressed in *Megarry on the Rent Acts* 11th edn, vol 3, p55, and he was apparently influenced by the tenant's counsel's submission that, since the Rent Act 1977 has not been repealed, one has first to consider whether a tenancy comes within the ambit of the Rent Act 1977, and then whether or not Housing Act 1988 s34(1)(b) removes the tenancy from Rent Act protection.

CHAPTER D

Exceptions to security of tenure and the right to buy

D1   **Introduction**

All three statutory regimes giving security of tenure (Housing Act 1985, Housing Act 1988 and Rent Act 1977) contain exceptions. If the tenancy, or in some cases, the tenant, comes within one of the exceptions, full security of tenure cannot exist. In most cases the tenant has 'a common-law' tenancy which can be terminated by notice to quit. The exceptions are to be found in Housing Act 1985 Sch 1, Housing Act 1988 Sch 1 and Rent Act 1977 ss4–16 and 24. Housing Act 1985 Sch 5 lists exceptions to the right to buy.

For introductory and demoted tenancies (Housing Act 1985 Sch 1 paras 1A and 1B), see chapter J.

D2   **Employees (Housing Act 1985 Sch 1 para 2)**

Housing Act 1985 Sch 1 para 2 excepts from security of tenure tenants who are employees of public sector landlords where their contract of employment requires occupation of the accommodation for the better performance of employment duties. The requirement may arise expressly or by implication from the contract of employment (para 2(5)).

The exception to the right to buy is set out in Sch 5 para 5 and applies where a dwelling-house is let in connection with employment and is within the curtilage of a building held for mainly non-housing purposes. The precedents followed in the Scottish cases are well summarised in 'Tenant employees and the right to buy' by Paul Watchman in March 1990 *Scolag* 36. The meaning of curtilage is explored in 'Curtilage – a lack of certainty' by Neil Stanley in [1996] Conv 352. Note also the following cases on the exception to the right to buy which were included in *Housing Law Casebook* 3rd edn but have been omitted from this edition:

E7.3 *Coleman v Ipswich BC* [2001] EWCA Civ 852; August 2001 *Legal Action* 23

E7.10 *Campbell v City of Edinburgh DC* 1987 SLT 51, Court of Session (2nd Division)

E7.11 *De Fontenay v Strathclyde Regional Council* 1990 SLT (Ex Div) 605, Court of Session (Extra Division of Inner House)

E7.12 *Fisher v Fife Regional Council* 1989 SLT (Lands Tr) 26, Lands Tribunal

E7.13 *Gilmour v City of Glasgow DC* 1989 SLT (Lands Tr) 74, Lands Tribunal

E7.14 *Jack v Strathclyde BC* 1992 SLT (Lands Tr) 29, Lands Tribunal

E7.15 *Little v Borders Regional Council* 1990 SLT (Lands Tr) 2, Lands Tribunal

E7.16 *McEwan v Annandale and Eskdale DC* 1989 SLT (Lands Tr) 95, Lands Tribunal

E7.17 *McKay v Livingston Development Corporation* 1990 SLT (Lands Tr) 54, Lands Tribunal

E7.18 *McTurk v Fife Regional Council* 1990 SLT (Lands Tr) 49, Lands Tribunal.

House of Lords

D2.1 *Hughes v Greenwich LBC*

[1994] 1 AC 170; [1993] 3 WLR 821; [1993] 4 All ER 577; (1995) 60 P&CR 487; (1994) 26 HLR 99; (1993) 92 LGR 61, HL

'Compelling reason' required to imply term that premises occupied for better performance of duties

A headmaster was provided with accommodation in the grounds of a special boarding school for children with physical handicaps. The express terms of his contract of employment (dating from 1967), provided for free board and lodging, but made no reference to the need to occupy any specific accommodation. On his retirement, he claimed that he was a secure tenant with the right to buy. A county court judge found that Housing Act 1985 Sch 1 para 2 did not apply because the headmaster could have fulfilled all the requirements of his employment if he had lived near to the school but not in the school grounds. He was granted a declaration that he was entitled to exercise the right to buy. The council appealed, contending that a term that he was required to occupy the house for the better performance of his duties should be implied into his contract.

The House of Lords rejected the council's assertion that a term to such effect should be implied. This should be done only for a 'compelling reason', ie, if the council could prove that the employee could not perform his duties unless he occupied the particular accommodation.

Court of Appeal

D2.2 *Brent LBC v Charles*

(1997) 29 HLR 876, CA

Employee who was resident key-holder not secure; requirement to live in accommodation means no more than it is a term of the contract; redundancy irrelevant

The appellant worked for Brent Council from 1984. In early 1988 his duties included acting as key-holder for a sports centre. Later in 1988, a flat at the centre became vacant and, in January 1989, he moved into it by agreement with the council. A charge was deducted from his wages as 'service tenancy rent'. From 1989 to 1990 the council gave him leave of absence from his job but he continued living in the flat. In 1991 he was made redundant but remained in occupation. Notice to quit was served in 1993 and in 1996 a possession order was granted. The appellant sought leave to appeal on the grounds that: (a) his contract of employment had never 'required' him to reside in the flat so as to apply Housing Act 1985 Sch 1 para 2 and thereby exclude him from security of tenure, (b) in any event, no such requirement was in place during his leave of absence and (c), by leaving him undisturbed from 1991 to 1993, the landlords must have given him a right to possession not associated with his employment.

Dismissing the application, the Court of Appeal held:

1) The judge had been entitled to find on the facts an express agreement to a term requiring the appellant to be a resident key-holder. The word

'requires' means no more than that it was a term of the contract of employment with which the employee was required as a matter of fact to comply in order to perform his duty.

2) The question of whether the employment remained on such terms during the leave of absence was a matter of fact on which the judge, having doubted the credibility of the appellant's evidence, was entitled to find against him.

3) The inaction of both the appellant and respondent for two years from 1991 to 1993 did not of itself give substance to a claim that a new tenancy could be implied.

D2.3   ## Dyer v Dorset CC
[1989] QB 346; [1988] 3 WLR 213; (1988) 20 HLR 490, CA (see D6.2)

Whether premises within curtilage of another building a question of fact and degree

D2.4   ## Elvidge v Coventry CC
[1994] QB 241; [1993] 3 WLR 976; [1993] 4 All ER 903; (1994) 26 HLR 281; (1993) 92 LGR 237, CA

Tenant lost secure status when promoted and new employment contract required him to occupy his (existing) home

The tenant began his employment with the council in 1978. He was offered and accepted the tenancy of a cottage in 1979. There was no express or implied term of his contract of employment requiring him to occupy the cottage and he therefore became a secure tenant on the introduction of the Housing Act 1980. In 1983, he was promoted and accepted a new employment contract which expressly required him to occupy the cottage for the better performance of his duties.

The Court of Appeal held that his tenancy was not secure. Housing Act 1985 Sch 1 para 2 uses the present tense 'is' in setting out the conditions for exemption from security. The question is therefore whether the conditions are presently satisfied. As there was now a contractual requirement to occupy the cottage, the tenant was not secure. He had effectively lost his security of tenure by taking the new employment contract, although the contractual tenancy itself had continued throughout.

D2.5   ## Greenfield v Berkshire CC
(1996) 28 HLR 691; (1997) 73 P&CR 280; (1997) 96 LGR 327, CA

Where requirement to occupy a particular property ended, tenant became secure

The council let a bungalow in school grounds to the school caretaker for the better performance of his duties. In those circumstances, his tenancy was not secure (Housing Act 1985 Sch 1 para 2(1)). He was then made redundant but found another job with the council at a different school. He was allowed to stay in the bungalow until accommodation at the new school became available. He later resigned and received notice to quit. In the county court, the council was granted possession.

The tenant's appeal was allowed. By the date of the termination of the tenancy it was no longer a condition of his employment that he should occupy the particular property. His current occupation of the bungalow was not 'referable' back to his last job because he had had new and different employment (distinguishing *South Glamorgan CC v Griffiths* (D2.6)).

D2.6 **South Glamorgan CC v Griffiths**
(1992) 24 HLR 334; [1992] 2 EGLR 232; [1992] NPC 13, CA

Retirement did not result in tenancy becoming secure

The council bought a house on a housing estate near a school, for occupation by the school caretaker. The caretaker occupied the house as his home until his retirement. The council then gave notice to quit, relying on Housing Act 1985 Sch 1 para 2 to deny security of tenure.

The Court of Appeal upheld a possession order. It had been an implied term of the employment contract that the tenant would take the house 'for the better performance of his duties' and so para 2 excluded secure status. The tenant's retirement did not revive the security that parliament had taken away.

D2.7 **Surrey CC v Lamond**
(1999) 31 HLR 1051; [1999] 12 EG 170; (1999) 78 P&CR D3, CA

Term implied that school caretaker required to occupy premises for his employment

Mr Lamond began work for the council as a school caretaker in 1970. He moved into accommodation owned by the council near the school. After he stopped working for the council a possession order was made. HHJ Catlin held that he was not a secure tenant and that the court could imply into Mr Lamond's contract a term that he should live at the premises for the better performance of his duties within the meaning of Housing Act 1985 Sch 1 para 2(1).

Mr Lamond appealed unsuccessfully to the Court of Appeal. The correct approach to be taken by a court in the light of *Hughes v Greenwich LBC* (D2.1) is to find out what duties the employee was required to perform. Having regard to the nature of these duties, the court should then ask itself the question whether or not it was practicable for those duties to be carried out if the employee did not live on the premises in question. A term that an employee was required to live in a property for the better performance of his duties should only be implied if there are compelling reasons to do so. Where, as on the present facts, there was a requirement to attend at the premises where the occupant was employed both in and out of hours and where it would not be practicable to carry out those duties without living at the provided premises, because there was no other accommodation nearby, such occupation was 'for the better performance of his duties'. The court took into account the fact that he was required to be on call for security reasons, deliveries, supervising contract workers and week end and evening work. There was a clear distinction between the position of a caretaker and that of a headmaster as in *Hughes v Greenwich LBC* (D2.1).

High Court

D2.8   *Godsmark v Greenwich LBC*
[2004] EWHC 1286 (Ch); [2004] HLR 53

Requirement not a sham and applied despite change of accommodation and employer

Mr Godsmark was employed from 1990 at a local authority residential special school. His conditions of employment required him to reside in accommodation on the school site for the better performance of his duties. In 1993 and 1995 he moved to other properties also owned by the local authority on the school site. In January 2003 a trust company took over the running of the school from the local authority and Mr Godsmark's employment was transferred to it. The trust went into occupation of the school and Mr Godsmark's rent for the accommodation was paid to the trust. In April 2003 Mr Godsmark issued proceedings claiming that he had the right to buy the accommodation as a secure tenant. The local authority denied that he was a secure tenant, relying on Housing Act 1985 Sch 1 para 2. HHJ Welchman held that (a) the requirement for Mr Godsmark to live in a property at the school was not a sham; (b) there had been an implied variation of his employment so as to require him to live in the accommodation to which he moved in 1993 and 1995; and (c) although Mr Godsmark had ceased to be employed by the local authority after the transfer, his occupation of the accommodation was still referable to his employment so that he remained within the exception.

Hart J dismissed his appeal. There was no doubt that there was a consensual variation of the terms of the employment contract when Mr Godsmark moved. The requirement that he live in the first accommodation plainly did not remain following his move. 'Slender as the evidence appears to have been', the judge was entitled to draw the inference that the variation did not expunge completely the requirement to live in the first accommodation and that the offer was to substitute the new accommodation in the existing terms of employment. Furthermore, Mr Godsmark's occupation of the property at the date when he issued his proceedings was still referable to his former employment by the local authority. As a result the exception in Sch 1 para 2 continued to apply. Mr Godsmark was not a secure tenant and was not entitled to exercise the right to buy.

D3   **Temporary use pending development (Housing Act 1985 Sch 1 para 3)**

Housing Act 1985 Sch 1 para 3 provides that a tenancy of premises acquired for development and temporarily used as housing accommodation pending that or other development is not secure.

Court of Appeal

D3.1   *Attley v Cherwell DC*
(1989) 21 HLR 613, CA

Where accommodation acquired for development exclusion continued to apply despite change in ownership and proposed development

The tenant lived in a house acquired by a board of health in 1879 for sewage works. It was appropriated by a borough council in 1972 under the Town and Country Planning Acts and transferred to the present council on local government reorganisation in 1974.

The Court of Appeal held that: (a) the land had been acquired in 1974; (b) Local Government Act 1972 s254(3) had the effect of continuing the original purpose of acquisition, ie, development; and (c), on the evidence, development was intended, even though it might not be the same type of development as had originally been envisaged. All the requirements of Housing Act 1985 Sch 1 para 3 were present and so the tenant was not secure.

D3.2   *Hyde Housing Association Ltd v Harrison*
(1991) 23 HLR 57; [1991] 1 EGLR 51; [1991] 07 EG 131, CA

Exclusion did not require immediate landlord to have acquired land for development

The Department of Transport acquired property for a road-widening scheme and then granted the association the right to use it for housing purposes.

The Court of Appeal rejected the argument that Housing Act 1985 Sch 1 para 3 required that the immediate landlord be the body which acquired the land for development. There are two distinct requirements: first, that the premises are on land acquired for development and, second, that they are used as temporary accommodation pending development. The conditions of the paragraph were fulfilled and the occupier was not secure.

D3.3   *Lillieshall Road Housing Co-operative Ltd v Brennan*
(1992) 24 HLR 193, CA

Occupiers became secure after change in plans and redevelopment no longer pending

In 1969, Lambeth LBC declared a clearance area and, in 1971, compulsorily purchased properties within it with a view to demolishing them. Later, the council decided to rehabilitate the properties and so passed them to the co-operative to use as housing accommodation. The council was never able to finance the rehabilitation scheme. However, in possession proceedings, the co-operative contended that the original acquisition for demolition was an acquisition for 'development' and that the tenancies were excluded from security of tenure by Housing Act 1985 Sch 1 para 3. Its evidence about the prospect of development of the house occupied by the defendants or the land around it in the foreseeable future was, however, vague, with the relevant council officer stating that he was 'not sure' what the council's plans were, except that retention and improvement of the housing were more likely than demolition and clearance.

The Court of Appeal held that the evidence was insufficient to support a finding that the land was still held pending redevelopment. Accordingly, the occupiers were secure tenants.

D4   # Private sector leasing (Housing Act 1985 Sch 1 para 6)

Housing Act 1985 Sch 1 para 6 excepts from the security provisions what is commonly called 'private sector leasing'. It applies when a private owner leases a property with vacant possession for use as temporary housing to a public landlord, which then sublets to an individual occupier. The subtenancy is excepted from secure status to ensure that vacant possession can be obtained at the expiry of the head lease.

Court of Appeal

D4.1   *Hackney LBC v Lambourne*
(1993) 25 HLR 172; [1993] COD 231, CA (see L1.5)

Occupant could not raise defence of non-performance of homlessness duties in possession proceedings based on Housing Act 1985 Sch 1 para 6

D4.2   *Haringey LBC v Hickey*
[2006] EWCA 373; [2006] HLR 36; (2006) *Times* 5 June

Tenant secure because not enough for lease to provide that lessee would yield up vacant possession at end or sooner determination of term

In 1996, Vinayak Patel leased a flat 'with vacant possession' to Haringey LBC for a term of one year nine months. The council covenanted not to use the flat except as 'temporary housing accommodation'. Although the lease included provision for Mr Patel to obtain vacant possession at the end of the term, it did not include provision for him to obtain vacant possession 'when required by him'. In January 1997 the council granted a subtenancy to Ms Hickey. It was described as a 'private sector leasing scheme: form for non-secure subtenancy' (see Housing Act 1985 Sch 1 para 6). Later, while Ms Hickey was still living in the flat, Mr Patel granted the council a further lease, this time for a term of three years from 19 September 1997. In August 2003 the council served a notice to quit on Ms Hickey and then, in December 2003, sued for possession and rent arrears of £5,358. Ms Hickey defended on the basis that she was a secure tenant because her subtenancy was outside the provisions of para 6 because (1) the flat was not leased with vacant possession when the 1997 lease was granted because she was then in lawful possession; and (2) the lease did not include provision for the lessor to obtain vacant possession 'when required'. District Judge Armon-Jones held that para 6 did apply and that Ms Hickey was not a secure tenant. He made a possession order. Ms Hickey appealed.

The Court of Appeal allowed the appeal. As between Mr Patel and the council the premises were let with vacant possession. Paragraph 6(a) was only concerned with the position as between Mr Patel and the council. The actual occupation of Ms Hickey at any given time was immaterial. However, the terms of the head lease did not 'include provision for the lessor to obtain vacant possession from the landlord on the expiry of a specified period or when required by the lessor' (para 6(b)). It was not sufficient for the lease simply to provide (as it did) that at 'the end or sooner determination of the term' the council would yield up the premises 'with vacant possession' to him.

D4.3 *Tower Hamlets LBC v Abdi*

(1993) 25 HLR 80; [1993] 1 EGLR 68; [1993] 06 EG 102; (1992) 91 LGR 300, CA

Arrangement gave council vacant possession and requirements of para 6 satisfied

Mrs Abdi was accepted by the council for rehousing as a homeless person and, pending an offer of permanent council accommodation, was placed in 'private sector leasing' accommodation. The council served notice to quit and began possession proceedings on the basis that Housing Act 1985 Sch 1 para 6 was satisfied and the premises were not secure. The tenant asserted that, on the true construction of the agreement between the private owner and the council, the latter had not been given 'vacant possession' and/or the former had not retained a power to recover possession, as required by para 6.

The Court of Appeal found that, although described as a 'licence', the arrangement gave the council vacant possession and, as a matter of construction, reserved a right to the owner to determine it when required. Paragraph 6 was satisfied, the tenant was therefore not secure and possession was granted.

D4.4 *Tower Hamlets LBC v Miah*

[1992] QB 622; [1992] 2 WLR 761; [1992] 2 All ER 667; (1992) 24 HLR 199; [1992] 1 EGLR 39; [1992] 18 EG 147; (1992) 90 LGR 151, CA

Para 6 exclusion did not require council to have a lease rather than a licence

The council took a property under licence from a private owner and then granted the defendant a licence to occupy. It later served notice to quit and sought possession. For the occupier, it was argued that a licence from a public landlord was the equivalent of a tenancy (Housing Act 1985 s79(3)) and that Housing Act 1985 Sch 1 para 6 could not apply because the council had taken a licence rather than a lease from the private owner.

The Court of Appeal held that para 6 was intended to apply to all arrangements by which a private owner granted lesser rights than the freehold to a council. Accordingly, the reference to 'lease' could be read as encompassing 'licence'. Possession was granted.

D5 **Business tenancies (Housing Act 1985 Sch 1 para 11, Housing Act 1988 Sch 1 para 4 and Rent Act 1977 s24)**

Housing Act 1985 Sch 1 para 11 provides that a tenancy is not a secure tenancy if it is one to which the business tenancy provisions of Landlord and Tenant Act 1954 Part II apply. There are similar provisions in Housing Act 1988 Sch 1 para 4 and Rent Act 1977 s24.

Court of Appeal

D5.1 *Broadway Investments Hackney Ltd v Grant*

[2006] EWCA Civ 1709; [2007] HLR 23; [2007] L&TR 11; [2007] 1 P&CR 18

Where tenant occupied part of premises for business purposes, the exception applied

In 1995 the claimant's predecessor in title granted a ten year lease to the defendant. The property comprised a basement, ground floor and first floor. The lease described the property as 'shop premises' and the 'permitted use' clause allowed for the use of 'the lower part of the premises for the sale and catering for fish, and the upper part for residential purposes only'. The lease also obliged the tenant 'to keep the premises open as a shop for carrying on the permitted use at all times of the year during the usual business hours of the locality, and at all times to maintain in good order an adequate and appropriate display in the shop windows'. The defendant sold fish and groceries in the lower part and lived upstairs. However, arrears accrued and the claimants issued proceedings for forfeiture, almost £25,000 of arrears, mesne profits, interest and costs. The defendant sought relief from forfeiture under County Courts Act 1984 s138. District Judge Manners found that the premises were occupied for the purposes of a business and made an order for possession in 28 days. On appeal, HHJ Cotran found that they were not occupied for business premises, allowed the defendant's appeal, set aside the absolute possession order and substituted an order suspended on terms that the defendant pay current rent and £1,000 per month towards the arrears.

The claimant appealed successfully to the Court of Appeal. Lloyd LJ, after considering Landlord and Tenant Act 1954 s23, said that the question posed by that section 'is a factual one. Does the tenant occupy all or part of the premises comprised in the tenancy, and if so does he occupy them, or part of them, for the purposes of a business carried on by him, or for those and other purposes?' He concluded that on the basis of the facts of this case 'it seems difficult to see how there could be any doubt as to that. Mr Grant does occupy the premises, and he does so, as regards the ground floor and basement, for the purposes of his shop business carried on in that part of the premises.' Following *Cheryl Investments v Saldanha* (D5.2), this was a tenancy under which the defendant was not only 'allowed to use the ground floor and basement for business purposes, and for no other purpose, but he was positively required to do so', by the lease. He had a business tenancy, not an assured tenancy. The Court of Appeal restored the absolute possession order. Obiter, Lloyd LJ, after pointing out that courts were obliged to consider whether or not the Rent Acts applied in any case. regardless of whether the tenant took the point at all, said:

> it seems to me that the court would be justified in taking the same stance as regards premises which may be held on an assured tenancy, still as an exception to the general rule [precluding the raising of points on appeal which had not been taken in the lower court] which continues to apply under the Civil Procedure Rules.

D5.2   ***Cheryl Investments Ltd v Saldanha***
[1978] 1 WLR 1329; [1979] 1 All ER 5; (1978) 37 P&CR 349; (1978) 248 EG 591, CA

Business activity must be a significant purpose of occupation for exception to apply

The Court of Appeal considered two cases. In the first, the tenant was a partner in a business which did not have a separate address. He operated from home, using business equipment, receiving visitors and having business notepaper with that telephone number. A considerable volume of trade was carried on from the address. In the second case, the tenant was a medical practitioner with consulting rooms nearby. However, he occasionally saw patients in the rented premises. His notepaper gave both addresses and telephone numbers.

The Court of Appeal held that in the first case the tenant was occupying for the purposes of a business within the meaning of Landlord and Tenant Act 1954 s23(1) but that in the second case the tenant was occupying as a residence within the meaning of Rent Act 1977 s2. Premises are only occupied 'for the purposes of a business' where the business activity on the premises is a significant purpose of the occupation or part of the reason for the occupation. Where, however, the business use is merely incidental to residential occupation, there is Rent Act protection.

D5.3   *Florent v Horez*

(1983) 12 HLR 1; (1984) 48 P&CR 166; (1983) 268 EG 807, CA (see G9.2)

'Business user' has a broad meaning

D5.4   *Gurton v Parrott*

(1991) 23 HLR 418; [1991] 18 EG 161, CA

Premises not occupied for purpose of business where business merely incidental

The court had to decide as a preliminary issue whether premises were occupied for business purposes, and so fell within the protection provided by Landlord and Tenant Act 1954 Part II, or for residential purposes, in which case they were within Rent Act protection. The tenant gave evidence that she had bred dogs and provided kennelling in timber outbuildings adjoining a two-bedroomed house until 1976. From 1976 to 1988 her son, who lived in a caravan on the premises, carried on these activities in his spare time, but there had been no kennelling, breeding or grooming at the premises since 1988. HHJ Paynter Reece, applying the test in *Cheryl Investments v Saldanha* (D5.2) found that the tenant occupied the premises as a residence and the running of the business was merely incidental.

The Court of Appeal held that this was essentially a question of fact for the trial judge. The landlord's appeal was dismissed.

D5.5   *Lewis v Weldcrest Ltd*

[1978] 1 WLR 1107; [1978] 3 All ER 1226; (1978) 37 P&CR 331, CA

Taking in of lodgers did not amount to a trade, profession or employment

The tenant took in lodgers who often stayed for long periods. At the time of the hearing she had five lodgers who occupied three rooms. She made little profit from them. The landlords claimed that the tenant had lost Rent Act protection and served notice under Landlord and Tenant Act 1954 s25, purporting to terminate the tenancy.

The Court of Appeal held that she had retained Rent Act protection. On the facts it could not be said that her activity of taking in lodgers amounted to a trade, profession or employment (see Landlord and Tenant Act 1954 s23).

D5.6   ## Pulleng v Curran

(1982) 44 P&CR 58, CA

Non-use of business part of premises did not bring tenancy within Rent Act 1977

The tenant rented a grocer's shop with residential accommodation above. The tenant claimed that he had acquired Rent Act protection because he lived in the residential part of the premises and the shop was unoccupied. A county court judge held that a small amount of business use was enough to take the tenancy outside the Rent Act and within the Landlord and Tenant Act 1954 and that the tenant had ceased to use the shop as a matter of convenience.

The Court of Appeal dismissed the tenant's appeal. Whether or not there is business use is a question of fact. The judge had been entitled to reach the conclusion that he had reached. The mere fact that a tenant leaves business premises fallow does not mean that the tenancy then comes within the Rent Act.

D5.7   ## Tan v Sitkowski

[2007] EWCA Civ 30; [2007] 1 WLR 1628; [2007] L&TR 17; (2007) *Times* 15 February

Premises let for mixed residential and business use not let as a dwelling for purposes of Rent Act 1977; tenancy not brought within Rent Act when business use ceased

In 1970, the Greater London Council granted Mr Sitkowski a tenancy of a building. He used the ground floor for his business and the first floor as a family residence. In 1989, he ceased using the ground floor for his business. He continued to occupy the first floor as his home, and he used the ground floor for storage in connection with his residential use of the first floor. In 1990, the freehold reversion was sold to Phaik Seang Tan and Kit Yeng Tan (the claimants). In 2003 they served notice to quit and brought a possession claim. HHJ Brian Knight QC made an order for possession, finding that, in 1970, Mr Sitkowski's tenancy enjoyed the protection of the Landlord and Tenant Act (LTA) 1954 Part II, that from 1989 the LTA no longer applied and that a tenant could not, simply by unilaterally ceasing business use, obtain protection under Rent Act 1977. Mr Sitkowski appealed.

After a detailed review of decisions concerning mixed business and residential use and the meaning of the phrase 'let as a separate dwelling' in Rent Acts from 1915, the Court of Appeal dismissed the appeal. In *Pulleng v Curran* (D5.6), the Court of Appeal held that premises let for a mixed use purpose were not 'let as a dwelling' for the purposes of Rent Act 1977. See too *Wagle v Trustees of Henry Smith's Charity Kensington* (D5.8) and *Webb v Barnet LBC* (C2.15). Although much of the reasoning in *Pulleng, Wagle* and *Webb* 'was either flawed or incomprehensible', those decisions had stood for over 15 years and there was a practical and rational justification for them. It would not be appropriate to overrule them simply because some of the reasoning was flawed and because another court might have reached a different decision. Furthermore, it would be anomalous and somewhat unfair to a landlord if a tenancy granted for mixed business and residential use could unilaterally be brought within the Rent Act simply by the tenant ceasing business use. The mere fact that business use of the premises had ceased 14 years before the notice to quit expired, and that the landlords continued to accept rent, could not amount to positive consent to the change of use (*Wolfe v Hogan* [1949] 2 KB 194). The fact that the landlords received rent in the form of housing benefit direct from the local housing authority did not mean that they were prevented from denying that they had consented to a change of use from mixed business and residential to purely residential since the Housing Benefit (General) Regulations 1987 reg.10(4) made it clear that housing benefit can be paid in respect of rent due under premises used for mixed business and residential purposes.

D5.8   *Wagle v Trustees of Henry Smith's Charity Kensington Estate*
[1990] 1 QB 42; [1989] 2 WLR 669; (1989) 21 HLR 177; [1989] 1 EGLR 124; [1989] 11 EG 75, CA

Tenant's unilateral acts could not change security of premises let for mixed use

Where a lease of business premises coming within Landlord and Tenant Act 1954 Part II contained a covenant by the tenant not to 'use the premises or any part thereof' for any other purpose than that of a sculptor's or artist's residential studio', the premises could not be converted into a Rent Act regulated tenancy by the unilateral acts of the tenant. The Court of Appeal reaffirmed that 'mixed premises' designed for both business and dwelling purposes come within the protection of the 1954 Act, not the Rent Act.

D5.9   *Webb v Barnet LBC*
(1989) 21 HLR 228; [1989] 1 EGLR 49; [1989] 11 EG 80, CA (see C2.15)

Premises let for business and residential use not secure on cessation of business use as premises had not been 'let as a separate dwelling'

D5.10   *Wright v Mortimer*
(1996) 28 HLR 719; (1996) 72 P&CR D36, CA

Where business activities never part of tenant's reason for occupying premises and incidental to residential occupation, Rent Act applied

A tenant of a maisonette with Rent Act protection became a self-employed art historian, making his living from writing books and articles on 17th-century painting, organising exhibitions and advising dealers and private collectors. He had no work address other than the maisonette and all his writing and some preparatory work was carried out at home. There was a registered rent, but subsequently the landlord claimed that the tenant was not occupying as a residence and served a notice under Landlord and Tenant Act 1954 s25 to terminate what he said was a business tenancy outside the protection of the Rent Act. Without prejudice to his contention that there was Rent Act protection, the tenant served a counter notice under Landlord and Tenant Act s29. The court considered the nature of the tenancy as a preliminary issue. Following *Cheryl Investments v Saldanha* (D5.2), HHJ Diamond QC asked whether the business activity was more than incidental to the residential occupation. He held that there was Rent Act protection. The business activities were never part of the tenant's reason for, or aim and object in, occupying the premises. The writing occupied only about 30 per cent of the tenant's professional time and accounted for only a small proportion of his income.

The Court of Appeal dismissed the landlord's application for leave to appeal. Whether or not business user was a significant element of the occupation was a question of fact and degree which was particularly within the trial judge's ability to decide. It was permissible for the judge to take into account the tenant's attachment to the flat and the fact that an informed or reasonable person would have concluded that the tenant was not carrying on a business at the premises.

D6   Within curtilage of building held for other purpose (Housing Act 1985 Sch 5 para 5)

The right to buy for secure tenants in England and Wales and security of tenure for public sector tenants in Scotland are lost if their homes form part of, or are within the curtilage of, buildings which are held mainly by landlords for purposes other than the provision of housing accommodation (Housing Act 1985 Sch 5 para 5 and Housing (Scotland) Act 1987 Sch 2 para 8, formerly Tenants' Rights, etc (Scotland) Act 1980 Sch 1 para 9, respectively). Similar wording also appears in some grounds for possession against secure tenants in England and Wales (Housing Act 1985 Sch 2 Grounds 7 and 12).

Note also the following cases which were included in *Housing Law Casebook* 3rd edn but have been omitted from this edition:

E13.3 *Allison v Tayside Regional Council* 1989 SLT (Lands Tr) 65, Lands Tribunal

E13.4 *Barron v Borders Regional Council* 1987 SLT (Lands Tr) 36, Lands Tribunal

E13.5 *Burns v Central Regional Council* 1988 SLT (Lands Tr) 46, Lands Tribunal

E13.7 *MacDonald v Strathclyde Regional Council* 1990 SLT (Lands Tr) 10, Lands Tribunal

E13.8 *Shipman v Lothian Regional Council* 1989 SLT (Lands Tr) 82, Lands Tribunal

E13.9 *Walker v Strathclyde Regional Council* 1990 SLT (Lands Tr) 17, Lands Tribunal.

Court of Appeal

D6.1   *Barwick v Kent CC*
(1992) 24 HLR 341, CA

Conveyancing history and function of property irrelevant to whether premises within curtilage of building

A former fireman tried to exercise the right to buy a house in the grounds of a fire station. If the house had been within the curtilage of the fire station, the right would have been excluded (Housing Act 1985 Sch 5 para 5). The judge found that the house and station had originally been conveyed together and the purpose of the house was to accommodate fire personnel near to the station to answer emergency calls.

The Court of Appeal held that the conveyancing history and function of the property were irrelevant. Applying *Dyer v Dorset CC* (D6.2), the court held that it was a simple question of fact and degree whether the home was within the curtilage of the building or not. Here, the house was enclosed with walls and a gate and had its own garden and garage. It was not within the curtilage of the station.

D6.2   **Dyer v Dorset CC**

[1989] QB 346; [1988] 3 WLR 213; (1988) 20 HLR 490, CA

Whether premises within curtilage of another building a question of fact and degree

The plaintiff was a college lecturer and tenant of a house within the college grounds. Although he was better able to perform his duties as a result of 'living in', there was no such requirement in his contract of employment. Therefore, he did not come within the exception for resident employees in Housing Act 1985 Sch 1 para 2 and he was a secure tenant. However, the landlords sought to deny him the right to buy on the ground that his home was within the curtilage of the college.

The Court of Appeal, while recognising that the house was within the grounds of the college as a whole, held that it was not within the curtilage of any one or more of the college buildings and was, therefore, not exempt from the right to buy. Whether or not a house is within the curtilage of another building is essentially a matter of fact and degree for the trial judge.

D7   **Specially designed or adapted houses (Housing Act 1985 Sch 5 paras 6–10)**

Under Housing Act 1985 Sch 5 paras 6–10, a secure tenant of a dwelling which is one of a group provided with facilities specially designed or adapted for the elderly or disabled is excepted from the right to buy and may in restricted circumstances be vulnerable to repossession (Housing Act 1985 Sch 2 Grounds 13 and 15).

Note also the following cases which were included in *Housing Law Casebook* 3rd edn but have been omitted from this edition:

E14.2 *Crilly v Motherwell DC* 1988 SLT (Lands Tr) 7, Lands Tribunal

E14.3 *Holloran v Dumbarton DC* 1992 SLT (Lands Tr) 73, Lands Tribunal

E14.4 *Martin v Motherwell DC* 1991 SLT (Lands Tr) 4, Lands Tribunal

E14.5 *Moonie v City of Dundee DC* 1992 SLT (Lands Tr) 103, Lands Tribunal.

See too *Davidson v Dundee CC* 2002 Hous LR 105 and *Forsyth v South Ayrshire Council* 2002 Hous LR 101.

Court of Appeal

D7.1   *Freeman v Wansbeck DC*
[1984] 2 All ER 746; (1983) 10 HLR 54; (1984) 82 LGR 131, CA

Downstairs lavatory installed for disabled occupier did not prevent tenancy from being secure

The installation of an indoor, downstairs lavatory was not a feature substantially different from those of ordinary houses, even though it had been provided as a result of the council's powers under the Chronically Sick and Disabled Persons Act 1970 for the benefit of the tenants' daughter, who suffered from spina bifida. Features which would not usually be found in ordinary dwelling-houses and which would exclude security include ramps, lifts, other mechanical contrivances (instead of staircases) and specially widened doors.

D8   # Holiday lets (Housing Act 1988 Sch 1 para 9 and Rent Act 1977 s9)

A tenancy cannot be an assured tenancy if the purpose of the tenancy is to confer on the tenant the right to occupy the premises for a holiday (Housing Act 1988 Sch 1 para 9). Similarly a holiday let cannot be a protected tenancy within the meaning of the Rent Act (Rent Act 1977 s9).

Court of Appeal

D8.1   *Buchmann v May*
[1978] 2 All ER 993; (1976) 7 HLR 1; (1976) 240 EG 49, CA

Courts should be 'astute to detect a sham' but for tenant to establish this

Mr May was a New Zealander. Mrs May, his wife, was an Australian. They were living and working in England on a series of temporary residence permits. In 1972 Mr Buchmann let premises to Mrs May for six months. This was followed by a succession of short-term tenancies which did not enjoy Rent Act protection because they were furnished and granted before the Rent Act 1974 came into force. Mr and Mrs May then went abroad. On their return they contacted Mr Buchmann, saying that they would be in the country for a few months before going abroad. They signed a three-month tenancy agreement which stated that the letting was for the purpose of a holiday. Mr and Mrs May, in subsequent possession proceedings, denied that the purpose of the tenancy was for a holiday.

The Court of Appeal held that the labels put on a transaction are not conclusive, but that where a tenancy agreement expressly states the purpose for which it is made, that statement is evidence of that purpose unless the tenant can establish that it does not correspond with the true purpose, either because the express label is a sham or because it is a false label. Although a court will be 'astute to detect a sham where it appears that a provision has been inserted for the purpose of depriving the tenant of statutory protection under the Rent Acts' ([1978] 2 All ER at 999), the burden of proof lies on the tenant. In this case there was no evidence which displaced the express purpose and, accordingly, there was no Rent Act protection. The court accepted the dictionary definition of a holiday as 'a period of cessation of work, or period of recreation'.

D8.2   *Killick v Roberts*

[1991] 1 WLR 1146; [1991] 4 All ER 289; (1991) 23 HLR 564; [1991] 2 EGLR 100; [1991] 41 EG 133, CA

Rescission available where tenancy entered into as a result of tenant's fraud

The tenant persuaded the landlord to grant a tenancy of a property, which she usually let as a holiday bungalow during the summer, by saying that he was having a house built and that it would be ready for occupation four months later.

   The Court of Appeal held that the remedy of rescission of a tenancy was available to a landlord who had been induced by fraud to enter into a tenancy agreement. The effect of rescission was to restore the parties to the position in which they would have been had the tenancy not been granted, ie, no statutory tenancy came into existence.

High Court

D8.3   *R v Rent Officer for Camden LBC ex p Plant*

(1980) 7 HLR 15; (1980) 257 EG 713, QBD

Holiday let agreement did not reflect reality of situation and tenancy protected

Four student nurses and two other students went to view a flat which was to let. At the landlord's request they filled out forms giving details of their present addresses, their parents' addresses, their employers and their banks. The nurses gave their addresses as a nearby nurses' home. One of the student nurses signed a tenancy agreement which stated that the purpose of the letting was for a holiday. All six then moved in. Six months later, when the tenancy expired, at the landlord's request one of the other occupants signed a further six-month 'holiday let' agreement.

   Glidewell J held that there was Rent Act protection, stating that the court should not only consider the written agreement, but was 'obliged to go on and consider other evidence to see whether [the written agreement] represents the reality of the situation' ((1983) 7 HLR at 27). He found that there was 'clear evidence that all the parties knew that [the applicants] were going to occupy it for the purpose of their work as students' and that that was 'conclusive of the matter'.

County courts

D8.4   *McHale v Daneham*

(1979) 249 EG 969, Bloomsbury and Marylebone County Court

'Working holiday' came within exception to security

HHJ Edwards held that, notwithstanding the dictionary definition of 'holiday' accepted in *Buchmann v May* (D8.1), there was 'no reason why a working holiday should not fall within the provisions of section 9 of the Rent Act'. (See also *Francke v Hakmi* [1984] CLY 1906, Bloomsbury and Marylebone County Court.)

D9   # Tenancies at a high or low rent (Housing Act 1988 Sch 1 paras 2 and 3 and Rent Act 1977 ss4–5)

A tenancy of a dwelling with a high rateable value cannot be an assured tenancy (Housing Act 1988 Sch 1 para 2). For tenancies entered into after 1 April 1990 this means a rent in excess of £25,000 per annum. A tenancy cannot be an assured tenancy if either no rent is payable or if it is at a low rent (Housing Act 1988 Sch 1 para 3). For tenancies granted after 1 April 1990 this means a rent less than £1,000 per annum in London or less than £250 per annum outside London. There are similar provisions in Rent Act 1977 ss4–5. See too the References to Rating (Housing) Regulations 1990.

Court of Appeal

D9.1   *Bankway Properties v Dunsford*
[2001] EWCA Civ 528; [2001] 1 WLR 1369; [2001] L&TR 339; [2001] 26 EG 164; [2002] HLR 42; (2001) *Times* 24 April (see E7.2)

Rent review clause unenforceable where it was a mere device for landlord to increase rent to level that would avoid statutory scheme for assured tenancy

D9.2   *Bostock v Bryant and Another*
(1990) 22 HLR 449; (1990) 61 P&CR 23; [1990] 2 EGLR 101; [1990] 39 EG 64, CA

Payment of gas and electricity bills was payment of expenses of house, not rent

The Court of Appeal considered whether or not payment of gas and electricity bills constituted rent. HHJ Barr held that an arrangement whereby the defendants had been given exclusive occupation of a house (with the exception of one room) and paid gas and electricity bills, while the owner paid general and water rates, was a periodic tenancy.

The Court of Appeal, reversing the county court decision, stated that 'if parties to an agreement describe a payment ... as rent, the court will normally accept that it is properly so described', but that in the present case 'the more natural inference to be drawn from the payments by the Bryants of the gas and electricity bills was that it was simply a payment of their part of the expenses incurred and a sharing of the expenses of the house' ((1990) 22 HLR at 452). In those circumstances, the inference should not be drawn that the payments were rent. The court made a possession order, holding that, because no rent was paid, there could be no Rent Act protection since the 'rent' was less than two-thirds of the rateable value.

D10   # Resident landlords (Housing Act 1988 Sch 1 para 10 and Rent Act 1977 s12)

In general, a tenancy granted by a landlord who was at that time living elsewhere in the building in which the premises are situated, and who has continued at all times to live in the premises since then, cannot be an assured or protected tenancy (Housing Act 1988 Sch 1 para 10 and Rent Act 1977 s12). There are, however, exceptions to this exception.

Court of Appeal

D10.1 *Bardrick v Haycock*

(1981) 2 HLR 118; (1976) 1 P&CR 420, CA

Landlord living in separate extension, not resident

The house in question was built in the early part of the twentieth century. In 1960 it was converted into six self-contained flats. In 1962 a number of lock-up garages were added. In 1968 one of the garages was demolished and a two-storey extension erected in its place. The extension was tied into the house, but there was no internal communication between the extension and the main building. The landlord lived in the extension. Tenants lived in the original house. The landlord claimed possession, relying on Rent Act 1974 s5A (now Rent Act 1977 s12). HHJ Barr held that the premises occupied by the landlord did not form part of the same building as that occupied by the tenants and dismissed claims for possession.

The landlord's appeals were dismissed. There was evidence on which the judge could reach his conclusion. What is a building is primarily a question of fact with which the Court of Appeal will only interfere if the judge errs in law.

D10.2 *Barnes v Goresuch*

(1976) 2 HLR 134; (1982) 43 P&CR 294; (1982) 263 EG 253, CA

Works of conversion not of a sufficient degree to render flats 'purpose-built'

A tenant sought a declaration that her tenancy was protected under the Rent Act 1977. Her landlord claimed that Rent Act 1977 s12 applied. The premises were a flat in a house which had been converted in 1959. A county court judge decided that the building was not a purpose-built block of flats, although in some circumstances a building which was wholly gutted and rebuilt could be considered a new and different building.

The Court of Appeal dismissed the tenant's appeal. The question was primarily one of fact. There were no grounds for interfering with the judge's decision that the works of conversion had not sufficiently changed the character of the building to make it a different building.

D10.3 *Cooper v Tait*

(1984) 15 HLR 98; (1984) 48 P&CR 460; (1984) 271 EG 105, CA

Residence by one joint landlord satisfies resident landlord exception

Three landlords jointly granted a tenancy. At the time of the grant and throughout the length of the tenancy, one of the three landlords lived elsewhere in the building. The other two lived at other addresses. The landlords took possession proceedings, claiming that they were resident landlords within the meaning of Rent Act 1977 s12.

The Court of Appeal held that the residence requirement may be fulfilled by just one out of several joint landlords and upheld the possession order which had been made in the county court.

D10.4 *Griffiths v English*

(1981) 2 HLR 134; (1982) 261 EG 257, CA

Landlord living in one extension was resident where tenant lived in another extension

The property in question was a neo-Georgian house. Two extensions had been built on to the main house. There was though no communication between either extension and the main house. The landlord lived in one extension. The tenant lived in the other extension. A county court judge, after visiting the premises, decided that the whole property comprised one building and that the landlord was a resident landlord within the meaning of Rent Act 1977 s12. He made a possession order.

The Court of Appeal dismissed the tenant's appeal. Whether or not the premises comprised one building was a question of fact. It could not be said that no reasonable person could come to the conclusion that the premises as a whole constituted one building.

D10.5 *Jackson v Pekic*
(1990) 22 HLR 9; [1989] 2 EGLR 104; [1989] 47 EG 141, CA

Residence test for landlord exception same as residence test in Rent Act 1977 s2

The Court of Appeal confirmed that, when courts are considering whether a landlord is a resident landlord within the meaning of Rent Act 1977 s12, they should use the same test as when deciding whether a statutory tenant continues to occupy premises as a residence for the purposes of Rent Act 1977 s2. Landlords who are temporarily absent must leave in the premises some personal and visible sign of their intention to return. In *Jackson* it was held that the landlord had not done this and her claim for possession was dismissed. Furniture was not a sufficiently personal sign and the fact that the landlord allowed the tenant's brother to use the only room in the house which she retained was more consistent with an intention not to reside.

D10.6 *Lewis-Graham v Conacher*
(1992) 24 HLR 132; [1992] 1 EGLR 111; [1992] 02 EG 171, CA

Borderline case but judge entitled to find landlord lived in same building as tenant

The landlords claimed to be resident within the meaning of Rent Act 1977 s12. The premises which were let (198a Nether Street) were an extension to the house in which the landlords lived (198 Nether Street) and had a common gas supply, a common electricity supply and a common water supply and were served by the same central heating system as the main house. Originally there had been interconnecting doors, but these had been blocked up. Further building works were carried out, but the county court judge found that, when the notice to quit served by the plaintiffs expired, 198 and 198a were still part of the same building and accordingly the tenants did not enjoy the protection of the Rent Act.

The Court of Appeal held that, although this was a borderline case, it was essentially a question of fact for the county court judge and declined to interfere with his finding.

D10.7 *O'Sullivan v Barnett*
[1994] 1 WLR 1667; (1995) 27 HLR 51; [1995] 1 EGLR 93; [1995] 04 EG 141, CA

Where intention that resident landlord and tenant move to another building exception still applied despite landlord actually moving into new building after tenant

During the 1960s the tenant began to rent a room in a house where the landlord was already living and, accordingly, had a restricted contract without full security (Rent Act 1977 ss12(1)(b)(i) and 19). The landlord later decided to convert the house into self-contained flats and it was agreed that both the landlord and the tenant would move into another neighbouring house. The tenant was the first to move. For four weeks after the tenant moved, the landlord did some work on the new house but still slept in the original house until works in the new house were completed, when he moved in. In 1992 the landlord served a notice to quit. The tenant defended possession proceedings, claiming that the landlord was not resident at the time when the new tenancy was granted and that, accordingly, she had acquired full Rent Act security. At first instance a possession order was made. The judge stated that he was not required to consider a 'fine matter of timing' and that the landlord's occupation had occurred either before or simultaneously with the creation of the new tenancy and that the tenant knew what was intended. The tenant appealed.

The Court of Appeal, dismissing the appeal, held that in reality it was a concerted move and that it was artificial to split up that co-ordinated transfer from one house to another. The judge was entitled to take into account the landlord's intention. The landlord's rights might be seriously frustrated if they were dependent on the very narrow distinctions which the tenant sought to make in this case.

D10.8 ## Palmer v McNamara
(1991) 23 HLR 168; [1991] 1 EGLR 121; [1991] 17 EG 88, CA

Landlord resided in premises despite not sleeping there (due to medical condition)

The landlord claimed to be a resident landlord within the meaning of Rent Act 1977 s12. He occupied a rear room in the flat and kept belongings there, including a fridge and a kettle. However, he had no cooker and, if he wished to eat there, he bought food that did not need to be cooked or take-away meals. As a result of a medical condition which prevented him from dressing or undressing himself, he did not sleep in the room, but went to stay with a friend each night.

The Court of Appeal held that these facts did not prevent the room from being a dwelling-house or the landlord from occupying it 'as his residence'. The court noted that all the landlord's possessions were in the room and found that, as a question of fact and degree, the county court judge was right to take the view that the landlord occupied the room as his home.

D10.9 ## Wolff v Waddington
(1990) 22 HLR 72; [1989] 2 EGLR 108; [1989] 47 EG 148, CA

Resident landlords under Rent Act 1977 can have two homes

A tenant appealed unsuccessfully against a possession order which had been made on the basis that he was outside the protection of the Rent Act 1977 because there had, at all times, been a resident landlord within the meaning of s12. The tenant claimed that, although part of his flat was above part of his landlady's accommodation, it was not part of the same building because there were separate entrances. He also claimed that, although his original landlady's daughter had moved into the building a fortnight before her mother's death and had lived in the premises for 13 months after the death, she was not resident because her real home was in the USA.

The Court of Appeal held that these were essentially matters of fact for the county court judge and saw no reasons to interfere with them. It followed *Langford Property Co v Athanassoglou* [1949] 1 KB 29, CA, and accepted that 'resident' landlords, like statutory tenants, could have two homes, although occupation merely 'as a convenience' or for occasional visits would not have been enough.

D11   Board and attendance

A tenancy cannot be a Rent Act protected tenancy if the rent includes 'payment in respect of board or attendance ... [and] the value of the attendance to the tenant forms a substantial part of the whole rent' (Rent Act 1977 s7). There is, however, no equivalent to section 7 in the Housing Act 1988 and a tenancy may be an assured tenancy even if substantial attendances or board are provided, so long as the occupant has exclusive possession.

House of Lords

D11.1   *Otter v Norman*
[1989] AC 129, [1988] 3 WLR 321; [1988] 2 All ER 897; (1988) 20 HLR 594; [1988] 2 EGLR 128; [1988] 39 EG 79, HL

Any amount of board satisfies requirement, provided not de minimus or a contrivance

The tenant claimed that he was a protected tenant and that a continental breakfast consisting of two bread rolls, butter, jam and marmalade, unlimited tea or coffee with milk and sugar and a glass of milk was not board within the meaning of Rent Act 1977 s7. The breakfast was served in a communal dining room by kitchen staff employed by the landlord.

Lord Bridge approved dicta in *Wilkes v Goodwin* [1923] 2 KB 86, CA (at 93–94 and 96) that any amount of board suffices, provided it is not de minimis, but stressed the need for the tenant's rent to include 'not only the cost of the food and drink provided but also all the housekeeping chores which must be undertaken in shopping for provisions, preparation and service of meals on the premises and cleaning and washing up after meals' ([1988] 2 All ER at 901). It is clear that the provision of a box of uncooked and unprepared groceries once a week is not sufficient to constitute board, although this might amount to an 'attendance'. Lord Bridge also pointed out that:

> ... courts have consistently set their face against artificial and contrived devices whereby landlords have sought to deny to tenants the protection intended to be conferred by the Rent Acts ([1988] 2 All ER at 901).

This general statement may be of assistance to other tenants or 'licensees' challenging Rent Act or Housing Act evasion.

Court of Appeal

D11.2 *Nelson Developments Ltd v Taboada*

(1992) 24 HLR 462; [1992] 2 EGLR 107; [1992] 34 EG 72, CA

Daily cleaning and weekly laundry of bed linen an 'attendance'

Mr Taboada rented a bed-sitting room. The landlords provided cleaning and refuse removal on a daily basis and clean bed linen weekly. In 1989 the rent officer assessed the value of the services at £12.97 when he registered a fair rent of £45 per week. In possession proceedings, the judge found that the provision of linen was an attendance and that the value of the services formed a substantial part of the rent.

The Court of Appeal, following *Palser v Grinling* [1948] AC 291; [1948] 1 All ER 1, HL, held that 'attendance' meant 'services personal to the tenant' and that the question of 'proportionality' was a question of fact for the judge. It upheld the possession order which had been made.

County courts

D11.3 *Rita Dale v Adrahill Ltd*

April 1982 *Legal Action* 39, Shoreditch County Court

Provision of breakfast in another house not 'board'

HHJ Stuckley held that the possibility of food (a breakfast of cereal, eggs, toast and tea or coffee) in another house was not 'board' within the meaning of the Rent Act.

Scottish courts

D11.4 *Gavin v Lindsay*

October 1985 *Scolag* 153, Glasgow and Strathkelvin Sheriff Court

Where breakfast not served to tenant at house, not 'board'

The 'board' offered by the landlord consisted of two alternative options. The tenant could either have breakfast at a particular café ('The Cup and Saucer') or collect the ingredients for breakfast from a shop.

Sheriff Kearney held that the concept of board should consist of two elements, 'substance' and 'service', both provided at or about the time of use. 'Substance' meant food and drink. Service meant the preparation and setting out of that food and drink. The service offered by the landlord was not 'board'.

Security of tenure: restrictions, rights and obligations

E1   Injunctions against tenants

Both landlords and tenants are bound by the covenants in their tenancy agreements. Landlords most commonly take possession proceedings if tenants breach their obligations, but they may also (or alternatively) bring claims for injunctions to prevent future breach and/or damages. Breach of an injunction may give rise to committal for contempt of court. In addition, Housing Act 1996 Part V, as amended, extended the law to enable local authorities and other social landlords to obtain injunctions against people engaging in anti-social behaviour. Courts may attach powers of arrest to such injunctions.

Court of Appeal

E1.1   *Accent Foundation Ltd v Lee*

[2007] EWCA Civ 665; 14 June 2007

Breach of injunction could not be waived by complainants

Mr Lee's mother and sister were tenants of Accent, a registered social landlord. After his sister had accused him of assaulting her, Accent obtained an injunction with a power of arrest under Housing Act 1996 s153A preventing Mr Lee from visiting either his mother or his sister or from entering the locality where they lived. Later, his sister contacted him and invited him to stay at her home. A few days later, Mr Lee was still staying at his sister's home, when he was arrested for breach of the injunction, and then released. His mother then invited him to stay at her home. The next day, he was arrested for breach of the injunction. A circuit judge imposed a 28-day custodial sentence, suspended until the expiry of the injunction. Mr Lee's mother again invited him to stay at her home. Again, he was arrested. There was evidence that his behaviour had affected other tenants of the housing association. A district judge activated the suspended sentence of 28 days, and imposed a further immediate consecutive custodial sentence of 28 days. The defendant appealed claiming that the contempt had been waived.

The Court of Appeal stated that although there are occasions when a person may waive a breach of an order, there may also be situations in which public policy requires the enforcement of the order. In this case, it was not open to Mr Lee's mother or sister to waive the breach. The order had been for the benefit of the neighbours and not simply for his mother and sister. There was evidence that the neighbours had been affected by his conduct. There had been no error by the district judge in taking into account the circumstances in passing sentence. However, the order was varied to replace the total sentence of two calendar months, with a total sentence of 56 days.

E1.2   *Caradon District Council v Paton*

(2001) 33 HLR 360; [2000] 35 EG 132, CA

Injunction to prevent holiday lettings of property with covenant against business user

Secure tenants exercised the right to buy. They covenanted not to use the properties for any purpose 'other than that of a private dwelling-house' and that 'no ... business of any kind shall be permitted to be set up or carried on ...' The defendants bought the properties, subject to the same restrictive covenants. They placed 'to let' signs in the windows and let them for short-term holiday lets for one or two weeks at a time. The council sought injunctions to prevent breaches of covenant.

The Court of Appeal held that there were breaches of covenant and granted injunctions. The purpose of the covenants was to protect the amenities of the surrounding neighbourhood and to ensure that the premises remained part of the housing stock available for people to live in within the district. To be used as 'a private dwelling-house' involved use as a home with some degree of permanence. Use by holiday-makers was not use as a private dwelling-house.

E1.3   *Enfield LBC v B (a minor)*
[2000] 1 WLR 2259; [2000] 1 All ER 255; (2000) 32 HLR 799; (1999) *Times* 7 September, CA

Injunctions with power of arrest against minors

In a case involving an application for an injunction under Housing Act 1996 s152 (now repealed) against the teenage son of a secure council tenant who was involved in a violent assault on council staff working in a social services office, the Court of Appeal doubted, but left open, the proposition that injunctions with powers of arrest could not be made against minors at all. (But see *H v H (a child) (occupation order: power of arrest)* (2001) *Times* 10 January, CA, where it was held that the court has the power to attach a power of arrest to an occupation order made against a minor under the similar provision in Family Law Act 1996 s47(2) and *Wookey v Wookey* [1991] 3 All ER 365, CA.)

E1.4   *Hillingdon LBC v Vijayatunga*
[2007] EWCA Civ 730; 28 June 2007

Committal proceedings not defective despite procedural defects of a technical nature

Ms Vijayatunga was the tenant of a first floor flat. Her tenancy agreement provided that she should not cause nuisance, annoyance or disturbance to other tenants. Hillingdon, her landlord, obtained an interim injunction to prevent her from going out on to the communal roof of the block to place food which had attracted birds and cats. She breached the injunction. Hillingdon made an application to commit her. After considering a number of witness statements, a judge found that she was in breach and ordered her to pay a fine and costs. She appealed, submitting that there had been a number of procedural defects – eg, evidence at the committal hearing had been in the form of witness statements, not affidavits.

The Court of Appeal dismissed the appeal. The procedural defects were of a most technical nature. Courts are entitled to waive defects if no injustice is caused (*Nicholls v Nicholls* [1997] 1 WLR 314. In this case, no complaint had been made at the committal hearing and no conceivable injustice had been caused. The committal proceedings could not be regarded as defective.

E1.5   **Lewisham LBC v Simba-Tola**

(1992) 24 HLR 644, CA

Only legal basis for injunction was breach of covenant

A council tenancy agreement included a term by which the tenant agreed not to cause nuisance 'to other people' either in or around the dwelling, or on the estate of which the dwelling formed part, or 'around any other housing property of the council'. In possession proceedings, the council applied for an injunction to restrain the defendant from entering two council offices and interfering with employees of the council working in those offices. The council alleged considerable harassment of its staff by the tenant, both in the offices and around them. HHJ James was not satisfied that such action would amount to breach of the tenancy provision on a strict construction but he decided to grant the application.

Allowing the tenant's appeal, Mann LJ held that the only legal basis for the injunction could be breach of the covenant. As the judge had expressly said that he could not found the injunction on that basis, the order had to be discharged. (But, in relation to the particular facts, see now, Housing Act 1996 s153A(4)(d).)

E1.6   *Manchester CC v Lawler*

(1999) 31 HLR 119; June 1998 *Legal Action* 11, CA

'In the locality' not too vague; shopping centre three streets away was in the locality

Following a history of anti-social behaviour in the course of which there had been 58 police visits to the tenant's home, the council began proceedings for possession. At a preliminary hearing the tenant gave six undertakings not to cause nuisance, use or threaten violence, etc 'in the locality' of her home. Following an incident in a shopping centre three streets away from the property, where the tenant threatened a child with a knife, the council applied to commit her for contempt. The judge found the incident proved but dismissed the application. He held that the words 'in the locality' were too vague and it was impossible to say precisely what they meant.

The Court of Appeal allowed the council's appeal. It held that the judge had erred in finding a well-recognised phrase such as 'locality' too vague. The phrase had been taken up and adopted by parliament (both in the revised Housing Act 1985 Sch 2 Ground 2 and in Housing Act 1996 s152). It was a matter of fact for the judge in each case to determine whether the conduct complained of had occurred in the locality. On the present facts it was clear that the shopping area was within the locality of the property.

E1.7   *Manchester CC v Lee*

[2003] EWCA Civ 1256; [2004] 1 WLR 349; [2004] HLR 11

Where allegations were of nuisance to a particular neighbour, injunction against persons in locality generally criticised

The defendant's grandparents lived next to a couple who owned their own home. The defendant abused one of the grandparents' neighbours, threatened to stab him, damage his car and burn down his house. He also made threats against the neighbour's young son and repeatedly kicked their front fence and gate. A district judge granted an injunction under

Housing Act 1996 s152 (now repealed) forbidding the defendant, 'from (1) engaging or threatening to engage in conduct causing, or likely to cause, a nuisance, annoyance or disturbance to any person residing in, visiting, or otherwise engaging in a lawful activity in the locality of [the neighbours' house]; (2) harassing any such person; (3) using abusive or insulting or threatening behaviour against any such person ; (4) using or threatening violence against any such person; (5) entering, or attempting to enter [the neighbour's house] and/or the front and/or the rear gardens thereof.'

In the Court of Appeal, Mummery LJ criticised the form of the injunction. Injunctions must be 'framed in terms appropriate and proportionate to the facts of the case'. If there is a risk of significant harm to a particular person or persons it would usually be appropriate for the injunction to identify that person or those persons. However, in order to justify granting a wider injunction, restraining someone from causing a nuisance or annoyance to, 'a person of a similar description', it would normally be necessary for the judge to make a finding that there had been use or threats of violence to persons of a similar description, and that there was a risk of significant harm to persons of a similar description if an injunction was not granted in respect of them.

E1.8   ***Medina Housing Association v Case***
[2002] EWCA Civ 2001; [2003] 1 All ER 1084; [2003] HLR 37

No basis for injunction restraining former tenant from entering street after possession order made

On 26 June 2002 Medina began a possession claim against Ms Case as a result of a number of breaches of the terms of her tenancy. A judge found that that the breaches alleged were made out and made an outright possession order. He also concluded that there was a continuing risk that she would carry on behaving anti-socially and granted the claimant an injunction restraining her from entering the vicinity of the street where the property was situated for five years. She appealed against the injunction on the ground that the judge had no power to make such an order after the tenancy had been terminated by the possession order.

The Court of Appeal allowed the appeal. The basis for Medina's application for the injunction was the contract for the tenancy agreement. In such circumstances:

> An injunction is granted in order to prevent future breaches of contract. The court has no power to grant an injunction which provides rights to a party that are not contractual rights unless a claim in tort can properly be made by that person.

The injunction was set aside. (But see Housing Act 1995 s153A where the grant of an injunction is not dependent on the defendant being a tenant.)

E1.9   ***Moat Housing Group South Ltd v Harris and Hartless***
[2005] EWCA Civ 287; [2006] QB 606; [2005] 3 WLR 691; [2005] 4 All ER 1051; [2005] HLR 33; (2005) *Times* 23 March

Grant of an injunction without notice an 'exceptional remedy'; guidance on grant of injunctions; approach to hearsay evidence; ASBOs

From May 2001 Ms Hartless rented a house from the claimant housing association on an assured tenancy. She lived there with her four children, who in October 2004 were aged between six and 14. She was estranged from Mr Harris, the children's father, but he visited frequently. On 29 October 2004, without any prior notice or other warning, Moat obtained without notice anti-social behaviour injunctions (ASBIs) under Housing Act 1996 ss153A–E (as amended) from District Judge Ackner. The orders provided that Ms Hartless should leave the house by 6.00 pm that day, should not enter part of the village where she lived and should exercise proper and reasonable parental control over the children to prevent them from behaving in an anti-social manner. A power of arrest (HA 1996 s153C) was attached. Similar orders were made against Mr Harris and two of Ms Hartless's neighbours. (The neighbours subsequently vacated their house and took no part in the proceedings.) Most of the evidence before the district judge related to the neighbours. There was some evidence that Ms Hartless and Mr Harris had made threats against other people living on the estate. There was also evidence that two of the children had been involved in some incidents with the neighbours' children. The claimant's representatives, accompanied by police and a television camera-man, called at the house at about 9 pm that evening to serve the orders. The police declined to enforce the order and Ms Hartless obtained a stay from Stanley Burnton J at 1.30 am that night. HH Anthony Thompson QC (sitting as a deputy circuit judge) made anti-social behaviour orders (ASBOs) against both defendants on 3 December 2004. An outright possession order was also made. On 16 December 2004, Brooke LJ granted permission to appeal and a stay (M7.4).

Brooke LJ gave the judgment of the court on the substantive appeals:

1) The grant of an injunction without notice is an exceptional remedy:

> It is hard to envisage a more intrusive 'without notice' order than one which requires a mother and her four young children to vacate their home immediately ... As a matter of principle no order should be made in civil or family proceedings without notice to the other side unless there is a very good reason for departing from the general rule that notice must be given. Needless to say, the more intrusive the order, the stronger must be the reasons for the departure. It is one thing to restrain a defendant from what would in any event be anti-social behaviour for a short time until a hearing can be arranged at which both sides can be heard. It is quite another thing to make a 'without notice' order directing defendants to leave their home immediately and banning them from re-entering a large part of the area where they live.

> After reviewing family law authorities on ouster injunctions, Brooke LJ said that when deciding whether to exercise their discretion to make ASBIs without notice, judges should follow the guidance given in Family Law Act 1996 s45(2)(a).

2) On the evidence, it would properly have been within the scope of the district judge's discretion to have made without notice non-molestation type orders restraining Mr Harris and/or Ms Hartless from contacting any witnesses; prohibiting them from causing nuisance or annoyance; and directing them to exercise proper and reasonable parental control over two of their children. However, it was neither necessary nor pro-

portionate to make the ouster and exclusion orders. Those elements of the district judge's order 'should never have been included'.

3) It is 'inconceivable that a court would grant an ASBI without notice unless there was both violence (or a threat of violence) in the past and a risk of significant harm to one of the relevant persons during the short period between the time of service of the order and the time of the court hearing on notice'.

4) The district judge was properly entitled to attach a power of arrest to the order protecting named persons from harm or for restraining acts of nuisance prior to the on notice hearing the following Thursday.

5) There is nothing wrong in a without notice order being for a duration of six months, provided that it is of a non-intrusive type (such as a typical non-molestation or non-nuisance order) and the on notice hearing takes place timeously.

6) Although courts have power to make ouster orders and/or exclusion orders without notice if the facts are sufficiently serious to warrant such a draconian order, very great care is needed. Furthermore, judges making such orders should generally be scrupulous to prescribe that the order may only be served at a reasonable time of the day (for example, between 9 am and 4.30 pm on a weekday).

7) It is now well established that hearsay evidence is available on an application for an ASBO or the trial of a possession action, but 'the willingness of a civil court to admit hearsay evidence carries with it inherent dangers in a case like this'. Rumours abound in small housing estates, and it is much more difficult for judges to assess the truth of what they are being told if the original makers of statements do not attend court to be cross-examined on their evidence. In this case, the large volume of hearsay evidence presented the judge with an unusually difficult problem. It might have been better if he had started his judgment with an analysis of the direct oral evidence he received, and made more transparently clear his approach to the evidence of the absent named witnesses and anonymous witnesses. More attention should be paid by claimants to the need to state, by convincing direct evidence, why it was not reasonable and practicable to produce the original makers of statements as witnesses. If statements involve multiple hearsay, the route by which the original statement came to the attention of the person attesting to it should be identified as far as practicable. However, there were no reasonable grounds for setting aside the possession order and ordering a retrial because of the hearsay point;

8) Although it was reasonable for the judge to make a possession order, having regard to the children's good school reports, the absence of any criminal records or any serious record of police involvement with this family, and favourable testimonies that were given about the defendants, the Court of Appeal concluded that it would be right to suspend the possession order on the terms that there are no further breaches of the tenancy agreement.

9) In relation to the ASBOs, the court expressed no view on 'the important question whether a failure to control one's children from being

a nuisance, although it may constitute a breach of a tenancy agreement, is an 'act' of the type referred to in' Crime and Disorder Act 1998 s1(1)(a).

10)ASBOs were inappropriate on the facts of the case, and some form of undertaking as to future conduct, backed by a penal notice was all that the situation required. In particular, the judge never identified the conduct on the part of Mr Harris which warranted the making of an ASBO against him. There was not the evidence of 'persistent and serious anti-social behaviour' on the part of Ms Hartless or Mr Harris which justified an ASBO. The judge's most serious explicit findings against either of them stemmed from the very unpleasant events of a single night. The ASBOs were accordingly set aside.

E1.10 **Nottingham CC v Zain (a minor)**

[2001] EWCA Civ 1248; [2002] 1 WLR 607; [2003] HLR 16; (2001) *Times* 29 August

Local authority can obtain injunctive relief to restrain a public nuisance

The local authority claimed that dealing in drugs was going on publicly on a housing estate and the defendant was associating there with well known drug dealers, had himself been in possession of drugs and had been arrested in suspicion of dealing in drugs. Relying on Local Government Act 1972 s222, they obtained an interim injunction restraining him from entering the estate. It was their case that what the defendant had been doing and threatened to continue to do amounted to a public nuisance and that s222 allowed them to issue civil proceedings 'for the promotion or protection of the interests of the inhabitants of their area'. HHJ Hall struck out the action holding that the court had no jurisdiction.

The local authority appealed successfully. The Court of Appeal held that a local authority has the power to institute proceedings in its own name for injunctive relief to restrain a public nuisance provided that it considers it expedient for the promotion and protection of the interests of the inhabitants of its area.

E1.11 **Sandwell BC v Preece**

[2007] EWCA Civ 1009; 28 September 2007

Importance of principle of totality when sentencing for contempt and activating earlier suspended sentence

The defendant had a long-standing relationship with a vulnerable council tenant and frequently visited her home. The council received complaints about his behaviour and applied for an injunction. An interim anti-social behaviour injunction was made. The defendant breached that injunction by attending at the property and shouting abuse. He was committed to prison for 28 days, but the sentence was suspended. After that time lapsed, he again attended at the property and banged on the door. A further injunction was granted, which, among other things, prohibited him from entering the area. He again attended at the address and was committed to prison for eight weeks. Four months later he went to the address and banged on the windows. He was committed to prison for three months. Some months later, he breached the injunction by visiting the property again. He was committed to prison for 16 weeks, suspended on condition that he complied with the injunction. One month later he visited the property. Complaints were received that there were raised voices. The defendant was arrested. The judge imposed a sentence of nine months' imprisonment, consecutive to the sixteen weeks suspended sentence which he activated.

The defendant's appeal was allowed. Sentences for contempt have two objectives: to mark the court's disapproval of the disobedience and to seek future compliance with the order. Although the judge was justified in imposing a consecutive sentence, he did not have regard to the totality of the sentence. Thirteen months' imprisonment was too long and out of proportion having regard to the mischief involved, which had not entailed any violence. The sentence of nine months' imprisonment was quashed. A sentence of four months' imprisonment to run consecutively with the suspended sentence of 16 weeks' imprisonment was substituted, making a total sentence of eight months.

E1.12   *Southwark LBC v Storrie*
June 1997 *Legal Action* 20; [1997] CLY 632, CA

On without notice injunction being discharged, damages in respect of council's undertaking in securing injunction to be considered

The council issued a writ action for a permanent injunction and at the same time sought and obtained an ex parte interlocutory injunction which restrained one of its tenants from returning to his home. It acted on reports that the tenant had forced entry to a neighbour's flat and made a racially motivated and violent assault with a knife. The tenant was subsequently arrested but the charges were dropped. The tenant's application to discharge the injunction was allowed and an inquiry ordered into damages in respect of the undertaking the council had given in securing the order. The council appealed, contending that: (a) the injunction ought not to have been discharged because the tenant was a violent man and the prosecution had been dropped only as a result of witness intimidation; and/or (b) the council had acted properly on the information received so the undertaking ought not to be enforced; and/or (c) any 'damages' suffered by the tenant were nominal because he had either been voluntarily staying away from the flat or had been on remand or in custody since the order was granted.

The Court of Appeal dismissed the appeal. There had been no evidence before the court below to suggest that the injunction should not be discharged. Leave to adduce such evidence in the Court of Appeal was refused since (a) it could have been adduced below and (b) it was all hearsay. The council was not in any special position with regard to undertakings in damages simply because it was a public housing authority (contrast *Coventry CC v Finnie* (1997) 29 HLR 658, QBD). As for damages, it was 'quite impossible' to suggest that a man kept out of his house for what turns out to be a mistaken reason would suffer only 'trivial' injury.

E1.13   *Sutton Housing Trust v Lawrence*
(1987) 19 HLR 520; (1988) 55 P&CR 320, CA

Wrong to refuse grant of injunction against keeping dog in breach of tenancy

The defendants were secure tenants. It was a term of their tenancy that they should 'not keep any animals of any kind on the premises'. Mr Lawrence suffered from multiple sclerosis and wanted the company of a dog. As a result, Mrs Lawrence's mother left her dog at the flat. The plaintiff sought an injunction. HHJ James refused to grant an injunction because it was unlikely that it would be enforced by committal proceedings and the defendants did not have the means to pay a fine.

The Court of Appeal allowed the plaintiff's appeal. There was ample evidence that the trust felt that the need for the proceedings was being forced on it. Eight other similar cases were pending. It was not a case where the granting of an injunction would be useless or unenforceable. It would serve a very clear purpose and there was no reason to suggest that it would be disobeyed. The Court of Appeal rejected the suggestion that the trust should use the alternative remedy of possession proceedings. The Court of Appeal allowed the plaintiff's appeal and granted an injunction.

High Court

E1.14 *Hampstead and Suburban Properties v Diomedous*

[1969] 1 Ch 248; [1968] 3 WLR 990; [1968] 3 All ER 545, ChD

Interim injunction appropriate where covenantor in clear breach of covenant

The lease of shop premises, which were adapted to a restaurant, contained a covenant that the defendant would not allow music to be played so as to cause a nuisance or annoyance to the occupiers of adjoining or neighbouring premises and that, if any reasonable complaints were received from occupiers of adjoining or neighbouring premises by the landlords, the defendant at the request of the plaintiffs would 'forthwith discontinue' the playing of music 'until such time as effective soundproofing works to the premises ... have been completed'. The defendant allowed music to be played in the restaurant and the plaintiffs received complaints. The music was not discontinued on the plaintiffs' request and they sought interlocutory injunctions to enforce the covenant.

Megarry J, in granting an injunction, stated that 'nuisance or annoyance' is to be determined by 'robust and common-sense standards'. 'Where there is a plain and uncontested breach of a clear covenant not to do a particular thing, and the covenantor promptly begins to do what he has promised not to do, then in the absence of special circumstances it seems to me that the sooner he is compelled to keep his promise the better ... I see no reason for allowing a covenantor who stands in clear breach of an express prohibition to have a holiday from the enforcement of his obligations until the trial.'

E1.15 *Harrow LBC v G*

[2004] EWHC 17 (QB); [2004] 1 P&CR DG17; 20 January 2004

Not appropriate to order injunction against minor which could not be effectively enforced

G was a schoolboy aged 14 who lived with his siblings and single mother in a property owned by the council. The council was seeking possession against his mother, a secure tenant, on the ground of rent arrears. The council and the police received numerous complaints about G's behaviour. The council sought an injunction against him under Housing Act 1996 s152 (now repealed). HHJ Dedman granted an injunction prohibiting G from engaging in behaviour likely to cause a nuisance in the locality where he lived. He also granted a power of arrest and included in his order a penal notice warning that if G did not obey the order, he would be guilty of contempt and liable to be committed to prison. G accepted that the court had jurisdiction to make the injunction against him and that the power of arrest was properly attached, but appealed, contending that effectively the injunction was unenforceable and so ought not to have been granted.

Roderick Evans J allowed the appeal. G was too young to be sent to prison for contempt. In the absence of evidence to the contrary, common sense and experience dictated that G would have no source of income or goods that could be sequestered. In the absence of any direct means of enforcement, it was not appropriate to rely on threats or fears of indirect consequences in related proceedings (eg, in the outstanding possession claim). The power of arrest should not be regarded as a sanction for breach of the injunction in its own right. The injunction could not be properly or effectively enforced and so should not have been granted. Roderick Evans J stated that if a council did seek an injunction against a minor, it should be in a position to place evidence before the judge of the minor's circumstances which would make enforcement by a way of a fine or sequestration of assets an effective sanction for breach.

E2

Committal for breach of injunctions

Breach of an injunction is a contempt of court and may be punished by committal. For cases involving breaches of injunctions by landlords, see chapter O.

Court of Appeal

E2.1 *Barnet LBC v Hurst*

[2002] EWCA Civ 1009; [2003] 1 WLR 722; [2002] 4 All ER 457; [2003] HLR 19; (2002) *Times* 12 August

Sentence of nine months excessive for activities encompassed in limited admissions

The defendant undertook not to assault, threaten, harass or cause nuisance to anyone residing in or visiting a block of flats where his father lived. He admitted breach of that undertaking in that he had been loud and noisy, disturbing the neighbours' sleep. The council also sought his committal for various other acts which were the subject of criminal proceedings at the time of the committal hearing. HHJ Bevington committed him to prison for nine months for the admitted breaches and adjourned the balance of the application to commit until after the criminal trial was over. The criminal proceedings were later withdrawn when the defendant and his father were reconciled shortly before the Crown Court trial. The defendant appealed against the length of the committal sentence and the council cross-appealed against the judge's decision to adjourn the balance of its application to commit until after the criminal trial was over.

The Court of Appeal allowed the defendant's appeal. The sentence was reduced to three months. Even when allowance was made for the fact that this was a serious breach of a court order, the original sentence was manifestly too long for the activities encompassed by the limited admissions. With regard to the council's appeal, once the criminal proceedings were discontinued, the council could restore the balance of its committal application for hearing. In those circumstances it was unnecessary for the Court of Appeal to make any order on the cross-appeal.

E2.2   *Leicester CC v Lewis*
(2001) 33 HLR 402, CA

Sentence of six months not excessive for breach of ouster injunction from estate

The defendant was a lodger living with a secure tenant. There were allegations that the flat was used for prostitution and that many visitors used the flat for the consumption of illegal drugs. There was also an allegation of assault on a neighbour. The local authority obtained an injunction under Housing Act 1996 s152 (now repealed) excluding the defendant from the flat and from part of the estate. The order was to remain in force for twelve months, with a power of arrest for six months. Five months later a police officer attended another flat on the estate to execute a search warrant under Misuse of Drugs Act 1971. The defendant was found in the flat and arrested as he was in breach of the injunction. He was brought before a judge the same day and sentenced to six months' imprisonment.

His appeal against sentence was dismissed. The sentence was not manifestly excessive. There was evidence of serious anti-social behaviour. There was a deliberate breach of the court's order, albeit on only one occasion. It was plain that consumption of drugs was going on in the premises and the defendant could not put himself forward as a man of good character.

E2.3   *Manchester CC v McCann*
[1999] QB 1214; (1999) 31 HLR 770; (1998) *Times* 26 November, CA

Committal for 'wilful insults' to a witness where husband abusive to witness

The council took possession proceedings against a tenant, Mrs McCann, on the grounds of anti-social behaviour by her children. At the conclusion of his evidence one of the council's witnesses – another tenant – was driven home by a housing officer. As he got out of the car, the defendant's husband shouted at him, 'I'll fucking have you, you bastard.' The council could have applied in the High Court to commit the husband for intimidation of a witness (RSC Ord 52) but instead applied in the county court for his committal under County Courts Act 1984 s118 which deals with 'wilful insults' to a witness.

Overturning the refusal of HHJ Holman to commit, the Court of Appeal held that s118 does give an immediate jurisdiction to punish in such circumstances since:

> If the court could deal with insults but not threats, the court would not be able to give immediate protection to those who needed it most. It would risk failing its users.

E2.4   *Manchester CC v Worthington*

October 1999 *Legal Action* 24, CA

Written particulars of alleged breaches should be available at committal proceedings despite limited time to prepare

The defendant was convicted of assault on a former partner and sentenced to a term of imprisonment. On his release he seriously assaulted his former partner and threatened her and her family. After he had kicked in their front door, in November 1998 the council obtained an injunction pursuant to Housing Act 1996 s152(3) (now repealed) restraining the defendant from anti-social behaviour, including violence and prohibiting him from entering certain geographical areas. There was a series of breaches of the injunction, including committal proceedings and imprisonment. On 12 March 1999 the police again found the defendant in the prohibited area being drunk and abusive. He was arrested and brought before a county court judge the same afternoon for three breaches of the injunction, all within the month after he had been released from prison for contempt. After a very short hearing HHJ MacMillan imposed a sentence of six weeks imprisonment suspended for 12 months. The council appealed, contending that if the history and evidence of the latest breaches had been fully considered an immediate custodial sentence would have been imposed.

The Court of Appeal allowed the appeal and remitted the matter. The council had been denied a fair hearing. Although a person arrested for breach of a s152 injunction had to be produced before a judge within 24 hours (s155(2)(a)) and there was not time for a formal application to commit or documentary evidence in support, 'it would be highly desirable' to have available for the judge and the defendant written particulars of the alleged breaches, even in manuscript form. As the liberty of the subject is at stake 'it is crucial' that the court establishes the relevant facts, gives time to consider proper disposal and delivers a judgment with reasons. Each breach should be considered separately. Judges giving suspended sentences of imprisonment should explain the consequences of breach.

E2.5   *Medina Housing Association v Connolly*

[2002] All ER (D) 397 (Jul); October 2002 *Legal Action* 27; 26 July 2002, CA

Appeal against committal dismissed despite procedural defects where no injustice; interim injunction 'until' trial date breached by actions on day of trial

The claimant landlord brought possession proceedings against the defendants. In the course of the proceedings the claimant obtained an interim injunction restraining the defendants from causing nuisance or annoyance or threatening residents on the estate where they lived. The injunction was to remain in force 'until 24 June 2002', the date of the trial. During the lunchtime adjournment on 24 July, the first defendant approached two of the claimant's witnesses outside court, stared at them, and then said 'I'm bad and I'm back'. The first defendant was arrested and brought before the court that afternoon. The judge told the first defendant's solicitor that he intended to deal with the matter as an alleged contempt, as breach of the injunction, but would reserve cross-examination of the witnesses to the following afternoon to allow the first defendant's solicitor time to prepare or instruct counsel. The judge found the contempt proved and sentenced

the first defendant to six months' imprisonment. The first defendant appealed, contending that (1) the judge had not followed the procedure laid
down in CCR Ord 29 r1 in that there was no notice of the breach and no
14-day period between service and the hearing of the matter; and (2) the
first defendant was not in breach because the injunction had expired.

The appeal was dismissed. Although judges are not to be encouraged
to proceed without following the procedure laid down in CCR Ord 29, the
court has power to waive procedural defects where there is no injustice.
The first defendant had a fair trial and was not prejudiced. Second, the
word 'until' in the interim injunction could mean nothing other than that
it included or excluded the whole day of 24 June. On the facts, as 24 June
was the trial date, and the time when a permanent injunction might be
granted, it would have been absurd to have a hiatus between the two injunctions. It must have been intended to include the whole of the day.

E2.6   *Middlesbrough BC v Turnbull*
[2003] EWCA Civ 1327; (2003) *Times* 15 September; 28 August 2003

*Maximum sentence should be reserved for worst cases; notice of committal
hearings*

In September 2002, the claimant local authority obtained an injunction
preventing the defendant, aged 19, from entering an area known as The
Triangle. He breached the order. In December 2002, he was arrested and
committed to prison for three months. He was released in January 2003,
after serving half of the sentence. Further complaints were made that he
had been riding a motorcycle irresponsibly, driving a vehicle dangerously, and selling cigarettes within The Triangle. The council applied to the
county court for his committal. A notice in Form N78 requiring him to
show cause why he should not be committed was served on the defendant's mother on 2 April and on him personally on 3 April. The hearing
was listed for 7 April, but that morning he was arrested for motoring
offences and held at the police station. He telephoned his solicitor and told
them he would be unable to attend the committal hearing. The court was
informed and confirmed with the police station that he was detained. He
was released without charge by 2.10 pm, but did not call his solicitor or ask
the police for assistance to attend court. His case was called at 3.25 pm.
No one was present on his behalf. The judge found that he had committed
the breaches as alleged and ordered that he be detained for the maximum
period of two years' imprisonment. The defendant appealed.

The Court of Appeal allowed his appeal. There was no excuse for not appearing at the committal hearing on 7 April, or for his solicitors not being
present on his behalf. Both had been fully aware of the timetable and could
have sought an adjournment had an appearance been entered. However,
the imposition of the maximum sentence was excessive. The maximum
sentence should be reserved for the worst cases. The judge should have
had regard to the facts that the defendant was only aged 19 and that his
conduct, although distressing to others, did not include personal hostility,
violence or abuse. It was true that the defendant had continued to engage
in conduct in breach of the order even after being imprisoned because of
earlier breaches, and that he showed no signs of desisting. It had to be

said, however, that the sentence imposed was manifestly excessive in all the circumstances. The Court of Appeal added that the practice in some county courts of listing applications for committal for contempt of court for hearing only seven days after the application was made, in breach of para 4.2 of the Practice Direction to CCR Ord 29 r1 (which provides for 14 clear days notice), is undesirable. A longer period should be given.

E2.7 *Newham LBC v Jones*

[2002] EWCA Civ 1779, 19 November 2002

County court has power to review decision to grant bail; appeal against refusal to grant bail by way of review not rehearing

Mr Jones was a council tenant. Newham issued a claim for possession based on allegations of rent arrears and nuisance and disturbance to a neighbour. There was an extensive history of abuse, threats and violence. The council also obtained an injunction under Housing Act 1996 s152 (now repealed). Mr Jones admitted breaching the injunction and on a (first) application to commit, a judge made no order regarding the admitted breach. The council then applied to commit Mr Jones for a second alleged breach of the injunction. HHJ Bradbury gave directions and then considered whether to remand the defendant in custody until the committal hearing or whether to release him on bail. Mr Jones sought bail and informed the judge that he would submit to any conditions imposed. However, no conditions were offered to the court. The judge referred to the serious nature of the allegations, in particular an allegation that he had made a threat to kill, and that he had previously admitted being in breach of the injunction. He refused bail on the grounds that the victim lived adjacent to the defendant and that there were plain difficulties particularly after the first breach of the injunction. The defendant appealed.

The Court of Appeal dismissed the appeal. (1) The county court has the power to review a decision to grant bail or to remand in custody, especially when there has been a change in circumstance. Accordingly, the Court of Appeal's task on appeal is one of review rather than rehearing. (2) The judge was fully aware of his power to grant bail and was alive to the fact that he could impose conditions if appropriate. Furthermore, although the judge did not specifically refer to the Bail Act 1976, he did express concerns over the seriousness of the allegations and the risk of further breaches of the injunction. The judge gave perfectly cogent reasons for his decision to refuse to grant bail. His exercise of discretion could not be said to have been plainly wrong. Nor could it be said that there were any serious procedural or other irregularities.

E2.8 *Nottingham CC v Cutts*

(2001) 33 HLR 83, CA

Where defendant made threats to kill committal for 12 months not manifestly unfair

The defendant tenant had been 'causing trouble' on his housing estate since 1995. In August 1998 the council obtained an injunction protecting neighbours, other residents and its own staff from further anti-social behaviour. Within a short time the order was breached and in October 1998 the defendant was committed to prison for 42 days. On a further application to commit heard in July 1999 a neighbour gave evidence that the defendant had threatened him with violence, tried to punch him and used racist and other foul language. Another witness gave evidence that on the day before the hearing the defendant had threatened to kill him and had kicked and banged at his door and used foul and threatening language. HHJ MacDuff QC committed the defendant to prison for 12 months.

The Court of Appeal dismissed his appeal. The judge 'was undoubtedly right in the case to impose a substantial term of imprisonment'. Although the sentence was 'a stiff one' it was not 'manifestly excessive'.

E2.9   *Poole BC v Hambridge*
[2007] EWCA Civ 990; 25 September 2007

Defendant committed to prison for contempt, but then purged contempt and released; council refused permission to appeal

The defendant's partner was an assured tenant. In 2004, he, his partner and their children conducted 'a campaign of anti-social behaviour', issuing threats, abuse and intimidation to other residents who complained to the council about the conduct of the family. The council obtained an anti-social behaviour injunction (Housing Act 1996 s153(A)) with a power of arrest. After a four-day hearing HHJ Meston QC made an outright possession order. The judge accepted that there was a high risk of recurrence of the behaviour and that the impact on neighbours and those who had given evidence would be severe. He continued the injunction. Within a fortnight of the possession order taking effect, Mr Hampton was arrested and admitted being in breach of the injunction by going into the street from which he was excluded and by intimidating one of the witnesses by banging on her door. HHJ Meston sentenced him to eight weeks' imprisonment, but suspended it for a period of one year. The following month Mr Hampton breached the injunction on four occasions. After stating that the victims found his behaviour alarming and upsetting, the judge activated the suspended sentence and imposed further consecutive sentences, so that the overall sentence became one of 20 weeks' imprisonment. Five days later, the defendant sought to purge his contempt. He wrote to the court stating that he was truly sorry, wanted to apologise to the court and all the people involved and stated that he would 'make sure that the residents ... can live their lives without having to worry about me or any of my family.' At the hearing to purge his contempt the defendant appeared in person and did not give evidence. The judge accepted that the apology was sincere, that the contempt had been purged and directed that the defendant should be released forthwith. The council sought to appeal.

The Court of Appeal, after considering CPR 52.3(1) and earlier conflicting authorities, held that permission to appeal was needed. It is only the alleged contemnor who can appeal without permission against a committal order. An applicant needs permission. With regard to the judge's decision on the merits, the Court of Appeal refused permission. Although committal, when the judge ordered it, was appropriate, two weeks had elapsed before the application to purge contempt was heard by the court. The judge was entitled to conclude that 14 days in custody (which, by virtue of Criminal Justice Act 2003 s253 amounted to a sentence of 28 days) was sufficient and that the contempt had been purged. Taken with the five days which had been served on remand, it was a sufficiently long period – a sufficient clang of the prison gates and a sufficient taste of custody – to persuade the defendant to behave himself. The judge had very considerable knowledge of the defendant and was in the best position to assess the effect which custody had had on him, and the significance of the statements made in the letter.

E2.10   *Stafford BC v Haynes*

[2003] EWCA Civ 159; [2003] HLR 46

Where admissions of acts amounting to contempt made, wrong to adjourn applications to commit

The council obtained without notice injunctions under Housing Act 1996 s152 (now repealed) against a couple, who were tenants on a housing estate, and their son, following threatening and abusive behaviour towards neighbours. When housing officers accompanied by police officers sought to serve the orders, they were met with abuse and violence from the defendants. The defendants were arrested and the council applied to commit them for breach of the injunctions. At the hearing, they admitted that they had behaved in the manner alleged. HHJ Mitchell expressed concern about a number of matters, including whether housing officers could come within the protection of s152, whether the breaches were deliberate, and whether the police intended to pursue criminal proceedings. He adjourned the applications to commit until such time as the defendants again breached the orders or criminal proceedings against them were determined. The council appealed.

The Court of Appeal allowed the appeal. The judge's decision was plainly wrong. Justice delayed was justice denied. If the matters admitted by the defendants amounted to contempt of court, then the council, on behalf of all those living on the estate, was entitled to have it acted on. The applications were remitted to the county court.

E2.11   *Tower Hamlets LBC v Long*

(2000) 32 HLR 219, CA

'Lynch mob behaviour' by tenant in breach of injunction required prison sentence

In June 1997 the council obtained an injunction restraining the defendant tenant from causing nuisance or annoyance to, or threatening or otherwise intimidating, other residents in his close. For nine months the defendant complied but in April 1998 he began a personal vendetta against the new tenant of an adjoining flat whom he believed to be a paedophile. He engaged in a course of conduct which involved shouting abuse, ranting and raving, threats of violence and spreading rumours about the neighbour that he was a paedophile. It was described as 'lynch mob behaviour' although no actual violence was used. Recorder White committed him to prison for three months for contempt.

The Court of Appeal, endorsing the sanction of immediate imprisonment, said:

... his bad behaviour as tenant, which is utterly unacceptable on a housing estate, is something to be viewed, and has been viewed by the court, as requiring a prison sentence.

However, since the defendant was a first-time offender and had initially complied with the injunction, the sentence was reduced to three weeks with a warning that 'the court will come down like a ton of bricks if he does it a second time'. Drink was not a mitigating factor.

E3   Assignments (secure tenants)

The Housing Act 1985 s91 provides that assignment of secure tenancies is, in general, prohibited but provides for a right to exercise mutual exchanges in some circumstances.

House of Lords

E3.1   *Burton v Camden LBC*
[2000] 2 AC 399; [2000] 2 WLR 427; [2000] 1 All ER 943; [2000] LGR 289; (2000) 32 HLR 625; [2000] L&TR 235; [2000] 14 EG 149; (2000) *Times* 23 February, HL

Joint tenant prevented from, in effect, assigning tenancy to other tenant

In 1994 the council granted a joint tenancy to the plaintiff and another tenant. In July 1996 the plaintiff gave notice to the council's housing benefit department that her joint tenant would be leaving and asked for her housing benefit to be increased so that it covered all of the rent. The council refused either to increase the benefit or to treat the plaintiff as a sole tenant of the property, since the flat had three bedrooms and was needed to accommodate families. However, the departing joint tenant completed a deed of release, releasing her interest to the plaintiff. The plaintiff sought a declaration that she had become the sole tenant of her council flat.

The House of Lords held that the deed of release was not effective. The prohibition on assignment in Housing Act 1985 s91(1) applied equally to deeds of assignment and deeds of release. Whatever the precise form of words chosen, the transaction would ordinarily be regarded as a transfer of one of the tenant's rights to the tenancy.

Court of Appeal

E3.2   *Camden LBC v Alexandrou*
(1998) 30 HLR 534, CA (see N4.7)

Surrender by operation of law made out where tenant had sought to assign his interest to other tenant

E3.3   *Camden LBC v Goldenberg*
(1996) 28 HLR 727; (1997) 73 P&CR 376; (1997) 95 LGR 693, CA

Residence test satisfied where occupant intended to return to grandmother's flat; intention not displaced by intention to set up home elsewhere if he could

In 1991 the defendant moved in to live with his grandmother in her one-bedroomed council flat in a block reserved for elderly people. In 1992 he married and moved out but he and his wife were unable to find permanent accommodation and after ten weeks he returned to live with his grandmother. In November 1992 she assigned her tenancy to him and moved to a nursing home. The council brought proceedings for possession. The defendant asserted that the assignment was valid as he would have been a person entitled to succeed his grandmother had she died (Housing Act 1985 s91(3)(c)). The council claimed that the ten-week absence broke the one-year period of residence required by s87 to qualify for succession.

A county court judge granted possession but the Court of Appeal allowed the defendant's appeal. It unanimously held that the defendant should be treated as continuing to reside at the flat during the ten-week absence, if there was sufficient physical manifestation of his occupation during that period. He had left his possessions there, it remained his postal address and he had throughout maintained an intention to return. By a majority, the court held that, although he and his wife had intended to establish a home for themselves if they could, that had been a distant prospect which qualified, but did not displace, the intention to return.

E3.4 **Croydon LBC v Buston and Triance**
(1992) 24 HLR 36, CA

Possession ordered where son unable to show tenancy properly assigned to him

A secure tenant left premises to live elsewhere and so lost her secure status (Housing Act 1985 s81). The council terminated the tenancy by notice to quit and began possession proceedings. The tenant had left her adult son behind in the premises. He argued that he had been qualified to succeed his mother (Housing Act 1985 s87) and had become the tenant by assignment before secure status had been lost (Housing Act 1985 s91). He had instructed solicitors to arrange for the tenancy to be transferred to him and had approached the council in good time.

The Court of Appeal granted possession. The son was unable to show either that the purported assignment had been made by deed or that there had been part performance of a parol agreement for an assignment.

E3.5 **Peabody Donation Fund v Higgins**
[1983] 1 WLR 1091; [1983] 3 All ER 122; (1983) 10 HLR 82, CA

Assignment in breach of tenancy nevertheless operated as an assignment

Mr Higgins was a secure tenant. He wanted to retire to Ireland. Although the tenancy agreement contained an absolute prohibition against assignment, he entered into a deed of assignment with his daughter. She was someone who could have succeeded to the tenancy if he had died (Housing Act 1980 s30, now Housing Act 1985 s87). Mr Higgins then left. Peabody served a notice to quit and brought possession proceedings, claiming that the tenancy was no longer secure because Mr Higgins had ceased to occupy as his only or principal home. HHJ Harris made a possession order.

The tenant's appeal was allowed. The effect of Housing Act 1980 s37 (now Housing Act 1985 s91(3)(c)) was that the instrument purporting to be an assignment did create a valid assignment, albeit in breach of the terms of the tenancy. Section 37 was not limited to 'lawful' assignments. Although the assignment in breach of the tenancy conditions gave rise to a ground for possession under Housing Act 1980 Sch 4 (now Housing Act 1985 Sch 2), it was effective in transferring the secure tenancy to Mr Higgins's daughter.

E3.6   *Sanctuary Housing Association v Baker*

(1998) 30 HLR 809; [1998] 1 EGLR 42; [1998] 09 EG 150, CA

Assignment effective despite consent to assign having been obtained by fraud; Fraud nullified consent; no implied surrender

Miss Scamp, an assured tenant of the housing association, sought and obtained the association's consent to a mutual exchange with a secure tenant of a local authority, Miss Baker. The local authority gave Miss Baker its consent to assign (under Housing Act 1985 s92(2A)). Miss Scamp then entered into a deed of assignment with Miss Baker, transferring the assured tenancy to her. Miss Baker moved into the association's property but never completed the assignment of her council tenancy to Miss Scamp. The association brought possession proceedings against Miss Baker, contending that its consent had been induced by misrepresentation, that the assignment was a nullity and that the original tenancy (under which the now departed Miss Scamp was alleged still to be the tenant) had been determined by a notice to quit which it had served subsequently. The trial judge found that the 'mutual exchange' had been a sham and a fraud from the beginning, as Miss Scamp had never intended to move to the council flat and had been paid by Miss Baker for her co-operation in the transactions. He directed himself that 'fraud unravels all' and granted a possession order.

The Court of Appeal allowed Miss Baker's appeal. It held that, even if the consent of the association had been fraudulently obtained, that did nothing to detract from the validity of the assignment by deed in which the two parties (the two tenants) had perfected their own agreement. The effect of nullifying the consent was simply to produce a situation in which a valid assignment had been made without valid consent, exposing the incoming tenant to a possible action for breach of covenant against assignment without consent. The court further held that, since there was no evidence that Miss Scamp had ever received the notice to quit and since the tenancy agreement did not incorporate Law of Property Act 1925 s196 allowing service of notice on the premises, the association could not prove that the original tenancy had been determined. The association could not claim that there had been a surrender because Miss Scamp's actions in assigning her tenancy were themselves a denial of any proposition that she intended to give up her tenancy to the plaintiff landlords.

E4   **Housing management and consultation (secure tenants)**

Housing Act 1985 s21 imposes a duty on local authorities for the general management, regulation and control of their housing. Housing Act 1985 s105 contains the mandatory requirements of the Tenants' Charter for consultation with council tenants on matters of housing management.

House of Lords

E4.1 *Akumah v Hackney LBC*

[2005] UKHL 17; [2005] 1 WLR 985; [2005] 2 All ER 148; [2005] HLR 26; (2005) *Times* 4 March

General management duty encompassed duty to control parking on housing estates

The claimant challenged the legality of a controlled parking scheme on a housing estate which had lead to the clamping and removal of his car. The Court of Appeal ([2002] EWCA Civ 582; [2003] HLR 5) held that the controlled parking scheme was lawful. The tenant appealed to the House of Lords.

The appeal was dismissed. Housing Act 1985 s21(1) imposes a duty on local authorities for the general management, regulation and control of their housing. It is inherent and incidental to that general management duty to control parking on housing estates for which they have responsibility. Unregulated parking can, in many housing estates, lead to congestion of the roads and the unavailability of places for residents to park their cars. It is also important to ensure access for service and emergency vehicles. Those factors are clearly capable of affecting the amenity of life for the residents and their access to and enjoyment of their houses and flats on the estate. Local authorities also have a subsidiary power contained in Local Government Act 1972 s111 to do anything incidental to the management of local authority business. Local authorities are accordingly entitled to introduce parking controls on estates without any need for bylaws to be made under Greater London Council (General Powers) Act 1975 s7.

Court of Appeal

E4.2 *R v Brent LBC ex p Morris*

(1998) 30 HLR 324; (1997) 74 P&CR D29, CA

Requirement to consult did not require notification of proposals to each tenant

The applicants were secure tenants on the Chalkhill Estate in Brent and members of the Chalkhill Residents Management Board, which had been established in 1991 as a result of consultations between tenants' representatives, the council and the Department of the Environment. In 1993, the council withdrew recognition from all tenants' and residents' associations on the estate and established 'area housing boards' as a mechanism for tenant consultation. McCullough J dismissed an application for judicial review.

The Court of Appeal dismissed the tenants' appeal. Section 105 does not require an authority to inform each tenant of its proposals. It is only required to make arrangements to enable tenants to be informed of its proposals. It was not necessary for there to be a specific determination by the authority that it considered the arrangements appropriate. That was implicit from the fact that they were in place.

E4.3   ***R v Secretary of State for the Environment ex p Walters***
(1998) 30 HLR 328, CA

Inadequate consultation of tenants; Secretary of state's consent wrong in law; refusal of relief

Brent LBC entered into arrangements to demolish the Chalkhill Estate and redevelop the land through a scheme of disposal to private companies. The consent of the secretary of state was required under Housing Act 1985 s32. The special consultation arrangements in Housing Act 1985 s106A and Sch 3A also applied. The secretary of state gave consent and a tenant applied for judicial review of that decision on the ground that there had been inadequate consultation.

Schiemann LJ, sitting as a High Court judge, found that there had been a failure to consult properly. Furthermore, the secretary of state had failed to appreciate that the whole of the estate was being disposed of. Therefore, his decision was flawed on both grounds and wrong in law. The 'deemed valid' provisions in Sch 3A para 6 could not save a consent given in error of law. However, the applicant was refused relief. The judge, in exercising that discretion, drew attention to the facts that: (a) the applicant was only one tenant; (b) he had waited almost three months before launching the challenge; (c) the effects on his personal rights would be minimal or non-existent; and (d) the clear majority of tenants wanted the scheme to proceed. He remarked, however, that 'the court will not lightly condone the bypassing of consultation requirements imposed by statute'.

The Court of Appeal dismissed an appeal by Mr Walters. It was perfectly within the discretion of the judge to refuse to grant relief despite finding that the consultation process was flawed.

E4.4   ***Short v Tower Hamlets LBC***
(1986) 18 HLR 171, CA

A decision 'in principle' did not require consultation

Tower Hamlets Council reached a decision 'in principle to sell and to authorise marketing' of certain council property before any consultation with tenants. Indeed, when the decision was taken (October 1983), the council had not even complied with its statutory duty to publish procedures for consultation by the deadline of 3 October 1981.

The Court of Appeal upheld the right of tenants to bring county court proceedings for injunctive relief to restrain the implementation of any decision which required consultation but about which they had not been consulted. However, on the specific facts of this case, it held that a decision reached 'in principle' to sell did not require consultation, as it did not pertain to 'housing management'.

High Court

E4.6   ***R v Gateshead MBC ex p Smith (Duncan)***
(1999) 31 HLR 97, QBD

Lawful decision despite 'somewhat false picture' of consultation results presented

The applicant sought judicial review of the council's decision to demolish its Saltmeadows Estate, which comprised about 200 rented homes. It was alleged that, although the council had consulted widely on future options for the estate, it had not sufficiently spelled out the demolition option and that, when the matter had been put to committee for decision, the results of the consultation exercise were misrepresented.

Collins J rejected the application. He held that: (a) there had been adequate consultation – the demolition option had at least been made clear as a 'possibility'; and (b) although the committee was given a 'somewhat false picture' of the consultation results, it was impossible to assert that the council was not aware of the alleged discrepancy because it had been drawn to its attention by a group lobbying against demolition.

E4.6 *R (Beale and Carty) v Camden LBC*
[2004] EWHC 6 (Admin); [2004] LGR 291; [2004] HLR 48

Section 105 duty is to inform; no requirement to set out arguments against proposals

Camden proposed to raise money by way of an arm's length management organisation (ALMO) to meet the government's target of improving its stock of council housing. Under Housing Act 1985 s27, the secretary of state's approval for such a scheme was required and guidance was issued. The guidance stated that the secretary of state would want to be satisfied that the proposal had the support of the majority of the authority's tenants and provided that authorities should give information about, and opportunity to comment on, the reasons for setting up the body. The authority sent documents containing information on the proposals which also set out the main case against them. The claimants applied for judicial review, arguing that Camden had failed to provide sufficient information setting out the arguments against the proposals. They submitted that Camden was required to ensure that the case against the proposals was made available to all voters and that information provided by the authority to voters should be balanced. Camden contended that there was no legal duty to do this. It relied on the absence of express words to that effect in Housing Act 1985 s105(1), in the guidance and in the Code of Recommended Practice on Local Authority Publicity.

Munby J dismissed the application. There is no legal requirement that a local authority should set out the case against its proposals in its publicity material. The obligation in s105(1) is to inform the relevant tenants of the authority's proposals and not to canvass the disadvantages of its proposals. Although failure to comply might fatally prejudice such an application for approval, it could not, of itself, render the consultation process unlawful. It was for the secretary of state to determine in the first place whether there had been compliance with the guidance. Furthermore, there was nothing in the guidance or the code to require the authority to advise its tenants of any matter that might lead them to vote against its proposals.

E5   # Variation of non-rent terms (secure tenants)

Variations to the non-rent terms of a secure tenancy can be achieved only by the notice and consultation procedures in Housing Act 1985 s103. The procedure for alteration of rent is that notice of variation must be given in accordance with the terms of the tenancy (Housing Act 1985 s102(1)(b)).

Court of Appeal

E5.1   ## Palmer v Sandwell MBC
(1988) 20 HLR 74; [1987] 2 EGLR 79; (1987) 284 EG 1487, CA

Variation of tenancy ineffective where no agreement and s103 not complied with

A county court judge awarded £2,000 for breach of a covenant to correct design defects set out in a revised tenancy agreement and tenants' handbook issued by the local authority. On appeal, that judgment was set aside.

The Court of Appeal found that simply sending existing tenants a revised tenancy agreement and handbook was insufficient to incorporate the terms set out in those documents into the secure tenancy. The procedure for variation of terms is set out in Housing Act 1985 s102 (formerly Housing Act 1980 s40), which provides that, except in relation to rent, the terms of a secure tenancy agreement can be varied only by (a) agreement between landlord and tenant or (b) the notice of variation procedure in Housing Act 1985 s103. The local authority was able to escape liability under the terms of the handbook and agreement because it had not used the s103 procedure and the tenant had not positively assented to the new terms (indeed, had not been invited to do so).

E5.2   ## R (Kilby) v Basildon DC
[2007] EWCA Civ 479; [2007] HLR 39

Housing Act 1985 ss102 and 103 provide a complete code for variation of tenancies

The claimant was a secure tenant. His tenancy agreement contained a clause which provided that the council could only vary the terms of the agreement if a majority of tenants' representatives agreed to the change. The council adopted a decision to implement a new form of agreement, which did not include that clause. It was of the opinion that the clause was ultra vires its powers and void in so far as it conflicted with the provisions of Housing Act 1985 ss102(1) and 103. The council purported to give preliminary notice of an intention to vary the agreement pursuant to s103. The claimant's application for judicial review was dismissed ([2006] EWHC 1892 (Admin); [2006] HLR 46). He appealed.

The Court of Appeal dismissed his appeal. The council was exercising its management powers under Housing Act 1985 s21 for the single purpose of regulating secure periodic tenancies. In that context ss102 and 103 constituted a complete code governing the variation of the terms of a secure tenancy. The terms of secure tenancies may only be varied by agreement, in some circumstances pursuant to existing contractual arrangements or by unilateral notice, following consultation. The council did not have the power to amend the statute by giving up its power of unilateral variation. The clause in the original tenancy agreement was incompatible with the council's statutory right and power to vary tenancies unilaterally under s103.

High Court

E5.3   *R v Brent LBC ex p Blatt*
(1992) 24 HLR 319, DC

Council could vary tenancy using s103 procedure despite covenant in agreement

The council had a standard tenancy agreement containing relatively generous terms on repairs and security of tenure, including a covenant that the council would not seek to vary those terms. Subsequently, the council sought to use the statutory procedures in Housing Act 1985 s103 to vary the tenancy agreement to incorporate less generous terms.

The Divisional Court held that the council was free to use the statutory variation procedure, notwithstanding the covenants in the tenancy agreement. The statute was of more recent origin than the contract and took precedence over it.

E6   Rents (secure tenants)

Housing Act 1985 s24 restricts councils to charging 'reasonable rents'.

Court of Appeal

E6.1   *R v Ealing LBC ex p Lewis*
(1992) 24 HLR 484; (1992) 90 LGR 571; [1992] COD 291, CA

Costs improperly included in Housing Revenue Account and rent set unlawful

The council charged to the Housing Revenue Account (HRA) the full cost of warden services to its sheltered accommodation and most of the cost of its homeless persons unit. Rents were set in order to meet these and other HRA costs.

The Court of Appeal held that only part of the cost of these services properly fell to be paid for by tenants alone. The rent levels were, therefore, unlawful and the application for judicial review succeeded.

E6.2   *Wandsworth LBC v Winder (No 2)*
(1988) 20 HLR 400, CA

Tenant failed in argument that rent levels too high

A tenant contended that the rents fixed by Wandsworth Council were unreasonably high, having regard to the financial resources of ratepayers and tenants in the borough, and the increases so large that in the private sector the 'phasing' provisions would have operated.

The Court of Appeal held that, although, in fixing rent levels under Housing Act 1957 s111 (now Housing Act 1985 s24), councils could make only 'such reasonable charges as they may determine', the consideration of the rent level could (but did not have to) take into account the relative financial circumstances of tenants and ratepayers. Wandsworth's rent charges were not '*Wednesbury* unlawful'.

High Court

E6.3 *Hemsted v Lees and Norwich CC*
(1986) 18 HLR 424, QBD

Ratepayer failed in argument that rent levels too low

A ratepayer asserted that the rents fixed by the local authority were too low, having regard to local market rent levels.

Dismissing an application for judicial review, McCowan J stated that the existing case-law establishes three principles: (a) a council has a wide discretion in fixing the rent level; (b) it is entitled to approach the matter as one of social policy; and (c) it is not obliged to make a profit from rents or relate them to market rent levels.

E7   Rent regulation (assured tenants)

Housing Act 1988 ss13 and 14 give rent assessment committees (RACs) power to determine the rent payable by assured periodic tenants in certain circumstances. The rent to be determined is the rent at which 'the dwelling-house concerned might reasonably be expected to be let in the open market by a willing landlord under an assured tenancy' (s14(1)).

House of Lords

E7.1 *Riverside Housing Association Ltd v White*
[2007] UKHL 20; [2007] 4 All ER 97; [2007] HLR 31; [2007] L&TR 22; (2007) *Times* 7 May; 25 April 2007

Notices of rent increases valid: tenancy provisions had to be interpreted in context

An assured tenancy agreement contained clauses providing that

> (6) Riverside may increase the rent by giving the tenant four (4) weeks notice in writing as set out in accordance with the provisions of this Agreement ...
> (7) The rent payable will be increased annually with effect from the first Monday of June each year. (This is known as the 'Rent Variation Date').

Another clause provided

> In this Agreement the term 'Rent Variation Date' refers to the annual increase in rent which will occur each year on the first Monday in June with four (4) weeks prior notice.

Tenants challenged the validity of a number of notices served which purported to increase the rent. One, served in February 2001, provided for a rent increase from 2 April 2001. In subsequent years, Riverside gave similar notices in February, purporting to increase the rent from a date in April. The tenants claimed that Riverside only had the right to increase the rent if it served a notice which took effect on the first Monday of June (ie, on the rent variation date) with 28 days' prior notice. HHJ Stewart QC found that notices were valid. The Court of Appeal held that they were not valid.

The House of Lords found that the notices were valid. Lord Neuberger stated that these rent review provisions, like any other contractual term, had to be interpreted by reference to the particular words used in their particular context. Although Riverside's argument that time was not of the essence when considering them was misconceived, the notion of a moveable rent review date, whereby Riverside could increase the rent once at any time during a year from the first Monday in June, provided that it first gives 28 days' notice, appeared sensible and fair. The House of Lords construed the relevant clauses in the tenancy agreement as meaning that Riverside was entitled to increase the rent once a year on 28 days' notice and that the notice could take effect any time on or after the first Monday in June.

Court of Appeal

E7.2 *Bankway Properties v Dunsford*
[2001] EWCA Civ 528; [2001] 1 WLR 1369; [2001] L&TR 339; [2001] 26 EG 164; [2002] HLR 42; (2001) *Times* 24 April

Rent review clause unenforceable where it was a device for landlord to increase rent to level that would avoid statutory scheme for assured tenancy

In 1994 the claimant landlord's predecessor in title granted the defendant an assured tenancy. The landlord knew that the rent would be paid through housing benefit. The rent was initially £4,680 per annum. However, the tenancy agreement provided that from the last review date, rent was payable at the rate of £25,000 per annum. The last review date was defined as 11 February 1996. In June 1998 Bankway Properties Limited became the landlord. Following a rent review, the defendants failed to pay the new rent of £25,000 per annum. The county court granted a possession order and gave judgment for the outstanding arrears of rent. The defendants appealed, arguing that since the claimant was aware that they were in receipt of housing benefit, it knew that there was no prospect of them being able to pay the increased rent. The rent review clause was a mere device or pretence inserted in order to regain possession and/or avoid the protection conferred by the assured tenancy.

The Court of Appeal allowed the appeal and dismissed the claim for possession. Arden LJ said that the rent review clause was inconsistent with the intention of the parties to grant an assured tenancy. In order to establish whether an agreement was intended to have its stated effect it was necessary to look at the substance and reality of the transaction entered into by the parties. For that purpose, the court could look at all the relevant circumstances, including the conduct of the parties after the creation of the tenancy. The rent of £25,000 could not be justified as a market rent and there was no explanation why, if it had genuinely intended that the rent of £25,000 should be payable, it was not immediately demanded on the review. If the clause was not in substance or reality a provision for the fixing of rent, but a provision for the landlord to recover possession otherwise than in accordance with the mandatory scheme, then the clause would amount to a contracting out of the statutory scheme for assured tenancies and would not be enforceable. That was a question of fact, which on the evidence as a whole was established. The clause was a mere device, which enabled the landlord, effectively when it chose, to recover possession. In those circumstances it was unenforceable as an unlawful contracting out of the Housing Act 1988. Pill LJ agreeing said that the clause was 'inconsistent with and repugnant to the statutory purpose' and that 'to permit enforcement of [the clause] would be to defeat the main purpose of the agreement.'

E7.3   ## Contour Homes Ltd v Rowen
[2007] EWCA Civ 842; (2007) *Times* 13 July; 26 June 2007

Exclusion from s13 not limited to rent review clause with prescripted increases; estoppel cannot give tribunal a jurisdiction it does not otherwise have

Mr Rowen was an assured tenant. His tenancy agreement contained a rent review clause. His landlords initiated a rent review by letter. Mr Rowen referred that letter to a rent assessment committee (RAC). The RAC decided that the letter was invalid because it failed to comply with the notice requirements in Housing Act 1988 s13(2). The landlords appealed, arguing that, in view of s13(1)(b), where the tenancy agreement contains its own provisions for rent reviews, s13(2) does not apply, and the RAC has no jurisdiction to review the rent increase. Irwin J found that the exclusion from s13 of any tenancy containing the provision for the rent review applied only to tenancy agreements with a fixed pre-agreed uplift. He concluded that the tenancy fell within s13(2). He also found that statements made in a tenants' handbook to the effect that a revised rent could be appealed to the RAC meant that the landlords were estopped from contending to the contrary. The landlords appealed.

The Court of Appeal allowed the appeal. There is nothing in the wording of s13(1)(b) which limits the exclusion to rent review clauses which provide for the increase of a fixed sum, as opposed to clauses that provide for unspecified amounts to be arrived at in a particular way. Both kinds of rent review clause fall within s13(1)(b). Second, estoppel cannot give a court or statutory tribunal jurisdiction that a statute says it is not to have. The jurisdiction of the RAC to determine the rent could have arisen only where notice had been required under s13(2). Where that requirement has not been satisfied, it is not possible to confer jurisdiction. Statutory jurisdiction cannot be reduced or enlarged by the consent of the parties, or by estoppel.

E7.4   ## R (Lester) v London Rent Assessment Committee
[2003] EWCA Civ 319; [2003] 1 WLR 1449; [2003] HLR 53; [2003] L&TR 406; (2003) *Times* 25 March

Referral must be received by (not merely sent to) RAC before beginning of period

Ms Lester's landlord served a notice pursuant to Housing Act 1988 s13 proposing a new rent which was due to take effect on 20 March 2002. Ms

Lester claimed that she sent an application referring the notice to a rent assessment committee (RAC) by first class post on 18 March 2002. It was common ground that the notice arrived at its office on 20 March 2002. The RAC took the view that the word 'refers' in s13 meant 'receive', and that it accordingly had no jurisdiction to hear an application referring the notice because it was received out of time. Ms Lester sought judicial review. Sir Richard Tucker dismissed her application for judicial review.

The Court of Appeal dismissed her appeal. The RAC was right to hold that in the context 'refer to' connotes 'receipt by'. Dictionary definitions tend to support that natural meaning where the question is one of referring a matter for adjudication. It would be highly inconvenient for the RAC if it had to consider whether it had jurisdiction over disputes about which it had no notice. The fact that there was no discretion to extend time or 'escape clause' for the tenant does not lead to the conclusion that 'refer' means 'send'. The subsidiary legislation prescribing the form of tenant's application could not be used as an aid to interpretation. The RAC has no jurisdiction to consider a tenant's application to determine the rent if it is not received before the date specified in the landlord's notice.

E7.5   *R (Morris) v London Rent Assessment Committee*
[2002] EWCA Civ 276, [2002] 24 EG 149; [2002] HLR 48; [2003] L&TR 5

Where notice not addressed to tenant not 'substantially to the like effect' as prescribed notice; RAC not prohibited from assessing rent at figure in excess of £25,000 limit

Mr Morris was the tenant under a long lease at a low rent under Landlord and Tenant Act 1954 Part I, which expired on 19 September 1995. Before that date the lessor served a notice proposing a statutory tenancy. However, the notice was not addressed to the current tenant, but to the original tenant. After expiry of the lease, the landlord contended that that notice was invalid, served a new notice and maintained that the tenant had become an assured tenant under Local Government and Housing Act (LGHA) 1989 Sch 10. The landlord then applied to a rent assessment committee (RAC), which determined a rent of £32,496 per annum. The tenant sought judicial review to quash the determination.

Upholding an Administrative Court decision, the Court of Appeal held that:

1) The notice was invalid because it did not name the tenant as required by the Landlord and Tenant (Notices) Regulations 1957 – even though Landlord and Tenant Act 1954 s4 provides that such a notice may be 'substantially to the like effect' as that required by the regulations. The failure to address the notice to the tenant was not a minor error or slip. The notice did not accomplish the statutory objective of serving a notice under s4. The reaction of a reasonable recipient would be to assume that the envelope and its contents were intended for the addressee, the previous tenant. [It is instructive to note that similar wording is used in the Secure Tenancies (Notices) Regulations 1987 SI No 755 and Assured Tenancies and Agricultural Occupancies (Forms) Regulations 1997 SI No 194 which deal with notices to be served on secure and assured tenants.]

2) As the notice was invalid, on expiry of the lease, the tenant became an assured tenant under Local Government and Housing Act 1989 Sch 10, rather than a statutory tenant.

3) Following *R v London Rent Assessment Panel ex p Cadogan Estates* (E7.9), a RAC is not prohibited from assessing the rent of an assured tenant at a figure in excess of the qualifying limit of £25,000 per annum. There is nothing in LGHA 1989 Sch 10 that supports a statutory principle of 'once an assured tenancy, always an assured tenancy' or which sets a ceiling of £25,000 on the amount of annual rent that may be validly determined by a RAC. If the RAC registers a rent in excess of £25,000, the tenancy ceases to qualify for protection as an assured tenancy.

E7.6   *Tadema Holdings v Ferguson*
(2000) 32 HLR 866; (1999) *Times* 25 November, CA

Older version notice 'substantially to the same effect' as prescribed notice; service of notice merely connoted delivery, no implication that it had to be understood

Mr Ferguson was an assured tenant by succession with a monthly rent of £200. His landlord, Tadema, purported to increase the rent to £800 per month by service of a Housing Act 1988 s13 notice. The form used, and which was delivered to his home, was an older version of the prescribed form since replaced by the Assured Tenancies and Agricultural Occupancies (Forms) Regulations 1997 Form 4. It gave the landlord's address as 'c/o the agent'. The notice gave an annualised figure of £9,600 per annum rather than a monthly figure for rent. It also stipulated the wrong date for the date on which each new period of tenancy started (the 20th of each month instead of the 24th, the date on the original lease). Arrears accrued. The landlord served a s8 notice and brought possession proceedings. The tenant defended claiming that the s13 notice was invalid and that that neither notice had been validly served because the tenant was suffering from a mental disability which prevented him from dealing with his own affairs properly. HHJ Rose made a possession order.

The tenant appealed unsuccessfully. Although the notice was not in the current prescribed form, it was 'substantially to the same effect' (Assured Tenancies and Agricultural Occupancies (Forms) Regulations 1997 reg 2). A s13 notice giving the landlord's address as a post office box number or care of an agent, where the agent was named and its address given, was perfectly valid. There was also nothing in the use of an annualised figure for rent or the 'wrong' date which had the effect of rendering the form not 'substantially to the same effect' as a form in the correct form. There was no basis for confusion. Second, the word 'service' in ss8 and 13 was an ordinary English word connoting delivery of a document to a particular person. It carried no implication that the document had to be read, understood or indeed known by the recipient to have been delivered as long as delivery was to the correct address. Such meaning did not change according to the capacity of the intended recipient. In addition there was nothing to put the landlord on notice in its dealings with the tenant that he was incapable of managing his own affairs by reason of mental disability. The position under contract was that such notice of mental disability was necessary in order to invalidate a contract. There was no reason why a more rigorous rule should apply to service of a notice on a tenant.

High Court

E7.7 *Ghani v London Rent Assessment Committee*

[2002] EWHC 1167 (Admin); 28 May 2002; August 2002 *Legal Action* 32

Reasons given by RAC adequate; more quantitative approach not required

Ms Ghani was an assured tenant of a maisonette above a restaurant. The property was in bad condition with an outstanding environmental health notice. In October 2001, the landlord served a notice pursuant to Housing Act 1988 s13 requiring a rent increase from £316 per month to £1,250. She objected and the matter was referred to a rent assessment committee (RAC). It was agreed that in determining the market rent under s14, the RAC was required to have regard to the condition of the premises as well as factors such as size, amenities and location. The RAC determined a rent of £848 per month. In its decision, it referred to the poor condition of the property and other aspects such as the location and noise level. It also stated that comparable properties referred to by both parties were not in any way comparable. Its reasons did not include mathematical calculations indicating how they had arrived at the rental figure. Ms Ghani appealed, contending that (1) the RAC had failed to give adequate reasons for its decision and (2) it should first have calculated the open market rental of the property in good condition, and then indicated by a figure or percentage discount what allowance had been made for the actual condition of the property.

The appeal was dismissed by Stanley Burnton J. Section 14 does not require the RAC to perform the two-stage process suggested by the tenant. There were no true comparable properties to assist in ascertaining the open market rent. Reasons given must deal with the substantial points in controversy between the parties. The reasoning of the committee in this case was sufficient. Had proper valuation evidence been submitted, a more quantitative approach to the giving of reasons would have been required.

E7.8 *N & D (London) Ltd v Gadson*

(1992) 24 HLR 64; [1992] 1 EGLR 112, QBD

Disregard of reduction in value due to failure by tenant meant failure by current tenant

Mr Gadson succeeded to the tenancy of a house after his father died. As a result of Housing Act 1988 s39 he became an assured tenant and the landlords applied to the rent assessment committee to fix 'a market rent'. The landlords sought a rent of £500 per month, but, taking into account the poor condition of the house, the RAC determined a rent of £5 per month. It found the house to be 'practically uninhabitable' with 'no water to bath, basin or WC ... no electricity to rear of house ... plaster has fallen off ceiling in rear ground floor room and off wall of kitchen and is defective around almost all windows'. The landlords challenged the RAC's decision, claiming that the committee had failed to take into account Mr Gadson's father's obligations to repair and decorate the premises and the fact that he had let the premises fall into disrepair.

Auld J held that Housing Act 1988 s14(2)(c), when stating that RACs should disregard 'any reduction in the value of the dwelling-house attributable to a failure by the tenant to comply with any terms of the tenancy' referred to default by the current tenant only. They were obliged to take into account the current condition of the premises, even if that had been brought about by the default of the tenant's father before his death.

E7.9 ### *R v London Rent Assessment Panel ex p Cadogan Estates*
[1998] QB 398; [1997] 3 WLR 833; (1998) 76 P&CR 410; (1998) 30 HLR 487; [1997] 33 EG 88, QBD

RAC could assess the rent without reference to the assured tenancy limit of £25,000

After the expiry of a fixed-term assured tenancy, landlords served a notice proposing that the rent under the statutory periodic tenancy be increased from £700 to £3,375 per month. In view of Housing Act 1988 Sch 1 para 2 (as amended by References to Rating (Housing) Regulations 1990 SI No 701 para 29 (tenancies at a high rent cannot be assured tenancies)), the RAC determined that since the notice proposed a rent in excess of £25,000 per annum, the RAC should determine the rent at £25,000.

Kay J held that the RAC could assess the rent without reference to the £25,000 limit. Housing Act 1988 s14(1) required the RAC to assess the rent at which 'the dwelling-house concerned might reasonably be expected to be let in the open market by a willing landlord under an assured tenancy'. Parliament had not intended the References to Rating (Housing) Regulations to introduce a rent cap. If the rent assessed by the RAC was in excess of £25,000, the assured tenancy would be at an end.

E7.10 ### *R (Innes) v Northern Rent Assessment Panel*
[2002] EWHC 2252 Admin; 17 October 2002

RAC did not have to accept evidence of comparables; use of personal experience

Ms Innes rented a flat in Firswood, Manchester on an assured tenancy. The rent was £520 per lunar month. Following an application under Housing Act 1988 s13, the rent assessment committee (RAC) increased the rent to £640 per lunar month. Ms Innes sought judicial review, challenging the decision on three grounds; (1) that although a RAC is entitled to use its own knowledge and experience, it can only do so after consideration of available evidence; (2) the RAC failed to give any, or any proper, reasons; and (3) it failed to have regard to her evidence that comparable properties were being let for £120 per week.

McCombe J dismissed her application. He accepted submissions of counsel for the RAC that there is no duty to accept valuation evidence by reference to comparables and that there is no necessity for the RAC to research such material if none has been presented to them by the parties. Second, the RAC's reasoning can only be reasoning that meets the cases of the parties as advanced, but it can use 'that imponderable element of personal experience of the Committee members when the evidence is otherwise wholly unsatisfactory'. Finally, it was clear that Ms Innes's evidence about other rents was considered because the RAC expressly said that it had considered all the submissions by the parties. It gave valid reasons during the course of arguments why such material was of limited value. In the light of the tenant's submissions it was not surprising that the RAC, having taken into account the oral material submitted to it, thought that there could not be any sensible alternative but to use its own experience, to reach the result that it did.

E7.11 *Rowe v South West Rent Assessment Panel*
[2001] EWHC 865 (Admin); February 2002 *Legal Action* 24; 23 October 2001

Increase in rent due to improvements carried out by tenants wrongly assessed

In 1994 tenants were granted an oral assured tenancy at a rent of £15 per week. They carried out improvements, including the installation of a new bathroom and a wood burning stove. The landlord served a notice pursuant to Housing Act 1988 s13 seeking to increase the rent to £360 per month. The tenants objected and the matter was referred to the Rent Assessment Panel (RAP). Under s14, the RAP's obligation was to consider the rent at which the premises 'might reasonably be expected to be let in the open market by a willing landlord under an assured tenancy'. In making such a determination the RAP must disregard any increase in value due to improvements carried out by the tenant (s14(2)). The RAP determined a market rent of £50 per week. The RAP arrived at this figure by assessing the current market rent with the improvements as £75 per week, and then deducted 10% of the notional cost of the works carried out.

The tenants appealed under Tribunals and Inquiries Act 1971 s13. Goldring J allowed their appeal. The RAP should not have applied a discount de-capitalised in the way that they did. It should simply have taken as the value of the house its current value, less the relevant improvements carried out. The matter was remitted to the RAP.

E8 **Rent regulation (Rent Act 1977 tenants)**

Where Rent Act 1977 protected or statutory tenancies are still in existence, 'fair rents' can still be determined by rent officers with appeals to rent assessment committees – see Rent Act 1977 Part IV. There have, over the years, been many cases in which these provisions have been considered, but none in the higher courts since publication of the last edition of the *Housing Law Casebook*. In view of this, those cases have not been reproduced in this edition – readers are referred to the third edition, paras C30.1 to C30.60.

E9 **Home loss and disturbance payments**

The Land Compensation Act 1973 gives tenants the right to apply for disturbance and/or home loss payments in certain circumstances where they are displaced. There have been no cases in the higher courts in which these provisions have been considered since publication of the 3rd edition of *Housing Law Casebook*. In view of this, those cases have not been reproduced in this edition – readers are referred to the third edition, section E40 where the following cases are noted:

Court of Appeal

E40.1 *Borg v Southwark LBC* June 1987 *Legal Action* 19, CA
Interpretation of tenancy agreement giving entitlement to discretionary payments

E40.2 *Gozra v Hackney LBC* (1989) 21 HLR 1; (1989) 57 P&CR 21; [1989] 2 EGLR 20; [1988] 46 EG 87, CA
Discretionary home loss payment to be at same rate as mandatory payment

E40.3 *Greater London Council v Holmes* [1986] QB 989; [1986] 2 WLR 628; [1986] 1 All ER 739; (1986) 18 HLR 131; [1986] 1 EGLR 22; (1985) 277 EG 641, CA
Redevelopment 'by' the council despite fact completed by private purchaser

E40.4 *Ingle v Scarborough BC* [2002] EWCA Civ 290; [2002] HLR 36; [2002] 08 EG 163 (CS); (2002) 12 February, CA
Where tenant within renovation programme transferred and had applied for a transfer not 'displaced' and not entitled to payment

E40.5 *Khan v Islington LBC* [2000] LGR 1; (2000) 32 HLR 534; (1999) *Times* 6 July; [1999] EGCS 87, CA
Rent arrears could be set off against payment

High Court

E40.6 *R v Islington LBC ex p Casale* (1986) 18 HLR 146, QBD
Question of fact and degree whether renovation rendered property something different

E10 # The right to buy

The right to buy provisions for secure tenants are contained in Housing Act 1985 Part V. See also 'Exceptions to security of tenure and the right to buy' (chapter D) and 'Death and the right to buy' (section E12).

E11 # Exercising the right to buy

House of Lords

E11.1 *Bristol CC v Lovell*
[1998] 1 WLR 446; [1998] 1 All ER 775; (1998) 30 HLR 770, HL
On competing applications to compel sale and for possession, court had wide discretion in deciding the order applications to heard

Mr Lovell, a secure tenant, gave notice that he intended to exercise the right to buy in April 1994. The council admitted the right and gave statutory notice of the proposed price and other terms on 30 June 1994. On 21 September 1994 the council issued possession proceedings, relying on Housing Act 1985 Sch 2 Ground 2 (nuisance or annoyance). Later it amended the pleadings to allege that Mr Lovell had used the premises for drug dealing. On 14 October 1994, before the case could be heard, he accepted the council's terms for his proposed purchase of the property. On 4 November his solicitors called for completion under Housing Act 1985 s138. Since the statutory conditions were satisfied, the council was under a duty to convey and Mr Lovell was entitled to enforce that duty by claiming an injunction under s138(3). Mr Lovell defended the possession proceedings and counterclaimed for an injunction. On 27 January 1995, a district judge refused his application for an injunction and directed that the claim for possession and the counterclaim for an injunction should be heard together. That decision was overturned by a circuit judge, who heard the tenant's application and granted an injunction. The Court of Appeal dismissed the council's appeal, following *Dance v Welwyn Hatfield DC* [1990] 1 WLR 1097; [1990] 3 All ER 572; (1990) 22 HLR 339, CA, and *Taylor v Newham LBC* (E11.16) and holding that there was no power to adjourn where the exercise of that power would prejudice the substance of the tenant's claim.

However, the Court of Appeal's decision was reversed by the House of Lords. Lord Hoffmann said that he could not think of an example where it would be proper to refuse an injunction under s138(3) but the question which arose was whether the judge was entitled to adjourn the application for an injunction once the conditions in s138 had been satisfied. The court had a broad discretion under CCR Ord 13 r3(1) to adjourn, a discretion which must be exercised judicially and not for the purpose of defeating the policy of the statute. Courts are entitled to use their discretion to hear applications at whatever time and in whichever order appears just and convenient. Although Mr Lovell would have succeeded if his case had been heard separately, that did not mean that he was entitled to insist that his application for an injunction be heard before the landlord's claim for possession. The case was remitted to the county court judge to rehear the appeal from the district judge. *Dance v Welwyn Hatfield DC* was overruled.

E11.2   **R (O'Byrne) v Secretary of State for Environment, Transport and Regions**
[2002] UKHL 45; [2002] 1 WLR 3250; [2003] 1 All ER 15; [2003] LGR 1; (2002) *Times* 18 November

Tenant entitled to exercise right to buy property in Green Belt

A secure tenant, formerly a landscape gardener employed by the council, exercised the right to buy her flat which had been granted under a service tenancy 'for the better performance of [her] duties'. The flat was above the stable block in a public park situated in the Green Belt. The council accepted the application and agreed terms of sale, but indicated that Green Belt (London and Home Counties) Act 1938 s5(1) prevented it from selling without the secretary of state's consent. An inquiry was held and the secretary of state accepted his Inspector's recommendation that consent be refused. Goldring J dismissed a claim for judicial review of that decision but the Court of Appeal allowed the tenant's appeal ([2001] EWCA Civ 499, [2002] HLR 30).

The House of Lords dismissed the secretary of state's appeal. Section 5 has no application to dispositions of 1938 Act Green Belt land brought about by the compulsory expropriation provisions of Housing Act 1985 Part V. The intention of s5 was to restrict the ability of local authorities to effect voluntary dispositions of Green Belt land. Ms O'Byrne was entitled to exercise the right to buy.

Court of Appeal

E11.3   *Basildon District Council v Wahlen*

[2006] EWCA Civ 326; [2006] 1 WLR 2744; [2007] 1 All ER 734; [2006] HLR 34; (2006) *Times* 17 April

On competing claims both should be considered and decision made which to prevail

Following his mother's death, Mr Wahlen succeeded to her secure tenancy. Basildon sought possession under Housing Act 1985 Sch 2 Ground 16 on the basis that he was living alone in a three-bedroom house. Mr Wahlen sought to exercise his right to buy under s118. He accepted Basildon's offer to sell him the freehold and refused their offer of alternative accommodation. Basildon issued possession proceedings. In his defence to the possession claim Mr Wahlen sought an injunction to enforce his right to buy. A district judge heard both claims at the same time and concluded that because the statutory requirements identified in s138 had been established the local authority was under a duty to grant the freehold to Mr Wahlen. The judge made no reference to Basildon's grounds for seeking possession, but dismissed its claim and granted the injunction sought. Basildon appealed, contending that the judge was bound to balance the competing claims and that he had failed to do so.

The Court of Appeal allowed the appeal. The Housing Act itself gives rise to the clash of competing claims as s121(1) does not include any provision for giving precedence to the possession claim, and s138(1) is silent as to the effect of an outstanding claim for possession on the landlord's obligation to grant an interest in the property. The conflict is not to be resolved by a race to judgment (*Bristol CC v Lovell* (E11.1)). If each claim is arguable, the judge should investigate the merits as a whole and consider both cases at the same time and then decide which should prevail. Accordingly, cases where it would be right not to hear both claims at the same time would be rare. Where claims are heard at the same time, the court has to consider how to resolve the conflict between the rival claims. It is not appropriate to suggest that any particular point might be likely to tip the balance. Each case must turn on its own particular facts, especially where there is no express statutory guidance on the factors to be taken into account. The local authority could pray in aid the fact that, if the tenant's application for an injunction prevailed, the property in question would be under-occupied, with all the disadvantages that that involved in the light of housing shortages. The local authority could not rely on the fact that it would lose property from its housing stock as the reason for the possession claim prevailing, as that was a consequence of the policy of the Housing Act. In this case, the judge had not carried out any balancing exercise and had made no reference to the local authority's competing claim. The balancing exercise had to be carried out, and it was an essential ingredient of any judgment that it contain some reasoning explaining how the balancing exercise was carried out and why the balance ultimately came down on one side. Although it appeared on the evidence that Mr Wahlen had a strong case, it was impossible to say that the judge had reached the only decision that could fairly have been reached. The matter was remitted to the county court for a retrial.

E11.4   *Copping v Surrey CC*
[2005] EWCA Civ 1604; [2006] HLR 16

'Relevant time' for the purposes of establishing price was date notice served

Mr Copping lived in accommodation provided by his employers, Surrey County Council. In 1991 he served notice on Surrey under Housing Act 1985 s122(1), seeking to exercise the right to buy. The council served a counter-notice denying the right to buy on the basis that the tenancy was not secure as Mr Copping was required to occupy the house for the better performance of his duties. In 2001 he again tried to exercise the right to buy. That application was denied on the same grounds. In 2002 he sought a declaration that he was entitled to exercise the right to buy. No reference was made to the 1991 application. HHJ Sleeman found that there was no express or implied term that he was obliged to occupy the house for the better performance of his duties and that he was entitled to exercise the right to buy. Subsequently Mr Copping claimed that the relevant valuation date was 1991. Surrey claimed that the earlier application had been abandoned and that the date for valuation was 2001. HH Michael Cook, sitting as deputy circuit judge, held that the 1991 notice was still extant and that Mr Copping could rely on it. Accordingly, the valuation date was 1991. Surrey appealed. Nelson J allowed the appeal ([2005] EWHC 754 (QB); 29 April 2005). Mr Copping appealed to the Court of Appeal.

The Court of Appeal dismissed his appeal. Although s118 grants a right to buy, it is expressly subject to the conditions set out in Part V. Section 138 expressly requires the right to be established before the duty to convey arises. It follows that the procedural provisions of s122 have to be complied with before the right can be effective. In the present case Mr Copping's right was established by the s181 proceedings before HHJ Sleeman. Those proceedings were based solely on the 2001 s122 notice. The procedure required by the Housing Act accordingly flowed from that notice and no other. When determining 'the relevant time' for the purposes of establishing the price pursuant to s126, it was inevitable that it was the date on which that notice was served. The suggestion made on behalf of Mr Copping that if a claim under s122 is denied, but not withdrawn in writing, it should remain effective, 'ignored reality'.

E11.5   *Dickinson v Enfield LBC*
(1997) 29 HLR 465; [1996] 2 EGLR 88; (1997) 96 LGR 379, CA

Tenants 'improvements' did not encompass repairs tenant contractually obliged to do

A tenant rented premises from the council under a long lease for a term of 20 years with full repairing obligations on his part. He covenanted to 'put and keep the property and grounds in tenantable repair to the satisfaction of the local authority'. He obtained consent to carry out alterations as well as the works of repair which were necessary to comply with the covenant. He then exercised the right to buy. Relying on Housing Act 1985 s127(1) ('the value of the dwelling-house ... [is] the price which at that time it would realise if sold on the open market by a willing vendor ... disregarding any improvements made by [the tenant]') the tenant claimed that all the works carried out were improvements and should be disregarded.

The Court of Appeal did not accept this contention. Housing Act 1985 s187 defines 'improvements' for the purposes of Part V as 'any alteration in or addition to the dwelling-house'. The word 'improvements' is not to be used in a 'wide, general or popular meaning' but has the specific meaning given by the 'exhaustive definition' in s187. As in the general law of landlord and tenant, the terms 'repairs' and 'improvements' are mutually exclusive.

E11.6   **Enfield LBC v McKeon**

[1986] 1 WLR 1007; [1986] 2 All ER 730; (1986) 18 HLR 330; (1987) 85 LGR 24, CA

Service of notice of right to buy did not prevent possession proceedings

The Court of Appeal held that service of a notice exercising the right to buy does not prevent a public sector landlord from seeking possession of the property on any of the grounds permitted by Housing Act 1985 Sch 2. However, if the ground requires the court to consider 'reasonableness', the fact that the tenant has exercised the right to buy is a circumstance to be taken into account.

E11.7   **Guinan v Enfield LBC**

(1997) 29 HLR 456, CA

Unreasonable terms in lease amended despite fact had been issued to other lessees

On a tenant's right to buy application, the council responded by offering a 125-year lease of his flat in the form of its 'standard draft'. It declined the tenant's suggestions for amendments or modifications, asserting that it was important that leases granted by the council were in uniform terms across the borough and most particularly in single blocks or estates. The tenant successfully applied in the county court for a declaration that certain of the terms of the lease were unreasonable (Housing Act 1985 Sch 6 para 5). He then appealed to the Court of Appeal, claiming that other terms were unreasonable.

While determining his appeal on the particular facts, the Court of Appeal considered the council's proposition that it should be entitled, not least for the purpose of administrative convenience, to have a uniform lease:

> If the standard form of a lease has terms that are unreasonable, they do not cease to be unreasonable because they apply to several thousand tenants

and because it is inconvenient for the council that Mr Guinan should have reasonable terms. The council may, if they wish, tell all other tenants that they will not insist upon those terms which have been held to be unreasonable. (Staughton LJ).

The court considered in detail the terms of the proposed lease and made various further amendments, including a provision that the landlord was only entitled to insist that the tenant comply with all 'reasonable' regulations made by the authority. As the tenant had been unsuccessful in relation to some of his contentions, the judge had been entitled to exercise his discretion to order the tenant to pay one third of the local authority's costs.

E11.8 **Jennings v Epping Forest DC**
(1993) 25 HLR 241, CA (see C3.8)
Secure status and right to buy lost when tenants left premises

E11.9 **Martin v Medina Housing Association Ltd**
[2006] EWCA Civ 367; [2007] 1 WLR 1965; [2007] 1 All ER 813; [2006] HLR 40; (2006) *Times* 20 April
Tenant could not rely on s122 notice where he had later abandoned the right generated

From 1969, the claimant's mother was a secure tenant of a local housing authority. In April 1989 she served a written notice pursuant to Housing Act 1985 s122 claiming the right to buy. She exercised the power given by s123 to require that her son should share that right with her. The council served on them notices admitting their right to buy at a price of £27,000. It informed them that if they wished to exercise their right to a mortgage, they should serve a written notice within three months. However, neither claimed the right to a mortgage. In February 1990 a council officer circulated an internal memorandum stating that 'the tenant ... no longer wishes to proceed with the purchase'. In 1990 the freehold interest was transferred to the defendant. The claimant's mother died in 2001, and in 2002 he indicated that he proposed to exercise the right to buy the property for £27,000 pursuant to the notice served in 1989. The defendant denied that it remained open for him to do so. The claimant sought an injunction under s138(3) requiring the defendant to convey the property. The judge found that there had been an oral notification of the intention not to proceed and dismissed the claim. The claimant appealed contending that any such notification had to be in writing (s122(3)).

The Court of Appeal dismissed the appeal. Although a withdrawal of the right to buy has to be by notice in writing (s122(3)), parliament had not sought to exclude from the armoury of the court the elementary principles of common law and equity relating to those who asserted rights which they had abandoned or waived or were estopped from asserting or which, in the light of their words or silences, actions or inactions, it would be inequitable for them to assert. In this case, there had been an express representation that the claimant and his mother did not intend to proceed with the purchase. Prima facie there was thus an express abandonment on their part of the right generated by the notice served under s122.

E11.10 *Milne-Berry v Tower Hamlets LBC*
(1998) 30 HLR 229, CA

Tenants could rely on council's waiver of notices to complete

Tenants gave notice to exercise their right to buy in 1985 but the statutory procedures and negotiations were long delayed as the tenants sought to have repairs problems addressed before completing. In 1989 the council served statutory notices to complete and, on their expiry, contended that the right to buy had been lost. The tenants sought and secured declarations that an officer of the council had waived the statutory notices (see at first instance (1996) 28 HLR 225).

The Court of Appeal rejected the council's appeal. The judge had been entitled to find on the facts that, after service of the notices, an officer of the council had given a 'clear and unqualified undertaking that the right to buy would proceed'. There was nothing in the statutory right to buy scheme which would prevent the doctrines of waiver or estoppel operating. Even if the judge had been wrong to hold that the case was one of waiver by election, all the ingredients of promissory estoppel were present and the council was bound by its undertaking not to rely on the notices.

E11.11 *Muir Group Housing Association Ltd v Thornley*
(1993) 25 HLR 89; [1993] 1 EGLR 51; [1993] 10 EG 144; (1992) 91 LGR 1, CA (see C3.12)

Tenancy must remain secure up to the moment of completion

E11.12 *R v Worthing BC ex p Bruce*
(1994) 26 HLR 223; [1994] 1 EGLR 116; [1994] 24 EG 149, CA (see H2.5)

Consent order stood as implied admission that tenant was not a secure tenant; compromise, including withdrawal of right to buy, effective

E11.13 *Southwark LBC v Dennett*
[2007] EWCA Civ 1091; 7 November 2007

No award of damages for misfeasance in public office where officials unnamed and unspecified

In June 2001, Mr Dennett, a secure tenant of Southwark, gave written notice under Housing Act 1985 s122(1) claiming to exercise the right to buy a long lease of his flat. In July 2001, Southwark served notice admitting his right to buy. Southwark's Valuation Service valued the flat at £145,000. Southwark should then have served a notice under s125 proposing a purchase price and other matters by early October 2001. It did not in fact do so until February 2002. In July 2003, Mr Dennett stopped paying rent in protest at the delay. Southwark issued a claim for arrears of rent. Mr Dennett quickly paid the rent arrears and the proceedings continued on his counterclaim. Mr Dennett served two initial notices of delay in form RTB6, but as a result of 'a catalogue of delay, in large part the result of inactivity and incompetence by Southwark' this routine and straightforward transaction was still not completed by January 2007. HHJ Bailey found, among other things, that unnamed and unspecified officials of Southwark had acted in bad faith and awarded damages for misfeasance in public office in the sum of £6,168, apparently calculated at the rate of

£2,000 a year from November 2003 to the date of trial. He also ordered Southwark to complete the conveyance by 26 February 2007. Southwark appealed in relation to a number of matters.

The Court of Appeal allowed the appeal against the award of damages for misfeasance in public office. For misfeasance in public office the public officer must act dishonestly or in bad faith in relation to the legality of his actions. Knowledge of, or subjective recklessness as to, the lawfulness of the public officer's acts and the consequences of them is necessary to establish the tort. Mere reckless indifference without the addition of subjective recklessness will not do. This element virtually requires the claimant to identify the person or people said to have acted with subjective recklessness and to establish their bad faith. An institution can only be reckless subjectively if one or more individuals acting on its behalf are subjectively reckless, and their subjective state of mind needs to be established. To that end, they need to be identified. The Court of Appeal also allowed the appeal in relation to issues arising out of the initial notices of delay.

E11.14   *Sutton LBC v Swann*

(1986) 18 HLR 140, CA (see C3.13)

Where security lost by subletting, tenant could not finalise exercise of right to buy

E11.15   *Tandridge DC v Bickers*

(1999) 31 HLR 432; [1998] 41 EG 220, CA

Judge properly exercised discretion in determining order to hear competing claims

In January 1997 the council began possession proceedings against joint secure tenants, alleging nuisance and other breaches of their tenancy agreement. In April 1997 the tenants gave notice exercising the right to buy. The council, notwithstanding the mandatory terms of Housing Act 1985 Part V, decided not to process the application until its proceedings were concluded. The tenants then initiated proceedings to compel the council to process the claim and applied for an adjournment of the possession proceedings. The adjournment was refused by the district judge and both cases were listed for trial on the same date. Recorder Cole held that he had a discretion to decide which to try first (see *Bristol CC v Lovell* (E11.1) and decided to try the council's claim first.

The Court of Appeal dismissed the tenant's appeal. The judge had properly directed himself to the relevant factors such as the sequence of events and the seriousness of the allegations. He was entitled to decide that if the council's claim had no merit it would be unsuccessful and the right to buy could proceed, whereas, if it did have merit but was not tried first it would have been pre-empted by the purchase. The fact that the tenants would lose their home if a possession order were made was a factor which was before the judge. He had met it by saying that if the tenants had behaved properly, there would have been no prejudice to them. The council's wrongful failure to comply with its Part V obligations was not 'fatal' to the exercise of discretion in its favour. When the case was remitted to the county court, HHJ Barnett made a possession order (February 1999 *Legal Action* 24).

E11.16 *Taylor v Newham LBC*

[1993] 1 WLR 444; [1993] 2 All ER 649; (1993) 25 HLR 290; [1993] 1 EGLR 54, CA

No discretion to refuse relief where all conditions for statutory entitlement existed

A tenant exercised the right to buy and all the stages except for the conveyance were completed. The tenant sought an injunction to compel completion (Housing Act 1985 s138(1)). The council was reluctant to complete because of the tenant's past misconduct and sought to defend the application on the basis that the grant of an injunction was a discretionary remedy and ought, on the facts, to be refused.

The Court of Appeal held that, once all the conditions for statutory entitlement to a mandatory order were in place, the court had no discretion to refuse relief. The council's defence had been properly struck out.

Note: This case was considered by the House of Lords in *Bristol CC v Lovell* (E11.1) but, unlike *Dance v Welwyn Hatfield DC* [1990] 1 WLR 1097; [1990] 3 All ER 572; (1990) 22 HLR 339, CA, was not overruled.

High Court

E11.17 *Barber v Southwark LBC*

[2002] EWHC 1497 (Ch); October 2002 *Legal Action* 28; 28 May 2002

Term in proposed lease unreasonable

The claimant was a secure tenant who wanted to exercise the right to buy. He objected to the council's standard form long-term lease which included a term that made the lessee's rights conditional on him complying with all his obligations under it.

Blackburne J held that the term was unreasonable and disproportionate. It would entitle the council to withhold all the lessee's rights because of the breach of an unimportant covenant. If a significant breach was committed by a tenant, the council could go to court to seek injunctive relief, re-entry or damages.

E11.18 *Hanoman v Southwark LBC*

[2004] EWHC 2039 (Ch); [2005] 1 All ER 795

Council had no power to treat application as withdrawn; continuing obligation to make decision

On 14 November 14 1999, Southwark received a right to buy application form signed by Mr Hanoman. On 17 January 2000, it wrote to him asking for further identification. He telephoned and asked for its housing officers to confirm his identity. He was told that an officer would revert to him. He heard nothing further. The council wrote to him giving a further seven days to provide necessary documentation, failing which it would withdraw the application. Mr Hanoman did not receive the letter and so did not reply. The council treated the application as withdrawn and closed its file. Mr Hanoman applied for relief under the Housing Act 1985 Part V against the decision. That application was refused at first instance. He appealed.

Peter Smith J allowed the appeal. Under Housing Act 1985 s124(2) the council was obliged to provide a decision on the application within four weeks of its receipt, ie, by 12 December 1999. It first communicated with Mr Hanoman on 17 January 2000. The council's failure to reach a decision was a breach of its statutory duty. There was no duty on Mr Hanoman's part to chase up the council. The council had no power under the statutory provisions to treat an application as withdrawn because an applicant failed to provide information within a short time period which was unilaterally imposed. It had a continuing obligation to make a decision on the application, either admitting or denying the right to buy. Mr Hanoman plainly had not withdrawn his application. Where a council breached its statutory duty, it was unfair to penalise an applicant and deny him his rights because he failed to remind the council that he was expecting a decision in discharge of the statutory duty. The council could not waive its statutory duties.

E11.19 *Islington LBC v Honeygan-Green*

[2007] EWHC 1270 (QB); [2007] 4 All ER 818; (2007) *Times* 29 June; 25 May 2007

Application to buy did not survive loss of tenancy, despite later revival of tenancy and right to buy

Ms Honeygan-Green was a secure tenant. In May 2000 she made an application to buy the property under the right to buy scheme. That application was admitted by Islington, her landlord. In July 2002, Islington began a possession claim based on arrears of rent. In the mean time, completion of the right to buy application was delayed because another tenant had encroached on Ms Honeygan-Green's garden and a wall had collapsed. She served notices of delay under Housing Act 1985 s153A. In October 2002 Islington obtained a suspended possession order in Form N28. It provided that the order was not to be enforced so long as Ms Honeygan-Green paid current rent and £50 per week. She failed to comply with the order and Islington wrote to her stating that she had become a tolerated trespasser. Ms Honeygan-Green then applied to set aside the possession order. By July 2003 she had paid all arrears and the possession order was discharged. In 2005 further arrears accrued. Islington again began a possession claim and Ms Honeygan-Green counterclaimed for a mandatory injunction ordering the council to convey the property to her. HHJ Marr-Johnson granted that order on the discharge of all arrears. Islington appealed.

Nelson J allowed the appeal. Ms Honeygan-Green's tenancy ended on the date specified in the October 2002 order. She then became a tolerated trespasser. However, in 2003 her secure tenancy was retrospectively revived, together with its covenants. Nevertheless, although the right to buy still existed, the 2000 application did not survive the possession order. Following *Sutton LBC v Swan* (C3.13)), the status of secure tenant has to exist not only at the time when the right to buy application is made, but also at the time when the grant comes to be made. If during the period between the claim to exercise the right to buy and the grant of the right to buy, the tenant ceases to be a secure tenancy, the right to the grant of a long lease is lost. The key to the interpretation of Housing Act 1985 s121 is that the right to buy is only exercisable through an application or claim under the statutory scheme. If the right to buy cannot be exercised or ceases to be exercisable, then the application or claim which established that right to buy must also cease to be exercisable. Furthermore, having regard to s138, it was inappropriate for an injunction to be granted as the area to be demised had not been determined. The case was remitted to the county court to determine further factual disputes.

E11.20 **R (Burrell) v Lambeth LBC**
[2006] EWHC 394 (Admin); 14 February 2006

On tenant failing to comply with statutory scheme, extension of time matter for council

The claimant was a secure tenant. In October 2001 she submitted a right to buy application. The council served notice of the purchase price pursuant to Housing Act 1985 s125. However, the claimant failed to serve a s125D notice within 12 weeks, as required. In August 2002 the council wrote giving the claimant a further 28 days, failing which the right to buy would be deemed to be withdrawn. Although the claimant wrote stating that she wished to pursue the matter and extensions of time were agreed, she did not serve any s125D notice. The council served notices to complete in accordance with ss140 and 141 in 2003. There was further correspondence and in July 2004 the claimant's then solicitors sought a further extension of time to complete. The council refused.

Bean J dismissed the claimant's application for judicial review of the council's decision to withdraw the right to buy. Once the claimant had failed to comply with the second notice to complete, s141(4) took effect and she no longer had the protection of the statutory scheme. Any extension of time granted by the council 'was a matter for them'. The council was entitled to say 'We have had enough, you have failed to complete in time, the deal is off.'

E11.21 **Sebanjor v Brent LBC**
[2001] LGR 339; (2001) *Times* 4 January, ChD

Notice to complete not effective where removal of joint purchaser had extended time

The claimant was entitled to exercise the right to buy. Her daughter also had the right to buy the property jointly with her because she was a close family member designated by the claimant. However, after commencing the right to buy procedure jointly, the claimant gave notification that she personally no longer intended to proceed with the purchase but that her daughter still wished to proceed to completion. The council served notice to complete pursuant to Housing Act 1985 s141.

Pumfrey J held that the claimant had not refused to complete the purchase, but had merely refused to complete the joint purchase with her daughter. An intending purchaser is free to remove any proposed joint purchaser from her application, with the consent of the joint purchaser. It followed therefore that s140 ought to allow for the removal of a joint purchaser who no longer wished to participate in the transaction when the other purchaser wished to proceed without her. The removal of a joint purchaser should be considered a relevant outstanding matter for the purposes of s140. Once the change of name had been accepted by the local authority the time for the remaining purchaser to complete the transaction under the existing s140 notice should begin to run again. As the remaining purchaser was ready and willing to proceed once that outstanding matter was resolved, there was no basis on which the local authority could validly serve a final notice to complete on the remaining purchaser pursuant to s141. The notice to complete, served pursuant to s141 could not have been validly served on the date on which it was served.

E11.22 *Terry v Tower Hamlets LBC*
[2005] EWHC 2783 (QB); 2 December 2005

On facts, form sent by tenant had been received by council in time

The claimant was a secure tenant who sought to exercise the right to buy. Although he maintained that he had sent form RTB1 by first class post on 6 March 2003, Tower Hamlets denied that it had received it by 26 March 2003, the date when the discount rules were changed. If it was received as Mr Terry claimed, he would have been entitled to the full statutory discount of £38,000, whereas if the form was not served until after the deadline the discount would have been capped at £16,000.

After hearing evidence, Michael Supperstone QC, sitting as a deputy High Court judge, was satisfied that Mr Terry sent the RTB1 form to Tower Hamlets by first class post on 6 March 2003 and that it was properly addressed. The judge found that Tower Hamlets had failed to show on a balance of probabilities that it did not receive the form RTB1 before 26 March 2003. Tower Hamlets was Mr Terry's landlord. If service on its home ownership department had been necessary (as Tower Hamlets claimed), then the driver who collected the home ownership department's mail from the local delivery office acted not only as the agent of Tower Hamlets, but also as the agent of its home ownership department in relation to the mail to be received by that department. On the balance of probabilities, it was much more likely that Tower Hamlets had mislaid the letter, given the number of steps from the collection of the form through its processing and delivery to the appropriate department. The form had, on the facts, been received by the authority in the relevant time.

Northern Irish courts

E11.23 *R (McDonnell and Lilly) v Northern Ireland Housing Executive*
[2004] NICA 7; 20 February 2004

Right to buy not within ambit of ECHR

The claimants were secure tenants of the NIHE. In 2001 they sought to exercise the right to buy under the statutory scheme made by the NIHE in 1983. Ground floor properties of fewer than two bedrooms, let to tenants who were aged 60 or over when the tenancy began, were exempted from the right to buy. Both claimants met those conditions and their applications were refused. They applied for judicial review and claimed that the rule represented unlawful discrimination against them (on grounds of 'age') contrary to ECHR article 14. The NIHE said that they could not rely on the Human Rights Act (HRA) 1998 as the provision of the scheme to which they objected had been made before commencement of that Act. Kerr J accepted that the subject of the complaint was within the ambit of article 8 and article 1 of the First Protocol, but dismissed the claims and the tenants appealed.

The Court of Appeal (NI) held that: (a) as the relevant decisions were made in 2001, the claimants were entitled to rely on their ECHR rights even in respect of a statutory scheme or provision made before commencement of the HRA; (b) the judge had been wrong to find that article 14 was applicable at all. Before that article could be relied on the subject matter of the discriminatory treatment had to be within the 'ambit' of another convention right. The 'right to buy' was not within the ambit of article 8 (applying *Strunjak v Croatia* ECtHR Application no 46934/99; 5 October 2000) as it represented no disruption of current home or family life nor to security of tenure. Nor was it within the ambit of article 1 of the First Protocol, which applies only to existing possessions and does not guarantee a right to acquire new ones (*Rudzinska v Poland* ECtHR Application no 45223/99; 7 September 1999); (c) even if that was wrong and there had been prima facie discriminatory treatment, the evidence of the NIHE had demonstrated that there was 'a reasonable, objective and proportionate justification for the policy that it has adopted'.

E12   ## Death and the right to buy

Court of Appeal

E12.1   *Bradford MDC v McMahon*

[1994] 1 WLR 52; [1993] 4 All ER 237; (1993) 25 HLR 534; (1993) 91 LGR 655, CA

On tenant's death, tenancy no longer secure and estate had no right to complete sale

A secure tenant exercised the right to buy and complied with all steps in the statutory procedure (Housing Act 1985 Part V). Before the actual completion of the conveyance, the secure tenant died. The council brought possession proceedings. The personal representative of the deceased defended and counterclaimed for an injunction to compel completion (Housing Act 1985 s138(1)).

The Court of Appeal held, following and applying *Muir Group Housing Association Ltd v Thornley* (C3.12), that a tenancy must remain a secure tenancy up to the moment of completion. As the tenant had died before completion, the tenancy was no longer secure (Housing Act 1985 s81) and the tenant's estate did not have the right to require completion of the sale.

E12.2   *Harrow LBC v Tonge*

(1993) 25 HLR 99; [1993] 1 EGLR 49; [1993] 09 EG 109, CA

Where co-purchaser procedure used, completion compelled despite tenant's death

A sole secure tenant died and his wife succeeded to the tenancy. She exercised both the right to buy and her right to join her daughter with her in the purchase (Housing Act 1985 s123). The council admitted the right to buy, the price, the discount and all other matters necessary for completion. The tenant then exercised the right to defer completion for up to three years. Within that period, she died intestate. The tenancy could not continue as a secure tenancy, because there is no provision for a second succession. The council served notice to quit and began proceedings for possession.

The Court of Appeal held that, because the tenant had used (and the landlord accepted) the s123 co-purchaser procedure, the daughter had attained the practical status of joint secure tenant. Accordingly, after the true tenant's death, she had a secure tenancy as sole secure tenant and could compel completion of the right to buy.

E12.3 *McIntyre v Merthyr Tydfil BC*
(1989) 21 HLR 320; (1989) 88 LGR 1, CA

Successor tenant entitled to discount based on former tenant's period of occupancy

A secure tenant who wished to exercise the right to buy served an RTC1 notice in 1984. The council admitted the right to buy and offered a sale at £14,000, less almost £8,000 discount based on 26 years' occupancy. Before completion, the tenant died and her daughter succeeded to the secure tenancy (Housing Act 1985 s89).

The Court of Appeal held that Housing Act 1985 s136(1) put the daughter in the same position as the tenant and enabled her to rely on the discount period accumulated by her mother, rather than on her own shorter period of occupancy.

High Court

E12.4 *Kensington and Chelsea RLBC v Hislop*
[2003] EWHC 2944 (Ch); [2004] 1 All ER 1036; [2004] HLR 26

History of right to buy application relevant to question of reasonableness

Ms Hislop lived with her mother in a three-bedroomed property owned by the council. She became a secure tenant by succession on the death of her mother in November 2001. She was then immediately entitled to exercise the right to buy (Housing Act 1985 Part V). She served a notice on the council claiming that right. The council admitted the right to buy in a notice served under s124 but then failed to process the application. However, following her mother's death, the council had served a s83 notice seeking possession on the ground that the accommodation afforded by the property was more extensive than was reasonably required by Ms Hislop (Sch 2 Ground 16). The council offered alternative accommodation for her and her sister who lived with her, and, when this was refused, commenced possession proceedings. Ms Hislop defended, alleging that she was living in the flat with both her sister and her nephew and, accordingly, the flat was not under-occupied. She also claimed that it would not be reasonable to make a possession order, as her application to exercise the right to buy had been accepted by the council, and she had a legitimate expectation of being able to exercise that right. The claim for possession was dismissed by HHJ Knight QC and the council appealed.

Lindsay J dismissed the appeal. There was no error in the approach taken by the judge. When faced, on the one hand, with a sound case by a tenant for further implementation of the right to buy and, on the other hand, with a good case for possession where reasonableness was a prerequisite for an order for possession, it was not right for the court to consider whether, but for the right to buy, it would have granted possession, nor, conversely, whether, but for the claim to possession, it would have allowed the right to buy process to continue to completion. Either course would be likely to create an onus of proof which should not be there. In determining such cases, relevant circumstances for consideration might include, in the tenant's favour, (1) whether the tenant had long been established at the property, (2) whether the claim to a right to buy was well-founded and genuine, rather than merely a device to delay possession, and (3) whether the landlord had deliberately failed to perform a statutory duty in processing the tenant's claim, thereby deliberately prolonging the period during which the right to buy claim was at risk of being negated by an order for possession. It might benefit the landlord if (1) the tenant were shown to be in serious or persistent breach of the terms of the tenancy or (2) the landlord was a public authority seeking possession and offering alternative accommodation in order the better to deploy its housing stock. If its claim to possession were shown to be merely a device to impede the right to buy, that would militate against the claim for possession being enabled to prevail. Questions as to the weight to be given to the various factors were best left to the judge who had heard all the evidence and seen the witnesses. In this case, it would have been wrong for the judge not to have considered the attempts by the council to thwart the tenant's claim to a right to buy.

E13   **After exercising the right to buy**

Court of Appeal

E13.1   *Berry v Newport BC*
[2000] EG 127; (2001) 33 HLR 197, CA

Damages for breach of duty to inform tenant property designated as defective

Ms Berry exercised the right to buy and bought her house with the benefit of a 59% discount in 1988. Unknown to her or the council the house was of a type which incorporated reinforced concrete columns which were defective. Such houses had been designated as defective houses under Housing Act 1985 s528. Under s563 the council owed Ms Berry a duty to inform her that the house was defective and that she would not be eligible for assistance under the Act. The council admitted a breach of duty. The judge awarded as damages the difference between what she had paid for the house (£10,000) and what she would have paid had she known of its defective condition (£3,485). She appealed.

The Court of Appeal dismissed the appeal. The scope of the council's duty was to inform Ms Berry that the house she was buying had been designated as defective. It was not a duty not to sell such a house nor to warrant that all houses being sold by the council were free of defects. The judge was right to follow the approach adopted by the courts in cases of negligent valuation such as *Perry v Sidney Phillips* [1982] 1 WLR 1297 and *South Australia Asset Management Corp v York Montague Ltd* [1997] AC 191. Had the duty been discharged, Ms Berry would either have declined to go ahead with the purchase or would have bought the house at the lower discounted price found by the judge. Since she did not seek rescission of the sale the judge was right to award damages on the latter basis.

E13.2 *Coventry CC v Cole*
[1994] 1 WLR 398; [1994] 1 All ER 997; (1993) 25 HLR 555; [1994] 1 EGLR 63; [1994] 06 EG 133; (1994) 92 LGR 18, CA

Restrictions on recovery of service charges not applicable to charges levied

The defendants exercised the right to buy. The lease granted to them included a provision that they should pay 'such sum (hereinafter called 'the service charge') as is specified in the fifth Schedule hereto'. The fifth schedule provided that that sum was £208 per annum, plus an additional charge calculated by reference to any increase in the Building Cost Information Service Tender Price Index published by the Royal Institution of Chartered Surveyors. The plaintiffs sued for alleged arrears of service charges. The defendants denied that they were liable, claiming that the council was not entitled to recover this sum because of Housing Act 1985 s125 and Sch 6 para 18(a) which restricts the amount of service charges recoverable within the initial period of the lease.

The Court of Appeal held that the money claimed by the council was not a 'service charge' within the meaning of the Housing Act 1985 and was not 'a reasonable part of the costs incurred by the landlord' within the meaning of Sch 6 para 16(a). The lessees were not able to rely on the restrictions on recovery of service charges contained in the Housing Act 1985 and were liable for the amount claimed.

E13.3 *Hodge v Newport BC*
(2001) 33 HLR 187, CA

Purchaser from former tenant could not rely on designated defective provisions

In 1987 Mr Hodge bought a former council house from a former secure tenant who had exercised the right to buy. The house incorporated reinforced concrete columns which were defective. Such houses had been designated as defective houses under Housing Act 1985 s528 in 1984. People who had purchased such houses prior to April 1985 were potentially eligible for assistance which was available for a ten-year period from 1984. The vendor would have been eligible for assistance but Mr Hodge was not. The council did not discover until 1989 that the house was of a kind which had been designated as defective. Mr Hodge brought proceedings against the council for damages for an alleged breach of statutory duty under s562(3). The judge held that although s562(3) could create private law rights Mr Hodge was not a person to whom the council owed a duty and that in any event there was no breach of duty. Mr Hodge appealed.

The Court of Appeal dismissed the appeal. The action was not based on a common-law duty of care and the question was not whether the appellant would foreseeably have suffered loss if the council were negligent. The question was to whom was the duty owed under the statute. The judge was right that the duty to give notice and provide information was imposed to enable those eligible for assistance to apply for assistance within the ten-year period. Parliament intended eligibility for assistance to end if there was a sale after April 1985. The duty under s562 was not owed to persons such as the appellant who bought houses after April 1985 when they were already in private hands. It was not necessary to decide whether there was also no breach of duty by the council.

E13.4   ## *Islington LBC v Dornan*

[2005] EWCA Civ 1372; (2005) *Times* 8 November

Proceedings based on former tenant's departure from property within 3 years of sale to be served on company that had arranged sale and had acquired title

Ms Dornan was a council tenant who exercised the right to buy. She vacated the premises within three years of the purchase as a result of an arrangement with Megaplace Ltd, a company which obtained title to the flat under a scheme plainly intended to enable council tenants to dispose of their properties before the three-year limit contained in Housing Act 1985 s155 in return for a comparatively modest sum: £12,000 in Miss Dornan's case. Islington sought possession of her current premises and repayment of the discount of £38,000 on the purchase price of her former flat. District Judge Armon-Jones found that the transaction was not a relevant disposal within s159 and that Ms Dornan was not obliged to repay the discount. The council appealed.

The Court of Appeal adjourned the appeal. The case would require the court to make decisions about difficult questions. The overwhelming impact of the documents was that Ms Dornan really knew nothing about the mechanisms of the matter and had no interest in the legal issues, save to the extent that she might be subject to a large financial burden. It was not satisfactory that proceedings had not been taken against Megaplace. The court directed that formal notification of the proceedings be given by Islington to Megaplace Ltd, via their solicitors. The council should give serious thought to enforcement of its charge on Ms Dornan's former premises.

E13.5   ## *Payne v Barnet LBC*

(1998) 76 LGR; 293(1998) 76 P&CR 293; (1998) 30 HLR 295, CA

Disclosure obligation on council no wider than that set out in s125

Mr and Mrs Payne served notice to exercise the right to buy their flat and, after the council had served a notice under Housing Act 1985 s125, proceeded with the purchase. Later they disputed whether the council had fulfilled its duty under s125(4A) to tell them of structural defects. An assistant recorder struck out the action as disclosing no cause of action.

The Court of Appeal held that, but for the statutory requirements, the ordinary principles of caveat emptor would apply. The effect of s125 was to impose a greater obligation than would usually be the case to tell the tenant in advance about usual service charges, improvements, ordinary external repairs and structural defects. The courts should not 'intervene in the delicately constructed statutory scheme' by imposing an additional common-law duty of care on the council's part. There was no wider obligation of disclosure than that set out in s125 and council tenants, like other purchasers, have to carry out their own searches and enquiries in the usual way. However, as the authority conceded that there were structural defects known to it which should have been included in the s125 notice, there were factual issues to be determined and it would be wrong to hold at the pre-discovery stage that there was no arguable case of breach of statutory duty or misrepresentation. (See also *Blake v Barking and Dagenham LBC* (E13.11)

E13.6 **Peckham v Ellison**
(1998) 79 P&CR 276; 31 HLR 1030; (1998) *Times* 4 December, CA

Reservation of right of way implied where not reserved in lease granted to former tenant

In a right to buy purchase of a former council house, the council failed expressly to reserve a right of way for the benefit of adjoining tenants.

The Court of Appeal, having reviewed the principles to be applied, dismissed an appeal from a finding that such reservation should be implied.

E13.7 **R v Braintree DC ex p Halls**
(2000) 32 HLR 770; [2000] 36 EG 164, CA

Restrictive covenant that property could not be developed unlawful

In 1987 a secure tenant exercised the right to buy under Housing Act 1985. In accordance with s128(1), the property was valued at its open market value not including any assessment of potential development value, less a discount. There was a restrictive covenant in the conveyance that provided that the property could only contain a single dwelling-house. In 1996, the applicant sought to build another dwelling in the garden of the property. He applied to the council for release from the terms of the restrictive covenant. The council indicated that it would require payment of 90% of the increased value of the property. The applicant sought judicial review on the basis that the demand for any payment was irrational and/ or unreasonable and that, in any event, the demand for a sum representing 90% of the value of the property was unreasonable (see Sch 2 paras 5 and 6).

The application was dismissed at first instance but allowed on appeal. The purpose of the right to buy legislation is to enable tenants exercising the right to buy to enjoy 'the ordinary fruits or advantages of home ownership, including a rise in the value of their property, whether that is because of the benefits of a later acquired planning permission or otherwise'. In view of sections 155 and 157, if it had been parliament's intention to allow local authorities to impose the kind of restriction imposed in this case, one 'would plainly expect to see it on the face of the statute'. A state of affairs where the local authority received the price fixed in the conveyance and then sought to recover a further price if the value of the property was enhanced by the potential for development was 'entirely outwith' the scheme of the Housing Act 1985. The covenant was unlawful.

E13.8   *R v Rushmoor BC ex p Barrett*

[1989] QB 60; [1988] 2 WLR 1271; [1988] 2 All ER 268; (1988) 20 HLR 366, CA

Tenants obliged to pay back discount despite sale being ordered on their divorce

Mr and Mrs Barrett exercised the right to buy. The purchase price was reduced by a discount of £12,650. In accordance with the provisions of the Housing Act 1980 (now Housing Act 1985), they covenanted to repay a proportion of the discount if the property was sold within five years of the purchase. After their marriage had broken down, an order was made in ancillary relief proceedings by consent for the sale of the property, with the proceeds to be divided equally between Mr and Mrs Barrett.

The Court of Appeal held that the sale had been directed under Matrimonial Causes Act 1973 s24A. As Housing Act 1985 s160(1)(c) does not refer to s24A, none of the exemptions from the obligation to repay discount applied. As the sale was not an exempt disposal, Mr and Mrs Barrett were obliged to pay back the discount.

E13.9   *Rushton v Worcester CC*

[2001] EWCA Civ 367; [2002] HLR 9, CA

Damages for failure to disclose structural defects

In 1991 the claimants bought their council house with a 60% discount under the right to buy scheme (Housing Act 1985 Part V). The house was of the Orlit type made using pre-cast reinforced concrete ('PRC') frames, joined by pre-cast beams, clad in pre-cast reinforced concrete panels with an inner block-work lining connected to the outer skin with metal cavity ties. These houses were known to have a problem with 'carbonation' of the concrete used in construction, leading to porosity and consequent corrosion of the steel reinforcement. They were designated as defective under the 1985 Act. A second defect likely to be found in PRC houses built with high alumina cement (HAC) was the 'conversion' of the cement which reduced its compressive strength and increased its porosity. A survey of the council's Orlit houses in 1984 revealed both carbonation and conversion of HAC. Before valuing the house for right to buy purposes the council advised the claimants of the carbonation defect but not of the presence of HAC. The council's notice pursuant to s125(1) indicated under structural defects that the property was designated as defective but did not mention HAC. In 1996 the council resolved to demolish the Orlit houses it still owned because of the continuing deterioration of the concrete. The claimants issued proceedings against the council for breach of its statutory duty to disclose structural defects under s125(4A) and for misrepresentation under Misrepresentation Act 1967 s2(1). The judge found for the claimants under both heads. He held that the measure of damages for breach of statutory duty was the difference between the discounted price paid and the value of the house (nil) plus interest since the purchase, totalling £16,397. He assessed damages for misrepresentation on the basis that if the seriousness of the HAC defect had been appreciated in 1991, the claimants would not have purchased then but would have exercised their right to buy only in 2000 after repairs had been effected. Damages for wasted purchase costs with interest, loss of the right to buy discount, and notional alternative accommodation while repairs were carried out amounted to nearly £30,000 and the judge gave judgment for the claimants in that sum.

The Court of Appeal held:

1) There was ample evidence to justify the finding that the council was aware of the HAC defect.

2) It was open to the judge to find that the council's statement of the market value of the house, while prima facie no more than a statement of opinion, carried with it the implication, given the council's duty to disclose defects within its knowledge, that the council knew of nothing which rendered its statement of value substantially inaccurate and/or that the council had reasonable grounds for its opinion. However, no claim lay against the council for misrepresentation under Misrepresentation Act 1967 s2 because the claimant never entered into a contract after the representation had been made. In a purchase under the right to buy provisions, no contract is entered into between the claimants and the council, and the claimants' right to transfer of the freehold was created by and derived from the Act itself. The 1985 Act contains an exhaustive statutory code, including a remedy for breach of statutory duty.

3) The judge was entitled to conclude that there was no contributory negligence.

4) The judge was entitled to find that the value of the house in 1991 was nil. The foreseeable measure of damage at the date of the council's breach in 1991 was the purchase costs wasted on a valueless asset (agreed at £13,720) plus the loss of the claimant's right to purchase the property in future. The judge assessed that as £22,800, being 60% of the value of a repaired house in 1991 (£38,000). The council wished to rely on Housing Act 1985 s131 and the Housing (Right to Buy) (Cost Floor) (England) Determination 1998 as reducing the value of the discount to nil on the basis that the cost of repairing (in this case demolishing and rebuilding) the house exceeded the 1991 repaired value of £38,000. However, the cost floor provisions of s131 had to be applied to the 2000 value of the house as to which there was no evidence. It was therefore too late for the council to rely on those provisions.

5) The judge erred in awarding the claimants sums for alternative accommodation, removal costs and inconvenience and disruption in the course of notional repairs, had the exercise of their right to buy been deferred. Such sums were not relevant to any valuation exercise in respect of the lost benefit of the discount, since they were not actually incurred. The claimants were only entitled to recover expenditure actually incurred and inconvenience actually suffered by them.

6) The judge was also wrong to award interest on the claimants' mortgage payments without crediting the council with the rental payments it would have received on the hypothesis that the claimants had remained tenants. The award of damages should be reduced by those amounts.

E13.10 *Sheffield CC v Jackson*

[1998] 1 WLR 1591; [1998] 3 All ER 260; (1999) 31 HLR 331, CA

Reasonableness of service charges only challengeable before execution of conveyance

Council tenants exercised the right to buy under Housing Act 1985 Part V. Before sale the council served a notice under Housing Act 1985 s125 which included estimates of service charges. The conveyance provided that the former tenants should pay service charges. Later the council sued for arrears of service charges in respect of costs incurred in the upkeep of play areas and the landscaping of gardens. The tenants who had exercised the right to buy defended, claiming that the sums were unreasonable. Astell J, hearing a preliminary point, held that the costs were unreasonable and contrary to Housing Act 1985 Sch 6 Part I para 5 and struck out the claim.

The Court of Appeal allowed the council's appeal. A covenant placing a burden on a tenant was a matter which was specifically required by s127 to be taken into account when assessing the price to be paid by the tenant on purchase. In view of this, the reasonableness of council service charges can only be challenged before execution of the conveyance. A tenant can only be released from such a covenant after purchase by applying to the secretary of state under ss167 and 168. Furthermore, there were no grounds for finding that the covenant was void for uncertainty.

High Court

E13.11 *Blake v Barking and Dagenham LBC*

(1998) 30 HLR 963, QBD

No duty of care on council in relation to valuation of property

The plaintiffs exercised their right to buy their high-rise flats on 125-year leases. They alleged that the council, in giving them notice of the purchase price, had been guilty of negligently supplying figures which grossly over-valued their homes.

Douglas Brown J dismissed their claims. He held that, in view of a tenant's right to challenge the purchase price proposed by the landlord – by referring it to the district valuer for independent determination (Housing Act 1985 s128), there was no place for a common-law duty of care. Even if that was wrong, the council had satisfied any such duty because it had relied on the valuation of a competent independent valuer in formulating the purchase price.

Note: See also *Payne v Barnet LBC* (E13.5) where this decision was approved.

Death and succession

E14   Succession to secure tenancies

On the death of a secure tenant, another person living in the dwelling as his or her only or principal home may succeed to the tenancy if he or she is either the spouse or civil partner of the tenant or a member of the tenant's family who has resided with the tenant throughout the 12 months ending with the death (Housing Act 1985 s87). 'Member of another's family' is defined by Housing Act 1985 s113.

Security of tenure is commonly lost when a tenant dies and there is no person qualified to succeed to the tenancy. In such circumstances, the tenancy passes to the late tenant's executors or administrators. In the case of intestacy (no will and no application for letters of administration), the tenancy now passes to the Public Trustee (Law of Property (Miscellaneous Provisions) Act 1994 s14).

House of Lords

E14.1 *Birmingham CC v Walker*

[2007] UKHL 22; [2007] 2 WLR 1057; [2007] 1 All ER 445; [2007] HLR 38; (2007) *Times* 17 May; 16 May 2007

Sole tenant by right of survivorship before Housing Act 1980 enacted not a successor

In 1965, Birmingham let a three-bedroomed property to Mr and Mrs Walker, the defendant's parents, on a joint contractual tenancy. In December 1969 Mr Walker senior died, and Mrs Walker became the sole contractual tenant by right of survivorship. She continued to live in the property with her son. In 1980, Mrs Walker became a secure tenant as result of the provisions of the Housing Act 1980. Mrs Walker died in February 2004, leaving her son in occupation. Birmingham served a notice to quit on her personal representatives, and claimed possession. In the county court, a district judge and a circuit judge held that Mr Walker junior was not entitled to succeed to the tenancy because Mrs Walker was herself a successor, and so made a possession order. The Court of Appeal ([2006] EWCA Civ 815; [2006] 1 WLR 2641) allowed Mr Walker's appeal on the basis that a person such as Mrs Walker who had been a joint tenant and had become a sole tenant by right of survivorship before the implementation of the Housing Act 1980 was not 'a successor' for the purposes of the Housing Act 1985 s88.

The House of Lords dismissed Birmingham's appeal. Although Housing Act 1985 s88(1) provides that 'the tenant is himself a successor if ... (b) he was a joint tenant and has become the sole tenant', those words do not apply to events which occurred before Housing Act 1980 came into force. The events to which s88(1) refers are events in relation to tenancies which have become secure tenancies and not to events which happened earlier. When Mrs Walker became the sole tenant, it was not of a secure tenancy and she was therefore not a successor.

E14.2 *Waltham Forest LBC v Thomas*

[1992] 2 AC 198; [1992] 3 WLR 131; [1992] 3 All ER 244; (1992) 24 HLR 622; [1992] 2 EGLR 40; (1992) 90 LGR 358, HL

Twelve-month residence with tenant satisfied despite deceased's transfer in that period

The defendant lived in his brother's council home for over two years. On 11 April 1991, his brother obtained a transfer to another council home, to which he moved with the defendant. On 21 April 1991, the brother died.

The Court of Appeal, following and applying *South Northamptonshire DC v Power* [1987] 1 WLR 1433, CA, held that the defendant could not succeed to the tenancy because he had not resided with his brother for 12 months in the particular home in which he wished to succeed.

Allowing the appeal, the House of Lords held that *Power* had been wrongly decided. The '12-month rule' can be satisfied by residence with the deceased council tenant in any premises or combination of premises (not necessarily subject to secure tenancies for the whole period) for the one year ending with the date of death.

Court of Appeal

E14.3   *Bassetlaw DC v Renshaw*

[1992] 1 All ER 925; (1991) 23 HLR 603; [1991] 2 EGLR 254; (1991) 90 LGR 145, CA

Joint tenant granted a sole tenancy on other tenant's departure not a successor

A husband and wife were joint secure tenants. The husband left, giving notice to quit to the council. The council granted the wife a new sole tenancy in her own name. On her death, one of her children claimed to be entitled to succeed to the tenancy. The council denied this, relying on Housing Act 1985 s88(1)(b) and claiming that there had already been one succession.

The Court of Appeal held that s88(1)(b) applied only when the joint tenancy became a sole tenancy. Here the joint tenancy had ended and been replaced by a new sole tenancy. The sole tenant was not a successor and so the child was entitled to succeed.

E14.4   *Brent LBC v Fofana*

September 1999 *Legal Action* 28, CA

'Member of family' only satisfied if within Housing Act 1985 s113

On the death of a secure tenant the defendant claimed to have succeeded as a member of his family who fulfilled the necessary residence conditions in Housing Act 1985 s87. He asserted that his mother and the deceased's mother had been sisters and according to his African culture he and the deceased were 'brothers'. The trial judge granted the council possession.

Refusing an application for permission to appeal, the Court of Appeal held that the term 'member of the family' could only be satisfied by the relationships listed in Housing Act 1985 s113. In law the defendant and the deceased were 'first cousins' and so not within the section at all.

E14.5   *Brent LBC v Knightley*

(1997) 29 HLR 857, CA (see I2.2)

Daughter could not succeed to mother's tenancy as it had been lost by breach of SPO

E14.6   *Epping Forest DC v Pomphrett*

(1990) 22 HLR 475; [1990] 2 EGLR 46; [1990] 35 EG 60, CA

Where tenant died before succession rules applied council's letter to deceased's wife 'transferring' tenancy interpreted as grant of new tenancy

A council tenant died in 1978 leaving no will. No one applied to administer his estate and so the tenancy vested in the President of the Family Division of the High Court. The tenant's wife and children continued in occupation but the 'succession' rules to be introduced by the Housing Act 1980 (now the Housing Act 1985) were not yet in force. The tenancy continued, therefore, but the council served no notice to quit. Balcombe LJ held that the President of the Family Division had no power to do anything but possibly receive notice to quit if any had been given. Despite the fact that the council had failed to determine the true tenancy and the President had no power to vest the tenancy in anyone, the council wrote to the deceased's spouse confirming that it would 'formally transfer' the tenancy to her. She continued in occupation until 1985 when she died and her children claimed the right to succeed.

The Court of Appeal held that: (a) the original tenancy had neither been determined nor vested in the widow for the purposes of Housing Act 1985 s88(1)(e); (b) the council's letter could, therefore, be interpreted only as the grant of a new tenancy to the widow; (c) the latter became secure under Housing Act 1980; and (d) the children were the first successors to the secure tenant and therefore the secure tenancy vested in one of them.

Note: Prior to July 1995 an intestate's interest vested in the President of the Family Division rather than the Public Trustee.

E14.7   *Kingston upon Thames RLBC v Prince*

[1999] LGR 333; (1999) 31 HLR 794; (1998) *Times* 7 December; [1998] EGCS 179, CA

Minor can succeed to tenancy

A secure tenant died and the council sought possession. The defendant claimed that she was the statutory successor. She was the late tenant's granddaughter and had been aged 13 at the date of death. The council claimed that, although the statutory conditions of family membership and periods of residence were satisfied, a minor could not rely on the statutory succession scheme in Housing Act 1985 s89. HHJ Bishop dismissed the possession claim.

The Court of Appeal dismissed the council's appeal. The court held that a secure tenancy in equity vests in a minor who satisfies the succession conditions. Nothing in Housing Act 1985 limits the provisions regarding succession to adults. It is well established that minors can succeed to statutory tenancies under Rent Act 1977. There is nothing that prevents a local authority from granting an equitable tenancy to a minor. The Trusts of Land and Appointment of Trustees Act 1996 Sch 1 operates in such a way that the legal tenancy to which the minor succeeded was held on trust for her and vested in her parent as trustee until she reached the age of majority. There is no policy objection to including minors within the succession provisions. Leave to appeal was refused.

E14.8   *Marsh v Lewisham LBC*

December 1989 *Legal Action* 14, CA

Where evidence that father lived on own, son found to fail residence requirement

The son of a secure tenant already had a council tenancy of another flat.

He claimed the right to succeed to the tenancy of his father's house on the basis that he had moved in and looked after his father for the year before his death. Although he had kept his own flat, he was able to call two neighbours as witnesses to his assertion that he had lived with his father. The authority produced evidence that (a) he had continued claiming housing benefit at his own flat and (b) shortly after he was alleged to have moved in, the father had written to the council for a grant, claiming to be a pensioner living alone.

The Court of Appeal held that weighing such evidence was essentially a matter for the county court judge. It declined to disturb a finding that Mr Marsh had not established the right to succeed. (See, by way of contrast, the Rent Act case of *Hildebrand v Moon* (E16.9).)

E14.9   *Michalak v Wandsworth LBC*

[2002] EWCA Civ 271; [2003] 1 WLR 617; [2002] HLR 39

Definition of family members in s113 exhaustive; restriction justified under ECHR art 8

Mr Michalak lived for 13 years with a secure council tenant, Mr Lul. They were distantly related. On Mr Lul's death the council served notice to quit on the Public Trustee and claimed possession. The judge held that: (1) the defendant had not been a 'member of the family' of Mr Lul; (2) even if he had been, the relationship was not in the list of relationships set out in Housing Act 1985 s113; and (3) nothing in ECHR art 8 prevented the court from granting possession. On appeal, Mr Michalak sought a declaration that if s113 contained an exhaustive list of relatives who could succeed, it was discriminatory (contrary to ECHR art 14) and should be declared incompatible.

The appeal was dismissed. The Court of Appeal held that: (1) s113 did contain an exhaustive list of categories of family members eligible to succeed a secure tenant; (2) the provision was discriminatory in relation to a matter within the scope of article 8 (the 'home') and so article 14 was engaged; (3) there was an objective justification for establishing a 'closed' list in s113 which was 'certainty' in determining which members of a secure tenant's family were eligible to succeed and accordingly article 14 was not infringed; (4) the fact that the Rent Acts contained no exhaustive definition of 'member of the family' could not assist the defendant because the schemes of the Rent Act and Housing Act tenancies were so different that a potential successor in one scheme had no 'comparator' in the other scheme; (5) on a claim for possession against a non-successor, the county court was not required to investigate the individual circumstances of the defendant in order to find the conditions of article 8(2) made out. Those conditions were satisfied by the common-law right to recover possession of property against a person who, under the relevant statutory scheme, had no right to remain following the death of the tenant.

E14.10   *Morris v Barnet LBC*

December 1995 *Legal Action* 18, CA

Implied admission that no secure tenancy existed where consent order gave possession

Following the death of a secure tenant, the council served notice to quit on her personal representative and claimed possession. Ms Morris defended on the basis that she had succeeded to the tenancy because she was the daughter of the deceased and had lived with her at the property for at least 12 months (Housing Act 1985 ss87 to 89). At the county court trial in 1987, both parties were represented by counsel. Counsel for the local authority opened the case and took the judge to the documents. He made it clear to his opponent that he intended not only to undermine the defence but to show that Ms Morris had forged one of the documents on which she relied. Over the lunch adjournment, Ms Morris became concerned about a possible prosecution for the alleged forgery and instructed her counsel to negotiate a compromise. Agreement was reached and the judge approved a consent order giving possession. Hutchison J dismissed an application for judicial review. He found that the submission to a consent order at that stage in the proceedings amounted to an implied admission by the defendant that she could not win on the only live issue in the case (whether she qualified to succeed).

The Court of Appeal dismissed her appeal. The judge had dealt with and determined correctly the only true issue, which was whether, on the facts, there had been an implied admission that there was no secure tenancy. (See also *R v Worthing BC ex p Bruce* (H2.5).)

E14.11 *Newham LBC v Phillips*
(1998) 96 LGR 788; (1997) 30 HLR 859, CA

Not possible for joint succession to secure tenancy

Mrs Iris Phillips was a secure tenant. Two of her daughters, Josephine and Beryl, were living with her at the time of her death. They agreed that Josephine should succeed to the tenancy. However, both sisters signed a form stating 'I am the successor ...'. Beryl asked if her name could be added to the rent book and the council and Josephine agreed on terms that she remained the sole successor tenant. Beryl then asked to be rehoused and served a notice to quit on the council. HHJ Hornby held that the notice to quit was invalid since Josephine was the sole successor and dismissed the council's claim for possession. The council appealed, claiming that the signing of its form amounted to a surrender of the secure tenancy and the grant of a new joint tenancy.

The appeal was dismissed. It is not possible for there to be a joint succession to a secure tenancy. Josephine had only agreed to Beryl's name being put on the rent book if she alone remained the tenant and so it was impossible to regard this as a surrender of the tenancy. The inclusion of Beryl's name on the book had no effect and Josephine remained the sole tenant. There was no act pointing unequivocally to surrender.

E14.12 *Newham LBC v Ria*
[2004] EWCA Civ 41; 15 January 2004

Common-law succession not suspended where statutory succession occurs

Sharmin Ria lived with her mother, a secure tenant. Her mother died in February 2001 when Sharmin was aged 15. She was qualified to succeed to her mother's tenancy under Housing Act 1985 s87. The mother had by her will appointed her sister trustee and left her entire estate to be held on trust for Sharmin. In August 2002 Newham began proceedings against Sharmin and her aunt to determine who held what estate in the tenancy after the mother's death. HHJ Marr-Johnson made a declaration that Sharmin had succeeded in equity to a secure periodic tenancy, but that that the legal estate in the tenancy vested in her aunt as trustee until Sharmin's majority. Sharmin appealed, claiming that where succession to a tenancy occurs under Housing Act 1985, common-law succession is suspended.

The Court of Appeal dismissed the appeal. The judge had not erred in making the declaration. There were no authorities to support Sharmin's submissions. The legal tenancy vested in Sharmin's aunt by the mother's will. Housing Act 1985 Part IV did not prevent the aunt from holding the legal tenancy (see *Kingston upon Thames RLBC v Prince* (E14.7)).

E14.13 *Peabody Donation Fund Governors v Grant*
(1982) 6 HLR 41; (1982) 264 EG 925, CA

For proposed successor to prove conditions for succession satisfied; issues are of fact

The defendant's father, who was a secure tenant, became ill. The defendant moved in to live with him for part of each week. After hearing evidence, a county court judge concluded that from 1980 the defendant was staying in her father's flat for four nights a week, that her clothes and books were there and that she regarded the flat as her home. He held that, after her father died in 1981, she succeeded to his tenancy.

The Court of Appeal dismissed the council's appeal. In 'family member' succession cases, the burden of proof is on successors to show that they are family members, that they lived with the tenant for the 12 months and that the dwelling is their only or principal home. These questions are primarily issues of fact. In this case, there was no basis for saying that the judge had erred in law or otherwise misdirected himself.

E14.14 *Sharp v Brent LBC*
[2003] EWCA Civ 779; [2003] HLR 65

Where daughter not entitled to succeed, no breach of ECHR art 8 in offering her different accommodation under Part VI after accepted as homeless under Part VII

Ms Sharp lived in a flat which her mother rented from Brent. In February 2000, following her mother's death, Ms Sharp applied to succeed as the tenant under the provisions of Housing Act 1985. Brent rejected that application, contending that Ms Sharp had lied about her entitlement to become a tenant by succession. Ms Sharp did not accept that she had deceived Brent, but did accept Brent's entitlement to find that she did not meet the necessary criteria. Accordingly, a possession order was made by consent. Ms Sharp then applied for housing as a homeless person. Brent made an offer of suitable accommodation which Ms Sharp rejected, claiming that the flat where she had lived with her mother was suitable accommodation, and that the property offered was unsuitable because it required her to move. Brent rejected that contention and upheld that decision on a Housing Act 1996 s202 review. HHJ Latham allowed Ms Sharp's s204 appeal, finding that the decision letter was irrational and that it confused the statutory scheme for succession of tenancies under Housing Act 1985 with Housing Act 1996 Parts 6 and 7. He also found that the eviction of Ms Sharp from her mother's flat breached her rights under ECHR article 8. He remitted the matter for a further s202 review.

The council appealed successfully. There was no confusion in the decision letter between Brent's obligations under Parts 6 and 7 and the purported deceit by Ms Sharp in relation to her application to succeed to the tenancy under Housing Act 1985. Second, the mother's flat was Ms Sharp's home for the purposes of ECHR article 8 and so Brent were wrong to argue that the article 8 issues were not relevant considerations for the judge. The requirement that she vacate that property, albeit with an offer of a new home, was on its face an interference with her article 8(1) rights. Ms Sharp did have a marginal complaint of interference, but Brent's decision, on the facts of the case, was well justified for the fulfilment of democratic rights and for the protection of the rights and freedoms of others (see article 8(2)). Accordingly, the judge fell into error in finding that Brent's decision was a violation of article 8. Finally, the judge further erred by 'blending' together Housing Act 1996 Parts 6 and 7. The duty of a local authority under s193 may be discharged by the allocation of housing under Part VI. However, the court was not entitled to reach the view that in reviewing the housing authority's decision under s204 a different result might have been reached had considerations been made under Part VI. The judge in the present case was not entitled to evaluate Brent's decision as falling under Part VI since he had no jurisdiction to go into Part VI matters. His decision was only on the legality of the decision letter as to the suitability of the housing offered. Accordingly, there was no foundation for the challenge to the decision letter.

E14.15 ### *Sheffield CC v Wall*

[2006] EWCA Civ 495; 23 March 2006

Foster child not within s113; where gap in actual residence consideration needed of whether residence requirement nevertheless satisfied

Mr Wall was fostered when he was six months old and by the time of the court hearing was aged 39. In 1986, his mother was granted a secure tenancy of a two-bedroom house on the basis that it was to be occupied by her and her 'son'. Mr Wall lived at the property with his foster mother continuously, apart from term time when he was a student. In September 1999, he obtained a training contract with solicitors in Sheffield and continued to live 'at home'. However, in September 2001, the solicitors gave him a temporary, six-month contract in London, which was later extended until June 2002. Accordingly, he leased a flat in London for one year as he was unable to find a tenancy for a shorter time. In November 2001, he was admitted as a solicitor. When his contract ended, he physically returned to live in the house in Sheffield and moved all of his belongings back on 6 July 2002. He continued to live there with his mother until she died on 21 June 2003. The council claimed possession. Mr Wall defended on the basis that he had succeeded to his foster mother's tenancy (Housing Act

1985 s87). The judge made a possession order because he was not satisfied that Mr Wall had been in residence for the 12 months immediately preceding his foster mother's death. Mr Wall appealed.

The Court of Appeal allowed the appeal and remitted the case for a rehearing. (1) Although a foster child is not a 'member of the family' for the purposes of ss113 and 87, Sheffield were, in the circumstances, estopped from claiming that Mr Wall was not a member of his foster mother's family. (2) Mr Wall had to establish residence between 22 June 2002 and 21 June 2003 to satisfy s87. The judge had failed to remind himself that he was only concerned with a period of absence of about two weeks (ie, prior to 6 July 2002). He made no reference to the case-law or the correct way in law to approach periods of absence from the property. In particular, the judge did not refer to the need for a person who sought to establish residence to show the necessary physical and mental elements of residence. The judge's determination was unfocused and he appeared to suggest that Mr Wall had been living elsewhere during periods when there was a great deal of evidence that suggested otherwise.

E14.16 *Wandsworth LBC v Michalak – see Michalak v Wandsworth LBC*
(E14.9)

E14.17 *Westminster CC v Peart*
(1992) 24 HLR 389, CA

Cohabitee required to have lived as 'husband and wife' with tenant for 12 months

The Court of Appeal held that Housing Act 1985 s87, when read together with the words 'living together as husband and wife' in s113, means that, in order to be entitled to succeed, a cohabitee must not only have lived with the deceased for a year but have lived as 'husband or wife' for the whole year. Succession cannot be established where the cohabitation 'as husband and wife' has been for only part of the 12 months of co-residence.

High Court

E14.18 *R (Gangera) v Hounslow LBC*
[2003] EWHC 794 Admin; [2003] HLR 68 (see L1.10)

Court not bound to consider whether possession in breach of art 8; defendant not entitled to raise public law arguments as defence in possession proceedings

E14.19 *Southwark LBC v O'Sullivan*
[2004] EWHC 75 Ch; 14 January 2004

Cogency of defendant's new evidence (doctor's letters) not such as to justify retrial

From 1993 Mr O'Sullivan senior rented premises from Southwark under a secure tenancy. When he died, Southwark began possession proceedings. His son defended, claiming that he had occupied the premises as his only or principal home during the 12 months prior to his father's death and that, accordingly, he had become the successor to his father's tenancy (Housing Act 1985 s89(2)). The court made a possession order, finding that the son had not made out his case on a balance of probabilities. He appealed, seeking permission to adduce evidence which had not been be-fore the county court, in the form of two letters written at different times by two different doctors who referred to the son having been registered at their surgeries and having lived at the premises for more than a year before his father's death.

Etherton J dismissed the appeal. There was no material before the court to justify the cost and delay to the parties in remitting the case for a fresh trial. In arriving at its conclusion, the court below had given a careful and comprehensive analysis of the relevant issues for determination and the evidence available from both sides. The court hearing the appeal had to consider that conclusion in the light of the new evidence. On consider-ation of that evidence, neither letter materially assisted in proving that the son's true home had been with his father during the critical period. The cogency of the new material was not such that it would have made any dif-ference to the outcome of the trial or have had a material influence on it.

County courts

E14.20 *Hereford CC v O'Callaghan*
[1996] CLY 3831, Worcester County Court

De facto child not entitled to succeed

A claim for possession was met by a defence that the secure tenancy had vested in the defendant on the death of the secure tenant. The late ten-ant had fostered the defendant throughout his childhood by arrangement with his natural parents. They had treated one another as mother and son. Housing Act 1985 permits succession by a 'member of the family'. That definition includes a 'child' (see s113). The county court judge granted possession, holding that the defendant was not the deceased's child for the purposes of the statutory definition. In so doing, the court expressly declined to follow the first instance decision in *Reading BC v Ilsley* [1981] CLY 1323, Reading County Court, that the statute was capable of embrac-ing a de facto child of the deceased.

Scottish courts

E14.21 *Monklands DC v Gallagher*
2000 Hous LR 112, Sheriff Court

Temporary absence did not negate residence

Ms Gallagher was the niece of the tenant. When the tenant died she claimed to be entitled to succeed to the tenancy. She had lived at the prop-erty from 1946 to 1983, when she moved out following a row. There was evidence that although she was staying elsewhere, she still stayed occa-sionally at the property, had her mail delivered there and attended to her uncle's requirements during his illness and generally ran the household. Following a reconciliation she lived at the property for 11½ months before her uncle's death in 1986.

Sheriff Stewart found that she was qualified to succeed. Temporary ab-sence did not destroy the fact that she regarded the property as her principal residence and ran the home, although she did not live there permanently.

E14.22 *Roxburgh DC v Collins*

1991 SLT (Sh Ct) 49; 1991 1 SCLR 575; 1991 8 GWD 483, Sheriff Court

Son succeeded to mother's tenancy despite living in lodgings elsewhere for 6 years

The tenant's son claimed to have succeeded to a secure tenancy of his mother's home in Newcastleton, Scotland. He lived with her throughout his adult life but in 1983 became unemployed and, unable to find local work, moved to London. He worked there until his mother's death in November 1989. In London, he had a single room in a lodging house with shared facilities. His clothes and possessions remained in his bedroom in his mother's home and he spent every Christmas and Easter and all holidays there with her. His GP and bank were in Newcastleton and he was not on the electoral register at either address.

Dismissing an appeal from the sheriff, Sheriff Principal Nicholson QC found that the son had succeeded. He held that the correct approach was to ask 'did the person concerned have such a real, tangible and substantial connection with the housing in question that it, rather than any other place or residence, can properly be described as having been his only or principal home?' On the facts, the son met that test.

E14.23 *Scottish Homes v Fairbairn*

2000 Hous LR 114, Sheriff Court

Fact that defendant not on HB form and claimed benefit from different address inconclusive

The defendant was the grandson of a tenant who had died. Scottish Homes brought possession proceedings claiming that he had not occupied the premises as his only or principal home throughout the requisite 12-month period before his grandfather's death. The defendant argued that he had lived at the property since 1996, taking care of his terminally ill grandfather. He was supported by a petition and by eye-witnesses. Scottish Homes rejected this, noting that he was not named on the tenant's housing benefit form, used a different address to claim income benefit and was not on the electoral register.

Sheriff Jandoo found that he was qualified to succeed. The defendant's evidence was credible and reliable. The tests relied on by the landlord were inconclusive and unreliable.

E15   Succession to assured tenancies

Housing Act 1988 s17 provides that spouses, civil partners or people who were living with tenants as their spouse or civil partner are entitled to succeed to assured tenancies if they were occupying the premises as their only or principal home immediately before the death of the assured tenant.

Court of Appeal

E15.1 *Southern Housing Group Ltd v Nutting*

[2004] EWHC 2982 (Ch); [2005] HLR 25; (2004) *Times* 5 January

Gay relationship did not satisfy living as 'husband and wife' requirement on facts

In 2001 the defendant moved into a flat to live with a man who had been an assured tenant since 1996. They had a volatile relationship, with both men drinking heavily. In January 2003, the tenant applied for a transfer to another of the landlord's flats. He moved out in February, but died from the effects of alcoholism in March 2003. The landlord claimed possession. In July 2003 the defendant claimed to be entitled to succeed to the assured tenancy under Housing Act 1988 s17, maintaining that his relationship with the tenant had been similar to a marriage. At trial, a recorder found that the tenant and the defendant had not committed themselves to each other for the rest of their lives and that their mutual companionship and partnership had not satisfied the requirement of s17(4) ('living with the tenant as his or her wife or husband'). The defendant was not entitled to succeed to the assured tenancy and the landlord was entitled to possession.

Evans-Lombe J dismissed the defendant's appeal. Without a lifetime commitment at least at some point in the relationship, there was no sufficient similarity to marriage. Such a relationship must be 'openly and unequivocally displayed to the outside world'. There were many ways in which a marriage relationship could be described but Evans-Lombe J was satisfied that the test applied by the recorder was an entirely adequate one that was consistent authority (eg, *Ghaidan v Godin-Mendoza* (E16.3)). On the findings of fact which he made, he was entitled to conclude that s17(4) was not satisfied.

E16 Succession to Rent Act tenancies

Rent Act 1977 s2 and Sch 1 (as amended by the Housing Act 1988 and the Civil Partnership Act 2004) provide that in some circumstances a spouse, civil partner or member of the tenant's family living with the tenant may succeed to the tenancy after the tenant's death and become a 'statutory tenant by succession'.

House of Lords

E16.1 *Carega Properties SA v Sharratt*
[1979] 1 WLR 928; [1979] 2 All ER 1084; (1979) 39 P&CR 76; (1979) 252 EG 163, HL

Two strangers could not become 'family members' despite close relationship

In 1959 Lady Salter, who was aged 75 and the widow of a High Court judge, met Mr Sharratt, who was then aged 24. They became close friends and the following year he moved in to the flat which she rented. The relationship was platonic and filial. He 'behaved as a dutiful and affectionate son and looked after her during her declining years'. They lived together in the flat until she died in 1976 aged 94. Mr Sharratt claimed that he was entitled to succeed to the statutory tenancy.

Lord Diplock declined to undertake a general consideration of what persons might be included in the expression 'a member of the original tenant's family' but approved comments by Russell LJ in *Ross v Collins* [1964] 1 WLR 425, CA, that there must be:

> ... at least a broadly recognisable de facto familial nexus. This may be capable of being found and recognised as such by the ordinary man – where the link would be strictly familial had there been a marriage, or where the link is through adoption of a minor, de jure or de facto, or where the link is 'step-', or where the link is 'in-law' or by marriage. But two strangers cannot, it seems to me, ever establish artificially for the purposes of this section a familial nexus by acting as brothers or as sisters, even if they call each other such and consider their relationship to be tantamount to that. Nor, in my view, can an adult man or woman who establish a platonic relationship establish a familial nexus by acting as a devoted brother and sister or father and daughter would act ...

Mr Sharratt was not entitled to succeed to the tenancy. The landlords were entitled to a possession order.

E16.2   *Fitzpatrick v Sterling Housing Association*
[2001] 1 AC 27; [1999] 3 WLR 1113; [1999] 4 All ER 705; [2000] UKHRR 25; (2000) 32 HLR 178; [2000] L&TR 44; (1999) *Times* 4 November, HL

Gay partners could not live as 'husband and wife' but were family members on facts

Mr Thompson was the statutory tenant of premises. Mr Fitzpatrick lived with him from 1976 in a 'long-standing, close, loving and faithful monogamous, homosexual relationship'. In 1986 Mr Thompson suffered severe head injuries and, as a result, Mr Fitzpatrick nursed him until his death in 1994. HHJ Colin Smith QC found that Mr Fitzpatrick was outside the statutory definition of a person entitled to succeed on the death of the statutory tenant since he was not a person who was a member of the original tenant's family residing with him for six months immediately before his death. The Court of Appeal, after a detailed consideration of various statutes and authorities, both from British and North American courts, by a majority, dismissed Mr Fitzpatrick's appeal.

His further appeal was, however, allowed by a majority of the House of Lords. Although gay partners could not live together as husband and wife, they could be members of the same family for the purposes of Rent Act succession. Since a man and a woman living together in a stable and permanent sexual relationship were capable of being members of a family, it could not make sense to say that a gay partnership of the same character could not. Lord Slynn of Hadley said:

> The hallmarks of the relationship were essentially that there should be a degree of mutual inter-dependence, of the sharing of lives, of caring and love, of commitment and support. In respect of legal relationships these are presumed, though evidently are not always present as the family law and criminal courts know only too well. In de facto relationships these are capable, if proved, of creating membership of the tenant's family.

A person claiming that he or she was a member of the same-sex original tenant's family had to establish, rather than merely assert, the necessary hallmarks of the relationship. All the cases stress the need for a permanent and stable relationship. A transient superficial relationship does not suffice if it was intimate. Mere cohabitation by friends as a matter of convenience is not sufficient either. In other statutes, in other contexts, the words may have a wider or a narrower meaning.

[See now Rent Act 1977 Schedule 1, which has been amended by the Civil Partnership Act 2004 to give rights of succession to civil partners.]

E16.3   *Ghaidan v Godin-Mendoza*

[2004] UKHL 30; [2004] 2 AC 557; [2004] 3 WLR 113; [2004] 3 All ER 411; [2004] HLR 46; [2005] L&TR 3; [2005] 1 P&CR 274; [2004] UKHRR 827; (2004) *Times* 24 June

Gay couple did live together as 'husband and wife'; ECHR arts 8 and 14

Mr Mendoza and Mr Walwyn-Jones lived together in a same sex relationship from 1972. There was overwhelming evidence that it was a loving and monogamous relationship. Mr Walwyn-Jones was granted a Rent Act tenancy in April 1983. Apart from the fact that the relationship was between two persons of the same sex, Mr Mendoza and Mr Walwyn-Jones were living together in the way that spouses live together. They continued living together in the premises until Mr Walwyn-Jones's death. If the relationship between Mr Mendoza and Mr Walwyn-Jones had been a heterosexual one, he would have been eligible to succeed to the statutory tenancy under Rent Act 1977 Sch 1 para 2(2) which provided that 'for the purposes of this paragraph, a person who was living with the original tenant as his or her wife or husband shall be treated as the spouse of the original tenant'. At first instance, the judge found that there had been no succession to the statutory tenancy, although the conditions for succession to an assured tenancy were satisfied. He was not persuaded that the construction of para 2 given in *Fitzpatrick v Sterling HA* (E16.2), which precluded a person in a same sex relationship with a deceased tenant from succeeding to a statutory tenancy, had to be reconsidered in the light of the Human Rights Act 1998. Mr Mendoza appealed successfully to the Court of Appeal.

The House of Lords (Lord Millett dissenting) dismissed the landlord's further appeal. A gay couple, as much as a heterosexual couple, share each other's life and make their home together. There is no rational or fair ground for distinguishing the one couple from the other. The difference in treatment flowing from the *Fitzpatrick* interpretation of para 2(2) infringed ECHR article 14 read in conjunction with article 8, since the distinction on grounds of sexual orientation had no legitimate aim and was made without good reason. The social policy underlying the 1988 extension of security of tenure to the survivor of couples living together as husband and wife was equally applicable to the survivor of homosexual couples living together in a close and stable relationship. Applying Human Rights Act 1998 s3, para 2 is to be read and given effect as though the survivor of such a homosexual couple is the surviving spouse of the original tenant. Reading para 2 in that way has the result that cohabiting heterosexual couples and cohabiting homosexual couples are treated alike for the purpose of succession as a statutory tenant.

[See now Rent Act 1977 Schedule 1, which has been amended by the Civil Partnership Act 2004 to give rights of succession to civil partners.]

Court of Appeal

E16.4   *Brock v Wollams*

[1949] 2 KB 388; [1949] 1 All ER 715, CA

De facto child entitled to succeed

The defendant, then a child of five or six years of age, came to live with the tenant in 1912. Apart from a period of three years, she lived with the tenant until his death in 1948. She was never formally adopted, but was treated throughout as if she was adopted.

The Court of Appeal held that she was entitled to succeed to the tenancy. Lord Denning stated that members of the tenant's family for the purposes of the Increase of Rent and Mortgage Interest (Restrictions) Act 1920 included 'not only legitimate children but also stepchildren, illegitimate children and adopted children, whether adopted in due form of law or not'.

Note: This case was referred to with apparent approval in *Fitzpatrick v Sterling Housing Association* (E16.2).

E16.5   *Chios Investment Property Co v Lopez*

(1988) 20 HLR 120; [1988] 1 EGLR 98; [1988] 05 EG 57, CA

Two-year relationship satisfied 'member of family' criterion

The defendant had had a relationship lasting two years with the original tenant before his death.

It was held that the relationship 'had reached a sufficient state of permanence and stability for it to be said that in all the circumstances' she was a member of the tenant's family and, therefore, entitled to succeed to the statutory tenancy.

E16.6   *Clore v MacNicol*

[2004] EWCA Civ 1055; 13 July 2004

Where brother found to have surrendered his tenancy by succession, sister did not obtain tenancy by assignment

Ms MacNicol's mother had a Rent Act statutory tenancy. She died in 1999. The claimant landlord accepted that Ms MacNicol's brother qualified under the Rent Act 1977 to take an assured periodic tenancy by succession. However, in negotiations for a new tenancy, the landlord and the brother failed to reach agreement. Ms MacNicol then made a claim to a tenancy by succession. The landlord claimed that she was not entitled to a tenancy. In the light of the landlord's stance, the brother wrote stating that he gave up 'all rights to the tenancy' to Ms MacNicol. The landlord sought possession. Ms MacNicol argued that the letter amounted to an effective transfer of the brother's assured periodic tenancy, despite Housing Act 1988 s15 which renders such a transfer a breach of the terms of the tenancy, so that she had become the tenant by assignment. A judge made a possession order, finding that there had been no assignment between the brother and Ms MacNicol and that his letter had represented a surrender of his rights rather than a transfer of them. Ms MacNicol appealed.

The Court of Appeal dismissed her appeal. The letter did not suggest an assignment. Any such assignment or transfer would have been sent to

Ms MacNicol herself and not to the landlord. Furthermore, the terms of letter suggested the giving up of rights under a tenancy. The judge had been correct to find that what the brother had done by the letter had been to surrender his rights under the tenancy. As a result Ms MacNicol had occupied the property as an assured shorthold tenant and the landlord was entitled to the possession order sought.

E16.7   *Daejan Properties Ltd v Mahoney*
(1996) 28 HLR 498; [1995] 2 EGLR 75, CA

Landlord estopped from denying daughter statutory tenant where assurance given

The defendant's father was the statutory tenant of a flat. After his death, in accordance with Rent Act 1977 Sch 1, his widow, the defendant's mother, became the statutory tenant by succession. The mother then had a stroke and the defendant gave up her career to look after her. In order to secure her daughter's position, the defendant's mother obtained a letter from the managing agents, stating that she and her daughter were joint tenants. Relying on that assurance, she refused an offer of rehousing by the local authority. After her mother's death, the landlords claimed that the defendant had succeeded to an assured tenancy at a market rent, rather than a statutory tenancy with a rent-officer registered rent (see Housing Act 1988 s39(3) and Sch 4 para 6).

    The Court of Appeal held that the landlords were estopped from denying that the defendant was a statutory tenant. Although there can only be one successor to a statutory tenancy, if joint tenants hold a protected tenancy, there is no reason why they should not both become statutory tenants on the expiry of the contractual term. The effect of the estoppel was to allow a transfer of the statutory tenancy without the written agreement between the outgoing tenant, the incoming tenant and the landlord which would usually be required by Rent Act 1977 Sch 1 para 13.

E16.8   *Hedgedale Ltd v Hards*
(1991) 23 HLR 158; [1991] 1 EGLR 118, CA

Residence requirement satisfied despite temporary absence of tenant in hospital

The Court of Appeal considered whether or not a grandson 'was residing with [the tenant] at the time of and for the period of six months immediately before [the tenant's] death' for the purposes of the succession provisions in Rent Act 1977 Sch 1 para 3. The defendant had lived in the premises for nine months before the tenant's death on 1 May 1988, but the tenant had been absent in hospital for three months in the middle of that period after breaking her arm. Allowing an appeal against a possession order, the court stated that, where both the statutory tenant and a member of the family intended that the non-tenant relative should become a permanent member of the tenant's household, the fact that the tenant was temporarily absent did not mean that the member of the family was not residing with the tenant.

Note: The result of the possession proceedings would have been different if the statutory tenant had died after 15 January 1989, since Housing Act

1988 Sch 4 para 3 amended Rent Act 1977 Sch 1 para 3 by increasing the required period of residence from six months to two years.

E16.9   *Hildebrand v Moon*

(1990) 22 HLR 1; [1989] 2 EGLR 100, CA

Daughter who moved in to nurse mother and had necessary intention entitled to succeed

A statutory tenant's daughter claimed that she had become a statutory tenant by succession and that she had been 'residing with' her mother before her death (Rent Act 1977 Sch 1 para 7). She had moved, from a flat which she owned, into premises rented by her mother to nurse her and had contemplated selling her own flat. The county court judge took the view that the daughter had not formed a sufficient intention to make her permanent home with her mother and decided that she had not become a statutory tenant by succession.

However, Mann LJ found that:

> ... all objective indicia are that [the daughter] had made her home with her mother. Her evidence as to permanency was accepted by the judge. All the indicia being as they are, the absence of specific evidence of contemporaneous intention cannot ... be decisive ((1990) 22 HLR at 5).

The Court of Appeal held that the daughter had become a statutory tenant by succession and dismissed the landlord's claim for possession.

E16.10   *Sefton Holdings Ltd v Cairns*

(1988) 20 HLR 124; [1988] 1 EGLR 99, CA

De facto daughter member of household but not member of family

The defendant came to live with the deceased tenant's family in 1941 when she was aged 23. She had lived in the premises ever since as a member of the household and had been 'treated as a daughter' by the original tenant.

However, Lloyd LJ stated that 'length of residence could not transform her into a member of the family'. There is a distinction between 'being a member of the family and being a member of the household, and [a] distinction between being a member of the family and living as a member of the family' ((1988) 20 HLR at 127). It was held that she was not a member of the family and so she was not entitled to succeed to the statutory tenancy.

E16.11   *Swanbrae Ltd v Elliott*

(1987) 19 HLR 86; [1987] 1 EGLR 99, CA

Daughter with home elsewhere living part time with mother not entitled to succeed

The defendant, although she had a 'secure home', stayed at her mother's house two miles away 'at least on a part-time basis' for over six months before her mother's death.

Her appeal against a county court decision that she was not residing with her mother and was therefore unable to succeed to the tenancy was dismissed. The Court of Appeal considered the meaning of 'residing with [the tenant]' in Rent Act 1977 Sch 1. Swinton Thomas J stated that the words meant that a person 'must show that he or she has made a home at the premises which they are claiming and has become in a true sense a part of the household'. Although it is possible for such a person to have two homes, the words mean more than merely 'living at' the premises. Essentially, such questions are matters of fact and degree which are best decided by judges of first instance.

E16.12 *Tennant v Hutton*

(1996) 73 P&CR D10, CA

On tenant's death during contractual term tenancy vested in her husband as surviving joint tenant; daughter did not succeed

Ms Tennant's parents were the lessees of a house. Following her mother's death in 1989, she and her father continued to live in the house. The contractual term came to an end in 1991. In 1994 her father left and went to live elsewhere. Ms Tennant claimed to be a protected tenant in succession to her mother and relied on Rent Act 1977 s2(1)(b) and Sch 1.

The Court of Appeal dismissed her claim. She was her parents' licensee. On her mother's death, the contractual term vested in her father as surviving joint tenant. On the expiry of the contractual term, he became the statutory tenant. When he left, the statutory tenancy came to an end and Ms Tennant had no legal right to remain in occupation. The Court of Appeal rejected Ms Tennant's contention that, since a literal application of the rules about joint tenancies produced an anomalous and capricious result, the court should adopt a purposive construction similar to that employed in *Lloyd v Sadler* [1978] QB 774; [1978] 2 WLR 721; [1978] 2 All ER 529; (1978) 35 P&CR 78, CA.

County courts

E16.13 *Portman Registrars v Mohammed Latif*

[1987] CLY 2239, Willesden County Court

Minor could succeed to statutory tenancy

The defendant lived with his mother in residential premises for ten years but, when she died, the landlords claimed that he was not entitled to succeed to her tenancy in accordance with the provisions of Rent Act 1977 Sch 1 because he was only 16.

HHJ Hill-Smith held that, because (a) a statutory tenancy is not an interest in land and (b) a contract for the provision of lodgings was a contract for the provision of necessaries, the son had the capacity to, and did, succeed to the statutory tenancy.

E17 # Disability Discrimination Act 1995

Court of Appeal

E17.1 *Williams v Richmond Court (Swansea) Ltd*

[2006] EWCA Civ 1719; [2007] HLR 23; [2007] L&TR 19; [2007] 1 P&CR 21; (2006) *Times* 29 December

Landlord did not discriminate against lessee as disabled person in refusing consent to install stairlift

Mrs Williams was aged 81 and had mobility problems. She was a long lessee and lived on the third floor of a block of flats. Her flat was served by stairs. She could get up and down the stairs only with the greatest difficulty. She needed a stair-lift. The defendants, her landlords, did not agree to the installation of a stair-lift, even though it would be installed at no expense to them. Mrs Williams claimed that their refusal to consent was discrimination. The defendants contended that they had done nothing to interfere with her right to use the stairs and had done nothing to her detriment. They said that they had merely failed to confer a benefit which was not covenanted in her lease and that her problem was caused by nature rather than any action on their part. Mrs Williams issued proceedings. The defendants applied for summary judgment. District Judge Evans refused the defendants' application and then determined a preliminary issue, namely whether the defendants' refusal of consent to the installation of a stair-lift at the claimant's expense constituted discrimination within Disability Discrimination Act 1995 s22(3), in favour of Mrs Williams. A circuit judge dismissed the defendants' appeal.

The Court of Appeal allowed their second appeal. The sole issue was whether the defendants had discriminated against Mrs Williams as a disabled person. None of the reasons for refusing consent (other tenants voting against it, aesthetics, the cost of repair and inconvenience to the residents as a while) related to Mrs Williams's disability. The Court of Appeal distinguished *Manchester CC v Romano* (H8.2) (where the reason for discrimination was assumed not to apply to comparators) and *Clark v Novacold Ltd* [1999] ICR 951, CA (where the critical reason for the claimant's absence from work was his disability). The effect of the judge's decision was to impose a positive duty on the manager of premises to do whatever was necessary (not just what was reasonable) to ensure that a disabled occupier was able to enjoy the relevant benefits or facilities to the same extent as relevant comparators. The judge had wrongly failed to carry out a two-stage test, first to identify the relevant act or omission on the part of the defendants and then to identify the relevant act or omission, if any, towards relevant comparators. The defendants had not treated the claimant less favourably than they had treated or would have treated anyone else within the meaning of s24(1). The Court of Appeal granted summary judgment to the defendants.

Scottish courts

E17.2　*Rose v Bouchet*

[1999] IRLR 463; 2000 SLT (Sh Ct) 170, Edinburgh Sheriff Court

Refusal to let property to blind man where steps a danger not discrimination

Mr Rose, who was blind, telephoned the defendant about accommodation and was told that there was a flat to rent. However, when he mentioned that he was blind, he was told that there were five steps without a hand rail leading up to the front door, which would be dangerous for a blind person. Mr Bouchet said that the flat would not be suitable. Mr Rose brought a claim under Disability Discrimination Act 1995 on the grounds that Mr Bouchet had contravened s22(1)(b) which provides that it 'is unlawful for a person with power to dispose of any premises to discriminate ... by refusing to dispose of those premises to [a] disabled person'. The defendant claimed that he was justified in treating Mr Rose less favourably because of his disability (s24(2)) because it 'was necessary in order not to endanger the health or safety of any person (which may include that of the disabled person)' (s24(3)(a)). Evidence was given that an inspector employed by the Environmental Health Department of the Council had advised that the steps constituted a danger to the public.

The Sheriff Principal, upholding the dismissal of the claim held that the test of justification is part subjective and part objective. The first part, that in the defendant's opinion one of the conditions in s24(3) was satisfied is subjective. The second part, that the opinion was one which it was reasonable to reach is objective.

Notices

F1   Introduction

Housing Act 1985 ss83, 83A and 84(3) and Housing Act 1988 ss8 and 8A contain provisions dealing with notices seeking possession ('NSPs'). Although the provisions are largely similar, there are still a few differences between the two types of statutory notice – and so cases relating to the two different regimes are summarised separately.

F2   Notices seeking possession (Housing Act 1985)

Housing Act 1985 s83 (as amended by Housing Act 1996) precludes a court from granting an order for possession against a secure tenant unless it is satisfied that a notice seeking possession (NSP) complying with the requirements of that section (and s83A where appropriate) has been served or that it is 'just and equitable' to dispense with the notice requirement. If it is not just and equitable to dispense with the need for a notice, the notice must state the ground for possession and give 'particulars' of the ground.

Court of Appeal

F2.1   *Braintree DC v Vincent*
[2004] EWCA Civ 415; 9 March 2004

NSP to be dispensed with in 'relatively exceptional circumstances'; sub-licensee's liability for mesne profits.

Mrs Vincent was an elderly lady. She was a secure tenant, living in a bungalow. In April 2002, she suffered an accident and was admitted to hospital, where she remained for a long time before being placed in a nursing home. From April 2003, one of her sons, the third defendant, lived in the bungalow. The council began possession proceedings against the sons as trespassers. A judge joined Mrs Vincent as a defendant. A possession order was made on the alternative bases that the mother was no longer a secure tenant and on the ground of rent arrears. On the latter basis, the judge considered that it was just and equitable to dispense with the requirement for a s83 notice. The judge also ordered one of the sons, the third defendant, to pay a sum equivalent to 22 weeks' rent for his use and occupation of the property. He appealed.

The Court of Appeal dismissed an appeal against the possession order. Although it is 'obviously only in relatively exceptional cases where the court should be prepared to dispense with a section 83 notice', in this case the circumstances were unusual in procedural terms. The tenant was only added as a defendant at the insistence of the judge. It was therefore understandable that no s83 notice had been served. Furthermore, a s83 notice would have been of no benefit to the tenant – indeed it would have been to her disadvantage because it would have postponed the date for possession and added to her liability for rent. The judge was entitled to dispense with the notice on the unusual facts of the case. However, the court allowed the appeal against the order for mesne profits. Until the order for possession was made, the third defendant had been Mrs Vincent's licensee. He had not become liable to the claimant until her tenancy came to an end. The money judgment against the third defendant was set aside.

F2.2 *Camden LBC v Oppong*
(1996) 28 HLR 701, CA

Power to give leave to alter grounds in NSP imports a power to give leave to alter particulars of ground. Power only to be exercised in exceptional circumstances.

Although Housing Act 1985 s83 expressly enables a court to give leave for a landlord to add to or alter the 'grounds' on which possession is claimed (s83(4)), it is silent about the addition or alteration of the 'particulars' required by the notice.

Allowing Camden Council's appeal against the dismissal of proceedings on the basis that the particulars in a notice were deficient, the Court of Appeal held that s83(4) imports a power to add to or alter the particulars. It cautioned that such leave would be granted only in circumstances where it would be just do so and that the nature and extent of the addition or alteration would always be a critical factor.

F2.3 *City of London Corporation v Devlin*
(1997) 29 HLR 58, CA

NSP not signed by Director of Housing; defence based on technical defects in notice defeated by procedural rulings.

At the hearing of a claim for possession for arrears of rent, a secure tenant raised two procedural points: (a) the notice seeking possession had not been signed by the 'Director of Housing' above that description on the printed form and (b) the proceedings had been issued three days before the date specified on the notice as the date on which they could first be issued. The trial judge held that the NSP was 'substantially to the same effect' as that prescribed and so valid. He gave the council leave to issue new court proceedings immediately. He dispensed with service for the new claim, abridged time and permitted the new action to be consolidated. This 'rescued' the otherwise defective proceedings. The judge made a possession order.

The Court of Appeal dismissed the tenant's application for leave to appeal. Simon Brown LJ said 'The reality here is that a series of aridly technical points raised by the applicant at trial were defeated by a series of creative, largely procedural rulings' which were not even arguably impermissible.

F2.4 *Dudley MBC v Bailey*
(1990) 22 HLR 424; [1991] 1 EGLR 53; [1991] 10 EG 140; (1990) 89 LGR 266, CA

NSP 'substantially to the same effect' as prescribed form; error in particulars of ground did not invalidate notice

In possession proceedings, the council conceded that general rates were not part of the rent. However, the court had to determine whether the possession action could proceed on the basis of the notice seeking possession (NSP) which the council had served in January 1989. The notice

had two potential flaws. First, it was not in the precise form prescribed by
the Secure Tenancies (Notices) Regulations 1987 SI No 755. Second, the
particulars referred to 'arrears of rent of £145.96' when the rent in arrears
was £72.88, the balance being general and water rates. HHJ Stuart-White
held that the notice was defective under Housing Act 1985 s83(2) and
dismissed the proceedings.

On appeal, Ralph Gibson LJ held that the NSP, although not precisely
in the prescribed form, was 'substantially to the same effect' (reg 2(1)).
With regard to the particulars contained in the notice, he stated that:

> The question is whether, at the date of the notice, the landlord has in
> good faith stated the ground and given the particulars of that ground. The
> requirement of particulars is satisfied, in my judgment, if the landlord
> has stated in summary form the facts which he then intends to prove in
> support of the stated ground for possession. Error in the particulars does
> not, in my judgment, invalidate the notice, although it may well affect the
> decision of the court on the merits. ((1990) 22 HLR at 431)

The council's appeal was allowed and the case remitted to the county
court.

F2.5   *Enfield LBC v Devonish and Sutton*
(1997) 29 HLR 691; (1997) 75 P&CR 288, CA (see N2.9)

Service of notice must satisfy common law or LPA 1925 s196(5)

F2.6   *Torridge DC v Jones*
(1986) 18 HLR 107; [1985] 2 EGLR 54, CA

*Particulars in NSP in rent arrears cases must at least show amount claimed;
NSPs in all cases must tell the tenant what to do to remedy the situation*

The council began possession proceedings based on arrears of rent, relying on Housing Act 1980 Sch 4 Ground 1 (now Housing Act 1985 Sch 2
Ground 1). The notice seeking possession (NSP) set out the ground in
full, but the particulars given were, 'The reasons for taking this action are
non-payment of rent'. The council's possession proceedings were struck
out on the basis that the particulars given in the NSP were insufficient.

The Court of Appeal dismissed the appeal. It held that in rent arrears
cases the particulars given must at least show the amount claimed, and
in all cases the NSP must be sufficiently particularised to 'tell the tenant
what he had to do to put matters right before proceedings are commenced'
((1986) 18 HLR at 114).

F2.7   *Wandsworth LBC v Attwell*
[1995] 3 WLR 95; (1995) 27 HLR 536; [1996] 1 EGLR 57; (1996) 94 LGR 419, CA (see
N2.22)

*LPA 1925 s196 does not apply to service of NTQs; express provision required in
tenancy for service at property*

County courts

F2.8   *East Devon DC v Williams and Mills*
December 1996 *Legal Action* 13, Exeter County Court

Proceedings struck out where particulars in NSP merely repeated the ground for possession and gave no details of the specific complaints

The council claimed possession for breach of the terms of the tenancy (Housing Act 1985 Sch 2 Ground 1). The notice seeking possession set out the relevant terms but in the section marked 'Particulars' it merely repeated the terms in full, without indicating what conduct was complained of.

Deputy District Judge Braga struck out the possession claim. He held that the function of the notice was to provide a 'warning shot across the bows' for a tenant (see *Torridge DC v Jones* (F2.6)). Here, the notice manifestly failed to detail what activity the tenant had to desist from.

F2.9   **Shaftesbury HA v Rickards**
Shelter's Housing Law Update, Issue 8; September 2005; 21 June 2005, Cheltenham County Court

Same NSP cannot be relied on for two separate claims for possession

Ms Rickards was an assured tenant. On 28 June 2004 her landlord served a Housing Act 1988 s8 notice seeking possession. On 7 December 2004 possession proceedings were issued on the basis of rent arrears. However, the defendant paid off the arrears before the hearing. The court made no order on the claim for possession but ordered the defendant to pay half the costs of issue. Later, the defendant fell into arrears again because of difficulties with housing benefit. Relying on the original notice, the landlord began new possession proceedings with a hearing on 21 June 2005.

A district judge accepted the defendant's submission that the same notice could not be used to found two separate claims for possession. He declined to strike out the claim but adjourned it generally on condition that the landlord 'got its house in order' with regards service of a notice, the defendant paid the original costs and sorted out her housing benefit claim.

F2.10   **Slough BC v Robbins**
[1996] CLY 3832, Slough County Court

Particulars in NSP need to state clearly nature of the case against the tenant

The council claimed possession relying on Housing Act 1985 Sch 2 Ground 2 (nuisance). The notice seeking possession gave particulars as follows:

> Numerous complaints have been received over a period of time that annoyance and nuisance is being caused to your neighbours by noise and disruptive behaviour. This nuisance and annoyance has been investigated by my staff and I believe the complaints to be substantiated.

District Judge Fortgang held that the purpose of a s83 notice was to ensure that the tenant knew very clearly the nature of the case against him. That was not achieved by the present notice, which was, accordingly, defective. The proceedings had to be struck out.

F2.11   **South Bucks DC v Francis**
[1985] CLY 1900, Slough County Court

Detailed particulars of nuisance and deterioration in condition of premises required in NSP; late request to amend NSP refused

The council took possession proceedings, claiming nuisance or annoyance to neighbours (now Housing Act 1985 Sch 2 Ground 2) and deterioration in the condition of the premises (now Housing Act 1985 Sch 2 Ground 3). However, the notice seeking possession (NSP) gave insufficient particulars of the grounds.

The court held that Housing Act 1980 s33(2) (now Housing Act 1985 s83(2)(c)) required detailed particulars, which should be similar to those required under Law of Property Act 1925 s146. It must be obvious to tenants what they must do. Although there was discretion to allow amendment of the NSP (now contained in Housing Act 1985 s84(3)), the council would not be permitted 'at a late stage' in the proceedings to amend the NSP to include a schedule of dilapidations and particulars of nuisance which ought to have been included in the original notice.

F2.12   *Waltham Forest LBC v England*
March 1994 *Legal Action* 11, Bow County Court

Particulars merely referring to 'major refurbishment scheme' defective

The council sought possession under Housing Act 1985 Sch 2 Ground 10 (redevelopment). The notice seeking possession recited the ground and set out as particulars 'major refurbishment scheme'.

HHJ Medawar QC dismissed the proceedings. The notice gave no particulars about the form of redevelopment proposed. It was no answer for the council to assert that the tenant's refusal of access has led to them being unable to be more precise until possession was recovered.

F3   ## Notice of proceedings for possession (Housing Act 1988)

Before bringing possession proceedings against assured tenants, landlords must either serve a 'notice of proceedings for possession' in accordance with Housing Act 1988 s8 or 8A, or (in cases other than Ground 8) persuade the court to dispense with that requirement on the ground that it is just and equitable to do so.. The relevant form is contained in the Assured Tenancies and Agricultural Occupancies (Forms) Regulations 1997 SI No 194 and states that the landlord must, among other things, 'give the full text of each ground which is being relied upon'. Regulation 2 of the Regulations provides that a notice may be in 'a form substantially to the same effect' as the prescribed form.

Court of Appeal

F3.1   *Kelsey Housing Association v King*
(1996) 28 HLR 270, CA

Discretion to dispense with NSP exercised; applications to strike out possession proceedings where failure to comply with notice provisions should be made promptly

The defendants were assured tenants of the plaintiff housing association. On 9 February 1994 the housing association served a notice to quit. No s8 notice was served. In May 1994 the association issued possession proceedings relying on Grounds 12 and 14 (breaches of obligations and nuisance and annoyance). In an appendix to the summons it set out the allegations of nuisance, including a reference to a conviction for actual bodily harm on a neighbour. At the trial of a preliminary issue, HHJ Kennedy held that there had been 'a virtually total failure to comply with' section 8. However, he also held that it was just and equitable to dispense with the notice, having regard, among other things, to the delay in objecting to the notice, the effect on neighbours and the effect on the defendants of not having been served with proper particulars. He concluded that they had known of the allegations for many months and that there had been no prejudice to them. The tenants appealed and argued that (a) as the court could not 'entertain' the proceedings unless it dispensed with the notice, in exercising its discretion it could only take account of events occurring before the possession claim was issued and (b) on the facts, the tenants had had insufficient notice of the nature of the complaints before the issue of proceedings to justify dispensing with the notice requirement.

The Court of Appeal dismissed the appeal. Butler-Sloss and Aldous LJJ held that the judge was not confined to considering matters before issue and his exercise of discretion would not be interfered with. In deciding whether it is just and equitable to dispense with service, a court should 'weigh all the factors before it' and 'take all the circumstances into account, both from the view of the landlord and the tenant'. In many cases, the fact that tenants had not been given 'an opportunity to put right what it is alleged had gone wrong' would be significant, but in this case they had had ample time. The attitude of the court in deciding what is just and equitable should be the same as in the Rent Act cases such as *Fernandes v Parvardin* (G24.5), and *Bradshaw and Martyn v Baldwin-Wiseman* (G24.3). Applications to strike out possession proceedings where there has been a failure to comply with section 8 should be made promptly.

F3.2   *Knowsley Housing Trust v Revell; Helena Housing Ltd v Curtis*
[2003] EWCA Civ 496; [2003] HLR 63; [2004] LGR 236; (2003) *Times* 17 April

Exercise of discretion to dispense with NSP (where stock transfer) needed to be given individual consideration on notice to the tenants

Local authority landlords served notices seeking possession under Housing Act 1985 s83 on a number of secure tenants and began county court possession claims. They then transferred their housing stock to registered social landlords. As a result of the stock transfers, the landlords were no longer within the landlord condition (Housing Act 1985 s80(1)). The tenancies ceased to be secure. By virtue of Housing Act 1988 s1(1) they became assured tenancies. The tenants contended that, subject to Housing Act 1988 s8(1)(b) (the power to dispense with notices), the court had no jurisdiction to entertain the possession proceedings unless the current landlords served s8 notices. The landlords applied to the court to dispense with the need for s8 notices and contended that it was appropriate for the dispensation to be granted in all of the cases, without having regard to the particular circumstances of individual cases. The judge accepted those submissions and granted the dispensation sought. The tenants appealed.

The Court of Appeal allowed the appeals. The court had no jurisdiction to entertain the claims unless s8 notices were served, or the court exercised the power to dispense with notice under s8(1)(b). The discretion was wide enough to allow substitution of the new landlord as claimant and dispensation of s8 notice where the reality was that the new landlord relied on the same breach of the same term and the relief sought was no different. However, it was not legitimate for a court to dispense with s8 notices without some consideration of any objection which might be taken by the tenant by reference to the facts of his or her case (see *Kelsey HA v King* (F3.1). If the landlords wished to continue with the possession proceedings, they would have to comply with CPR Pt 19.4 to obtain an order for substitution and apply to amend the pleadings, or consider commencing fresh proceedings. The cases were remitted to a district judge for a hearing to determine whether it was right to dispense with notice. Such consideration should not be dealt with on a without notice basis or without a hearing. The issue should be heard at the same hearing as to the possession claim.

F3.3   *Marath v MacGillivray*
(1996) 28 HLR 484; (1996) 72 P&CR D25, CA

NSP relying on Ground 8 (mandatory rent arrears ground); s8(2) allowed particulars, as well as grounds, to be amended with leave

The defendant was an assured tenant. After failure by the local authority to pay housing benefit, the landlords brought possession proceedings relying on rent arrears, including the mandatory ground in Housing Act 1988 Sch 2 Ground 8. A notice, purporting to comply with Housing Act 1988 s8, was served before the issue of proceedings, stating as particulars of the arrears, 'At a meeting between the landlord and tenant on 24 July 1994 the arrears were agreed at £103.29 ... Since that date no payments of rent have been made.' No figure for the arrears at the date of the notice was given.

The Court of Appeal held that a notice from a landlord to a tenant complies with Housing Act 1988 s8 provided that:

> ... it is made clear ... that more than three months' rent is at the date of that notice unpaid and due and provided also that in some way or other that notice makes it clear either how much, or how the tenant can ascertain how much, is alleged to be due.

It is not necessary for the notice to contain a schedule of the arrears. The Court of Appeal also indicated that: (a) under s8(2) a court may allow particulars to be added if they have not been given earlier; (b) the address of the landlord's agents in a s20 notice exhibited to an affidavit was sufficient to comply with Landlord and Tenant Act 1987 s48; and (c) the judge was entitled to find that over 13 weeks' rent was owing at the date of the hearing, despite the fact that housing benefit was owed by the local authority and was paid after the hearing, with the result that the arrears were reduced below the equivalent of 13 weeks' rent.

Note: Since amendments made by the Housing Act 1996, Ground 8 is satisfied by eight weeks or two months arrears, rather than 12 weeks or three months.

F3.4   *Mountain v Hastings*
(1993) 25 HLR 427; [1993] 2 EGLR 53, CA

Substance of grounds for possession must be set out; NSP relying on Ground 8 defective

A notice of intention to bring proceedings given by the landlord, under the heading 'Ground 8', simply stated, 'At least three months' rent is unpaid', although later, under 'Particulars of Ground', it did state the total of arrears claimed.

Ralph Gibson LJ held that, although the full text of the ground as set out in Housing Act 1988 Sch 2 might not have to be repeated verbatim:

> ... the words used [must] set out fully the substance of the ground so that the notice is adequate to achieve the legislative purpose of the provision. That purpose ... is to give ... information ... to enable the tenant to consider what she should do and, with or without advice, to do that which is in her power and which will best protect her against the loss of her home. ((1993) 25 HLR at 433)

The notice was defective because it had omitted the words 'both at the date of service of the Notice ... and at the date of the hearing' and the explanation that '"rent" means rent lawfully due from the tenant'. The Court of Appeal also held that the words in s8(2) which allow a court to alter or add to the grounds specified in a notice assume that there is a valid notice and are solely directed to the possibility of adding to or deleting grounds. The tenant's appeal was allowed and the case remitted to the county court for rehearing.

F3.5   *North British Housing Association v Sheridan*
[2000] L&TR 115; (2000) 32 HLR 346; (1999) 78 P&CR D38, CA

Landlord not limited by express terms in tenancy restricting the circumstances in which possession could be sought, but just and equitable to dispense with NSP

The defendant was an assured tenant. The tenancy agreement provided that (1) before bringing possession proceedings the landlord would give four weeks' notice and (2) that it would only rely on certain grounds for possession which were set out in full in the agreement. (At the time the tenancy was granted, these terms reflected the statutory requirements. These requirements were later amended.) The tenant was convicted of an arrestable offence under the Protection from Harassment Act 1997 in the locality of the dwelling-house. The victim was his daughter, who lived three streets away on the same estate. The landlord immediately served a s8 notice, which stated that proceedings would not be begun until after 15 June 1998, the date on which the notice was served. HHJ Appleton made a possession order. The defendant appealed contending that (1) the s8 notice did not give four weeks' notice and (2) that, although the conviction came within Housing Act 1988 Sch 2 Ground 14 as amended by Housing Act 1996, it did not come within the unamended version of the ground included in the tenancy agreement.

His appeal was dismissed. Although landlords are not precluded from giving their tenants additional rights, the parties to this agreement must have intended that the court should retain its power under s8(1)(b) to dispense with the need for a s8 notice if it were 'just and equitable'. Although the judge was not asked to consider this, the Court of Appeal has all the powers of the trial judge. It decided that it should entertain an application to dispense with the requirement and should grant that dispensation. Second, it had not been the intention of the parties to the tenancy agreement 'to restrict the landlord for ever to the statutory grounds for possession as they stood in the 1988 Act and the intention must have been that, if the statutory grounds for possession (or other related provisions) were amended, neither party would be disentitled from relying on the amended provisions'. Any other construction 'would fossilise the agreement'.

County courts

F3.6   *McShane v William Sutton Trust*
(1997) 1 L&T Rev D67; December 1997 Legal Action 13, Warrington County Court

Exercise of discretion to dispense with s8 notice

The tenant, who was aged 18, was granted an assured tenancy on 19 May 1997. There were allegations that she had breached many of the covenants against causing nuisance or annoyance almost immediately. On 28 May 1997 a solicitor for the landlord housing association appeared ex parte before a district judge and obtained orders that it was just and equitable to dispense with service of a Housing Act 1988 s8 notice and to abridge the time for service of possession proceedings. The judge also granted an injunction and listed the hearing of the possession claim on 4 June 1997. The housing association had made no attempt to serve a notice or the possession summons before the ex parte hearing, although it would have been quite easy for it to do so. At the hearing on 4 June the tenant appeared and applied for an adjournment so that she could obtain legal advice. The district judge refused that request, and, after hearing evidence, ordered the tenant to give up possession the following day. The tenant appealed.

HHJ Daley, granting the appeal, held: although (a) there is nothing to prevent a landlord from serving a s8 notice on the same day as proceedings are commenced and (b) there is nothing in the rules preventing a landlord from applying ex parte to dispense with service of a s8 notice, (c) following *Kelsey Housing Association v King* (F3.1), it was not possible for a judge deciding whether or not to dispense with service of a s8 notice to weigh up all factors from both points of view without the tenant being in court; (d) the decision to dispense with service was plainly wrong; (e) following *R v Kingston upon Thames Justices ex p Martin* [1994] Imm AR 172, DC, the matters to be considered in relation to the application for an adjournment included the importance of the proceedings, the risk of the applicant being prejudiced, the convenience of the court, the interests of justice, the desirability of not delaying future litigants by adjourning early and the extent to which the party applying for the adjournment had been responsible for creating the difficulty; (f) no reasonable judge in the circumstances should have refused this tenant the opportunity to have a short adjournment on strict terms. The decision not to adjourn was 'a wholly unreasonable exercise of his discretion, a breach of natural justice and plainly wrong.' The possession order was set aside and the action re-listed for trial on 11 July 1997.

F4 **Notices to quit served by tenants**

It is now settled law that, if there is a joint secure tenancy, one of the joint tenants, acting alone, may terminate the tenancy (and security of tenure) by serving a notice to quit on the landlord. A notice to quit must comply both with the statutory requirements of Protection from Eviction Act 1977 s5 and the common law.

House of Lords

F4.1 *Hammersmith and Fulham LBC v Monk*

[1992] 1 AC 478; [1991] 3 WLR 1144; [1992] 1 All ER 1; (1992) 24 HLR 207; (1991) 63 P&CR 373; [1992] 1 EGLR 65; (1992) 90 LGR 30; [1992] 09 EG 135, HL

Service of NTQ by one joint tenant terminates tenancy

The defendant had been one of two joint tenants. Without his knowledge, the other tenant gave notice to quit to the council to terminate the tenancy. The defendant did not leave and the council sought possession.

The House of Lords, upholding a series of Court of Appeal decisions, including *Greenwich LBC v McGrady* (F4.8), held that, in the absence of any express term of tenancy to the contrary, one joint tenant can unilaterally terminate a periodic joint tenancy by giving proper notice to quit. Lord Browne-Wilkinson doubted whether the tenant who gave the notice to quit was in breach of trust towards the other joint tenant, but even if she was, that did not make the notice to quit a nullity. Accordingly, possession was granted.

F4.2 *Harrow LBC v Johnstone*

[1997] 1 WLR 459; [1997] 1 All ER 929; (1997) 29 HLR 475; (1997) 95 LGR 470, HL

NTQ by one joint tenant terminated the tenancy despite a court order restraining that tenant from excluding the other tenant from the premises

On the separation of joint secure tenants who were married, the husband obtained an order that his wife must not 'exclude or attempt to exclude [him] from the [house]'. Later she served a notice to quit and was rehoused by the council. The council in turn asserted that the notice had determined the joint tenancy (see *Hammersmith and Fulham LBC v Monk* (F4.1) and sought possession from the husband. The trial judge refused the order and the council's appeal was dismissed by the Court of Appeal.

The House of Lords allowed the appeal. The wife had not been in 'contempt' of the earlier order in giving notice. The earlier order had not been made in any jurisdiction enabling the court to adjust or restrain dealing with property – it had not, for example, been made in matrimonial litigation. At best it had been concerned with rights of occupancy under the tenancy, not with the future of the tenancy itself. The council could not be criticised for acting on the notice it had received. It could not be said that permitting possession to be obtained against the background of the earlier order was an affront to the integrity of the judicial process which ought to be restrained.

F4.3   *Harrow LBC v Qazi*

[2003] UKHL 43; [2004] 1 AC 983; [2003] 3 WLR 792; [2003] 4 All ER 461; [2003] UKHRR 974; [2003] HLR 75; [2004] L&TR 9; [2004] 1 P&CR 19; (2003) *Times* 1 August (see L1.1)

Meaning of 'home' for purposes of ECHR art 8; art 8(1) not breached by un-qualified right to possession following service of NTQ by one joint tenant

F4.4   *Newlon Housing Trust v Al-Sulaimen*

[1999] 1 AC 313; [1998] 3 WLR 451; [1998] 4 All ER 1; (1998) 30 HLR 1132; (1998) *Times* 20 August, HL

As NTQ ended tenancy, there was no 'matrimonial asset' to dispose of; question of whether husband could restrain wife from serving NTQ left open

A married couple held a joint secure tenancy of their home. The wife left, a decree of divorce was pronounced (it is not clear from the report whether the decree was nisi or absolute) and she then gave unilateral notice to quit, which brought the tenancy to an end: *Hammersmith and Fulham LBC v Monk* (F4.1). The landlords sought possession against the ex-husband. He applied for an adjournment so that he could make an application in the divorce proceedings for (a) an order setting aside the notice to quit on the ground that it was the disposal of a matrimonial asset designed to defeat a transfer order (Matrimonial Causes Act 1973 s37) and (b) transfer into his sole name. HHJ Tibber refused the adjournment and ordered possession. In the Court of Appeal, counsel for the landlords conceded that the court could make an order setting aside the termination of the tenancy on the ground that it was a disposition. The appeal was allowed but the landlord appealed to the House of Lords. There, counsel for the landlord success-fully applied for leave to withdraw the concession.

The House of Lords, allowing the appeal, held that, although the sur-render of a subsisting proprietary interest could be a disposition, it is essential to the notion of a disposition of property that there should be property which can be disposed of. Here, as the tenancy had been termi-nated, it could not be revived and the husband had no defence to the pos-session claim. The question of whether an order could have been obtained to restrain the ex-wife from giving a notice to quit was left open.

Court of Appeal

F4.5   *Bater v Bater; Bater v Greenwich LBC*

[1999] 4 All ER 944; (2000) 32 HLR 127; [2000] L&TR 1; (1999) *Times* 28 September, CA

Court had no jurisdiction to set aside NTQ even if it also extinguished right to buy; joint tenant could seek an injunction under Matrimonial Causes Act (now Family Law Act) or Children Act 1989 restraining other tenant

Mr and Mrs Bater were joint secure tenants. They claimed the right to buy and the council made a discounted offer to them. However, their mar-riage later ran into difficulties and Mrs Bater gave notice to the council terminating the joint tenancy. The council began possession proceedings against Mr Bater. He made an application under Matrimonial Causes Act 1973 for the avoidance of a disposition of property. The council served a notice on Mr Bater denying that he had the right to buy as he was no longer a secure tenant.

The Court of Appeal, following *Newlon Housing Trust v Al-Sulaimen* (F4.4) held that the notice terminating the tenancy was not a disposition of property for the purposes of Matrimonial Causes Act 1973 s37(2)(b) and so the court had no jurisdiction to set it aside. The nature of the notice did not change because it ended the right to buy as well as the secure tenancy. It was not necessary for the court to decide whether the right to buy was property within the meaning of s37(2). The right to buy could not be brought to fruition unless the secure tenancy continued to the ultimate point of completion. However, where joint tenants are party to divorce proceedings, the court has wide inherent powers to control the acts or omissions of spouses if the act or omission would have the effect of harassing or molesting the other party or would adversely affect the welfare of any child. Equally, such inherent power can be exercised to prevent any act which would have the consequence of diminishing or curtailing the court's statutory powers to distribute or redistribute capital or income. Similar powers exist where parties are not married but have children under Children Act 1989 and wardship. Accordingly, where the unilateral act of one tenant could destroy the interests of both, the joint tenant who would be prejudiced by service of a notice should seek an undertaking or an injunction.

F4.6   *Bradney v Birmingham CC; Birmingham CC v McCann*
[2003] EWCA Civ 1783; [2004] HLR 27

ECHR art 8 is not available as a defence to possession proceedings brought by a local authority to enforce its ordinary property rights

Mr Bradney and Ms Bromwell were joint secure tenants. Ms Bromwell asked Birmingham, their landlord, to remove her name from the tenancy, leaving it in Mr Bradney's sole name. At Birmingham's request Ms Bromwell signed a notice to quit. There was no evidence that it was explained to her that by giving notice to quit she would bring to an end Mr Bradney's right to remain in the property. His subsequent request for a sole tenancy was refused and he was required to vacate. A possession order was made. Mr Bradney appealed.

Mr McCann and his wife were also joint tenants. Mrs McCann was rehoused by the council on the grounds of domestic violence. At the council's instigation, she signed a notice to quit. She did not realise that the notice to quit would bring the joint tenancy to an end. Mr McCann sought to transfer the tenancy into his own name, but was told that the tenancy had come to an end and given notice to vacate. However, the council's possession claim was dismissed. It appealed.

Following *Harrow LBC v Qazi* (L1.1), the Court of Appeal dismissed Mr Bradney's appeal and allowed the council's appeal in the McCann case. ECHR article 8 is not available as a defence to possession proceedings brought by a local authority to enforce its ordinary property rights. There was nothing exceptional about the circumstances of these cases, or improper or unlawful in the conduct of the local authority, which could give the former tenants a defence under article 8 to prevent the local authority from enforcing its right to immediate possession of the properties. The fact that the council had procured the termination of the tenancy by one joint tenant against the wishes of both joint tenants was not a ground for distinguishing *Qazi*. Nothing had happened after the service of the notice to quit which fundamentally altered the rights and wrongs of the proposed evictions so that the local authority might be required to justify its claim to override article 8.

The House of Lords subsequently refused a petition for leave to appeal.

F4.7   **Crawley BC v Ure**
[1996] QB 13; [1995] 3 WLR 95; [1996] 1 All ER 724; (1995) 27 HLR 524; (1996) 71 P&CR 12, CA

Service of NTQ by one joint tenant was not breach of trust for sale

Mr Ure defended the council's possession claim on the grounds that: (a) in giving unilateral notice to quit, his wife had acted in breach of the 'trust for sale' under which their joint tenancy was held because she had not consulted him (Law of Property Act 1925 s26(3)); and (b) the council could not rely on the notice, because it had been party to the breach of trust in advising and encouraging her to give notice.

The Court of Appeal dismissed his appeal against a possession order. It held that Mrs Ure's decision to give notice to quit because she no longer wished to be bound was not a 'positive act' attracting the consultation requirements of s26(3).

F4.8   **Greenwich LBC v McGrady**
(1982) 6 HLR 36; (1982) 46 P&CR 223; (1982) 267 EG 515; (1982) 81 LGR 288, CA

NTQ served by one joint tenant is effective; Housing Act did not apply to protect the former tenant

Mr and Mrs McGrady were joint tenants. They divorced. Mrs McGrady left the premises but later served a notice to quit on the council. Mr McGrady stayed in the premises and the council took possession proceedings.

The Court of Appeal held that, although all joint tenants have to agree to a surrender of a tenancy, a notice to quit served by one tenant is effective. Furthermore, once the tenancy had been determined, Mr McGrady was not entitled to the protection of the Housing Act 1980 (now the Housing Act 1985) because the Act operates to give security where landlords serve notices to quit, not where tenants give notice to quit.

F4.9   **Hackney LBC v Snowden**
[2001] L&TR 60; (2001) 33 HLR 554, CA

Open to landlord and tenant to agree to treat NTQ as valid and thereby waive the requirement of four weeks' notice

Ms Pidcock, a secure tenant, made allegations of domestic violence against Mr Snowden, her husband. As a result, the council agreed to rehouse her temporarily. She then signed a notice to quit expressed to take effect three days later and confirmed that she would vacate the premises from that date.

She paid no further rent and was then rehoused. Mr Snowden requested that the council transfer the original tenancy to him. The council refused to recognise him as a tenant and sought possession of the premises. In his defence Mt Snowden contended that the tenancy had never been validly terminated as the notice had not complied with Protection from Eviction Act 1977 s5(1). He counterclaimed for a declaration that he occupied the premises as a tenant. HHJ Graham made a possession order, holding that the principle in *Elsden v Pick* [1980] 1 WLR 898 applied. The parties had agreed to treat the invalid notice as effective and the tenancy had, accordingly, been determined by service of the notice. He made no finding on when the agreement had been made. Mr Snowden appealed, contending that it was necessary to show that the agreement had been reached before the time expressed for the notice to take effect.

His appeal was dismissed. It did not matter when the agreement was reached provided that agreement was reached that the notice would take effect and that such agreement was not invalidated by being made before the notice was given. Section 5(1) was for the benefit of the tenant. It was open to the parties to agree after service to treat the notice as valid and thereby waive the requirement of four weeks' notice. The fact that the tenant's spouse had rights under Matrimonial Homes Act 1983 s1 (now Family Law Act 1996 s30) did not restrict the tenant's right to bring the tenancy to an end. There was sufficient evidence of such agreement. Evidence that the authority had voided the rent account, had not sought further rent and had rehoused the tenant provided sufficient evidence to show that the authority considered the tenancy terminated. The notice served by Ms Pidcock was effective to terminate the tenancy.

F4.10   *Hounslow LBC v Pilling*

[1993] 1 WLR 1242; [1994] 1 All ER 432; (1993) 25 HLR 305; (1993) 66 P&CR 22; [1993] 2 EGLR 59; (1993) 91 LGR 573; [1993] 26 EG 123, CA

NTQ served by one joint tenant which did not comply with the statutory requirements was ineffective despite waiver clause

One joint secure tenant, without informing the other, delivered to the council on Friday 6 December 1991 a letter stating, 'I wish to terminate my tenancy held on the above mentioned property with immediate effect'. The council treated the letter as a notice to quit, terminating the tenancy from the following rent day (Monday 9 December 1991) and brought proceedings to claim possession from the other joint tenant. A clause in the standard-form tenancy permitted the council to waive the usual requirement of four weeks' notice.

The Court of Appeal held that: (a) the other joint tenant was entitled to rely on the Protection from Eviction Act 1977 (requiring a tenant's notice to quit to be of a minimum duration of four weeks) – the 'waiver' clause in the agreement could not be used by the council and the notice-giver to contract out of that protection; and (b) the attempt to bring the tenancy to an end 'immediately' with less than even the minimum common-law notice of one week was akin to an attempt to activate a break clause in the tenancy and, as such, required the participation of both joint tenants. The notice was bad and the appeal against a possession order was allowed.

F4.11   *Kensington and Chelsea RLBC v O'Sullivan*
[2003] EWCA Civ 371; [2003] 1 FCR 687; [2003] HLR 58; (2003) *Times* 27 March

Possession order did not violate occupant's ECHR art 8 and art 14 rights

In 1970 Mr O'Sullivan was granted a sole weekly tenancy of a five-bedroomed house. It became a secure tenancy under Housing Act 1985. In 2001 he served a notice to quit on the landlord council and moved into sheltered accommodation. He informed the council that his marriage had broken down and that he had been living in the property on his own. In fact, his wife and one of her grandchildren had also been living with him. The council brought possession proceedings against her. She defended, contending that (a) the grant of a sole tenancy to Mr O'Sullivan was an act of discrimination contrary to ECHR article 14; and (b) she was entitled to relief under ECHR article 8. HHJ Green QC made an order for possession finding that article 14 was not engaged.

Mrs O'Sullivan's appeal was dismissed. There was no discrimination contrary to article 14. It was an important part of the council's housing allocation policy only to grant one tenancy on the termination of a joint tenancy – either of the property in which the former tenant remained or, if that property was not of the right size, by transfer to another property. It was contrary to the policy to grant two tenancies because that would enable one of the previous occupiers to jump the housing queue. There was no breach of the ECHR, either when the original tenancy was granted in 1970, because the property was not then Mrs O'Sullivan's home, or between 1983 and 1991 when she could have been made a joint tenant without objection from Mr O'Sullivan, because there was no positive obligation on the council to make her a joint tenant. Second, the possession order did not violate any of Mrs O'Sullivan's rights under article 8. The council's decision was not vulnerable to successful challenge by way of judicial review on public law grounds. It was not open to Mrs O'Sullivan to argue that there was some defence to the possession proceedings based on an assertion that, although the council was otherwise entitled to possession, a possession order was not necessary for the protection of the rights and freedoms of others. (See *Sheffield CC v Smart* (T55.7) and *Michalak v Wandsworth LBC* (E14.9).)

F4.12   *Newham LBC v Kibata*
[2003] EWCA Civ 1785; [2004] 15 EG 106; [2004] HLR 28

Council had not acted in breach of its public law duties in obtaining possession after service of NTQ

Newham let a flat to Ms Nkurkiye on an introductory tenancy, which, after a year, became a secure tenancy. She lived there with her son and Mr Kibata, whom she later married. However, after making serious allegations of domestic violence against Mr Kibata, she left the flat with her son and applied to be rehoused. Mr Kibata disputed the allegations and remained in the property. The council warned him it would be seeking possession. Ms Nkurkiye was required to serve a notice to quit which validly terminated the tenancy. Deputy District Judge Backhouse dismissed Newham's claim for possession and held that the council had been in breach of its public law duties and standards in failing to act fairly towards Mr Kibata.

The Court of Appeal allowed the council's appeal. After considering *Harrow LBC v Qazi* (L1.1), Mummery LJ said that the service of the notice to quit was a lawful exercise of Ms Nkurkiye's rights as a tenant. It was not procured by the council in an unlawful, unfair or underhand sense, nor was it a device in the sense of an inappropriate procedure improperly used by the council to avoid having to establish Housing Act 1985 Sch 2 Ground 2A. The council could have acted with more concern for Mr Kibata's situation, but its conduct did not involve a breach of any of its public law duties or give Mr Kibata a defence to a claim for possession in the county court. The council had acted in accordance with the law, both in respect of the formulation and application of its domestic violence policy and in respect of its part in the decision of Ms Nkurkiye to exercise her right to terminate the tenancy. There was no duty to await a judicial determination of the truth of his wife's allegations before deciding whether or not to issue possession proceedings. On the facts before the county court, there was nothing incompatible with the ECHR in the court making a possession order. Furthermore, the council had not acted in breach of article 6. The obtaining of a notice to quit from Ms Nkurkiye did not amount to a 'determination' of Mr Kibata's civil rights. A possession order was made.

F4.13   *Notting Hill Housing Trust v Brackley*
[2001] EWCA Civ 601; [2002] HLR 212; [2001] 35 EG 106; [2001] L&TR 467; (2001) 82 P&CR D48; (2001) *Times* 15 June; [2001] 18 EGCS 175(CS), CA

Service of NTQ by one joint tenant was not a breach of trust

Mr and Mrs Brackley were joint tenants of a property let by the claimant landlord in March 1997 as a periodic tenancy. The tenancy was terminable on four weeks' notice. In May 1999 Mrs Brackley left the property and, on the advice of the landlord, served a notice to quit terminating the tenancy. She did not consult Mr Brackley before doing so. The tenancy duly determined and the landlord sought possession of the property, relying on the notice to quit. At trial, Mr Brackley argued that, since the joint tenancy had been held under a trust for land, his wife had acted in breach of trust by not consulting him, a beneficiary under the trust, before giving notice to quit: the giving of the notice to quit was a 'function' of a trustee of land within the meaning of the word as used in the Trusts of Land and Appointment of Trustees Act 1996 s11; that section imposed on a trustee of land an obligation to consult with beneficiaries before executing a relevant function. On 16 November 2000, HHJ Cowell ordered possession of the property, having held as a preliminary issue that the giving of the notice to quit was not a function for the purposes of s11. Mr Brackley appealed.

His appeal was dismissed. The reasoning in *Hammersmith and Fulham LBC v Monk* (F4.1) and *Crawley BC v Ure* (F4.7), decided under the Law of Property Act 1925, applied. The giving of a notice to quit by a joint tenant was an indication by that joint tenant of his or her unwillingness that the tenancy should continue beyond the end of the period when the notice took effect. It was not the exercise by a trustee of a power or duty or 'function' within the meaning of the word in s11. It was no more than the exercise by one joint tenant of his right to withhold his consent to the tenancy continuing into a further period. The 1996 Act had not affected, nor was there any evidence that it had ever been intended to affect, the operation of a periodic tenancy or the consequences of giving a notice to quit in circumstances such as the present.

CHAPTER G

Security of tenure: grounds for possession

continued

G1 **Introduction**

This chapter includes cases on the ambit of grounds for possession against all types of tenants with full security of tenure: secure tenants under Housing Act 1985, assured tenants under Housing Act 1988 and protected or statutory tenants under Rent Act 1977.

G2 **Rent arrears**

Housing Act 1985 Sch 2 Ground 1 provides a discretionary ground for possession where 'rent lawfully due from the tenant has not been paid'.

Housing Act 1988 Sch 2 contains three grounds for possession against assured and assured shorthand tenants based on rent arrears. Ground 8, a mandatory ground, applies where there are eight weeks, or two months, arrears both at the date of service of the s8 notice and at the date of the hearing. Ground 10, which is discretionary, applies where there were rent arrears both at the date when proceedings were begun and, unless the court considers it 'just and equitable' to dispense with the need for service of a notice prior to issue, when the s8 notice was served. Ground 11, which is also discretionary, applies where there has been persistent delay in paying rent which is due.

Rent Act 1977 Sch 15 Case 1 gives a discretionary ground for possession where any rent lawfully due from the tenant has not been paid.

G3 **Rent arrears (Housing Act 1985 Sch 2 Ground 1)**

Court of Appeal

G3.1 *Notting Hill Housing Trust v Jones*
[1999] L&TR 397, CA

Landlord could not rely on arrears of rent incurred before assignment of tenancy

Mr Jones was a secure tenant. Mrs Jones obtained an order for the transfer of the tenancy and it was assigned to her in January 1997. Her husband's rent account had been in arrears and in February 1997 she made a written agreement to discharge those arrears. Thereafter, she paid sufficient to cover her own rent but the trust obtained a suspended order for possession based on over £400 arrears still outstanding.

The Court of Appeal allowed Mrs Jones's appeal. On the claim for possession, the court held that Housing Act 1985 Sch 2 Ground 1 ('rent lawfully due from the tenant has not been paid or an obligation of the tenancy has been broken or not performed') was not made out. The general rule is that an assignee tenant is not liable for an assignor tenant's arrears and so the rent was not 'lawfully due' from Mrs Jones. There was no breach of obligation 'of the tenancy' as the agreement made in February 1997 was no part of the tenancy and was at most a personal obligation 'of the tenant'. The money claim could not be sustained because the agreement relied on had been made after the assignment and so without consideration. It was unenforceable. The action for possession and the money claim were dismissed.

County courts

G3.2   *Lewisham LBC v Simba-Tola*

June 1993 *Legal Action* 14, Bromley County Court

'Rent' means the indebtedness arising under the tenancy and includes water rates etc

The council claimed possession under the first limb of Housing Act 1985 Sch 2 Ground 1 ('rent lawfully due has not been paid') and relied on a notice seeking possession containing the words 'Arrears of rent which at 22/1/90 amounted to £714.54.' That amount, and the higher amount owing at trial, was entirely attributable to non-payment of general rates, water rates and other sundry charges, the tenant having received full housing benefit for rent throughout most of the tenancy.

HHJ Colyer QC reviewed the Rent Act and common-law authorities on the meaning of 'rent' and held that in Ground 1 it means 'the indebtedness arising under the tenancy'. Accordingly, the notice was valid and the ground fulfilled. In the light of the specific facts of the case, possession was granted, suspended on terms.

Local government ombudsman reports

G3.3   *Investigation 90/B/1546 (Birmingham CC)*

11 October 1991

Maladministration where direct payments not sought from DSS

A tenant in rent arrears and receiving income support agreed to make small regular repayments. Birmingham City Council failed to seek 'arrears direct' payments from the DSS but applied for a possession order. The tenant was advised 'not to worry' about attending court and did not attend. A suspended possession order and costs were granted.

The ombudsman found this to be maladministration and decided that the council should refund the costs of the court hearing and pay the tenant £250.

G3.4   *Investigation 90/B/2514 (Wychavon DC)*

23 March 1992

Overpayment of housing benefit should not be shown as rent arrears

A tenant was overpaid housing benefit. Wychavon District Council decided to recover the overpayment but did not notify the tenant promptly or comply with the notice requirements (Housing Benefit (General) Regulations 1987 SI No 1971 Sch 6). The overpayment was entered as 'arrears' on the tenant's rent account.

The ombudsman directed that the overpayment should not be shown as rent arrears, that the correct information about recovery must be issued and that £250 compensation should be paid.

G3.5 *Local Government Ombudsman Complaint no 05/B/16773*
(Northampton BC)
27 June 2007

Maladministration where arrears action taken while benefits claim outstanding

Northampton BC took possession proceedings and instructed bailiffs to collect council tax arrears from a woman while her benefits entitlement was unresolved.

The local government ombudsman found that there had been maladministration in that the council delayed excessively in processing benefit claims and appeals and pursued recovery of rent and council tax arrears while benefit claims and appeals were outstanding. He referred to 'serious failings in the Council's administration of housing and council tax benefit and in the recovery of rent and council tax arrears'. The council agreed to apologise, write off an outstanding housing benefit overpayment of £79.46, write off an outstanding balance of £187 on the council tax account, make a payment of one week's housing and council tax benefit and pay additional compensation of £1,865.

G4 Rent arrears (Housing Act 1988 Sch 2 Grounds 8, 10 and 11)

Court of Appeal

G4.1 *Artesian Residential Investments Ltd v Beck*
[2000] QB 541; [2000] 2 WLR 357; [1999] 3 All ER 113; (2000) 32 HLR 107, CA

Relief from forfeiture not available to assured tenant

A fixed-term assured tenancy agreement included a proviso for re-entry and determination if the rent was at any stage 14 days in arrears. The defendant fell into rent arrears before the expiry of the term and the landlord brought possession proceedings relying on Housing Act 1988 Sch 2 Grounds 8 and 10. A possession order was made, but the defendant later paid all the arrears and applied for suspension of the possession order, relying on the relief from forfeiture provisions of County Courts Act 1984 s138.

HHJ Mitchell granted relief but the Court of Appeal held that Housing Act 1988 s5(1) sets out the only routes for bringing an assured tenancy to an end. There is no need for a parallel claim for forfeiture to prevent the contractual tenancy continuing after the granting of an order for possession under the Act. By its express words, s5(1) makes it abundantly clear that an order for possession brings a tenancy to an end. This construction is also borne out by s7(7) which provides that, when the court makes an order for possession on grounds relating to a fixed-term tenancy which has come to an end, any ensuing statutory periodic tenancy which arises on the ending of the fixed-term tenancy ends (without any notice or regardless of the period) on the day on which the order takes effect. Furthermore, s7(3) is explicit, obliging the court mandatorily to make an order for possession if satisfied that any of the grounds in Sch 2 is established subject to, among other things, s6. Section 7(6)(b) does no more than require provision for, eg, forfeiture to be included in the terms of the tenancy, and does not set up forfeiture as an independent ground for terminating the tenancy. As a matter of principle, there is no room for applying County Courts Act 1984 s138. As there is no exercise of a right of re-entry or forfeiture for non-payment of rent, its requirements are not met.

G4.2   **Baygreen Properties Ltd v Gil**

[2002] EWCA Civ 1340; [2002] 49 EG 126; [2003] HLR 12; [2003] L&TR 1; (2002) *Times* 17 July

No jurisdiction to make order unless ground established, by admission or otherwise

The defendant was an assured shorthold tenant. The claimant landlord claimed that she owed at least eight weeks' rent and sought possession, inter alia, under Housing Act 1988 Sch 2 Ground 8. The tenant, by a defence and counterclaim, did not admit that rent had been lawfully due because the landlord had been in breach of its duties to keep the property in repair and to allow quiet enjoyment. The proceedings were compromised at court by a consent order, which provided that the landlord recover possession, all future proceedings be stayed, and the landlord pay the tenant £2,500 before she left the property. A circuit judge enquired of the tenant whether she consented to the order, before approving it. The tenant subsequently appealed against the order for possession on the ground that the judge had not had jurisdiction to make it in the absence of an admission by the tenant that one of the grounds in Sch 2 was satisfied.

The Court of Appeal allowed the tenant's appeal and set aside the possession order. The jurisdiction of the court to make an order for possession under s7 is limited. If the court is not satisfied that a ground under Sch 2 has been established it does not have jurisdiction to make the order. A court is under a duty to determine whether the relevant ground has been established, whether or not it has been raised by the parties. Where a court lacks jurisdiction, it cannot be conferred merely by consent. To confer jurisdiction, an admission that a ground is satisfied, either express or implied, has to be clearly shown. Any consent order should clearly spell out in express terms the admission made by the tenant, or the court should ask the tenant what admission was being made, so that there can be no room for confusion or doubt in the future. In this case, the judge had not asked the tenant whether she was making an admission of at least eight weeks' rent arrears, only whether she had consented to the order.

G4.3   **Bessa Plus v Lancaster**

(1998) 30 HLR 48, CA

Landlord can reject tender of rent from third party unless paying as tenant's agent

A house was let to a tenant on an assured tenancy allowing for direct payment of rent by the council's housing benefit department. One term of the tenancy was that the tenant would not share occupation. Five months after the grant of the tenancy the landlords received a cheque in respect of housing benefit awarded to the tenant's partner who, by this time, was living with her. When the cheque was returned by the landlords, the local authority informed them that the partner was claiming income support 'for the family' but undertook to issue a new cheque in the name of the tenant. However, the council later issued a second cheque in the name of the partner, which was also returned by the landlords. The landlords claimed that the two returned cheques did not count as rent and that they were entitled to a mandatory order for possession under Ground 8 (non-payment of rent).

The Court of Appeal made a possession order, holding that landlords are entitled to reject a tender of rent from a stranger unless that person is paying as agent for the tenant. The plaintiff had not acted unreasonably since acceptance might have constituted a waiver of the covenant against sharing occupation and, as a result, the partner might have had claims to the tenancy as successor to the tenant.

G4.4 *Capital Prime Plus plc v Wills*
(1999) 31 HLR 926, CA

Order did not indicate possession ordered on Ground 8; court should not go behind prima facie meaning of possession order

A landlord brought possession proceedings under Housing Act 1988 Sch 2 Grounds 8, 10 and 11. The defendant filed a defence, denying receipt of a s8 notice seeking possession. At the hearing, Ground 8 would have been made out if the landlord could have proved service of the s8 notice, but a suspended possession order was made, apparently by consent, without any evidence being called. The terms of the order were breached and a warrant was issued. Deputy District Judge Dabezies dismissed an application to suspend the warrant, holding that, in view of Housing Act 1988 s9(6), he had no power to suspend because when the possession order was made the court must have been satisfied that Ground 8 was made out. The tenant's appeal to Recorder Pawlak was dismissed.

The Court of Appeal allowed the tenant's further appeal. It was clear that neither the judge who made the suspended possession order nor Recorder Pawlak gave any thought to whether the landlord had served a s8 notice. There was nothing in the suspended possession order to show that the landlord was entitled to a possession order under Ground 8. At execution stage the court cannot revisit factual issues which were or should have been resolved at the original hearing. At a later stage a court should not go behind the prima facie meaning of the possession order in question. As the order had not been made under Ground 8, the court had power to suspend the warrant. The case was remitted to the county court to consider the merits of the application to suspend.

G4.5 *Day v Coltrane*
[2003] EWCA Civ 342; [2003] 1 WLR 1379; [2003] HLR 56; [2003] L&TR 359

Where payment may be made by cheque, delivery of cheque is conditional payment

In February 2001 the defendant was granted an assured tenancy of a flat in London. He paid his rent by cheque, posted the day before it was due, to the landlord in Daventry. However, he failed to pay his rent from May 2002 because of housing benefit problems. When 11 weeks' rent was outstanding, the landlord served a notice under Housing Act 1988 s8 and began proceedings relying on Ground 8. When housing benefit was finally paid, the tenant's advisers sought details of the landlord's bank account so that rent could be paid directly into the account. No reply was received, and so, five days before the hearing, the tenant's cheque was sent via the document exchange to the landlord's solicitors. It was not dealt with immediately by the solicitors but, on the day of the hearing, the landlord was handed the cheque for the full amount of the arrears by his solicitor advocate. He accepted the cheque. At the hearing, the landlord said that, since the cheque had not cleared, the district judge hearing the case had no power to adjourn the proceedings (s9(1) and (6)). The district judge did adjourn to give the cheque time to clear but gave the landlord permission to appeal. A circuit judge held that the rent was unpaid on the day of the hearing and made an order for possession. The tenant appealed.

The Court of Appeal allowed the appeal. Delivery of a cheque is a conditional payment. If it is agreed (either expressly or through a course of dealing) that payment may be made by cheque, 'where a cheque is offered in payment it amounts to a conditional payment ... from the time when the cheque was delivered' provided that it clears (*Homes v Smith* [2000] Lloyd's Law Rep Banking 139). That principle applies to Ground 8. If the cheque cleared on presentation, the debt was paid when the cheque was delivered. An un-cleared cheque delivered to the landlord at or before the hearing and which was accepted by him, or which he was bound by an earlier agreement to accept, is to be treated as payment on the date of delivery provided it was subsequently paid on first presentation. At the date of the hearing, therefore, the district judge had jurisdiction to adjourn the claim to see whether the cheque would be paid. The circuit judge was wrong to make a possession order and it was set aside.

G4.6   *Leadenhall Residential 2 Ltd v Stirling*
[2001] EWCA Civ 1011; [2002] 1 WLR 499; [2001] 3 All ER 645; [2002] HLR 3; [2002] L&TR 14; (2001) *Times* 25 July, CA

Agreement to remain after order under Ground 8 did not create new tenancy

Mr Stirling was an assured tenant. As a result of rent arrears his landlord obtained an order under mandatory Ground 8 that he give up possession on 19 July 1996. Before the date for giving up possession, Mr Stirling offered to pay off the arrears at £100 per month. The landlord agreed to that proposal and Mr Stirling remained in occupation. Mr Stirling argued that in all the circumstances there was an agreement to create a new assured tenancy.

That contention was rejected by a deputy district judge, a circuit judge and the Court of Appeal. The tenancy came to an end on the date for giving possession. Without the agreement, Mr Stirling would have continued as a trespasser with the landlord receiving the amount of the rent by way of mesne profits. The landlord had done nothing to affect the legal relations between the parties. No new or different terms were come to. The parties did not intend to create a new tenancy (*Street v Mountford* (B2.4) and *Burrows v Brent LBC* (I2.1)). The legal relations between the parties were governed by the terms of the order until the landlord took a position inconsistent with the order. Until such time, Mr Stirling's occupation was referable only to forbearance on the part of the landlord and not to the grant of any new entitlement to exclusive possession.

G4.7 **North British Housing Association Limited v Matthews**
[2004] EWCA Civ 1736; [2005] 1 WLR 3133; [2005] 2 All ER 667; [2005] HLR 17; [2005] CP Rep 16; (2005) *Times* 11 January

Court cannot adjourn Ground 8 claim to allow tenant to pay arrears unless exceptional circumstances

The defendants in four separate possession claims were assured tenants of housing associations who had fallen into arrears of rent. The landlords relied on mandatory Housing Act 1988 Sch 2 Ground 8. There was no dispute that, both at the date of the service of s8 notices and at the date of the hearings before district judges, the arrears exceeded the eight weeks' limit specified in Ground 8. On the face of it, therefore, in each case the court was obliged by s7 to make a possession order. However, all the defendants said that they owed rent as a result of housing benefit problems. They applied for adjournments so that they could have time to resolve those problems and obtain money towards the arrears. In all four cases, district judges refused adjournments on the grounds that they had no jurisdiction to grant them, or that, if jurisdiction existed, it would have been wrong to exercise it.

The Court of Appeal dismissed the tenants' appeals. It held:

- The court cannot be satisfied that the landlord is entitled to possession before the date of the hearing. The date of the hearing is the date when the claim is heard. It is not the date fixed for the hearing if, on that date, an adjournment is granted without a hearing taking place at all.
- There is no doubt that it is a perfectly proper exercise of the court's discretion to adjourn if a case has to be taken out of the list because there is no judge available, because there has been over-listing, or because the defendant is prevented by ill health from attending court.
- The court retains jurisdiction to grant an adjournment before it is satisfied that the landlord is entitled to possession. It may be a proper exercise of discretion to adjourn the hearing before the court is satisfied that the landlord is entitled to possession, eg, where there is an arguable claim for damages which can be set off against arrears; where the tenant shows that there is an arguable defence based on accord and satisfaction or estoppel arising from an agreement whereby the landlord accepts an offer by the tenant to pay off the current rent and arrears at a certain rate in return for not pursuing the claim for possession; or where the court is satisfied that there is a real chance that the tenant would be given permission to apply for judicial review of the landlord's decision to claim possession because of abuse of power.
- However, it is not legitimate to adjourn to enable the tenant to pay off arrears and so defeat the claim for possession, unless there are exceptional circumstances, eg, if a tenant is robbed on the way to court or if a computer failure prevents the housing benefit authority from being able to pay benefit due until the day after the hearing date. The fact that arrears are attributable to maladministration on the part of the housing benefit authority is not an exceptional circumstance.

- Once the court has expressed the conclusion that it is satisfied that the landlord is entitled to possession, there is no power to grant an adjournment in any circumstances (see s9(6)). The court cannot be 'satisfied' within the meaning of s9(6) until the judge has given a judgment and effect is given to that judgment in a perfected order of the court.

- The Housing Corporation may consider it wise to expand its advice in Regulatory Circular 07/04 (see November 2004 *Legal Action* 23) about the need for effective liaison between landlords and housing benefit departments right up to the time when a possession claim for rent arrears is heard.

High Court

G4.8   *Diab v Countrywide Rentals 1 plc*
October 2001 Legal Action 15; (2001) 10 July, ChD

Order made on mandatory grounds must state this on the face of the order

The defendant was an assured tenant. In November 2000 her landlords served a section 8 notice relying on all three rent arrears grounds, ie, Grounds 8, 10 and 11. Possession proceedings were issued, but the defendant did not attend the hearing in March 2001. At that time the rent arrears were £1,095 which was the equivalent of 3.4 months' rent. An outright possession order was made. The order was in 'a common form' and did not specify the ground on which possession was ordered. Later, an application to suspend the warrant was issued and heard by the same judge. He 'decided' that the possession order had been made under Ground 8 and that, accordingly, he had no discretion to suspend.

Pumfrey J allowed the tenant's appeal. He was not satisfied that the possession order had been made on a mandatory ground. Where an order for possession is made under one of the mandatory grounds in Housing Act 1988 Sch 2, then that ground should be stated on the face of the order. It is not proper for the judge at a later date to determine whether the order was made on the ground claimed by the landlord or on some other ground. Accordingly, where an order for possession made under Sch 2 failed to state the ground on the face of the order, it could be regarded as having been granted on uncertain grounds and, in those circumstances, a court could revisit the exercise of discretion by the previous judge.

G4.9   *Etherington v Burt*
[2004] EWHC 95 (QB); 5 February 2004

Defendant's counterclaim and payment into court reduced arrears to below 2 months

In 1993 the claimants let a house to the defendant on an assured tenancy. The claimants brought a possession claim relying on arrears of rent. The defendant counterclaimed for lack of hot water. At trial HHJ Cook found that there were arrears of £2,069, but deducted from this £500 which he awarded as damages for the lack of hot water and £1,100 which the defendant had been ordered to pay into court to abide the event at an earlier hearing. This reduced the arrears to £469, slightly over four weeks' arrears. Accordingly, the judge found that Housing Act 1988 Sch 2 Ground 8 was not proved. Furthermore, exercising his discretion in relation to Grounds 10 and 11, he dismissed the claim for possession, on the basis that it was not reasonable to make an order. The claimants appealed, arguing that the judge had been wrong (1) to take into account the payment into court since it still belonged to the defendant and they were not free to take the money out of court; and (2) because failure by the local authority in connection with housing benefit ought to have been equated with non-payment of rent.

Fulford J dismissed the appeal. On the day of the hearing, the sum paid into court was available 'on account of rent arrears', subject only to determination of the counterclaim. To ignore that sum would have led to an artificial and inequitable result. With regards the discretionary grounds, most of the accumulated arrears were explicable by fault on the part of the local authority and the decision of the tenant to withhold rent 'following the wilful default on the part' of the landlords. *Marath v MacGillivray* (F3.3) is not authority for the proposition that an administrative failure by a local authority is to be equated with a deliberate withholding of rent by a tenant. The judge addressed the three main issues (fault by the local authority, reasons for deliberate non-payment and the general history of the amount and length of arrears) relevant to the discretionary grounds for possession. He gave wholly sustainable and undoubtedly adequate reasons for his conclusions. Neither party argued for a suspended order and it was not incumbent on the judge to impose such an order. A three-year period for repayment in a money judgment was not, given the history of a relatively long tenancy, an unreasonable time frame.

G4.10 *Milecastle Housing Ltd v Walton*
14 June 2005, High Court of Justice, Newcastle on Tyne District Registry

Court had power to adjourn where discretionary grounds relied on

The defendant was an assured tenant. Arrears accrued when he stopped receiving housing benefit because the housing benefit authorities formed the view that he had ceased to occupy the premises. The claimants sought possession under Housing Act 1988 Sch 2 Grounds 10 and 12 – discretionary grounds based on rent arrears. At the hearing, the defendant's representative sought an adjournment to try to sort out the defendant's housing benefit position. A district judge refused the application, referring to *North British Housing Association Ltd v Matthews* (G4.7). He made a 28-day possession order. The defendant appealed.

HHJ Langan QC, sitting as a deputy High Court judge, allowed the appeal. The effect of *Matthews* is that the power to adjourn in Housing Act 1988 s9(1) must not be used when possession has been sought on one of the *mandatory* grounds. 'The decision has nothing whatever to do with cases such as the present, where possession is sought on one of the discretionary grounds.' The district judge had, by error of law, debarred himself from giving proper consideration to a matter which he should have considered, namely whether he should exercise the power to adjourn. The possession order was set aside and a new trial ordered.

G5   Rent arrears (Rent Act 1977 Case 1)

Court of Appeal

G5.1   *Bird v Hildage*
[1948] 1 KB 91; [1947] 2 All ER 7, CA
Rent not lawfully due if tendered
If rent is tendered after the due date but before the commencement of proceedings, that prevents rent from being 'lawfully due' unless time has been made the essence of the contract. The words 'lawfully due' mean that the obligation to pay rent must have arisen and not been discharged.

G5.2   *Dellenty v Pellow*
[1951] 2 KB 858; [1951] 2 All ER 716, CA
Reasonable to make a possession order despite payment of arrears
The landlord brought possession proceedings, claiming arrears of rent. The tenant paid the rent the day before the hearing. The Court of Appeal held that, once a landlord had shown that there were arrears of rent at the commencement of proceedings, the court had jurisdiction to make a possession order. If rent arrears were paid before the hearing, prima facie it would not ordinarily be reasonable to make a possession order. However, in this case, where the tenant had frequently been in arrears and proceedings had been issued on a number of occasions, it was reasonable to make a possession order.

G5.3   *Shaw v Groom*
[1970] 2 QB 504; [1970] 2 WLR 299; [1970] 1 All ER 702; (1970) 21 P&CR 137, CA
Failure to provide rent book does not disentitle landlord from recovering rent
Failure to provide a rent book did not disentitle the landlord from recovering rent.

G6   **Breach of obligation**

Housing Act 1985 Sch 2 Ground 1, Housing Act 1988 Sch 2 Ground 12 and Rent Act 1977 Sch 15 Case 1 all provide discretionary grounds for possession where an obligation of the tenancy has been broken or not performed.

G7   Breach of obligation (Housing Act 1985 Sch 2 Ground 1)

Court of Appeal

G7.1   *Kensington and Chelsea RLBC v Simmonds*
(1997) 29 HLR 507, CA
SPO appropriate despite tenant not being able to control son
The tenant, a single parent, lived with her two children aged 5 and 13. The teenage son and his friends caused considerable nuisance to neighbours, including racial abuse. The council brought possession proceedings relying on Ground 1 (breach of a covenant on the tenant's part 'not [to] ... allow members of his household ... to commit any act which may ... cause offence

to any other tenant ... by reason of his race, colour, ethnic origin or nationality' and Ground 2 (nuisance or annoyance). The tenant claimed that her son was beyond her control and therefore she was not responsible for his behaviour. Recorder Bevington made a suspended possession order (SPO).

Dismissing the tenant's appeal, the Court of Appeal held that, although one incident of racial abuse by the son on one unheralded occasion would not have amounted to a breach of the covenant, since the conduct had persisted over a number of months, there was ample basis for the judge's findings that the tenant had allowed her son to abuse the neighbours. The court also rejected the argument that it was necessary to show 'fault' on the part of the tenant before a possession order could be made. The court had to consider not only the interests of the tenant but also those of neighbours. It would be quite intolerable if neighbours were deprived of the possibility of relief because the tenant was incapable of controlling her son.

G7.2   *Lambeth LBC v Thomas*
(1998) 30 HLR 89; (1997) 74 P&CR 189, CA (see H3.9)

Wrong to refuse to make order on ground not reasonable merely because arrears related to water charges

G7.3   *Northampton BC v Lovatt*
(1998) 30 HLR 875; (1998) 96 LGR 548; [1998] 1 EGLR 15, CA

Meaning of 'neighbours'; conduct does not have to take place in dwelling-house

Mr and Mrs Lovatt were secure tenants of the council. Their tenancy agreement imposed an obligation to ensure that no nuisance or annoyance was caused to neighbours. Their teenage sons ran wild on the council estate. Other residents were frightened. It appeared that the parents were not trying to restrain the boys. The council sought an order for possession of the house on the ground that the boys who were residing in the house were a nuisance or annoyance to neighbours. The judge found that numerous acts of criminal or anti-social behaviour had been proved and granted a possession order. The Lovatts appealed on two grounds: first, that the boys' behaviour had taken place away from the dwelling-house and, second, that the nearest identified victim lived further than 100 metres away and so could not be classified as a neighbour.

Their appeal was dismissed. Following *Kensington and Chelsea RLBC v Simmonds* (G7.1), the court held that a tenant can be responsible for the acts of a minor child, although there must be a link between the behaviour of the tenant or the tenant's family and the fact that they live in the area. The word 'neighbours' means those living or working in the neighbourhood and includes all persons sufficiently close to be affected by the conduct. Conduct does not have to take place in the dwelling-house. Landlords have a legitimate interest in requiring their tenants to respect the neighbourhood in which they live and the quiet enjoyment of their homes by those who live there.

G7.4   *Southwark LBC v O'Sullivan*
[2006] EWCA Civ 124; 27 January 2006

Possession order could not stand where preliminary issue determined on facts without a fact-finding exercise

Mrs O'Sullivan was a secure tenant. She lived in the property with Mr O'Sullivan, her husband, who was not a party to the tenancy, and their children. Mrs O'Sullivan moved out and sought alternative housing, alleging that she had been the victim of domestic violence. After she left the property, she served a notice to quit on Southwark. Mr O'Sullivan remained in the property. Condition 3.1 of the tenancy agreement provided that occupiers should be living together as a couple but that, if the relationship broke down, Southwark would provide suitable alternative accommodation to the person vacating the property and grant a tenancy to the remaining person. However, if the breakdown was due to domestic violence, Southwark was not obliged to grant a tenancy to the remaining person. Southwark brought possession proceedings against Mr O'Sullivan. He counterclaimed, alleging that Southwark was obliged to grant him a tenancy. A judge ordered the trial of preliminary issues, one of which was whether the tenancy was capable of enforcement by Mr O'Sullivan after its termination by his wife. The judge did not hear any evidence and regarded the issues before him as questions of law. He recorded that there might be an issue as to whether Mr O'Sullivan had operated a trigger of condition 3.1 by asking for a rent card, but then determined that any claim for a tenancy had to be made by Mr O'Sullivan before the tenancy had expired. He made a possession order.

The Court of Appeal allowed Mr O'Sullivan's appeal against the possession order. By making a possession order, the judge had pre-empted the question of whether or not Mr O'Sullvian's request for a rent card had operated as a trigger of condition 3.1. The decision to have a trial on preliminary issues had been a false economy. The court should not embark on a question of construction in advance of the fact-finding exercise. The issue determined by the judge had been decided on facts which were not ordered to be assumed and which were not decided by him. The possession order could not stand.

County courts

G7.5   *Camden LBC v McBride*

January 1999 *Legal Action* 26, Clerkenwell County Court

Term where breach was to be determined subjectively by council unfair

The council brought possession proceedings against a secure tenant, relying on Housing Act 1985 Sch 2 Grounds 1 (breach of term) and 2 (nuisance). The term relied on prohibited 'anything ... which in the opinion of the Council may be or become a nuisance'.

HHJ Tibber held that the term was unfair and so unenforceable (Unfair Terms in Consumer Contracts Regulations 1994 SI No 3159 reg 4 – see now Unfair Terms in Consumer Contracts Regulations 1999 SI No 2083) because any question of its breach was to be determined subjectively by the council. Possession was granted on Ground 2 on the facts.

G7.6   *Newham LBC v Anwar Ali*

27 November 2003, Bow County Court

Landlord could not rely on breach of terms of tenancy relating to overcrowding and was restricted to relying on overcrowding ground

Mr Ali was granted a secure tenancy of a bed-sit in sheltered accommodation in April 2000. One clause of the tenancy agreement provided: 'The tenant's responsibilities: Not to overcrowd the premises in contravention of sections 324–328 and 330–331 of the Housing Act 1985.' In August 2002, his wife and four children came from Bangladesh to join him. The bed-sit became overcrowded within the meaning of Housing Act 1985 Part X. Newham brought possession proceedings, not under Housing Act 1985 Sch 2 Ground 9 (which requires that there be suitable alternative accommodation available) but on Ground 1 for breach of the overcrowding clause in the tenancy agreement, in an attempt to avoid the obligation to make suitable alternative accommodation available.

HHJ Roberts dismissed the claim for possession. Applying *RMR Housing Society v Combs* [1951] 1 All ER 16 CA, it was not possible to contract out of the provisions of the Housing Act so as to diminish the tenant's protection. The Housing Act provides a complete code for possession and the part of the code which deals with overcrowding is Ground 9. Landlords can only claim possession on the basis of overcrowding where the criteria for Ground 9 apply. The landlord must use Ground 9 to claim possession on the basis of overcrowding. To allow the landlord to rely on Ground 1 in such circumstances would be to drive a coach and horses through the scheme of the Act. The judge went on to hold that, even if he were wrong on this point, it would never be reasonable to grant possession under Ground 1 in these circumstances unless the requirements of Ground 9 were met with regard to the availability of suitable alternative accommodation.

G8 Breach of obligation (Housing Act 1988 Sch 2 Ground 12)

Court of Appeal

G8.1 *Pollards Hill HA v Marsh*
[2002] EWCA Civ 199, [2002] HLR 35

Landlord bound by more restrictive grounds for possession in tenancy agreement

Ms Marsh was an assured tenant. The tenancy agreement provided that the landlord could issue possession proceedings on a number of grounds. One particular clause stated that the housing association had a ground to serve a notice of possession if 'you have been convicted of using the premises for immoral or illegal purposes or of an arrestable offence' at or in the locality of the premises. In January 2000 Ms Marsh and her partner were arrested after drugs were found at the premises. At trial her partner pleaded guilty to offences involving the supply of controlled drugs. The prosecution dropped charges against Ms Marsh. In January 2001 the housing association issued possession proceedings against her relying on Housing Act 1988 Sch 2 Ground 14 ('The tenant or a person residing in or visiting the dwelling-house ... has been convicted of ... an arrestable offence committed in, or in the locality of, the dwelling-house.'). A suspended possession order was made.

The Court of Appeal allowed Ms Marsh's appeal. The language of the clause was simple and straightforward. The inclusion of the word 'you' can only have been intended to refer to the criminal conviction of the tenant. The use of the word 'you' was wholly unnecessary if it was to be given exactly the same meaning as that used in Ground 14. Second, the reference to the only grounds and circumstances in which the housing association would seek to recover possession was not, as it claimed, merely descriptive of the statutory rights. The agreement set out contractual rights that were more restricted than those under the statute. The claim for possession was not within the terms of the tenancy agreement and so no order for possession could be made.

G8.2   *Sanctuary Housing Association v Baker (No 2)*
(1999) 31 HLR 746; (1999) 78 P&CR D15, CA

Breach of tenancy agreement res judicata in second possession proceedings

Miss Scamp, an assured tenant of the housing association, and Miss Baker, a local authority tenant, entered into a mutual exchange. Miss Baker moved into the association's property but never completed the assignment of her council tenancy to Miss Scamp. A county court judge found that the 'mutual exchange' had been a sham and a fraud from the beginning, as Miss Scamp had never intended to move to the council flat and had been paid by Miss Baker for her co-operation in the transactions. However, the Court of Appeal dismissed the association's initial claim for possession, which had been based on the contention that the assignment was a nullity (see *Sanctuary Housing Association v Baker* (E3.6). The housing association then began a second action against the defendant for possession on the ground of breach of covenant not to assign without the landlord's consent. The defendant argued that the plaintiff was estopped from pursuing this point which should have been taken earlier. HHJ Poulton rejected this and made a possession order.

The defendant appealed successfully to the Court of Appeal. The alleged breach of covenant was res judicata. Miss Baker's fraud did not amount to special circumstances justifying the dis-application of this doctrine. Early on in the present litigation the defendant had pleaded the validity of the assignment. The plaintiff had been put on notice and had had ample time to serve a s8 notice (Housing Act 1988). The subject of the litigation in the first action was possession of the property. No reason was given for not serving a notice or for not applying to dispense with the requirement. It was not necessary to confine the rule to a strict and formal analysis of what constituted a cause of action. The rule was wide enough to include within its ambit issues which were clearly part of the subject matter. The proceedings were sufficiently obvious and were well covered by the rule in *Henderson v Henderson* (1843) 3 Hare 100. Given the public policy of not wasting time, this prolixity of litigation should not be permitted.

County courts

G8.3 *Paddington Churches Housing Association v Boateng*
January 1999 *Legal Action* 27, Central London Civil Trial Centre

Clause in tenancy requiring tenant to take up support merely a personal obligation

An assured tenancy agreement included a term stating: '[The tenant agrees to] participate in groups and individual programmes designed to assist with the tenant's resettlement and to comply with the agent's move-on policies and procedures as set out in the preamble to this agreement. The project is not intended to provide permanent accommodation for the tenant, therefore, the tenant also agrees to move into other accommodation if notified in writing by the agent that other accommodation is available.' The landlords brought possession proceedings under Housing Act 1988 Sch 2 Ground 12, claiming that this term had been broken.

HHJ Colin Smith QC dismissed the claim for possession. The clause was merely a personal obligation, not a term binding on the tenant (see *RMR Housing Society v Combs* [1951] 1 KB 486, CA). The clause was also unenforceable in view of Housing Act 1988 s5(5).

G9 **Breach of obligation (Rent Act 1977 Case 1)**

House of Lords

G9.1 *Cadogan Estates Ltd v McMahon*
[2001] AC 378; [2000] 3 WLR 1555; [2000] 4 All ER 897; [2001] 06 EG 164; [2001] L&TR 12; (2001) 33 HLR 462; (2001) 81 P&CR D24; (2000) *Times* 1 November, HL

Obligation of tenancy broken when tenant became bankrupt

Cadogan granted Mr McMahon a 14-year lease in March 1979. When it expired he became a statutory tenant (Rent Act 1977 s2). On 17 March 1998, he was made bankrupt. Although the covenants in the lease made no reference to bankruptcy, the re-entry clause gave the landlord a right of re-entry if the tenant became bankrupt. The landlord issued possession proceedings under Sch 15 Case 1, claiming breach of that proviso. A possession order was made. Mr McMahon's appeal to the Court of Appeal was dismissed ([1999] 1 WLR 1689). It held that the proviso was a condition and created an obligation not to become bankrupt. In view of s3(1) it was an obligation under the statutory tenancy within the meaning of Case 1.

After considering 'the broad policy' of the Rent Acts dating back to 1919, the House of Lords, by a majority, held that that the circuit judge and the Court of Appeal reached the right conclusion for the right reasons. The tenant was 'obliged' not to become a bankrupt if he wished to remain in possession of the house. By becoming bankrupt he had broken 'an obligation of the previous protected tenancy' within the meaning of Case 1 para (b). It was not inconsistent with the provisions of the Rent Act.

Court of Appeal

G9.2 *Florent v Horez*
(1984) 12 HLR 1; (1984) 48 P&CR 166; (1983) 268 EG 807, CA

'Business user' has broad meaning

The landlords claimed possession, relying on Rent Act 1977 Sch 15 Case 1 (breach of obligation, in this instance a breach of covenant not to carry on profession, trade or business) and Case 2 (nuisance or annoyance to adjoining occupiers). The main allegation was that the tenant had used the premises, where he was a statutory tenant, to carry out work for the British Turkish Cyprus Committee, which he had set up. The landlords alleged that the tenant, as chair of the committee, had authorised people, including members of the committee, to come to the premises at all hours of the day and night. They had been given keys to the external door, slammed doors and whistled. Although the noise nuisance had abated over a year before the trial, the county court judge found that the plaintiff's allegations had been made out and that it was reasonable to make a possession order. The tenant appealed, principally on the ground that there was no business use.

The Court of Appeal stated that the phrase 'business user' has a broad meaning and approved a statement by Lindley LJ in *Rolls v Miller* (1884) 27 ChD 71 at 88, that business:

> ... means almost anything which is an occupation, as distinguished from a pleasure – anything which is an occupation or duty which requires attention is a business.

Covenants against business user:

> ... are designed to preserve the amenities of residential premises and neighbourhoods, and if the word 'business' is not given as wide a meaning as possible, the purpose of the covenant could readily be defeated.

It is a question of fact and degree in any case whether the tenant's activities constitute the carrying on of a business or are merely ancillary to the main residential user. Furthermore, in the light of the judge's findings, it was also reasonable to make an order under Case 2 (nuisance).

G10   Nuisance or annoyance

Since amendment by Housing Act 1996, Housing Act 1985 Sch 2 Ground 2 and Housing Act 1985 Sch 2 Ground 14 apply if:

> the tenant or a person residing in or visiting the dwelling-house
> (a) has been guilty of conduct causing or likely to cause a nuisance or annoyance to a person residing, visiting or otherwise engaging in lawful activity in the locality, or
> (b) has been convicted of
>   (i) using the dwelling-house or allowing it to be used for immoral or illegal purposes, or
>   (ii) an arrestable offence committed in, or in the locality of, the dwelling-house.

Rent Act 1977 Sch 15 Case 2 provides a discretionary ground for possession where the tenant or any person residing or lodging with him or her or any subtenant of his or hers has been guilty of conduct which is a nuisance or annoyance to adjoining occupiers, or has been convicted of using the dwelling-house or allowing the dwelling-house to be used for immoral or illegal purposes.

G11 Nuisance or annoyance (Housing Act 1985 Sch 2 Ground 2)

Court of Appeal

G11.1 *Harlow DC v Sewell*
[2000] EHLR 122, CA

'Nuisance' to be interpreted broadly; having 38 cats a nuisance

The council brought proceedings under Housing Act 1985 Sch 2 Ground 2 (nuisance and annoyance) against the defendant, a long-standing secure tenant. The tenant allowed large numbers of cats to live in her house (38 at date of trial). Neighbours complained that the cats defecated in their gardens and elsewhere in the locality. HHJ Sennit found Ground 2 made out and granted a suspended possession order on terms that the number of cats be reduced to six or fewer within six weeks. The tenant sought permission to appeal, contending that Ground 2 could not as a matter of law have been made out because neither she not any human resident or visitor was causing a nuisance. The cats had a 'right to roam' and the tenant could not at common law be liable in nuisance if they chose to defecate on someone else's property.

Pill LJ dismissed the application. He held that it was not arguable that common-law considerations of the general scope of the tort of nuisance were to be superimposed on the specific statutory provisions of Sch 2. In the context of the grounds for possession in Housing Act 1985, the word 'nuisance' should be interpreted broadly. The judge was entitled to hold that there was a breach of Ground 2, which would cease if the number of cats were reduced.

G11.2 *Kensington Housing Trust v Oliver*
[1997] NPC 119, CA

Court has power to release a party from an undertaking when just to do so

Landlords brought an action for possession against a secure tenant on the ground of nuisance (Housing Act 1985 Sch 2 Ground 2). Those proceedings were adjourned in March 1995 on undertakings by the tenant about her future conduct. The undertakings were broken and the action restored. In September 1995, on an express admission that (a) the ground had been proved and (b) it was reasonable to order possession, a possession order was made by consent. However, the order recorded undertakings, first, by the tenant about her future conduct and, second, by the landlords to the effect that they would not execute the order without first offering alternative accommodation. The tenant later failed to comply with her undertakings. The landlords applied to be released from their undertakings and for execution of the possession order. The recorder held that the landlords' undertakings were part of a consent order and so not capable of being varied or discharged by the court.

Allowing the landlords' appeal, the Court of Appeal held that, in all civil litigation, the court has the power to release from an undertaking, even one recorded in a final order made by consent. That power can be exercised when it is just to do so. In this case, a release from the undertakings was just, in the light of the tenant's breach of her own undertakings.

G11.3   *Leeds CC v Harte*

April 1999 *Legal Action* 27; [1999] 4 CLD 470, CA

Nuisance can be proved by hearsay evidence

The council sought possession from a secure tenant under Housing Act 1985 Sch 2 Ground 1 (breach of tenancy) and Ground 2 (nuisance) relying on acts of nuisance, annoyance and criminal activities by her partner and eldest children. The two eldest children had committed hundreds of arrestable offences, mainly house burglaries. The council called evidence from various council officials and police officers about what had been going on in the neighbourhood and relied on memoranda of conviction to prove the criminal offences. All the evidence led was hearsay. None of the victims of the nuisance was called. The judge granted possession.

The Court of Appeal refused an application for leave to appeal. The judge had not erred in finding the grounds proved. He had directed himself to the fact that all the evidence was hearsay and that he should be cautious about the weight to be placed on it. Not only was he entitled to reach the conclusion that the case was proved on the evidence called but it would have been perverse had he not done so.

G11.4   *Manchester CC v Lawler*

(1999) 31 HLR 119; June 1998 *Legal Action* 11, CA (see E1.6)

'In the locality' not too vague; Shopping centre three streets away was in the locality

G11.5   *Portsmouth CC v Bryant*

(2000) 32 HLR 906; [2000] EHLR 287, CA

Tenant 'allowed' misconduct by failing to prevent it or by 'closing her mind' to it; 22-month SPO not wrong in principle

The defendant secure tenant occupied her council home for nearly 30 years. She raised her grandsons at her home. They were aged 15 and 17 at the date of trial. It was alleged that the grandsons sprayed graffiti, used abusive and threatening language, and threw stones at and spat at neighbours. In November 1997 the council served a NSP relying on Grounds 1 and 2 (as amended in 1997) and giving as particulars of breach of the Grounds that the tenant had 'allowed' her grandchildren to behave in this way. After a two day trial a District Judge made a suspended possession order (SPO). A circuit judge dismissed an appeal by the tenant.

On appeal to the Court of Appeal it was contended that (1) the judge had misdirected himself that Ground 2 was a ground of 'strict liability' requiring no personal fault on the part of the tenant; (2) on the evidence the tenant had not 'allowed' the misconduct and no other matter was particularised in the NSP; (3) the judge had erred in his approach to 'reasonableness'; and (4) the 22-month period of suspension was too long. The Court of Appeal dealt with all four grounds:

1) Following and applying *Kensington and Chelsea RLBC v Simmonds* (G7.1) and *West Kent HA v Davies* (H4.26) 'no personal fault on the tenants' part is required to bring a case within Ground 2', especially in its enlarged and amended form. By confining the permissible limits of 'locality' and exercising a sensible discretion of 'reasonableness',

judges could be trusted to deal with individual cases 'appropriately'. In Sedley LJ's view '[I]t may very well be unreasonable to make even a suspended order against somebody who will be powerless to rectify the situation and it will almost certainly be unreasonable to make an outright order against such a person'. (But see now the comments on this passage in *Knowsley Housing Trust v McMullen* (H4.12).)

2) The NSP had only alleged 'allowing' and had not been amended or dispensed with. Simon Brown LJ and Sir Christopher Staughton held that the tenant had either 'allowed' the misconduct (in the sense that she had failed to prevent it) or she had had sufficient 'notice' of the reasons for which the council was actually seeking possession by setting out Ground 2 in full in the NSP or by the particulars given well before trial. Sedley LJ found himself bound by *Simmonds* and *West Kent* to hold that by 'closing her mind' to the misconduct, the tenant had 'allowed' it.

3) An order for possession was necessary to protect neighbours from the 'objectionable rude and arrogant' conduct of the grandsons. The judge had been right to find it 'reasonable' to make an order.

4) Having regard to the fact that the Court of Appeal had itself imposed a 2-year suspended order in *West Kent* it could not be said that a 22-month suspension was wrong in principle.

G11.6 *Sandwell MBC v Hensley*

[2007] EWCA Civ 1425; 1 November 2007

Where tenant commits criminal offence, possession order should be suspended only in exceptional circumstances

The defendant was a secure tenant. In 2005, police officers found an extensive and sophisticated cannabis cultivation operation involving the use of hydroponics in his home. He pleaded guilty to a charge of being knowingly concerned with the cultivation of cannabis. Sandwell sought possession on Sch 2 Grounds 1 (breach of an obligation of the tenancy) and 2 (conviction for arrestable offence). A judge made a possession order, but suspended it for two years, referring to evidence that the defendant appeared to have ceased his offending behaviour.

The Court of Appeal allowed Sandwell's appeal and substituted an outright order. Where an individual commits a criminal offence, a possession order should only be suspended in exceptional circumstances where there is cogent evidence to demonstrate that the offender's particular conduct had ceased (*Bristol CC v Mousah* (H4.4)). The judge's reasons for suspending the order did not stand up to scrutiny since they were sparse and provided little explanation of which facts she considered were relevant. It was of particular concern that the decision was made without hearing oral evidence from the defendant. Although the judge made a passing reference to the defendant's previous convictions, she did so without referring to the impact they had had on her decision. In the circumstances, the judge had exercised her discretion poorly, as the defendant had run a sophisticated operation with complete disregard for his tenancy agreement and those around him. Local authorities and providers of social housing have a duty to keep areas free of criminal conduct where possible and, unless a court is provided with evidence demonstrating real hope that an individual has changed his or her ways, those landlords are entitled to an outright possession order.

G11.7 *Watford BC v Simpson*

(2000) 32 HLR 901, CA

Judge had no power to order council to make proposals to rehouse tenant

A local authority took possession proceedings against a secure tenant because of anti-social behaviour, principally caused by her three children. On the date fixed for trial, there was insufficient time to hear the case and the circuit judge adjourned, giving directions. He directed that, unless the local authority wrote to Ms Simpson's solicitors setting out their best proposals for rehousing, they would have to pay the costs of the action, unless ordered otherwise by the trial judge. He took the view that if a possession order were made, the local authority would be bound to rehouse Ms Simpson and her children as homeless persons and that the order would promote a compromise.

The Court of Appeal allowed the authority's appeal. The judge had no power to make the order. He had misunderstood the authority's duties under Housing Act 1996 Part VII and his powers under County Courts Act 1984.

G12 Nuisance or annoyance (Housing Act 1988 Sch 2 Ground 14)

High Court

G12.1 *Raglan Housing Association Ltd v Fairclough*

[2007] EWCA Civ 1087; (2007) *Times* 28 November; 1 November 2007

Ground 14 is not restricted to offences committed during currency of the tenancy; it applies to offences committed in the neighbourhood before the tenancy if the conviction occurred after commencement of the tenancy

The defendant was an assured tenant. In May 2004, he was arrested on suspicion of offences under the Protection of Children Act 1978, but he was not charged with any offence until January 2006. Meanwhile, in 2005, he 'transferred' his tenancy to a neighbouring property owned by the same landlord. In March 2006, he pleaded guilty to 15 counts of making indecent photographs of children by downloading them on to his computer from the internet and a further four counts of possessing indecent photographs of children. All the offences had been committed between May 2001 and May 2004 while he was still living at the former property. He was sentenced to an extended sentence of four years' imprisonment comprising a custodial period of 12 months and an extended licence period of three years. His landlord sought possession under Housing Act 1988 Sch 2 Ground 14 (conviction for indictable offence in locality). HHJ Burford QC made a possession order. He rejected a submission that Ground 14(b)(ii) relates only to offences committed during the currency of the tenancy agreement and does not extend to offences committed before the tenancy began. Mr Fairclough appealed.

The Court of Appeal dismissed the appeal. Ground 14 applies to those who have committed indictable offences in the neighbourhood where they live. In view of this, there is no reason to think that Parliament intended to restrict the ground to offences committed during the currency of the tenancy. A tenant who is convicted of supplying illegal drugs or of burgling his neighbours' houses poses no less of a continuing threat if the offences were committed before he became a tenant than he would if they had been committed afterwards. The Court of Appeal was not agreed on whether the ground could be satisfied only if the conviction itself (though not the facts on which it was based) occurred during the currency of the tenancy, but did not have to decide that point.

G12.2   *Kensington Housing Trust v Borkwood*
CC/2005/PTA/1033; July 2005 *Legal Action* 28; 19 May 2005, QBD

Nuisance to be given broad meaning; motive or intention to harass irrelevant; test of harassment subjective

Mr Borkwood was an assured tenant. His tenancy agreement included clauses prohibiting 'nuisance or annoyance' and 'racial or other harassment'. His landlord claimed that Mr Borkwood had made racially offensive comments at a tenants' conference and that he had included racially offensive passages in correspondence. It sought interim injunctive relief. A judge refused that application. The landlord appealed.

Cox J allowed the appeal. The phrase 'nuisance or annoyance' should be construed broadly and with common sense. It is not confined to activities which would amount to an actionable nuisance at common law. Its aim was to address the behaviour of tenants in the relevant neighbourhood. The behaviour alleged on the part of the tenant was capable of amounting to a breach of the tenancy agreement. Second, the word 'harassment' is capable of including unintended conduct of a racist nature, and the existence of an intention or motive to harass is irrelevant in determining whether any particular conduct amounts to harassment. So long as the conduct in question is capable objectively of amounting to harassment, the test as to whether a person was actually harassed is essentially a subjective one. It is not appropriate to equate the word 'harassment' in the tenancy agreement with the criminal offence of harassment.

G12.3   *Washington Housing Company Ltd v Morson*
[2005] EWHC 3407 (ChD); 25 October 2005 (see J2.2)

Hearsay evidence comprising anonymous complaint forms could be considered

G13   Nuisance or annoyance (Rent Act 1977 Case 2)

Court of Appeal

G13.1   *Abrahams v Wilson*
[1971] 2 QB 88; [1971] 2 WLR 923; [1971] 2 All ER 1114; (1971) 22 P&CR 407, CA

Conviction for possession of cannabis did not satisfy ground of using premises for illegal purposes

The tenant was convicted of possession of 66 grains [sic] of cannabis resin in the premises that he rented. His landlord claimed possession on the ground that he had been convicted of using the premises for illegal purposes.

The Court of Appeal dismissed the landlord's appeal against a first instance decision refusing a possession order. Although Case 2 can be relied on even if there was no reference in the charge itself to using the premises, it is necessary to show that the crime had actually been committed on the premises and that the premises had been used for the purpose of committing the offence. There is a difference between drugs being in the defendant's immediate possession, on the one hand, and, on the other hand, the tenant using the premises to store drugs.

G13.2   **Cobstone Investments Ltd v Maxim**

[1985] QB 140; [1984] 3 WLR 563; [1984] 2 All ER 635; (1984) 15 HLR 113; (1984) 49 P&CR 173; (1984) 272 EG 429, CA

'Adjoining occupiers' used in sense of neighbouring occupiers

A possession order was made on the ground that the tenant had been guilty of nuisance or annoyance to adjoining occupiers. On appeal, counsel for the tenant submitted that some of the plaintiff's witnesses were not 'adjoining occupiers' because their premises were not contiguous in the sense that they were not physically joined to the defendant's flat.

The tenant's appeal was dismissed. The word 'adjoining' is used in the wider sense of 'neighbouring'. See also *Northampton BC v Lovatt* (G7.3).

G13.3   **Florent v Horez**

(1984) 12 HLR 1; (1984) 48 P&CR 166; (1983) 268 EG 807, CA (see G9.2)

Use of premises by British Turkish Cyprus Committee members caused a nuisance

G13.4   **Frederick Platts Co Ltd v Grigor**

[1950] 1 All ER 941, CA

Judge can infer nuisance caused to occupiers without evidence from them

In a claim for possession based on nuisance or annoyance to adjoining occupiers, a judge may infer that adjoining occupiers have been affected, even if none of them gives evidence of actual nuisance to them.

G14   **Domestic violence**

Housing Act 1985 Sch 2 Ground 2A and Housing Act 1988 Sch 2 Ground 14A, which were inserted by Housing Act 1996, apply where one or both partners is a tenant and (a) one partner has left because of violence or threats of violence by the other towards that partner or a member of that partner's family; and (b) the court is satisfied that the partner who has left is unlikely to return.

Court of Appeal

G14.1   **Camden LBC v Mallett**

(2001) 33 HLR 204, CA

Domestic violence must be the dominant cause of the departure

In 1991 the council granted the defendants, a married couple, a secure tenancy of a flat. Their marriage broke down. In 1997 Mrs Mallett left the property, alleging that her husband had harassed her and been violent towards her throughout their marriage. The parties later divorced. The council served notice on Mr Mallett, who remained in the property, stating that it was seeking possession of the flat pursuant Housing Act 1985 Sch 2 Ground 2A. HHJ Cotran refused the council possession of the flat on the ground that Ground 2A required that the violence or threat of violence was 'the real reason, the effective reason, the immediate and causative reason'. He held that the wife left the flat to live with her then boyfriend and that on those facts Ground 2A was not made out. The council appealed.

The Court of Appeal dismissed the appeal. Where possession is sought from a tenant pursuant to Ground 2A, it is not sufficient that the alleged violence or threats of violence was merely one of a range of causes of equal efficacy in the victim's departure from the property. For the ground to be made out it has to be established that the alleged violence or threat of violence was the dominant, principal and real cause of the departure. Accordingly, the judge had not misdirected himself in expounding the test that he did. Moreover, on the evidence before him he was entitled to make the findings of fact that he did about the wife's true reason for leaving the council's property.

G15 Tenancy obtained by false statement

Housing Act 1985 Sch 2 Ground 5 and Housing Act 1988 Sch 2 Ground 17, as amended by Housing Act 1996 s146, give grounds for possession when the tenant is the person, or one of the persons, to whom the tenancy was granted and the landlord was induced to grant the tenancy by a false statement made knowingly or recklessly by (a) the tenant, or (b) a person acting at the tenant's instigation.

Court of Appeal

G15.1 *Islington LBC v Uckac*
[2006] EWCA Civ 340; [2006] 1 WLR 1303; [2006] L&TR 10; [2006] HLR 35; (2006) *Times* 19 April

Ground 5 could not be used where tenancy had been assigned by misrepresentor

Mr and Mrs Uckac applied to Islington as homeless persons under Housing Act 1996 Part VII. In their application they stated that they had left their previous address in Islington owing to overcrowding and because they had been given seven days' notice to leave. Islington accepted that they had not been intentionally homeless and granted Mr Uckac a tenancy, which he later assigned to Mrs Uckac. Islington later sought rescission of the tenancy on the ground of fraudulent misrepresentation and an order for possession, relying on Housing Act 1985 Sch 2 Ground 5, claiming that the defendants had been living in Essex. HHJ Simpson dismissed the claim on the basis that Ground 5 is only available where the defendant is the person to whom the tenancy was granted. Islington appealed.

The appeal was dismissed. (1) Dyson LJ said that the language of Ground 5 is clear and unambiguous and only refers to the current tenant – the person against whom possession is sought. The first 17 words of Ground 5 make it clear that the word 'tenant' does not include any predecessor in title who made the misrepresentation relied on. (2) Furthermore, Islington was not entitled to claim rescission of the tenancy on the grounds of fraudulent misrepresentation because Housing Act 1985 s82 specifies the only ways in which a landlord can bring a secure tenancy to an end. The relevant provisions of the Act provide a complete code for the termination of secure tenancies and so the private law remedy of rescission is not available.

G15.2   *Merton LBC v Richards*

[2005] EWCA Civ 639; [2005] HLR 44

Possession refused where tenant's mother had not acted on tenant's instigation

In 1994 Ms Richards was both an employee and a tenant of Merton. She wanted to move to larger accommodation. With the help of her mother, who worked in the council's housing department, she entered into a mutual exchange with a Mrs Mahon. In fact, Mrs Mahon had no intention of moving into the flat previously occupied by Ms Richards. Instead she went to live with her daughter. The council sought possession against Ms Richards, relying on Housing Act 1985 Sch 2 Ground 5. A recorder dismissed the claim for possession. He found that Ms Richards did not, herself, know that Mrs Mahon's statement that she would move into Ms Richards's flat on exchange was false at the time when the tenancy was granted. The defendant's mother, who did know, was not 'a person acting at the tenant's instigation'. Merton appealed, contending that on the facts Ms Richards had instigated her mother's acts and that the recorder had misconstrued the word 'instigated' in Ground 5.

The Court of Appeal dismissed the appeal. The word 'instigate' means 'to bring about or initiate'. The Latin source of the word is instigare, to urge or incite. The Ground refers to 'instigation' and not merely to someone 'acting on behalf of the tenant'. On the recorder's findings of fact, there was no instigation by Ms Richards. Furthermore, the instigation must be of the false statement and not merely instigation of action in general on behalf of the tenant. Although the court could 'understand the sense of grievance which the appellants may feel about the judge's findings of fact on the evidence in this case', those findings of fact could not be disturbed.

G15.3   *Rushcliffe BC v Watson*

(1992) 24 HLR 123, CA (see H5.3)

Burden of proof under Ground 5 akin to criminal standard because of seriousness of the allegation

G15.4   *Waltham Forest LBC v Roberts*

[2004] EWCA Civ 940; [2005] HLR 2

Fair inference that obviously material misrepresentation induced grant of tenancy

Ms Roberts was employed as a warden of sheltered housing. She was required to retire and vacate the accommodation provided in connection with her employment. She applied to be rehoused by Waltham Forest. On her application, she stated that she did not own any property. In fact, she was a joint legal owner of a property. After being granted a council tenancy, she applied for housing benefit. She again failed to disclose her interest in the other property and also failed to disclose that she received rent from that property. After investigations, the council stopped payment of benefit and sought recovery of the overpayment. It also sought possession under Housing Act 1985 Sch 2 Grounds 1 and 5. At the date of the issue of proceedings, there were arrears of rent of over £7,000. The judge dismissed the claim. He found that no ground for possession had been established. In relation to Ground 5, although Ms Roberts had knowingly made a false statement in her housing application, as there was no evidence from the actual decision maker, he could not find that the council had been induced to grant the tenancy as a result. In relation to Ground 1, he concluded that the arrears had arisen only because Ms Roberts had been wrongfully denied housing benefit by the council.

The Court of Appeal allowed the council's appeal. When considering whether a misstatement has induced a misrepresentee to act to its detriment, it is helpful to start by considering the materiality of the misstatement. The applicant's ownership of another property is obviously material to a housing application. The judge did not consider the materiality of the false statement as it affected the responsibilities of the council in the discharge of its public functions. Once materiality had been established, it was a 'fair inference' of fact that the misrepresentee had been influenced by the statement. The judge had erred in law in his approach to the evidence of inducement. Had he applied the correct test and approach, he would have been bound to conclude that the local authority had established that the false statement induced the grant of the tenancy. With regards Ground 1, the council had followed the prescribed scheme for the determination of a housing benefit claim and on appeal to the review board it was held that Ms Roberts had no entitlement. It was not apparent how the judge was able to conclude that there was an entitlement to housing benefit, for he neither applied public law principles to the review board's determination, nor applied the regulations that governed entitlement. In the circumstances, the judge's conclusion that the local authority had acted wrongfully could not stand. The judge had exceeded his powers and reached a determination of Ms Robert's entitlement to housing benefit which was not open to him. The case was remitted to a different county court judge to determine whether it was reasonable to make an order for possession as both Grounds 1 and 5 were established.

G16 ## Property required for demolition or redevelopment

This ground for possession under Housing Act 1985 Sch 2 Ground 10 may arise if a landlord of a secure tenant requires possession in order to carry out demolition or redevelopment work and cannot reasonably carry out the work without obtaining possession. There is a similar provision in Housing Act 1988 Sch 2 Ground 6.

Court of Appeal

G16.1   *Wansbeck DC v Marley*

(1988) 20 HLR 247, CA

Landlord to prove intent to carry out works and that works could not reasonable be done without obtaining possession

The council relied on Housing Act 1985 Sch 2 Ground 10, claiming that it needed possession of a cottage in order to carry out works. The council did not produce to the trial judge any minutes or resolution of a council committee which showed precisely what works were intended or that possession would be needed before they could be carried out. The only evidence was given by a council officer, who stated that a building would be built in the garden and that this would be attached to the cottage by a doorway.

The Court of Appeal held that it was for the landlord to prove (a) that it intended to carry out works and (b) that such work could not reasonably be done without obtaining possession. In this case, there was no evidence on which the judge could have reached such conclusions. The tenant's appeal against a possession order was allowed.

County courts

G16.2   *Sugarwhite v Afridi*

[2002] 5 CL 425, Central London Civil Justice Centre

Ground 6 applied only where legal rather than merely physical possession required

The claimant landlord sought possession against an assured tenant pursuant to Housing Act 1988 Sch 2 Ground 6. He produced a complex programme of works to be carried out at the premises. It was common ground that part of the programme included works that the landlord was obliged to carry out under Landlord and Tenant Act 1985 s11. The tenant contended that the landlord already had a right of access under Housing Act 1988 s16 and that, by analogy with cases such as *Heath v Drown* [1973] AC 498 decided under Landlord and Tenant Act 1954 s30(1)(f), the landlord was entitled to possession only if he could prove that he required legal possession, as opposed to physical possession, to carry out the works.

HHJ Collins dismissed the claim for possession. The cases decided under s30(1)(f) were authority for matters decided under Ground 6. To succeed under Ground 6, the landlord was required to satisfy the court that the proposed works not only fell outside s11, but also that they were of such a nature that legal, rather than physical possession of the property was necessary for them to be carried out.

G17   # Death of tenant

Housing Act 1988 Sch 2 Ground 7 applies where an assured periodic tenancy has devolved under the will or intestacy of the former tenant and the proceedings for the recovery of possession are begun not later than 12 months after the death of the former tenant or, if the court so directs, after the date on which, in the opinion of the court, the landlord or, in the case of joint landlords, any one of them became aware of the former tenant's death. Housing Act 1985 Sch 2 Ground 16 provides a ground for possession where a tenancy vested, on the former tenant's death, in a successor who is a member of the tenant's family, other than a partner. The accommodation must be underoccupied and notice requirements complied with.

Court of Appeal

G17.1 *Shepping v Osada*

(2001) 33 HLR 146; [2000] 30 EG 125; [2001] L&TR 489; (2000) *Times* 23 March, CA

Service of 8 notice did not amount to proceedings for recovery of possession

The defendant succeeded to a periodic assured tenancy on the death of the former tenant. The landlords knew of the death of the former tenant by 31 May 1998. They served a notice pursuant to Housing Act 1988 s8 on 17 February 1999 relying on Sch 2 Ground 7. A county court summons was issued on 2 June 1999. A possession order was made. Although Ground 7 provides that proceedings must be begun 'not later than 12 months after the death of the former tenant or, if the court so directs, after the date on which, in the opinion of the court, the landlord became aware of the former tenant's death', a recorder held that 'proceedings for the recovery of possession' were constituted by the service of the s8 notice rather than by the subsequent issue of proceedings.

The tenant's appeal was allowed. It was clear that the references in s8 to 'proceedings for possession' meant court proceedings rather than service of a s8 notice. Much the same followed from a reading of Ground 10. There was no valid reason for distinguishing between the use of the expression 'proceedings for possession' in s8 and Ground 10 and the use of 'proceedings for the recovery of possession' in Ground 7. The clear indication was that where the 1988 Act referred to proceedings for possession, it meant court proceedings.

G17.2 *Wandsworth LBC v Randall*

[2007] EWCA Civ 1126; 7 November 2007

Correct date for establishing whether family members are residing with tenant who has succeeded to a secure tenancy is date of hearing before the court

Mr Randall's grandfather was a secure tenant. Mr Randall lived alone in the property with him. On 31 December 2004, the grandfather died. Mr Randall succeeded to the tenancy. In August 2005, at his request, his mother and half-sister moved into the property. In April 2006, Wandsworth issued possession proceedings relying on Housing Act 1985 Sch 2 Ground 16. A deputy district judge made an order for possession, holding that: (1) the accommodation afforded by the property was more extensive than was reasonably required by Mr Randall; (2) suitable alternative accommodation in the form of a one-bedroom flat had been offered; and (3) it was reasonable to make an order for possession. In reaching this conclusion, he left out of account the needs of Mr Randall's mother and half-sister, since they were not members of his family at the date of Mr Randall's succession to his grandfather's tenancy. HHJ Birtles allowed an appeal.

The Court of Appeal dismissed a second appeal by Wandsworth. The correct date for establishing whether family members are residing with a tenant who has succeeded to a secure tenancy is the date of the hearing before the court, not the date of succession. Dyson LJ found it impossible to construe s84(2)(c), which provides that the court shall not make a possession order unless it both considers it reasonable to make the order and is satisfied that suitable accommodation will be available for the tenant when the order takes effect, as requiring a consideration of whether the accommodation is reasonably suitable to the needs of the tenant and his family as they were at the date of succession. It would be odd if the question of reasonableness were to be judged at the date of the hearing, the issue of the availability of suitable alternative accommodation were to be judged at a date later than the hearing, but the issue of whether the accommodation is more extensive than is reasonably required were to be judged as at the date of succession. The case was remitted to a district judge to decide whether, when the order took effect, there would be available to Mr Randall, his mother and half-sister accommodation that was reasonably suitable to their needs. The Court of Appeal said that it would be open to Wandsworth to establish that a three-bedroom flat would be sufficient for their needs.

G18   Subletting the whole of premises

Housing Act 1985 s93(2) provides that secure tenancies cease to be secure if the tenant sublets the whole of the premises. An assured tenancy also ceases to be an assured tenancy of the whole of the premises are sublet (see Housing Act 1988 s1(1)). In such circumstances, the landlord need only serve a notice to quit and bring a possession claim. There is no need to prove any ground for possession. Rent Act statutory tenancies also come to an end if the tenant ceases to occupy the premises as a residence (see section C4). There is no equivalent provision for Rent Act protected tenancies. However, Rent Act 1977 Sch 15 Case 6 provides a discretionary ground for possession, where, 'without the consent of the landlord, the tenant has ... assigned or sublet the whole of the dwelling-house or sublet part of the dwelling-house, the remainder being already sublet'.

Court of Appeal

G18.1 *Leith Properties Ltd v Springer*
[1982] 3 All ER 731; (1982) 4 HLR 33, CA

Case 6 could be relied on where tenant had lawfully sublet premises without consent

Landlords let a flat on a quarterly tenancy to Mrs Byrne. There was no prohibition against subletting. She sublet the whole of the flat to Mr Springer. Mrs Byrne did not live in the flat. The landlords served notice to quit and brought possession proceedings, claiming possession under Case 6. Mr Springer defended, relying on Rent Act 1977 s137(1) (which states that nothing in a possession order against a protected or statutory tenant shall affect the right of any subtenant to whom the dwelling-house has been lawfully sublet) and s137(2) (which states that where a statutorily protected tenancy is determined, any lawful subtenant shall become the tenant of the landlord). The tenant appealed against the possession order that was made in the county court.

The Court of Appeal accepted the tenant's submission that the flat had not been unlawfully sublet and that, accordingly, Rent Act 1977 s137(2) applied. However, the subtenant still remained vulnerable to proceedings where the landlord could establish against him one of the conditions set out in s98 and Sch 15. The Court of Appeal held that the landlord could rely on Case 6 against Mr Springer, but remitted the case to the county court to decide whether or not it was reasonable to make a possession order against him.

G18.2   *Pazgate Ltd v McGrath*
(1984) 17 HLR 127; (1984) 272 EG 1069, CA

Case 6 applied where tenancy had been assigned without consent

Mr McGrath took a tenancy for a term of five years so that his daughter-in-law and her two young children could live in the flat. The tenancy agreement contained covenants which prohibited subletting and assignment. Mr McGrath died and his executors executed a vesting assent transferring the tenancy to his daughter-in-law. The landlords denied that the assent was effective in vesting the tenancy on Mrs McGrath and refused to accept rent. They then sold the flat to the plaintiffs, who began possession proceedings based on Cases 1 and 6.

The Court of Appeal held that the assent was effective, that Mrs McGrath had become the tenant and that, on expiry of the fixed term, she became the statutory tenant. However, the landlords had not consented to the assignment. Although the old landlords took no steps to evict the tenant before sale of the property, there was no reason why they should have done. The correspondence between the solicitors was a clear contemporary record of the attitude of the parties and showed that the landlords had not consented. The county court judge's finding that there was no consent was correct. The Court of Appeal also declined to interfere with the judge's finding that it was reasonable to make a possession order.

G18.3   *RC Glaze Properties Ltd v Alabdinboni*
(1993) 25 HLR 150, CA

Case 6 applied where rent book contained prohibition against subletting

The tenants had been granted an oral tenancy. The rent book used consistently by the managing agents contained a prohibition against subletting. In possession proceedings in the county court, no evidence was given about the terms of the original letting, but the judge drew the inference from the rent book that the tenants had agreed to the inclusion in their tenancy of a prohibition against subletting and that, when they became statutory tenants, that term continued to apply (see Rent Act 1977 s3(1)).

The Court of Appeal dismissed the tenants' appeal, holding that there was ample evidence to justify the judge's finding of fact.

G19   Former employees

Housing Act 1985 Sch 2 Ground 12 and Housing Act 1988 Sch 2 Ground 16 both provide grounds for possession against former employees. Rent Act 1977 Sch 15 Case 8 gives a discretionary ground for possession 'where the dwelling-house is reasonably required by the landlord for occupation as a residence for some person engaged in his whole-time employment, or in the whole-time employment of some tenant from him or with whom, conditional on housing being provided, a contract for such employment has been entered into, and the tenant was in the employment of the landlord or a former landlord, and the dwelling-house was let to him in consequence of that employment and he has ceased to be in that employment'.

Court of Appeal

G19.1   *Duncan v Hay*
[1956] 1 WLR 1329; [1956] 3 All ER 555, CA

Case 8 did not apply where tenant remained an employee in a different capacity

Hospital authorities let a cottage on their farm to their farm foreman as a Rent Act tenant, as a consequence of his employment. Later the hospital decided to give up possession of the farm. It gave the tenant notice to quit but employed him in a new capacity as a laundry machine operator in the hospital. The new landlord of the farm brought possession proceedings.

The Court of Appeal held that the landlord was not entitled to a possession order because the tenant had not ceased to be in the employment of the former landlords within the meaning of the predecessor to Case 8. 'Employment' in this context meant the relationship of employer and employee. Changing the nature of the work that the tenant had been performing did not mean that he had ceased to be in the employment of the hospital. The words 'in a particular capacity' could not be implied as a qualification of the reference to the cessation of employment.

G20   Agricultural employees

Rent Act 1977 Sch 15 Case 16 gives a mandatory ground for possession 'where the dwelling-house was at any time occupied by a person under the terms of his employment as a person employed in agriculture, and (a) the tenant neither is nor at any time was so employed by the landlord and is not the widow of a person who was so employed, and (b) not later than the relevant date, the tenant was given notice in writing that possession might be recovered under this Case, and (c) the court is satisfied that the dwelling-house is required for occupation by a person employed, or to be employed, by the landlord in agriculture'.

Cases involving the notice provisions under Case 16 may be relevant to other grounds for possession.

Court of Appeal

G20.1 *Fowler v Minchin*

(1987) 19 HLR 224; [1987] 1 EGLR 108; (1987) 282 EG 1534, CA

Notice that did not state 'that possession might be recovered under this case' invalid

A landlord let a former tied agricultural cottage under a tenancy agreement which included a term that the tenant would vacate on 28 days' notice if the landlord required it for a farmworker.

The Court of Appeal held that this did not satisfy the Case 16 requirement that a landlord seeking possession must have given 'notice in writing that possession might be recovered under this Case' under the provisions of the Rent Act 1977. The same principles would seem to apply to the other cases in Rent Act 1977 Sch 15 Part II, although courts hearing claims brought under Cases 11 and 12 have power to dispense with written notice.

G20.2 *Springfield Investments Ltd v Bell*

(1990) 22 HLR 440; [1991] 02 EG 157, CA

Notice valid provided made clear that possession might be recovered for agricultural worker

A tenant appealed unsuccessfully against a possession order made under Case 16. HHJ McNaught had found that a certificate of fair rent which stated that the letting was to be one pursuant to Case 16, which had been handed by the landlord to the tenant before commencement of the tenancy, satisfied the requirements of Case 16.

The Court of Appeal agreed, stating that a Case 16 notice did not have to be in any specific form, but merely had to make it clear that possession might be recovered for an agricultural worker.

G21 **Owner-occupiers**

Housing Act 1988 Sch 2 Ground 1 and Rent Act 1977 Sch 15 Cases 9 and 11 contain provisions which may allow owner-occupiers and others to recover possession in a wide range of differing situations.

G22 **Returning owner-occupier (Housing Act 1988 Sch 2 Ground 1)**

Court of Appeal

G22.1 *Boyle v Verrall*

(1997) 29 HLR 436; [1997] 1 EGLR 25, CA

Judge wrong to hold must be 'exceptional case' before dispensing with notice; persistent late payment of rent relevant to reasonableness

The plaintiff landlord sought possession against the defendant who was an assured tenant, under Ground 1 (owner-occupier), claiming that she required the property as a principal home for her husband. No written notice that she intended to rely on that ground had been given before the grant of the tenancy and so she sought to persuade the court that it was just and equitable to dispense with the notice requirement. She relied on the fact that she had served a blank (and therefore invalid) s20 notice, stating that the tenancy would be an assured shorthold tenancy. At first instance, the judge heard evidence that the landlord's husband had an urgent need for a London home because he worked long unsocial hours and that the tenants, who received income support, were unable to afford the expense of moving home. He found that the landlord had not told the tenants that the flat would be required for herself or her husband, although there had been some conversation about her husband's intentions. He held that it would have to be an 'exceptional case' to justify dispensing with the written notice and so dismissed the claim for possession. The landlord appealed.

Allowing her appeal and making a possession order, Auld LJ stated that, in determining whether it was just and equitable to dispense with notice, the court should look at all the circumstances of the case. If oral notice was given when a tenancy was granted, it may be an important factor favouring dispensation. However, it does not follow that oral notice is a prerequisite for such a decision. On the other hand, absence of oral notice is not a reason for restricting dispensation to circumstances where there is an 'exceptional case'. The judge had given the wrong weight to some of the circumstances and had wrongly applied a test of exceptionality to them. Auld LJ also held that the tenant's persistent late payment of rent was a relevant circumstance.

G22.2 **Hegab v Shamash**
June 1998 *Legal Action* 13, CA

All relevant matters to be considered when deciding whether to dispense with notice

Dr Hegab brought possession proceedings relying on Housing Act 1988 Sch 2 Ground 1 (owner-occupier). Although he had occupied the flat before Mr Shamash entered into possession, he had not served a notice before the grant of the tenancy indicating that he intended to rely on this ground. The trial judge dispensed with the need for such a notice on the ground that it was just and equitable to do so. He expressly took into account the fact that no tenancy had been intended because the defendant had intended to purchase the premises from the plaintiff and the fact that the landlord had later 'behaved in a disgraceful way' by illegally evicting the tenant and disobeying an injunction.

The Court of Appeal stated that it was 'inherent in the way the judge proceeded that he was deciding what was just and equitable by taking into account all the circumstances'. However, it allowed the tenant's appeal because the judge had failed to take into account two matters: (a) the tenant had paid a deposit of £4,000 in relation to the proposed purchase, which had not been refunded, and (b) the landlord had not paid the costs of the earlier proceedings concerning the illegal eviction.

G22.3 *Mustafa v Ruddock*
(1998) 30 HLR 495, CA

Failure to notify tenant that possession might be required important but not conclusive

In 1991 the plaintiff landlord lived in premises which he owned. In 1994 agents acting on his behalf let the property to the defendant under what purported to be a one-year assured shorthold tenancy but was in fact an assured tenancy because no Housing Act 1988 s20 notice was served. The agent was later made bankrupt. The landlord brought possession proceedings under Ground 1 (owner-occupier), contending that it was just and equitable to dispense with the requirement for a notice. The defendant did not appear at trial, but the county court judge held that it was not just and equitable to dispense with the notice requirement since no indication had been given to the tenant at the outset that the landlord might require the premises for his own occupation.

The Court of Appeal allowed the landlord's appeal. Although the Court of Appeal will rarely interfere with the exercise of judicial discretion, the judge would certainly have decided the case differently if *Boyle v Verrall* (G22.1) had been cited to him. The Court of Appeal stated that in this case the following matters were relevant to the exercise of discretion:

1) The original letting purported to be an assured shorthold.
2) The proceedings were undefended. There was no evidence of hardship to the tenant.
3) There was genuine hardship to the landlord.
4) The error arose through the mistake of the landlord's agent who was now bankrupt.

The failure to notify the tenant that possession might be required was an important factor but in no way conclusive. If *Boyle v Verrall* had been drawn to his attention, the judge would have given greater weight to the landlord's family situation and to the fact that the tenancy agreement warned the tenant that no security of tenure would be given. Given the failure of the tenant to advance her case (either at first instance or in the Court of Appeal), there were no valid reasons for refusing an order for possession.

G23 **Premises required for landlord or member of family (Rent Act 1977 Sch 15 Case 9)**

Court of Appeal

G23.1 *Alexander v Mohamadzadeh*
(1986) 18 HLR 90; (1985) 51 P&CR 41; [1985] 2 EGLR 161, CA

No evidence given by tenant of attempts to find other accommodation

The landlady of a flat brought possession proceedings, relying on Case 9, claiming that she reasonably required it for her own occupation. Following *Smith v McGoldrick* (H2.6) and *Kidder v Birch* (G23.10), it was held that the relevant date for deciding whether the premises were required was the date of the hearing, not the date of commencement of proceedings. Furthermore, the tenant had not proved that greater hardship would be caused by making the order than by not making it, because no evidence had been given by her of any attempts to find other accommodation.

G23.2 *Amaddio v Dalton*

(1991) 23 HLR 332, CA

Landlord by purchase could not rely on Case 9

The former landlady, before she died, expressed a wish that her executors would offer the premises in question to the plaintiff, who had been employed by her, and, if he wanted to purchase them, provide the necessary money. It was held that, once these wishes had been carried out, the plaintiff was a landlord by purchase and accordingly was not entitled to possession under Case 9.

G23.3 *Baker v MacIver*

(1990) 22 HLR 328; [1990] 2 EGLR 104, CA

Greater hardship to tenant where less prospect of finding alternative accommodation

A landlord brought possession proceedings against a protected tenant, claiming that he and his wife reasonably required the premises for occupation by themselves as a residence (Case 9). The landlord was himself a protected tenant of other accommodation which had been let by his employer, but had been offered either £20,000 to vacate or alternative accommodation. Notwithstanding this, a county court judge made an order for possession. The tenant appealed, contending that the judge had not properly considered the question of greater hardship.

The Court of Appeal allowed the appeal, stating that, although the tenant had to discharge the burden of proving greater hardship, the judge had not 'considered the disparity of the positions of landlord and tenant in finding alternative accommodation'. There would be greater hardship to the tenant in making a possession order because he did not have the same prospect of finding alternative accommodation as the landlord.

G23.4 *Bassett v Fraser*

(1981) 9 HLR 105, CA

Judicial notice taken of difficulty in renting furnished accommodation

The landlady, who was in her early 70s, took possession proceedings under Case 9 against the tenant, who was aged 83. The county court judge refused an order for possession on the basis that greater hardship would be caused to the tenant. The landlady appealed, contending, among other things, that the tenant had not herself looked for other accommodation.

The Court of Appeal, dismissing the appeal, held that the judge was able to take judicial notice that:

> ... it is in fact common knowledge from one end of the United Kingdom to another that in nearly all areas it is almost impossible to rent furnished accommodation.

G23.5 *Bostock v Tacher de la Pagerie*

(1987) 19 HLR 358; [1987] 1 EGLR 104, CA

Premises required for landlord's daughter who was equitable tenant in common

A court can make a possession order under Case 9 where a landlord reasonably requires accommodation as a residence for an adult daughter, even if the daughter is an equitable tenant in common of the house and so entitled to require the landlord to transfer the premises into their joint names. (If the property had been in joint names, a possession order could not have been made, because all joint owners must require the premises as a residence if they are to rely on Case 9, see *McIntyre v Hardcastle* (G23.13).) The Court of Appeal also stated that, although in the usual case it might well be that any judgment on a claim for arrears of rent should be stayed pending the hearing of the tenant's counterclaim, in this case the counterclaim was so nebulous and ill-drafted that the judge was entitled to give judgment on the claim for rent arrears without a stay.

G23.6 **Coombes v Parry**

(1987) 19 HLR 384, CA

Prospect of landlord obtaining alterative accommodation needed consideration

A county court judge found that a landlord reasonably required possession of a dwelling-house under Case 9 and that greater hardship would not be caused to the tenant by making an order. However, he dismissed the landlord's claim for possession because he found that the potential future development of property owned by trustees under the landlord's father's will would improve the financial position of the landlord and so enable him to purchase another home.

The Court of Appeal granted the landlord's appeal because there was insufficient evidence that the development would take place. The case was remitted to the county court for rehearing because, since trial, another property owned by the trust had become vacant.

G23.7 **Evans v Engelson**

(1979) 253 EG 577, CA

Possession ordered where landlord acquired property from company he owned

The plaintiff, Mr Evans, held all the shares in FC Property Co, a corporate body. The company let premises to the defendant tenant. Later the company sold the house to Mr Evans for a price which was well below the market value. Mr Evans then claimed possession under Case 9 for occupation as a residence for himself and his future wife and stepson.

The Court of Appeal held that the company was merely a nominee for Mr Evans, that it was a mere shell and that it was therefore irrelevant for the analysis of Rent Act rights. The landlord for Rent Act purposes was, and had at all material times been, Mr Evans. The possession order made in the county court was confirmed.

G23.8 **Ghelani v Bowie**

[1988] 2 EGLR 130; (1988) 42 EG 119, CA

House obtained as investment property not required for landlord's own occupation

This case is an example of how difficult it is for either a landlord or a tenant to appeal against a county court judge's finding that premises either are or are not required as a residence by a landlord or a member of the landlord's family. HHJ Hill-Smith, sitting at Willesden County Court, dismissed the landlord's claim for possession, holding that a house which had been let to five trainee surveyors was 'an investment property' and was not required for the landlord's own occupation.

The Court of Appeal found no grounds which would justify disturbing the judge's conclusions or for saying that they were wrong.

G23.9   *Hodges v Blee*

(1988) 20 HLR 32; [1987] 2 EGLR 119, CA

Tenant had not discharged the burden of proving greater hardship

The landlord reasonably required possession of a maisonette for two sons who were living in cramped and unsatisfactory accommodation. The tenant had lived in the maisonette for 15 years, was aged 57 and received supplementary benefit. The county court judge concluded that hardship would be caused whatever order he made, but held that the tenant had not discharged the burden of proving that greater hardship would be caused to him by making a possession order. On appeal, it was contended for the tenant that the judge had failed to take into account that he would be homeless and would not have a right to be rehoused by the local authority, whereas the landlord's sons, with a total income of £165 per week, would be more able to find other accommodation.

Dismissing the appeal, Stocker LJ stressed that questions of greater hardship are essentially matters for county court judges, and their findings will usually be overturned only if no reasonable county court judge could have reached the same conclusion or if the decision was perverse.

Note, however, *Manaton v Edwards* (G23.11), where, unusually, a county court judge's finding on greater hardship was overturned on appeal.

G23.10   *Kidder v Birch*

(1982) 5 HLR 28; (1983) 46 P&CR 362; (1983) 265 EG 773, CA

Case 9 could be relied on where need for accommodation in the ascertainable future

The landlord claimed possession under Case 9 on the basis that she wanted to modernise the premises and move into them when her mother, who was aged 86 and in bad health, died. The judge made a possession order, but directed that the warrant for possession should lie in the court office until the death of the plaintiff's mother.

The Court of Appeal refused to set aside the possession order, holding that it is perfectly proper for a landlord to seek possession under Case 9 where the need for accommodation is in the ascertainable and not distant future. However, it directed that a warrant for possession was to issue if the plaintiff's mother died within 12 months, but that otherwise it was not to issue at all.

G23.11   *Manaton v Edwards*

(1986) 18 HLR 116; [1985] 2 EGLR 159, CA

Where tenant would be rehoused by council, landlord's appeal successful

The landlord, who had recently married, brought possession proceedings under Case 9. The tenant conceded that the landlord, who was living in a rented caravan, reasonably required the premises, but claimed that greater hardship would be caused by making an order for possession. He asserted that, although there was a letter before the court from the local authority stating that it would consider an application from him for housing under the Housing (Homeless Persons) Act 1977 (now Housing Act 1996 Part VII), there was no guarantee of the nature or location of accommodation which would be offered.

After accepting that the local authority had an obligation under the 1977 Act to secure that accommodation was available, the Court of Appeal decided that, although some hardship would be caused to the tenant in the short term if a possession order were made, there was no evidence to justify the county court's decision that greater hardship would be caused to the tenant and so an order should have been made. The onus of proving greater hardship lies on the tenant. The court stressed, in accordance with a long line of authorities, that, notwithstanding the decision in this case, it is only in exceptional circumstances that the Court of Appeal interferes with a trial judge's finding on greater hardship.

G23.12 **Mansukhani v Sharkey**

(1992) 24 HLR 600; [1992] 33 EG 65, CA

Landlord who received property as a gift, and not by purchase, could rely on Case 9

After they had granted a tenancy to Ms Sharkey, Mr Mansukhani's parents transferred the premises to him 'in consideration of mutual love and affection and of the covenants hereinafter contained'. One of the covenants provided that he was to make all payments due under the mortgage taken out by his parents.

The Court of Appeal held that the arrangement was a gift and that, since Mr Mansukhani was therefore not a landlord by purchase, he was entitled to claim possession under Case 9.

G23.13 **McIntyre v Hardcastle**

[1948] 2 KB 82; [1948] 1 All ER 696, CA

Case 9 requires all joint beneficial owners to require property as residence

Where there are two or more joint beneficial owners, possession can be claimed under what is now Case 9 only if possession is required for occupation as a residence for all or both of them. The position is different under Case 11 (see *Tilling v Whiteman* (G24.1)).

G23.14 **Patel v Patel**

[1981] 1 WLR 1342; [1982] 1 All ER 68; (1982) 43 P&CR 243, CA

Personal representatives can rely on Case 9

Personal representatives can be landlords of properties for the purposes of Case 9 and can claim possession even if they have no beneficial interest. Usually, however, to do so would be a breach of trust, but that is not the case where the personal representatives are trustees for their children and are claiming possession in order to live in the house with the children.

G23.15 *Potsos v Theodotou*

(1991) 23 HLR 356; [1991] 2 EGLR 93, CA

Case 9 applied where possession required for illegitimate son of one of joint owners

It was held that a husband and wife who were joint owners of a house were entitled to claim possession under Case 9 where premises were required for the 'illegitimate son' of the wife, even though the husband was not his father and had not adopted him.

G23.16 *Rowe v Truelove*

(1976) 241 EG 533, CA

Possession refused where landlord only intended to live in property until sold

It was held that a landlord who only established an intention to sell as quickly as possible, but decided to live in the premises temporarily pending sale, could not claim that premises were reasonably required as a residence under the predecessor to Case 9.

G23.17 *Thomas v Fryer*

[1970] 1 WLR 845; [1970] 2 All ER 1; (1970) 21 P&CR 398, CA

Daughter who inherited part share in mother's estate not a landlord by purchase

The owner of a rented house died. She left the residue of her estate, including the house, to four children in equal shares. The children agreed that one daughter, the plaintiff, should take the house in part satisfaction of her share, but that she should pay three-quarters of the value of the house to her siblings to achieve equality of benefit. The Court of Appeal held that the plaintiff was not a landlord by purchase and so was entitled to claim possession under the predecessor to Case 9.

G24 **Premises required for landlord or member of family (Rent Act 1977 Sch 15 Case 11)**

House of Lords

G24.1 *Tilling v Whiteman*

[1980] AC 1; [1979] 2 WLR 401; [1979] 1 All ER 737; (1979) 38 P&CR 341; (1979) 250 EG 51, HL

Only one of two joint landlords need require property as residence for Case 11

Mrs Tilling and Miss Dossett jointly owned a house. Before letting it on a Rent Act protected tenancy, they served a notice under the predecessor to Case 11. At the end of the fixed-term tenancy, they brought possession proceedings on the basis that it was required as a residence for Mrs Tilling.

The House of Lords held that one of two joint owners of a dwelling-house who together let it was entitled to recover possession even though the house was required as a residence for only one of them. The term 'owner-occupier' is shorthand for 'a person who occupied the house as his residence and let it' ([1979] 1 All ER at 741). The position is different where proceedings are brought under Case 9 (see *McIntyre v Hardcastle* (G23.13)).

Court of Appeal

G24.2   *Bissessar v Ghosn*

(1986) 18 HLR 486, CA

Where landlord intended to sell property and use proceeds to build new house in Trinidad possession ordered

The landlord went to work in the West Indies. He served a Case 11 notice before letting his house in London to the defendant. After the tenant had applied to the rent officer, the landlord brought possession proceedings and, at trial, contended that the house was not suitable having regard to his place of work and that he required possession in order to dispose of it and to use the proceeds of sale to buy a house that was more suitable to his needs (see Rent Act 1977 Sch 15 Part V para 2(f)).

The Court of Appeal held that there must be a connection between the acquisition of a new house by a landlord as a residence and the use of the proceeds of sale of his or her existing house for that purpose. It is not sufficient for the landlord merely to say that at some time in the future the proceeds of sale might be used to purchase a new property. However, in the present case there was ample evidence to show that the landlord intended to use the proceeds of sale to acquire a new house in Trinidad. The fact that the landlord intended to build a house rather than purchase a house which was already standing made no difference. The Court of Appeal upheld the possession order made in the county court.

G24.3   *Bradshaw and Martyn v Baldwin-Wiseman*

(1985) 17 HLR 260; (1985) 49 P&CR 382; [1985] 1 EGLR 123, CA

Not just and equitable to dispense with notice where no indication possession might be required

The plaintiff's mother let a flat to the defendant's husband. A Case 11 notice was not served and there was no suggestion that the plaintiff's mother might wish to recover possession for her own use. The plaintiff's mother and the defendant's husband then died. Later the plaintiff began possession proceedings based on Cases 9 and 11 but, in the light of the hardship which would be caused to the defendant, who was aged 73, abandoned the claim under Case 9. The county court judge found it just and equitable to dispense with the requirement for notice under Case 11 and made a possession order.

The Court of Appeal allowed the tenant's appeal. Griffiths LJ stated that it is '... of the utmost importance to a tenant that he should appreciate when he takes rented property whether or not he is obtaining a secure tenure ...', and that it cannot have been the intention of parliament '... to apply Case 11 to a letting which was not in the first place intended to be a temporary letting, and which was a letting which was intended to carry with it the security of the Rent Act' ((1985) 17 HLR at 267). The words 'just and equitable' have a wide import and when considering whether it is just and equitable to dispense with the notice requirement, courts should consider the circumstances affecting the landlord, or his successors in title, and the circumstances of the tenant, and, of course, the circumstances in which the failure to give written notice arose (cf, *Fernandes v Parvardin* (G24.5)).

G24.4 *Davies v Peterson*

(1989) 21 HLR 63; [1989] 06 EG 130, CA (see also P11.6)

Landlord's intention to occupy premises intermittently could satisfy ground

The tenant submitted that a county court judge had been wrong to hold that it was 'just and equitable' to dispense with service of a Case 11 notice before commencement of the tenancy, and to find that the landlord required the premises as 'a residence' because it was his intention to stay in the house for only a few months of the year.

The Court of Appeal dismissed the appeal and followed *Naish v Curzon* (G24.10), in which it was held that even an intention on a landlord's part to occupy premises 'intermittently' is enough to satisfy the ground for possession.

G24.5 *Fernandes v Parvardin*

(1982) 5 HLR 33; (1982) 264 EG 49, CA

Possession ordered where tenants had been given oral notice

Before premises were let, the tenants were informed orally that the landlord had formerly occupied the property as his home. However, no written Case 11 notice was served. The landlord brought possession proceedings under Cases 9 and 11 and contended that it was just and equitable for the court to dispense with the need for written notice. The county court judge made an order for possession and the tenants appealed.

The appeal was dismissed. There was no suggestion of any misunderstanding on the part of the tenants and, in practical terms, oral notice was just as effective in notifying the tenants of the landlord's intention as written notice would have been (cf, *Bradshaw and Martyn v Baldwin-Wiseman* (G24.3)).

G24.6 *Ibie v Trubshaw*

(1990) 22 HLR 191, CA

Judge entitled to conclude landlord had not occupied as a residence in visiting girlfriend

A landlord appealed against the refusal of HHJ Krikler to make an order for possession. The landlord had claimed that periodic visits to stay with a girlfriend in the house which he owned amounted to 'occupation as a residence' and that, accordingly, he was entitled to rely on Case 11 as a 'returning owner-occupier'.

The Court of Appeal refused to overturn the judge's findings. Staughton LJ stated that although 'occupation as a residence' could exist even if a person was temporarily absent, the judge was fully entitled to conclude that the landlord had not resided in the premises. Staughton LJ also stated that, even if the landlord had occupied them as a residence, it would not have been 'just and equitable' for the judge to have dispensed with the need for a Case 11 notice before commencement of the tenancy, simply because the tenants had signed what purported (wrongly) to be merely temporary 'licence agreements'.

G24.7 **Kennealy v Dunne**

[1977] QB 837; [1977] 2 WLR 421; [1977] 2 All ER 16; (1976) 34 P&CR 316; (1976) 242 EG 623, CA

Landlords 'required' flat where genuinely intended to occupy it

Landlords claimed possession under the predecessor to Case 11, even though there were two other properties that they could occupy. The county court judge dismissed their claim because he did not consider that they 'required' the flat which was let. The landlords appealed.

Allowing their appeal, Stephenson LJ stated that all that landlords who sought possession under the predecessor to Case 11 had to prove was that they really wanted to occupy and genuinely had the intention of occupying the premises which were let as a residence at once or within a reasonable period. The word 'required' was not qualified by any need for reasonableness on the landlord's part.

G24.8 **Lipton v Whitworth**

(1994) 26 HLR 293, CA

Intention to occupy residence until sold consistent with occupying as a residence

Possession proceedings were brought against regulated tenants, relying on Case 11. In the county court, it was claimed that the premises were required as a residence by the plaintiff's wife and daughter, who were returning from abroad. A possession order was made, but the wife stayed in the house for a few weeks only. She found it difficult to adjust and went to live with relatives. The property was put on the market and sold. The tenants claimed that the wife had never intended to live in the house and obtained leave to appeal out of time.

The Court of Appeal held that occupation for a short time did not negate residence. An intention by a landlord to live in a house until it could be sold was consistent with occupying a house as a residence under Case 11.

G24.9 **Mistry v Isidore**

(1990) 22 HLR 281; [1990] 2 EGLR 97, CA

Previous occupation by landlord could be temporary and intermittent

The Court of Appeal dismissed a protected tenant's appeal against a possession order made under Case 11. The tenant had contended that the judge had applied the wrong tests in deciding whether the landlord had occupied the flat before the grant of the tenancy and whether he had an intention to occupy the flat within a reasonable time. The Court of Appeal followed *Naish v Curzon* (G24.10) in finding that, for the purposes of Case 11, a landlord's previous occupation was a question of fact and could be temporary and intermittent. The court also declined to interfere with the judge's finding that the landlord required the premises for his occupation.

G24.10 **Naish v Curzon**

(1985) 17 HLR 220; (1985) 51 P&CR 229; [1985] 1 EGLR 117, CA

Case 11 did not require any permanence of occupation as a residence

The plaintiff, who lived mainly in South Africa, bought a house in 1971 and lived in it from time to time until 1980, when he let it to the defendant. Subsequently he obtained a possession order, relying on Case 11. The tenant appealed, contending that, since the plaintiff only visited the country for short periods, he did not require the house for the purposes of 'residence'.

The Court of Appeal dismissed the appeal, holding that there was nothing in Case 11 that required any permanence of occupation as a residence. Occupation which is temporary or intermittent is sufficient to establish residence. It is a question of fact and the judge was entitled to take the view that he did.

G24.11   *White v Jones*

(1994) 26 HLR 477, CA

Not just and equitable to dispense with notice despite oral notice having been given

The plaintiff landlords, who had last lived in the house in 1964 before going abroad, brought possession proceedings under Case 11 against the tenants, who had moved in during 1972. No written notice had been given, but on the grant of the tenancy the plaintiffs had said that they might return to the United Kingdom and require possession. The tenancy originally lacked full security of tenure because the house was furnished, but the tenancy became protected as a result of the Rent Act 1974. The landlords claimed that it was 'just and equitable' to dispense with written notice under Case 11. At first instance a possession order was made.

On appeal, it was held that the oral notice was not of great significance because no one believed that there was security of tenure. The relatively limited residential requirements of the plaintiffs, the length of time that the defendants had lived in the premises and the hardship which would result from eviction all outweighed the significance of the 1972 oral notice. It was not 'just and equitable' to dispense with the requirement for written notice in this case and the claim for possession was dismissed.

High Court

G24.12   *Clements v Simmonds*

[2002] EWHC 1652 (QB), [2002] 41 EG 178

Landlord who sold property after obtaining possession under Case 11 ordered to compensate former tenant under s102

Mr and Mrs Simmonds, the owners of a large Victorian house, lived in the property during World War II but then moved to California. Miss Clements moved into a ground floor flat in the building in 1975 as a Rent Act protected tenant. After her husband's death in 1996 Mrs Simmonds served a notice to quit and began proceedings under Rent Act 1977 Sch 15 Case 9 (dwelling reasonably required as a residence for her). After protracted litigation, HHJ Rowntree made a possession order. Miss Clements vacated on 22 November 2000. Mrs Simmonds did not move into the property, but within a couple of weeks instructed agents to put it on the market. The house was sold in the early part of 2001 for approximately £1.25 million. Miss Clements began proceedings under s102 seeking compensation.

Burton J held that it had to be shown that any representation was false when made. The mere fact that the property was put on the market when possession was obtained did not mean automatically that the statements made in the possession claim were false. There was, however, an evidential burden on Mrs Simmonds to explain what had occurred in November and why it was inconsistent with the original statements. If that was done, as in this case, the legal burden remained with the claimant. Although she had to show on the balance of probabilities that the claim was made out, the burden was higher than normal because of the seriousness of the allegations. Burton J rejected Mrs Simmonds's explanation that when she recovered possession, the property was in such a disastrously bad state that she was unable to contemplate moving in. He found that she had misstated the position about her finances to improve her case on greater hardship and had no intention of moving into the property and that her aim was to achieve vacant possession.

As to compensation, Burton J, following *Murray v Lloyd* (O9.11), stated that 'the measure of damages is in general the sum required to put an injured party in the same position he would have been in if he had not suffered the wrong for which compensation is being awarded'. Although a jointly instructed expert had placed a value of £100,000 on the statutory tenancy, Burton J rejected Miss Clements's evidence that she would have remained in the property – by the time of the trial of the s102 claim, she was in fact living in Australia. He found that the parties would have negotiated a deal whereby Miss Clements would have been paid £60,000 in return for the giving of vacant possession and that that was her loss. Although the claimant pursued a claim in addition for general damages for distress and inconvenience, no such loss was proved.

G25 ## Suitable alternative accommodation

Housing Act 1988 Sch 2 Ground 9 provides a ground for possession where 'suitable alternative accommodation is available for the tenant or will be available for him when the order for possession takes effect'. Rent Act 1977 s98(1)(a) is in almost identical terms. See too Housing Act 1988 Sch 2 Part III and Rent Act 1977 Sch 15 Part IV. Housing Act 1985 does not provide that the mere existence of suitable alternative accommodation is a ground for possession, but it is, in relation to certain grounds for possession, a requirement that suitable alternative accommodation is available for a secure tenant (see Housing Act 1985 s84(2)(b) and Sch 2 Part IV).

Court of Appeal

G25.1 *Akram v Adam*

[2002] EWCA Civ 1679; [2005] 1 WLR 2762 [2005] 1 All ER 741; [2003] HLR 27; (2002) *Times* 19 November

Alternative accommodation to be available at time order made/came into force

The defendant tenant occupied a room in the landlord's house under a Rent Act statutory tenancy. The landlord proposed to convert the tenant's accommodation into a self-contained unit. This would require the landlord to have access to the tenant's accommodation to undertake works. The tenant would not give consent to such access. The landlord applied for orders that his proposal be deemed acceptable alternative accommodation within the meaning of Rent Act 1977 s98(1)(a) and that the tenant provide him with such access as was required to undertake the works. A judge made the orders sought. The tenant appealed on the ground that the judge could not make an order requiring him to provide the landlord with access, since he was a statutory tenant and could accordingly only be required to give access where the conditions within s116 of the Act were satisfied.

The Court of Appeal allowed the appeal. The case did not satisfy the conditions of s116. The judge had not considered that he had been exercising his power under s116 when he made the order. Furthermore, the court could not have made an order under s98(1)(a) for possession of the tenant's accommodation since that required suitable alternative accommodation to be available at the time the order was made, or to be available by the time the order would come into force. That could not be the case where the order would have been made so as to enable works to be done which, when completed, would have given suitable alternative accommodation. Accordingly, without the consent of the tenant or the provision by the landlord of suitable alternative accommodation in the interim, there had been no basis on which the judge could make the order that he had.

G25.2   *Amrit Holdings Co Ltd v Shahbakhti*

[2005] EWCA Civ 339; [2005] HLR 30; [2006] L&TR 18

Balancing financial hardship of parties not reasonable to force tenant to move

Mr Shahbakti lived in rented accommodation which had been let to him in 1978 as a Rent Act 1977 regulated tenant. The claimants sought possession on the basis that alternative accommodation was available. That alternative accommodation was one of many residential properties owned by Mr Shahbakti, which he let as investment properties. It had been held on an assured shorthold tenancy by one of his tenants. That tenancy had come to an end, but the tenant was still in possession. HHJ Lindsay QC dismissed the claim for possession, after balancing the financial consequences to Mr Shahbakti of making a possession order (he would have had to rearrange his financial investment affairs) against the lack of any financial hardship caused to the landlord in dismissing the claim for possession.

The Court of Appeal dismissed the appeal. It was open to the judge to take the view that it was not reasonable to force Mr Shahbakti to move to the alternative accommodation, even on an assumption that it was available, and that was a decision which could not be interfered with.

G25.3   *Dawncar Investments Ltd v Plews*

(1993) 25 HLR 639; [1994] 1 EGLR 141; [1994] 13 EG 110, CA (see H6.3)

Possession refused as neighbourhood of proposed accommodation very different

G25.4 *Fennbend Ltd v Millar*

(1988) 20 HLR 19, CA

No power to order injunction to prevent tenant from disposing of property she owned

The tenant rented a flat in Chelsea. The landlords brought possession proceedings claiming, among other things, that a house which the tenant owned in Putney was suitable alternative accommodation. The landlords sought an interlocutory injunction to prevent the tenant from disposing of the house that she owned or from letting it. A county court judge granted an injunction and the tenant appealed.

The Court of Appeal allowed the appeal, holding that the court's power to grant an injunction could 'only be exercised in support of a right which the plaintiff has or ... probably has' (at 22). The landlord had a right to possession only if there was suitable alternative accommodation available at the time of the hearing and, in the meantime, the tenant had an untrammelled right to deal with her own property as she thought fit. Subsequently, the tenant let her house in Putney on a five-year 'company let'. At the trial of the claim for possession of the Chelsea flat, HHJ Hordern held that the Putney house was not available and, accordingly, could not be suitable alternative accommodation (see September 1987 *Legal Action* 14).

G25.5 *Hill v Rochard*

[1983] 1 WLR 478; [1983] 2 All ER 21; (1983) 8 HLR 140; (1983) 46 P&CR 194; (1983) 266 EG 628, CA

Environment and standard of existing accommodation relevant

The tenants rented a large period country house in an isolated position with a staff flat, outbuildings, stable, large garden and adjoining field. The landlords brought possession proceedings, offering as an alternative a modern house with four bedrooms, two living rooms, double garage and garden, situated on a pleasant estate on the outskirts of a country village. The county court judge made a possession order, holding that he need only have regard to the needs of the tenants as regards extent and character.

The tenants appealed, but their appeal was dismissed. The environment and standard of living to which the tenants were accustomed in their existing accommodation were relevant but, since the alternative accommodation offered was in a country environment which would enable them to enjoy the amenities of country life and was of a sufficiently high standard to provide for their housing needs, it was suitable alternative accommodation.

G25.6 *Jones v Cook*

(1990) 22 HLR 319; [1990] 2 EGLR 108, CA

Judge to consider whether accommodation offered similar to type referred to in local authority certificate

The tenant challenged the validity of a certificate provided by a local authority and used by a landlord in possession proceedings, based on the alleged availability of suitable alternative accommodation which he was offering (see Rent Act 1977 Sch 15 Part IV para 5(1)(a)). The certificate in question stated that the 'property is similar in extent to council-owned dwelling-houses which may be provided in the neighbourhood for families consisting of husband, wife and three children'.

The Court of Appeal set aside the possession order because HHJ Mc-Naught had not himself decided whether the accommodation offered was similar to that which would be offered in similar circumstances by the local authority, having regard to the certificate. He should have considered whether or not the alternative accommodation offered was similar to the type of premises referred to in the certificate.

G25.7 *Laimond Properties Ltd v Al-Shakarchi*
(1998) 30 HLR 1099; (1998) *Times* 23 February; [1998] EGCS 21, CA (see C7.1)

Where possession ordered against protected tenant on basis of suitable alternative accommodation, the new tenancy did not have to be protected

G25.8 *Montross Associated Investments v Stone*
March 2000 *Legal Action* 29, CA

'Needs' meant 'the needs for housing': superb view not a housing need

The defendant rented 'a beautiful flat' overlooking Hyde Park. It was 'a superb flat with spacious accommodation ... a magnificent living room and magnificent views from the bedroom'. The judge described 'the brilliance of light in the living room as truly magnificent'. The claimant, who wanted to develop the site sought possession, offering suitable alternative accommodation under Rent Act 1977 s98(1)(a). In making an order for possession, the judge held that the superb view was not a housing need. He said that his task was not simply that of comparing one place with another, but, rather to decide whether the property offered satisfied the statutory test contained in s98(1)(a) and Sch 15 Part IV.

Following *Hill v Rochard* (G25.5), the Court of Appeal held that the judge had not erred in law and that 'needs' must mean 'the needs for housing' or 'need for accommodation for the purpose of habitation'.

G25.9 *Mykolyshyn v Noah*
[1970] 1 WLR 1271; [1971] 1 All ER 48; (1970) 21 P&CR 679, CA

Part of tenant's existing accommodation could be alternative accommodation

The tenant rented four rooms. The landlords offered the same accommodation as suitable alternative accommodation, but minus one sitting room. It was the landlord's case that the tenant did not use the sitting room except to store furniture in it.

The Court of Appeal upheld a possession order. First, it was settled law that part of the tenant's existing accommodation could amount to suitable alternative accommodation (see *Thompson v Rolls* [1926] 2 KB 426; *Parmee v Mitchell* [1950] 2 KB 199, CA, *McIntyre v Hardcastle* (G23.13) and *Scrace v Windust* [1955] 1 WLR 475, CA). Second, the premises were not made unsuitable merely because there was no room for furniture for which the tenant had no foreseeable need. However, in considering whether accommodation offered is reasonably suitable to the needs of the tenant, courts should consider, among other things, whether it is large enough to take the tenant's furniture in so far as that furniture is required to enable the tenant to live in reasonable comfort.

G25.10 *Redspring v Francis*

[1973] 1 WLR 134; [1973] 1 All ER 640; (1972) 25 P&CR 8, CA

Environmental factors relevant to suitability and reasonableness

The tenant rented a small flat in a quiet residential road with use of a garden. The landlords offered alternative accommodation with no garden on a busy thoroughfare, next door to 'a fried fish shop', near to a hospital, cinema and public house and with an open space to the rear which the local authority proposed to use as a transport depot. The judge made a possession order stating that in considering whether the alternative accommodation was suitable, he had to disregard environmental factors such as the smell from the fish and chip shop, noise from traffic and the public house, etc.

The tenant's appeal was allowed. The court could properly take into account environmental matters, both when considering suitability to the tenant's needs and reasonableness. The flat offered was not suitable.

G25.11 *Siddiqui v Rashid*

[1980] 1 WLR 1018; [1980] 3 All ER 184; (1980) 40 P&CR 504; (1980) 256 EG 169, CA

Environmental factors only relevant to extent they relate to the property

The Court of Appeal held that, in determining whether accommodation is suitable to the tenant's needs as regards character, environmental matters can be taken into account only in so far as they relate to the property itself. This does not extend to matters such as the location of his friends, his mosque or cultural interests.

G25.12 *Yewbright Properties Ltd v Stone*

(1980) 40 P&CR 402; (1980) 254 EG 863, CA

Proximity to work and suitability to be construed in common sense way

The landlords claimed that suitable alternative accommodation in Dulwich, London SE22 had been offered to a freelance clothes designer. Most of her customers were in Fulham, London SW6. A county court judge held that the accommodation was not reasonably suitable to her needs with regards to proximity to her work.

The Court of Appeal allowed the landlord's appeal, holding that where a tenant's work required travel from a home base to a number of places in the surrounding area, that surrounding area could be a 'place of work' for the purposes of Rent Act 1977 Sch 15 para 5(1). Proximity and suitability should be construed in a commonsense way, taking into account not only the distance as the crow flies, but also the means of transport available and the journey time.

G25.13 *Yoland Ltd v Reddington*

(1982) 5 HLR 41; (1982) 263 EG 157, CA

Alternative accommodation may be part only of premises already rented by tenant

Suitable alternative accommodation may be part only of premises already rented by the tenant.

County courts

G25.14 *Rosemary Estates Ltd v Connolly*
March 1987 *Legal Action* 20, Clerkenwell County Court

Not suitable where tenant would have to wait much longer for bus to work

Possession proceedings were brought on the basis that suitable alternative accommodation was available at either of two other properties. One property was held not to be suitable because a s9(1)(a) (now Housing Act 1985 s190(1)) notice, listing major works, was outstanding and so HHJ Aron Owen could not be satisfied that the property 'is ... or will be available' to the tenant (Rent Act 1977 s98(1)(a)). A suggestion by the landlords that there should be an adjournment found no favour because the landlords had appealed against some of the works in the notice and were not able to say when the works would be completed. The second property was held not to be suitable 'as regards proximity to place of work' (Rent Act 1977 Sch 15 Part IV para 5(1)). The defendant's evidence that at present he had to wait three to four minutes for a bus, whereas from the other property he would have to wait 16 to 17 minutes, was accepted. HHJ Aron Owen also found that it would not be reasonable to make an order, in view of the length of the tenant's residence and the fact that the landlords' motives were purely financial.

G26 **Overcrowding**

Housing Act 1985 Sch 2 Ground 9 applies where 'the dwelling-house is overcrowded, within the meaning of Part X, in such circumstances as to render the occupier guilty of an offence'. Rent Act 1977 s101 provides that, if premises are statutorily overcrowded, 'nothing shall prevent the immediate landlord of the occupier from obtaining possession'.

G27 **Overcrowding (Rent Act 1977 s101)**

Court of Appeal

G27.1 *Henry Smith's Charity Trustees v Bartosiak-Jentys*
(1992) 24 HLR 627; [1991] 2 EGLR 276, CA

Overcrowding a state of affairs and possession ordered where evidence that it continued

In possession proceedings, HHJ Simpson QC found that four people, including the statutory tenant, were living in a bed-sitting room which measured 28 feet by 18 feet. It was, therefore, statutorily overcrowded. Relying on Rent Act 1977 s101, the landlord sought, and was granted, an outright order for possession. The tenant appealed, contending that, although there was evidence on which the judge could find that there were four people living in the room, the judge had to be satisfied that there was overcrowding on the actual day when the order was made, and that the evidence was that, on the morning of the trial, only two beds were made up.

The Court of Appeal held that overcrowding is a state of affairs, and that there was overwhelming evidence that this was continuing. There was no evidence, apart perhaps from on the morning of the trial, that this had ceased to be the case. The tenant's appeal was dismissed. The Court of Appeal also held that, in such circumstances, there was no jurisdiction to make a suspended possession order, although the court left open the question of whether the original order could have been varied.

CHAPTER H

Reasonableness

H1   Introduction and general considerations

Where a landlord claims possession on a discretionary ground against a secure tenant (Housing Act 1985 Sch 2 Grounds 1–8 and 12–16), an assured tenant (Housing Act 1988 Sch 2 Grounds 9–17) or a protected or statutory tenant (Rent Act 1977 s98(1)(a) or Sch 15 Cases 1–10), the court may make an order for possession only if it considers that it is reasonable to do so (Housing Act 1985 s84(2)(a), Housing Act 1988 s7(4) and Rent Act 1977 s98(1)).

For cases where the reasonableness of making a possession order has been considered in the context of a secure tenant's exercise of the right to buy, see chapter E.

It should also be remembered that, even if a ground for possession is proved, courts may have to take into account the Disability Discrimination Act 1995. The effect of s22(3)(c) is that it is unlawful to discriminate 'by evicting the disabled person or subjecting him to any other detriment'. According to the Act, courts should consider whether the defendant is a 'disabled person' within the meaning of Disability Discrimination Act 1995 ss1–3, whether or not there has been discrimination, ie, treating a disabled person less favourably for a reason which relates to the disabled person's disability – and whether the landlord's treatment of the tenant and the making of a possession order is justified – see H8 below.

Court of Appeal

H1.1   *Cumming v Danson*
[1942] 2 All ER 653, CA

All relevant circumstances to be taken into account when considering reasonableness

At page 655, Lord Greene MR said:

> in considering reasonableness . . . it is, in my opinion, perfectly clear that the duty of the Judge is to take into account all relevant circumstances as they exist at the date of the hearing. That he must do in what I venture to call a broad common-sense way as a man of the world, and come to his conclusion giving such weight as he thinks right to the various factors in the situation. Some factors may have little or no weight, others may be decisive, but it is quite wrong for him to exclude from his consideration matters which he ought to take into account.

H1.2   *Manchester CC v Green*
January 1999 *Legal Action* 26, CA

Judges should refer to question of reasonableness and how they resolve it in their judgments

The defendant was a secure tenant. The council obtained a suspended possession order in 1993, and an injunction under Housing Act 1996 s152 in May 1998. Later the defendant was committed for breach of the injunction. The council then brought proceedings for possession under Housing Act 1985 Sch 2 Ground 2 arising from the conduct of the tenant's children. HHJ Tetlow granted a 28-day outright order.

The Court of Appeal, refusing an application for leave to appeal, observed that it would helpful if trial judges expressly referred in their judgments to the question of 'reasonableness' (Housing Act 1985 s84) and how they had resolved that question. As this judge had in fact considered whether it would be reasonable to grant possession there was no prospect of his order being disturbed.

H1.3   *Shrimpton v Rabbits*
(1924) 131 LT 478, KBD

Where landlord's wish is reasonable it does not follow that it is reasonable to gratify it

In a case involving possession proceedings under the Increase of Rent and Mortgage Interest (Restrictions) Act 1920, Swift J said that, in relation to the question of reasonableness, the court 'must consider all the circumstances affecting the holding of the premises by the person who holds them and as they relate to the landlord who wants to hold them'. Acton J said, 'Because a [landlord's] wish is reasonable, it does not follow that it is reasonable in a court to gratify it.'

H2   'Consent orders'

Court of Appeal

H2.1   *Appleton v Aspin*
[1988] 1 WLR 410; [1988] 1 All ER 905; (1988) 20 HLR 182; (1988) 56 P&CR 22; [1988] 1 EGLR 95, CA

Ground and reasonableness have to be satisfied despite tenant's prior agreement to leave

The vendor and purchaser of a freehold property both agreed with a Rent Act protected tenant that the purchaser would acquire the property with vacant possession. The tenant specifically agreed not to make any claim to occupy the premises against the purchaser.

In subsequent possession proceedings brought by the purchaser, the Court of Appeal held that no possession order could be made unless the conditions in Rent Act 1977 s98(1) (ie, a ground for possession and reasonableness) were satisfied.

H2.2   *Hounslow LBC v McBride*
(1999) 31 HLR 143, CA

Possession order cannot be made 'by consent' unless admission that ground for possession and 'reasonableness' satisfied

Ms McBride rented a flat from the council on a secure tenancy. She lived there with her four sons aged between 13 and 22. In December 1993 the council began possession proceedings relying on Housing Act 1985 Sch 2 Ground 1 (non-payment of rent) and Ground 2 (in this case serious criminal conduct causing nuisance or annoyance). Before the hearing of the claim in January 1997 the parties agreed that a suspended possession order should be made. At a brief hearing lasting no more than five minutes, which was attended by solicitors but not the defendant, the district judge made the order sought. Before making the order she checked that the figure for the arrears was agreed and that the defendant understood the implications of the order. In a later affidavit it was stated that both solicitors 'assumed that the district judge would simply rubber stamp the order'. Later the council alleged that Ms McBride had broken the conditions of the suspended order and applied for a warrant of possession. Ms McBride applied to have both the possession order and the warrant set aside, claiming that the district judge had not had sufficient material before her to enable her to reach the conclusion that it was reasonable to make the order. A circuit judge allowed the defendant's application. The council appealed.

The appeal was dismissed. Simon Brown LJ said that 'an order such as this is not in law capable of being consented to unless the terms of the Act are satisfied'. A distinction has to be drawn between a form of order which contains an admission about those matters on which the jurisdiction to make the order rests (eg, reasonableness) and an order such as this one which did not. The bar against appealing against an order made by consent contained in CCR Ord 37 r6(1) did not apply and the judge had jurisdiction to set aside the order. Nothing in the order itself or in the circumstances surrounding the making of the order indicated that Ms McBride had admitted that it was reasonable to make the order. Nor had the district judge taken sufficient steps to satisfy herself of the reasonableness of making the order. Simon Brown LJ said:

> Whilst acknowledging that the case falls close to the border-line, it seems to me in the end that that there really never was here any admission of any sort, implied or otherwise, with regard to the reasonableness of making an order on the nuisance and annoyance ground. ... In my judgment the reasonableness of an order on that ground really was something about which the district judge ought specifically to have sought assurance.

H2.3   *Plaschkes v Jones*
(1982) 9 HLR 110, CA

Possession order should not be made merely on basis tenant said would like to leave

A landlord served a notice to quit and brought possession proceedings against Rent Act protected tenants. Their solicitor advised that the notice to quit was invalid and applied for legal aid. That application was refused on the ground that, since the notice was invalid, no order would be made. However, at court, the tenants, when asked, said that they would like to leave the property. A possession order was made.

The tenants' appeal was allowed. The court had not considered the validity of the notice to quit or whether it was reasonable to make a possession order.

H2.4   *R v Bloomsbury and Marylebone County Court ex p Blackburne*
(1985) 275 EG 1273, CA

Order quashed despite tenant's consent to order on payment of £11,000

Mr Blackburne was a statutory tenant. His landlords brought possession proceedings, claiming that he was not occupying the premises as a residence and that he owed rent. He denied these allegations and counterclaimed for breach of repairing obligations. At court, negotiations took place and a consent order was made whereby Mr Blackburne was to receive £11,000 in return for him consenting to a possession order. He subsequently changed his mind and instructed new solicitors to apply for judicial review and to quash the possession order.

The Court of Appeal granted his application, approving Glidewell J's conclusion that:

> ... if there is before the court a claim that the defendant is entitled to the benefit of the Rent Acts, the court may not make an order for possession unless it is satisfied, either by evidence or by admission by or on behalf of the defendant, that he is not entitled to that protection. ((1984) HLR 56 at 67)

The court can only make a possession order if it is satisfied that the conditions set out in Rent Act 1977 s98 (ie, a ground for possession and, where necessary, that it is reasonable) are met. The fact that Mr Blackburne had received and spent some of the money due under the order did not raise an estoppel.

H2.5   *R v Worthing BC ex p Bruce*
(1994) 26 HLR 223; [1994] 1 EGLR 116; [1994] 24 EG 149, CA

Consent order stood as implied admission that tenant was not a secure tenant

The occupier unsuccessfully appealed against the refusal of his application for judicial review of the making of a consent order in possession proceedings. Initially he had exercised the right to buy. That right had been admitted and completion deferred. On his application to complete, the council refused to do so and asserted that he had not been a secure tenant. He then began proceedings for a declaration and the council counterclaimed for possession. With the case part heard, the action was compromised on terms that the tenant would withdraw the right to buy claim and give up possession.

The Court of Appeal held that the implied admission in the consent order that the tenant was not a secure tenant taken together with the fact that the order was made by the judge after at least some evidence was heard, enabled the order to stand despite the general rule that statutory protection cannot be undermined by a simple order based on consent. (See also *Morris v Barnet LBC* (E14.10).)

H2.6   *Smith v McGoldrick*
(1976) 242 EG 1047, CA

Defendant should have been allowed to withdraw admission given prior to hearing date

Landlords claimed possession under the predecessor to Case 9 (premises reasonably required as residence for landlord or family). The tenant thought that she would be offered a council house and instructed solicitors to write to the court admitting the claim to possession. Subsequently, she found that the council would not offer accommodation and tried to withdraw the admission. The county court judge refused to allow her to do so and found that, since she had already admitted the plaintiff's claim, it was reasonable to make a possession order.

The Court of Appeal allowed the tenant's appeal. The county court judge was wrong in refusing to allow the defendant to withdraw the admission made or to lodge a defence out of time. Furthermore, it said that courts must consider whether it is reasonable to make an order for possession at the date of the hearing and not at an earlier stage.

H2.7 **Wandsworth LBC v Fadayomi**
[1987] 1 WLR 1473; [1987] 3 All ER 474; (1987) 19 HLR 512; (1988) 86 LGR 176, CA

'Consent order' set aside on application by tenant's wife

The council brought possession proceedings under Housing Act 1985 Sch 2 Ground 10 (possession needed for carrying out of works), which requires that suitable alternative accommodation be available for the tenant and his or her family. The tenant's marriage had broken down and initially the council had offered to rehouse the parties separately. At the date of hearing, however, Mr Fadayomi accepted accommodation offered and undertook to allow the rest of his family to live with him there. A possession order was made 'by consent'.

On appeal by Mrs Fadayomi, the Court of Appeal set aside the possession order and held that (a) the wife had an interest in the proceedings as a member of the family for whom the new accommodation was required to be suitable (she should therefore have leave to intervene and be joined as a defendant) and (b) 'consent orders' have no place in public sector proceedings, because the court must be satisfied that the appropriate grounds and conditions (eg, reasonableness) are made out. The court can have jurisdiction only if the necessary matters are proved by evidence or if there is express admission of the relevant facts.

High Court

H2.8 **R v Birmingham CC ex p Foley**
March 2001 *Legal Action* 29; 14 December 2000, QBD

Order made 'by consent' following compromise set aside

The council brought possession proceedings under Housing Act 1985 Sch 2 Ground 2 (nuisance). After a day's argument the claim was compromised on terms, including an undertaking that the council would rehouse the tenant. A possession order was made, expressed to be 'by consent'.

In proceedings for judicial review Longmore J set aside the order on the basis that it was granted without jurisdiction. An order for possession can be made only if the court is satisfied both that a ground for possession is made out and that it is reasonable to order possession. Applying *Hounslow LBC v McBride* (H2.2) in the absence of any express or implied admission of those matters, there was no basis on which the order could be sustained.

H2.9 **R v Newcastle upon Tyne County Court ex p Thompson**
(1988) 20 HLR 430; [1988] 26 EG 112, QBD

Order set aside where conditions for making order not proved or admitted

A landlord brought possession proceedings based on Rent Act 1977 Sch 15 Case 9 (premises reasonably required as residence for landlord or family).

The tenant consented to a possession order, but later applied for judicial review.

Quashing the possession order, McNeill J held that, before a court can make a possession order under Case 9, three conditions have to be satisfied. First, the court must consider it reasonable to make an order. Second, it must be shown that the property is reasonably required. Third, the court must be satisfied on the question of greater hardship. The court has jurisdiction to make a consent order only where those conditions are proved or the tenant has plainly and expressly admitted them.

H3   Rent arrears

Court of Appeal

H3.1   *Brent LBC v Marks*
(1999) 31 HLR 343, CA

Order set aside where tenant paying arrears, although quarterly due to DSS payment system

In 1993 the defendant tenant was granted a secure tenancy. Arrears of rent for temporary accommodation were transferred to the rent account. Housing benefit was then credited weekly to the rent account from 1996 to meet current rent. Deductions were made by the DSS from income support and paid to the council in respect of (a) the charges which were ineligible for housing benefit and (b) £2.50 per week towards the arrears. These payments were made quarterly in arrears and so the pattern of the rent account was of regularly accruing arrears which were only reduced four times a year. The council served a notice of intention to seek possession in 1997. Legal aid was not granted to the tenant, but her solicitors wrote to the court drawing attention to the pattern of payment and the reasonableness condition. A circuit judge granted a possession order, suspended on terms that the tenant pay current rent and £2.50.

The Court of Appeal allowed the tenant's appeal and remitted the case to the county court. Following *Second WRVS Housing Society v Blair* (H3.11) the judge ought to have had more regard to the fact that current rent was being paid and that the benefit system was both causing and then dealing with the arrears. Looking at the overall position, this was a responsible tenant whose position had stabilised. The tenant should not be penalised for the fact that the Benefits Agency paid the council quarterly in arrears. On a new exercise of the court's discretion, a possession order might not be made.

H3.2   *Burgoyne v Griffiths*
(1991) 23 HLR 303; [1991] 1 EGLR 14; [1991] 12 EG 164, CA

Order not overturned on appeal; judge 'must have applied his mind' to reasonableness

From 1960 Mr Griffiths, who was employed as an agricultural foreman or bailiff by the plaintiff's predecessors in title, lived with his wife in a farm cottage provided by his employers rent free. The employers paid the rates. In 1985 Mr Griffiths retired because of ill health, but he and his wife continued to live in the cottage rent free. In 1987 the plaintiff applied to the rent officer. He registered a rent of £27 per week but the defendants refused to pay any rent. The plaintiff sought possession on the ground of non-payment. Mr Griffiths claimed that he had been granted a licence to occupy rent free for the rest of his life. The trial judge disbelieved this. He accepted the plaintiff's submissions that the licence was part and parcel of the employment and coterminous with it and that, when his employment came to an end, Mr Griffiths became a statutory tenant in accordance with Rent (Agriculture) Act 1976 s4. He made a suspended order for possession.

The defendant's appeal was dismissed. The Court of Appeal held that, on the evidence, the judge was entitled to come to the conclusion that there was a service occupancy which came to an end at the same time as Mr Griffiths's employment, see *Ivory v Palmer* [1975] ICR 340, CA. Second, although the judge did not specifically refer to the question of reasonableness (Rent (Agriculture) Act 1976 s7(2)), the Court of Appeal was satisfied that:

> Whilst unexpressed, the learned judge must have applied his mind in the circumstances of this case to the question of reasonableness.

The Court of Appeal noted that the judge had listened to the case over a period of three days and that the defendant had not been as frank as he might have been and had made no effort to make any payment once a fair rent had been assessed.

H3.3   *Dellenty v Pellow*

[1951] 2 KB 858; [1951] 2 All ER 716, CA (see G5.2)

Reasonable to make possession order, despite tenant paying off arrears the day before the hearing, in light of tenant's payment history

H3.4   *Drew-Morgan v Hamid-Zadeh*

(2000) 32 HLR 316; [1999] 26 EG 156, CA (see Q4.2)

Reasonable to make order despite payment of arrears during hearing where non-payment 'plainly deliberate and avoidable'

H3.5   *Haringey LBC v Stewart*

(1991) 23 HLR 557; [1991] 2 EGLR 252, CA

Reasonable to make possession order where counterclaim failed and no arrangement made to pay off arrears

In possession proceedings based on rent arrears, the tenant's counterclaim for breach of repairing obligations was dismissed. The judge made an immediate possession order. On appeal, the tenant argued that it was not reasonable (Housing Act 1985 s84) for an order to have been made.

The Court of Appeal held that a reasonable tenant would have put aside the rent money to meet the eventuality of the counterclaim failing. The judge had rightly looked at the tenant's history of late rent payment, his failure to make any provision to meet the arrears, and the fact that he was single and under-occupying premises in an area of great housing need. In answer to the assertion that it was not reasonable to make an absolute order and that the judge ought to have suspended any order made (Housing Act 1985 s85), Waite J stated that, in ordinary circumstances, it would not have been reasonable if the tenant had made arrangements, in the event of the failure of his counterclaim, for the early discharge of the arrears. However, in exceptional circumstances where there was a bad history of persistent delay in paying rent, it could be reasonable to do so. The appeal was dismissed and illustrates the difficulty of appealing first instance decisions on reasonableness.

H3.6   *Hayman v Rowlands*

[1957] 1 WLR 317; [1957] 1 All ER 321, CA

'Everyday practice' to suspend order for possession on terms where tenant in arrears

Denning LJ stated:

> It would be very unusual indeed for the tenant to be ordered out on the ground of non-payment of rent when the full amount was already paid into court. If the tenant is in arrear, in these cases under the Rent Restriction Acts the everyday practice is to make an order for possession, but to suspend it so long as the current weekly rent and a payment on account of the rent in arrear are paid. ([1957] 1 All ER at 323).

H3.7   *Laimond Properties Ltd v Raeuchle*

[2000] L&TR 319; December 1999 *Legal Action* 21; (2001) 33 HLR 113; April 2000 *Legal Action* 31, CA

Judge wrong to make outright order where tenant offered to pay off arrears; matters not pleaded should not be taken into account

A property company brought possession proceedings against an elderly Rent Act tenant in circumstances in which she would be voluntarily homeless and ineligible for local authority accommodation if she was evicted. Although she was described as a 'cantankerous and extremely difficult tenant', she had been justified in the past in withholding large sums from rent which were set off against damages for disrepair. At the date of trial in the current proceedings there were arrears of £511.10. This was the difference between the registered rent and housing benefit paid direct to the landlord. Judgment was also awarded for £3,200 for trespass for the unauthorised use of a storage room. The trial judge was sceptical about the defendant's offer to pay £10 per week and made an outright order, stating that it would be futile to make a suspended possession order.

Sedley LJ gave permission to appeal, saying that, in his experience

> ... it would have been unique to find an outright order made in circumstances such as these, even against a tenant as difficult as this one where there was no history (and there was none) of breaches of the conditions upon which previous orders have been suspended. There was indeed no history of suspended possession orders.

He noted that one factor not mentioned by the judge was the considerable length of time that the applicant had been a tenant, although she had very rarely been up to date with her rent. By the time of the hearing of the tenant's appeal the landlords had succeeded in garnisheeing the tenant's bank account and all arrears had been paid.

The Court of Appeal allowed the tenant's appeal and discharged the possession order. Chadwick LJ said that the first requirement for a judge who had found a ground for possession to be proved was to ask whether it was reasonable to make a possession order at all and then, second, to ask whether the order should be stayed or suspended under s100(2). He held that the trial judge had erred in law in holding that any suspended possession order should include terms about paying the licence fee and giving access. The correct approach was to determine the extent of the rent arrears and how quickly those were likely to be paid. If a suspended possession order had been made on the tenant's offer of £10 per week the arrears would have been discharged within a year. Section 100(4) contemplates that it is usual to discharge a suspended possession order once arrears have been paid off. In those circumstances it would not have been futile to make a suspended possession order. The Vice-Chancellor indicated that the judge had been wrong to take into account matters which had not been pleaded (eg, the fact that the tenant had made it difficult for the landlord to carry out repairs). He should have constrained himself to those matters properly pleaded by the landlord to establish whether the order for possession should have been suspended. He said:

> In considering whether it is reasonable to make an order ... the judge should consider all the relevant circumstances: but that is not a consideration at large. It is, or should be, a consideration in accordance with the pleadings. In my judgment, the matters proposed to be relied upon by the landlord in support of the contention that it would be reasonable to make an order for possession ... must be pleaded by the landlord.

H3.8   *Lambeth LBC v Henry*
(2000) 32 HLR 874, CA

SPO 'obvious' order to make despite fact that tenant would have order hanging over her for 23 years

The defendant was a secure tenant. In 1990 the council obtained an order for possession and judgment for arrears and costs of £2,375. The order was suspended on terms that the tenant pay current rent plus £1.85 per week towards the arrears. The tenant did not attend the hearing, was not represented and, having been notified of the order, did not seek to appeal it. By October 1995 the arrears had reached £3,600 and the council obtained a warrant. The tenant then agreed to increase instalment payments to £2.41 per week and to have the amount deducted from her income support. The warrant was withdrawn. By August 1998 arrears were still £3,500. The council sought permission to issue a warrant since six years had elapsed since judgment (CCR Ord 26 r5(1)(a) and 17(6))). The tenant cross-applied to set aside the possession order: CCR Ord 37 r2. HHJ Cox dismissed both applications. The tenant appealed, contending among other things, that the original order had been wrong in principle because its terms would involve a suspended order hanging over the tenant for 23 years with the tenancy liable to be lost automatically on any breach.

The Court of Appeal dismissed the appeal. A suspended possession order (SPO) had been the obvious order to make. Although the court practice was to be merciful to tenants and to give them a realistic opportunity to pay arrears, the question of whether it was appropriate for Ms Henry, who owed substantial arrears, to have the threat of losing her home hanging over her for years was a political question and did not go to the correctness of making the order. The order was fully permitted under the Housing Act as it stood. There were, in any event, cases in which long-term suspension of orders was appropriate and this was such a case.

H3.9 **Lambeth LBC v Thomas**
(1998) 30 HLR 89; (1997) 74 P&CR 189, CA

Wrong to refuse to make order on ground not reasonable merely because arrears related to water charges

A secure tenancy granted in 1984 contained an express obligation that the tenant should pay rent and 'other charges' promptly when due. In August 1994 the council served a notice seeking possession on the basis that there were 'rent and other charges' of £701.11 outstanding. Most of these were unpaid water charges. The balance was unpaid general rates. The net rent was fully paid up. The council sought an order for possession relying on Housing Act 1985 Sch 2 Ground 1 (rent arrears or other breach of tenancy agreement). The judge found the ground proved but held that it would not be reasonable to order possession (see Housing Act 1985 s84) as a penalty for failure to pay charges for water supplied by a privatised utility.

The court held that the judge had erred in principle in failing to make any order for possession. The tenant was in clear breach and the bulk of the debt had been outstanding since 1992. Nothing had been put aside in case she was found liable to pay. The council was out of pocket and tenants as a whole were disadvantaged by non-payments. The fact that the bulk of the money would ultimately go to a privatised utility company was irrelevant. A suspended possession order should have been made. However, the Court of Appeal decided that no order should now be made because deductions in respect of small repayments towards the arrears were being made directly from the tenant's welfare benefits.

H3.10 **Lee-Steere v Jennings**
(1988) 20 HLR 1, CA

On appeal, tenant could not adduce matters which could have been put at first hearing

A possession order was made against a statutory tenant on the ground of persistent rent arrears, even though the tenant paid all rent outstanding the day before the county court hearing. The tenant appealed and sought leave to adduce further evidence dealing with the local authority's decision not to provide accommodation because he was intentionally homeless and the difficulties he would have in obtaining a mortgage in view of the judgment relating to non-payment of rent.

Dismissing the appeal, the Court of Appeal held that these were both matters which could have been put before the trial judge and that it was unlikely that they would have had an important influence on the result of the case.

H3.11   *Second WRVS Housing Society v Blair*
(1987) 19 HLR 104, CA

Order set aside where judge refused to adjourn to ascertain more clearly the benefits position and the possibility of direct payments to the landlord

The defendant was a secure tenant, who had lived in the property for seven years when he became affected by a psychiatric illness. His life 'fell apart' and rent arrears mounted. He received supplementary benefit towards the housing costs but spent it on food. A county court judge, finding that there were arrears of £1,198 and that the tenant was still in receipt of supplementary benefit, ordered possession (suspended for two months in case the debt could be cleared in that time) and costs of £140.

The Court of Appeal set aside the order because the judge had failed to consider in detail the question of reasonableness and, in particular, the available welfare benefits. The case was sent back for reconsideration to ascertain 'more fully the benefits which could be obtained from the DHSS in relation to arrears and more generally in relation to [the tenant's] condition'. Dillon LJ stated:

> It is well known that arrangements can be made with the DHSS when housing benefit is payable to see that the rent is paid direct to the landlord and I feel that is a matter which should have been taken into account.

H3.12   *Sopwith v Stutchbury*
(1985) 17 HLR 50, CA

Judge wrong in ordering outright possession where low arrears and conduct of tenant not such as to make outright order reasonable

A country house was let to Mr Stutchbury for a term of seven years from 15 March 1975 at a rent of £600 per annum. He surrendered the tenancy and became a statutory tenant. Later, in divorce proceedings, the statutory tenancy was transferred to Mrs Stutchbury under Matrimonial Homes Act 1983 s7(3). The landlord then took possession proceedings based on arrears of rent. Although Mrs Stutchbury had tendered rent in the form of cheques, they had not been cashed by the landlord and by the time that proceedings were issued, some were out of date and Mrs Stutchbury had 'dipped into' the money, with the result that, by the time of the hearing, there were arrears of £75. The judge, after weighing up a number of matters, made an order for possession, but delayed it for six months until the defendant's youngest daughter had left school. In considering reasonableness he took into account a number of factors, including that Mrs Stutchbury was not the tenant of the landlord's choice, that the parties had entered into a 'gentleman's agreement' about vacation which had been broken, Mrs Stutchbury's suspect financial standing and that the house was too big for her.

The Court of Appeal found that the judge had erred and that it was not reasonable to make a possession order and allowed Mrs Stutchbury's appeal. The judge was not entitled to take into consideration against her the fact that she had relied on her statutory rights. Kerr LJ approved the following passage in *Woodfall* volume 3, para 3-0166:

> In practice the court will rarely consider it reasonable to make an absolute order for possession on this ground unless the arrears still unpaid at the

date of the hearing are substantial or unless there is something in the conduct of the tenant which makes it reasonable to make an absolute order.

H3.13 *Taj v Ali (No 1)*
(2001) 33 HLR 253; [2000] 43 EG 183, CA

SPO replaced with outright order where it would take 55 years to pay off arrears
A Rent Act tenant withheld rent because of disrepair. No rent was paid from 1992. Agreement was reached that the sum of £10,000 should be set off against the rent as compensation for the disrepair. In possession proceedings a judge entered judgment for £14,503 in respect of the remaining rent arrears and interest and made a possession order, suspended on payment of current rent and £5 per week. Under the order, the debt would not be paid off for more than 55 years. The judge said that, although he realised that the effect of his order was that most of the debt would be written off, he was suspending possession because the landlord had allowed the matter to run on for a long time without carrying out any repairs and because the landlord was at fault for not getting the trial on earlier. The landlord appealed.

The appeal was allowed. Any suspension should be for a definite period of time and should not extend into the mists of time. The judge had been wrong to attach too much importance to the history of the matter and why the arrears had arisen and too little to the fundamental purpose of a suspended possession order which is to enable the arrears to be paid off within a reasonable time. Robert Walker LJ said

> The judge may also be open to criticism for having apparently approached the issue in two steps: first should I suspend the order and, second, if so on what terms? That appears to be an inappropriate approach in a case where there were arguably no sensible terms on which the order could be suspended.

The Court of Appeal substituted a possession order to take effect within 28 days.

H3.14 *Televantos v McCulloch*
(1991) 23 HLR 412; [1991] 1 EGLR 123; [1991] 19 EG 18, CA (see P12.7)

Not reasonable to make a possession order to take effect five months later (in any event tenant had a complete defence by way of set-off for disrepair)

H3.15 *Woodspring DC v Taylor*
(1982) 4 HLR 95, CA

Not reasonable to make possession order where current rent and arrears being paid

The defendants, who were in their mid-fifties, had been tenants of the council for 24 years. They had a good rent record. However, Mr Taylor was made redundant and received a large tax demand. His wife became ill. As a result, rent arrears accrued. They owed £557 at the launch of possession proceedings and £700 at the date of the hearing. By this time, they were receiving benefit and the DHSS was paying current rent plus £1 per week off the arrears. In the county court, a registrar made an absolute possession order.

The Court of Appeal set aside the order, finding that no reasonable registrar (now district judge) could have found that it was reasonable to make the order. Waller LJ stated that it was 'hard to understand a conclusion that it was reasonable to make an order turning them out of their house' (at p99).

Scottish courts

H3.16   *Edinburgh DC v Stirling*
1993 SCLR 587; 1993 GWD 16-1069, Sheriff Court

If true intention of landlord was solely to recover rent, possession could be refused

The council brought possession proceedings for rent arrears against three tenants, J, L and S. Tenant S's arrears were £186. She told the court that she received income support and had applied to the DSS for direct deductions to be made and paid to the council. The council asked for an adjournment to investigate that assertion. It was refused and the claim was dismissed. Tenant L's arrears were £297. The tenant said that she received income support, cared for her terminally ill brother and knew nothing of the arrears. The sheriff dismissed the claim, noting that the council had done nothing to collect the arrears by way of applying for direct deduction itself or by any means other than possession proceedings. In both cases, he held that it would not be reasonable to order possession. Tenant J's arrears were only £65 and the council could not prove service. The sheriff refused an application to re-serve and dismissed the claim. The council appealed in all three cases, asserting that (a) it should have been given an opportunity by an adjournment to consider issues raised by tenants at the hearings and to re-serve in the case of J and (b) the sheriff seemed to be taking a uniform approach that it could never be reasonable to evict tenants who were in receipt of income support.

Allowing the appeals and remitting each case for rehearing, the Sheriff Principal (C G B Nicholson QC) held that an adjournment should have been granted to such a large municipal landlord to enable it to investigate issues first raised by the tenant at a hearing and, in the case of J, an opportunity should have been given to effect proper service. He acknowledged the concern that some local authority landlords were said to be making excessive and inappropriate use of possession proceedings, but said that:

> I am in absolutely no doubt that if a sheriff were satisfied on reasonable grounds that the true intention of the landlords in a particular case [was solely to recover the rent arrears] he would be well entitled to refuse [an order] for recovery of possession as not being reasonable in the circumstances ... (1993 SCLR at 587)

H3.17   *Glasgow DC v Erhaigagnoma*
1993 SCLR 592; [1993] CLY 5473, Court of Session

Appeal dismissed even though not pleaded that it was reasonable to make order

The council claimed possession, relying on rent arrears of over £1,000. The proceedings were adjourned on four occasions to give the tenant time to pay but, because of the tenant's continuing default, the council eventually pressed for and secured an order for possession. The tenant appealed on the ground that the council had not expressly pleaded that it was reasonable for possession to be ordered and so the proceedings were a nullity.

The appeal was dismissed on the grounds that: (a) there had been material before the sheriff from which he could have concluded that it was reasonable to order possession; (b) on the facts, what had been set out in the pleading either amounted to a prima facie assertion of reasonableness or was a failure to comply with only formal rather than substantial requirements; and (c) in any event, the tenant was not prejudiced by any deficiency. However, the Court of Session went on to hold that usually a pleading in this type of case should expressly recite the proposition that it would be reasonable to order possession and refer to the relevant statutory provision containing that requirement.

H3.18   *Midlothian DC v Brown*
1990 SCLR 765; 1991 SLT (Sh Ct) 80; [1991] CLY 5193, Sheriff Court

Money judgment granted but possession order refused where reasonableness not pleaded or proved

A routine possession claim was brought for arrears of rent. The court granted a money judgment for the arrears but dismissed the possession claim on the basis that: (a) the pleadings did not particularise the landlord's case about why it was reasonable to have possession; (b) the landlord had not exercised its right to obtain rent arrears by direct deduction from the DSS; (c) even if an order for possession were granted, the landlord was intending to keep the defendant as its tenant; and (d) the ordinary remedies for debt should not include loss of a home. The court not only applied the leading English authorities on rent arrears and 'reasonableness' (*Woodspring DC v Taylor* (H3.15) and *Second WRVS Housing Society v Blair* (H3.11), but in its judgment brought to light a series of previously unreported Scottish decisions, in which the courts had refused possession in undefended cases on the basis that the council had neither pleaded nor proved satisfaction of the 'reasonableness' requirement (see, eg, *Midlothian DC v Drummond* 1991 SLT (Sh Ct) 67, Sheriff Court).

H3.19   *Moray DC v Lyon*
1992 GWD 14-824; June 1992 *Scolag* 91, Sheriff Court

Order set aside where tenant had cleared arrears by time of hearing of application

A council tenant had repeatedly fallen into arrears since taking a tenancy in 1986. On each occasion, the council took enforcement action and the tenant raised the sums due just in time to stave off eviction. In May 1991, the arrears had again reached £300 and the council applied for possession. The tenant failed to attend the hearing and possession was granted. An application made to set aside that order was heard on 13 December 1991, by which time the tenant had again cleared the arrears. The sheriff (after considering the equivalent of the 'reasonableness condition' in Housing Act 1985 s84) stated that:

> At present, the defender is in advance with her rent. Eviction would render her and her family homeless. I did not consider it reasonable to make an

order with such drastic consequences when the tenant is not currently in default, notwithstanding her previous history.

He dismissed the possession claim.

On the council's appeal, the sheriff principal held that the decision was a proper exercise of the statutory discretion vested in the court and dismissed the appeal.

H4   Breach of obligation and anti-social behaviour

Court of Appeal

H4.1   *Barking and Dagenham LBC v Hyatt and Hyatt*
(1992) 24 HLR 406, CA

Issue is reasonableness, not the propriety or impropriety of policy regarding caravan parking

The tenancy agreement prohibited caravan parking in front gardens, without express permission from the council. The defendant joint tenants owned a caravan because Mrs Hyatt was severely disabled and it was convenient for giving her a break. The caravan was parked in their front garden because the tenants received benefit and could not afford parking fees for a site and because it was easier to maintain and keep it clean near the house. The council refused to waive the tenancy condition and took proceedings for possession. HHJ Medawar QC dismissed the proceedings, holding, among other things, that the council had failed to satisfy the reasonableness test, because the policy never to grant consent for caravans prohibited housing staff from exercising discretion in exceptional cases.

The Court of Appeal held that the propriety of the council's policy was not a factor relevant to the exercise of discretion. The judge should not have been concerned with the propriety or impropriety of the policy rule. His concern should have been with the reasonableness in the particular case of ordering possession. The case was remitted for retrial.

H4.2   *Brent LBC v Doughan*
[2007] EWCA Civ 135; [2007] HLR 28

Judge could take into account conditions of urban living and fact that landlord had placed two sensitive tenants next to each other

Mr Doughan was a secure tenant. After complaints from neighbours that he had been shouting, swearing and playing loud music when drunk, Brent applied for and was granted an interim anti-social behaviour injunction with a power of arrest under Housing Act 1996 s153. It was alleged that he then breached the terms of the injunction by slamming a door and shouting. He was made the subject of a suspended order for committal to prison subject to conditions, which again he was alleged to have breached. A further injunction was made on the same terms, but it was then alleged that Mr Doughan verbally abused one of his neighbours at a railway station. Brent applied for a possession order and for his committal. HHJ Bevington was satisfied that Mr Doughan had been noisy and had caused annoyance but dismissed the possession claim on the grounds that the noise was not greatly beyond what was to be expected from normal urban conditions and that the housing department had been at fault in placing Mr Doughan and his neighbour, both of whom were of a sensitive nature, in the same building. She also found that the premises were poorly insulated against noise. She dismissed the committal application on the grounds that the evidence of his behaviour did not satisfy the criminal standard of proof and that the incident at the railway station did not breach the terms of the injunction as it had taken place outside the area determined by the order. Brent appealed.

The Court of Appeal dismissed the appeal. May LJ stated 'The judgment as to reasonableness is intrinsically one of judicial balance akin to the exercise of a judicial discretion. It is the kind of judgment with which [the Court of Appeal] is likely to be slow to interfere for well trodden reasons.' He continued:

> Eviction is likely to be a draconian step because the spectre of intentional homelessness under Part VII of the Housing Act 1996 looms over it. On the other hand the legislative policy is to enforce good behaviour between neighbours by court orders and thereby to protect others who may well be vulnerable from socially unacceptable behaviour ...

The judge's finding was perhaps unusual but 'intellectually an entirely tenable composite decision'. It was entirely rational to find that Mr Doughan had caused annoyance under the civil standard of proof but not under the criminal standard. She was plainly aware of, and had expressly considered, the effect which his behaviour had had on his neighbours. Conditions of urban living and the perceived shortcomings of the housing department were not wholly irrelevant considerations and in any event they were not determinative in the judge's decision. She had implicitly considered the risk of repetition and was entitled to conclude that the risk was small. That risk had to be seen in the context of the fact that there had only been two or three incidents over a period of 18 months. The incident at the railway station was of some relevance but it was put forward as a breach of the conditions of the suspended committal order, which, given where it occurred, it was not.

H4.3   *Bristol CC v Grimmer*

[2003] EWCA Civ 1582; 22 October 2003

No prospect of interfering with judge's exercise of discretion on appeal

Mrs Grimmer was a secure tenant. The claimant brought a possession claim under Housing Act 1985 Sch 2 Grounds 1 and 2, relying on a large number of incidents of anti-social behaviour by her, her husband and her elder sons. It was conceded that the ground for possession was made out, but argued that it was not reasonable to make a possession order, or alternatively, if made, an order should be suspended. District Judge Frenkel made an outright possession order.

The defendant's renewed application for permission to appeal was refused. Hale LJ said that whether or not to make an outright possession order 'is pre-eminently a difficult judgment that has to be made by the judge who is hearing the evidence and seeing the parties'. There was no prospect of the Court of Appeal interfering with the exercise of the judge's discretion.

H4.4   *Bristol CC v Mousah*

(1998) 30 HLR 32, CA

Where very serious breach of tenancy, reasonable to order possession in absence of exceptional circumstances

It was an express term of the council's standard tenancy agreement that the tenant must not 'supply from or in the neighbourhood of the premises any controlled drug'. In 1993 the defendant tenant took a tenancy which was subject to those terms. Within nine months, the premises were subject to repeated police raids as a result of drug use. Surveillance established a steady stream of visitors calling at the house. Many people were arrested (in the absence of the tenant) and drugs, including crack cocaine, were found hidden on the premises, together with the accessories of dealing, such as foil, pipes and cling-film. The council sought possession under Housing Act 1985 Sch 2 Ground 1 (breach of the tenancy agreement). The judge found the ground proved – even on the higher standard required to establish illegal behaviour – and rejected the tenant's assertion of ignorance about what had been going on. However, after considering the passage of time between the last alleged wrongdoing and the trial, the personal medical circumstances of the tenant, and that, as a single man, he would be unlikely to be rehoused as a homeless person, the judge refused to make an order on the ground that it would not be reasonable to grant possession.

The Court of Appeal allowed the council's appeal. The judge had misdirected himself. Whether the tenant would be rehoused was a matter for the council. The delay between the last allegation and the trial had largely been caused by the tenant's failure to comply with the court's directions. The proper approach in a case of the commission of a most serious breach of the tenancy agreement was that it would be reasonable to order possession in the absence of some exceptional circumstance. There were no exceptional circumstances and possession should be ordered.

H4.5   *Camden LBC v Gilsenan*

(1999) 31 HLR 81, CA

Judge considered reasonableness and differentiated between acts done by tenant and those of her visitors

The council took possession proceedings against a secure tenant under Housing Act 1985 Sch 2 Ground 1 (rent arrears) and Ground 2 (nuisance or annoyance). The tenant repeatedly allowed visitors to cause severe disruption to other occupants. Incidents complained of included throwing rubbish from balconies, loud music, loitering and drunkenness. In a fracas between the defendant's boyfriend and her sister's boyfriend there was an attack with a machete which led to bloodshed. In another incident an estate co-ordinator was locked in a boiler room. The tenant was debarred from defending for failing to comply with an 'unless' order. After hearing evidence from the defendant, an assistant recorder made an absolute order for possession.

The tenant appealed unsuccessfully to the Court of Appeal. It was clear that the judge had been fully aware that he had to consider reasonableness.

He had differentiated between acts done by the defendant and acts done by her visitors. His approach had been fully consistent with *Kensington and Chelsea RLBC v Simmonds* (G7.1).

H4.6   *Canterbury CC v Lowe*

[2001] L&TR 152; (2001) 33 HLR 583, CA

Judge wrong to take account of availability of injunction when suspending order

Mrs Lowe was a secure tenant who lived in a property with two of her children and her partner. In possession proceedings based on breach of the express terms of the tenancy (Housing Act 1985 Sch 2 Ground 1), it was alleged that they had physically assaulted a neighbour's 11-year-old daughter, engaged in severe verbal abuse and threatening behaviour and had made threats to kill. The grounds were proved. The judge found it reasonable to make a possession order, but suspended it. The council appealed successfully against the suspension of the possession order.

The Court of Appeal held that (1) what had happened after the making of the possession order was irrelevant when deciding the appeal; (2) the trial judge had erred in taking into account the availability of an injunction which had been made when considering making a suspended order; (3) reliance by the council on *Bristol CC v Mousah* (H4.4) was misplaced because the circumstances were very different; but (4) taking all the evidence into account, and in particular the effect on the neighbouring family, it was not a case in which a possession order ought to have been suspended. An outright possession order was made.

H4.7   *Castle Vale Housing Action Trust v Gallagher*

(2001) 33 HLR 810, CA

Outright order disproportionate where tenant's daughter to move out; consideration of ECHR art 8

The first defendant was a secure tenant. The landlord sought possession of the property on the grounds of nuisance and annoyance and convictions for arrestable offences (Housing Act 1985 Sch 2 Ground 2). The allegations related to the anti-social conduct and criminal convictions of the tenant's daughter, who resided at the property, and her daughter's boyfriend, who was a frequent visitor. At first instance an outright order for possession was made. The tenant appealed, submitting that the judge had failed to consider whether the conduct was likely to continue, in the light of the evidence that the daughter had, by the date of judgment, bought her own property to which she intended to move. She also claimed that the judge had failed to apply properly ECHR article 8 in making a decision about the reasonableness of eviction. The council submitted that County Courts Act 1984 s77(6) prevented an appeal on the issue of the reasonableness of the order.

The Court of Appeal, allowing the appeal in part, held that:

1) Although s77(6) excluded an appeal against the judge's findings of fact, it did not exclude, in a proper case, the possibility of an appeal against a finding of reasonableness.

2) It was to be doubted whether article 8 made any difference to the way the court had always approached the question of the reasonableness of making a possession order. It did, however, reinforce the importance of only making an order depriving someone of his or her home in circumstances where a clear case was made out.

3) The difficulty in the present case was that, having decided that it was reasonable to make a possession order, it was not apparent why the judge had thought that the appropriate order was an outright one. It was not clear whether the judge had failed to consider altogether whether some other order was appropriate or whether he had considered the possibility, in which case he had failed to make clear his reasons for rejecting the less draconian alternatives. It was not for the court to speculate.

Exercising the discretion afresh, the following factors were relevant: the length of time the tenant had occupied the property; the arrestable offences had not been committed by the tenant; the tenant was guilty of omission, being unable or unwilling to prevent the anti-social behaviour; the chances of recurrence were reduced by the daughter's moving. This represented a significant change. Given these factors, an outright possession order was wholly disproportionate. The appropriate order was an order for possession suspended for two years on condition that there was no further significant breach of the tenancy agreement.

H4.8   *Croydon LBC v Moody*
(1999) 31 HLR 738; (1999) 2 CCLR 92, CA

Judge not entitled to reject psychiatric evidence; prospects of homeless application relevant

The council sought possession on the grounds of breach of express terms of tenancy prohibiting nuisance and other anti-social conduct (Housing Act 1985 Sch 2 Ground 1). In the course of a trial over six days the defence called a consultant psychiatrist who described the tenant as '... an elderly, vulnerable man who suffers from a complex personality disorder which could be described as a hybrid of schizotypal and obsessional personality disorders'. The council called no contrary medical evidence. The recorder found all the factual complaints of the council's witnesses proved and made an outright possession order. He described the psychiatric evidence as 'to a great extent unsatisfactory' and was unconvinced that the tenant was suffering from any mental ill health.

The Court of Appeal allowed the tenant's appeal. The recorder was not entitled to reject the medical evidence and it should have been taken into account in considering reasonableness (Housing Act 1985 s84), particularly if there was a prospect of the tenant being treated so that his behaviour improved. In the alternative, the evidence was relevant to the question of whether any order should be suspended. Furthermore, the court doubted whether (notwithstanding *Shrewsbury and Atcham BC v Evans* (H5.4) and *Bristol CC v Mousah* (H4.4)) a trial judge was precluded, when considering reasonableness, from considering the likelihood of a finding of intentional homelessness and the question of whether the tenant would be left without any accommodation at all.

H4.9 *Darlington BC v Sterling*

(1997) 29 HLR 309, CA

Not permissible for court to require alternative accommodation to be provided to tenant

The council sought possession, relying on Housing Act 1985 Sch 2 Ground 2. The nuisance alleged was that the tenant's young son (aged 13) had been guilty of throwing stones, lighting fires, using knives, assaults and other aggressive behaviour. A district judge found that the ground was proved and, after considering a range of factors including the circumstances of the tenant, her difficulty in controlling her son, the effect on the other residents and the consequences of a possession order (ie, the prospective homelessness of the tenant), decided that it would be reasonable to grant an order. He strongly expressed the view that (although recognising it was not a matter for him) the tenant herself could not be described as 'intentionally homeless'. The tenant appealed successfully to a circuit judge. The circuit judge held that, since the district judge had formed the view that the tenant ought not to be roofless, he should not have ordered possession unless the council could show that it would provide suitable alternative accommodation.

The Court of Appeal allowed the council's appeal. The district judge's judgment had not been vitiated by any error and there were no grounds on which the circuit judge, in exercising his appellate jurisdiction, was entitled to set it aside. It was not permissible for the court to require suitable alternative accommodation to be provided in a Ground 2 case when parliament had imposed only a requirement of reasonableness.

H4.10 *Greenwich LBC v Grogan*

(2001) 33 HLR 140; (2000) *Times* 28 March; (2000) 80 P&CR D7, CA

Wider public interest relevant when considering reasonableness in relation to possession against care leaver convicted of criminal offence

The council granted a secure tenancy to the defendant when he was 17. He had previously been in care. While still 17 he was arrested and pleaded guilty to handling stolen goods on the premises. He was sentenced to six months' youth custody. The council sought possession. By the date of the hearing there were no further matters of complaint against him. The judge made a possession order.

The tenant appealed on the ground that the judge ought to have suspended the order. The Court of Appeal allowed the appeal and suspended the possession order for 12 months. In exercising its discretion, the court could take into account the wider public interest. The tenant was a young man trying to live a life free of crime and there was a serious possibility that that attempt would fail if he lost his flat. It was in the public interest generally, and more likely in the interests of the community that he would live an honest life if he remained in the flat. The council had a duty to consider its other tenants and people on its waiting list, but the balance was in favour of suspending the order. If Mr Grogan committed any other offences, the chances of him remaining a tenant in Greenwich were very small indeed, whether the criminal conduct was before or after the period of suspension.

H4.11 *Kensington and Chelsea RLBC v Simmonds*
(1997) 29 HLR 507, CA (see G7.1)

Not necessary to show fault on part of tenant incapable of controlling sons

H4.12 *Knowsley Housing Trust v McMullen*
[2006] EWCA Civ 539; [2006] HLR 43; [2006] L&TR 21; (2006) *Times* 22 May

SPO where tenant could not control behaviour of household upheld but order made that landlord to apply on notice before seeking warrant as case exceptional

The defendant was an assured tenant. She lived with her 19-year-old son. Possession proceedings were brought under Housing Act 1988 Sch 2 Grounds 12, 13 and 14. The claimants relied on admitted acts of nuisance by the defendant and her son and damage to the property. It was accepted that the son was 'a recidivist young offender with a string of convictions and a history of relapsing into misconduct'. He had been sentenced to 12 months in a young offender institution and on his release an ASBO was made against him. The author of a psychiatric report said that Ms McMullen had a low IQ and was 'an immature and vulnerable person'. The claimants also relied on damage to a door and furniture being thrown into the back yard of the house. The claimants sought a suspended possession order. HHJ Platts found that the defendant's own acts of nuisance were relatively slight and historic. It would not have been reasonable to make an order for possession if they had been the sole basis of the claim. However, in view of the damage to the house and, more importantly, the nuisance for which the son was responsible, a suspended possession order was justified. Ms McMullen appealed.

The Court of Appeal dismissed the appeal but amended the order to provide that the claimant should apply on notice before seeking a warrant. It held that:

1) It is clear that the court can make an outright or suspended order for possession on the ground that a person living with the tenant has been guilty of nuisance. There is no restriction on the making of an order for possession simply because the tenant cannot control the other person's behaviour. Dicta by Sedley LJ in *Portsmouth CC v Bryant* (G11.5) that 'it will almost certainly be unreasonable to make an outright order against such a person' went 'further than is justified by principle or authority. It ... [is] wrong in principle to rule out an outright order for possession' in such circumstances. The fact that a tenant cannot control the nuisance-maker may help the tenant in resisting an order in relation to past breaches if the nuisance-maker has vacated or is about to vacate, but otherwise may assist the landlord.

2) There is 'no intrinsic reason why the existence of an ASBO against the person responsible for the nuisance should prevent the making of an order for possession, whether outright or suspended', although the existence of an ASBO may be a relevant matter when deciding whether to suspend an order. (See too *London and Quadrant HT v Root* (H4.14), *Manchester CC v Higgins* (H4.15) and *Moat Housing Group South Ltd v Harris* (E1.9).) The weight given to the evidence of an ASBO must inevitably turn on the particular facts of the case in question.

3) It was 'a rational and proper, indeed a proportionate, exercise of the Judge's powers to have made the suspension of the order dependent on [the son's] good behaviour, as well as that of the defendant'.

4) However, on the facts of this case, Knowsley should not be entitled to apply for a warrant without first applying on notice to the court for permission to do so. Such a restriction is not appropriate in the 'normal run of cases' but in the light of the defendant's disability and the existence of the ASBO, this was an 'exceptional' case where it was justified. The Court of Appeal also stated that Housing Act 1988 s9A does 'not in practice alter the previous approach of the court, at any rate in the great majority of such cases: its effect is to codify and mandate the already existing jurisprudence'.

H4.13   *Lambeth LBC v Howard*
[2001] EWCA Civ 468; (2001) 33 HLR 636, CA

Outright order necessary because of past obsessive behaviour in relation to neighbour

Mr Howard was convicted at Horseferry Road Magistrates' Court of a course of conduct contrary to Protection from Harassment Act 1997 s2(1) and (2). The conduct involved harassment of a female neighbour and her daughter. He was sentenced to three months' imprisonment and was made the subject of a restraining order preventing him from going within 50 yards of the property. His appeal against conviction was dismissed but the sentence was varied to a three-year probation order. A restraining order was also enforced preventing him from going within 50 yards of the property. An application for judicial review of the restraining order was dismissed. In possession proceedings HHJ Medawar QC made an outright possession order. On appeal to the Court of Appeal the defendant submitted that the possession order breached ECHR article 8 and should have been suspended.

The appeal was dismissed. There comes a point when anti-social tenants must face the consequences of their actions. Mr Howard's past obsessive harassment meant that he was in no position to dispel the fear that he had instilled in his neighbour and her daughter by any undertakings. The order for possession was appropriate and proportionate. Second, the county court judge was not obliged to consider the Human Rights Act 1998 because at the time it was not in force. However, because of its imminent arrival, the judge did consider whether or not an order for possession would conform with the 1998 Act. As the judge pointed out, there was a need to find a fair balance and accordingly protect the rights of the neighbours and other members of the public. The judge's findings on this issue could not arguably be regarded as incompatible with the 1998 Act. The eviction had to be in accordance with the law in this case and had to be balanced against the neighbours' right to live in peace. An outright possession order was necessary in consequence of the past obsessive harassment. There is nothing in article 8 that should carry county courts to materially different outcomes when considering whether it is reasonable to make a possession order. The judge's reasons, findings and conclusions could not be criticised.

H4.14   *London and Quadrant Housing Trust v Root*
[2005] EWCA Civ 43; [2005] HLR 28; [2006] L&TR 23

Outright order despite tenant's partner having left premises in accordance with ASBO

Ms Root was an assured tenant of a house on a small estate in a quiet residential neighbourhood. Her landlords received many complaints from other tenants about the behaviour of her partner, who was running a car repair business from the property in breach of the tenancy agreement. He had also terrorised neighbours by intimidation and threats. A housing officer witnessed his behaviour and felt unable to carry out her duties on the estate because of it. London and Quadrant began possession proceedings on the grounds of Ms Root's partner's behaviour and breaches of the tenancy agreement concerning the condition of the exterior of the property and its use for running a business. The local authority obtained an interim anti-social behaviour order (ASBO) against the partner, and he was joined as a defendant to the possession proceedings. He left the property after the making of the ASBO, but he continued to come as close as possible to the boundary of the area covered by the ASBO in order to see Ms Root's youngest child, of whom he was the father. The condition of the exterior of the property did not improve. The judge, after considering Housing Act 1988 s9A, made an outright possession order. Ms Root appealed, contending that the judge should have suspended the possession order.

The Court of Appeal dismissed the appeal. It could not be said that the judge's decision to make a final order was clearly wrong. It was a very bad case. Although it was Ms Root's partner who caused it to be so bad, the relationship between Ms Root and her landlord had totally broken down and there was a limit to the extent to which the court could tolerate such behaviour for the sake of the tenant and her three children. Although the judge could have spelt out the reasons for his decision in more detail, it was clear that he had directed himself correctly on the law and had taken the correct matters into account.

H4.15   *Manchester CC v Higgins*
[2005] EWCA Civ 1423; [2006] 1 All ER 841; [2006] HLR 14; [2006] L&TR 11; (2005) *Times* 14 December

Outright order where tenant without remorse and indifferent to effect of children's behaviour; interrelationship of ASBOs and possession orders

Ms Higgins was a secure tenant and a single mother of three children, a daughter aged nearly 16, a son aged 13, and a daughter aged two. Her tenancy included terms which made her responsible for the behaviour of every person (including children) living in or visiting the premises, and prohibited her or anyone living in or visiting the premises from causing a nuisance, annoyance or disturbance to any other person, or harassing any other person. Her son, and to a lesser extent, her elder daughter, caused distress to a widow who lived nearby with three sons, all of whom suffered from a mental disability. They swore at the widow and her children, bullied the children and damaged her property. In May 2004, Manchester required Ms Higgins to attend a formal neighbourhood nuisance interview. She was warned in writing that, if her son's behaviour did not change, Manchester would have no alternative but to begin proceedings. That had no effect and Manchester obtained a without notice injunction. On the return date in September 2004 Ms Higgins gave undertakings, but at the end of September Manchester applied to the magistrates' court for an anti-social behaviour order (ASBO) against her son. The son was arrested in December 2004 after a further incident involving criminal damage. In February 2005 Manchester began possession proceedings under Housing Act 1985 Sch 2 Grounds 1 and 2. Ms Higgins' son was placed under supervision for two years for the offences of criminal damage and assault but he continued to harass the widow and her family. In May 2005 a recorder made a possession order, but suspended it for 18 months. Manchester appealed.

The Court of Appeal allowed the appeal. The discretion of the court to make a possession order under Housing Act 1985 s85 is unfettered, but it has to be exercised judicially. It follows that all the circumstances of the case which are material are to be borne in mind. In one case, the facts giving rise to the making of an ASBO might be so serious that both the making of a possession order and the refusal to suspend it would be self evident. In another case, making an ASBO might have served its purpose of restraining future misbehaviour so that, although past conduct might make it reasonable to order possession, suspension might still be possible. If the misconduct by the tenant or even by a member of the household is serious and persistent enough to justify an ASBO, that is strong but not conclusive evidence that the tenant would have forfeited any entitlement to retain possession. Since the court would already have found that it was reasonable to make a possession order, the question whether or not to suspend its execution has to be very much a question of the future. Previous unheeded warnings point one way, genuine remorse the other. The level of support available to a parent who is making proper efforts to control an errant child is relevant. However, there has always to be a sound basis for the hope that the anti-social behaviour will cease. Ultimately, given the respect for a tenant's home, guaranteed by ECHR article 8, the question is whether an immediate possession order is necessary in order to meet the need to protect the rights and freedoms of others, the neighbours, and is proportionate. In this case, the behaviour of Ms Higgins and her children, especially the son, had been quite intolerable. The son had shown himself unrepentantly anti-social. In the absence of any expression of remorse or any well-founded expectation of improvement, it was disproportionate not to make an immediate possession order. The mere fact that the ASBO would remain in force until the son attained the age of 16 would not give the neighbours sufficient protection. Ms Higgins was without remorse and totally indifferent to the effect her children's behaviour was having on her neighbours. She had forfeited her right to respect for her home. The recorder should have made an order for possession in 28 days.

H4.16 *Mansfield DC v Langridge*

[2007] EWCA Civ 303; 31 January 2007

No real prospect of success of appeal against outright order

Mr Langridge was a secure tenant. He suffered from learning disability and had Tourette's Syndrome, reactive changes in his mood, and anxiety and personality disorder. He was 'in a highly unstable state of mind'. The council sought possession, claiming that he had breached terms of his tenancy relating to payment of charges, anti-social behaviour, repairs, bad hygiene, the keeping of animals and/or that he was guilty of conduct causing, or likely to cause, a nuisance or annoyance to his neighbours. HHJ Mithani made a forthwith order for possession.

Auld LJ refused an oral renewal of Mr Langridge's application for permission to appeal. Although it was argued that there had only been findings of acts of nuisance and annoyance on 17 out of almost 700 days and that this was not enough to justify a possession order, Auld LJ could not say that the trial judge's reasoning was so wrong as to give Mr Langridge a real prospect of success if the matter were to go forward to appeal. Although another judge might have taken a different view, the proposed grounds for appeal were simply an attempt to re-argue the case on the facts.

H4.17 *Matthews v Ahmed*
[1985] 7 CL 3, CA

Appeal against order allowed where incidents merely a pretext for gaining possession

In proceedings which a tenant brought against his landlord for nuisance, the landlord counterclaimed for possession under Rent Act 1977 Sch 15 Case 2. The county court judge found that the tenant had thrown a hammer at the landlord during a quarrel and broken a window and that, during another quarrel with his girlfriend, she had called the police to the premises late at night. Although the tenant had lived in the premises for ten years, the judge made an order for possession.

The Court of Appeal allowed the tenant's appeal on the ground that it was not reasonable to make an order for possession. The incidents were, 'on the history, fairly to be regarded as no more than a pretext for enabling the landlord to expand the overcrowded accommodation which he occupied'.

H4.18 *New Charter Housing (North) Ltd v Ashcroft*
[2004] EWCA Civ 310; [2004] HLR 36

SPO inappropriate, despite son's imprisonment, where tenant showed no regret

Ms Ashcroft was an assured tenant. After a long history of harassment towards neighbours, her 17-year-old son was the subject of an interim anti-social behaviour order. He breached that order and was sentenced to a six-month detention and training order. As a direct result of the conduct of Ms Ashcroft (threats) and her son (eg, smashing windows and slashing car tyres), four neighbours who had made complaints about their conduct moved away from the area. Ms Ashcroft's landlord claimed possession under Housing Act 1988 Sch 2 Ground 14, relying on 28 incidents of nuisance. HHJ Armitage QC found that there was 'the clearest possible case made out under Ground 14', but decided that Ms Ashcroft should have the opportunity to demonstrate that she was able to curb her son's conduct on his release, and that it was reasonable to suspend the possession order. The landlord appealed.

The Court of Appeal allowed the appeal. There was no reason to suppose that Ms Ashcroft would take the opportunity to curb her son's conduct. She had herself uttered threats to neighbours about what would happen if she was evicted. She failed to show any regret for her son's conduct or any basis on which she sought to put it right. The judge had failed properly to consider the position and rights of the neighbours. It was appropriate to interfere with the judge's exercise of discretion and set aside the order suspending the order for possession.

H4.19   *Newcastle upon Tyne CC v Morrison*
(2000) 32 HLR 891; [2000] L&TR 333, CA

Outright order where 'reign of terror' by tenant's sons

The council claimed possession under Housing Act 1985 Sch 2 Ground 1 (breach of tenancy) and Ground 2 (nuisance). They relied on the anti-social behaviour of the tenant's teenage sons. The judge found the grounds made out but refused the possession order on the ground that it was not reasonable to make one (Housing Act 1985 s84).

The Court of Appeal allowed the council's appeal. The court noted that the tenant herself had not been involved, had been a secure tenant of the house for ten years and, as a single parent with another younger child, had been unable to control her eldest 'rampaging, destructive, intimidating and sometimes dangerous sons'. However, there had been a catalogue of 'quite appalling behaviour over a period of more than six years' involving 'plain, repeated and grave breaches of the tenancy agreement, numerous offences affecting the neighbourhood and a dreadful catalogue of incidents' which was like 'a reign of terror'. On those facts the case 'obviously' called for the making of an order. The judge had been wrong to consider that the council could have controlled the activities of the sons by the alternative remedy of an injunction (applying *Sheffield CC v Jepson* (H4.22)). Equally it had been wrong to take account of the fact that the sons might continue to cause mayhem in the locality even if their mother were evicted (applying *West Kent HA v Davies* (H4.26)). The Court of Appeal substituted a 28-day possession order.

H4.20   *Norwich CC v Famuyiwa*
[2004] EWCA Civ 1770; (2005) *Times* 24 January; 21 December 2004

Judge wrong in dismissing claim and viewing SPO as pointless

The defendant was the secure tenant of a flat. Norwich brought a possession claim on the ground that the defendant's conduct was causing nuisance or annoyance to, and constituted harassment of, her neighbours. The judge found that Housing Act 1985 Sch 2 Grounds 1 and 2 were made out but concluded that it would be unfair to the defendant, and therefore not reasonable, to make an outright order for possession. He also decided that a suspended order would be pointless and 'a recipe for disaster' because there was an unfortunate deteriorating relationship between the defendant and three other tenants. He therefore dismissed the claim but granted an injunction restraining the defendant from insulting, abusing, threatening or harassing any person in her block of flats or its locality, for a period of two years or until further order. Norwich appealed.

The Court of Appeal allowed the appeal. The judge was wrong, when deciding whether it was reasonable to make a possession order, to rule out the possibility that the court could meet the circumstances of the case by postponing the date for possession and imposing conditions (ie, a suspended possession order). It was wrong to assume that a suspended order would be absolutely pointless and a recipe for disaster. The judge had overlooked the possibility that, by postponing the date for possession on appropriate conditions, the situation could be controlled by the court. In exercising his discretion in this way, he had therefore erred in principle. The Court of Appeal, exercising the discretion itself, decided that it was reasonable to make an order for possession, but the date for possession would be postponed. The case was remitted to the county court to consider what terms should be imposed under Housing Act 1985 s85(3).

H4.20A *Sandwell MBC v Hensley*
[2007] EWCA Civ 1425; 1 November 2007 (see G11.6)

Where tenant commits criminal offence, possession order should be suspended only in exceptional circumstances

H4.21 *Sheffield CC v Green*
(1994) 26 HLR 349, CA

Where there was an admitted breach (keeping a dog) and intention to continue possession order appropriate

The tenant kept a dog, in breach of the express terms of the tenancy. He was not present at the hearing of possession proceedings brought under Housing Act 1985 Sch 2 Ground 1 and was unsuccessful in his application to set aside the possession order (CCR Ord 37 r2). He, therefore, lodged an appeal against the original order and sought to adduce evidence about why he had acquired the dog (for protection) and why he should be allowed to retain it (the advanced age of the dog, letters of support from neighbouring tenants, etc).

The Court of Appeal held that: (a) the matters of evidence should have been, but were not, put before the trial judge and the court could not consider them afresh; (b) where there was an admitted breach of covenant and an intention to continue with the breach, a landlord should only be refused possession in a 'very special case' (*Bell London and Provincial Properties Ltd v Reuben* [1947] KB 157, CA); and (c) in those circumstances, there was nothing the court could do to assist the appellant, who could only seek the 'mercy' of the council to waive the breach.

H4.22 *Sheffield CC v Jepson*
(1993) 25 HLR 299, CA

Rehearing directed where order refused despite deliberate breach of agreement (dog)

A secure tenant kept a dog, in breach of an express term of the tenancy agreement. Although the council produced evidence about nuisance caused generally by dogs in the flats, there was little evidence about the defendant's dog in particular. The county court judge refused to grant possession, on the ground that to do so would not be reasonable in all the circumstances.

The Court of Appeal directed a rehearing, because there had been no evidence at trial in the county court to justify the judge in so exercising his discretion. The term in the tenancy agreement was necessary and the breach of the term was deliberate and persisted in after requests that it cease. It is in the public interest that necessary and reasonable conditions in tenancy agreements are enforced fairly and effectively. Although the council could have obtained an injunction, there was no reason why it should be expected to do so. A suspended possession order which can be extended or set aside is in many cases a better remedy than a fine or imprisonment.

H4.23   *Sheffield CC v Shaw*
[2006] EWCA Civ 1671; 15 November 2006
[2007] EWCA Civ 42; [2007] HLR 25; 12 January 2007

Judge not wrong to refuse outright order despite serious harassment of young girl

Mr Shaw was a secure tenant, aged about 65. In 2000, he became obsessed with a 12-year-old girl living in the same neighbourhood. For many years, he stalked her, pestered her, threw cigarettes at her and touched her. In 2002, he was found guilty in Sheffield Magistrates' Court of harassing the girl. The magistrates made a restraining order prohibiting Mr Shaw from contacting the girl directly or indirectly for five years. In 2003, he was again found guilty of harassing her and breaching the terms of the restraining order. He was sentenced to four months' imprisonment. Later that year, he was again found guilty of the same offences and sentenced to 14 months' imprisonment. In August 2004 he was convicted at Sheffield Crown Court of the same offences and sentenced to two years' imprisonment. In April 2005, Sheffield issued proceedings claiming possession, based on breach of a covenant against harassment in Mr Shaw's tenancy agreement, and an ASBO. An interim ASBO was made. When the claim was tried Mr Shaw was in custody on remand facing a charge of breach of the interim ASBO. At trial of the possession claim, Mr Shaw's probation officer said that she was still greatly concerned that his behaviour would continue and that in her professional opinion, she believed that the situation was so bad that there was no reasonable alternative to turning Mr Shaw out of his house. HHJ Moore found that the defendant was in breach of the covenant in his tenancy agreement but, after considering the question of reasonableness, made an indefinite suspended possession order and an ASBO excluding the defendant from a particular part of Sheffield.

The council's appeal was dismissed. There is no general principle that, where the harassment of neighbours is such that the fear and tension cannot be dispelled, an immediate possession order must be made. That is simply a possible judgment to take depending on the facts of the case. Judging sincerity is the province of the trial judge. Mr Shaw's potential homelessness was not the judge's sole consideration. There were various other considerations in his judgment, primarily the optimism shown that Mr Shaw was capable of reform. In this case, the previous opportunistic apology by the defendant to the police, and the fact that he had denied all or most of the historic allegations at the hearing, did not compel the conclusion that the judge's assessment for the future had to have been wrong. Although the defendant might have shown no more than embryonic remorse, and had failed, for many years, to understand the effect of his conduct, that did not preclude the assessment that proper psychiatric help could help him mend his ways. In that regard, the judge had not misunderstood the evidence of the probation officer. Although she had expressed reservations about whether he would continue his unacceptable behaviour, she had said that Mr Shaw was capable of reform, and had been prepared to back that judgment in her proposals to the sentencing judge. It was, moreover, a matter of fact that the girl no longer lived close to the defendant. It followed that the order had not been made outside the judge's discretion, and was not plainly wrong. The judge had made no error of law.

H4.24 *Solon South West Housing Association Ltd v James*
[2004] EWCA Civ 1847; [2005] HLR 24

No error in admitting hearsay evidence and making order despite improvement

Solon sought possession on the grounds of rent arrears, breaches of other obligations of the tenancy, and conduct amounting to anti-social behaviour to persons residing in the locality. The defendants admitted non-payment of rent and one incident of nuisance or annoyance. The judge found that other allegations of anti-social behaviour, including acts of violence and racist abuse, were proved. He made an outright possession order. The defendants appealed, contending that the judge had erred in admitting hearsay evidence without a reason being given for the non-attendance of the witnesses at trial, and that he had failed to apply the correct criteria when deciding what weight to place on that evidence. Second, they claimed that the judge had failed to consider evidence that there had been an improvement in their conduct, so that a suspended, rather than an outright, order for possession should have been imposed.

The Court of Appeal dismissed the appeal. There was no error in the way in which the judge had admitted the hearsay evidence, or the weight he had given to it. The reason for not adducing live evidence was the witnesses' fear of reprisals. That was clearly a reason that the judge had been entitled to put into the balance in deciding what weight to give to the evidence. Second, when deciding whether to suspend an order for possession, the court has to consider whether the anti-social behaviour is likely to happen again. It is relevant that it may be difficult to prove breach of a suspended order, or who was responsible for an alleged breach. The suspension of an order may not diminish the fear that neighbours feel but that fear may be removed by an immediate order for possession. Furthermore, the Court of Appeal will not interfere with a judge's discretion unless it is plainly wrong. In this case, the judge was entitled to make the order that he had made. The severity of the conduct which he found proved overlaid any subsequent improvement in the defendants' conduct, and they had, in any case, been unrepentant about their behaviour.

H4.25 *Wandsworth LBC v Hargreaves*
(1995) 27 HLR 142, CA

No error in refusing order where one-off incident (petrol bomb) and tenant not directly involved

The defendant had been a tenant since 1987. The tenancy agreement provided that he should 'not permit to be done anything which may increase the risk of fire'. In 1991 a visitor brought petrol into the flat to make petrol bombs, which were thrown from the window. A fire started in the flat from spilt petrol, causing £14,000 worth of damage. The tenant was out of occupation from March 1991 to June 1992 while the flat was repaired.

The Court of Appeal dismissed the council's appeal against a refusal of the county court judge to order possession. The court held that: (a) the judge had to take into account all the circumstances; (b) that would include the risks to other tenants, the landlord's duty towards those other tenants, and the effect on each party of a possession order; and (c) since the judge had expressly found that the tenant had not taken an active part in the events leading to the fire and there had been no problems since his return, the judge had not erred in dismissing the claim on the basis that it was not reasonable to make the order.

H4.26 *West Kent Housing Association v Davies*
(1999) 31 HLR 415; [1998] EGCS 103, CA

Dismissal of possession order on basis of son's racial harassment wrong

The landlord brought possession proceedings against assured tenants under Housing Act 1988 Sch 2 Grounds 12 (breach of obligations within the tenancy agreement) and 14 (nuisance). The judge found that the tenants had caused nuisance by carrying out car repairs late at night and that the tenants' eldest son had made racially abusive remarks and been a party to racial harassment of neighbours. However, he found that the tenants (ie, the parents) did not approve or encourage the son's behaviour and were not a party to it. He declined to make a possession order or a suspended possession order.

The Court of Appeal allowed the landlord's appeal. The covenant in the tenancy agreement prohibited not only 'permitting' but also 'allowing' racial harassment. Similarly, Ground 14 clearly covered the conduct of the son. Knowledge or approval of the conduct was not an essential factor in the statutory ground. The tenants had failed to prevent their son's behaviour (see *Kensington and Chelsea RLBC v Simmonds* (G7.1)). The judge should have considered whether it was reasonable to make an order for possession in all the circumstances (Housing Act 1988 s7). He had seriously underestimated the effects of the behaviour on the neighbours and on a socially responsible landlord. In circumstances such as this, it would usually be unreasonable not to order possession. Such an order was necessary to preserve the interests of the landlord and its other tenants in the quality of life and in the maintenance of physical and mental health on the estate. The fact that a number of the tenants who had been threatened were no longer on the estate did not make the matter less serious. The Court of Appeal made a possession order, suspended on terms, for two years.

H4.27   *Woking BC v Bistram*

(1995) 27 HLR 1, CA

Dismissal of order on basis of abusive and menacing language wrong

The council sought possession under Housing Act 1985 Sch 2 Ground 2, relying on nuisance to other occupiers. The claim based on noise nuisance was withdrawn but the council proceeded on the basis of complaints from long-standing tenants (both immediate neighbours and those in adjoining blocks of flats) that the tenant had been guilty of foul, abusive and menacing language, which had continued right up to the date of hearing. The judge refused to grant an order for possession and held that such language was 'no doubt very much a common experience' in certain areas.

On the council's appeal, the Court of Appeal held: (a) the judge's finding could not be sustained, as there had been no evidence of the character of the neighbourhood and its occupants; (b) insufficient emphasis had been given to the highly relevant fact that the nuisance was continuing and to the obligations which the council had to the other tenants; and (c) the appropriate course was to make a suspended order for possession on terms that any further such conduct would lead to repossession in 28 days.

High Court

H4.28   *Sheffield CC v Fletcher*

[2007] EWHC 419; (Ch); [2007] HLR 26; 12 January 2007

High Court has jurisdiction to hear application under HA 1985 s85(1); refusal to set aside where outright order inevitable

Ms Fletcher had been a secure tenant since 2001. She lived in the premises with a number of children. As a result of complaints about noise and verbal abuse by a neighbour, the council wrote letters, served a notice seeking possession and began possession proceedings. Ms Fletcher did not attend the hearing and a forthwith possession order was made. She later applied to set aside the order on the ground that the trial had taken place in her absence and, in the alternative, she applied for postponement or a stay on the possession order. The evidence placed before the judge contained no expression of remorse, stated that none of the incidents had happened and that, if they had, they were not as serious as alleged. The judge found that Ms Fletcher had no reasonable prospect of success in defending the claim if the order were to be set aside and that the overwhelming likelihood was that, even if she had given evidence, the same order would have been made. He dismissed the application, but Ms Fletcher appealed. On appeal, the council argued that the High Court did not have jurisdiction to entertain any application under s85(1), because s110 conferred exclusive jurisdiction under s85 on the county court.

Lewison J rejected that contention. Although s110 confers jurisdiction on the county court in relation to matters arising under Housing Act 1985 Part 4, it does not oust the jurisdiction of the High Court. However, he dismissed Ms Fletcher's appeal. When considering whether to postpone or suspend a possession order that had been obtained on the basis of anti-social behaviour, the court was required to take into account the effect that a continuation of that behaviour would have, or might have, on neighbours. That required the court to look to the future (*Manchester CC v Higgins* (H4.15). The judge had not erred in principle or reached a decision which was outside his ambit. Past unheeded warnings tell against a suspension of the possession order. Furthermore, the evidence put before the judge showed no expression of remorse or any assurances for the future. Although the defendant had children, there was nothing about them to which the judge ought to have paid special attention. The fact that the defendant had lived in the area for 16 years was of little weight because of the seriousness of the allegations of anti-social behaviour. Although there had been no previous proceedings against the defendant, the judge had been entitled to form the view that, in light of the degree of anti-social behaviour, an immediate order had been inevitable.

H5

Tenancy obtained by false statement

Court of Appeal

H5.1 *Lewisham LBC v Adeyemi/Lewisham LBC v Akinsola*
(2000) 32 HLR 414; [1999] EGCS 74, CA

Not for judge to pre-empt outcome of homelessness application under HA 1996 Part VII

Proceedings were brought under Housing Act 1985 Sch 2 Ground 5. The defendant did not dispute that the local authority had been induced into granting the tenancy by a false statement. A county court judge held that the ground had been made out and that it was reasonable to make a possession order. The tenant appealed, claiming that the judge, when considering reasonableness, had failed to take into account whether the local authority would have a duty to rehouse under Housing Act 1996 Part VII.

The appeal was dismissed. It is not for the court to make a pre-emptive decision on the possible outcome of an application that might or might not be made to the local authority. Entitlement to Part VII accommodation is confined to the judgment of the local authority. It is not for the court to anticipate the outcome of that decision. The judge was well aware of the self-evident consequence of a possession order. The legal and practical consequences of homelessness, however, were not before the court, nor need they have been as they were for the local authority to determine. (See also *Rushcliffe BC v Watson* (H5.3).)

H5.2 *North Herts DC v Carthy*
[2003] EWCA Civ 20; 17 January 2003

Reasonableness needed consideration where false statements made under Part 7

The claimant landlord sought possession under Housing Act 1985 Sch 2 Ground 5. The defendants had intended to settle in the Philippines and to build a house there. However, owing to financial difficulties, they were unable to finish building their house, and returned to England. The council housed them in temporary accommodation and then granted them a secure tenancy. When he initially applied for accommodation, Mr Carthy signed a form which stated that they knew that they were liable under Housing Act 1996 s214 if they did not inform the council of any change in circumstances. The tenants' financial situation then improved, and they were able to finish building their house in the Philippines, but failed to tell the council that the house was habitable. In the possession claim, the council submitted that the tenants' statement that they had nowhere to live was a continuing representation which became untrue and which, because they failed to correct it, resulted in the secure tenancy. A recorder accepted that the tenants had failed to furnish the new information but concluded that the false representation had not induced the council to grant the tenancy. He dismissed the claim. The recorder made no reference to whether it was reasonable to make the possession order.

On appeal, the tenants conceded that the recorder had been wrong. The Court of Appeal held that it was by no means a foregone conclusion that, if the council had been told of the house in the Philippines, such information would not have affected the position. It was the false representation that the tenants were still in need of housing that induced the grant of the secure tenancy. The reasonableness of making a possession order needed very careful appraisal. The case was remitted to a different judge.

H5.3 *Rushcliffe BC v Watson*
(1992) 24 HLR 124, CA

Prospects of tenant's application under Part VII relevant to reasonableness

Possession was sought under Housing Act 1985 Sch 2 Ground 5 following the discovery that the defendant had not been a lodger in her former home but a housing association tenant.

The Court of Appeal confirmed that, when considering whether or not to grant possession, the county court should bear in mind that Housing Act 1985 s84(2)(a) applies a test of reasonableness to Ground 5. A very real consideration in applying that test is the prospect that, if evicted, the tenant would probably be found to be intentionally homeless. However, the judge's finding that she could cope with her homelessness and that it was otherwise reasonable to grant possession was upheld. Dealing with the standard of proof required in cases brought under Sch 2 Ground 5, Nourse LJ approved comments made by the judge at first instance that the burden of proof was akin to the criminal standard because of the seriousness of the allegation.

H5.4 *Shrewsbury and Atcham BC v Evans*
(1998) 30 HLR 123, CA

Where deliberate lying to obtain council housing, effect of application under Part VII only relevant in exceptional circumstances

Mrs Evans owned a farm house jointly with her husband. In 1988 she applied to Shrewsbury and Atcham BC for accommodation, stating (falsely) that she was living with her parents in overcrowded conditions. In 1991 Shrewsbury and Atcham BC granted her a tenancy of the premises which were later to become the subject matter of this action. In 1992 the mortgagees began possession proceedings in respect of the farm house. Mrs Evans then applied to North Shropshire DC for accommodation. In 1992 North Shropshire granted her a tenancy of other accommodation. In 1993 North Shropshire heard about the premises which she still rented from Shrewsbury and Atcham BC and brought possession proceedings. Mrs Evans handed back the keys before the possession hearing. Shrewsbury and Atcham BC meanwhile heard about this and then brought possession proceedings under Housing Act 1985 Sch 2 Ground 5, relying on the false statement that she had been living with her parents when she originally applied for accommodation. Mrs Evans was debarred from defending because she failed to comply with an order that she give discovery of papers relating to her divorce proceedings. Mrs Evans, who had five children, asserted that it would not be reasonable to order possession (Housing Act 1985 s84). HHJ Northcote found that she had 'flagrantly and deliberately lied about her circumstances' in order to obtain council housing and that it was reasonable to make a possession order. She appealed against a possession order on the basis that the trial judge had misunderstood or failed to satisfy himself about evidence on the prospects of her being rehoused if evicted.

The Court of Appeal dismissed her appeal. Beldam LJ, after considering earlier authorities (including *Darlington BC v Sterling* (H4.9) and *Bristol CC v Mousah* (H4.4), said (at 132):

> The effect of these decisions, in my view, is that in a case such as this, where there has been a deliberate lying to obtain public housing that only in exceptional circumstances would the court consider the effect of the homelessness legislation. It is not the function of the court to decide whether or not a person is intentionally homeless. That is the function of the local authority and has been entrusted to the local authority by parliament.
>
> Those who are on the housing list who have an equal or even greater claim to public housing would, in my view, justly be indignant to find that the court did not think it reasonable in circumstances where someone had obtained accommodation by a deliberate and flagrant lie, to make an order for possession merely because the effect of the order would result in the occupant having to be considered by the local authority as homeless or intentionally homeless.

The court was entitled to take into account the fact that the defendant's attitude was 'to lie and lie again to deny completely that she had made the application to the District Council'. Beldam LJ referred to 'the great importance to be attached to honesty in making application for public housing'.

High Court

H5.5 *Southwark LBC v Erekin*

[2003] EWHC 1765 (Ch D); 24 June 2003

Possession refused despite tenant having obtained housing fraudulently

Ms Erekin fraudulently obtained housing from Southwark. She was prosecuted and, for this and other offences, received a sentence of 18 months' imprisonment. Southwark issued possession proceedings. A judge found the ground for possession (Housing Act 1985 Sch 2 Ground 5) proved, but refused to make a possession order on the basis that it was not reasonable to do so. Southwark appealed.

Laddie J dismissed the appeal. Appeals against the exercise of discretion by a judge should succeed only if it can be shown that the judge exceeded the generous ambit of his discretion. It is not the role of the appellate court to substitute its views for the judge at first instance. There was nothing to suggest that the judge had exceeded the ambit of his discretion. His decision should stand.

H6   Suitable alternative accommodation

Court of Appeal

H6.1   *Battlespring Ltd v Gates*
(1983) 11 HLR 6; (1983) 268 EG 355, CA

Order refused where tenant had been living in accommodation for 35 years

The defendant, an elderly lady, had lived in a maisonette for 35 years. A property company bought the building and offered her suitable alternative accommodation. They claimed that the property offered was a modern flat in a more comfortable and congenial area at a lower rent. The defendant claimed that it was unreasonable for anyone to expect her to move from the flat where she had brought up her family and which had 'very tender memories for her'. The county court judge decided that it was unreasonable to make a possession order.

The Court of Appeal dismissed the landlord's appeal, holding that it was impossible to fault the exercise of the judge's discretion.

H6.2   *Dame Margaret Hungerford Charity Trustees v Beazeley*
(1994) 26 HLR 269; [1993] 2 EGLR 143; [1993] 29 EG 100, CA (see also P5.5)

Appeal refused; assumed judge had taken all relevant matters into consideration

Landlords instituted possession proceedings, relying on a certificate of the local housing authority that it would provide accommodation for the tenant (Rent Act 1977 Sch 15 Part IV para 3). After taking into account the plaintiff's circumstances (a charity with limited income) and the defendant's submissions on why it would not be reasonable to make an order (residence in the property since 1978, size of the alternative accommodation, effect on health and lack of adequate parking for cars), the judge made an order for possession.

Dismissing the tenant's appeal, Roch LJ stated that the court would only overrule a county court judge on the question of reasonableness 'on very strong grounds' and would 'assume that the county court judge has taken all the relevant matters into account unless the contrary is clearly shown'.

H6.3   *Dawncar Investments Ltd v Plews*
(1993) 25 HLR 639; [1994] 1 EGLR 141; [1994] 13 EG 110, CA

Possession refused as neighbourhood of proposed accommodation very different

The plaintiffs brought possession proceedings against the defendant, who was a Rent Act protected tenant, based on the availability of alternative accommodation in accordance with Rent Act 1977 s98. The tenant's existing flat was in a quiet road in a pleasant part of Hampstead near good quality shops. The proposed alternative accommodation was on a busy commercial road in Kilburn, with heavy lorries turning into a timber yard nearby. There was a railway to the front and rear of the alternative accommodation and two public houses nearby. The county court judge visited both flats and indicated that, if he had been able to ignore the neighbourhood, the alternative accommodation would have been superior. However, in view of the environmental considerations, he found that it was not reasonable to make a possession order.

The Court of Appeal refused to overturn the judge's finding. It held that the environmental considerations were relevant in deciding between the two flats and that it was difficult to imagine a case where the court would interfere because a judge had given too much weight to one factor and not enough to another factor.

H6.4   *Minchburn Estates Ltd v Fernandez*
(1987) 19 HLR 29; [1986] 2 EGLR 103; (1986) 280 EG 770, CA
Order a nullity where judge had failed to consider reasonableness

A county court judge held that alternative accommodation offered by landlords was suitable and made a possession order. He referred only to matters concerning the two properties in question and did not consider whether or not it was reasonable to make a possession order.

The Court of Appeal allowed the tenant's appeal, holding that the judge's failure to consider reasonableness made the order a nullity. Slade LJ stated that he would have expected the judge to refer to other factors 'which would appear to have been relevant in relation to the context of reasonableness', including:

> ... the great length of time for which the defendant had been living in these premises, the effect which a move might have on her personal situation and, on the other side of the scale, the landlords' reasons for desiring to obtain possession of the property ((1987) 19 HLR at 33).

(See May 1985 *Legal Action* 66 for a note of earlier proceedings between the parties.)

H7   Other grounds for possession

Court of Appeal

H7.1   *Empson v Forde*
[1990] 1 EGLR 131; [1990] 18 EG 99, CA
Possession refused where tenants had not refused access to do repairs

The landlord sought possession of Rent Act protected premises, relying on Cases 1 and 3 on the ground that the tenants had refused to move out to allow the landlord to carry out repairs. The tenants indicated that they believed that the works could be carried out with them in possession and that they were concerned not only that the landlord might carry out improvements which they did not want, but also that they might not be able to regain possession. HHJ Goldstone held that the tenants had not refused to allow the landlord 'to carry out the repairs and only the repairs for which a landlord was entitled to obtain access to carry out, that is repairs without improvement'. He also indicated that it was not a case in which it would be reasonable to make a possession order.

Woolf LJ held that the issue 'was essentially one of fact for the learned judge' and that his judgment 'was one which could not possibly be impugned' by the Court of Appeal.

H7.2   *Enfield LBC v French*
(1985) 17 HLR 211; (1984) 49 P&CR 223; (1984) 83 LGR 750, CA

Weight to be given to tenant's needs (garden) a matter of degree; council's policy relevant to reasonableness

The son of a secure tenant succeeded to a two-bedroomed property with a living room, kitchen, etc, and use of a garden. It was his hobby to cultivate the garden. The council offered him a one-bedroomed flat on a housing estate with no garden and, when he refused that offer, brought possession proceedings under Housing Act 1980 Sch 4 Ground 13 (now Housing Act 1985 Sch 2 Ground 16). In the county court, a possession order was made.

The Court of Appeal dismissed the tenant's appeal. In cases such as this, judges should take into account the potential loss of the garden and all other circumstances in assessing whether the accommodation offered is 'suitable alternative accommodation'. The weight to be given to the tenant's needs is a matter of degree in each case and some needs are more important than others. In considering the reasonableness of ordering possession, judges should also take into account the housing allocation policy of the authority if it is a reasonable one.

H7.3   *Holloway v Povey*
(1984) 15 HLR 104; (1984) 271 EG 195, CA

Successor to tenancy not liable for deterioration of garden until becoming a tenant

The defendant's father was the statutory tenant of a cottage with a garden. When he died, the defendant's mother succeeded to the tenancy and then, on her death, the defendant became the tenant. From the death of the father, the garden was neglected and became overgrown. The judge found that it was reasonable to make an order for possession under Case 3 (deterioration). The tenant appealed and, before the hearing of the appeal, tidied up the garden.

The tenant's appeal was allowed. The Court of Appeal held that he had been under no legal obligation to do anything to the garden until he became the tenant. The Court of Appeal reiterated that it can only intervene in relation to a county court judge's finding on reasonableness if the judge has taken something irrelevant into account, has failed to take something relevant into account or has reached a perverse decision. In this case, the judge had failed to distinguish between the tenant's moral responsibility before he became a tenant and his legal responsibility after his mother's death. It was not reasonable to make a possession order without giving the tenant the opportunity to tidy up the garden. The Court of Appeal made a suspended possession order requiring the tenant to keep the garden in a reasonable condition of tidiness for one year.

H8   Disability Discrimination Act 1995

Court of Appeal

H8.1   *Gloucester CC v Simmonds*
[2006] EWCA Civ 254; 14 February 2006

Issues to be taken into account when considering reasonableness and DDA

The defendant was a secure tenant. The council sought possession on the grounds of nuisance or annoyance. It relied on 35 separate incidents over a period of over two years, including banging, shouting, abusive language and loud music, often for prolonged periods late at night. Ms Simmonds accepted that the ground for possession was made out, but denied that it was reasonable to make a possession order or, alternatively, argued that any possession order should be suspended. She relied on a medical report which confirmed that she was suffering from a disability in the shape of mental impairment comprising an emotionally unstable personality disorder and that her behaviour was a result of her 'disability' since 'poor impulse control is a feature of her personality disorder'. Notwithstanding this, District Judge Thomas found that her 'conduct which gave rise to the claim for possession did not relate to her disability ... since the legislation excludes from mental impairment a number of things, including addiction to alcohol or drugs'. He was satisfied that the conduct was caused by 'other character defects, deliberate conduct knowingly done, conduct caused by the use of alcohol and/or drugs, and conduct cause[d] by her relationship with [her partner] which she could easily cease'. He made an outright possession order. Ms Simmonds sought permission to appeal on the basis that that finding was perverse.

Tuckey LJ refused a renewed application for permission to appeal. After referring to Disability Discrimination Act 1995 and *Manchester CC v Romano* (H8.2), he stated:

> the broad issues which arose were: (i) was the applicant suffering from a disability within the meaning of the Act, (ii) if she was, was the Council's claim for possession against her related to that disability, (iii) if so, could the discrimination be justified because the Council was of the opinion that the claim was necessary in order not to endanger the health or safety of any person and it was reasonable for it to hold that opinion? If there had been discrimination which could not be justified, this was something which was very relevant to whether it was reasonable to make an order for possession.

With regards the medical evidence, he stated that issues of causation are primarily questions of fact for the judge, who may be assisted by expert evidence but is by no means bound to accept it. There was nothing in this case which compelled the judge to accept the doctor's view. Tuckey LJ could not characterise the judge's finding as perverse. It was open to the judge on the evidence and was a finding of fact which there was no real prospect of the Court of Appeal disturbing. Turning to the defendant's 'general attack on the judge's conclusion that it was reasonable to make an immediate order for possession', Tuckey LJ stated that Housing Act 1985 gives the trial judge a very wide discretion with which the Court of Appeal will seldom interfere. There was no error of approach in the way in which the judge exercised it in this case.

H8.1A   *Lewisham LBC v Malcolm and the Disability Rights Commission*
[2007] EWCA Civ 763; (2007) *Times* 28 August; 25 July 2007 (see L2.1)

Claim for possession unlawful discrimination under DDA where causal relationship between tenant's disability and reason for issue of proceedings

H8.2   *Manchester CC v Romano*
[2004] EWCA (Civ) 834; [2005] 1 WLR 2775; [2004] HLR 47; [2005] L&TR 13; [2005] LGR 282; (2004) *Times* 27 July

DDA relevant to issue of reasonableness; possession justified where neighbour's health affected

Possession orders were made against two secure tenants under Housing Act 1985 Sch 2 para 2 (nuisance or annoyance). One order was suspended, but after further allegations of nuisance, a district judge refused an application to suspend a warrant. The tenant appealed, relying on Disability Discrimination Act 1995. HHJ Armitage dismissed the appeal. He was satisfied, having regard to expert evidence, that the tenant's mental impairment (depression) did not have a substantial effect on her ability to carry out any day to day activities and that she did not therefore have a disability for the purpose of s1(1). The other order, also made by HHJ Armitage, after finding that the defendant was not disabled and considering reasonableness, was an outright order. The tenants appealed.

The Court of Appeal, in a very thorough review of the legislation, stated that, when a court considers the Disability Discrimination Act 1995 in the context of possession proceedings, the first matter which has to be determined is whether the person who complains about disability discrimination is a 'disabled person' within the meaning of ss1–3, Sch 1, the Disability Discrimination (Meaning of Disability) Regulations 1996 SI No 1455 and the *Guidance on matters to be taking into account in determining questions relating to the definition of disability* issued by the secretary of state. Second, the court should consider whether or not there has been discrimination, ie, treating a disabled person less favourably for a reason which relates to the disabled person's disability. Third, the court should consider whether the landlord's treatment of the tenant is justified. It is only justified if in the landlord's opinion the treatment (viz the decision to set in motion proceedings for possession) is necessary in order not to endanger the health or safety of any of the people living in neighbouring houses and it is reasonable, in all the circumstances, for the landlord to hold that opinion. The landlord must prove that if it does not take this action someone's health or safety would be endangered. It does not have to prove that that person's health or safety has actually been damaged.

The 1995 Act does not explicitly provide a defence for disabled persons who wish to assert that the reason why their landlord brought possession proceedings related to disability. It is, though, open to such disabled persons to counterclaim for a declaration that they have been unlawfully discriminated against and/or to counterclaim for injunctive relief. Furthermore, if tenants can prove that the landlord's conduct amounts to unlawful discrimination, this is bound to be a relevant factor when the court is determining whether it is reasonable to make an order for possession. The Court of Appeal stated that it is preferable, in cases involving a secure tenancy or an assured tenancy, for tenants to assert that it is unreasonable for the court to make a possession order, rather than to complicate the proceedings by adding a formalistic counterclaim for a declaration or an injunction. Landlords whose tenants hold secure or assured tenancies must consider the position carefully before they decide to serve a notice seeking possession or to embark on possession proceedings against a tenant who is or might be mentally impaired. They should liaise closely with local social services authorities at an early stage

The first appeal was dismissed because the neighbour's evidence that he was stressed and tired due to noise nuisance led properly to a conclusion that his health was endangered by his frequent loss of sleep. In any event, it was difficult to relate some of the nuisance (loud hammering during DIY work and loud music played by the tenant's sons) to the tenant's mental impairment. In the light of those conclusions, it was not necessary to decide whether the judge was wrong to conclude that the tenant was not a disabled person within the meaning of the Act.

The second appeal was also dismissed. In view of a neighbour's evidence that she was at the end of her tether and felt that she could no longer cope with the behaviour of the defendant and her family, the judge was entitled to conclude on the evidence that the council held the opinion that the continuation of eviction proceedings was justified in order not to endanger the neighbour's health and that it was reasonable in all the circumstances for the council to hold that opinion.

The Court of Appeal called for parliament to review the legislation at an early date.

High Court

H8.3   *North Devon Homes Ltd v Brazier*

[2003] EWHC 574 (QB); [2003] HLR 59; [2003] L&TR 398; [2003] 22 EG 141

Appeal against order allowed where tenant's breach of tenancy related to disability

Ms Brazier was an assured tenant who suffered from a paranoid psychosis, possibly schizophrenia. Her landlord served a notice pursuant to Housing Act 1988 s8 alleging breach of the tenancy agreement, which contained a covenant not to cause nuisance, annoyance, inconvenience or harassment to neighbours or to the public. In the subsequent possession claim, Ms Brazier admitted that she had been involved in persistent anti-social behaviour, including shouting at neighbouring residents, keeping neighbours awake at night by banging and shouting and using foul language and making rude gestures to neighbours. Her landlord accepted that she was a disabled person within the meaning of Disability Discrimination Act 1995. Her disability arose from a 'mental impairment, which has a substantial and long-term effect on her ability to carry out normal day-to-day activity'. A recorder found that she was unable to prevent herself from behaving in a manner which was a breach of the tenancy agreement and made a possession order.

David Steel J allowed her appeal. The effect of Disability Discrimination Act 1995 s22(3)(c) is that it is unlawful to discriminate 'by evicting the disabled person or subjecting him to any other detriment'. He rejected the landlord's contention that they were not evicting Ms Brazier. After considering *Clark v Novacold Ltd* [1999] ICR 951, CA he held that it was an issue of fact whether the breach of the terms of the tenancy was caused by disability. If it was, then Ms Brazier, as a disabled person, could not be treated less favourably than someone who was not similarly disabled. David Steel J stated that any fair reading of the material demonstrated that the overwhelming preponderance of Ms Brazier's bizarre and unwelcome behaviour was attributable to her mental illness. He rejected the landlord's contention that the discrimination was justified on the basis that eviction was necessary in order not to endanger the health or safety of any person (s24(3)), as there was no evidence of any actual physical risk. Although unlawfulness under the Disability Discrimination Act was not a bar to the landlord seeking a possession order under the Housing Act, the fact that the eviction was unlawful and not justified was a highly relevant consideration for the s7 discretion of whether or not to make a possession order. The Disability Discrimination Act contains its own code for justified eviction which requires a higher threshold than the Housing Act. It was not appropriate to make an order for possession.

County courts

H8.4   *Community Housing Association Ltd v Wye*

17 February 2007, Edmonton County Court (see K5.1)

Where possession claim against assured shorthold tenant unlawful under DDA, injunction granted to restrain landlord from continuing proceedings

H8.5   *Liverpool CC v Slavin*

July 2005 *Legal Action* 28, 29 April 2005, Liverpool County Court

Discrimination not justified as failure to pay rent did not endanger health of others

The council obtained a possession order suspended on terms that the defendant pay current rent and £2.65 per week towards arrears of just under £3,000. She breached it almost immediately and the arrears began to increase. The defendant suffered from depression from at least 1989. Her mental health deteriorated and she failed to reapply for housing benefit. Arrears continued to accrue and a bailiff's appointment was obtained. An application to suspend the warrant was made before District Judge Wright. The application was supported by a report from a psychiatrist who confirmed that the defendant suffered from a moderate depressive episode bordering severe classifiable under F32.1–32.2 of the ICD-10 Classification of Mental and Behavioural Disorders. The psychiatrist stated that this condition had a substantial and long-term adverse effect on the defendant's ability to carry out normal day-to-day activities including her ability to apply for housing benefit and pay her rent.

District Judge Wright considered *Manchester CC v Romano* (H8.2) and *North Devon Homes Limited v Brazier* (H8.3) and found that the council had acted unlawfully under Disability Discrimination Act 1995 ss22–24 in deciding to evict the defendant. That decision was not justified on the ground that it was necessary in order not to endanger the health or safety of any person. She rejected the assertion that the council had not acted unlawfully on the basis that they did not know that the defendant suffered from a disability. The fact that the decision was unlawful was just as relevant to the exercise of the court's discretion under Housing Act 1985 s85 as it was to considerations of reasonableness under Housing Act 1985 s84. She suspended execution on payment of current rent and £2.85 per week and ordered the council to pay the defendant's costs of the application, to be assessed if not agreed.

CHAPTER I

After the possession order

I1   The effect of possession orders – in general

Court of Appeal

I1.1   *Church Commissioners for England v Al-Emarah*

[1997] Fam 34; [1996] 3 WLR 633; (1997) 29 HLR 351, CA

Tenancy transferred to wife under MHA 1983 was subject to terms of SPO against husband, but possession order not enforceable against wife

Mr Al-Emarah was the sole statutory (Rent Act) tenant of the matrimonial home. On the breakdown of his marriage, he moved out and arrears accrued. The landlords obtained a possession order, suspended on terms that he pay current rent and £1,000 per month off the arrears. Mrs Al-Emarah then obtained housing benefit which covered all of the rent apart from £8–10 per week. Mr Al-Emarah was subsequently made bankrupt. In proceedings brought under Matrimonial Homes Act 1983 Sch 1 para 3(1), Connell J made an order that Mrs Al-Emarah was deemed to be the sole statutory tenant, but subject to the terms of the suspended possession order.

Mrs Al-Emarah's appeal, on the ground that para 3(1) conferred on her anew all the rights which her husband had originally enjoyed without regard to the suspended possession order, was dismissed. However, in view of *Sherrin v Brand* [1956] 1 QB 403, CA, the possession order, as opposed to the conditions of its suspension, was not enforceable against her. If the landlords wished to evict her, they would have to bring new proceedings.

I1.2   *Kensington and Chelsea RLBC v Richmond*

[2006] EWCA Civ 68; [2006] 1 WLR 1693; [2006] HLR 25; [2006] LGR 407; (2006) *Times* 27 February

Order on application of landlord to extend the period of suspension of a possession order did not revive the tenancy

Mr Richmond was a secure tenant of a flat. Kensington and Chelsea sought possession on the ground that he was causing a nuisance to and harassing his neighbours (Housing Act 1985 Sch 2 Ground 2). On 17 December 2003 the trial judge made an order for possession but suspended it on condition that Mr Richmond complied with the terms of his tenancy agreement. The order also provided 'No warrant to issue without permission of Circuit Judge. Order possession to remain in existence until 17 December 2004. Permission to Claimant to apply for extension.' It was alleged that Mr Richmond broke the terms of the order. On 1 November 2004 Kensington and Chelsea applied for permission to issue a warrant for possession and, if the application and/or execution was not dealt with before 17 December 2004, an order that the suspended possession order be extended for a period of six months. The application was listed on 10 December 2004. Mr Richmond did not attend. HHJ Mackie QC ordered that the suspended possession order be extended for a further six months and that the application for a warrant be adjourned. It was subsequently argued on behalf of Mr Richmond that the order had the effect of (1) changing the date on which Mr Richmond was obliged to give up possession; (2) reviving the original tenancy; (3) wiping the slate clean in respect of the alleged breaches up to the date of the order; and (4) meaning that if Kensington and Chelsea wanted to rely on breaches after the order, it would need to start new proceedings. HHJ Faber rejected that submission, holding that HHJ Mackie had simply been exercising case management powers.

The Court of Appeal dismissed Mr Richmond's appeal. The effect of HHJ Mackie's order was to keep in place the application to enforce the sanction imposed for the original breaches of the tenancy. The last thing that he saw himself as doing was to relieve the tenant from the consequence of those breaches. It was impossible to see this as an extension of the date on which possession must be given. Accordingly, the order did not have the effect of reviving the tenancy. Buxton LJ went on to say 'If on [10 December 2004] Mr Richmond was indeed already in breach [of the suspended possession order], then the judge's order could not have the effect of changing the date on which possession was to be given, because that date had already accrued.'

11.3   *Merton LBC v Hashmi*
September 1995 Legal Action 13, CA (CAT 94/1147)

Execution of warrant set aside where tenant paid off the arrears prior to execution and the possession order had provided that it would then cease to be enforceable

The defendant was a secure tenant. The council was granted a suspended possession order in proceedings based on arrears of rent. The order in the pre-1994 County Court Form N28 stated, '... the judgment shall cease to be enforceable when the arrears of rent, mesne profits and costs ... are satisfied'. The tenants failed to comply with the terms of the order and the council applied for and obtained a warrant for possession. The tenants successfully applied for it to be suspended on terms. Further arrears accrued and the council obtained a second warrant. On the eve of execution of the warrant, the tenants supplied a cheque for £300 towards the arrears and asked how they could stop the eviction the following day. A council officer told them that only a cash payment or a banker's draft could prevent it. The tenants raised the cash and paid it into the council offices the next morning. They returned home with the receipt to find the bailiffs already at the property. Their application to the county court to set aside the execution was dismissed.

The Court of Appeal allowed the tenants' appeal, holding that the order became unenforceable at the moment that the balance was paid. The council's contention that the judgment had not been satisfied because the cheque for £300 had not cleared before execution was rejected, since the tenants had been told that the further payment would satisfy all that was owed.

Note: Much the same result would probably follow under the wording of the 1994 to 2001 Form N28, which stated: 'When you have paid the total amount mentioned, the plaintiff will not be able to take any steps to evict you as a result of this order.' There is no such proviso on the post-Civil Procedure Rules N28.

I1.4   *R v Wandsworth County Court ex p Wandsworth LBC*
[1975] 1 WLR 1314; [1975] 3 All ER 390; (1975) 74 LGR 62, CA (see M5.4)

Warrant entitles bailiffs to evict any person on premises, whether or not a party to proceedings

I2   Outright orders and breach of suspended or postponed orders

House of Lords

I2.1   *Burrows v Brent LBC*
[1996] 1 WLR 1448; [1996] 4 All ER 577; (1997) 29 HLR 167; [1997] 1 EGLR 32; [1997] 11 EG 150, HL

Tenant remaining in possession after absolute possession order effective was a 'tolerated trespasser'

In proceedings against a secure tenant based on arrears of rent, the council obtained an absolute order for possession in 14 days. Before that period expired, the council's officers and the tenant reached an agreement that she would pay future rent, together with instalments towards the arrears. She failed to comply with the agreement and was evicted. She brought proceedings for a declaration that the effect of the agreement had been to grant her a new tenancy and for a mandatory injunction to restore her to the flat. Both were granted in the county court.

Brent Council's appeal was dismissed in the Court of Appeal but allowed in the House of Lords. The House of Lords noted that the agreement was one by which the landlords would forbear from executing the possession order. The absolute order (or breach of a suspended order) ended the secure tenancy: Housing Act 1985 s82 and *Thompson v Elmbridge BC* (I2.16). An agreement to forbear does not restore the old tenancy but simply means that the occupier is in a legal limbo as a 'tolerated trespasser' until either the agreement to forbear is broken (in which case the landlord can seek a warrant) or the former tenant applies successfully to the court to discharge, rescind or modify the order so as to revive the earlier tenancy: Housing Act 1985 s85. In this 'limbo' period there is neither a tenancy nor a licence. Accordingly, there can be no breach of any express or implied obligations or duties relevant to tenancies or licences (eg, to repair). Occupiers are not, however, homeless because they continue in occupation by 'rule of law': s58(2)(c) (now Housing Act 1996 s175(1)(c)). If either party wishes to revive the old tenancy for the purpose of enforcing its express or implied terms, they can apply to the court for an order varying the date on which possession be given so that the old tenancy can be resurrected: s85. See also *Greenwich LBC v Regan* (I2.4).

Court of Appeal

I2.2   *Brent LBC v Knightley*
(1997) 29 HLR 857, CA

Daughter could not succeed to mother's tenancy as it had been lost by breach of SPO

Brent Council obtained a possession order against a secure tenant, suspended on condition that she paid current rent and £2.50 per week towards arrears. She failed to comply with the terms of the suspended possession order and then died. The defendant, the tenant's daughter who had been living with her, claimed the right to succeed to the tenancy (Housing Act 1985 s87).

The Court of Appeal held that the tenancy had ended when the terms of the order were breached. A subsequent order suspending a warrant did not revive the tenancy. The right to succeed applies only where a secure tenancy is still in existence. In this case, there was nothing for the defendant to succeed to. The right to apply for a postponement of an order for possession under Housing Act 1985 s85 is not an interest in land which is capable of being inherited. It is only available to the tenant, the tenant's spouse or former spouse.

12.3 *Bristol CC v Hassan; Bristol CC v Glastonbury*
[2006] EWCA Civ 656; [2006] 1 WLR 2582; [2006] 4 All ER 420; [2006] HLR 31

Courts have jurisdiction to make SPO without specifying a date for possession

A solicitor representing secure tenants in possession claims based on rent arrears argued that suspended possession orders should be in a form which did not specify a date for possession, in order to avoid the tenants becoming tolerated trespassers immediately on any breach. Two district judges held that the court had no jurisdiction to make suspended possession orders in any form other than Form N28. The defendants appealed. HHJ Darlow transferred the appeals for hearing in the Court of Appeal under CPR 52.14 because the cases raised important points of principle.

The Court of Appeal allowed the tenants' appeals. After reviewing a number of authorities (including *McPhail v Persons Unknown* (L3.5) and *American Economic Laundry Ltd v Little* [1950] 2 All ER 1186, CA) and statutes, the Court held that:

1) It is not obligatory for the court to use Form N28 in any given case. CPR 4 provides that 'a form may be varied by the court or a party if the variation is required by the circumstances of a particular case'.

2) Judges are not obliged to set out an absolute date for possession on the face of their orders.

3) Although it is not 'necessary or appropriate to give a fair wind to any procedure which will require a further hearing before a date for possession can be fixed, with all the attendant expense and delay that this might involve, [it] would ... be sufficient for possession to be postponed on the terms that if a claimant landlord wishes a date to be fixed, it must write to the defendant giving details of the current arrears and its intention to request a date to be fixed at least 14 days before it makes that application. If the tenant does not respond, or if the landlord wishes to apply for a date to be fixed notwithstanding the tenant's response, it will then be at liberty to apply to the court on a "without notice" basis requesting a date to be fixed. With its application the landlord must submit to the court a copy of its letter (and the tenant's response, if any), together with a copy of the rent account since the date of the order postponing possession. Other evidence will seldom be required.'

(para 37). It is both lawful and appropriate to make an order along the following lines:

1. The defendant is to give up possession of [address] to the claimant.
2. The date on which the defendant is to give up possession of the property to the claimant is postponed to a date to be fixed by the court on an application by the claimant.
3. The defendant must pay the claimant £[   ] for rent arrears and £[   ] for costs. The total judgment debt is £[   ] to be paid by instalments as specified in paragraph 4 below.
4. The claimant shall not be entitled to make an application for a date to be fixed for the giving up of possession and the termination of the defendant's tenancy so long as the defendant pays the claimant the current rent together with instalments of £[   ] per week towards the judgment debt.
5. The first payment of the current rent and the instalment must be made on or before [date].
6. Any application to fix the date on which the defendant is to give up possession may be determined on the papers without a hearing (unless the district judge considers that such a hearing is appropriate) provided that
    (a) the claimant has written to the defendant at least 14 days before making its application giving details of the current arrears and its intention to request that a date be fixed; and
    (b) a copy of that letter (and the defendant's response, if any) together with the rent account showing any transactions since the date of this order are attached to the application.
7. This order shall cease to be enforceable [on [date]] [when the judgment debt is satisfied].

What order the court will in fact make in any case will be a matter for the discretion of the judge on that occasion, although the [DCA] working party (and in due course the Rules Committee) will no doubt wish to prescribe or recommend simple forms of alternative order for the use of courts. If a tenant has a particularly bad record of payment, for instance, but is not yet deserving of an outright possession order, the court might wish to make an order along the lines of the current form N28, although the use of the phrase 'in addition to your current *rent*' would be inapposite since the contractual tenancy would have been brought to an end by the making of the order. (para 43)

Note: The Court of Appeal did not address the problem of those former secure tenants who are the subject of N28 orders made between October 2001 and the decision in *Harlow DC v Hall* (12.6). However, 'The court has an inherent power to vary its own orders to make the meaning and intention of the court clear.' (PD40B para 4.5.) Alternatively, it is possible to apply retrospectively to postpone the date for possession (Housing Act 1985 s85(2)).

12.4   *Greenwich LBC v Regan*
(1996) 28 HLR 469; (1996) 72 P&CR 507, CA

Agreement for former tenant to remain in possession following breach of SPO did not create new tenancy

The defendant was a secure tenant. In 1989 the council obtained an order for possession suspended on terms that the tenant pay current rent plus £1.75 per week towards arrears of £1,370. By 1994 the arrears exceeded £5,000. The tenant then made an agreement to clear the arrears at the rate of £10 a week but failed to comply. By May 1995, £5,500 was owing and the council applied for a warrant. The tenant applied to a district judge for a stay of execution, contending that (a) on his first breach of the suspended order the tenancy had determined (Housing Act 1985 s82 and *Thompson v Elmbridge BC* (12.16)) and (b) by the subsequent agreements the council had entered into a new tenancy with him which had not been determined (*Burrows v Brent LBC* (12.1)).

The tenant's application and subsequent appeals to the circuit judge and Court of Appeal were all dismissed. The tenancy had come to an end on the first breach of the suspended order. Where a tenant holds over after the expiry of an existing tenancy, it is a question of fact whether or not the parties have agreed a new tenancy. It depends on the intention of the parties (see *Vaughan-Armatrading v Sarsah* (B3.6)). Courts will be reluctant to conclude that councils are at risk of creating new tenancies because they accept payments following suspended possession orders without the court's sanction. In this case, no new tenancy arose because the agreement on repayment was referable to the tenant's right to apply to the court under Housing Act 1985 s85 for a stay or further suspension. Viewed objectively, there was no intention on the part of either party to create a new tenancy or licence (cf, *Burrows v Brent LBC* (12.1)).

12.5 **Hackney LBC v Porter**
(1997) 29 HLR 401, CA

Acceptance of payment by tenant after breach of SPO did not evidence a new tenancy

The defendant was a secure tenant. Following breach of a suspended possession order, the council applied for a warrant. The tenant successfully obtained a stay on terms. Arrears continued to accrue. The council obtained and executed a new warrant. The tenant successfully applied for readmission to the premises on the basis that a payment accepted after the breach evidenced the grant of a new tenancy. The council appealed.

The Court of Appeal, applying *Greenwich LBC v Regan* (12.4), held that, although the tenancy had ended on breach of the suspended order and although the parties had agreed no variation to the terms and conditions of that order so as to resurrect it, the acceptance of the subsequent payment did not evidence a new tenancy. It was acceptance of a part-payment of the money judgment and no more.

12.6 **Harlow DC v Hall**
[2006] EWCA Civ 156; [2006] 1 WLR 2116; [2006] HLR 27; [2006] 2 P&CR 16; (2006) *Times* 15 March

SPO does not postpone the date for possession, merely enforcement; tenancy ends after period of suspension regardless of breach; possession orders and bankruptcy

Mr Hall was a secure tenant. He fell into rent arrears. Harlow obtained a suspended possession order in Form N28 which provided that he 'give possession ... on or before 9 February 2005' and pay arrears of rent and costs totalling £1,919. The order also stated that the order was not to be enforced so long as Mr Hall made payments of £10 per week in addition to the rent. The first payment was to be made by 9 February 2005. He did not make the first payment and on 10 February 2005 he was made bankrupt. On 28 May 2005 Mr Hall applied to discharge the possession order, arguing that the rent arrears were a debt provable in his bankruptcy and that the order for possession was precluded by Insolvency Act 1986 s285(3)(a) because it was a remedy against the property of a bankrupt. That application was dismissed by a district judge and, on appeal, by a circuit judge.

The Court of Appeal dismissed Mr Hall's second appeal. The fact that the debts became provable in the bankruptcy did not have the effect of paying them off. Liability remained although the means of enforcement changed. Furthermore, the Chancellor said:

> ... the order required Mr Hall to give possession on 9th February 2005 ... it was suspended in the sense that it was to take effect on a specified future date, but the obligation to give possession on or before 9th February was not qualified by the postponement of its enforcement .... The distinction between suspending the execution of the order and postponing the date for possession is also made in s85(2). Accordingly it is ... plain that the date on which the tenant 'is to give up possession ... in pursuance of the order' for the purposes of s.82(2) was 9th February 2005 whether or not the conditions prescribed by paragraph 5 for the postponement of its enforcement were observed. It follows that the secure tenancy had ended before the bankruptcy order was made on 10th February 2005.

Chadwick LJ said

> ... it is not possible to treat the order made in the present case as an order which postpones the date on which possession is to be given beyond the date specified in paragraph 1; that is to say, to any date after 9 February 2005. It follows that the secure tenancy ended on 9 February 2005, the day before the bankruptcy order was made.

While it subsisted, the tenancy was property, but it did not subsist at the time the bankruptcy order was made and so s285 did not apply.

12.7   *Knowsley Housing Trust v White*

[2007] EWCA Civ 404; [2007] 4 All ER 800

Assured tenants under Housing Act 1988 become tolerated trespassers on breach of SPO

Mrs White was initially a secure tenant of Knowsley MBC but, as a result of a large-scale stock transfer, she became an assured tenant of the claimant. She fell into rent arrears. A 'suspended possession order' was made on 8 June 2004 in Form N28 which provided 'The Defendant gives the Claimant possession of [the property] on or before 06 July 2004 ... This Order is not to be enforced so long as Defendant pays the Claimant the rent arrears and the amount for use, occupation and costs, totalling £2,262.52 by the payments set out below in addition to the current rent.' Largely owing to housing benefit difficulties, Mrs White breached the terms of the order. Later, she sought to exercise her preserved right to buy, but Knowsley HT informed her that she was not entitled to exercise that right because her tenancy had come to an end on the breach of the 'suspended possession order'. They asserted that she occupied the property as a tolerated trespasser. She sought a declaration that she was still an assured tenant and entitled to exercise the right to buy. HHJ Mackay dismissed her claim.

The Court of Appeal dismissed her appeal. After referring to 'the formidable complexity' of housing legislation, Buxton LJ rejected Mrs White's contention that an assured tenancy can only terminate when possession is given up. Housing Act 1988 does 'not mandate any particular solution' to the question of when an assured tenancy comes to an end. '[T]he answer must be found in the construction of the order made by the county court.' That is particularly so when the court exercises its powers under Housing Act 1988 s9(2)–(4) to suspend execution or postpone the date of possession. Following *Harlow DC v Hall* (12.6), the effect of the order made was that Mrs White's assured tenancy expired on the last date for giving possession, ie, 6 July 2004. Longmore LJ stated that the absence of an equivalent in Housing Act 1988 to Housing Act 1985 s82(2) made no difference to the proper construction of an order for possession made against an assured tenant. He continued 'If a tenant wishes to retain her tenancy until she is evicted, she can always ask the court not to insert in the order any date on which she is to give up possession. It would then be in the discretion of the court whether to make an order in that form.'

12.8   *Lambeth LBC v O'Kane; Helena Housing v Pinder*
[2005] EWCA Civ 1010; [2006] HLR 2; (2005) *Times* 22 September

Notice of increase of rent sent to tolerated trespassers did not create new tenancies

The defendants were secure tenants. Their landlords obtained suspended possession orders based on rent arrears. The terms of the suspended possession orders were breached and the defendants became tolerated trespassers.

In the Lambeth case, the former tenant, a Mr Kennedy, was living in a same-sex relationship with Mr O'Kane. Mr Kennedy died. Mr O'Kane sought to succeed to the tenancy. Before his death, but after the terms of the suspended possession order had been breached, Lambeth sent Mr Kennedy notice of variation of tenancy conditions and four notices of revision of rent and water charges. They referred to rent and not mesne profits. Mr O'Kane argued that, by its actions, Lambeth had either waived the breaches of the suspended possession order or entered into a new tenancy. HHJ Welchman rejected those arguments.

In the Helena Housing cases, after breach of the suspended possession orders, the landlord sent new rent cards with an increased 'rent'. Relying on this, the 'tenants' applied to the court to discharge warrants for possession on the basis that new tenancies had been created. HHJ Mackay rejected their applications.

The Court of Appeal rejected appeals by all the occupants. It concluded that it was not possible to argue that breaches had been waived in view of the decision of the Court of Appeal in *Marshall v Bradford MDC* (12.11).

The question of whether or not a new tenancy has been created is a question of fact for the trial judge. The rent increases in the O'Kane case were consistent with the former landlord's desire to increase mesne profits. There was nothing in those increases 'to force the conclusion that the [former] landlord intended to create a new tenancy. The full context of fact must be considered, and that context includes the fact that Mr Kennedy still owed significant arrears.' The same applied in the Helena cases. The position is no different where the original tenancy was granted to joint tenants.

12.9   ### Lambeth LBC v Rogers

[2000] 03 EG 127; (2000) 32 HLR 361; [2000] LGR 191; [2000] L&TR 319; (1999) *Times* 10 November, CA

Effect of court postponing possession, after SPO breached, was to revive the tenancy and, retrospectively, the repairing obligation

In February 1992 the council granted the defendant a secure tenancy. In October 1992 it obtained a possession order for arrears of rent of £871 suspended on terms that the defendant pay current rent and £5 per week towards the arrears. By December 1992 the tenant had breached the terms. In May 1994 she reached an agreement with the council for further repayments but broke those terms. In September 1996 she brought an action for damages for breach of repairing obligations. The council did not apply to strike out her claim but put in a defence, asserting the loss of the tenancy from the date of breach of the order and the consequent loss of any obligation to repair. In September 1997 the defendant issued an application that the date for possession under the possession order be postponed. In April 1998, when the arrears had reached over £2,000, she agreed a further repayment arrangement with the council, with which she thereafter complied. At trial HHJ Gibson found that her compliance with the latest agreement enabled him to exercise the discretion to postpone the date for possession (Housing Act 1985 s85(2)(a)) with the effect that the tenancy and its repairing obligations revived. On the disrepair claim, he awarded damages in a sum exceeding the arrears and, as the arrears were thereby satisfied, he discharged the possession order altogether (s85(4)).

The Court of Appeal dismissed the council's appeal. It held that from the date of breach in 1992 the former tenant had been a 'tolerated trespasser' enjoying only the prospect that at some date in the future her former tenancy might be revived by a successful s85 application. In that 'limbo period' she did not have the benefit of any contractual repairing obligations and could not enforce them. Her claim in 1996 could have been struck out on the council's application but it did not apply. The agreements with the council in May 1994 and April 1998 did not revive the tenancy or amount to new tenancies. However, the effect of the defendant's successful application for postponement of the possession date was to revive the tenancy and with it, retrospectively, the obligations on each party under the tenancy (unless the court otherwise directed (s85(3)(b)). There was no error of principle in the judge's exercise of his discretion. (See too *Routh v Leeds CC* (13.6).)

12.9A *Leadenhall Residential 2 Ltd v Stirling*

[2001] EWCA Civ 1011; [2002] 1 WLR 499; [2001] 3 All ER 645; [2002] HLR 3; [2002] L&TR 14; (2001) *Times* 25 July, CA (see G4.6)

Agreement to remain after order under Ground 8 did not create new tenancy

12.10 *London and Quadrant Housing Trust v Ansell*

[2007] EWCA Civ 326; [2007] HLR 37; (2007) *Times* 25 April

Warrant of possession cannot be obtained against a tolerated trespasser where a possession order has ceased to be enforceable; a new possession order can be sought on basis of trespass

Ms Ansell was a secure tenant. In 2000 her landlord began possession proceedings based on arrears of rent of just under £1,050. A judge made a suspended possession order in 2001. The order provided 'When you have paid the total amount mentioned the claimant will not be able to take any steps to evict you as a result of this order.' Ms Ansell failed to comply with its terms and so became a tolerated trespasser. In October 2004 she paid all the arrears and her rent account went into credit. Five years after the original order, and after allegations of anti-social behaviour, her landlord took the view that it was no longer possible to enforce the earlier possession order and issued a new possession claim on the basis that Ms Ansell was a trespasser. HHJ Birtles held that, in accordance with its terms, the first possession order could no longer be enforced once the arrears and costs had been paid. Accordingly, the landlord was entitled to bring a new possession claim. Ms Ansell had no good defence.

The Court of Appeal dismissed Ms Ansell's appeal. If it had been open to the landlord to issue and execute a warrant of possession under the earlier order, the present proceedings would be misconceived. It would be wrong to allow the protection afforded by s85(2) to be circumvented by proceeding otherwise than under that order. However, all sums due under the suspended possession order had been paid. That meant that the original order for possession was not enforceable and the court's powers under s85 were no longer exercisable in relation to enforcement under that order (*Swindon BC v Aston* (12.15)). The judge was entitled to conclude that Ms Ansell had become a trespasser, that the landlord was required to bring a new claim for possession, and that that was a valid and lawful claim for possession which succeeded. He did not fall into the error of allowing a possession order to be enforced in a manner which circumvented the provisions of s85(2). The extended discretion conferred on the court by those provisions had ceased to be exercisable.

12.11 *Marshall v Bradford MDC*

[2001] EWCA Civ 594; [2002] HLR 22; [2001] 19 EG 140 (CS), CA

Payment of all arrears following SPO did not revive a tenancy; exercise of court's discretion regarding application for reinstatement considered

Mr and Mrs Marshall were granted a secure tenancy in 1984. In 1989 the council obtained a possession order suspended on condition that they pay the current rent and £1.70 per week towards the arrears, which then amounted to £490.60. Mr and Mrs Marshall separated in 1996 and he left the property. Payments were made fitfully over a number of years but by April 1999 payments of the current rent were up to date and the arrears stood at £5.82. In April 1999 Mrs Marshall brought proceedings in her sole name against the council for breach of its repairing obligations. In May 1999 the council applied to have the proceedings struck out. On 15 June 1999, shortly before the hearing of the council's strike out application, Mrs Marshall paid off the outstanding arrears The district judge concluded that the tenancy had terminated on the occasion of the first failure by Mr and Mrs Marshall to abide by the terms of the suspended order in 1990. On appeal a circuit judge accepted that reasoning, and rejected an argument that the tenancy had revived on discharge of the arrears in June 1999. Mrs Marshall appealed.

The appeal was dismissed. The council had not waived its right to treat the tenancy as terminated. An agreement permitting a former tenant to remain in occupation on terms does not of itself have the effect of reviving the secure tenancy. Nor was there any automatic revival of the tenancy once the whole of the arrears had been paid off. The order provided for possession of the property to be given to the council. Enforcement of the order was suspended on certain conditions. Compliance with the conditions did not have the effect of discharging or rescinding the possession order. For that, a further order under Housing Act 1985 s85(2) or (4) was required. It followed that the present proceedings were commenced long after the tenancy had come to an end and Mrs Marshall had not made a cross-application for reinstatement of the tenancy. In exercising the discretion to strike out or to entertain an application or the possibility of an application for reinstatement, the court should bear in mind: (1) the tenant's previous payment record; (2) whether all parties were before the court; and (3) whether the tenant was seeking merely the execution of works of repair or also damages for past disrepair. Having regard to all those factors there was no basis for interfering with the exercise of discretion below.

Note: Following *London and Quadrant Housing Trust v Ansell* (I2.10) it is not possible to reinstate a tenancy where arrears have been cleared under a pre-CPR SPO (see note to *Merton LBC v Hashmi* (I1.3)) nor where the premises have been vacated (see *Dunn v Bradford MDC; Marston v Leeds* (I3.1)).

I2.12   *Newham LBC v Hawkins*

[2005] EWCA Civ 451; [2005] HLR 42; [2005] LGR 750; (2005) *Times* 3 May

No new tenancy created after SPO breached despite council treating tenancy as having been reinstated after payment of arrears

Mr Hawkins was a secure tenant. On his death his widow succeeded to the tenancy under Housing Act 1985 s87. She fell into arrears with the rent. A suspended possession order was made. She breached that order but later a substantial payment of arrears was made. Newham treated it as having cleared the account so that the widow was reinstated to the original tenancy. However, the possession order did not provide in terms that it would come to an end once the arrears were paid off. When the widow died, Newham sought possession on the ground that her sons had no right to succeed to the tenancy because their mother was herself a successor. The judge found that the local authority had not created a new tenancy and that the widow occupied the property either as a tolerated trespasser or, if Newham had waived her breaches of the suspended possession order, under her original secure tenancy, so that in either case the sons had no right of succession. The sons claimed that their mother's tenancy had come to an end because of s82(2) after she had breached the suspended possession order, and that the conduct of Newham was consistent with an agreement for a new tenancy.

The Court of Appeal held that where a suspended possession order is made and breached, but the local authority permits a person to remain in occupation, that person is a 'tolerated trespasser'. In the ordinary case of a tolerated trespasser there is no creation of a new secure tenancy. In this case all that happened was that Newham agreed after the suspended possession order was breached that the widow could continue to remain in occupation provided that she made satisfactory payments of rent thereafter. There was no offer of new terms or demand for an increased rent which might have shown that the intention of the parties was to create a new tenancy. The widow could have applied under s85(2) for possession to be postponed. That would have revived her original tenancy retrospectively. This case was not exceptional and there were no facts on which the judge could have found that a new tenancy had arisen. (cf *Swindon BC v Aston* (12.15)

12.13 *Pemberton v Southwark LBC*
[2000] 1 WLR 1672; [2000] 3 All ER 924; (2000) 32 HLR 784; [2000] 21 EG 135; (2000) *Times* 26 April, CA

Tolerated trespassers have sufficient interest in land to claim in nuisance

The claimant was a secure tenant but fell into rent arrears. A suspended possession order was made but breached. She became a tolerated trespasser. In October 1997 she began proceedings against the council in nuisance, alleging that her flat was infested with cockroaches from common parts of the building in the ownership of the council. The defendant claimed that the claimant had no cause of action because she was not a tenant and did not have sufficient interest in the premises to support an action in nuisance.

The Court of Appeal held that she did have sufficient interest in the premises to bring an action in nuisance. Tolerated trespassers cannot require landlords to carry out repairs or bring proceedings under Defective Premises Act 1972. Landlords cannot evict for breach of covenants in the former tenancy agreements. However, the policy considerations that had led to the special status of tolerated trespassers were not good reasons for depriving such people of all rights and remedies in trespass and nuisance. Possession or occupation by tolerated trespassers may be precarious but it is not wrongful and is exclusive. Although the council was under no obligation to repair, there was no reason why it should not be obliged to conduct itself in relation to the remainder of the premises so as not to create a nuisance. A petition by the defendants for leave to appeal to the House of Lords was dismissed: [2001] 1 WLR 538.

12.14   *Rogers v Lambeth LBC*
see *Lambeth LBC v Rogers* (12.9)

12.15   *Swindon BC v Aston*
[2002] EWCA Civ 1850; [2003] HLR 42; [2003] L&TR 18; [2003] 2 P&CR 22

Facts supported creation of new tenancy after breach of SPO

Mr Aston was a secure tenant. His landlord, Thamesdown Borough Council, obtained a possession order, suspended on condition that he pay current rent and arrears by instalments. The order provided that it would 'cease to be enforceable when the [arrears of rent] are satisfied'. Mr Aston breached the conditions of the order, but on several occasions paid off all the arrears. Thamesdown BC then ceased to exist, and its functions were taken over by Swindon Borough Council. It provided him with a copy of its tenancy agreement. Some time later, neighbours complained about the state of Mr Aston's garden. As a result, Swindon served both a simple notice to quit, on the basis that there was no subsisting tenancy at the date of the notice, and a 'without prejudice' notice seeking possession (Housing Act 1985 s83). In possession proceedings a district judge held that the tenancy had determined on the breach of the conditions attached to the possession order, and that thereafter Mr Aston remained in the property as a 'tolerated trespasser'. He appealed against that decision to a circuit judge, but his appeal was dismissed. He then applied under Housing Act 1985 s85(4) to rescind the first possession order on the ground that he had complied with the conditions by paying off all the arrears. Recorder Ralphs dismissed that application. Mr Aston appealed.

   The appeal was allowed. On breach of the suspended possession order Mr Aston became a 'tolerated trespasser'. Although 'the court will be extremely reluctant to infer the creation of a new secure tenancy during the limbo period', viewed objectively, the conduct of both landlord and tenant was sensibly referable only to the existence of a new tenancy. That was confirmed by the way in which the landlord relied on the terms of his 'tenancy agreement' to coerce him into keeping the garden in proper order, and by the provision of the new tenancy agreement. Mr Aston was, accordingly, a secure tenant from approximately three months after he cleared the arrears. It was neither possible nor necessary to rescind the original order. Mr Aston was entitled to security of tenure under the new secure tenancy. The possession claim was remitted to be considered on the basis that Mr Aston was a secure tenant.

12.16   *Thompson v Elmbridge BC*
[1987] 1 WLR 1425; (1987) 19 HLR 526; (1988) 86 LGR 245, CA

Secure tenancy ends on breach of SPO

Mrs Thompson was a sole tenant. A possession order was made on grounds including arrears of rent. The order was suspended on terms including payment of £10 per week towards the arrears. Further arrears accrued and Mrs Thompson departed, leaving her husband in possession. The council sought to execute the possession order. Mr Thompson (who was paying current rent by way of certificated housing benefit) applied for a transfer of the tenancy to him under the Matrimonial Homes Act 1983.

The Court of Appeal held that the secure tenancy had come to an end on the first occasion that the terms of the suspended possession order had been breached by failing to pay the current rent or instalments towards the arrears. Accordingly, the court found that there was no tenancy to transfer under the Matrimonial Homes Act.

High Court

12.17 *R v Sheffield CC ex p Creaser and Jarvis*
September 1991 *Legal Action* 15, QBD

Former tenants not entitled to contractual internal review of decision to evict

Suspended possession orders were made against two tenants, which were then breached. The council intended to apply for warrants for possession. The tenants asked for an internal review to be held, as apparently required by the council's standard tenancy agreement. When refused, the tenants applied for judicial review of the council's refusal.

Kennedy J considered that he was bound by *Thompson v Elmbridge BC* (12.16) to find that both tenancies had ended on breach of the respective orders. Accordingly, even if the tenancy agreement referred to an internal review, the occupiers were no longer tenants and so were unable to rely on it. Alternatively, the right to an internal review or lack of it could be dealt with by an application for declaratory relief in the county court (Housing Act 1985 s110) rather than by way of judicial review. The application was dismissed.

13 Variation and suspension of possession orders after their creation

Court of Appeal

13.1 *Dunn v Bradford MDC; Marston v Leeds CC*
[2002] EWCA Civ 1137; [2003] HLR 15; [2003] L&TR 11; (2002) *Times* 5 September

Extended discretion cannot be exercised to revive tenancy where former tenants have vacated premises

In both cases the landlord local authority obtained a suspended possession order against secure tenants. The tenants failed to comply with the terms and their tenancies came to an end. They remained in the premises for some time with the knowledge and acquiescence of the council, before voluntarily giving up possession prior to execution of the orders. The tenants then applied under Housing Act 1985 s85(2) to postpone the date for possession so as to enhance claims which they wished to bring against the local authorities for breach of their repairing covenants.

The Court of Appeal held that there is no power under s85(2) to stay or postpone the date for giving up possession under an existing possession order if tenants have already given up possession without the need for execution of the order. The words 'at any time before the execution of the order' in s85(2) have to be read subject to the qualification 'and for so long as execution is required to give effect to that order'. It could not be right to attribute to parliament an intention that the intended discretionary powers conferred by s85(2) should continue to be exercisable once the former tenant had given up possession. Furthermore, the trial judges had rightly rejected one tenant's plea of estoppel and attempted reliance on the Supply of Goods and Services Act 1982 and/or the Defective Premises Act 1972.

13.2   *Lambeth LBC v Rogers*

[2000] 03 EG 127; (2000) 32 HLR 361; [2000] LGR 191; [2000] L&TR 319; (1999) *Times* 10 November, CA (see 12.9)

Effect of postponement of possession, after SPO breached, was to revive the tenancy and, retrospectively, repairing obligations

13.3   *Manchester CC v Finn*

[2002] EWCA Civ 1998; [2003] HLR 41

Postponed possession order (on basis of rent arrears) can be varied to outright possession order (on basis of nuisance)

In February 2000 a possession order was made against Ms Finn, a secure tenant, as a result of arrears of rent of over £1,860. The order was postponed on terms as to the payment of rent and instalments of £2.60 per week towards the arrears. Ms Finn complied with the terms of the order. In November 2000 the police found stolen property valued at £28,000 at the property. In August 2001 the police found five stolen microwaves at the property. On each occasion the defendant received a non-custodial sentence. In December 2001 the council applied to have the possession order varied and for the substitution of a forthwith order. A district judge dismissed the application on the ground that he did not have jurisdiction. On appeal HHJ Holman allowed the council's appeal and remitted the matter to a district judge. Ms Finn appealed to the Court of Appeal contending that, once an order for possession is made and postponed by the court, the court is functus officio and there is no jurisdiction to vary or revoke it.

The appeal was dismissed. The important words in Housing Act 1985 s85(2) are 'at any time'. The court has to give a sensible meaning to those words. A purposive construction has to be adopted. Since the order was still running, liberty to apply to the court was implicit, without the need to start new proceedings for possession. The court could make a new order, even if the old order had not expired or if the new order would provide for possession to be given up forthwith. The court had, on such an application, to bear in mind the guidance given in cases such as *Sheffield CC v Hopkins* (15.2), as to the exercise of its discretion in such a situation, and should be astute to ensure that tenants are not taken by surprise. However, that does not necessarily extend to insisting that the proceedings be delayed by the equivalent of the extra time that would have been taken if the landlord had had to begin new proceedings. Courts can ensure that any notice of application gives the grounds and particulars which put the tenant to no greater disadvantage than envisaged by s84(3). Courts should determine any application to vary a possession order in exactly the same way as they would determine an original claim.

13.4   *Marshall v Bradford MDC*

[2001] EWCA Civ 594; [2002] HLR 22; [2001] 19 EG 140 (CS), CA (see 12.11)

Payment of all arrears following SPO did not revive a tenancy; exercise of court's discretion regarding application for reinstatement considered

13.5   *Plymouth CC v Hoskin*

[2002] EWCA Civ 684; August 2002 *Legal Action* 32; 1 May 2002

No compelling reason for second appeal where a continuing remedy existed in the county court after outright possession order made

In possession proceedings based on anti-social behaviour, a district judge made an outright possession order. The defendant sought permission to appeal, claiming that the district judge had misunderstood the provisions of the Housing Acts in stating that the local authority had 'a broad duty to house' Mr Hoskin, rather than the more limited duty contained in Housing Act 1996 s190.

Although the language used by the circuit judge could have been 'clearer' the Court of Appeal found that he had refused permission to appeal, rather than dismissed the appeal. In any event, even if the appeal had been dismissed, there was no compelling reason for a second appeal. The changed circumstances could be brought to the attention of the district judge since 'there is a continuing remedy in the county court'. Clarke LJ said that Mr Hoskin was entitled to make a fresh application to a district judge to stay or suspend execution. Such an application:

> ... is not in any way affected or fettered by the reasons given by [the district judge who heard the possession claim] ... on such an application the district judge can take all relevant circumstances into account as they appear at the time of the application. Those will include any medical evidence which is before the court, any evidence as to the defendant's behaviour since the original order and the effect of an immediate order for possession which is not suspended upon the likelihood of the applicant being rehoused under the Housing Act 1996.

13.6   *Routh v Leeds CC*

June 1998 *Legal Action* 11, CA

Reinstatement of tenancy, to allow action for disrepair, would be unjust

The plaintiff was a secure tenant. In May 1990 the council obtained a suspended possession order against the plaintiff on the ground of rent arrears. The terms were breached. In 1994 the plaintiff, who had remained in possession, brought an action for damages for disrepair. In defence, the council pleaded that the tenancy had come to an end on breach of the possession order and with it the covenant to repair (see *Thompson v Elmbridge BC* (12.16). The plaintiff then applied to have the original possession order set aside or the date for possession stated in it extended. Either application, if successful, would have retrospectively revived the tenancy (see *Burrows v Brent LBC* (12.1)). The judge refused both applications. The plaintiff sought leave to appeal against the refusal to postpone the date for possession (Housing Act 1985 s85(2)(b)).

Leave was refused. Sir John Vinelott said:

Not only was [the judge] entitled to exercise his discretion in the way he did but, in my judgment, he was bound to take the view that it would be unjust to the council to reinstate the tenancy retrospectively with the result that they would have obligations to a tenant imposed upon them, although the tenant was one who had never consistently discharged her obligations to pay rent to them.

13.7   *Vandermolen v Toma*
(1981) 9 HLR 91, CA

Extended discretion of court exercisable on more than one occasion; indefinite suspension of possession on payment of current rent, if no arrears, inappropriate

On 17 December 1980, the plaintiff, the landlord of a Rent Act protected tenant, obtained an order for possession, suspended on payment of arrears of £771 and costs of £50 by 7 January 1981. On 13 January 1981, the landlord issued a warrant. The tenant applied to suspend the warrant on the ground that all arrears had been paid. That application was refused. The tenant made a further application and the warrant was suspended for 21 days, subject to an enquiry by the registrar (now district judge) about whether the tenant had complied with the terms of the possession order. The enquiry was completed outside the 21-day period. The registrar found that the tenant owed £73. A cheque for the outstanding money was sent 17 days later. The tenant then applied to discharge the possession order and the warrant. The court suspended the possession order on condition that the tenant paid the current rent. The landlord appealed.

The Court of Appeal dismissed the appeal. Under Rent Act 1977 s100 the court may suspend on more than one occasion. In any event, the court had power under County Court Rules 1936 Ord 13 r5 (now CPR 3.1(2)(a)) to enlarge time. Although the court may suspend indefinitely, such an order should only be made in very special circumstances. Templeman LJ said

... an order for possession should, in general, either be enforced, or be discharged, or it can be suspended, but it should only be suspended for a defined period. If the order is suspended for a defined period, that period should not extend into the mists of time, but should have some relevance to the facts existing at the date when the order for suspension is made.

In the present case, suspension was not a proper exercise of discretion. The Court of Appeal retrospectively enlarged the time for compliance and discharged the order.

High Court

13.8   *Barnet LBC v Hurley*
[2003] EWHC 751 (Ch), 11 March 2003 (see 15.3)

Further suspension of possession allowed where excluded husband had caused breach and no further breaches in 11 months prior to listing of appeal

13.9   *Ujima Housing Association v Smith*
April 2001 *Legal Action* 21; 16 October 2000, ChD

Outright order for possession varied to SPO where circumstances had changed

In possession proceedings HHJ Sitch found that the defendant, an assured tenant, had been responsible for serious damage to a shared kitchen, including ripping units away from the wall and smashing base units with a hammer. He found that these incidents 'constituted serious breaches of the relevant tenancy agreement' and that the defendant was 'in effect accusing the housing officers of lying and trying to 'frame' her'. In those circumstances, it was 'difficult to see how any relationship can continue' and, as a result, he found it reasonable to make an outright order for possession. Subsequently, the defendant made an application to HHJ Zucker QC to suspend the order. She offered to pay £150 towards the damage to the kitchen. HHJ Zucker, finding that it 'was one incident', granted her application, suspending the possession order on terms that she cause no damage to the property and pay £150.

Ujima appealed unsuccessfully. Ferris J found that Housing Act 1988 s9 'gives a wide power to stay or suspend an order for possession which is applicable to all cases except those where it is expressly excluded by statute'. There was no sustainable argument that HHJ Zucker had no jurisdiction to suspend. He found that circumstances had changed since the original hearing because the defendant was now accepting her legal responsibility for the incident and that marked a change from her earlier attitude. The new factors were sufficient to give HHJ Zucker an independent discretion under s9.

14 Setting aside possession orders

If a tenant fails to attend court when a possession order is made, there may be grounds to apply to set aside the order. The jurisdiction to set aside an order where one party was absent is now contained in Civil Procedure Rule 39.3(5). The jurisdiction may only be exercised '... if the applicant (a) acted promptly when he found out that the court had exercised its power ... to enter judgment or make an order against him; (b) had good reason for not attending the trial; and (c) has a reasonable prospect of success at the trial.

To succeed in having a possession order set aside on the basis of non-attendance, a tenant must satisfy all three requirements. These are different criteria from those formerly exercisable under CCR Ord 37 r2, but some of the cases decided under CCR Ord 37 r2 are retained in this section because they illustrate the effect of a successful application to set aside. If a tenant was present when a possession order was made it may be possible to appeal (see CPR Part 52).

Court of Appeal

14.1 *Governors of Peabody Donation Fund v Hay*
(1987) 19 HLR 145, CA

Where possession order set aside, any execution also ceased to have effect

In county court possession proceedings, the landlords obtained an order for possession in 14 days and a money judgment. On the fourteenth day, the tenant paid all the money due into court. The following day, a warrant for possession was issued. The tenant's solicitors told the landlords' solicitors that they would issue an application to set aside the possession order and to suspend the warrant the next day. However, the warrant was executed and the locks were changed before the application was issued. Later in the day that the locks had been changed, a county court judge heard the tenant's application and set aside the judgment and the warrant. The landlords appealed.

The Court of Appeal, dismissing the appeal, held that the effect of CCR Ord 37 r8(3) was that, where a judgment or order is set aside, any execution that has been issued, whether completed or not, ceases to have effect unless the court orders otherwise.

14.2   *Tower Hamlets LBC v Abadie*
(1990) 22 HLR 264, CA

Order set aside despite delay where council would not be prejudiced

A possession order was made against a secure tenant under Housing Act 1985 Sch 2 Ground 8 (repossession of temporary accommodation where the tenant's original home is available again after improvement work). After a long delay, the tenant applied to set the order aside, presumably under CCR Ord 37 r2, on the basis that he had not been present in court when the possession order was made. The application was dismissed and the order for possession executed. The council prepared to re-let.

On the tenant's appeal, the Court of Appeal held that: (a) the order could be set aside even after it had been executed (CCR Ord 37 r8(3) and *Governors of Peabody Donation Fund v Hay* (14.1)); (b) despite the delay the council would not actually be prejudiced if the order were set aside; and (c) the tenant had an arguable defence to the original proceedings which had not been put (that his original accommodation was not being offered to him). The judgment was set aside and the case sent back for retrial.

High Court

14.3   *Clapton Community Housing Trust v McGrath*
January 2004 *Legal Action* 30; 31 October 2003, QBD

Order set aside where tenant had been told wrong time of hearing

Ms McGrath was a secure tenant from 1990. As a result of a stock transfer in 1999 she became an assured tenant. On 18 June 2003 she attended her landlord's housing office and was interviewed regarding a transfer. She lost her temper and assaulted a female allocations officer. She pulled her hair and punched her. The allocations officer fell to the floor. Ms McGrath pleaded guilty to common assault in the magistrates' court and was fined £100. CCHT issued a claim for possession, relying on that one incident, and sought an injunction. The case was listed for hearing on 23 July. Ms McGrath arrived at 10.00 am as the case was listed for 10.30 am but was informed that the hearing had been moved to the afternoon. She understood that she should return about 4.00 pm. CCHT had been told the day before that the case was listed for 3.00 pm. The case was heard without Ms McGrath being present and an order for possession was made to take effect by 25 July. Ms McGrath came back to court later in the afternoon, after the case had been dealt with. A district judge called Ms McGrath into her chambers with CCHT's housing officer and listened to Ms McGrath but confirmed that the order stood. On 24 July, Ms McGrath applied to vary the order, but was sent a letter by the court saying that there was no date for her eviction and she should come back when she had notice from the bailiffs. On or about 9 August she received a bailiff's notice that she was to be evicted on 23 September. CCHT were unhappy with this date and requested an earlier date. The court issued a new notice of eviction bringing the eviction forward to 22 August. The notice had a hand-written note, stating that the earlier date was in error and the new date was correct. CCHT wrote to Ms McGrath on 14 August, stating that her eviction would occur on 22 August 2003 and claiming she had breached the injunction. The letter did not advise her of her rights to stay the process. Ms McGrath became aware of the new date for her eviction on 15 August. She approached solicitors the following week but none could see her before the eviction date. She was evicted on 22 August and applied to re-enter that day. HHJ Cotran heard her application on 26 August. He set aside the possession order under CPR 39.3 and held that there was oppression in the execution of the warrant, mainly because advancing the date of eviction by a month meant that Ms McGrath was unable to obtain legal advice in order to protect her position. CCHT appealed.

McKinnon J dismissed the appeal. He held that the judge's decision under CPR 39.3 was correct. Ms McGrath had applied promptly. There was a good reason not to attend at 3 pm as on facts she was given the wrong time for the hearing. Finally, she had reasonable prospects of success. There were arguments on the issue of 'locality' and reasonableness (given that it was a single incident of assault in a tenancy that commenced in 1990 and there were no other complaints against her) and there was a clear issue over whether to suspend any order for possession. Although not necessary, McKinnon J agreed that there was oppression in giving six weeks' notice and then reducing it unilaterally to four days' notice when Ms McGrath could not get legal advice. He was also critical of both CCHT and the bailiff for failing to inform Ms McGrath why the date had been changed.

14.4   *Lewisham LBC v Gurbuz*

[2003] EWHC 2078 (Ch); 24 July 2003

Courts should not be over critical about evidence where defendant acted in good faith

Ms Gurbuz was a secure tenant. Lewisham sought possession against her on the basis that she had ceased to occupy as her residence the property let by them. She disputed this allegation. On the afternoon of the day before the trial, the court switched the hearing of the case from Woolwich County Court to Mayor's and City County Court. The court did not manage to inform Ms Gurbuz or the litigation friend who was acting for her of the change. The council did deliver a letter to Ms Gurbuz notifying her of the change of court but she did not receive it until 8 pm. She was unable to speak to her litigation friend and did not know what to do. In the morning she went to his office, while he went to Woolwich County Court. When he learnt of the transfer of the case, he telephoned Mayor's and City County Court to say that he was making his way to that court. However, the judge proceeded with the hearing and made an order for possession. Ms Gurbuz applied to set aside the possession order (CPR 39.3(5)). HHJ Gibson refused her application. He considered that there was a triable issue but declined to determine whether there was a reasonable prospect of success because witness statements dealing with this issue were not attached to the defendant's application

Patten J allowed Ms Gurbuz's appeal, set aside the possession order and remitted the case to the county court. Late notification of the change of venue led to a muddle. Unless it can be shown that a defendant who fails to attend trial has done so either deliberately or in a clearly dilatory way, not caring really about the consequences, courts should not be over critical about reasons for not attending trial. The defendant acted in good faith and had a good reason for not attending trial. Second, as the judge had, quite rightly, concluded that there was a triable issue, he was wrong to have refused to determine whether there was a reasonable prospect of success simply because the witness statements were not formally part of the application. 'Reasonable prospect of success' does not mean that the defence will succeed. What it means is that there is enough material before the court to establish a viable defence if that evidence is accepted.

15   Suspension of warrants before execution

Where tenants enjoy statutory security of tenure, courts have wide powers to stay or suspend execution of any possession order or to postpone the date of possession – see Housing Act 1985 s85(2) and the comparable provisions in Rent Act 1977 s100(2) and Housing Act 1988 s9(2), These powers can be exercised after the making of a possession order 'at any time *before the execution* of such an order', even if an absolute possession order was originally made or if the original order was made by consent. More than one application can be made. However, once eviction has taken place, the court no longer has any power to stay, suspend or set aside a warrant under Rent Act 1977 s100(2), Housing Act 1985 s85(2) or Housing Act 1988 s9(2), since those powers are expressly limited by the words 'at any time before the execution of the order'.

Court of Appeal

15.1   *Haringey LBC v Powell*
(1996) 28 HLR 798, CA

Where there is a substantial dispute about compliance with SPO, position should be clarified before determining application to suspend warrant

In 1992 the council obtained a suspended possession order. At the time the tenant's arrears were £3,500. By November 1994 the arrears had increased by £1,000 and the council obtained a warrant. On the tenant's application to stay the warrant, she argued that the figures claimed in the rent account were wrong and that she was owed approximately £1,000 in respect of housing benefit. After a short adjournment, during which it was not possible to clarify the position, her application was dismissed.

The Court of Appeal allowed the tenant's appeal and ordered a further adjournment of the application for a stay. Where there is a substantial dispute about the amount claimed and the tenant's compliance with the order, the up-to-date position has to be clearly and accurately established. If what the defendant said about benefit was correct, the arrears would have been similar to those at the date of the possession order. Although the defendant would still not have complied with the terms of the possession order, the difference in the level of the arrears would have had a substantial effect on the exercise of the court's discretion under Housing Act 1985 s85(2). The council was ordered to set out its housing benefit decisions within 14 days and to supply an updated rent account statement.

15.2 *Sheffield CC v Hopkins*
[2001] EWCA Civ 1023; [2002] HLR 12; (2001) *Times* 23 July, CA

When exercising discretion to suspend warrant, judge can take account of nuisance despite fact that possession order made on basis of rent arrears

In proceedings against a secure tenant based on rent arrears, the landlord obtained a suspended possession order. Later a warrant for possession was issued. The tenant applied to suspend the warrant (Housing Act 1985 s85). At the hearing of the application, the landlord sought to adduce evidence of nuisance caused by the tenant. The parties agreed that the issue of whether such evidence could be admitted should be heard as a preliminary point. District Judge Oldham ruled that matters other than rent could not be raised on the application to suspend the warrant for possession. HHJ Bartfield upheld that ruling on appeal.

The landlord appealed successfully. The court, exercising its discretion under s85, can take into account matters other than those relied on as grounds for making the original possession order – although it is not always right to do so. Whilst not attempting to fetter the discretion of district judges, the Court of Appeal stated that the following points are relevant.

1) The discretion should be used so as to further the policy of Housing Act 1985 Part IV, reinforced by ECHR article 8. The policy is only to evict after a serious breach of an obligation, where it is reasonable to do so and where the tenant is proved to have breached any condition of suspension.

2) The overriding objective of the Civil Procedure Rules, especially the need for applications to be dealt with in a summary and proportionate way, means that wider issues may not be able to be dealt with on an application to suspend or vary. They may need to be dealt with in some other way.

3) The tenant should have clear evidence of what is alleged, especially where the allegations were not contained in the original claim.

4) The fact that the landlord had or had not included the allegations as part of the original proceedings is relevant.

5) The discretion to consider other allegations should generally be exercised more readily in respect of matters occurring after commencement of the proceedings.

6) The court should also consider the practicalities of dealing with matters on the execution of a warrant.

7) The fact that the tenant is at the mercy of the court and the responsibilities of a public landlord to its other tenants.

The list is not exhaustive. District judges have to exercise the discretion bearing in mind the importance of the issue to the tenant, at risk of losing his home, and the responsibilities of social landlords to their other tenants. The case was remitted to the county court for reconsideration of the application to suspend the warrant.

High Court

15.3   *Barnet LBC v Hurley*

[2003] EWHC 751 (Ch), 11 March 2003

Further suspension of possession allowed where excluded husband had caused breach and no further breaches in 11 months prior to listing of appeal

Mrs Hurley was a secure tenant from 1975. In 1997, after a long history of racial and other abuse and extensive intimidation, a recorder made a suspended possession order. In 2002, after there had been 97 instances of contempt of court by Mr Hurley, the council applied to have the suspension lifted. Mrs Hurley, and other members of the family, gave evidence denying all the allegations. However, a circuit judge found that they had all lied and that the allegations against Mr Hurley were proved. He also found that Mrs Hurley had no part in the matters proved and did not condone or support them. The judge further suspended the possession order on terms that Mr Hurley should move out of the premises by 9 April 2002 and would not return and that Mrs Hurley would comply with provisions in the tenancy agreement dealing with nuisance and annoyance to others. Mr Hurley remained in the house for about a week after the date by which he was ordered to depart and was imprisoned for a short period for contempt for breaching non-molestation orders. The council appealed against the further suspension. As the circuit judge had given no reasons for not lifting the suspension, Mrs Hurley accepted that the judge's decision could not be sustained.

By the time of the hearing of the appeal (some 11 months later) there had been no further breaches. After considering the discretion whether or not to suspend afresh, and referring to *Canterbury CC v Lowe* (H4.6), Peter Smith J further suspended the order on terms that Mr Hurley did not enter the premises or attempt to do so. He also asked for and received an undertaking from Mrs Hurley that she would prevent him from doing so in so far as she was able to. He stated that he had to balance 'the overriding need ... to ensure that perfectly innocent people can enjoy the use of their property free from harassment, racial abuse and intimidation' against 'the legitimate rights of Mrs Hurley to enjoy the property'. Reluctantly he concluded that 'it would be disproportionate and unduly punishing of Mrs Hurley to throw her out of a house which she had occupied since 1975'. He was reluctant to suspend because 'the bonds of marriage ... [did] not justify going to court and telling lies to save her husband'.

15.4 *Hackney LBC v Side by Side (Kids) Ltd*

[2003] EWHC 1813 (QBD); [2004] 1 WLR 363; [2004] 2 All ER 373; (2003) *Times* 5 August (see M5.8)

Housing Act 1980 s89 applies to orders made in the High Court; court had no jurisdiction to suspend possession beyond limits in s89, even by consent

15.5 *R v Ilkeston County Court ex p Kruza*

(1985) 17 HLR 539, QBD

County court had jurisdiction to suspend warrant following breach of SPO

In county court possession proceedings based on rent arrears, the court made an order for possession which was suspended for seven days and thereafter for so long as the tenant paid her rent. The tenant later failed to pay rent and the council accordingly obtained a warrant for possession. Two days before the warrant was due to be executed, the tenant issued an application to suspend the warrant. The county court refused to grant the application on the ground that there was no jurisdiction to suspend the warrant further.

Tudor Evans J held that, in view of CCR Ord 13 r4, 'generally speaking there is unquestionably power in the County Court to extend time generally'. The suspended possession order was not to be read as an order that enabled the landlord to execute the order as soon as rent was not paid, with the result that no application for suspension could be entertained. Accordingly, the county court registrar (now district judge) had jurisdiction to entertain the application for suspension of the warrant for possession. An order of mandamus was issued to require the registrar to hear and determine the application.

15.6 *Stonebridge HAT v Gabbidon*

[2002] EWHC 2091 ChD; (2002) *Times* 13 December; 21 November 2002

Drug issues, breaches and arrears did not compel court to refuse to suspend warrant

In February 1997 the claimant housing trust obtained a suspended possession order on the ground of rent arrears against the second defendant, who was a secure tenant. She failed to comply with the terms of suspension and a warrant for possession was obtained. The second defendant applied to stay the warrant or to suspend the possession order further. The court was satisfied that further rent arrears had accrued and that she had, on five occasions, allowed the premises to be used for drug use. The judge ruled that the arrears of rent were insufficient to justify immediate possession. Furthermore, although all five allegations of drug use were serious and amounted to a nuisance, and would have been grounds for making a possession order, there were two mitigating factors: (1) the judge was not satisfied that the second defendant had been involved personally in drug dealing; and (2) nothing recent had been proved. He also took into account the fact that the second defendant had a 7-month-old child, and, having regard to the overall requirement of reasonableness and ECHR article 8, further suspended the order. The claimant appealed, submitting that immediate possession should have been ordered.

Lloyd J dismissed the appeal. The judge had taken into account both the second defendant's conduct with the drugs and her financial breaches and had paid clear regard to ECHR article 8. Such considerations were not irrelevant factors to which the judge should not have had regard. The claimant's contention that allowing the second defendant to remain in occupation despite the breaches and nuisance would set a precedent for other tenants was not supportable. No other tenant would be able to resist an application for a possession order by drawing an analogy with this case. The drug matters, the nuisance and the further rent arrears did not compel the court when exercising its discretion under Housing Act 1985 s85 to reach only one possible answer, namely that immediate possession had to be granted.

County courts

15.7   *Sheffield CC v Gosling*
December 1989 *Legal Action* 14, Sheffield County Court

Court cannot place fetter on tenant's right to apply under Housing Act 1985 s85(2)

Following breach of a suspended possession order, the landlords obtained a warrant for possession. The tenant succeeded in an application for a stay but Registrar Lambert directed that no further applications be accepted. On a later further breach of the order, the council again obtained a warrant, which met with another application for a stay by the tenant. Registrar Vincent adjourned the second application to the circuit judge for consideration of whether or not it could be entertained, in the light of the previous direction.

HHJ Bentley held that the court could not place a fetter on the tenant's right to apply under Housing Act 1985 s85(2), and the direction was set aside. Each successive application should be dealt with on its merits.

16   Setting aside warrants after execution

Once eviction has taken place, the court no longer has any power to stay, suspend or set aside a warrant under Rent Act 1977 s100(2), Housing Act 1985 s85(2) or Housing Act 1988 s9(2), since those powers are expressly limited by the words 'at any time before the execution of the order'. A warrant can be set aside after execution if the possession order itself is set aside, the warrant has been obtained by fraud or there has been an abuse of the process or oppression in its execution.

Court of Appeal

16.1   *Barking and Dagenham LBC v Saint*
see *Saint v Barking and Dagenham LBC* (16.13)

16.2   *Camden LBC v Akanni*
(1997) 29 HLR 845, CA

Cases where the execution of a warrant is an abuse of process are 'rare'

A former tenant applied to set aside a warrant on the basis that the circumstances of its execution were oppressive. He alleged that, shortly before the application for the warrant was made, he took a lump sum of £400 to the council and a housing officer received it with the words 'that will do for now'. He took no further steps and made no further payment because he thought that the council would be in touch with him. HHJ White found it 'difficult to believe' in all the circumstances that the tenant had genuinely formed the belief that he had simply to wait for the council to contact him. He preferred the evidence of the housing officer and rejected the allegation of 'oppressive' conduct.

The Court of Appeal dismissed the former tenant's application for leave to appeal. It held that there was no arguable case that the council landlords had been guilty of 'oppression' in executing by warrant a suspended possession order. Brooke LJ's judgment offers a helpful indication of the sorts of 'rare, but appropriate, cases' in which it could be suggested that execution of a warrant had been an abuse of process which the court should, in its inherent jurisdiction, control. He referred to 'the general principle that the Court can and will interfere whenever there is a vexation and oppression to prevent the administration of justice being perverted for an unjust end. I would rather do that than attempt to define what vexation and oppression mean; they must vary with the circumstances of the case.'

16.3   *Circle 33 Housing Trust v Ellis*
[2005] EWCA Civ 1233; [2006] HLR 7

Landlord had not acted oppressively in executing warrant in light of information it had been given by housing benefits department at the time

The defendant was an assured tenant. He was in receipt of income support and housing benefit. Housing benefit was paid direct to Circle 33. The tenancy agreement included an express term that Circle 33 should make every effort to make direct contact with the housing benefit department before taking enforcement action in respect of rent arrears. After some time, housing benefit payments ceased. Circle 33 sought possession on the ground of arrears of £1,739 at the date of the hearing. Mr Ellis did not attend the hearing and an outright order was made. Mr Ellis was evicted. After eviction, he made inquiries and was given a letter from the local social security office, confirming that he had been in receipt of income support during the relevant periods. The housing benefit department reassessed his claim and confirmed that he had in fact been entitled to benefits at all material times. His rent account was accordingly credited with the benefit payments, leaving arrears of £203. HHJ Ansell refused Mr Ellis's application to set aside the warrant and to be reinstated. Holland J, on appeal, found that execution of the warrant was oppressive. He allowed the defendant's appeal, quashed the eviction and ordered that re-entry be permitted.

The Court of Appeal allowed Circle 33's further appeal. A finding of oppression in the execution of an order cannot be made unless the court's process has been misused. Circle 33 made enquiries of the housing benefit department and was informed that the defendant was not eligible for housing benefit. That view persisted until the defendant himself made enquiries of the housing benefit department following his eviction. It was impossible to say that the claimant had been doing less than it was required to do. Its conduct did not amount to oppression. Holland J's order was set aside.

16.4   *Dunn v Bradford MDC; Marston v Leeds CC*
[2002] EWCA Civ 1137; [2003] HLR 15; [2003] L&TR 11; (2002) *Times* 5 September (see 13.1)

Extended discretion cannot be exercised to revive tenancy where former tenants have vacated premises

16.5   *Hackney LBC v White*
(1996) 28 HLR 219, CA

Abuse of process where leave to issue warrant more than six years after possession order not obtained

The defendant was a secure tenant. In 1986 the council obtained judgment for arrears of rent and a suspended possession order. Despite the order, arrears continued to accrue and warrants for possession were issued but stayed or suspended on the tenant's applications. In April 1995 a further warrant was issued and the tenant was evicted.

Her application to set aside execution was dismissed by the county court judge but allowed on appeal by the Court of Appeal, which confirmed that, after execution an occupier can be restored to possession only if either the whole proceedings are set aside (see *Governors of Peabody Donation Fund v Hay* (14.1) or the warrant was obtained by fraud, abuse of process or oppression (see, eg, *Hammersmith and Fulham LBC v Hill* (16.6). Here, the council had failed to apply for the leave of the court before issuing the warrant, despite the fact that more than six years had elapsed since judgment (CCR Ord 26 r5). The Court of Appeal held that the purpose of that rule was that stale judgments for possession should not be enforced without judicial intervention in the form of leave. Here, none had been obtained, the execution pursuant to the improperly issued warrant was an abuse of process and it could not be saved by the provisions for ignoring simple irregularities under CCR Ord 37 r5.

16.6   *Hammersmith and Fulham LBC v Hill*
(1995) 27 HLR 368; [1994] 2 EGLR 51; (1995) 92 LGR 665, CA

After eviction possession can only be recovered by setting aside possession order or warrant (on basis of fraud or abuse of process by 'oppressive conduct')

The defendant was a secure tenant. The council obtained a suspended possession order in 1990 for non-payment of rent. In 1993 it applied ex parte for a warrant following breach of the order. The warrant was executed. After eviction in March 1993 the defendant applied for the warrant to be suspended and the county court judge granted her application. She was readmitted to the property.

The Court of Appeal allowed the council's appeal and held that there was no power to stay or suspend the warrant further, because it had been executed. The tenant could only lawfully recover possession if: (a) the original order were set aside on application under CCR Ord 37 (now CPR 39.3(5)); (b) the warrant had been obtained by fraud; or (c) there had been abuse of the process in the sense of 'oppressive conduct' by the plaintiff. The Court of Appeal remitted to the county court for trial of the issue of whether the council had behaved 'oppressively', as alleged. (It was claimed that after issue of the warrant, but before execution, council officers had said that the defendant would have no chance of having the warrant suspended unless she was able to pay £1,000 within 24 hours.)

16.7   *Hammersmith and Fulham LBC v Lemeh*
[2001] L&TR 423; (2001) 33 HLR 231, CA

Oppression can result from action of court

The defendant was a secure tenant. He had a poor rent payment record and the council obtained a warrant for possession, which was due to be executed on 30 September 1999. On 29 September 1999 the defendant went to the county court offices, where he informed a member of the court staff that he was due to be evicted the next day. He did not know the case number and did not inform the member of staff that there were in fact three sets of proceedings between him and the council. Using the court computer, the officer saw one of the actions but not the present case. She said that there was no warrant and told the defendant to contact the council. As a result he left the court. The warrant for possession was executed the following morning. The defendant applied to set aside execution of the warrant on the ground of oppression having regard to *Hammersmith and Fulham LBC v Hill* (16.6). The judge granted the application and the council appealed, contending that oppression had to be caused by the landlord and not by the court.

The Court of Appeal dismissed the council's appeal. It is well established that in order to set aside execution of a warrant for possession a tenant had to show that: (1) the warrant is defective; or (2) the warrant has been obtained by fraud; or (3) there has been an abuse of process or oppression in its execution. Once a warrant for possession has been obtained, its execution is a matter between the tenant and the court. There is no reason why misleading information from a court office, depriving a tenant of taking steps to have execution of a warrant for possession stayed prior to execution, cannot amount to oppression, thereby entitling the court to set aside execution of the warrant. As to whether the misleading information constituted oppression in the present case, that was a question of fact. It was clear that, if the member of the court staff had not given the wrong information, the defendant would have been able to make his application, and undoubtedly had the application heard, before execution.

16.8   *Islington LBC v Harridge*
(1993) *Times* 30 June, CA

Court has jurisdiction to suspend warrant where application made but (wrongly) not heard prior to execution

Possession was granted against a secure tenant and the warrant was due to be executed on 13 May 1993. On 12 May the tenant's solicitor attended court to make an emergency application to stay the warrant, relying on Housing Act 1985 s85. The court staff said that the judge had finished his list for the day and it was too late for the application to be heard. The judge, who was in the court building, was not informed. When he heard the application on 20 May, the warrant had been executed and he declined to make an order suspending it.

The Court of Appeal allowed the tenant's appeal. It was arguable that the application was made on 12 May (ie, prior to execution) and should have been heard then. The solicitor had been wrongly turned away. Accordingly, the judge did have jurisdiction to make an order further staying the warrant.

16.9   *Jephson Homes HA v Moisejevs*
[2001] 2 All ER 901; (2001) 33 HLR 594; [2001] 41 EG 186; [2001] L&TR 202; (2001) *Times* 2 January, CA

Oppression and abuse of process required fault by someone; no general requirement for notice of eviction

Ms Moisejevs was a secure tenant. In August 1999 the court made a suspended possession order requiring her to pay arrears of rent and costs by instalments. She fell further into arrears, and in March 2000 the landlord applied to the court for a warrant for possession. Notice of issue of the warrant was sent by the bailiff to Ms Moisejevs. She contacted the Citizens' Advice Bureau, which prepared, but never issued, an application to suspend the warrant under Housing Act 1985 s85(2). The landlord then wrote to her, stating that the outstanding arrears stood at £1,280.64 together with £80 court costs, and advised that eviction could be cancelled by payment of the debt. On 20 March she paid £876 off the arrears, and a few days later she paid the court costs. After learning that there would be a housing benefit shortfall of £433.64 the landlord proceeded with execution of the warrant and Ms Moisejevs was evicted. She applied to set aside the warrant but her application was refused by HHJ McNaught. Ms Moisejevs appealed, contending that she had genuinely believed, albeit not as the result of anything said or done by the landlord, that she had done all that she needed to do in order to avoid eviction. She claimed that it was no longer necessary, as a prerequisite to the exercise by the court of its jurisdiction to set aside a warrant for possession after its execution, to identify someone who acted oppressively towards the tenant, provided that it could be established that the end result was from the tenant's viewpoint 'manifestly unfair'. She argued that the warrant should be set aside under the court's inherent jurisdiction and that natural justice, or alternatively the practice of the High Court, as imported by County Courts Act 1984 s76, required that a tenant should in all cases be given notice of a request for the issue of a warrant.

The appeal was dismissed. A possession warrant obtained and executed against a secure tenant without fault on anyone's part cannot properly be set aside as oppressive or an abuse of process. Oppression cannot exist without the unfair use of court procedures. In all of the cases where oppression has been found, the tenant was misled or obstructed (even if inadvertently) in the exercise of his or her rights. Something more than the mere use of the eviction process – some action on someone's part which is open to criticism – is required before the court's procedures can be said to have been unfairly used. An eviction cannot be regarded as oppressive or abusive merely because it is appreciated after the event that the tenant would have been well advised to make a s85(2) application. There is no requirement that a tenant should be given notice of a request for the issue of a possession warrant in all cases. The absence of such a provision in the County Court Rules had been noted in *Peachey Property Corporation Ltd v Robinson* [1967] 2 QB 543. There had been two new sets of Rules since then, without any such requirement being thought necessary. However, cases may arise when the landlord can properly be held to have acted oppressively if the tenant never received any notice whatever of the impending eviction.

16.10   *Lambeth LBC v Hughes*
(2001) 33 HLR 350, CA

Oppression where council advised that only way to stop eviction was by full payment of arrears and court failed to advise properly

The defendant was a secure tenant. Following breach of a suspended possession order, the council was granted a warrant for possession. The council wrote to the defendant giving him the date of eviction (28 October 1999). The letter stated that the only way to stop eviction would be to pay all the arrears in full. The defendant went to see his housing officer, who told him the same thing but said that he could take legal advice. The defendant tried but failed to secure such advice and went to the court office. His file could not be found and he was told to await receipt of a letter from the court bailiff, which would contain both the eviction date and details of how to stop the eviction. The bailiff's letter was dated 22 October 1999 but was not posted until 23 October 1999 by second-class post and arrived on 28 October 1999 as the eviction was taking place. HHJ Cox dismissed an application to set aside execution.

The Court of Appeal allowed an appeal. Following a review of the authorities from *Hammersmith and Fulham LBC v Hill* (16.6) to *Hammersmith and Fulham LBC v Lemeh* (16.7), the court held that what amounts to oppression must depend on the circumstances. In this case: (1) the council's message conveyed by its letter and the housing officer to the effect that only payment in full could prevent eviction was misleading and 'oppressive' in the absence of any reference to the possibility of an application to the court; (2) that was not cured by advising the defendant of the possibility of taking legal advice without indicating what he could seek advice about; (3) the failure of the court office to advise the defendant of the procedure when he sought assistance in person was oppressive and (4) the failure to despatch the bailiff's letter in sufficient time for it to be received and acted on again made the execution oppressive.

16.11   *Leicester CC v Aldwinkle*
(1992) 24 HLR 40, CA

No abuse of process in not giving notice of warrant where rules did not require this

The defendant was a secure tenant. A suspended possession order was made in 1983. By 1988, the tenant was in breach of its terms as a result of non-payment of rent following a period of illness. In view of *Thompson v Elmbridge BC* (12.16), this breach brought her tenancy to an end. In early

1989, the ex-tenant, although often away from the property for hospital and other treatment, was in contact with the housing benefit department of the council in an attempt to clear the arrears in part by a backdated housing benefit claim. Despite this, in July 1989, the council applied for and obtained a warrant and executed the possession order by recovering possession in August 1989. The ex-tenant returned to her flat in November to find the property secured and all her possessions removed. She applied to have the warrant stayed or suspended. However, the power to suspend or stay is available only before actual execution of the order (Housing Act 1985 s85). It was therefore argued in the alternative either that the grant of the warrant was a nullity, as it had been applied for in breach of natural justice, or that by obtaining it without notice (as provided for in CCR Ord 26 r17) the council had engaged in abuse of process.

The Court of Appeal held that (a) application without notice for a warrant was provided for by rules of court and use of the rules was not an abuse of process and (b) the court could not 'write in' to the rules a requirement for notice to cure a perceived breach of natural justice. Leggatt LJ, giving the judgment, urged that consideration be given to the introduction in the county court of an equivalent to RSC Ord 46 r3, which requires that leave be sought before a possession order can be executed.

16.12   *Merton LBC v Hashmi*
September 1995 *Legal Action* 13, CA (CAT 94/1147) (see I1.3)

Execution of warrant set aside where tenant paid off the arrears prior to execution and the possession order had provided that it would then cease to be enforceable

16.13   *Saint v Barking and Dagenham LBC*
(1999) 31 HLR 620; November 1998 *Legal Action* 25, CA

Warrant oppressive where council knew applicant was in prison and had not sent housing benefit forms to him; application for warrant stated wrong amount owing

A former secure tenant sought to set aside an executed warrant for possession. His application was refused by a district judge and by a circuit judge on appeal. The applicant had been the subject of a suspended possession order for arrears of rent but failed to comply with its terms during a short period while he was held on remand in custody. He notified the council about his detention and whereabouts. The council, without notice to him, applied ex parte for, obtained, and executed the warrant during his absence.

The Court of Appeal set aside the warrant and directed reinstatement. Peter Gibson LJ held that the conduct of the council in obtaining and executing the warrant had, in the circumstances, been 'oppressive'. The council had been under a duty 'promptly' to invite the applicant to renew his housing benefit under Housing Benefit (General) Regulations 1987 reg 72(14). This obligation required the council to send the renewal form to an address where it was likely to come to the applicant's attention (ie, his prison address). The council was relying on its own wrongdoing in obtaining the warrant to the extent that non-payment of housing benefit had caused the suspended order to be breached. Second, before the applicant's arrest, his level of arrears had fallen below the level required to comply with the suspended order and when the warrant was applied for his outstanding debt was small (£336). In these circumstances, if he had been given an opportunity to apply to suspend the warrant of possession he should have succeeded. Third, there was an egregious error by the council in that its warrant application had sought a sum £270 greater than that to which it was entitled. Finally, the council had indicated that its motive for evicting him had nothing to do with his conduct as a tenant.

16.14   *Southwark LBC v Sarfo*
(2000) 32 HLR 602, CA

Categories of oppression 'not closed'; relief refused despite oppression, due to delay

The defendant was a secure tenant. Southwark were granted a possession order in October 1991, suspended on terms that Ms Sarfo pay the monthly rent plus £2 towards arrears. She failed to maintain payments and Southwark applied for a warrant. In July 1994 the warrant was suspended on terms that she continue paying the rent plus £2.20 towards arrears which then stood at £5,275. In July 1995 payments to the rent account stopped. In August 1995 Ms Sarfo applied for income support and housing benefit. In September and October 1995 she made two further applications for housing benefit. All three application forms were lost by the council. In December 1995, the council applied for a warrant, informing her of the action it was taking. In January 1996, Southwark sent her a letter stating that the council was arranging for bailiffs to evict her. Later she received notice that the eviction would take place on 6 March 1996. On 20 February 1996, Ms Sarfo was informed that all the application forms for income support and housing benefit had been lost and she duly made a further application. On the eve of the eviction, Southwark's housing officer rang to enquire whether she had applied to the court to stop the eviction. She confirmed that she had not made any such application and was given the number of the court offices which she rang. The court rang Southwark to ask whether it would agree to a stay. Southwark refused. The court rang Ms Sarfo to inform her that the bailiffs would be coming at 9 am the following morning and that she should consequently pack up and be ready to leave. On 6 March 1996, she was evicted. On 26 January 1998, Ms Sarfo made an application to set aside the warrant of eviction on the ground that the authority had acted oppressively. Recorder Jolles dismissed her application.

The Court of Appeal, following and applying *Camden LBC v Akanni* (16.2) and *Saint v Barking and Dagenham LBC* (16.13) held that an executed warrant could be set aside if there had been oppression in the execution. Roch LJ said:

> [O]ppression may be very difficult if not impossible to define, but it is not difficult to recognise. It is the insistence by a public authority on its strict rights in circumstances which make that insistence manifestly unfair. The categories of oppression are not closed because no one can envisage all the sets of circumstances which could make the execution of a warrant oppressive.

On the facts, the tenant had been entitled to conclude that no further step would be taken until her housing benefit applications had been decided and, against a background of maladministration, the execution of the warrant had been manifestly unfair. However, as the application was late and the block had been demolished, the court would not – in exercise of its discretion – set aside the execution, notwithstanding the finding of 'oppression'.

16.15 ### Southwark LBC v St Brice

[2001] EWCA Civ 1138; [2002] 1 WLR 1537; [2002] HLR 26; [2002] L&TR 11; [2002] 1 P&CR 27; [2002] LGR 117; (2001) *Times* 6 August

Issue of warrant as an administrative act without a hearing not in breach of ECHR

In 1997 the council obtained a suspended possession order against Mr St Brice, who was a secure tenant with rent arrears of £3,700. When the arrears increased to over £4,000 the council, using Form N325 and without notice to Mr St Brice, obtained a warrant for eviction. In December 2000 the court and the council separately wrote to the defendant to give him notice of the eviction date and explaining what steps he could take. On 31 January 2001 he was evicted. He then applied to set aside the warrant contending that the procedure enabling the council to obtain a warrant on an application made without notice and without either a hearing or opportunity to make written representations was in breach of his ECHR rights under articles 8 and 6(1). He argued that the issue of the warrant should have been a judicial act, as opposed to an administrative act. HHJ Cox dismissed the application but gave permission to appeal direct to the Court of Appeal (CPR 52.14).

The Court of Appeal dismissed his appeal. The procedure which allowed the court to issue a warrant for possession and arrangements for execution following non-compliance by a tenant with a suspended possession order do not infringe tenants' rights under ECHR articles 6, 8 or 14. Mr Brice's right to possession of the premises had already been determined, when the suspended possession order was made. That hearing complied fully with ECHR article 6. Although enforcement may be regarded as part of the trial for the purposes of article 6, enforcement need not involve the determination of civil rights and obligations in such a way as to necessitate a further hearing. The issue of the warrant for possession was simply a step authorised to be taken to enforce the earlier order. It did not alter the legal status of the tenant or make any kind of decision in relation to his rights, and so was not required to be the subject of a separate hearing. It was not unreasonable to expect the tenant to bring the matter back before the court if there had been a change of circumstances. Second, although the possession proceedings undoubtedly interfered with Mr St Brice's right to respect for his home, they were clearly in accordance with the law and they were a legitimate and proportionate response to his non-payment of rent. Proportionality was considered when the possession order was made. Article 14 was not engaged. He was not treated less favourably than a defendant in the High Court and had an equal opportunity to require the court to hear him before eviction. There was no aspect of his personal characteristics or status that was discriminated against by the council's choice of forum for the possession proceedings. Referring to Form N54, now used by courts to notify tenants of dates for eviction, Kennedy LJ said:

> It is important that so far as possible tenants should receive such notice in time to enable time to take advice and, if so advised, bring the matter back to the court before the date fixed for eviction.

16.16 *Tower Hamlets LBC v Azad*
(1998) 30 HLR 241, CA

Warrant not defective despite alleged errors in application for warrant

In October 1994 the council obtained a suspended possession order and a money judgment for arrears of rent of over £600. By October 1996 the terms of the order had not been complied with and arrears had reached over £1,100. The council applied for and obtained a warrant scheduled for execution on 3 December. On 2 December, galvanised into action by the impending eviction, the former tenant sought advice and then tried to lodge an application to stay or suspend the warrant. He was delayed by traffic and arrived to find the court shut. The following morning the warrant was executed at 9 am but, as soon as the court office opened at 10 am, he lodged his application. The judge held that he had no jurisdiction to grant a stay or further suspension as the warrant had been executed.

The Court of Appeal dismissed the tenant's application for leave to appeal. It held that, once physical execution of a warrant has taken place, the court has no further power to stay or suspend it under Housing Act 1985 s85(2) (or the equivalents in Rent Act 1977 s100(2) and Housing Act 1988 s9(2)), even if the application is made and heard on the very day of execution. The Court of Appeal also rejected an assertion that the warrant itself should be set aside as defective on the grounds that (a) the words 'and the balance now due is as shown' had not been deleted from the application for a warrant, even though only possession was to be recovered, and (b) the amount stated on the application as outstanding (see CCR Ord 26 r17(3A)) was not simply the amount for which judgment had been entered but subsequent indebtedness. It held that (a) the non-deletion of the surplus words was immaterial and (b) where judgment had been given for arrears of rent and an order made requiring payment of 'current rent', the amount to be inserted on the application could properly be the total amount owed by the tenant, including missed payments since judgment, costs and the warrant fee.

High Court

16.17 *Rendham Holdings Ltd v Patel*
[2002] EWHC 320; [2002] All ER (D) 132 (Oct); December 2002 *Legal Action* 21; 10 October 2002, ChD (see N3.28)

Warrant oppressive where court failed to consider application for stay of execution

County courts

16.18   *Barking and Dagenham LBC v Marquis*
October 2002 *Legal Action* 28; 9 May 2002, Ilford County Court

Oppression by landlord where housing benefit issues outstanding and advice not given that applicant could apply for suspension of warrant

The defendant was a secure tenant. He fell into arrears and the claimants obtained a suspended possession order in August 2000. He breached the terms of suspension and the claimants applied for a possession warrant in December 2001. The eviction was fixed for the morning of 29 January 2002. On 28 January 2002 the defendant issued an application for suspension of the possession warrant. The application was heard by a district judge at 9.55 am on 29 January and dismissed. Almost immediately thereafter the warrant was executed. The defendant then consulted solicitors and issued an appeal notice and application for permission to appeal.

In the appeal the defendant argued that CPR 52.10 ('the appeal court has all the powers of the lower court') meant that the circuit judge had jurisdiction to suspend the warrant after eviction. HHJ Platt rejected this contention in the light of authorities such as *Leicester CC v Aldwinkle* (16.11), *Hammersmith and Fulham LBC v Hill* (16.6) and *Jephson Homes Housing Association v Moisejevs* (16.9), where the Court of Appeal has held that, after eviction, a warrant can only be suspended if either (1) the order on which it is issued is itself set aside; (2) the warrant has been obtained by fraud; or (3) there has been an abuse of process or oppression in its execution. The judge then considered whether or not there had been oppression. He was not persuaded that the failure of the district judge to ask the defendant if he wanted to appeal and to outline the appeal procedure amounted as a matter of law to oppression.

However, the judge found that there had been oppression by the local authority due to:

a) a letter claiming that the defendant was behind with his payments under the court order when he was still in fact ahead of schedule;

b) the issue of a warrant for possession one day before the expiry of the time allowed for the defendant to produce documents in support of his claim for housing benefit;

c) the issue of a warrant for possession at a time when the arrears which had accrued on the account were simply the result of an administrative decision to suspend the defendant's housing benefit;

d) the failure to inform the defendant of his right to apply under Housing Act 1985 s85(2) at the time when the application for the warrant was made;

e) the decision to oppose the application to suspend when the time for challenging the claimant's refusal to determine his first application had yet not expired; and

f) the failure to inform the District Judge of the true position over housing benefit.

The warrant was accordingly set aside.

16.19   *Southwark LBC v Augustus*

24 November 2006, Lambeth County Court

Warrant oppressive and so set aside where council failed to have regard to its own rent arrears policy and arrears were low

The defendant was a secure tenant. Southwark obtained a suspended possession order as result of rent arrears. The defendant breached the terms and the claimant applied for a warrant. The defendant failed to open the letter notifying her of the impending eviction. The warrant was executed while she was out at work.

HHJ Welchman set aside execution of the warrant. The claimant had acted oppressively. The court could consider public law issues where the claimant was a public authority. The claimant had failed to have regard to its own rent arrears policy requiring it to use eviction only as a last resort. The defendant was in work and had been making some payments. The arrears were £274 at the date of the request for the warrant. The claimant had failed to consider applying for an attachment of earnings order.

Introductory and demoted tenancies

J1   **Introductory tenancies**

Introductory tenancies are a form of probationary tenancy introduced by Housing Act 1996 and granted by some local authorities. Initially, they lack security of tenure. Where a local housing authority elects to operate an introductory tenancy regime in accordance with Housing Act 1996 s124, all new periodic tenancies and licences which would otherwise be secure tenancies are introductory tenancies or licences unless, immediately before the new tenancy, one or more of the tenants was either a secure tenant or an assured tenant of a registered social landlord. Tenancies remain introductory tenancies until the end of the 'trial period', which generally lasts for one year, unless the landlord applies for an extension.

Court of Appeal

J1.1   *Cardiff CC v Stone*
[2002] EWCA Civ 298; [2003] HLR 47; (2002) *Times* 19 February

No requirement for second notice where conditions imposed on previous review breached

The defendant was an introductory tenant of the council. In April 1999 she received a s128 notice of possession proceedings alleging that she had arrears of rent of over £400. She applied for a review. That resulted in her being told that proceedings would not be issued if she cleared the arrears at the rate of £3 per week. The arrears later increased to over £500 and the council claimed possession without giving a further (or 'second') notice of proceedings. The judge granted possession and the tenant appealed.

The Court of Appeal held that there is no requirement to give a further or second notice. Housing Act 1996 s127 imposes a mandatory duty on the court to grant possession if 'a' notice has been served in compliance with s128. A requirement to serve a further notice would introduce unnecessary formality and might deter an authority from taking a humane 'wait and see' approach before issuing proceedings.

J1.2   *Manchester CC v Cochrane*
[1999] 1 WLR 809; [1999] LGR 626; (1999) 31 HLR 810; (1999) *Times* 12 January, CA

Court must order possession if notice provisions in s128 complied with; Invalidity of review matter of public law

On 15 April 1997 the council granted an introductory tenancy. On 9 March 1998 the council served a notice of proceedings for possession for breach of the terms of the tenancy (Housing Act 1996 s128). An oral review was carried out on 1 April 1998 but the council confirmed the decision and issued possession proceedings. The tenants tried to defend the proceedings and were allowed to file a defence denying the alleged breaches of the tenancy agreement and alleging that there had been a denial of natural justice.

The Court of Appeal held that the county court is not able to entertain such a defence. The word 'shall' in s127(2) means that once the requirements of s128 have been complied with, the county court has no discretion but to make an order for possession. The private law right of tenants under an introductory tenancy is no more than a right to remain in possession until an order for possession is made. Tenants are not entitled to raise by way of private law defence any alleged invalidity of the review. That is a matter of public law.

J1.3 **Merton LBC v Williams**

[2002] EWCA Civ 980; [2003] HLR 20

Courts have general duty to ensure statutory procedure followed and compliance with ECHR; jurisdiction to adjourn pending judicial review; no prospect of success on facts

On 3 April 2000 Mr Williams was granted an introductory tenancy. On 26 June 2000 Merton served notice of proceedings for possession because he had not taken up occupation of the flat and was in arrears with his rent payments. Mr Williams sought a review of the decision to seek possession (Housing Act 1996 s129), but failed to appear at the review hearing. Merton's decision was confirmed. Mr Williams later claimed that the rent arrears had arisen because of difficulties in his application for housing benefit. A possession claim was issued and a district judge made a possession order. On appeal HHJ Ellis held that Merton had failed to give any adequate reasons for its decision to seek possession, and that the district judge had failed to consider whether Merton's decision to seek possession was necessary and proportionate (*R (McLellan) v Bracknell Forest BC* (J1.4)).

The Court of Appeal allowed Merton's second tier appeal and restored the order for possession. In the light of Mr Williams's failure to attend the review hearing, Merton's ability to give fuller reasons for its decision was considerably restricted. The judge's criticism in this respect was not appropriate. The Court of Appeal accepted that courts have a general duty in possession proceedings against introductory tenants to consider the procedure that has been followed and to ensure that it complies both with the statutory procedure and the tenant's rights under the European Convention on Human Rights. There is an inherent jurisdiction to adjourn and power to draw to the attention of a litigant in person the possibility of applying for relief from infringement of ECHR rights by seeking judicial review. However, in this case there was no realistic prospect that any judicial review proceedings would succeed. Mr Williams's excuse for non-payment of rent was unsustainable, and his non-payment clearly demonstrated his unsuitability as a tenant. There was no basis on which Merton's decision to terminate the tenancy could be described as other than necessary and proportionate.

J1.4 **R (McLellan) v Bracknell Forest DC**

[2001] EWCA 1510; [2002] QB 1129; [2002] 2 WLR 1448; [2002] 1 ALL ER 899; [2002] UKHRR 45; [2002] LGR 191; (2001) *Times* 3 December

Introductory tenancy regime not incompatible with ECHR; county court has power to consider whether breach in individual cases; court can order limited adjournment

Bracknell Forest gave an introductory tenant notice of proceedings for possession (Housing Act 1996 s128) because of arrears of rent. In an application for judicial review she argued that the introductory tenancy regime was incompatible with ECHR articles 6 and 8. Longmore J dismissed her application.

The Court of Appeal dismissed her appeal. It held that

1) Eviction of a tenant falls within ECHR article 8(1) (*Lambeth LBC v Howard* (H4.13). Accordingly, it is necessary to consider under article 8(2) whether an eviction is in accordance with the law and whether it is necessary for the protection of the rights of others. A tenant with an introductory tenancy has the right to raise the question whether it is reasonable in the particular case to insist on eviction, ie, whether the eviction can be justified under article 8(2) (*Poplar HARCA v Donoghue* (K2.1) and Human Rights Act 1998 s7(1)(b)). The review procedure taken together with the availability of judicial review provides adequate protection. Section 127 does not prevent tenants from relying on ECHR rights if the procedure in *Manchester CC v Cochrane* (J1.2) is followed. The fact that the tenant has failed to seek judicial review of the decision to seek possession does not deprive the county court of the power to consider whether there is arguably a breach of the ECHR and to adjourn if necessary. Therefore, the introductory tenancy scheme is not as such incompatible with article 8 and there is no reason to think that individuals' rights will be infringed without remedy from the courts. If the pace of eviction is too fast the court may grant a limited extension of time under Housing Act 1980 s89(1). Section 89 is not itself incompatible with article 8.

2) The decision of the review panel involves the determination of an introductory tenant's civil rights and so ECHR article 6 is engaged. However, the combination of the review panel plus judicial review is enough to meet the requirements of article 6. There is no requirement that a council must be satisfied that there has been a breach of the terms of the tenancy before serving notice – the question is whether, in the light of allegation and counter-allegation, it was reasonable for the council to take a decision to proceed with termination of the tenancy. There is no reason to believe that the review procedure will not be operated fairly, nor any reason to believe that judicial review will not provide an adequate safeguard to tenants, enabling them to challenge any unfairness or infringement of their ECHR rights, bearing in mind that the courts will 'examine the decision maker's actions more rigorously' where a discretionary power is liable to interfere with fundamental human rights. Where a review has taken place, it should be the norm for the council to set out in an affidavit before the county court how the review procedure was operated in each case so that the court has the necessary information to decide whether to adjourn pending an application for judicial review.

The House of Lords granted leave to appeal: [2002] 1 WLR 2321 but it ws not pursued

J1.5   *Salford CC v Garner*

[2004] EWCA Civ 364; [2004] HLR 35; (2004) *Times* 10 March

Proceedings started when claim form issued; tenancy started when keys handed over

Mr Garner's introductory tenancy agreement stated that the tenancy was to begin on 12 November 2001. However, he was handed the keys and told he could take immediate possession on 9 November 2001. He began to occupy the premises on 10 November. Salford sought possession on the ground of rent arrears. It lodged the claim form at the county court on 7 November 2002, but the proceedings were not issued by the court until 11 November. Mr Garner defended, contending that his tenancy had become a secure tenancy after one year which, he claimed, was 9 November 2002. A district judge dismissed the claim but a circuit judge allowed the council's appeal.

The Court of Appeal allowed Mr Garner's appeal. (1) Proceedings are started by the issue of the claim form by the court (CPR 7.2 and PD7, para 5.1). In this case that took place on 11 November 2002. That was the date when the council began the proceedings for the purposes of Housing Act 1996 s130. (2) The housing officer's decision to hand over the keys of the property passed possession to Mr Garner and therefore the tenancy started on 9 November 2001. Furthermore, Mr Garner had provided the council with sufficient consideration for the three days that the property had been occupied prior to 12 November 2001, as (a) he would have been obliged to pay rent for that period, and even if that was not the case, (b) the council would have been bound to observe the obligations contained in the tenancy agreement that he had agreed to on 9 November 2001.

High Court

J1.6 *R (Chelfat) v Tower Hamlets LBC*
[2006] EWHC 313 (Admin); 10 February 2006

Relief refused in judicial review proceedings where would be unjust; no prescribed manner to request a review; Whether failure to carry out review fatal turns on facts

Ms Chelfat was an introductory tenant. On 5 March 2004 Tower Hamlets served a Housing Act 1996 s128 notice of proceedings for possession on the ground that she was in arrears of rent. The notice stated that she had a right to seek a review of the decision and that any request had to be made within 14 days and be sent to the rent arrears section. Ms Chelfat did not write to the housing officer named in the notice but instead wrote to Tower Hamlets' housing benefits section complaining of the decision and requesting a review. The benefits section assumed that her letter referred to a refusal of a claim for housing benefit. It carried out a review of that refusal. Tower Hamlets then began possession proceedings and obtained a possession order. Ms Chelfat was aware of the proceedings but made no attempt to defend them or appeal the possession order. A warrant of possession was issued. Her solicitors wrote to the authority requesting a review of the decision. The possession warrant was suspended by consent so that the review could be carried out. On 19 August 2005 a review was held but it was concluded that Tower Hamlets were entitled to seek possession. Ms Chelfat sought judicial review of the decision to continue to seek possession, relying on the fact that the review had not been carried out before the date specified in the notice as the date after which proceedings might be begun (Housing Act 1996 s129(6)).

Sullivan J dismissed her application. The decision whether or not to grant relief in the Administrative Court is essentially a matter for the court's discretion. In this case Ms Chelfat's own former solicitors positively asked Tower Hamlets to carry out a review. In the light of the express agreement that there should be a review and that the warrant for possession should be suspended to enable that to be carried out, it was wholly inconsistent for Ms Chelfat to argue that the possession proceedings should not have been issued at all because there had not been any review within the timescale prescribed by s129(6). Against that background, as a matter of the court's discretion, it would be wholly unjust to allow Ms Chelfat's application. Sullivan J also stated (1) s128 does not require a tenant requesting a review of a s128 notice to complete any particular form or to make such a request in any particular manner; and (2) since s129(6) is silent about the consequences of any failure to carry out a review within the time specified, the question of whether such delay was fatal to a landlord's decision would turn on the facts. If the failure was due to a genuine oversight capable of being remedied, there seemed to be no good reason to prevent a landlord from remedying the position.

J1.7   *R (Chowdhury) v Newham LBC*
[2003] EWHC 2837 (Admin); 27 November 2003
Council entitled to make judgment that tenants not suitable

The claimants were granted an introductory tenancy. They applied for housing benefit. The application for housing benefit was incorrectly filled in by them. Newham wrote requiring information but there was no response and a further letter was sent. The claimants then supplied some of the necessary information but, because they had not supplied it all, their application for housing benefit was refused. Benefit was granted at a later date but the council refused to backdate it to the beginning of the tenancy. As a result of the arrears, Newham served a s128 notice. There was no request for a statutory review, but Newham held one. The claimants did not attend and made no written representations. The panel decided that the council had acted correctly in serving a notice to terminate on the basis that the claimants had broken their tenancy conditions by accruing arrears. Newham began possession proceedings but they were adjourned to allow the claimants to apply for judicial review.

Grigson J dismissed the application. In view of the history of the dealings between the claimants and the council, the council had been entitled to make a judgment that they were not suitable tenants. It was fully justified in pursuing possession proceedings. The role of a tenant was not a passive one. Mr Chowdhury had been advised repeatedly of the rent arrears and had failed to respond. If he did not understand the obligations that he was undertaking when entering into a tenancy agreement he should have taken steps to discover what they were. Furthermore, if he wanted housing benefit it was incumbent on him to deal with the application efficiently. If there were problems in providing the necessary information he should have notified the housing benefit department. If he ignored correspondence and requests for further information, the failure lay at his door.

J1.8   **R (Forbes) v Lambeth LBC**

[2003] EWHC 222 (Admin); [2003] HLR 49; (2003) *Times* 10 March

On facts review did not uphold decision in s128 notice but reversed it, albeit with a warning; tenant ought to have opportunity to review where reasons changed

On 3 March 2000 Lambeth granted Mr Forbes, a 62-year-old vulnerable homeless person, an introductory tenancy commencing on 20 March 2000. On 28 September 2000 the police raided the property and found drugs. On 13 October 2000 they served a s128 notice indicating that they intended to apply to court for possession because the premises were being used for selling drugs and immoral purposes. Mr Forbes requested a review. After the review the council wrote stating that it had 'decided not to proceed with terminating your tenancy but will be monitoring your tenancy for a period of 12 months and then will review the situation and advise you'. On 9 March 2001 the council wrote stating that in view of continuing complaints of noise nuisance it had 'no alternative but to continue the legal proceedings commenced when the Notice of Proceedings for Possession was served'. A possession claim was issued on 14 March 2001. Recorder Atkins adjourned the possession claim to enable Mr Forbes to apply for judicial review.

Crane J heard the application for judicial review and Lambeth's appeal against the decision to adjourn. He held that, in the light of *Cardiff CC v Stone* (J1.1), a council may uphold a notice but suspend or defer the actual taking of proceedings. However, the letter sent to Mr Forbes after the review did not have the same effect as the letter in *Stone*, which made it clear that the decision was being upheld. Here, the original decision was not confirmed. There was in reality a decision to reverse or quash the original decision, albeit with a warning about future conduct. That conclusion was supported by the absence of any reasons, which would have been required if the decision had been confirmed (s129(5)). Second, in a case such as this, where the reasons for the decision have changed, the tenant ought at least to be given an opportunity to seek a review, not only to question the alleged facts, but also, crucially, to argue that it was not reasonable to require possession. If that were not done, the scheme of the Act would not be ECHR compliant. The possession claim was dismissed.

J1.9   **R (Laporte) v Newham LBC**

[2004] EWHC 227 (Admin); [2004] 2 All ER 874

Where additional grounds relied on in review, additional s128 notice should be served

Ms Laporte was granted an introductory tenancy of a flat by Newham in November 2001. Her rent account fell into arrears. In June 2002, Newham served a Housing Act 1996 s128 notice of proceedings for possession relying on the arrears. Ms Laporte requested a review hearing. Before the hearing, Newham sent her a letter which cited the grounds for the initial decision, and stated that there had been allegations of nuisance against her son which would be an issue at the review hearing. On review the original decision was upheld because insufficient payments had been made towards the arrears, there had been additional complaints against her son and Ms Laporte did not attend. Ms Laporte applied for judicial review, arguing that the grounds relied on at the review included the allegations of nuisance, which were not part of the original grounds in the s128 notice.

McCombe J dismissed the application. It was clear that the review decision took into account both the allegations of nuisance and the rent arrears. Although the correct procedure would normally be for a landlord to serve an additional notice under s128, in this case this Ms Laporte had not suffered any prejudice. Newham's evidence, which was accepted, was that, in view of the arrears, the same decision would have been reached, even without the allegations of nuisance.

J1.10   *R (McDonagh) v Salisbury DC*
(2001) *Times* 15 August, QBD Admin Ct

Review hearing valid; review not a nullity simply because late; possession proceedings can continue at same time as review

On 22 May 2000 Salisbury District Council granted Ms McDonagh an introductory tenancy under Housing Act 1996 s124. Complaints were made by neighbours and the police were called. On 5 September 2000 the council served a s128 notice of proceedings for possession. Ms McDonagh sought a review of the council's decision (s129(1)). On 18 October 2000 the review took place before the Introductory Tenancy Review Board, which decided that the parties should go to court for the matter to be decided. Permission was given for Ms McDonagh to apply for judicial review by Richards J who felt that the review board had adopted the wrong test of the council's decision by using a *Wednesbury* reasonable test instead of a substantive merits approach. A second review was then fixed for 17 May 2001 but Ms McDonagh declined to attend. At this review, the members of the review board had no knowledge of the case and there was a different clerk. The findings were against Ms McDonagh but she refused to accept that that review board's hearing had cured the council's errors.

Jackson J held that:

1) In view of the Introductory Tenants (Review) Regulations 1997, the review board hearing on 18 October 2000 had been faulty.
2) (a) It was implicit under reg 5 that Ms McDonagh should have had a proper opportunity to read the documents of the case and be properly prepared but she had not attended the proceedings on 17 May 2001.
   (b) All the evidence indicated that the review board had properly sorted and sifted through the information before it.
   (c) The review board was entitled to consider events both before 18 October 2000 and after.
   (d) The review board had applied the correct standard of proof.
   (e) Ms McDonagh's personal circumstances would not have changed the overall picture.
   Accordingly the second review hearing was not invalid.
3) Sections 128 and 129 were not incompatible with ECHR article 6.
4) A s128 review is not a nullity simply because it is carried out after the date specified in the notice.
5) There is nothing to prevent possession proceedings continuing at the same time as the review.

The warrant for possession was stayed for 28 days from 5 July 2001 and until the outcome of any appeal to the Court of Appeal.

County courts

J1.11   *Lambeth LBC v Azu*

June 2002 *Legal Action* 25; 4 February 2002, Lambeth County Court

Warrant set aside where tenant complied with conditions for stopping eviction in council's letter warning her of eviction

The council obtained an outright possession order against an introductory tenant and then applied for a warrant. It sent the defendant a standard letter that read 'The Council will only agree to the eviction not taking place if all the rent arrears and legal costs are paid by the day before the eviction is due to take place.' The defendant promptly paid all the arrears and legal costs and the costs of the warrant. Despite this, the council indicated that it would proceed with the eviction. The defendant applied to suspend or set aside the warrant.

HHJ Cox held that the letter contained an 'offer' which the defendant had 'accepted' and the payment he had made amounted to 'consideration'. That constituted a contract that the council would not enforce the warrant. He further held that to allow execution of the warrant would be oppressive. He ordered that the warrant be set aside.

J1.12   *Lambeth LBC v Dearie*

April 2001 *Legal Action* 20, Lambeth County Court

Notice arguably defective where reasons simply that tenant had failed to pay rent

An introductory tenant applied to set aside a possession order made in her absence (CPR 39.3). She contended that she had an arguable defence arising from a deficiency in the Housing Act 1996 s128 notice of proceedings served by the council. No form of notice is prescribed but the section requires that the notice set out, among other things, 'the reasons' for the decision to take proceedings. The notice gave as a reason that the 'tenant had failed to pay the rent due' but did not indicate the amounts of the rent or of the alleged arrears.

District Judge Zimmels allowed the application. Although s128 does not require 'particulars', the notice was arguably defective and unfair (having regard to ECHR article 6). It did not give the tenant enough information either to identify how to rectify matters or to make representations in support of a request for review.

J1.13   *Salford CC v Entwistle*

October 2002 *Legal Action* 28; 15 October 2001, Salford County Court

Service of s128 notice did not commence proceedings or extend trial period

On 15 May 2000 the defendant was granted an introductory tenancy. On 26 September 2000 the claimant landlord served notice of intention to seek possession. Possession proceedings were issued on 5 June 2001. The tenant defended the claim by arguing that, as a year had elapsed since the grant of the tenancy, he had become a secure tenant. The council argued that service of the notice amounted to commencement of proceedings.

District Judge Chapman dismissed the claim. Service of the notice was simply the prerequisite to the issue of a claim and not the first step in proceedings. Service of the notice did not have the effect of extending the introductory tenancy (See Housing Act 1996 s130 and *Torridge DC v Jones* (F2.6) and *Shepping v Osada* (G17.1).)

J2   Demoted tenancies

Anti-Social Behaviour Act 2003 gives county courts power to change secure or assured tenancies into demoted tenancies, lacking the rights that are associated with secure and assured tenancies. Under new Housing Act 1985 s82A and new Housing Act 1988 s6A, local housing authorities, housing action trusts and registered social landlords may apply to a county court for demotion orders. The court can only grant a demotion order if (a) a notice seeking a demotion order has been served or it is just and equitable to dispense with that requirement; (b) it is satisfied that the tenant or a person residing in or visiting the dwelling-house has engaged or has threatened to engage in conduct to which section 153A or 153B of the Housing Act 1996 (anti-social behaviour or use of premises for unlawful purposes) applies, and (c) it is reasonable to make the order.

High Court

J2.1   *R (Gilboy) v Liverpool CC*
[2007] EWHC 2335 (Admin); 15 October 2007

Demoted tenancy provisions not incompatible with ECHR

Ms Gilboy was a secure tenant. In June 2006 Recorder Moran QC granted a demotion order on the ground that Ms Gilboy's son had been responsible for anti-social behaviour whilst living at the property and because of the son's criminal convictions. Later, the council received further allegations of anti-social behaviour and a decision was made to terminate the claimant's demoted tenancy. Ms Gilboy contested the allegations and made a request for a review of the decision to terminate. At the review hearing, a council official heard evidence from a solicitor representing the council and Ms Gilboy who disputed all of the allegations. After referring to the son's conviction for offences of unauthorised taking of a motor vehicle, breaching an anti-social behaviour order and using a vehicle without insurance or a licence and two witness statements, the official concluded that there had been further breaches of the tenancy within the 12-month period of the demoted tenancy. In December 2006, the council issued a claim for possession. Ms Gilboy sought judicial review, challenging the compatibility of the Demoted Tenancies (Review of Decisions) (England) Regulations 2004 SI No 1679 with ECHR article 6.

Stanley Burnton J dismissed the claim for judicial review. Although it was common ground that the demoted tenancy conferred civil rights and imposed obligations to which article 6 applied, he questioned whether the decision of the reviewing officer engaged article 6, saying:

It seems to me that the decision by the reviewing officer does not determine any right or liability. It is a decision that the local authority should exercise its right to apply to the county court for an order for possession. The determination of the demoted tenant's rights is made by the decision of the county court. Unless and until the county court makes an order for possession, the tenant's tenancy continues unaffected by the reviewing officer's decision.

However, in any event, the regulations relating to demoted tenancies were materially indistinguishable from the Introductory Tenants (Review) Regulations 1997 SI No 72 and in *R (McLellan) v Bracknell Forest BC* (J1.4), the Court of Appeal decided that the provisions relating to the internal local authority review of the decision to seek possession of the property held under the introductory tenancy, together with the judicial review jurisdiction, satisfied the requirements of article 6. The decision of the ECtHR in *Tsfayo v UK* (A2.8), would not have led to a different conclusion, even if it were binding on the court. Stanley Burnton J concluded that the contention that the proceedings conducted or the decision made by the council official infringed the claimant's rights under article 6 was ill founded. Ms Gilboy has lodged an appeal to the Court of Appeal.

J2.2 *Washington Housing Company Ltd v Morson*
[2005] EWHC 3407 (ChD); 25 October 2005

Hearsay evidence comprising anonymous complaint forms could be considered

Mrs Morson was an assured tenant. Her tenancy agreement included an express term requiring her to take all reasonable steps to prevent persons, such as her own children, from committing any acts of nuisance. After allegations of anti-social behaviour, her landlords sought possession under Housing Act 1988 Sch 2 Grounds 12 and 14 or, alternatively, a demotion order. All but one of the allegations involved her children. It was admitted that some of them had committed criminal offences. HHJ Carr found that Mrs Morson's daughter was the leader of a group of young people who drank and shouted 'at all hours of the day and night', congregated around the premises, used foul and abusive language and smashed windows. He made a demotion order. Mrs Morson sought permission to appeal, complaining that the judge had taken into account hearsay evidence comprising complaint forms filled in by local residents, mainly anonymously.

Patten J refused permission to appeal. When confronted with hearsay evidence, judges should

> ... in weighing up the strength and weight to be attributed to it, have regard to the various factors set out in section 4(2) of the Civil Evidence Act, but ... assessment of that evidence will necessarily depend on the view which [the judge] takes of the case overall and, in particular, on whether the hearsay evidence is corroborated by any live evidence given by other witnesses. (para 53)

In this case the judge was entitled to weigh up the hearsay evidence having regard to the admitted background. It was impossible for Patten J to conclude that it was not open to the judge to accept the veracity of the hearsay allegations, having regard to the state of the evidence as a whole.

He also found that the judge was entitled to come to the conclusion that a demotion order was necessary and reasonable.

> [The] children in this case are faced with a choice: they either conform their behaviour to what is acceptable, or their parents lose their home. Although that is obviously a Draconian sanction, it is not as Draconian as an immediate order for possession, and the Judge, although pessimistic perhaps about what the future holds, judged it to be a reasonable way of balancing the parents' rights and entitlement to a secure home with the public interest in preventing this sort of behaviour in the future. (para 67)

Assured shorthold tenancies

K1   **Introduction**

Assured shorthand tenancies lack security of tenure. Landlords seeking possession do not have to satisfy the court that any ground for possession exists. They need only give two months' notice in accordance with Housing Act 1988 s21. In addition landlords may seek possession on the same basis as fully assured tenancies by relying on grounds for possession – see chapter G. Landlords seeking possession during a fixed term (where there is no break clause) must rely on this procedure. The grounds on which they can rely are restricted, as for other fixed-term assured tenancies, by Housing Act 1998 s7(6)).

K2   **Assured shorthold tenancies and the ECHR**

Court of Appeal

K2.1   *Poplar Housing and Regeneration Community Association Ltd v Donoghue*
[2001] EWCA Civ 595; [2002] QB 48; [2001] 3 WLR 183; [2001] 4 All ER 606; (2001) 33 HLR 823; [2001] UKHRR 693; [2001] LGR 489; (2001) *Times* 21 June, CA

Housing association acting as a 'functional public authority' within meaning of Human Rights Act 1998; mandatory nature of possession for AST does not conflict with tenants' right to family life.

Tower Hamlets LBC granted Ms Donoghue a weekly non-secure tenancy, acting under Housing Act 1985 Sch 1 para 4, pending a decision as to whether she was intentionally homeless. The property was later transferred to Poplar HARCA, which was created by the council to administer some of its former housing stock. Ms Donoghue became an assured shorthold tenant. The council decided that Ms Donoghue was intentionally homeless and Poplar commenced proceedings for possession, having served notice under Housing Act 1988 s21(4). Before a district judge Ms Donoghue argued that s21 was incompatible with her rights under ECHR article 8. The district judge declined to adjourn the hearing in order to allow Ms Donoghue to adduce evidence on the issue of incompatibility. He dismissed her arguments in relation to the ECHR. She appealed directly to the Court of Appeal under CPR 52.14.

The Court of Appeal dismissed her appeal. While the activities of a housing association need not involve the performance of public functions, in providing accommodation to Ms Donoghue and seeking possession in this case, Poplar HARCA's functions were so closely assimilated to the council that it was properly to be regarded as a functional public authority within the meaning of Human Rights Act 1998 s6(1). Second, notwithstanding its mandatory terms, the right to possession contained in s21(4) did not conflict with the tenant's right to family life under ECHR article 8. The section was clearly necessary in a democratic society in so far as there had to be a procedure for recovering possession of property at the end of a tenancy. The court would defer to parliament as to whether the restricted power of the court under that section was legitimate and proportionate.

Note that this decision was disapproved in *YL v Birmingham CC* (U2.1). where Baroness Hale and Lord Mance both criticised the Court of Appeal's reasoning for relying too heavily on the historical links between the local authority and the registered social landlord, rather than on the nature of the function itself, which was the provision of social housing.

K3 # Requirements for assured shorthold tenancy

Until 28 February 1997, when amendments to Housing Act 1988 introduced by Housing Act 1996 s96 came into force, it was a mandatory requirement for the creation of an assured shorthold tenancy that the tenancy be for a fixed term of not less than six months and that the landlord should, before the tenancy was entered into, serve a notice in the prescribed form stating that the tenancy would be an assured shorthold tenancy (a 's20 notice') (see Housing Act 1988 s20(2) and the Assured Tenancies and Agricultural Occupancies (Forms) Regulations 1988 SI No 2203). However, for tenancies granted on or after 28 February 1997, these formalities do not apply. There is now no requirement for a statutory notice before the grant of an assured shorthold tenancy. All tenancies, even if granted orally, for periodic terms or for fixed terms of less than six months, are likely to be assured shorthold tenancies unless landlords specify otherwise (see Housing Act 1988 s19A).

As it is now over ten years since s20 applied to the grant of new assured shorthand tenancies, almost all the cases on the validity of s20 notices have been omitted form this edition – for full details, see *Housing Law Casebook*, 3rd edn, section D7.

Court of Appeal

K3.1 *Andrews v Cunningham*
[2007] EWCA Civ 762; 23 July 2007

Words 'assured tenancy' on cover of rent book not a statement that tenancy would not be an assured shorthold tenancy

Mr Cunningham was granted an oral tenancy of a ground floor flat. His landlord gave him a rent book which had the words 'Assured Tenancy' on the cover. After the landlord's death, his executors claimed that Mr Cunningham was an assured shorthold tenant and served a Housing Act 1988 s21 notice. District Judge Pollard dismissed a possession claim, holding that the rent book was a notice under Sch 2A para 1. On appeal, HHJ Hayward held that he was an assured shorthold tenant and made an order for possession of the flat. Mr Cunningham appealed

The Court of Appeal dismissed his appeal. The words on the cover of the rent book were not a notice under para 1 or para 2. The words 'assured tenancy' on the cover were not a statement 'that the assured tenancy to which it relates is not to be an assured shorthold tenancy' (para 1(2)(c)), because an assured shorthold tenancy is itself a type of assured tenancy. Second, if there were any doubt about that, the schedule to the rent book contained a notice to the tenant that, if the rent was payable weekly (which was not the case), the rent book had to contain the notice properly filled in. The significance of that notice was that it confirmed that the expression 'assured tenancy' on the first page was not confined to non-shorthold tenancies, since it said 'if you have an assured tenancy, including an assured shorthold tenancy ...'. Third, the reference in para 1 to 'a notice' being 'served' was a reference to the service of a written notice. The rent book was clearly intended and used simply to record the payment of rent.

K3.2   **Bedding v McCarthy**
(1995) 27 HLR 103; [1994] 41 EG 151, CA

Section 20 notice could be served on the same day as tenancy entered into; tenancy entered into, and to start, on 18 December 1990 and expiring 17 June 1991 was for six months

The tenant entered into an 'assured shorthold' tenancy for a term of six months commencing on 18 December 1990 and expiring on 17 June 1991. The notice of assured shorthold tenancy was given to the tenant on the morning of 18 December. The tenancy agreement was signed on the same day and the tenant went into possession on that afternoon. It was contended by the tenant that it could only be an assured shorthold tenancy if the term of the tenancy included the whole of that day. Otherwise it was not a tenancy 'of not less than six months' within the meaning of Housing Act 1988 s20(1)(a) because the tenancy was only granted part way through the day. Alternatively, if the tenancy was deemed to date back to the beginning of 18 December, the notice was not served before 'the tenancy was entered into' in accordance with s20.

The Court of Appeal dismissed these submissions, holding that in ascertaining when a term commences, fractions of days are disregarded and that it was a pure question of fact whether the notice was served before the tenant entered into the tenancy. Service earlier on the day when the tenancy commences is sufficient.

K3.3   **Bhopal v Walia**
(2000) 32 HLR 302, CA

Written agreement for assured shorthold tenancy with a higher rent was a sham

Mr Walia entered into an oral assured shorthold tenancy with a rent of £300 per calendar month. Later he signed an agreement which falsely stated that the rent was £450 per month, because the landlords wanted to mislead their bank about their income. The landlords then sold the property with vacant possession. Mr Walia refused to move out and the new landlord brought possession proceedings claiming arrears of rent, calculated at the rate of £450 per month. HHJ Hague QC made a suspended possession order.

Mr Walia appealed successfully. The written agreement was a sham in the sense described by Diplock LJ in *Snook v London and West Riding Investments Ltd* [1967] 2 QB 786 at 802D. It was a document intended to give to third parties or to the court an appearance of creating between the parties legal rights and obligations different from the actual legal rights and obligations which the parties intended to create. As a sham document it gave rise to no legal rights or obligations and did not have the effect of varying the existing oral tenancy agreement. The purchasers could be in no better position than the original landlord through whom they claimed. The tenant was not estopped from asserting a tenancy agreement other than that contained in the sham agreement against his original landlord's successors in title. The new landlords had not placed any reliance on the written agreement when purchasing, since they had contracted for vacant possession, and had made no enquiry about the terms of occupation. Furthermore, the written agreement had not been designed to mislead the purchasers.

K3.4   *Manel v Memon*
(2001) 33 HLR 235; [2000] 33 EG 74; [2000] 2 EGLR 40; (2000) *Times* 20 April, CA

Validity of s20 notice; need for district judges to consider documents rigorously when landlords use accelerated possession procedure

The claimant landlord brought proceedings under the accelerated possession procedure (CCR Ord 49 r6A) against the defendant, claiming that he was a pre-1997 assured shorthold tenant. The tenant filed a reply, denying that the landlord had served a valid s20 notice because the notice served omitted the four bullet points with instructions and advice to the tenant set out in Form 7 of the Assured Tenancies and Agricultural Occupancies (Forms) Regulations 1988 SI No 2203.

   The Court of Appeal held that the bullet points and, in particular, the exhortation to take legal advice and the statement that the giving of the notice did not commit the tenant to take the tenancy were part of the substance of the notice. Without them, the notice was not 'substantially to the same effect' as the prescribed form within the meaning of para 2 of the regulations. The notice was defective and a possession order made by the district judge was set aside. The Court of Appeal expressed concern that the district judge adopted the accelerated possession procedure and made a possession order without giving the tenant the opportunity to make representations at an oral hearing. Holman J said:

> [The accelerated possession procedure] is a robust machinery. It depends upon district judges rigorously considering the documents which have been filed. Some replies may be little more than a plea, however genuine for mercy. But if, on the face of the reply, a matter has been raised which, if true, might arguably raise a defence; or if the documents filed by the claimant might arguably disclose a defect in his claim, then the district judge must necessarily be 'not satisfied' within the meaning of CCR Ord 49 r6A(16) and a hearing on notice must be fixed.

K3.5   *Osborn and Co Ltd v Dior*
[2003] EWCA Civ 281; [2003] HLR 45

Omission of particulars of landlords in s20 notice not fatal

In two cases landlords served notices which they claimed complied with Housing Act 1988 s20. In one case, the notice was in Form 7 of the Assured Tenancies and Agricultural Occupancies (Forms) Regulations 1988 SI No 2203, but was signed by the landlord's agent. The spaces on the form for entry of the particulars of the landlord were left blank, and the requisite particulars of the agents were entered in the appropriate box. In the other case, Form 7 was again used, but the spaces for the particulars of the landlord were completed with the details of a company which was not in fact the landlord. In both cases, circuit judges made possession orders and the tenants appealed.

The Court of Appeal dismissed both appeals. The test that the court has to apply is whether, notwithstanding any error or omission, the notice is substantially to the same effect as that prescribed by the regulations. Although parliament had clearly attributed importance to the formality of s20 notices, it could not have intended the omission of the particulars of the landlord to be fatal. Tenants can take steps to identify the landlord by enquiries with the agents or by reference to the tenancy agreement. Even if the particulars of the landlord are absent, a notice is still substantially to the same effect where the agent has signed and given its particulars.

K3.6   *Ravenseft Properties Ltd v Hall*
[2001] EWCA Civ 2034; [2002] HLR 33; [2002] 11 EG 156; (2002) *Times* 15 January

Applying a purposive approach, s20 notice was valid despite incorrect start date

In August 1996 Ravenseft granted Ms Hall a tenancy of a flat purporting to commence in June 1996 and expiring in June 2000. The tenancy agreement provided that the landlord intended to create an assured shorthold tenancy (Housing Act 1988 s20(1)) and that the lessee acknowledged that she had been served with a notice complying with s20(2). In August 2000 Ravenseft issued a possession claim. Ms Hall defended on the basis that the s20 notice was defective as it was not in the form prescribed by the Assured Tenancies and Agricultural Occupancies (Forms) Regulations 1988 SI No 2203 or a form 'substantially to the same effect', because it gave the June date as the date of the commencement of the tenancy rather than the date on which the tenancy agreement had been executed (ie, in August). The judge held that the notice was valid.

Ms Hall appealed unsuccessfully. The start date of the tenancy was not correctly stated in the notice. The date which should have been inserted in the 'from' box was the date of the tenancy and not the date from which the term to be created by it was calculated. The tenancy created by the tenancy agreement could not begin before the date of execution of the agreement (*Roberts v Church Commissioners for England* [1972] Ch 278). The decision in *Panayi v Roberts* (1993) 25 HLR 421, [1993] 2 EGLR 51, CA was to the effect that a notice which gave the wrong date (in that case the termination date) was not 'substantially to the same effect' as one which gave the correct date, at least in a case where the mistake was not obvious. However, in the light of the purposive approach sanctioned in *Manel v Memon* (K3.4) and *Mannai Investment Co Ltd v Eagle Star Life Assurance Co Ltd* (N2.3), the question was simply whether, notwithstanding any errors or omissions, the notice was substantially to the same effect in accomplishing the statutory purpose of telling the proposed tenant of the special nature of an assured shorthold tenancy. Despite the error as to the start date, the present notice had done that. It was therefore valid.

K3.7   *White v Chubb; Kasseer v Freeman*

[2001] EWCA Civ 2034; [2002] 11 EG 156; (2002) *Times* 15 January

Despite errors s20 notices were valid as they were substantially to the same effect as the prescribed form

In 1993 Mr White granted Mr Chubb an assured shorthold tenancy for a term of six months commencing on 1 October 1993. Mr White gave Mr Chubb a notice under Housing Act 1988 s20(2) giving an incorrect end date of 1 May 1994 instead of 1 April 1994. Mr White took possession proceedings and the judge held that the notice was defective as it was not in the form prescribed by the Assured Tenancies and Agricultural Occupancies (Forms) Regulations 1988 SI No 2203 or a form 'substantially to the same effect' because of the incorrect end date. Mr White appealed.

In 1994 Ms Freeman granted Mr Kasseer a one-year tenancy. When Ms Freeman sought possession, Mr Kasseer argued that the notice under s20 was invalid because it misstated the rent assessment committee's power of investigation and misstated the tenant's rights. The judge upheld the notice on the basis that, considered as a whole, it had substantially the same effect as a notice in the prescribed form despite the errors. Mr Kasseer appealed.

The Court of Appeal held that both notices were valid and that, accordingly, the tenancies were assured shorthold tenancies. There is no statutory or common-law doctrine of 'obvious mistake' or any requirement to apply a two-stage test in which the court has first to consider whether the error in the notice is obvious or evident before proceeding to consider whether the notice read in context is sufficiently clear to leave a reasonable recipient in no reasonable doubt about the terms of the notice. There is only one statutory question, which is whether, notwithstanding any errors or omissions, the notice is 'substantially to the same effect' as a correct notice in accomplishing the purpose of telling the proposed tenant of the special nature of an assured shorthold tenancy (*Mannai Investment Co Ltd v Eagle Star Life Assurance Co Ltd* (N2.3)). This is a matter of fact and degree in each case. The resolution of that question is not a decision on a point of law that is binding on later courts. The notice served on Mr Chubb satisfied that test because the mistaken end date, even if not obvious to the reasonable recipient, did not prevent the notice when read by the reasonable reader from fulfilling the function it was meant to perform. The notice served on Mr Kasseer, despite inaccurately stating the law in a misleading way, had conveyed to the tenant the substance of the prescribed form and satisfied the statutory objective.

K4   **Notice requiring possession (Housing Act 1988 s21)**

Landlords of assured shorthold tenants who wish to recover possession relying on Housing Act 1988 s21 must give at least two months' notice to tenants that possession is required. If landlords comply with this requirement, they are automatically entitled to possession. The court has no power to suspend possession orders, apart from Housing Act 1980 s89(1), which provides that orders for possession must take effect no later than 14 days after the court order, unless exceptional hardship would be caused. The s21 notice (1) may be given before any fixed term expires or even at the beginning of the tenancy (s21(2)); (2) need not be in any particular form, although it must be in writing (s21(1)(b), s21(4)(a)); and (3) may be given by only one of several joint landlords (s21(1)(b), s21(4)(a)). There is no power to dispense with service of s21 notices.

Court of Appeal

K4.1   *Aylward v Fawaz*

(1997) 29 HLR 408, CA

Section 21 notice was effective in operating a break clause

An assured shorthold tenancy granted for a term of one year from 1 July 1995 included a break clause enabling the landlord to give one month's notice to determine the tenancy after the expiry of the first six months. On 13 February 1996 the landlord simply served a s21(1)(b) notice requiring possession on 13 April 1996.

The Court of Appeal held that that notice was sufficient to determine the tenancy under the terms of the break clause. It was clear and unambiguous and indicated in terms that possession was required. The court rejected the tenant's contention that a separate notice was necessary to activate the break clause. To require a tenant to give up possession was, in substance, no different from giving him notice of a decision to determine the tenancy.

K4.2   *Barker v Hands*

[2007] EWCA Civ 869; 26 June 2007

Possession order where s21 notice unsigned; permission to appeal refused

A landlord served a Housing Act 1988 s21 notice on an assured shorthold tenant. The notice was not signed. The tenant defended subsequent possession proceedings, arguing that because the notice was unsigned, it was invalid. District Judge Shroder found that the notice was valid and made a possession order. HHJ Rubery dismissed an appeal.

Sir Henry Brooke, sitting as a judge of the Court of Appeal, refused an application for permission to bring a second appeal on the papers. He stated, 'This second appeal raises no important point of principle or practice, and in any event the judge's decision was clearly right.'

K4.3   *Church Commissioners for England v Meya*

[2006] EWCA Civ 821; [2007] HLR 4; [2007] L&TR 3; (2006) *Times* 4 July

Whether a statutory periodic tenancy is quarterly or annual is determined by the period for which rent was last payable under the contractual tenancy

The Church Commissioners initially granted Ms Meya a two-year fixed-term assured shorthold tenancy. It was subsequently renewed. The last agreement was for a term commencing on 1 January 2004 and expiring on 30 December 2004. The rent was expressed to be 'a clear yearly rent of £17,680 per annum'. The obligation to pay the rent was expressed to be 'to pay the rent to the landlords by equal quarterly payments in advance on the usual quarter days (the first such payment or a proportion to be made on the date of this agreement)'. No further tenancy was agreed and on 31 December 2004 Ms Meya became a statutory periodic assured shorthold tenant (Housing Act 1988 s5(2)). On 2 March 2005 the Church Commissioners served a s21(4) notice stating 'the landlord requires possession of the property after the thirtieth day of May 2005 or at the end of that period of your tenancy which will end after the expiry of two months from the giving of this notice whichever is the later'. A possession claim was issued on 4 July 2005. Ms Meya accepted that, if the landlord only had to give a quarter's notice requiring possession, the notice was good. However, she claimed that she had an annual tenancy, insufficient notice had been given and that the issue of proceedings was premature. A deputy district judge dismissed the possession claim. The Church Commissioners appealed.

The Court of Appeal allowed the appeal. When deciding the period of a statutory periodic tenancy, what matters is the period for which rent was last payable – see Housing Act 1988 s5(3)(d). In this case, the tenancy agreement provided for the rent to be paid by instalments. The last instalment became payable in September 2004 and was payable for a quarterly period. The statutory periodic tenancy was, accordingly, a quarterly tenancy and sufficient notice had been given. (The position would have been different if this had been a common-law tenancy and s5(3)(d) had not applied. As the rent was expressed to be an annual rent, an annual tenancy, not a quarterly tenancy, would have arisen when the tenant held over.)

K4.4   *Fernandez v McDonald*

[2003] EWCA Civ 1219; [2004] 1 WLR 1027; [2003] 4 All ER 1033; [2004] HLR 13; [2004] L&TR 5; [2003] 42 EG 128; (2003) *Times* 9 October

Section 21 to be strictly applied; s21(4)(a) notice must specify the last day of a period of the tenancy, not the first day.

The landlord granted an assured shorthold tenancy for six months from September 1999 to March 2000. After its expiry, the tenants remained as statutory periodic tenants from the 4th of each month to the 3rd of the following month. On 24 October 2002, the landlord gave them a notice headed 'Section 21(4)(a) Assured Shorthold Tenancy: Notice Requiring Possession Periodic Tenancy' stating 'I give you notice that I require possession of the dwelling-house known as ... on 4th January 2003'. The tenants did not leave and the landlord began possession proceedings. The tenants defended, claiming that the date specified in the notice was not 'the last day of a period of the tenancy' in accordance with s21(4)(a). A district judge struck out the tenants' defence and they appealed unsuccessfully to a circuit judge.

The Court of Appeal allowed a second appeal. It rejected the landlord's contention that s21 should be construed in the same way as the common-law rules relating to notices to quit. It might be possible to give a notice to quit that expired on either the first day or the last day of a period of the tenancy, but that was not because there were two last days. It was because the last day ended at midnight and the first day of the new period would begin thereafter. A section 21 notice is not a notice to quit. The niceties of contractual notices to quit should not be imported into the plain words of the statute. Section 21(4)(a) requires the notice to specify the last date of the period. It is not a situation where the legislation permits the form to be substantially to the same effect. The subsection is clear and precise. The notice did not comply with s21(4)(a) and was defective.

Note: The outcome would have been different if the notice had included a 'savings clause', stating, after the date, 'or at the end of the period of your tenancy which will end next after the expiration of two months from the service upon you of this notice'.

K4.5   *Gracechurch International v Tribhovan and Abdul*
(2001) 33 HLR 263, CA

Section 21 notice was invalid because it did not expire on the last day of a period of statutory periodic tenancy

Landlords granted a tenancy which they claimed was an assured shorthold tenancy for a term of six months from 12 June 1996. On 26 June 1998 they served a notice requiring possession, purportedly in accordance with Housing Act 1988 s21. A circuit judge dismissed possession proceedings on the basis that the notice was invalid because it did not expire on the last day of a period of the tenancy (see s21(4)). The landlords did not contest that finding.

Simon Brown LJ, while delivering judgment on another issue, described that holding as 'clearly correct'.

K4.6   *Lower Street Properties v Jones*
(1996) 28 HLR 877; [1996] 2 EGLR 67, CA

Landlord cannot bring possession proceedings until after s21 notice has expired; no date need be specified in s21 notice provided it can be ascertained

On 28 March 1989 an assured shorthold tenancy was granted to Mr van Praag. That tenancy expired by effluxion of time on 27 September 1989. In the years that followed, there were two further fixed-term agreements which purported to create assured shorthold tenancies. The defendant lived with Mr van Praag in the premises. Mr van Praag died in 1992 and whatever tenancy he had vested in the defendant in accordance with Housing Act 1988 s18. The landlord began possession proceedings. However, the claim for possession was dismissed because proceedings were started the day before the s21 notice expired.

In the Court of Appeal, Schiemann LJ stated that it is 'implicit that the landlord cannot bring proceedings until after [the date specified in the notice]'. Kennedy LJ reached his decision on the ground that the notice served stated 'The landlord cannot apply for such an order before the notice has run out', and left open whether, with a different wording, proceedings could have been begun before expiry.

The occupant had also challenged the s21 notice served on two other grounds, namely that (a) it did not specify the date on which possession was required (the wording used was 'at the end of your period of tenancy which will end next after the expiration of two months from the service upon you of this notice') and (b) although dated, it did not state the date on which it was served. Both these contentions were rejected by the Court of Appeal. No date need be specified in a s21 notice provided that:

> ... the tenant knows or can easily ascertain the date referred to ... The word 'specified' ... means no more than 'made clear'.

K4.7 **Notting Hill Housing Trust v Roomus**
[2006] EWCA Civ 407; [2006] 1 WLR 1375; [2006] L&TR 23; [2007] HLR 2

The phrase 'at the end of your tenancy' has the same meaning as 'after the end of your tenancy'

The defendant was granted a periodic assured shorthold tenancy. Notting Hill served a Housing Act 1988 s21 notice which stated 'Possession is required (by virtue of section 21(4) Housing Act 1988 of [the property] which you hold as tenant at the end of the period of your tenancy which will end after expiry of two months from the service upon you of this notice'. A possession order was made, but the tenant applied to set it aside on the ground that the s21 notice was invalid because of the use of the word 'at' in the phrase 'at the end of the period' instead of 'after' (s21(4)(a)). District Judge Plaskow found that the words 'at the end of' had the same effect as the word 'after', and dismissed the application to set aside. The defendant appealed.

The Court of Appeal dismissed the appeal. The phrase 'at the end of the tenancy' in a notice given pursuant to s21 means 'after the end of the tenancy' and so complies with the requirements of s21(4)(a). A request to an audience that they remove all their belongings 'at the end of the concert' is not asking them to do something in the split second when the last note is played. It is asking them to do something after the end of the concert. Similarly, to say that soldiers came home 'at the end of the war' means that they came home after the war had ended, not the split second when the enemy surrendered.

K4.8 **Singh v Emmanuel**
(1997) 74 P&CR D18, CA

Section 21 notice given three months into three-year term was valid

On 6 March 1996 the plaintiff granted the defendant an assured short-hold tenancy for a term of three years. The written agreement provided that 'the landlord may bring the tenancy to an end at any time ... (but not earlier than six months from the commencement date ...) by giving to the tenant not less than two months' written notice stating that the landlord requires possession of the premises'. On 6 June 1996 the landlord gave notice that he required possession on 6 September 1996. The landlord brought possession proceedings. The tenant argued that the notice was invalid because it was given only three months into the term and so fell foul of the provision in the tenancy agreement allowing termination. A recorder made a possession order.

The Court of Appeal dismissed the tenant's appeal. Sir Patrick Russell stated that he regarded the appeal as 'basically unarguable', holding that the landlord had given 'a perfectly valid notice'.

County courts

K4.9   *Dovetail Estates Ltd v Mazrekaj*

31 January 2006, Clerkenwell County Court

Claim issued prematurely; saving clause was not effective

On 13 May 2004, F Q Sidney & Co granted Mr and Mrs Mazrekaj a joint assured shorthold tenancy of a three-bedroom flat. The tenancy was for a fixed term of six months at a weekly rent, payable on the first day of each week. Mr and Mrs Mazrekaj continued to occupy the flat when the fixed term expired on Friday 12 November 2004. Thereafter, by Housing Act 1988 s5, they occupied the flat under a joint periodic assured shorthold tenancy, which 'renewed itself' every Saturday. On 5 September 2005, Dovetail Estates, who claimed to be successors in title to the original landlords, sent Mr and Mrs Mazrekaj a notice requiring possession of the flat under Housing Act 1988 s21(4)). The tenants received the notice in the post on 9 September 2005. It required them to give possession of the flat 'on 7th November 2005 or on the day ending on the last day of a period of your tenancy'. 7 November 2005 was a Monday. Possession was not given up and, on 8 November 2005, the claimants began possession proceedings, using the accelerated procedure (CPR 55 Part II). The claimant did not provide proof of its entitlement to possession when it issued the claim. The defendants argued that (1) the earliest date after which they could have been required to give up possession of the flat was Friday 11 November 2005 and that the claim had been issued prematurely (*Lower Street Properties Ltd v Jones* (K4.6)); and (2) the notice was invalid because 7 November 2005 was not the last day of a period of the tenancy and, applying *Mannai Investment Co Ltd v Eagle Star Life Assurance Co Ltd* (N2.3), considered objectively, the saving clause in the notice would not enable a reasonable recipient to ascertain the date after which he or she would be required to give up possession of the flat. In particular, it did not specify a period of notice or a date from which notice was intended to run.

District Judge Stary found that (1) the claim was an abuse of the court's process, having been issued before the requisite notice period had expired; (2) for the reasons advanced by the defendants, the notice was invalid, and (3) in any event, the claimant had not proved its entitlement to possession of the flat. She dismissed the claim and ordered the claimant to pay the defendants' costs.

K4.10   *Gloucestershire HA v Phelps*

10 February 2003, Gloucester County Court

Possession cannot be ordered under s21 within a fixed term (in absence of break clause)

The claimant granted the defendant an assured shorthold tenancy on 4 February 2002 for a fixed term of 12 months. It was described as a 'Starter Tenancy' and included a clause that it would cease to be an assured shorthold after 12 months conditional on no possession proceedings having been brought. On 4 September 2002, the claimant served a s21 notice but cited rent arrears and anti-social behaviour, although no such behaviour was specified. The claimant brought a possession claim under the accelerated possession procedure. A possession order was made by a district judge without a hearing on 11 December 2002.

The tenant appealed successfully because the possession order had become effective before the 12-month fixed-term tenancy had ended. HHJ Hutton stated that s21 specifically provides that possession may be granted only if the assured shorthold tenancy has actually come to an end at the time of the order. In this case it had not come to an end. The application and the possession order were premature. Although anti-social behaviour was raised in the claim, this was irrelevant because this action was not commenced under Housing Act 1988 s8.

K4.11   *Paddington Churches Housing Association v Khan*
(1) 25 July 2003; [2004] 3 CLD 328; (2) 29 October 2003, Willesden County Court

Section 21 notice could be relied on in possession proceedings despite having been served three years earlier

The defendant was an assured shorthold tenant. In March 2000 his landlord served a Housing Act 1988 s21 notice. No possession claim was issued until April 2003. A deputy district judge dismissed the claim for possession, finding that the claimant landlord had waived its right to proceed under the March 2000 notice because it had allowed the defendant to remain in the property for so long after serving the notice.

HHJ Copley allowed the landlord's appeal and made a possession order. There was no statutory basis for the deputy district judge's decision. He was wrong in law to rule that the s21 notice had expired.

K5   # Assured shorthold tenancies and Disability Discrimination Act

K5.1   *Community Housing Association Ltd v Wye*
17 February 2007, Edmonton County Court

Where possession claim against assured shorthold tenant unlawful under DDA, injunction granted to restrain landlord from continuing proceedings

Mr Wye was an assured shorthold tenant. As a result of acts of nuisance and anti-social behaviour, which included playing loud music during the day and night, harassment and intimidation of neighbours, threats to stab the police, banging doors, loud parties involving the consumption of drugs and excessive amounts of alcohol, in March 2006 the claimant (CHA) served notice pursuant to Housing Act 1988 s21 and sought possession. Mr Wye defended and counterclaimed for damages and an injunction ordering the claimant to take no further steps in the proceedings, on the basis that he was a disabled person within the meaning of Disability Discrimination Act 1995 Part I, that the service of the s21 notice was discriminatory and, therefore, unlawful, as was the issue and continuation of the proceedings to trial. CHA admitted that the defendant was a 'disabled person' in that he suffered from a borderline personality disorder. CHA also conceded that the behaviour complained of was symptomatic of the disability.

District Judge Silverman initially determined that the s21 notice was valid. Although the defendant's assured shorthold tenancy was a statutory periodic tenancy, the s21 notice was headed 'Housing Act 1988 Section 21 (1)(b)' (rather than referring to s21(4)(a)) and did not state, as s21(4)(a) requires, that possession 'is required by virtue of this section'. He held that the fact that the wrong subsection was quoted was irrelevant since s21(4)(a) only requires the section to be stated, not the subsection. Since the notice clearly quoted s21 'it must be taken that the notice requires possession by virtue of that section and, therefore, complies with the statutory requirements'. As regards the allegations of nuisance, the judge found that the acts complained of did occur, but that the evidence fell short of establishing that Mr Wye was a danger to anyone other than himself. After considering *Manchester CC v Romano* (H8.2), he noted that there was no evidence before him to explain why possession was necessary so as not to put identified persons at risk. Furthermore, there had been no further incidents of harassment or intimidation towards neighbours since a meeting on 9 February 2006. The judge found that there was insufficient evidence at the date of service of the s21 notice or issue of proceedings to show that CHA held the opinion that it was necessary to obtain possession, and that any such opinion, if in fact held, could not be objectively justified by the evidence. Accordingly, he found that the service of the s21 notice, the issue of proceedings and continuing to trial were unlawful. He concluded that the award of damages on the counterclaim would not be an adequate remedy and that the appropriate course was to grant a final injunction restraining CHA from continuing the proceedings. District Judge Silverman granted permission to appeal and requested that his judgment be forwarded to the Court of Appeal by CHA, if deciding to appeal, so that the Court of Appeal might have the opportunity of considering whether to accept the appeal direct.

K6   Rent regulation

High Court

K6.1   *Park Lane Properties Ltd v Northern Rent Assessment Committee*
[2003] EWHC 1837 (Admin); 2 July 2003

Rent set by RAC pursuant to Housing Act 1988 s22 application was lawful

In July 2002 Park Lane Properties granted an assured shorthold tenancy to five students for a rent of approximately £58.50 per person per week. In November 2002, the tenants applied to a rent assessment committee (RAC) under Housing Act 1988 s22. The RAC considered comparable rents put forward by all parties. It also had regard to its local knowledge of the area in question. It concluded that the rent payable by the tenants was significantly higher than the rent that the landlord might reasonably be expected to obtain, and reduced it to approximately £52.50 per person per week. Park Lane Properties appealed under Tribunals and Inquires Act 1992 s11.

Davis J rejected the appeal. A complaint that the RAC had not given proper weight to the comparables put forward was misplaced. The RAC had not discounted Park Lane's comparables, but had been eminently justified in taking into account the fact that (a) there had been selectivity in its use of a limited internet search and (b) the comparables were in respect of rents advertised rather than in fact obtained. Second, the RAC's local knowledge had not been used in an impermissible way. It had not used its local knowledge alone, but in addition to all the other evidence and representations. Its approach had been proper. Third, the RAC had given adequate reasons. It had clearly considered all the evidence. It had not plucked a figure out of the air but had given a reasoned decision of 39 paragraphs.

CHAPTER L

Tenants without security of tenure and trespassers

L1   # Administrative law and human rights defences

A tenant of a local authority or other registered social landlord who does not have a secure or assured tenancy may be able to defend possession proceedings by claiming that the proceedings are improperly brought. Defendants may wish to rely on administrative law defences (eg, bad faith or *Wednesbury* unreasonableness (see *Associated Provincial Picture Houses v Wednesbury Corporation* [1948] 1 KB 223, CA)). Alternatively, they may try to mount challenges to decisions to bring possession claims relying on alleged breaches of occupants' rights under the ECHR. It is rare for such defences to succeed.

House of Lords

L1.1   ### Harrow LBC v Qazi
[2003] UKHL 43; [2004] 1 AC 983; [2003] 3 WLR 792; [2003] 4 All ER 461; [2003] UKHRR 974; [2003] HLR 75; [2004] L&TR 9; [2004] 1 P&CR 19; (2003) *Times* 1 August

Art 8(1) not breached by unqualified right to possession following service of NTQ by one joint tenant; property rights cannot be defeated by defence based on art 8; in exceptional cases defendants can apply to High Court for judicial review

From 1992 Mr and Mrs Qazi were joint secure tenants of a council house. In 1998 Mrs Qazi left and in 1999 she gave notice to quit, bringing the tenancy to an end. Mr Qazi applied for a new tenancy of the property in his sole name but his request was refused. The council brought possession proceedings. Mr Qazi based his defence on the contentions that (a) in seeking a possession order the council had failed to give effect to his right to respect for his home as required by ECHR article 8; (b) the council's interference with his right was not justified under article 8(2); and (c) the making of a possession order would be a breach of article 8. A recorder found that Mr Qazi had had no legal or equitable right or interest in the house and so it was not his home within the meaning of article 8(1). He made the possession order sought. Mr Qazi appealed successfully to the Court of Appeal ([2001] EWCA Civ 1834; [2002] HLR 276) and the council appealed to the House of Lords.

The House of Lords allowed the appeal. It held unanimously that residential accommodation occupied by a former tenant whose tenancy has come to an end by the operation of law is that person's 'home' within the meaning of ECHR article 8(1). Lord Bingham stated that the general approach of the Strasbourg institutions has been to apply a simple, factual and untechnical test, taking full account of the factual circumstances but very little of legal niceties. Whether a particular property is a person's home is a question of fact (Lord Millett). When the possession proceedings were issued Mr Qazi had lived in the property continuously for eight years. The house had been his home and he had no other. The expiry of his wife's notice to quit brought his right to occupy the house as a tenant to an end, but it did not bring his occupation to an end. The house continued to be the place where he lived and so his home. Lord Hope described his links with the premises as 'sufficient and continuous'. Furthermore, the effect of an order for possession would be to require Mr Qazi to leave his 'home'. Lord Hope said that removal from his home was bound to interfere with his enjoyment of that right at least to some extent. In that sense, article 8 was 'engaged'. However, the Strasbourg Court has repeatedly said that article 8(1) does not guarantee a right to a home. What it guarantees to the individual is respect for his home. This is an entirely different concept. Respect for the home is one of 'various things that affect a person's right to privacy'. By a majority (Lord Bingham and Lord Steyn dissenting), the House of Lords held that the law enabling a public authority landlord to exercise its unqualified right to recover possession, following service of a notice to quit which has terminated the tenancy, with a view to making the premises available for letting to others on its housing list, does not violate the essence of the right to respect for the home under article 8(1). Contractual and property rights cannot be defeated by a defence based on article 8 (Lord Hope and Lord Scott), although, in exceptional cases where defendants believe that local authorities are acting unfairly or from improper notices, they can apply to the High Court for judicial review (Lord Millett).

On 11 March 2004 the European Court of Human Rights (ECtHR) decided that Mr Qazi's application to the ECtHR was inadmissible.

L1.2 *Lambeth LBC v Kay; Leeds CC v Price*

[2006] UKHL 10; [2006] 2 AC 465; [2006] 2 WLR 570; [2006] 4 All ER 128; [2006] UKHRR 640; [2006] HLR 22; [2006] L&TR 8; [2006] LGR 323; [2006] P&CR 323; (2006) *Times* 10 March

Qazi considered in light of Connors in ECtHR; defence to possession claim based on occupier's personal circumstances should be struck out

In *Lambeth LBC v Kay*, the council licensed and later leased 'short-life' premises to London and Quadrant Housing Trust (LQHT) who purported to grant licences to those allowed into occupation. In fact those 'licences' created a relationship of landlord and tenant as between LQHT and the sub-occupants (*Bruton v London and Quadrant Housing Trust* (B2.1)). However, Lambeth gave notice to end the LQHT leases and brought possession claims. Defences based on ECHR article 8 were struck out and possession orders were made. The defendants appealed to the Court of Appeal, but the Court of Appeal ([2004] EWCA Civ 926; [2004] HLR 56) dismissed the appeal.

In *Leeds CC v Price*, the council sought possession of land which had been unlawfully occupied two days earlier by the defendant trespassers, who were Gypsies. The claim was transferred to the High Court for determination of the preliminary issue of whether the defendants could rely on article 8. The judge, applying *Harrow LBC v Qazi* (L1.1), held that they could not and made a possession order. On appeal ([2005] EWCA Civ 289; [2005] 3 All ER 573) the Court of Appeal held that domestic courts should follow and apply *Qazi* until it had been reconsidered by the House of Lords and gave leave to appeal to the House of Lords.

The appeals were joined and heard together by an appellate committee comprising seven law lords which reconsidered *Qazi* in the light of *Connors v UK* (A3.3). The appeals were dismissed in both cases.

The House of Lords did not consider the position as it affects private landlords (para 64). All the law lords agreed that article 8 does not in terms give a right to be provided with a home and does not guarantee the right to have one's housing problem solved by the authorities.

Lord Hope, giving the leading speech of the majority, said that Strasbourg jurisprudence indicates that three requirements must be met under article 8(2). The first question is whether the interference brought about by the possession claim is 'in accordance with the law'. The second question is whether it has an aim that is identified as a legitimate one. Satisfaction of the housing needs of others is regarded as a legitimate aim for this purpose. The third question is whether interference in pursuit of that aim is 'necessary in a democratic society'. The notion of necessity implies a pressing social need, and the measure employed must be proportionate to the legitimate aim pursued (para 66). He pointed out that *Connors* is the only case where the ECtHR has held that the making of a possession order against an occupier in favour of a public authority in accordance with the requirements of domestic property law has failed to meet the third requirement in article 8(2). 'It failed to do so in that case because the making of the order was not attended by the procedural safeguards that were required to establish that there was a proper justification for the interference with the applicant's right to respect for his private and family life and his home.' It was the law itself that was defective. In his opinion, it left untouched cases, such as *Qazi*, where the judgment of the legislature on issues of property law met the third requirement of article 8.

Lord Hope explained that the effect of *Qazi* is that, where an order for possession is made by the court in accordance with domestic property law, the essence of the article 8(1) right to respect for the home will not be violated. So the question whether the interference is permitted by article 8(2) is not a matter that need be considered by the county court. The law itself provides the answer to that question. The only matter which the court needs to consider is whether the requirements of the law and the procedural safeguards which it lays down for the protection of the occupier have been satisfied (para 72). The absence of any statutory protection in such cases is the result of a deliberate decision by parliament that the owner's right to recover possession should be unqualified, other than by the requirement that an order for possession must be sought from the court, which ensures that procedures are in place to safeguard the rights of the occupier.

Referring to the ECtHR's decision that Mr Qazi's application to the ECtHR was inadmissible, Lord Hope said that it was reasonable to think that the ECtHR accepted that Mr Qazi had established that the house was his home for the purposes of article 8 and that the enjoyment of his right to respect for his home was interfered with at least to some extent by the possession order sought. To that extent there was an issue to be considered under article 8(2). However, it was reasonable also to think that the ECtHR was satisfied that the requirements of article 8(2) were so obviously met by the law 'that there was nothing more to be said in Mr Qazi's case'. The tenancy had come to an end, and he no longer had any right to remain in occupation of the premises. His personal circumstances were irrelevant (para 107). There are some cases 'of a special and unusual kind' such as *Connors*, where the interference with the right to respect for the home which results from the making of a possession order needs to be justified by a decision-making process that ensures that 'some special consideration' is given to the interests safeguarded by article 8. If there is such a defect, the law will need to be amended to provide the necessary safeguards. But there will be many other cases where there are no such special circumstances – where the person's right to occupy the premises as his home has simply been brought to an end by the operation of law and his eviction is necessary to protect the rights under the law of the land-owner. In these cases it is enough that the eviction is in accordance with what the law itself requires.

In the key passage in Lord Hope's speech (para 110), with which the other members of the majority expressly agreed, he said

> a defence which does not challenge the law under which the possession order is sought as being incompatible with the article 8 but is based only on the occupier's personal circumstances should be struck out ... [If] the requirements of the law have been established and the right to recover pos-session is unqualified, the only situations in which it would be open to the court to refrain from proceeding to summary judgment and making the possession order are these: (a) if a seriously arguable point is raised that the law which enables the court to make the possession order is incom-patible with article 8, the county court in the exercise of its jurisdiction under the Human Rights Act 1998 should deal with the argument in one or other of two ways: (i) by giving effect to the law, so far as it is possible for it do so under section 3, in a way that is compatible with article 8, or (ii) by adjourning the proceedings to enable the compatibility issue to be dealt with in the High Court; (b) if the defendant wishes to challenge the decision of a public authority to recover possession as an improper exercise of its powers at common law on the ground that it was a decision that no reasonable person would consider justifiable, he should be permitted to do this provided again that the point is seriously arguable: *Wandsworth LBC v Winder* [1985] AC 461.

He concluded that the decision in *Connors* was not incompatible with *Qazi*. Lord Scott said that any inconsistencies between *Qazi* and *Connors* were 'minor'.

Lord Scott suggested that it could not 'credibly be suggested that in the two days between the entry by [the Gypsies] on the recreation ground and the commencement by Leeds of possession proceedings [they] had established 'sufficient and continuous links" so as to make that land their home. Baroness Hale also said that 'it cannot plausibly be asserted that [the Gypsies] had established a home on the recreation ground'. Lord Scott also said that parliament's omission to provide any statutory secure of tenure to home occupiers in the position of the Lambeth sub-occupants was well within the wide margin of appreciation referred to in *Blecic v Croatia* (A3.1). He agreed that the article 8 defences were rightly struck out. Where a home occupier has no contractual or proprietary right to remain in possession as against the owner of the property, an article 8 defence based on no more than the personal circumstances of the occu-pier and his family can never succeed. Lord Scott also said that 'no court, domestic or in Strasbourg, has ever suggested that a person who enters and remains on land as a trespasser can assert an article 8 right to respect for the home he has unlawfully established on the land as a defence to the owner's eviction proceedings ... An article 8 defence in such a case could not ever succeed.'

Note: See now *Stanková v Slovakia* (A3.13). Although *Qazi* and *Kay* are binding on all English and Welsh courts, up to and including the Court of Appeal, it is arguable whether these cases are now consistent with Strasbourg jurisprudence.

Court of Appeal

L1.3   *Avon CC v Buscott*

[1988] QB 656; [1988] 2 WLR 788; [1988] 1 All ER 841; (1988) 20 HLR 385, CA (see L3.1)

Public law rights cannot be raised as defence in possession proceedings, although court may adjourn to allow application for judicial review

L1.4   *Birmingham CC v Doherty*

[2006] EWCA Civ 1739; [2007] HLR 32; [2007] LGR 165

'Conventional' judicial review grounds can be raised as defence in possession claim, but only if seriously arguable challenge under art 8 to the law or seriously arguable challenge on conventional judicial review grounds

The defendant was a Traveller. From 1987 he and his family occupied a site as their home under a licence agreement with Birmingham City Council. In March 2004 the council served notice to quit, which expired in May 2004. The council began possession proceedings, asserting that the family's occupation was not protected under any relevant legislation, that possession was required to carry out essential improvements, and that the site would then be managed as temporary accommodation for Travellers coming to the city. It was said that the family's presence on the site 'deterred' other Travellers from going there, that it was 'severely under-utilised', and that this caused unauthorised encampments elsewhere in the city. The defendant accepted that he had no enforceable right to remain under English property law, but relied on the protection of ECHR article 8, claiming that the grant of summary possession would not be reasonable or proportionate. In December 2004 HHJ McKenna gave summary judgment for the council and made an order for possession. The defendant appealed.

The Court of Appeal dismissed the appeal. After referring to *Harrow LBC v Qazi* (L1.1), and *Connors v United Kingdom* (A3.3), the Court of Appeal carried out a detailed and helpful analysis of the speeches in *Lambeth LBC v Kay; Leeds CC v Price* (L1.2). The Court of Appeal noted that all the law lords 'seem to have accepted it as settled law under [*Wandsworth LBC v Winder* [1985] AC 461] that 'conventional' judicial review grounds can be raised by way of defence to possession proceedings in the county court.' However,

> there are only two possible 'gateways' ... for a successful defence to summary judgment in such cases: (a) a seriously arguable challenge under

article 8 to *the law* under which the possession order is made, but only where it is possible (with the interpretative aids of the Human Rights Act) to adapt the domestic law to make it more compliant; (b) a seriously arguable challenge on conventional judicial review grounds ... to *the authority's decision* to recover possession. (paras 26–40)

The Court of Appeal accepted the council's submission in *Doherty* that gateway (a) was closed because the authority's claim to possession was in accordance with a statutory scheme, which, whether compatible or not with the ECHR, had to be applied by the county court as it stood. The court rejected the defendant's contention that the authority's claim to possession depended on its common-law rights, not on any statutory entitlement. The Court of Appeal distinguished *Connors* on the basis that the council's decision in *Doherty* depended, not on a factual allegation of nuisance or misconduct, or 'the bald ground that the family were trespassers', but on an administrative judgment about the appropriate use of its land in the public interest. The Court of Appeal reached the clear and unanimous conclusion that the judge was right to make an order for possession.

L1.5   *Hackney LBC v Lambourne*
(1993) 25 HLR 172; [1993] COD 231, CA

Occupant could not raise defence based on non-performance of homelessness duties in possession proceedings based on HA 1985 Sch 1 para 6

The defendants were accepted by the council for rehousing as homeless people. Pending an offer of permanent council housing, they were placed in 'private sector leasing' accommodation, lacking security of tenure, on a joint tenancy. The council served notice to quit and began possession proceedings on the basis that Housing Act 1985 Sch 1 para 6 was satisfied and the premises were not secure. The tenants asserted that the council had served the notice in the erroneous belief that it had discharged its duty to make an offer of suitable accommodation (because no offer of any specific accommodation had been made by the date of service of the notice and the council did not propose to provide further temporary accommodation). The council's application to strike out that aspect of the defence was dismissed by a county court judge but allowed on appeal.

    The Court of Appeal dismissed an appeal by the defendant. On termination of the tenancy, the defendants had no private law right to remain in the temporary accommodation let to them. The proper way to exercise their public law rights to challenge the council's decision was by way of judicial review; to raise it in county court proceedings was 'abusive'. Evans LJ referred to the decision in *O'Reilly v Mackman* [1983] 2 AC 237, HL, where the House of Lords held that, since all remedies for the infringement of rights protected by public law can be obtained on an application for judicial review, as a general rule it is contrary to public policy and an abuse of process for someone complaining of a public authority's infringement of his or her public law rights to seek redress by ordinary action.

L1.6   *R v Westminster CC ex p Parkins*
(1994) 68 P&CR 253, CA

Judicial review of decision to serve NTQ refused

Mr Parkins was employed at a school. Accommodation was provided as part of his job. Following his dismissal, the council served a notice to quit. Mr Parkins applied for judicial review of that decision.

The Court of Appeal held that any rights which he enjoyed in relation to the accommodation arose in private law and should be determined in ordinary civil proceedings. The application for judicial review had been rightly refused. The case was wholly distinguishable from *West Glamorgan CC v Rafferty* (L1.8).

L1.6A   *Sheffield CC v Smart*

[2002] EWCA Civ 04; [2002] HLR 34; [2002] LGR 467; (2002) *Times* 20 February (see T55.7)

County court does not have to consider art 8 when determining possession claim against non-secure tenant housed under s193

L1.7   *Tower Hamlets LBC v Begum (Rahanara)*

[2005] EWCA Civ 116; [2006] HLR 9; [2005] LGR 580; (2005) *Times* 22 February (see T55.8) (see T55.8)

No role for county court, within possession proceedings against homeless applicant, to consider challenge under Part VII; court has power to adjourn proceedings pending judicial review of decision to claim possession

L1.8   *West Glamorgan CC v Rafferty*

[1987] 1 WLR 457; [1987] 1 All ER 1005; (1986) 18 HLR 375; (1987) 85 LGR 793, CA

Decision to evict Gypsies and Travellers quashed where council had failed to comply with duties to provide accommodation for Gypsies and Travellers

The county council obtained a possession order by using RSC Ord 113 against large numbers of 'Gypsies' who had parked caravans on a disused industrial site. The Gypsies and Travellers obtained orders setting aside the possession order and quashing the council's decision to bring proceedings. The council, claiming that severe nuisance and damage were being caused to neighbouring occupiers, appealed against both orders.

After hearing that the council had failed for over 15 years to comply with its duties under the Caravan Sites Act 1968 to provide accommodation for Gypsies and Travellers, that there was no site in West Glamorgan and that evictions would cause considerable hardship, the Court of Appeal dismissed the appeal. It held that the 'only reasonable conclusion would be against eviction, if eviction was to be carried out with no provision for alternative accommodation' ([1987] 1 All ER at 1021).

High Court

L1.9   *R v Hammersmith and Fulham LBC ex p Quigley*

(2000) 32 HLR 379; (1999) *Independent* 24 May, QBD

Council's decision to bring possession claim quashed; no implied surrender

A secure tenant of a local authority fled the country, abandoning his children in the property. His partner, from whom he was separated, moved into the premises to care for the children.

Ognall J quashed a decision by the local authority to bring a possession claim. The local authority, when deciding whether to serve a notice to quit, should have considered the fact that the partner could have applied for a transfer of the tenancy under Children Act 1989 s15. Its alternative contention that the tenancy had already been surrendered by operation of law could not survive the absence of any unequivocal acceptance of surrender by the council. Indeed, the council had itself thought the tenancy was continuing. This was evidenced by giving a notice to quit and the subsequent pleaded assertion in possession proceedings that the tenancy had continued up to the expiry of that notice.

L1.10 ## R (Gangera) v Hounslow LBC
[2003] EWHC 794 Admin; [2003] HLR 68

Court not bound to consider whether possession in breach of art 8; defendant not entitled to raise public law arguments as defence in possession proceedings

The claimant entered the UK as a visitor from Tanzania in 1989. He went to live with his parents at premises rented by them from Hounslow under a joint weekly secure tenancy. His father died in 1995 and his mother then succeeded to the secure tenancy. She died intestate in November 2001. The council's housing department told the claimant that he was not entitled to succeed to her tenancy and asked him to vacate. In December 2001 a deportation order was made against the claimant and he applied for leave to remain in the UK relying on ECHR article 8. On 23 January 2002 the council served notice to quit at the premises and on the public trustee. In April 2002 a possession claim was issued in Brentford County Court. In May 2002 the claimant requested that the council's social services department provide support and financial assistance. The possession claim was adjourned and the council undertook an assessment of the claimant pursuant to National Health Service and Community Care Act 1990 s47. However, the social worker who conducted the assessment took the view that the claimant fell within the lowest priority group within the council's eligibility criteria and was entitled to be provided with information and guidance but did not attain the threshold for entitlement to accommodation under National Assistance Act 1948 s21. In December 2002 the possession claim was transferred to the Administrative Court and the claimant issued fresh proceedings for judicial review.

Moses J granted permission to apply for judicial review, but refused the application. (1) In view of Housing Act 1985 ss87 and 88(1)(b), the claimant could not succeed to his parents' joint tenancy. On the death of his father, the claimant's mother became the sole tenant by virtue of the principle of survivorship within s88(1)(b). Accordingly, although the claimant was another member of the tenant's family, since the tenant, his mother, was herself a successor as defined in s88, he was not qualified to succeed her by virtue of s87. (2) The provisions prohibiting the claimant from succeeding to his mother's secure tenancy did not infringe ECHR article 14 read with article 8. Parliament had to strike a balance between security of tenure and the wider need for systematic allocation of the local authority's housing resources in circumstances where those housing resources are not unlimited. The striking of such a balance was pre-eminently a matter of policy for the legislature. The court should respect the legislative judgment on what was in the general interest unless that judgment was manifestly without reasonable foundation (see *Mellacher v Austria* (A5.14) and *Poplar HARCA v Donoghue* (K2.1)). There was no basis for contending that the statutory scheme amounted to a disproportionate interference with a person's right to respect for his home. For article 14 purposes, there was no dispute that there was a difference of treatment between Mr Gangera and two other comparators. First, if his mother had been the sole tenant from the commencement of the tenancy he would have been entitled to succeed. Second, where there is no spouse, and a secure tenant was not formerly a joint tenant, the tenant's nephew by marriage could succeed to the secure tenancy so long as he fulfilled the requirement of residing with the tenant for a period of 12 months ending with the tenant's death. However, Moses J found that the chosen comparators were not in an analogous situation to the complainant's position and were not true comparisons at all. The legislation did not discriminate against the claimant on the basis of his status. The difference in treatment followed from the fact of the previous succession, not from the status of the claimant. (3) The fact that the court is required to intervene when a landlord seeks to enforce rights of possession does not lead to the conclusion that the court is bound, in each case, to consider whether an order for possession would, in the circumstances of the individual case, be disproportionate and contrary to article 8. In proceedings between private parties, when a court enforces a possession order without considering proportionality, it does not act incompatibly with ECHR rights because it is merely giving effect to a domestic system of law which itself is not disproportionate. So long as the system as a whole is compatible with the ECHR, it is not for the court to arrogate to itself a discretion in other cases. It is not open to an individual such as the claimant to resurrect arguments about necessity and proportionality in an individual case. Courts are not required to adjudicate on compatibility in each case. (These observations were endorsed by Lord Millett in *Harrow LBC v Qazi* (L1.1); (4) Mr Gangera was not entitled to raise the public law arguments under article 8 and about rationality as a defence in possession proceedings. He fell within the same category as *Michalak v Wandsworth LBC* (E14.9) and could, therefore, rely on his rights enshrined in article 8 and arguments about rationality only by challenging the council's decision in judicial review proceedings following service of the notice to quit. (5) The contention that the claimant was entitled to be provided with accommodation to meet his needs pursuant to s21 was premature. There was nothing disproportionate or irrational in the council's decision to institute possession proceedings without any further assessment of his needs other than that undertaken in June 2002.

L2   Disability Discrimination Act 1995

For other cases on the Disability Discrimination Act, see sections H8 and K5.

Court of Appeal

L2.1   *Lewisham LBC v Malcolm and the Disability Rights Commission*
[2007] EWCA Civ 763; (2007) *Times* 28 August; 25 July 2007

Claim for possession unlawful discrimination under DDA where causal relationship between tenant's disability and reason for issue of proceedings

Mr Malcolm, a secure tenant, was diagnosed with schizophrenia. Although he was admitted to hospital on numerous occasions, his condition was stabilised by medication. Later, he exercised the right to buy his flat but, before completion, he sublet it. Lewisham did not consent to that subletting and so he ceased to be a secure tenant (Housing Act 1985 s93). He said that his decision to sublet the flat related to his schizophrenia. Lewisham gave notice to quit and issued proceedings for possession. HHJ Hallon held that the provisions of Disability Discrimination Act (DDA) 1995 preventing discrimination by eviction did not apply because Mr Malcolm had lost his security of tenure and so the court had no discretion to withhold a possession order. She also held that he was not a disabled person and that his actions had not been caused by his disability. Mr Malcolm appealed against the possession order.

The Court of Appeal allowed his appeal and dismissed the possession claim. On the evidence, Mr Malcolm's mental impairment did have a substantial (ie, more than minor or trivial) effect on his ability to carry out normal day-to-day activities and, accordingly, he was disabled within DDA s1. The requirement that a reason for discrimination related to a person's disability implied an appropriate causal relationship between the subletting and the disability. Mr Malcolm did not have to establish that the disability was the actual cause of the subletting. In this case, the necessary causal relationship did exist. Lewisham's reason for starting possession proceedings, namely the subletting, was 'related' to his disability for the purposes of s24(1)(a). In bringing proceedings for possession, the local authority unlawfully discriminated against Mr Malcolm. DDA s22(3)(c) is unqualified and does not apply only where a tenant has security of tenure. There is no exception where the tenant has lost security of tenure under s93. If a court is satisfied that eviction would discriminate against an occupier – regardless of his or her status – then the decision to evict is unlawful unless the discrimination can be justified. DDA s24 does not require the alleged discriminator to be aware of the claimant's disability and such lack of knowledge does not preclude a finding of discrimination although it may be relevant to a defence of justification. It followed that both the service of the notice to quit and the claim for possession constituted unlawful discrimination.

On 4 December 2007, the House of Lords gave leave to appeal.

L3   # Claims for possession and injunctions against alleged trespassers

A trespasser is someone who is in possession of land or premises without the owner's permission or, in traditional legal language, 'without licence or consent'. Before statutory intervention, landowners could always use reasonable force to eject a trespasser, without the need for court proceedings. That common-law position has been modified by several statutes, principally the Protection from Eviction Act 1977 and the Criminal Law Act 1977.

Special procedures have been developed by the courts for proceedings against trespassers. Both Rules of the Supreme Court (RSC) Ord 113 and County Court Rules (CCR) Ord 24 allowed proceedings against trespassers to be brought against persons unknown and for far shorter periods than usual between service of proceedings and the hearing. These differences have been retained in Civil Procedure Rules (CPR) Part 55 which has replaced RSC Ord 113 and CCR Ord 24.

Court of Appeal

L3.1   *Avon CC v Buscott*
[1988] QB 656; [1988] 2 WLR 788; [1988] 1 All ER 841; (1988) 20 HLR 385, CA

Public law rights cannot be raised as defence in possession proceedings, although court may adjourn to allow application for judicial review

The council brought possession proceedings under RSC Ord 113 against people living in 'benders' or improvised shelters. The defendants did not deny that they were trespassers, but sought an adjournment so that they could call evidence that they were Gypsies and that the council was in breach of its duties under the Caravan Sites Act 1968 to provide accommodation.

The Court of Appeal held that this challenge did not stem from a private law right and so could not be raised as a defence in the possession proceedings. Public law rights such as this should only be advanced in applications for judicial review. Although defendants may request adjournments of possession proceedings in order to make an application for judicial review, to succeed in obtaining an adjournment they must be able to show that the application for leave to apply for judicial review has a real chance of being granted.

L3.2   *Camden LBC v Person Unknown*
[1987] 3 CL 133c, CA

No jurisdiction to order warrant not to be executed until council rehoused occupant

In possession proceedings brought under CCR Ord 24, a Miss Ford appeared at court, admitted that she was in occupation of premises 'without licence or consent' but said that she was on the council's waiting list and had no other place to live. The judge made a possession order but directed that the warrant for possession should not be executed until the council offered Miss Ford alternative accommodation.

The council's appeal was allowed. The judge had no jurisdiction to make the order he made. The lawful owner was entitled to an immediate order for possession.

L3.3   *Countryside Residential (North Thames) Ltd v Tugwell*
[2000] 34 EG 87; (2000) 81 P&CR 2, CA

Claimant with right of access but not effective control of land did not have sufficient interest to issue proceedings against trespassers

Ms Tugwell and her friends set up a protest camp in woodland. The claimant, a developer, had an option to purchase part of the land for residential development. The option agreement gave the claimant a licence permitting access to carry out surveys. The claimant brought possession proceedings under RSC Ord 113 and obtained a possession order.

Ms Tugwell appealed successfully. The Court of Appeal accepted a submission that the only licensees who have the right of possession required to eject trespassers are those with a right of 'effective control' of land. In this case, the claimant had only a right of access, not a right to effective control. It was important not to confuse contractual rights with the right of possession which is the foundation of an Order 113 remedy. The position might have been different if the developer had occupied land before the setting up of the protest camps, in which case it might have been able to argue that it had effective control. The Court of Appeal distinguished *Manchester Airport plc v Dutton* (L3.4).

L3.4 **Manchester Airport plc v Dutton**
[2000] QB 133; [1999] 3 WLR 524; [1999] 2 All ER 675; (2000) 79 P&CR 536; (1999) *Times* 5 March, CA

Licensee could bring possession proceedings against trespassers

The Court of Appeal held that a licensee had power to bring possession proceedings against trespassers under RSC Ord 113. It was not necessary for an applicant in such proceedings to have a title or estate in land or even a right to exclusive possession.

L3.5 **McPhail v Persons Unknown**
[1973] Ch 447; [1973] 3 WLR 71; [1973] 3 All ER 393, CA

Court has no discretion to suspend possession against trespassers

In proceedings brought against trespassers under RSC Ord 113, a judge made an immediate possession order. The respondents appealed, seeking a stay for four weeks.

Their appeal was dismissed. Where an owner seeks a possession order against squatters, the court is bound to grant the order sought and has no discretion to suspend it. Lord Denning MR, referring to the summary procedure, stated:

> There is no provision for giving any time. The court cannot give any time. It must, at the behest of the owner, make an order for recovery of possession. It is then for the owner to give such time as he thinks right to the squatters. They must make their appeal to his goodwill and consideration, and not to the courts. ([1973] 3 All ER at 398)

L3.6 **Preston BC v Fairclough**
(1983) 8 HLR 70, CA (see N4.16)

For landlord to establish surrender; tenant leaving premises owing rent insufficient

L3.7 **Secretary of State for the Environment, Food and Rural Affairs v Drury**
[2004] EWCA Civ 200; (2004) *Times* 15 March; 26 February 2004

Inclusion of unoccupied area in possession order against trespassers should be exceptional

The secretary of state owned woodlands which were managed by the Forestry Commission. Eleven travellers, including Ms Drury and her children, wrongfully began to occupy Fermyn Woods, one of the woodlands. The secretary of state sought a possession order. A judge made a possession order, not just in respect of the Fermyn Woods, but also in respect of 30 other areas of woodland owned by the secretary of state and managed by the Forestry Commission, lying in a 20-mile radius of Fermyn Woods. Ms Drury appealed.

The Court of Appeal allowed the appeal. Although the law recognises that even an anticipated trespass may give rise to a right of action, it is nugatory unless an effective remedy is also offered. In a claim against trespassers (CPR 55.1(b)), a separate unoccupied area should be included in a possession order if, and only if, the land owner is entitled to an injunction quia timet against occupants in relation to the separate area (*Ministry of Agriculture, Fisheries and Food v Heyman* (1990) 59 P&CR 48, QBD and *University of Essex v Djemal* (L3.10). The threshold requirement is for convincing evidence of a real danger of actual violation. The inclusion in a possession order of an unoccupied area should be exceptional. Factors to be considered are the imminence of the threat to move, the history of former illegal occupations and the frequency and timing of them, and evidence that the same people are involved. The necessary evidence should usually take the form of an intention to decamp to the other area, of a history of movement between the two areas from which a real danger of repetition can be inferred, or of such propinquity and similarity between the two areas as to command the inference of a real danger of decampment from one to the other. In this case the evidence adduced to demonstrate the risk of decampment was insufficient to convince the court that there was a real danger that Ms Drury would decamp to one or other of the 30 other areas of woodland.

L3.8   *South Cambridgeshire DC v Gammell; Bromley LBC v Maughan*
[2005] EWCA Civ 1429; (2005) *Times* 3 November

Injunctions against persons unknown should only be granted where impossible to identify occupants

Where an injunction has been granted under Town and Country Planning Act 1990 s187B in respect of the occupation of land in breach of planning control by persons unknown, a person moving on to the land who learns of the injunction is in breach of it and in contempt of court. However, the court must balance environmental and other public interest considerations against the defendant's ECHR article 8 rights to a private and family life. Accordingly, courts should grant such injunctions only where it was impossible for the applicant to identify the persons concerned or likely to be concerned. In those circumstances, the proper course for anyone finding out that occupation is in breach of such an injunction is to apply for the injunction to be varied or set aside. Then the court can take into consideration both the public interest issues and the personal circumstances of the applicant. See *South Bucks DC v Porter* (T38.1) and *Mid-Bedfordshire DC v Brown* [2004] EWCA Civ 1709; [2005] 1 WLR 1460.

L3.9   *Swordheath Properties Ltd v Floydd*
[1978] 1 WLR 550; [1978] 1 All ER 721; (1977) 36 P&CR 181; (1977) 249 EG 657, CA

No power to suspend order for possession for 14 days against squatters

A county court judge made an order for possession under CCR Ord 26 (predecessor of CCR Ord 24) which was not to be executed for 14 days.

The Court of Appeal allowed the owners' appeal. In the absence of consent, a county court judge has no power to grant a suspension of an order for possession against squatters.

L3.10   *University of Essex v Djemal*
[1980] 1 WLR 1301; [1980] 2 All ER 742; (1980) 41 P&CR 340, CA

Summary order for possession can extend beyond areas occupied

In proceedings brought under CCR Ord 26 (predecessor of CCR Ord 24) or RSC Ord 113, the court could make a summary order for possession which extended to areas beyond the particular area adversely occupied by trespassers if there was convincing evidence to establish a real danger of actual violation of all the areas in question. (See also *Ministry of Agriculture, Fisheries and Food v Heyman* (1990) 59 P&CR 48 QBD.)

L3.11   *West Glamorgan CC v Rafferty*
[1987] 1 WLR 457; [1987] 1 All ER 1005; (1986) 18 HLR 375; (1987) 85 LGR 793, CA
(see L1.8)

Decision to evict Gypsies and Travellers quashed where council had failed to comply with duties to provide accommodation for Gypsies and Travellers

L3.12   *Whitbread West Pennines Ltd v Reedy*
(1988) 20 HLR 642, CA

Former employee could not defend possession claim on basis of claim for unfair dismissal and reinstatement

Mr Reedy, a manager of a public house, was sacked and possession proceedings were instituted.

Although the possession proceedings were dismissed at first instance, the Court of Appeal allowed the brewery's appeal and made a possession order. Dismissed service licensees who have occupied premises for the better performance of their jobs cannot defend possession proceedings by arguing that claims for unfair dismissal and reinstatement have been submitted to an industrial tribunal.

L3.13   *Wirral MBC v Smith*
(1982) 4 HLR 81; (1982) 43 P&CR 312; (1982) 80 LGR 628; (1982) 262 EG 1298, CA
(see N2.23)

NTQ must be served to end deceased's tenancy

High Court

L3.14   *Hampshire Waste Services Ltd v Persons Unknown*
[2003] EWHC 1738 (ChD); [2004] Env LR 9; [2003] 42 EGCS 126

Injunction granted where protesters intended to trespass; no requirement for defendants to be named

The claimants owned and operated several waste incineration sites. Environmental protestors had in the past invaded those sites with the result that plants were shut down, causing considerable loss to the claimants and danger to the protestors and others. Information from the internet indicated that 14 July 2003, a 'Global Day of Action Against Incinerators' was the next date designated for such activity. The claimants sought an injunction restraining any people from entering or remaining on any of the sites without their consent.

Sir Andrew Morritt V-C granted the injunction. Damages were an inadequate remedy and, if one of the plants was invaded, the claimants would suffer substantial and irrevocable damage. Although they were unable to name any of the protestors who might be involved, under the Civil Procedure Rules there was no requirement that a defendant had to be named. (*Bloomsbury Publishing v News Group Newspapers Ltd* (2003) EWHC 1205 (Ch)) The overriding objective and the obligations cast on the court were inconsistent with undue reliance on form over substance. Where there is a clear case for an injunction, any difficulty envisaged in enforcing it is not a ground for refusing it.

L3.15 **R v Brighton and Hove Council ex p Marmont**
(1998) 30 HLR 1046; (1998) *Times* 15 January, QBD

Council had considered all relevant matters before deciding to evict Travellers

The applicants were Travellers and single mothers who were encamped without permission on land owned by the local authority. After complaints from local residents and the holding of a 'rave', the authority decided to bring possession proceedings under RSC Ord 113. Two of the occupants sought judicial review of the decision to bring possession proceedings, contending that the local authority had failed, among other things, (1) to apply the considerations set out in Department of the Environment Circular 18/94 (Gypsy Sites Policy and Unauthorised Camping); (2) to take reasonable steps to acquire necessary information; (3) to consider whether duties under Children Act 1989 could arise; and (4) to have regard to the health of children.

The application was dismissed. Tucker J held that the circular had no application where authorities brought proceedings to recover their own land under RSC Ord 113. Although the welfare of the mothers and children had to be the authority's primary concern, it had given proper consideration to those matters before applying for a possession order and in offering time before enforcing it. The council had not acted unfairly or unreasonably.

L3.16 **R v Hillingdon LBC ex p McDonagh**
[1999] LGR 459; (1999) 31 HLR 531; (1998) *Times* 9 November, QBD

Authority seeking possession against trespassers not obliged to carry out Children Act or homeless person assessments

Carnwath J held that a local authority seeking to obtain possession against trespassers under CCR Ord 24 had no obligation to carry out investigations under Children Act 1989 Part III or Housing Act 1996 Part VII, as recommended in Department of the Environment Circular 18/94. Landowners have a right to obtain possession against trespassers. The circular was an indication of good practice but did not impose any legally binding obligation on local authorities seeking to evict trespassers. It was, however, a relevant matter which is material for the purpose of deciding whether the exercise of that power is *Wednesbury* unreasonable.

L3.17 **R v Leeds CC ex p Maloney**
(1999) 31 HLR 552, QBD

Council lawfully decided to evict Travellers

The Maloneys were a family of Travellers. A number of them suffered from severe health problems. Mrs Maloney had cancer. Mr Maloney's 85-year-old mother was sick, infirm and suffered from arthritis. She also had heart and circulation problems. One of the children was deaf. They were evicted from the council's authorised site because of disturbances. They moved on to industrial land owned by the authority which was already the subject of county court proceedings to evict other Travellers who were unauthorised occupiers on that site. The authority's Travellers liaison officer made enquires and found that none of the Travellers already living there was in apparent need of help. He visited again after the Maloneys had moved on to the land and decided that there was nothing to cause him to change his decision to proceed with the eviction.

The Maloneys' application for judicial review was dismissed. Enquiries are a safety net for the families of Travellers. It is crucial for authorities to ensure that none of the occupiers has a pressing need which would make it inhumane to proceed with the eviction. In this case there was nothing unlawful in the way that the decision was made. The authority had made an offer of permanent accommodation to the Maloneys and the Education department had made arrangements to meet the educational needs of the children.

L3.18 **R v Minister of Agriculture, Fisheries and Food ex p Callaghan**
(1999) 32 HLR 8, QBD

Government departments not under obligations owed by council when deciding to evict Travellers

The applicants were Travellers camped on land owned by the respondent. The respondent's solicitors wrote to the district council for the area stating that the respondent wanted to remove the applicants from the land and asking it to make enquiries to ascertain whether there were any people on the land to whom the council might owe obligations under any of the enactments listed in the Department of the Environment Circular 18/94, *Gypsy Sites Policy and Unauthorised Camping*. The applicants sought judicial review of the respondent's decision to evict.

Turner J dismissed the application. Although the respondent accepted that it owed a common duty of humanity towards the applicants, it had not acted in breach of any relevant guidance. Its letter to the council showed that it had given consideration to all relevant matters before deciding to issue proceedings. There was no basis for extending the obligations owed by local authorities towards travellers to government departments in respect of possession of their own land.

L3.19 **R (Casey) v Crawley BC**
[2006] EWHC 301 (Admin); [2006] LGR 239

Council had taken all relevant matters into account in deciding to evict Travellers

The claimants were Irish Travellers. They camped in two unauthorised places in Crawley. Crawley BC began possession proceedings on the basis that the Travellers were trespassers and the council had an absolute legal entitlement to the land. It was not under any statutory duty to supply caravan sites and in any event had no such sites, either temporary or permanent. The Travellers sought judicial review of the decision to bring possession proceedings.

Burton J dismissed the application. Crawley had taken into account all material considerations and had not acted perversely, or *Wednesbury* unreasonably, in reaching its decisions first to issue and then to continue proceedings for possession. ECHR article 8 made no difference to that outcome. On the assumption that there was some interference with the claimants' article 8 rights, such an interference was very much at the lower end of the spectrum, given the powerful case for the entitlement of a local authority landowner to enforce its ownership rights and its planning duties.

Local government ombudsman reports

L3.20   *Investigation 88/A/858 (Tower Hamlets LBC)*

No legal basis for council's use of protected intending occupier certificates

The local government ombudsman found maladministration by Tower Hamlets LBC in its use of certificates under Criminal Law Act 1977 s7, by which squatters can be evicted without court proceedings on the basis that the premises are required for protected intending occupiers (PIOs). The local commissioner found that one certificate was issued at a time when there was no PIO. He found that 'there was no legal basis' for the resulting eviction carried out by council officers and the police and that 'indeed it appears that an offence under s6 of the Criminal Law Act may have been committed when the complainants were turned out'. He recommended that compensation should be paid to the squatters and that immediate steps should be taken to train all officers dealing with evictions to use the Criminal Law Act 1977 provisions properly.

L4   Interim possession orders and removal directions

Criminal Justice and Public Order Act 1994 creates criminal offences where trespassers fail to comply with interim possession orders (IPOs). The procedure (formerly CCR Ord 24 Part II) is now contained in Civil Procedure Rules Part 55, paras 20 to 28.

High Court

L4.1   *Metropolitan Housing Trust v Ali and Persons Unknown*
December 2001 *Legal Action* 23; 16 August 2001, ChD
No discretion not to make IPO where conditions satisfied

The claimant owned a block of flats which it intended to demolish. It secured possession on one flat in July 2000, but on 9 July 2001 learnt that squatters had entered the premises. It applied for an interim possession order (IPO) under Criminal Justice and Public Order Act 1994 and CCR Ord 24 Part II. One squatter attended court and relied on an affidavit in which she stated that a housing officer had told her that, as a squatter, she could reside in the flat until the court ordered otherwise. HHJ Cotran refused to make an IPO on the ground that (1) the claimant had given consent to the squatters being in the premises (and so the condition in CCR Ord 49 r9(c) was not met) and (2), in any event, he had a discretion whether or not to make an IPO. The squatters should be allowed to leave without the threat of being arrested. He made a forthwith possession order under CCR Ord 24 Part I.

Park J allowed the claimant's appeal. The claimant had not given consent. The housing officer's statement could only be construed as meaning that the claimant would have to obtain a court order to evict the squatters (see Criminal Law Act 1977 s6). All the conditions for making an order were satisfied and the judge therefore had no discretion: he was bound to make an order (CCR Ord 24 r12(5)). There was no violation of the ECHR in making an IPO.

L4.2 *R v Wealden DC ex p Wales; R v Lincolnshire CC ex p Atkinson*
[1995] NPC 145, QBD

Statutory and humanitarian considerations required to be taken into account when deciding whether to make directions for removal of Gypsies and Travellers

The local authorities made directions under Criminal Justice and Public Order Act 1994 s77 for the removal of Travellers who had been unlawfully camped on land. In the first applications for judicial review under the Act, the applicants sought to quash the directions, on the basis that the respondents had failed to carry out enquiries before making them.

Sedley J granted the applications sought against Wealden DC, but dismissed those involving Lincolnshire. He held that local authorities at the initial stage of deciding whether and to whom to give a removal direction under s77 have to consider the relationship of their proposed action to various statutory and humanitarian considerations and make their decision accordingly. Such decisions should be reviewed by local authorities if there is a change in circumstances. They must strike a balance between the competing and conflicting needs of those encamped illegally and of residents in the area. Counsel for the respondents conceded that local authorities have to take into account the contents of DoE Circular 18/94, *Gypsy sites and unauthorised camping*. A removal direction, once made, can apply only to people who were on the land at the time when the direction was made and, therefore, can only be contravened by such persons.

L4.3 *R v Wolverhampton MBC ex p Dunne*
(1997) 29 HLR 745; [1997] COD 210, QBD

Enquiries into personal circumstances of Gypsies and Travellers to be made before, not after, making order under s77(1); magistrates to consider only formalities, not merits

The council made a decision to issue a notice under Criminal Justice and Public Order Act 1994 s77(1), requiring Travellers to leave land, without first making enquiries about their circumstances. A magistrate adjourned the subsequent proceedings so that enquiries could be made.

The High Court quashed both the council's decision to issue the s77 notice and the magistrate's subsequent decision upholding the complaint. Local authorities should make enquiries into the personal circumstances of travellers before, and not after, the making of an order under s77(1) (see *R v Wealden DC ex p Wales; R v Lincolnshire CC ex p Atkinson* (L4.2). When making such an order, magistrates are restricted to considering whether the formalities under the Act have been carried out and should not review the merits of the local authority's decision to give the notice. If Travellers wish to challenge a direction (unless the challenge concerns the form of the direction), the appropriate course of action is to seek a stay in the magistrates' court and to make a speedy application for leave for judicial review.

L4.4   *R (Fuller) v Chief Constable of Dorset Police*
[2001] EWHC Admin 1057; February 2002 *Legal Action* 27; 12 December 2001

Section 61 notice invalid where Travellers had not been first asked to leave; ss61 and 62 complied with ECHR

Travellers moved on to a rubbish tip site owned by a borough council in July 2001 and camped there without permission. After a number of meetings involving the county council's Gypsy and Traveller Liaison Service, the police and the Travellers, a representative of the borough council informed the Travellers that they were being treated as trespassers and that they were required to leave two days later, on 31 August 2001. At the same time, the police gave notice under Criminal Justice and Public Order Act 1994 s61 (power to remove trespassers) to leave on 31 August 2001.

The Travellers applied for judicial review. Stanley Burnton J rejected the Travellers' proposition that the s61 direction necessarily breached ECHR articles 3, 6, 8 and article 1 of the First Protocol. Article 3 (torture and inhuman or degrading treatment) was not engaged. Article 6 (right to a fair hearing) would not be infringed if parliament made all trespass a criminal offence and so a law making it a criminal offence to fail to comply with a direction by a police officer to leave did not engage article 6. Article 8 (right to respect for home) was not necessarily breached because s61 satisfied the tests of necessity and proportionality. Article 1 of the First Protocol was not breached because the trespassers were free to enjoy their possessions elsewhere. Stanley Burnton J accordingly held that ss61 and 62 are compatible with ECHR rights.

So far as the police's decision was concerned, they were entitled, in the absence of any challenge, to assume that the borough council's decision to require the Travellers to leave was lawful and valid. The decision to serve the s61 notice did not breach article 8 because the concept of a 'home' in article 8 involved a degree of continuity (see *Gillow v UK* (1986) 11 EHRR 335). That was absent in the present case. The Travellers had only arrived in July and had been told at an early stage that they would need to move in

August. In any event, even if article 8(1) were engaged, the unlawfulness of the establishment of the encampment was a relevant and significant factor when considering the justifications for infringement in article 8(2) (*Chapman v UK* (A3.2)).

However, Stanley Burnton J found that it is implicit in s61 that trespassers must have failed to comply with steps taken by the occupier of the land to ask them to leave before the power to give a direction can be lawfully exercised. He held that the direction was not valid or lawful because (1) it was premature – the Travellers had not been given the opportunity to comply with the borough council's direction to leave; and (2) it did not require the Travellers to leave immediately or as soon as reasonably practicable, but rather in two days' time.

L4.5   *Shropshire CC v Wynne*
(1998) 96 LGR 689; (1997) *Times* 22 July, DC
Magistrate has no discretion to review council's decision

The respondent lived for several years in a caravan on land which was part of the highway. The council, relying on Criminal Justice and Public Order Act 1994 s77, asked him to leave. When he did not do so, they sought an order in the magistrates' court under s78. A stipendiary magistrate declined to make an order, stating that, on the facts, it was unreasonable to do so and that he had a discretion not to make an order.

The Divisional Court allowed the council's appeal. The question of reasonableness was for the council to decide. A magistrate has no discretion to review that decision.

L4.6   *Ward v Hillingdon LBC*
(2001) 15 February, QBD AdminCt
Removal directions lawful and justified under ECHR art 8(2)

Mr Ward, a Traveller, challenged the local authority's decision to issue removal directions against him and his family under Criminal Justice and Public Order Act 1994 s77(1), requiring them to vacate a plot in a caravan site owned and operated for occupation by Travellers. He claimed that the local authority had failed to make any or sufficient enquiries into his and his family's situation and needs, that the decision was *Wednesbury* unreasonable, that s77 violated ECHR articles 6 and 7 because it reversed the burden of proof, and that an implementation of the decision would amount to a disproportionate infringement of his human rights when compared to the benefit to the local authority.

Stanley Burnton J dismissed the application. The enquiries were sufficient. The council was entitled to take a decision and act on it swiftly because of the social tension that would be caused by Mr Ward being allowed to jump the queue for a plot. Furthermore, it was entitled to require the plots to be granted in accordance with the existing site policy. In view of the interests of the council, the other dwellers on the site and those on the waiting list, the decision was not disproportionate. The decision was lawful, necessary and justified within the meaning of ECHR article 8(2). Section 77 of the Criminal Justice and Public Order Act 1994 did not reverse the burden of proof for the purpose of ECHR article 6(1) or 7.

However, human rights issues could not be determined formally without notice to the Crown and in this case they did not have to be determined because of the intention to evict under s78.

L5   Mesne profits

Landowners are entitled to claim damages for use and occupation against trespassers. If a possession order is made after a tenancy has been terminated, a landlord is entitled to seek mesne profits from the termination of the tenancy until possession is given up. Usually they are calculated according to the fair value of the premises. Often that is the amount of rent which the tenant has been paying.

Court of Appeal

L5.1   *Braintree DC v Vincent*
[2004] EWCA Civ 415; 9 March 2004 (see F2.1)

Sub-licensee not liable for mesne profits until order for possession against tenant takes effect

L5.2   *Ministry of Defence v Ashman*
(1993) 25 HLR 513; (1993) 66 P&CR 195; [1993] 2 EGLR 102, CA

Open market value usually appropriate rate for mesne profits; special circumstances where occupants would never have had to pay full market rent

The defendants lived in RAF married quarters. The open market rental value of the premises was £472 per month, but, as a serviceman, Mr Ashman was charged a 'concessionary licence fee' of £95 per month. After he became estranged from his wife, the Ministry of Defence obtained an order for possession. In the county court it was held that the Ministry of Defence was estopped from claiming the full market rental value for the period after termination.

   On appeal, it was held that this was not so and the case was remitted to the county court. Although the open market value would usually be the appropriate rate for mesne profits, there were special circumstances in this case which the county court should take into account. In particular, the defendants would probably never have occupied the premises in the first place if they had had to pay the full market rent. In order to ascertain the value to the wife (after the husband had left), more assistance would have been gained by examining how much she would have had to pay for suitable local authority housing if she could have been immediately rehoused.

L5.3   *Ministry of Defence v Thompson*
(1993) 25 HLR 552; [1993] 2 EGLR 107; [1993] 40 EG 148, CA

Principles of basis of calculation of mesne profits; rate for occupant of army quarters awaiting rehousing by council is concessionary rate or council rate

An army sergeant and his wife occupied service quarters for which they paid a licence fee of £104 per month. Possession proceedings were brought against the wife after her husband had left home. The trial judge disregarded evidence given by the Ministry of Defence about the market rent and instead calculated the rate of mesne profits by reference to the previous concessionary rent. There was no evidence before the court about what the defendant would have paid had she been rehoused by the local authority.

The Court of Appeal dismissed the Ministry of Defence's appeal. Hoffmann LJ summarised the position as follows:

> First, an owner of land which is occupied without his consent may elect whether to claim damages for the loss which he has been caused or restitution of the value of the benefit which the defendant has received.
>
> Second, the fact that the owner, if he had obtained possession, would have let the premises at a concessionary rent, or even would not have let them at all, is irrelevant to the calculation of the benefit for the purposes of the restitutionary claim. What matters is the benefit which the defendant has received.
>
> Third, a benefit may be worth less to an involuntary recipient than to one who has a free choice as to whether to remain in occupation or move elsewhere.
>
> Where, as in this case, a former licensee has continued to occupy premises because she is awaiting local authority rehousing, the amount of mesne profits would either be the former concessionary rent or the rent which the local authority would charge, whichever is the higher.

L5.4   **Swordheath Properties Ltd v Tabet**

[1979] 1 WLR 285; [1979] 1 All ER 240; (1978) 37 P&CR 327; (1978) 249 EG 439, CA

Measure of damages for trespass is value to trespasser; ordinarily this is letting value

Where a person remains as a trespasser on residential property, the owner is entitled to damages for trespass without bringing evidence that it could or would have let the property to someone else if the trespasser had not been there. The measure of damages is the value to the trespasser of the use of the property. In most cases, that is the ordinary letting value of the property.

L5.5   **Viscount Chelsea v Hutchinson**

(1996) 28 HLR 17; [1994] 43 EG 153, CA

Landlord entitled to mesne profits against former head lessee

It is settled law that forfeiture of a head lease also terminates the interests of any underlessees. In such circumstances, a landlord is entitled to mesne profits by way of damages for being kept out of the property, whether or not the actual lessee is physically present on the premises. A claim for mesne profits against a former head lessee is not undermined by the occupation of parts of a property by underlessees. Following *Swordheath Properties Ltd v Tabet* (L5.4), the Court of Appeal assessed the mesne profits as the letting value of the premises, without the landlord having to prove that the property would have been let if there had been vacant possession.

Possession procedure

M1   **Introduction**

Civil Procedure Rules (CPR) Part 55 applies to all possession claims. It contains one general procedure for claims against tenants, long lessees, mortgagors and trespassers, although there are modifications for claims against different categories of defendants (eg, different claim forms, different methods of service, different times between service and hearing, etc). In addition, there are completely different procedures (albeit within CPR 55) which may be used where landlords claim possession against assured shorthold tenants following service of a Housing Act 1988 s21 notice (the accelerated possession procedure CPR 55 paras 11 to 19) and where land owners seek interim possession orders (IPOs) against trespassers (CPR 55 paras 20 to 28). Any cases on IPOs are included in chapter L.

M2   **Commencement of proceedings**

Court of Appeal

M2.1   *Alamo Housing Co-operative Ltd v Meredith*
[2003] EWCA Civ 495; [2003] HLR 62; [2004] LGR 81; (2003) *Times* 21 April
Landlord had sufficient interest after service of NTQ to evict subtenants

Islington Council, as freehold owner, let certain properties to Alamo, a housing association. Alamo sublet them. The lease between the council and Alamo was for a term of two years but permitted the council to serve notice to determine Alamo's interest 'except for the purpose of enabling eviction if required by the council'. The council served notices to quit on Alamo, which then served notices to quit on the subtenants. After the expiry of the council's notices to quit, Alamo took possession proceedings. The subtenants argued that, when proceedings were commenced, Alamo did not have a sufficient interest in the properties to entitle it to possession as against the subtenants. A district judge gave judgment for Alamo on that preliminary issue. The subtenants appealed.

The appeals were dismissed. The effect of the exception was to confer on Alamo a continuing right to possession for the purpose of evicting the tenants. (See *Manchester Airport v Dutton* (L3.4) and *Countryside Residential (North Thames) Ltd v A Child* (2001) 81 P&CR 10.)

M2.2   *Chesters Accommodation Agency Ltd v Abebrese*
(1997) *Times* 28 July, CA
Agent does not have locus standi to obtain possession order

A managing agent does not have locus standi to obtain a possession order of a property against a tenant. Only a landlord can obtain such an order. The Court of Appeal allowed the tenant's appeal against a possession order.

M2.3   *Patel v Smeaton*
(2000) 24 October, CA
Order set aside where no evidence that court had sent summons to tenant

Landlords' solicitors issued proceedings against an assured shorthold tenant, claiming arrears of rent. They wrote to the court enclosing the summons in triplicate, asking for a sealed copy to be returned to them. The tenant did not appear at the hearing and a forthwith possession order was made. He then applied to set aside the order, claiming that he had not received the summons. The application was dismissed. HHJ Krikler stated that it was 'assumed that if service of court proceedings is the court's job then they will have served the relevant documents to the parties involved'.

The Court of Appeal granted the tenant's appeal and set aside the possession order. On examining the county court file, the Court of Appeal found that it contained the summons in triplicate. The top copy had not been endorsed on the reverse of the first page with any details of service. The computer records of the county court contained no record that the summons had been served. Hale LJ said that, if there is evidence that something has been posted, then it is for the addressee to show that it is not received. However, where there is no evidence that the court has posted a summons, there is no presumption of service. There is no presumption that, if it is the court's job to serve, it has done so. There has to be some record to indicate that the summons has been posted.

High Court

M2.4   *Barnet Primary Care Trust v X*
[2006] EWHC 787 (QB); 6 March 2006

Possession proceedings in High Court appropriate in relation to patient in hospital

The defendant was admitted to Finchley Memorial Hospital as an in-patient in December 2002. By March 2006 he had three medical problems, namely, severe chronic obstructive pulmonary disease (which was stable and did not significantly impair his activities of daily living), hernias (which were extremely large and caused discomfort) and a left foot drop (which was helped by a foot splint). However, he required no treatment by trained medical staff and was generally capable of taking care of himself. The hospital sought to facilitate the orderly discharge of the patient to an alternative setting where there would be an appropriate social package of care which would meet his needs. Three residential homes indicated that they were willing to take him. However, the patient refused to leave hospital. The Primary Care Trust took possession proceedings in the High Court. The defendant did not acknowledge the proceedings, produce any evidence or argument against the claimant's case, or appear in court.

Wilkie J indicated that the claimants were right to bring proceedings in the High Court 'given the sensitivities involved'. He granted a declaration that the patient was not entitled to occupy his bed in the ward or any other part of the hospital and made a possession order.

County courts

M2.5   *Birmingham CC v Hosey*
December 2002 *Legal Action* 20; 2 October 2002, Birmingham County Court

Statement of truth required to be signed not merely rubber stamped

The claimant brought a possession claim based on arrears of rent. The statement of truth in the claim form was not signed personally by anyone on behalf of the claimant. It bore the rubber stamp of a signature of a Mr Tatlow, an employee in Birmingham's legal services department. He had no personal knowledge of the case. He never saw the papers. He never checked the facts nor read any of the source documents. He merely authorised more junior employees, who applied the rubber stamp to the paper. District Judge O'Regan found that the statement of truth had not been signed within the meaning of CPR 22.1 and adjourned the claim to enable the defect to be remedied. Birmingham appealed.

HHJ MacDuff QC dismissed the appeal. The requirement in CPR 22.1(a) for the statement of case to be signed was not a mere technicality or a matter of form. Courts need to be able to rely on documents bearing statements of truth. It is essential that statements of case should be properly verified. The statement of truth had not been signed. CPR 5.3, which allows a document to be signed by 'printing or other technical means', did not apply because the statement of truth was not a document but rather a statement in a document.

M2.6   *Camden LBC v M*
29 July 2005, Central London Civil Justice Centre
Possession orders set aside due to tenant's incapacity

Camden issued possession proceedings against a secure tenant in July 2004 based on arrears of £540.78, which related entirely to non-payment of water and gas charges. The defendant refused to pay because he had found cheaper providers. The defendant did not attend the hearing and Camden obtained an outright possession order. Later, the order was varied to a suspended order. The defendant breached the suspended order. He was evicted in March 2005. A certificate of incapacity was obtained. It concluded that the defendant had had a mental disorder since April 2003. The Official Solicitor was instructed on his behalf. He applied to set aside the possession orders and for re-entry for the defendant on the basis that the orders were without effect as the defendant had no litigation friend when they were made (CPR 21.3(4)). Documentation showed that, from at least October 2004, Camden was concerned that the defendant had underlying mental health problems. He had been banned from writing more than one letter per week to the council. There were records of phone calls which he had made which were not rational. Records also showed that the police and neighbours considered that he had mental health problems

HHJ Medawar QC set aside the possession orders. The evidence drove him to conclude that the defendant's incapacity probably flowed from April 2003 but at least from the start of 2004.

M3   **Adjournments**

Court of Appeal

M3.1   *Bates v Croydon LBC*
[2001] EWCA Civ 134; (2001) 33 HLR 792, CA
Wrong to refuse adjournment to allow tenant to obtain legal aid and representation

In September 1999, the council issued possession proceedings against Ms Bates, relying on 53 allegations of nuisance to neighbours. She sought legal aid but her application was initially refused owing to insufficient information. She made a further application. At an interlocutory hearing in February 2000, she applied for an adjournment because her legal aid entitlement had not been determined. That application was refused and the substantive hearing date set. That hearing date was, however, moved forward, with the result that Ms Bates was given three days to read witness statements produced by the council and to prepare for the hearing. She disclosed witness statements from herself and her brother, which questioned the credibility of the council's witnesses. At the substantive hearing, she represented herself and a possession order was made. She appealed to a circuit judge, but that appeal was dismissed because the judge concluded that Ms Bates did not have a reasonable prospect of successfully defending the claim.

Ms Bates appealed successfully to the Court of Appeal, which held that it was a case in which legal representation would have been of a considerable benefit in relation to, among other things, cross-examination. The case turned essentially on the credibility of witnesses. Ms Bates had been put on very short notice to deal with the documentation, exhibits and witness statements. She was required to respond in writing to lengthy details and then conduct her own case in person. While the court accepted the desirability of conducting litigation with proper dispatch, and was reluctant to review interlocutory decisions of district judges, the decision reached in this case was wrong. An adjournment was appropriate for Ms Bates to finalise her legal aid application and enable her to be represented.

M3.2 **Brent LBC v Aniedobe**

September 1997 *Legal Action* 13, CA

Wrong to give landlord permission to rely on evidence produced at hearing without granting tenant adjournment

The council sought possession on the basis that the tenant was not occupying his home in London NW6 as his only or principal home (as required in order to preserve secure status by Housing Act 1985 s81 – see section C3) but was in fact living in London NW10. At the hearing, it produced and was given leave to rely on, documentary evidence not previously disclosed to the tenant. The judge granted possession.

The Court of Appeal allowed the tenant's appeal and ordered a rehearing. The tenant had clearly been taken by surprise by the new material and had no opportunity to muster evidence in rebuttal. If the trial judge was properly to admit the material, he should have at least granted the adjournment that the tenant had requested.

M3.3 **Kingscastle Ltd v Owen-Owen**

(1999) *Times* 18 March, CA

Court can adjourn case pending the outcome of an appeal in another case

A recorder adjourned possession proceedings pending the outcome of the appeal to the House of Lords in *Fitzpatrick v Sterling HA* (E16.2).

The Court of Appeal dismissed the landlord's appeal. A court can in appropriate cases adjourn pending the outcome of an appeal provided that it correctly exercises its discretion and takes into account prejudice to both parties. CCR Ord 13 r3 gave the court a complete discretion.

Note: See now CPR 3.1(2)(b)

M3.4   *North British Housing Association Limited v Matthews*

[2004] EWCA Civ 1736; [2005] 1 WLR 3133; [2005] 2 All ER 667; [2005] HLR 17; [2005] CP Rep 16; (2005) *Times* 11 January (see G4.7)

Court cannot adjourn Ground 8 claim to allow tenant to pay arrears unless exceptional circumstances

M3.5   *Spitaliotis v Morgan*

[1986] 1 EGLR 50, CA

No adjournment granted for landlord to adduce evidence in rebuttal of tenant's evidence where evidence had not taken landlord by surprise

The landlord brought possession proceedings, claiming that the tenant had abandoned the premises and that he had assigned or sublet in breach of the terms of the tenancy agreement and without the landlord's consent. At the hearing the original tenant gave evidence that the agent of the previous landlord had agreed to the transfer of the tenancy to the current occupants. Counsel for the landlord applied for an adjournment to call the previous landlord's agent. The application was refused and the claim for possession dismissed.

The Court of Appeal, following *Ladd v Marshall* [1954] 1 WLR 1489, CA, held that the landlord had not been taken by surprise by the tenant's evidence and that the landlord's solicitors should have arranged for the former agent to be present at court. Accordingly, the landlord's appeal was dismissed.

M3.6   *Verrilli v Idigoras*

[1990] EGCS 3, CA

Possession order set aside where tenant unrepresented and spoke little English

A landlord brought possession proceedings against a tenant, who was Spanish and spoke little English, alleging arrears of £912. Although the tenant consulted solicitors, he was not represented at the hearing because his solicitor was ill. The tenant's request for an adjournment was refused and a possession order made. The tenant appealed, submitting that the assistant recorder should have granted an adjournment and did not consider reasonableness.

In the Court of Appeal, Sir Roualeyn Cumming-Bruce said that he was satisfied that there was a miscarriage of justice and that, if the judge had understood what the real circumstances were, he would have granted an adjournment unhesitatingly. The possession order was set aside and a new trial ordered.

High Court

M3.7   *Birmingham Citizens Permanent Building Society v Caunt*
[1962] Ch 883; [1962] 2 WLR 323; [1962] 1 All ER 163, ChD (see R2.24)

Limited power to adjourn mortgage possession proceedings pre-Administration of Justice Act

M3.8   *R v A Circuit Judge (sitting at Norwich County Court) ex p Wathen*
(1976) 33 P&CR 423, QBD

If landlord establishes a claim for forfeiture, the judge should proceed forthwith to judgment, although it might be permissible to adjourn once for arrears to be paid

A lessor brought county court proceedings seeking forfeiture of a lease granted for a term of 25 years, on the ground of rent arrears. At the initial hearing on 2 October 1975, the lessee admitted the arrears. The lessee did not defend the proceedings or seek an adjournment. However, the judge, of his own motion and without the plaintiffs' consent, adjourned the proceedings generally because the defendant had an expectancy of receiving money under a trust. The plaintiffs restored the hearing on 4 December 1975 and the judge, again of his own motion and without the plaintiffs' consent, adjourned to 6 February 1976. The landlords sought an order of mandamus requiring the judge to hear and determine the case.

The court held that, in view of the word 'shall' in County Courts Act 1959 s191(1)(b) (now County Courts Act 1984 s138(3)), if a plaintiff establishes a claim for forfeiture, the judge should proceed forthwith to judgment for the plaintiff. However, Watkins J added:

> Despite what I have just said, I do not believe that a judge can inevitably be criticised for not proceeding to judgment forthwith, for example, on the first occasion when the matter comes before him if something of real materiality remains uncertain as a matter of evidence. To adjourn a case on virtually the same ground again is, however, I think, impermissible.

However, the court thought it unnecessary to grant an order of mandamus.

M4   **Representation**

County courts

M4.1   *Hackney LBC v Spring*
January 2007 *Legal Action* 23; 18 September 2006, Clerkenwell and Shoreditch County Court

Exercise of power to allow lay representation in rent arrears possession cases

Hackney LBC, 'a very busy housing authority', brings at least 3,000 possession claims each year in Clerkenwell and Shoreditch County Court. In late 1998, as a cost saving exercise, it began developing the practice of housing officers presenting cases to the court without the use of solicitors. Between 1999 and 2004, the council entered into housing management contracts. The effect of these contracts was effectively to pass the housing management role, and in particular key responsibility for arrears recovery, to 'housing partner organisations'. In 2006, Hackney's housing directorate became Hackney Homes Ltd, an arm's length management organisation (ALMO), which was a 'not for profit' organisation wholly owned by Hackney LBC. This change offered opportunities for increased central government funding which were not available to local government. The result was to transfer the housing management role from the council to Hackney Homes, including all matters relating to possession claims and the responsibility for presenting cases in court. Hackney sought permission under the Courts and Legal Services Act 1990 for employees of Hackney Homes, their agents, or employees of sub-contractors to appear in rent arrears possession cases without instructing lawyers.

After considering Courts and Legal Services Act (CLSA) 1990 s11 (the Lord Chancellor's power to allow lay representation in rent possession cases which has not been exercised) and s27, Local Government Act 1972 s223, County Courts Act 1984 s60(2) and *Paragon Finance plc v Noueiri*, [2001] EWCA Civ 1402, HHJ Mitchell noted that employees of the ALMO and employees of the ALMO's partners were not employees of the local authority. Furthermore, although Hackney Homes was wholly owned by Hackney LBC, it was a separate legal entity. In addition, although a local authority may in fact authorise people to act on its behalf, it cannot delegate the power to authorise to people who are not employed by it. He held that the right of audience given by s60(2) can 'exist only as granted within the terms of the statute and, in my judgment, does not extend to other bodies who take over housing functions from the local authority'. It followed that any rights of audience could only result from the court exercising its discretion under CLSA s27(2)(c). In exercising that discretion, HHJ Mitchell stated that it is for the court to decide whether or not to allow an individual to represent a body. It is not for the other party to consent. It is also 'for the court to assess the competence and probity of the person they are authorising ... [T]here must be exceptional circumstances justifying the grant of a right of audience and it is not a right to be given lightly ... In my judgment, there is no good reason and no exceptional reason why this authorisation should be given, and very good reasons for not giving it.' Hackney LBC subsequently obtained an opinion from leading counsel on whether or not to appeal, but decided not to.

M5   # Possession orders and enforcement

Court of Appeal

M5.1   *Boyland & Sons Ltd v Rand*
[2006] EWCA Civ 1860; [2007] HLR 24; (2007) *Times* 18 January

Housing Act 1980 s89 does not give squatters additional rights to postpone possession

The defendant travellers moved on to a site owned by the claimants without permission. They were accordingly trespassers. A possession order was subsequently made. The defendants' application to postpone the date for possession was refused. They appealed, contending that, although previous authorities stated that trespassers could not be given time to vacate by the court unless the land owner agreed, different considerations applied under Housing Act 1980 s89. The application was dismissed and the defendants appealed.

The Court of Appeal refused permission to appeal. Section 89 does not create a free-standing power to postpone the date of possession. The purpose of s89 is to provide a statutory time limit to the extent of courts' common-law discretion to postpone possession. Section 89 was not intended to grant squatters rights which they did not previously have. Although this is a decision on permission, and therefore not otherwise citable under the Practice Direction (Citation of Authorities) 2001 [2001] 1 WLR 1001, the Court of Appeal made an express statement under para.6.1 of the Practice Direction that the decision is capable of being cited.

M5.2   *Bristol & West Investments plc v Tompkins*
[2006] EWCA Civ 977; 26 June 2006

Committal for contempt where cattle not removed from land in accordance with order

Bristol and West were mortgagees of farmland. After lengthy possession proceedings, HHJ Harris QC ordered Mr Tomkins to remove 60 head of cattle from the farmland. He refused to do this or hand over the necessary documentation or 'passports' which would enable their sale. Without the passports, the only option on the removal of the cattle was for their slaughter, under licence. The judge made a further order committing Mr Tomkins to prison for 28 days for contempt of court unless he removed the cattle by a specified date. Mr Tomkins appealed.

The Court of Appeal dismissed his appeal as 'hopeless'. He had failed to comply with the conditions in the committal order and had taken no steps to correct the matter which had led the judge to commit him.

M5.3   *De Grey v Ford*
[2005] EWCA Civ 1223; 30 September 2005

Committal for failure to comply with possession order appropriate in exceptional cases

The claimants obtained a possession order. They attempted to execute a warrant of possession but the bailiffs did not obtain possession. A further copy of the possession order, now with a penal notice attached, was served. The defendants remained in possession and, as a result, the claimants applied for a committal order. The judge found that the defendants had been in flagrant breach of the terms of the possession order, had understood the penal notice and by their conduct had indicated their intention not to leave at any cost. A suspended committal order for 28 days was made.

The Court of Appeal dismissed the defendants' appeal. Following *Bell v Tuohy* [2002] EWCA Civ 423; [2002] 3 All ER 975, committal for failure to comply with a possession order can be ordered in exceptional cases where the court is left with little alternative but to commit a defendant to prison simply for the purpose of enabling the court's order to be executed effectively and peacefully. The defendants were in continuing contumelious breach of the court's order. Faced with their continuous and resolute defiance of the possession order, the judge was plainly justified in making a committal order and the suspended order was a merciful one. There was no basis for the appeal.

M5.4   *R v Wandsworth County Court ex p Wandsworth LBC*
[1975] 1 WLR 1314; [1975] 3 All ER 390; (1975) 74 LGR 62, CA

Bailiffs executing warrant for possession can evict anyone on premises
Possession proceedings were brought against squatters under CCR Ord 26. After the possession order was made, the original squatters moved out and a new squatter moved in. The registrar directed the bailiffs not to execute the warrant and to wait until new proceedings were issued.

The Court of Appeal held that the registrar's direction was wrong. Bailiffs or sheriffs executing a warrant for possession can evict anyone they find on premises, even if that person was not a party to the possession proceedings or moved in after the order was made.

M5.5   *Trustee in Bankruptcy of Canty v Canty*
[2007] EWCA Civ 241; 5 March 2007

Imprisonment for six months where defendant failed to vacate premises after possession order with penal notice attached

The trustee in bankruptcy obtained a possession order in respect of a property owned by the defendant and his mother. They appealed unsuccessfully. After the defendant's mother died, the trustee in bankruptcy sought to enforce the order. The defendant refused to comply. He left the property, but occupied the roof. The possession order was amended to include a penal notice, and, when the defendant remained on the roof, he was committed for contempt of court, and sentenced to an immediate term of six months' imprisonment. He appealed.

The appeal was dismissed. It was clear that the defendant was in breach of the possession order, as well as various obligations arising under the Insolvency Act 1986, including ss312, 333 and 363. It was a wilful and deliberate breach, motivated by a belief that the possession and bankruptcy orders should not have been made, and that he should not have to comply with them. There was no point in any order other than an immediate custodial sentence. In the circumstances, a sentence of six months' imprisonment was not manifestly excessive. The defendant's appeal was totally without merit.

M5.6   *Tuohy v Bell*
[2002] EWCA Civ 423; [2002] 1 WLR 2783; [2002] 3 All ER 975

Warrant issued prior to date of possession a nullity; Failure to comply with order for possession contempt

Mr Bell was the trustee in bankruptcy for Mr and Mrs Tuohy. In July 2001 he obtained an order for the sale of their matrimonial home, with possession to be given by 11 October 2001. He obtained a warrant for possession in August 2001 and the bailiff tried to execute it on 15 October 2001 but Mr and Mrs Tuohy refused to leave. Mr Bell applied for them to be committed to prison. The application was heard on 22 October 2001. By that time Mrs Tuohy had left. The hearing was adjourned to 5 November 2001 to enable Mr Tuohy to obtain legal representation. At the adjourned hearing, Mr Tuohy was committed to prison for seven days because he had failed to comply with the possession order, had impeded the bailiff, and had told the judge that he had no intention of complying with the possession order. The committal was made despite the lack of a penal notice on the possession order. Mr Tuohy appealed unsuccessfully.

The Court of Appeal held that a warrant cannot be issued before the date on which it is ordered that possession be given. If a warrant is issued in such circumstances, it is a nullity. Accordingly, Mr Tuohy could not be guilty of contempt in refusing to comply with it. However, the failure to comply with the order for possession meant that he was prima facie guilty of contempt of court. As he had said that he would not give up possession, the judge was not wrong to imprison him because it was the only way that the court's order could be executed effectively and peacefully. Although there were procedural defects in the application to commit, there was no prejudice to Mr Tuohy because the judge had warned him in clear and uncertain terms of the possible consequences of failure to comply with the order.

High Court

M5.7   *Anchor HA v Person Unknown*
October 2002 *Legal Action* 29; 28 June 2002, QBD

Where vacant possession obtained and premises subsequently reoccupied by persons with no connection to original unlawful occupants; owner cannot merely enforce writ

The claimant was the owner of an empty property formerly used as an old people's home. The property was squatted in 2001 by persons unknown. The claimant obtained a possession order under RSC Ord 113 on 24 May 2001. A warrant for possession was issued on 1 June 2001. The warrant was never executed because the squatters vacated the property before execution. The claimant obtained vacant possession and secured the property. The property was squatted again in February 2002. It was agreed that this group of squatters had no connection with the previous squatters. The claimant sought to execute the writ for possession. One of the squatters applied to set aside the writ for possession. District Judge Exton dismissed his application and extended the writ for possession to 1 June 2003, holding that *R v Wandsworth County Court ex p Wandsworth LBC* (M5.4) was authority for the proposition that the bailiff was entitled to evict anyone on the premises even though that person was not a party to the proceedings. She decided that the fact that the claimant had obtained vacant possession of the property did not curtail its right to use the writ.

On appeal, HHJ Weekes QC, sitting as a High Court judge, set aside the order. He held that where vacant possession has been obtained and a property is subsequently reoccupied by persons with no connection to the original unlawful occupants, the remedy available to the owner is to bring fresh possession proceedings, not enforcement of a writ. The important dividing line was the recovery of possession by the claimant.

M5.8   *Hackney LBC v Side by Side (Kids) Ltd*

[2003] EWHC 1813 (QBD); [2004] 1 WLR 363; [2004] 2 All ER 373; (2003) *Times* 5 August

Housing Act 1980 s89 applied to High Court and to consent orders

The defendant charity operated a nursery for mentally handicapped children. The council sought possession of the site. The parties agreed a consent order that the charity would give up possession in return for the grant of an alternative site. However, the council could not make the new site fit and as a result the charity refused to give up possession of the existing site. A deputy master stayed execution of Hackney's writ of possession and the council appealed.

Stanley Burnton J held that Housing Act 1980 s89 applies as much to orders made in the High Court as to those made in the county court. The decision of Harman J in *Bain and Co v Church Commissioners for England* [1989] 1 WLR 24, ChD that a 'a court' meant 'a county court' was clearly wrong. Furthermore, the general words of s89 'did not permit him to find that it did not apply to consent orders'. The deputy master did not have jurisdiction to make the consent order staying execution of the writ.

M5.9   *Polarpark Enterprises Inc v Allason*

[2007] EWHC (Ch) 1088; (2007) *Times* 26 June; 18 April 2007

PEA 1977 requires proceedings for possession to be taken in county court

In 1980, Polarpark became the owner of a property pursuant to a tax saving scheme under which its shares were held by the trustees of a discretionary settlement. The main beneficiaries were Mr and Mrs Allason's children. Mr and Mrs Allason used the property as licensees as one of their homes with the oral permission of the trustees until they divorced in 1996. Mrs Allason then left the property, but Mr Allason remained there. The trustees gave notice to quit and obtained a possession order in the High Court (CPR 55.3(2), 55.5 and 55.8). Subsequently, Briggs J made an order by which he permitted the claimants to issue a writ of possession. Mr Allason then made an application under CPR 3.1(7) for that part of the order to be revoked on the ground that it had been made without jurisdiction. He relied on County Courts Act 1984 s21 which gives the county court jurisdiction in relation to claims for possession, Protection from Eviction Act 1977 (PEA) s3 which makes it unlawful in such circumstances to enforce a right to recover possession otherwise than by proceedings in court and PEA s9(1) which provides that for the purposes of PEA Part I, 'the court' means the county court.

Briggs J granted the application and found that his earlier order had been made without jurisdiction. Mr Allason's contention was not an abuse of process. The licence granted to Mrs Allason was for money's worth. The quid pro quo for the licence was that Mrs Allason would keep the premises repaired and insured. In those circumstances, Mr Allason was in lawful occupation when the licence was terminated. As it was not an excluded licence, ss3 and 9(1) applied. Briggs J transferred the action to the county court for enforcement.

M5.10 *Six Arlington Street Investments v Persons Unknown*
[1987] 1 WLR 188; [1987] 1 All ER 474, ChD

Sheriff not required to evict trespassers 'at once'

After obtaining an order for possession, landowners sought an injunction against the Sheriff for Greater London to compel him to evict trespassers 'forthwith'.

Knox J refused to issue an injunction, stating that the sheriff's duty on receiving a writ of possession was to enforce it 'as soon as was reasonably practicable', not 'at once'.

M5.11 *Wiltshire CC v Frazer (No 2)*
[1986] 1 WLR 108; [1986] 1 All ER 65; (1986) 52 P&CR 46, QBD

Writ of restitution where close nexus between current and past occupiers

In 1983 the plaintiffs obtained orders for possession against a number of named defendant trespassers. Executing the order, the sheriff gained possession of the premises. Over the next two years, groups of trespassers, including some of the original defendants, returned to the site. The landowners applied for a writ of restitution.

On appeal, Simon Brown J found that:

> ... the picture here is one of a cohesive group of nomadic, gypsy-like squatters who are ready to flout the orders of the Court and who habitually live unlawfully on the property of others, moving from one parcel of land to another as and when they are evicted. ([1986] 1 All ER at 66)

He held that a writ of restitution could be issued even though some of the current occupiers of the land were not among the original defendants, because there was a 'close nexus' between the current occupiers and the trespassers who were dispossessed in the 1983 action. In reality, the current occupation was 'part and parcel of the same transaction'. (The effect of a writ of restitution is to enable the sheriff to evict again without the landowners issuing new proceedings.)

M6 # Costs

Court of Appeal

M6.1 *Church Commissioners for England v Ibrahim*
[1997] 1 EGLR 13, CA

Party not to be deprived of contractual right to indemnity costs unless good reason

An assured shorthold tenancy included a clause that the tenant would 'pay and compensate the landlords fully for any costs, expense, loss or damage incurred or suffered by the landlords as a consequence of any breach of the agreements on the part of the tenant in this agreement'. After the tenant had fallen into arrears with the rent, the landlords obtained a possession order. Relying on the terms of the tenancy agreement, they sought costs on an indemnity basis. However, they were only awarded costs to be taxed on Scale 1. They appealed.

Allowing their appeal, the Court of Appeal held that the principles set out in *Gomba Holdings (UK) Ltd v Minories Finance Ltd (No 2)* (R6.1) are not confined to mortgage cases. Although the award of costs is always a discretionary order, a party is not to be deprived of a contractual right to costs unless there is a good reason to do so. The mere fact that it was a straightforward possession action was not a good reason. Similarly, the bargaining strength of the landlord did not justify departing from the contractual basis for taxation. The plaintiffs were entitled to an order for costs on Scale 2, to be taxed on an indemnity basis.

Note: See, however, the dicta of Lord Templeman in *Billson v Residential Apartments Ltd* (N3.1) where he indicated that the practice of awarding indemnity costs as a condition of granting relief was ripe for reconsideration. See now CPR 48.3 and section 50 of the Costs Practice Direction.

M6.2   ## Contractreal Ltd v Davies
[2001] EWCA Civ 928; 17 May 2001, CA

Assessment of costs too low

The claimant landlord and the defendant long lessee entered into a consent order which provided that the defendant owed service charges of £5,459.72. However, the parties could not agree costs. The claimants sought costs of £21,388.57. HHJ Poulton held that it was inappropriate for the claimant to have issued forfeiture proceedings and that as cheques totalling slightly over £2,200 had been tendered but not cashed, they could simply have issued a small claim for the money outstanding. He assessed costs summarily in the sum of £1,000.

The claimants appealed. The Court of Appeal rejected the claimant's contention that the judge had been wrong to assess costs summarily and accepted that summary assessment is a 'relatively rough and ready process'. However, the judge had been wrong to fail to draw a distinction between costs incurred before and after 26 April 1999. Second, he had been wrong to state that the landlord could have recovered the sums due via county court small claims arbitration, since at the time the maximum limit was £3,000. Third, the amount assessed for costs was far too low. The Court of Appeal set aside the summary assessment and ordered a detailed assessment on the standard basis.

M6.3   ## Hackney LBC v Campbell
[2005] EWCA Civ 613; 28 April 2005

Defendant's costs where he had failed on all but one claim inappropriate

Hackney claimed possession of a flat against a tenant and her son. The tenant defended and counterclaimed, saying that she had exercised her right to buy. Her son made a number of counterclaims, including the right to buy, and alleging nuisance, breach of repairing covenants, trespass and human rights violations. The trial judge dismissed Hackney's possession claim and upheld the counterclaim in respect of the tenant's right to buy. He dismissed all of the son's counterclaims except the one relating to the right to buy. He ordered Hackney to pay the costs of both defendants. Hackney appealed.

The Court of Appeal allowed the appeal. The judge had failed to follow the basic rule in CPR 44.3 that costs should follow the event. He appeared to have treated the tenant and the son as if they were in the same legal position. The son had failed to establish the right to buy and failed on all but one of the claims raised in his counterclaim. The right course was to set aside the judge's order and exercise the discretion afresh. The appropriate order was that there be no order as to costs on the son's defence and counterclaim.

M7 Appeals

The procedure for appeals is now set out in CPR Part 52.

Court of Appeal

M7.1 *Alamo Housing Co-operative Ltd v O'Daly and Thompson*
[2004] EWCA Civ 1583; 5 November 2004

Extension of time to appeal refused where not case of ignorance or oversight

A district judge made a possession order on 26 February 2004. Time to appeal expired on 13 March 2004. The defendants deliberately decided not to appeal, because, at that time, they believed that they would be rehoused through a scheme being propounded by Solon, a registered social landlord, and that any appeal might prejudice that scheme. However, the Solon scheme foundered. As a result, the defendants filed notices of appeal on 10 May 2004, some two months out of time, and sought extensions of time.

The Court of Appeal refused to grant extensions of time. First, there was no suggestion that the particular questions raised by the case were of any general importance. Second, a decision would not bind any person other than the parties to the proceedings and, for one of the defendants, the case was of academic interest only since he was guaranteed rehousing. Furthermore, when considering the factors that have to be taken into account on an application for relief from sanctions (CPR 3.9), the failure to comply with the time limit was intentional and there was no good explanation for the failure. It was not a case of ignorance or oversight.

M7.2 *Ealing LBC v Richardson*
[2005] EWCA Civ 1798; [2006] HLR 13; [2006] CP Rep 19; (2005) 14 *Times* December

To justify a rehearing some injustice is necessary; in this case, no injustice – judge's decision to suspend generous but not outside ambit of her discretion

Ms Richardson was a secure tenant. Substantial rent arrears accrued. Ealing obtained a possession order and then made eight applications for execution of the order. On each occasion Ms Richardson successfully applied to suspend. The rent arrears again increased and a further warrant of execution was obtained. Ms Richardson again applied for suspension of the warrant. District Judge Allen suspended on terms that Ms Richardson paid £588 by the end of the day and £10 per week to reduce her rent arrears. Ealing appealed and sought to have a rehearing on the ground that the court file, giving details of all the previous proceedings, had not been before the district judge. HHJ Oppenheimer reheard the matter and set aside the suspension. Ms Richardson appealed, contending that the judge had been wrong to order a rehearing.

The Court of Appeal allowed Ms Richardson's appeal. When allowing the rehearing the judge had not considered CPR 52.11(1)(b). A rehearing is the exception to the general rule that an appeal is limited to a review of the decision of the lower court. To justify a rehearing some injustice has to have occurred. In this case there was no injustice in the way that the district judge handled the case and no injustice that compelled a rehearing. At the rehearing the judge concentrated solely on the history of the matter. However, an application to suspend a warrant should involve inquiries into various matters, including whether payments to reduce arrears can be maintained. Whilst the district judge's decision was very generous, it was not outside the ambit of her discretion. Accordingly, the decision of the district judge was restored.

M7.3   **Law Land v Sinclair**
(1992) 24 HLR 57, CA

Striking out of appeals confined to clear cases where notice of appeal hopeless

The landlord respondent made an application to strike out the tenant's appeal against a possession order based on the availability of suitable alternative accommodation, on the ground that it was frivolous and vexatious. Refusing the landlord's application, Purchas LJ stated:

> I find it difficult to see how an attack on the discretion of a judge in the special circumstances of Schedule 15 cases under section 98 of the Rent Act 1977 can be vexatious or an abuse of the court. I consider this regardless of whether there is a good chance of success.

Butler-Sloss LJ confirmed that the striking out of appeals should be confined to 'clear obvious cases' where the notice of appeal is 'frivolous, unarguable or hopeless'.

M7.4   **Moat Housing Group South Ltd v Harris and Hartless**
[2004] EWCA Civ 1852; (2005) *Times* 13 January

Stay pending appeal ordered having regard to the potential prejudice to the parties

Ms Hartless was an assured tenant of rented premises where she lived with her four children aged six to 14. Mr Harris was the children's father and, although separated from Ms Hartless, was deeply involved in his children's lives. The claimants brought possession proceedings after a history of neighbour disputes. On 3 December 2004 HHJ Thompson QC made an order for possession with the effect that Ms Hartless and the four children had to leave their home by 4 pm on 17 December. He also made an ASBO excluding Ms Hartless and Mr Harris from properties owned by the claimant and a wide area of their home town. The defendants appealed and sought a stay.

The Court of Appeal granted the stay. Brooke LJ stated that the court had to look at the reasonableness of the process by which it was considered appropriate to make a possession order 'effectively abandoning four young children' where there appeared to have been no previous discussion between their social landlord and the relevant education authorities. Regard had to be had to the potential prejudice to the parties and in particular

- if the stay were to be refused, the risk of the appeal being stifled;
- if the stay were granted and the appeal failed, the risk that the landlord would be unable to enforce the judgment; and
- if the stay were refused and the appeal succeeded, but the judgment was enforced in the meantime, the risks to the family.

The risk to the family, especially the young children, and practical matters such as the children's schooling and the risk that the defendants might end up in bed and breakfast in another town, led to the conclusion that a stay should be granted pending the hearing of the appeal. The stay was granted on terms, including undertakings that the defendants must use their best endeavours to control the children.

M7.5   *Taj v Ali (No 2)*
(2001) 33 HLR 259, CA

Application to suspend possession refused where tenant only took matter seriously after Court of Appeal made outright order; new material not sufficiently unexpected

At an earlier hearing the Court of Appeal allowed the landlord's appeal against a suspended possession order and substituted a 28-day outright order (*Taj v Ali (No 1)* (H3.13)). The day before the order was due to take effect the tenant applied to the Court of Appeal, seeking to suspend the possession order and produced new evidence that he could pay money regularly towards the arrears. Although not formally deciding the issue, Robert Walker LJ considered that the Court of Appeal probably has a residual power to review an unexecuted order for possession which it has made, just as a lower court would under Rent Act 1977 s100(2). However, he did not wish to encourage repeated applications to stave off the execution of possession orders and indicated that the power should 'be exercised only if there is some unexpected and significant change in circumstances of which the Court of Appeal has proper evidence ... It may be that the rule as to the admission of new evidence in *Ladd v Marshall* [1954] 1 WLR 1489, no longer strictly applies. But, under the new procedure also, the court will always be reluctant to look at new and late evidence and inquire as to why it was not produced before'.

Robert Walker LJ dismissed the defendant's application. Although the court 'is always extremely reluctant to see possession orders executed if the result is that disadvantaged persons are evicted and a new problem is created for hard-pressed housing departments', it 'was only when the Court of Appeal made an almost immediate order for possession that the tenant took this matter seriously and cast about to consider whether it was possible to put forward proposals for the arrears of rent to be paid off within a reasonable time ... the new material put forward does not amount to anything sufficiently new or unexpected for it to be appropriate for this court to reopen the matter and to exercise its discretion afresh'.

High Court

M7.6   *R (Mills) v Airways Housing Society Ltd*
[2005] EWHC 328 (Admin); 14 January 2005

Judicial review of decision to bring possession proceedings refused; county court could take into account allegations that proceedings contrary to regulatory guidance

Ms Mills was an assured tenant, renting from Airways. After allegations of anti-social behaviour, Airways, a registered social landlord, claimed possession under Housing Act 1988 Sch 2 Grounds 12 and 14. A defence was filed and witness statements were due to be exchanged. However, the claimant sought judicial review of the decision to bring the possession claim, alleging that Airways was a public body for the purposes of judicial review and that the institution of the possession proceedings was unlawful. Collins J refused permission on the papers, stating that 'whether or not the defendant is a public body is indeed arguable, but in the context of this case, the argument is academic ... There is a dispute of fact which can be resolved in the county court and cannot be resolved in the Administrative Court.'

Bennett J also refused permission on a renewed application to bring judicial review proceedings. Collins J's decision was correct. The county court proceedings were well advanced. Issues of fact can be explored in the county court, but not in the Administrative Court. A county court judge would be able to take into account allegations that the institution of proceedings might have been unlawful and contrary to regulatory guidance when considering the issue of reasonableness. Judicial review proceedings would be completely otiose.

Termination of tenancies at common law

Introduction

Before a landlord can succeed in obtaining a possession order against an unprotected tenant or any kind of Rent Act protected tenant, the original contractual tenancy must be terminated.

Notices to quit

A notice to quit must comply with the statutory requirements of the Protection from Eviction Act 1977 s5, common-law requirements and any contractual requirements.

House of Lords

N2.1 ### Hammersmith and Fulham LBC v Monk

[1992] 1 AC 478; [1991] 3 WLR 1144; [1992] 1 All ER 1; (1992) 24 HLR 207; (1991) 63 P&CR 373; [1992] 1 EGLR 65; (1992) 90 LGR 30; [1992] 09 EG 135, HL (see F4.1)

Service of NTQ by one joint tenant terminates tenancy

N2.2 ### Harrow LBC v Johnstone

[1997] 1 WLR 459; [1997] 1 All ER 929; (1997) 29 HLR 475; (1997) 95 LGR 470, HL (see F4.2)

NTQ by one joint tenant terminates tenancy despite court order restraining that tenant from excluding the other tenant from the premises

N2.3 ### Mannai Investment Co Ltd v Eagle Star Life Assurance Co Ltd

[1997] AC 749; [1997] 2 WLR 945; [1997] 3 All ER 352; [1997] 1 EGLR 57; [1997] 25 EG 138, HL

Where date one day out, valid; reasonable recipient test applied

A ten-year fixed-term tenancy allowed the tenant to terminate by giving six months' notice expiring on 13 January 1995. The tenant gave notice expiring on 12 January 1995.

The House of Lords held that the notice was effective in determining the tenancy. Looked at objectively, a reasonable recipient with knowledge of the terms of the lease would have been in no doubt that the tenant wished to determine the lease on 13 January, but had wrongly described it as 12 January. The House of Lords approved the test applied in *Carradine Properties Ltd v Aslam* (N2.24).

Court of Appeal

N2.4 ### Addis v Burrows

[1948] 1 KB 444; [1948] 1 All ER 177, CA

NTQ valid despite not giving date, as date could be ascertained by tenant

A landlord served a notice 'to quit and deliver up at the expiration of your tenancy which will expire next after the end of one half year from the service of this notice ...' The Court of Appeal held that the notice was valid. Landlords have a duty:

> ... to give notices in terms which are sufficiently clear and unambiguous in that the right date is either stated or can be ascertained by the tenant

by reference to his tenancy agreement with the terms of which he must be taken to be familiar. ([1948] 1 All ER 177 at 182)

N2.5 *Beckerman v Durling*

(1981) 6 HLR 87, CA

Notice valid despite old prescribed form being used

A landlord served a notice to quit in the form prescribed by the Notices to Quit (Prescribed Information) Regulations 1975 SI No 2196 after the Notices to Quit (Prescribed Information) Regulations 1980 SI No 1624 had come into force.

The Court of Appeal held that since, on the tenant's admission, in substance all the information required by the 1980 regulations was contained in the notice, it was valid. It was not necessary that the precise form of wording of the 1980 Regulations should be set out. See also *Swansea CC v Hearn* (N2.20).

N2.6 *Blunden v Frogmore Investments Ltd*

[2002] EWCA Civ 573; [2002] 2 All ER 668; [2002] L&TR 31; [2002] 29 EG 153

Service by post good despite not coming to recipient's attention

The only issue on the appeal was the validity of service of a notice by Frogmore terminating Mr Blunden's lease of a shop. The notice was served in the aftermath of the IRA bombing of the Arndale Centre in Manchester. As a result of the explosion, Mr Blunden's shop had been rendered substantially unfit for occupation. His lease provided that:

• If any destruction or damage shall render the Demised Premises ... wholly or substantially unfit for occupation the Landlord may by giving to the Tenant ... notice in writing determine this Demise ...
• In addition to any other prescribed mode of service any notices requiring to be served hereunder shall be validly served if served in accordance with Section 197 of the Law of Property Act 1925 as amended by the Recorded Delivery Service Act 1962 or in the case of the Tenant if left addressed to it or if there shall be more than one to any of them on the Demised Premises or sent to it him or any of them by post or left at the last known address or addresses of it him or any of them in Great Britain.

(It was common ground that the reference to s197 was an obvious error and that s196 was intended.) Frogmore posted by recorded delivery three letters containing notices addressed to Mr Blunden, one to the demised premises and the other two to private addresses, one of which was the latest given by him. However, all three letters were returned by the Post Office. Mr Blunden's evidence was that he was unable to visit two of the addresses because of the police security cordon. He did not visit the third address until after the time for collection of the recorded delivery letter had expired. The court accordingly considered the case on the basis that he had no knowledge of the notices.

The Court of Appeal, after reviewing a number of authorities, held that there had been good postal service of the notices, even though they did not come to Mr Blunden's attention. Robert Walker LJ said that 'Notice is not the same as knowledge. ... It is possible for valid notice to be given even though the intended recipient does not know of the notice (and is not at fault in not knowing about it).' However, it was recognised that there may be exceptions to this rule where a notice was not left at a tenant's house 'in a proper way ... but in a way which was deceptive and illusory' or where the sender of the notice had intentionally taken steps which ensured that it did not come to the attention of the addressee.

Note: Although this case involves consideration of service of notices under Landlord and Tenant Act 1954 Part II, the same rules may apply in certain circumstances to service of notices to quit.

N2.7   ### Crate v Miller

[1947] KB 946; [1947] 2 All ER 45, CA

NTQ may expire on last day or first day of period of tenancy

A notice to quit a weekly tenancy may expire either on the same day as the date on which the tenancy commenced or on the day before.

N2.8   ### Crawley BC v Ure

[1996] QB 13; [1995] 3 WLR 95; [1996] 1 All ER 724; (1995) 27 HLR 524, (1996) 71 P&CR 12, CA (see F4.7)

Service of a NTQ by one joint tenant was not in breach of 'trust for sale'

N2.9   ### Enfield LBC v Devonish and Sutton

(1997) 29 HLR 691; (1997) 75 P&CR 288, CA

Service of notice required to satisfy common law or LPA 1925 s196(5)

Mr Devonish, a council tenant, moved out, leaving his former cohabitee Ms Sutton in possession. The tenancy ceased to be secure because the tenant was not in occupation (Housing Act 1985 s81). The council sought to end the tenancy and 'served' a notice to quit by putting it through the letterbox of the property, although the council knew that the tenant was not there. A county court judge granted possession. Ms Sutton appealed, contending that the tenancy had not ended because the council could not prove that the notice had come to Mr Devonish's attention.

The Court of Appeal allowed the appeal and discharged the possession order. At common law, service of a notice to quit can be effected either by actual delivery to the tenant (or spouse or servant) or by evidence that the notice has come to the tenant's attention. The landlords could establish neither and were therefore forced to rely on statute. By Law of Property Act 1925 s196(5), a notice can be served by being left at the premises if that method is required by the lease or tenancy agreement itself. Mr Devonish's tenancy contained no express provision to that effect (cf *Wandsworth LBC v Attwell* (N2.22)) and the Court of Appeal declined to imply one).

By Local Government Act 1972 s233 a local authority landlord may serve any notice required or authorised by statute to be served by leaving it at the recipient's address. The Court of Appeal found that here the notice to quit was given in exercise of the council's powers at common law to end a contractual tenancy, not pursuant to statute and that, accordingly, s233 had no application. Although leave to appeal was refused, the court suggested that social landlords might seek from parliament some express statutory authority to serve notices in the manner which this council had sought to adopt.

N2.10   *Fletcher v Brent LBC*

[2006] EWCA Civ 960; [2007] HLR 12; 7 July 2006 (see also T5.1)

NTQ with wrong date but with savings clause valid

Mr and Mrs Fletcher were joint secure tenants of the council. On the breakdown of their relationship, Mrs Fletcher obtained a court order ousting her husband. She later gave notice to quit, ending the tenancy, and was rehoused. The notice was expressed to expire on the same day that it was given or 'on the first Monday after that date being at least 4 clear weeks after service'. On his application for homelessness assistance under Housing Act 1996 Part 7, Brent decided that Mr Fletcher was not homeless because the notice was ineffective to end the tenancy and he was still a tenant. The decision was upheld on review and on appeal to the county court.

The Court of Appeal allowed a second appeal. The notice to quit had been valid and had ended the joint tenancy. The question of whether Mr Fletcher had any other right to occupy the property (eg, under a subsequent express or implied licence from the council) – which had not been addressed in the council's decision-making – was remitted to the council's reviewing officer to consider.

N2.11   *Garston v Scottish Widows*

[1998] 1 WLR 1583; [1998] 3 All ER 596; [1998] L&TR 230; [1998] 32 EG 88; (1998) *Times* 14 July, CA

Notice valid applying reasonable recipient test

By a lease dated 10 July 1985-, office premises were demised for a term of 20 years from 24 June 1985. The lease contained a break clause enabling the tenant to determine the term 'at the expiration of the tenth year of the term' by giving to the landlord 'at least six months' previous notice in writing'. On 14 September 1994, the tenant gave notice of its desire to determine the term on 9 July 1995. It was accepted by both parties that the tenant had made a mistake in specifying the date of termination as the expiration of the tenth anniversary of the date of the lease (10 July 1985) instead of the tenth year of the term (24 June 1985). The landlord did not accept that the lease had been validly determined.

Following *Mannai Investment Co Ltd v Eagle Star Life Assurance Co Ltd* (N2.3), the Court of Appeal held that a reasonable recipient of the notice would have known that 24 June 1995 was the only date on which the lease could be determined and that the landlords intended to break the lease on the correct date but had wrongly specified 9 July 1995. The lease had been validly determined.

N2.12   *Greenwich LBC v McGrady*

(1982) 6 HLR 36; (1982) 46 P&CR 223; (1982) 267 EG 515; (1982) 81 LGR 288, CA (see F4.8)

NTQ served by one joint tenant effective and Housing Act 1985 did not apply to protect the former tenant.

N2.13   *Harler v Calder*

(1989) 21 HLR 214; [1989] 1 EGLR 88; [1989] 25 EG 95, CA

Contractual requirement did not oust common-law rule

A clause in a monthly tenancy agreement provided that, if either party wished to terminate the tenancy, not less than one month's written notice should be given in accordance with the statutory requirements, but that 'no other formality will be required'. It was held that the clause did not have the effect of ousting the common-law rule that, to be valid, a notice to quit must expire on the rent day or the day before the rent day.

N2.14   *Hounslow LBC v Pilling*

[1993] 1 WLR 1242; [1994] 1 All ER 432; (1993) 25 HLR 305; (1993) 66 P&CR 22; [1993] 2 EGLR 59; (1993) 91 LGR 573; [1993] 26 EG 123, CA (see F4.10)

A NTQ served by one joint tenant which did not comply with the statutory requirements ineffective; waiver clause did not render it effective

N2.15   *Manorlike Ltd v Le Vitas Travel Agency*

[1986] 1 All ER 573; [1986] 1 EGLR 79; (1986) 278 EG 412, CA

Notice valid despite notice 'within 3 months' rather than 'not less than 3 months'

A lease provided that it could be terminated by the landlord giving 'not less than three months' previous notice'. The landlord's solicitors wrote giving notice to quit 'within a period of three months from the date of service of this notice'. The notice was valid.

N2.16   *National Trust for Places of Historic Interest v Knipe*

[1997] 4 All ER 627; (1998) 30 HLR 449; [1997] 2 EGLR 9, CA

Agricultural holding not a dwelling and PEA 1977 s5 did not apply

The Court of Appeal held that premises let as an agricultural holding, even if there was a dwelling on the holding, did not constitute premises let as a dwelling for the purposes of Protection from Eviction Act 1977. A notice to quit such premises was not invalid for failure to include the prescribed information required by the Notices to Quit (Prescribed Information) Regulations 1988. The prescribed information is inappropriate in the case of an agricultural tenancy.

N2.17   *Notting Hill Housing Trust v Brackley*

[2001] EWCA Civ 601; [2002] HLR 212; [2001] 35 EG 106; [2001] L&TR 467; (2001) 82 P&CR D48; (2001) *Times* 15 June; [2001] 18 EGCS 175(CS), CA (see F4.13)

Service of NTQ by one joint tenant not a breach of trust

N2.18   *Pennell v Payne*

[1995] QB 192; [1995] 2 WLR 261; [1995] 2 All ER 592; [1995] 1 EGLR 6, CA

Service of NTQ by tenant on landlord also ended subtenancy

The tenant of a farm sublet without consent. The tenant subsequently served an upward notice to quit on the landlord.

The Court of Appeal, overruling *Brown v Wilson* (1949) 208 LT 144, held that service of the notice to quit meant that the subtenancy also came to an end and that the landlord was entitled to possession against the subtenant.

N2.19   *Schnabel v Allard*

[1967] 1 QB 627; [1966] 3 WLR 1295; [1966] 3 All ER 816, CA

NTQ does not require 28 clear days; Friday to Friday 4 weeks later satisfactory

A flat was rented on a weekly tenancy. The tenant received a notice to quit on Friday 4 March 1966, purporting to terminate the tenancy on Friday 1 April.

The Court of Appeal held that the notice was valid at common law and complied with Rent Act 1957 s16 (now Protection from Eviction Act 1977 s5). The statutory four-week period should be reckoned as a period which included the first day of the notice but excluded the last day. The requirement for a minimum of four weeks' notice does not mean '28 clear days'.

N2.20   *Swansea CC v Hearn*
(1991) 23 HLR 284, CA

NTQ in old prescribed form valid

The defendant was a homeless person in priority need whom the council had found to be intentionally homeless. He was provided with temporary accommodation in accordance with Housing Act 1985 s63(3) (now Housing Act 1996 s190(2)). The council served a notice to quit. It was in the form prescribed by the Notices to Quit (Prescribed Information) Regulations 1980 SI No 1624, not that prescribed by the Notices to Quit (Prescribed Information) Regulations 1988 SI No 2201, which were in force at the time of service. The tenant claimed that the notice was invalid.

In the county court, the council's claim for possession was dismissed but its appeal to the Court of Appeal was allowed. The information given in the old form of notice to quit was sufficient to comply with the current regulations.

N2.21   *Trustees of the Gift of Thomas Pocklington v Hill*
(1989) 21 HLR 391; [1989] 2 EGLR 97, CA

In absence of firm evidence, not inferred that deceased's tenancy terminated

The Court of Appeal refused to overturn a county court judge's decision that, in the absence of any firm evidence, it could not be inferred that a contractual tenancy had been determined at some stage before the tenant's death. The deceased tenant's daughter was able to establish that the contractual tenancy had been assigned to her by the administrator of the tenant's estate and, consequently, when a notice of increase of rent later terminated the contractual tenancy in accordance with Rent Act 1977 s49(4), she became the statutory tenant.

N2.22   *Wandsworth LBC v Attwell*
[1995] 3 WLR 95; (1995) 27 HLR 536; [1996] 1 EGLR 57; (1996) 94 LGR 419, CA

LPA 1925 s196 does not apply to service of NTQs; express provision required in tenancy for service at property

A secure council tenant went abroad to work and left his half-brother to take care of his home and pay the rent. The council claimed to have ended the tenancy by leaving a notice to quit at the property and by sending another notice to quit to the address overseas given by the half-brother. In possession proceedings, the judge found that the tenant had ceased to occupy the premises as his only or principal residence and that the tenancy had ceased to be secure. However, the tenant and his half-brother claimed that the contractual tenancy had not been terminated because the tenant had not received the notice to quit. The council claimed that a notice to quit was a document 'required to be served' within the meaning of Law of Property Act 1925 s196 and so it was 'sufficiently served if ... left at the last known place of abode ... of the lessee' (s196(3)). In the county court, possession was granted on the basis that the council had taken 'all the steps which were available' to give notice to the tenant.

The Court of Appeal allowed the tenant's appeal and held that a land-lord can rely on service by delivery to the premises only if there is an express provision for that method of service in the tenancy agreement. A notice to quit is not a document required to be served by any instrument or by Law of Property Act 1925 and so s196 does not apply. In the absence of any express provision in a tenancy agreement, a landlord must prove that a notice to quit has come to the attention of the tenant.

Cf: *Enfield LBC v Devonish and Sutton* (N2.9)

N2.23 *Wirral MBC v Smith*

(1982) 4 HLR 81; (1982) 43 P&CR 312; (1982) 80 LGR 628; (1982) 262 EG 1298, CA

NTQ must be served to end deceased's tenancy

Mrs Horne, a council tenant, died intestate in hospital. Shortly after she had gone into hospital, but two months before her death, Mr Smith moved into the house to look after it. Four months later, without determining the tenancy, the council began possession proceedings in the county court under the summary procedure.

The Court of Appeal allowed Mr Smith's appeal against a possession order. On the tenant's death, the tenancy had vested in the possession of the President of the Family Division. No notice to quit had been served on the President and so the tenancy had not been terminated. Ormrod LJ confirmed that: 'An action for trespass can only be maintained by some-one who has a right to immediate possession.'

Note: From 1 July 1995, any such tenancy vests in the Public Trustee rather than the President: Law of Property (Miscellaneous Provisions) Act 1994 s14. Any notice to quit relating to property rented by a deceased person has to be addressed to the personal representatives of the deceased and left or posted to the last known place of residence. In addition a copy must be served on the Public Trustee at PO Box 3010, London WC2A 1AX. The Public Trustee (Notices Affecting Land) (Title on Death) Regulations 1995 SI No 1330 deal with the Public Trustee's functions and prescribe fees. A Practice Note, originally issued by the Public Trust Office, which can be obtained by telephoning 020 7911 7100 or 020 7911 7127, describes how searches of the register can be made.

High Court

N2.24 *Carradine Properties Ltd v Aslam*

[1976] 1 WLR 442; [1976] 1 All ER 573; (1975) 32 P&CR 12, ChD

Test is: 'Is the notice quite clear to a reasonable tenant reading it?'; notice valid where obvious mistake

A lease for a term of 21 years included a provision entitling the landlord to terminate it on giving 12 months' notice. On 6 September 1974, the landlords served a notice stating that they intended to terminate the lease on 27 September 1973. Their intention had been to determine it on 27 September 1975, but the reference to 1973 was a clerical error.

Goulding J held that the notice was valid. He stated that the test generally applicable when interpreting a notice to quit is: 'Is the notice quite clear to a reasonable tenant reading it? Is it plain that he cannot be misled by it?' The tenant reading the notice must have seen the mistake and realised that it was 'obvious' that the landlord meant 1975.

Note: This decision was approved by the House of Lords in *Mannai Investment Co Ltd v Eagle Star Life Assurance Co Ltd* (N2.3).

N2.25 *Kinch v Bollard*
[1999] ! WLR 423; [1998] 4 All ER 650; [1998] 47 EG 140 (1998) *Times* 16 September, ChD

LPA 1925 s196(3) applied to service of LPA s36(2) notice

Neuberger J held that a notice of severance sent pursuant to Law of Property Act 1925 s36(2) was validly served even though it was not received by the addressee. As Law of Property Act s196(3) applied, service had been effected since the notice had been posted by ordinary first class post and delivered to the property.

N2.26 *Leckhampton Dairies Ltd v Artus Whitfield Ltd*
(1986) 130 SJ 27; (1986) 83 LSG 875, QBD

NTQ served by one joint tenant valid

A notice to quit served by one joint landlord without the knowledge or agreement of the other is valid.

Note: Although this case concerned a notice served to terminate a business tenancy, the same principle applies to residential tenancies. See also *Annen v Rattee* (1985) 17 HLR 323, CA.

N2.27 *Precious v Reedie*
[1924] 2 KB 149, KBD

Period of notice in monthly tenancy is month; notice must end at end of period

A house was let on a monthly tenancy which began on the first day of the month. On 5 September 1923, the tenant received a notice to quit dated 1 September 1923, giving 'one month's notice to quit'. In possession proceedings, a county court judge held that the notice was a good notice for 31 October 1923, which was the earliest possible date on which the tenancy could be terminated.

The tenant's appeal was allowed. In a monthly as in a weekly tenancy, the period of the notice to quit must correspond with the length of the tenancy and must determine at the end of a periodic month from the commencement of the tenancy. A notice to quit should be strictly construed by the court. If it is invalid, it cannot be amended. However, if the notice to quit had included additional words such as 'or so soon thereafter as the tenancy would expire' it would have been valid.

N3   # Forfeiture

Forfeiture is the procedure which allows a landlord to bring to an end a contractual fixed-term tenancy or lease before the fixed period of time for which the lease was originally granted expires. In view of the various forms of relief available to lessees (see below), the lease is not actually terminated until a court order is made, but the effect of an order is that forfeiture takes effect from the date when proceedings were served (*Borzak v Ahmed* [1965] 2 QB 320, QBD). Forfeiture does not apply to assured tenancies.

House of Lords

N3.1   ## *Billson v Residential Apartments Ltd*
[1992] 1 AC 494; [1992] 2 WLR 15; [1992] 1 All ER 141; (1992) 24 HLR 218; (1991) 63 P&CR 122; [1992] 1 EGLR 43; [1992] 91 EG 91, HL

Tenant can apply for relief from forfeiture after forfeiture by re-entry without court order

Major alterations were carried out by a lessee in breach of covenant. The freeholder served a Law of Property Act 1925 s146 notice and peaceably re-entered – the flat was vacant and so Protection from Eviction Act 1977 s2 did not apply. The tenant applied for relief from forfeiture.

The House of Lords held that a tenant may apply for relief against forfeiture under Law of Property Act 1925 s146 after the landlord has forfeited by re-entry without a court order. Lord Templeman stated:

> A tenant may apply for ... relief from forfeiture under section 146(2) after the issue of a section 146 notice but he is not prejudiced if he does not do so. A tenant cannot apply for relief after a landlord has forfeited a lease by issuing and serving a writ, has recovered judgment and has entered into possession pursuant to that judgment. If the judgment is set aside or successfully appealed, the tenant will be able to apply for relief in the landlord's action but the court in deciding whether to grant relief will take into account any consequences of the original order and repossession and the delay of the tenant. A tenant may apply for relief after a landlord has forfeited by re-entry without first obtaining a court order for that purpose, but the court in deciding whether to grant relief will take into account all the circumstances including delay on the part of the tenant ([1992] 1 All ER at 149).

Lord Templeman also indicated that he considered the practice of awarding indemnity costs as a condition of granting relief was ripe for reconsideration. The case was remitted for reconsideration by the High Court (see N3.24).

Court of Appeal

N3.2   ## *Adagio Properties v Ansari*
[1998] 35 EG 86, CA

Section 146 notice did not require particulars of each defect

A Law of Property Act 1925 s146 notice stated that the tenant had breached his obligations by 'making alterations so as to divide [the flat] into two separate studio flats without permission'. The Court of Appeal held that it fulfilled the statutory purpose of giving the tenant the opportunity to remedy the breach and was valid. A notice served under s146 does not require the landlord to give particulars of each defect. The Court of Appeal followed a passage in *Fox v Jolly* [1916] AC 1, HL, where Lord Buckmaster, LC said:

> All that the landlord is bound to do is to state particulars of breaches of covenants of which he complains and call upon the lessee to remedy them. The means by which the breach is to be remedied is a matter for the lessee and not for the lessor. In many cases specification of the breach will of itself suggest the only possible remedy.

In *Adagio Properties* the notice did comply with these requirements. There is no need to overburden a notice with detail when the alleged breach is perfectly clear. The tenant knew what he had done in order to make the alteration, and so knew what was required to turn it back again into a single dwelling.

N3.3 *Belgravia Property Investment and Development Co Ltd v Webb*
[2001] EWCA Civ 2075; 18 December 2001

Unlawful to forfeit lease where premises lawfully occupied

On 7 November 1986, the first claimant purchased the freehold reversionary interest in a block of residential flats. The purchase was subject to the existing leasehold interests of the residential occupiers of the flats. The first defendant was one of those leaseholders and his lease was for a term of 199 years from 1 January 1972. On 17 January 1988, the first defendant sublet the property to the second defendant under a protected shorthold tenancy, expiring on 16 January 1990. The agreed rent was £375 per month, to be paid to the first defendant via a rent collector. The first defendant disappeared in 1990 and in doing so, stopped paying the ground rent and service charges due to the first claimant. The rent collector also ceased to collect the rent due from the second defendant, who remained living in the property. On 7 July 1994, in the absence of the second defendant, the first claimant re-entered the property, pursuant to a forfeiture clause in the lease, and changed the locks. On the same day, the first claimant granted a new long lease of the property to the second claimant at a premium of £30,000 under the same terms as the first defendant's lease. The second defendant returned to the property in late July 1994 to discover that the locks had been changed. He took legal advice and on 30 July 1994 he attended the property with police officers and obtained re-entry. On 3 August 1994 he obtained an injunction forbidding the first claimant from re-entering the property. In proceedings begun in 1999, the first and second claimants sought a declaration that the second defendant's lease had been forfeited on 7 July 1994. HHJ Dedman dismissed the claim for possession, made no order on the money claim and made a declaration that the second defendant was a statutorily protected tenant of the property, whose tenancy had not been lawfully determined. The second claimant appealed.

The appeal was dismissed. Protection from Eviction Act 1977 s2 provides that it is unlawful to forfeit a lease if a property is lawfully occupied, as was the case here. Furthermore, the second defendant was a tenant entitled to the statutory protection of the Rent Act 1977. The position was that the second claimant had been the second defendant's immediate landlord only since the judge's order. The second defendant was only liable to pay rent from that date onwards. The second defendant owed no arrears of rent and the judge was right to have refused possession of the property. There could be no criticism of the way in which the judge exercised his discretion in refusing to make an order for possession. The second claimant had not properly identified itself as the second defendant's new landlord and in any event, as the judge found, had taken several years to bring an action for possession.

N3.4   *British Petroleum Pension Trust v Behrendt*
(1986) 18 HLR 42; (1985) 52 P&CR 117; [1985] 2 EGLR 97, CA

Relief from forfeiture properly refused where premises had been used for prostitution

The Court of Appeal held that a trial judge had properly exercised his discretion in not granting relief from forfeiture where premises had been used for prostitution over a number of years, in breach of a covenant against immoral user. Even though the prostitution had ceased, the 'stigma' which attached to the premises remained.

N3.5   *Central Estates (Belgravia) Ltd v Woolgar (No 2)*
[1972] 1 WLR 1048; [1972] 3 All ER 610; (1972) 24 P&CR 103, CA

Breach waived by acceptance of rent; relief would otherwise be granted on facts

A lease contained a covenant on the tenant's part not to cause nuisance, damage, annoyance, inconvenience or disturbance. The tenant was convicted of allowing the premises to be used as a brothel and, as a result, the landlords' agents served a Law of Property Act 1925 s146 notice. Staff were instructed not to demand rent, but the memorandum did not reach a junior member of staff who was responsible for sending out rent demands. As a result, the tenant paid rent.

The Court of Appeal held that the breach had been waived. To constitute waiver it is sufficient if there is an unequivocal act done by the landlord which recognises the existence of the lease after having knowledge of the ground for forfeiture. The intentions of the parties are irrelevant. The landlords were not entitled to claim possession. In any event, if the breach had not been waived, the Court of Appeal would have granted relief from forfeiture. The lessee was sick and aged and, apart from the short period of immoral user, a respectable person. The value of the house and the estate on which it was situated had not diminished as a result of the immoral user.

N3.6   *Chrisdell Ltd v Johnson and Tickner*
(1987) 19 HLR 406; (1987) 54 P&CR 257; [1987] 2 EGLR 123, CA

No waiver despite acceptance of rent where breach not fully known by landlord

Landlords suspected that, in contravention of an absolute prohibition against assignment, the tenant had assigned his tenancy. They did not, however, know 'all necessary facts to establish a breach' and continued to accept rent.

The Court of Appeal held that they had not waived the breach of covenant against assignment.

N3.7 *Cooper v Henderson*

(1982) 5 HLR 1; (1982) 263 EG 592, CA

Breach of covenant regarding user only waived for past breaches

A tenant covenanted not to use premises as a private residence. The landlord brought forfeiture proceedings alleging breach of that covenant. The tenant defended, claiming that the landlord knew from the commencement of the tenancy that he had been occupying as a residence and that the breach had been waived.

The Court of Appeal dismissed his appeal against a possession order. A breach of covenant requiring or prohibiting a particular user is a continuing breach. Waiver by conduct applies only to past breaches. A landlord may at any time bring forfeiture proceedings relying on any continuing breach which has occurred after the waiver.

N3.8 *Cornillie v Saha and Bradford and Bingley Building Society*

(1996) 28 HLR 561; (1996) 72 P&CR 147, CA

Waiver of breach

The landlord of a flat held on a long lease was aware of illegal subletting at the time when she commenced proceedings against the lessee seeking access to the flat.

The Court of Appeal held that the commencement of such proceedings with knowledge amounted to a waiver. In determining whether there has been waiver of a breach of covenant against subletting, a court should ask (a) whether the alleged act of waiver unequivocally recognises the subsistence of the lease; (b) whether the landlord had knowledge of the breach of covenant at the time of the alleged act of waiver; and (c) whether the act of recognition was communicated to the lessee.

N3.9 *Courtney Lodge Management Ltd v Blake*

[2004] EWCA Civ 975; [2005] L&TR 2; (2005) 1 P&CR 264; (2004) *Times* 15 July

Four days not reasonable period to respond to breach; nuisance by subtenant

The claimant landlord leased a flat to Mr Blake. The lease contained a covenant on Mr Blake's part not to cause a nuisance to the landlord or any other residents in the block. Mr Blake granted an underlease to Atlantic Lodge Management Ltd for use of the flat as temporary accommodation. Atlantic Lodge granted a sub-underlease to a local housing authority which granted a non-secure tenancy. Neither the underlease nor the sub-underlease contained covenants similar to those contained in the head lease preventing nuisance. From March 2003 there were complaints of nuisance caused by the tenants of the flat. On 2 September 2003 the landlord served a Law of Property Act 1925 s146 notice on Mr Blake. On 8 September 2003 Mr Blake instructed Atlantic Lodge to terminate the non-secure tenancy agreement with the tenants. As a result, a notice to quit was subsequently served. The claimant landlord issued proceedings on 2

October 2003 seeking forfeiture and damages based on the disturbances by the tenants. In the county court a recorder found that Mr Blake had been in breach of the terms of the head lease since his inaction amounted to 'suffering' a nuisance to continue. The claimant was therefore entitled to forfeiture. Mr Blake appealed that decision.

The Court of Appeal allowed his appeal. A covenantee may suffer (ie, allow) a nuisance, even if there is no legal power to prevent it, if the covenantee fails to exert influence to prevent breach if, on the balance of probabilities, exertion of influence would have brought to an end the offending state of affairs. The evidence in this case showed that Mr Blake had power to influence an abatement of the nuisance. Furthermore, a lessee, bound by covenants contained within a head lease to prevent a nuisance, is not entitled to rely on inability to prevent a sublessee from causing a nuisance where he failed to mirror the provisions of the head lease in the sublease. However, the order for forfeiture should be set aside. As the s146 notice had been served on 2 September, and Mr Blake had taken action to abate the nuisance on 8 September, Mr Blake had not been afforded enough time to respond and remedy the breach. Four working days is not a reasonable period to respond to a s146 notice.

N3.10   *Croydon (Unique) Ltd v Wright*

[2001] ChD 318; [2000] 2 WLR 683; [1999] 4 All ER 257; [2000] L&TR 20; [1999] 40 EG 189; (2000) 32 HLR 670; (1999) *Times* 24 August, CA

Creditors with charging orders to be given notice of possession proceedings

The defendant was a lessee with a 125-year lease. Creditors obtained a charging order nisi to secure the payment of a debt of £233,887 and a caution to protect the charging order was registered at the Land Registry. Later the lessee fell into arrears with the rent and judgment was obtained against him. The order obtained was in fact wrong in that it provided for possession on the same day, rather than allowing a period of not less than four weeks before the order took effect in accordance with County Courts Act 1984 s138. The creditors were not notified of the proceedings and only learnt about the possession order when the landlord attempted to remove the caution over a year later. They then applied to be joined to the landlord's action. They offered to discharge the arrears of rent if there was relief from forfeiture. That offer was rejected by the landlords. As there had been no application for relief within six months (s139(9A)), the creditors applied to set aside the possession order.

The Court of Appeal, by a majority, set aside the possession order, holding:

1) It was defective in not giving four weeks for the outstanding rent to be paid. The court had had no jurisdiction to make that order.
2) Section 138(9C) allows holders of charging orders to seek relief from forfeiture. In view of this, CCR Ord 6 r3(2) required such persons to be given notice of possession proceedings. It would be manifestly unjust to deprive the holder of a charging order who had registered his interest of any right to apply for relief from forfeiture.

Note: All of these points apply equally to mortgagees of long leases.

N3.11 *Eaton Square Properties Ltd v Beveridge*
[1993] EGCS 91, CA

After lease forfeited, occupant not in occupation at date of forfeiture not protected by PEA 1977

A tenant assigned a 12-year lease of residential premises. The landlord took proceedings for forfeiture against the assignee, relying on rent arrears, obtained an order for forfeiture and regained possession after executing a warrant for possession. By consent, the assignor then obtained an order for possession against the assignee and went into possession. The landlords then took proceedings against the assignor under CCR Ord 24 and obtained a possession order. The assignor appealed.

The Court of Appeal dismissed the appeal, holding that the lease had already been forfeited and that the assignor had not been entitled to rely on the Protection from Eviction Act 1977 at the date of forfeiture, because at that date she was not residing in the premises.

N3.12 *Escalus Properties Ltd v Robinson*
[1996] QB 231; [1995] 3 WLR 524; [1995] 4 All ER 852; (1996) 28 HLR 338; (1996) 71 P&CR 47; [1995] 2 EGLR 23, CA

Relief available to mortgagees

The Court of Appeal held that relief against forfeiture can be granted to mortgage lenders retrospectively on terms that the lenders pay all rent and service charges due. Such relief is available under County Courts Act 1984 s138 (in the county court) or Supreme Court Act 1981 s38 (in the High Court). In such circumstances, mortgage lenders are not obliged to pay mesne profits from the date of forfeiture, which will generally be higher than rent and service charges.

N3.13 *Fairview Investments Ltd v Sharma*
11 January 2000, CA

Where contractual right to costs, court should exercise discretion to reflect right

A lessee covenanted to pay all the lessor's properly incurred expenses incidental to the preparation and service of any notices and other costs incurred in contemplation of or in proceedings under Law of Property Act 1925 s146. In 1997 the first defendant completed the sale of the flat to the second defendant without obtaining licence to assign. Fairview served a notice under s146 and brought possession proceedings. The second defendant claimed relief from forfeiture. The parties compromised the proceedings at trial by way of a Tomlin order granting the second defendant a retrospective licence. HHJ Cotran ruled that the second defendant should pay the lessor's costs up to and including an earlier hearing and that Fairview should bear its costs thereafter. Fairview appealed.

In allowing the appeal, the Court of Appeal stated that, although costs are in the court's discretion, where there is a contractual right to costs the discretion should ordinarily be exercised so as to reflect that contractual right (*Gomba Holdings (UK) Ltd v Minories Finance Ltd (No 2)* (R6.1) [1993] Ch 171 at page 194B). If a lessee is to be relieved from forfeiture, it should be on terms that reflect the lessee's breach of covenant and the lessor should not be left out of pocket by taking proper steps to protect his interests. Where a lessor has bargained for the protection afforded by a clause providing for payment of costs, a court should be slow to deprive him or her of that protection and should not do so without good reason. On the facts, the judge failed to determine the extent of the lessor's contractual rights and gave no explanation why the lessor should be deprived of its contractual rights.

N3.14   *Hynes v Twinsectra Ltd*
(1996) 28 HLR 183; [1995] 2 EGLR 69; [1995] 35 EG 136, CA

Where forfeiture proceedings dismissed, no need to apply for relief from forfeiture.

Where a claim for forfeiture of a lease is dismissed, the lease is restored to its full existence and the lessee is entitled to apply to acquire the freehold under the Leasehold Reform Act 1967. When the forfeiture proceedings are dismissed, there is no need to apply for relief from forfeiture.

N3.15   *Khar v Delbounty Ltd*
(1998) 75 P&CR 232; [1996] NPC 163, CA

Terms of relief from forfeiture varied

Over a period of six years the lessor of a flat let on a 99-year lease started five sets of proceedings for arrears of rent and maintenance charges. After a further default and service of a Law of Property Act 1925 s146 notice, the landlord forfeited the lease and re-let the flat on an assured shorthold tenancy. Eleven months later, the lessees sought relief from forfeiture, which was granted.

The Court of Appeal held that:

- Unless a lease states that maintenance charges are to be treated as rent, they are not rent.
- In the context of relief from forfeiture there is no difference in substance between a covenant to pay rent and a covenant to pay maintenance charges.
- The master had been right to grant relief from forfeiture, but the terms of relief were varied to provide for the flat to be sold and for the landlord to take out the arrears of maintenance charges from the proceeds of sale. Completion was to be delayed until the tenant left.

N3.16   *Maryland Estates v Bar-Joseph*
[1999] 1 WLR 83; [1998] 3 All ER 193; (1999) 77 P&CR 150; (1999) 31 HLR 269; [1998] 27 EG 142, CA

'All the rent in arrear' means the rent payable up to the date stated in the order for relief, not just the arrears but the continuing liability as well

The plaintiffs, freehold owners of premises held on a long lease, brought forfeiture proceedings in the High Court based on arrears of rent and service charges. The lease provided that the service charges were deemed to be sums due by way of additional rent. The action was transferred to the county court. By 15 August 1996, the lessees had paid into court an amount equivalent to the arrears claimed in the writ, interest and costs, but did not pay into court sums which had fallen due after the service of the writ. On 28 October 1996, the landlord applied for possession unless within 28 days the tenants paid rent and service charges including sums which had fallen due since issue. HHJ Diamond QC made an order for possession ([1997] 46 EG 155) but gave automatic relief from forfeiture provided that 'all the rent in arrear' and costs of the action were paid (County Courts Act 1984 s138(3)). He held that 'all the rent in arrear' referred to the rent due at the date of forfeiture – ie, the date of service of the summons – not at the date of payment.

The Court of Appeal, allowing an appeal by the landlords, held that the words used in s138(3), which provides that relief from forfeiture may be granted if 'the lessee pays into court … all the rent in arrear' were not to be construed to mean that the court could order payment only of the rent in arrears at the date of the summons. It was to be assumed that the lease continued after service of the summons, that the tenant remained under an obligation to pay the sum reserved in the lease as rent and that 'all the rent in arrear' means the rent payable up to the date stated in the order.

N3.17   **Reichman v Beveridge**

[2006] EWCA Civ 1659; [2007] L&TR 18; (2007) *Times* 4 January; 13 December 2006

Landlord not under duty to mitigate loss

The claimants let office premises to the defendants, who were solicitors, on a five-year lease. The defendants ceased to practice as solicitors. They did not pay rent from March 2003. The claimants sued for those arrears. The defendants served a defence asserting that the claimants had failed to mitigate their loss by failing to instruct agents to market the premises, failing to accept the offer of a prospective tenant who wanted to take an assignment or a new lease, and failing to accept an offer from one of the defendants to negotiate payment of a consideration for surrender of the defendants' lease. District Judge Kubiak was asked to determine as a preliminary issue 'whether it is necessary as a matter of law for a landlord to mitigate his loss when seeking to recover arrears of rent'. She held that there was no such duty. An appeal by one of the defendants was dismissed by HHJ Reid QC.

The Court of Appeal dismissed a second appeal. After reviewing authorities from courts in this country and the Commonwealth, it held that the defendants' defence was 'not open' to them.

N3.18   **Savva v Houssein**

(1997)73 P&CR 150; [1996] 2 EGLR 65; [1996] 47 EG 138, CA

Tenant's breach of a negative covenant may be capable of remedy

In breach of a covenant in his lease, the tenant put up signs outside his property and altered the premises. Before issuing forfeiture proceedings, the landlord served a Law of Property Act 1925 s146 notice stating that the breach was incapable of remedy. The claim for possession was dismissed because the county court judge found that the breach was capable of remedy and the notice was invalid because it did not require the tenant to remedy the breach.

The Court of Appeal dismissed the landlord's appeal. A tenant's breach of a negative covenant is capable of remedy for the purposes of Law of Property Act 1925 s146(1) if the effect of the breach can be effectively removed.

N3.19 *Sinclair Gardens Investments (Kensington) v Walsh*
[1996] QB 231; [1995] 3 WLR 524; [1995] 4 All ER 852; (1996) 28 HLR 338; (1996) 71
P&CR 47; [1995] 2 EGLR 23, CA

Date from which relief should be granted

Mortgagees sought relief from forfeiture. Although the lessors accepted that relief was available, a dispute arose over the date from which relief should be granted.

The Court of Appeal held that:

1) Sums claimed as service charges are 'rent' where leases state that service charges are deemed to be due as additional rent.
2) In rent-only cases, mortgagees are automatically entitled to retrospective relief from forfeiture under County Courts Act 1984 s138 – see also *United Dominions Trust v Shellpoint Trustees* [1993] 4 All ER 310, CA.
3) The position is exactly the same under Supreme Court Act 1981 s38 where proceedings are commenced in the High Court.
4) In one of the cases where service charges were not recoverable as rent, the mortgagee was entitled to relief under Law of Property Act 1925 s146(2) or (4). Relief was no longer restricted under s146(2) to those with privity of contract or estate with the lessor.

N3.20 *Smith v Spaul*
[2002] EWCA Civ 1830; [2003] QB 983; [2003] 2 WLR 495, [2003] 1 All ER 509; [2003] 17
EG 148; [2003] HLR 38; [2003] L&TR 17; [2003] 2 P&CR 21; (2002) *Times* 28 December

Lessee required to be served under s146(1) is person bound to remedy a breach

The Halifax Building Society obtained possession of a flat from a lessee who had defaulted under the terms of a mortgage. Smith, the freeholder of the block, served a notice on Halifax under Law of Property Act 1925 s146 as a result of alleged breaches of covenant to keep the property in repair. Spaul subsequently bought the flat at auction from Halifax.

The Court of Appeal held that, even if a mortgagee is in possession, it is not the appropriate recipient of a notice under s146(1). Although the expression 'the lessee' is defined in very wide terms by s146(5)(b), the lessee required to be served under s146(1) is the person who vis-à-vis the lessor is bound to remedy a breach or to make compensation in money. The relationship of lessor and lessee is unaffected by the mortgage, even if the mortgagee takes possession. *Target Home Loans Ltd v Izza Ltd* [2000] 1 EGLR 23 was disapproved.

N3.21 *Swordheath Properties Ltd v Bolt*
[1992] 2 EGLR 68; [1992] 38 EG 154, CA

'The return day' in forfeiture proceedings is date fixed for first hearing

County Courts Act 1984 s138(2) provides that if, in forfeiture proceedings in a county court, a lessee pays all arrears and costs into court not less than five clear days before the return day, the lessee is entitled automatically to relief from forfeiture.

The Court of Appeal held that 'the return day' is the date of the first hearing which is typed on the summons. In this case, the first hearing was treated as a hearing for directions. The defendants subsequently paid the arrears of rent, but not the costs. It was held that the action had not 'ceased' within the meaning of s138(2) and that the plaintiffs were entitled to the costs of a subsequent hearing, but, in the light of comments made by Lord Templeman in *Billson v Residential Apartments Ltd* (N3.1), not automatically on an indemnity basis.

N3.22 **Thomas v Ken Thomas Ltd**
[2006] EWCA 1594; [2007] L&TR 21; 9 October 2006

Payment of rent operated to waive breach where landlord did not return rent

In May 2004, the claimant let a warehouse to the defendant on a ten-year lease. The defendant paid rent until October 2004, but without the VAT which was due. Owing to financial difficulties, it did not pay the rent which was due on 1 November 2004. Payments of some sums were made by CHAPS in December 2004 and January 2005. They were not returned by the claimant. In February 2005 the claimant began forfeiture proceedings, based on non-payment of November's rent and the VAT. The defendant argued that, by not returning the sums paid in December and January, the claimant had waived the breaches of covenant and so was unable to rely on them for forfeiture of the lease. HHJ Darroch found for the claimant.

The Court of Appeal allowed the defendant's appeal. Subsequent demands for and acceptance of rent are classic ways in which a landlord can waive the right to forfeit. It is not necessary that the landlord should intend to waive the right to forfeit. Where rent is paid into a landlord's bank account despite his instruction to the bank not to receive it, if the landlord takes no steps to repay it to the tenant, that is sufficient acceptance to amount to a waiver.

High Court

N3.23 **Ashton v Sobelman**
[1987] 1 WLR 177; [1987] 1 All ER 755; [1987] 1 EGLR 33; (1987) 231 EG 303, ChD

Landlord cannot forfeit head lease by agreement with subtenant

A landlord cannot forfeit a head lease merely by coming to an agreement with an existing subtenant that locks should be changed and that the subtenant can remain in occupation on the same terms as the head lease. The landlord must show an unequivocal intention to re-enter the premises.

N3.24 **Billson v Residential Apartments Ltd (No 2)**
[1993] EGCS 150, ChD

Relief refused where nine planning enforcement notices served

Although the House of Lords had held that the courts do have power to grant relief from forfeiture under Law of Property Act 1925 s146 after re-entry where the landlord has not taken court proceedings (N3.1), on the lessee's remitted application, relief from forfeiture was refused. Mr Morrison QC, sitting as a deputy High Court judge, took into account nine enforcement notices which had been served alleging breaches of planning permission and the lack of any reliable evidence that the lessees would comply with the terms of the lease in future.

N3.25 *Church Commissioners for England v Nodjoumi*
(1986) 51 P&CR 155, ChD

Right to forfeit for rent arrears not waived by s146 notice regarding assignment

Where a tenant already owed arrears of rent, service of a notice in accordance with Law of Property Act 1925 s146, relating to an alleged unlawful assignment, did not amount to an unequivocal affirmation of the continuing existence of the lease. The landlord had not waived its rights to forfeit based on the arrears of rent.

N3.26 *Iperion Investments Corporation v Broadwalk House Residents*
[1992] EGLR 235, Official Referees' Business

Right to forfeit waived by acceptance of rent

A lease contained a covenant prohibiting the tenant from carrying out works which would alter the structure of the building. The tenant broke the covenant. Although the landlords were aware of the breach, they continued to accept rent. It was held that the landlords had waived their right to forfeit the lease.

N3.27 *Re Debtors Nos 13A10 and 14A10 of 1994*
[1996] 1 All ER 691; [1995] 41 EG 142, ChD

Demands for rent had not waived landlord's right to forfeit

During December 1994, the landlord of business premises wrote demanding rent arrears which had been accruing since September. The rent was not paid and in January the landlord re-entered and forfeited the lease. The tenant claimed that the landlord had, by demanding the rent, waived the right to forfeit. The landlord conceded that the demand waived the right to forfeit for the rental periods which had passed but contended that the right to forfeit for the arrears due in the current rental period had not been waived.

Rattee J accepted the landlord's argument. Once an instalment of rent has not been paid in the period allowed in the lease for payment, there is nothing inconsistent in the landlord claiming and even receiving the rent concerned and seeking to forfeit the lease.

N3.28 *Rendham Holdings Ltd v Patel*
[2002] EWHC 320; [2002] All ER (D) 132 (Oct); December 2002 *Legal Action* 21; 10 October 2002, ChD

Warrant oppressive where court failed to consider application for stay of execution

A landlord of commercial and residential premises let under a long lease obtained a possession order from a district judge as a result of arrears of ground rent and management charges. The tenant lodged an appeal against the decision of the district judge as well as an application for a stay of execution. Owing to an oversight, the application for a stay of execution was not put before a circuit judge. A warrant for possession was issued and executed. The tenant applied to set aside the warrant on the basis that the circumstances in which it was issued and executed were oppressive. A circuit judge set aside the warrant for possession and granted relief from forfeiture. The claimant appealed against that decision on the ground that the judge was not entitled to find that there had been oppression.

Etherton J dismissed the appeal. The tenant was entitled to believe that the court would not issue the warrant for possession or allow its execution before considering her application for a stay. It was likely that, had that application come before the circuit judge, he would have granted a stay pending the hearing of the second defendant's appeal as it was unlikely, on a cursory appraisal, that he would have viewed the appeal as having no substance. In all the circumstances of the case, it was the court's failure to deal properly and promptly with the application that deprived the tenant of the opportunity to procure a stay prior to the execution of the warrant for possession. It was the court's failure to process the application which was oppressive and caused injustice in respect of the issue and application of the warrant. That causative oppression entitled the judge to exercise his discretion to set aside the execution of the warrant for possession.

N3.29 **Sambrin Investments v Taborn**
[1990] 1 EGLR 61, ChD

Tenant's claim for relief from forfeiture an equitable counterclaim.

A landlord bringing forfeiture proceedings based on arrears of rent and dilapidations sought summary judgment under RSC Ord 14 (now CPR 24).

Gibson J gave unconditional leave to defend, holding that the tenant's claim for relief from forfeiture was an equitable counterclaim inextricably involved in the claim.

N3.30 **Southern Depot Co Ltd v British Railways Board**
[1990] 2 EGLR 39, ChD

Relief not limited to 'exceptional circumstances'

In a case involving commercial premises, Morritt J examined the circumstances in which relief against forfeiture should be given under Law of Property Act 1925 s146. He stated that it was not limited to 'exceptional circumstances' and that it was permissible to have regard to the interests of a company which was not a party to the lease and which had been allowed into possession in breach of a covenant in the lease.

N3.31 **Van Haarlam v Kasner Charitable Trust**
(1992) 64 P&CR 214; [1992] 2 EGLR 59; [1992] 36 EG 135, ChD

Demand for rent after knowledge of lessee's arrest amounted to a waiver of breach

The freeholders sought to forfeit a long lease for breach of a covenant not to use premises for 'illegal or immoral user'. The lessee was arrested for spying for Czechoslovakia and sentenced to ten years' imprisonment. He had 'spying equipment' on the premises and had received secret radio transmissions there. The freeholder had, however, sent a demand for rent after the lessee's arrest, but before his conviction. After the lessee had been imprisoned, a Law of Property Act 1925 s146 notice was sent to him at the property.

Harman J held that, in view of Law of Property Act 1925 s196, which provides that service may be effected by sending any notice to the property in question, the s146 notice was validly served even though it did not come to the lessee's attention. However, the demand for rent after knowledge of the lessee's arrest amounted to a waiver of the breach of covenant. Accordingly, the lessor was not entitled to forfeit the lease. In any event, Harman J indicated that, even if there had not been a waiver of the breach, he would have granted relief from forfeiture.

N4 Surrender

A surrender is a voluntary agreement by both landlord and tenant that a tenancy should come to an end. A surrender should be by deed, although an oral agreement to surrender may be effective as a surrender by operation of law.

House of Lords

N4.1 *Barrett v Morgan*
[2000] 2 AC 264; [2000] 2 WLR 284; [2000] 1 All ER 481; [2000] 1 EGLR 8; (2000) *Times* 28 January

Arrangement concerning NTQ not tantamount to consensual surrender of tenancy

Freeholders of agricultural land agreed with their tenants that they would serve a notice to quit and that the tenants would not serve a counter notice under Agricultural Holdings Act 1986. The purpose of this agreement was to enable the freeholders to obtain possession against a subtenant. The Court of Appeal held that this arrangement was tantamount to a consensual surrender of the tenancy and so did not determine the subtenancy.

The House of Lords allowed a further appeal. Service of a notice to quit by either a tenant or a landlord by pre-arrangement with the other was not tantamount to a surrender of the tenancy as, unlike a surrender, it did not need the consent of the receiving party to have effect. In this case, the tenants' consent was unnecessary and the freeholders were only doing with their consent what they were entitled to do without it.

Court of Appeal

N4.2 *Basingstoke and Deane BC v Paice*
(1995) 27 HLR 433; [1995] 2 EGLR 9, CA

Unlawful subtenant became council's tenant on surrender of lease

The council granted a 15-year fixed-term lease of commercial garage premises to Mr L'Heureux. Without the council's knowledge or consent, he converted part of the garage offices into a self-contained flat and let it to Mr Paice. The council then accepted a surrender of the lease.

The Court of Appeal allowed Mr Paice's appeal against a possession order and substituted a declaration that he was the council's tenant and, since all the conditions of Housing Act 1985 ss79 to 81 were satisfied, that he was a secure tenant.

N4.3 *Belcourt Estates Ltd v Adesina*
[2005] EWCA Civ 208; 18 February 2005

*Surrender by operation of law requires unequivocal conduct by parties consist-
ent with termination of tenancy such that inequitable for parties to dispute
termination*

In August 2000 Belcourt Estates let three dilapidated houses with what
had been shops or businesses on the ground floor to Ms Adesina. She did
not pay any rent because she decided that she did not want the premises
and left in November 2000. She did not inform Belcourt of this. Belcourt
did not take any action until the local authority sought payment of business rates. As a result, in January 2002 it issued proceedings against Ms
Adesina. A judge found that Belcourt had not exercised its right to re-enter
the premises, and that it had done nothing to collect the rent until January
2002. He held that that conduct amounted to evidence that the tenancy
no longer existed and that it had been surrendered in November 2000.
Accordingly no rent was due. Belcourt appealed.

The Court of Appeal allowed the appeal. Surrender of a lease by operation of law requires that the conduct of the parties has to amount unequivocally to acceptance that the tenancy has ended. There must either
be relinquishment of possession and its acceptance by the landlord or
other conduct consistent only with the cesser of the tenancy and the
circumstances must be such as to render it inequitable for the tenant to
dispute that the tenancy has ceased or such as to render it inequitable
for the landlord to dispute that the tenancy has ceased. Mere inaction, or
acts of omission, cannot be unequivocal conduct. In this case, although
Belcourt had failed to act in taking possession or pursuing payments of
rent, that conduct had not unequivocally amounted to acceptance that the
tenancy had ended. Belcourt was entitled to the arrears of rent claimed.

N4.4 *Bolnore Properties Ltd v Cobb*
(1997) 29 HLR 202; (1996) 75 P&CR 127, CA

Tenant vacating flat for 24 hours and handing over keys operated as surrender

The landlord brought possession proceedings against a statutory tenant,
relying on arrears of rent. After the tenant had failed to comply with a suspended possession order, the landlord issued a warrant. In or about 1987,
execution of the warrant was suspended on terms that the tenant would
pay all arrears and agree to substitute a protected shorthold tenancy. In
order to avoid the effect of Housing Act 1980 s52(2) (which prevented
the creation of a protected shorthold tenancy if the tenancy was 'granted
to a person who, immediately before it was granted, was a protected or
statutory tenant of that dwelling-house') and as part of the agreement,
the tenant agreed to vacate the flat for 24 hours and to hand over the keys.
At first instance, the judge decided that the previous tenancy had determined. Delivery of the keys was indicative of the tenant's intention to
bring the tenancy to an end.

The Court of Appeal dismissed the tenant's appeal. A Rent Act tenancy
can be brought to an end by the creation of a new tenancy which is inconsistent with the old one. It is a question of fact and degree whether the

grantee of a new tenancy is a protected or statutory tenant immediately before its grant. There is no rule of law 'precluding a 24-hour period' out of occupation. It was impossible to state that the parties' actions were a device to avoid the impact of the Rent Act.

N4.5   **Bone v Bone**

[1992] EGCS 81, CA

Licence not terminated merely by licensees moving out

The defendants (the parents) owned an early 19th-century farmhouse where they lived with their son (the plaintiff). They also owned a coach house and four acres of grounds. The parents sold the house to the son in 1985 for £35,000, but continued to live there as licensees. The judge found that the sale was at an undervalue and that the continuing provision of living accommodation for the parents was an important part of the consideration. A year later the parents moved out. Claiming that they had abandoned their licence, the son put the house on the market for £350,000. The parents registered land charges to protect their rights of occupation and, as a result, the son sought a declaration that they had abandoned their licence. Before the hearing, the son exchanged contracts for the sale of the house for £450,000. In the High Court, it was held that the parents had not abandoned their licence and they were awarded damages of £70,000.

On appeal, it was held that, although no formalities were required for the abandonment of a contractual licence, it had not been reasonable for the son to assume that, merely by moving out, the parents had abandoned their licence. Therefore, the parents' licence had not been determined. The Court of Appeal took into account the fact that the parents had refused to sign a deed of surrender which had been prepared by the son. The damages award was upheld.

N4.6   **Brent LBC v Sharma and Vyas**

(1993) 25 HLR 257, CA

Tenant's letter regarding transfer of tenancy operated as surrender

Mr Sharma was granted a tenancy in 1984. Later Ms Vyas came to live with him. In 1987 Mr Sharma moved out and surrendered his tenancy. The council then granted a tenancy to Ms Vyas. Mr Sharma apparently moved back into the premises with his two children. Ms Vyas wrote saying that she had no objection to the tenancy being transferred into his name. There were rent arrears of about £4,000. The council did not transfer the tenancy and did not treat Mr Sharma as a tenant. They no longer debited any rent to the account of Ms Vyas. They delivered a notice to quit addressed to Ms Vyas at the property, but it was clear that it never came to her attention and so was ineffective. HHJ Rowntree found that the letter was an unequivocal act showing that Ms Vyas wished to surrender the tenancy and that this had been accepted by the council.

The Court of Appeal dismissed Mr Sharma's appeal. It was plain by the time that proceedings were issued that the council accepted by its conduct that the tenancy no longer existed. There was a surrender by operation of law. Stuart-Smith LJ cited with approval the following passage in *Woodfall* vol 1 p822, para 1-1849:

The term 'surrender by operation of law' or 'implied surrender' (there being no distinction) is the expression used to describe all those cases where the law implies a surrender from unequivocal conduct of both parties which is inconsistent with the continuance of the existing tenancy.

N4.7   *Camden LBC v Alexandrou*

(1998) 30 HLR 534, CA

Surrender by operation of law where tenant sought to assign interest to other tenant

Mr Alexandrou was a secure tenant. He wrote to the council stating, 'The above flat is no longer my responsibility as I am unable to pay for the upkeep. My wife wishes to keep the said flat and pay the rent to which I agree.' The council treated the tenancy as having been assigned to the wife. She later gave notice to quit and the council took proceedings for possession against Mr Alexandrou on the basis that he no longer had an interest in the property. The trial judge granted possession, holding that the notice had been validly given by the wife as the sole tenant and had determined her tenancy. He further held that she had either obtained the tenancy from her husband by assignment or following a surrender by him. Mr Alexandrou sought leave to appeal on the grounds that (a) there was no assignment because there was no deed (see *Crago v Julian* [1992] 1 WLR 372, CA) and (b) no case for surrender had been pleaded or made out by evidence.

The Court of Appeal was satisfied that, notwithstanding the absence of a deed of either surrender or assignment, a surrender by operation of law had been made out on the evidence even though the tenant had not given vacant possession at the date of his letter or thereafter. Accordingly, the court refused an application for leave to appeal.

N4.8   *Chamberlain v Scalley*

(1994) 26 HLR 26, CA

Surrender not to be implied by absence unless long absence with large arrears

The defendant was a joint tenant with a Miss Butler. In 1990 Miss Butler moved out, but left her belongings and two cats behind. The landlord argued that this was unequivocal evidence that there had been an implied surrender by operation of law. A county court judge made an order for possession and Mr Scalley appealed.

The Court of Appeal held that, for there to be an implied surrender, there had to be unequivocal conduct on the part of both the landlord and the tenant which was inconsistent with the continuance of a tenancy. A surrender was not to be implied unless there had been a long absence with large arrears of rent. The tenant's conduct was equivocal because she had left her belongings and cats behind and so there had been no surrender. The possession order was set aside.

N4.9   *Climping Park Ltd v Barritt*

(1989) *Independent* 15 May, CA

Where parties enter into new agreement old agreement surrendered

When an existing tenancy between the same parties is replaced by a new agreement which operates as a surrender of the old tenancy by the tenant and a re-grant by the landlord, the latter is good consideration for the surrender by the tenant and all new obligations which the tenant takes on.

N4.10   *Ealing Housing Association v McKenzie*

[2003] EWCA Civ 1602; [2004] HLR 21; [2004] L&TR 15; (2003) *Times* 30 October

Where ineffective NTQ served by departing tenant who was rehoused by land-lord there was an implied surrender

Ealing Housing Association let a flat to Mrs McKenzie on an assured tenancy. In February 2000 she moved out, leaving her husband, Mr McKenzie, who enjoyed matrimonial home rights under Family Law Act 1996 s30, in occupation. She informed Ealing that she did not intend to return because of domestic violence and applied for a transfer to a new property. She was offered alternative accommodation on condition that she terminated her existing tenancy of the flat. On 11 July 2000 she signed a notice to quit. Ealing later accepted that it was invalid because it gave insufficient notice. Ealing brought possession proceedings, claiming that Mr McKenzie was a trespasser. HHJ Oppenheimer held that there had been an implied surrender and made a possession order.

The Court of Appeal dismissed Mr McKenzie's appeal. There was no express surrender because there was nothing in writing within the meaning of Law of Property (Miscellaneous Provisions) Act 1989 s2. There was no implied surrender by operation of law simply as a result of Mrs McKenzie moving out without an intention to return because the flat was still occupied by Mr McKenzie pursuant to Family Law Act 1996 s30. However, there was evidence that from 17 July 2000 Ealing had transferred Mrs McKenzie's rent account to the new flat and ceased to charge her rent for the old flat. There was an unequivocal inference that Ealing accepted that the tenancy had been terminated. The notice to quit was an act by the tenant manifesting an intention to terminate the tenancy immediately. From 17 July 2000 both sides conducted themselves on the basis that the tenancy was terminated. Accordingly the judge was entitled to find that there had been an implied surrender of the tenancy.

N4.11   *Foster v Robinson*

[1951] 1 KB 149; [1950] 2 All ER 342, CA

Agreement that retired farm worker need no longer pay rent operated as sur-render; son estopped from claiming tenancy still existed

A cottage was occupied by a farm worker who paid a yearly rent of £6 10s (£6.50). When, as a result of age and infirmity, he stopped working, his landlord and former employer agreed that he need not pay any further rent but could live in the cottage for the rest of his life.

The Court of Appeal held that this agreement was an effective surren-der by operation of law and that the former tenant's son was estopped from claiming that the old tenancy still existed. The Court of Appeal approved the following passage in *Foa's General Law of Landlord and Tenant*:

> It has been laid down that in order to constitute a surrender by operation of law there must be, first, an act of purported surrender invalid per se by

reason of non-compliance with statutory or other formalities, and secondly, some change of circumstances supervening on, or arising from, the purported surrender, which, by reason of the doctrine of estoppel or part performance, makes it inequitable and fraudulent for any of the parties to rely upon the invalidity of the purported surrender.

N4.12 *Hackney LBC v Snowden*

[2001] L&TR 60, (2001) 33 HLR 554, CA (see F4.9)

Open to landlord and tenant to agree to treat NTQ as valid and thereby waive the requirement of four weeks' notice

N4.13 *Laine v Cadwallader*

(2001) 33 HLR 397, [2001] L&TR 77, CA

Return of keys an offer of surrender, not a surrender

The claimant granted the defendants an assured shorthold tenancy for a term of six months from 19 January 1998. The tenants held over at the end of the fixed term and became statutory periodic tenants. On 10 September 1998 they left and put the keys through the landlord's letter box. The landlord sued, among other things, for four weeks' rent in lieu of notice.

Her claim was dismissed in the county court, but allowed in the Court of Appeal. Under Protection from Eviction Act 1977 s5 any notice to quit by a tenant is invalid unless it is given not less than four weeks before the date on which it is due to take effect. The dropping off of the keys was not a surrender, but an offer to surrender. There was no express acceptance of the offer. The landlord had agreed to terminate the tenancy at the end of the minimum period for which a proper notice could have been given. The landlord was accordingly entitled to recover the rent for that four-week period.

N4.14 *Leek and Moorlands Building Society v Clark*

[1952] 2 QB 788; [1952] 2 All ER 492, CA

One of two joint tenants cannot surrender a joint tenancy

Unless there is express agreement, one of two joint tenants cannot validly surrender a joint tenancy.

N4.15 *Mattey Securities Ltd v Ervin*

[1998] 34 EG 91, CA

Payment of rent by non-tenant did not amount to surrender and re-grant to payer

In a case involving commercial premises, the court considered the circumstances in which a surrender by operation of law may occur. Bracewell J said:

> The conduct of the parties must unequivocally amount to an acceptance that the tenancy is ended for the doctrine to apply. Although a surrender by operation of law does not require that there is an intention of the parties to surrender the lease, it does however require that there is some unequivocal act which has the effect of estopping the parties from asserting that the lease is still extant.

Payment of rent by a company other than the tenant which had entered into occupation did not operate as a surrender by operation of law and re-grant to the company which was paying the rent.

N4.16   *Preston BC v Fairclough*
(1983) 8 HLR 70, CA

For landlord to establish surrender; tenant leaving premises owing rent insufficient

The tenants of a council house allowed Mrs Fairclough to move in with them. Later the tenants left, leaving Mrs Fairclough in occupation. The council, without taking any steps to terminate the tenants' tenancy (such as serving a notice to quit), brought possession proceedings under County Court Rules Ord 24. A county court judge held that the tenancy had been terminated by operation of law and made a possession order.

Mrs Fairclough's appeal was allowed. Griffiths LJ stated:

> ... it is for the Council to establish on such an application that they are entitled to possession of the premises. As they have taken no steps to deter-mine the tenancy of [the tenants], they would only be able to establish that they were entitled to possession of the premises if there was material from which the learned judge could draw the inference that there had been a surrender by law of the tenancy. It is for the Council to establish a sur-render by law. They have placed virtually no material before the judge which would entitle him to draw such an inference. The bare fact that a tenant leaves premises at a time when he owes rent is certainly insufficient to enable a court to draw the inference that there has been a surrender.

N4.17   *Proudreed Ltd v Microgen Holdings plc*
[1996] 1 EGLR 89; [1996] 12 EG 127, CA

No surrender by return of keys

Although the return of keys by a tenant to a landlord may amount to a sur-render, this is not so if there is no other evidence that the landlord intends to resume possession. In this case, the landlord held the keys for six days before returning them to the tenant's receiver.

The Court of Appeal held that on these particular facts there had been no surrender.

N4.18   *R v Croydon LBC ex p Toth*
(1988) 20 HLR 576, CA (see T12.2)

Tenancy surrendered where tenant left premises taking all belongings; facts at time landlord accepted surrender relevant; later assertion by tenant that did not intend to leave permanently irrelevant

N4.19   *Sanctuary Housing Association v Baker*
(1998) 30 HLR 809; [1998] 1 EGLR 42; [1998] 09 EG 150, CA (see E3.6)

Assignment effective despite consent to assign having been obtained by fraud; fraud nullified consent; no implied surrender

N4.20   *Sanctuary Housing Association v Campbell*
[1999] 1 WLR 1279; [1999] 3 All ER 460; (2000) 32 HLR 100; [1999] 18 EG 162; (1999) *Times* 1 April, CA

*Where tenant left premises and rehoused herself actions unequivocal; MHA
did not restrict tenant's rights to terminate tenancy*

The plaintiff housing association granted Ms Shaw a secure weekly
tenancy of a dwelling. She occupied the house with her children and her
co-habitee, Mr Campbell. Later she married Mr Campbell, but then left
the house as a result of domestic violence and purported to surrender
possession. However, Mr Campbell remained in the house and refused to
leave. The housing association began proceedings to gain possession of
the house. In his defence, Mr Campbell relied on rights conferred on him
by Matrimonial Homes Act 1983. An assistant recorder decided that the
tenancy had been expressly surrendered.

Mr Campbell appealed unsuccessfully. On appeal it was conceded that
any surrender could only have been by operation of law. The Court of
Appeal held that there had been a surrender by operation of law. After
rehousing herself, Ms Shaw had done all that she could to comply with the
housing association's stipulation that she should vacate the premises and
return the keys. Her conduct was unequivocal. The court distinguished
Hoggett v Hoggett (1980) 39 P&CR 121, CA. Furthermore, there is nothing
in Matrimonial Homes Act 1983 s1 which restricts a tenant's right to terminate her contractual relationship with the landlord. Nothing in s1 gave
Mr Campbell indefinite rights of occupation of the former matrimonial
home which were only terminable by an order under s1(2)(a) or otherwise within the court's jurisdiction derived from the suit. The section was
plainly intended to regulate the rights of spouses between themselves.

N4.21   *Zionmor v Islington LBC*

(1998) 30 HLR 822; March 1998 *Legal Action* 10, CA

*Tenant leaving note to other tenants that he was leaving did not amount to
offer of surrender to landlord*

In 1992 the council let the plaintiff a flat on a secure tenancy. In October
1995, the tenant gave notice of the right to buy. This was admitted by
the council. Before completion the tenant left the flat, leaving behind a
friend. When he left, he put up a notice in the common parts indicating
that because graffiti had been written on the walls of his flat, his windows smashed and his door locks broken, he would no longer be residing
at the property. Later he explained that the note was intended to make
those who had been harassing him think that he had left the property for
good. The council was informed of the note by other tenants and the council's caretaker could not find the tenant. The council decided that the flat
had been abandoned and changed the locks to the front door. The tenant
sought orders readmitting him to the property and restraining the landlord's further interference with it. The council claimed that the departure
of the tenant amounted to a surrender and thereby determination of the
tenancy. The county court judge rejected the council's defence and held
that the tenancy had not been determined.

The council's appeal was dismissed by the Court of Appeal. The court
held that the county court judge had properly directed himself that the
question was whether the acts of the tenant amounted to an implied offer
of surrender of the tenancy. If the acts could not amount to such an implied

offer of surrender, then there was no offer for the landlords to accept. The Court of Appeal agreed with the judge that, as the tenant had left a friend in possession together with at least some of his belongings, no inference could properly be drawn that he had intended to give up the tenancy. The council could not place reliance on the notice affixed to the notice-board because it was not directed to the landlord and did not suggest that the tenant was giving up possession in any legal or technical sense so as to surrender the tenancy. There had been no unequivocal relinquishment of possession and no implied offer of surrender.

High Court

N4.22   *Barakat v Ealing LBC*
[1996] COD 502, QBD

Return of keys and landlord's acceptance with intention of taking possession a surrender

In a case involving liability for non-domestic rates, Brooke J held that a surrender by operation of law occurs where one party does and the other assents to an act which is inconsistent with the continuance of the lease or tenancy. The tenant's return of the keys and the landlord's acceptance of them with the intention of taking possession was sufficient to effect a surrender. There are four preconditions to surrender by operation of law:

1) the doing of an act by a party;
2) that the act is inconsistent with the continuation of the tenancy;
3) the assent of the other party; and
4) the intention of the landlord to take possession and accept the termination of the tenancy.

N4.23   *Coker v London Rent Assessment Panel*
[2006] EWHC 2367 (Admin); 19 May 2006

Variation to terms of tenancy did not amount to surrender of tenancy and re-grant

Mr Coker was the tenant of a flat. For many years there were substantial disputes between him and his landlord. In October 2004 these were settled by a Tomlin order which had the effect of varying the rent, rendering insurance rent non-payable, modifying the covenant against alterations and changing the contract from a business tenancy to an assured tenancy. The rent payable was £950 per month. Later the landlord served a notice of increase of rent under Housing Act 1988 s13. Mr Coker referred the notice to the rent assessment panel (RAP), arguing that it was invalid because the Tomlin order amounted to the surrender of the old tenancy and grant of a new tenancy. The RAP rejected that argument on the basis that the amendments created by the order could not amount to a new tenancy as they were not sufficiently substantial. The RAP inspected the flat and concluded that £1,120 per month was the rent for which the flat could reasonably be expected to be let on the open market in accordance with s14. Mr Coker appealed against that decision.

James Goudie QC, sitting as a deputy High Court judge, dismissed the appeal. The Tomlin order had not resulted in any increase in the premises demised or in the length of term. The absence of both features did not mean that there could never be a surrender, but that there would only exceptionally be one. At the date of the Tomlin order, it was common ground that Mr Coker had an assured tenancy and not a business tenancy. The only variations to the tenancy agreement (ie, agreement by the land-lord not to enforce the insurance rent and a modification to the covenant against alterations) 'came nowhere near, individually or cumulatively, to being sufficient to imply a surrender and re-grant'.

N4.24   *R v Hammersmith and Fulham LBC ex p Quigley*
(2000) 32 HLR 379; (1999) *Independent* 24 May, QBD (see L1.9)

Council's decision to bring possession claim quashed. No implied surrender

County courts

N4.25   *Hackney LBC v Ampratum*
7 April 2003, Central London Civil Trial Centre

Not possible to infer surrender where tenant left unwillingly (due to deportation)

Ms Bonney-Offei, the second defendant, was a secure tenant. She was deported to Ghana in 1993. In 1994 the council agreed to the assign-ment of the tenancy to the first defendant. However, that assignment was invalid because the written consent of Ms Bonney-Offei was not obtained. In 2000 Ms Bonney-Offei returned from Ghana and went back into occu-pation of the premises. The council began possession proceedings, claim-ing that Ms Bonney-Offei's tenancy had been surrendered by operation of law and that the first defendant had unlawfully sublet.

Bell J, sitting as a judge of the county court, dismissed the claim. There was nothing in the circumstances to justify the inference that there had been a surrender. Ms Bonney-Offei had left unwillingly and could be expected to return, if able, in due course. She had left her family in occu-pation. It was not possible to infer surrender from her deportation. Her actions did not amount to an unequivocal acceptance that the tenancy had ended.

CHAPTER O

Harassment and illegal eviction

01 Civil proceedings

An occupant who has been harassed or unlawfully evicted can rely on a number of causes of action in civil proceedings, in both contract and tort. These are outlined below. For a more detailed analysis of the law, see Arden, Carter and Dymond *Quiet Enjoyment* 6th edn (LAG, 2002).

In order to establish what causes of action an occupant may have it will be necessary to consider their status in premises. See the earlier chapters in this book regarding security of tenure and the termination of agreements. Note that once an occupier is outside Housing Act protection the lease/licence distinction (section B2) may not be important because protection under Protection from Eviction Act ss3 and 5 applies to licences and tenancies. However, the covenant of quiet enjoyment strictly only applies to tenancies.

Contract

In contract, a claim may be brought for breach of express terms or implied terms, including the covenant of quiet enjoyment and the covenant not to derogate from grant.

The covenant of quiet enjoyment is implied into every tenancy. It requires a landlord not to interfere with a tenant's lawful possession of the premises. Anything which is an invasion of a tenant's right to remain in possession of premises undisturbed can amount to a breach of this covenant, even if there is no direct physical interference.

Tort

There are a number of torts that may be of relevance. These include nuisance, trespass to land, trespass to goods, trespass to the person, deceit, intimidation and breaches of: Protection from Harassment Act 1997 s3, Housing Act 1988 s27 (O4), Protection from Eviction Act 1977 s3 (O3).

Nuisance arises where an activity or state of affairs exists on premises which unreasonably interferes with another's use or enjoyment of land. The person affected must have a sufficient interest in the land to have a cause of action (eg, a tenant or licensee with exclusive possession).

Trespass to land is caused by any unlawful entry on to land or unlawful placing of something on to land. Tenants are entitled to exclusive possession of premises let and the unauthorised entry (or failure to leave or actions outside that for which permission to enter was granted) of any person constitutes a trespass. Landlords may be liable for trespass on premises of their own tenants (see *Street v Mountford* (B2.4) and *Borg v Rogers* [1981] CAT 330 (UB)).

02 General

House of Lords

02.1 *Southwark LBC v Mills; Southwark LBC v Tanner; Baxter v Camden LBC*
[2001] 1 AC 1; [1999] 3 WLR 939; [1999] 4 All ER 449; [2000] LGR 138; [1999] 45 EG 179; (2000) 32 HLR 148; [2000] L&TR 159; (1999) *Times* 22 October, HL (see P4.2)

Ordinary use of residential premises cannot amount to a nuisance; no breach of covenant of quiet enjoyment where sound insulation inadequate

Court of Appeal

02.2   *Botu v Brent LBC*

(2001) 33 HLR 151, CA

Eviction pursuant to court order not rendered unlawful when order subsequently set aside

Mr Botu was a secure tenant. In 1996 he was arrested and remanded in custody. On 14 July 1997, at a hearing which Mr Botu did not attend, Brent obtained an outright possession order which was then enforced. On 21 November 1997 Brent granted a new tenancy to a third party. Later Mr Botu succeeded in setting aside the possession order pursuant to CCR Ord 37 (now see CPR 39.3) and on 3 July 1998 Brent granted him a new tenancy of an alternative property. He began proceedings against Brent for damages for breach of the implied covenant for quiet enjoyment for the period from 14 July 1997 to 3 July 1998. HHJ Hornby upheld the claim in relation to the period from 21 November 1997 until 3 July 1998, but rejected the claim for the earlier period. Brent appealed against the finding of liability and Mr Botu cross-appealed against the finding that breach of covenant prior to 21 November had not been established.

The Court of Appeal allowed Brent's appeal and dismissed the cross-appeal. *Burrows v Brent LBC* (12.1) and *Lambeth LBC v Rogers* (12.9) were not on point. The case of *Hillgate House Ltd v Expert Clothing Service and Sales Ltd* [1987] 1 EGLR 65; (1987) 282 EG 715, ChD held that while an order of the court is in force it is to be obeyed, and acts done under it are lawful. Sir Nicholas Browne-Wilkinson V-C, dealing with a claim for breach of the covenant of quiet enjoyment, had decided that any interruption by the landlord acting under an order of the court had been lawful at the time it took place and could not retrospectively be made unlawful when the order was reversed on appeal. The present case was concerned with an order by a court setting aside its own earlier order. The two cases were indistinguishable. Like the landlord in *Hillgate*, Brent had been acting on the basis of a valid existing order of the court (see also the decision in *Isaacs v Robertson* [1985] AC 97). There is no distinction between orders set aside on application to the court which made them and those set aside by an appellate court.

02.3   *Cowan v Chief Constable for Avon and Somerset Constabulary*

[2001] EWCA Civ 1699; [2002] HLR 43; (2001) *Times* 11 December

Police did not owe duty of care to tenant to prevent unlawful eviction

Mr Cowan was an assured tenant. He received a letter from his landlord stating that he wanted him to leave. Several weeks later two men called at the property and told him that they would break his legs if he was not out of the property by 6 pm. Mr Cowan telephoned the police. Two officers called and told him to telephone again if the men returned. At about 6 pm Mr Cowan saw four men removing his belongings into the street. He called the police and the same two officers returned. The men told the police that they had bought the property and that Mr Cowan had been given notice to leave. The police advised both sides to seek legal advice and then left. Neither of the officers knew about the Protection from Eviction Act 1977. Mr Cowan brought proceedings against the chief constable, claiming that he was liable in negligence because the police officers failed to prevent an offence being committed. HHJ Jack dismissed the claim, finding that the officers owed no duty of care to Mr Cowan, but that if he was wrong, any duty had not been broken.

The Court of Appeal dismissed Mr Cowan's appeal. It is only if a particular responsibility towards an individual arises, establishing a sufficiently close relationship, that the police may owe a duty of care to that individual. The trial judge was entitled to make the finding of fact that the police had attended to prevent a breach of the peace. The police fulfilled that purpose. They did not assume a responsibility towards Mr Cowan to prevent his eviction. Mere presence at the scene was not sufficient to give rise to the necessary special relationship. On the facts, the police did not assume any responsibility to prevent his eviction. Accordingly they owed no duty of care to Mr Cowan.

02.4 *Guppys (Bridport) Ltd v Brookling*
(1984) 14 HLR 1; (1984) 269 EG 846, CA

Disruption caused by major building works amounted to nuisance

The local authority served notices on the landlord of a house in multiple occupation for works to be carried out. The landlord decided to convert the house into self-contained flats and carried out major building works while two tenants remained in occupation. The works caused serious disruption to the tenants. The tenants were forced into leaving the property and were offered alternative accommodation by the local authority. The county court held that (1) the occupants were tenants (2) the facts amounted to a trespass and (3) the tenants were entitled to exemplary damages of £1,000.

The Court of Appeal dismissed an appeal by the landlord. The occupants were tenants: they had been described and treated as such and it was very difficult for a landlord to claim later that they were no more than licensees. Whether or not the landlord's actions amounted to trespass, there clearly was a nuisance. The interferences with the comfort of the tenants went beyond what was reasonably necessary. It was open to a tenant to sue his own landlord in nuisance. Furthermore, there was evidence which justified the award of exemplary damages: the landlord's motive to get rid of the tenants and make a profit; the failure to find alternative accommodation or to keep to a minimum the interference with the comfort and enjoyment of the premises and the breach of an undertaking given to the county court.

See also *Mira v Aylmer Square Investments Ltd* (P11.15)

02.5 *Haniff v Robinson*
[1993] QB 419; [1992] 3 WLR 875; [1993] 1 All ER 185; (1994) 26 HLR 386, CA

Eviction without using court bailiffs after possession order obtained unlawful

A landlord, relying on Rent Act 1977 Sch 15 Case 11 (returning owner-occupier), obtained a possession order while a tenant was away on holiday. The tenant applied to set aside the possession order but, before the application could be heard, the landlord evicted her. The tenant claimed damages under Housing Act 1988 ss27 and 28. The landlord contended that the eviction was lawful because he had obtained a possession order.

The Court of Appeal held that a possession order made against a protected tenant can be executed only by issuing a warrant for possession directed to the bailiff (see CCR Ord 26 r17(1)) and that to decide otherwise would have the result of depriving Rent Act 1977 s100 (the court's power to suspend execution etc) of any value. The eviction was unlawful and the awards of damages made in the county court were upheld, namely £26,000 under ss27/28, approximately £2,000 for aggravation of post-viral fatigue syndrome from which the tenant suffered, and £700 for loss of property. Rent arrears of approximately £4,000 were set off against these damages.

Note: In *R (Sacupima) v Newham LBC* (T5.2) it was held that, where a court order was required to recover possession (in *Sacupima*, under Housing Act 1988 s5), the effect of CCR Ord 26 r17 was that an order for possession was enforceable only by warrant of possession. CCR Ord 26 r17 remains in force despite the introduction of the CPR.

02.6 *Kenny v Preen*

[1963] 1 QB 499; [1962] 3 WLR 1233; [1962] 3 All ER 814, CA

Covenant of quiet enjoyment can be breached without direct physical interference

A landlord sent letters to a tenant threatening physical eviction and removal of her belongings. He called at her room repeatedly, knocked on her door and shouted threats at her.

It was held that this course of action, which was a deliberate attempt to drive her out, amounted to breach of covenant for quiet enjoyment even though there was no direct physical interference with the tenant's possession or enjoyment of the room. The landlord's conduct had seriously interfered with her proper freedom of action in exercising her right to remain in possession undisturbed.

02.7 *Khorasandjian v Bush*

[1993] QB 727; [1993] 3 WLR 476; [1993] 3 All ER 669; (1993) 25 HLR 392, CA

Harassing telephone calls amounted to a nuisance of bare licensee

The plaintiff lived with her parents. The defendant pestered her with telephone calls to her at her parents' home. He also stole her handbag so as to have a memento to keep and was sent to prison for making threats to kill her. However, he continued to behave aggressively towards her and to pester and harass.

It was held that the harassing telephone calls amounted to a nuisance because they interfered with the plaintiff's ordinary and reasonable use of her home. The campaign of harassment was clearly intended to cause harm to the plaintiff and could be restrained quia timet (because some actionable event is likely to occur) by an injunction.

Note: In *Hunter v Canary Wharf Ltd* (P7.3) the House of Lords held that a licensee without exclusive occupation, such as a member of a tenant's family, did not have a sufficient interest in land to found an action in private nuisance and overruled *Khorasandjian* to this extent. The plaintiff could now, however, rely on Protection from Harassment Act 1997.

02.8   *Mafo v Adams*

[1970] 1 QB 548; [1970] 2 WLR 72; [1969] 3 All ER 1404, CA (see O9.6)

Landlord can be liable in tort of deceit

02.9   *McCall v Abelesz*

[1976] 1 QB 585; [1976] 2 WLR 151; [1976] 1 All ER 727; (1976) 31 P&CR 256, CA (see O3.4)

Implied covenant to supply gas and electricity

02.10   *Pemberton v Southwark LBC*

[2000] 1 WLR 1672; [2000] 3 All ER 924; (2000) 32 HLR 784; [2000] 21 EG 135; (2000) *Times* 26 April, CA (see I2.13)

A tolerated trespasser has a sufficient interest in land to claim in nuisance

02.11   *Queensway Marketing Ltd v Associated Restaurants Ltd*

[1988] 2 EGLR 49; [1988] 32 EG 41, CA

Erection of scaffolding could breach covenant of quite enjoyment

It was confirmed that the erection of scaffolding round a building may amount to breach of covenant for quiet enjoyment.

02.12   *Sampson v Floyd*

[1989] 2 EGLR 49; [1989] 33 EG 41, CA

Physical eviction not necessary for breach of covenant of quiet enjoyment

The plaintiff was the lessee of a chalet and a restaurant on a complex including a caravan park and holiday homes in Devon. The landlord refused to pay for a meal at the restaurant, 'abused' the tenant and there was an 'exchange of fists'. After finding his 'frightened wife hiding under a caravan', the tenant left the property and recovered his possessions under police escort. The tenant issued proceedings and was awarded £11,364, which included £10,000 which he had paid for the lease, conveyancing costs and £750 for mental distress to himself and his wife.

The Court of Appeal dismissed the landlord's appeal. There was no reason to disagree with the county court judge's conclusions. Physical eviction is not necessary to constitute breach of covenant for quiet enjoyment. The award of damages was upheld.

02.13   *Sampson v Hodson-Pressinger*

[1981] 3 All ER 701; (1984) 12 HLR 40; (1982) 261 EG 891, CA

Landlord liable for leasing a flat where ordinary use would cause a nuisance

The plaintiff held a long lease of his flat. The freeholder then built a terrace on the flat roof above the flat. Use of the terrace by the lessee who later lived above the plaintiff caused nuisance which interfered with the plaintiff's reasonable use and enjoyment of his premises. The plaintiff sued the successor in title to the original freeholder in nuisance. He was refused an injunction but awarded damages of £2,000.

The Court of Appeal dismissed the freeholder's appeal. The upper flat had been leased in such a condition that its ordinary use would cause nuisance to the plaintiff. The purchaser of the freehold was legally in the same position as the original landlord and was liable both in nuisance and for breach of covenant for quiet enjoyment.

Note: See though *Southwark LBC v Mills* (P4.2)

02.14 **Smith v Nottinghamshire CC**
(1981) *Times* 13 November, CA

Implied term in licence not to disturb students while studying

Law students in a hall of residence at Trent Polytechnic were disturbed by building works. They were unable to study in their rooms.

The Court of Appeal held that there was an implied term in their contractual licences that the council, which owned the halls of residence, would 'do nothing without just cause to disturb the students from getting on with their studies in their rooms in reasonable quietude'.

02.15 **Speiro Lechouritis v Goldmile Properties Ltd**
[2003] EWCA Civ 49; [2003] 15 EG 143; [2003] 2 P&CR 1; [2003] L&TR 390 (also known as *Goldmile Properties Ltd v Speiro Lechouritis*)

Covenant of quiet enjoyment not breached by a disturbance caused by necessary building works

A lease of a restaurant contained a covenant for quiet enjoyment in favour of the tenant and a covenant by the landlord to repair the parts of the building which were not the responsibility of the tenant. The landlord engaged contractors to clean the external walls and windows of the building and to repair the seals between the frames and the walls. The work was completed within six months but required scaffolding and sheeting to be fixed to the outside of the building. The tenant's restaurant business was seriously disrupted. As a result the tenant made a claim against the landlord for loss of profit. A district judge dismissed the claim on the basis that the landlord was necessarily carrying out repairing obligations under the lease and that it took all reasonable steps to minimise the potential risks, and so there was no breach of the covenant for quiet enjoyment.

A circuit judge allowed the tenant's appeal but the Court of Appeal allowed the landlord's second appeal. The test adopted and applied by the district judge was right. The threshold for disturbance by repairs was all reasonable precautions rather than all possible precautions. The covenant of quiet enjoyment was qualified by the phrase 'except as herein provided' and the effect was that the ways in which the tenant's quiet enjoyment could be disturbed included the execution of structural repairs and maintenance. The district judge was entitled to find that the landlord had taken all reasonable steps and his judgment was restored.

Cf *Guppys (Bridport) Ltd v Brookling* (O2.4)

Local government ombudsman reports

02.15 *Investigation 88/A/858 (Tower Hamlets LBC)*
(see L3.20)

No legal basis for council's use of protected intending occupier certificates

03   **Protection from Eviction Act 1977 (civil provisions)**

Breach of Protection from Eviction Act 1977 s3 gives rise to the tort of breach of statutory duty (*Warder v Cooper* [1970] 1 All ER 1112, CA). It applies where a landlord evicts an occupier whose tenancy or licence has come to an end, without obtaining a court order. It does not apply to excluded tenancies or licences as defined by s3A, eg, where there is a resident landlord, the grant is not for money or money's worth or the premises are a council/housing association run hostel. Furthermore, s3 does not apply to tenancies or licences that are statutorily protected, as defined by s8(1), eg, assured tenancies.

Section 3 (1) provides:

Where any premises have been let as a dwelling under a tenancy which is neither a statutorily protected tenancy nor an excluded tenancy and –
(a) the tenancy... has come to an end, but
(b) the occupier continues to reside in the premises...
it shall not be lawful for the owner to enforce against the occupier, otherwise than by proceedings in the court, his right to recover possession of the premises.'

An 'occupier' is any person lawfully residing in the premises at the termination of the former tenancy (s3(2)). Section s3(2B) provides that s3(1) also applies to premises occupied as a dwelling under a licence, other than an excluded licence.

Section 5 prescribes that a notice to quit a non-excluded tenancy or licence must, among other requirements, be of at least 28 days. See N2.2–N2.27 for notices to quit.

Court of Appeal

03.1   *Brennan v Lambeth LBC*
(1998) 30 HLR 481, CA (see B2.6)

Provision enabling residents (homeless applicants) to be moved from room to room resulted in licence; accommodation was a 'hostel' within PEA 1977(3A)(8)

03.2   *Brillouet v Landless*
(1996) 28 HLR 836, CA (see B2.8)

Hotel resident does not occupy premises 'let as a dwelling' and PEA 1977 s3 does not apply

03.3   *Desnousse v Newham LBC*
[2006] EWCA Civ 547; [2006] 1 QB 831; [2006] 3 WLR 349; [2007] 2 All ER 218; [2006] HLR 38; [2007] LGR 368; (2006) *Times* 28 June; 17 May 2006

Accommodation of homeless applicant under HA 1996 s188 or s190 not 'let as a dwelling'

Mrs Desnousse applied to Newham as a homeless person under Housing Act 1996 Part VII. After being accommodated in bed and breakfast accommodation, she was granted a licence of self-contained accommodation owned by Veni Properties Ltd and managed by Paddington Churches

Housing Association on behalf of Newham. Five months later Newham decided that Mrs Desnousse was intentionally homeless and informed her that her accommodation booking would be cancelled four weeks later. When Mrs Desnousse discovered that Veni was planning to evict her summarily she obtained an interim injunction restraining Veni from evicting her without a court order. However, at trial, following *Mohamed v Manek and Kensington and Chelsea RLBC* (O3.5), HHJ Roberts dismissed her claim.

The Court of Appeal dismissed Mrs Desnousse's appeal (Lloyd LJ dissenting). All three judges held that *Manek* was binding authority that Protection from Eviction Act 1977 s3(2B) does not apply to a licence of accommodation secured for a homeless person in discharge of its duty under s188(1) or 190(2)(a). Mrs Desnousse's case did not fall within any of the exceptions in *Manek*. The accommodation was not 'let as a dwelling'. It was not necessary to decide the position in relation to tenancies of such accommodation. Tuckey and Pill LJJ both held that, once a decision has been taken that no duty is owed, local authorities should not have to take proceedings to evict any applicant who refuses to vacate. They rejected Mrs Desnousse's submission that a reading of Protection From Eviction Act s3 that did not allow it to extend to the recovery of possession from someone in her position was incompatible with ECHR article 8. Any eviction in these circumstances is in accordance with the law. The question is one of proportionality – whether the possibility of eviction without the procedural safeguards contained in the Act can be justified. Tuckey and Pill LJJ held that it could. Evictions are likely to be under the local authority control. They can be trusted to act lawfully and responsibly.

03.4   ## McCall v Abelesz
[1976] 1 QB 585; [1976] 2 WLR 151; [1976] 1 All ER 727; (1976) 31 P&CR 256, CA

Breach of PEA s1(3) does not give rise to civil cause of action; implied covenant to supply gas and electricity

A landlord failed to pay the gas bill for the house where the claimant tenant lived and the gas board disconnected the gas supply. For a time the electricity and water supplies were also cut off. The tenant brought county court proceedings claiming damages solely under Rent Act 1965 s30(2) (the precursor of Protection from Eviction Act 1977 s1(3), unlawful harassment, see section O10).

The Court of Appeal held that s30(2) did not give rise to a civil remedy for damages for harassment in addition to imposing a criminal sanction. The tenant should have sued for breach of the implied covenant to supply gas and electricity and the covenant for quiet enjoyment.

03.5   ## Mohamed v Manek and Kensington and Chelsea RLBC
(1995) 27 HLR 439; (1995) 94 LGR 211, CA

Temporary accommodation of homeless applicants not covered by PEA 1977 s3

A homeless applicant was booked into Mr Manek's hotel by the council pending enquiries into his application. Three days later the council notified the applicant of its decision that he was not in priority need and that his booking was terminated. It was made clear that the applicant would be excluded from the hotel and he applied for an injunction to prevent either the hotelier or the council from evicting him without a court order obtained in proceedings for possession (Protection from Eviction Act 1977 s3(2B)).

Allowing the council's appeal against an injunction granted in the county court, the Court of Appeal held that (a) the 1977 Act was not intended to apply to temporary housing provided by local authorities under Housing Act 1985 s63 (now Housing Act 1996 s188) and (b) temporary accommodation in a hotel or hostel could not be 'premises occupied as a dwelling under a licence' for the purposes of s3(2B).

03.6   *National Trust for Places of Historic Interest v Knipe*

[1997] 4 All ER 627; (1998) 30 HLR 449; [1997] 2 EGLR 9, CA (see N2.16)

Agricultural holding not 'let as a dwelling' and PEA 1977 s5 did not apply

03.7   *Pirabakaran v Patel*

[2006] EWCA Civ 685; [2006] 1 WLR 3112; [2006] All ER 506; [2006] HLR 39; [2006] L&TR 24; (2006) *Times* 19 July; 26 May 2006

Mixed residential/business premises covered by PEA 1977 s2

The claimant landlords let premises which comprised a shop on the ground floor and a residential flat on the first floor to Mr Pirabakaran. He lived in the flat. He fell into arrears and the landlords exercised their right of re-entry to forfeit the lease by taking possession of the shop premises. Mr Pirabakaran continued to live in the flat and so the landlords began possession proceedings, claiming that as a result of their re-entry, the lease had become forfeit. Later the landlords excluded Mr Pirabakaran from the flat. He issued a claim for an injunction against the landlord, relying on Protection from Eviction Act 1977 s2 and claiming that the purported forfeiture of the lease was unlawful. HHJ Oppenheimer found that the demised premises were not let 'as a dwelling', that accordingly the landlords were not constrained by s2 and that therefore the lease had been lawfully forfeited.

The Court of Appeal allowed an appeal. After extensive consideration of the Rent Acts and the effect of the Protection from Eviction Act s8, it held that the phrase 'let as a dwelling' in s2 means 'let wholly or partly as a dwelling'. It therefore applies to premises which are let for mixed residential and business purposes. Furthermore, ECHR article 8 supports this interpretation.

03.8   *Sumeghova v McMahon*

[2002] EWCA Civ 1581; [2003] HLR 26; (2002) *Times* 6 November

Excluded tenancy where landlord shared accommodation temporarily with tenant

The defendant granted the claimant tenant a tenancy of a room in a house in April 1998. In August 1998 he informed the tenant that he needed her to vacate the room on 9 September 1998. On 18 September 1998 he evicted her and threw her belongings on to the pavement outside. In a claim for unlawful eviction, the defendant maintained that he had lived in the same house as the tenant throughout the period of her tenancy, using one room as a living room and another room as a bedroom. His defence was that the tenancy was an excluded tenancy under Protection from Eviction Act 1977 s3A(2) because the tenant had shared accommodation with him and, immediately before the tenancy was granted and at the time it came to an end, he occupied part of those premises as his only or principal home. Recorder Hurst found that although the accommodation was shared both immediately before the tenancy was granted and at the time it came to an end, this was a 'temporary arrangement' and that the landlord's principal residence was in the house next door. As a result the tenancy was not an excluded tenancy. The defendant appealed, complaining that the judge had made no finding as to when he started to sleep in the premises.

The Court of Appeal allowed the defendant's appeal. The defendant was using the premises as his only or principal home in April and September even though it may have been a temporary arrangement. The place where a person sleeps is of the utmost importance. Circumstances may well arise where that would not be a decisive factor but it is a matter which would influence any court considerably. Having rejected the judge's finding in relation to the 'temporary arrangement' on which he had relied, it was necessary for the court to consider whether the property was the defendant's only or principal home in April and September 1998. In the circumstances, it was clear that it was his only or principal home and that the tenancy was therefore excluded.

High Court

03.9 *Polarpark Enterprises Inc v Allason*
[2007] EWHC (Ch) 1088; (2007) *Times* 26 June; 18 April 2007 (see M5.9)

Licence was for money's worth where licensee was to keep the premises repaired and insured; possession order could only be enforced in the county court

03.10 *Rogerson v Wigan MBC*
[2004] EWHC (QB) 1677; [2005] HLR 10; [2005] LGR 549

Licence in council-run hostel excluded under PEA 1977 s3A; accommodation provided to a homeless applicant which is no longer referable to the temporary accommodation duty is 'a dwelling' for the purposes of s3

In November 2002 the council accepted that it owed the claimant a duty to provide interim accommodation under Housing Act 1996 s188 pending a decision on his homelessness application. It placed him and his partner in a room in its 'hostel' for the homeless. This was not a purpose-built hostel but a building constructed as a block of flats. There were seven two-bedroom flats, a single-bedroomed flat and a warden's flat on the ground floor. Each flat contained bedrooms as well as a living room, kitchen and bathroom. Residents were allocated bedrooms (with their own locks) but shared the facilities of the flat with other residents. The terms of occupation included a nightly curfew, a prohibition on alcohol and drugs and a facility enabling the occupier to be required to move from one flat or bedroom to another. The warden had a master key for all the flats and bedrooms. The licence agreement provided for seven days' notice. The day after the claimant moved in, the council accepted that it owed him the full housing duty (Housing Act 1996 s193). He remained in occupation of the hostel. On 17 February 2003 he was evicted on the expiry of ten days' notice given by the council following an investigation into alleged breach of the licence conditions. He asserted that the Protection from Eviction Act 1977 required the council to give a minimum of four weeks' notice (s5) and to obtain a court order for possession (s3). He brought a claim for damages for unlawful eviction. The council contended that either: (1) the licence of the hostel accommodation was expressly excluded from protection by s3A(8) or; (2) the premises did not constitute a 'dwelling' protected by ss3 and 5 because they had only been provided as stop-gap housing for a homeless person (see *Mohamed v Manek and Kensington and Chelsea RLBC* (O3.5). HHJ McMillan accepted both of the council's defences and dismissed the claim.

On appeal, Elias J held that the hostel met the statutory definition of a hostel in Housing Act 1985 s622 in that it provided residential accommodation with facilities for preparation of food 'otherwise than in separate or self-contained sets of premises'. The sharing requirement in the licence agreement prevented the accommodation occupied by the claimant from being 'separate'. The claimant's own bedroom did not amount to separate 'residential accommodation' and although the flats were self-contained it was 'not appropriate to describe someone as being in separate accommodation if they are being compelled to share some of the facilities with someone they have not chosen' [26]. Because the hostel was provided by the council, the licence was excluded from protection by s3A(8) and there had not been an unlawful eviction. However, if the premises had not been a council-provided hostel, the licence would not have been excluded. Although premises provided as short-term interim accommodation do not normally count as a 'dwelling' for the purposes of that Act (see *Manek*), that judicial exception to the scope of the Act was strictly limited in time. Elias J said that 'if the Council permits the occupier to remain in the premises for a period which is no longer reasonably referable to the decision to accommodate him temporarily pending the decision as to whether there is a duty to house him, then *Manek* is no longer applicable' [33]. On the facts, by the date of notice in February 2003 the premises had become the claimant's 'dwelling' for PEA purposes.

03.11   *West Wiltshire DC v Snelgrove*
(1998) 30 HLR 57, DC (see O10.12)

Occupier excluded from protection by s3A as grant was otherwise than for money's worth

County courts

03.12   *Evans v Copping*
January 2008 *Legal Action* 30, Ashford County Court, 14 November 2007 (see O9.19A)

Tenancy not excluded under s3A where laundry room shared with landlord

04   # Housing Act 1988 ss27 and 28

Housing Act 1988 s27 creates a cause of action in tort against a landlord where the landlord, or anyone acting on his or her behalf, 'unlawfully deprives the residential occupier of any premises of his occupation of the whole or the part of the premises' (s27(1)). The tort also applies where a residential occupier gives up occupation of premises as a result of conduct falling short of an actual eviction (see s27(2)).

A 'residential occupier' has the same meaning as in Protection From Eviction Act 1977 s1 (s27(9)(a)). See O10.

A landlord means 'the person who, but for the occupier's right to occupy, would be entitled to occupation of the premises' (s27(9)(c)).

The liability is in addition to any liability arising apart from s27 (s27(4)) but damages are not be awarded both in respect of a liability for loss of a right to occupy premises as a residence and in respect of a liability arising under s27 (s27(5)).

No liability arises if the occupier is reinstated in the premises before proceedings are finally disposed of, whether by court order or otherwise (s27(6)).

Damages can be reduced under s27(7) where:

(a) the residential occupier's conduct prior to eviction was such that it is reasonable to mitigate the damages, or

(b) the residential occupier unreasonably refuses an offer of reinstatement made prior to the commencement of proceedings.

It is a defence if the landlord proves that he or she believed, and had reasonable cause to believe, that the residential occupier had abandoned the premises or, in relation to s27(2), the landlord had reasonable grounds for withholding or withdrawing services (s27(8)).

Section 27 is modelled on Protection from Eviction Act 1977 s1 (which creates criminal offences relating to unlawful eviction and harassment) and case-law relating to those offences may be relevant to s27 (eg, cases concerning the constituent elements of unlawful eviction and defences – see O10).

The real significance of s27 is not the scope of the cause of action, which is narrower than the covenant for quiet enjoyment (although applying to a wider class of occupant), but the way in which damages are to be assessed. Section 28 provides that the basis for the assessment of damages is the difference, at the time immediately before the residential occupier left the premises, between the value of the landlord's interest *with*, and the value of the landlord's interest *without*, the residential occupier in occupation. It is, therefore, essential in all cases brought under s28 to produce expert evidence from a valuer. The status of the residential occupier and the use of the rest of the landlord's premises (if any) will be very relevant to the valuation exercise.

Court of Appeal

04.1   *Abbott v Bayley*
        (2000) 32 HLR 72 CA

Landlord liable under s27(2) although tenant not physically excluded; damages in addition to s28 damages

Mr Bayley owned a two-bedroomed flat. In September 1994 he granted Mr Abbott an assured (non-shorthold) tenancy of one bedroom with shared use of the sitting room, kitchen and bathroom. At this time the other bedroom was occupied by a friend of the landlord but she moved out in November 1994. In January 1995 Mr Bayley wrote to Mr Abbott asking him to leave. The landlord purported to let the whole of the flat to two other people and in February 1995 Mr Abbott returned from holiday to find the new tenants in the flat and one of them occupying his bedroom. Mr Abbott was allowed back into his bedroom and for three months all three lived in the flat, with one of the new tenants sleeping on the sofa in the sitting room. In a telephone conversation Mr Bayley was threatening and abusive to Mr Abbott and in March 1995 Mr Bayley's father threatened forcibly to evict Mr Abbott and his belongings. Mr Abbott could not stand the unpleasant social and physical conditions and on 2 May 1995 he left and brought a claim for damages. HHJ Green QC awarded damages of £6,750 plus interest under Housing Act 1988 s27, and £2,050 for breach of the covenant for quiet enjoyment.

Mr Bayley appealed, contending that s27 only applies where 'the seriousness of the landlord's conduct is established to a high degree and where he makes the tenant's position so intolerable that he is driven out of the property'. The Court of Appeal rejected that submission. The judge had been correct in finding that the landlord's letter asking Mr Abbott to leave and unwarranted and offensive remarks in letters did not amount to acts likely to interfere with his peace and comfort. However, the judge had also been correct in finding that the purported letting of the entire flat, including Mr Abbott's bedroom, and the threat by Mr Bayley's father did come within s27. Section 27 did not require a landlord's conduct to have been of such a degree as to have made a tenant's continued occupation intolerable. The Court of Appeal also rejected the landlord's submission that the common-law damages were too high – in awarding such damages in addition to ss27/28 damages, the judge had considered Mr Abbott's inconvenience and distress both in the period before and in the period after he vacated the premises and s27(5) did not preclude such an award. The appeal was dismissed.

04.2   *Francis v Brown*
(1998) 30 HLR 143, CA

Intended purchaser is not a landlord for the purposes of s27(9)(c)

A landlord and her daughter unlawfully evicted the plaintiff. The daughter was convicted of an offence under Protection from Eviction Act 1977 s1(2), fined and ordered to pay compensation of £2,500 and costs. The tenant brought county court proceedings for damages against both the landlord and her daughter. The judge awarded damages under ss27/28 of £40,000 against the daughter. He found that, although there was no contract for sale, it had been the intention of both defendants that the freehold interest was to be conveyed from the mother to the daughter and that, following *Jones v Miah* (O4.4), the daughter was the landlord within the meaning of Housing Act 1988 s27(9)(c) because she was 'entitled to occupation of the premises'. He indicated that, if he had not awarded such damages, he would have awarded 'aggravated damages' against the daughter in the same sum. He awarded 'aggravated damages' of £40,000 against the mother. He awarded £1,500 special damages and £1,000 'exemplary damages' against both defendants.

The Court of Appeal allowed the daughter's appeal.

1) The county court judge had confused aggravated damages with exemplary damages. References by the judge to aggravated damages were to be read as exemplary damages and vice versa.

2) The award of ss27/28 damages was set aside because there was no evidence that the intention to transfer the freehold had been translated into a right of occupation.

3) The judge's indication that, if he had not awarded ss27/28 damages of £40,000, he would have awarded exemplary damages against the daughter in the same sum was criticised. In *Broome v Cassell and Co* [1972] AC 1027, the House of Lords held that awards of punitive damages against joint tortfeasors should reflect the lowest figure for which any of the defendants could be held liable. No exemplary damages could be awarded against the mother since she had not intended to profit from the eviction and therefore no exemplary damages could be awarded against the daughter. £40,000 was, on any view, a wholly excessive sum to award here by way of exemplary damages, even had there been no award against the mother.

4) Per Sir Iain Glidewell: Sections 27/28 provide a mechanism by which the award of damages may deprive the landlord of any increase in value of the property which has resulted from the eviction '... where damages have been awarded to the tenant against the landlord under sections 27 and 28, there is no place for a further award of exemplary damages against either the landlord or against the person who assisted her in the eviction...'. However, that principle does not prevent the award of aggravated damages.

The total award of damages against the daughter was reduced to £2,500.

Note: The type of tenancy granted to the claimant is not expressed in the judgment. The background to this case was that the mother was no longer in the UK and any award against her was unlikely to be enforceable.

04.3 *Haniff v Robinson*
[1993] QB 419; [1992] 3 WLR 875; [1993] 1 All ER 185; (1994) 26 HLR 386, CA (see O2.5)

Section 27 applied where eviction took place following possession order but without using court bailiffs; £26,000 damages awarded under ss27/28 to protected tenant

04.4 *Jones v Miah*
(1992) 24 HLR 578; [1992] 2 EGLR 50, CA

Purchasers let into occupation prior to completion were 'landlords'

Two tenants were 'brutally evicted' on 18 October 1988, not by the owners of the property but by purchasers of a leasehold term, who were let into occupation as licensees before completion of the sale. The tenants brought proceedings under s27 for damages against the purchasers.

The Court of Appeal held that the purchasers came within the definition of 'landlord' in s27(9)(c). They became the owners in equity of the leasehold term when they entered into the contract to purchase it and, pursuant to a provision in the contract under condition 8 of the National Conditions of Sale, were let into occupation by the vendors before completion. The court rejected a submission made on behalf of the defendants that ss27 and 28 are criminal in nature and that, since the sections operated retrospectively, they were void under EEC law. (The Act received royal assent on 15 November 1988, but ss27 and 28 are expressed to take effect from 9 June 1988.) However, the damages awarded were reduced because of defects in the valuation evidence.

04.5   *Kaur v Gill*

(1995) *Times* 15 June, CA

Damages other than for the loss of the right to occupy not to be set off against s28 damages

HHJ Orme awarded common-law damages of £500 for breach of covenant for quiet enjoyment and £15,000 statutory damages under Housing Act 1988 ss27/28. The landlord appealed, contending that, in view of the decision of the Court of Appeal in *Nwokorie v Mason* (O4.9), the common-law damages should have been set off against the statutory damages.

The Court of Appeal dismissed the appeal, distinguishing *Nwokorie v Mason* on the basis that in *Kaur* the common-law damages had not been awarded for any loss of right to occupy, but rather for breaches of the covenant for quiet enjoyment.

04.6   *King v Jackson*

(1998) 30 HLR 541; [1998] 1 EGLR 30; [1998] 03 EG 138, CA

Assessment of damages under s28 to take account of a tenant's right to occupy being limited by her agreement to leave

A landlord let a flat to a tenant on an assured shorthold tenancy on 20 March 1994. The tenant later orally gave four weeks' notice to quit, expiring on 12 May 1994. The landlord agreed to this. The landlady advertised the room and showed round a prospective new tenant. On 5 May the landlady wrote to the tenant asking her to leave that day as she was in arrears of rent. The next day the landlord changed the locks when the tenant was out. The premises were let to the new tenant at the same rent. The tenant who was evicted sued for unlawful eviction and breach of covenant of quiet enjoyment. The judge assessed damages under Housing Act 1988 ss27/28 as the difference between the tenanted value and the value with vacant possession and awarded £11,000 in accordance with the valuation evidence. The landlord appealed.

The Court of Appeal allowed the appeal. The tenant had an assured shorthold tenancy but the landlord had relied on the conversation with the tenant to the effect that she would vacate the flat. But for this, she would have begun proceedings for possession and the tenant would have been estopped if she had sought to resile from her agreement. Accordingly, even though there was an agreed valuation difference of £11,000 between the vacant possession and tenanted value, it was based on a right to occupy which did not exist. The award of £11,000 damages for a right of six days' occupation was manifestly wrong. The Court of Appeal rejected the tenant's contention that it was not possible to look behind the valuation. Given the very limited nature of the tenant's right of occupation, it was very unlikely that the proper application of s28(1) would have produced a higher figure than the award of £1,500 which the county court judge would have made for breach of covenant. If judgment was entered for that, the question of the statutory measure of damages did not arise and the absence of proper statutory valuations was immaterial.

04.7   *Melville v Bruton*
(1997) 29 HLR 319, CA

No damages under ss27/28 for assured shorthold tenant

The plaintiff was an assured shorthold tenant. She was unlawfully evicted when the landlord changed the locks. She claimed statutory damages under ss27/28 and common-law damages. Valuation evidence was given in which both valuers had assumed that there was vacant possession throughout the property. They disregarded two other tenancies which had been granted in breach of a restrictive covenant against user of the premises except as a private dwelling-house in single occupation.

The Court of Appeal held that this notional approach was wrong. The valuation evidence should have taken into account the other tenancies and, had that been the case, the evidence was that there would have been no increase in value to the landlord as a result of the eviction. Ordinarily, where premises are let at a market rent on a shorthold tenancy, it is difficult to see why there should be any significant difference in value for the purposes of s28. Where a tenant is wrongfully evicted, but the eviction makes no difference to the value of the landlord's interest in the property, no damages can be awarded under ss27/28. An award of £15,000 made in the county court was set aside and replaced with common-law damages of £500 for inconvenience, discomfort and distress. It was considered, obiter, that the judge at first instance had been correct in not invoking s27(7)(a), although the tenant was in rent arrears.

04.8   *Murray v Aslam*
(1995) 27 HLR 284, CA

Award of s28 damages set aside where it was doubtful that the landlord's actions had caused the tenant's departure (s27(2))

The landlord excluded the tenant by changing the locks and putting her possessions into the street. The tenant and her son had to wait in the rain for two hours before police persuaded the landlord to let her back in. Her possessions were damaged and her son was ill. Although the landlord did not harass her further, she left two weeks later. She commenced proceedings under s27. The landlord did not file or serve a defence and judgment was entered in default. Although the landlord was informed of the date for assessment of damages, he did not attend. The tenant was awarded special damages of £5,703 and damages assessed under s28 of £34,560. An application to set aside the judgment was refused and the landlord appealed.

The Court of Appeal considered that it was highly questionable whether the case fell within s27. The landlord had a strong argument that the tenant had been reinstated and should be allowed to defend the action. The award of damages under ss27/28 was set aside. However, the award of special damages was allowed to stand and the tenant was awarded the costs of the appeal.

04.9 ## Nwokorie v Mason
(1994) 26 HLR 60; [1994] 1 EGLR 59; [1994] 05 EG 155, CA

Set-off of damages

The plaintiff occupied a room in a shared house with a resident landlord. His status at that time was such that he was entitled to 28 days' notice to quit and could not be evicted without a court order. After a series of disagreements, the landlord gave the plaintiff 14 days' notice to leave and then evicted him, placing his belongings in black dustbin bags. At first instance the plaintiff was awarded damages of £6,000, comprising general damages of £500, exemplary damages of £1,000 and damages of £4,500 under ss27/28.

The Court of Appeal allowed the appeal in part. It was not open to the court to interfere with the award of £4,500 under ss27/28. However, in the context of the case, the general damages were essentially damages for the loss of the right of occupation and should be set off against the ss27/28 damages (s27(5)). It was accepted that the landlord had not acted for financial gain and it was not appropriate to award exemplary damages. However, the landlord had acted in a way to humiliate the plaintiff and the award of exemplary damages should be treated as an award of aggravated damages. Such damages were also for the loss of the right of occupation and were similarly to be set off. The total award was reduced to £4,500.

Note: It is significant that damages were awarded under ss27/28 even though the tenant had no long-term security of tenure. They were based on a surveyor's evidence of the diminished value of the property with a tenant who could lawfully be removed within six months (28 days' notice to quit and the time it would have taken for a possession order to come before the court) cf *Melville v Bruton* (O4.7).

04.10 ## Regalgrand Ltd v Dickerson
(1997) 29 HLR 620; (1997) 75 P&CR 312, CA

Section 28 damages reduced by tenant's conduct (including non-payment of rent)

In July 1990 the landlord granted a joint assured tenancy to the tenants. Later in the year the tenants complained of a lack of hot water and other matters. In December 1990 they stopped paying the rent. The landlord, believing the tenancy to be an assured shorthold tenancy, served a notice requiring possession on 15 February 1991. One of the tenants moved out and the other tenant did not spend much time in the flat. On 6 February 1991 the landlord entered the flat and changed the locks, asserting that it had been abandoned. He sued for arrears of rent. The tenants counter-claimed for damages under ss27/28.

The judge decided that the tenancy was an assured tenancy, that it had not been abandoned and that the tenants were entitled to damages under s28. The agreed figure for the difference in value of the landlord's interest was £12,000. The judge reduced the damages from £12,000 to £1,500 under s27(7)(a) because their conduct 'was such that it [was] reasonable to mitigate the damages'. The relevant conduct which she took into account was (a) withholding rent without giving prior notice and without justification because they had failed to inform the landlord of the continuing problems with the premises, and (b) their intention to vacate in any event. The tenants appealed on the grounds that the landlord had failed to plead mitigation, that the judge had failed to specify how she had arrived at the figure of £1,500, that their omissions were not 'conduct', and that the judge had been wrong to take into account the arrears of rent as serious misconduct was required under s27(7)(a).

The Court of Appeal dismissed the appeal. Failure to pay rent was conduct that could fall within the ambit of s27(7)(a). Although a mere intention to leave could not amount to conduct, here the intention to leave had been partly acted on because the tenants had moved some of their belongings out and only very occasionally resided in the flat. The Court of Appeal refused to have regard to *Hansard* (see *Pepper v Hart* [1993] AC 593, HL) in construing s27 since there was no ambiguity in the section.

04.11 *Sampson v Wilson*

[1996] Ch 39; [1995] 3 WLR 455; (1997)29 HLR 18; (1995) 70 P&CR 359, CA

Only landlord liable under s27; landlord liable for acts of agent

In the absence of the landlord abroad, his agent managed the property. The agent in turn handed over management to a third party, Mitchell. Mitchell harassed and threatened the tenants. He served a notice to quit. The tenants left and brought proceedings for damages under ss27/28 against the landlord, the agent and Mitchell.

At first instance ((1994) 26 HLR 486, ChD) the plaintiffs were awarded damages against the agents, but the claim against the landlord was dismissed. The tenants' appeal to the Court of Appeal was allowed. Section s27(3) referred to a liability on a landlord, not those acting on his behalf, and the basis for awarding damages was on the value of the landlord's interest. This indicated that s27 imposed a liability on landlords alone. In reaching this conclusion, the court differed from views expressed obiter in *Jones v Miah* (O4.4) to the contrary.

04.12 *Tagro v Cafane and Patel*

[1991] 1 WLR 378; [1991] 2 All ER 235; (1991) 23 HLR 250; [1991] 1 EGLR 279, CA

An offer of a key to a room that had been wrecked did not amount to reinstatement

The tenant occupied one of four bed-sitting rooms in a property leased to the landlord by the council and from which he ran a secondhand furniture business from the ground floor. The landlord seriously harassed the tenant and then changed the locks to her flat. The tenant obtained an injunction to be readmitted but when she was finally given a key to her room she found that the lock was broken and her room wrecked. She did not move back in. She amended her claim to include a claim for damages under ss27/28. A surveyor gave evidence on her behalf that the difference between the value of the landlord's interest with vacant possession and the value with her in occupation was £31,000. The landlord did not submit valuation evidence. HHJ Simpson QC awarded s28 damages of £31,000 against the landlord and damages of £15,538 against the landlord and his agent for trespass to the tenant's personal belongings. The landlord appealed against the award of statutory damages.

The Court of Appeal dismissed the appeal:

1) The landlord's submission that no liability arose because the tenant had been reinstated in accordance with s27(6) was rejected. 'Reinstatement does not consist in merely handing the tenant a key to a lock which does not work and inviting her to resume occupation of a room which has been totally wrecked.'

2) In any event, a tenant had a right to decide not to be reinstated under s27(6).

3) In relation to mitigation of damages under s27(7)(b), for refusal of an offer of reinstatement prior to proceedings being commenced, it was held that an offer of reinstatement prior to the amendment to include a claim under ss27/28 would qualify. However, here the facts did not amount to an offer of reinstatement in any realistic sense.

4) In relation to the quantum of damages it was held that, although the landlord's tenancy was terminable on one month's notice by the council, the reality was that the Landlord and Tenant Act 1954 applied and his tenancy could go on virtually for ever. Although the award of damages was high it was not so high that it should be disturbed. An argument that the value of the landlord's interest without the tenant in occupation was virtually nil as the landlord's lease contained a prohibition against assignment and subletting was rejected. The Act contemplated, by the notion of the 'willing buyer' in s28(3), that the purchaser would take a lease from the council on the same terms as the landlord and the issue of forfeiture would not arise.

Note: It is not clear what the tenant's security of tenure was – reference is made to her as 'a sitting tenant'.

04.13 *Wandsworth LBC v Osei-Bonsu*

[1999] 1 All ER 265; [1999] 11 EG 167; (1999) 31 HLR 515; (1998) *Times* 4 November, CA

Mitigation of s28 damages based on domestic violence against co-tenant; s28 damages should take account fact that co-tenant wanted to end tenancy

Mr Osei-Bonsu and his wife were joint secure tenants of a council property. He left after his wife obtained an ouster order based on his violence. She was offered alternative accommodation by the council. As a result she served a notice to quit seeking to determine the joint tenancy. The notice gave insufficient notice but the council treated it as valid. After Mrs Osei-Bonsu had been rehoused, the ouster order was discharged by consent but the council refused to readmit Mr Osei-Bonsu to the property. He commenced proceedings and, following *Hounslow LBC v Pilling* (F4.10), the council accepted that the short notice to quit was not effective to determine the joint tenancy. However, at the council's instigation, Mrs Osei-Bonsu served a second notice to quit, which was valid. Mr Osei-Bonsu took further proceedings claiming damages under ss27/28. In the county court he was awarded damages of £30,000 and a declaration that he remained a tenant of the property. The council appealed, although it accepted that its initial refusal to readmit the respondent to the property constituted unlawful eviction under s27(1) and gave rise to a claim for damages to be assessed under s28(1).

The Court of Appeal allowed the council's appeal in part and held that:

1) The council had no defence under s27(8)(a) because it had no reasonable cause for its belief that the wife's short notice had ended the joint tenancy. In any event, as the respondent was claiming a right to be readmitted to the property, the council should have issued proceedings for possession.

2) The judge's view that Mr Osei-Bonsu's conduct was not relevant to mitigate damages because it did not involve the council was too narrow. His violence broke up the family and started an unbroken chain of events which culminated in his wrongful eviction. Following *Regalgrand Ltd v Dickerson* (O4.10), it was appropriate to mitigate the damages substantially. The damages were reduced by two-thirds to £10,000.

3) The tenancy had been precarious because it was dependent on Mrs Osei-Bonsu not serving a valid notice to quit, which she was clearly anxious to do. On that basis statutory damages should have been assessed at no more than £2,000, but this point was not open to the council because specific agreement on quantum in the court below had to be treated as sacrosanct.

4) A tenant cannot be entitled to statutory damages and a continuing right to possession. By electing to accept the statutory damages, Mr Osei-Bonsu had given up his entitlement to damages at common law and any claim to rights of occupation.

5) The second notice to quit was effective. It was properly served on the council rather than on the then tenant of the property.

High Court

04.14 *Mehta v Royal Bank of Scotland*
(2000) 32 HLR 45; [1999] 3 EGLR 153; (1999) *Times* 25 January, QBD (see O9.10)

Temporary occupation of accommodation after eviction did not amount to reinstatement; £45,000 s28 damages for contractual licensee of hotel room entitled to 4 months' notice

County courts

04.15 *White v Lambeth LBC*
June 1995 *Legal Action* 20, Lambeth County Court (see O9.29)

£18,000 (1995) s28 damages for loss of secure tenancy

Scottish courts

04.16 *Scott v Thomson*
2003 SLT 99 Court of Session, Ex Div

Landlord liable for the actions of his son who managed his property

Ms Scott was evicted by her landlord's son, who changed the locks while she was away on holiday. She sought police assistance, but was unable to regain entry. She took proceedings against the landlord for damages under Housing (Scotland) Act 1988 ss36 and 37 (the Scottish equivalent to Housing Act 1988 ss27 and 28). A sheriff awarded damages, but the decision was overturned by the sheriff principal because the expression 'acting on [the landlord's] behalf' in s36 was ambiguous and should be read as imposing liability only where a landlord instigated or at least connived at his agent's illegitimate activities. Ms Scott had failed to prove this.

The Court of Session allowed Ms Scott's appeal. The sheriff principal's approach was misconceived and unnecessary. The expression 'acting on his behalf' was clear and unambiguous and encompassed anyone who was acting either as direct agent of the landlord or as someone employed to do a particular act or to undertake the management of the property with no particular fetter. The sheriff had found that, throughout the time that the property was owned by the landlord, his son had absolute authority to manage and administer it as he saw fit. He could have been acting for no one but the landlord.

05   Landlord's failure to take action against other occupants

Where an occupier is disturbed by the actions of a neighbour, they may have a cause of action against that neighbour. Where the neighbour's premises are owned by another person, sometimes a more effective remedy will be to get the landowner to take action against their tenant/licensee. However, there are only limited circumstances in which an occupier can force a landowner to take such action. In cases involving local authority landlords or registered social landlords, a complaint to the relevant ombudsman for failure to take action may result in a finding of maladministration.

Court of Appeal

05.1 *Hussain v Lancaster CC*
[2000] QB 1; [1999] 2 WLR 1142; [1999] 4 All ER 125; (1999)31 HLR 164; (1999) 77 P&CR 89; (1998) LGR 663; (1998) *Times* 26 May, CA

Council not liable for anti-social behaviour of its tenants

The plaintiffs were joint owners of a shop and residential premises on a council housing estate. They alleged that the council was liable in negligence or nuisance for failing to prevent council tenants and/or members of their households from committing criminal acts of harassment against them. The harassment included threats, racist abuse and the throwing of stones. The council applied to strike out the claim.

The Court of Appeal held that the claim should be struck out. The council was not liable in negligence or nuisance because:

1) Although the acts complained of unquestionably interfered intolerably with the plaintiffs' enjoyment of the plaintiffs land they did not involve the tenants' use of the tenants land and therefore fell outside the scope of the tort of nuisance.
2) Even if there had been such nuisance, the council was not liable for it unless it authorised the tenants to commit the nuisance, either expressly or by letting premises in circumstances where nuisance was certain to result (approving *Smith v Scott* [1973] 1 Ch 314, ChD).
3) In relation to negligence, it was not fair, just and reasonable to impose a duty of care on the council to control its tenants. This was not a case which could be brought within the category of negligent performance of statutory functions. Hirst LJ referred to Lord Browne-Wilkinson's concluding words in *X v Bedfordshire CC (minors)* [1995] 2 AC 633, HL, that:

> ... the courts should proceed with great care before holding liable in negligence those who have been charged by parliament with the task of protecting society from the wrong doings of others.

The decision in *O'Leary v Islington LBC* (O5.4) was approved. A petition for leave to appeal to the House of Lords was dismissed ([1999] 1 WLR 1359).

O5.2   *Lippiatt v South Gloucestershire Council*
[2000] QB 51; [1999] 3 WLR 137; [1999] 4 All ER 149; [1999] LGR 562; (1999) 31 HLR 1114; (1999) *Times* 9 April, CA

Landlord can be liable for acts of nuisance of licensees

Travellers occupied a strip of land owned by the council. The council decided to tolerate their 'unauthorised encampment' and provided toilet, water and other facilities. Neighbouring tenant farmers took proceedings against the council alleging repeated acts of nuisance by the travellers. They complained of trespass on their land, obstruction of access to fields, dumping of rubbish, theft of timber, gates and fences, damage to a stone wall and dogs chasing sheep. HHJ Weeks QC, following *Hussain v Lancaster CC* (O5.1), struck out the claim as disclosing no cause of action.

The Court of Appeal allowed the farmers' appeal. There is no rule of law that prevents an owner or occupier of land being held liable for the tort of nuisance as a result of the activities of licensees which take place off the land occupied by them. *Hussain* was distinguished because the disturbance there was a public nuisance and the conduct was not linked to, or did not emanate from, the homes where the perpetrators lived. The evidence in this case was that the travellers were allowed to congregate on the council's land and that they used it as a base for the unlawful activities of which the plaintiffs complained. The travellers 'emanated' from the land. Nothing in *Hussain* precludes a court from holding that an occupier of land may be held liable for nuisance consisting of a continuing state of affairs on land where acts are to the knowledge of the occupier committed by persons based on the land and interfere with the use and enjoyment of the plaintiff's land. The case was reasonably arguable in law and the judge should not have struck out the claim.

05.3   *Mowan v Wandsworth LBC*
(2001) 33 HLR 616; [2001] LGR 110, CA

Landlord not liable for tenant's nuisance

The claimant was a long lessee of the council. She brought an action against the council complaining of nuisance committed by a secure tenant who occupied the flat above her and who suffered from a mental disorder. The nuisance complained of included regularly blocking the toilet causing sewage floods, leaving taps running, noise nuisance and threats to kill. The particulars of claim alleged that the defendant knew or ought to have known about the nuisance and had breached its duty to the claimant by adopting it or failing to abate it. In particular, the council had failed to institute possession or injunction proceedings. The claim concerned events prior to 2 October 2000 when Human Rights Act 1998 came into force. The claim was struck out on the basis that it was bound to fail. The claimant appealed unsuccessfully.

The Court of Appeal held that neither a claim in nuisance nor in negligence could succeed. Landlords are only liable for the nuisance of their tenants if they authorise the nuisance (*Hussain v Lancaster CC* (O5.1)). The claimant's argument that a landlord could authorise nuisance simply by failing to take action to prevent it and that it was no longer necessary to show consent or active participation by the landlord was rejected. *Lippiatt v South Gloucestershire Council* (O5.2) was a different type of case where the landlord had been the occupier of the land on which, or from which, a nuisance had been created by others. As the claim concerned events before 2 October 2000, reliance could be placed on the European Convention on Human Rights only if the common law was uncertain (*DPP v Jones* [1999] 2 WLR 625). Neither was the defendant liable in negligence. The fact that negligence had not been pleaded or particularised was not fatal. If the case were put on the basis of breach of a duty of care to protect the claimant as its tenant from nuisance created by other tenants, the allegation was not one of carelessness but of a failure to do what it should have done, which was simply the argument of nuisance by another name. The claim should be struck out.

05.4   *O'Leary v Islington LBC*
(1983) 9 HLR 83, CA

No implied term in tenancy agreement to enforce terms in another tenancy

The plaintiff's neighbour breached the terms of his tenancy agreement not to cause nuisance. The plaintiff took proceedings against Islington Council, the common landlord, to compel it to enforce the clause in the neighbour's tenancy agreement.

The Court of Appeal held that there was no implied term in the plaintiff's tenancy agreement that the landlord would enforce the nuisance clause in the other tenancy agreement. There was no need to imply such a term where a tenant had a cause in action in nuisance against the other tenant.

Note: This case was referred to with approval in *Hussain v Lancaster CC* (O5.1).

High Court

05.5 *Winch v Mid Bedfordshire DC*
October 2002 *Legal Action* 29, 22 July 2002, QBD
Landlord liable for nuisance of licensees

The claimants owned a house which was less than 200 metres from a travellers' site leased and managed by the defendant council. The claimants sued in nuisance and negligence, complaining that the occupants of the site were responsible for the dumping of rubbish, abandoning vehicles, fires and smoke, racing of motor cars, noise and police response to criminal activity. Some of the activities took place on-site and some off-site. They sought damages for distress and inconvenience and for the reduction in the value of their house. The defendants conceded that a catalogue of mis-management and non-management by their employees amounted to negligence, but submitted that the claimants' claim must fail because it was not liable for off-site activities since they could not be said to emanate from the defendant's land and because the evidence did not support nuisance from on-site activities.

Astill J found that most of the activities complained of were directly linked to licensees and that most emanated from the site, whether on-site or off-site activities. Occupiers of land are liable for acts of nuisance unless they prove that they have not caused the nuisance or have done all that they reasonably can to prevent the acts. In this case there were persistent and numerous acts amounting to nuisance which emanated from the site occupied by the defendant. The defendant was aware of the emanations, had the means to abate the nuisance but failed to take steps that would have done so in a reasonable time. It was therefore liable to the claimants.

Ombudsman complaints

05.6 *Local Government Ombudsman Complaint 04/B/05253 (Southwark LBC); 24 October 2005*
Failure to deal with complaints of noise nuisance

The complainant lived in a maisonette in a council-owned block. He made complaints about noise nuisance from an upstairs neighbour. No action was taken.

The local government ombudsman found that there had been maladministration. As a result, the complainant suffered almost a year of avoidable noise nuisance. The council agreed to apologise, to provide training for its staff in dealing with noise nuisance and to pay £1,000 to the complainant.

05.7 *Local Government Ombudsman Complaint No 05/A/02280 (Milton Keynes Council); 8 January 2007*
Failure to deal with complaints and treat transfer request as urgent

The complainant was a secure tenant who had cystic fibrosis. In 2001 he had a heart and lung transplant. He started to have problems with an upstairs neighbour almost as soon as he returned to his flat after the transplant. He experienced episodes of rudeness, abuse, threatening behaviour, harassment and general noise nuisance for over three years. He complained to the council about the neighbour's behaviour and, when this did not improve, asked the council to move him as his health was deteriorating.

The Local Government Ombudsman found that there had been maladministration in that the council had failed to deal with the tenant's complaints of anti-social behaviour properly or to treat his transfer request with the urgency it required. There were frequent changes of staff and a failure to keep records. Officers promised action and then failed to follow through with that action. The ombudsman recommended that the council should compensate the tenant for the delay of approximately two years before he was able to move at the rate of £1,750 per annum (total £3,500) and pay his mother £750 for the impact on her and to recognise her dogged pursuit of the complaint on behalf of her son.

05.8   *Report for Public Service Ombudsman for Wales 2004/0537/AC/382 (Conwy CBC); 10 August 1996*

Tenant should have right to buy comparable property if nuisance not resolved

Mrs Walker, a council tenant, suffered unacceptable behaviour and acts of nuisance from neighbours, including racist verbal abuse, noise, foul smells and acts of intimidation for two to three years. The council did not have a racial harassment policy or any specific procedures for dealing with anti-social behaviour. Despite a substantial body of evidence, in the form of log sheets, letters and witness statements, over a lengthy period, it failed to recognise the severity of the situation or take appropriate action. When it eventually took legal action against the perpetrators, this was dilatory and ineffectual. As a direct result, Mrs Walker withdrew her right to buy application. The situation also had an impact on her employment and health.

The Public Service Ombudsman for Wales found that there was extensive systematic maladministration leading to personal injustice. He recommended that the council bring its procedures up to date and take appropriate action against the perpetrators. He recommended that the council allow Mrs Walker a further opportunity to buy her property at the original offer price. If the council failed to resolve the nuisance within 12 months, the council should enable Mrs Walker to buy a comparable property. He also recommended that it should pay her £2,500 per year from January 2003 until the issue was resolved.

06   **Injunctions and committal**

Interim injunctions may be sought without notice or on notice. The grant of an interim injunction is a discretionary remedy. Except where the right to be protected is clearly established, it is necessary, in accordance with the principles laid down by the House of Lords in *American Cyanamid Co v Ethicon Ltd* [1975] AC 396, HL, for the applicant to show that:

1) damages are not a sufficient remedy;

2) there is a serious issue to be tried (although not necessarily a prima facie case); and

3) the balance of convenience favours the grant of an injunction (eg, to maintain the status quo).

Breach of an injunction amounts to contempt of court. Contempt may be punished by imprisonment. However, particular care has to be taken by applicants when drafting and serving injunctions and when making applications to commit, since committal orders are likely to be refused if there are any procedural defects.

See also sections E1 and E2 regarding injunctions and committal.

07 Injunctions

Court of Appeal

07.1 *Lewis v Lewis*

[1991] 1 WLR 235; [1991] 3 All ER 251, CA

Retrospective dispensation with service of injunction

On applications to commit for contempt for breach of a mandatory injunction, county courts cannot dispense with the need for service of the order retrospectively. However, there is nothing to prevent them from doing so where the purpose of the injunction is to restrain a party from doing something. In this case there was evidence that the defendant had been deliberately evading service.

07.2 *Love v Herrity*

(1991) 23 HLR 217; [1991] 2 EGLR 44; [1991] 32 EG 55, CA

American Cyanamid principles not applicable where clear right; tenants denied injunction where landlord had re-let premises

The appellants were joint assured tenants of a flat owned by the landlord. They fell into arrears with their rent and received a notice purporting to terminate their tenancy on 5 January 1990. In mid December the tenants left the premises temporarily. The landlord changed the locks and re-let the premises. The tenants obtained an ex parte injunction requiring the landlord to readmit them. This was subsequently discharged because although, following *American Cyanamid Co v Ethicon Ltd* [1975] AC 396, HL, the judge found that there was a serious issue to be tried and that damages would not be an adequate remedy, the fact that the premises had been re-let meant that the balance of convenience was that it was more appropriate to await trial than to continue the interlocutory injunction. The tenants appealed.

The Court of Appeal allowed the appeal. It was agreed that the tenants were assured tenants. Consequently, their right to occupy could only be brought to an end by a court order or by their unequivocally giving up possession to the landlord. The notice was not effective and the evidence of the tenants' conduct fell far short of establishing that they had given up possession. The tenants had left belongings in the premises and the landlord's conduct in changing the locks showed that he expected them to return. Consequently, the matter was clear and there was not a serious issue to be tried. The further questions referred to in *American Cyanamid* did not require consideration.

However, an injunction to be readmitted could not be enforced owing to the letting of the flat to a third party. The proper order was to make a declaration that, as against the landlord, the tenants were entitled to possession of the flat on an assured tenancy, with liberty to apply. If the tenants applied to add the third party as a party to the proceedings for the purpose of obtaining possession of the flat, the court would then reconsider the matter.

Note: It is likely that the tenants would have recovered possession more quickly if they had, from the outset, taken possession proceedings against the new 'tenant' on the basis that, since they were entitled to exclusive possession, the new 'tenant' was merely a trespasser as against them (see *Street v Mountford* (B2.4) and *Borg v Rogers* [1981] CAT 330 (UB)).

07.3   *Parsons v Nasar*

(1991) 23 HLR 1, CA

Injunction must clearly set out what landlord needs to do to readmit tenant where premises had been re-let

After a tenant had been evicted, she obtained an ex parte injunction that 'the Defendant do permit the Plaintiff to re-enter the premises at 135, Tenby Drive and do have quiet enjoyment thereof until the hearing of this claim'. The landlord did not allow the tenant back into the premises and was sentenced to 14 days' imprisonment for contempt. He appealed.

The Court of Appeal held that the injunction was defective in that, because the landlord had already re-let the premises, it failed to set out clearly what he should have done. The order should have specified what positive steps the landlord was required to take. It was also defective in that it failed to state by what date the landlord had to comply with it. The trial judge had also erred in refusing to hear the application to discharge the injunction before the application to commit.

07.4   *Patel v W H Smith (Eziot) Ltd*

[1987] 1 WLR 853; [1987] 2 All ER 569, CA

Prima facie right to injunction against trespass to land

Landowners are prima facie entitled to injunctions preventing trespass to their land where title is not in issue, even where the acts complained of cause no harm. In such circumstances it is unnecessary to consider the balance of convenience (cf *American Cyanamid Co v Ethicon Ltd* [1975] AC 396, HL).

08   Committal

Court of Appeal

08.1   *Howes v Howes*

[1992] 2 FCR 287; (1992) 142 NLJ 753, CA

Proper service of committal order necessary

Where an injunction has been breached, a person cannot be committed by the county court pursuant to a committal order unless a copy of the committal order has been served in accordance with the provisions of CCR Ord 29 r1(5).

08.2 *O'Neill v Murray*
(1990) *Times* 15 October, CA
Committal order must set out breaches

A committal order which fails to set out the breaches of an injunction which have been proved is defective and should be set aside.

08.3 *Parsons v Nasar*
(1991) 23 HLR 1, CA (see O7.3)
Injunction defective for failing to specify clearly what landlord should do

Note: For other cases where committal orders have been set aside for procedural defects, see *Clarke v Clarke* [1990] 2 FLR 115, CA (order not in Form N29 and delay in serving it) and *Temporal v Temporal* [1990] 2 FLR 98, CA (no time specified for compliance with order). Although these were both matrimonial cases, the same principles apply in cases involving landlords and tenants.

08.4 *Saxby v McKinley*
(1997) 29 HLR 569, CA
Immediate custodial sentence for disregard of injunction to readmit tenants

A landlord evicted two tenants who were in arrears with their rent by changing the locks while they were away. He knew that what he had done was unlawful and a criminal offence. After they had been deprived of their accommodation for 30 days, he disregarded an injunction ordering him to readmit them.

The Court of Appeal held that he was properly committed to prison for 28 days for contempt of court. The contempt was serious and the consequences of his actions were potentially disastrous for the tenants. An immediate custodial sentence was not wrong in principle and was fully justified.

08.5 *Wright v Jess*
[1987] 1 WLR 1076; [1987] 2 All ER 1067, CA
In exceptional circumstances committal can be ordered ex parte

In exceptional circumstances a court may commit a contemnor on an ex parte application if it is the only way to uphold the authority of the court or to protect the applicant. Here, the respondent was jailed for two years.

Note: Although this was a domestic violence case, the same principles apply in breach of covenant for quiet enjoyment cases. See also CCR Ord 29 r1 and *Warwick Corporation v Russell* [1964] 1 WLR 613, ChD.

09 **Damages at common law**

The general aim of the courts is to put tenants into the position that they would have been in if there had been no breach of contract or if there had been no tort. However, exemplary damages are punitive in nature and statutory damages under Housing Act 1988 ss27/28 are based on the landlord's gain resulting from an eviction.

Tenants bringing civil proceedings following acts of harassment or unlawful eviction may be entitled to six different categories of damages:

1) **Special damages**. These are compensation for any identifiable loss that is quantifiable in monetary terms, eg, loss of earnings, second-hand value of lost items, additional cost of meals, cost of alternative accommodation. Any expenditure must be reasonable, proper and necessary.

2) **General damages**. These are compensation for losses that are not quantifiable in monetary terms and can be claimed for such matters as discomfort, inconvenience, loss of enjoyment, loss of occupancy, shock, personal injury, pain and suffering.

3) **Aggravated damages**. These are compensation for especially severe suffering or to demonstrate the outrage and indignation at the way a person has been treated. They are compensatory in nature and reflect the victim's suffering. They are only available in tort.

4) **Exemplary damages**. These are punitive and are awarded to punish or deter a defendant. They may be awarded where the defendant's behaviour was calculated to make a profit. They are only available in tort. In the words of Lord Devlin:

   > Where a defendant with a cynical disregard for a plaintiff's rights has calculated that the money to be made out of his wrongdoing will probably exceed the damages at risk, it is necessary for the law to show that it cannot be broken with impunity.... Exemplary damages can properly be awarded whenever it is necessary to teach a wrongdoer that tort does not pay. (*Rookes v Barnard* [1964] AC 1129 at 1227)

   Exemplary damages are not confined to money making in the strict sense. Obtaining possession without the trouble and expense of going to court falls within this category.

5) **Nominal damages**. These are awarded in respect of those torts where it is not necessary to show that damage has occurred (eg, trespass to land).

6) **Statutory damages under Housing Act 1988 ss27/28**. See O4 for examples of such damages. Any common-law damages for loss of occupancy must be set off against any damages under Housing Act 1988 ss27/28 (s27(5)), or vice versa.

Exemplary and aggravated damages should now be expressly pleaded – see CPR Part 16.4(1)(c).

When considering levels of damages awarded, account should be taken of the year of the award and subsequent inflation. See P11 for how to calculate an updated figure.

Court of Appeal

09.1   *Asghar v Ahmed*
(1985) 17 HLR 25, CA

Aggravated and exemplary damages awarded in addition to fine in criminal court

The tenant and his family were unlawfully evicted by their landlord, who threw all their belongings on to the street. Despite the tenant obtaining an injunction, the landlord delayed in readmitting him. The landlord was convicted under Protection from Eviction Act 1977 and fined £750 and ordered to pay £250 costs. In the county court, the judge awarded aggravated damages of £500 and exemplary damages of £1,000 in addition to special damages.

The landlord's appeal was dismissed. It was as 'plain a case for aggravated damages as one would expect to find'. The Court of Appeal declined to overturn the award of exemplary damages even though the landlord had been fined in the Crown Court. There was a great deal more to the landlord's conduct that followed the eviction which justified the finding that this was an outrageous example of persecution by a landlord of a tenant.

09.2   **Branchett v Beaney**
[1992] 3 All ER 910; (1992) 24 HLR 348; [1992] 2 EGLR 33; [1992] 28 EG 107, CA

Exemplary damages covered all elements of compensation

Workmen employed by the landlord bulldozed a way across the tenant's front garden and constructed a private road to an adjoining property where they were building a house. The tenant brought a claim for damages for trespass and breach of covenant for quiet enjoyment. Although the county court judge awarded exemplary damages for trespass of £3,250, he held that the tenant was not entitled to damages for mental distress arising from the breach of the covenant for quiet enjoyment.

The Court of Appeal dismissed the tenant's appeal. The award of exemplary damages for trespass covered all elements of compensation, including compensation for injured feelings and mental distress, to which the appellant was entitled for invasion of her garden and use of the road. The judge was right not to extricate the punitive from the non-punitive element in his award. Such an award had given the tenant all and more than she could recover in a claim for damages for breach of the covenant of quiet enjoyment. Obiter, in a contractual claim for damages for breach of covenant for quiet enjoyment, a tenant is not entitled to compensation for 'injured feelings and mental distress'. (See *Addis v Gramophone Co Ltd* [1909] AC 488, HL; cf, comments of Lord Denning MR in *McCall v Abelesz* (O3.4)).

09.3   **Drane v Evangelou**
[1978] 1 WLR 455; [1978] 2 All ER 437; (1977) 36 P&CR 270; (1977) 246 EG 137, CA

Exemplary damages appropriate for unlawful eviction

The tenant's rent was reduced following an application to the rent officer. As a result, the landlord moved other people into the premises, moved the tenant's belongings into the back yard and changed the locks. The tenant obtained an injunction but was only able to return to the premises ten weeks later after two further court hearings. A county court judge held that 'the monstrous behaviour called for exemplary damages of £1,000'.

The landlord's appeal was dismissed. Lord Denning MR, referring to *Rookes v Barnard* [1964] AC 1129, HL, which held that exemplary damages may be awarded where the defendant's conduct has been calculated to make a profit which might well exceed the compensation ordinarily payable to the plaintiff, stated 'To my mind this category includes cases of unlawful eviction of a tenant. The landlord seeks to gain possession at the expense of the tenant ...' Lawton LJ said 'To deprive a man of a roof over his head in my judgment is one of the worst torts which can be committed. It causes stress, worry and anxiety.'

09.4   *Francis v Brown*

(1998) 30 HLR 143, CA (see O4.2)

Award of exemplary damages should reflect the lowest figure that one of joint tortfeasors liable for; aggravated and exemplary damages considered

09.5   *Lord and Haslewood-Ogram v Jessop*

August 1999 *Legal Action* 28, CA

Damages for unlawful eviction and harassment

The claimants occupied bed-sitting rooms with shared use of bathroom and toilet. They signed 'licence agreements', but HHJ Milligan held that they had assured tenancies. Ms Lord fell into arrears because of reductions in the amount of housing benefit received. The defendant landlord constantly threatened her with eviction, telephoned almost daily, entered her room without permission, was aggressive and implied that there might be violence. He changed the locks and did not give her a key. Ms Lord suffered from stress and anxiety and her health deteriorated. These events culminated in a suicide attempt. Ms Haslewood-Ogram complained about a lack of heating and, while she was out, the landlord changed the locks. Her possessions were either locked in the house or thrown out of the rear and she was left in the clothes that she was wearing. She was extremely upset.

HHJ Milligan described the landlord's behaviour as 'discourteous, insulting, humiliating and threatening' and 'disgraceful, self-interested and bullying.' He awarded Ms Lord damages of £5,716.99 comprising £1,000 damages for breach of covenant for quiet enjoyment up to the eviction, £2,000 damages for unlawful eviction, aggravated damages of £2,000, special damages of £420 and interest of £647.82. He awarded Ms Haslewood-Ogram damages of £4,948.95 comprising £1,000 damages for breach of covenant for quiet enjoyment up to the eviction, £2,000 damages for unlawful eviction, aggravated damages of £1,000, special damages of £430 and interest of £518.95. The defendant's appeal was dismissed. The judge's findings could not properly be challenged in the Court of Appeal.

09.6   *Mafo v Adams*

[1970] 1 QB 548; [1970] 2 WLR 72; [1969] 3 All ER 1404, CA

Landlord's motives not established to justify an award of exemplary damages

A landlord tricked his tenant into leaving premises by falsely informing him that alternative accommodation was available at another address. The tenant suffered physical inconvenience but no financial damage. The tenant was awarded £100 damages for breach of the covenant of quiet enjoyment and £100 exemplary damages in deceit.

The Court of Appeal upheld the award for breach of the covenant of quiet enjoyment. However, it held that, assuming exemplary damages could be awarded in an action for deceit, the tenant was not entitled to such damages because there was no finding that the landlord had acted so as to justify an award. The county court judge had described the landlord's reasons for evicting the tenant as 'obscure' and his motives had not been established.

09.7   **McMillan v Singh**

(1985) 17 HLR 120, CA

Tenant's conduct irrelevant to award of exemplary damages

A landlord removed a tenant's belongings from his room. The next day the tenant met the landlord, who excluded him from the house and threatened him. The landlord let the room for a higher rent. After six or seven weeks the tenant obtained an injunction reinstating him. When the plaintiff's claim for damages was heard, the judge declined to award exemplary damages because the tenant had rent arrears.

The Court of Appeal allowed the tenant's appeal. The concept of 'coming to court with clean hands' had never been applied to the assessment of damages. The proper approach was to assess the loss suffered to the tenant's property or person, then consider aggravated damages for injury to feelings and then, finally, to consider whether an award of exemplary damages was appropriate. The Court of Appeal awarded exemplary damages of £250, approximately four times more than the increased rent which the landlord had gained while the tenant was out of occupation.

Note: Conduct of a claimant is, by virtue of s27(7), relevant to statutory damages under Housing Act 1988 ss27/28.

09.8   **Melville v Bruton**

(1997) 29 HLR 319, CA (see O4.7)

Common-law damages of £500 for inconvenience, discomfort and distress of eviction for assured shorthold tenant where s28 statutory damages not appropriate

09.9   **Ramdath v Daley**

(1993) 25 HLR 273; [1993] 1 EGLR 82; [1993] 20 EG 123, CA

Exemplary damages against agent who did not profit from eviction wrong

Following a dispute over rent, and despite the fact that the landlord had been advised about the need for court proceedings, the plaintiff was evicted by his landlord and the landlord's son, who acted as his agent. The locks were changed and the tenant was threatened with violence. In the county court Mr Recorder Bridge Adams described the eviction as 'extremely bad' and 'brutal'. The landlord's son had acted with 'flagrant disregard for the law'. The way in which the tenant's possessions were treated and the threats which were made were primarily the responsibility of the son. Damages were awarded against both defendants. The award against the father comprised general damages of £2,000, special damages of £510 and exemplary damages of £1,000 (because he had been warned about the legal position before eviction). These sums were not overturned on appeal. There were also awards of general damages (£1,250) and exemplary damages (£2,500) against the son. He appealed, claiming that it had not been established that his conduct had been calculated to make a profit for himself (see *Rookes v Barnard* [1964] AC 1129, HL).

The Court of Appeal, allowing the appeal in part, held that, in a case of unlawful eviction, the payment of exemplary damages cannot be ordered against a defendant acting as the landlord's agent unless it can be proved that he himself stood to benefit from the eviction. The tenant's damages were reduced accordingly.

High Court

09.10   *Mehta v Royal Bank of Scotland*
(2000) 32 HLR 45; [1999] 3 EGLR 153; (1999) *Times* 25 January, QBD

Damages for unlawful eviction of long-term licensee of hotel

Mr Ramji owned a hotel. The property was subject to two charges in favour of a bank. In 1992 the bank demanded various sums which were due and, when these were not paid, appointed a receiver pursuant to Law of Property Act 1925 ss101 and 109. Under s109 the receiver was deemed to be the agent of Mr Ramji. In 1993 the manager of the hotel, acting as agent for the receiver, agreed orally that Mr Mehta was to have exclusive possession of Room 418 of the hotel 'on a long-term basis', that he would not share facilities with other hotel occupants except for the common parts of the hotel for access, that he would pay a monthly rent and that the hotel maids would clean the room and Mr Mehta's sheets at no extra charge. In 1994 the receiver contracted to sell the hotel. On completion, Mr Mehta was evicted by the receiver and his managing agent. He obtained an interim injunction allowing him readmission to his room but this injunction was discharged a few days later and he was forced again to leave the hotel. Mr Mehta issued proceedings against Mr Ramji, the receiver and the managing agent.

Richard Southwell QC, sitting as a High Court judge, held that Mr Mehta was a contractual licensee and not a tenant. Although the three hallmarks of a tenancy identified by Lord Templeman in *Street v Mountford* (B2.4) were present (exclusive possession, monthly payments and a periodical term) in this case, there were other equally important factors to be taken into account. There was no simple all-embracing test for the distinction between a contractual tenancy and a contractual licence. The agreement was clearly intended to be terminable by either party on reasonable notice. What length of notice was reasonable had to be determined with regard to the facts at the time when the notice was given, having regard to all the relevant circumstances. Four months' notice represented the reasonable period of notice for either party to give.

The receiver and the managing agent were acting as agents for Mr Ramji, not for the bank. The interim injunction did not constitute reinstatement for the purposes of Housing Act 1988 s27(6) as it only gave Mr Mehta temporary occupation and he was entitled to statutory damages against Mr Ramji under s27. With Mr Mehta in occupation any purchaser would have required a substantial discount assessed at £45,000. The plaintiff was, as against all three defendants, entitled to an award of compensatory damages for trespass to land and goods of £10,000, aggravated damages of £10,000 and exemplary damages of £7,500. There had been exceptional conduct and motive on the part of the receiver and managing agent acting on Mr Ramji's behalf, their conduct was designed solely for profit (their fees) and, furthermore, Mr Ramji would have profited. The awards of general, aggravated and exemplary damages against Mr Ramji were set off under Housing Act 1988 s27(5) against the award of statutory damages.

09.11   *Murray v Lloyd*
[1989] 1 WLR 1060; [1990] 2 All ER 92; [1990] 1 EGLR 274; (1989) 21 HLR 525, ChD
Statutory tenancy led to 25% reduction in value of the freehold

An occupier of residential premises claimed that the City firm of solicitors, Theodore Goddard, had been negligent in advising her that a tenancy, for which she paid a substantial premium, should be in the name of a company registered in the Virgin Islands for tax reasons. They wrongly advised that, by assigning the tenancy to herself, she would be able to obtain a statutory tenancy, even though the lease contained an absolute covenant against assignment.

John Mummery, sitting as deputy High Court judge, after accepting expert evidence that freehold property values were generally discounted by 25 per cent to reflect the existence of statutory tenancies, awarded the plaintiff damages of £115,000, assessed at 25 per cent of the freehold vacant possession value of the property (£460,000), even though there was evidence that the freeholder would not have been prepared to sell the freehold to her at a discount nor 'buy her out'.

County courts
The following are examples of awards in the county court for harassment and unlawful eviction. For examples of more cases see *Housing Law Casebook* 3rd edition.

09.12   *Ahmed v Bains*
September 2001 *Legal Action* 25; 18 June 2001, Brentford County Court
£100 per day general damages for unlawful eviction, £3,000 aggravated and exemplary damages

The defendants granted the claimant an oral assured shorthold tenancy in May 1997 of one bedroom, plus shared use of living room, bathroom and kitchen. There were two other assured shorthold tenants in the property. The defendants lived elsewhere. In September 1997 the male defendant started to occupy the living room, making noise and depriving the tenants of its use. When the claimant complained, he was threatened with violence. He called the police, complaining of noise and threats of violence, on eight occasions. The defendants served the claimant with a notice of intention to seek possession. On the day that the notice expired, the male defendant and another male assaulted the claimant as he was leaving his room, grabbing him from behind and taking his keys out of his hand. The defendants then disposed of the claimant's property. The claimant called the police, who took no action. He stayed with friends on a casual basis until the end of December 1997. In December 1997, he issued proceedings for unlawful eviction.

After a contested trial HHJ Marcus Edwards awarded: (1) special damages for loss of possessions: £1,695; (2) general damages for acts of harassment in September: £1,000; (3) general damages for the unlawful eviction and homelessness from 14 October 1997 to the end of December 1997 at £100 per day: £7,800; (4) aggravated damages: £1,500; and (5) exemplary damages as the defendants plainly knew that the eviction was unlawful and had arranged to re-let the whole of the premises from 14 October 1997: £1,500. The total damages were £13,495.

09.12A *Arabhalvaei v Rezaeipoor*

January 2008 *Legal Action* 36; 7 November 2007, Central London County Court

£188,000 damages for harassment and disrepair

Mr Rezaeipoor was a protected tenant of a one-bedroom flat which he shared with his wife. From 1995 until January 2006, when the claimant, his landlord, transferred the property to his former wife, Mr Rezaeipoor and his wife suffered as a result of disrepair at the flat and harassment from the claimant. The disrepair included penetrating damp, cracks to various internal walls and a leaking toilet and sink. The heating system was out of order at various times over the period in question, with the result that the property was without heating and hot water. The harassment comprised verbal abuse, disconnection of the water supply, nuisance telephone calls, locks to the property being filled with glue and, on one occasion, a window being smashed by a bottle. The defendant ignored four statutory abatement notices served by the authority in respect of the disrepair and letters from Mr Rezaeipoor's tenancy relations officer warning him that his actions could amount to harassment. In 2000 Mr Rezaeipoor lost his job as a radio presenter with the BBC's World Service as he was finding it increasingly difficult to leave his wife alone in the property. In 2004, the claimant issued possession proceedings based on rent arrears, and Mr Rezaeipoor counterclaimed for damages for harassment and disrepair. In August 2007 the claimant's claim was struck out and the claimant was debarred from defending the counterclaim.

District Judge Taylor awarded damages of £188,526.21, calculated as follows:

- Disrepair (50% of the rental value of £455 pm over the period in question) £22,500.00;
- Harassment (at the rate of £6,000 per annum) £46,500.00
- Loss of employment £67,500.00
- Special damages £2,601.68
- Additional special damages for heating, cleaning and related damages £2,325
- Aggravated damages £5,000
- Exemplary damages £5,000, and
- Interest £37,099.53.

09.13 *Bamberger v Swaby*

December 2005 *Legal Action* 19; 27 September 2005, Lambeth County Court

£300 per day general damages, £3,000 aggravated and exemplary damages

Ms Bamberger was an assured shorthold tenant. In March/April 2004 there were difficulties with housing benefit leading to rent arrears. As a result, Mr Swaby, her landlord, visited the premises and confronted one of Ms Bamberger's sons, making it clear that he wanted Ms Bamberger out and that he was prepared to go to any lengths to achieve that. He served an invalid notice to quit, which he delivered just after midnight, and removed the fuses to the premises so that there was no power and food in the freezer was spoilt. A tenancy relations officer wrote stating that the landlord's action amounted to a criminal offence and that he should take immediate steps to restore power. This had no effect. However, the electricity was restored on 30 April 2004 after Ms Bamberger obtained an injunction. Mr Swaby inspected the property on 17 May 2004 and was offensive, abusive and unnecessarily intrusive. These matters unsettled Ms Bamberger. As a result of the landlord's behaviour, Ms Bamberger and her two sons left the property. Ms Bamberger claimed damages for trespass and unlawful eviction. The defendant did not appear at trial.

HHJ Welchman found that Ms Bamberger was out of her home for eight days in circumstances where there was a great deal of stress. The defendant's conduct was highly inappropriate and alarming. He awarded general damages of £3,000 on the basis that 'damages should be awarded at somewhere in the region of £300 per day and there is in addition the anxiety concerning departure. That is an added element. I arrive there not by strict mathematics. £2400 for general damages and loading it with an additional sum to take account of events which caused it.' Special damages of £25 for the contents of the freezer and £25 for additional catering were also awarded. The judge also awarded aggravated damages of £1,000 and exemplary damages of £2,000.

09.14   *Biga v Martin*

June 2001 *Legal Action* 25; 16 November 2000, Ilford County Court

Damages of £10,000 for PTSD after violent eviction

The claimant was an assured shorthold tenant. His landlord refused to provide documentary evidence to enable him to obtain housing benefit and told him to leave. Notwithstanding a letter from solicitors warning the landlord of the consequences of taking the law into his own hands, the landlord changed the locks and placed the tenant's belongings in a corridor. Although the claimant obtained an injunction ordering the landlord to readmit him, the landlord attended at the premises, armed with a sledgehammer. He was accompanied by three men. He tried unsuccessfully to break in through the barricaded front door and then broke in through the living room window. The tenant was assaulted. Although he suffered no significant physical injury, he was very distressed and frightened. He spent three nights in a night shelter before being provided with bed and breakfast accommodation by the local authority. He was diagnosed as suffering from post-traumatic stress disorder (PTSD) at the lower end of the scale of the 'moderate' category within the Judicial Studies Board guidelines.

HHJ Platt awarded £10,000 general damages (including personal injury and aggravated damages), £900 special damages and £2,500 exemplary damages.

09.15   *Cooper v Sharma*

October 2005 Legal Action 15; 5 July 2005, Brentford County Court

Damages for disconnection of utilities, interference with post and unsatisfactory accommodation after eviction

Ms Cooper was the assured shorthold tenant of a one-bedroom flat. The defendant landlord interfered with her mail from the beginning of the tenancy. On 28 April 2003, after Ms Cooper had applied for housing benefit, the landlord disconnected the electricity supply to her lights. On 2 May he disconnected the gas, electricity and hot water supplies. On 5 May he cut off the cold water supply. On 5 May Ms Cooper obtained an injunction ordering the landlord to reconnect the utilities. He did not comply until 19 May. On 4 July he obtained a possession order, although he never gave her any notice of proceedings. On 16 July he changed the locks and threw Ms Cooper's belongings, and those of her son, on to the pavement. On 22 July Ms Cooper obtained an order setting aside the possession order and an injunction that the defendant readmit her, but he refused to comply. He was committed to prison for four months for contempt on 29 August. Ms Cooper and her son slept on a friend's floor until 5 August when they were given bed and breakfast accommodation. On 13 October the local authority granted her a non-secure tenancy of a flat. In a claim for damages, the defendant was debarred from defending for non-compliance with directions. District Judge Plashkow awarded general damages of £23,350, aggravated damages of £4,000 and exemplary damages of £2,500. The general damages were assessed on the following basis: £4,600 for the disconnection of the utilities (23 days at £200) and £400 for interference with post; £4,750 for the period sleeping on the friend's floor (19 days at £250); £10,500 for the period in bed and breakfast accommodation (70 days at £150); and £3,100 for the period after moving into non-secure accommodation (31 days at £100, the 31 days representing the balance of the time that it would have taken the defendant to repossess the flat using the Housing Act 1988 s21 procedure). The defendant appealed.

HHJ Marcus Edwards allowed the appeal in part. There was no basis for saying that the district judge's awards of special, aggravated or exemplary damages were wrong. However, the district judge was wrong to assess damages for inconvenience for disconnection of utilities at £200 per day. HHJ Edwards reduced them to £100 per day. He also reduced damages for unlawful eviction from £250 per day to £200 per day and, for the period of 70 days when the claimant was in bed and breakfast accommodation allowed a lump sum of £500 rather than £100 per day. Total damages were reduced to £21,459.24 including interest.

09.16   *Daley, James, Wiseman and Reynolds v Mahmoood and Rahman*

[2006] 1 P&CR D29; 12 July 2005, Central London Civil Justice Centre

£100,000 common-law damages for harassment and unlawful eviction of four occupants

The claimants lived in a house in multiple occupation from the late 1980s. Three had Rent Act protected tenancies of their own rooms, with shared use of common parts. The fourth claimant had acquired the freehold interest of his room by adverse possession. He had no legal rights of way into his room, or use of the common parts, but rights of way and use of the common parts were acknowledged in a court order recording that the landlord would not seek to withdraw them except on 24 days' written notice. There were three empty rooms in the house. In 2003, the first defendant acquired the house at auction for £100,000. The second defendant was her uncle. He represented to the claimants, the police, the local authority and others that he was the landlord and used the first defendant's name as his own. In May 2003, the second defendant and three men forced entry into the house by smashing a window pane in the front room. They were abusive, threatening and intimidating to the claimants. They told the first claimant to move rooms and handed the fourth claimant a letter purporting to withdraw his rights of way on seven days' notice. They stood over him and shouted at him in the hallway. Later that day, he collapsed and was taken to hospital. A few days later, the second defendant and three men came to the property with a skip. They forced entry. They began to clear one of the empty rooms, where the claimants had stored some of their possessions. They threw away the possessions and stripped the room. They stripped the fourth claimant's kitchen of its furniture and fittings. They cut off his gas and electricity supply. They threw out the first claimant's possessions and continued to insist that he moved rooms. In the course of the next four days, they removed the first claimant's kitchen and bathroom furniture and fittings, demolished internal walls and the banisters, and rendered the entire house uninhabitable. The claimants felt that they had no choice but to leave. The fourth claimant was a vulnerable person, suffering from depression. He and the first claimant, as his carer, were given bed and breakfast accommodation for eight weeks by the local authority and then two-bedroom accommodation held on a non-secure tenancy. The second and third claimants lived on a campsite for three months. The eviction had a devastating effect on each of them.

HHJ Medawar QC found that 'there was a deliberate campaign of intimidation, harassment and threats designed to make them leave. The actions were wrongful and, at times, criminal. This is one of the most serious cases of harassment followed by unlawful eviction.' The second defendant was the prime mover. The defendants' intention was to obtain vacant possession to maximise the profit by converting the house into three self-contained flats, yielding a profit of £100,000–£150,000. The judge preferred to award exemplary damages instead of damages under Housing Act 1988 ss27 and 28. The judge awarded:

1) Against both defendants jointly and severally: general damages for harassment prior to vacation: £3,500 each for the second and third claimants, £5,000 each for the first and fourth claimants (who were more vulnerable); aggravated damages for the harassment leading up to vacation: £1,500 for each claimant; general damages for the eviction: £10,000 for each claimant; aggravated damages for the eviction: £2,500 for each claimant; exemplary damages for the eviction: £7,500 for each claimant; damages for personal injury suffered by the fourth claimant as a result of the harassment and eviction (exacerbation of

pre-existing depressive illness and alcoholism, resulting in brain damage and dementia, by 100%): £16,000.

2) Against the second defendant alone: £1,250 for assault on the fourth
   claimant; special damages: each claimant's loss of goods at replacement value (*McGreal v Wake* (P11.13)) plus interest.

09.17 *Daramy v Streeks*

June 2007 *Legal Action* 37; 15 November 2006, Lambeth County Court

Damages for eviction of assured shorthold tenant without using court bailiffs

The claimant was an assured shorthold tenant. He lost his employment
and fell into two months' rent arrears. His landlord then began harassing
him for the rent and assaulted his wife. He obtained a possession order,
but evicted the tenant without obtaining a warrant. He also took the tenant's belongings to sell in order to recover the rent that was due to him.
The tenant brought a claim for damages.

HHJ Crawford Lindsay awarded damages of £1,500 for the harassment
leading up to the eviction, £2,500 for the actual eviction and for the time
spent out of the property and £1,250 in aggravated damages, to reflect the
landlord's conduct.

09.18 *Diallo v Brosnan*

January 2007 *Legal Action* 21; 29 September 2006, Willesden County Court

£2,000 damages for four nights' eviction and aggravating features

The claimant rented a room in a flat from a man called Nick. It transpired
that Nick was in fact the assured shorthold tenant of the first defendant landlord. That tenancy agreement was still extant. Two weeks after the claimant moved in, the first defendant attended the premises and discovered
that Nick was no longer in occupation. He requested that all the occupants
leave. Five of the seven occupants left. The claimant and another occupant
remained in the premises after agreeing to pay rent to the first defendant. The claimant paid rent for a number of months but then requested a
written tenancy agreement so that he could apply for housing benefit. The
landlord refused. The claimant did not pay rent for three weeks and came
back one Friday to find the locks to the flat changed. He broke back into
the premises. The next morning the landlord and another tenant forcibly
evicted the claimant at knife point. The claimant reported the matter to the
police. He spent three nights at his partner's flat and one night sleeping in
a car. An injunction for re-entry was subsequently obtained.

In a claim for damages for unlawful eviction, District Judge Morris
held that the arrangement between the claimant and the first defendant
was one of tenant and landlord. The claimant was therefore an assured
shorthold tenant of the landlord from 2 April 2006. On the evidence, rent
was paid to the landlord. District Judge Morris awarded general damages
of £1,000 and £1,000 'exemplary' (aggravated) damages. 'The use of the
knife was a particularly aggravating factor.'

09.19 *Dorival v Simmons*

August 2003 Legal Action 30; 10 April 2003, Lambeth County Court

Damages for harassment and unlawful eviction

The claimant was the assured shorthold tenant of the defendant landlord. Her tenancy of one room on the first floor with shared use of kitchen, toilet and bathroom was granted in May 2000 for a fixed term of six months, at a rent of £60 per week. The defendant had an office in the premises and rented out the ground floor as a newsagents. For the first three weeks of the tenancy, the cooker and the bathroom were unusable (due to the defendant's failure to repair them) and the claimant cooked and took baths at the defendant's home (immediately opposite the premises). The newsagent, at the deliberate instigation of the defendant, turned off the electricity supply. Three weeks into the tenancy, the claimant complained to the defendant that the taps to the bath could not be turned off and water was flooding from the bath. The defendant's response was to abuse the claimant, and then to assault her, beating her about the face as she was held by the defendant's son and various friends. The defendant turned off the water supply. The claimant complained to the local authority's tenancy relations officer, who wrote to the defendant. The water supply was reinstated four days after the assault. There continued to be difficulties with the electricity supply. After a threat by the defendant to evict the claimant, the tenancy relations officer wrote again to the defendant reminding her of the provisions of Protection from Eviction Act 1977 and interviewed her under caution. On 2 January 2001, the claimant, who was by then four months pregnant, was unable to enter the property as the front door had been locked from the inside by a mortice lock. The defendant refused to readmit her, despite the attendance of the tenancy relations officer. As a result, the local authority provided emergency bed and breakfast accommodation where the claimant remained for six months. The defendant finally allowed the claimant access to collect her possessions six days after receipt of a solicitor's letter.

HHJ Cox found that the defendant had interfered with the claimant's right to quiet enjoyment by the constant interference with the electricity and water supply and harassment from her and her family. He also found that the defendant deliberately set out summarily to exclude the claimant on 2 January 2001, knowing that she was not entitled to do so. He held that general damages for the period after 2 January 2001 should be limited to a period of three months, the length of time it would have taken for the defendant to obtain and enforce a possession order through the accelerated possession procedure. He awarded aggravated damages, holding that the claimant had suffered particularly, had been subject to deliberate harassment and was deliberately evicted in circumstances calculated to cause maximum distress. He awarded exemplary damages, holding that the defendant had chosen deliberately to short-circuit the possession procedure. The damages comprised: £1,500 for the breaches of quiet enjoyment prior to 2 January 2001; £750 for the assault; £2,000 for the eviction; £1,000 for distress and inconvenience of temporary accommodation for three months; £2,000 aggravated damages; £1,000 exemplary damages; total: £8,250. As the defendant had rejected a Part 36 offer of £5,500, HHJ Cox awarded the claimant her costs, and ordered that the defendant pay 10% per annum interest on costs accrued after the last date for acceptance of the offer.

09.19A *Evans v Copping*

January 2008 *Legal Action* 30; 14 November 2007, Ashford County Court

Damages for unlawful eviction including deceit

The defendant landlord and his wife lived in the ground floor flat of a Victorian conversion. The defendant's stepdaughter lived in the basement flat. The claimant lived in the top floor flat and was entitled to use a laundry room which was on a mezzanine floor. It was a very small room housing a washing machine and tumble dryer. During ongoing refurbishment works the defendant's wife and stepdaughter used the laundry facilities. The claimant was excluded from the property when he returned from shopping and discovered all the locks had been changed. He applied for an injunction permitting re-entry, but the defendant misled the court by indicating that the flat had been re-let whereas, in fact, there was just an agreement to re-let in a fortnight's time. Between eviction and the trial three months later the claimant stayed with friends. The claimant sought damages.

Deputy District Judge Cagney held that the tenancy was not excluded under Protection from Eviction Act 1977 s3A. The defendant's wife's use of the laundry room was only temporary and transitory and so there was no shared accommodation through her activities. He also doubted whether the laundry room could amount to accommodation for the purposes of s3A. He awarded general damages of £2,500; aggravated damages of £500; special damages of £240; and exemplary damages of £1,500 to condemn the deception of the court.

09.20 *Festusi Porbeni v Abdellaziz Chaabdiss*

11 September 2001, Willesden County Court (see P11.31)

£2,500 pa (2001) for 7 years' harassment

09.21 *Garcia v Khan*

March 2005 *Legal Action* 21; 17 December 2004, Bow County Court

£100 per night and £4,500 aggravated/exemplary damages for eviction

The claimant was an assured shorthold tenant of a flat. He lived there with his wife. After they had complained of disrepair, the landlord sold the property to the defendant without informing the claimant. Four months later, on a Monday, the defendant's husband, pretending that he was acting on the previous landlord's behalf, told the claimant's wife that works were to start, but could not start while she and their one-year-old child were in the premises. The claimant's wife was six months pregnant. It was agreed that the wife and child would stay with family for three or four days, while the claimant would stay each night in the premises. The claimant locked his valuable possessions away. On the Tuesday night, the defendant's husband bolted the premises from the inside and refused the claimant access. On the Thursday, the claimant's wife was refused access. On the Friday, the claimant and his wife went to the premises and found that the premises were stripped bare of all their possessions. The lock to the room where they had left their valuable possessions appeared to have been tampered with. The defendant, whom they had never met, was sleeping on their bed. The police were called. The defendant told the police that she was the owner and insisted that the claimant and his wife leave. During the following week, the defendant claimed that the claimant had been subletting the premises and accused him of housing benefit fraud. She claimed that she had bought with vacant possession. She refused to reinstate the claimant and his wife. At the end of the second week, the local authority confirmed that it would make an offer of a secure tenancy. The claimant and his wife spent the following five weeks staying with relatives, sleeping on the floor with their one-year-old child.

HHJ Hornby held that there had been an unlawful exclusion, probably from the Tuesday. He rejected a submission that the claimant had failed to mitigate his loss by failing to apply for an injunction. He awarded general damages of £100 per night (£5,500); aggravated damages of £2,000 to reflect pain and suffering, and the outrage and indignation of the court; and exemplary damages of £2,500 to penalise the defendant's attempt to make a profit by obtaining vacant possession earlier than she would have done if she had used the accelerated possession procedure.

09.22   ### Grillo v Cant and Bassairi Ltd

March 1998 *Legal Action* 13, Central London County Court

Damages for loss of assured tenancy

The plaintiff was an assured tenant of a room. Six months after the grant of the tenancy and shortly after the second defendant had bought the property, the first defendant, the company secretary, evicted the tenant and left her belongings on the communal staircase in black dustbin bags. The tenant spent two nights sleeping on the communal staircase to look after her belongings and then two weeks on a friend's sofa. She was then only able to find accommodation let on an assured shorthold tenancy. The first defendant was fined £250 for illegal eviction.

HHJ Butter QC awarded £6,000 damages for loss of the assured tenancy, £2,000 for the manner of the eviction, £1,000 exemplary damages and £45 special damages.

09.23   ### Hadden v Nicholson

November 2006 *Legal Action* 32; 15 August 2006, Carlisle County Court

£1,000 general damages for one night on the street and four nights in a hostel

Mr Hadden was an assured shorthold tenant of a bed-sit from December 2003. In April 2005 Mr Nicholson acquired the property and granted a new assured shorthold tenancy to Mr Hadden. In September and October 2005 Mr Nicholson wrote to Mr Hadden informing him that urgent repairs were required to the electrical system, that Mr Hadden would have to leave the property as soon as possible; that the electricity supply would be switched off on 10 October 2005 and that Mr Hadden would be able to return once the repairs had been carried out. No evidence was presented at court that there ever was a problem with the electricity supply or that any repairs were carried out. Mr Hadden agreed to move out temporarily into alternative accommodation provided by Mr Nicholson. On 10 October 2005 Mr Hadden loaded his belongings into a van and attempted to move into the temporary alternative accommodation. When he arrived at the alternative accommodation Mr Nicholson's agent refused to allow him admission unless he paid a week's rent (£40) in advance, which he was unable to do. He returned to his original property but was unable to gain entrance as the lock there had been changed. Mr Hadden was unable to find any alternative accommodation on 10 October 2005 and so spent the night on the streets. He suffered the indignity of being moved on by security guards and the police. On 11 October 2005, he was admitted to a homeless shelter, and stayed there for a total of four nights. Mr Hadden's belongings remained in a van for five days. On 14 October 2005 an injunction ordering Mr Hadden's readmittance to the original bed-sit, or to suitable alternative property, was served on Mr Nicholson. Mr Nicholson admitted Mr Hadden into an alternative property which was suitable.

In county court proceedings, a judge found that Mr Hadden had been unlawfully evicted. When he moved out on 10 October 2005 he had no intention of surrendering his tenancy. He was merely responding as best he could to Mr Nicholson's threat to switch off the electricity. The judge held that that in itself was enough to make out a claim for unlawful eviction, but indicated that the matter was made worse by Mr Nicholson's refusal to allow Mr Hadden to enter the alternative accommodation. The judge awarded Mr Hadden £1,000 in general damages for the night on the streets and the four nights in the shelter. Mr Hadden was awarded £350 in aggravated damages as he had never spent a night on the streets before, was moved on by the police, and had never stayed in a hostel before. Mr Hadden was also awarded £1,000 in exemplary damages, chiefly because Mr Nicholson had made a profit by evicting him.

09.24 *Naveed v Raja*
July 2007 *Legal Action* 32; 10 May 2007, Willesden County Court

£27,000 common-law damages for assaulted assured shorthold tenant
Mr Naveed was an assured shorthold tenant. In December 2005 he was injured in a car accident and had no means of paying rent. He asked the defendant, his landlord, to provide him with a new tenancy agreement so that he could claim housing benefit. The defendant refused and, instead, served a Housing Act 1988 s21 notice. On the day that the notice expired, the defendant's father, who was managing the property, and three other men assaulted the claimant and evicted him. They took all his property. He slept for three nights in a car. After obtaining an injunction, he was readmitted to the property, but his belongings were not returned. Three weeks later he was again assaulted by three men, one of whom had been with the defendant's father on the previous occasion. Mr Naveed was beaten with sticks, and sustained injuries to his head, body and legs. He was kept in hospital overnight. He was too scared to return to the property.

HHJ Copley awarded £10,000 general damages, £15,000 aggravated and exemplary damages and £2,000 special damages for lost possessions.

09.25 *Neil v Kingsnorth*
March 1988 *Legal Action* 21, Shoreditch County Court

Quantum of damages for misrepresentation

The landlord brought possession proceedings under Rent Act 1977 Sch 15 Case 9, claiming that she intended to live in the premises. However, after a possession order was made, she sold the property and it was converted into four flats. In proceedings brought under Rent Act 1977 s102, interlocutory judgment was obtained in default of a defence and, at the hearing for assessment of damages, the court heard from a local estate agent that the likely profit which the landlord had gained by obtaining vacant possession was in the region of £10,000.

Registrar Lipton awarded the plaintiff special damages of £170, general damages of £750 for worry and inconvenience (she subsequently found better accommodation) and exemplary damages of £5,000.

09.26 **Pillai v Amendra**

October 2000 *Legal Action* 24; 27 July 2000, Central London County Court

Damages for bad case of eviction, but not at top end of scale as no violence/ vulnerability

The claimant was a single man and a weekly assured shorthold tenant of a one-bedroomed flat. The rent was £300 per month. He refused to move to alternative accommodation for two weeks to enable the landlord to reinstate a previous tenant and so defeat a housing benefit fraud investigation. The claimant returned from holiday to find himself locked out and his possessions in the front garden. He secured re-entry with the assistance of the police. His car windscreen was smashed and a threatening note left for him. He was then locked out for a second time and his goods were again left in the garden. The landlord ignored an injunction. The tenant was too frightened to return. He stayed with a friend for six months in cramped conditions before finding another flat. Time which the tenant was obliged to take off work was a contributory factor in his employer's decision to sack him from his job as an accountant. (He was awarded £3,000 compensation for unfair dismissal by an industrial tribunal.) The defendant landlord signed a statement of truth in his defence denying the claimant's case entirely, ignored orders for disclosure and exchange of witness statements and gave a misleading address for service. The landlord did not give evidence at trial but cross-examined the claimant.

HHJ Green QC considered the matter 'a bad case, but not at the very top end' because there was no actual violence and the claimant was not a vulnerable member of the community. He awarded general damages for trespass to land in the sum of £6,000, £10,000 aggravated and exemplary damages for trespass to land and £3,000 aggravated damages for trespass to goods. Special damages for loss of goods and incidental expenditure were assessed at £17,000 (total damages £36,000). Costs were awarded on the indemnity basis.

09.27 **Poku-Awuah v Lenton**

February 2006 *Legal Action* 28; 5 December 2005, Lambeth County Court

£300 per day for exclusion of 17 days; £3,000 aggravated/exemplary damages

Mrs Poku-Awuah was an assured shorthold tenant from April 2004. On 2 February 2005 her landlord attended the property late at night with four men and two women and knocked on her door. When she opened it they went into her room and started packing her belongings into black bags. One of the group changed the locks to the property and she was forcibly removed. She slept in her car that night, followed by a night at her daughter's accommodation and 15 nights in a hotel. On 19 February 2005, following the court award of an interim injunction, her landlord allowed her to stay at a neighbouring property. Following a breach of directions, the landlord's defence and Part 20 claim (rent arrears) were struck out, judgment was entered for Mrs Poku-Awuah and the matter was set down to decide quantum.

District Judge Jacey found that the whole episode on 2 February must have been very distressing for Mrs Poku-Awuah. He had particular regard to *Bamberger v Swaby* (O9.13), although he also considered *Drane v Evangelou* (O9.3) (exemplary damages), *Asghar v Ahmed* (O9.1) (aggravated damages) and *Tvrtkovic v Tomas* (O9.28). He awarded Mrs Poku-Awuah £5,100 (ie, general damages of £300 per day), £390 special damages (including hotel costs), £1,000 aggravated damages and £2,000 exemplary damages. He also awarded interest from the date of re-admission at the rate of 8% having taken into account that Mrs Poku-Awuah had beaten the CPR Part 36 offer she had made in August 2005. This totalled £537.78. He also awarded costs against the landlord, including costs on the indemnity basis from the date of expiry of the Part 36 offer.

09.28   *Tvrtkovic v Tomas*
August 1999 *Legal Action* 29, Brentford County Court

Damages for unlawful eviction when landlord demanded tenant left

In February 1996 the claimant was granted an assured tenancy of a double room in a shared house with shared use of kitchen, living room and bathroom at a rent of £120 per week. In May 1996 the defendant landlord demanded an extra £5 per week, backdated to the commencement of the tenancy. The claimant paid a cheque for some of the additional rent into the landlord's bank account, but at 11.30 pm one night the landlord came round, demanded cash and told her to get out and give him the keys. The claimant was frightened, started to cry, gave him the keys and left. She spent one night sharing a bed with a female friend and then three nights in a hotel. Then she obtained rent-free accommodation with a family. She had law exams to sit the day following the eviction and for several days thereafter. When she returned to collect belongings left at the property she found that the defendant had disposed of them. The defendant did not attend trial.

HHJ Oppenheimer found that it was a clear case of unlawful eviction and said 'This eviction was severe and this young woman subjected to wholly unwarranted treatment. She was a girl on her own, in the middle of her examination and the eviction took place in circumstances in which she could not remove her own belongings and at 11.30 at night.' He awarded general damages of £250 per night for the four nights before the claimant found alternative accommodation, aggravated damages of £1,250, exemplary damages of £1,250, special damages of £4,198.25 and interest of £505.17.

09.29 **White v Lambeth LBC**

June 1995 *Legal Action* 20, Lambeth County Court

£10,000 common-law damages for council tenant evicted for 15 weeks

An absolute possession order was obtained against Mr White, a secure tenant, but then set aside under CCR Ord 37 r2 (see now CPR 39.3). In July 1992, believing that the order was still in force and that Mr White had abandoned the flat, Lambeth Council authorised contractors to force the door in order to carry out works. When Mr White next called at the flat, he found that it was a building site and most of his possessions had disappeared. Subsequently he was offered and accepted another flat, but was unable to gain access to it for some time. He was without accommodation for 15 weeks.

Mr Recorder Rylance awarded damages under Housing Act 1988 ss27 and 28 of £18,000, and for interference with goods of £1,500. He assessed damages for trespass to land and breach of covenant for quiet enjoyment as £8,000 and aggravated damages of £2,000, but in view of the fact that these sums were less than the award of Housing Act damages, the total amount of damages (excluding interest) was limited to £19,500.

09.30 **Youziel v Andrews**

March 2003 *Legal Action* 29; 23 January 2003, Lambeth County Court

Damages of £20,000 for personal injury and assault

The claimant was the assured shorthold tenant of a one-bedroom flat in Peckham. The defendant was initially his landlord but then transferred his interest to a third party. However, no notification of the transfer was given to the claimant in accordance with Landlord and Tenant Act 1985 s3 and the defendant continued to manage the property. Rent arrears accrued because the claimant was an asylum-seeker who was not eligible for housing benefit. Over a period of six weeks, the defendant subjected him to a campaign of harassment. There were some ten occasions when the defendant threatened the claimant by telephoning, entering the flat without permission and shouting threats, including that the claimant 'would pay with his life'. On one occasion, the claimant was assaulted by the defendant and two friends. He was slapped, kicked and thrown to the ground. The defendant was prosecuted for assault and was bound over to keep the peace. As a result of the assault, the claimant sustained an injury to his knee found by the judge to fall within the upper end of the scale of the 'moderate' category within the *Judicial Studies Board Guidelines for the assessment of general damages in personal injury cases* (p48: £7,750 to £14,000). He was caused stress and anxiety, as a result of which he lost 12 lb in weight. Six months later, he vacated the premises voluntarily.

District Judge Jacey awarded damages of £20,000, comprising damages for the personal injury assessed at £13,000, aggravated damages in tort for the assault at £4,300, and contractual damages for the breach of covenant of quiet enjoyment arising from the other incidents of harassment at £2,700. Interest of £200 was also awarded.

010   **Criminal offences**

Protection from Eviction Act 1977 s1 creates offences relating to acts of
unlawful eviction and harassment of residential occupiers. There are various other offences specific to the landlord and tenant context (eg, Criminal Law Act 1977 s6 and Landlord and Tenant Act 1985 s1). The ordinary
criminal law may also be relevant (eg, assault, theft).

For the purposes of Protection from Eviction Act 1977, a residential
occupier means 'a person occupying the premises as a residence, whether
under a contract or by virtue of any enactment or rule of law giving him
the right to remain in occupation or restricting the right of any other person to recover possession of the premises' (s1(1)). This includes those who
are, or were, secure or assured tenants and also those who are, or were,
non-protected tenants and licensees that are not excluded (Protection from
Eviction Act 1977 ss3 and 3A, see O3) and their households up to the point
of eviction by the court bailiffs. Residence is not defined but has been held
to have the same meaning as under Rent Act 1977 (*Schon v Camden LBC*
(1986) 18 HLR 341; (1987) 53 P&CR 361; [1986] 2 EGLR 219, DC).

Section 1(2) provides:

> If any person unlawfully deprives the residential occupier of any premises
> of his occupation of the premises or of any part thereof, or attempts to do
> so, he shall be guilty of an offence unless he proves that he believed, and
> had reasonable cause to believe, that the residential occupier had ceased to
> reside in the premises.

Section 1(3) provides:

> If any person with intent to cause the residential occupier of any
> premises –
> (a) to give up the occupation of the premises or any part thereof; or
> (b) to refrain from exercising any right or pursuing any remedy in respect
> of the premises or part thereof;
> does acts likely to interfere with the peace or comfort of the residential
> occupier or members of his household, or persistently withdraws or with-
> holds services reasonably required for the occupation of the premises as a
> residence, he shall be guilty of an offence.'

Section 1(3A), inserted by Housing Act 1988, creates a further offence
which does not require intent to be proved. It applies if the conduct set out
in s1(3) is done by a landlord/agent who knows, or has reasonable cause to
believe, that that conduct is likely to cause the residential occupier to give
up the occupation or to refrain from exercising any right or pursuing any
remedy. It is a defence if there are reasonable grounds for doing the acts
or withholding/withdrawing the services (s1(3B)).

Section 6 provides that prosecutions for offences under the Act may by
instituted by district councils and London boroughs.

House of Lords

010.1   *R v Burke*
[1991] 1 AC 135; [1990] 2 WLR 1313; (1990) 91 Cr App R 384; [1990] 2 All ER 385;
(1991) 22 HLR 433, HL
Offence of harassment can arise despite no breach of civil law

The House of Lords upheld convictions under Protection from Eviction Act 1977 s1(3) where a landlord had padlocked a lavatory, disconnected the front doorbells and cut off water supplies to one of the toilets and one of the bathrooms. It was not necessary for an act by a landlord to be actionable in civil law in order for it to be an offence under s1(3). The House of Lords approved the Court of Appeal decision in *R v Yuthiwattana* (O10.7). In his speech Lord Griffiths referred to harassment as a 'social evil'.

Court of Appeal

010.2 *R v Ahmad*

(1987) 84 Cr App R 64; (1986) 18 HLR 416; (1986) 52 P&CR 346, CA

Intentional failure to rectify damage not an offence

The defendant landlord started building works and removed all of the tenant's bathroom fittings. After a meeting at the tenancy relations office, he agreed not to do any further works until firm agreement was reached on, among other things, storage of the tenant's belongings. Over the next year, he carried out no further works and the bathroom remained out of use. He was charged alternatively with offences under Protection from Eviction Act 1977 s1(3)(a) and s1(3)(b). There was evidence that, once the landlord had removed the bathroom fittings, he formed the intention of evicting the tenant.

On appeal, the landlord's conviction was quashed because, after he formed the necessary intention, he did not do acts, but merely failed to rectify damage caused. Where a landlord 'innocently' causes damage, an intentional failure to rectify that damage is not a crime.

010.3 *R v Brennan and Brennan*

(1979) 1 Cr App R(S) 103, CA

Immediate custodial sentence for threats to evict tenants correct in principle

The appellants pleaded guilty to offences of depriving residential occupiers of occupation of premises under Protection from Eviction Act 1977 s1(2). They came to the premises in question one afternoon with a large man and an Alsatian dog and told the students who lived there to leave. They were sentenced to one year's imprisonment.

The Court of Appeal stated that the use of threats and force to get tenants out was one of the worst forms of the offence, and a sentence of immediate imprisonment was correct in principle. Loss of liberty should be the usual penalty where landlords used threats or force in the absence of unusual mitigation. However, in view of the good character of the appellants, the sentences were too long. They were reduced to three months' imprisonment.

010.4 *R v Khan (Jahinger)*

[2001] EWCA Crim 912; [2001] 2 Cr App R (S) 129, CA

15 months' imprisonment for landlord of previous good character upheld

The victim, a single mother, rented a flat owned by the defendant landlord. There was a delay in paying rent as a result of an application for housing benefit. The defendant went to the flat with four associates. They kicked in the door, broke the door-frame and then went through the flat, disturbing and breaking much of the contents. The stereo was smashed, the television was broken, beds were turned upside down and the baby's cot and toys were broken. Some items were stolen. The tenant did not return. When her boyfriend went to collect some baby's clothes he was told that if she returned her face would be 'rearranged'. The defendant was charged with offences of interfering with the tenant's peace and comfort (s1(3)) and unlawful eviction (s1(2)) and found guilty. He was sentenced to 15 months' imprisonment, concurrent, on each of those offences, with other sentences for theft and attempting to pervert the course of justice to run consecutively. The total sentence was two years.

The Court of Appeal dismissed the defendant's appeal. The offences under Protection from Eviction Act clearly merited a custodial sentence. The court noted aggravating factors such as the wanton damage, theft and the number of men used to intimidate. The court also took into account the defendant's age (26) and good character but concluded that it was a case that merited more than just a short term of imprisonment.

010.5   *R v Phekoo*

[1981] 1 WLR 1117; [1981] 3 All ER 84; (1981) 73 Cr App R 107, CA

Defence where honest belief that victim was not a residential occupier

The defendant owner of a house believed that two men were squatters and had no right to be there. He was abusive and threatened them with violence if they did not leave. He was charged with an offence contrary to Protection from Eviction Act 1977 s1(3)(a). At the conclusion of the evidence, the defence conceded that the men were in fact residential occupiers within the meaning of the Act. The judge directed the jury that, if the person harassed by a defendant was a residential occupier, the defendant's belief regarding the status of the occupier was irrelevant.

The defendant's appeal against conviction was allowed. This was not an offence of strict liability. The prosecution was required to prove an intent on the part of the defendant to harass someone he knew to be a residential occupier and also to prove that his belief that the person was not a residential occupier was not an honest belief. Hollings J also indicated that, where a defendant asserts a belief that a person is not a residential occupier, the jury should be directed that there must be reasonable grounds for that belief.

010.6   *R v Polycarpu*

(1978) 9 HLR 129, CA

A single act can constitute an offence despite reference in s1 to 'acts' in the plural

The landlord removed a gas ring which was the tenant's sole source of heat. He also erected a partition, which had the effect of forcing the tenant to go out and re-enter the house each time he wanted to go from one room to another. The landlord was charged with two separate offences of harassment under Rent Act 1965 s30(2) (now Protection from Eviction Act 1977 s1(3)). He appealed, contending that the use of the word 'acts' in the statute did not include a single act.

The appeal was dismissed. Interpretation Act 1889 s1(2), which provides that whenever a word is used in the plural it covers the singular, applied.

010.7 *R v Yuthiwattana*

(1984) 80 Cr App R 55; (1984) 16 HLR 49, CA

Exclusion for one night did not amount to unlawful eviction; harassment can occur without landlord being in breach of the civil law

Mr Nelson, a residential occupier, found that his key was missing. He asked his landlord for a replacement. She refused to give him one. He was, accordingly, dependent on someone being in the premises to open the door for him. From time to time he had difficulty getting in and had to spend one night at a unit for homeless persons. The landlord wrote letters requiring him to leave. Mr Nelson eventually left the premises because he thought that he would otherwise be thrown out. The landlord was charged with harassment and illegal eviction.

The defendant's appeal against conviction for harassment was dismissed but his conviction for illegal eviction was quashed. It is not necessary for a landlord's act to amount to a breach of contract before it can constitute an act of harassment for Protection from Eviction Act 1977 s1(3). However, for the purposes of s1(2), the deprivation of occupation has to have the character of an eviction. Exclusion need not be permanent, but exclusion for weeks or months would be sufficient. The exclusion for one night could not be regarded as deprivation of occupation within s1(2).

Note: Approved by the House of Lords in *R v Burke* (O10.1).

High Court

010.8 *Costelloe v Camden LBC*

[1986] Crim LR 249, DC

Question was whether exclusion was designed to evict tenant or merely to deprive of occupation for a short time

The defendant landlord told a tenant that she had to be out of her room by 13 May. On 9 May, at 11.30 pm, he refused to allow her into the room. She called the police and, an hour later, he allowed her into her room. She collected her property and left. The landlord was convicted of depriving the tenant of occupation of her room contrary to Protection from Eviction Act 1977 s1(2).

His appeal was allowed because there was no finding on whether the tenant was being excluded permanently or for a short time. Where a defendant's intention was to exclude a tenant for a short time then the exclusion did not amount to an eviction. However, where the defendant's intention was to evict the tenant permanently it was an unlawful eviction, regardless of whether the exclusion was for a short or a long time. If a prosecutor is in doubt about whether facts constitute an offence under s1(2) or s1(3) the offences may be charged in the alternative.

010.9 *R (Dewa) v Marylebone Magistrates' Court*

[2004] EWHC 1022 (Admin); 28 April 2004; [2004] All ER (D) 289 (Apr)

Offence of failure to provide rent book

Mr Dewa was the tenant of residential premises from 1973. He laid an information in a magistrates' court against his landlord, alleging a failure to provide a rent book contrary to Landlord and Tenant Act 1985 ss4(1) and 7(1). The defendant made a submission that there was no case to answer, claiming that from 1992 the rent had been paid fortnightly and that more recently it had been paid monthly by the local authority. A district judge accepted that submission. The claimant applied for judicial review.

The application was allowed. The words 'in consideration of a rent payable weekly' in s4(1) meant rent that was payable as a matter of obligation under the tenancy agreement. A distinction may have to be drawn between the basis on which rent became payable and when it was in fact paid. The decision was quashed and remitted to be heard by a different district judge.

010.10 *R (McGowan) v Brent Justices*
[2001] EWHC Admin 814; [2002] HLR 55

Landlord had cause to believe that building works likely to cause tenant to leave

Mr McGowan bought a building, which included a disused bank, with the intention of converting it into a pub. Ms Harris, a protected tenant, occupied the first floor. Over a three-year period Mr McGowan performed a series of acts connected with the conversion which, it was alleged, amounted to harassment of Ms Harris contrary to Protection from Eviction Act 1977. These included allowing dust to penetrate into her flat, removing the staircase twice, placing a noisy banner outside her flat and interrupting the gas supply. These acts made the tenant suicidal and eventually she left. The magistrates found that Mr McGowan did the acts complained of, that they were likely to interfere with Ms Harris's peace and comfort and that Mr McGowan knew or had reasonable cause to believe that the conduct was likely to cause her to give up occupation of the premises. They found him guilty of an offence contrary to s1(3A).

Mr McGowan applied for judicial review, contending that the magistrates had failed to give adequate reasons and that they had applied an objective test when the section requires a subjective test. The application was dismissed. The magistrates' essential finding was that the cumulative effect of the acts 'was such as to cause Mr McGowan to know or believe that they were likely to cause Ms Harris to leave the premises'.

010.11 *Westminster CC v Peart*
(1968) 19 P&CR 736, DC

'Persistently' applied to withholding as well as withdrawal of services

The prosecution alleged that the defendant landlord had committed three offences contrary to Rent Act 1965 s30(2) (now Protection from Eviction Act 1977 s1(3)). Two of the allegations were that he had withheld the gas and electricity supplies on one day.

Lord Parker CJ held that the word 'persistently' in s30(2) referred to the offence of withholding as well as withdrawing services. The allegation of an element of persistency is material in connection with that offence. The information was defective and the prosecution's appeal dismissed.

The court found it unnecessary to decide whether a landlord's failure to pay for the gas and electricity supply amounted to withholding a service.

010.12 *West Wiltshire DC v Snelgrove*

(1998) 30 HLR 57, DC

Occupier was excluded from protection by s3A as grant was otherwise than for money's worth

The defendants entered into a casual arrangement to allow a Mr Lacey and his two sons to use their house for two weeks. Mr Lacey was not obliged to pay any rent, but it was agreed that he would pay for use of water, electricity, gas and some food left in the fridge at the rate of £10 per day. He did not leave at the end of the two weeks and, after an argument, was arrested for damage to property. The defendants were, at a later date, prosecuted under Protection from Eviction Act 1977 s1(3). The magistrates found that there had been 'an act of charity' which gave rise to a licence, not a tenancy, and that Mr Lacey was not a residential occupier within the meaning of s1(1). They dismissed the charge and the council appealed.

The Divisional Court decided that it was not necessary to determine whether or not Mr Lacey was a residential occupier and dismissed the appeal, finding that the arrangement with him was excluded under s3A(7)(b) because the 'grant was otherwise than for money'. Such money that was paid was for services only and not a charge for the occupation of the property.

Crown Court

010.13 *Lewisham LBC v Ranaweera*

[2000] 2 CL 385, Crown Court

Offence of failing to provide name and address of landlord

Mr Ranaweera was convicted of failing to comply with a notice requiring him, for the purpose of proceedings brought or intended to be brought, to disclose the name and address of the landlord of premises contrary to Protection from Eviction Act 1977 s7(2). The notice was served following a complaint of an alleged unlawful eviction and stated that there would be a meeting the following week with the council's legal representatives to discuss the matter but that, in the meantime, if any attempt to evict the tenant unlawfully was made, an injunction would be sought.

HHJ Norris found that there was no intention to bring proceedings at the time when the notice was served and allowed Mr Ranaweera's appeal.

CHAPTER P

Disrepair

P1   General

Court of Appeal

P1.1   *Chin v Hackney LBC*

[1996] 1 All ER 973; (1996) 28 HLR 423, CA

PI claim, brought by daughter of tenant who had settled disrepair claim, not res judicata

A tenant brought an action for damages for disrepair in contract (Landlord and Tenant Act 1985 s11) and tort (Defective Premises Act 1972 s4). In October 1992 the claim was compromised on terms that the council would carry out agreed works and pay damages of £15,000. The tenant's disabled daughter (acting by her next friend) then issued new proceedings against the council for damages for personal injury caused to her by the conditions in her mother's home. The council applied to strike out the daughter's action as an abuse of process of the court. HHJ Graham QC allowed the council's application, applying the doctrine of res judicata.

The Court of Appeal allowed the daughter's appeal. It was a cardinal principle of res judicata that the second issue or action must arise between the same parties as the first. Here, the plaintiff was different. No exception to the rule arose simply from the fact that the second plaintiff was a member of the same family as the first or dependent on her. Therefore, the doctrine of 'res judicata' had no application to the case. The council's alternative proposition, that the settlement included a compensatory element for the child, was similarly rejected. No settlement including an award for a child or other person suffering from a disability could be made without proceedings by a next friend and the approval of the court: CCR Ord 10 rr10 and 11 (now CPR Part 21). However, Simon Brown LJ stated:

> As the judge rightly recognised, in circumstances such as these, it is plainly in the public interest to have a single action in which the claims of all affected members of the household are included rather than a multiplicity of actions. If, unjustifiably, separate actions are brought and the fault is found to lie with the solicitor, a wasted costs order may well be appropriate.

P1.2   *Lambeth LBC v Rogers*

[2000] 03 EG 127; (2000) 32 HLR 361; [2000] LGR 191; [2000] L&TR 319; (1999) *Times* 10 November, CA (see I2.9)

Effect of court postponing possession, after SPO breached, was to revive the tenancy and, retrospectively, the repairing obligation

P1.3   *Routh v Leeds CC*

June 1998 *Legal Action* 11, CA (see I3.6)

Reinstatement of tenancy to allow action for disrepair would be unjust

See also *Marshall v Bradford MDC* (I2.11) and *Dunn v Bradford MDC* (I3.1).

County courts

P1.4   *Bibi v Southwark LBC*

November 2004 *Legal Action* 26, Lambeth County Court

Parties could not be forced to adopt ADR

Southwark sought a stay of a number of claims where damages were sought for disrepair on the basis that they should be transferred and dealt with under the Southwark Arbitration Scheme.

HHJ Cox decided that arbitration or any other form of alternative dispute resolution could not be forced on reluctant parties, in the light of the decision in *Halsey v Milton Keynes General NHS Trust* [2004] EWCA Civ 576, [2004] 1 WLR 3002. The judge rejected Southwark's assertion that claimants have to satisfy the court that they have considered alternative dispute resolution, and justify their decision not to use it except in relation to costs. Southwark was ordered to pay costs on an indemnity basis.

Note: See now *Practice Direction – Protocols and Pre-Action Protocol for Housing Disrepair Cases* regarding the conduct expected of parties prior to issue of proceedings.

P1.5 *Hussein v Mehlman*

[1992] 2 EGLR 87; [1992] 32 EG 59, Wood Green Trial Centre

Serious disrepair can amount to repudiatory breach; plaster part of 'structure'

Joint tenants of premises in serious disrepair left during a fixed-term tenancy and claimed damages for disrepair. The landlord counterclaimed for arrears of rent. Assistant Recorder Sedley held:

1) Serious failure to repair is capable of amounting to repudiatory breach of contract, entitling the tenants to accept the repudiation and leave.
2) On the facts, there had been a repudiatory breach which the tenants had accepted and there was no liability for rent following their departure.
3) Defective plaster on a bedroom ceiling was part of the 'structure' for the purposes of Landlord and Tenant Act 1985 s11.

Cf *Irvine v Moran* (P5.23) on the point regarding plaster.

P1.6 *Millington v Islington LBC*

August 1999 *Legal Action* 25, Clerkenwell County Court

Where disrepair claim included a PI claim, limitation period extended for non-PI element

A tenant experienced repeated water penetration to her home from 1979 (for which she claimed general damages) culminating in a serious flood in 1995 (for which she claimed damages for personal injury – severe anxiety state and nocturnal bruxism (excessive grinding of teeth)). The proceedings were issued in August 1997. As a 'personal injury action' by virtue of the inclusion of a claim for personal injury damages, a three-year limitation period applied to the whole claim. The tenant applied under Limitation Act 1980 s33 to extend the limitation period on the non-personal injury aspects of her claim.

HHJ Marr-Johnson QC allowed the application. He held that there was no reason why the tenant should not benefit from the normal six-year limitation period on her non-personal injury claim. If the application were not allowed the tenant would have had to start two separate proceedings (PI and non-PI) and apply for them to be tried together in order to have her whole claim considered.

P1.7   *Murphy and Peers v Stockport MBC*
August 2002 *Legal Action* 27; 26 April 2002, Stockport County Court

Tenant's children did not have separate causes of action from tenant

The first claimant brought an action for damages for disrepair against her council landlord. The second and third claimants were her minor children. The question of whether the children had a separate cause of action was tried as a preliminary issue.

Recorder Marriot held that, in the absence of any claim for personal injury or damage to their personal property, the children could not rely on the duty of care in Defective Premises Act 1972 s4. They could not sue in nuisance as they had no proprietory interest in their home. They could not rely on any express term as they were not parties to the tenancy agreement with the council and the Contract (Rights of Third Parties) Act 1999 did not apply as the children were not identified by name, class or description in the agreement. They could not rely on the implied term in Landlord and Tenant Act 1985 s11 and, applying *Lee v Leeds CC* (P4.9), that statute was not to be read as in any way extended by the Human Rights Act and ECHR article 8. In relation to these matters, parliament had already struck a fair balance between the competing interests of the individual and the community as a whole by the legislative provision it had made. The best that the children could expect would be to have some element of a remedy on the coat-tails of the first claimant, by application of the rule in *Jackson v Horizon Holidays* [1975] 1 WLR 1468.

P2   Liability in contract

The starting point when considering whether a landlord or tenant has any liability for disrepair should always be the tenancy agreement or lease and any express covenants to carry out repairs. In addition there may be covenants which are implied by statute (see P5) or at common law (see P4).

P3   Express covenants

Court of Appeal

P3.1   *Creska Ltd v Hammersmith and Fulham LBC*
[1998] 3 EGLR 35; [1999] L&TR 207, CA

Repair obligation not satisfied by installing different heating system

The express terms of a lease required the repair and maintenance of 'all electrical heating ... installations'. The building had an electric underfloor heating system with cables buried in concrete. The cables had become corrupted and repair to the system was required. The party subject to the repairing obligation proposed to introduce a new modern electric heating system using night storage wall heater units and producing equivalent heat.

The Court of Appeal held that the other party was entitled to insist on 'repair' to the existing underfloor heating system even though that work would be comparatively much more expensive and would necessarily incorporate some improvement.

P3.2   *Elmcroft Developments Ltd v Tankersley-Sawyer*
(1984) 15 HLR 63; (1984) 270 EG 140, CA

Replacement of damp-proof course within repairing covenant

Tenants occupied basement flats in a purpose-built Victorian mansion block. Their leases contained an express covenant by the landlord 'to maintain and keep the exterior of the building and the roof, the main walls, timbers and drains thereof in good and tenantable repair and condition'. The building had been constructed with a slate damp-proof course. It was, however, ineffectual because it was below ground level. As a result, rising damp caused damage to plaster, decoration and woodwork. The judge at first instance found that the remedial work required was the installation of a new damp-proof course by silicone injection and that such work fell within the repairing covenant. The landlord appealed.

The Court of Appeal held that whether or not remedial works were within the repairing covenant was a matter of degree. The judge had been entitled to decide that the installation of a new damp-proof course would not involve a change in the nature and character of the flats. The landlord's obligation was not 'repetitively to carry out futile work instead of doing the job properly once and for all' (per Ackner LJ)

Note: The distinction between this case and *Eyre v McCracken* (P3.3) and *Wainwright v Leeds CC* (P5.19) is that the property had been built with a damp-proof course.

P3.3   *Eyre v McCracken*
(2000) 80 P&CR 220; [2001] L&TR 411; (2001) 33 HLR 169, CA

Installation of damp-proof course was an improvement rather than a repair

A tenancy agreement obliged a tenant to 'put the premises ... in good and substantial repair and condition'. The property lacked a damp-proof course.

The Court of Appeal held that in every case it was a matter of fact and degree, having regard to the age and design of the premises, as to whether works fell within a particular covenant. In this case the insertion of a damp-proof course would radically alter the character of the premises. It was an improvement, not a repair, and so not part of the tenant's repairing obligations.

Cf *Elmcroft Developments Ltd v Tankersley-Sawyer* (P3.2)

P3.4   *Fincar SRL v 109/113 Mount Street Management Co Ltd*
August 1999 *Legal Action* 23, CA

Render part of 'structure' of wall; false wall not structure

A lease imposed an obligation to 'keep the exterior in a proper state of structural ... repair ... and in particular to carry out ... repair of the exterior walls ... and generally of the exterior and structure of the building'. The building included cellars and basements which prior to the lease being taken had been 'tanked' by the application of an impermeable render to the inner face of most of the walls. A smaller area of the cellar walls had been covered by a plasterboard 'false wall' with battens behind it nailed to the wall surface and a layer of polythene sheeting stretched across.

Repairs were required when dampness penetrated both areas of the cellar walls.

By a majority, the Court of Appeal held that the impermeable render had become part of the 'structure' of the building and repair to it was within the express term. The 'false wall' was not within the term as it had been affixed to the structural wall rather than become part of it.

P3.5   *Holding and Barnes plc v Hill House Hammond*
[2001] EWCA Civ 1334; [2002] L&TR 7

Construction of conflicting repairing covenants required common sense approach

A lease of a building contained two repairing obligations. The first required the tenant to keep the property in good internal repair. The second required the landlord to keep in repair the structure and exterior of the building (other than the parts comprised in the demised property). The terms had been transposed from the drafts of other leases between the parties. Neither party sought rectification of the lease but invited the court to determine how the repairing obligations were to be construed given that the literal wording of the lease made no sense.

The Court of Appeal held that the modern authorities on the proper approach to the construction of contracts require a common sense approach having regard to the background factual matrix in which the contract was produced and disregarding the 'old intellectual baggage of "legal" interpretation'. Applying this test, the true construction of the repairing covenants was that the tenant was responsible for only internal repairs and the landlord was responsible for repairing the structure and exterior. The bracketed words in the second repairing obligation were to be treated as having no effect.

P3.6   *Long v Southwark LBC*
[2002] EWCA Civ 403; [2002] 47 EG 150; [2002] HLR 56; [2002] LGR 530; (2002) *Times* 16 April

Obligation not satisfied merely by appointing contractors to perform task

The claimant's flat was next to a large paladin bin into which a rubbish chute ran. The chute was inadequate in size and tenants frequently left rubbish outside the bin. The tenant complained of noise from other tenants banging the chute, of smells and maggot infestation. The tenancy agreement obliged the landlord 'to take reasonable steps to keep the estate and common parts clean and tidy'. HHJ Goldstein found that the common parts were not kept clean and there was unchallenged evidence that rubbish piled up outside the tenant's door. He found that the council was in breach of its obligations under the tenancy agreement and awarded damages of £13,500. The council appealed, submitting that: (1) it had taken reasonable steps by appointing contractors and instructing them to clean the common parts; and (2) it had given notice to tenants reminding them of their obligations.

The Court of Appeal dismissed the appeal. The obligation could not be satisfied by delegation to contractors unless there was an adequate system for monitoring their performance. Inadequate supervision of the contractors was a failure to take reasonable steps for the purpose of the obligation in the tenancy. Furthermore, giving notice to tenants about their obligations did not necessarily exhaust the duty to take reasonable steps. There was no room for compromise on basic standards of cleanliness. The award of damages should stand.

P3.7 *Marlborough Park Services Ltd v Rowe and another*
[2006] EWCA Civ 436; 7 March 2006

Structure not limited to items in ownership of landlord; floor joists part of structure

The tenant, a long leaseholder, was liable to keep his two-storey maisonette in good repair. His landlord was liable to repair the main structure of the property. The tenant's property suffered from cracking due to deflection of intermediate timber floor joists. The judge held that the works fell within the landlord's repairing obligation (with the costs being shared equally among all the tenants of the building).

The Court of Appeal held that the judge's construction of the lease had been correct. A landlord's obligation under a lease to repair the main structure of a property included an obligation to repair floor joists in a tenant's property as the joists played a significant part in keeping the structure sound. The main structure was not limited to items in the ownership and control of the landlord or items which served more than one unit. Such qualification of the landlord's obligation was neither obvious nor necessary.

P3.8 *Palmer v Sandwell MBC*
(1988) 20 HLR 74; [1987] 2 EGLR 79; (1987) 284 EG 1487, CA (see E5.1)

Replacement tenancy agreement not effective where council had merely sent out revised agreement to tenants

P3.9 *Petersson v Pitt Place (Epsom) Ltd*
[2001] EWCA Civ 86; [2002] HLR 52; [2001] L&TR 238; (2001) 82 P&CR 276, CA

Leases to be construed to avoid conflicting repairing obligations between parties

In construing repairing covenants in leases, a judge found that roof terraces were within the repairing covenants of both the landlord and tenants and that both were responsible.

The Court of Appeal held that this would lead to the absurd result that each party would have a remedy against the other for failure to do works. The practical result of this would be to stultify both obligations. Leases have to be construed so as to avoid overlapping covenants if possible.

P3.10 *Post Office v Aquarius Properties Ltd*
[1987] 1 All ER 1055; (1987) 54 P&CR 61; [1987] 1 EGLR 40; (1987) 281 EG 798, CA

Where defect present at time of construction, defect was not disrepair

The property concerned had been poorly constructed or designed to such a degree that when, in the ordinary course of events, the water table rose, the concrete basement floor became soaked and water covered the surface to ankle depth.

The Court of Appeal held that the first question to be addressed was whether the property was in disrepair. If, as in this case, the defect had been present since both the date of construction and the date of letting, there was no disrepair – the building was in its original state. The doctrine in *Proudfoot v Hart* (1890) 25 QBD 42 (that a covenant to 'keep in repair' also means 'put in repair') was confined to cases in which the property was not, when let, in the condition in which it was originally constructed. As there was no evidence in the present case of damage to the property itself (eg, corrupted wall plaster, rotten woodwork, etc), disrepair was not established and no work under the covenant to keep in repair was required. The Court of Appeal went on to consider the test which would be applied if disrepair were later proved. It upheld the line of authorities deriving from *Ravenseft Properties Ltd v Davstone (Holdings) Ltd* (P3.16) and adopted the proposition that whether the works required to remedy the disrepair were works of repair, renewal or improvement was a matter of degree.

P3.11   **Smedley v Chumley and Hawkes Ltd**
(1982) 44 P&CR 50; (1982) 261 EG 775, CA

Covenant to maintain structure of walls required repair when walls sank due to subsidence

The Court of Appeal held that landlords who built a new building which they let in 1972 under a 21-year lease for use as a restaurant were liable for breach of their covenant 'to keep the main walls and roof in good structural repair and condition ...' when the building developed grave defects (including cracking to the walls and sinking of the floor) caused by subsidence, which was itself a result of defective foundations. The intention of the covenant was to place on the landlords an unqualified obligation to keep the walls and roof in good structural condition. The court rejected the landlord's contention that the works which were required were outside the covenant because they would result in an improvement to the building. The landlords were liable to carry out such works to the foundations as were necessary to give the walls a stable base.

P3.12   **Welsh v Greenwich LBC**
[2000] 49 EG 118; (2001) 33 HLR 40; [2001] L&TR 115; (2001) 81 P&CR 144; (2000) *Times* 4 August, CA

Express covenant to keep premises 'in good condition' wider than 'to repair'

Mrs Welsh was a secure tenant. The tenancy contained an express covenant by the landlord 'to maintain the dwelling in good condition and repair', except for such items of repair which were the responsibility of the tenant under a clause which included an obligation 'to keep the dwelling clean, in good condition and to prevent damage ...'. The dwelling-house suffered from damp which gave rise to severe black spot mould growth inside, particularly at the base of the windows and external walls, under the carpets and also affecting the soft furnishings. The damp was caused by excessive condensation, which in turn was due to the lack of thermal insulation to the walls of the dwelling-house. Mrs Welsh sought damages from the council for alleged breach of its obligations under the express covenant. HHJ Gibson awarded her agreed damages of £9,000, having held that the council had breached its obligations by failing to take steps to prevent the damp by the installation of thermal insulation. It was conceded at first instance that, on the facts of the case, Landlord and Tenant Act 1985 s11 did not apply to the problems complained of.

The council appealed unsuccessfully. The contract was one between a local authority and a tenant in circumstances in which the latter would not be expected to take legal advice. Against that background, it was right as far as possible to construe the phrase 'good condition' so as to give it the meaning that the ordinary person in the street would accept as normal. The phrase was intended to mark a separate concept and to make a significant addition to what was conveyed by the word 'repair'. It was a more extensive obligation than that implied by Housing Act 1985 s11. The judge was right to conclude that by failing to provide thermal insulation or dry lining for external walls, Greenwich had allowed excessive condensation and mould to continue and so had failed to maintain the flat in good condition. Severe black spots owing to excessive condensation, in turn causing severe mould growth, could not be regarded as simply a matter of amenity, dissociated from physical condition, even in the absence of structural damage. The House of Lords subsequently refused the council's petition for permission to appeal.

P3.13 *Yeomans Row Management Ltd v Bodentien-Meyrick*
[2002] EWCA Civ 860; [2002] 34 EG 84; [2003] L&TR 10

Construction of lease; tenant could refuse access to landlord to carry out improvements where clause in tenancy provided merely for right of entry to carry out repairs

The defendant was the successor to a statutory tenancy. A clause of the original contractual tenancy agreement provided that the tenant was to 'permit the landlords to execute any repairs or work to the said flat and for the purpose of executing any repairs or work to or in connection with any flats above or below or adjoining the said flat'. The claimant wanted to enter the flat to carry out a variety of improvements. The defendant did not want to allow access and argued that, when read in the context of other provisions in the lease, 'work' in the clause merely meant works of repair and that the proposed improvements did not fall into that category and would constitute a breach of quiet enjoyment. Furthermore, given the intention in the lease to grant exclusive possession, in the absence of a clear provision, to require the defendant to permit the claimant access to carry out the extensive proposed works would constitute a derogation from grant. HHJ Cowell held that the defendant was not required to permit access. Pumfrey J dismissed the claimant's appeal.

The claimant's second tier appeal was also dismissed. If the meaning of words in a lease is not clear, the approach in *Investors Compensation Scheme Ltd v West Bromwich Building Society* [1998] 1 WLR 896 should be adopted to identify the meaning which the document would convey to a reasonable person with the background knowledge reasonably available to the parties. In this case, given the passage of time since the grant of the lease, it was necessary to identify the nature of the restriction within the four corners of the lease, including the covenant for quiet enjoyment. It was clear from the terms of the lease that the relevant clause gave a right of entry only in the event of a failure to repair or where works of repair or works akin to repair were required to be carried out. Since it was possible to construe the words 'repairs or work' as being limited to that clear function, it would require equally clear words to extend the meaning of the clause in issue. Those clear words were not present in the lease and, accordingly, the clause did not require the defendant to permit access to the claimant to carry out improvements.

High Court

P3.14   *Hallisey v Petmoor Developments Ltd*
(2000) *Times* 7 November; [2000] EGCS 124, ChD

'Structure' included not only bare concrete walls but also additional surfaces

In 1993 Mr Hallisey bought a long lease of a flat on the seventh floor of a modern block of residential flats. The ceiling of the bedrooms of the flat was made up of a horizontal concrete slab. Its underside was plastered to form the bedroom ceilings. Above the slab were various layers of block insulation, polythene membrane, sand and cement screed and asphalt. On top of them there were tiles which formed the floor surface of a roof terrace to one of the flats on the eighth floor of the building. It was common ground that the asphalt layer had failed, and that as a consequence water and damp were percolating through the various layers below and into the bedrooms of the flat. Mr Hallisey's lease contained a covenant on the part of the landlord to 'maintain and keep in good and substantial repair and condition ... the main structure of the building including ... the roof of the building ...'. The landlord conceded that the concrete slab above the bedrooms of the flat was within the term 'main structure', but contended that the layers above it were properly to be construed as part of the demise of the flat above.

Patten J, granting an order for summary judgment that the defendant carry out works to repair the terrace and damages, held that the 'main structure' of the building was to be construed as including not only its bare concrete shell but also whatever additional surfaces were created by the landlord in order to make that shell a complete and effective structure for the purpose of maintaining the physical integrity of the flats within it.

P3.15   *Ibrahim v Dovecorn Reversions Ltd*
(2001) 82 P&CR 362; [2001] 30 EG 116, ChD

'Main structure' of building included whole of roof terraces of flats except tiled surfaces

The express terms of leases placed liability for repair of the structure on the landlord and responsibility for each flat on the lessees. The claimant brought proceedings against the landlord and other lessees as a result of damp penetration through roof terraces of two flats above his.

Rimer J, on appeal, held that the reference in the leases to the 'main structure' included the whole of the roof terrace, except for its tiled surface area, which was demised to the lessees who used it. The landlord was accordingly responsible for its repair.

P3.16   *Ravenseft Properties Ltd v Davstone (Holdings) Ltd*
[1980] QB 12; [1979] 2 WLR 897; [1979] 1 All ER 929; (1978) 37 P&CR 502; (1979) 249 EG 51, 247, QBD

Repair due to inherent defect could fall within repairing covenant

The underlease of a block of maisonettes included a covenant on the tenant's part to repair the building, including the walls. The building had been constructed without expansion joints and the stones had not been tied in properly. As a result of expansion and contraction the exterior stone cladding became so defective that it had to be replaced. The tenant denied liability to remedy this, claiming that rectification of an inherent defect did not come within the repairing covenant and that there was no obligation to insert expansion joints which would amount to an improvement.

Forbes J held that there was no doctrine that want of repair due to an inherent defect in the demised premises could not fall within the ambit of a covenant to repair. It is a question of degree whether works are repairs or works which so change the character of a building. The insertion of expansion joints would not amount to a changing of the character of the building. The joints formed a trivial part of the building as a whole and the cost of inserting them was trivial when compared with the value of the building. The works came within the repairing covenant and the landlord was entitled to recover the cost of carrying out the works from the tenant.

County courts

P3.17   *Islington LBC v Keane*
November 2005 *Legal Action* 28; 20 January 2005, Clerkenwell County Court (see P5.27)

Express obligation on tenant to replace washers ineffective as came within s11

P4   Implied covenants

Tenancies and leases are types of contract. In the absence of express terms, the common law may imply terms and obligations, but only where it is necessary to give business efficacy to the contract or where the term represents the obvious but unexpressed intention of the parties – sometimes called the 'reasonable bystander' test, in the sense that if a bystander listening to the parties making their contract were to suggest incorporation of an express provision, they would both say 'of course'. See *Chitty on Contracts*, 29th edn. For the statutorily implied covenant to repair under Landlord and Tenant Act 1985 s11, see P5.

House of Lords

P4.1   *Liverpool CC v Irwin*
[1977] AC 239; [1976] 2 All ER 39; (1976) 13 HLR 38, HL

Implied obligation to take reasonable care to maintain common parts

A tenant lived in a tower block containing 70 flats. There was a common staircase and two lifts. There were defects to the common parts including continual failure of the lifts, lack of proper lighting on the stairs and blockage of rubbish chutes. The tenant claimed that there was an implied covenant to keep the common parts in repair and properly lighted.

The House of Lords found that, since the stairs, lifts and rubbish chutes were necessary for tenants occupying the block, there was an implied obligation on the landlord's part to take reasonable care to maintain the common parts in a state of reasonable repair and efficiency.

Note: See also now Landlord and Tenant Act 1985 s11(1A) (P5) relating to common parts.

P4.2   *Southwark LBC v Mills; Southwark LBC v Tanner; Baxter v Camden LBC*
[2001] 1 AC 1; [1999] 3 WLR 939; [1999] 4 All ER 449; [2000] LGR 138; [1999] 45 EG 179; (2000) 32 HLR 148; [2000] L&TR 159; (1999) *Times* 22 October, HL

No obligation to provide soundproofing; no implied warranty as to fitness; covenant for quiet enjoyment not applicable to things done before grant of tenancy; normal use of residential flat cannot be a nuisance to neighbours

In *Southwark LBC v Mills* secure tenants rented council flats constructed in 1919 which had, by modern standards, inadequate sound insulation. They complained about noise emanating from adjacent premises. Their tenancy agreements contained covenants for quiet enjoyment. The complaints were referred to the Southwark Arbitration Tribunal, which held that the council was 'obliged to carry out effective soundproofing of the tenants' flats'. The council appealed. Laddie J held that the covenants for quiet enjoyment imposed obligations to improve the property to meet modern building standards. The council appealed to the Court of Appeal which allowed the appeal by a majority.

In *Baxter v Camden LBC* the plaintiff was disturbed by the sounds of ordinary domestic noise coming from the tenanted flat above hers in a converted house. She brought an action in contract (breach of covenant for quiet enjoyment) and tort (nuisance) against the defendant council which was both her landlord and the landlord of the upstairs tenant. Neither tenancy agreement contained a warranty on the part of the landlord that the flats had sound insulation or were in any other way fit to live in.

The tenants' appeals in both cases to the House of Lords were dismissed. In relation to covenants, it was held that:

a) In granting a tenancy a landlord does not give an implied warranty as to the condition or fitness of the premises. Caveat lessee.

b) A covenant to keep in repair imposes an obligation to remedy disrepair. It obliges a landlord only to restore premises to their previous good condition. A landlord does not have to make it a better house than it originally was. (Lord Hoffmann)

c) The covenant for quiet enjoyment is broken if the landlord or someone claiming under the landlord does anything that substantially interferes with the tenant's title to or possession of the demised premises or with his or her ordinary and lawful enjoyment of the demised premises The interference need not be direct or physical. (Lords Slynn and Millett) Excessive noise, in principle, may constitute a substantial interference with the possession or ordinary enjoyment of demised premises and so can amount to a breach of the covenant for quiet enjoyment. (Lords Slynn and Hoffmann)

d) The covenant for quiet enjoyment is prospective in nature. It does not apply to things done before the grant of the tenancy, even though they may have continuing consequences for the tenant (Lords Hoffmann and Millett). *Sampson v Hodson-Pressinger* (O2.13) was distinguished. Lord Hoffmann described that case as 'possibly correct on the facts'.

In relation to private nuisance it was held that:

e) Nuisance involves doing something on adjoining or nearby land which constitutes an unreasonable interference with the utility of the claimant's land. The primary defendant is the person who causes the nuisance by doing the acts in question. (Lord Hoffmann)

f) The normal use of a residential flat cannot be a nuisance to the neighbours. (Lords Hoffmann and Millett)

g) In addition a person who authorises nuisance may be liable. On this basis landlords may be liable for nuisances caused by their tenants. To be liable they must either participate directly in the commission of the nuisance or they must have been taken to have authorised it by letting the property (Lord Millett). However, a landlord cannot be liable in nuisance for conduct which is not a nuisance on the part of the tenant (Lords Slynn, Hoffmann and Millett).

h) Parliament has dealt extensively with the problem of substandard housing over many years but has declined to impose an obligation to install soundproofing in existing dwellings. The courts should not attempt to fill the gap by creating a common-law remedy.

Court of Appeal

P4.3   *Adami v Lincoln Grange Management Ltd*
(1998) 30 HLR 982; [1998] 1 EGLR 58; [1998] 17 EG 148, CA

No implied covenant for lessor to maintain structure of block of flats

A long lease contained detailed provisions governing the repair of individual properties, the levying of service charges to meet maintenance costs and for the lessees to effect and maintain insurance policies to cover damage for any catastrophe affecting the block as a whole. There appears to have been no express covenant requiring the lessor to maintain the structure of the block in a proper state of repair. HHJ Martineau held that the lessor was not liable to carry out such repairs.

    The lessee's appeal was dismissed by the Court of Appeal. The contention that there was an implied term was untenable. It was impossible to presume an intention that the lessor should maintain the structure of the block. A covenant to permit the lessor to inspect did not affect this. *Barrett v Lounova* (P4.4) was decided on its own special facts.

P4.4   *Barrett v Lounova (1982) Ltd*
[1990] 1 QB 348; [1989] 2 WLR 137; [1989] 1 All ER 351; (1988) 20 HLR 584; (1989) 57 P&CR 216; [1988] 2 EGLR 54; [1988] 36 EG 184, CA

Obligation on landlord to repair exterior implied where tenant liable to repair interior

A tenancy was granted in 1941 and contained an obligation on the tenant to do 'all inside repairs'. The agreement was silent about responsibilities for repair of the exterior or structure. At first instance, Recorder D Keane QC held that the landlord was liable to pay damages for disrepair in both contract and tort. In contract, he found that, because of the tenant's covenant, it was an implied term that the landlord would attend to structural repairs under both the 'reasonable bystander' and the 'business efficacy' tests. In the alternative, he held that, as the landlord had a right to enter and carry out repairs (even in the absence of any obligation to do so), under both Rent Act 1977 s3(2) and the tenancy agreement itself, Defective Premises Act 1972 s4 imposed a duty to take care that no damage resulted to the tenant or property from disrepair, and the landlord was in breach of duty. The measure of damages was calculated under either head as £1,250 for two years of disrepair, and works costing £10,000 to £12,000 were ordered.

On the landlord's appeal, that decision was upheld by the Court of Appeal. Kerr LJ held that an obligation on the landlord to repair the exterior could be implied as it gave 'business efficacy' to the tenancy. The award of £1,250 damages for breach of the implied term and an injunction requiring repairs were upheld.

Cf *Adami v Lincoln Grange Management Ltd* (P4.3).

P4.5   *Demetriou v Poolaction Ltd*
(1990) 63 P&CR 536; [1991] 1 EGLR 100; [1991] 25 EG 113, CA

No implied covenant on landlord where no correlative obligation on tenant

Premises were let for use as a commercial lodging-house. There were no express contractual repairing obligations. The repairing obligations in Landlord and Tenant Act 1985 s11 did not apply because the lease was for more than seven years (s13(1)). The tenant sought to require the landlord to carry out repairs.

The Court of Appeal held that, in the absence of a 'correlative obligation' (requiring the tenant to undertake internal repairs), no obligation would be implied requiring the landlord to repair the structure or exterior.

P4.6   *Gordon and Texeira v Selico Ltd and Select Managements Ltd*
(1986) 18 HLR 219; [1986] 1 EGLR 71; (1986) 278 EG 53, CA

Implied term on landlord to take reasonable care in relation to common parts

The plaintiff lessees bought a flat on a long lease in a block owned by Selico. The managing agents appointed by the lessor company took virtually no steps to carry out repairs, to manage the building or to budget in a proper manner for its maintenance. Statutory notices were served by the local authority, which carried out works in default. A few months after the lessees had purchased their lease, extensive dry rot was discovered. The local authority served a dangerous structure notice and carried out works to remedy the dry rot. The lessees brought proceedings for damages and an order of specific performance, requiring the lessor to carry out outstanding, necessary works. At first instance, Goulding J held:

1) The lessor's builder had deliberately covered up existing dry rot when carrying out works to the flat before the lessees bought it. In hiding 'so sinister and menacing a defect' the lessor had made a fraudulent misrepresentation that the flat did not suffer from dry rot and, accordingly, was liable to the lessees in damages for deceit.

2) The failure to keep the premises watertight amounted to a breach of the covenant for quiet enjoyment.

3) The lessees were justified in not paying service charges because of the 'complete and obvious unwillingness or inability of the defendants to carry out the scheme of the lease [as regards maintenance and repairs] in such a way as to keep the building in repair', and those charges were irrecoverable under the provisions of Housing Act 1980 Sch 19 (now Landlord and Tenant Act 1985 s19). The services provided were not of a 'reasonable standard' and the statutory provisions relating to obtaining estimates had not been complied with.

4) The lessor had an implied duty to take reasonable care that the condition of the parts of the building retained within its control did not cause damage to the lessees or their flat. This duty was better regarded as an implied term of the lease than as a duty of care, breach of which could give rise to an action in negligence (see *Duke of Westminster v Guild* [1985] QB 688, CA).

He held that the lessees were entitled to an order for specific performance and damages.

The landlord's appeal was dismissed. The Court of Appeal confirmed that although the courts will not usually imply a condition requiring repair which does not appear in the lease, the lessees were entitled to recover damages for deceit and breach of express covenants in these circumstances.

P4.7   *Habinteg Housing Association v James*
(1995) 27 HLR 299, CA (see P7.8)

No implied term that landlord should take reasonable care to abate an infestation

P4.8   *King v South Northamptonshire DC*
(1992) 24 HLR 284; (1991) 64 P&CR 35; [1992] 1 EGLR 53; [1992] 06 EG 152, CA

Implied term to maintain rear path

The plaintiff was the tenant of a terraced house with front, side and rear access. The council landlord was prepared to repair the front path but denied responsibility for the side and rear paths, which had been neglected and had become dangerous. The express terms of the tenancy imposed obligations on the tenant but none on the council.

The Court of Appeal held that, although the rear and side paths were not part of the 'exterior' of the dwelling and Landlord and Tenant Act 1985 s11 did not apply (see section P5), there was a necessary implied contractual requirement to maintain the path, since the house could not be enjoyed without use of the rear access (which was needed for the removal of rubbish, the delivery of coal, etc). The plaintiff was entitled to an injunction and damages.

P4.9   *Lee v Leeds CC*

[2002] EWCA Civ 6; [2002] 1 WLR 1488; [2002] HLR 17; [2002] L&TR 35;[2002] LGR 305; (2002) *Times* 29 January, CA

Human Rights Act did not impose a general obligation to keep premises in good condition

Ms Lee was the council tenant of a two-storey semi-detached house of traditional brick construction which, owing to a defect in design, suffered from condensation, mould and damp. A number of areas of plaster became damp and mouldy through condensation. The plaster did not need to be replaced but needed to be treated with a fungicide and redecorated. On the basis that the condition of the property was prejudicial to health, Ms Lee commenced county court proceedings for an order requiring the council to remedy the defects, relying on the council's duty to keep the structure of the property in good repair. The judge held that there was no implied term in the tenancy to ensure that the house was fit for human habitation, as the rent was below the limit in Landlord and Tenant Act 1985 s8. Following *Quick v Taff Ely BC* (P5.16), the exterior and structure were not out of repair because internal condensation unrelated to water penetration made the house unfit for human habitation. He rejected the contention that Human Rights Act 1998 s3 required Landlord and Tenant Act 1985 s11 to be read so as to impose liability on the council for the mould to give effect to rights to home and family life under ECHR article 8.

The Court of Appeal dismissed the claimant's appeal.

1) Human Rights Act 1998 s6 imposes an obligation on local authority landlords to take steps to ensure that the condition of dwelling-houses which they let for social housing are such that the tenants' rights to respect for home and family life under article 8 are not infringed. However, rights under article 8 are not unqualified (*Southwark LBC v Tanner* (P4.2)) and there is nothing in the Strasbourg jurisprudence to support the proposition that s6 and article 8 impose a general and unqualified obligation on local authorities in relation to the condition of their housing stock. There might though be cases where a local authority that had let a property that was unfit for human habitation or prejudicial to health would be in breach of the positive duty imposed by s6 and article 8. In this case there was no such breach of duty. The conditions complained of did not seem to be sufficiently serious (*López Ostra v Spain* (A3.8)).

2) *Quick* was not decided per incuriam because of a failure to consider the meaning given to 'repair' in *Proudfoot v Hart* (1890) 25 QBD 42. Even if *Quick* was decided in ignorance of *Proudfoot*, both cases were before the court in *Post Office v Aquarius Properties Ltd* (P3.10) and the court did not regard them as inconsistent.

3) In view of an express covenant to keep the structure in repair and the similar covenant which was otherwise implied under s11, the court would not imply into local authority tenancies a term that the landlord was to keep the property 'in good condition'.

4) Works required to remedy a defect in design are not works of 'repair', giving that word the meaning that it has to bear in this context. It followed that Defective Premises Act 1972 s4 was not engaged.

P4.10 **McAuley v Bristol CC**

[1992] QB 134; [1991] 3 WLR 968; [1992] 1 All ER 749; (1991) 23 HLR 586; [1991] 2 EGLR 64; [1991] 46 EG 155; (1991) 89 LGR 931, CA (see P10.5)

Right of entry reserved to landlord gave rise to implied right to enter to repair any defect

P4.11 **McGreal v Wake**

(1984) 13 HLR 107; (1984) 269 EG 1254, CA (see P11.13)

Landlord liable to clear up and redecorate after repairs

High Court

P4.12 **Berry v Wrexham BC**

30 April 2001, QBD

Only terms essential to living on Gypsy site to be implied

In 1985 Gypsies moved on to land owned by the council. Although the council obtained a possession order, it consented to the order being set aside and made some basic provision for the people occupying the site (central standpipe, mobile lavatories, hardcore standing etc). In 1994 the council wrote giving occupiers temporary licences to occupy pitches. The letters provided for payment of licence fees but did not impose any express contractual obligations on the council. Conditions on the site were poor and a number of occupants brought proceedings for damages for breach of terms which they said were to be implied into the licences. HHJ G O Edwards QC found that there were implied terms that the council should (1) provide a WC connected to a sewer for each caravan; (2) supply running water to each caravan; and (3) employ a warden. He awarded damages. The council appealed.

Thomas J held that terms can only be implied where it is necessary to do so. In doing so, it is useful to apply either the 'officious bystander' or the 'business efficacy' test (*Lloyd's v Clemenson* [1995] Lloyd's Reinsurance Reports 307 at 330). It was necessary to imply terms that the council provide that which was essential to living on the site. However, in determining what was necessary, regard had to be had to the written agreement. He found that it was not necessary to provide running water to each pitch. Furthermore, although the council was clearly under an obligation to control access to the site, clean the central facilities, remove rubbish, and generally manage the site, it was not necessary for a warden to be appointed to perform those obligations. However, it was clear on the findings made by the judge that the council was in breach of its obligation to manage the site. The case was remitted to the county court for the judge to reassess the damages payable.

County courts

P4.13 **Walton v Lewisham LBC**

May 1997 *Legal Action* 20, Tunbridge Wells County Court

Implied term to carry out repairs with reasonable care and skill

On 13 February 1995 the council removed the tenant's roof to replace it, using a sarking felt-and-batons temporary cover. On 20 February 1995 rain poured into the house. The following day roofers arrived and one put his foot through the ceiling. On 28 February 1995 there was a further flood. Re-roofing was only completed weeks later and the consequential redecoration of the interior of the house was not completed until June 1995. The council denied liability on the tenant's claim for damages for loss caused by the flooding. It argued that: (a) there was no implied term that work would be carried out with reasonable skill and care; (b) if there was, it was met by the provision of a temporary cover, and (c) any liability would arise only after a reasonable time had passed from notification of the temporary cover leaking.

HHJ Hargrove found for the tenant. There was an implied term not only to repair (Landlord and Tenant Act 1985 s11) but to do so with reasonable care and skill and proper materials. The temporary cover was inadequate – at least a flying 'crinkly tin' roof cover should have been used. Since the council was in 'actual occupation' of the roof from the start to finish of the works, liability was strict and immediate, ie, not contingent on notice or the expiry of a reasonable period. He awarded £750 general damages plus special damages and interest at 8 per cent.

Northern Ireland courts

P4.14   *Collins v Northern Ireland Housing Executive*
[1987] 2 NIJB 27, CA(NI)

Landlord liable to maintain heating system under collateral contract

A housing estate was provided with hot water and heating services through a central system operated by the landlord authority. The tenancy agreement required the tenants to pay standing charges and amounts for consumption, but contained no express obligation on the landlords to provide or maintain the system. The tenants claimed damages for the cost of providing alternative heating for periods when the system was broken or deficient.

O'Donnell LJ, in the Court of Appeal (Northern Ireland), held that there existed a collateral contract between the parties for the supply of the heating system services and that a term would be implied into that contract that the landlords would provide and maintain sufficient heat for the comfort of tenants and their families 'so far as reasonable skill and care could provide the same'. The court was unwilling to disturb the judge's findings of fact that, since most repairs were attended to within 24 to 48 hours of complaint, no breach of the implied term had been made out. Modest damages were awarded for a delay of four weeks in attending to a single defective radiator.

Note: See now Landlord and Tenant Act 1985 s11(1A) (P5) relating to communal heating systems.

P5   ## Landlord and Tenant Act 1985 s11

Landlord and Tenant Act 1985 s11 implies into every lease of a dwelling-house to which the section applies a covenant requiring a landlord:

   (a) keep in repair the structure and exterior of dwelling-house (including drains, gutters and external pipes);

(b) to keep in repair and proper working order the installations in dwelling-house for supplying water, gas and electricity and for sanitation (including basins, baths and sanitary conveniences but not other fixtures and fittings and appliances for making use of the supply of water, gas or electricity);

(c) to keep in repair and proper working order the installations in the dwelling-house for space heating and heating water.

To be in breach of the contractual duty, where the defect is within the demised premises, landlords must (a) have knowledge of the defect and (b) then fail to carry out the repair within a reasonable period (see P6). The repairing obligation cannot be transferred to tenants by express terms in the tenancy agreement (s11(4)). It does not apply to tenancies for a term of seven years or more.

Two important amendments, introduced by Housing Act 1988, were made to s11. First, the covenant to repair the 'structure and exterior' was extended beyond the tenant's dwelling to cover 'any part of the same building in which the lessor has an estate or interest'. Second, the obligation to repair and maintain installations is extended from those in the dwelling to any installation which 'directly or indirectly' serves the dwelling and is either part of the same building or owned by the landlord. Only tenancies granted after the implementation of the Housing Act 1988 on 15 January 1989 are affected by these changes.

Court of Appeal

P5.1   *Bradley v Chorley BC*
(1985) 17 HLR 305; [1985] 2 EGLR 49; (1985) 275 EG 801; (1985) 83 LGR 628, CA

Landlord required to make good after repairs, including decorations

Mr Bradley rented a house from the local authority. The tenancy was subject to the obligations implied by Housing Act 1961 s32 (now Landlord and Tenant Act 1985 s11). The agreement provided that Mr Bradley was responsible for decorations. When he moved in, the house was in a poor state of decoration and it appears that he did little to improve this state. The local authority decided to rewire the house, and in doing so some damage was caused to decorations. The local authority took the view that it had no obligation to decorate following completion of the rewiring. The plaintiff claimed the cost of carrying out such decorations. A county court judge held that, because Mr Bradley had not carried out his own obligations under the tenancy agreement, it would be inequitable for the local authority to have to decorate. Alternatively, he had forfeited any such right because of his own failure.

On appeal it was held that, even if a landlord is not at fault in carrying out its repairing obligations, it has an obligation to reinstate the property after completion of works to a reasonable standard, and that includes putting right damage done to decorations. The tenant's appeal was allowed and judgment given for £220, the cost of decorating.

P5.2   *Brikom Investments Ltd v Seaford*
[1981] 1 WLR 863; [1981] 2 All ER 783; (1982) 1 HLR 21; (1981) 42 P&CR 190; (1981) 258 EG 750, CA

*Landlord estopped from denying implied covenant to repair where rent regis-
tered on basis of covenant*

A tenant was allowed into possession in accordance with an agreement for
a lease on 1 November. The lease was executed some days later but provided for a term of seven years commencing on 1 November. The landlord
contended that Housing Act 1961 s32 (now Landlord and Tenant Act 1985
s11) did not apply because it was not 'for a term of less than seven years'
(s32(1)).

The Court of Appeal held that, in view of Housing Act 1961 s33(5)
(now Landlord and Tenant Act 1985 s13(2)(a)), the commencement of
the term was 1 November (compare *Roberts v Church Commissioners for
England* [1972] 1 QB 278, CA). However, the landlord was estopped from
denying that s32 (now s11) applied where the rent officer had registered a
rent on the basis that the implied covenant applied, the rent registered had
not been challenged or rectified and the landlord had been receiving the
higher rent.

P5.3   ## Brown v Liverpool Corporation
[1969] 3 All ER 1345; (1984) 13 HLR 1, CA

Path to front door part of 'exterior'

A tenant rented a terraced house. Access to the house from the street was
via a gate, four shallow steps and a path made of flagstones which was
seven feet in length. The steps were broken. As a result, the tenant fell
and was injured.

The Court of Appeal held that a county court judge was entitled to find
that the steps were not part of the structure of the house but were part of
the exterior and so within the covenant implied by Housing Act 1961 s32
(now Landlord and Tenant Act 1985 s11).

P5.4   ## Campden Hill Towers Ltd v Gardner
[1977] QB 823; [1977] 2 WLR 159; [1977] 1 All ER 739; (1976) 13 HLR 64; (1976) 34
P&CR 175; (1976) 242 EG 375, CA

Outside walls part of 'structure' of flat

A lease expressly excluded the outside walls of a flat from the demise.

The Court of Appeal held that for the purposes of Housing Act 1961 s32
(now Landlord and Tenant Act 1985 s11), the phrase 'structure and exterior'
applied to anything which, in the ordinary use of words, would be considered as part of the structure and exterior, not merely that which is included
in the demise. It included 'Anything which, in the ordinary use of words,
would be regarded as part of the structure, or the exterior ... the outside
wall or walls of the flat; the outside of inner party walls of the flat, the outer
side of horizontal division between [the flat] and flats above and below; the
structural framework and beams directly supporting floors, ceilings and
walls of the flat'. The outside walls were part of the structure and so covered
by the implied covenant, even though they were outside the demise.

Note: These cases relate to tenancies granted before amendments to s11
were made by Housing Act 1988 s116, the effect of which was to extend the
ambit of s11 to cover the structure and exterior of the whole of the building in which the landlord has an interest, not just the demised premises.

P5.5 *Dame Margaret Hungerford Charity Trustees v Beazeley*
(1994) 26 HLR 269; [1993] 2 EGLR 143; [1993] 29 EG 100, CA (see also H6.2)

Patch repairs to old roof not in breach of repairing covenant

In possession proceedings, a tenant counterclaimed for damages for breach of Landlord and Tenant Act 1985 s11. The main allegation was that the landlords had failed to keep in repair a stone tile and wooden peg roof, which was probably 150 to 180 years old. The trial judge was satisfied that by 1989 the roof was in need of complete repair but that since that date the landlords had simply undertaken 'running repairs' by replacing individual rotten pegs and slipped tiles. Preferring the evidence of the landlords' expert, and having regard to the age, character and prospective life of the dwelling (s11(3)), he held that the landlords were not in breach of the repairing covenant. Although replacing the roof would be ideal, it was no breach simply to keep patching up the old roof.

The Court of Appeal rejected the tenant's appeal, declining to interfere with the judge's findings of fact.

See also: *Riverside Property Investments Ltd v Blackhawk Automotive* [2004] EWHC 3052 (TCC); [2004] 1 EGLR 114 QBD (repair rather than replacement of roof satisfied covenant); *Elite Investments v Bainbridge Silencers* [1986] 2 EGLR 43; (1986) 280 EG 1001, ChD (see *Housing Law Casebook* 3rd edition) (replacement of roof a repair not improvement); *Carmel Southend Ltd v Strachan & Henshaw Ltd* [2007] EWHC 1289 (TCC); December 2007 *Legal Action* 29; 24 May 2007.

P5.6 *Department of Transport v Egoroff*
(1986) 18 HLR 326; [1986] 1 EGLR 89; (1986) 278 EG 1361, CA

Housing Act 1961 s32 (now Landlord and Tenant Act 1985 s11) does not apply where the Crown is the landlord

P5.7 *Douglas-Scott v Scorgie*
[1984] 1 WLR 716; [1984] 1 All ER 1086; (1984) 13 HLR 97; (1984) 48 P&CR 109; (1984) 269 EG 1164, CA

Roof part of structure and exterior

A tenant rented a top-floor flat. The roof above the flat was defective. The Court of Appeal held that the roof above the flat was capable of being part of 'the structure and exterior' of the dwelling comprising the flat within the meaning of Housing Act 1961 s32 (now Landlord and Tenant Act 1985 s11), whether or not the roof was part of the demised premises.

P5.8 *Hopwood v Cannock Chase DC (formerly Rugeley UDC)*
[1975] 1 WLR 373; [1975] 1 All ER 796; (1974) 13 HLR 31; (1974) 29 P&CR 1256, CA

Yard not part of 'exterior'

The widow of the tenant tripped and fell on the edge of a paving slab in the yard behind the house. The Court of Appeal held that the yard did not form part of the essential means of access to the property and so was not part of the structure or exterior of the dwelling-house for the purposes of Housing Act 1961 s32 (now Landlord and Tenant Act 1985 s11).

See: *King v South Northamptonshire DC* (P4.8) (common law implied term to maintain rear path) and *McAuley v Bristol CC* (P10.5) (landlord liable under DPA 1972 s4 for injury resulting from a defective garden step).

P5.9   *King v South Northamptonshire DC*
(1992) 24 HLR 284; (1991) 64 P&CR 35; [1992] 1 EGLR 53; [1992] 06 EG 152, CA (see P4.8)

Rear and side paths not part of 'exterior' for purposes of s11 but common law implied term to maintain rear path

P5.10   *McClean v Liverpool CC*
(1988) 20 HLR 25; [1987] 2 EGLR 56; (1987) 283 EG 1395, CA

Age and character of premises such that repairs were required

A tenant was paying a modest rent for a property which was not near the end of its life, had been in disrepair for three years and would cost only £1,200 to repair. The council successfully defended proceedings brought under Landlord and Tenant Act 1985 s11, relying on s11(3), which states that, when determining the standard of repair required, regard should be had to the age, character, locality and prospective life of the property.

The Court of Appeal allowed the tenant's appeal and directed a retrial, holding that the county court judge had taken too restrictive a view of the matter in the light of *Newham LBC v Patel* (P5.13).

P5.11   *McDougall v Easington DC*
(1989) 21 HLR 310; (1989) 58 P&CR 201; [1989] 1 EGLR 93; (1989) 87 LGR 527, CA

Improvement/repair distinction; tenants liable to make good decorations after improvements

A number of council houses had serious design faults. The council undertook works which involved reducing each property to its original concrete framework and then fitting new roofs, windows, internal fittings and re-tiling the floors.

The Court of Appeal held that these works were not repairs but improvements. Accordingly, they had not been undertaken under the repairing covenant imposed by Landlord and Tenant Act 1985 s11 and the landlord was not liable for the cost of redecoration after the works. As the works were improvements, the tenants should have negotiated compensation for redecoration as a condition of granting the landlord permission to do the improvement works on their properties. The court reviewed authorities on the distinction between works of repair and works of improvement. After considering precedents up to and including *Stent v Monmouth DC* (P5.18), Mustill LJ stated that:

> ... three different tests may be discerned, which may be applied separately or concurrently as the circumstances of the individual case may demand, but all to be approached in the light of the nature and age of the premises, their condition when the tenant went into occupation, and the other express terms of the tenancy:
> - whether the alterations went to the whole of the structure or only to a subsidiary part;
> - whether the effect of the alterations was to produce a building of a wholly different character than that which had been let;
> - what was the cost of the works in relation to the previous value of the

building, and what was their effect on the value and lifespan of the building [(1989) 21 HLR at 316].

Note: See *Yeomans Row Management Ltd v Bodentien-Meyrick* (P3.13) where the express right of entry was held to be limited to a right to enter to carry out works of repair not improvements.

P5.12   *Murray v Birmingham CC*
(1988) 20 HLR 39; [1987] 2 EGLR 53; (1987) 283 EG 962, CA

Patch repairs to roof rather than replacement adequate

The roof of a rented property built in 1908 failed repeatedly, causing six incidents of rainwater penetration in six years. Although each had 'sooner or later' been repaired by retiling or other minor work, the tenant pressed for complete replacement.

The Court of Appeal dismissed the tenant's appeal against a county court finding in favour of the landlord. Slade LJ said:

> I accept that in any case where a landlord or a tenant for that matter is under an obligation to keep in repair an old roof, the stage may come where the only practicable way of performing that covenant is to replace the roof altogether. ((1988) 20 HLR at 43)

However, the Court of Appeal found that by the end of the tenancy in 1982 that stage had not been reached. If a tenant wanted to make good the assertion that the whole roof should be replaced, it would require evidence about the roof's general condition, its construction, the condition of battens and joists, the fixing of slates and expert evidence about why piecemeal repair was no longer practicable.

See also *Dame Margaret Hungerford Charity Trustees v Beazeley* (P5.5).

P5.13   *Newham LBC v Patel*
(1978) 13 HLR 77, CA

Age and character of premises such that it could be demolished rather than repaired

A tenant rented a house in a short-life housing scheme at a low rent. It suffered from dampness and other defects. An environmental health officer reported that it was unfit for human habitation. The council took the view that it could not be put into good repair by carrying out temporary repairs and that, accordingly, it would have to rehouse the tenant and demolish the property. The landlord brought possession proceedings and the tenant defended, counterclaiming for breach of repairing obligations in Housing Act 1961 s32 (now Landlord and Tenant Act 1985 s11).

The Court of Appeal held that, in view of s32(3) (now s11(3)) and the fact that the prospective life of the house was very short, there was no breach of s32.

P5.14   *Niazi Services Ltd v Van der Loo*
[2004] EWCA Civ 53; [2004] 1 WLR 1254; [2004] 17 EG 130; [2004] HLR 34

Landlord not liable for poor water pressure where this due to works in part of building in which landlord had no interest

The claimant leased a top floor flat in a building with a restaurant on the ground floor. It sublet the flat to the defendant. The rent was £34,800 per annum. The claimant sued for rent arrears. The tenant counterclaimed for disrepair, relying on the covenants implied by Landlord and Tenant Act 1985 s11. HHJ Ryland found that there was a period of 33 months during which the water pressure in the flat was inadequate, leading either to a trickle or no supply of water. This was caused by works in the restaurant on the ground floor and basement in which the claimant had no interest. The judge held the claimant liable for the poor water pressure, a failure to paint parts of the flat and a number of lesser matters. He awarded damages of £48,000, based on a notional reduction of 40% of the rent for a 33-month period, by way of a global assessment for the defects, and added a minor amount for the repainting claim. The claimant appealed.

The Court of Appeal allowed the appeal. Under s11(1A)(b)(i), a landlord's liability for maintenance and repair extends only to an installation, or the defective portion of an installation, in that part of the building in which the landlord has an estate or interest. The implied covenant to repair does not extend to installations located in parts of a building in which the lessor does not have an estate or interest, even if the lessor has an estate or interest in other parts of the same building. In this case, the landlord had no estate or interest in any part of the building except for the top floor flat let to the defendant. The judge was entitled to assess the damages for the other admitted breaches by taking a global figure based on a notional reduction in rent. The appropriate sum for damages for the other breaches amounted to £5,000. Taking into account a small reduction to the damages awarded for the repainting claim, the overall damages were reduced to £9,050.

P5.15   *O'Connor v Old Etonians Housing Association Ltd*
[2002] EWCA Civ 150; [2002] Ch 295; [2002] 2 WLR 1133; [2002] 2 All ER 1015; [2002] HLR 37; [2002] L&TR 36; [2002] 14 EG 127; (2002) *Times* 6 March

Distinction between duty to keep in repair and duty to keep in proper working order

In 1986 the landlord of a block of flats replaced the water pipe-work with pipes of a smaller bore (one inch). The smaller pipes successfully carried water to the top floor of the relevant premises until there was a fall in the water pressure in the summer of 1992. The previous pipe-work (one and a quarter inches) would have been able to carry water to the third floor successfully. From 1998, once the Water Authority had constructed a new pumping station, water was carried successfully to the third floor flats by the smaller pipes. Tenants of the top floor flats claimed that there was in that period a breach of the obligation to keep the water pipes in proper working order as required by Landlord and Tenant Act 1985 s11(1)(b). In a trial of a preliminary issue, a circuit judge held that there was no breach. Blackburne J allowed an appeal but the Court of Appeal allowed a further appeal and remitted the claim to the circuit judge.

The Court of Appeal stated that there is a distinction between the duty to keep in repair and the duty to keep in proper working order. The court was concerned only with the latter. An installation could not be said to be in proper working order if, by reason of a defect in construction or design, it was incapable of working properly: see *Liverpool CC v Irwin* (P4.1). The characteristics of the supply of water, gas and electricity were all capable of varying, whether by accident or design. An obligation requiring the landlord to provide installations, which would function regardless of the vagaries of supply, would be manifestly unreasonable. Equally unreasonable would be an obligation which enabled the landlord to supply installations which would accommodate no changes in the character of supply after the date of installation, even though some variations were reasonably to be anticipated. So far as installations for the supply of water, gas and electricity were concerned, an installation would be in proper working order if it was able to function under those conditions of supply that it was reasonable to anticipate would prevail. Whether supply variations should be reasonably anticipated and provided for would depend on the particular facts. If, after a tenancy had commenced, a variation occurred to the supply which could not reasonably have been anticipated but which required some alteration to the installation if the installation was to continue to function properly, was the landlord obliged to make that change or modification? It was not possible to give a categorical answer. An unanticipated change in the nature of the supply of a utility might occur in a variety of circumstances. Some-*Times* the change was imposed deliberately because of some scientific or technical advance, for example, a change in the voltage of electrical supply, or the change from coal gas to natural gas. In such circumstances, the change was likely to be introduced in a manner and subject to conditions under which it was reasonable to expect customers to modify their installations to accommodate the change, and business efficacy would suggest that the landlord's duty to keep installations in proper working order would require him to make necessary modifications. In other circumstances, the change might be forced on the undertaker by some unforeseen event – eg, the collapse of a reservoir or a drought, resulting in a drop in water pressure. If the change was likely to be short-lived, the cost of modification might be disproportionate. Where the changed circumstances were likely to persist for a lengthy period it might seem wholly unreasonable for the landlord to leave his tenants deprived of a satisfactory supply of water for want of relatively modest expenditure on modifications.

P5.16 ### *Quick v Taff-Ely BC*
[1986] 1 QB 809; [1985] 3 WLR 981; [1985] 3 All ER 321; (1986) 18 HLR 66; [1985] 2 EGLR 50; (1985) 276 EG 152, CA

Severe condensation was not disrepair to structure or exterior

The plaintiff rented a terraced house to which Housing Act 1961 s32 (now Landlord and Tenant Act 1985 s11) applied. The house suffered from very severe condensation which made living conditions for the plaintiff and his family appalling. Paper peeled off walls. Wood rotted. Fungus and mould growth appeared. There was a persistent and offensive smell of damp. The house was virtually unfit for human habitation. The plaintiff's expert witness said that the condensation was caused by cold bridging, sweating from single-glazed metal windows and inadequate heating.

The Court of Appeal found that there was no disrepair to the structure or exterior and that accordingly the condensation-related dampness was not a breach of the s32 covenant. Dillon LJ stated:

In the present case the liability of the local authority was to keep the structure and exterior of the house in repair, not the decorations. Though there is ample evidence of damage to the decorations and to bedding, clothing and other fabrics, evidence of damage to the subject matter of the covenant, the structure and exterior of the house, is far to seek ... there is no evidence at all of physical damage to the walls, as opposed to the decorations, or the windows. [[1985] 3 All ER at 326]

Lawton LJ stated:

It follows that, on the evidence in this case, the trial judge should first have identified the parts of the exterior and structure of the house which were out of repair and then have gone on to decide whether, in order to remedy the defects, it was reasonably necessary to replace the concrete lintels over the windows, which caused 'cold bridging', and the single-glazed metal windows ... [ibid at 328]

P5.17   *Staves v Leeds CC*

(1991) 23 HLR 107; [1992] 2 EGLR 37; [1992] 29 EG 119, CA

Saturated plasterwork was in disrepair

Condensation was so bad that the wall plaster had become saturated in places. The council conceded: (a) that the internal plasterwork was part of the structure; (b) that there had been considerable condensation; and (c) that the house was possibly unfit for human habitation. It argued, however, that, although the plaster was saturated, the patches concerned were minimal and the plaster was not in 'disrepair'.

The Court of Appeal upheld HHJ Coles QC's finding that plaster when saturated is in disrepair and dismissed the de minimis argument. The plaster was in such poor condition that it required complete renewal. An award of £5,000 general damages (see December 1990 *Legal Action* 17) was not disturbed.

Cf *Irvine v Moran* (P5.23)

P5.18   *Stent v Monmouth DC*

(1987) 19 HLR 269; (1987) 54 P&CR 193; [1987] 1 EGLR 59; (1987) 282 EG 705, CA

Where repair required replacement of door, there was an obligation to make good the inherent design defect of door

A tenancy included an express term 'to repair and maintain the structure and exterior'. The tenant's house was built in 1953 to design specifications which would not be acceptable at the date of trial. In particular, the front door, which faced directly into the prevailing wind, had no barrier in front or behind its base. There was a history of 30 years' difficulty with the door. Rainwater not only blew in under the door but also formed puddles under it. The accumulation of water caused parts of the door to warp and eventually rot. The fitting of a new door did not remedy the problem.

The Court of Appeal held that if the only defect had been that the door did not perform its primary function of keeping out rain, but was otherwise undamaged, there would have been no defect which breached the repairing covenant. The property would have been in the same state as it was when it was built. However, because the door itself became damaged it needed to be replaced. Stocker LJ said:

... in my view the obligation under the covenant in this case was one which called upon [the council] to carry out repairs which not only effected the repair of the manifestly damaged parts but also achieved the object of rendering it unnecessary in the future for the continual repair of this door.

Sir John Arnold P said:

... on the true construction of the covenant to repair there is required to be done, not only the making [good] of the immediate occasion of disrepair, but also, if this is what a sensible, practical man, would do, the elimination of the cause of that disrepair through the making good of an inherent design defect at least where the making good of that defect does not involve a substantial rebuilding of the whole.

The defendants were liable for breach of the repairing covenant.

P5.19 *Wainwright v Leeds CC*

(1984) 13 HLR 117; (1984) 270 EG 1289; (1984) 82 LGR 657, CA

Insertion of damp-proof course not required where house had been built without one

The plaintiff rented a house which did not have a damp-proof course. There was rising damp. The plaintiff claimed that the defendants were in breach of Housing Act 1961 s32 (now Landlord and Tenant Act 1985 s11) because they failed to install a damp-proof course.

The Court of Appeal rejected this contention. The landlord had no obligation to go beyond repairing the subject-matter of the demise, namely a house with no damp-proof course. The plaintiff was seeking something completely different, namely a house with a damp-proof course. Furthermore, the court could see no reason why a local authority owed a higher repairing obligation than any other landlord.

Cf *Elmcroft Developments Ltd v Tankersley-Sawyer* (P3.2)

P5.20 *Welsh v Greenwich LBC*

[2000] 49 EG 118; (2001) 33 HLR 40; [2001] L&TR 115; (2001) 81 P&CR 144; (2000) *Times* 4 August, CA (see P3.12)

Express covenant to keep premises 'in good condition' wider than s11

P5.21 *Wycombe Area Health Authority v Barnett*

(1982) 5 HLR 84; (1982) 264 EG 619, CA

Section 11 did not require landlord to lag pipes; tenant not acting in tenant-like manner

The Court of Appeal held that landlords were not obliged by Housing Act 1961 s32 (now Landlord and Tenant Act 1985 s11) to lag pipes which functioned satisfactorily in all but the most extreme weather conditions. Accordingly, there is no liability on the part of landlords for damage caused by the bursting of an unlagged pipe in very severe cold. In this case, the Court of Appeal found that the tenant had not acted in a tenant-like manner by failing to lag the pipes or to turn off the water at the mains and to drain the system before going away. She was liable for the cost of repairing the damage.

Cf *Stockley v Knowsley MBC* (P7.16)

High Court

P5.22   *Ball and Ball v Plymouth CC*

[2004] EWHC 134 (QB); November 2004 *Legal Action* 27; 4 February 2004

Damp not due to defect in structure or exterior

The claimants sought damages for breach of implied repairing obligations under Landlord and Tenant Act 1985 s11 and Defective Premises Act 1972 s4. They claimed that the premises were damp owing to an actionable defect in the structure and exterior of the building. The council's expert gave evidence that the dampness was due to an inherent design defect or the ordinary incidents of everyday life. In the county court, the judge accepted the defendant's evidence that the damp was not caused by an actionable defect and dismissed the claim.

The claimants' appeal was dismissed. The claimant had failed to discharge the burden of proof.

P5.23   *Irvine v Moran*

(1992) 24 HLR 1; [1991] 1 EGLR 261, QBD

Ambit of 'structure and exterior' of premises; plaster decorative

A landlord sought to enforce an agreement imposing very extensive repairing obligations on the tenant of a house. It was conceded that the landlord could enforce only those obligations not covered by Landlord and Tenant Act 1985 s11.

The question of which repairs were within that section was tried as a preliminary issue. The tenants conceded that works required to the gardens, grounds and driveway were beyond the section and were their responsibility. As to the other works, Recorder Thayne Forbes QC held that the words 'structure and exterior' did not mean that the landlord was liable to repair the whole of the house. On the other hand, 'structure' was not limited to the load-bearing parts. It consists of those elements of the overall dwelling-house which give it its essential stability and shape. The expression does not extend to the many and various ways in which the dwelling-house will be fitted out, equipped, decorated and generally made habitable. Applying that test to the specific items, he held that:

1) the separate garage and gates were not within the section;
2) internal wall plaster and door furniture were decorative and therefore not part of the structure;
3) external windows and doors and their constituent parts (including sashes) were either part of the structure or exterior;
4) external painting was part of the obligation to repair the exterior;
5) internal decorative painting of installations such as radiators was purely decorative and not part of the implied covenant.

Note: On the issue of whether plasterwork is part of the structure or exterior, see also *Hussein v Mehlman* (P1.5); *Fincar SRL v 109/113 Mount Street Management Co Ltd* (P3.4); *Hallisey v Petmoor Developments Ltd* (P3.14); *Staves v Leeds CC* (P5.17); *Willis and Willis v Fuller* (P5.30) and *Hyde Southbank Homes v Oronsaye and Obadiara* (P11.36).

P5.24 *Southwark LBC v McIntosh*

[2002] 08 EG 164; 9 November 2001, ChD

Disrepair to structure or exterior required physical damage; damp alone not disrepair

The claimant's flat was damp. She brought a claim alleging that Southwark were liable under the covenant for repair implied in her tenancy by Landlord and Tenant Act 1985 s11. HHJ Cox awarded general damages of £7,500, for breach of covenant in respect of discomfort arising from the damp condition of the demised premises over a five-year period, and special damages of £350.

Southwark appealed successfully. Lightman J held that it was established by the Court of Appeal in *Quick v Taff Ely BC* (P5.16) and succeeding cases that 'disrepair' was established for the purposes of s11 if, and only if, there was physical damage to the structure or exterior of the premises which did not arise by reason of the tenant's default. A landlord was not liable under the covenant merely because there was very serious damp in the demised premises. In a case such as the present, the tenant must establish either that the damp arose from a breach of the covenant (ie, physical damage to the structure or exterior of the premises) or that the damp had itself caused damage to the structure or exterior and that this damage in turn had caused the damp. There was no particularised allegation in the particulars of claim of any physical damage to the structure or exterior of the property or that such damage caused the damp for which damages were sought. All that was pleaded and particularised was the damp itself. The judge was wrong to decide the case on the basis that the existence of the damp constituted a breach of covenant and cause of action in itself for which damages should be and were awarded. The appeal was allowed and the action dismissed.

County courts

P5.25 *Churchill v Nottingham CC*

January 2001 *Legal Action* 25, Nottingham County Court

Keeping chimneys in proper working order generally within s11

HHJ MacDuff QC held that, following *Warren v Keen* [1954] 1 QB 15, CA, cleaning chimneys may still be part of tenants' duties to act in a tenant-like manner (s11(2)(a)) if the premises are small cottages on the moors where wood or coal is still burned and the chimney is used in an old-fashioned way. However, in modern housing, tenants' duties do not extend to disconnecting fixed gas fires, removing back plates, inspecting flues and cleaning chimneys of any blockages. In such circumstances, keeping chimneys in repair and proper working order is part of the landlord's responsibilities under Landlord and Tenant Act 1985 s11.

P5.26 *Hussein v Mehlman*

[1992] 2 EGLR 87; [1992] 32 EG 59, Wood Green Trial Centre (see P1.5)

Plaster part of 'structure'

P5.27   *Islington LBC v Keane*

November 2005 *Legal Action* 28; 20 January 2005, Clerkenwell County Court

Express obligation on tenant to replace washers ineffective as came within s11; limitation period for disrepair counterclaim ran from date of possession claim

Islington sought possession, relying on arrears of rent. Mr Keane brought a Part 20 counterclaim on the basis that he had been left without a cold water supply from his kitchen tap for several years. It was agreed that the likely cause of the defect was a defective or perished washer. Islington disputed liability, claiming that tenants are obliged to replace tap washers under the express terms of their standard tenancy agreement and that the defect did not fall within the implied obligation under Landlord and Tenant Act 1985 s11(1)(b) to keep in repair and proper working order the installations in the dwelling-house for the supply of water (see also s11(2)(a)).

District Judge Stary rejected both these arguments. She decided that the repairing obligation covers the whole of the installation which supplies water including the tap and its component parts. Replacing a defective washer was not one of the little jobs about the place which a reasonable tenant must do as most people would call in a plumber to do it. Accordingly, given that it was covered by the implied obligation on Islington to repair under s11(1)(b), the council could not transfer liability for the repair on to the tenant by way of the express terms of the tenancy agreement. In so far as the tenancy sought to impose liability on the tenant for replacing washers other then those installed for washing machines and dishwashers, the repairing obligation was void. District Judge Stary accepted that, as this was a Part 20 counterclaim, the limitation period ran from the date of the original possession claim rather than from the date of the Part 20 counterclaim. Therefore, this gave the tenant an extra year of claim.

P5.28   *Walker v Nottingham CC*

May 1997 *Legal Action* 20, Nottingham County Court (see P7.21)

Banister not part of 'structure'

P5.29   *Walton v Lewisham LBC*

May 1997 *Legal Action* 20, Tunbridge Wells County Court (see P4.13)

Implied term to carry out s11 repairs with reasonable care and skill – council liable for damage caused when carrying out repairs to roof

P5.30   *Willis and Willis v Fuller*

May 1997 *Legal Action* 20; (1996) H&HI(1) 3:0, Hastings County Court

Plaster normally part of structure and wet plaster was in disrepair

The plaintiffs had a Rent Act tenancy of a self-contained, two-bedroomed ground floor flat in substantial disrepair. The landlord, relying on *Irvine v Moran* (P5.23), contended that wall and ceiling plaster was not part of the 'structure' of the flat for the purposes of Landlord and Tenant Act 1985 s11 and, even if the plaster was 'wet' as claimed, it was not in disrepair. The tenant relied on *Hussein v Mehlman* (P1.5).

Recorder Gault held that plaster might in some cases be a non-structural decorative finish but that for most houses most plaster would be part of the structure and would have a function of supporting a decorative finish.

In this dwelling, that was the case and, furthermore, the 'wet' plaster was perished and required repair. However, he rejected the tenant's contention that a mechanical ventilator in the bathroom window was an installation for 'sanitation' within s11. Nor was the landlord liable in respect of an 'ill-fitting door' because the tenants had not discharged the burden of showing that it had once fitted properly but was now in disrepair. General damages were assessed at £1,000 per annum for a case described by the recorder as 'at the lower end of the range'.

P5.31   *Windever v Liverpool CC*

[1994] CLY 2816, Liverpool County Court

Floors which became uneven could not perform function for which constructed and in disrepair

A council tenant brought proceedings for breach of the obligation in Landlord and Tenant Act 1985 s11 to keep the structure of her home in repair. As a result of settlement, the floors of the kitchen and living room had sunk and were no longer level, causing furniture to wobble and occasionally floorboards to rise under the carpets. The council denied breach of covenant, asserting that, in the absence of any hazard, the floors did not warrant expenditure by way of repairs.

    Recorder Stockdale found that the floors were in disrepair. The correct test was not whether they were hazardous but whether they could still perform the function for which they were constructed. They did not provide an adequate surface for seating or other normal use and were thus in disrepair.

P6   ## Notice and delay in carrying out repairs

Most repairing obligations require (expressly or by implication) that the landlord has knowledge of disrepair within the demised premises before any liability arises. The most usual way of fixing the landlord with knowledge is to show that the tenant has given notice of the defect. However, it is also possible to establish knowledge indirectly. Where notice is required, the landlord then has a reasonable time within which to carry out the repairs before liability will arise.

    The requirement for notice does not apply if the defects are to parts of the building other than those demised, eg, to the outer walls and roof of a block of flats, or to common parts. Furthermore, the requirement of notice for cases brought within the Defective Premises Act 1972 is that the landlord knows or ought to know of the existence of a defect (see P8).

House of Lords

P6.1   *O'Brien v Robinson*

[1973] AC 912; [1973] 2 WLR 393; [1973] 1 All ER 583; (1973) 13 HLR 7; (1973) 25 P&CR 239, HL

No liability arose until landlord had knowledge of defect

The tenant and his wife were in bed one night when the bedroom ceiling collapsed on them. The fall was caused by a latent defect. Neither the tenant nor the landlord was aware of the defect until the collapse occurred.

The House of Lords held that no liability under Housing Act 1961 s32 (now Landlord and Tenant Act 1985 s11) arose until the landlord had information about the existence of a defect in the premises which would put a reasonable person on enquiry about whether works of repair were needed. The landlord was only liable to repair the ceiling and not liable for damage resulting from the collapse.

Court of Appeal

P6.2   *Al Hassani v Merrigan*

(1988) 20 HLR 238; [1988] 1 EGLR 93; [1988] 03 EG 88, CA

Solicitor's letter was such that it did not satisfy the notice requirement

A tenant consulted solicitors about disrepair. The solicitors wrote to the landlord mentioning 'countless occasions' on which the landlord's agent had been notified of the need to repair and saying that 'estimates' covering the work presently required would be submitted in due course. Estimates were not submitted. The landlord commenced possession proceedings. In response, a counterclaim for damages was served – before the landlord was given particulars of the disrepair. Indeed, a surveyor's report prepared a year earlier, detailing the defects (which was the only pleaded 'notice' of defect) was not served on the landlord until a week after the counterclaim was lodged. Although the trial judge gave leave to amend, the evidence of notice at trial amounted to only a single report of failed hot water, which had in fact been attended to. The counterclaim was dismissed. A possession order was made on the ground of rent arrears, which had accrued partly because of legal advice to withhold the rent on account of repairs.

The Court of Appeal held that: (a) notice of disrepair need not specify the precise nature or degree of want of repair; (b) the letter from the solicitors would usually be sufficient to put the landlord under an obligation to attend and inspect and thereafter carry out the repair; but (c) the letter could be construed as saying that the landlord was 'being told that he would be told what was necessary in due course and he could then either do it or have the cost deducted from rent', which was not of itself sufficient notice. The judge had considered all the matters relevant to the issue of reasonableness and there was no basis to interfere with his exercise of discretion in making the possession order.

P6.3   *British Telecommunications plc v Sun Life Assurance Society plc*

[1996] Ch 69; [1995] 3 WLR 622; [1995] 4 All ER 44; (1997) 73 P&CR 475; [1995] 2 EGLR 44; [1995] 45 EG 133, CA

Notice not required where defect was not in premises let

Tenants occupied offices in a large block. The landlord expressly covenanted to 'keep [it] in complete good and substantial repair'. In 1986 the external faces of the block began to bulge. Remedial works were started by the landlord in 1988. The tenant sought damages for breach of covenant from 1986. The claim was defended on the basis that no liability arose until a reasonable time after the landlord first had knowledge of the need for repair. Aldous J held that the landlords were liable from the time that the defect arose. They appealed.

The Court of Appeal dismissed the appeal. After an extensive review of the authorities, Nourse LJ stated:

> The general rule is that a covenant to keep premises in repair obliges the covenantor to keep them in repair at all *Times*, so that there is breach of the obligation immediately a defect occurs. There is an exception where the obligation is the landlord's and the defect occurs in the demised premises themselves, in which case he is in breach of his obligation only when he has information about the existence of a defect such as would put a reasonable landlord on enquiry as to whether works of repair are needed and he has failed to carry out the works with reasonable expedition thereafter. ([1995] 4 All ER at 52)

Here the defect was not 'in' the part let and so the landlords were immediately liable.

It was suggested by Nourse LJ that a further exception to the general rule that a landlord is liable immediately a defect occurs is where the cause of the defect is an occurrence wholly outside the landlord's control, eg, where a roof retained in control of the landlord is damaged by a tree standing on a neighbouring property.

P6.4   *Charalambous v Earle (Addendum to Judgment)*
[2006] EWCA Civ 1338; 12 October 2006

Where common ground that date of notice of defect was the starting point for damages it was logical to add a reasonable time for works to be done

The tenant, a long leaseholder, brought a claim for damages for disrepair due to defects to the roof above his top-floor flat. On an appeal in respect of damages (see *Earle v Charlambous* (P11.7)), the Court of Appeal reduced the damages awarded partly on the basis that the judge had failed to make any allowance for the time needed for the landlord to carry out repairs.

Having heard further submissions on this point, the Court of Appeal, in this addendum judgment, upheld its reduction in the level of damages. It accepted that the defects were principally within the roof and therefore arguably within the general rule in *British Telecommunications plc v Sun Life Assurance Society plc* (P6.3), namely that, in respect of disrepair in parts of the building within the landlord's control, the landlord was in breach immediately a defect occurred. However, the court held that as it had been common ground before the trial judge that, for the purposes of assessing damages, the date of the notice of the defects should be taken as the starting point, it was illogical not to allow the landlord a reasonable time to respond. Carnwath LJ raised the possibility of a further amendment to the notice rule as he held that: 'In a future case, it may have to be considered whether the "general rule" as laid down by BT requires some modification to take account of the practicalities of the modern relationship of residential lessors and lessees.' It should be borne in mind that this was said in the context of long leases, where there is a reciprocal obligation on lessees to contribute to the costs of the works.

P6.5   *Dinefwr BC v Jones*
(1987) 19 HLR 445; [1987] 2 EGLR 88; (1987) 284 EG 58, CA

Knowledge of disrepair, other than by direct complaint, satisfied requirement of notice

A tenancy agreement indicated that notice of disrepair should be given direct to the architectural service of the council. The tenant gave no such notice but instead relied on the knowledge of the landlord authority in that: (a) an officer of the environmental health department had visited the property and seen the defects; and (b) the chief executive had received a report from the district valuer – prepared after a right to buy application – which drew attention to the defects.

The Court of Appeal was satisfied that either of these fixed the landlord with knowledge. The environmental health officer was:

> ... a responsible official of the local authority and certain items of disrepair were brought to his attention. In my view, when that was done that was notice to the local authority ... (per Bush J (1987) 19 HLR at 449)

However, this extended only to disrepair that the environmental health officer had in fact observed. As regards the chief executive, Bush J failed:

> ... to see how, when the Chief Executive, in that capacity, receives a report which relates to one of the properties owned by the local authority and for which they have responsibility, that can be distinguished in terms merely on the basis that the report was for a different purpose. The report is quite clear. It is specifying defects and indicating that the external doors and windows require immediate attention as do certain ceilings and skirtings. (ibid at 450)

In the light of these findings, the court more than doubled the damages which had been awarded in the county court.

P6.6 *Hall v Howard*

(1988) 20 HLR 566; [1988] 2 EGLR 75, CA

Details of defects in tenant's surveyor's valuation report constituted notice

A sitting tenant began negotiations to purchase the landlord's interest. The tenant's surveyor produced an inspection report which set out items of disrepair taken into account in reaching a valuation of the property. This was sent to the landlord's agents. Later the tenant began an action based on breach of repairing obligations. The landlord denied knowledge of the need for repair.

Following and applying *Dinefwr BC v Jones* (P6.5), the Court of Appeal held that the details contained in the valuer's report constituted sufficient notice once served on the landlord's agent. The landlord was, accordingly, liable in damages to the tenant for disrepair.

P6.7 *Morris v Liverpool CC*

(1988) 20 HLR 498; [1988] 1 EGLR 47; (1988) 14 EG 59, CA

Onus on tenant to prove unreasonable delay in front door being secured properly

On 15 January the tenant's door and doorframe were broken down by firemen attending to a fire. That same day, the council arranged to board it up with thin plywood sheeting. On 16 January the tenant reported the need for repair and a workman called, but he did not repair the door and it remained sheeted. No further work was done and seven days later the property was burgled. Entry was forced through the sheeting. The issue was whether the council was in breach of the obligation to repair on that date and therefore liable for the loss (the court was satisfied that the loss through the actions of a third party was not too remote to be recoverable). The trial judge did not expressly deal with the question of unreasonable delay in dismissing the claim and little evidence was recorded on the point – indeed the tenant 'did not give evidence on this issue' (per Stocker LJ).

Slade LJ held that the onus of proving that a reasonable period had passed was on the tenant. On the evidence it had not been proved that a delay of seven days between notice and any permanent repair was unreasonable. Such evidence would have included: the difficulty or otherwise of obtaining the proper quality and size of door and frame, the council's workload, the fact that the tenant was temporarily absent from the property and the fact that the temporary repair had been carried out. The claim was originally pleaded in the alternative as negligence but this was not pursued on appeal. Balcombe LJ expressly left open the question of any liability which might have arisen had the case been argued on the basis that the landlords owed a duty of care to make the premises secure pending the necessary repairs. No reference to the duty of care under the Defective Premises Act 1972 appears in the judgment.

P6.8   *Passley v Wandsworth LBC*
[1998] 30 HLR 165, CA

Landlord liable without notice for flooding from pipes in common parts

During freezing weather in early 1991, water pipes in the roof over a block of flats burst, flooding the plaintiff tenant's flat. The council attended promptly to effect repairs but the tenant claimed compensation for the damage caused by the flooding itself, arguing that the disrepair arose in a common part retained in the ownership and management of the landlord (the roof) and that the statutorily implied covenant to 'keep in repair' imposed an absolute obligation on the landlord to keep the pipes in good order at all *Times*

The Court of Appeal held that the general rule that the landlord was liable immediately a defect occurred applied (*British Telecommunications plc v Sun Life Assurance Society plc* (P6.3)). Severe weather was not so uncommon an occurrence in the UK that it cannot be forseen and suitable precautions taken. None of the exceptions to the rule in *British Telecommunications* applied.

P6.9   *Sheldon v West Bromwich Corporation*
(1973) 13 HLR 23; (1973) 25 P&CR 360, CA

Discolouration of water in old tank sufficient to give landlord knowledge of need to repair

The plaintiff rented a house from the defendants. He claimed damages for breach of repairing obligations in Housing Act 1961 s32 (now Landlord and Tenant Act 1985 s11) following a burst water tank which caused damage to his property. As a result of discolouration of the water supply and 'hammering', there had been six inspections of the tank by plumbers employed by the defendants.

The Court of Appeal, allowing the tenant's appeal against the dismissal of his claim in the county court, held that the state of discolouration of the water and the tank's age were sufficient to give the landlords actual knowledge of the need to repair. Information about the existence of such a defect, which would put a reasonable person on enquiry about whether works of repair are needed, is sufficient for the landlord's repairing obligation to commence.

High Court

P6.10   *Loria v Hammer*

[1989] 2 EGLR 249, ChD

No notice required where defect in water tanks in roof not in tenant's letting

The cause of dampness was a failure to keep in repair the water tanks in the roof space and gutters around the roof. The landlord was held to be liable to repair, irrespective of any notice, because these were in the common parts of the building. Since they were not part of the tenant's letting, they remained the responsibility of the landlord, who was liable for the consequential damage when the dampness affected the tenant's own flat.

County courts

P6.11   *Bavage v Southwark LBC*

[1998] 12 CL 313, Lambeth County Court

Landlord liable without notice for backsurge in central sewage stack in block of flats

The plaintiff was a secure tenant who lived in a nine-storey block containing forty flats. A central sewage stack which ran down the roof of the block was vandalised, causing a blockage and a backsurge. The plaintiff's flat was flooded by raw sewage. This continued for 48 hours until the problem was dealt with. The plaintiff lived with her mother for seven weeks while her flat was cleaned and redecorated. Redecoration was completed three weeks later.

HHJ Cox held that, where an event giving rise to liability occurs entirely on land in the possession or control of the landlord, the landlord is liable, irrespective of notice. In this case there was no exception to the general rule identified in *British Telecommunications plc v Sun Alliance Assurance Society plc* (P6.3). The plaintiff was entitled to the replacement cost of all items lost or damaged in the flood, less a 25% reduction for depreciation. General damages of £350 were awarded for loss of rent together with an additional £1,250 reflecting the undoubted trauma and distress experienced.

P6.12   *Walton v Lewisham LBC*

May 1997 *Legal Action* 20, Tunbridge Wells County Court (see P4.13)

Council liable for damage caused when carrying out works to roof without notice as in actual occupation of roof when carrying out repairs

Northern Ireland courts

P6.13 *Collins v Northern Ireland Housing Executive*
[1987] 2 NIJB 27, CA(NI) (see P4.14)

No breach of obligation to maintain heating system where repairs done within 24/48 hours

Liability in tort

P7 ## Negligence and nuisance

Landlords do not owe a general duty of care to tenants with regard to the condition of the premises when they are let: 'A landlord who lets a house in a dangerous state is not liable to the tenant's customers or guests for accidents happening during the term: for, fraud apart, there is no law against letting a tumbledown house and the tenant's remedy is upon his contract, if any'. (*Cavalier v Pope* [1906] AC 428, HL)

The courts have, however, held that a landlord does have a duty of care in some prescribed circumstances. Furthermore, a landlord who designs and builds a premises may be liable in that capacity (see *Rimmer v Liverpool CC* (P7.13)). Section 4 of the Defective Premises Act 1972 also places a statutory duty of care on a landlord in defined circumstances (see P8).

Landlords are liable for any common-law nuisance arising from ancillary property owned by them, including common parts, impinging on the tenant's dwelling-house.

House of Lords

P7.1 *D & F Estates Ltd v Church Commissioners*
[1989] AC 177; [1988] 3 WLR 368; [1988] 2 All ER 992; [1988] 2 EGLR 263, HL

Builder not liable for negligence of subcontractor

A long leaseholder claimed damages for the cost of repair work to wall plaster in an action for negligence against the building contractor who built his home. The contractor had subcontracted the plastering work.

The House of Lords held that (a) in the absence of any contractual relationship, the contractor was not liable for any negligence committed by an independent subcontractor and (b) in any event, the cost of the repairs was irrecoverable as pure 'economic loss'.

P7.2 *Delaware Mansions Ltd v City of Westminster*
[2001] UKHL 55; [2002] 1 AC 321; [2001] 3 WLR 1007; [2001] 4 All ER 737

Council as highway authority liable for damage caused by roots of trees

A five-storey block of flats was let on long leases. There was structural cracking and other disrepair caused by the roots of a large plane tree growing in the pavement of the street outside the block. The tenant management company and the freeholders claimed damages from the council as the highway authority responsible for the pavement and the tree. The Court of Appeal awarded damages of £835,000 – the cost of remedial works.

The House of Lords dismissed the council's appeal. Lord Cooke said that 'the concern of the common law lies in working out the fair and just incidents of a neighbour's duty rather than affixing a label [such as "nuisance" or "negligence"] and inferring the extent of the duty from it'. Where a tree owner was notified of root damage, he was entitled to a reasonable opportunity to abate the nuisance. The council had had both notice and opportunity but failed to prevent further damage and so was liable for the full cost of the subsequent remedial work.

P7.3   *Hunter v Canary Wharf Ltd*
[1997] AC 655; [1997] 2 All ER 426; (1998) 30 HLR 409; [1997] Env LR 488; 24 April 1997, HL

Disruption to television reception not a nuisance; exclusive possession of land necessary to sue in nuisance

Residents claimed that the construction of the Canary Wharf Tower interfered with their television reception. The House of Lords held that (a) the creation or presence of a building between a television transmitter and other properties was not capable of constituting an actionable private nuisance and (b) ordinarily, only a person with a right to exclusive possession of land may bring an action in private nuisance.

P7.4   *Southwark LBC v Mills; Southwark LBC v Tanner; Baxter v Camden LBC*
[2001] 1 AC 1; [1999] 3 WLR 939; [1999] 4 All ER 449; [2000] LGR 138; [1999] 45 EG 179; (2000) 32 HLR 148; [2000] L&TR 159; (1999) *Times* 22 October, HL (see P4.2)

Normal use of residential flat cannot be a nuisance to neighbours; landlord cannot be liable in nuisance for conduct of neighbouring tenants, which is not a nuisance on their part

Court of Appeal

P7.5   *Adams v Rhymney Valley DC*
(2001) 33 HLR 446, CA (see P10.1)

Council not in breach of duty of care in installing windows according to standards at time of installation

P7.6   *Boateng v Camden LBC*
(1999) 31 HLR 41; May 1998 *Legal Action* 22, CA (see P10.3)

Landlord not liable for burns to baby caused by hot pipes

P7.7   *Boldack (minor) v East Lindsey DC*
(1999) 31 HLR 41; May 1998 *Legal Action* 22, CA (see P10.4)

Landlord not liable in negligence for injury to non-tenants

P7.8   *Habinteg Housing Association v James*
(1995) 27 HLR 299, CA

No liability for cockroach infestation where no common parts retained by landlord

In February 1986 the plaintiff took a tenancy of the middle flat of three flats stacked vertically in a single block. She claimed that from spring or summer 1986 her flat had been infested by cockroaches. Some temporary remedial treatment was undertaken by the pest control service of the local council, but that ceased in 1990. Following a residents' association survey, the council served notice on the landlords to abate the nuisance and then undertook its own survey and block treatment programme which eradicated the cockroaches in 1991. The tenant sought damages from her landlord. Recorder Lipton dismissed her claim, but indicated that, if she had succeeded, he would have awarded damages of £10,000.

The Court of Appeal dismissed the tenant's appeal. Waite LJ held that:

1) There was no implied term that the landlord should take reasonable care to abate an infestation, even if block treatment would be the only effective treatment.

2) There was no liability in nuisance because:
   a) there were no common parts retained by the landlords and no conclusive evidence about the source of the infestation;
   b) the reserved rights of entry over tenanted flats did not give the landlords sufficient control over them to be liable for failure to treat any infestation emanating from them.

3) There was no liability in negligence because there is no duty of care on the part of lessors to block-treat infestations where there are no legal means for the lessors to force others on the estate to participate.

P7.9   *Hawkins v Dhawan*
(1987) 19 HLR 232; [1987] 2 EGLR 157; (1987) 283 EG 1388, CA

Tenant owed duty of care to neighbour but not breached by unexpected overflow

Water penetrated the ceiling of the tenant's flat, causing damage to possessions. The problem was caused by a blocked overflow pipe to the bathroom basin of the tenant on the floor above. The tenant's claim for damages against the landlord was dismissed and he continued with the action against the neighbouring tenant. Since he was unable to base a claim in contract, nuisance or the rule in *Rylands v Fletcher* (1868) LR 3 HL 330, the plaintiff was forced to rely on negligence.

Although the Court of Appeal held that the upstairs tenant owed a duty of care to the downstairs tenant, it was not prepared to find any breach of that duty unless it could be shown that the circumstances should have alerted the upstairs tenant to the possibility of a blockage. In the absence of any such circumstances (such as a previous incident), no liability arose from a first, unexpected overflow.

P7.10   *Issa v Hackney LBC*
[1997] 1 WLR 956; [1997] 1 All ER 999; (1997) 29 HLR 640; (1997) 95 LGR 671, CA
(see P16.3)

A statutory nuisance under Environmental Protection Act 1990 does not give rise to a civil cause of action

P7.11   *McNerny v Lambeth LBC*
(1989) 21 HLR 188; [1989] 1 EGLR 81; [1989] 19 EG 77, CA

Council not liable in negligence for low standard accommodation

A tenant relied on various causes of action in a claim for compensation for the effects of living in a flat plagued with condensation dampness. The premises were a third-floor flat in a typical five-storey council block built in the 1940s or 50s with solid walls and metal window frames. The court was told that the problems arose from lack of permanent ventilation, single glazing to the windows and lack of insulation to the solid walls. The result of normal production of water vapour in the dwelling (from washing machine, tumble drier, etc) was condensation, causing discoloured decorations, fungal mould growth, deterioration to fabrics and furnishing and a history of colds and minor ailments among the occupiers. The remedy recommended was the replacement of the metal window frames with wood or plastic, double-glazing, external cladding of walls with insulating material and more effective heating. Dillon LJ commented, 'I would not be at all surprised to find that there is the same problem in the areas of very many other housing authorities throughout the country.' In the county court the judge had rejected assertions that the landlord was liable under: (a) the repairing covenant (following *Quick v Taff-Ely BC* (P5.16)); (b) nuisance (nuisance at common law was not established on the facts); or (c) negligence. The tenant appealed against the decision on negligence only.

The Court of Appeal dismissed the appeal. There was no evidence that the properties had been negligently constructed having regard to the standards of that time. The tenant therefore had to establish that the landlord owed a duty of care as the landlord of an unfurnished letting, notwithstanding the decision in *Cavalier v Pope* [1906] AC 428, HL. The Court of Appeal rejected the argument that public sector landlords should owe such a duty by virtue of their other housing powers and responsibilities. The rule in *Cavalier v Pope* still binds the Court of Appeal (see *Rimmer v Liverpool CC* (P7.13)). The Court of Appeal also held that, even if there were a duty of care, it would be unlikely to extend beyond the scope of a repairing covenant, as parliament had already circumscribed liability in that way (Defective Premises Act 1972 s4). Dillon LJ stated that:

> It is for Parliament to extend the duties imposed on landlords of council houses or flats or other low standard accommodation. It is not for the courts.

P7.12   *Pemberton v Southwark LBC*

[2000] 1 WLR 1672; [2000] 3 All ER 924; (2000) 32 HLR 784; [2000] 21 EG 135; (2000) *Times* 26 April, CA (see I2.13)

Tolerated trespasser could sue in nuisance (cockroach infestation)

P7.13   *Rimmer v Liverpool CC*

[1985] QB 1; [1984] 2 WLR 426; [1984] 1 All ER 930; (1984) 12 HLR 23; (1984) 47 P&CR 516; (1983) 269 EG 319; (1984) 82 LGR 424, CA

Landlord as designer and builder of premises liable for faults in design and construction

The plaintiff rented a flat which had been designed and built by the council. An internal wall of a passage included a thin panel of glass which was unprotected. The tenant complained to the housing department about the potential danger to his young son, but was told that it was a standard installation and could not be changed. Later the plaintiff tripped, put out his hand to steady himself and cut his hand on the glass. He claimed damages in negligence.

The Court of Appeal held that, although landlords of unfurnished premises owe no duty of care to tenants with regards the condition of the premises when they are let, landlords who also designed and built premises owe a duty of care in their capacity as designer or builder to all persons who might reasonably be expected to be affected by faults in the design or construction of the premises. The council was liable.

P7.14 **Sharpe v Manchester MDC**

(1977) 5 HLR 71, CA

Council liable in nuisance and negligence for failure to treat cockroach infestation

Mr Sharpe's council flat suffered from a cockroach infestation. The cockroaches probably came into the flat through service ducts. No other tenants suffered from any infestation and the council decided not to treat the service ducts. The plaintiff's claim for damages in the county court was dismissed.

The Court of Appeal allowed his appeal. The infestation was a nuisance. The council's failure to treat the service ducts and its continuing use of DDT, which was known to be ineffective, meant that it was also liable in negligence.

P7.15 **Stevens v Blaenau Gwent CBC**

[2004] EWCA Civ 715; [2004] HLR 54

Council not liable for injury to child falling where no locks on windows

The infant claimant fell from the first-floor window of a house rented by his mother from the council and sustained serious injury. He had managed to open a window that could only be opened by a small child using a piece of furniture as a stepping stone. The claimant's mother had requested that window locks be fitted, but had been told by the council that this could not be done because of the fire risk they created. After the accident, the council fitted a safety catch to the window, which prevented it from being opened more than two or three inches by a small child. The judge found the council liable by analogy with the decision in *Stockley v Knowsley MBC* (P7.16) .

The Court of Appeal allowed the council's appeal. The judge was wrong to derive assistance from the decision in *Stockley* as there was no emergency or external threat which called for action by the council.

P7.16 **Stockley v Knowsley MBC**

[1986] 2 EGLR 141; (1986) 279 EG 677, CA

Landlord owed duty of care to tenant and breached duty where aware of frozen pipes

A tenant telephoned twice to report frozen pipes but was not told to turn off the stopcock nor told where the stopcock was. When the pipes burst, flooding was so severe that the tenant had to leave the property for one night and thereafter part of the property was unusable for ten months.

The Court of Appeal upheld a finding of negligence based on breach of the duty of care and awarded £250 general damages (in addition to a further £100 general damages for failure to repair a window under Housing Act 1961 s32 (now Landlord and Tenant Act 1985 s11)) and £75 special damages. The Court of Appeal held that landlords owe a duty of care to any tenant and that once they:

> ... were appraised of the fact that a pipe was frozen and were aware, or should have been aware, that when the pipe thawed it would be likely to burst and cause water to flow out into the property below, they were under a duty to do whatever was reasonable in the circumstances, having regard ... to their capacity to act and their ability to abate or deal with the hazard.

Cf *Wycombe Area Health Authority v Barnett* (P5.21)

P7.17   *Targett v Torfaen BC*
[1992] 3 All ER 27; (1992) 24 HLR 164; [1992] 1 EGLR 274, CA

Landlord who undertakes design and construction of premises liable for damage caused by inherently dangerous steps

The plaintiff tenant was injured falling from stone steps leading up to his house. There were two flights of steps over sloping land. They had been constructed by the council with no handrail and no lighting. At first instance, the construction was found as a fact to have been inherently dangerous.

The Court of Appeal held that:

1) The *Donoghue v Stevenson* [1932] AC 562, HL, duty of care was owed by a landlord who had undertaken the design and construction of premises let to all persons who might reasonably be expected to use the property.

2) No immunity attached to the defendant as a result of its status as 'landlord' (applying *Rimmer v Liverpool CC* (P7.13)). *Rimmer* had not been overruled by *Murphy v Brentwood DC* [1991] 1 AC 398, HL, and was still good law.

3) The defendant council could not claim that the tenant's opportunity to inspect prior to or after letting relieved it of the duty, unless the tenant was free to remove or avoid the danger and it was reasonable to expect him to do so.

The tenant had been injured by a defect manufactured, designed or created by the landlord and liability followed. A finding of contributory negligence on the part of the tenant reduced the damages by 25 per cent.

High Court

P7.18   *Lips v Older*
[2004] EWHC 1686 (QB); 16 June 2004

Landlord liable in negligence for dangerous pathway

The tenant claimed damages for paraplegia sustained when he fell over a wall leading up to the front door of the premises owned by his landlord on to a concrete basement area.

Mackay J held that the landlord was in breach of his duty of care to his tenant, in common-law negligence, to take such care as was reasonable so that people who he could contemplate using the path, namely, a floating population of tenants, including students and Mr Lips, were safe to do so. It was reasonable to expect such tenants to return to the house in a state of inebriation on occasion, and it was relevant to the standard of care that the landlord was a professional property-owner and had access to advice. The erection of a handrail was cheap and would have returned the house to its original condition. Damages were reduced by two-thirds for Mr Lips's contributory negligence in being drunk at the time of the accident, and carrying a very heavy load which caused him to lose his balance.

County courts

P7.19   *Clark v Wandsworth LBC*
June 1994 *Legal Action* 15, Wandsworth County Court

Council liable in nuisance or negligence for cockroach infestation

The plaintiff, a single parent with two children aged ten and three, occupied a two-bedroomed maisonette in a system-built block with ducted warm air heating. From January 1991 until June 1992 the property was infested with cockroaches. HHJ Sumner, following *Leakey v National Trust* [1980] QB 485, CA, held that the council, whether sued in nuisance or negligence, owed a duty to do 'all that is reasonable to prevent risk of damage and injury to a neighbour's property'. Proper treatment should have involved a survey to ascertain the extent of infestation, systematic block-control treatment repeated after three or four weeks and monitoring after completion. He rejected the council's contention that the ducting was only a means of access, not a breeding ground, and that therefore there was no nuisance emanating from the common parts. He described the effect of the infestation as being worse than damp and awarded general damages of £3,500 for the physical, mental and emotional effects on the family.

    The council's application for leave to appeal to the Court of Appeal was refused (June 1995 *Legal Action* 23). Hoffmann LJ stated that there was 'ample evidence' to support the judge's findings.

P7.20   *Murphy and Peers v Stockport MBC*
August 2002 *Legal Action* 27; 26 April 2002, Stockport County Court (see P1.7)

Tenant's children could not sue in nuisance as they had no proprietory interest in their home

P7.21   *Walker v Nottingham CC*
May 1997 *Legal Action* 20, Nottingham County Court

Council liable in negligence for injury from failed banister it had refixed

In 1990 the council as landlords repaired a handrail to the stairs in the plaintiff tenant's council house. In May 1991 the tenant was ascending the stairs relying on the handrail for support when it gave way. He fell and was badly injured.

    At trial, the judge rejected the contention that the handrail was part of the 'structure' for the purposes of Landlord and Tenant Act 1985 s11 (or

Defective Premises Act 1972 s4) but held that the council was liable in common-law negligence because it had refixed the handrail in 1990 without exercising proper skill and care. He dismissed a claim of contributory negligence (based on an assertion of excess of alcohol) and awarded: (a) £38,000 general damages for pain and suffering; (b) £63,000 for loss of earnings and (c) interest of £2,600.

Scottish courts

P7.22 *Scott v Glasgow DC*

1997 Hous LR 107; August 1997 *Scolag* 135, Glasgow Sheriff Court

Tenant's children could not sue in negligence for personal injury

Three children sued their mother's local authority landlord in negligence for damages for personal injury. They claimed that they had developed asthmatic conditions as a result of the mould growth and dampness in their home.

After a trial extending over 25 days, Sheriff Wilkinson dismissed their claim. He held himself bound by the decision of the House of Lords in *Cameron v Young* 1908 SC (HL) 7, which was delivered shortly after *Cavalier v Pope* [1906] AC 428, HL. In that case, the House of Lords had decided that the law of Scotland on a landlord's common-law liability in negligence was the same as that in England, ie, landlords are not liable for defects in the premises causing injury to non-tenants and, contractual obligations apart, are entitled to allow their houses to 'fall to pieces'. Since the children could not sue in contract and the landlord owed them no obligation at common law, they could not recover damages. The sheriff rejected an attempt to distinguish *Cameron v Young* or to argue that it had been overruled by *Donoghue v Stevenson* [1932] AC 562, HL. Indeed, the House of Lords did not assume the power to overrule its own decisions until 1966.

Ombudsman complaints

P7.23 *Complaint against Dudley MBC*

06/B/13743, 26 November 2007

Council liable where damage caused by its contractors

Council contractors unnecessarily destroyed three ornamental trees and a rose shrub in a long lessee's garden when replacing a fence. The work was carried out without the lessee's knowledge or consent. The council failed to accept liability for its contractor's actions and told the lessee to pursue her complaint against the contractors. The contractors offered her £200 compensation. The ornamental trees had matured for 25 years and the replacement cost had been estimated at £3,250.

The ombudsman found the council liable for its contractor's actions and recommended that it compensate the lessee for the damage caused and a sum of £250 for the time and trouble in pursuing her complaint. How the council wished to apportion between itself and its contractors was a matter for itself and the contractors. The council's buck-passing was unacceptable.

P8   Defective Premises Act 1972

Work undertaken on dwellings: s1 provides that:

> A person taking on work for or in connection with the provision of a dwell-ing ... owes a duty ... to see that the work which he takes on is done in a workman-like or ... professional manner, with proper materials and so as regards that work, the dwelling shall be fit for habitation when completed.

Duty to take reasonable care to avoid personal injury or damage to property: s4 provides:

> (1) Where premises are let under a tenancy which puts on the landlord an obligation to the tenant for the maintenance or repair of the premises, the landlord owes to all persons who might reasonably be expected to be affected by defects in the state of the premises a duty to take such care as is reasonable in all the circumstances to see that they are reason-ably safe from personal injury or from damage to their property caused by a relevant defect.
>
> (2) The said duty is owed if the landlord knows (whether as the result of being notified by the tenant or otherwise) or if he ought in all the cir-cumstances to have known of the relevant defect.
>
> (3) ... 'relevant defect' means a defect in the state of the premises ... aris-ing from, or continuing because of, an act or omission by the landlord which constitutes or would if he had had notice of the defect have con-stituted a failure by him to carry out his obligation to the tenant for the maintenance or repair of the premises; ...

P9   *Defective Premises Act 1972 s1*

Court of Appeal

P9.1   *Alderson v Beetham Organisation Ltd*
[2003] EWCA Civ 408; 2 April 2003

Limitation period under s1 extended where works undertaken to rectify damage

The claimants bought long leases of basement flats in the defendant's residential development, which was completed in 1994. They complained of damp and remedial works were undertaken. The works did not pre-vent the damp. In 1995 a chartered surveyor reported that the flats had been constructed in breach of the Defective Premises Act 1972 in that the below-ground accommodation did not have adequate damp proofing. The claimants took no legal action until January 2001. Their claim was that the respondent was in breach of the duty owed to them under the Defective Premises Act 1972 s1. The defendant applied to strike out on the basis that the cause of action accrued on completion of the dwelling in 1994 and that the claim commenced in January 2001 was accordingly statute-barred since it was commenced more than six years after accrual of the cause of action. The claimants relied on s1(5), which provides that any cause of action in respect of a breach of the duty imposed by s1 should be deemed to have accrued at the time when the dwelling was completed, but that, if after that time a person did further work to rectify the work he had already done, any such cause of action in respect of that further work accrued at the time when the further work was finished. The judge granted the application.

The Court of Appeal allowed the claimant's appeal. Parliament intended that there should be a fresh cause of action for breach of the duty to provide a dwelling fit for habitation when further work did not rectify the original defect as intended. The action was only in respect of that further work, but the further work was for the purpose of rectifying the original work carried out in breach of duty. The claimants' action was in respect of the work carried out in 1995 and therefore the six-year limitation period in the proviso to s1(5) had not expired when the action was brought.

P9.2   *Andrews v Schooling*

[1991] 1 WLR 783; [1991] 3 All ER 723; (1991) 23 HLR 316, CA

Section 1 breached where failure to carry out necessary works when constructing premises

The landlords converted a house and let out the separate flats. The tenant of the ground-floor flat complained of dampness permeating from the cellar below. The landlords denied any liability under Defective Premises Act 1972 s1 because they had undertaken no works to the cellar. It was held on an application for an award of interim damages that s1 applies to both damage caused by the actual work and damage caused by failure to undertake necessary works.

See also *Mirza v Bhandal* August 1999 *Legal Action* 24, QBD.

County courts

P9.3   *Tillott v Jackson*

[1999] 5 CL 530, Birmingham County Court

Section 1 does not apply to fixtures added to property after it was built

The defendant sold a house to the plaintiff. Soon after the sale was completed the purchaser alleged that the boiler, which had been fitted long after the construction of the house, had been negligently installed by the defendant's agent.

HHJ Durman dismissed the claim. Defective Premises Act 1972 s1 does not apply to fixtures added to a property after it was built.

P10   *Defective Premises Act 1972 s4*

Court of Appeal

P10.1   *Adams v Rhymney Valley DC*

(2001) 33 HLR 446, CA

Council not in breach of duty of care in installing windows according to standards at time of installation

The council installed double-glazing with locks that had removable keys rather than button locks. The claimant tenant's family kept the windows locked as a safety measure and hung the key in the kitchen. In the course of a fire, the family was unable to escape through the locked windows and three children died. The council owed a duty of care because they had fitted the windows (*Rimmer v Liverpool CC* (P7.13)). The claimant took proceedings for damages for negligence and breach of statutory duty.

The Court of Appeal held that the landlord was not in breach of duty. The council was to be judged according to the standards of the reasonably skilful window designer and installer at the date of installation. At the time of installation button locks and key locks were not negligent choices for window security. There was no breach in opting for one rather than the other. The design of the windows did not oblige the local authority to install a smoke alarm.

P10.2 **Alker v Collingwood Housing Association**

[2007] EWCA Civ 343; [2007] HLR 29; [2007] L&TR 23; 7 February 2007, CA

A duty to maintain and repair did not encompass a duty to make property safe

The claimant was a tenant of the defendant landlord. Her front door contained a glass panel. When having difficulties opening the door one day she pushed the glass panel with her hand. The glass broke and she received serious injuries to her forearm. A clause in the tenancy agreement required the claimant to grant entry to her landlord to inspect and carry out repairs and improvements. A repairing covenant included the provision that her landlord must keep the property 'in good condition'. The claimant made a claim for breach of Landlord and Tenant Act 1985 s11 and breach of statutory duty under Defective Premises Act 1972 s4.

In the county court, Recorder Clayton QC found that: the glass panel in the door was not safety glass but ordinary annealed glass; it was not broken or in disrepair; the use of ordinary annealed glass in doors presents a safety hazard and that had been understood since at least 1963; the property had been constructed in accordance with the building regulations in existence at the time. He held that the landlord was not on actual notice of any disrepair to the front door and dismissed the claim under s11 but held the landlord liable for breach of the statutory duty of care under s4. The landlord appealed.

The Court of Appeal allowed the appeal. The issue was whether the state of the glass panel constituted a 'relevant defect' for the purposes of s4(3). The glass panel was not in disrepair. The court rejected the claimant's submission that it was nevertheless a relevant defect because it was dangerous and the obligation to maintain and to keep in good condition included an obligation to make the property safe. A duty to repair, maintain or keep in good condition did not equate to a duty to put in a safe condition. A property may offer many hazards, but s4 does not necessarily require a landlord to make safe a dangerous feature. Parliament, when enacting the Defective Premises Act 1972, chose to link the duty of care imposed by s4(1) to the landlord's failure to carry out an obligation 'for the maintenance or repair' of the premises rather than link the duty of care to a failure to remedy defects in any more general sense.

P10.3 **Boateng v Camden LBC**

July 2001 *Legal Action* 22, 17 March 2000, CA

Landlord not liable for burns to baby caused by hot pipes

The claimant, then a nine-month-old baby, fell from his bed and became trapped against hot central heating pipes. He suffered disfiguring burns to his face. He claimed damages for personal injuries which it was alleged were sustained due to the defendant landlord's negligence and/or breach of Defective Premises Act 1972 s4. It was claimed that the central heating system was on constantly and was operating at a temperature some ten degrees in excess of that to which it had been set and that the pipes should have been protected so as to prevent accidental contact resulting in injury.

Nelson J dismissed the claim. A local authority could reasonably assume that the parents of a small baby, able to crawl, would take reasonable care to protect that baby from injury from unprotected pipes. To have the heating system on 24 hours amounted neither to negligence nor to a defect under the 1972 Act. Any excess of temperature could not have been prevented and did not cause the accident. Despite the identical case of *Ryan v Camden LBC* (1982) 8 HLR 75, the local authority had been reasonable to conclude that the risk of injury was so slight that it need not take the step of protecting the pipe work. The court noted that no British Standard Code of Practice required that such pipes should be protected.

P10.4 ## Boldack (minor) v East Lindsey DC
(1999) 31 HLR 41; May 1998 *Legal Action* 22, CA

Paving slab left leaning upright in garden not a 'relevant defect'

A council tenant had been in her new home for only four days when her five-year-old child was injured in the back yard by a two-foot-square paving slab, which had been left resting against the rear wall of the house. The plaintiff child sued for damages for personal injury, which were agreed at £5,000, but the council denied liability. The claim was based on Defective Premises Act 1972 s4 and/or common-law negligence.

The Court of Appeal rejected both claims. First, there was no want of 'maintenance or repair' which could trigger the duty under s4 to prevent harm being caused by a 'relevant defect'. Furthermore, even the express covenant in the tenancy agreement was only to repair the structure or exterior of the dwelling. The slab was simply resting against the rear wall. Even if s4 did apply, the duty under it would be triggered only if the council knew or ought to have known of the presence of the paving slab, and that could not be proved on the evidence. Second, on negligence, the Court of Appeal held itself bound by *Cavalier v Pope* [1906] AC 428, HL, in which the House of Lords had held landlords immune from liability to non-tenants coming on to the premises and being injured by defects. The Court of Appeal decided that this decision still represented the law and had not been overruled by subsequent decisions such as *Donoghue v Stevenson* [1932] AC 562, HL. Even if there were a duty at common law arising from a pre-letting inspection, or responsibility to conduct one, there was no evidence to support a contention that the council's visiting officer had been negligent in failing to ensure the removal of the slab.

P10.5 ## McAuley v Bristol CC
[1992] QB 134; [1991] 3 WLR 968; [1992] 1 All ER 749; (1991) 23 HLR 586; [1991] 2 EGLR 64; [1991] 46 EG 155; (1991) 89 LGR 931, CA

Landlord liable under s4 for damage resulting from defective garden step where implied right to enter for purposes of repairing any defect

The tenant was injured falling on a defective step in the rear garden. Under the tenancy agreement, the tenant was expressly required to 'give the council's agents and workmen all reasonable facilities for entering upon the premises at all reasonable hours for any purposes which may from time to time be required by the council'.

The Court of Appeal held that this led to the proper inference of an implied right to enter for the purpose of repair to remedy any defects which might cause injury to lawful visitors or to the tenant himself. Accordingly, the council owed a duty of care in respect of the whole premises. As it had known of the defective step and not repaired it, it was in breach of duty.

P10.6   **Morley v Knowsley BC**
May 1998 *Legal Action* 22, CA

Landlord ought to have known of defect by carrying out a pre-letting inspection

The tenant moved into her council home, a two-storey house, on 21 November 1994. On 23 December 1994 she fell down the stairs because a piece of wood broke off the leading edge of one of the steps. She brought an action for personal injury damages. Assistant Recorder Knopf awarded damages of £2,500 under Defective Premises Act 1972 s4 (including interest). He held that, given the age of the house and the fact that the accident happened so soon after the tenant had moved in, the landlord 'ought in all the circumstances to have known of the relevant defect' for the purposes of s4(2). Accordingly, the council owed a duty to take reasonable care. On the facts, that required a pre-letting inspection, including a check of the state of the staircase. The council had called no evidence of any such inspection and could not show that it had taken any care at all.

The Court of Appeal described the findings as 'more stringent than some judges would have made', but refused the council leave to appeal.

P10.7   **Smith v Bradford MDC**
(1982) 4 HLR 86; (1982) 44 P&CR 171; (1982) 80 LGR 713, CA

Landlord liable for damage caused by fall from patio

Mr Smith, a council tenant, fell from a paved patio area in his garden on to a grassed area four or five feet below and injured himself. The patio had been built by a former tenant. Mr Smith had complained previously about its dangerous state and it had been inspected by a council official.

The Court of Appeal held that the word 'premises' included the paved area. As the council had reserved a right to enter and repair, it was liable under Defective Premises Act 1972 s4.

P10.8   **Sykes v Harry**
[2001] EWCA Civ 167; [2001] QB 1014; [2001] 3 WLR 62; (2001) 33 HLR 908; [2001] 17 EG 221; (2001) 82 P&CR 446; (2001) *Times* 27 February, CA

Not necessary to establish actual or constructive notice of defect under s4

The claimant was an assured shorthold tenant. The tenancy was subject to Landlord and Tenant Act 1985 s11 and the tenant was obliged to give access to carry out repairs. In 1994 the claimant was taken to hospital where he was diagnosed as suffering from carbon monoxide poisoning, which was admitted at trial to have been caused by emissions from a gas fire. In proceedings for personal injuries, the judge found that the gas fire and flue were defective as they had not been serviced for a long period. The defendant knew of the need for servicing and the lack of servicing and should have been put on enquiry of the risk of development of defects. The defendant's obligation under s11 was to keep the gas fire in repair and proper working order. The judge held that the landlord was not liable under s11 in the absence of knowledge of the defects, applying *O'Brien v Robinson* (P6.1). The landlord also owed a duty of care under Defective Premises Act 1972 s4. The judge held that the duty in tort was no more extensive than the obligation under s11 and that accordingly, in the absence of actual knowledge of a particular defect, the landlord was not liable. The claimant appealed against the finding under s4.

The Court of Appeal held that the judge erred in equating the task of the claimant as tenant in establishing a breach of duty under s4 with the need under s11 to demonstrate notice (actual or constructive) of the actual defect giving rise to injury. Section 4(3), when defining a relevant defect by reference to an act or omission by the landlord which constituted or would, if he had notice of the defect, have constituted a failure by him to carry out his obligation, showed that the duty under s4 was not to be confined in the same way as the contractual obligation was under *O'Brien v Robinson*. A claimant under s4 merely had to show a failure on the part of the landlord to take such care as was reasonable in the circumstances to see that the claimant was reasonably safe from personal injury. That duty was owed if the landlord 'ought in all the circumstances' to have known of the relevant defect. That was a general test of negligence. There was no express or implied exclusion of the tenant from the category of persons who might be affected. Accordingly the test was whether the landlord by his failure to service the gas fire regularly or at all or otherwise to take steps to check or make appropriate enquiries of the tenant as to the state of the gas fire, failed in his duty to take such care as was reasonable to see that the claimant was reasonably safe from injury. On that test and the judge's findings of fact, the landlord was in breach of duty under s4. The judge's finding of 80% contributory negligence because the claimant knew of the defects in the fire would not be disturbed.

The House of Lords refused leave to appeal: [2002] 1 WLR 2286.

Note: See now duties under Gas Safety (Installation and Use) Regulations 1998 SI No 2451.

High Court

P10.9   *Clarke v Taff Ely BC*
(1983) 10 HLR 44, QBD

Council liable under s4 where it had failed to make proper inspections of property

The plaintiff's sister and brother-in-law were tenants of the council. She went to help them decorate. As she stood on a table to wash down the ceiling, a leg of the table went through the floorboards, throwing her to the ground. The area where the house had been built was well known to be damp and there was no ventilation under the floorboards. Evidence was given by expert witnesses for both sides that, as a result of the manner of construction and the presence of damp, it was foreseeable that floors were likely to give way without notice.

Wood J held that, in failing to make proper arrangements for inspection, the council had failed to take reasonable care to ensure that the plaintiff was reasonably safe from personal injury. Damages were awarded.

P10.10 *Wadsworth v Nagle*

[2005] EWHC 26 (QB); November 2005 *Legal Action* 28

Landlord had no express or implied right of entry to repair defect and not liable under s4

Mr Wadsworth claimed damages from his landlord, Mr Nagle, for breach of his duty of care under the Defective Premises Act 1972 s4. Mr Nagle owned a property which contained two flats, one leased to Mr Wadsworth and a flat above which was also leased. The sealant at the edge of the bath in the upper flat was defective. This resulted in water leaking into the claimant's flat. He complained to Mr Nagle but nothing was done. Mr Wadsworth started proceedings against Mr Nagle for damages on the basis that Mr Nagle had a duty under the Defective Premises Act to repair the leak as he had an express or implied right under the tenancy agreement to enter the upper flat to repair it.

Mr Wadsworth's claim was dismissed both in the county court and on appeal to the High Court. It was held that the lease had to be construed in the context of the relationship between landlord and tenant. Clause 2(5) of the upper flat lease obliged the lessee to pay all costs and charges and expenses incurred by the lessor in abating a nuisance at the flat. However, it did not give the lessor an express right to enter that flat to abate any nuisance, only a right to recover the cost of abating a nuisance by entering the flat, where such a right to enter would arise at common law. Clause 2(13) of the lease of the upper flat permitted the lessor to enter the flat for the purposes of 'laying down, maintaining, repairing and testing drainage, gas and water pipes and electric wires and cable and for similar purposes'. These purposes did not include repairing bath sealant, as that was not similar to the other purposes listed in clause 2(13). The sealant had a connection with water but that was all, and entry for the purpose of repairing the bath sealant alone was not covered by clause 2(13).

County courts

P10.11 *Harman v Greenwich LBC*

August 1999 *Legal Action* 24, Woolwich County Court

Landlords ought to have known of defects in roof despite no notice being given

A tenant was injured by slipping on a puddle of rainwater which had accumulated on his kitchen floor. The source was a defective flat roof. The landlords did not know of, and had been given no notice of, the defect. On the issue of whether they 'ought to have known' the tenant led expert evidence that given the type of roof, the roof covering and the age of the roof, any reasonable property owner would have realised that it was well beyond the point at which it could be relied on and that it was vulnerable to fail. The landlords owned 33,000 properties and operated a responsive repairs service when defects were reported. They had no systematic programme for the inspection of their stock or the older stock in particular.

HHJ Gibson held (1) the landlords ought on the evidence reasonably to have known of the defects, (2) accordingly they owed a duty of care, (3) the extent of the landlord's resources (or lack of them) was a relevant factor in determining whether 'reasonable' care had been taken, but (4) so was the fact that the tenant was blind. In the particular circumstances the landlords had not taken reasonable care. The occasion of a letting to a blind person ought to have prompted the replacement (or at least thorough inspection) of a worn-out roof. The judge rejected a contention that, where the tenant was blind and known to be so by the landlord, the implied contractual requirement that the landlord should have knowledge or notice of the defect was modified or disapplied. He held that, if the case of a blind person provided an exception from the general rule, 'an infinite variety of tenant's circumstances might be deployed in an attempt to circumvent' it.

Civil proceedings

P11   Damages

The basic principle in awarding damages in both contract and tort is to put a person, so far as money can do so, in the position he or she would have been in had they not suffered the wrong. Principles such as causation of damage, remoteness of damage, mitigation of loss and contributory negligence need to be considered.

General damages may include claims for inconvenience and discomfort, diminution of value and injury to health caused or aggravated by disrepair. Special damages claimed may include the value of belongings or furniture damaged or ruined, the cost of rectifying the disrepair, including the cost of redecorating, the additional cost of heating damp premises, the cost of alternative accommodation if the tenant moves out, etc.

It is important when relying on previous awards of compensation to update the amount to account for inflation. A table of the latest retail price indices is available at www.statistics.gov.uk (use quick link 'virtual bookshelf', 'economy', 'focus on consumer price indices' and download the latest guide. The required table is under Consumer price inflation – RPI long run series (Table 5.1)).

$$\text{Updated current value} = £[\text{old value}] \times \frac{\text{Later date index}}{\text{Earlier date index}}$$

So £1,000 awarded in 1990 was, in 2006, the equivalent of £1,000 x 781.5 (annual average RPI in 2006) divided by 497.5 (annual average RPI in 1990), ie £1,570.85. Monthly RPI figures are also available on the table.

Court of Appeal

P11.1   *Ahmed v Southwark LBC*
(1999) 31 HLR 286, CA

Arbitration tribunal could not revisit decision on liability when later assessing damages

The council's tenancy agreement provided that disputes about alleged breaches of the agreement could be referred to an arbitration tribunal operated by the council. In 1991 tenants complained about disrepair to the bedroom, which comprised an area above the window that needed replastering, defects to the window and condensation dampness. In 1995 the tribunal ordered the authority to rectify all defects within 28 days. The council failed to do this. The tenants applied for compensation in the county court for the delays in carrying out repairs. The application was remitted to the tribunal. The tribunal awarded compensation for the disrepair to the window, but decided that the council had not been in breach of the covenant in respect of condensation dampness.

The Court of Appeal allowed the tenants' appeal. At the second hearing the tribunal could not go behind the finding at the first hearing that the council had been in breach of contract and find that there was no breach. At the second hearing the tribunal was simply concerned with assessing the compensation which was due as a consequence of the breach.

P11.2   *Berryman v Hounslow LBC*
(1998) 30 HLR 567, CA

Council's failure to maintain lift did not make it liable for tenant's injury on stairs

In breach of an express covenant, the council failed to maintain the lifts in an 18-storey block of flats. As a result, the lifts broke down and were immobilised. The plaintiff tenant was forced to use the stairs and stumbled and fell, suffering serious personal injury. She was awarded damages of over £25,000.

The Court of Appeal allowed the council's appeal on liability. The breach of covenant had immobilised the lift which was, accordingly, 'safe'. The stairs were 'safe'. The plaintiff's stumbling and falling on the stairs was not a reasonably foreseeable consequence of the breach of covenant in respect of the lift. Stairs are an ordinary feature of life and there is no more than a bare possibility of extra or added risk of injury in climbing stairs.

P11.3   *Brent LBC v Carmel (sued as Murphy)*
(1996) 28 HLR 203, CA

Permission to appeal award of damages refused; award not manifestly excessive

The council claimed possession and a money judgment for arrears of rent of over £13,000. The tenant counterclaimed for damages for disrepair and pleaded a set-off. At trial the council abandoned its claim for possession and £3,858 of the rent claim (which was a charge for heating which had not in fact been provided). HHJ Charles QC found that the tenant had first complained of dampness and a defective central heating system in 1981.

The condition of her home 'became progressively worse and from 1986 onwards was appalling and intolerable'. The home was so cold and damp that the tenant and her two children had to sleep in outdoor clothes. For part of that time they had to share one bedroom. He awarded: (a) damages for discomfort and inconvenience of £1,000 per annum from 1981 to 1986 and £1,500 per annum from 1987 to 1993 (£14,000 in all); (b) damages for loss of value of the premises assessed at 30 per cent of the rent for 1986/87 and 50 per cent from 1988 to 1993 (leaving the council rent claim worth only £1,570); and (c) special damages of £19,320 with interest at 13.5 per cent from 1986 to trial. After setting-off and extinguishing the rent claim, the tenant obtained judgment on the counterclaim for £50,004.

The Court of Appeal refused the council's application for leave to appeal. Roch LJ stated that there was 'no reasonable prospect of a successful appeal'. The award was 'not wrong in principle or manifestly excessive'.

P11.4   *Calabar Properties Ltd v Stitcher*

[1984] 1 WLR 287; [1983] 3 All ER 759, (1983) 11 HLR 20; (1983) 268 EG 697, CA

Damages for dimunition in value of flat not appropriate where repairs to be carried out

In October 1975 Mrs Stitcher bought the long lease of a flat in a block of flats with the intention of living there permanently. In January 1976 she complained that, in breach of the landlords' repairing covenant, rainwater was penetrating the flat and causing damage. Apparently ignoring the contents of their own expert's report, the landlords took the view that they had no responsibility and failed to carry out the necessary repairs. The dampness affected Mr Stitcher's health and he suffered from bronchitis and pleurisy. In January 1981 the flat became uninhabitable and the Stitchers moved out temporarily into rented accommodation. The landlords sued for arrears of ground rent (£100 per annum) and service charges, and the tenant counterclaimed for damages for breach of repairing obligations. An official referee found that the damage to the flat was due to the breach of the landlords' repairing obligations. He awarded damages of (a) £4,606.44, being the cost of making good and redecorating the flat, plus 10 per cent for supervision, plus VAT, and (b) £3,000 for 'disappointment, discomfort, loss of enjoyment, and bouts of ill health' which Mr Stitcher had suffered. The landlord did not appeal against the finding of liability or the quantum of damages. Mrs Stitcher, however, appealed against the refusal of the official referee to make an award in respect of (a) the rates, rent and running costs, including the service charges, during the period when the flat was uninhabitable and (b) further damages for diminution in the capital or rack rental value of the flat.

The Court of Appeal dismissed her appeal. The running costs were not recoverable because they were 'a necessary consequence of retaining the lease of the flat and would have been offset by the outgoings included in the award for alternative accommodation if that had been claimed' (no claim for the cost of alternative accommodation was pleaded, but the Court of Appeal indicated that such costs could have been recovered if they had been pleaded). Damages for diminution in capital value were not recoverable because the lessee had not acquired the premises with the intention of reselling and there would be no long-term diminution in value when the disrepair had been rectified. Griffiths LJ stated:

> The object of awarding damages against a landlord for breach of his coven-
> ant to repair is not to punish the landlord but, so far as money can, to
> restore the tenant to the position he would have been in had there been no
> breach. This object will not be achieved by applying one set of rules to all
> cases regardless of particular circumstances of the case. The facts of each
> case must be looked at carefully to see what damage the tenant has suf-
> fered and how he may be fairly compensated by a monetary award. ([1983]
> 3 All ER at 768)

P11.5   *Chiodi v De Marney*
(1989) 21 HLR 6; [1988] 2 EGLR 64; [1988] 41 EG 80, CA

General damages of £30 pw (where rent was £8 pw) not disturbed on appeal

The tenant, Miss De Marney, was a statutory tenant by succession. She rented a flat consisting of a living room, a bedroom, and a kitchen with shared use of a bathroom. She was aged 32. A fair rent of £8 per week was registered. Miss De Marney complained about disrepair in October 1980 and stopped paying rent later the same year. There were several items of disrepair. An Ascot water heater broke down, with the result that there was no hot water supply to the bathroom. A disintegrating bedroom window was not replaced and panes of glass fell from it. Water penetration through holes in the roof caused electrical wiring to deteriorate. Ceilings fell in, and there was rubble in the bath. As a consequence, Miss De Marney's arthritis was exacerbated and she suffered colds and influenza. In 1981 a Public Health Act notice was served and in September 1983 Miss De Marney was rehoused temporarily by the local authority while works were carried out in default. She moved back into the flat in March 1985. Later in the year the landlord's personal representatives brought proceedings alleging rent arrears and Miss De Marney counterclaimed for breach of repairing obligations. A recorder sitting at West London County Court assessed damages on the counterclaim under three heads:

1) general damages for inconvenience and distress at the rate of £30 per week for the period of three and a half years from the date when notice was given until the time when Miss De Marney moved out so that the local authority could carry out works – damages under this head totalled £5,460;
2) special damages for furniture, clothing, decorations, etc, which amounted to £4,657; and
3) damages for injury to Miss De Marney's health, which were assessed at £1,500.

The landlord's personal representatives appealed to the Court of Appeal, but only against the award of £5,460 for general damages.

The appeal was dismissed. Although Ralph Gibson LJ described the award as being 'at least at the very top of any appropriate range of mon-
etary awards for such a case', he stated that the recorder's approach to damages was right and that he had not erred in failing to take account of the rent as a prima facie indication in the level of damages. The award of damages was not 'so high as by itself to indicate error'.

P11.6   *Davies v Peterson*

(1989) 21 HLR 63; [1989] 06 EG 130, CA (see also G24.4)

Award of damages was 'little more than nominal' and increased on appeal

The landlord brought possession proceedings (see G24.4) The tenant not only defended these claims (unsuccessfully), but also counterclaimed for damages for breach of repairing obligations. HHJ Lipfriend, sitting at Westminster County Court, awarded damages of £858, mainly in respect of special damages, but with an award of £250 for discomfort, anxiety and inconvenience. Although there were few specific findings relating to this, it was clear 'to a limited extent in point of time that one of the bedrooms and the living room of this house were uninhabitable because of damp'. This state 'extended over a period of at least 12 months'.

In the Court of Appeal, Russell LJ stated that in 1988 'the sum of £250 must ... be regarded, when awarded by way of compensation for inconvenience, anxiety and discomfort, as little more than nominal'. He did not regard it as a case in which nominal damages were appropriate and, although recognising that the Court of Appeal will not interfere with an award of damages unless it is wholly out of keeping with established authority, increased the award of general damages from £250 to £1,000. He stated:

> It is plain that in this day and age the courts are prepared to award substantial sums to tenants who are the victims of defaulting landlords where disrepair occurs. ((1989) 21 HLR at 70)

Kerr LJ described an award of £250 as:

> ... just the sort of sum which ... should not be awarded, because it is little more than nominal or cosmetic. (ibid at 71)

In the light of the uncertain findings, he agreed that £1,000 was an appropriate figure 'though it might well have been higher'.

P11.7   *Earle v Charalambous*

[2006] EWCA Civ 1090; [2007] HLR 8; 28 July 2006

Assessment of damages based on reduction in notional rental value appropriate starting point

The tenant was a long leaseholder of a top-floor flat. There was disrepair to the roof which resulted in damp and water penetration into the tenant's flat. It was accepted that the landlord was on notice of the problem from January 2000. By March 2001 water was entering the flat in '20 different places'. In December 2002 the kitchen ceiling partially collapsed, at which point the tenant had to move out. He stayed with his parents until the completion of works in September 2004. He brought a claim for damages for breach of the landlord's covenant to repair under the terms of the lease.

Liability was agreed. The county court judge awarded £20,000 general damages for the 35-month period from January 2000 to December 2002 (period 1) when the tenant was in occupation, and £10,000 for the 21 months from December 2002 to September 2004 (period 2), when he lived with his parents. The judge determined a global figure for general damages and cross-checked his awards against a notional rental value of £1,000 per month.

The landlord appealed, contending that it was wrong in principle to base damages on a notional reduction in the market rent where the flat was the tenant's home and not an investment property and the only rent payable was a ground rent. He submitted that the awards (equivalent to £6,800 pa and £5,700 pa respectively for periods 1 and 2) were excessive, particularly when compared to damages awarded in other housing disrepair cases (which indicated a 'tariff' of not more that £3,300 pa 'in a worst case').

The Court of Appeal held that assessment of damages based on market rent was not wrong. *Wallace v Manchester CC* (P11.20) permitted this approach. Furthermore, a long lease of a residential property was not only a home but a valuable property asset. Distress and inconvenience caused by disrepair were not free-standing heads of claim, but were symptomatic of interference with the tenant's enjoyment of that asset. Where the landlord's breach of covenant had the effect of depriving a tenant of that enjoyment, wholly or partially, for a significant period, a notional judgment of the resulting reduction in rental value was likely to be the most appropriate starting point for assessment of damages. That reduction would not be capable of precise estimate but was a matter for the court rather than for expert valuation evidence. The award in respect of the first period was not supported by adequate reasoning and was excessive when viewed against the tenant's own claim. This award was reduced to £13,500. The award of £10,000 in respect of the second period was upheld. The award was just under half the rental value for that period and was not open to criticism in principle. In the addendum judgment (see P6.4), given after consideration of further submissions in relation to notice, the Court of Appeal decided that the landlord should pay 50 per cent of the tenant's appeal costs, given that the tenant had succeeded on all the major issues but the landlord had achieved a significant reduction in the damages awarded for the first period.

P11.8 *Ezekiel v McDade*

[1995] 2 EGLR 107; [1995] 47 EG 150, CA

Damages for living in unsuitable temporary accommodation

The plaintiff bought a former council house, which had been constructed with Bison reinforced pre-cast concrete panels. The purchase was part-financed by a building society loan and the society's valuer negligently overlooked a major structural defect. The plaintiff then tried to sell but a purchaser withdrew once the defect was discovered. The plaintiff fell behind with payments, partly as a result of his inability to sell and partly as a result of being made redundant, and was evicted. He spent almost 18 months with his family in unsatisfactory temporary accommodation until rehoused by the council in a house without central heating. The judge at first instance awarded £6,000 damages against the valuer for discomfort and inconvenience.

The Court of Appeal held that the judge had overlooked the fact that the plaintiff's financial difficulties had started before he had tried to sell but, nevertheless, held the claim for discomfort to be a 'valuable' one and substituted £4,000.

P11.9   *Irontrain Investments Ltd v Ansari*

[2005] EWCA Civ 1681; 15 November 2005

Claimant entitled to damages for loss of rent caused by disrepair

The defendant was a long lessee of a flat. He carried out works to his flat and, as a result, water leaked through the ceiling damaging the flat below. That flat was rented out by the claimant lessor on an assured shorthold tenancy. The claimant claimed breach of covenant to keep the flat in good repair and maintenance, and in tort for breach of duty. It sought damages for the damage caused to the flat and for loss suffered as a result of the tenants of the flat making a reduced payment of rent due to the quality of the flat. A judge found for the claimant and the defendant appealed.

The Court of Appeal dismissed the lessor's appeal. Following *Ehlmer v Hall* (1993) EG 115 the lessor was entitled to claim damages to recover the loss in rent payable by the tenants below as a result of the damage caused to the flat by the lessee's negligence, or the negligence of his agents.

P11.10   *Lavimizadeh v Lambeth LBC*

August 1999 *Legal Action* 25, CA

Once glass in window broken, risk of injury was reasonably forseeable

At the end of May 1994 the tenant's wife reported to the landlords by telephone that the glass in a strip of window of their flat had broken and needed repair. The council responded that the item was in a 'Priority 3' category and would be repaired within 28 days. On 26 July 1994 the tenant tripped on his balcony and fell, lacerating his right wrist and hand on the broken strip of glazing. He had been permanently disabled by the injury and unable to work since. HHJ Butter QC found the council liable in contract and tort and held that, once a report of broken glass in a domestic dwelling had been made, it was reasonably forseeable that there might be a risk of injury. He reduced damages by 40% on account of contributory negligence (carelessly tripping), producing £54,500 including interest.

On appeal, the landlords contended that the judge had erred on causation. Their expert evidence suggested that, even if the glass had not already been broken, the impact of a fall would still have shattered it and caused injury. The Court of Appeal dismissed the appeal. The expert evidence was based on a factual premise as to the manner of the fall and the likely impact on the glass. The judge had been entitled to make his own assessment of the facts on all the evidence. His implicit finding that undamaged glass would probably not have been broken by the particular fall or would have caused a less serious injury would not be disturbed.

P11.11   *Lubren v Lambeth LBC*

(1988) 20 HLR 165, CA

Offers of alternative accommodation did not affect damages

The condition of the tenant's accommodation started to deteriorate from 1979 and by 1984 had become 'appalling'. Two offers of alternative accommodation were made by the local authority but refused by the tenant. A county court judge awarded: (a) special damages of £500; (b) general damages for the period from 1979 to 1984 of £4,000 (ie, £800 per annum); and (c) general damages of £500 for the period from October 1984 to the end of 1985 when the tenant was living in temporary accommodation while the landlords repaired her home. The local authority did not appeal against the award of special damages, but did appeal against the award of general damages.

The appeal was dismissed. Parker LJ stated that the fact that offers of alternative accommodation were made but not taken up 'cannot ... affect the question of damages'.

P11.12 *Marshall v Rubypoint Ltd*
(1997) 29 HLR 850; [1997] 1 EGLR 69; [1997] 25 EG 142, CA

Landlord liable for burglary resulting from failure to repair communal front door

A flat was repeatedly burgled by intruders breaking through a common front door and then an internal door leading to the flat. The landlords admitted breach of an express repairing covenant in relation to the common front door but denied liability for the loss. They claimed that the forcing of the internal door was a 'novus actus interveniens' and/or the resultant loss was too remote from the breach of covenant.

The Court of Appeal upheld the trial judge's finding in favour of the tenant. The nature of the building, the visible disrepair and the admitted breach of covenant entitled the judge to find that criminal damage after forced entry through the defective front door was a 'not unlikely' consequence. A door which is obviously broken and dilapidated is an invitation to would-be burglars. The forcing of the main door was, as a matter of common sense, a substantial cause of the eventual loss, even though the most proximate cause was the forcing of the inner door. *Stansbie v Trowman* [1948] 2 KB 528, CA, was followed and applied – an attempt to distinguish it as a 'one-door' case failed. A burglar who has gained access through the main front door is out of sight of passers-by and more likely to force an internal door.

P11.13 *McGreal v Wake*
(1984) 13 HLR 107; (1984) 269 EG 1254, CA

Landlord liable to clear up and redecorate after repairs; alternative accommodation

The house which the plaintiff rented was in disrepair, but no notice of the disrepair was given to the landlord until the local authority served a notice under Housing Act 1957 s9(1A) (subsequently Housing Act 1985 s190, see now Housing Act 2004 Part 1) in November 1979. Notwithstanding the service of the statutory notice, the landlord did not carry out any repairs. The local authority carried out works in default. In order to facilitate this, the plaintiff moved out of the house for 15 weeks into rented accommodation where she paid £10 per week. She continued to pay rent and rates on the house. She spent £127.50 in arranging for furniture and carpets to be stored and £30 to have her carpets refitted. The council, although it completed repairs, did not carry out any decorative work and the plaintiff spent £608.51 decorating after completion of repairs. She claimed these sums from the landlord, together with general damages for having to live in a house which was less habitable and pleasant than would have been the case had the landlord carried out his repairing obligations. Her claim was dismissed by a county court judge.

The Court of Appeal allowed her appeal and remitted the case to the county court judge for damages to be assessed. The Court of Appeal indicated that there was no breach of covenant by a landlord until expiration of a reasonable time for putting the house into adequate repair. In view of the local authority's notice, it concluded that such time had expired by 1 January 1980. For the following seven months the plaintiff was either living in an unrepaired house or living in alternative accommodation. Damages for such inconvenience could not 'be described as "negligible"'. The Court of Appeal stated that the plaintiff was entitled to recover the cost of re-decorating even though the tenancy agreement contained no obligation to decorate on the landlord's part. She should also be compensated for the work of clearing up debris and cleaning up after the completion of building works. She was also entitled to the cost of renting alternative accommodation and storing furniture.

P11.14   *Minchburn v Peck*
(1988) 20 HLR 392; [1988] 1 EGLR 53, CA

Damages reduced because of tenant's failure to give notice

A 99-year lease contained very wide repairing covenants on the landlord's part. There was no requirement that the tenant give notice of the particular defects that existed. However, there was a possibility that the landlord would have carried out works earlier if notice had been given.

The Court of Appeal decided that some allowance should be given by way of mitigation and reduced general damages for discomfort and dampness from £800 to £700.

P11.15   *Mira v Aylmer Square Investments Ltd*
(1990) 22 HLR 182; [1990] 1 EGLR 45; [1990] 22 EG 61, CA

Loss of rental income due to premises being in disrepair forseeable

The freeholders of three blocks of flats entered into an agreement with developers to construct new penthouse flats in the roof apexes above existing flats. Tenants and long lessees of top floor flats suffered from holes being made in ceilings, ingress of water and physical damage to furniture, carpets and other property. There were also problems of dust, dirt, noise, loss of privacy, interference with television reception, deterioration of the common parts and general inconvenience. The tenants and long lessees brought proceedings for, among other things, breach of repairing covenants and breach of the covenant for quiet enjoyment. The defendants agreed a scale of general damages using a benchmark of £2,000 per annum per top floor lessee, with additional sums where residents' health had been adversely affected, but with reductions where inconvenience was less. However, the defendants did not concede that those long lessees, who would have sublet their flats had it not been for the breaches of covenant,

were entitled to recover sums equal to the rent which they would have
received from subletting less deductions for outgoings and tax.

After reviewing cases on damages for breach of covenant, including
Lock v Furze (1866) LR 1 CP 441; *Calabar Properties Ltd v Stitcher* (P11.4)
and *City and Metropolitan Properties v Greycroft Ltd* (see *Housing Law Casebook* 3rd edition), the Court of Appeal held that the plaintiffs were entitled
to recover loss of rent. The damage occurring (ie, loss of rental income)
was 'not very unusual and was easily foreseeable' within the first rule in
Hadley v Baxendale (1854) 9 Ex 341.

P11.16 **Niazi Services Ltd v Van der Loo**

[2004] EWCA Civ 53; [2004] 1 WLR 1254; [2004] 17 EG 130; [2004] HLR 34 (see
P5.14)

*Judge entitled to assess damages on basis of notional reduction of high rent
(40%)*

P11.17 **Shine v English Churches Housing Group**

[2004] EWCA Civ 434; [2004] HLR 42; [2005] L&TR 7; (2004) *Times* 2 June

Basic rule of thumb that damages should not exceed rent payable
Mr Shine, a secure tenant, sought damages under Landlord and Tenant
Act 1985 s11. Liability was not in dispute. The only substantive issue was
the amount of damages. The premises suffered from extensive dampness
following a leak beneath a bath which had not been repaired. At trial HHJ
Cotran awarded damages of £19,000 for a period of approximately seven
years, including £16,000 for a period from May 1999 to June 2003. He also
refused the landlord's application for permission to set off an interlocutory award of costs (£1,500) against the damages. The landlord appealed,
claiming that the judge had failed to follow the guidance given in *Wallace
v Manchester CC* (P11.20) to cross-check a global award of damages against
the rent to ensure that the award is not disproportionate, had failed to give
reasons and had failed to take into account the tenant's refusal to move out
of the premises (despite offers of temporary alternative accommodation)
to allow repairs to be carried out.

The Court of Appeal allowed the appeal. Although the guidelines in
Wallace 'are not to be applied in a mechanistic or dogmatic way', and that
there are cases 'where the level of distress or inconvenience experienced
by a tenant may require an award in excess of the level of rent payable' if
an award is made in excess of the rent payable, 'clear reasons need to be
given'. The facts of the case, notably the landlord's conduct, must warrant
such an award. HHJ Cotran's award was manifestly excessive. No explanation was given by the judge about how he arrived at the award. The court
accepted the submissions of counsel for the landlord that the maximum
award should be broadly equivalent to the rental value of the premises.
The court referred to 'a basic rule of thumb that – all other things being
equal – the maximum award of damages should be the rental value of the
premises'. It substituted a figure equivalent to 75% of the rent for a period
when Mr Shine was living in very poor conditions, without a bathroom
and with no gas supply. For a later period of two and a half years, when
conditions were worse, the court took the full rental value, but reduced
damages by 75% to take into account the fact that works would have been

completed within six to nine months if the tenant had co-operated. Damages were reduced to £8,000. The Court of Appeal also held that the landlord was entitled to set off the interlocutory costs against the damages.

P11.18 *Sturolson and Co v Mauroux*
(1988) 20 HLR 332; [1988] 1 EGLR 66; [1988] 24 EG 102, CA

Tenant could claim damages for disrepair despite registration of fair rent

A landlord brought possession proceedings, alleging rent arrears of £2,988. The tenant counterclaimed for breach of repairing obligations. A county court judge dismissed the claim for rent arrears and awarded damages on the counterclaim of £5,895 with interest of £1,250. The landlords appealed, contending that, since a fair rent had been registered by the rent officer under Rent Act 1977 s70, the tenant was precluded from obtaining damages for the breaches of the implied covenant to repair.

The landlords' appeal was dismissed. Glidewell LJ stated that rent officers value premises taking into account not only the condition of the premises, but also the landlord's covenant to repair, which is obviously of value to the tenant. The rent officer would not assume that the covenant would not be carried out.

P11.19 *Taylor v Knowsley BC*
(1985) 17 HLR 376, CA

Damages for loss of hot water not too low in tenant's circumstances

Mr Taylor was a local authority tenant. In 1982, as a result of a burst pipe, he was without any supply of hot water for five months. In addition, as a result of the burst pipe, he was without a central ceiling light in his living room for three months. There was also a leak from the bathroom ceiling, causing dripping and damp for a period of eight months in 1983/84. As a result of the lack of hot water, he had to go to relatives' homes to bath and to the launderette to wash his clothes. In the county court he was awarded (a) £100 for loss of hot water and the absence of the ceiling light, of which £68 was attributed to launderette costs and (b) £59 for the dripping in the bathroom.

The Court of Appeal dismissed the tenant's appeal, stating that the level of damages awarded was 'not so clearly low that this Court should interfere with it'. In particular, the Court of Appeal noted that the tenant was a young man in his 20s with relatives in the neighbourhood. It implied that its decision might have been different in a case of a woman with a young family.

P11.20 *Wallace v Manchester CC*
(1998) 30 HLR 1111; [1998] 41 EG 223; (1998) *Times* 23 July, CA

Damages need not be assessed for both discomfort and diminution of value; fact rent paid by housing benefit irrelevant; unofficial tariff for disrepair

The plaintiff was a secure weekly tenant. Landlord and Tenant Act 1985 s11 and Defective Premises Act 1972 s4 applied. In 1996, a surveyor reported that the premises were in a state of disrepair. In particular, an external wall had partially collapsed, the windows were rotten and the house suffered from a constant infestation of rats. The landlord remedied some of the defects. The tenant began proceedings for breach of covenant against the landlord on behalf of herself and her two children. She claimed specific performance of the repairing obligations and sought damages for diminution in the value of her rent, the inconvenience to her and her children and the ill health suffered by the children. The judge at first instance awarded her £2,000 in respect of the last head and a sum of special damages for her ruined property. For the other two heads of damage the judge awarded £3,500 general damages on the basis of a global figure designed to compensate the tenant for her distress and the inconvenience and disruption caused to her life and that of her children. The judge considered that this was the best approach to take and, in any event, doubted whether he could have made an award related to the diminution in the value of the tenant's rent since she was in receipt of housing benefit. The tenant appealed.

The Court of Appeal dismissed the tenant's appeal. Morritt LJ said:

> First, the question in all cases of damages for breach of obligation to repair is what sum will, so far as money can, place the tenant in the position he would have been in if the obligation to repair had been duly performed by the landlord. Second, the answer to that question inevitably involves a comparison of the property as it was for the period when the landlord was in breach of his obligation with what it would have been if the obligation had been performed. Third, for the periods when the tenant remained in occupation of the property, notwithstanding the breach of the obligation to repair the loss to him requiring compensation is the loss of comfort and convenience which results from living in a property which was not in the state of repair it ought to have been if the landlord performed his obligation ... Fourth, if the tenant does not remain in occupation but, being entitled to do so, is forced by the landlord's failure to repair to sell or sublet the property he may recover for the diminution of the price or recoverable rent occasioned by the landlord's failure to perform his covenant to repair.

In relation to the third proposition:

> ... the sum required to compensate the tenant for the distress and inconvenience ... may be ascertained in a number of different ways, including but not limited to a notional reduction in the rent. Some judges may prefer to use that method alone ... some may prefer a global award for discomfort and inconvenience (*Calabar Properties Ltd v Stitcher* (P11.4) and *Chiodi v De Marney* (P11.5)) and others may prefer a mixture of the two (... and *Brent LBC v Carmel Murphy* (P11.3)). But, in my judgment, they are not bound to assess damages separately under heads of both diminution in value and discomfort because in cases within the third proposition those heads are alternative ways of expressing the same concept.

Morritt LJ considered that expert valuation evidence is not needed when assessing such damages and that 'a judge who seeks to assess the monetary compensation to be awarded for discomfort and inconvenience on a global basis would be well advised to cross-check his prospective award by reference to the rent payable for the period equivalent to the duration of the landlord's breach of covenant'. He also said that the source of the money with which the tenant pays the rent (eg, housing benefit) is irrelevant to the extent of the discomfort and inconvenience suffered by the tenant and what would be proper monetary compensation for it. Counsel had referred to 'an unofficial tariff of damages for discomfort and inconvenience of

£2,750 per annum at the top to £1,000 per annum at the bottom'. Morritt LJ, 'assuming, but without deciding' that there was such a tariff, found that the award of £3,500 for approximately three years of disrepair, did not fall outside it. There was no error of principle which entitled the court to interfere with the judge's award.

High Court

P11.21 *Electricity Supply Nominees Ltd v National Magazine Co Ltd*
[1999] 1 EGLR 130, ORB

Damages for breach of covenant to repair lift could be assessed by reference to rent

In a counterclaim for damages for breach of a covenant to keep in repair (and proper working order) lifts and an air conditioning system, the tenant specifically pleaded for damages assessed by reference to the rent. Whether that was the correct measure for damages was tried as a preliminary issue.

HHJ Hicks QC, having referred to his own experience in the county court, to the reported cases cited with approval in *Wallace v Manchester CC* (P11.20), to *Wallace* itself, and to the notes of cases appearing in *Legal Action*, held that the reason why damages were often assessed for breach of covenant to repair by reference to rent was that:

> ... rack rents are some evidence, and often sufficiently good evidence, of the value of fully enjoyed occupation to tenants. In which case consideration of diminution in that value can properly start from there and may often helpfully be approached in terms of its proportional reduction.

He held that the tenant was entitled to press its claim on the basis of loss of value measured by reference to (although not exclusively to) the difference between the rent actually payable and the rent that would be payable for the premises in disrepair.

County courts

P11.22 *Alienus v Tower Hamlets LBC*
[1998] 1 CL 312, Central London County Court

Damages assessed on finding 50% condensation caused by disrepair and 50% by design defect

Premises suffered from substantial mould growth, severe damp and excessive condensation from about 1986. The plaintiff's expert said that 50 per cent of the condensation was caused by the construction, which included concrete cladding which was unsuitable for the retention of heat, and 50 per cent by long-term persistent water penetration. He considered that the premises were unfit. The plaintiff and his family left in 1993, when the whole block was decanted following a decision to demolish it. The defendants were debarred from calling expert evidence. The plaintiff and his family suffered from asthma. One of his children, whose asthma was severe, was admitted to hospital for a week and his schooling was affected.

Mr Recorder Haines awarded general damages of £1,250 per annum (half of what would have been awarded if the dampness had been caused solely by water penetration), diminution of rent of 50 per cent to the tenant and personal injury damages of £11,000 to the plaintiff's son.

P11.23 *Angelidis and Sellers v Hastereel Ltd*

May 1997 *Legal Action* 20; (1997) H&HI(2) 1:4, Central London County Court

Damages for disruption caused by refurbishment work

The plaintiffs were the last remaining statutory tenants in a block of 16 flats when in 1991/92 the landlords began a programme of refurbishment of the block. Minimal notice was given and the work lasted for 11 months. Only injunctive relief prevented disconnection of the communal heating and hot water system. The tenants alleged that there was: (a) no lift service (their flats were on the fifth and sixth floors) for 21 weeks; (b) no entry-phone for 22 weeks; (c) no TV aerial for 19 weeks; (d) no refuse collection for 40 weeks; (e) no post or milk deliveries for 18 weeks; and (f) through-out the period of the works, noise, failure to clean or light common parts, working at unreasonable hours, lack of security, unexplained floods of water and malicious damage to their property.

HHJ Green QC awarded each plaintiff £7,000 general damages for 'the grossest breaches of covenant' and 'a programme of harassment'. Special damages in excess of £5,000 each were also awarded. No claim was made for diminution in value as the rent officer had already adjusted the rent for the duration of the works (Rent Act 1977 s67(3)(a)).

P11.23A *Arabhalvaei v Rezaeipoor*

January 2008 *Legal Action* 36; 7 November 2007, Central London County Court (see O9.12A)

£188,000 damages for harassment and disrepair

P11.24 *Bavage v Southwark LBC*

[1998] 12 CL 313, Lambeth County Court (see P6.11)

Damages of £1,250 reflecting the distress experienced by backsurge of sewage

P11.25 *Bird v Hackney LBC*

July 2001 *Legal Action* 25, Central London County Court

Damages for disruption caused by works including loss of heating and personal injury (respiratory problems) to children

In 1993 the claimant was granted a secure tenancy in a block scheduled for demolition. The rest of the estate was undergoing complete rehabilita-tion and the block was an island in a building site. Balcony doors and win-dows were ill-fitting allowing in dust and noise. The block heating system was inefficient and often broke down. From December 1996 to February 1997 there was no heating at all. The floor of the flat was holed. There were cockroaches in the common parts. For nine months the block was covered in plastic sheeting which made such a noise in windy conditions that the tenant and her family could not sleep.

Recorder Lawson QC found that there had been a serious breach of repairing obligations under Landlord and Tenant Act 1985 s11 and awarded general damages of £2,500 for the period from December 1996 to February 1997 and damages of £1,800 per annum for the remaining period. He awarded personal injury damages of £2,500 per child for respiratory problems. Special damages of £5 per week for six months of the year were awarded for extra heating costs.

P11.26 *Brongard Limited v Sowerby*

May 2007 *Legal Action* 30, Manchester County Court

Damages of £2,700 pa for over 7 years' disrepair awarded on counterclaim

The claimant sought possession of a three-bedroom house let on a Rent Act tenancy. It relied on arrears of rent of £7,351. The claimant did not serve a notice to quit before starting the claim because it believed that the tenancy was a statutory tenancy following past rent increases. The defendant counterclaimed for disrepair, including defects to the roof, an unstable chimney, defective and rotten windows, a rotten front door, high levels of dampness in the walls of the kitchen, dining room, and two of the bedrooms, water penetration from the roof space into two of the bedrooms and rotten floor joists in the kitchen and dining room. In addition, there had been no gas certificates since before 1999. There was also a small personal injury claim for the defendant's wife who had grazed her ankle when falling through the floor of the kitchen in 2006. The defendant also counterclaimed for the costs of works that he had had to undertake, including the replacement of kitchen units which had been damaged by the damp and rotten conditions in the property. The land-lord had been on notice from July 1999 and had during that time failed to undertake any works at all. The landlord accepted liability and notice but argued that the defendant had refused access for the entirety of the period concerned.

Recorder Clayton gave a money judgment for the rent arrears but found that the possession claim was misplaced as the claimant had not demonstrated on a balance of probabilities that the tenancy was a statu-tory tenancy. A 'cautious' landlord would have served a notice to quit. The possession proceedings were dismissed. (See *Thomas Pocklington's Gift Trustees v Hill* (1989) 21 HLR 391.) On the counterclaim, he found that the landlord had failed in its repairing obligations and awarded the defendant special damages of £8,319 (incorporating the costs of certain works in-cluding the kitchen units) and general damages of £2,700 pa for 7.3 years (October 1999–January 2007), totalling £19,710. The total award of dam-ages (once the rent arrears had been taken into account) was £20,658.

P11.27 *Brydon v Islington LBC*

May 1997 *Legal Action* 18; [1997] CLY 1754, Clerkenwell County Court

Damages for leak in corner of kitchen

Water leaked into the tenant's kitchen pantry from a defect in the bath-room plumbing above. The pantry cupboard was damaged by water and the wallplaster became damp and defective. The tenant kept a bucket in one corner, which was checked daily but three *Times* overspilled during the night. The council's plumbers investigating the leak removed, but did not replace, the bath panel and smashed tiling in the WC. The experts disagreed about the cause of the leak.

HHJ Gibson found the council liable and accepted an undertaking to carry out repairs within eight weeks. He awarded damages of £4,009.56 comprising: (a) diminution in value assessed as a percentage of the rent over a period of three years, ranging from 10 to 20 per cent and totalling £1,508.56; (b) special damages of £15; (c) general damages of £2,250 (spanning three years) and (d) interest of £236.

P11.28 **Clark v Wandsworth LBC**
June 1994 *Legal Action* 15, Wandsworth County Court (see P7.19)

Effect of cockroach infestation considered worse than damp; £3,500 for the physical, mental and emotional effects on family for a period of a year and a half

P11.29 **Conroy v Hire Token Ltd**
February 2002 *Legal Action* 22, Manchester County Court

Children awarded £650 for general coughs and colds over six-month period
The first claimant was an assured shorthold tenant but she left after six months because her landlord failed to carry out repairs to the premises, which were subject to severe dampness and related mould growth. The second and third claimants were her children. They sought damages from the landlord for personal injury arising from breach of the duty of care imposed by Defective Premises Act 1972 s4. Both the children, who were aged under five, had suffered from general coughs and colds over the six-month period. There was no diagnosis of asthma and they had not been taken to a GP or for hospital treatment.

HHJ Holman awarded damages of £650 to each child.

P11.30 **Cook v Horford Investment Ltd and Mohammed Taj**
September 1993 *Legal Action* 16, West London County Court

Damages for disrepair including exemplary damages and amount for works to be done

The flat was in serious disrepair, with water penetrating through the roof and defective windows. Statutory notices served on the landlords were not complied with. On the tenant's claim for damages and specific performance, interlocutory judgment was entered and neither defendant appeared at the hearing.

On the claim for specific performance, HHJ Phelan found that, given the attitude of the defendants, it would be immensely difficult to enforce a mandatory order. It was also impossible to assess the final extent of the works that would be required. He gave directions for the assessment of damages in lieu of specific performance and made an interim award of £11,500 to enable the tenant's surveyor to put remedial works in hand. He awarded the following damages for the failure to repair: (a) diminution in value assessed at 50 per cent of the rent (£1,958); (b) special damages of £2,095; (c) damages for inconvenience etc at £1,500 per annum (£5,250); (d) exemplary damages of £3,000; and (e) interest at 15 per cent on special damages, 2 per cent on general damages; total £13,200.

P11.31 **Festusi Porbeni v Abdellaziz Chaabdiss**
11 September 2001, Willesden County Court

£2,500 pa for 7 years' harassment

The tenant first occupied the flat in 1985 under what was found to be a Rent Act protected tenancy. There were serious acts of harassment, including actual and threatened violence, threats to kill, racial abuse, regular trespass and invasion of privacy, and commencing possession proceedings on a blatantly false basis. These acts contributed to the tenant's depression and the breakdown of his marriage. There was a report about disrepair which adversely affected the safety and comfort of the tenant and his family. The disrepair included rising and penetrating damp, loose and fallen plaster, rotten doors and windows, fire hazards, trip hazards, dangerous gas and electrical items, and broken toilet, sinks and drains. The landlord ignored five local authority notices as well as the expert's report.

HHJ Bevington awarded damages:

a) for disrepair at £2,500 per annum for 7.1 years totalling £17,750;
b) for harassment/breach of covenant for quiet enjoyment at £2,500 per annum for seven years totalling £17,750;
c) aggravated damages of £10,000;
d) exemplary damages of £12,500 (this being described as a 'classic case' for exemplary damages);
e) interest.

The total award including interest amounted to £62,060. The judge also awarded costs on the indemnity basis.

P11.32 *Hallett v Camden LBC*

August 1994 *Legal Action* 17, Central London County Court

Council not liable to repair cracks; £300 pa for draughty windows

A tenant occupied a Victorian house and complained of two items of disrepair: (a) cracks to walls and ceilings and (b) defective sash windows, which had been outstanding for two and a half years. The council defended on the basis that the cracks were minor and could be dealt with by application of filler and redecoration by the tenant and that the windows would be dealt with during cyclical external redecoration.

Recorder Behar held that, having regard to the age, character and prospective life of the dwelling (Landlord and Tenant Act 1985 s11(3)), the cracking was so minor as not to be actionable at all. However, he found the council in breach in respect of the windows, which had caused the premises to be draughty. He awarded damages at a rate of £300 per annum, producing an award of £750. The problem was 'low in the scale of possible defects'

P11.33 *Hannant and Curran v Harrison*

[1995] CLY 1562, Hull County Court

£1,000 for loss of bedroom for six months

As a result of defective workmanship during improvement works, the owners of a bungalow lost the use of their bedroom for six months. During that time they slept in the lounge and were obliged to change in the bathroom. They recovered general damages of £1,000.

P11.34 *Hassib v Hackney LBC*

[2003] 3 CL 281, Shoreditch County Court

Damages awarded by reference to scale guide in Wallace

Mr Hassib, aged 65, was the sole occupier of premises consisting of a bathroom, a bedroom and a bed-sitting room. From December 1999 the premises suffered from high levels of penetrating dampness in all the rooms owing to a faulty roof. In the bed-sitting room Mr Hassib used a bucket to collect water when it rained. The gas central heating system was disconnected because it was faulty and he had no means of heating other than a small electric heater. The premises were cold, damp and unsightly.

HHJ Cotran awarded general damages of £3,600 for three years of disrepair and £872 for the cost of additional heating. He said that, when assessing damages for disrepair, diminution in value was not a very useful method. It was better to have regard to 'the scale guide' in *Wallace v Manchester CC* (P11.20).

P11.35 *Hughes v Liverpool CC*

August 1999 *Legal Action* 27, Liverpool County Court

General damages £2,500 pa for damp that had deteriorated over 6 years to be very bad

Most of the rooms in the tenant's house were affected by either rising or penetrating dampness. Fungus grew on the kitchen wall and vermin, attracted to damp conditions, entered. Dampness had affected the clothing, carpets and curtains over many years. After heavy rain, the water penetration was some*Times* so bad that the tenant had to stay with relatives temporarily.

Recorder Stockdale accepted the tenant's evidence that conditions in the house were 'barely tolerable' but directed himself that conditions would have deteriorated over time to reach their state as at the date of issue of proceedings. He assessed general damages as averaging £2,500 per annum over 6 years. Total: £15,000.

P11.36 *Hyde Southbank Homes v Oronsaye and Obadiara*

November 2005 *Legal Action* 28; 18 February 2005, Bow County Court

£900 for 4–5 months damage to plaster caused by leak from neighbour's flat

The claimant sought possession on the basis of rent arrears. The tenant brought a Part 20 counterclaim for water penetration to her flat which resulted from the tenant of the flat above carelessly hammering a nail through a central heating pipe. The claim was defended on the basis that the disrepair was due to the default of the tenant above.

Recorder Nathan found Hyde Southbank Homes liable for four and a half months of water penetration on the basis that this had caused damage to the plaster, which he considered was structural and, therefore, within Hyde's repairing obligation. He awarded damages of £900.

Cf *Irvine v Moran* (P5.23) on the point about plaster.

P11.37 *Islam v Begum*

[2000] 7 CLD 361, Bow County Court

Damages for no heat and hot water and no carpets, in breach of agreement

For nine months the claimant and her five children occupied a four-bedroomed house let by the defendant. In breach of contract, the defendant failed to provide furniture and carpets, carry out internal decorations or mend ill-fitting windows. Also for about half of the period of occupation there was no heating or hot water. There was penetrating dampness. Halfway through the tenancy the landlord removed the bath, wash-hand basin and toilet from the bathroom and did not replace them.

District Judge Gregory awarded general damages of £2,160 (representing 30% diminution in rental value), £400 for distress and inconvenience and a further £360 (5% diminution) for failure to provide carpets.

P11.38 *Islington LBC v Spence*

July 2001 *Legal Action* 26, Clerkenwell County Court

£1,500 for six months without heating and hot water

In a rent arrears possession case, the defendant counterclaimed for damages for disrepair. For the first six months of the defendant's tenancy of a one-bedroom flat, there was no heating or hot water. As a result he stayed with a friend for three months. Once heating was restored, the radiators failed to heat up properly and the living room gas fire was defective and inoperable. The living room window was defective and allowed drafts to penetrate.

District Judge Stary awarded general damages of £4,250 (£1,500 for the first six months, and £1,100 per annum thereafter).

P11.39 *Joyce v Southwark LBC*

May 1997 *Legal Action* 20, Lambeth County Court

Damages for failure to collect refuse and sleeping difficulties resulting from fear of fire

Joint council tenants claimed damages for breach of express and implied terms of their tenancy relating to collection and removal of refuse. Between 1979 and 1981, refuse from 16 flats was infrequently collected from just eight dustbins stored in a communal back garden. For the next 11 years, rubbish was stored and infrequently removed from an unsecured converted washroom, which was also used by schoolchildren as a smoking area and urinal. Dozens of small fires were started in the refuse, many extinguished personally by the plaintiffs. On one occasion there was a serious fire at night immediately under their flat. For the last two years, the council provided large infrequently emptied 'wheelie bins'. For over 16 years the accumulations of rubbish looked unsightly, smelled and attracted pests. The plaintiffs were prevented from opening their rear windows or using the garden. The council was debarred from defending.

District Judge Jacey assessed general damages at £600 per annum for 16 years and £1,000 in respect of the fear and subsequent sleeping difficulties resulting from the serious fire. With interest and special damages, the total award was £12,250.

P11.40 *Lally v Whiteley*

[1995] CLY 1852, Liverpool County Court

Damages for unsatisfactory temporary accommodation

The tenant of a four-bedroomed privately rented house brought an action for damages for disrepair. Among other heads, he recovered damages of £500 for a period of eight weeks which he had been forced to spend in an otherwise satisfactory one-bedroomed council flat while the works were carried out.

P11.41 *Lambeth LBC v Martin*

August 1999 *Legal Action* 26, Lambeth County Court

Damages for damp and flooding

In proceedings for possession for arrears of rent the tenant counterclaimed for damages for disrepair. She had lived in the maisonette with her four sons from March 1995. Penetrating dampness affected at least three parts of the maisonette throughout the tenancy. Additionally, there was a problem with water building up on a defectively constructed balcony, which in 1997 flooded into the premises. At the date of trial, notwithstanding some remedial work, there was still significant dampness.

HHJ Cox awarded general damages of £4,500 for the first two and a quarter years of the tenancy and a further £3,500 for the 18 months from the flooding to the trial. In arriving at both figures he took into account the rent payable rather than awarding a separate sum for diminution in value. Then, adopting the approach suggested in *Wallace v Manchester CC* (P11.20) he tested the level of compensation against the rent and, finding it equated to broadly 50% of the rent over the period of tenancy, confirmed the award. He also awarded special damages of £1,950 (£455 extra heating costs, £750 for redecoration, £745 for damaged possessions) and interest of £118.33. Total: £10,021.44 (after £51.89 set-off for arrears of rent).

P11.42 *Lewis v Courtney*

December 2006 *Legal Action* 24, Barnet County Court

Damages for 18 weeks of water penetration resulting in severe damp in bathroom

In a possession claim for rent arrears, the tenant counterclaimed damages for disrepair because of water penetration due to a defective roof for an 18-week period.

HHJ Viljoen found that, on the facts (namely, that there had been severe damp in the bathroom but that it had remained usable and some dampness in the kitchen, living room and bedroom), this was not a particularly serious case of disrepair. He awarded damages of 20 per cent of the rent of £1,300 per month. The claim for special damages was dismissed as the tenant failed to persuade the judge that he had suffered any damage to his possessions.

P11.43 *McCaffrey v Lambeth LBC*

August 1994 *Legal Action* 18; [1994] CLY 1635, Wandsworth County Court

Damages awarded to children for personal injury (chestiness etc)

The plaintiffs were three children (aged nine, seven and four). Their parents, the tenants, had already taken proceedings in respect of serious dampness in their two-bedroomed flat and had settled for £9,500, to include the inconvenience suffered by all family members. This second action was for recovery of damages for injury to health. The three children had required no hospital treatment but had each had chestiness and wheezing to varying degrees, requiring medication.

After consideration of the precise suffering and extent of treatment in each case, HHJ Compston assessed damages at £2,700 for the 7-year-old (£600 per annum), £2,475 for the 9-year-old (£450 per annum) and £900 for the 4-year-old (£400 per annum).

P11.44 McCarthy v Khosla

(1997) H&HI(2) 1:3; May 1997 Legal Action 19, Bristol County Court

Damages for ill health where tenant developed a serious depressive disorder

A tenant rented a three-bedroomed flat on an assured shorthold tenancy for nearly three years. Throughout, there was a range of disrepair, including defective central heating, leaking radiators and toilet, dampness in the kitchen, ill-fitting windows and defective electrical installations. In a reserved judgment, District Judge Stuart Brown awarded damages of £8,654 comprising: (a) diminution in value assessed at 20 per cent of rent for the period of the tenancy (£2,238); (b) general damages for inconvenience and discomfort at £750 per annum (£2,062); (c) general damages for ill health of £4,000 (the judge was satisfied that the adverse living conditions had played a part in the development of a serious depressive disorder which only began to lift slowly after rehousing); and (d) interest of £354.

P11.45 McCue v Hemingway

[2000] 12 CLD 392, Central London County Court

Damages for loss of amenity arising from stain on ceiling and fear of collapse after leak

The defendant admitted liability for a leak through the claimant's ceiling. The leak stopped after a few hours, but a stain grew on the ceiling and a settee and rug were damaged. The claimant sought administration costs associated with repair works and waiting for builders. She also sought damages for loss of amenity, saying that she lived in fear of the ceiling collapsing, had very restricted use of her living room and had to move some furniture into her bedroom.

District Judge Lightman held that the claimant was not entitled to administration costs. However, he awarded damages for loss of amenity of £25 per week for one period and £5 per week for another period. The total award for loss of amenity was £106.21.

P11.46 McGuigan v Southwark LBC

March 1996 Legal Action 14; [1996] CLY 3721, Central London County Court

Damages for cockroach infestation

A tenant claimed damages for ant and cockroach infestation and failure to maintain the common parts of a block of flats. Judgment was entered in default of a defence and the hearing was simply concerned with the assessment of damages. From 1986 the tenant's flat had severe ant infestation, especially in the kitchen. There were ants in food packets, clothes, sheets and towels. The council eradicated the ants after about a year. The cockroaches also began to appear in 1986. The council knew that there was a problem in the block but no action was taken. By 1988 conditions had deteriorated and by 1990 an extremely serious infestation existed. The cockroaches were in the fridge, the freezer and the oven. No food could be kept in the house by 1990/91. The plaintiff stopped eating at the premises and always ate out. The furniture had cockroaches nesting in it. No one could sit on the sofa or walk across the living room floor without wearing their shoes because of the infestation. The cockroaches crawled out of the TV and the telephone. The bedding had to be checked every day. On entering the premises, the plaintiff and her daughter would bang on the walls before they turned the lights on. The plaintiff used no heating in an attempt to prevent the infestation from increasing. By mid-1991 the plaintiff began to stay elsewhere, preferring to sleep on friends' floors rather than in her own bed. She became profoundly depressed and then suicidal because of the housing conditions. She was referred for psychiatric assistance. She was offered alternative accommodation in December 1991 and moved at once. She was advised by her new landlords and by her environmental health officer not to take her possessions with her, as they could infest her new premises. The new landlord stated that she would be liable for any infestation at the new flat. She abandoned all her possessions and could not afford to refurbish her new flat to any significant extent. With regard to the failure to maintain the common parts, her case was that during the tenancy she had complained of drug-taking on the estate and the presence of discarded needles which were not cleaned up by the defendant. In 1989 her daughter picked up a dirty syringe and pricked herself. She had to have a hepatitis B injection and after three months an HIV test. This was a traumatic period for the plaintiff.

Recorder Rose adopted the level of damages and reasoning of HHJ Sumner in *Clark v Wandsworth LBC* (P7.19). General damages were awarded as follows: 1986–87, £2,000; 1987–88, £1,000; 1988–89, £2,500 per annum, ie, £5,000; 1990–91: £3,500 per annum, ie, £7,000; 1991–95, £500 per annum (for period without replacement furniture), ie, £1,500. The judge took the tenant's figure of £11,250 for the possessions discarded as the starting point for special damages. He deducted 20 per cent from this figure on the basis that there was some depreciation of some items, but in relation to other items he accepted that there was no second-hand market. The special damages awarded were £9,000. Interest of £3,150 was also awarded under both heads, producing a total award of £28,650.

P11.47 *Mzae v Abigo*

November 2004 *Legal Action* 29; 12 August 2004, Bow County Court

Damages assessed at £4,000 pa

Throughout her tenancy, which commenced in March 2001, an assured shorthold tenant of a two-bedroom flat suffered from disrepair, including dampness, cracked and loose plaster work, water penetration, overflowing drains, mice infestation from 2003, and consistent problems with the boiler from April 2001. One bedroom was unusable because of the conditions.

HHJ Bradbury accepted that the landlord was not acting deliberately or maliciously in failing to carry out the repairs. The judge was referred to the decisions in *Wallace v Manchester CC* (P11.20) and *Shine v English Churches Housing Group* (P11.17) and, in particular, the recommended approach of assessment damages by way of a putative rent reduction. He made a global assessment of damages in the sum of £14,000 where the annual rent was £10,400. This figure equates to approximately £4,000 per annum (or 40 per cent of the annual rent) taking a three and a half year period of liability.

P11.48 *O'Beirne v Lambeth LBC*

July 2001 *Legal Action* 26, Central London County Court

Joint tenants separately entitled to general damages for water penetration

From September 1993 the claimants' converted flat was subject to water penetration through roofs and windows. The kitchen was worst affected. The claimants punctured holes in the ceiling to allow accumulated water to escape into buckets. There was less severe water penetration in both bedrooms, the bathroom, WC, landing and living room. Decorations were damaged and the claimants became ashamed and embarrassed. There were also problems with the boiler.

HHJ Colin Smith QC held that each joint tenant was separately entitled to general damages for inconvenience and distress, but as they were in a relationship and gave each other support, a discount of 20% was appropriate. He awarded damages from October 1993 to March 2000 in the sum of £7,550 and interest for each claimant (total award £17,400). He cross-checked this award by reference to the rent payable and was satisfied that the damages (equivalent to one-third of the rent) were correctly assessed.

P11.49 *Ogefere v Islington LBC*

[1999] CLD 109, Clerkenwell County Court

Damages for damp

In November 1996 the plaintiff complained of rising damp that exacerbated condensation damp. The rising damp spread from the hallway and bathroom to the bedroom and kitchen. The only room not affected was the living room. Plaster and decorations were ruined. Carpets and personal possessions were damaged. In January 1997 a surveyor inspected but simply told the tenant to remove the wallpaper and to redecorate. Despite complaints via the tenant's councillor, the ombudsman and solicitors, no works were carried out. The plaintiff and her young daughter were forced to sleep on the living room floor. In June 1998 she was transferred because of the conditions. The plaintiff suffered from coughs, colds and depression.

District Judge Southcombe awarded damages for (1) diminution in value at 30% of the rent for the first year, 50% for the following six months and 60% for the last year; (2) damages for inconvenience and discomfort of £1,250 for the first year, £700 for the following six months and £1500 for the last year; (3) £750 for the effect on health; and (4) special damages of £1,918. The total award was £8,415 excluding interest.

P11.50 *Pierce v Westminster CC*

[2001] 9 CLD 431; July 2001 *Legal Action* 27, Willesden County Court

Damages for cracks

Subsidence caused the tenant's three-bedroom house to develop cracks to walls and ceilings. The worst crack was 12 mm wide. Daylight could be seen around the lounge window. The cracks made the house cold and plaster fell. The tenant was unable to redecorate and was upset by the worsening state of her home. Although the interference was to the lower end of the scale, there was real disruption to the tenant.

HHJ Sich awarded general damages of between £500 and £1,000 for a period of seven and a quarter years, producing an award of £5,450.

P11.50A *Pirachia v Mavadia*

December 2007 *Legal Action* 30; 12 July 2007, Lambeth County Court

Reduction in registered rent did fully compensate Rent Act tenant for disrepair

In a possession claim for rent arrears, a Rent Act-protected tenant of a three-bedroom house counterclaimed damages for disrepair. The landlord argued that the registered rent reflected the fact that the property was in disrepair at the time of registration, and therefore the tenant had already been compensated and his damages should be nil.

HHJ Welchman, relying on *Sturolson & Co v Mauroux* (P11.18) rejected this submission but held that his global award reflected, in part, the fact that the registered rent was lower than it would have been otherwise because of the disrepair. The judge awarded total damages of £11,425 based on a global figure per annum but had regard to the rent payable at the date of the counterclaim of £133.50 per week. The judge made the following awards:

1) £2,500 per annum for 3.5 years from May 1999 to November 2002 when the property was in a 'lamentable state of disrepair' with severe wood rot to windows, general dampness with mould growth, particularly in the living room, bathroom and one of the three bedrooms, which was unusable. The estimated cost of repairs during this period was £21,000.

2) £750 per annum from December 2002 to December 2005 when works had been carried out so that the overall state of the flat had improved markedly but there were still 'substantial defects', namely some dampness to the living room and to the third bedroom, water penetration to the kitchen door and cracked ceilings. For this period, the cost of repair was estimated at just under £2,000 and the judge used this as a measure of how the situation had improved since 2002.

3) £300 per annum for the 18-month period from January 2006 to July 2007 when there was still some water penetration into the third bedroom and through the kitchen door, but in the judge's view there had been a 'sea change' at the property.

P11.51 *Sarmad v Okello*

November 2004 *Legal Action* 27; 24 October 2003, Shoreditch County Court

Damages for deficiency in heating and hot water and rat infestation

The tenant of a one-bedroom flat above a takeaway restaurant made a Part 20 claim for damages for nuisance and disrepair in a possession action brought by his landlord. He complained of disrepair throughout his tenancy, which lasted from February 1999 to November 2002. The supply of heating and hot water was intermittent for the first three years of the tenancy and, in 2002, the heating broke down altogether. In addition, there was water penetration to the bathroom, hallway and, from April 2002, to the bedroom. From 2001, there was an infestation of rats from the restaurant below, which gained access through holes in the floors and walls.

District Judge Manners found the conditions intolerable and awarded damages totalling £14,250, as follows:

- £2,000 per annum for the intermittent heating and hot water supply from February 1999 to February 2002;
- £1,750 for the lack of heating and intermittent hot water supply from February 2002 to November 2002;
- £1,500 per annum in respect of all other defects between February 1999 and February 2001; and
- £2,000 per annum, from February 2001 to November 2002, when the rat infestation arose.

P11.52 *Shawyer v Hackney LBC*

[1997] CLY 2722, Shoreditch County Court

Damages of £750 for four months where bedroom unusable

In January 1995 a waste pipe in the bathroom of the flat above the tenant's flat caused a leak into the tenant's bedroom. The resulting smell made it unusable. The tenant, who was elderly and suffered from osteoporosis and depression, had to sleep in the living room. Water leaked into the hall. The defendant landlords failed to find the cause of the leak. In April 1995 the plaintiff asked workmen working on a neighbouring property to inspect. They identified the source of the leak and repaired it.

Deputy District Judge Naqvi awarded general damages for the period from January to May of £750 and special damages (for redecoration) of £750.

P11.53 *Shefford v Nofax Enterprises (Acton) Ltd*

December 2006 *Legal Action* 24, Central London County Court

Damages of 50% of rent for extensive damp

Three joint tenants rented a split-level basement/ground floor flat which was advertised as a three-bedroom property. Within a short time of moving in, all three bedrooms became damp and the whole flat started to smell. Three months later the landlord asked the tenants to sign a document confirming that the property was let as a one-bedroom flat, but they refused to do so. They subsequently learnt from an environmental health officer (EHO) that notices had been served before the tenancy prohibiting the landlord from letting the flat as other than a one-bedroom flat. They were advised that the other bedrooms lacked adequate ventilation and natural light and it was the EHO's view that it was inevitable that dampness would occur. After four months the tenants moved out and sought damages from the landlord.

District Judge Gilchrist found the landlord liable in nuisance, misrepresentation, and for breaches of LTA 1985 s11 and the covenant implied in *Smith v Marrable* [1843] 11 M&W 5, namely, that a furnished dwelling should be fit for human habitation at the start of the tenancy. He awarded general damages of £2,750, based on the fact that the tenants had bargained for a three-bedroom flat, but had only received a one-bedroom flat and even that bedroom was in disrepair. The damages awarded equated to approximately 50 per cent of the rent of £1,300 per month.

P11.54 **Southwark LBC v Bente**

[1998] 2 CL 181, Lambeth County Court

£2,500 pa for mid range disrepair

The plaintiff lived in a three-storey, five-bedroomed terraced house with her six children for five years. She complained of disrepair from the outset. The main problems were a continual leak from her bathroom, which caused part of her kitchen ceiling to collapse; water penetration from an outside pipe into the dining room, which meant that she could not use the room; drains which leaked detritus into the back garden for three years; and a dangerous garden wall, which meant that her children could not play in the garden.

HHJ Cox found that the conditions were extremely unpleasant and that the tenant must have been continually frustrated by the council's failure to carry out effective repairs. Although it was not the most serious case of its kind, the premises deteriorated with time. HHJ Cox awarded general damages of £2,500 per annum for five years and special damages for ruined goods of £2,000.

P11.55 **Stone and Stone (minor) v Redair Mersey Agencies**

May 1997 *Legal Action* 18; [1996] CLY 2244, Liverpool County Court

£500 pa for child who suffered chest infections and asthma

A tenant rented a converted upper-floor flat in a Victorian house. For the duration of her occupation (four years) the landlord had notice of disrepair. The rooms were all affected by penetrating damp. The windows were draughty. The banister spindles were missing. The electrical installations were faulty. Drainage problems caused sewage overflows. Both the tenant and her young daughter suffered chest infections and their asthma was exacerbated by the damp.

District Judge Knopf awarded damages assessed at £2,500 per annum for the tenant (£10,000) and £500 per annum (£2,000) for the child. Total: £12,000.

P11.56 **Switzer v Law**

[1998] CLD 380, Southport County Court

Damages for condensation exacerbated by water penetration; order for extractor fans

A landlord brought proceedings for rent arrears. The tenant counterclaimed for damages for breach of the implied repairing covenant under Landlord and Tenant Act 1985 s11, alleging that she had complained about various items of disrepair for more than six years. It was agreed that the flat was affected by disrepair in the form of rotten window frames which allowed moisture ingress, open mortar joints, defects to external gutters and penetrating dampness to the lounge. The principal problem was one of condensation, particularly in the bathroom and kitchen, which was caused by inadequate levels of heating and ventilation and which had led to mould growth and damage to decorations. The tenant conceded that the condensation was not caused by any disrepair to the structure and exterior of the flat, but claimed that the condensation had been exacerbated by the ingress of water through rotten windows. The tenant's expert claimed that, if the cause of the condensation was not effectively dealt with, it would result in considerable damage to plaster, which would have to be hacked off and replaced. He also said that the problem could have been addressed by the installation of extractor fans in the kitchen and bathroom at a cost of £150 for each room.

HHJ Morgan awarded general damages of £5,500 to compensate for the inconvenience and discomfort over a period of eight years (from service of counterclaim to date of trial). He said that the cost of installing extractor fans, set against the value of the premises and the alternative of repeated piecemeal repairs, was clearly one which any reasonable property owner would regard as the obvious and practical course for disposing of the problem of condensation and dampness (*Elmcroft Developments Ltd v Tankersley-Sawyer* (P3.2) and *Stent v Monmouth DC* (P5.18)). The landlord was obliged to install fans as part of his obligation to keep the structure of the premises in repair.

P11.57 *Symons v Warren*

[1995] CLY 3039, Clerkenwell County Court

Damages for disrepair to extractor fan and light in bathroom

An assured shorthold tenant of a flat, paying a rent of £175 per week, counterclaimed for breach of covenant to repair in possession proceedings. For a period of five months the light and extractor fan in the bathroom/WC did not work. The bathroom had no natural light or ventilation. The tenant bathed and shaved by candlelight and odours from the lavatory would not clear, causing inconvenience and embarrassment.

District Judge Armon Jones awarded: (a) 10 per cent of the rent (£17.50) for loss of value – the bathroom was one of five rooms in the flat and the tenant had 'enjoyed' at least partial use of it (100 per cent divided by five divided in half); and (b) general damages at £30 per week. Total: £1,000.

P11.58 *Thornton and Jarrett v Birmingham CC*

November 2004 *Legal Action* 27; 23 February 2004, Birmingham County Court

Damages equivalent to £4,500 pa for severe dampness

Ms Thornton complained of severe dampness and condensation affecting her home, which she occupied with her two children aged 9 and 11, from June to October 1998. She also complained that, in carrying out a modernisation plan, including the installation of UPVC windows and a new kitchen and bathroom, from October 1998 to March 1999, the council took too long to carry out the works and interfered with her everyday life so as to constitute a breach of the covenant of quiet enjoyment. The premises were much improved from March 1999, but some defects remained.

HHJ McKenna rejected the claim that it was reasonable to delay all repairs until the modernisation programme began in October 1998. He found that the works should have been undertaken by the end of July 1998. He accepted that the works were very noisy, dirty and disruptive (Ms Thornton was confined to one bedroom for over three months) but that no specific criticism could be made of the manner in which the council carried out the modernisation and repairs. Applying the test of whether there had been a breach of the covenant of quiet enjoyment as set out in *Speiro Lechouritis v Goldmile Properties Ltd* (O2.15), namely, whether the defendant had taken all reasonable steps to minimise the potential risks, the judge found that the council had breached the covenant. He was not satisfied that the council had taken all reasonable steps: it should have rehoused Ms Thornton, particularly given the ages of her two children, and it was irrelevant that she did not ask to be rehoused. He also found that the council was unable to rely on Ms Thornton's failure to continue to complain after the works were done to avoid liability after March 1999. A claim for damages by Ms Thornton's children, who had suffered no personal injury, on the basis of a breach of ECHR article 8 was rejected. There would only be a breach of article 8 in the most serious cases where a minimum level of interference had been reached. The interference in this case came nowhere near the appropriate threshold.

Damages of £3,000 were awarded for the period from August 1998 to March 1999 (equivalent to an annual award of £4,500), and £1,000 per annum was awarded for the period from March 1999 to the trial date. These sums amounted to an award of £7,667 plus £280 special damages.

P11.59 *Ujima Housing Association v Aboasu*
July 2001 *Legal Action* 26, Willesden County Court

Damages assessed on basis of number of rooms affected by damp; damages for period in temporary accommodation without garden

In a rent arrears possession case, the defendant counterclaimed for damages for disrepair. Her two-bedroom house was affected by damp caused by structural disrepair.

HHJ Copley awarded damages of £1,500 per annum for a period when only the children's bedroom was severely affected. He awarded £2,250 for a period of one year and two weeks when the damp affected both bedrooms and the hall, causing the family to sleep in the living room. He also awarded damages of £1,000 for a period of 22 months when the family was in temporary accommodation with no garden.

P11.60 *Vergara v Lambeth LBC and Hyde Southbank Homes*
August 2002 *Legal Action* 30, Lambeth County Court

General damages of £4,500 pa for bad case of disrepair and nuisance

The tenants, their elderly mother and their two sons, occupied a three-bedroom, ground-floor flat in a converted terraced house owned successively by the two defendants. They claimed damages for disrepair from July 1994 (the beginning of the limitation period). Water penetrated various rooms. Windows were in disrepair. The hot water supply to both the kitchen and bathroom failed for several periods. The living room gas heater was not serviced. When the rest of the terrace was decanted of tenants in 1997, the claimants were left in occupation. The properties had been allowed to fall into a state of dereliction. There was rubbish accumulation and squatting. The drains were blocked and, by 1999, there were vermin infestations, particularly by rats. Both liability and quantum were disputed.

HHJ Cox found for the claimants and described it as the worst disrepair and nuisance action he had tried. He assessed damages on the basis that there had been a progressive deterioration in conditions. He awarded £2,500 per annum for the first three years, £3,500 per annum for the next two years and £4,500 per annum for the final two years. He assessed damages for six months' inconvenience in temporary accommodation at £1,500. The total damages amounted to £25,000 plus £625 interest.

P11.61 ## Wakefield v Lambeth LBC

August 1999 *Legal Action* 25, Lambeth County Court

Damage caused by dog entering tenant's garden through broken fence foreseeable

The express terms of the plaintiff's tenancy imposed an obligation on the landlords to repair 'fences'. In high wind, part of the garden fence, which had become rotten, fell down. The tenant reported the need for repair and was given a receipt indicating that the repair would be dealt with within a month. Many months later, the fence had not been repaired and a vicious dog owned by a neighbour (about which the tenant had earlier expressed concerns to the landlord) entered the garden, bit the tenant and damaged his garden furniture.

Damages (including damages for personal injury and special damages) were agreed at £5,000. The landlords denied liability on the basis that the disrepair did not cause the injury and/or that the type of damage incurred was not foreseeable or was too remote. HHJ Gibson held: (1) on causation, although no one had seen the dog enter the garden on the day of the incident, the gap in the fence was the 'obvious' route for entry and it was not sufficient for the landlords to assert that the dog 'might' have bounded over or burrowed under some other part of the fence; (2) on foreseeability, the function of a fence was not merely 'cosmetic' or to demonstrate the location of a boundary but was primarily to keep things in and keep things out and therefore 'it was foreseeable as a serious possibility that a dog would get through the broken fence and that having got in it would cause damage' (applying *Marshall v Rubypoint Ltd* (P11.12)).

P11.62 ## Walker v Lambeth LBC

September 1992 *Legal Action* 21, Lambeth County Court

Damages for breach of covenant to maintain lift where tenant on 15th floor

The plaintiff was the tenant of a council flat on the 15th floor of a 21-storey block, served by two lifts and a concrete staircase. For a period of 18 months, one or other of the lifts was out of operation and the other was subject to frequent breakdowns. When the second lift was working, it was often commandeered by the council's builders to carry materials for work on site. The plaintiff had on occasion been trapped in the lift and was frequently forced to use the stairs at a time when she had a young child (aged two) and was pregnant.

HHJ James awarded general damages of £3,750 for breach of the implied term for reasonable maintenance of the means of access (see *Liverpool CC v Irwin* (P4.1)).

P11.63 **Yates v Elaby**

November 2004 *Legal Action* 29; 23 March 2004, Manchester County Court

General damages of £1,125 pa for mid range disrepair

Throughout her two-year tenancy, the assured tenant of a house suffered from disrepair, including rotten window frames allowing water penetration, episodes of flooding, dampness, a defective heating and hot-water system and a wood lice infestation in the kitchen.

Recorder Berkley QC found that this was not, by any means, a case of the most serious disrepair, He took into account the facts that the claimant lived in the premises with a young baby but had, on two occasions, confirmed the tenancy relationship by further agreement. The tenant was awarded general damages of £2,250.

Scottish courts

P11.64 **Craig v Strathclyde RC**

1998 Hous LR 104 (Sheriff Court)

Damages for injury on stairs with no lighting

The council was responsible for maintaining lighting in common parts. It was to give priority to complaints in relation to dark staircases and was required to attend to such complaints within 24 hours. The plaintiff, a nine-year-old child, injured his ankle while carrying a mountain bike down a dark stairway. The stairway had no lighting at all. This defect had been notified to the council on a number of occasions during the preceding four weeks. The plaintiff's injuries meant that he was unable to participate in many sporting activities and suffered a loss of movement which was likely to be permanent.

Sheriff I Peebles QC held that there were serious breaches and it was reasonably foreseeable that they would lead to an accident like that suffered by the plaintiff. He awarded damages of £8,000.

Ombudsman complaints

P11.65 **Complaint against Basildon DC**

06/A/13667; December 2007 *Legal Action* 31; 19 April 2007

Maladministration where delay in carrying out repairs

Mr and Mrs B complained that the council took over 19 months to repair roof leaks, rotten windows and the shed at their bungalow. For some of that time, Mr and Mrs B were unable to use their lounge because of the roof leaks. Mr B had severe arthritis that was affected by cold or damp conditions.

The ombudsman found maladministration. There were unacceptable delays in completing the repairs that must have impacted on Mr and Mrs B's ability to enjoy living in their home, which was both cold and damp for at least 19 months. The council agreed the following:

1) to complete the works needed as soon as possible;
2) to review the recently revised and improved monitoring and record-keeping procedures within its repairs team to ensure incidents such as these would not occur in future; and
3) to pay Mr and Mrs B £1,000 compensation to reflect the injustice that they were caused when living in unsatisfactory housing conditions for 19 months longer than they otherwise should have done.

Comment: This award equates to an annual award of £630, which appears to be less than would have been recovered through litigation through the courts.

P11.65A *Complaint against Stonebridge Housing Action Trust*
05/A/7668, 13 September 2006

Award for disrepair included part of solicitors' costs

The tenant complained that the Housing Action Trust (HAT) had failed to identify the source of a roof leak which caused water penetration into her premises for a period of 18 months from August 2004 until January 2006, although ineffective remedial works were carried out in April and November 2005. The ombudsman found that it should have taken no longer than six months to rectify the problem and the HAT's delay amounted to maladministration. The ombudsman approved an offer of compensation of £1,250, of which £750 was to remedy the injustice to the tenant and £500 was to go towards her legal costs, which she had incurred by using solicitors to make her complaint to the ombudsman. The ombudsman questioned whether it was essential for the tenant's solicitors to have embarked on the statutory charge procedure (by applying for public funding to instruct an environmental health consultant) once they had referred the complaint to him in August 2005, but considered it appropriate in the circumstances of this case to ask the HAT to make a contribution towards the solicitors' costs. The award amounted to half of the solicitors' costs, with the tenant being obliged to pay the rest from the compensation awarded to her.

Note: This report highlights the dangers for tenants in pursuing alternative dispute resolution at the same time as having a public funding certificate.

P12 **Set-off and counterclaim**

Tenants may defend claims for arrears of rent by counterclaiming for damages for breach of repairing obligations. In such cases, any damages awarded on the counterclaim may be set off against the arrears and so reduce or extinguish them. Procedurally, a counterclaim is a Part 20 claim within the Civil Procedure Rules and should be filed and served at the same time as the defence, otherwise permission from the court is required (CPR Part 20.4(2)).

It is possible to exclude a right of set-off by agreement but the agreement must be unambiguous. Furthermore, although the Unfair Contract Terms Act 1977 does not apply to tenancy agreements, the more recent Unfair Terms in Consumer Contract Regulations 1999 do apply and an anti-set-off clause in a standard agreement may be struck out as unfair.

Court of Appeal

P12.1   *Connaught Restaurants Ltd v Indoor Leisure Ltd*

[1994] 1 WLR 501; [1994] 4 All ER 834; [1993] 2 EGLR 108; [1993] 46 EG 184, CA

Set-off can only be excluded by an unambiguous express term

A lease provided that rent was to be paid 'without any deductions'. The tenants withheld rent on account of disrepair and, in a claim for arrears, counterclaimed for damages for disrepair. The trial judge separately gave judgment for damages on both the claim and counterclaim but held that the term of the lease must be construed to exclude the tenants' right to an equitable set-off of their damages against the rent.

Allowing the tenants' appeal, the Court of Appeal held that the term was too wide and ambiguous to exclude a right of equitable set-off, which could only properly be excluded by an explicit express term.

See also *Edlington Properties Ltd v Fenner & Co Ltd* (P12.2) [66–75].

See now Unfair Terms in Consumer Contract Regulations 1999 and *Cody v Philps* (P12.11)

P12.2   *Edlington Properties Ltd v Fenner & Co Ltd*

[2006] EWCA Civ 403, 22 March 2006

Tenant not entitled to set off damages against original landlord in claim by new landlord

The assignee of a tenant's original landlord made a claim for rent arrears and insurance premiums, that fell due after the assignment, against the tenant. The tenant sought to set off its damages claim against the original landlord. (This was for breaches of an agreement to build a factory, for the defendant's use, on the land – the factory was built but suffered from significant defects.) The lease was silent on this issue.

The Court of Appeal, after a thorough review of the law, held that the tenant's right to claim damages against a predecessor in title of a present landlord by way of equitable set-off was a personal right, not a right which ran with the land so as to entitle the tenant to claim against arrears that had accrued to the present landlord.

Note: The decision did not rest on the fact that the building contract was separate from the lease. The same principle would apply to disallow a tenant from setting off a claim for damages against an original landlord in a claim by an assignee landlord. See, however, *Muscat v Smith* (P12.6).

P12.3   *Filross Securities v Midgeley*

(1999) 31 HLR 465; [1998] 43 EG 124, CA

Usual limitation periods do not apply to equitable jurisdiction

The defendant was a long lessee. In 1987 the freeholder issued proceedings for arrears of service charges. The defendant counterclaimed for breach of repairing obligations. In 1997 the defendant successfully applied to strike out the claim for want of prosecution. The freeholder applied to strike out the counterclaim on the same ground. That application was also successful, except for parts of the counterclaim which were not time-barred under Limitation Act 1980 s8. The freeholder then served a defence to counterclaim which, among other things, sought to set off the arrears of service charges. A district judge struck out that part of the freeholder's defence to counterclaim under CCR Ord 13 r5 (see now CPR 3.4).

The Court of Appeal allowed the freeholder's appeal. It would be unjust in the eyes of equity for the defendant's claim to succeed if he had not paid service charges. The freeholder was entitled to an equitable set-off. In view of Limitation Act 1980 s36(2), whereby the usual time limits do not affect any equitable jurisdiction to refuse relief, that part of the defence was not statute-barred.

P12.4   *Maunder Taylor v Blaquiere*

[2002] EWCA Civ 1633; [2003] 1 WLR 379; [2003] 07 EG 138; [2003] HLR 43; (2002) *Times* 21 November

Set-off not available where claimant is a manager appointed under LTA 1987 Part II

The claimant was appointed manager of a block of flats by a leasehold valuation tribunal in accordance with the provisions of Landlord and Tenant Act 1987 Part II. He sued for arrears of service charges. The defendant lessee sought to set off and counterclaim for breach of repairing obligations. Recorder Hamlin held that, although there was a connection between the claim for arrears and the breaches of the landlord's repairing covenant, it would be inequitable to allow a set-off.

The defendant appealed unsuccessfully to the Court of Appeal. The purpose of Part II was to provide a scheme for the appointment of a manager who would carry out the functions required by the court. He did that in his own right as a court-appointed official. The claimant had not been appointed as manager of the landlord or of the landlord's obligations under the lease. The manager should, when appointed, 'come in with a clean sheet and be able to collect service charges due from the tenants and use the money so obtained for repair of the premises'. The defendant was not entitled to set off ([2002] 30 EG 135).

P12.5   *Mortgage Corporation v Ubah*

(1997) 29 HLR 489; (1997) 73 P&CR 500, CA (see C2.10)

Tenant could not, after repossession by mortgagees, set off money spent on works which landlord had agreed to reimburse; agreement not binding on successor in title where works did not relate to landlord's obligation to repair

P12.6   *Muscat v Smith*

[2003] EWCA Civ 962; [2003] 1 WLR 2853; [2004] HLR 6; [2004] L&TR 7; [2003] 40 EG 148; (2003) *Times* 12 August

Tenant can set off damages for disrepair against landlord's successor in title where arrears assigned

Mr Smith had been the statutory tenant of a small house for over 40 years. In 1995 the local authority served a repairs notice on the landlord under Housing Act 1985 s189 (see now improvement notices, Housing Act 2004 s11). From June 1995 to February 1997 the landlord's builders carried out remedial work on the house, causing major disruption. Mr Smith withheld rent. In October 1999 the freehold was purchased by Mr Muscat subject to the ongoing disrepair problems. Mr Muscat was assigned the rent arrears. By this time 128 weeks' rent was in arrears. Mr Smith continued to withhold rent. In September 2001 Mr Muscat began possession proceedings based on arrears of rent due both before and after the transfer of title. The judge held that no right of set-off existed at law or, inferentially, in equity against Mr Muscat in relation to breaches of covenant to repair by the previous landlord. An outright possession order was stayed pending appeal.

The Court of Appeal allowed Mr Smith's appeal. This was a case in which the rules of equity must prevail. The view taken by Lightman J in *Lotteryking Ltd v AMEC Properties Ltd* [1995] 2 EGLR 13 was correct – a tenant's right to set off his claim for damages for breach of a provision in a collateral contract which ran with the reversion was exercisable not merely against the person entitled to the reversion at the date of the breach but also against any successor in title. The successor in title acquired the reversion and the benefit of all covenants contained in the lease subject to all equities at the date of his acquisition. Second, if the law was as held by the judge, it would be asymmetrical and anomalous and would distinguish on no just basis between the tenant who, faced with breaches of his landlord's repairing covenant, could find the money and obtain access to do the works and the tenant who, in the same situation, was forced by lack of means or want of access to put up with the consequences of repair. Rent today is correctly regarded as consideration not merely for granting possession but for undertaking obligations that go with the reversion. Provided that the nexus between the rent and the breach is appropriately close, what the common law recognised as an abatement of rent where the damage had been quantified in expenditure is treated by equity as the potential subject matter of a set-off where the damage required quantification. Mr Smith was therefore entitled to set off against Mr Muscat's claim for damages for breach of his repairing obligations, because the debt, a chose in action, vested in Mr Muscat as assignee subject to all equities which were available to Mr Smith against the previous landlord. These included the previous landlord's liability to pay unliquidated damages for disrepair. The claim and counterclaim were remitted for trial in the county court.

P12.7   *Televantos v McCulloch*
(1991) 23 HLR 412; [1991] 1 EGLR 123; [1991] 19 EG 18, CA

Tenant entitled to set off damages on counterclaim against arrears, resulting in complete defence to possession claim

A Rent Act tenant withheld rent because of her landlord's failure to carry out repairs. The landlord brought possession proceedings based on rent arrears of £2,274 and the tenant counterclaimed for breach of repairing obligations. HHJ Hill-Smith awarded damages of £2,700 on the counterclaim but found the claim for rent arrears proved and made an order for possession. The tenant appealed.

The Court of Appeal, following *British Anzani (Felixstowe) Ltd v International Marine Management (UK) Ltd* (P12.9) held that the tenant was entitled to set off the damages and that she had a complete defence to the claim for arrears of rent. The county court judge's findings in relation to reasonableness were, therefore, immaterial but the Court of Appeal went on to indicate that he had been 'plainly wrong' in finding it reasonable to make a possession order to take effect five months later. The tenant's appeal was allowed.

P12.8   *Unchained Growth III plc v Granby Village (Manchester) Management Co Ltd*

[2000] L&TR 186; (1999) *Times* 4 November; [1999] EGCS 116, CA (see Q2.23)

Anti set-off clause (service charges payable 'without any deduction by way of set-off') effective and UCTA 1977 not applicable to contract for creation of an interest in land

See now Unfair Terms in Consumer Contract Regulations 1999 and *Cody v Philps* (P12.11).

High Court

P12.9   *British Anzani (Felixstowe) Ltd v International Marine Management (UK) Ltd*

[1980] QB 637; [1979] 3 WLR 451; [1979] 2 All ER 1063; (1978) 39 P&CR 189; (1978) 250 EG 1183, QBD

Unliquidated counterclaim can give rise to set-off against claim for rent

In a claim for rent for warehouses which had become unusable as a result of serious defects to floors, Forbes J held that an unliquidated counterclaim can give rise to an equitable set-off against a claim for rent. The fact that a counterclaim for unliquidated damages remains unquantified until an award is made does not prevent it from being used as a set-off. If there is a bona fide counterclaim which exceeds the amount of the plaintiff's claim, the set-off amounts to a complete defence.

Note: approved by Court of Appeal in a number of cases, most recently *Edlington Properties Ltd v Fenner & Co Ltd* (P12.2).

P12.10   *Lee-Parker v Izzet*

[1971] 1 WLR 1688; [1971] 3 All ER 1099; (1971) 22 P&CR 1098, ChD

Tenant's expenses in carrying out repairs in default can be set off against rent

The tenant spent money in carrying out repairs to remedy a breach of the landlord's repairing covenant. The landlord's interest was assigned to the claimant. The tenant, in an action by the plaintiff for rent arrears, claimed to be able to deduct the cost of the repairs from future rent payments. Goff J stated that:

> ... so far as repairs are within the express or implied covenants of the lessor, [tenants] are entitled to recoup themselves out of future rents and defend any action for payment thereof. It does not follow however that the full amount expended by the [tenants] on such repairs can properly be treated

as payment of rent. It is a question of fact in every case whether and to what extent the expenditure was proper ... [The] right can only be exercised when and so far as the landlord is in breach and any necessary notice must have been given to him. ([1971] 3 All ER at 1107)

Note: Another way of analysing the case is to view the expenditure on repairs as payment of rent (see *Edlington Properties Ltd v Fenner & Co Ltd* (P12.2) at para 53).

Cf *Mortgage Corporation v Ubah* (C2.10)

County courts

P12.11 *Cody v Philps*
December 2005 *Legal Action* 28; 4 November 2004, West London County Court

Anti-set-off clause struck out under Unfair Terms in Consumer Contract Regulations 1999

A landlord of residential premises sought to recover rent arrears. The rent was £1,473 per month. The tenant, who had left the premises by the time of proceedings, accepted that rent arrears were ostensibly owed, but counterclaimed for damages for disrepair. The landlord sought to rely on a clause in the tenancy agreement preventing any set-off or deduction whatsoever against rent. The tenancy agreement was a standard agreement used by the letting agents. The tenant sought to strike out the no set-off clause under the Unfair Terms in Consumer Contract Regulations 1999 SI 2083.

After considering the Office of Fair Trading guidance on Unfair Terms in Tenancy Agreements and *Khatun, Zeb and Iqbal v Newham LBC and OFT* (T53.4), District Judge Wright struck out the no-set-off clause on the basis that it failed the test of fairness and was contrary to the requirements of good faith. (See *Director General of Fair Trading v First National Bank plc* [2001] 3 WLR 1297, HL.) It therefore fell foul of the regulations. The judge allowed the counterclaim and awarded damages of £1,500 for the six-month period of occupation. Although the actual disrepair was not substantial, reference had to be made to the fairly substantial rent for these particular premises.

P12.12 *Islington LBC v Keane*
November 2005 *Legal Action* 28; 20 January 2005, Clerkenwell County Court (see P5.27)

Limitation period for disrepair counterclaim ran from date of possession claim

P13 Court orders and undertakings to carry out works

Court of Appeal

P13.1 *Connell v Hackney LBC*
March 1987 *Legal Action* 20, CA (CAT 85/316)

Fine of £1,000 and costs for breach of undertaking

Proceedings in the county court were settled on an undertaking to start works 'no later than 56 days from date of order with completion by 1 March

1985'. The landlord then did nothing. 'A vital memorandum got stuck somewhere in the bureaucratic machinery' and no single responsible officer knew of the undertaking. The council received an indication that the tenant would apply to the court and then sent four wholly inappropriate letters to the tenant, the tenor of which 'left a lot to be desired'. The tenant applied to enforce the undertaking and the necessary works (to the value of £14,000) were carried out before 1 March. On appeal against the penalty imposed for breach, the landlord admitted contempt and apologised.

The Court of Appeal held that, even if the landlord had been incompetent or negligent, there had not been a deliberate flouting of the court's order. The appropriate penalty was a fine of £1,000 and payment of the tenant's costs on a common fund basis.

P13.2   *Mullen v Hackney LBC*

[1997] 1 WLR 1103; [1997] 2 All ER 906; (1997) 29 HLR 592; (1997) 95 LGR 587, CA

Fine of £5,000 where judicial knowledge taken of council's failure to honour undertakings

On 24 July 1994 the council, in proceedings for breach of repairing covenants, gave an undertaking to commence works on or before 1 December 1994 and to complete them by 31 March 1995. The works had still not been commenced by 4 March 1996 when HHJ Graham QC ordered the council to pay a fine of £5,000 in respect of the breach. He noted that it was not 'an exceptional case' but:

> ... one of numerous examples of the failure on the part of Hackney Council to take with sufficient seriousness promises which are made to the court. Time and again in repairing cases undertakings are given to the court which are not honoured, and as a result applications are made to commit.

The council's appeal was dismissed. A judge may rely on his own local knowledge where he does so 'properly and within reasonable limits'. Otton LJ stated that he was satisfied that:

> ... the judge was entitled to take judicial notice of his 'special (or local) knowledge' of how the council had conducted itself in relation to undertakings given to the court in similar cases.

Counsel for the council conceded that he could not maintain that the fine was manifestly excessive.

High Court

P13.3   *R v Wandsworth County Court ex p Munn*

(1994) 26 HLR 697, QBD

Endorsement of penal notice required on mandatory injunction against council

In a disrepair action, the council landlord consented to a mandatory order for repairs but objected to the endorsement of a penal notice on the order itself. The county court office refused to endorse the penal notice on the order.

In judicial review proceedings, Sedley J held that the court staff had no discretion. CCR Ord 29 r1(3) requires the chief clerk, as the proper officer, to endorse a penal notice. In the case of a local authority landlord, he held that Form N77 would need to be adapted and also that it was not necessary for the notice to specify a particular officer.

The matter was remitted and the county court office (on advice from the Lord Chancellor's Department) endorsed a penal notice in the following terms:

> To the [name of local authority]
> If the [name of local authority] neglect to obey this order by the time stated above, any officer of the [name of local authority] may be held in contempt of court and may be liable to imprisonment.

P13.4   *Rainbow Estates v Tokenhold Ltd*

[1999] Ch 64; [1998] 3 WLR 980; (1998) *Times* 3 March, ChD

No prohibition on specific performance in repairs cases

The High Court held that there is no longer a common-law prohibition on the grant of specific performance to either landlord or tenant to enforce a repairing obligation and that *Hill v Barclay* (1810) 16 Ves 402, is no longer to be followed on this point.

Note: However, tenants can in any event take advantage of the statutory provision for specific performance in Landlord and Tenant Act 1985 s17.

P14   Interlocutory injunctions

Tenants who claim for breach of repairing obligations may seek interlocutory injunctions to require landlords to carry out urgent repairs before trial. However, strictly speaking, they ought to be granted only in 'very rare cases' (per Lord Donaldson MR) or 'in the most exceptional circumstances' (per Browne Wilkinson LJ) or as 'an exceptional measure' (per Mustill LJ), in *Parker v Camden LBC* (P14.3).

House of Lords

P14.1   *Redland Bricks Ltd v Morris*

[1970] AC 652; [1969] 2 WLR 1437; [1969] 2 All ER 576, HL

General principles relating to grant of interlocutory mandatory injunctions

In a case involving land slips caused by brick-makers who had been digging clay, Lord Upjohn laid down some general principles relating to the grant of interlocutory mandatory injunctions:

1) A mandatory injunction can only be granted where the plaintiff shows a very strong probability on the facts that grave damage will accrue in future. It is a jurisdiction to be exercised sparingly and with caution but, in a proper case, unhesitatingly.
2) Such an injunction should only be granted where damages would not be a sufficient or adequate remedy if such damage does happen.
3) The cost of carrying out works has to be taken into account.
4) The court must be careful to see that the defendant knows exactly what he or she has to do.

Court of Appeal

P14.2   *Knight v Lambeth LBC*
[1995] CLY 3969, CA

Costs should usually follow event on interim injunction applications

The tenant applied for and succeeded in obtaining a mandatory interim repairing injunction at short notice. The county court judge refused to award her the costs of the application because she had legal aid and the council was a public authority well known to be short of funds.

The Court of Appeal allowed the tenant's appeal and awarded her the costs. It found that there was no reason to justify departure from the usual rule that a successful applicant for relief should have her costs. The fact that she had legal aid was an irrelevant consideration of which account ought not to have been taken.

P14.3   *Parker v Camden LBC*
[1985] Ch 162; [1985] 3 WLR 47, [1985] 2 All ER 141; (1985) 17 HLR 380; (1985) 84 LGR 16, CA

Mandatory interim injunction to be granted in exceptional circumstances

In February 1985 boilermen employed by the London Borough of Camden went on strike. This meant that, when communal boilers which supplied hot water and heating on large estates broke down, Camden Council was unable to repair them. On one estate, 220 properties housing about 1,000 people were without heating and hot water. On another estate, 500 properties were without heating and hot water. Representative actions were brought by tenants on each estate. Camden Council readily admitted that it was in breach of its repairing obligations. Its representatives said that they were doing all that they could by providing electric heaters and individual hot water boilers to tenants but that, if they brought in outside contractors to repair the boilers, the industrial dispute would be widened and far more tenants would be deprived of heating. The two separate actions were heard by different judges at first instance. Scott J refused to order the council to restore the space heating and hot water, but appointed a receiver and manager to receive rents, to manage the properties and to take steps to repair the heating and hot water system. Walton J, on the other hand, refused to make either order. He recognised that the situation was 'pretty catastrophic' and would have liked to have appointed a receiver, but considered that he did not have jurisdiction to do so.

Interlocutory appeals in both actions were heard together. The Court of Appeal accepted that the court's power to appoint a receiver was unlimited, provided that it was exercised judicially. However, it is improper for the court, by the appointment of a receiver and manager who acts as agent of the court, to assume powers and duties which parliament has expressly conferred on another body (*Gardner v London, Chatham and Dover Railway Co (No 1)* (1867) LR 2 Ch App 201). In the case of council tenants, parliament had by Housing Act 1957 s111 (now Housing Act 1985 s21) given local authorities the duty of maintaining such accommodation. Accordingly, the Court of Appeal held that it was wrong to appoint a receiver to manage local authority housing accommodation. The court did, however, state that mandatory interlocutory injunctions may be granted in such cases, but only in rare or exceptional cases, for example where there is:

> ... an undoubted breach of covenant giving rise to actual and immediate major discomfort and inconvenience and to a real risk of damage to health flowing from the admitted breach ([1985] 2 All ER at 149).

County courts

P14.4   *Hooton v Liverpool CC*

August 1999 *Legal Action* 25, Liverpool County Court

Injunction granted where disrepair serious and threat to the welfare of children

The tenant occupied a four-bedroomed house with her seven children. A surveyor's report identified penetrating damp as the cause of saturated wall plaster in the living room and first-floor bedroom. There was fungal growth on the living room wall and the dampness made the property smell 'appalling'. The tenant brought county court proceedings for damages and specific performance and applied for an interim mandatory injunction.

District Judge Frost found the tests for the grant of such relief set out in *Redland Bricks v Morris* (P14.1) to be satisfied. The disrepair was serious and (notwithstanding the absence of specific medical evidence) was a sufficient threat to the welfare and safety of the children who had all been forced to live 'in conditions that one would not let an animal live in'. The council was ordered to do the essential works within seven days.

P14.5   *Sheriden v Broadbridge*

September 1995 *Legal Action* 16, Clerkenwell County Court

Staircase in danger of collapse justified injunction

A landlord accepted that a range of remedial work should be undertaken but did not accept that the works should be subject to injunctive relief.

HHJ Marr-Johnson was satisfied that at least one item (a rear staircase in danger of collapse) was sufficiently serious to pass the tests set out in *Parker v Camden LBC* (P14.3) and so made a mandatory order in respect of that and all the other outstanding works. He expressly held that, provided at least one item justified the making of an order, the injunction should cover all the work agreed to be required.

Public health and environmental protection

P15   Local authority enforcement

Housing Act 2004 Part 1 replaced the housing fitness standard contained in Housing Act 1985 s604 with a new Housing Health and Safety Rating System (HHSRS). The concept of a 'hazard' is introduced, the definition of which is broader that the fitness standard. Hazards are assessed on the effect of a defect, rather than the defect itself. The Act also adapted the enforcement powers available to local authorities. The repairs notice, closing order and deferred action notice contained in Housing Act 1985 and Housing Grants, Construction and Regeneration Act 1996 were replaced by the improvement notice, prohibition notice and hazard awareness notice in Housing Act 2004. Demolition orders and clearance areas contained in Housing Act 1985 were retained, with amendments, as were compulsory purchase orders.

Housing Act 2004 Part 2 contains provisions relating to Houses in Multiple Occupation (HMOs), including compulsory licensing of larger HMOs. The previous provisions in Housing Act 1985 Part XI were repealed. The definition of an HMO was changed as was the regulatory regime.

For an overview of the changes introduced by Housing Act 2004 Parts 1 and 2, see article by Beatrice Prevatt and Marina Sergides in December 2005 *Legal Action* 25.

See section P16 regarding local authority enforcement under Environmental Protection Act 1990.

House of Lords

P15.1   *Pollway Nominees Ltd v Croydon LBC*
[1987] AC 79; [1986] 3 WLR 277; [1986] 2 All ER 849, (1986) 18 HLR 443; [1986] 2 EGLR 27; (1986) 280 EG 87; (1987) 88 LGR 1, HL

Repairs notice served on wrong person a nullity and challengeable in the High Court

Pollway Nominees, a company which owned the freehold of a block of flats let on long leases at low rents, was served with a repair notice (Housing Act 1957 s9, subsequently Housing Act 1985 s189, see now improvement notices: Housing Act 2004 s11) compelling it to carry out, among other things, repairs to the roof. Under the leases Pollway retained control of the structure of the block, was responsible for carrying out repairs and received ground rents. It did not appeal to the county court against the notice, but sought a declaration in the High Court that the notice was not valid since it was not the 'person having control of the premises'. Croydon Council contended that the notice was on its face valid and that, accordingly, the proper course would have been for Pollway to appeal to the county court.

The Court of Appeal held that Pollway was not the person in control and the council's appeal to the House of Lords was dismissed. As all the flats were already leased at low rents, Pollway could not receive a rack rent (ie, at least two-thirds of the full rent) or let them at a rack rent, as required by Housing Act 1957 s39(2). In view of this, the notice was a nullity, and there was no obligation on the company to challenge it by appealing to the county court.

Note: Under Housing Act 2004, although the concept of 'person having control' is retained (defined in s263) the provisions in relation to who should be served with notices are different (see Schedule 1 regarding service of improvement notices).

Court of Appeal

P15.2   *Gwynedd CC v Grunshaw*
[2000] 1 WLR 494; (2000) 32 HLR 610; (1999) *Times* 30 August, CA

Appeal filed when delivered to court, despite court managers refusal to accept it

Mrs Grunshaw lived in Lincolnshire. She owned a house in Gwynedd. The council considered that the house was unfit and on 18 July 1998 served a demolition order. Mrs Grunshaw had 21 days after that date to appeal to the county court. She attempted to file notice of appeal in Skegness County Court, but was told by the court manager that under CCR Ord 4 r9 she had to file her notice of appeal in Caernarfon County Court. She faxed a notice of appeal to Caernarfon County Court on Saturday 8 August and posted a copy, even though she knew that it would not arrive in time.

The Court of Appeal held that (1) as there was no provision in the County Court Rules for filing by fax, faxing the notice of appeal was insufficient; but (2) under CCR Ord 2 r4 the duty of the proper officer of the court was to enter the document in the records of the court. In determining that Skegness was not the correct county court, the court manager had taken on a judicial function and made a determination that he did not have power to make. He had failed to comply with CCR Ord 2 r4. That failure was an irregularity that did not nullify the proceedings. Mrs Grunshaw had done all that was necessary to file her appeal when she had handed or attempted to hand her notice to the proper officer. As a matter of fact, not deeming, she had appealed to the county court within 21 days as required by Housing Act 1985 s269(1). Her appeal was allowed.

Note: Although this case was decided on the interpretation of the County Court Rules 1981, there are similarities between CCR Ord 2 r4 and CPR 2.3(1) where 'filing' is defined as 'delivering it, by post or otherwise to the court office'.

P15.3   *Kenny v Kingston upon Thames RLBC*
(1985) 17 HLR 344; [1985] 1 EGLR 26; (1985) 274 EG 395, CA

Judge entitled to put stronger emphasis on policy considerations than expense of repairs

See *Housing Law Casebook* 3rd edition.

P15.4   *Kensington and Chelsea RLBC v Khan*
[2002] EWCA Civ 279; [2002] HLR 47; [2003] 1 P&CR 11

Time for recovering cost of works in default run from expiration of demand for payment

See *Housing Law Casebook* 3rd edition.

P15.5   *Nolan v Leeds CC*
(1991) 23 HLR 135; (1990) 89 LGR 385, CA

Definition of HMO can be dealt with in county court

On an appeal against notices served on owners of houses in multiple occupation under Housing Act 1985 Part X, it was held that the county court could deal with the question of whether the building was 'a house in multiple occupation' as a preliminary issue. The owner did not have to commence judicial review proceedings to have the notices quashed in order to raise that point.

P15.6   *R v Cardiff CC ex p Cross*
(1982) 6 HLR 1; (1983) 81 LGR 105, CA

Repair notice provisions do not apply to houses owned by local authority

Housing Act 1957 Part II (subsequently Housing Act 1985 Part VI, see now Housing Act 2004 Part 1) does not apply to homes owned by local authorities. Accordingly, it is not possible for formal repairs notices to be served where a local authority has control of premises.

See also *R (Erskine) v Lambeth LBC* (P15.16)

P15.7   *R v Woking BC ex p Adam*
(1996) 28 HLR 513, CA

Tenant's standing to challenge notices served by council on landlord

A council declared the tenant's home unfit for habitation and served a statutory repairs notice on the landlord. The landlord appealed. After the council had been advised by counsel not to resist the appeal, the court declared that the most satisfactory course of action was a closing order. The council made such an order and the tenant unsuccessfully applied for leave for judicial review, contending that the council should not have conceded the appeal and should now reissue repairs notices.

The Court of Appeal dismissed the renewed application for leave. Glidewell LJ expressed concern about the standing of the tenant, stating that such a tenant had no right of appeal under the Housing Act 1985 and that it would not be right for judicial review to be used as an appeal by the 'side-door'.

Note: The applicant was unrepresented in the Court of Appeal. It is not settled whether a tenant has a right of appeal under the statutory scheme and other tenants have brought successful judicial review proceedings: see *R v Ealing LBC ex p Richardson* (1982) 4 HLR 125, CA. See also *R v Forest of Dean DC ex p Trigg* (1990) 22 HLR 167; [1990] 2 EGLR 29; [1990] 30 EG 95, QBD, reported in *Housing Law Casebook* 3rd edition.

P15.8   *Reynolds v Brent LBC*
[2001] EWCA Civ 1843; [2002] HLR 15; [2001] 50 EG 89 (CS); (2001) *Times* 18 December, CA

Applicant not a 'fit and proper person' to control HMO

Pursuant to the Housing Act 1985, Brent operated a registration scheme regulating the control of houses in multiple occupation (HMOs) within its area. The terms of the scheme, which mirrored the control provisions in Housing Act 1985 s348(1), permitted Brent to refuse an application for registration where the person having or intended to have control of an HMO was 'not a fit and proper person' (see now Housing Act 2004 Part 2 s64(3)(b)) and empowered Brent to impose such conditions relating to the management of an HMO during the period of registration as it might determine. Brent refused Mr Reynolds' application for registration of the house on the ground that he had six prior convictions in relation to HMOs and so could not be regarded as a fit and proper person to have control. He appealed to the county court on the grounds that Brent had failed to consider whether it would be appropriate to accept his registration (a) for a probationary period and/or (b) subject to conditions. The judge allowed the appeal, holding that Brent should have gone on to consider whether the position could be ameliorated by the imposition of conditions.

The Court of Appeal allowed Brent's appeal. The judge was wrong to characterise Housing Act 1985 s348(1)(d) (introduced by Housing Act 1996 and allowing conditions to be imposed where an HMO is registered) as a proviso to the rest of the subsection. It was a free-standing and separate provision that added to, rather than imposed qualifications on, the powers conferred on a local housing authority by the rest of s348(1). If a local housing authority concluded that a person was unfit to have control of a house in multiple occupation, it did not have to go on to consider whether the situation could be ameliorated by the imposition of conditions. The Court of Appeal substituted for the judge's order an order that the application be approved subject to the appointment by Mr Reynolds of a manager who was, and whose terms of appointment were, acceptable to the council. It would further be open to the council to arrange for such monitoring of and reporting in relation to the property as seemed reasonably necessary. That would be in accordance with the council's policy of encouraging landlords to appoint able and responsible managers wherever possible when registration was refused.

P15.9 **Rogers v Islington LBC**
(2000) 32 HLR 138; [1999] 37 EG 178; (1999) *Times* 30 August, CA

Occupants not a 'household' where not a sufficient relationship between them

See *Housing Law Casebook* 3rd edition. See the new definition of an HMO in Housing Act 2004 Part 7 which now prescribes who may form a single household.

P15.10 **Stanley v Ealing LBC (No 2)**
[2003] EWCA Civ 679; [2003] HLR 71

HMO provisions did not breach art 1 of ECHR First Protocol

The claimant owned a house which had been built in the 1850s. In 1992 he converted it into 11 self-contained flats, including three flats in a new extension which was independent of the house but with access through the original building. The local authority served a notice to carry out amenity and safety works on the basis that the building was a house in multiple occupation (HMO) and that the independent extension formed part of the building. The claimant contended that a building containing separate self-contained flats could not be an HMO. A judge held that it was an HMO.

The claimant appealed unsuccessfully. The expression 'house in multiple occupation' in Housing Act 1985 Part XI s345(2) includes any part of a building which 'was originally constructed or subsequently adapted for occupation by a single household'. Although internally divided and externally added to, the building was a 'house'. (See too *Okereke v Brent LBC* [1966] 1 All ER 150, CA.) Furthermore, there was no contravention of ECHR article 1 of the First Protocol. The provisions in Part XI were in the public interest. If the local authority exercises its powers in a disproportionate or unreasonable way, the owner has a right of appeal to a court.

In any event, states had a wide margin of discretion in relation to matters concerning public health and control.

See also *Norwich CC v Billings* (1997) 29 HLR 679, DC (house with extension was an HMO), reported in *Housing Law Casebook* 3rd edition.

Note: Under Housing Act 2004 Part 7 a house converted into flats is only within the definition of an HMO if it is in breach of building standards and fewer than two-thirds of the occupiers are owner-occupiers (Housing Act 2004 s257).

P15.11 *Webb v Ipswich BC*
(1989) 21 HLR 325; (1989) 88 LGR 165, CA

Control order invalid where made without proper authority

See *Housing Law Casebook* 3rd edition.

High Court

P15.12 *Bell v Secretary of State for Environment and Brent LBC*
[1989] 1 EGLR 27; [1989] 12 EG 70, QBD

CPO justified and no evidence of ulterior motive

See *Housing Law Casebook* 3rd edition.

P15.13 *Jacques v Liverpool CC*
(1997) 29 HLR 82, DC

Collection of meter money meant defendant did receive 'rents and other payments'

The director of a company which owned the freehold of a house in multiple occupation (HMO) asked the defendant to collect rent. Subsequently the house was leased to a partnership formed between two other companies. The defendant stopped receiving the rent in 1990 but continued to collect money from the gas and electric meters and to receive cheques for housing benefit which were payable to the lessee. The local authority prosecuted the defendant for breaches of the Housing (Management of Houses in Multiple Occupation) Regulations 1990 SI No 830 (see now Housing Act 2004 s72) contending that he was a 'person managing' the premises within Housing Act 1985 s398(6) (see now Housing Act 2004 s263(3)) because he received 'rents and other payments'.

The Divisional Court held that:

1) The collection of cheques for housing benefit made out to the leaseholder and the payment of those cheques into the leaseholder's bank account did not amount to the receipt of rent for the purposes of s398(6).

2) It was not open to the magistrate to infer from the earlier receipt of rent payments that the defendant was still receiving those payments some three or four years later.

3) However, having regard to the context, the phrase 'other payments' in s398(6) does include the collection of meter money.

The appeal against conviction was dismissed.

P15.14 *Pascoe v First Secretary of State and Others*
[2006] EWHC 2356 (Admin); 27 September 2006.

CPO quashed where statutory test not satisfied

The claimant was an owner-occupier of a house in Liverpool. English Partnerships adopted a regeneration scheme for an area which included her house and made compulsory purchase orders (CPOs) in respect of the homes of the claimant and her neighbours. It relied on its powers under the Leasehold Reform, Housing and Urban Development Act 1993 s159(2)(b) to deal with 'land which ... is under-used or ineffectively used'. The orders were confirmed by an inspector and by the secretary of state on the basis that the regeneration area was 'predominantly' one of under-used or ineffectively used land.

Forbes J allowed an application made under Land Acquisition Act 1981 and quashed the orders. He held that the statutory test was only satisfied if the land in question was, taken as a whole, ineffectively used or under-used. The references to 'predominantly' in the inspector's report and the secretary of state's decision had been a misdirection of law. The judge rejected a claim that, had there not been such misdirection, the orders would have infringed the claimant's right to respect for her home (ECHR article 8).

P15.15 *R v Mansfield DC ex p Ashfield Nominees*
(1999) 31 HLR 805; (1998) 26 November, QBD

Judicial review not available where right to appeal to county court

The applicants sought judicial review to quash repair notices served under Housing Act 1985 s189 (see now improvements notices Housing Act 2004 s11). The application was dismissed. It is a well-known principle that the judicial review jurisdiction cannot be exercised where an alternative remedy exists (see *R v Birmingham CC ex p Ferrero* [1993] 1 All ER 53). An alternative right to appeal was provided by Housing Act 1985 s191. All matters raised were capable of resolution by the county court. The fact that a point of law was to be decided did not amount to an exceptional circumstance which would justify the acceptance of jurisdiction.

Cf *Pollway Nominees Ltd v Croydon LBC* (P15.1) where the validity of a notice was held to be challengeable in High Court.

P15.16 *R (Erskine) v Lambeth LBC*
[2003] EWHC 2479 (Admin); 14 October 2003

Fact that council could not serve notice on itself not discriminatory under ECHR

Ms Erskine rented a flat from Lambeth. In the kitchen there was a single electrical socket over a work surface and a double socket that had no work surface beneath it. Ms Erskine employed a gang socket that hung freely by its own wire to use her electrical appliances. An environmental report stated that the 'whole set-up' was extremely dangerous to the extent that it rendered the flat unfit for human habitation under Housing Act 1985 s604(1)(f) (see now Housing Act 2004 Part 1). As Lambeth could not serve a notice to repair under s189 (see now improvement notices Housing Act

12004 s11) on itself, Ms Erskine argued that ECHR article 8 was engaged for the purposes of considering whether or not Lambeth's failure to repair amounted to discrimination under article 14 because s189 notices could have been served on private landlords. She sought a declaration that ss189 and 604 were incompatible with articles 8 and 14.

Mitting J held that the provisions of the Act had not been introduced to protect individuals or promote that protection, but to promote and protect public health and the condition of low-cost housing. Sections 189 and 604 had no sufficient link with article 8 for article 14 to be engaged. The application was refused.

P16   Criminal proceedings under Environmental Protection Act 1990

The Environmental Protection Act 1990 obliges local authorities to serve enforcement notices where they are satisfied that there is a 'statutory nuisance'. This includes any premises which are such a state as to be prejudicial to health or a nuisance (s79(1)(a)). Alternatively, tenants themselves may prosecute landlords in the magistrates' court if there is a statutory nuisance. Under s82 magistrates may make mandatory orders for remedial work. They can also award compensation (up to a maximum of £5,000).

House of Lords

P16.1   *Birmingham CC v Oakley*
[2001] 1 AC 617; [2000] 3 WLR 1936; [2001] 1 All ER 385; (2001) 33 HLR 283; [2001] LGR 110; (2000) *Times* 30 November, HL

Arrangement of rooms (toilet without a basin next to kitchen) could not render premises in a 'state' so as to be prejudicial to health

A tenant rented a three-bedroom council house. The kitchen led, via a small lobby, to a small WC which had no hand basin and no room to install one. On the other side of the kitchen there was a bathroom. The only way for the family who occupied the premises to wash their hands after using the WC was to use the sink in the kitchen or in the bathroom. The justices held the premises were in such a state as to be likely to cause injury to health. An order was made under Environmental Protection Act 1990 s82 requiring the council to resite the toilet in the bathroom. An appeal to the Divisional Court failed.

The House of Lords allowed the council's further appeal. The arrangement of rooms, which were not in themselves insanitary, did not fall within s79(1)(a). There was nothing wrong with the WC, drain or basin and so nothing in the premises themselves that was prejudicial to health. It was not sufficient to render the house itself 'in such a state' as to be prejudicial to health that the WC and basin were in separate rooms or that to get from one to the other it was necessary to pass through the kitchen where food was prepared. The prejudice to health resulted from the failure to wash hands or to wash hands in the sink or the basin after access through the kitchen. Undesirable though this arrangement was, it was not permissible to give an extended meaning to the words in s79(1)(a), however socially or hygienically desirable that might be. They were directed to some feature in itself prejudicial to health in that it was a source of possible infection or disease or illness such as dampness, mould, dirt or evil smelling accumulation or the presence of rats. It was for parliament, the government or the local authority to take steps to remedy the problem and not for the courts to give an unjustified extension to words which had a different meaning and a different context. The object of s79(1)(a) of the 1990 Act and its predecessors was to provide a means for the summary removal of noxious matters. Where there was a defective drain or WC it was obvious that that in itself could constitute a statutory nuisance and render the premises in such a state as to be prejudicial to health. That was not the present case. Lords Steyn and Clyde dissented, holding that the Act was intended to protect the public's health and the words 'prejudicial to health' should be given a wide meaning.

Court of Appeal

P16.2 **Budd v Colchester BC**
[1999] LGR 601; (1999) *Times* 14 April, CA

Notice requiring abatement of nuisance (dog barking) need not specify steps to be taken

On 31 March 1994 the council served an abatement notice on the appellant pursuant to Environmental Protection Act 1990 s80. The notice identified the nuisance as 'dog barking' and required the appellant to abate the nuisance within 21 days. The dog owner appealed, contending that the notice did not identify clearly and precisely the nuisance complained of or state what steps were required to abate the nuisance.

The Court of Appeal, in dismissing the appeal, held that there was no conflict between *Network Housing Association v Westminster CC* (P16.24), *R v Wheatley ex p Cowburn* (1885) 16 QBD 34 and *SFI Group plc v Gosport BC* (1998) *Times* 13 February, DC (P16.5 – in the Court of Appeal). Section 80(1) makes it clear that local authorities have a choice. They are required to serve a notice 'imposing all or any of the following requirements', namely 'requiring the abatement of the nuisance' or 'requiring other steps as may be necessary'. Depending on the circumstances, it is open to them to take one or other course when serving the notice. Furthermore, they are under no obligation when exercising their discretion in making such choice to be more precise either as to the nature of the nuisance or the steps required to abate it. The course taken by the council was wholly appropriate. There is no obligation to specify a manner of abatement or the level of barking which would constitute a nuisance or the level that would be acceptable.

P16.3 **Issa v Hackney LBC**
[1997] 1 WLR 956; [1997] 1 All ER 999; (1997) 29 HLR 640; (1997) 95 LGR 671, CA

EPA 1990 does not give rise to civil cause of action

The council was convicted of allowing its tenant's home to become 'prejudicial to health' and so a statutory nuisance contrary to Environmental Protection Act 1990, even though there was no actionable disrepair. It was fined and ordered to carry out remedial works. The tenant's children then brought civil proceedings against the landlord for damages for injury to their health and asserted as their cause of action the council's failure to comply with the Environmental Protection Act and the conviction.

The Court of Appeal held that the Act introduced a self-contained criminal code giving rise to no private law right of action. Until parliament sees fit expressly to impose a civil liability on landlords to keep premises fit or healthy, non-tenant plaintiffs such as those in this case are without a private law remedy, unless Defective Premises Act 1972 s4 applies (which it did not here because there was no actionable disrepair).

P16.4   *R v Bristol CC ex p Everett*
[1999] 1 WLR 1170; [1999] 2 All ER 193; [1999] LGR 513; (1999) 31 HLR 1102; (1999) *Times* 9 March, CA

'Prejudicial to health' refers to likelihood of illness, not risk of injury by accident; councils can withdraw abatement notice

A tenant claimed that a steep staircase in the 19th century house that she rented was a statutory nuisance under Environmental Protection Act 1990 s79(1)(a). She suffered from a back injury, experienced difficulty negotiating the stairs and was worried that she might fall and injure herself. In 1994 the council served an abatement notice on her landlords requiring them to take out the existing staircase and to construct a new one. However, in 1996 the council decided that the staircase could not be considered a statutory nuisance and withdrew the notice. The tenant sought judicial review of that decision. Richards J refused her application. He held that s79(1) was not intended to apply in cases where the sole concern was that, because of the state of the premises, there was a likelihood of an accident causing personal injury, as opposed to an injury to health caused by disease, vermin etc.

The Court of Appeal dismissed her appeal. The same expression 'injury to health' was used in the 1990 Act as had been used in earlier 'sanitary statutes'. Parliament had intended to produce the same result as in earlier Public Health Acts. That expression had been interpreted in the sense of a 'threat of disease, vermin or the like'. It was probable that parliament intended to leave the risk of injury by accident to be dealt with by local authorities under other available statutory powers such as the Building Act 1984 and the building regulations. The council did have power to withdraw an abatement notice once served.

P16.5   *SFI Group plc v Gosport BC*
[1999] LGR 610; (1999) *Times* 5 April, CA

Issue is whether nuisance existed or was likely to recur at time s80 abatement notice served, not date of court hearing

On 25 August 1995 the local authority served an abatement notice under Environmental Protection Act 1990 s80(1). The appellant appealed first to the magistrates' court, which dismissed the appeal, and then to the Crown Court. The Crown Court found that there had been a statutory nuisance at the date of the service of the notice and that it was likely to recur at the date of the magistrates' court hearing. However, by the time of the Crown

Court hearing, works had been carried out, the nuisance did not exist and it was unlikely to recur. The Crown Court quashed the notice.

The Divisional Court held that the correct date at which both the magistrates' court and the Crown Court had to view the justification for and validity of the s80 notice was the date when the notice was served. The question of whether a statutory nuisance existed or was likely to recur should, in the context of an appeal to the Crown Court, be answered by reference to the position at the date of service of the notice. *Johnson News of London v Ealing LBC* [1990] COD 135, QBD was wrongly decided. A subsequent appeal to the Court of Appeal was also dismissed. The Court of Appeal agreed that the *Johnson News* case was wrongly decided. The use of the present tense in the phrase 'is not justified by s80' in reg 2(2)(a) of the Statutory Nuisance (Appeals) Regulations 1995 SI No 2644 is indicative of nothing more than an intention to cross-refer to the provisions of Environmental Protection Act 1990 s80(1) which, on its true construction, requires the situation to be tested at the time of service of the notice. In any event it is not permissible to use secondary legislation as an aid to construction of primary legislation. The procedure under s80 is quite different from that under Public Health Act 1936. The Court of Appeal noted that the 1990 Act provides for a single stage process and an appeal (whereas the 1936 Act did not), daily fines for the contravention of an abatement notice and grounds of appeal specified by regulations. There is also an absence of comparable language requiring the magistrates' court to consider whether the nuisance has abated. It is also notable that the regulations contain the very strong word 'quash' and provide for a variation to have retrospective effect, as opposed to using the weaker word 'set aside', which acknowledged the validity of the notice until such time as it was set aside. There is also the striking deliberate omission in s80 of the 1990 Act of any comparable provision to that contained in s94(3) of the 1936 Act in relation to costs. Any other construction would lead to the unsatisfactory situation of a defendant being able to defer abating the nuisance until the very last moment before an appeal to the magistrates' court. Furthermore, if it were correct that the notice had to be quashed so long as there was no existing nuisance or likely recurrence when the appeal came before the magistrates or Crown Court, any conviction which might have been made would be at least arguably equally open to being quashed.

High Court

P16.6 *Botross v Hammersmith and Fulham LBC*
(1995) 16 Cr App R(S) 622; (1995) 27 HLR 179; (1995) 93 LGR 269, DC

Proceedings under s82 are criminal and carry power to make compensation order

A council tenant issued proceedings under Environmental Protection Act 1990 s82. On the day set for trial, the council changed its plea to 'guilty' and the magistrates made an order for works. They were then advised by their clerk that the proceedings were civil, so they refused to make a criminal compensation order or an order for costs.

The Divisional Court allowed the tenant's appeal by way of case stated.

Beldam LJ said that, although the statute referred to commencement of proceedings by the civil process (complaint), that simply arose from a legislative oversight. Proceedings under s82 were plainly criminal, should be commenced by the criminal process (information) and gave rise to a power to make a compensation order.

P16.7   *Camden LBC v Gunby*

[2000] 1 WLR 465; [1999] 4 All ER 602; (2000) 32 HLR 572; [1999] 44 EG 147; (1999) *Times* 12 July, QBD

'Owner' is the person receiving the rent

The defendant was a partner in a firm of surveyors who were managing agents for the freeholder. The council served an abatement notice relating to a statutory nuisance arising from structural defects. Environmental Protection Act 1990 s80(2) provides that such a notice must be served on the owner, but does not define 'owner'. After considering s81A(9), the Statutory Nuisance (Appeals) Regulations 1995 SI No 2644 and the legislative history of previous related Acts, the Divisional Court 'applying common sense', held that an owner of premises for the purposes of Environmental Protection Act 1990 s80(2) is the person for the time being receiving the rack rent of premises, whether on his own account or as agent or trustee for another person, or who would so receive the rack rent if the premises were let out on a rack rent. No injustice was caused because a managing agent could appeal against the notice or recover expenses by making deductions from rent collected on behalf of the landlord. The case was remitted to the Crown Court.

See also *Pollway Nominees Ltd v Croydon LBC* (P15.1) regarding receipt of rent where premises let on long leases.

P16.8   *Canterbury CC v Ferris*

[1997] Env LR D14; [1997] JPL B45, DC

Magistrates have discretion whether or not to impose a daily rate of fine for continued non-compliance with abatement order

The council served an abatement notice with which the defendant failed to comply. The defendant was prosecuted under Environmental Protection Act 1990 s80(4) and convicted. The council sought, but the magistrates refused, an order that the defendant be fined a further £50 for each day of non-compliance after conviction, in accordance with s80(5).

On appeal, the Divisional Court held that Magistrates' Courts Act 1980 s34(1) gave the magistrates a discretion on the amount of the fine. Section 80(5), stipulating a daily fine of one-tenth of Scale 5, was not sufficient contra-indication to oust the statutory discretion.

P16.9   *Carr v Hackney LBC*

(1996) 28 HLR 747; [1995] Env LR 372, DC

Condensation not likely to recur where council were to install heaters

On an Environmental Protection Act 1990 s82 prosecution, the council accepted that there had been a statutory nuisance arising from condensation and mould growth, but that it had been abated. The tenant contended that the offence had been proved because the dampness was likely to recur without the installation of gas central heating. The stipendiary magistrate acquitted the council, having found that any recurrence would arise only from the tenant's failure to allow the council to install electric convector heaters, which it wished to provide.

The tenant appealed, contending that if parliament had intended such a defence to be available it would have enacted one, as it had in the Public Health Act 1936. The Divisional Court dismissed the appeal and held that such a defence was 'obviously' available, despite the absence of specific provision in the 1990 Act.

P16.10 *Carr v Leeds CC; Wells and Coles v Barnsley MBC*
(2000) 32 HLR 753; (1999) *Times* 12 November, DC

Costs agreements between tenants and their solicitors not 'shams'

Tenants sought to compel their respective council landlords to carry out certain works pursuant to the Environmental Protection Act 1990. The councils were both held liable for the works and the only remaining issue in the cases related to costs. The tenants had instructed solicitors and signed costs agreements, the terms of which made them liable, should they have failed in their actions, both for their costs and for those of their landlords. The councils resisted costs orders against them, arguing that the costs agreements were shams as the tenants were impecunious and it had never been the intention of the solicitors to claim their fees. The councils also claimed that the arrangements were contingency fee agreements prohibited under Solicitors' Practice Rules r8. They submitted that, since the tenants would have had no liability to pay their own costs if they had been unsuccessful, equally no liability could lie against the landlords on their success in the action.

The Divisional Court held that, outside certain statutory exceptions, if it were shown that a contingency fee arrangement had been made, a successful party's costs would be irrecoverable. However, there was no contingency fee arrangement in either case. It was evident that the tenants had at all relevant *Times* believed that they would be held liable for their own costs in the event that they failed in their actions. Without consulting their clients, the solicitors decided, of their own accord, not to pursue them for fees. There were no contingency fee agreements since the solicitors could, at any time have decided to sue their clients for their costs. In that event the clients would have had no defence to such claims. The arrangements were clearly distinguishable from contingency fee agreements.

Note: See also *Hughes v Kingston upon Hull Council* (P16.19) and note thereto.

P16.11 *Cunningham v Birmingham CC*
(1998) 96 LGR 231; (1998) 30 HLR 158, DC

Objective test applied in assessing whether a statutory nuisance existed

Ms Cunningham laid an information under Environmental Protection Act 1990 s82, claiming that her kitchen was too small and dangerous, having regard to the fact that she had an autistic son who was fascinated by doors. She contended that the court should have regard to her subjective requirements when considering whether or not a statutory nuisance was prejudicial to health.

The Divisional Court rejected this contention. An objective test has to be applied when construing both limbs of s79(1)(a).

P16.12   *Davenport v Walsall MBC*

(1996) 28 HLR 754; [1997] Env LR 24, DC

No award of compensation where guilty plea but quantum and causation disputed; costs payable

In proceedings under the Environmental Protection Act 1990 a tenant sought, among other things, compensation. The council disputed the quantum of the specific and general heads of loss claimed and denied that the statutory nuisance (to which it had pleaded guilty) had caused the loss. The justices heard lengthy submissions on whether they should entertain consideration of the compensation claim by hearing witness evidence and cross-examination on each side. They then dismissed the compensation claim and refused the tenant the costs of the hearing.

On the tenant's appeal, the Divisional Court held that the principles for the award of criminal compensation in statutory nuisance cases established under the Public Health Act 1936 (see *Herbert v Lambeth LBC* (P16.18)) apply equally to Environmental Protection Act 1990 proceedings. Justices can and should award compensation in clear or straightforward cases. The Divisional Court rejected the contention that the justices had wrongly exercised their discretion on compensation on the specific facts. The fact that a tenant might not succeed in bringing successful civil proceedings in respect of damage caused by condensation mould growth was something to be taken into account by magistrates when deciding whether or not to make a compensation order. However, the absence of a civil remedy does not automatically mean that magistrates should award compensation. The Divisional Court allowed the tenant's appeal against the magistrates' refusal to award costs. Environmental Protection Act 1990 s82(12) entitles a tenant to costs 'properly incurred' and there was nothing improper in making the application for compensation.

P16.13   *East Staffordshire BC v Fairless*

(1999) 31 HLR 677; (1998) *Times* 26 October, QBD

No requirement for notice of statutory nuisance under s82 to specify works

On 18 April 1997 a tenant wrote to his council landlord informing it of a statutory nuisance and enclosing a surveyor's report which referred to disrepair, dampness and mould growth. An information was laid on 30 May 1997, but the nuisance was remedied between that date and the issue of the summons. Although the council agreed that there had been a statutory nuisance as defined by Environmental Protection Act (EPA) 1990 s79(7), it appealed against an order that it should pay the tenant's costs, claiming that the letter and report had not complied with s82(6) (notice of intention to bring statutory nuisance proceedings) because they had not stated why the council was in breach of EPA 1990 and had not stated what needed to be done to abate the nuisance.

The appeal was dismissed. Sullivan J said that EPA 1990 sets out a detailed statutory framework and states what has to be included in a s82(6) notice, namely the matter complained of. It does not have to specify the works which are necessary to remedy the complaint. There is no reason to import additional requirements which are not set out in the Act. It would be unfortunate if magistrates' courts were deprived of jurisdiction purely because of technical defects in s82(6) notices. The letter and the report were a valid notice of intention to bring proceedings under s82(6) and the magistrates were entitled to make a costs order under s82(12) – see *R v Liverpool Crown Court ex p Cooke* (P16.32).

See also *Pearshouse v Birmingham* [1999] LGR 169; (1999) 31 HLR 756, QBD, reported in *Housing Law Casebook* 3rd edition.

P16.14 **Farrar v Dover CC**
(1982) 2 HLR 32, DC

No statutory nuisance where condensation due to tenants' failure to use heating

Houses on an estate which were heated by an electric warm air system suffered from condensation dampness. Six tenants laid informations under Public Health Act 1936 s99 alleging that their homes were statutory nuisances which were prejudicial to health. The magistrates found that: (a) the tenants did not understand that the heating was to be used as background heating; (b) the electric heating was too expensive for the tenants to use; and (c) if heated as intended, the houses would not suffer from condensation. The magistrates made a nuisance order.

The council appealed successfully. Notwithstanding the condensation dampness, the heating was not defective and the construction and method of heating supplied were adequate and not unsuitable. The state of the premises arose from the act or default of the tenants in failing to use the system provided.

See also *Pike v Sefton MBC* (P16.26); *Greater London Council v Tower Hamlets LBC* (P16.15); *Earl v Kingston upon Hull CC* (P16.43); *Pringle v Hackney LBC* (P16.46); *Robb v Dundee CC* (P16.49).

P16.15 **Greater London Council v Tower Hamlets LBC**
(1983) 15 HLR 57, DC

Statutory nuisance where heating inadequate

A flat suffered from dampness and mould growth. It was at a raised level and three sides of the structure underneath were exposed to the elements. A coal fire, which would have provided ventilation, was taken out and replaced with a storage heater which was not sufficient to combat condensation. Magistrates found that the condensation was caused by lack of proper ventilation and insulation and lack of heating. They made an order requiring the landlord to abate the nuisance.

The Divisional Court found that there was ample evidence to entitle the magistrates to come to the conclusion that the state of the premises was a statutory nuisance which was prejudicial to health. If the construction of a building is so unusual as to require some special form of heating to combat condensation, it is reasonable to expect the landlord to install it.

P16.16 *Haringey LBC v Jowett*
[1999] LGR 667; (2000) 32 HLR 308; [1999] EGCS 64; (1999) *Times* 20 May, DC

Traffic noise could not be a statutory nuisance under s79(1)(a) in light of s79(1)(ga)

See *Housing Law Casebook* 3rd edition.

P16.17 *Hazlett v Sefton MBC*
[2000] Env LR 416, QBD

Assumption that where solicitor on record tenant liable to pay his costs

Ms Hazlett, a council tenant, complained to the magistrates' court that the condition of her home constituted a statutory nuisance under Environmental Protection Act 1990 s79(1)(a). The council accepted that there was a nuisance at the time of the complaint and she accepted that it had been abated and was unlikely to recur. The only issue was therefore the question of costs. The council argued that despite the wording of s82(12) the tenant was not entitled to her costs because she had entered into an unlawful and unenforceable conditional fee agreement with her solicitor and accordingly would not be liable for her solicitor's costs. She produced a letter from her solicitor which stated that if the claim was successful costs would be paid by the council and no payment would be sought from her. The magistrate decided that in the absence of admissible evidence he could not assume that she had incurred any expenses within s82(12) and was not entitled to a costs order.

The tenant appealed successfully. There was a presumption that since she had a solicitor on the record she was liable to pay his costs (*R v Miller; R v Glennie* [1983] 1 WLR 1056). Section 82(12) provided that if the nuisance existed at the date of the complaint the court should order the defendant to pay the complainant's expenses. The complainant did not have to adduce evidence to support that presumption. The magistrate erred in deciding that he could not assume that Ms Hazlett had incurred costs. If the defendant simply put the complainant to proof of his or her entitlement to costs, the complainant would be justified in relying on the presumption. Where the defendant raised a genuine issue as to whether the complainant had incurred costs, the complainant should be given notice that the issue would be raised. It was then for the magistrate to decide whether it required proof by the complainant of the liability to pay or whether the respondent's case was insufficient to displace the presumption. If the complainant sought to adduce evidence in support of the presumption, he or she had to do so by admissible evidence. In this case, the solicitor's letter would have to have been proved by a relevant witness who could be cross-examined on relevant matters. The case was remitted to the magistrate.

P16.18 *Herbert v Lambeth LBC*
(1992) 13 Cr App R(S) 489; (1992) 24 HLR 299; (1991) 90 LGR 310, DC

Principles for awarding compensation

Magistrates made a nuisance order in proceedings brought under Public Health Act 1936 s99, but held that they did not have the power to make a compensation order under Powers of Criminal Courts Act 1973 s35, since no offence had been committed.

The Divisional Court allowed an appeal by way of case stated, and remitted the case for the justices to fix the amount of compensation. If the justices were satisfied that a nuisance existed, they were convicting for an offence and the power to award compensation followed. On the appropriate quantum, the court said that substantial sums should not be awarded where these could be recovered in civil proceedings (especially where the claim was for 'personal injury'). However, where a civil court could not award damages (eg, because the conditions did not arise from disrepair), magistrates should take that into account in making an award. The Divisional Court expressly held that the provisions in the Environmental Protection Act 1990 are not materially different from those in the Public Health Act 1936.

P16.19   **Hughes v Kingston upon Hull Council**

[1999] QB 1193; [1999] 1 All ER 49; (1999) 31 HLR 779; (1998) *Times* 20 November, QBD

Tenant not entitled to costs where contingency fee arrangement existed

Solicitors acting for Mr Hughes brought proceedings alleging that his premises constituted a statutory nuisance under Environmental Protection Act 1990 s79(1)(a). A deputy stipendiary magistrate found that Mr Hughes was not aware of any liability for costs of the proceedings and was unaware that he might have to pay the council's costs should his prosecution fail. As Mr Hughes was a pensioner in receipt of state benefit, his solicitors should have been aware of his impecuniosity.

The Court of Appeal held that Mr Hughes was unable to seek an order for costs against the council even if he was successful in establishing liability under s82, because the agreement with his solicitors was a contingency fee contrary to public policy. The decision of the Court of Appeal in *Thai Trading Co v Taylor* [1998] 2 WLR 893, CA was undermined by the failure to cite the House of Lords case of *Swain v The Law Society* [1983] 1 AC 598, HL.

Note: The scope for conditional fee agreements has now been widened by Access to Justice Act 1999

P16.20   **Jones v Walsall MBC**

[2002] EWHC 1232 (Admin) [2003] Env LR 5; (2002) 10 May, QBD Admin Ct

Tenant not entitled to costs where access not given to abate nuisance

Ms Jones was the tenant of a flat owned by the council. In December 1999, the flat was flooded following an escape of water from an empty flat above. Ms Jones reported the flooding immediately. The council unsuccessfully attempted to dry out the flat with heaters. In February 2000, Ms Jones's solicitors wrote to the council threatening proceedings under the Environmental Protection Act 1990 unless the dampness and certain other matters were rectified. A schedule of works was promised by the council. In March and April 2000 council officials attended at the flat in order to produce such a schedule, but were unable to gain access. On 31 May 2000, Ms Jones laid a complaint before the magistrates, alleging statutory nuisance.

Following service of the summons, the council gained access to the flat and carried out the required works. At the hearing before the magistrates it was common ground that the summons should be dismissed, and the only live issue was as to costs. The justices held that Ms Jones was not entitled to costs because the council had done all that could reasonably be expected to gain access. It was not liable for the continuation of the nuisance.

Ms Jones's appeal was dismissed. The magistrates had properly considered the process as a whole, and had properly concluded that the council had done all that could reasonably be expected to gain access to abate the nuisance. They were right to conclude that Ms Jones was responsible for the continuance of the nuisance at the time that the information was laid.

P16.21   *Leeds v Islington LBC*

(1999) 31 HLR 545; [1998] EGCS 15, DC

Section 82 notice required to be served on clerk to local authority

The appellant, an Islington tenant, sent the council a notice pursuant to Environmental Protection Act 1990 s82, complaining of a pharaoh ant infestation. It was addressed to the senior estate manager at the local neighbourhood office, at the address given on the rent card for service of notices in accordance with Landlord and Tenant Act 1985 s48. It was not sent to the principal office of the authority. The magistrates' court dismissed the complaint because failure to send the notice to the correct address meant that it had not been properly given.

The tenant's appeal was dismissed. Service on the senior estate manager did not comply with Environmental Protection Act 1990 s160 which provides that a notice must be served on a clerk to a local authority. Compliance with s48 did not amount to authorisation for all documents connected with legal proceedings to be sent there. A liberal interpretation of what constituted notice was not appropriate to the Environmental Protection Act, which involved possible criminal penalties.

Cf *R v Birmingham CC ex p Ireland; Baker v Birmingham CC; Hall v Kingston upon Hull* (P16.28)

P16.22   *Lewisham LBC v Hall*

[2002] EWHC 960 (Admin); [2003] Env LR 4; 7 May 2002

Acoustic evidence not required for conviction in relation to noise nuisance

A local authority served a noise abatement notice under Environmental Protection Act 1990 s80(4) in respect of loud music and/or anti-social behaviour. After further complaints by neighbours, environmental enforcement officers from the local authority attended the property and, based on their experience decided that there was a statutory nuisance in breach of the notice. However, they did not take any acoustic measurements. On a subsequent prosecution the magistrates were not satisfied that the level of noise amounted to a nuisance, concluding that it was unsatisfactory that the officers had taken no acoustic measurements.

The local authority's appeal was allowed. It would be wrong to refuse to convict merely on the basis that no reliable acoustic evidence had been produced. The evidence of an environmental enforcement officer or any other lay witness could be relied on.

P16.23 *Liverpool CC v Worthington*

(1998) *Times* 16 June, DC

Time limit for appeal by way of case stated

The time for making an appeal by way of case stated under Magistrates' Courts Act 1980 s111(3) runs from 'the day on which the court sentences or otherwise deals with the offender'. When the court makes an abatement order under Environmental Protection Act 1990 s82(12), if the decision on costs is the final termination of proceedings, an aggrieved party has 21 days from that date to ask the magistrate to state a case.

P16.24 *Network Housing Association v Westminster CC*

(1995) 27 HLR 189; (1995) 93 LGR 280, DC

Council should specify nature of works in difficult sound transmission cases

See *Housing Law Casebook* 3rd edition.

P16.25 *O'Toole v Knowlsley MBC*

(2000) 32 HLR 420; (1999) *Times* 21 May, QBD

EHOs qualified to assess whether premises prejudicial to health

A tenant brought proceedings under Environmental Protection Act 1990 s79(1)(a). At the hearing she called two environmental health officers (EHOs), who concluded that the premises were prejudicial to health. The justices found that the officers were 'sufficiently qualified and experienced to be regarded as expert witnesses' but, in the absence of medical evidence about the tenant's state of health, decided that they could not accept the officers' evidence. They held that the tenant had failed to discharge the burden of proof to establish a prima facie case.

The Divisional Court quashed the justices' finding. It is not necessary for EHOs to have medical qualifications to assess whether premises are prejudicial to health. The magistrates had wrongly substituted their own views for those of an appropriate expert. As there was no contradictory evidence and the issue was in fact one for expert evidence, the justices should have taken the EHOs' evidence into account and accepted it. (See *Southwark LBC v Simpson* (P16.36).)

P16.26 *Pike v Sefton MBC*

September 2002 *Legal Action* 18, DC

Condensation arose from tenant's failure to use heating

The tenant occupied a three-bedroom terraced council house with a gas fire in the living room and electric sockets in the upper rooms. The property suffered from condensation dampness and mould growth. The tenant's prosecution under Environmental Protection Act 1990 s82 was dismissed by the magistrates' court. It found that the condensation arose not from any default of the council, but by reason of the tenant's failure to provide sufficient heat input 'for his own cogent reason, namely the cost of that heating'. The tenant appealed by case stated.

The Divisional Court dismissed the appeal. It would only be in an exceptional case that the council would be liable on such facts (eg, where the building had been designed or provided by the council in such condition, or so modified, as to be 'doomed' to dampness: *Greater London Council v Tower Hamlets LBC* (P16.15)). In the case of an ordinary house which could, with objectively reasonable heat input, avoid condensation dampness, the council would not be liable if such dampness arose: *Farrar v Dover DC* (P16.14).

P16.27 ## Quigley v Liverpool Housing Trust
[1999] EGCS 94, QBD

Defence where tenant refuses to move out while works undertaken

Ms Quigley wrote to her landlords sending notice of intention to bring proceedings under Environmental Protection Act 1990 and requesting that they abate a statutory nuisance affecting the premises. The landlords claimed that they were ready to carry out works, but had been unable to do so because she had refused offers of suitable alternative temporary accommodation. They said that they would carry out works as soon as she left. She then brought proceedings under s82. The magistrate found that any nuisance was caused by Ms Quigley's unreasonable refusal of the offers of alternative accommodation and dismissed the claim.

Ms Quigley's appeal was dismissed. There was no evidence of a statutory nuisance and, if there had been a statutory nuisance, she had unreasonably refused alternative accommodation that was clearly suitable. Under s82(4)(a) a landlord can assert that he is not the person responsible for the nuisance where a tenant has refused an offer of suitable alternative accommodation while works are done. That defence can be relied on even where the refusal of accommodation occurred before the landlord was put on notice under s82(6) and (7). The 1990 Act should be used responsibly, and not capriciously and irresponsibly as it had been in bringing this appeal.

P16.28 ## R v Birmingham CC ex p Ireland, Baker v Birmingham CC, Hall v Kingston upon Hull CC
[1999] 2 All ER 609; (1999) 31 HLR 1078; [1999] LGR 184, QBD

Service of notices under s79 on local authorities

Council tenants served notices on their landlords under Environmental Protection Act 1990 s82 to abate statutory nuisances under s79. In three separate cases, magistrates dismissed informations on the basis that the notices were ineffective under s82 because they were not served on the clerks to the authorities at their principal offices within the meaning of s160(3) or at another address given by the council.

The tenants' appeals were allowed. The councils had been properly served. The notices had been sent to the councils as landlords and 'the person to be served' in s160(5) was the council. Section 160(3) did not mean that the 'secretary or clerk' of a council was the only person who could specify another address for service. Another person could specify on behalf of a council an address for service of s82 notices and in these cases had done so. The procedure under ss79 and 82 was supposed to be simple and speedy. The councils had informed tenants how and where to report statutory nuisances and the s82 notices were accordingly served in accordance with s160(5). The court added

If in any particular local authority area there is uncertainty on the part of either the local authority's tenants or their legal advisers as to where and to whom section 82(6) notices should be sent, it seems to us in everyone's interests for the local authority to inform its tenants precisely how to proceed.

Note: Cf *Leeds v Islington LBC* (P16.21).

P16.29 *R v Dudley Magistrates' Court ex p Hollis*
[1998] 1 All ER 759; [1998] 1 All ER 759; [1998] 18 EG 133; (1998) 30 HLR 902, DC

Costs mandatory if nuisance existed at time of complaint; no power to adjourn simply to allow for works to be done

Tenants complained that premises rented by them were prejudicial to health. Informations were laid under Environmental Protection Act 1990 s82. The council submitted that work would have been carried out without the need for a summons and that the proceedings were unnecessary. In the case of Ms Hollis the court adjourned the case to give the council the opportunity to complete the works. The magistrates accepted the council's submissions and refused to award the tenants their costs.

The Divisional Court allowed the tenants' appeals. Environmental Protection Act 1990 s82(12), which provides that the court 'shall order the defendant ... to pay to the person bringing the proceedings such amount as the court considers is reasonably sufficient to compensate him for any expenses properly incurred by him in the proceedings', is a mandatory provision. Magistrates are not entitled to refuse costs if they are satisfied that a nuisance existed at the time of the complaint. There was no power to disallow costs where the court thought that proceedings need not have been brought. The only discretion vested in magistrates is to decide whether or not costs are excessive. The court also stated that the power to grant adjournments should not be exercised in such a way as to deprive a litigant of rights conferred by statute. The effect of the adjournment in Ms Hollis's case had been to deprive her of the right to compensation under the Powers of Criminal Courts Act 1973 s35. The court has no power to adjourn without taking a plea simply to allow the landlord to carry out works.

P16.30 *R v Enfield Justices ex p Whittle*
June 1993 *Legal Action* 15, DC

Costs order against tenants quashed

Tenants withdrew statutory nuisance proceedings brought under Public Health Act 1936 s99, as a result of difficulties with witnesses. On the formal dismissal of the proceedings, magistrates ordered the tenants to pay the council's costs of £6,000.

Granting certiorari to quash the costs order, the Divisional Court (Watkins LJ and Rougier J) held that, following the repeal of the Costs in Criminal Cases Act 1973 s2(1), the justices had no general discretion on the question of costs. Provisions relating to costs are now to be found in Prosecution of Offences Act 1985 ss16 to 19. Section 19 (which was not relied on by the justices) restricts awards for payment of costs from tenant to council to cases of 'unnecessary or improper' conduct by the tenant. Accordingly, the costs order had been made without jurisdiction.

P16.31 *R v Highbury Corner Magistrates' Court ex p Edwards*
(1994) 26 HLR 682, DC

Not vexatious to issue summons under s82 as well as issue civil proceedings

A council tenant laid an information under Environmental Protection Act 1990 s82 seeking a summons against Hackney LBC. The information alleged statutory nuisance arising from substantial dampness due to condensation. The chief clerk refused to issue the summons on the grounds that the tenant already had a civil legal aid certificate to take proceedings for disrepair and that to subject the council to proceedings in which they might be fined was vexatious.

The Divisional Court granted an order of mandamus to compel the issue of the summons. After considering *Quick v Taff Ely BC* (P5.16), the court was satisfied that s82 proceedings would enable the court to make orders for improvement works to remedy condensation dampness which could not be achieved in civil proceedings.

P16.32 *R v Liverpool Crown Court ex p Cooke*
[1997] 1 WLR 700; [1996] 4 All ER 589; [1997] 1 Cr App R(S) 7; (1997) 29 HLR 249; (1997) 96 LGR 379, QBD

Earliest date that could be subject of compensation is date of expiry of notice

In Environmental Protection Act 1990 s82 proceedings, a tenant claimed that her home was prejudicial to health because of dampness, mould and fungi growth, a leaking hot water cylinder and broken and missing bathroom tiles, among other things. She also relied on the 'nuisance' limb of s79(1)(a) because of the effects of the discharge of foul water from, and accumulation of rubbish and putrescible material in and about, a vacant council flat below her own. The council entered a guilty plea. The court made an order for remedial works, and awarded compensation of £3,000 (£1,000 for property damaged by damp), and costs of £2,170. No evidence was heard on the question of compensation and no figure was agreed. The award was based on the premise that the nuisance had been present at the dwelling for two and a half years. The council appealed to the Crown Court, which varied the compensation order to £250 and imposed a fine of £500.

The complainant sought judicial review. Dismissing the application, the court held that there is no 'offence' for s82 purposes unless a nuisance is proved to exist on the date of hearing. It followed that compensation could be awarded only in respect of that offence as alleged in the information. The earliest date that could be the subject of compensation would be the date of expiry of a 21-day notice (s82(6)) if the complaint had not by that date been rectified, because that was the first date on which the prospective offence could be prosecuted. The latest date would be the date of hearing.

Note: Since *Cooke* it has, therefore, become important for tenants to allege in the information that the statutory nuisance existed at the date of expiry of the notice.

P16.33 *R v Southend Stipendiary Magistrate ex p Rochford DC*
[1994] Env LR D15, QBD

No formal procedure on assessment of costs

On an application for judicial review in respect of a magistrate's decision on costs, Judge J held that magistrates have a wide jurisdiction on the assessment of costs. There were no arrangements for taxation or for referral for taxation to another court. No formal procedure on assessment was expected and therefore a decision on costs, even where the sums claimed were large, could be reached in summary form without pleadings or formal bills.

P16.34 *R (Anne) v Test Valley BC*
[2001] EWHC Admin 1019; 16 November 2001

Refusal to serve abatement notice upheld

In March 2001, homeowners formally complained to the council that a large lime tree in a neighbour's garden was a statutory nuisance. It harboured aphids which excreted honeydew droplets on to their house and drive, and was a source of mould and mould spores adversely affecting their property and their health. As no inspection was scheduled in response to the complaint, the claimants threatened judicial review and an environmental health officer (EHO) then visited. On 18 April 2001, the council's executive committee noted that 'the issue of statutory nuisance is still being investigated'. On 1 June 2001, the claim for judicial review was served and, on 11 July 2001, permission was granted. The council then made further inspections and specialist investigations and its EHO concluded that there was 'insufficient evidence found to indicate that the lime tree is affecting the property to such an extent as to be considered a statutory nuisance'. Judicial review was then sought of that decision.

Forbes J held that, applying *R v Carrick DC ex p Shelley* [1996] Env LR 273, the issues under Environmental Protection Act 1990 ss79 and 80 were matters of fact not discretion and if the authority was satisfied, on the balance of probability, that there was a statutory nuisance then it was under a duty to serve an abatement notice. In considering the rationality of the decision taken, the court would review the way in which the relevant investigations were carried out and their adequacy. As the subject matter was the claimant's home and private life (each protected by ECHR article 8(1)), the court would subject the rationality of the decision and the process leading up to it to 'anxious scrutiny'. Applying *Cunningham v Birmingham CC* (P16.11), the test in measuring prejudice to health was an objective one (ie, not whether the claimant had been made ill, but 'whether the health of the average person would be prejudiced'). On the facts, the investigations into the complaint were properly conducted, the conclusions were adequately reasoned and the decision made was neither irrational nor unreasonable.

P16.35 *R (Vella) v Lambeth LBC and London and Quadrant Housing Trust*
[2005] EWHC 2473; [2006] HLR 12; [2005] Env LR 33; (2005) *Times* 23 November, QBD

Lack of sound insulation cannot cause premises to be prejudicial to health

From December 2000 Mr Vella was a tenant of a flat in a converted house, let by London and Quadrant Housing Trust. From January 2001 he complained about noise transference from the flat above and the communal hallway and stairs. He said that the noise was not due to unreasonable behaviour but to inadequate sound insulation. He could hear footsteps, conversations, flushing toilets, activity with pots and pans in the kitchen, bed squeaks, and water running through the main pipes, as well as television and radio. He described the noise as incessant. He argued that, as a result, the premises were in such a state that they were prejudicial to health and that Lambeth had to serve an abatement notice under Environmental Protection Act 1990 s80. Lambeth refused to do so and Mr Vella sought judicial review of that decision.

His application was dismissed. The contention that a lack of adequate sound insulation could cause premises to be in such a state as to be prejudicial to health for the purposes of 79(1)(a) was no longer sustainable following *R v Bristol CC ex p Everett* (P16.4) and *Birmingham CC v Oakley* (P16.1). The premises in the present case were not themselves in such a state as to be injurious or likely to cause injury to health. They were not defective, unwholesome, filthy, verminous etc. It was simply that, when noise was caused in adjoining premises, they did not prevent the transmission of that noise. Parliament had provided for a separate statutory code under which local authorities had express powers and, in the most serious cases, duties to deal with sound insulation. In addition, the government had introduced the decent homes scheme by which planned improvements to the social and private housing stock would be made by 2010. The immense financial burden that would be imposed on social and private landlords if the court were, by the statutory nuisance route, to require the immediate upgrading of properties generally to a standard of sound insulation not required when they were constructed or adapted was also very real. Imposing burdens on that scale was a matter of housing management not environmental health. The council's decision not to serve an abatement notice on the housing trust was not merely lawful, but legally correct.

Note: This decision overtakes the decisions in *Southwark LBC v Ince* (1989) 21 HLR 504, DC (see *Housing Law Casebook* 3rd edition) and *Network Housing Association v Westminster CC* (P16.24).

P16.36 *Southwark LBC v Simpson*
(1999) 31 HLR 725; [1999] Env LR 553, QBD

Chartered surveyor not expert on issue of prejudice to health

A tenant brought successful proceedings under Environmental Protection Act 1990 against the council. In the magistrates' court the case turned on whether the premises occupied by her were so damp as to be injurious and prejudicial to health. A chartered surveyor gave evidence for her that, although he had no specific medical knowledge, his opinion was that the conditions were prejudicial to health. He said that his opinion was not based on direct knowledge but on reading certain articles, none of which was available at court.

The council's appeal was allowed. The magistrates were not entitled to have regard to the hearsay evidence adduced by the chartered surveyor. Although they were entitled to consider questions of fact and, in doing so, to use their own knowledge, the question of whether a property was prejudicial to health required expert opinion and was not something on which they could draw their own opinion (see *Patel v Metab* (1982) 5 HLR 80). Experts are not required to have any medical expertise, simply expertise in their particular field. Surveyors are capable of being experts for these purposes if they have first-hand expertise in the field but, in this case, the chartered surveyor had specifically disavowed himself of any such experience and was simply relying on hearsay evidence.

Note: See *O'Toole v Knowlsey MBC* (P16.25) regarding EHOs.

P16.37 **Taylor v Walsall and District Property and Investment Co**
(1998) 30 HLR 1062; (1998) *Times* 5 February, DC
Advance notice of costs should be given

As a matter of routine, in all cases of statutory nuisance under Environmental Protection Act 1990 s82(12), complainants should give advance notice of any claim for costs and the respondent should indicate in advance whether that claim is accepted or challenged. Even though s82(12) calls for a broad brush approach and requires only the crudest form of taxation process, justices have to take proper steps to investigate how the claim is arrived at and the detailed grounds sought to challenge it. The concept of *Calderbank* offers should be introduced to protect respondents who accept some responsibility and to resolve the matter of costs with the least expense (see *Calderbank v Calderbank* [1975] 3 WLR 586, CA).

Crown Court

P16.38 **Dent v Haringey LBC**
December 1999 *Legal Action* 18; 25 November 1997, Wood Green Crown Court
Council liable for infestation arising from defects in roof

A tenant's home was infested with flying hide beetles (dermestes peruvianus). The tenant called a leading specialist entomologist who gave evidence that the beetles fed on, and bred in, the rotting mummified carcasses of dead pigeons. Pigeons had gained access through defects in the roof covering, which was over 100 years old but had been patch repaired to 40% of its area, and had been nesting there.

HHJ Binning and justices dismissed the council's appeal against conviction. The court was satisfied by the expert evidence of the link between the beetles and the pigeon carcasses and rejected the proposition that the council was not 'responsible for' the infestation. A nuisance order was made requiring a complete re-roofing within six months. The magistrate's orders for compensation of £1,000, a fine of £50 and costs of £12,250 were confirmed.

P16.39 **Ozmus v West Hampstead Housing Association**
December 1999 *Legal Action* 18; 10 October 1998, Wood Green Crown Court
Housing association was 'person responsible'

The association took a lease of privately owned accommodation and sublet it to the prosecutor. She complained that, owing to an infestation of mice, the premises were in such a state as to be a statutory nuisance. The association defended on the basis that it was not 'responsible for' the infestation because (1) it did not own the property (see Environmental Protection Act 1990 s82(4)(b)), (2) the subtenancy agreement cast no liability on it for infestations, and (3) the tenant's handbook stated that the occupier was liable for 'pest control'. The justices convicted and the association appealed.

HHJ Connor and justices dismissed the appeal. The association was the 'person responsible for' the premises within s82(4)(a). The conviction and abatement order were upheld and a further £4,000 was added to the costs payable.

Magistrates' courts

P16.40 *Ashard v Islington LBC*

June 1995 *Legal Action* 23, Highbury Corner Magistrates' Court

Compensation for failure to carry out abatement works in accordance with order

A tenant took Environmental Protection Act 1990 s82(1) proceedings. The council pleaded guilty. On 2 August 1994 it was ordered to carry out abatement works by 25 October. It was also fined £500, and ordered to pay compensation of £2,600 and costs of £1,285. The work was not carried out and so the tenant laid a fresh information alleging an offence contrary to s82(8). The council again pleaded guilty, was fined £750 and ordered to pay costs of £655. On the tenant's application for compensation, the council argued that any assessment should run only from 25 October.

The justices disagreed and awarded the tenant compensation of £1,119, representing £36.10 per week from 2 August.

Note: The compensation of £2,600 must be considered in light of fact that the case was decided before *R v Liverpool Crown Court ex p Cooke* (P16.32).

P16.41 *Brown v Brent LBC*

May 1997 *Legal Action* 21, Brent Magistrates' Court

£650 compensation for anxiety and stress for four months

Environmental Protection Act 1990 proceedings were brought in relation to a flat which suffered dampness due to leaking pipes as well as condensation and mould growth on aluminium window frames. The council initially denied liability but pleaded guilty at trial. Following *R v Liverpool Crown Court ex p Cooke* (P16.32) the tenant sought compensation only from the date of expiry of the s82(6) notice to the date of hearing (four months). The claim was not in respect of any specific damage but for the 'anxiety and distress' occasioned by the offence itself (see *Bond v Chief Constable of Kent* [1983] 1 WLR 40; [1983] 1 All ER 456, DC).

Lay justices made a compensation order of £650 and a costs order for £3,172.

P16.42 *Crowe v Tower Hamlets LBC*

May 1997 *Legal Action* 21; (1996) H&HI(1) 1:0, Thames Magistrates' Court

£600 for anxiety and stress for three and a half months

Environmental Protection Act 1990 proceedings were brought in relation to a flat which suffered dampness and a range of other defects. The council denied liability but undertook some works and after the trial had started (and during an adjournment to a later date) undertook further works. It then argued at the resumed trial that it could not be convicted of any offence because the statutory nuisance had been eliminated before the conclusion of the trial. The tenant argued that the relevant date was the date the trial commenced (*Coventry CC v Doyle* [1981] 1 WLR 1325, [1981] 2 All ER 184, DC).

The justices convicted. Following *R v Liverpool Crown Court ex p Cooke* (P16.32), the tenant sought compensation only from the date of issue of the information (the earliest date specified in it) to the date of the resumed hearing (3 months 2 weeks). The claim was not in respect of any specific damage but for the 'anxiety and distress' (see *Bond v Chief Constable of Kent* [1983] 1 WLR 40; [1983] 1 All ER 456, DC). They made a compensation order of £600 and a costs order for £4,044.

P16.43 *Earl v Kingston upon Hull CC*

May 1997 *Legal Action* 21, Kingston Magistrates' Court

Nuisance where tenant would have to put in heating at wholly disproportionate expense

The tenants alleged prejudice to health arising from condensation mould growth due to lack of heating. Their council home was fitted only with a single gas fire. Before issue of the summons the council removed the mould and applied fungicidal paint. It alleged that the mould had arisen from the tenant's failure to supplement the heating provided. The tenant's independent environmental health officer gave evidence based on electronic temperature and humidity monitoring to show that the mould and proliferating dust mites would return and thus the nuisance recur.

Stipendiary Magistrate White convicted, holding that to prevent recurrence the tenants would have to put in 'wholly disproportionate effort and expense'. The council agreed an order for extensive works, including full gas central heating, and paid the tenants' costs.

P16.44 *Ogunlowo v Southwark LBC*

December 2005 *Legal Action* 29; 25 January 2005, Camberwell Magistrates' Court

£2,500 compensation for condensation and cockroach infestation

Ms Ogunlowo was a tolerated trespasser of her flat following her breach of a suspended possession order. She brought a prosecution alleging that the council had allowed dampness, due to condensation and water penetration, and an infestation of cockroaches to render her premises prejudicial to health. The complaint was defended on the basis that Ms Ogunlowo had caused the damp and cockroaches.

After a six-day hearing, between March 2004 and January 2005, the magistrates upheld the complaint and found that a statutory nuisance existed and was likely to recur. They ordered the council to abate the nuisance in eight weeks, to pay Ms Ogunlowo and her family compensation of £2,500 and costs which totalled many thousands of pounds.

P16.45 *Parry v Walsall MBC*

May 1997 *Legal Action* 21, Aldridge and Brownhills Magistrates' Court

Fines for failure to carry out works

On 20 May 1996 the council was ordered to carry out works following a successful Environmental Protection Act 1990 s82 prosecution. The work was not done and the tenant issued proceedings under s82(8). At trial on 15 October 1996, the justices convicted the council and ordered it to complete the original works within a further 21 days but imposed no financial penalty. The work was still not done. The tenant issued further s82(8) proceedings, seeking a fine and a continuing daily fine. The work was finally completed on 4 February 1997.

The justices found that s82(8) in mandatory terms required both a fixed initial and a continuing daily fine from the date of conviction (15 October 1996). It imposed fines totalling £45,500

See also *Queeney v Wolverhampton BC* (P16.47)

P16.46 *Pringle v Hackney LBC*

September 1995 *Legal Action* 16, Wells Street Magistrates' Court

Condensation likely to recur without background heating

Following a complaint of condensation dampness, the council had provided adequate ventilation and an electric convector heater in the living room and so at the date of the hearing the nuisance had abated. The tenant contended that the council was nonetheless guilty of an offence contrary to Environmental Protection Act 1990 Part III because, in the absence of provision for background heating, the nuisance was likely to recur. The council argued that, if the living room heater were used 24 hours a day, the base temperature of the walls would rise sufficiently to prevent condensation arising.

Applying *Greater London Council v Tower Hamlets LBC* (P16.15) and rejecting the council's evidence, Metropolitan Stipendiary Magistrate Bates held that without background heating the condensation was liable to recur. He entered a conviction, awarded costs of £3,500 and made a nuisance order requiring the provision of background heating. On the tenant's application for a compensation order, the council argued that, as Environmental Protection Act 1990 Part III created no 'offence' until it had been established that there was a nuisance at the date of hearing or the likelihood of recurrence, there should be no compensation order in respect of loss suffered before the hearing. The magistrate rejected the submission and awarded £3,000 compensation.

Note: See now *R v Liverpool Crown Court ex p Cooke* (P16.32) regarding compensation.

P16.47 *Queeney v Wolverhampton BC*

September 1995 *Legal Action* 16, Wolverhampton Magistrates' Court

Fine at daily rate of £500

By a nuisance order made in Environmental Protection Act 1990 proceedings, the council was required to complete remedial works by 13 March 1995. The tenant laid an information under s82(8), complaining that the council had failed to comply. On 12 April 1995 the council pleaded guilty and was fined £2,500 and ordered to pay £1,100 costs. The work was still not carried out. A second information was laid and on 7 June 1995 the council pleaded guilty. It was again fined £4,000 and ordered to pay £1,500 costs. The work was still not completed. The tenant laid a third information and on 19 July 1995 the council pleaded guilty yet again.

On this last occasion the council was fined £1,000, ordered to pay costs of £800 and made the subject of a daily fine of £500 (the amount prescribed by s82(8)). The justices directed that the tenant should restore the matter to court on completion of the works so that the number of days for which payment was due could be ascertained.

County courts

P16.48 *Middlemast v Hammersmith and Fulham LBC*

May 1997 *Legal Action* 20, West London County Court

Compromise in criminal proceedings did not prevent civil claim

In 1993, Environmental Protection Act 1990 proceedings brought by a tenant of a damp flat were met with a 'not guilty' plea. They were adjourned and then compromised on the basis that the council would, without admission of any liability, install central heating. The tenant then brought a civil claim for damages for disrepair, annexing to the particulars of claim the same inspection report which had featured in the Environmental Protection Act proceedings. The council applied to strike out the action as an abuse of process (CCR Ord 13 r5(1)(d)) on the basis that the compromise in the Environmental Protection Act proceedings determined all liability of the council for the conditions set out in the inspection report.

Deputy District Judge Lightman refused to strike out and the council appealed. HHJ Reynolds dismissed the appeal. He held that the clearest evidence would be needed to establish that the compromise extended not simply to the criminal proceedings but to any prospective civil claims arising from the same matters. On construction of the documents, such an extensive compromise was not made out.

Scottish courts

P16.49 *Robb v Dundee CC*

2002 SLT 853, Court of Session, Extra Division

Condensation arose due to inadequate heat input by tenant

The appellant was a secure council tenant whose home was very badly affected by condensation dampness and mould growth. She brought a prosecution under EPA s82 alleging that the premises were prejudicial to health or a nuisance and so a statutory nuisance. The local sheriff decided that she had failed to establish a statutory nuisance (as another sheriff had decided on similar facts in *Anderson v Dundee CC* 2000 SLT (Sh Ct) 134) and the sheriff principal dismissed her appeal. She appealed to the Court of Session.

All three members of the court were satisfied that the available evidence established that the state of the premises was such as to be prejudicial to health (although not a nuisance) and that, accordingly, a statutory nuisance existed. However, the majority held that the appellant had failed to establish that the nuisance had arisen through the act, default or sufferance of the council (EPA s82(4)(a)). The flat had an electric radiant heater in the living room and electric sockets in the other rooms into which heating appliances could be plugged. The condensation resulted primarily from the lack of adequate heat input. The evidence was that the cost of providing the necessary heating was neither 'abnormal nor extravagant from an objective point of view' even though it was well beyond the modest means of the tenant. It was for the tenant to provide the heat input. The majority also held that the tenant could not rely on the council's strict liability as owner because there were no structural defects (EPA s82(4)(b)). Inadequate insulation was not a defect of a structural character. Lady Panton, dissenting, would have held that the provision by the council of 'premises which, as a result of their component materials, design and construction, have an inherent defect, namely a particularly pronounced vulnerability to condensation dampness' rendered it liable both as owner and as the person by whose act default or sufferance the nuisance had arisen. No appeal to the House of Lords was pursued because the tenant obtained alternative accommodation.

Ombudsman complaints

P16.50 *X Council*

Case reference confidential; December 2007 *Legal Action* 30

Maladministration in failing to respond to mould growth and condensation

Ms H complained that a council failed to deal properly with a dampness problem to her home. Ms H complained of damp, including water dripping around the windows, black mould on the walls and dangerously slippery wooden floors. Initially, the council responded promptly: it inspected the property and decided to apply anti-fungal paint to the affected walls and seek further advice. Approximately one year later, a further report on the property confirmed that it suffered from condensation and persistent mould growth because of its position and the design of the building. As a result, secondary glazing was installed but it made the problem worse. Specialist consultants inspected the property and concluded that there was severe condensation because of a general lack of ventilation and heating, and because of problems caused by the construction of the building. The consultants recommended thermal dry lining to all affected rooms. However, when the council wrote to Ms H to tell her the outcome, it blamed poor ventilation and lack of heating; it failed to mention the structural problem and the recommendation to install dry lining. In response to Ms H's MP, the director of housing indicated that the damp problem was the result of the tenant's lifestyle. A subsequent report following an inspection by the council's environmental health service concluded that the persistent condensation was the result primarily of the design and construction of the building, rather than the lifestyle of its occupants. The report declared the flat unfit for human habitation and recommended works to make it habitable, including installing extractor fans, a ventilation unit, checking the central heating and dry lining the external walls to provide thermal insulation. One year later, only some of the recommended measures had been undertaken and the property was still considered to be unfit for habitation.

The ombudsman found that the council had failed to deal properly with Ms H's complaints about dampness. It had delayed in identifying the cause of the damp problems and had failed to follow its own good practice guide which recommended a thorough and systematic investigation of complaints about mould growth and condensation. These failings led to a delay of around 12 months in making the appropriate finding that the problem was largely structural and recommending appropriate remedial works. There was a further delay of 12 months in agreeing to carry out the works that the environmental health department identified as necessary to make the property fit. During this latter period, one bedroom was un-inhabitable because of the damp conditions. The council agreed to settle the complaint by:

1) providing a detailed schedule of works to implement the package of measures recommended by the environmental health department;
2) considering whether Ms H and her family needed to be moved out for the duration of the works, which was subsequently arranged; and
3) paying Ms H £4,000 to compensate her and her family for having to live in unhealthy and unsuitable conditions for two years longer than they should have done.

P17   Grants

The Regulatory Reform (Housing Assistance) Order 2002 SI No 1860 gives local authorities a broad general power to provide assistance for home repair, improvement and adaptation, subject only to limited constraints. It repeals much of Housing Grants, Construction and Regeneration Act 1996 Part I but retains, with amendment, the provisions for Disabled Facilities Grants, which are mandatory.

Court of Appeal

P17.1   *R v Greenwich LBC ex p Glen International*
(2001) 33 HLR 1023; (2000) *Times* 29 March, CA

Application for grant not required to be made before works completed nor with estimates

See *Housing Law Casebook* 3rd edition.

P17.2   *R v Tower Hamlets LBC ex p Von Goetz*
[1999] QB 1019; [1999] 2 WLR 582; [1999] LGR 135; (1999) 31 HLR 669, CA

Renovation grant – equitable lease was an 'owner's interest'

See *Housing Law Casebook* 3rd edition.

P17.3   *R (B) v Calderdale MBC*
[2004] EWCA Civ 134; [2004] 1 WLR 2017; [2004] HLR 19

Refusal of grant to build extra room for child with Asperger's syndrome unlawful

B's eldest son suffered from Asperger's syndrome, a disability which resulted in aggressive behaviour towards his sibling. The eldest son shared a bedroom with his younger brother, and regularly attacked him and interrupted his sleep during the night. B applied for a grant to provide for a separate bedroom for each child. The council refused the grant. Stanley Burnton J dismissed an application for judicial review ([2003] EWHC 1832 (Admin); (2003) *Times* 11 September), but B appealed.

The Court of Appeal allowed the appeal. Under Housing Grants, Construction and Regeneration Act 1996 s23(1) one of the purposes for which a grant application must be approved is making a dwelling safe for a disabled occupant and other persons residing with him. In this case, the building of an extra bedroom was a practical way of reducing the risk to the eldest son and the rest of the family. The fact that the house would not be made entirely safe did not matter.

P17.4   **Trustees of Dennis Rye Pension Fund v Sheffield CC**
[1998] 1 WLR 840; [1997] 4 All ER 747; (1998) 30 HLR 645, CA

Private law right crystallised on making of decision to award grant

See *Housing Law Casebook* 3rd edition.

High Court

P17.5   **Brent LBC v Patel**
[2001] 1 WLR 897; [2001] LGR 285; (2000) *Times* 30 November, ChD

Grant repayable with interest where conditions not complied with

Mr Patel and his sister Ms Patel applied for a house in multiple occupation grant in respect of works which they certified, as required by Local Government and Housing Act 1989 s106(7), would be let as a residence to someone who was not a member of the family. The grant was made subject to conditions restricting the occupation of the property to persons unconnected with the family. The conditions were imposed in accordance with Local Government and Housing Act 1989 s122(2).

Patten J held that they related to the whole of the property, so that Ms Patel's occupation of part of the property was in breach of those conditions. Mr and Ms Patel lost their entitlement to the grant. The grant awarded was repayable to the council with interest.

P17.6   **Qazi v Waltham Forest LBC**
(2000) 32 HLR 689; April 2000 *Legal Action* 19, QBD

Local authorities owe no private law duty to advise about statutory provisions concerning grants.

P17.7   **R v Birmingham CC ex p Mohammed**
[1999] 1 WLR 33; [1998] 3 All ER 788; (1998) 1 CCLR 441; (1999) 31 HLR 392, QBD

Council not entitled to have regard to finances in determining disabled facilities grant

Mr Mohammed was disabled within the meaning of the Housing Grants, Construction and Regeneration Act 1996. He made an application to the respondent for a disabled facilities grant under s2. On 15 April 1997, the housing department refused his application on the ground that he did not meet the criteria. He instituted judicial review proceedings. On 9 April 1998, the respondent agreed to reconsider its decision. The respondent had not made a further decision but indicated it would do so on the basis that it was obliged, or alternatively entitled, to have regard to its financial resources in determining the application.

Dyson J held that local housing authorities are not entitled to have regard to their resources in determining whether or not to approve an application for a disabled facilities grant for the purposes of s23(1). They should consider objectively whether, having regard to the applicants' needs and the nature of the works proposed, those works would achieve their intended purpose. Such a purpose must come within s23(1).

P17.8   *R v Bradford MDC ex p Pickering*
(2001) 33 HLR 409, QBD

Purchasers under purchase rental agreement had 'owner's interest'

See *Housing Law Casebook* 3rd edition.

P17.9   *R v Newham LBC ex p Trendgrove Properties Ltd*
(2000) 32 HLR 424, QBD

Discretion to revoke grant valid where works completed late

See *Housing Law Casebook* 3rd edition.

Ombudsman complaints

P17.10   *Ombudsman complaint against Trafford MBC*
Complaint No 04/C/17057; 30 November 2006

Failure to explain significant change in renovation grants amounted to maladministration

W was a home-owner who had mental health problems. Her property was declared unfit for human habitation. She was allocated a social worker to assist her in bringing her house back into a habitable state. In February 1996, W made an enquiry about a renovation grant which she did not pursue. In January 1998, while detained in the psychiatric ward of a local hospital W signed an application form for a renovation grant. This application was granted and the renovation work took place at a cost of over £33,000. Subsequently, W's condition worsened and it was decided that she should sell her house and move into supported accommodation. She sold the house in April 2003. The council set about recovering the renovation costs from W.

In December 1996, the conditions regarding the repayment of grants when a property was sold had changed, with the possibility of a repayment being sought if the property was sold within three years being extended to five years. W knew about the three-year condition but claimed that the extension to five years was not explained to her. The local authority had the discretion to waive the repayment but refused to do so.

The ombudsman found maladministration. There was no doubt that W would not have sold the house when she did if she had known of the change. The ombudsman was not satisfied that when council officers met W in hospital she was told of the change of the grant conditions period from three to five years, despite an assertion that they would have told her. The fact that W had severely impaired mental capacity meant that the council should have made particular efforts to ensure that she understood every aspect of what she was agreeing to. The failure to ensure that W was aware of a new, vital condition of her grant was maladministration. The injustice was her inability then to delay the sale of their house and avoid any repayment of the grant. During investigations the ombudsman also found that the council's policy was invariably to recommend refusals.

To remedy the injustice that arose, the ombudsman recommended that the Council (1) waive repayment of the W's grant in full, (2) devise an appropriate policy on how to deal with waivers of repayments of renovation grants, and (3) make sure that all of the lessons that emerged from this complaint were learnt.

Long leases: service charges

Q1   Service charges

It is usual for long leases of residential flats to include provisions enabling the lessor to recover from the lessee a proportion of the expenditure spent in maintaining, repairing and managing the building. The amount of service charges recoverable depends on two factors, first, the provisions of the lease in question and, second, the statutory restrictions on the recovery of service charges, now contained in the Landlord and Tenant Act 1985. For example, s19 provides that service charges are recoverable only to 'the extent that they are reasonably incurred' and where 'services or works are of a reasonable standard'. Section 20 provides that, where lessors wish to recover a proportion of the cost of major works from lessees, they should first serve a notice giving details of estimates obtained, and then consult with the lessees. 'Major works' are defined as either works costing more than £1,000 or more than £50 multiplied by the number of flats, whichever is the greater (see Service Charge (Estimates and Consultation) Order 1988 SI No 1285).

Q2   Construction of service charges provisions

Court of Appeal

Q2.1   *Adelphi (Estates) Ltd v Christie*
(1984) 269 EG 221, CA

'Lessor' in lease included anyone standing in lessor's shoes

A long lease provided that lessors were entitled to recover as service charges 2.9 per cent of the amount spent by them. The question to be decided by the court was whether this included expenditure by both the head landlord and, after grant of a concurrent lease, the mesne landlord.

The Court of Appeal held that it did, and that the word 'lessor' included anyone standing in the lessor's shoes.

Q2.2   *Berrycroft Management Co Ltd v Sinclair Gardens Investments*
(1998) 75 P&CR 210; (1997) 29 HLR 444; [1997] 1 EGLR 47, CA

Landlord's right to nominate insurance company unqualified

Lessees challenged insurance charges passed on to them by their landlord under the terms of their leases, apparently claiming that cheaper insurance could have been found with other companies.

The Court of Appeal held that there was no reason to imply any term into the covenants that the landlord's right to nominate either the company or the agency through which the insurance was to be placed should be restricted. The insurance had been arranged in the normal course of business through an agency of repute. The right of the landlord to nominate the insurance company and agency was unqualified.

Q2.3   *Billson v Tristrem*
[2000] L&TR 220, CA

Where lease poorly drafted function of court is to ascertain terms in accordance with intentions of parties; lease to be read as a whole

In a dispute about unpaid service charges, the Court of Appeal held that, although the lease was 'unhappily drafted', the function of the court was to ascertain the terms of the lease in accordance with the whole intentions of the parties evinced from the terms regardless of the use of inept words. The lease should be read as a whole.

Q2.4   **Blatherwick (Services) Ltd v King**
[1991] Ch 218; [1991] 2 WLR 848; [1991] 2 All ER 874; (1991) 23 HLR 188; (1990) 62 P&CR 18; [1991] 2 EGLR 39, CA

Liability under lease continued when lease expired and lessee became statutory tenant

It was held that a covenant in a long lease requiring a lessee to pay service charges was a term of the tenancy 'relating to' the property within the meaning of Landlord and Tenant Act 1954 s10(1). Accordingly, when the lease expired and the lessee became a statutory tenant, that liability was not extinguished. Service charges (including a proportion of the cost of insurance, lighting, cleaning, maintenance, employment of porter, etc) were payable, in addition to the rent registered by the rent officer.

Q2.5   **Boldmark Ltd v Cohen**
(1987) 19 HLR 135; [1986] 1 EGLR 47; (1986) 277 EG 745, CA

Clear words necessary to charge interest on money borrowed to provide services

The Court of Appeal held that a landlord is not entitled to charge to lessees interest payments on money borrowed to finance the provision of services, unless the lease contains clear and unambiguous words to this effect. It was, however, recognised that such express provision might be sensible and that 'in some contexts a reference in general terms to expenditure in respect of the general administration of a block of flats might perhaps, on a liberal construction, be capable of including an interest element' ((1987) 19 HLR at 142).

Q2.6   **Coventry CC v Cole**
[1994] 1 WLR 398; [1994] 1 All ER 997; (1993) 25 HLR 555; [1994] 1 EGLR 63; [1994] 06 EG 133; (1994) 92 LGR 18, CA (see E13.2)

Restrictions on recovery of service charges where right to buy exercised did not apply to particular charges levied

Q2.7   **Embassy Court Residents' Association Ltd v Lipman**
(1984) 271 EG 545, CA

Term implied that expenses of employing management company could be recovered

The residents' association, which had become leasehold owners of the block, claimed as service charges from lessees a contribution towards the cost of employing managing agents. The leases contained a covenant that the lessees should pay 'a due proportion of the cost and expenses incurred ... in carrying out works of maintenance, repair and renewal of the main structure' etc, but did not contain any express provision requiring the lessee to pay anything towards the cost of employing managing agents.

The Court of Appeal held that, in view of the fact that the lessor was a residents' association,

> ... it was necessary in order to give business efficacy to this transaction to imply a term that the reasonably necessary administrative expenses of the Management Association (a) should be incurred by the Association and (b) should be recovered from individual lessees pro rata pursuant to an implied covenant to do so.

However, Cumming-Bruce LJ qualified this by stating:

> No doubt in the case of leases entered into between a landlord and tenant it is necessary for the landlord to spell out specifically in the terms of the lease, and in some detail, a sufficient description of every financial obligation imposed upon the tenant in addition to the tenant's obligation for rent ...

The former landlord, who was a private individual, would not have been entitled to recover a proportion of the cost of employing managing agents.

Q2.8   *Finchbourne Ltd v Rodrigues*

[1976] 3 All ER 581, CA

Implied term that costs recoverable should be 'fair and reasonable'

A clause in a lease stated that the lessor was entitled to recover as service charges a proportion of the money 'expended' in maintaining and running the block. The amount was to be 'ascertained and certified by the [plaintiffs'] Managing Agents acting as experts and not as arbitrators'.

The Court of Appeal held that:

1) The certificate had to be prepared by someone other than the lessor. As the real lessor was in fact the managing agent who certified the amount due, there was no valid certificate and the sums claimed were not due.

2) In order to give business efficacy to the lease, there had to be implied a term that the costs recoverable from the lessee should be 'fair and reasonable'. It could not have been intended that the lessors should have an unfettered discretion to adopt the highest conceivable standard of maintenance and to charge the lessees accordingly (cf, *Bandar Property Holdings Ltd v J S Darwen (Successors) Ltd* [1968] 2 All ER 305, QBD and *Havenridge Ltd v Boston Dyers Ltd* [1994] 2 EGLR 73; [1994] 49 EG 111, CA).

Q2.9   *Gilje v Charlegrove Securities Ltd*

[2001] EWCA Civ 1777, [2002] 16 EG 182, [2002] L&TR 33, [2000] 44 EG 148, [2001] L&TR 197, Central London County Court and Lands Tribunal

Obligations on tenants for service charges construed restrictively (contra proferentem)

Leases of four flats in a building included covenants that the landlord would provide a resident caretaker and that the lessees would pay service charges. A dispute arose as to whether lessees were liable to pay a notional rent of £7,800 charged in respect of the caretaker's flat.

The Court of Appeal noted that the construction sought by the landlords was that the tenants were obliged to pay a service charge. For such an obligation to exist, its terms have to be clearly set out. Obligations on tenants for service charges are construed restrictively (contra proferentem) and are not likely to include ambiguous clauses. Mummery LJ approved the 'obvious' proposition that 'courts tend to construe service charge provision restrictively and are unlikely to allow recovery for items which are not clearly included'. The leases in this case did not provide any criteria for how the notional rent would be calculated and were ambiguous in terms of the caretaker's residence. A reasonable tenant or prospective tenant reading the leases would not perceive that the provisions for service charges obliged the tenant to contribute towards the notional cost of providing the caretaker's flat. Such a construction did not arise clearly and plainly form the words used.

Q2.10 **Gordon and Texeira v Selico Ltd and Select Managements Ltd**
(1986) 18 HLR 219; [1986] 1 EGLR 71; (1986) 278 EG 53, CA (see P4.6)

Service charges not recoverable where maintenance and repair not carried out and services provided not of reasonable standard

Q2.11 **Hackney LBC v Thompson**
[2001] L&TR 69, CA

Covenant to pay service charges not void for uncertainty

The defendant exercised the right to buy under Housing Act 1985 Part V and covenanted to pay the council annual service charges in a sum representing the 'due proportion' of costs incurred in lighting, cleaning and maintaining the surrounding estate and 'a reasonable and fair proportion' of its management expenses. A district judge found that the covenant to pay service charges was void for uncertainty.

The Court of Appeal held that the correct approach was to ascertain the intention of the parties, having regard to the background. The covenant to pay service charges was not void for uncertainty. The term 'due' was sufficiently wide to embrace what was 'fitting', 'proper' or 'reasonable'. It could not be suggested that the parties had intended that anything other than what was reasonable should have been due. The court was reluctant to hold void for uncertainty a provision that was intended by both parties to have legal effect. While it might not have been easy to determine what was reasonable, courts had nevertheless been obliged to do so in other similar cases – see eg *Sheffield CC v Jackson* (E13.10) and *Brown v Gould* [1972] 1 Ch 53.

Q2.12 **Heinemann v Cooper**
(1987) 19 HLR 262; [1987] 2 EGLR 154, CA

Damages for misrepresentation of amount of service charges

A purchaser of a long lease claimed damages for misrepresentation. Before exchange of contracts, the vendor's solicitor had indicated that service charges would be in the region of £250 per annum. They turned out to be £625. A county court judge accepted evidence given by a surveyor who appeared on behalf of the lessee that the higher service charges would make a difference of £3,000 to the sale price of the flat. Damages in that sum were awarded.

The Court of Appeal dismissed the vendor's appeal, finding no reason for interfering with the county court judgment.

Q2.13   *Hi-Lift Elevator Services v Temple*
(1996) 28 HLR 1; (1995) 70 P&CR 620, CA

No right for lessee to obtain injunction restraining lessor from carrying out works

Under the terms of his lease, a lessee was liable to pay half of the lessor's expenses in maintaining the main structure of the building. This included the roof. The lessors obtained three tenders for works to the roof. The cheapest of these cost £10,840. The lessee's surveyor thought that only minor works, costing between £1,500 and £2,000, were necessary. The tenant applied for and obtained an ex parte injunction restraining the lessor from carrying out any works to the roof pending a determination on whether or not the works were necessary.

The Court of Appeal allowed the lessor's appeal. If there is a landlord's repairing covenant, it is for the landlord to decide what works to carry out and so there is no common-law right for a lessee to apply for an injunction to restrain a lessor from carrying out works under the covenant. There was no 'serious issue to be tried' within the meaning of *American Cyanamid Co v Ethicon Ltd* [1975] AC 396, HL. In any event the lessee had an alternative remedy in that he could challenge the reasonableness of his service charges (Landlord and Tenant Act 1985 s19).

Q2.14   *Holding and Management Ltd v Property Holding and Investment Trust plc*
[1989] 1 WLR 1313; [1990] 1 All ER 938; (1989) 21 HLR 596; [1990] 05 EG 75, CA

Proceedings to enforce repairing covenants; costs; repair/improvement distinction

A maintenance trustee managed a block of flats on behalf of the landlord and held a maintenance fund which was provided by contributions from the lessees. The tenants brought proceedings against both the landlord and the maintenance trustee to enforce repairing covenants.

The proceedings were largely successful. It was held by Mervyn Davies J that the maintenance trustee, in defending the proceedings, had acted as agent for the landlord and not as trustee for the tenants, and so was not entitled to recover from the maintenance fund its legal costs in unsuccessfully defending proceedings brought by lessees. He also found that a proposed scheme, which involved the complete removal of the brick skin to the building, was not a repair but part of a scheme of improvements. The Court of Appeal dismissed appeals and cross-appeals.

Q2.15   *Northways Flats Management Co (Camden) Ltd v Wimpey Pension Trustees Ltd*
[1992] 2 EGLR 42, CA

Provisions in lease a condition precedent to recovery of costs of works

The Court of Appeal considered the construction of various clauses in a lease relating to the payment of service charges, and, in particular, a covenant requiring the landlord to submit a copy of the specifications of proposed works and estimates before starting work.

The Court of Appeal held that this obligation was an essential part of the mechanism whereby disputes between the parties regarding works could be resolved and held that the obligation created a condition precedent to the recovery of a contribution towards the costs of works. As the plaintiffs had failed to comply with this provision, they were not able to recover money which they had spent on the exterior of the block.

Q2.16 **Parkside Knightsbridge Ltd v Horwitz**
(1983) 268 EG 49, CA

Management charges reasonable

The provisions of the lease entitled the landlords to include as service charges an amount for management and supervision.

The Court of Appeal considered whether or not the amount claimed was reasonable and, having seen quotations from four other estate agents, found that it was.

Q2.17 **Pole Properties Ltd v Feinberg**
(1981) 43 P&CR 121; (1981) 259 EG 417, CA

Where situation envisaged in lease had changed radically, terms of the lease regarding heating charges disregarded and court adopted a fair and reasonable approach

The landlords sued for service charges resulting from the provision of heating and hot water.

The Court of Appeal found that the situation originally envisaged in the lease had been changed radically by the construction of further flats and the installation of a new central heating system for both the old and the new flats. In view of this, the court disregarded the terms of the lease and adopted 'a fair and reasonable approach', calculating the amount due as the proportion of the directly heated volume in the defendant's maisonette to the entirety of the directly heated volume of the whole of the block.

Q2.18 **Sella House Ltd v Mears**
(1989) 21 HLR 147; [1989] 1 EGLR 65; [1989] 12 EG 67, CA

Cost of employing solicitors to recover arrears from other lessees not recoverable unless clear and unambiguous clause

Construing a service charges covenant in a long lease, the Court of Appeal held that a freeholder was not entitled to pass on to lessees as a whole the cost of employing solicitors and counsel to recover arrears of rent and service charges from particular lessees, since the clause in question did not contain any specific mention of lawyers, proceedings or legal costs, but was, rather, concerned with maintenance, safety and administration. There must be a clear and unambiguous clause to persuade the court that costs of such proceedings can be recovered from lessees as a whole.

Q2.19 **Sheffield CC v Jackson**
[1998] 1 WLR 1591; [1998] 3 All ER 260; (1999) 31 HLR 331, CA (see E13.10)

When exercising right to buy reasonableness of service charges only challengeable before execution of conveyance

Q2.20 *Sinclair Gardens Investments (Kensington) v Walsh*

[1996] QB 231; [1995] 3 WLR 524; [1995] 4 All ER 852; (1996) 28 HLR 338; (1996) 71 P&CR 47; [1995] 2 EGLR 23, CA (see N3.19)

Sums claimed as service charges are 'rent' where so defined in lease

Q2.21 *Skilleter v Charles*

(1992) 24 HLR 421; [1992] 1 EGLR 73; [1992] 13 EG 113, CA

Interest chargeable on arrears of service charges; recovery of cost of employ-ing managing agent allowed despite freeholder and wife being directors of company

Long lessees appealed against a county court judge's refusal to grant declar-ations which they sought about the non-recoverability of service charges under their long leases.

The Court of Appeal dismissed the appeal. It held that, on the con-struction of the leases, interest was chargeable by the landlord on arrears of service charges but, even in the absence of any express provision, such a term could be implied, either to give business efficacy to the lease or on the basis of the 'officious bystander' test. A paragraph in the lease which entitled the landlord to recover through service charges 'the cost of em-ploying a managing agent' permitted him to claim the fees of a company which managed the property, even though he and his wife were the direc-tors of the company. The position would have been different if the com-pany was a sham or where the managing agent was a mere nominee of the landlord (cf, *Finchbourne Ltd v Rodrigues* (Q2.8)).

Q2.22 *St Mary's Mansions Ltd v Limegate Investment Co Ltd*

[2002] EWCA Civ 1491, [2002] 05 EG 146; [2003] HLR 24; (2002) *Times* 13 November

Construction of lease; detailed accounting of overpayments required

Leases of flats provided for the payment of service charges. Although no proper mechanism for the establishment of a reserve fund existed in the terms of the leases, lessees paid into a reserve fund sums to be used for improvements and repairs. Payments into the reserve fund regularly ex-ceeded expenditure. The landlord kept the outstanding balance in the fund and used it to ameliorate any cash flow problems.

The Court of Appeal held that:

- The terms of the leases allowed the landlord to establish and main-tain a reserve fund. However, detailed accounting should be provided and appropriate provision made for overpayments to be repaid to the lessees at the end of each year. Landlord and Tenant Act 1987 s42 pro-vides that service charge contributions are held on trust. It is a breach of that provision for landlords to retain such over payments in respect of one identified expense for other, unidentified future expenses.
- The natural and ordinary meaning of words in the leases meant that interest on late payment of ground rent and service charges should be paid to the landlord.
- On a proper construction of the leases, the landlord was not able to charge legal costs as part of the service charge.

Q2.23 *Unchained Growth III plc v Granby Village (Manchester) Management Co Ltd*

[2000] 1 WLR 739; [2000] L&TR 186; (1999) *Times* 4 November; [1999] EGCS 116, CA

Prohibition of set-off against maintenance charges valid

The plaintiffs were the management company for a block of flats. The defendants were the long lessees of 51 flats within the block. The leases provided that maintenance charges were payable to the plaintiffs 'without any deduction by way of set-off'. The defendants claimed that service charges for the years 1993 to 1996 were unreasonable and that they were entitled to set off alleged overpayment during those years against the plaintiffs' current claim. They claimed that the exclusion clause was unreasonable because of Unfair Contract Terms Act 1977 ss3 and 13. The plaintiffs sought summary judgment under RSC Ord 14 (now CPR 24). HHJ Howarth, sitting as a High Court judge, granted summary judgment. A right of set-off can be excluded by contract. If the service charges had been payable to the landlord, rather than to the management company, the set-off clause could not have been challenged under Unfair Contract Terms Act 1977 since the Act had no application to a contract relating to the creation of an interest in land (see Sch 1 para 1(b)). In this connection it made no difference that the service charges were payable to a management company where that company was a party to the lease.

The Court of Appeal dismissed the lessees' appeal. The obligation to pay maintenance charges was plainly a provision which related to the creation of the leasehold interest. It was an integral part of the lease, providing the administrative mechanism for the enjoyment of the leasehold interest in common with, and for the benefit of, the other tenants of the development. Even if the statutory test applied, there was no ground for saying that the prohibition was unreasonable.

Q2.24 *Universities Superannuation Scheme Ltd v Marks & Spencer plc*

[1999] 04 EG 158, CA

Where error in sums charged by freeholder, lessee liable to pay additional sums

A lease provided for payment of service charges calculated according to rateable values. The tenant paid the service charges demanded by the landlord for years 1992 and 1993. The landlord then discovered that it had been mistaken as to the rateable values and sent the tenant new demands.

The Court of Appeal held that the lessee was liable for the additional sums. Payment of a lesser sum incorrectly calculated was not a performance by the tenant of its contractual obligation.

High Court

Q2.25 *Capital and Counties Freehold Equity Trust Ltd v BL plc*

[1987] 2 EGLR 49; (1987) 283 EG 563, ChD

Lessee not obliged to pay proportion of costs of building contract entered into before lease expired when works not started

A lease included a covenant to pay a proportion of 'all amounts sums costs and expenses of each and every kind whatsoever which may from time to time during the said term be expended or incurred or become payable by the landlord'. Before the expiry of the lease, the landlord entered into a building contract for works to be carried out, but no works were started and no sums paid by the landlord until after the lease had terminated.

It was held that the lessee was not obliged to pay a proportion of the cost of those works, as the word 'incurred' was synonymous with 'expended' or 'become payable'.

Q2.26   *Frobisher (Second Investments) Ltd v Kiloran Trust Co Ltd*
[1980] 1 WLR 425; [1980] 1 All ER 488; (1979) 40 P&CR 442; (1979) 253 EG 1231, ChD

Construction of lease; landlord must have incurred liability before it could be recovered

The service charges clause in the lease included the words 'to the extent that the liability incurred or amount defrayed by the landlord in respect of such items is reasonable ...'

Walton J held that 'the landlord must have defrayed the cost, or at any rate incurred liability to pay the cost, before it can be recovered from the tenant' (at 492).

Q2.27   *Lloyds Bank v Bowker Orford*
[1992] 2 EGLR 44, ChD

Ambit of 'any other beneficial services ... by the lessors' considered

A lease included a provision for the payment of service charges in respect of a number of specified services, such as cleaning, caretaking, lighting, etc, and 'any other beneficial services which may properly be provided by the lessors'.

David Neuberger QC, sitting as a deputy High Court judge, held that these provisions did not allow the freeholders to pass on the cost of major external repairs and internal decorations, but did allow them to recover the cost of employing managing agents and a proportion of the notional cost of providing accommodation for the caretaker.

Q2.28   *Mullaney v Maybourne Grange (Croydon) Management Co Ltd*
[1986] 1 EGLR 70, ChD

Works done improvement not repair and not covered by covenant

A landlord covenanted to 'repair maintain ... and otherwise provide services and amenities to the structure and common parts'. The lessee covenanted to pay a percentage of the landlord's costs of performing this obligation and of providing and maintaining additional services or amenities. The landlord replaced defective wooden-framed windows with new double-glazed windows.

It was held that this amounted to an improvement, not a repair, and that the new windows could not be regarded as an additional amenity. Accordingly, the lessee had no obligation to contribute towards their cost (cf, *Manor House Drive Ltd v Shahbazian* (1965) 195 EG 283, CA).

Q2.29   *New England Properties plc v Portsmouth News Shops Ltd*
[1993] 1 EGLR 84, ChD

New and improved roof covered by terms of lease; new roof in any event a repair

A roof which had been defectively designed was damaged in the great storm of 1987. There was a risk of collapse. The landlords carried out works which resulted in a different and improved roof structure. They sought to recover the cost of the works from the lessees. The service charges provision in the lease enabled the landlord to recover the 'cost and expense of constructing, repairing, rebuilding ... and maintaining all things' connected with the premises. Another covenant obliged the landlord 'to keep and maintain ... and to renew or replace' the building's exterior and structure.

Terence Cullen QC, sitting as a deputy High Court judge, held that the inclusion of the words 'renew or replace' entitled the landlord to recover the cost of the works. Furthermore, following *Post Office v Aquarius Properties Ltd* (P3.10), he held that, even if the covenant had not included those words, the works were repairs and so the landlords would have been able to pass on the cost. (cf *Scottish Mutual Ass plc v Jardine Public Relations* [1999] EGCS 43, Technology and Construction Court (costs of replacing roof not recoverable from short-term lessees).

Q2.30   *Primeridge Ltd v Jean Muir Ltd*
[1992] 1 EGLR 273, Official Referees' Business

'All proper costs' did not entitle lessor to indemnity costs

Underlessees who had been defending a claim for service charges made a payment into court, which was accepted by the plaintiff landlord. As a result, in accordance with RSC Ord 62 r5 (see now CPR 36.13) the plaintiff was entitled to the costs of the action 'up to the time of giving notice of acceptance'. The plaintiffs, relying on a provision in the underlease which entitled them to recover 'all proper costs charges and expenses ... incurred ... in connection with any breach of covenant' sought those costs on an indemnity basis.

HHJ Esyr Lewis QC held that the contractual term did not 'plainly and unambiguously' entitle the plaintiffs to indemnity costs rather than costs on the standard basis. The words 'all proper costs' meant no more than such costs as may be recovered under an order of the court. The plaintiffs were, accordingly, not awarded costs on an indemnity basis.

Q2.31   *Reston Ltd v Hudson*
[1990] 2 EGLR 51; [1990] 37 EG 86, ChD

Construction of lease; reasonable to replace all windows where some were rotting

HHJ Hague QC, sitting as a High Court judge, held that, on the true construction of leases of flats in a block, replacement of rotten window frames was the landlords' responsibility and that it was reasonable for all the windows to be replaced at the same time. He also granted declarations that, subject to the works being of a reasonable quality, the landlords were entitled to recover as service charges both the cost of the replacement windows and the costs incurred in taking the proceedings for a declaration.

Q2.32   **Woodtrek Ltd v Jezek**
(1982) 261 EG 571, QBD

Four matters to be satisfied in order for charges to be due

A lease included a provision that the landlords were entitled to recover, under management expenses, the 'total expenditure ... in carrying out their obligations under clause 5(4) of this lease and any other costs and expenses reasonably and properly incurred in connection with the building ...'.

Walton J found that, in order for charges to be due, four matters had to be satisfied: first, that charges had been incurred in the accounting year, second, that they were reasonable, third, that they had actually been incurred and, fourth, that they came within the list of chargeable items set out in the lease. He held that the mere collection of rent did not come within the chargeable items.

Q3   Service charges – statutory provisions

Court of Appeal

Q3.1   **Aylesbond Estates Ltd v Macmillan and Garg**
(2000) 32 HLR 1; [1999] 2 L&TR 127, CA

Not appropriate to transfer case to LVT

Landlords sought forfeiture of a long lease for arrears of ground rent and service charges. The lessees defended on the basis that the service charges were excessive and unreasonable and counterclaimed for breach of covenant for quiet enjoyment and/or nuisance, including the cost of the installation of sound insulation. During an interlocutory appeal, the Court of Appeal considered whether the case should be transferred to the Leasehold Valuation Tribunal (LVT) under Landlord and Tenant Act 1985 s19(2A).

The Court of Appeal, in refusing to transfer, noted that not all the disputes between the parties were capable of being referred to the LVT, which only had jurisdiction to determine the reasonableness of service charges. The LVT could not consider relief from forfeiture, disputes about ground rent or the counterclaim. Although 'the question of costs is of course uppermost', in view of Landlord and Tenant Act 1985 s20C (power of court to order that costs in proceedings should not be added to service charges), there were no good costs reasons why the case should be sent to the LVT. Although the LVT is 'an expert tribunal' and 'following an inspection ... could reach a decision on the service charge dispute more quickly and easily, and therefore perhaps less expensively, than a judge who does not have that experience', the court noted that there were not currently any proceedings before the LVT. Proceedings before the LVT could be a 'somewhat lengthy and a somewhat costly exercise' whereas the court case was ready for trial.

Q3.2   **Broadwater Court Management Co Ltd v Jackson-Mann**
[1997] EGCS 145, CA

Exercise of discretion under LTA 1985 s20 to dispense with notice

Although the plaintiff failed to comply with the requirements of Landlord and Tenant Act 1985 s20 with regard to estimates and consultation, a quotation for works had been sent to the defendant's predecessor in title, the lowest tender was chosen, the costs were reasonable and the plaintiffs were a management company, not a building company or commercial landlord. A recorder dispensed with the requirement for a s20 notice and gave judgment for the plaintiffs on their claim for service charges.

The Court of Appeal held that the judge had exercised his discretion under Landlord and Tenant Act 1985 s20(9) to dispense with the notice on a proper appreciation of the facts and in accordance with the proper principles and so there was no cause to interfere with that exercise of discretion.

Q3.3   *Cinnamon Ltd v Morgan*
[2001] EWCA Civ 1616; [2002] 2 P&CR 10; [2002] L&TR 20

LTA 1985 s19 applied to costs incurred by management company

The defendant's lease included a provision that she should pay service charges calculated by reference to expenditure by a management company, rather than by her landlord. She claimed that the sums charged were not reasonable and that accordingly, in view of Landlord and Tenant Act 1985 s19, she had no obligation to pay them. In a trial of a preliminary issue, HHJ Oppenheimer held that the statutory regime did not apply where service charges were incurred by a management company, rather than by the landlord. The defendant appealed.

The appeal was allowed by consent. Although s18 defines relevant costs for service charges as 'costs incurred or to be incurred by or on behalf of the landlord', the definition of 'landlord' in s30 includes 'any person who has a right to enforce payment of a service charge.' In so far as there were comments to the contrary by the Court of Appeal in *Berrycroft Management Co Ltd v Sinclair Gardens Investments (Kensington Ltd* (Q2.2) they were obiter and distinguishable.

Q3.4   *Iperion Investments Corporation v Broadwalk House Residents Ltd*
(1995) 27 HLR 196; (1996) 71 P&CR 34; [1995] 2 EGLR 47; [1995] 46 EG 188, CA

Where tenant had successfully challenged service charge, order made that costs of proceedings not to added to service charge

The Court of Appeal upheld an order made under Landlord and Tenant Act 1985 s20C by a deputy judge sitting on Official Referee's Business (see N3.26) that the costs of the proceedings were not to be taken into account in determining the amount of any service charge payable by the tenant or any other person, even though on the construction of the lease those costs could in usual circumstances have been recovered as service charges. Peter Gibson LJ said that, in general, the landlord should not 'get through the back door what has been refused at the front'. It was unattractive that a tenant who had been substantially successful in litigation against his landlord and who had not only been told by the court that he need pay no part of his landlord's costs but also had an award of costs in his favour should find himself having to pay the landlord's costs through service charges.

Note: See also *Holding and Management Ltd v Property Holding and Investment Trust plc* (Q2.14).

Q3.5   *Martin (and Seale) v Maryland Estates Ltd*
[1999] 26 EG 151; (2000) 32 HLR 116, CA

Cost of additional works not included in s20 notice disallowed

The claimants were long lessees in a house which had been divided into flats. In 1994 the landlord's surveyor wrote enclosing a specification of proposed works. Later a notice complying with Landlord and Tenant Act 1985 s20 was served with accompanying estimates. The claimants' solicitors wrote suggesting that the works should be put on hold while the tenants exercised their right to acquire the freehold under the Leasehold Reform, Housing and Urban Development Act 1993 and that works should be attended to after the tenants had acquired the freehold. On 21 March 1995 the landlord commenced works. The builders also carried out additional work that they identified and which had not been included in the s20 notice. The tenants accepted that the landlords were entitled to recover the cost of the original works, but not the additional costs. An assistant recorder hearing a claim for service charges refused to grant the landlord a dispensation under s20(9), holding that the landlord had not acted reasonably in failing to inform the tenants of the need for additional works.

The landlord's appeal was dismissed. The cost of all the works, including the additional items, was almost double the amount estimated in the s20 notice. Although it had not been practical for the landlord to comply with all the requirements, that did not justify a total disregard of the requirements and a deliberate decision not to tell the lessees what was going on. A reasonable landlord would have informed the lessees of the extra work that it proposed to carry out. The assistant recorder was entitled to conclude that the landlord had not acted reasonably. The Court of Appeal also held that the assistant recorder had been correct to dismiss the landlords' claim under s20(1) for £1,000 towards the cost of the additional works. A common sense approach is required when deciding how one batch of 'qualifying works' is to be divided from another for the purposes of s20(1).

Q3.6   *Mohammadi v Anston Investments Ltd*
[2003] EWCA Civ 981; [2004] HLR 8; [2004] L&TR 6

Court should consider Housing Act 1996 s81 restriction on right of re-entry where service charges disputed

Ms Mohammadi was a long lessee. In 1993 she brought proceedings against the defendant lessor alleging breach of repairing covenants. She withheld payment of ground rent and service charges. In May 1996 Anston served a notice under Law of Property Act 1925 s146 indicating an intention to re-enter the property and forfeit the lease if Ms Mohammadi failed to pay outstanding ground rent, legal fees and service charges. In November 1996 Anston amended its defence and brought a counterclaim in an action begun by Ms Mohammadi for arrears of ground rent and service charges and possession of the flat. Service of the counterclaim amounted to re-entry by the landlord. Ms Mohammadi sought relief from forfeiture, questioning the reasonableness of the service charges. A judge gave judgment for the arrears of ground rent and service charges and made an order for possession but granted relief from forfeiture on the condition that Ms Mohammadi made certain payments, including the outstanding service charges and the cost of preparing the s146 notice. The judge refused to allow her to rely on Housing Act 1996 s81 (forfeiture for service charges not allowed unless previously agreed or determined) because it had not been sufficiently pleaded or relied on at trial as a substantive defence.

Ms Mohammadi's appeal to the Court of Appeal was allowed in part. The judge erred in refusing to allow her to rely on s81. The point was sufficiently raised in pleadings. In any event, although it was not necessary to decide the point, the court is probably obliged to take s81 into account even if it is not pleaded. Re-entry was effected by the service of the counterclaim on the ground of arrears of ground rent. However, re-entry for failure to pay service charges was forbidden by s81 because the arrears of service charges were neither admitted nor determined at that time. Accordingly, the county court action fell within County Courts Act 1984 s138 and the court was obliged to make an order for possession within the terms of s138(3)(b). The terms of relief from forfeiture had to be that the lessee paid into the court 'all the rent in arrears and the costs of the action'. The terms of relief should not have included payment of the outstanding service charges nor the cost of preparing the s146 notice. The costs of the counterclaim would have included costs referable to the claim for outstanding service charges. Those costs should not be included in the 'costs of the action' under s138(3).

Q3.7   *R (Daejan Properties Ltd) v London Leasehold Valuation Tribunal*
[2001] EWCA Civ 1095; [2001] 43 EG 187; [2002] HLR 25; [2002] L&TR 5; (2001) *Times* 10 August, CA

LVT's jurisdiction under s19(2A) applies only to unpaid service charges

Daejan were the owners of a block of flats. Many of the flats in the block were held under long leases which included provisions for the payment of service charges. Between 1989 and 1999 Daejan carried out major works projects in relation to the flats. In 1999 a lessee of one of the flats applied to the London Leasehold Valuation Tribunal (LVT) under Landlord and Tenant Act 1985 s19(2A) contending that management fees charged by Daejan for the works projects were excessive. He had not taken action in relation to the management fees until 1999 because he had feared the forfeiture of his lease. At the hearing Daejan submitted that the LVT had no jurisdiction under s19(2A) to investigate the reasonableness of the management fees as they had already been paid, and that, if that was not the case, the LVT only had jurisdiction to investigate service charges paid within the past six years. The LVT held that it had jurisdiction to determine whether the service charges actually paid in the past were reasonably incurred and that the limitation period applicable to the application was 12 years, not six years under Limitation Act 1980 s8. Daejan sought judicial review of the decision of the LVT.

Their application was dismissed by Sullivan J but allowed by the Court of Appeal. The wording of s19(2A) connoted an element of futurity by referring to a service charge which was 'alleged to be payable'. The natural and ordinary meaning of those words referred to a dispute about service charges that were claimed by the landlord and unpaid by the tenant. Moreover, to allow a tenant to reopen service charges paid many years previously would be a recipe for never ending litigation. Accordingly, the tribunal's jurisdiction under s19(2A) applies only to unpaid service charges. This includes the position where payments were made under an interim contractual arrangement for repayment if the charge was found to be excessive. It followed that the issue of limitation was irrelevant.

Q3.8   **R (Sinclair Gardens Investments (Kensington) Ltd) v The Lands Tribunal**
[2005] EWCA Civ 1305; [2006] 3 All ER 650; [2006] HLR 11

Judicial review of Lands Tribunal's refusal of permission to appeal only to be granted in exceptional circumstances

After a hearing before the LVT about disputed service charges, the landlord applied to the Lands Tribunal for permission to appeal. This was refused because there were no reasonable grounds for concluding that the LVT's decision was wrong. The landlord then applied for permission to apply for judicial review of the Lands Tribunal's decision. Sullivan J dismissed the application.

The Court of Appeal dismissed the landlord's appeal. In view of Lands Tribunal Act 1949 s3(4), it is in principle open to someone who has been refused permission to appeal by the Lands Tribunal to seek judicial review of that refusal. However, as the statutory scheme for appealing decisions of the LVT on service charge issues contained in the Lands Tribunal Act, the Landlord and Tenant Act 1985, and the regulations made thereunder is an adequate system for reviewing the merits of the first instance decision, and to involve fair, adequate and proportionate protection against the risk that the first instance tribunal acted without jurisdiction or fell into error, judicial review of a refusal of permission to appeal should only be granted in exceptional circumstances. This does not amount to a breach of ECHR article 6 since both the LVT and the Lands Tribunal satisfy the requirements of a 'court' for article 6 purposes. They are both independent judicial bodies with the additional advantage of specialising in service charge disputes.

Q3.9   *Ruddy v Oakfern Properties Ltd*
[2006] EWCA Civ 1389; [2007] L&TR 9

Subtenant could challenge maintenance charge of freeholder in LVT

Oakfern Properties Ltd was the freeholder of a building comprising, on different floors, commercial and residential premises. The upper floors contained 24 separate residential flats which were let to Publicshield Property Management Ltd, a non-profit making company, which sublet flats individually on long leases. Publicshield was owned by 15 of the subtenants. Mr Ruddy was a subtenant who was not a member of Publicshield. Under the head lease Oakfern was responsible for keeping the building in good repair, and Publicshield was obliged to pay Oakfern a maintenance charge equal to 90% of the costs incurred in discharging the repairing obligations. Each subtenant was obliged to pay Publicshield one twenty-fourth of the maintenance charge. Mr Ruddy challenged the amount of the maintenance charge on the basis that it was unreasonable and applied to a leasehold valuation tribunal (LVT) for a determination of the amount properly payable. The only respondent to the application was Oakfern. The LVT determined that the maintenance charge was a service charge within the meaning of Landlord and Tenant 1985 s18 and that Mr Ruddy, in his capacity as a subtenant, had the requisite status in law to challenge the amount of the maintenance charge as against Oakfern, even though the obligation to pay Oakfern lay not on him, as subtenant, but on Publicshield as headlessee. Oakfern appealed to the Lands Tribunal, which dismissed the appeal. Oakfern appealed further to the Court of Appeal.

The Court of Appeal dismissed the appeal. First, the definition of 'service charge' in s18 as 'an amount payable by a tenant of a dwelling' applied. Publicshield was tenant of part of the building. The fact that Publicshield was also the tenant of other flats and common parts did not take the charge outside the s18 definition. Following *Heron Maple House Ltd v Central Estates Ltd* (2002) 13 EG 102, Jonathan Parker LJ said that the section referred to 'tenant of a dwelling' and not 'tenant of a dwelling and nothing else'. Furthermore, s38, which defines 'dwelling,' does not require that the tenant be in occupation of the dwelling. Second, there was no justification for implying any restriction into the general words of s27A which give LVTs jurisdiction to determine the amount of service charge payable.

Q3.10   *Sutton (Hastoe) Housing Association v Williams*
(1988) 20 HLR 321; [1988] 1 EGLR 56, CA

Recovery for costs of repairs/improvements under Housing Act 1980

The defendants exercised the right to buy their flat, which had been held on a secure tenancy. Under the lease, the housing association covenanted to keep the block of flats in repair and 'to carry out such additional works ... as may be considered necessary by the lessor in its absolute discretion'. The lease also provided for the recovery as service charges of all expenditure incurred in complying with covenants. In view of the fact that the estate as a whole suffered from a problem of rotting window joinery, the housing association decided to replace all windows with new UPVC double-glazed windows. The defendants took the view that these works were not necessary and refused to pay service charges.

The Court of Appeal held that the lease complied with Housing Act 1980 Sch 2 (now Housing Act 1985 Sch 6) and so was not void. If the works were repairs within the repairing covenant, they were reasonably incurred and the cost was reasonable (see Housing Act 1980 Sch 19 – now Landlord and Tenant Act 1985 s19). However, if they were improvements, the restrictions on recovery contained in Housing Act 1980 Sch 19 did not apply.

Q3.11   *Yorkbrook Investments Ltd v Batten*
(1986) 18 HLR 25; (1985) 52 P&CR 51; [1985] 2 EGLR 100, CA

Approach to deduction from service charges where services not of reasonable standard; lessor obliged to comply with covenants despite non-payment of charges

The plaintiff company owned an estate consisting of about 280 flats. The defendant long lessee complained about the inadequate provision of services and withheld service charge contributions. The plaintiff claimed possession. Although the county court judge deducted some amounts from the money claimed as a result of the defendant's defence and counter-claim, some arrears remained. An order for forfeiture was made but suspended.

On the lessee's appeal, the Court of Appeal held:

1) Where services provided do not reach a reasonable standard (see now Landlord and Tenant Act 1985 s19, formerly Housing Act 1980 Sch 19 para 3), the judge is not bound to disallow the whole amount claimed by the freeholder, but may deduct a proportion. In this case the judge had deducted one-seventh of the lessee's contribution towards expenditure on the garden.

2) Only in exceptional circumstances should such reductions be disallowed because they are de minimis. Although such matters may be 'small in quantum [they] may be of considerable moment to the parties'.

3) If landlords covenant 'to provide a good, sufficient and constant supply of hot water and an adequate supply of heating in the hot water radiators', they must do so. The court rejected arguments that the covenant should be construed in the light of the inadequacies of the central heating system when the lessee bought the flat. It is implicit from the judgment handed down by Wood J that the lessor could and should have expended capital sums to update the system.

4) Some of the lessor's covenants were expressed to be 'subject to the lessees paying the maintenance contribution pursuant to the obligations' in the lease. The lessor argued that this was a condition precedent and, as the lessee was in arrears, it had no obligation to comply with its own covenants. This approach was rejected.

As a result of these findings, the lessee's counterclaim exceeded the arrears claimed. The order for forfeiture was set aside and the lessor ordered to pay £1,213 to the lessee.

High Court

Q3.12 *Gilje v Charlegrove Securities Ltd*
[2003] EWHC 1284 (Ch); [2004] 1 All ER 91; [2004] 1 All ER 91; [2004] HLR 1; [2004] L&TR 3; [2003] 36 EG 110

LTA 1985 s20B did not apply to payments on account

Etherton J held that Landlord and Tenant Act 1985 s20B does not apply to payments on account. It applies where costs are incurred more than 18 months before a demand for payment.

Q3.13 *R v Marylebone Magistrates' Court ex p Westminster CC*
(2000) 32 HLR 266, QBD

LTA s21 not limited to cases of 'wilful and inexcusable' failure to produce documents

Mrs Munns, a landlady of six flats, was summonsed for failing without reasonable cause to perform a duty imposed by Landlord and Tenant Act 1985 s21. A summary of relevant costs incurred in providing services which she sent to a tenant failed to comply with the statutory provisions. A stipendiary magistrate stayed the summons because he was satisfied that the offence allegedly committed was 'so trivial that it did not justify the bringing of proceedings'. Westminster, who had prosecuted the case, applied for judicial review. Although leave was refused because the case was 'extremely old' and 'stale', Collins J said:

> ... it would be wrong for a court to decide that it was an abuse of the process of the court to prosecute if the summary did not contain all that was required by parliament. Of course, the court might take the view that no penalty should follow. It might even take the view in an appropriate case that that be coupled with some sort of costs sanction.

Section 21 is not limited to cases where there is a 'wilful and inexcusable' failure to produce documents. Collins J also said that it is better for such challenges to be brought by way of case stated rather than by judicial review since it would mean that the court was provided with the magistrates' reasons in every case.

Q3.14   *Taber v MacDonald*
(1999) 31 HLR 73, QBD

Landlord had reasonable excuse for not producing documents under LTA 1985 s21

The landlord gave a written summary of the relevant costs of service charges for the accounting year to the end of 1996. A lessee gave written notice to the landlord requesting to inspect accounts in accordance with Landlord and Tenant Act 1985 s21. Later he contended that the landlord did not provide all the documentation and launched a prosecution under s25. The justices acquitted the landlord. The lessee appealed.

The Divisional Court held that a landlord has to make available all documentation, receipts and vouchers which have been stated in the written summary, including those which relate to composite expenditure on overheads for other properties owned by the same landlord (eg, 'direct labour, including national insurance', 'legal and financial charges', 'secretarial costs', 'communication costs', etc). On the other hand, landlords are not obliged to produce documents which do not relate to relevant costs even if details of such costs are voluntarily supplied in the summary. The landlords had not made available 'the underlying books and records'. However, in this case, the landlord had a reasonable excuse for not producing documentation regarding the composite charge because the lease provided that the lessee could refer the matter to arbitration. As he had not availed himself of that opportunity, the landlords had a reasonable excuse for not producing the documents. The appeal was dismissed.

County courts

Q3.15   *Westminster CC v Hammond*
December 1995 *Legal Action* 19, Central London County Court

Section 20B requirements mandatory

The defendants were long lessees of flats owned by the council. The council entered into a rolling programme of major building works. Every six months the council sent the lessees estimated service charge demands for management and maintenance, which did not include any share of the cost of the building works. At the same time the council purported to notify lessees in accordance with Landlord and Tenant Act 1985 s20B of their intention to pass on the cost of the building works which had been incurred but not yet billed. The notifications did not, however, state how much the cost of the building works was. Contrary to the provisions of s20B, the council did not notify the lessees of the amount which they were to pay for most of the work until more than 18 months after the lessees claimed that sums had been incurred.

HHJ Martin Reynolds held that s20B is mandatory and that landlords 'are required to adhere strictly to the code' contained in ss18–30. He found that costs were 'incurred' at the time when the council was obliged to pay them, ie, when each interim certificate was issued in accordance with the JCT building works contract which governed the works. The notifications sent every six months did not comply with s20B since they did not give sufficient detail. In order to be effective, such notices should state the nature of the works, the amount of the costs incurred and the proportion attributable to each individual lessee.

Lands Tribunal

Q3.16   *Hyams v Wilfred East Housing Co-Operative Ltd*
[2006] EWLands LRX_102_2005; 14 November 2006

Costs were 'incurred' when they 'became payable'

Assured tenants exercised the right to buy their flats under Housing Act 1985 Part V. They claimed in applications to the Leasehold Valuation Tribunal (LVT) that they were not liable to pay some of the service charges demanded because the charges related to costs incurred before their liability commenced. Invoices for works reflected seven stage payments due under an external work contract between November 2002 and March 2004 and a final payment.

On appeal from the LVT, George Bartlett QC, President of the Lands Tribunal, after considering Housing Act 1985 Sch 6 para 16C(1), and following *Capital and Counties Freehold Equity Trust Ltd v BL plc* (Q2.25), construed the word 'incurred' in a lease to be synonymous with 'expended' or 'become payable'. The amount in each invoice became payable on the date stated in that invoice. He rejected the landlord's contention that, since this was a single project, the amount due under it was a single overall sum and it was this that constituted the costs incurred. Some of the stage payments were 'incurred' before the lessees' liability commenced. The lessees' liability was reduced accordingly.

Q4   ## Landlord's name and address

Landlord and Tenant Act (LTA) 1987 s47 provides that any written demand for rent or other sums payable under a tenancy which is not a business tenancy must contain the name and address of the landlord and, if that address is outside England and Wales, an address in England and Wales at which notices may be served on the landlord. If the demand relates to a claim for service charges and the required information is missing, the amount demanded is treated as not being due.

Similarly, LTA 1987 s48 provides that landlords must furnish tenants with an address in England and Wales at which notices may be served. Failure to provide that information means that any rent or service charges claimed is treated as not being due.

Court of Appeal

Q4.1 *Dallhold Estates (UK) Pty Ltd v Lindsey Trading Properties Inc*
(1995) P&CR 332; [1994] 1 EGLR 93; [1994] 17 EG 148, CA

Section 48 does apply to agricultural tenancies which include a dwelling-house

At first instance it was held that Landlord and Tenant Act 1987 s48 applied to an agricultural holding which consisted of 940 acres, including an Elizabethan manor house and a number of cottages. Although rent demands were served by solicitors, they did not expressly state that they were authorised to accept service of notices on behalf of the landlord, which was a company registered in Panama.

On appeal, it was confirmed that, in view of the contents of s46, the requirements of s48 do apply to agricultural tenancies which include a dwelling-house. The word 'premises' means the subject matter of the letting and may include land which is the subject matter of the same letting.

Q4.2 *Drew-Morgan v Hamid-Zadeh*
(2000) 32 HLR 316; [1999] 26 EG 156, CA

Information in notice requiring possession could satisfy s48

In possession proceedings based on arrears of rent, a judge rejected a submission by the tenant that the landlord had failed to comply with Landlord and Tenant Act 1987 s48(1) in that he had not furnished the tenant with an address for service of notices.

The Court of Appeal dismissed the tenant's appeal against the possession order. Until a notice is furnished there is no right to rent. However, following *Rogan v Woodfield Building Services Ltd* (Q4.5) and *Marath v MacGillivray* (F3.3), a notice within the meaning of s48(1) was furnished when the landlord served a notice under Housing Act 1988 s21, whether or not it was valid in its own right as a s21 notice. It informed the tenant of the name and address of the landlord's agent without limitation or qualification. The fact that it was not served for the purposes of s48(1) and that it did not state that the address was one at which 'notices (including notices in proceedings) may be served' on the landlord was irrelevant. There might be cases where a suitably worded possession summons served with another document might constitute notice within s48, but in this case the summons did not itself constitute sufficient notice.

In relation to reasonableness, the judge was entitled to conclude that it was reasonable to make a possession order in the light of persistent non-payment, which was inexcusable because the tenant had received housing benefit. The non-payment was plainly deliberate and avoidable. The fact that the tenant paid arrears during the hearing underlined the fact that she had been in a position to pay, but had chosen not to do so until the last moment. The judge was also entitled to take into account false allegations made by the tenant.

Q4.3   *Glen International Ltd v Triplerose Ltd*
[2007] EWCA Civ 388; 23 March 2007

Letter with address for correspondence on particular matter was not notice under s48

A tenant sought to exercise its right to a new lease under Leasehold Reform, Housing and Urban Development Act 1993 s42. Under s99(3)(ii), such a notice should be sent to the address last furnished to the tenant as the landlord's address for service, in accordance with a notice under Landlord and Tenant Act 1987 s48. The landlord disputed service of the requisite notice, claiming that it had been sent to the wrong address, claiming that its agents had furnished the claimant with an address for service pursuant to s48, but that the tenant had sent the notice to a different address. The landlord relied on one specific letter in which its agents had indicated an address for correspondence. The tenant argued that the solicitors to whom that letter had been written had been acting for it only in relation to dilapidations and insurance, and that the letter had been understood as giving an address for correspondence between the landlord's agents and the solicitors on those discrete issues, not for the service of notices on the landlord. A county court judge found for the tenant, holding that the letter had not been a valid s48 notice.

The Court of Appeal dismissed the landlord's appeal. The correspondence, although referable to the lease and the relationship of landlord and tenant, was specifically focussed initially on matters of dilapidations, and subsequently on questions of insurance, and dealt with nothing else. There was nothing in the correspondence which either explicitly or implicitly indicated that the solicitors had any more general retainer in relation to either the property or the landlord and tenant relationship. Neither the terms of the specific letter relied on nor that letter read in the context of the correspondence as a whole could reasonably have been regarded by the recipient agents of the tenant as conveying that message. It followed that, for the purposes of s48, the letter did not constitute notice of an address for service on the landlord.

Q4.4   *Hussain v Singh*
[1993] 2 EGLR 70; [1993] 31 EG 75, CA

Section 48 applies to tenancies and rent arrears in existence before LTA 1987

The Court of Appeal held that Landlord and Tenant Act 1987 s48, which requires landlords to furnish tenants with addresses at which notices may be served, applies to tenancies created and rent arrears in existence before the Act came into force on 1 February 1988. As a result, the landlord in question was unable to recover the arrears claimed.

Q4.5   *Rogan v Woodfield Building Services Ltd*
(1995) 27 HLR 78; [1995] 1 EGLR 72; [1995] 20 EG 132, CA

Where landlord's address in tenancy agreement s48 satisfied

The plaintiff was a regulated tenant under Rent Act 1977, renting a furnished flat. The tenancy agreement dated 31 October 1986 gave the landlord company's name and registered office. When the tenant applied to the rent officer, he used the same address for the landlord and, when the landlord served notice increasing the rent, the same address was given. The proceedings concerned a claim for overpaid rent under Rent Act 1977 s57(3)(b) and a counterclaim for arrears of rent. Although the tenant had not pleaded Landlord and Tenant Act 1987 s48, at trial his counsel raised the section as a defence to the counterclaim. Although the landlord had not served any notice which specifically stated that the registered office was the address at which notices might be served, at first instance, it was held that the landlord had complied with s48.

The tenant's appeal was dismissed, although the Court of Appeal rejected the landlord's contention that a s48 notice could be oral. In this case, there was nothing in the tenancy agreement to suggest that the registered office was not the address at which proceedings might be served. Ralph Gibson LJ said:

> In the ordinary case, where the address of the landlord is stated without qualification in the written tenancy agreement, the requirement of section 48(1) is thereby satisfied provided that the address is an address in England and Wales.

Stuart-Smith LJ agreed, saying that in such circumstances it is a necessary implication that the landlord 'can be communicated with at that address and hence it is an address to which notices can be sent'. He distinguished *Dallhold Estates (UK) Pty Ltd v Lindsey Trading Properties Inc* (Q4.1), where Ralph Gibson LJ had said that a s48 notice must state at what address notices 'including notices in proceedings' must be served on two grounds – first, that in *Dallhold* the company was registered and incorporated in Panama and, second, that the only address in the jurisdiction was that of the landlord's solicitors. He said that the decision in *Dallhold* should be confined to its own facts.

Russell LJ said in *Rogan* that the test is:

> ... whether the circumstances of the individual case are such that a reasonable tenant must be taken to understand the purport and purpose of the notice.

Mortgage possession proceedings

Mortgage possession proceedings generally

Court of Appeal

R1.1   *Abbey National v Gibson*
September 1997 *Legal Action* 15, CA

Warrant need not specify amount outstanding when enforcing order that did not include money judgment

On 8 April 1992 a suspended possession order was made in mortgage possession proceedings. The defendant failed to comply with the terms and on 31 January 1996 the lenders applied for a warrant, which was executed on 12 March 1996. The defendant subsequently applied to set it aside on the ground that the request for the warrant failed to specify the amount remaining due under the judgment or order. HHJ Graham dismissed this application. The defendant appealed to the Court of Appeal, but subsequently attempted to withdraw his appeal. However, the appeal proceeded, without him being present or addressing the court.

The Court of Appeal dismissed the appeal. The pre-1993 version of Form N31 (suspended possession order) used, made an order for possession suspended on terms, but did not include an order for repayment of the balance outstanding or the arrears. Singer J held that it was 'impossible to construe that as a money judgment [within the meaning of CCR Ord 26 r17(3A)(a)]. It is not an order to pay money that can be enforced by execution or any other means'. There was, accordingly, no need to insert the amount of money outstanding in the request for the warrant. That was enough to dispose of the appeal, but he also stated that he could find no error in HHJ Graham's view that, even if the amount should have been inserted, failure to include it was an irregularity which could be cured under CCR Ord 37 r5 (see now CPR 3.10).

R1.2   *Albany Home Loans Ltd v Massey*
[1997] 2 All ER 609; (1997) 29 HLR 902; (1997) P&CR 509, CA

Ordinarily, order for possession not to be made against one of two joint borrowers

Possession proceedings were brought against Mr and Mrs Massey, who were joint borrowers. Mr Massey defended, alleging that he had a claim for wrongful dismissal by an associated company of the lender. A district judge found that Mr Massey had no defence and the Court of Appeal, although not required to rule on whether his case was arguable, noted that Mr Massey's counsel did not produce to the court any material on which it appeared that he would recover the outstanding amount. However, the district judge did find that Mrs Massey had an arguable defence on the ground that the mortgage should be set aside for undue influence. The claim against her was listed for trial, but a possession order was made against Mr Massey. By the time of the hearing of the appeal, no order had been made against Mrs Massey. Mr Massey appealed, arguing that the court had no power to make a possession order against one of two joint mortgagors.

The Court of Appeal held that, although the court has power to make such an order, in general an order for possession ought not to be made against one of two joint borrowers where it is not necessary and there would be no advantage to the lender because the other joint borrower would be entitled to remain in possession. Schiemann LJ approved and followed the statement by Lord Denning MR in *Quennell v Maltby* [1979] 1 WLR 318; [1979] 1 All ER 568, CA, that:

> A mortgagee will be restrained from getting possession except when it is sought bona fide and reasonably for the purpose of enforcing the security and then only subject to such conditions as the court thinks fit to impose.

The court should have disposed of the case in such a way that Mr Massey was not required to leave until Mrs Massey left. However, Mr Massey's appeal was dismissed because the lender undertook not to enforce the possession order until an order for possession was made against Mrs Massey or she left voluntarily.

R1.3   *Bank of Scotland v Ladjadj*
[2000] 2 All ER (Comm) 583, CA

Mortgage documents to be construed according to contra preferentem rule

In mortgage possession proceedings the defendant disputed the mortgage arrears and in particular the basis on which interest had been calculated. In December 1998 the bank claimed arrears of £82,032, whereas the defendant said that they were no more than £40,000. The agreement between the bank and the borrower was contained in four separate agreements which were not easy to reconcile.

Law LJ criticised the bank's documentation as 'disgracefully sloppy'. He said:

> What a lay person would be supposed to make of them I cannot begin to imagine. In such a situation I consider that the contra preferentem rule of construction possesses special force. I regard it as nothing short of scandalous that a major lending institution should foist this jigsaw puzzle of a contract on the borrowing public.

As the question of interpretation of the contract had only been gone into in the Court of Appeal, a retrial was directed.

R1.4   *Cheltenham and Gloucester Building Society v Grattidge*
(1993) 25 HLR 454, CA

Building society entitled to money judgment when SPO made

A district judge in possession proceedings based on mortgage arrears made a suspended possession order. The building society also sought a money judgment but the judge made no order in respect of the money claim. The building society appealed.

The Court of Appeal held that the building society was entitled to a money judgment. There was no inconsistency between the making of a suspended possession order and a concurrent money judgment for the whole of the mortgage debt, suspended for as long as the possession order remained suspended. Although it is for the judge in every case to decide whether or not to exercise the discretion given by County Courts Act 1984 s71(2), usually the money judgment should be suspended for as long as the possession order is suspended.

R1.5   ## Cheltenham and Gloucester Building Society v Johnson

(1996) 28 HLR 885; (1996) 73 P&CR 293, CA

Special circumstances required to justify no money judgment on making of SPO

In mortgage possession proceedings, a district judge made a suspended possession order and adjourned the money claim generally with liberty to restore. The building society successfully appealed to the Court of Appeal. Mortgagees are entitled as of right to money judgments for whatever sum of money is due and payable under the terms of the mortgage (see *Cheltenham and Gloucester Building Society v Grattidge* (R1.4). The Court of Appeal stated, however, that there may be special circumstances which would justify a departure from the practice set out in *Grattidge*, eg, where there is evidence that a sale will take place within a reasonable time. In the usual course of events, if a judge thinks it right to suspend a possession order, then the proper exercise of the discretion given by County Courts Act 1984 s71(2) would require suspension of the money judgment on the same terms. The court also followed *National and Provincial Building Society v Lloyd* (R2.16) in holding that there is no rule of law that mortgage possession claims can be adjourned or orders suspended only if a sale will take place within a short period of time.

R1.6   ## Citibank International plc v Kessler

[1999] 1 Lloyd's Rep (Banking); (1999) 78 P&CR D7; (1999) *Times* 24 March; [1999] EGCS 40, CA

Prohibition in mortgage deed against subletting not in breach of European Community rights

A covenant in a mortgage deed that a borrower would not, without the prior written consent of the mortgagee, lease the whole or any part of the property is not incompatible with article 48 of the European Community Treaty (see now the Consolidated Treaty Establishing the European Community article 49, which guarantees the freedom of movement of workers).

R1.7   ## Credit & Mercantile plc v Marks

[2004] EWCA Civ 568; [2005] Ch 81; [2004] 3 WLR 489

Mortgagee has right to possession on execution of mortgage despite subcharge

As soon as a mortgage is executed, a mortgagee has a right to go into possession unless the mortgage expressly or impliedly provides otherwise. The mere existence of a subcharge does not, regardless of the construction of the relevant contractual documents divest a principal mortgagee of that right to possession or suspend that right during the currency of the subcharge. There is no reason why both a mortgagee and a submortgagee should not both have rights to possession

R1.8   ## Emery v UCB Bank plc

December 1997 *Legal Action* 14, CA

Where bank went back on agreement to accept weekly instalments, borrowers had arguable claim in promissory estoppel

The bank lent money under an all moneys charge. After the borrowers had failed to make agreed payments, the bank made an arrangement whereby it would accept payments of £700 per week. However, nine weeks later, with no further correspondence, the bank wrote requiring the full balance of £259,000 within two days. The borrowers brought proceedings relying on promissory estoppel. The bank applied to strike out those proceedings on the ground that they were frivolous and vexatious.

The Court of Appeal held that the borrowers had an arguable case and that, pending trial, the bank was not entitled to enforce its charge.

R1.9 *Halifax plc v Alexander*
April 2000 *Legal Action* 15, CA

Mortgagees should have documentary evidence at court to show how sums calculated

The plaintiffs obtained a money judgment for £133.000.

Evans LJ said that where mortgagees are claiming large sums, it should be normal practice for building societies and similar organisations to have documentary evidence giving details of how the figure was calculated at court in order to avoid adjournments.

R1.10 *Halifax plc v Taffs*
April 2000 *Legal Action* 15, CA

Where arrears paid off, practice of adjourning generally desirable

After the issue of possession proceedings, the borrower paid the outstanding arrears and a district judge ordered that the claim should be adjourned generally with liberty to restore. The defendant again fell into arrears and a district judge made an order for possession. The defendant appealed, contending that on payment of the arrears the case should not have been adjourned generally.

The Court of Appeal dismissed the appeal. The practice of adjourning generally in such circumstances is desirable because it saves court fees that will ultimately be added to the mortgage debt.

R1.11 *Lloyds Bank plc v Dix*
[2000] All ER (D) 1533, CA

Where merits of case hopeless court did not have to consider some failing of fairness

In a mortgage possession claim where no procedural guarantees or indulgences could save a party from an inevitable conclusion on the merits that his case was truly hopeless, the court was not required by the Civil Procedure Rules to allow him to go back into the fray because there had been some failure of fairness along the way, nor did ECHR article 6 require it do so.

R1.12 *Paragon Finance Ltd v Nash; Paragon Finance plc v Staunton*
[2001] EWCA Civ 1466; [2002] 2 All ER 248; [2002] 2 P&CR 20

Power to vary interest rates not completely unfettered; whether loan an extortionate credit bargain to be judged at time loan agreed

Mortgages granted to the defendants contained variable interest rates. Throughout the term of the mortgage the bank's interest rate had significantly exceeded the Bank of England base rate and prevailing market rates. The defendants fell into arrears and the bank brought possession proceedings.

The Court of Appeal held that:

1   A power given to a lender in a mortgage deed to vary interest rates from time to time was not completely unfettered. To give effect to the reasonable expectations of the parties, it was necessary to imply into the agreements a term that the rates of interest would not be set dishonestly, for an improper purpose, capriciously or arbitrarily. Although it was an implied term that rates of interest would not be set unreasonably in the *Wednesbury* sense, that did not mean that there was a term not to set unreasonable rates.

2) When deciding whether a loan agreement was an extortionate credit bargain within Consumer Credit Act 1974 s138, the time to consider the relevant factors was the date when the agreement was entered into. Subsequent changes in interest rates were irrelevant.

3) The setting of interest rates under a discretion given by contract was not 'contractual performance' within the meaning of Unfair Contract Terms Act 1977 s3(2)(b)(i).

The House of Lords refused leave to appeal: [2002] 1 WLR 2263.

R1.13   *Ropaigelach v Barclays Bank plc*
[2000] 1 QB 263; [1999] 3 WLR 17; [1999] 4 All ER 235; (1999) *Times* 6 January, CA

Mortgagees have common-law right to take possession without court order

The plaintiff defaulted on his mortgage with the defendant bank. The bank demanded repayment of the monies owed and wrote to the plaintiff at the property to inform him that it was taking steps to sell the property. However, he was not living there. The property was empty and in the process of being renovated. It was sold at auction on 26 November 1996 and the sale was completed. On 6 January 1997, the plaintiff issued an originating summons for the determination of the question whether the defendant as mortgagee was entitled by law to take possession without having an order of the court. The application was dismissed and the plaintiff appealed.

The appeal was dismissed. Administration of Justice Act 1970 s36 has not abrogated the mortgagee's common-law right to take possession of property (see *Western Bank v Schindler* (R2.23)). Parliament had not intended that s36 should give mortgagors protection from mortgagees who took possession without the assistance of the court (cf Criminal Law Act 1977 s6 and Consumer Credit Act 1974 s126 where specific protection has been given to mortgagors from forcible re-entry). The protection given by s36 applies only where possession proceedings are taken.

R1.14   *UCB Bank plc v Chandler*
[1999] EGCS 56, CA

Money claim not res judicata where only possession order made in earlier proceedings

The bank brought proceedings claiming possession, repayment of the debt and interest. The proceedings were not opposed and a possession order was made, although no money judgment was obtained. After the borrower moved out, the lender issued new proceedings for the recovery of the debt. An order was made. The borrower argued that the lender was prevented from raising the money claim again because it had been part of the previous proceedings.

The Court of Appeal held that the claim was not res judicata in the strict sense because no money judgment had been obtained. The borrower could only claim that the lender was estopped from claiming the money because of the previous default judgment for possession. When it is asserted that a judgment which has been obtained unopposed estops a party from bringing a claim, it is essential to ascertain the scope of the judgment. The lender could have brought a separate action for recovery of the arrears rather than issuing a claim for possession and arrears. The lender could not be said to have behaved inequitably by not pursuing the money claim at the same time as the previous proceedings. The borrower could not reasonably have believed that he would be released from the debt by agreeing to the making of the earlier order.

R1.15 *Yorkshire Bank plc v Hall*
[1999] 1 WLR 1713; [1999] 1 All ER 879, CA

Outside London only county courts can hear mortgage possession claims

County Courts Act 1984 s21(3) gives county courts outside London exclusive jurisdiction to hear mortgage possession cases.

The Court of Appeal held that a High Court judge sitting at Leeds District Registry did not have jurisdiction to make mortgage possession orders in cases which had been consolidated with High Court actions, without first deconsolidating them and then transferring the possession claims to the county court.

High Court

R1.16 *Birmingham Citizens Permanent Building Society v Caunt*
[1962] Ch 883; [1962] 2 WLR 323; [1962] 1 All ER 163, ChD (see R2.24)

Limited power to adjourn mortgage possession proceedings pre-Administration of Justice Act

R1.17 *Mortgage Express v Da Rocha-Afodu*
[2007] EWHC 297 (QB); 22 February 2007

Court had no jurisdiction to grant stay of execution in circumstances of case

A possession order was made against mortgage borrowers with arrears of approximately £18,000. They were described as having a 'very poor payment history.' It was also said that they had overstretched themselves financially and that they did not have the ability to maintain regular payments on the mortgage. In September 2006, they unsuccessfully applied to suspend the warrant. The following day they were evicted. In December 2006, they filed an appellants' notice seeking to appeal the dismissal of their application, for an order to extend time for filing the appellants' notice, for a stay of enforcement and for an order that they be reinstated into the property. The stay was granted by the court on the papers. The lender applied for an order lifting the stay.

Tugendhat J held that the court had no jurisdiction to grant a stay in the circumstances of the case. If the security was being marketed at an undervalue as the defendants asserted that might provide the basis for a claim against the lender. It could not on any view amount to oppression in the execution of the warrant. Still less did the court have any jurisdiction to permit the defendants to re-enter the security by way of an interim measure pending the hearing of an application for permission to appeal out of time. The claimant's application for the stay to be lifted was allowed.

R1.18   *Rahman v Sterling Credit Ltd*
[2002] EWHC 3008 (Ch); 17 December 2002
No implied term to reduce interest rate as prevailing market rate fell

Sterling claimed possession for failure to make payments on a secured loan. The original counterclaim contended that the loan agreement was an extortionate credit bargain. The Rahmans were refused permission to amend their pleadings to include a claim that there was an implied term that the company had a positive obligation to reduce the interest rate on the loan as the prevailing market rate fell.

Park J dismissed their appeal. There was no such implied term.

R1.19   *Securum Finance Ltd v Ashton*
[2001] ChD 291; (1999) 22 June, ChD
Limitation period 12 years; claim not statute-barred or abuse of process

The claimant brought proceedings claiming possession, sale and foreclosure. The defendants applied to strike out the action on the basis that the cause of action was subject to a six-year limitation period or on the ground that the action was an abuse of process.

I Hunter QC (sitting as a deputy High Court judge) found that the mortgage contained an all moneys covenant to pay which was subject to a 12-year limitation period under Limitation Act 1980 ss8 and 20(1). The mortgage provided in terms that it was in addition to all other security held by the bank for the mortgagor's obligations and was not to merge with or prejudice such other security. The 12-year period in s8 was not cut down by the six-year period in s5 since the two sections were mutually exclusive. The covenant contained in the mortgage was not statute-barred. *Birkett v James* [1978] AC 297 was a complete answer to the application to strike out because that case confined the power to strike out to cases where the limitation period had expired, except in the case of contumelious default or other abuse of process.

R1.20   *Target Holdings Ltd v Priestley*
(1999) Vol 143 No 21 *Solicitors Journal* (28 May) LB 121, ChD
Agreement to pay off arrears need not be in writing

The defendants obtained a mortgage of £160,000 but fell into arrears. In October 1993 they agreed to pay the plaintiff £160,000 by direct debit of £1,000 per month in settlement of all liability for principal and interest. That agreement was never reduced to writing. The plaintiffs brought proceedings for all outstanding sums, claiming that the agreement was void because it failed to comply with the requirements of Law of Property (Miscellaneous Provisions) Act 1989 s2.

HHJ Hicks QC held that contracts for disposition, as distinct from executory contracts for disposition, were not caught by s2. He found that the contract entered into in October 1993 remained valid and enforceable. He dismissed the claim.

R2   Power to adjourn, stay, suspend or postpone

Administration of Justice Act 1970 s36 and Administration of Justice Act 1973 s8 give courts in mortgage possession proceedings power to adjourn, stay, suspend or postpone the date for giving up possession if it is likely that the arrears of instalments and interest can be repaid during a reasonable period. It is, therefore, crucially important to determine what is 'a reasonable period'.

Court of Appeal

R2.1   *Abbey National Building Society v Mewton*
[1995] CLY 3598, CA

Application to suspend warrant dismissed and order that no further application be made

The defendant in mortgage possession proceedings successfully applied to set aside judgment, then for possession to be suspended, and then on two occasions for the possession warrant to be suspended. On each occasion, he failed to make payments which he had promised. On a further application to suspend the warrant, the district judge dismissed his application and ordered that he make no further application to suspend in any circumstances.

The Court of Appeal dismissed the defendant's appeal, stating that:

> It seems to be clear that [the defendant], having failed to comply with the conditions on which the suspension of possession is granted, is not in a position to complain about the orders and warrants for possession made. His record of payment is deplorable ... The district judge was fully entitled to order as he did.

R2.2   *Abbey National Mortgages v Bernard*
(1996) 71 P&CR 257, CA

Court cannot suspend order if there is no prospect of the borrower reducing the arrears

The defendant bought a new house with a National House Builders' Council (NHBC) guarantee. Structural problems appeared, which made it difficult to sell the house in 1990. In 1991 an order for possession was obtained, suspended on terms. In 1992 the lender's application to vary the terms of the order on the ground that the arrears were increasing was refused. A further application by the lender in 1994 to vary the order for possession under Administration of Justice Act 1970 s36 was dismissed, as the judge considered that he had no jurisdiction to do so because the application was in the same terms as the 1992 application.

The Court of Appeal allowed the lender's appeal and made an order for possession. The judge below did have jurisdiction although he could reject what amounted to a repeat application if it was an abuse of process. However, the court cannot suspend an order for possession under s36, however hard the circumstances, if there is no prospect of the borrower reducing the arrears. Negotiations with NHBC were still not concluded and any compensation was unlikely to cover the debt.

R2.3   ***Bank of Scotland v Grimes***

[1985] QB 1179; [1985] 3 WLR 294; [1985] 2 All ER 254, CA

AJA s36 applies to mortgagors with endowment mortgages

Administration of Justice Act (AJA) 1973 s8 extends the possibility of relief under Administration of Justice Act 1970 s36 to mortgagors with endowment mortgages from banks as well as to instalment mortgages from building societies.

R2.4   ***Barclays Bank v Alcorn***

[2002] EWCA Civ 817; October 2002 *Legal Action* 29; 17 June 2002

AJA struck right balance of interests and law not inconsistent with ECHR rights under art 8 or art 1 of the First Protocol

The bank obtained a possession order in respect of mortgaged property which comprised a main house and a cottage. In the first instance hearing, Hart J rejected the defendants' contention that Administration of Justice Act (AJA) 1970 s36 should be interpreted in such a way as to allow them to remain in the cottage. The evidence indicated that there would be insufficient funds realisable from the sale of the main property alone to repay the claimant. Second, an order under s36 could not apply in respect of part only of the property. A literal reading of the statute indicated that s36 conferred a power only in relation to the whole of a mortgaged property. The bank entered into possession of the main house but Mr and Mrs Alcorn continued to reside in the cottage. Mrs Alcorn sought permission to appeal, arguing that the Court of Appeal could consider (1) the interaction between ECHR article 8 and article 1 of the First Protocol and s36; (2) the existence and extent of any obligation on a mortgagee to repair the mortgaged property in order to maximise its return from the property; and (3) whether s36 could be invoked where the possession order had already been executed in part.

The Court of Appeal refused permission to appeal. There was no compelling reason to consider the issues said to arise under the ECHR. A mortgagee proceeding by action to obtain possession of a dwelling-house was plainly proceeding in accordance with the law. The question whether it was necessary for the mortgagee to have possession so that the property could be sold was addressed directly by s36. The court had to consider whether it was likely that if possession was postponed the mortgagor would within a reasonable time pay off the debt or arrears. That was the balance struck between the right of the mortgagor to remain in his home and the right of the mortgagee to repayment within a reasonable time. There was no inconsistency with the ECHR rights under article 8 or article 1 of the First Protocol. There could be no obligation on a mortgagee to repair in circumstances where the cost of effecting the repair would exceed the resulting increase in the value of the property. There was no real prospect that the Court of Appeal would interfere with that exercise of discretion under s 36.

R2.5   **Bristol and West Building Society v Ellis**

(1997) 29 HLR 282; (1996) 73 P&CR 158, CA

Reasonable period for sale depends on individual circumstances of case

Mr and Mrs Ellis borrowed £60,000 under an endowment mortgage. By August 1990 there were arrears of £8,449. In possession proceedings a suspended possession order was made, but Mr and Mrs Ellis did not comply with it. By January 1995 the arrears were over £16,000 and the balance outstanding under the mortgage was over £76,000. In April 1995 Mrs Ellis applied to suspend a warrant for possession. In an affidavit she stated that she was in receipt of income support, the DSS would make interest payments, she could make an immediate payment of £5,000, but thereafter could only pay £10 per month towards the arrears. She offered, however, to sell the property in approximately three to five years when her children would have finished university education. The warrant was suspended and the building society appealed.

The Court of Appeal allowed the appeal. What is a reasonable period for sale depends on the individual circumstances of each case, particularly the extent to which the mortgage and arrears are secured by the value of the property. The comments by Neill LJ in *National and Provincial Building Society v Lloyd* (R2.16) that sale 'could take place in six or nine months or even a year' did not establish a year as the maximum period 'as a rule of law or as a matter of general guidance'. However, in this case there was insufficient evidence that Mrs Ellis could or would sell the property within three to five years or that the proceeds of sale would be sufficient to discharge the mortgage debt and arrears. Although there were letters from two estate agents, courts should approach such estimates with 'reserve'.

R2.6   **Cheltenham and Gloucester Building Society v Grant**

(1994) 26 HLR 703, CA

Possible for judge to act without formal evidence from mortgagors

The Cheltenham and Gloucester Building Society challenged the common practice of district judges who exercise their discretion under the Administration of Justice Act 1970 s36 on the basis of information given to them by defendants, without necessarily hearing sworn evidence from them.

The Court of Appeal declined to lay down rigid rules on how busy district judges should satisfy themselves about the requirements in s36 and upheld the original order made by the district judge that a possession order should not be enforced without leave of the court while regular payments were made. Nourse LJ stated that:

> It must be possible for [judges] to act without evidence, especially where, as here, the mortgagor was present in court and available to be questioned and no objection to the reception of informal material is made by the mortgagee. Clearly, it will sometimes be prudent for the mortgagor to put in an affidavit before the hearing. ((1994) 26 HLR at 707)

If a lender disputes the truth of what a borrower has said, formal evidence will be necessary. In practice, that will usually require an adjournment.

R2.7   *Cheltenham and Gloucester Building Society v Johnson*
(1996) 28 HLR 885; (1996) 73 P&CR 293, CA (see R1.5)
On making SPO, suspension of money judgment on the same terms usual

R2.8   *Cheltenham and Gloucester Building Society v Krausz*
[1997] 1 WLR 1558; [1997] 1 All ER 21; (1997) 29 HLR 597; (1997) P&CR D16, CA (see R4.5)
Court could not suspend warrant to enable mortgagor to apply to the High Court for an order under section 91

R2.9   *Cheltenham and Gloucester Building Society v Norgan*
[1996] 1 WLR 343; [1996] 1 All ER 449; (1996) 28 HLR 443; (1996) 72 P&CR 46, CA
Starting point for 'reasonable period' for purposes of AJA is full term of the mortgage

In May 1990, when arrears of instalments and interest stood at £7,216, the building society obtained a possession order suspended for 28 days. The borrower had said that she was hoping to refinance the mortgage and the district judge indicated that, if the arrears were not paid within 28 days, she was at liberty to apply for a further suspension. In December 1990 the terms of the suspension were varied, but not complied with, and the building society obtained a warrant. The warrant was twice suspended on terms, but when the borrower failed to comply, the building society applied to reissue the warrant and the borrower cross-applied for a further suspension. A district judge gave leave to reissue the warrant and refused any further suspension. By the time the appeal came on before the circuit judge, the arrears were in the region of £20,000. He dismissed the borrower's appeal and she appealed to the Court of Appeal.

Allowing her appeal, Waite LJ followed dicta in *First Middlesbrough Trading and Mortgage Co Ltd v Cunningham* (R2.12) and *Western Bank v Schindler* (R2.23) and stated that in determining 'a reasonable period' for the purposes of Administration of Justice Acts 1970 s36 and 1973 s8,

> ... the court should take as its starting point the full term of the mortgage and pose at the outset the question: would it be possible for the mortgagor to maintain payment-off of the arrears by instalments over that period? ([1996] 1 All ER at 458)

Evans LJ set out a number of considerations which are likely to be relevant when establishing what is a reasonable period. They include:

a) How much can the borrower reasonably afford to pay, both now and in the future?
b) If the borrower has a temporary difficulty in meeting his obligations, how long is the difficulty likely to last?
c) What was the reason for the arrears which have accumulated?
d) How much remains of the original term?
e) What are the relevant contractual terms, and what type of mortgage is it, ie, when is the principal due to be repaid?

Other matters which may be relevant include family circumstances and the income of other members of the family. If arrears have accrued as a result of matrimonial breakdown, are any proceedings for ancillary relief likely to result in an order which will enable arrears to be paid off? Is the Benefits Agency (or should it be) paying anything towards the interest due on the mortgage?

This was a case where the lender's security was not at risk and Waite LJ recognised that there would be cases where evidence might 'be required to see if and when the lender's security will become liable to be put at risk as a result of imposing postponement of payments in arrear'. ([1996] 1 All ER at 459)

R2.10   *Cheltenham and Gloucester Building Society v Obi*
(1996) 28 HLR 22, CA

Powers under AJA cease after warrant executed

It was held that the court's power under Administration of Justice Act (AJA) 1970 s36 to adjourn mortgage possession proceedings, stay or suspend execution or postpone the date for delivery of possession ceases after a warrant has been executed. The principles set out by the Court of Appeal in *Hammersmith and Fulham LBC v Hill* (I6.6) apply equally to mortgage possession proceedings.

R2.11   *Cheltenham and Gloucester plc v Booker*
(1997) 29 HLR 634; (1997) 73 P&CR 412; [1997] 1 EGLR 142; [1997] 19 EG 155, CA

Court has residual inherent jurisdiction where AJA s36 not available to suspend warrant to enable lender to sell the property

The Court of Appeal held that, in mortgage possession proceedings, where the power to suspend execution under Administration of Justice Act 1970 s36 cannot be exercised because it is unlikely that the borrower can repay arrears within a reasonable period, the county court still has a residual inherent jurisdiction to defer the date of giving up possession in order to enable the lender to sell the property. The court may give conduct of the sale of premises to the lender while postponing execution of a warrant for possession until completion of the sale, thus allowing the borrower to remain in occupation. There is no reason in principle for the court to accede to a lender's insistence on immediate possession if:

1) possession will only be required on completion;
2) the presence of the borrowers pending completion will enhance, or at least not depress, the sale price;
3) the borrowers will co-operate in the sale; and
4) they will give possession to the purchasers on completion.

However, Millett LJ stated that these conditions are seldom likely to be satisfied and the circumstances in which such a course would be appropriate are hard to imagine. Such an order would 'certainly be a rarity'.

R2.12   *First Middlesbrough Trading and Mortgage Co Ltd v Cunningham*
(1974) 28 P&CR 69, CA

Powerful presumption in favour of term of the mortgage being 'reasonable period'.

In mortgage possession proceedings, there was evidence that the borrower could pay off arrears of £142 by instalments of £3 per week. Such instalments would clear the arrears well within the outstanding term of the mortgage.

The lender's appeal was dismissed. Scarman LJ, when considering what is a 'reasonable period' within Administration of Justice Act 1970 s36, stated:

> Since the object of the instalment mortgage was, with the consent of the mortgagee, to give the mortgagor the period of the mortgage to repay the capital sum and interest, one begins with a powerful presumption of fact in favour of the period of the mortgage being the 'reasonable period'. ((1974) 28 P&CR at 75)

R2.13   *Habib Bank v Tailor*

[1982] 1 WLR 1218; [1982] 3 All ER 561, CA

AJA 1973 s8 does not apply to all moneys charge

The bank allowed the defendant an overdraft of up to £6,000 on his current account. It was secured by a charge on his home. The charge contained a covenant in the usual bankers' form by which he agreed to pay, on written demand, the balance due in respect of 'all moneys' owing to the bank. The bank made a written demand for repayment. Mr Taylor did not comply and the bank brought possession proceedings. A circuit judge held that s36 applied and postponed the operation of the possession order for a reasonable time to enable the defendant to pay the amount by which the overdraft limit had been exceeded.

The Court of Appeal held that, although Administration of Justice Act (AJA) 1970 s36 applies to all moneys charges, Mr Tailor could not rely on AJA 1973 s8 because he could not 'pay any sums due under the mortgage' (ie, the whole outstanding balance) within a reasonable period. The court could not exercise the s36(2) discretion to stay suspend or postpone the date for possession because s8 does not apply to 'all moneys' charges, since (a) the principal does not become due and cannot be sued on until a written demand has been made and (b) such charges do not provide for deferment after a written demand has been made. Oliver LJ stated that:

> Deferment ... involves the deferment of payment after it has become due, and quite clearly in this case there appears to me to be no provision, either in the agreement between the parties or in the mortgage itself, by which, on any realistic construction, it can be said that payment by the customer was to be 'deferred'. ([1982] 3 All ER at 566)

R2.14   *Mortgage Agency Services v Bal*

(1998) LSG 15 July p32, CA

AJA 1970 s36 ceases to apply after execution

After a possession order was made in mortgage possession proceedings, a warrant for possession was issued, but suspended on eight occasions. The warrant was executed on 28 May 1998. By an application dated 4 June, the defendant applied for reinstatement. A district judge ordered that 'a warrant of restitution be granted on payment of £4,000'.

Although a circuit judge dismissed the plaintiff's appeal, it was allowed by the Court of Appeal. The judges' decisions had been based, wrongly, on the premise that the protection given by Administration of Justice Act 1970 s36 continues to apply after execution. Once a warrant has been executed, the statutory jurisdiction ceases to be exercisable. The court can then act under its inherent jurisdiction only if the judgment is set aside or if execution amounts to abuse of the process or oppression (*Governors of Peabody Donation Fund v Hay* (I4.1) and *Hammersmith and Fulham LBC v Hill* (I6.6)).

R2.15 ## *Mortgage Service Funding plc v Steele*
(1996) 72 P&CR D40, CA

If property has to be sold, it can just as well be sold by mortgagee

The borrower was loaned £207,546 under the terms of a mortgage. Although the borrower received housing benefit, there was a shortfall of over £1,000 per month. Arrears of £24,000 accrued and a possession order was made. Nothing was said in the county court about the possibility of sale. The borrower sought leave to appeal, contending that he had found a buyer willing to pay £310,000. However, no details were given.

The Court of Appeal dismissed the application for leave. Nourse LJ said:

> If the property has to be sold, it can just as well be sold by the mortgagee, whose duty is always to obtain the best price ... at the date of sale. If there is a potential purchaser at hand, then all the mortgagor has to do is put the mortgagee in touch with him and the matter can proceed from there. Unless there is firm evidence that a particular sale is about to be completed, it is not the practice of the court to prevent the mortgagee from enforcing his remedy of obtaining possession and exercising his own power of sale over the property.

Note: *Target Home Loans v Clothier* (R22.2) was not cited.

R2.16 ## *National and Provincial Building Society v Lloyd*
[1996] 1 All ER 630; (1996) 28 HLR 459, CA

If sale of property 'could take place in six or nine months or even a year', court may conclude likely that arrears would be repaid within reasonable period

The Court of Appeal considered an appeal against a decision to suspend a possession order to give the borrower time to sell premises and so clear mortgage arrears. The building society argued that any such suspension should only be for a short period.

Neill LJ rejected this submission. If there is clear evidence that completion of the sale of a property 'could take place in six or nine months or even a year', there is no reason why the court should not come to the conclusion that it is likely that the arrears would be repaid within a reasonable period. What is 'a reasonable period' is a question for the court in each individual case. However, in *Lloyd* there was insufficient evidence before the judge to show that the arrears would be paid within a reasonable period. Much of it was 'a mere expression of hope' and so the building society's appeal against the suspension was allowed.

R2.17   *Nationwide Building Society v Purvis*
[1998] BPIR 625, CA

Bankrupt has locus standi

A bankrupt has locus standi to make an application to the court for relief under Administration of Justice Acts 1970 and 1973.

R2.18   *Ropaigelach v Barclays Bank plc*
[2000] 1 QB 263; [1999] 3 WLR 17; [1999] 4 All ER 235; (1999) *Times* 6 January; [1998] EGCS 189, CA (see R1.13)

Mortgagees have common-law right to take possession without court order

R2.19   *Royal Bank of Scotland v Miller*
[2001] EWCA Civ 344; [2002] QB 255; [2001] 3 WLR 523; (2001) 82 P&CR 396, CA

Whether premises consist of or include a dwelling-house to be decided at time when mortgagee brings possession claim

Ms Miller was the freeholder of a night club with living accommodation above. In 1993 she granted a legal charge in favour of the bank to secure her obligations to the bank. The loan agreement provided for repayment of the principal sum after ten years from the proceeds of personal equity plans. Arrears accrued and a district judge made a possession order. On appeal HHJ Appleton held that it was an all moneys charge and that he had no power to postpone possession (*Birmingham Citizens Permanent Building Society v Caunt* (R2.24)).

Ms Miller appealed to the Court of Appeal. The first question considered by the Court of Appeal was whether the premises consisted of or included a dwelling-house within the meaning of Administration of Justice Act 1970 s36. The bank contended that the relevant date for deciding this was the date when the charge was entered into. That submission was rejected. Dyson LJ held that

> ... the true interpretation of section 36(1) is that the time when the land is required to consist of or include a dwelling-house so as to attract the benefits of the subsection, is the time when the mortgagee brings an action in which he claims possession of the mortgaged property. ... The present tense is intended to indicate what condition is required to be met at the very time when the mortgagee starts proceedings for possession.

Breach of a term of the mortgage (eg, occupation by a third party without consent) would not prevent s36 from applying. Second, the Court of Appeal held that it was not an 'all moneys' charge. Following *Bank of Scotland v Grimes* (R2.3), the loan agreement did provide for the borrower to 'defer payment' of the principal sum within the meaning of Administration of Justice Act 1973 s8(1) and so Ms Miller enjoyed the protection of s36. The appeal was allowed and the case was remitted for hearing before a district judge.

R2.20   *Royal Bank of Scotland v O'Shea*
April 1998 *Legal Action* 11, CA

Counterclaim may operate as set-off to money claim

The Court of Appeal held that a borrowers' counterclaim against the lender was available as a set-off against the money claim. Applying dicta in *Ashley Guarantee plc v Zacaria* [1993] 1 WLR 62, CA, although a counter-claim is no defence to a possession claim, it can be a defence to a money claim. If the borrowers applied under Administration of Justice Act 1970 s36, the court could take into account that there might be a valid counter-claim which would be sufficient to satisfy the money judgment. In those circumstances, the court could use its s36 discretion to deny or stay the possession order. The borrowers' appeal was allowed and directions were given for the defence to be argued in the county court.

R2.21 *Royal Trust Co of Canada v Markham*
[1975] 1 WLR 1416; [1975] 3 All ER 433; (1975) 30 P&CR 317, CA

Wrong to suspend in general terms without fixing any period for length of the suspension

Where the court exercises its power under Administration of Justice Act 1970 s36 to stay or suspend execution for such period as the court thinks reasonable, that period must be defined or rendered ascertainable.

The Court of Appeal allowed a lender's appeal against an order for possession which was not to be enforced without leave of the court. It was wrong to suspend in general terms without fixing any period for the length of the suspension.

R2.22 *Target Home Loans v Clothier*
[1994] 1 All ER 439; (1993) 25 HLR 48, CA

Prospects of early sale meant interests of mortgagee and borrower best served by deferring an order for possession

Borrowers paid no mortgage instalments for over 15 months and when possession proceedings came to court there were arrears of £46,000. The lenders sought an immediate possession order, but the district judge adjourned for 56 days under Administration of Justice Act 1970 s36. The lenders appealed to an assistant recorder against the decision to adjourn. By the time that the appeal was heard, no further payments had been made and the arrears were over £64,000. At the hearing of the appeal the borrowers produced a banker's draft for £10,000, indicated that they were seeking planning permission and stated that, after the grant of planning permission, they would be able to sell part of the garden for £40,000. The assistant recorder adjourned the appeal for four months. The lenders appealed against that decision to the Court of Appeal.

When the Court of Appeal heard the appeal, planning permission had been granted but the sale of the garden had not taken place. Instead, there was a letter from estate agents indicating that an offer of £450,000 for the house had been received. Nolan LJ, after asking whether there was a prospect of an early sale, stated:

> If so, is it better in the interests of all concerned for that to be effected by [the borrower] and his wife or by the mortgage company? If the view is that the prospects of an early sale for the mortgagees as well as for [the borrower] are best served by deferring an order for possession, then it seems to me that that is a solid reason for making such an order but the deferment should be short. ([1994] 1 All ER at 447)

The Court of Appeal made a possession order to take effect in three months' time.

R2.23   *Western Bank v Schindler*
[1977] Ch 1; [1976] 3 WLR 341; [1976] 2 All ER 393; (1976) 32 P&CR 352, CA

What is reasonable depends on circumstances of case

The Court of Appeal held that, on its true construction, Administration of Justice Act 1970 s36 gave the court a discretion to delay for a reasonable period making an order in all cases where a lender was seeking possession of a dwelling-house, whether or not the borrower was in arrears or otherwise in default. In exercising that discretion, the judge was entitled to take into account all relevant surrounding circumstances, including the fact that the debt might be inadequately secured. Buckley LJ stated:

> What must be reasonable must depend on the circumstances of the case. This may involve, amongst other things, considering why the mortgagee is anxious to obtain possession and what degree of urgency may exist in relation to any particular aspect of the case. It might, perhaps, also involve consideration of whether the mortgagor is likely to be able to pay sums accruing due from time to time under the mortgage punctually as and when they should become due ... If on the true interpretation of the section the period [of adjournment, suspension or postponement] must be defined or ascertainable, the court might, if it thought it reasonable to do so, keep control of the matter by holding it in abeyance for a specified period with liberty to apply in the meantime, and reconsider the situation at the end of that period or on an earlier application by either party. In a suitable case the specified period might even be the whole remaining prospective life of the mortgage. I would not myself dissent from the view that the court could, if it thought it reasonable to do so, grant an adjournment, suspension or postponement for an indefinite period (eg, until further order) with liberty for either party to apply. ([1976] 2 All ER at 400)

Scarman LJ, however, doubted whether s36 gave the court power to adjourn indefinitely or generally.

High Court

R2.24   *Birmingham Citizens Permanent Building Society v Caunt*
[1962] Ch 883; [1962] 2 WLR 323; [1962] 1 All ER 163, ChD

Limited power to adjourn mortgage possession proceedings pre-Administration of Justice Act

Before there was any statutory power to adjourn or postpone possession, a district registrar adjourned mortgage possession proceedings on terms that the borrower make weekly payments of 30 shillings (£1.50) towards arrears of £71. Russell J, allowing the building society's appeal, held that:

> Where (as here) the legal mortgagee under an instalment mortgage under which by reason of default the whole money has become payable, is entitled to possession, the court has no jurisdiction to decline the order or to adjourn the hearing, whether on terms of keeping up payments or paying arrears, if the mortgagee cannot be persuaded to agree to this course. To this the sole exception is that the application may be adjourned for a short time to afford the mortgagor a chance of paying off the mortgagee in full

or otherwise satisfying him; but this should not be done if there is no reasonable prospect of this occurring. When I say the sole exception, I do not, of course, intend to exclude adjournments which in the ordinary course of procedure may be desirable in circumstances such as temporary inability of a party to attend, and so forth. ([1962] Ch at 912)

Russell J made a 28-day possession order.

Note: The decision on the facts of this case would no longer be the same since the passing of the Administration of Justice Act 1970, but Russell J's statement is still good law in circumstances where the Act does not apply or the court is not satisfied that arrears are likely to be paid off within a reasonable period.

R2.25   *Centrax Trustees v Ross*
[1979] 2 All ER 952, ChD

In light of terms of mortgage, suspension of execution ordered

The defendant covenanted to repay a loan of £27,500, which was secured by a mortgage on his home, within six months. However, the mortgage deed also provided that he was 'permitted to defer payment of [the principal sum] in whole or part' and provision was made for earlier payment in default. He fell into arrears with interest payments and the lender brought possession proceedings.

Goulding J held that, for the purposes of Administration of Justice Act 1970 s36, in ascertaining the terms of the mortgage, the court should take into account not only the legal stipulations in the mortgage but also their practical effect. On its true construction, the mortgage contemplated an indefinite loan with the right of redemption being kept alive indefinitely. In view of the fact that the defendant's financial position was improving, he stated that 'some further indulgence' was justified and suspended execution of the order for possession. In assessing how long a reasonable period might be, the court must 'bear in mind the rights and obligations of both parties, including [the lender's] right to recover their money by selling the property, if necessary, and the full past history of the security'.

R2.26   *Citibank Trust Ltd v Ayivor*
[1987] 1 WLR 1157; [1987] 3 All ER 241; (1987) 19 HLR 463, ChD

Contention that arrears would be paid in reasonable time on basis of cause of action against surveyors rejected

The plaintiff lender brought mortgage possession proceedings. The defendants counterclaimed for damages for the cost of putting right defects (including dry rot), which were apparently referred to in a surveyor's report obtained by the lender but not disclosed to them before purchase. Mervyn Davies J held that:

> In this particular case, I do not, on the evidence, find myself able to say that the existence of the counterclaim means that the defendants are likely 'to be able within a reasonable period' to pay off the arrears. Even if I assume that the defendants' prospects of success on the counterclaim are good, that does not justify me in concluding that the defendants are likely soon to reduce the arrears by paying over any damages that they may recover. ([1987] 3 All ER at 246)

R2.27 *Rees Investments Ltd v Groves*

(2001) 27 June, ChD

No jurisdiction to exercise discretion under s36 where overdraft facility secured on property

In 1988 the defendants drew down £140,000 from an overdraft facility provided by Allied Irish to finance a business. The facility was secured by a second charge on a property. By 1992 the balance of the defendants' account was £155,068.29 overdrawn. Agreements were made for the payment of monthly instalments, but these were broken. The debt was assigned to the claimant who sought an order for possession of the property. At a hearing before a master, an order for possession was made but suspended, purportedly under Administration of Justice Act 1970 s36 and Administration of Justice Act 1973 s8. He held that the agreements came within s8 because payment of the principal sum secured could be made by instalments or could otherwise be deferred, but earlier payment was required in the event of default.

The claimant appealed successfully against the suspension of the order. Neuberger J held that the master had no jurisdiction to exercise his discretion under s36. It would be unfair to the claimant if, by granting an indulgence of this kind, its customers were given rights which they would not otherwise have enjoyed. Since, until 1992, possession of the property could have been sought at any time and there had been a failure to follow either of the two agreements, the order for possession would no longer be suspended (see *Habib Bank v Tailor* [1982] 1 WLR 1218, CA (R2.13)).

County courts

R2.28 *Cheltenham and Gloucester Building Society v Frasca*

April 2004 *Legal Action* 15; 16 June 2003, Gloucester County Court

Refusal to suspend warrant to allow sale 'palpably wrong'

The lender commenced possession proceedings against Ms Frasca in February 2003. She was separated from her husband who had left her with financial difficulties. The claimant obtained a possession order suspended on payments, which became unsustainable. By this time, no payment had been made over a period of 15 months. The claimant applied for a warrant. The defendant applied for a suspension of the warrant to market the property and protect her equity of some £80,000. A district judge dismissed the application. The defendant appealed.

HHJ Roach allowed the appeal. It was a matter of history that the defendant had done her best to deal with the mortgage but the Benefits Agency and her ex-husband had been against her. The claimant would not be prejudiced except by loss of monthly instalments rightly owed, which would be recovered with interest following sale. The decision of the district judge was palpably wrong and no reasonable district judge would have made such a decision in these circumstances. It was appropriate to follow the dictum of Nolan LJ in *Target Home Loans v Clothier* (R2.22) because in this case there was no intention to apply for an order for sale rather than *Cheltenham and Gloucester Building Society v Krausz* (R4.5). The warrant was stayed for three months. No costs were allowed to the claimant.

R2.29 *Hyde Park Funding Ltd v Ioannou*

April 2000 *Legal Action* 15; [1999] 3 CLD 428, Barnet County Court

Appeal against refusal to suspend warrant can succeed despite execution of warrant

Mortgagees were granted a possession order. Later they obtained a warrant. On the morning of the proposed eviction the borrower applied to a district judge to suspend the warrant. That application was dismissed and the borrower was evicted. The borrower appealed to a circuit judge. The lender contended that, as the warrant had been executed, the court no longer had jurisdiction to suspend under Administration of Justice Act 1970 s36.

HHJ Connor allowed the appeal. On appeal from a district judge, a circuit judge can exercise all the jurisdiction that the district judge had and can make any order that the district judge could have made. In view of new evidence adduced on the appeal, the correct order was to suspend on terms. The district judge's order was set aside and possession restored.

Note: See now CPR 52.10 'the appeal court has all the powers of the lower court'.

R2.30 *Royal Bank of Scotland v Elmes*

April 1998 *Legal Action* 11, Clerkenwell County Court

Court could suspend warrant on payment of less than current monthly instalments

A district judge suspended a warrant for possession for three months on terms that the defendant pay £250 one month and thereafter £500 per month for two months, whereupon the case would be further considered. The defendant could command a high salary and stood a good prospect of obtaining fresh employment in the three-month period. The lender appealed on the basis that the court had no power to suspend the warrant on terms of payments less than the current instalments.

Assistant Recorder Thomas QC dismissed the appeal, holding that Administration of Justice Act 1970 s36 enables the court to impose any terms about payments so long as the borrower would, within a reasonable period, be able to clear the arrears and pay the current instalments. The lender's contention that the current instalments had to continue to be paid throughout was rejected. The assistant recorder relied instead on the criteria considered by Evans LJ in *Cheltenham and Gloucester Building Society v Norgan* (R2.9).

R2.31 *Skandia Financial Services Ltd v Greenfield*

[1997] CLY 4248, Horsham County Court

Power to adjourn where at adjourned hearing likely that mortgagor would be in position to pay arrears within reasonable time

In mortgage possession proceedings based on arrears, the defendant stated that she was completing a course of studies and that her employment prospects would be better once she had obtained qualifications. She sought an adjournment. A district judge held that, at the time of the request for an adjournment, it was not likely that the arrears would be cleared within a reasonable period, but adjourned the case for six months, stating that it was likely that at the adjourned hearing the defendant would be able to pay off the arrears within a reasonable period. The plaintiff appealed, contending that the district judge had erred in law and that under Administration of Justice Act 1970 s36 the court did not have power to 'wait and see'.

Recorder Wilson dismissed the appeal. Section 36 allows the court to adjourn if by doing so it is likely that the defendant will be able to pay off sums due within a reasonable period.

R3   # Consumer Credit Act 1974

If a loan is a regulated agreement, Consumer Credit Act 1974 s129 provides that the court may make a time order, rescheduling the rate of repayment and, if appropriate, the amount of interest charged. A 'regulated agreement' is one which is not exempt (ss8 and 16) where the amount of the loan was less than £15,000 if the agreement was entered into before 1 May 1998 or less than £25,000 if the agreement was entered into on or after 1 May 1998 (see Consumer Credit (Increase of Monetary Limits) (Amendment) Order 1998 SI No 996).

Court of Appeal

R3.1   *Broadwick Financial Services Ltd v Spencer*
[2002] EWCA Civ 35; 30 January 2002

Agreement properly executed under CCA 1974; not an extortionate credit bargain

The claimant granted a loan to the defendants. The claimant registered a legal charge against the property. The claimant sent various documents to the defendants including a concessionary letter providing that, in the absence of default, the lenders would accept a reduced monthly sum instead of the contractual amount and also a loan agreement. The annual percentage rate (APR) on the loan was 29.78%. The total of the loan was £4,840 repayable by 180 monthly instalments. The defendants later borrowed further sums of money from another finance company. The benefit of the second company's legal charge was transferred to the claimant. The defendants defaulted and the claimant issued possession proceedings. The defendants contended that the agreement could not be enforced as it had not been properly executed in accordance with Consumer Credit Act 1974 Part V. They sought to reopen the agreement and the legal charge as extortionate credit agreements under ss137–140. The judge granted the possession order and the defendants appealed.

The Court of Appeal dismissed their appeal. (1) The loan agreement had been properly executed. The agreement was a 'regulated agreement' within the meaning of s189(1). Section 61 provided that a regulated agreement was not properly executed unless its contents conformed to the Consumer Credit (Agreements) Regulations 1983 SI No 1553. The signed loan agreement contained terms stating how the defendants were to discharge their obligations and those terms satisfied the requirements of Sch 6 of the Consumer Credit (Agreements) Regulations. The wording of the concessionary letter made it clear that its terms were ex gratia and 'not intended to be contractually binding'. Therefore, its terms were not part of the agreement and consequently did not have to satisfy the Sch 6 requirements. (2) The loan agreement was not an extortionate credit bargain within s138. The statutory test of 'extortionate' was a high one. The payments required had to be grossly exorbitant and/or the bargain had otherwise to contravene ordinary principles of fair dealing.

R3.2   *First National Bank v Syed*
[1991] 2 All ER 250, CA

Exercise of power to order payment by instalments

The plaintiffs were second mortgagees. A loan of £5,000 was granted to the defendants. It was a regulated agreement under the Consumer Credit Act 1974. Arrears accrued and possession proceedings were begun. A district judge made a possession order suspended on condition that the defendants paid the arrears within 28 days, a sum which the Court of Appeal found 'was manifestly beyond the means of the defendants, who were living on supplementary benefit'. The plaintiffs appealed to the circuit judge and then to the Court of Appeal, which considered whether or not a time order should be made under s129 of the Act. Dillon LJ stated:

> Under this section, then, the court is empowered to order payment by instalments which are reasonable having regard to the means of the debtor. But the court can only exercise the power if it appears, or is considered, just to do so. But consideration of what is just does not exclude consideration of the creditor's position. I cannot think that it is just, in the circumstances of this case, and in the light in particular of the fairly long history of default and merely sporadic payments on the defendants' part, and in the absence of any realistic, as opposed to merely speculative, prospect of improvement in the defendants' finances, to require the plaintiff to accept the instalments the defendants can afford, when those will be too little even to keep down the accruing interest on the defendants' account. ([1991] 2 All ER at 256)

The appeal was dismissed.

R3.3   *Paragon Finance Ltd v Nash; Paragon Finance plc v Staunton*
[2001] EWCA Civ 1466; [2002] 2 All ER 248; [2002] 2 P&CR 20 (see R1.12)

Whether loan an extortionate credit bargain to be judged at time loan agreed

R3.4   *Rahman v Sterling Credit Ltd*
[2001] 1 WLR 496; (2001) 33 HLR 708; (2000) *Times* 17 October, CA

Application to file defence and counterclaim 8 years after possession order made allowed where limitation period of 12 years applied

Sterling were the assignees of a legal charge on Mr and Mrs Rahman's matrimonial home. The initial amount loaned was £5,000 to be repaid by monthly instalments of capital and interest at a rate of 32.1%. Mr and Mrs Rahman defaulted and Sterling obtained a possession order. The order remained unexecuted. Eight years later Mr Rahman applied to set aside the order and the warrant for possession and for leave to file a defence and counterclaim alleging for the first time that the loan was an extortionate credit bargain under Consumer Credit Act 1974 s139(2).

The Court of Appeal held that

1) The statutory limitation period for a claim under s139(2) was 12 years. The cause of action arose out of the provisions of the 1974 Act. The claim was therefore an 'action upon a specialty' within the meaning of Limitation Act 1980 s8. Mr Rahman's claim, whether brought by counterclaim or separate action, to reopen the loan agreement under Consumer Credit Act 1974 s139 was not statute barred.

2) The fact that a possession order had been made and that there was no present claim did not affect the power of the court to permit the making of the counterclaim. The question was whether the action was at an end so that there were no longer any proceedings by the claimant to which the defendant could respond. The action was not at an end. Mr and Mrs Rahman were still living in the property. Sterling continued to accept monthly instalments and had not obtained possession. It would have to apply for a warrant of execution and such an application would be proceedings to enforce the security relating to the credit bargain, within the meaning of s139(1)(b).

3) The overriding objective made it appropriate to grant permission to make a counterclaim rather than direct the claim to be made by separate action because the counterclaim was related to the original claim and savings of time and expense would be made.

R3.5 ***Southern and District Finance plc v Barnes***
(1995) 27 HLR 691, CA

Principles relevant to exercise of discretion to make time order

The Court of Appeal considered three appeals relating to time orders which had been made in county courts. Dismissing one appeal by a lender and allowing two appeals by borrowers, the Court of Appeal stated that:

1) When an application is made for a time order, the court must consider whether or not it is just to make it. That involves considering all of the circumstances of the case, including the position of the lender as well as that of the borrower.

2) A time order should normally be made for a stipulated period on account of temporary financial difficulty. If, despite being given more time, the borrower is unlikely to be able to resume payment of the whole indebtedness by at least the amount of the contractual instalments, no time order should be made. In such circumstances it is more equitable to allow the regulated agreement to be enforced.

3) When a time order is made following financial default, the 'sum owed' means every sum which is due and owing. In possession proceedings, that usually comprises the whole indebtedness. The court must consider what instalments would be reasonable, both in amount and their timing, having regard to the borrower's means.

4) Courts may vary the contractual interest rate.

If justice requires the making of a time order, the court should suspend any possession order for so long as the terms of the time order are complied with.

High Court

R3.6 *Barclays Bank plc v Brooks*
[1997] CCLR 60, QBD

Proceedings relating to CCA agreement struck out where brought in High Court

The bank issued High Court proceedings to enforce an overdraft agreement which was a regulated agreement. The borrower sought to have the proceedings transferred to the county court but the district judge of his own motion struck out the claim, referring to Consumer Credit Act (CCA) 1974 s141(1), which provides that proceedings to enforce a regulated agreement should not be brought in any court other than a county court.

Dismissing the bank's appeal, the judge held that, while s141(2) provides that such an action brought in the High Court should not be treated as improperly brought, the court had jurisdiction under County Courts Act 1984 s40(1), as substituted by Courts and Legal Services Act 1990 s2(1), to strike out the proceedings if the bank knew or ought to have known that they should have been brought in the county court. Given that the bank had offered no reason for having initiated High Court proceedings (the choice appears to have been a matter of policy), the district judge had properly exercised the court's discretion to strike out the claim.

County courts

R3.7 *Cedar Holdings v Jenkins*
October 1987 *Legal Action* 19, Sheffield County Court

Power when making time order to reduce interest rate and monthly instalments

Mr Jenkins borrowed £2,258 from the plaintiffs. The loan was secured as a second mortgage. Monthly repayments were £52.56. The monthly interest rate was 1.9 per cent, the equivalent of an APR of 25.34 per cent. Some payments were missed and possession proceedings brought. Mr Jenkins applied for a time order under Consumer Credit Act 1974 s129. The registrar ordered that the monthly repayments should be reduced to £45 per month and the interest rate to 1.45 per cent per month. The lender appealed.

HHJ Cotton dismissed the appeal. The powers in ss129 and 136 were sufficient to allow the court to reduce both the monthly payment and the rate of interest. Since there was no error of law (see CCR Ord 37 r6), the appeal was dismissed with costs.

R3.8 *City Mortgage Corp Ltd v Baptiste*
[1997] CCLR 64; [1998] 1 CL 57, Bow County Court

Extortionate credit bargain counterclaim to be heard at same time as possession claim

In mortgage possession proceedings, the borrower defended and counterclaimed, seeking under Consumer Credit Act 1974 ss137–140 to reopen the agreement as an extortionate credit bargain. A district judge made an order for possession and directed that the counterclaim be heard within six weeks. The defendant appealed.

Recorder Russell held that the defendant had a good arguable case on the extortionate credit bargain and that, although generally a counterclaim is not a good reason to adjourn possession proceedings, an application to reopen the agreement was akin to an application for rescission. That issue and the claim for possession should be tried at the same time.

R4   # Orders for sale and claims for mortgage shortfall

Under Law of Property Act 1925 s91 the court (which includes the county court if the amount owing in respect of the mortgage at the commencement of proceedings does not exceed £30,000) may direct the sale of the premises on such terms as it thinks fit. The court has a wide discretion and may order a sale of mortgaged property against the wishes of the lender where it would be unfair to the borrower to postpone sale, even if the mortgage would not be redeemed.

House of Lords

R4.1   ## *Bradford and Bingley plc v Rashid*
[2006] UKHL 37; [2006] 1 WLR 2066; [2006] 4 All ER 705; (2006) *Times* 14 July

Letters offering to settle mortgage debt extended limitation period; analysis of without prejudice correspondence

Bradford and Bingley were mortgagees under a legal mortgage granted to Mr Rashid to secure repayment of a sum of £50,300 advanced towards its purchase. Payments fell into arrears. The last payment was made in January 1991. In October 1991, after Bradford and Bingley had obtained a possession order, the property was sold for £47,000 leaving a shortfall of £15,583. Bradford and Bingley then had difficulty in tracing Mr Rashid. In 2001 they asked him to make an offer of repayment. In September 2001, an advice centre wrote on his behalf stating '... at present, he is not in a position to repay the outstanding balance, owed to you.' In October 2001 they wrote, 'He is willing to pay approximately £500 towards the outstanding amount as a final settlement.' None of the correspondence was marked 'without prejudice'. In June 2003, Bradford and Bingley began county court proceedings claiming £15,583 and statutory interest. The sole defence was that the limitation period had expired (Limitation Act 1980 s20(1) and (5)). Bradford and Bingley relied on the letters written in September and October 2001 as acknowledgments of the debt under s29(5).

The House of Lords held that letters not written in the context of any dispute regarding the debt did not attract the without-prejudice privilege. (See *Rush and Tompkins Ltd v Greater London Council* [1989] AC 1280, 1299.) The 'without prejudice' rule has no application to apparently open communications, designed only to discuss the repayment of an admitted liability rather than to negotiate and compromise a disputed liability. The references in the letters to an 'outstanding balance' and an 'outstanding amount' were plain acknowledgments of the existence of a debt. Each letter constituted a clear acknowledgment of the debt and therefore the claim was not statute barred.

R4.2   *West Bromwich Building Society v Wilkinson*
[2005] UKHL 44; [2005] 1 WLR 2303; [2005] 4 All ER 97

Mortgagee's right to recover shortfall of mortgage advance accrued on date mortgagors defaulted on monthly instalment payments; 12-year limitation

The claimant building society was the mortgagee of a house owned by the defendants. The mortgage deed expressly provided for repayment of the advance by monthly instalments, but did not include any covenant that the borrowers would repay the balance of the advance on a specified date or on a specified event (eg, default in payment of the instalments). The defendants fell into arrears. The claimant obtained possession and sold the house on 14 November 1990. On 12 November 2002 it began proceedings to recover the shortfall. The defendants claimed that the proceedings were statute barred on the basis that time started to run on the date of the last repayment of a monthly instalment (31 July 1989). The building society claimed that time started to run when the amount of the shortfall was actually ascertained, ie, on sale of the house (14 November 1990). The Court of Appeal found that a covenant to repay the balance of the advance was to be implied into the legal charge and that the whole of the balance would become immediately repayable if the borrowers defaulted in payment of instalments. Accordingly, more than 12 years had elapsed from the accrual of the right of the claimant to receive the balance of the mortgage debt and the commencement of the action and the claim was statute barred within the meaning of Limitation Act 1980 ss8 (action 'upon a specialty') and 20 (advance 'secured by a mortgage on property').

The House of Lords dismissed the building society's appeal. For the purposes of the Limitation Act 1980 ss8 and s20, the date on which a building society's right accrued to recover the shortfall of a mortgage advance from the mortgagors was the date when the mortgagors defaulted in the monthly instalment payments.

Court of Appeal

R4.3   *Bradford and Bingley plc v Ross*
[2005] EWCA Civ 394

Burden on mortgagees who sold to connected company to show attained best price

Bradford and Bingley issued proceedings for the recovery of a shortfall on the sale of the security. On appeal, the defendant argued that evidence had come to light which showed that the lender had sold the property to a connected company and that the claimant had failed to disclose this to the trial judge.

The Court of Appeal allowed the appeal. Although there is no hard and fast rule that a lender may not sell a property to a company in which it has an interest, a party seeking to uphold such a transaction has to show that it was done in good faith, and that reasonable precautions had been taken to show that it had attained the best price reasonably obtainable at the time of sale.

R4.4   **Bristol and West plc v Bartlett**
[2002] EWCA Civ 1181; [2002] 4 All ER 544; [2003] 01 EG 69; [2003] HLR 22; (2002) *Times* 9 September

Limitation period: 12 years for recovery of principal sum, 6 years for interest

Mr and Mrs Bartlett borrowed £89,750 from Bristol and West to assist in the purchase of their home. It was secured by a mortgage. The mortgage deed provided that the debt would become repayable immediately if arrears exceeded three monthly payments. Mr and Mrs Bartlett defaulted on repayments in 1993. The lenders obtained possession in March 1994 and sold the property in July 1994 for £63,000. There was a mortgage shortfall of £64,961. Bristol and West began court proceedings to recover that sum in May 2001. The defendants argued that the claim was statute barred by the Limitation Act 1980. Section 5 provides that an action brought on a simple contract shall not be brought after the expiration of six years from the date on which the cause of action accrued. Section 8 provides that the limitation period for an action on a specialty is 12 years. Section 20 provides that the limitation period for an action to recover any principal sum of money secured by a mortgage is 12 years, but six years for the recovery of interest on any sum secured by a mortgage. HHJ Havelock-Allan QC held that the claim fell within s8. The defendants appealed.

The Court of Appeal, allowing the appeal in part, held that the true cause of action was still for the mortgage debt arising on default under the terms of the deed. Section 20(1) applies to any action to recover any principal sum of money secured by a mortgage which existed when the right to recover the money accrued, even if the mortgagee has exercised a power of sale before issuing proceedings. The limitation period for recovery of the principal sum is accordingly twelve years. The claim for interest is governed by s20(5), with a six-year limitation period.

Note: This decision was approved by the House of Lords in *West Bromwich Building Society v Wilkinson* (R4.2).

R4.5   **Cheltenham and Gloucester Building Society v Krausz**
[1997] 1 WLR 1558; [1997] 1 All ER 21; (1997) 29 HLR 597, CA

Court could not suspend warrant to enable mortgagor to apply to the High Court for order for sale under LPA s91

On 25 July 1991 a possession order was made as a result of mortgage arrears. Four warrants for possession were issued and on each occasion agreement was reached, with the result that the warrant was not enforced. A fifth warrant was due to be executed on 12 June 1995. The borrowers' valuer estimated that the property was worth £65,000. On 9 June 1995 the borrowers applied to suspend the warrant so that they could apply in the High Court for an order for sale under Law of Property Act 1925 s91(2). By this time the mortgage debt amounted to £83,000. A district judge dismissed their application, but a circuit judge allowed their appeal. The building society appealed to the Court of Appeal, contending that the district judge had no jurisdiction to suspend in these circumstances.

The Court of Appeal accepted this submission, allowed the appeal and dismissed the application to suspend the warrant. Phillips LJ stated that he:

... [did not consider] that the County Court, as part of its inherent jurisdiction, can properly suspend an order or warrant for possession in order to enable a mortgagor to apply to the High Court for an order under section 91. It [is] incumbent on the mortgagor to seek from the High Court any relief which the court is empowered to give before the warrant takes effect.

He noted that Administration of Justice Act 1970 s36 (see section R2) makes it clear that parliament did not intend that the court should have power to curtail mortgagees' rights to possession unless the proceeds of sale were likely to discharge the mortgage debt. Millett LJ expressed serious doubts about whether *Barrett v Halifax Building Society* (R4.10), where an order was made allowing the borrowers to sell even though the proceeds of sale would not discharge the mortgage debt, was correctly decided.

R4.6   ## Cheltenham and Gloucester plc v Booker
(1997) 29 HLR 634; (1997) 73 P&CR 412; [1997] 1 EGLR 142; [1997] 19 EG 155, CA (see R2.11)

Court has residual inherent jurisdiction where AJA s36 not available to defer date of giving up possession to enable the lender to sell the property

R4.7   ## Mortgage Express v Mardner
[2004] EWCA Civ 1859; 17 December 2004

Evidential burden on mortgagee where sale is to associated company

The claimant company obtained a possession order after the defendant failed to meet his mortgage repayments. It obtained three valuations of the property and placed it on the market for three months. A single offer was made but that sale fell through. The claimant then sold the property to an associated company for £68,000 and sought the shortfall from the defendant. The defendant counterclaimed, alleging that the property had been sold at an undervalue. A jointly appointed expert valued the property at a figure higher than that which the claimant had obtained. The judge found that the claimant had not discharged its duty to obtain the best price reasonably obtainable and dismissed its claim. The claimant appealed.

The Court of Appeal allowed the appeal in part. On the sale of a repossessed property by a mortgagee to an associated company, the evidential burden is on the mortgagee to show that it has taken all reasonable steps to comply with its duty to obtain the best price reasonably obtainable for the property. On the limited evidence before the judge, it was clear that the claimant had not discharged its duty. However, the judge had erred in dismissing the claim in its entirety. He should have found that the expert's valuation figure was the best price reasonably obtainable for the property. The claimant was entitled to the difference between that figure, as reduced to reflect estate agent's fees, mortgage interest and conveyancing savings made by the original sale, and the mortgage debt.

R4.8   ## Palk v Mortgage Services Funding
[1993] Ch 330; [1993] 2 WLR 415; [1993] 2 All ER 481; (1993) 25 HLR 56; (1992) 65 P&CR 207, CA

Court has an unfettered jurisdiction to order sale of mortgaged property

Mr Palk obtained an advance of £300,000 secured on the matrimonial home. He made three monthly payments, but then his business started to founder and he was unable to make any further payments. He negotiated to sell the house and received an offer of £283,000. By this time the balance outstanding under the mortgage was £358,587. The finance company obtained a possession order which was suspended to enable Mrs Palk to apply for an order, under Law of Property Act 1925 s91(2) for sale of the property.

The Court of Appeal held that the court has an unfettered jurisdiction to order a sale of mortgaged property against the wishes of the lender where it would be unfair to the borrower to postpone sale. This was so despite the fact that the mortgage would not be redeemed. In exercising that discretion, the court should have regard to the interests of all concerned and to what was just and equitable. This was an exceptional case and it would be just and equitable for the court to direct a sale. If the property was rented, as the lender proposed, the rent would fall short of the interest which would accrue and the likelihood that Mrs Palk would suffer further loss if the property were let far outweighed the prospect of any gain which the finance company might make.

R4.9   *Scottish Equitable v Thompson*
[2003] EWCA Civ 225; [2003] HLR 48

Limitations periods 12 years under s20(1) and 6 years under s20(5)

Scottish Equitable lent £15,000, secured by a second legal charge. The mortgage deed contained an express covenant to pay the interest, but not the principal. Arrears accrued. The first mortgagee obtained possession in 1991 and sold the property, but Scottish Equitable did not receive any of the proceeds. In March 1999 it began proceedings claiming the principal and interest owing.

Following *Bristol and West plc v Bartlett* (R4.4), the Court of Appeal held that Limitation Act 1980 s20(1) (12-year limitation period) applied to the claim for the principal and that s20(5) (six-year limitation period) applied to the claim for the interest.

High Court

R4.10   *Barrett v Halifax Building Society*
(1996) 28 HLR 634, ChD

Mortgagors given leave to sell even though would leave a mortgage shortfall

The Barretts remortgaged their house for £189,000 but subsequently fell into arrears. By the time of the court proceedings, there was negative equity with an outstanding balance of over £300,000. The mortgagors found a purchaser who would pay £252,000, more than an independent valuation, but the building society refused to allow the sale to proceed. In court, the mortgagors argued that the building society would not obtain such a high price under a forced sale.

Evans-Lombe J gave the mortgagors leave to sell their house, even though the proceeds of sale would not clear the mortgage debt.

Note: In view of *Cheltenham and Gloucester Building Society v Krausz* (R4.5) there are now serious doubts about whether this case was correctly decided.

R4.11   *Polonski v Lloyds Bank Mortgages Ltd*

(1999) 31 HLR 721; [1998] 1 FCR 282; (1997) *Times* 6 May, ChD

Court can take account of social as well as financial factors in ordering sale

The plaintiff owned a property in a run-down area in Mitcham. Her partner left her with two young children. She was in receipt of income support. Although there was no suggestion that she had been financially irresponsible, mortgage arrears accrued. By the date of the hearing there was a negative equity of approximately £12,000. She sought an order for sale at a proper value (not an undervalue) to a housing association because she wanted to move to Salisbury for strong social reasons. Her affidavit gave graphic accounts of the neighbourhood in Mitcham where she lived, including problem families, drug dealers, violence nearby and condoms and spirit bottles being thrown into her back yard. She believed that schooling would be better in Salisbury and that she stood some chance of gaining employment there. The bank, however, took the view that if she stayed in Mitcham, with state benefits meeting her mortgage payments, the arrears would remain fairly constant and, in time, the increase in house prices would take the property out of negative equity.

Jacobs J, following *Palk v Mortgage Services Funding* (R4.8) granted the plaintiff an order permitting sale under Law of Property Act 1925 s91(2). He stated that, when ordering a sale, the court can take into account an applicant's pressing social needs as well as purely financial matters. What the plaintiff 'wanted to do ... was to exercise, perfectly legitimately, her undoubted right to live where she wanted'.

R4.12   *Raja v Lloyds TSB*

[2001] 19 EG 143; (2001) 82 P&CR 191; (2000) *Times* 16 May, ChD

Six-year limitation for claim for breach of duty to obtain best price

The duty of a mortgagee to obtain a proper price after recovering possession of a mortgaged property does not arise under the deed of charge, but in equity. A claim for damages for breach of duty in equity corresponds with the remedy for breach of duty of care in tort and accordingly the limitation period is the six-year period in Limitation Act 1980 s2.

R4.13   *Woolwich Building Society v Brown*

[1996] CLC 625; March 1996 *Legal Action* 13, Commercial Court

Payments under lender's insurance policy did not reduce sums due from borrower

In an action by a lender for the shortfall on sale of the security, the court held that the borrower was not entitled to claim a credit for the amount which the lender had received from an insurance company under a mortgage indemnity policy. The lender was entitled to recoup the full sum from the borrower. The indemnity insurance policy was not for the benefit of the borrower but for the benefit of the lender.

R5   Tenants of mortgagors

Most mortgage deeds exclude the lender's power to let the property. In those circumstances, a tenancy granted after the date of the mortgage, and without the consent of the lender, is not binding on the lender. The position is, however, different if the tenancy pre-dates the mortgage. In that case, the tenancy is binding on the lender.

Court of Appeal

R5.1   *Berkshire Capital Funding Ltd v Street*
(2000) 32 HLR 373; (1999) 78 P&CR 321, CA

Second mortgagee could not obtain possession to destroy tenancy granted by prior mortgagee

Mr Street mortgaged a property to the Nationwide Building Society. Then in 1992 he granted a tenancy to the second defendants. In 1996, Mr Street entered into a second mortgage to the plaintiffs' predecessor in title. It was a term of the second mortgage that Mr Street was prohibited from granting any tenancy of the property without the plaintiffs' prior consent. Later he fell into arrears on both mortgages. Possession proceedings were brought by the plaintiffs against him. District Judge Hughes decided that he had no jurisdiction to make an order for possession where there was a superior mortgagee in possession. The plaintiffs appealed on the grounds that they were not bound by the tenancy entered into by Nationwide with the tenants, the second defendants, since Law of Property Act 1925 s99(2) bound only prior incumbrancers and not subsequent mortgagees.

The Court of Appeal held that the plaintiff could not obtain possession to destroy a valid tenancy granted by a prior mortgagee. A mortgagee in possession has to be able to exercise powers of management over a charged property, including the ability to grant tenancies both at common law and pursuant to s99(2). Section 99 was drafted on the basis that a subsequent incumbrancer could not do anything to affect the interests of a prior mortgagee adversely. Such interests included the interests of a prior mortgagee as landlord in respect of a lease granted under the section. Therefore, any order made in favour of the second mortgagee must respect the interests of the prior mortgagee, including his interests as a landlord of valid tenancy. It was probable that if an order were made in those terms, a second mortgagee would not be entitled to a warrant of possession since CCR Ord 26 r17(2) required that the land had not been vacated in accordance with the judgment order for the recovery of the land.

R5.2   *Britannia Building Society v Earl*
[1990] 1 WLR 422; [1990] 2 All ER 469; (1990) 22 HLR 98; [1990] 1 EGLR 133; [1990] 25 EG 72, CA

Mortgagee not bound by subsequent unauthorised tenancy

After taking out a mortgage, a flat owner granted a nine-month fixed-term protected tenancy, in breach of the terms of the mortgage and without obtaining the building society's consent. When the building society brought possession proceedings, the tenants contended that, since they had become statutory tenants, irrespective of whether proceedings were brought by the landlord or the building society, a possession order could only be made in accordance with Rent Act 1977.

Dismissing the tenants' appeal, the Court of Appeal confirmed that a mortgagee is not bound by a subsequent unauthorised tenancy. It held that, because the tenants merely enjoyed a statutory tenancy, they were not 'persons deriving title' from the mortgagor and so the court did not have power under Administration of Justice Act 1970 s36 to grant an adjournment on terms.

R5.3 **Lloyds Bank plc v Doyle and Others**
April 1996 *Legal Action* 17, CA

Mortgagee not bound by subsequent tenancies where no consent despite fact property of type used for letting

In 1985 and 1987 the first defendant bought two adjacent properties which were already let to tenants and contained many bedsits and small flats. Each of the properties was subject to a mortgage in favour of the plaintiffs, containing the standard clause precluding the granting of tenancies without the written consent of the bank. No consent was ever sought or given. After the issue of possession proceedings on the first defendant's default, ten of the occupiers who had taken tenancies after the mortgages were joined as defendants and sought leave to defend. Evidence was available that the bank knew at the time of the mortgage advances that the building was to continue to be used for letting and the generation of rental income from a flow of different occupiers.

Refusing leave to appeal against a refusal of leave to defend, the Court of Appeal rejected the arguments (a) that the bank could be taken in the circumstances to have given 'umbrella consent' to the use of the property for multiple letting in the future and (b) that the clause in the legal charge prohibiting letting without consent did not accurately reflect the true agreement reached by the owner and the bank.

R5.4 **Mann v Nijar**
(2000) 32 HLR 223; [1998] EGCS 188, CA

Where mortgagee's receivers collected rent, tenancy was confirmed

Mrs Caine bought a property with the aid of a mortgage from the National Westminster Bank. It was a term of the mortgage not to grant a tenancy of the property without the prior written consent of the bank. Despite this, she granted the plaintiff an assured tenancy of a flat in the building. Later Mrs Caine fell into arrears with the mortgage repayments, handed over the keys and surrendered the property to the bank. Receivers were appointed who collected rent and paid it to the bank. The property was offered for sale by the bank. It was bought by the defendants who disconnected the electricity and water supplies. The plaintiff then found that his flat was occupied by the defendant's builders and that his furniture and possessions had been removed. He successfully claimed damages under Housing Act 1988 ss27 and 28.

The defendants appealed but their appeal was dismissed. A prohibition against letting in the mortgage deed entitles a lender to treat such a tenancy as a nullity. However, a mortgagee can confirm the tenancy by its conduct, although knowledge of the tenancy is not enough by itself to do this. It is necessary to look at all the facts in order to get a picture of whether the mortgagee has accepted the tenant as his own. The question of rent collection by the receivers was relevant since Law of Property Act 1925 s109(2) deems a receiver appointed under the Act to be the agent of the mortgagor. It was clear that the bank knew of the tenancy although it was not certain at first whether it was bound by it. It was also aware that acceptance of rent by it could give rise to a new tenancy. In view of the fact that it instructed the receivers to collect the rent, the bank created, or was held to have created, a new tenancy with the plaintiff. That new tenancy was binding on the defendants. (See too *Iron Trades Employers Insurance Association Ltd v Union Land and House Investors Ltd* [1937] 1 Ch 313, *Parker v Braithwaite* [1960] 2 All ER 837, *Stroud Building Society v Delamont* [1960] 1 WLR 431 and *Chatsworth Building Society v Effion* [1971] 1 WLR 144.)

R5.5   **Sadiq v Hussain**
[1997] NPC 19, CA

Tenancy granted without consent void unless illegality waived

The Court of Appeal held that a lease granted after a property had been mortgaged and in breach of a covenant in the mortgage not to lease or part with possession without consent was void unless the mortgagee waived the illegality.

R5.6   **Starling v Lloyds TSB**
[2000] 01 EG 89, CA

Borrower not entitled to complain of unreasonable decision to withhold consent

A mortgage excluded the mortgagor's powers of leasing and prevented the mortgagor leasing the property without the bank's consent in writing. In 1992 the borrower asked the bank for permission to let the property. That request was dismissed 'out of hand'. The borrower took proceedings against the bank for damages for negligence and breach of duty on the basis that the bank owed a duty in equity properly to consider the request for permission to let the property.

The Court of Appeal held that the master who had struck out the claim was right that the statement of claim disclosed no reasonable cause of action. The borrower was not entitled to complain of an unreasonable decision to withhold consent. Breach of an implied term that the bank's consent would not be unreasonably withheld did not give rise to a claim for damages. To establish breach of the duty of good faith, the borrower had to show dishonesty or an improper notice. In this case the manager could have had a variety of honest reasons for the rejection.

R5.7   **Walthamstow Building Society v Davies**
(1990) 22 HLR 60; (1989) 60 P&CR 99, CA

Where second mortgage executed to replace earlier defective charge, existing tenancy not thereby granted prior to the mortgage

Mr Davies let premises in breach of the terms of his mortgage and without the consent of the building society. Subsequently, the building society found that the charge executed was defective and arranged for him to execute a second mortgage. The tenants argued that there was a moment in time between the discharge of the first mortgage and the grant of the second mortgage during which they were in lawful occupation against the building society.

The Court of Appeal rejected this contention and upheld a deputy registrar's order refusing the tenants' application to be joined as parties in the possession proceedings. The Court of Appeal left open the question of whether or not the position would have been different if the further mortgage had been in favour of a different building society or bank.

R5.8 **Woolwich Building Society v Dickman**
[1996] 3 All ER 204; (1996) 28 HLR 661; (1996) 72 P&CR 470, CA

Mortgagee not entitled to possession despite tenants having signed rights away

The building society made it a requirement of a mortgage advance that tenants of the proposed borrower who were already living in the property should sign written consents to their rights of occupation being subordinated to the rights and powers of the lender. The borrower subsequently defaulted and did not defend possession proceedings. However, the tenants defended, arguing that their tenancy was binding on the building society.

The Court of Appeal held that the society was not entitled to possession. The tenancy was an overriding interest under Land Registration Act 1925 s70(1)(g) and so the building society's charge took subject to the tenancy. In those circumstances, the tenants had protection under Rent Act 1977 and the effect of s98(1) was to prevent a possession order being made against the tenants unless there was a ground for possession and it was reasonable to make an order.

High Court

R5.9 **Barclays Bank plc v Zaroovabli**
[1997] Ch 321; [1997] 2 WLR 729; [1997] 2 All ER 19, ChD

Tenancy binding on mortgagee where charge not registered until after tenancy granted

In May 1988 the purchaser of premises charged them by way of legal mortgage to the bank. In July 1988 she granted Mrs Pourdanay a six-month protected tenancy. The bank did not register its charge until 1994, by which time Mrs Pourdanay had a statutory tenancy.

Sir Richard Scott V-C held that the statutory tenancy was binding on the bank. Following *Abbey National Building Society v Cann* [1991] AC 56, HL, the relevant date for determining the existence of overriding interests is the date of registration. If a contractual tenancy, when granted, is binding on a mortgagee, any statutory tenancy which comes into existence on the termination of the contractual tenancy is also binding on the lender. The bank was not entitled to possession.

R5.10 **Pourdanay v Barclays Bank plc**
see *Barclays Bank plc v Zaroovabli* (R5.9)

R5.11 *Woolwich Equitable Building Society v Marshall and Long*
[1952] Ch 1; [1951] 2 All ER 769; (1951) 158 EG 344, ChD

Tenancy binding as overriding interest

Mr Long was first granted a tenancy in 1946. The building society's charge
was executed in 1948. Mr Marshall, the borrower, fell into arrears and the
building society brought possession proceedings.

Danckwerts J held that the tenancy to Mr Long was binding on the
building society as an overriding interest within the meaning of Land
Registration Act 1925 s70. He made a possession order, subject to Mr
Long's tenancy.

County courts

R5.12 *Abbey National plc v Yusuf*
June 1993 *Legal Action* 12, Shoreditch County Court

Tenants came within definition of 'mortgagor'; possession suspended on terms

Three tenants applied to be joined as parties in mortgage possession proceedings. Although their tenancy post-dated the date of the mortgage, the
arrears were relatively low and they were in a position not only to pay
current instalments but also all the arrears. They were all post-graduate
students who wished to stay in the property until September 1993 in order
to complete their exams.

A district judge accepted that the tenants came within the definition
of 'mortgagor' in Administration of Justice Act 1970 s39, since they were
'persons deriving title under the original mortgagor'. Despite the opposition of the plaintiff, he joined the students as parties to the action and suspended the possession order on terms until the end of September 1993.

R5.13 *National Westminster Home Loans v Riches*
[1996] CLY 4998, Hertford County Court

Possession suspended to allow tenant to redeem mortgage

A possession warrant was suspended to enable a tenant of the borrower to
pursue a claim to redeem the mortgage herself (Law of Property Act 1925
s91(2)).

R6 # Costs

Where mortgagees bring proceedings concerning mortgaged property
(eg, possession proceedings where there are mortgage arrears), the usual
rule is that they are entitled to 'reimburse [themselves] out of the mortgaged property for all costs, charges and expenses reasonably and properly
incurred in enforcing or preserving [their] security'. (See *Parker-Tweedale
v Dunbar Bank plc (No 2)* (R6.2).) Costs are usually added to the sum outstanding under the mortgage. However, this rule does not apply if costs
have been unreasonably incurred. The principles which were set out by
the Court of Appeal in *Gomba Holdings (UK) Ltd v Minories Finance Ltd
(No 2)* (R6.1) are now contained in CPR 48.3 and PD 48 section 50.

Court of Appeal

R6.1 *Gomba Holdings (UK) Ltd v Minories Finance Ltd (No 2)*
[1993] Ch 171; [1992] 3 WLR 723; [1992] 4 All ER 588, CA

Principles relating to orders for costs in mortgage cases

After default on mortgage payments, receivers were appointed by the lenders. However, the borrowers were able to raise sufficient sums to meet their liabilities. The lenders, in accordance with the terms of the mortgage, submitted mortgage accounts and receivers' costs to the borrowers. These included costs, charges and expenses involved in litigation. The total amount challenged was £1.8 million.

The Court of Appeal set out the following principles:

1) An order for the payment of costs of proceedings by one party to another party is always a discretionary order.

2) Where there is a contractual right to costs, the discretion should normally be exercised to reflect that contractual right.

3) The power of a court to disallow a mortgagee's costs sought to be added to the mortgage security is a power which does not derive from Supreme Court Act 1981 s51. It derives from the power of courts of equity to fix the terms on which redemption should be allowed. A mortgagor is required to show a clear case of unreasonableness if any of the mortgagee's actual costs, charges and expenses are to be disallowed.

4) A mortgagee is not to be deprived of the right to add costs to the security merely because of an order for payment of costs made without reference to the contractual provisions.

(See too Civil Procedure Rules Part 48.3 and the Practice Direction on Cost, section 50.)

R6.2 *Parker-Tweedale v Dunbar Bank plc (No 2)*
[1991] Ch 26; [1990] 3 WLR 780; [1990] 2 All ER 588, CA

Costs against mortgagor's husband could not be added to security but mortgagee generally entitled to reimbursement for costs in preserving security

The borrower's husband unsuccessfully sought to set aside an order in favour of the bank for sale of the premises. The Court of Appeal held that the mortgagee bank could not add the costs of that action to the security but confirmed that, as a general rule, a lender is entitled 'to reimburse himself out of the mortgaged property for all costs, charges and expenses reasonably and properly incurred in enforcing or preserving his security'. That right occurs as a result of the relationship between lender and borrower and not out of the proceedings. Any dispute is usually determined on the taking of an account between the lender and the borrower although, if the borrower is involved in the proceedings, it may be convenient for any questions arising to be determined by the judge who tried the proceedings.

Note: There is an exception to this general rule that costs may be added to security where, as in *Parker-Tweedale*, a mortgagee incurs costs in an action brought by a third party who seeks to impugn the title to the mortgage.

Allocation and transfer

S1   # General

Housing Act 1985 s22 provided that, in selecting their tenants, local author-ities should give a 'reasonable preference' to various categories of people, including those in unsatisfactory housing conditions and those found to be homeless under Part III of the Act.

Housing Act 1996 repealed s22 and introduced Housing Act 1996 Part VI. This was intended to create a 'single route into social housing', cover-ing not only the manner in which authorities selected people to be tenants of their own stock but also the nomination of people to be tenants of reg-istered social landlords. (Part VI does not, however, otherwise apply to the allocation by registered social landlords of their housing stock.) The Act was designed to remove what was perceived as an automatic priority for the statutory homeless. Part VI retained the notion of 'reasonable preference' but omitted the homeless as a category to which preference was required to be given. This was reversed by regulation by the incoming Labour gov-ernment in 1997. Significant amendments to Part VI were subsequently made by Homelessness Act 2002. These included bringing applications for transfers by existing local authority tenants within the ambit of Part VI and limiting the circumstances in which applicants could be excluded from an allocation scheme (although still allowing an applicant's behav-iour to be an important factor in determining priority). Further amend-ments were made with the intention of promoting and facilitating the policy of allowing applicants to exercise an element of choice in the al-location process. Although the legal requirements relating to choice are not strong, there is an ongoing policy imperative for choice-based lettings schemes to become universal.

Many of the reported cases concern the legislation before amendment by Homelessness Act 2002. While many of the concepts of Part VI remain unchanged, some aspects of such cases are specific to the pre-amended Part VI. (The amendments introduced to Part VI by Homelessness Act 2002 came into force on 31 January 2003 in England and 27 January 2003 in Wales.)

The framework of Part VI

Section 159(1) provides that an authority shall comply with the provisions of Part VI in allocating housing accommodation. Section 159(7) provides that subject to Part VI, an authority may allocate housing in such manner as it considers appropriate. Sections 159–160 define what is, and is not, an allocation for the purposes of Part VI.

Section 160A provides that an allocation can only be made to an eligible person. It prescribes that certain 'persons from abroad' are not eligible and that an authority may decide to treat a person 'unsuitable to be a tenant' as ineligible. Subject to this, any person may be allocated accommodation. The provisions regarding persons from abroad and eligibility are the same as for Housing Act 1996 Part VII (see T2) except that asylum-seekers, a dwindling number of whom are eligible under Part VII, are never eligible under Part VI. The eligibility exclusion does not apply to a person who is already a secure or introductory tenant or an assured tenant of accommo-dation allocated by an authority.

Section 167 deals with the allocation scheme itself. Section 167(1) provides that every housing authority shall have an allocation scheme for determining priorities, specifying the procedure to be followed in allocating housing accommodation. 'Procedure' includes all aspects of the allocation process, including the descriptions of the persons who are to make decisions.

Subsection 167(2) requires the scheme to be framed so as to secure that reasonable preference is given to:

a) people who are homeless;
b) people owed certain homelessness duties under Housing Act 1996 Part VII;
c) people living in unsatisfactory housing conditions (including insanitary or overcrowded housing);
d) people with a particular need to move on medical or welfare grounds; and
e) people with a particular need to move to avoid hardship to themselves or others.

Additional preference may be given to those within the above categories with urgent housing needs.

Subsection 167(2A) provides that schemes may contain provisions for determining priorities between applicants who fall within the reasonable and additional preference categories. The factors which the scheme may allow to be taken into account include:

a) the financial resources available to a person to meet his or her housing costs;
b) any behaviour of a person (or a member of his or her household) which affects his or her suitability to be a tenant;
c) any local connection which a person has with the local authority district.

No preference need be given to those who are 'unsuitable to be a tenant'(s167(2B)), if indeed they are not excluded from the scheme under s160A.

Subsection 167(6) provides that, subject to the provisions in s167, an authority may decide on what principles the scheme is to be framed.

Subsection 167(8) provides that a local housing authority shall not allocate housing accommodation except in accordance with their allocation scheme.

Section 166 governs advice and assistance and the making of an application; s168 provides for information to be provided about an allocation scheme and s169 requires authorities to have regard to guidance issued by the secretary of state. Renewed guidance was issued following the amendments introduced by Homelessness Act 2002 (published in November 2002 for England and March 2003 for Wales; available on www.communities.gov. uk and www.wales.gov.uk). Subsection 167(4A) provides for a right of review in limited circumstances. There is no right of appeal to the county court; challenges are by way of judicial review or local ombudsman complaint.

Local authorities must have allocation schemes which give reasonable preference to the statutory categories and then allocate accommodation in accordance with the scheme. A composite assessment of a household's needs, taking account of multiple needs, must be reflected in the priorities within a scheme. Allocation schemes must not be so rigid that they amount to rules which exclude the consideration of individual cases, as this would amount to a fettering of discretion.

High Court

S1.1   *Dixon v Wandsworth LBC*
[2007] EWHC 3075 (Admin), 20 December 2007

Council entitled to find claimant ineligible on basis unsuitable to be a tenant

The claimant was a joint tenant of council flat with his sister. The property became unsuitable for his sister and she was required to serve a Notice to Quit in order to be re-housed by the council. The claimant applied to the council for alternative accommodation and was informed that he would be granted a tenancy of a one-bed flat when one became available. He remained in the original flat awaiting an offer. Following a subsequent police raid on 10 February 2006, the claimant was convicted for possession of a small amount of cocaine, a Class A drug. On 16 March 2006 a further police raid resulted in the claimant being cautioned for possession of a small amount of herbal cannabis. The council then decided that the claimant was ineligible for the allocation of accommodation under Housing Act 1996 Part VI on the basis that he was guilty of unacceptable behaviour (s160A). He applied for a review of that decision under s167(4)(d). During the course of further enquiries police records indicated that the claimant had previously been cautioned for similar offences in 1996. In a detailed letter the review officer informed the claimant that he considered that all the elements for exclusion for unacceptable behaviour under s160A were satisfied. In accordance with the Code of Guidance (in force 31 January 2003) he found that the county court would grant an outright possession order. The claimant was told that he would be evicted from his original flat. He applied for judicial review.

Michael Supperstone QC dismissed his application. He found little assistance on whether an outright order for possession would be made on the basis of the established case-law. It was necessary to examine the facts of the individual case with care. He found that the review officer's decision was not unlawful. Furthermore, the decision under challenge, concerning as it did the system for allocating accommodation in the future, did not interfere with the claimant's right to respect for his home under ECHR article 8. The possession order that had been obtained and that was now to be enforced resulted from the service of the Notice to Quit.

S1.1A   *El Yemlahi v Lambeth LBC*
[2002] EWHC 1187, Admin; 29 May 2002

Policy designed to prevent leapfrogging within queues not unlawful

The applicant and his partner applied under Lambeth's allocation scheme and were placed in the queue for one-bedroom accommodation. His partner then became pregnant and Lambeth reassessed his needs and placed him in the two-bedroom queue (which he chose over remaining in the one-bedroom queue). Under the scheme, his waiting time on the two-bedroom list ran from the date of the reassessment, rather than from the date of his initial application. He had nearly reached the top of the one-bedroom queue but would have to wait a minimum of two years for a two-bedroom property. He sought judicial review of the allocation policy, claiming that it was unreasonable because a family could be constantly relegated to the bottom of the housing queue as it grew.

Sullivan J dismissed his application. Lambeth's policy of linking priority to waiting time for a particular size accommodation rather than date of application was designed to prevent leapfrogging within queues. This was not in principle unreasonable. What the applicant perceived as unfair might be regarded as entirely fair when considered from the perspective of other applicants. Lambeth's approach was within the ambit of its discretion under Housing Act 1996 s167. It could not be said that its approach was irrational.

S1.2 *R v Canterbury CC ex p Gillespie*
(1986) 19 HLR 7, QBD

Policy which excluded consideration of individual circumstances unlawful

The council, following a policy not to accept on to its housing waiting list anyone who held a tenancy with another local authority, refused the applicant's request to be put on its waiting list.

Granting an order of mandamus requiring the council to reconsider its decision, Simon Brown J held that its policy, which allowed 'no exceptions beyond those expressly provided for', had been 'applied without proper consideration of the individual considerations of the applicant's case'. The policy, although not 'intrinsically irrational', was a 'rule which requires to be followed slavishly rather than merely a stated general approach which is always subject to an exceptional case and which permits each application to be individually considered'.

Note: Exclusions are now permitted only in the circumstances set out in s160A.

S1.3 *R v Lambeth LBC ex p Njomo*
(1996) 28 HLR 737, QBD

Rigid application of policy relating to rent arrears unlawful

The council's policy of not approving transfer requests from people in arrears of rent was subject to a number of exceptions. Examples of them were set out in the policy.

It was held that there was nothing inherently wrong in this approach. However, the evidence showed that the council's consideration of the claimant's application had been confined to a consideration of whether she came within the specified exceptions set out in the policy, which she did not. The claimant's particular individual circumstances warranted consideration by the council but had not been considered. The council, in rigidly applying its policy, had failed to take a relevant matter into consideration. The decision was quashed.

See comment in *R v Wolverhampton MBC ex p Watters* (S2.1). See also *R v Southwark LBC ex p Melak* (1997) 29 HLR 223 QBD.

S1.4   *R v Lambeth LBC ex p Trabi*
(1998) 30 HLR 975, QBD

Applicant had legitimate expectation that policy (to grant tenancies to child-caring partners left in possession) would be applied

See *Housing Law Casebook* 3rd edition.

S1.5   *R v Macclesfield BC ex p Duddy*
[2001] JHL D16, 17 October 2000, QBD

Allocation made outside the published rules unlawful

A resident warden of sheltered accommodation occupied council accommodation as a licensee. In July 1997 she decided to leave the council's employment and the council's then chief housing and environmental health officer granted her a secure tenancy of other premises. It was claimed that the allocation was made under an informal policy or practice on the part of the council (that former employees who had been living in non-secure accommodation should be transferred to secure accommodation on the cessation of their employment) rather than in accordance with its official allocation scheme. The official scheme, devised under Housing Act 1996 s167, was a waiting list system based on points. Although the warden had been on the council's waiting list for a number of years, she had no points. No question as to the propriety of the allocation was raised until February 1999, when the former warden applied to buy the property under the 'right to buy' provisions. The leader of the council sought to quash the allocation decision.

Harrison J held that it was clear that the property had been allocated in breach of the statutory duty under Housing Act 1996 s167. The informal policy or practice was unlawful. However, there had been very considerable delay in bringing the application for judicial review. The circumstances had been known to the council since 1997. The council alone was to blame for the failure to bring the proceedings expeditiously. Given those circumstances the tenant would suffer considerable financial hardship and/or prejudice if forced to give the property back. This was an appropriate case in which the court would refuse the relief sought. The application was dismissed.

S1.6   *R v Newham LBC ex p Miah (Askir)*
(1996) 28 HLR 279, QBD (see T51.16)

Policy not to move people with rent arrears to permanent accommodation lawful

S1.7   *R v Tower Hamlets LBC ex p Bradford*
(1998) 1 CCLR 294; (1997) 29 HLR 756, QBD (see U3.6)

Child with special educational needs entitled to Children Act 1989 s17 assessment addressing housing needs (in circumstances where parents did not obtain a transfer)

S1.8   *R v Tower Hamlets LBC ex p Khalique*
(1994) 26 HLR 517, QBD (see T51.17)

Policy to defer allocation of permanent accommodation unlawfully made and rigidly applied

S1.9   *R (Bibi) v Camden LBC*

[2004] EWHC 2527 (Admin); [2005] HLR 18; (2004) *Times* 25 October

Allocation decision failed to address issue of whether children were part of applicant's household as required by allocation policy

The claimant and her husband were joint tenants of council accommodation where they lived with their two children. Their relationship broke down and they divorced. The ex-husband applied to Camden for rehousing under Housing Act 1996 Part VI. He claimed that he had sole care of the children and he was allocated a three-bedroomed property. He gave notice to quit to end the joint tenancy and Camden began possession proceedings against the claimant, which were adjourned pending the determination of her application under Part VI. Meanwhile, in proceedings in the Family Court, a joint residence order was made by consent under Children Act 1989 s8. The order provided that the children would spend alternate weeks with each parent. That was how it actually operated in practice. Camden accepted the claimant for rehousing under Part VI but decided it would only offer one-bedroom accommodation stating, inter alia, that the children were adequately housed with her ex-husband. The council's allocation scheme specified that the size of accommodation offered would depend on 'the number of people in your family' and the number of bedrooms 'each household needs'

Davis J, allowed the claimant's application for judicial review. He held that:

1) Although the making of a residence order in favour of an applicant was a relevant consideration which an authority must consider, it could not dictate the outcome of an allocation decision (applying *R v Oxford CC ex p Doyle* (T16.11)). A housing authority had different factual, policy and statutory considerations to apply compared with the Family Court;

2) The council's decision did not address whether the children were part of the claimant's 'family' or what the 'household' required. While it may have been relevant to consider the position of the children with regard to her ex-husband, the position of the children with regard to the claimant herself had to be addressed in order to assess her own housing needs. The council's own rehousing manual recognised that, exceptionally, children might be spending 50% of the time with each parent and thus be in two households.

3) The defendant's witness statement did not remedy this deficiency. It was illogical for Camden to assert that the ex-husband was the primary carer on the basis that he worked. No explanation was given as to why the children were not considered to be part of the applicant's household, despite the residence order. Camden was entitled to take into account such factors as its shortage of housing stock and the partial under-occupation that would occur, but such factors could not of themselves displace the policy and provisions of the allocation scheme.

The decision was quashed and remitted for reconsideration. Davis J commented that his decision was very much dependent on the precise '50/50' shared residence order and the fact that this was operated in practice. This was a relatively rare situation.

S1.10   **R (Bibi (No 1) and Al-Nashed) v Newham LBC**

[2001] EWCA Civ 607; [2002] 1 WLR 237; (2001) 33 HLR 84; (2001) *Times* 10 May, CA
(see T51.10)

Legitimate expectation resulting from the promise of council accommodation to homeless applicants required to be considered

S1.11   **R (Bilverstone) v Oxford CC**

[2003] EWHC 2434 (Admin); 10 October 2003

Refusal to consider application for transfer under Part VI because applicant accepted under Part VII unlawful

Ms Bilverstone was a council tenant. She requested a transfer under Housing Act 1996 Part VI because of domestic violence. The council referred her case to its exceptional circumstances panel (ECP) which had a discretion to award an 'urgent' category to her application. In the meantime, Ms Bilverstone also made an application under Housing Act 1996 Part VII. The day before the ECP was to consider her case she was accepted for the main housing duty under Housing Act 1996 s193. The ECP decided that it was consequently precluded from considering her transfer application. Her acceptance as a homeless person was said to have provided a satisfactory resolution of her housing problems. It was contended that the Part VII route was an alternative to the Part VI route and that Ms Bilverstone had elected the former.

Maurice Kay J allowed her application for judicial review. It was wrong to conclude that the fact that a favourable decision had been taken under Part VII meant that the ECP was precluded from considering the application for a transfer. Ms Bilverstone could pursue an application under both parts. The ECP's decision was unlawful and would be quashed.

S1.12   **R (Heaney) v Lambeth LBC**

[2006] EWHC Admin 3332; 17 November 2006

Decision not to admit claimant into emergency category not unlawful

The claimant was a tenant of Lambeth. Her 6-year-old daughter died suddenly and unexpectedly in her home. The death had had a devastating effect on the claimant and her other children. She applied for a transfer, supported by medical opinion and a social services assessment. The council's allocation scheme had eight priority groups (A–H). The claimant asked to be placed in group B which dealt with emergencies and which gave priority over all other groups. Group B included five categories, one of which allowed the director of housing to recognise emergency cases that were not covered by the other four categories (into which the applicant did not fit). Lambeth refused to place the claimant in group B.

Collins J dismissed an application for judicial review. Lambeth had, eventually, considered all the relevant material. It had been entitled to conclude that the high threshold for group B had not been reached. Even if the final decision were to have been viewed as irregular, granting relief would have brought no advantage to the claimant as it was 'quite impossible to envisage' that the claimant could qualify for group B, given the very high threshold.

S1.13   *R (Kimvono) v Tower Hamlets LBC*
(2001) 33 HLR 78, QBD

Unlawful to ignore ineligible members of eligible applicant's household when allocating accommodation

The council's allocation scheme provided that three-bedroomed accommodation would be allocated if a household comprised children of the opposite sex at least one of whom was aged seven or over. The applicant fulfilled those criteria but one of his children was still waiting for her application for indefinite leave to remain in the UK to be granted. The council considered that, because she was not a 'qualifying person' as a result of her immigration status, it was prevented by Housing Act 1996 s161 from including her as part of the applicant's household when assessing his housing needs and allocating accommodation. It advised him that he would only be offered two-bedroomed accommodation.

Collins J quashed the decision. On a true construction, s161 was only concerned with whether an applicant for accommodation (rather than another member of his household) was a qualifying person. The immigration status of the applicant's daughter was irrelevant and she was to be taken into account by the council when making an allocation to the applicant.

Note: The same outcome would apply now under Housing Act 1996 s160A (eligible persons), as amended by Homelessness Act 2002.

S1.14   *R (Maali) v Lambeth LBC*
[2003] EWHC 2231 (Admin); [2004] HLR 12

Decision irrational

The claimant was the secure tenant of a second/third floor maisonette which she occupied with her four young children. There was no lift. She and her eldest daughter suffered from severe asthma. She applied to Lambeth for a transfer. Her doctor stated that 'when [her] asthma is bad, it would be impossible for her to climb stairs alone, let alone with children and shopping'. She was assessed as being within group D of Lambeth's allocation scheme, a 'mainstream' group which covered a number of the categories of applicants listed in Housing Act 1996 s167(2). She asserted that she should be in group B, covering emergencies, and applied for judicial review asserting that the assessment was unlawful.

Crane J allowed the application. The medical assessment of whether the claimant was eligible for inclusion in group B contained assumptions which rendered the assessment flawed. The council's medical adviser had attributed the claimant's stays with friends to the need for assistance with child care, rather than to her difficulty at times in climbing the stairs, as she had asserted. There was no basis for the medical adviser's substitution of different reasons. Furthermore, there was no basis for concluding that, because exercise was beneficial for asthma sufferers, the climbing of stairs was a positive aspect. The fact that the claimant might climb the stairs carrying a child and shopping had been ignored. The assessment was so flawed as to be irrational and *Wednesbury* unreasonable. It was quashed and an order made for the claimant to be reassessed in relation to the group B criteria.

See also *R (Wakie) v Haringey LBC* [2003] EWHC 2107 (Admin), 2 July 2003 (medical assessment not irrational); *R v Westminster CC ex p Hussain* (1999) 31 HLR 645, QBD (offer of bedsit failed to have regard to community care assessment) (see *Housing Law Casebook* 3rd edition); *R v Oxford CC ex p Crowder* (1999) 31 HLR 485, QBD (decision that applicant's daughter no longer lived with her based on inadequate enquiries) (see *Housing Law Casebook* 3rd edition); *R (Sleith) v Camden LBC* [2003] EWCA Civ 347 (refusal of tenancy to carer of deceased tenant justified under policy).

S1.15   **R (Mays) v Brent LBC**

[2003] EWHC 481 (Admin); May 2003 *Legal Action* 34; 3 March 2003

Possession against daughter of deceased tolerated trespasser did not breach ECHR

Scottish cases

S1.16   *Gallacher v Stirling Council*

2001 SLT 94, CS (OH)

Policy of allocating low demand housing to homeless applicants not within published scheme and unlawful

The applicant applied to the council for accommodation as a homeless person. She was provided with temporary accommodation. The council then made an offer of permanent accommodation from its own stock. The applicant considered the property unacceptable and sought judicial review. She contended that the council had adopted a policy or practice of only considering homeless persons for low-demand high-turnover housing but that this policy did not appear in the council's published housing allocations scheme. (See Housing Act 1996 s167 for the equivalent obligation of English and Welsh authorities to have a published scheme and to allocate only in accordance with its terms.) Additionally, it was contended that the published scheme failed to give a reasonable preference to homeless persons (see Housing Act 1996 s167(2) for the equivalent provision in England and Wales). The council admitted that the particular arrangements for allocations to the homeless were not set out in the published scheme but were contained in a 'de facto' policy.

Lord Macfadyen quashed the allocation decision. He held that the council's

> de facto policy, insofar as it purports (a) to render inapplicable to homeless applicants provisions of the housing allocations policy and (b) to apply special rules to such applications, is invalid, and any decision made in reliance on the unpublished elements of the de facto policy is likewise invalid.

About the failure to publish, he said:

> [I]t would in my view be destructive of the value of the requirement for publication, if an unpublished rule or a decision based on an unpublished rule were nevertheless treated as valid.

Local government ombudsman reports

S1.17 *Complaint against Croydon LBC*
Investigation 05/B/00679, 17 October 2006

Delay in medical assessment for transfer

A Croydon tenant applied for a transfer on medical grounds. The council's officers decided that there should be a visit and assessment by an occupational therapist (OT). No such visit was scheduled for seven months and only then undertaken in response to the ombudsman's request. That delay – compounded by a failure to tell the tenant what was (not) going on – amounted to maladministration. When the OT's report was received it was not considered properly by the council in assessing the tenant's needs and the council took two months to correct that mistake.

The ombudsman recommended £500 compensation and a review of the council's procedures.

S1.17A *Complaint against Havering LBC*
Investigation 06/A/10428, 31 October 2007

£10,000 recommended where transfer policy operated inflexibly and tenant's mother confined to her home

A secure tenant applied in September 2000 for a transfer from her council maisonette, which had internal stairs and was reached by three flights of steps from the street. Her mother, aged 86, who lived with her, had bronchial asthma and arthritis in all major joints and was deaf and partially sighted. The family needed ground floor accommodation. Most ground floor accommodation constituted properties with gardens and the council's allocation policy provided that properties with gardens should be let to families with children or with proven medical need for use of a garden. After a home visit in 2003, a council officer reported that the complainant's mother was 'practically a prisoner in the home'. Despite the involvement of an MP, no transfer offer was made and the application was not placed in the highest priority band for the council's choice-based lettings scheme until November 2006. The council told the tenant that she could keep bidding for level access properties but that her bids 'would never be successful' even though she had the highest possible banding. Its initial response to the complainant's complaint was to offer £50 compensation for not returning her telephone calls. By the time the ombudsman concluded his investigation, the tenant's mother had died.

The ombudsman found that the council had failed to consider any flexibility in its policy by the exercise of discretion. No consideration was given to the special circumstances of the tenant's mother or to her article 8 rights. Although the council had known that the mother was effectively confined to the home (and only parts of it) that 'tragic, deplorable and wholly preventable circumstance' had not been addressed. The ombudsman found that the family had suffered injustice for five years, that the impact on the mother and the family 'must have been terrible' and that the mother's quality of life had been severely affected. He recommended payment of £10,000 compensation.

S1.18 *Complaint against Hounslow LBC*
Investigation No 06/A/14890, 7 August 2007

Wrong priority date recorded; practice of date priority not in written policy

Hounslow maintained a choice-based lettings scheme operated by Locata. Available properties were advertised and let to the highest banded bidder (bands A–D) and, within bands, to the bidder with the oldest 'priority date'. As applicants moved up bands they were given new priority dates (to avoid leapfrogging those already in that band) but, if moved-down, resumed their previous priority date. The complainant, who had first applied for an allocation in 1999, was aggrieved that, having been moved up a band in November 2005 (as homeless) and then down in December 2005 (having had suitable temporary accommodation secured for her), she had not resumed her old priority date. The council said that its practice was that homeless applicants (dealt with under Part VII) were treated as having a new 'priority date', ie, the date of their homelessness application. The practice was not reflected in the council's published allocation scheme. Moreover, in the complainant's case the council had wrongly recorded her, until June 2007, as having an April 2006 priority date. A sampling exercise showed that 15 out of 20 homeless applicants had also been given the wrong priority dates.

The ombudsman found maladministration by the council in:

- not correctly recording the complainant's priority date until June 2007;
- adopting and operating a practice which was not part of its published scheme; and
- failing to recognise earlier a need either to change the practice or amend the scheme.

He recommended £500 compensation and cautioned that, if the allocation scheme was amended to reflect the practice (rather than the practice changed to comply with the scheme), issues might arise about whether the scheme gave homeless applicants the 'reasonable preference' to which they were entitled by s167. He sent copies of his report to other local authorities operating the Locata scheme.

S1.19 *Complaint against Nottingham Council*
Investigation 05/C/02965, 19 April 2007

Offer of accommodation in 'stomach turning' condition

On her homelessness application, a young single parent was given priority for an urgent allocation of council accommodation. She was made a single offer of a house from which the previous tenant had been evicted for failing to maintain the premises and his garden. At the date of letting, the floors were soaked in urine, the walls were smeared with human faeces and the garden was completely overgrown. A ward councillor who visited the property described the condition of the house as 'stomach turning'. The complainant felt she had had no option but to take it. Subsequently, the council's contractor estimated that £11,500 of remedial works were needed.

The ombudsman was 'appalled' that anyone should be invited to view a house in this 'dreadful condition'. Compensation of £2,450 was recommended.

S1.20 **Complaint against Vale of Glamorgan Council**
Investigation 2005/01724, 26 February 2007

No proper assessment of housing need

The complainants were elderly owner-occupiers of a holiday chalet. They were required to vacate for two months each year. From 2003 their health deteriorated significantly. One developed a substantial visual impairment and the other had severely reduced mobility. In 2004 they applied to join the council's housing register and were placed in the bronze category (the lowest priority group) because the council considered them adequately housed. They unsuccessfully sought 'medical priority' which would have significantly improved their prospects of being rehoused.

The Public Sector Ombudsman for Wales found maladministration in the council's handling of the housing application and, in particular, the applications for medical priority. Contrary to the statutory code of guidance, there had been a failure to carry out any form of enquiries, which meant that the council was not in a position to undertake a proper and considered assessment. There was also failure to give sufficient consideration to whether homelessness was an issue. A proper assessment would have led to the complainants being deemed to be statutorily homeless no later than the end of September 2005, leading to their application for permanent housing being given greater priority. Compensation of £2,500 was recommended for the 15 months unfairly and avoidably spent in 'unacceptable housing conditions'.

S2   **Reasonable preference**

Court of Appeal

S2.1 *R v Wolverhampton MBC ex p Watters*
(1997) 29 HLR 931

Reasonable preference can be nullified by other factors including rent arrears

The applicant was married with five children. She was evicted from her council home because of rent arrears. She obtained accommodation in the private rented sector which was overcrowded and unsatisfactory. She applied to go on the council's waiting list but was excluded because of its policy to exclude those who owed more than two weeks' rent arrears. She appealed to an appeals panel that could reverse a decision where there was a social or medical need or substantial efforts had been made to reduce the arrears or 'exceptional circumstances' applied. Her appeal failed. Sh⸍ applied for judicial review, contending that, despite falling within thr⸍ the statutory reasonable preference categories in Housing Act 1⁹⸍ she had not been granted a preference.

Her application and her appeal to the Court of Appeal ᶠ 22 did not require 'preference' to be given but merely ⸍ erence'. That envisaged that other factors could weigh ⸍

diminish and even nullify the preference. Rent arrears could properly be taken into account in the process of selecting tenants and a council could decide that an applicant's rent arrears were such as to outweigh a reasonable preference. Sedley J's comment in *R v Lambeth LBC ex p Njomo* (S1.3) that a council must not 'eclipse or distort' the priority that s22 accords was wrong if he meant that statutory preference cannot be outweighed by other relevant considerations. The scope of 'exceptional circumstances' in the council's policy was unfettered and the policy was sufficiently flexible to comply with Housing Act 1985 s22. The council's appeals panel had not erred in balancing against the applicant's obvious housing need the history of past rent default, very substantial arrears and eviction from an earlier council tenancy.

Note: Following amendments by Homelessness Act 2002, an applicant can be excluded from an allocation scheme only in the circumstances set out in s160A. New s167(2A) specifically allows behaviour which affects a person's suitability to be a tenant to be taken into account in determining priorities among those with preference.

S2.2   *R (A) v Lambeth LBC; R (Lindsay) v Lambeth LBC*
[2002] EWCA Civ 1084; [2002] HLR 57

Allocation scheme which failed to distinguish between applicants with and without statutory preference unlawful; variation in procedure unlawful

Lambeth revised its allocation scheme in July 2000 with a view to introducing a greater degree of choice, in line with government policy. Applicants were placed in one of a number of allocation groups. Groups A–C related to management transfers, group D 'mainstream allocations', group E 'homeless households' and group F 'referrals'. The scheme provided for offers to be made to those in group A then B then C and, if not accepted by them, to the other groups according to targets set for each group, which could be changed if necessary. Offers were made in date order within each group to those with matching property preferences. The time within which an offer was made might, in practice, be reduced by applicants assessing the size and type and location of property they would accept, within limits. (Lambeth asserted that this allowed for a composite assessment of need within a group because those in most need would widen the types of property they were prepared to accept in order to receive a quicker offer.)

In September 2000, in view of very high numbers of homeless people, the director of housing changed the basis on which allocations were to be made. Offers were to be made first to group A and then B, with the remainder being split between E (80%) and C (20%). No offers were to be made to the other groups which had zero targets.

'A' was a single parent in unsatisfactory accommodation who suffered from physical and mental health problems. She qualified under all but one of the reasonable preference categories set out in Housing Act 1996 s167(2). She was referred by social services and placed in group F (referrals).

Lindsay was a single homeless man. He qualified for a reasonable preference under two of the s167(2) categories. He was placed in group G (mainstream allocations), which contained 85% of applicants.

The fact that A and Lindsay were in more than one of the statutory 'reasonable preference' categories gave them no extra priority within the group. The register contained a small percentage (4%) of people within the allocation groups who had no statutory preference.

The claimants succeeded on applications for judicial review and Lambeth appealed. The Court of Appeal held that:

1) In order to confer reasonable preference under s167(2), allocation schemes must be framed in such a way that applicants with preferences do not compete on equal terms with those without a preference. The presence in the groups of applicants without a statutory preference contravened this principle. 4% was not de minimus.

2) The scheme did not allow for composite assessment to identify those in greatest need within groups (even if those without reasonable preference were ignored).

3) In so far as Lambeth's scheme relied on an applicant's self-assessment of his or her housing need, to confer a preference and identify those in greatest need it was irrational.

4) The scheme sufficiently set out the process and criteria to be applied in making decisions. The basis for the targets and adjustments to the quotas was explained. The figures did not need to be set out in the scheme. The variation of the targets was provided for in the scheme and was lawful. The variation in the order of allocations would have been lawful if the scheme had provided for it, but was unlawful because it did not.

The case came back before the Court of Appeal on 3 July 2003 (*R (Lindsay) v Lambeth LBC* [2003] EWCA Civ 919). The council had difficulty formulating a replacement allocation scheme and sought an extension of time. The claimant pressed for his reassessment. The Court of Appeal heard those cross applications and the council's evidence that it would not be able to implement a new allocation scheme before February 2004. It expressed 'grave misgivings about the passage of time and the continued application of a scheme which the court had declared unlawful, for so long a period.' The council undertook to reassess the claimant and was ordered to pay his costs. The court pointed out that 'the consent order now made does not seek to prevent, and does not prevent, other applicants taking points on the lawfulness of the current conduct of the council in the light of the judgments of the Court'.

S2.3 ### *R (Lin) v Barnet LBC*
[2007] EWCA Civ 132; [2007] HLR 30; [2007] LGR 454; 22 February 2007

Scheme did not fail to accord reasonable preference to homeless applicants; points granted to transfer applicants unlawful; scheme failed to set out procedures clearly

Barnet accepted that it owed the claimant the main housing duty under Housing Act 1996 s193. It placed her in private sector leasing (PSL) accommodation. Barnet's allocation scheme provided, inter alia, for applicants to be awarded: 200 local residency points, 100 income points, 100 transfer points and 10 points for each year waiting up to a maximum of 50.

Furthermore, homeless applicants waiting for family size accommodation were also awarded 10 points, with 300 points being awarded when their PSL accommodation was about to be returned to the landlord. In the context of the scheme, the claimant, with 350 points in total, was unable to be in a position to bid successfully for a property until she received 300 points at the end of her lease (which was of ten years).

At first instance ([2006] EWHC 1041 (Admin)) the scheme was held unlawful for granting 100 points to transfer applicants, as they would always defeat a homeless person who otherwise shared the same characteristics. In that respect the scheme failed to accord a reasonable preference to the homeless. The claimant appealed, contending that the grant of 10 points for her homeless status created no more than an illusion of preference.

The Court of Appeal held that 10 points, even in a scheme requiring successful bidders to have hundreds of points, was capable of giving a reasonable preference. The council had been entitled to take into account in setting those points the fact that a person owed the main homelessness duty would, by definition, be occupying 'suitable' accommodation. When such accommodation came to an end, the scheme reflected that new housing need by an additional 300 points.

Although some applicants outside the reasonable preference categories might have accumulated more points than the statutory homeless, that was not unlawful 'provided that such non-statutory preferences do not dominate the scheme at the expense of the statutory preference categories' (para [36]). It was necessary to look at how the scheme operated as a whole, rather than individual cases, in assessing this.

However, the scheme did not clearly set out the procedure whereby a withdrawal of PSL accommodation would trigger the 300 extra points. That was a failure to comply with the requirement in s167(1) that a published scheme must spell out procedures relating to allocation and to that extent the appeal was allowed.

Note: The claimant's application for leave to appeal to the House of Lords was refused.

High Court

S2.4   *R (Ahmad) v Newham LBC*
[2007] EWHC 2332 (Admin); 11 September 2007
Scheme failed to give reasonable preference or account for cumulative needs

The claimant, his wife and four children lived in a two-bedroom housing association property. He suffered from chronic depression. He shared a bedroom with his wife and youngest child. The other children, one of whom was severely disabled, shared the other bedroom. His eldest son, who suffered from a behavioural disorder and allergies, was badly affected by having to share a room with his disabled sister. The claimant applied to Newham under Housing Act 1996 Part VI. Newham accepted that the property was overcrowded and that the claimant was in priority need but a medical officer assessed that neither he nor his son came within the reasonable preference categories in s167. Newham's allocation scheme had two aspects: choice-based lettings (CBL) and direct offers. Under the CBL part, property details were circulated to all priority homeseekers and to a limited percentage of transfer applicants. Properties were awarded to the bidder who had been waiting the longest. Direct offers were made available to those with additional preference, including those with multiple needs. The claimant sought judicial review.

Nicholas Blake QC, sitting as deputy High Court judge, allowed the claim. The medical assessments were flawed as they were insufficiently reasoned. The scheme did not comply with the requirement to afford reasonable preference and account for cumulative needs. Under the CBL the claimant, despite his reasonable preference, was on the same footing as a selected transfer applicant in bidding for a property. It therefore failed to accord reasonable preference, despite the limited selection of transfer applicants. The provision relating to direct offers did not cure this defect as an applicant needed three or more medical or social needs to qualify. Furthermore, Newham's policy of only considering statutorily overcrowded properties as unsatisfactory for the purposes of reasonable preference was unlawful. Section 167(2)(c) included those in unsatisfactory accommodation and was not limited to those statutorily overcrowded.

S2.5 **R (Aweys and Others) v Birmingham**

[2007] EWHC 52 (Admin); 18 January 2007 (see T51.19)

Allocation scheme that gave homeless people accepted under Part VII lower priority if 'homeless at home' rather than in temporary accommodation unlawful

S2.6 **R (Giles) v Fareham BC**

[2002] EWHC 2951 (Admin); [2003] HLR 36; (2003) *Times* 11 February; 13 December 2002

Reasonable preference negated by anti-social behaviour; scheme did not fetter authority's discretion; best practice was for guidance on exercise of discretion; reasons not required

In 1999 a possession order was made against Mrs Giles and her husband on the grounds of neighbour nuisance. She applied to Fareham under Housing Act 1996 Part VII and was assessed as being intentionally homeless. Her appeal to the county court was unsuccessful. She was informed that her addition to the housing register might be deferred for a period of up to five years. The council's allocations policy was that applications for assistance from people found to be intentionally homeless would be deferred for one year, and that applications from those who had been evicted might be deferred for a period of up to five years. Following correspondence, the matter was referred to the housing committee, which concluded that Mrs Giles' entry on the housing register would be deferred for a period of five years and that the position would be reviewed in one year. Mrs Giles applied for judicial review.

Her application was dismissed. Housing Act 1996 ss159(7) and 167(6) give authorities wide discretionary powers to include in allocation schemes such additional rules (eg, former tenant misconduct) as are appropriate to give effect to reasonable preference. The duty in s167(2) to give reasonable preference does not mean that other factors cannot extinguish that duty. The material part of the policy did not fetter discretion and was not unlawful because it was discretionary and did not suggest any minimum period of deferment. The committee had exercised its discretion on the material before it and had imposed a requirement for review after one year. Although the allocations policy did not include any guidelines on the exercise of the discretion to defer making offers this did not render the policy irrational. Best practice, however, was to include such guidance. There was no basis for imposing an obligation to give reasons in this case, particularly when the decision had been reached following an extra-statutory review.

S2.7   **R (Onuegbu) v Hackney LBC**
[2005] EWHC 1277 (Admin); 22 June 2005

Decision whether to reduce preference on basis of rent arrears could be deferred until applicant at top of waiting list

The claimant was a tenant of a council flat which was overcrowded. He applied for a transfer. He was witholding rent on account of alleged disrepair and court proceedings were pending. The council's policy was that a transfer application from a tenant in rent arrears would receive prioritisation in the normal way but if it reached the top of any particular list it would be 'by-passed' for an offer unless the arrears were cleared or an acceptable repayment arrangement made.

Wilson J found that no decision had yet been taken in respect of the claimant's application for transfer. As the claimant did not assert that the policy was unlawful and as no discrete decision had been made which was amenable to judicial review, the claim was dismissed.

Note: The claimant (who acted in person) made no challenge to the policy. Its terms were, on the face of it, difficult to reconcile with the arrangements envisaged by the statutory regime for allocation now found in HA 1996 Part VI and with the need to relet *promptly* any available void to the person at the top of the allocation scheme. See also *Local Government Ombudsman Complaint against Ealing LBC*, 06/A/11660, December 2007 *Legal Action* 37, 22 October 2007, regarding delays due to failing to explain verification of address policy.

S3   **Composite assessment**

High Court

S3.1   **R v Islington LBC ex p Reilly and Mannix**
(1999) 31 HLR 651, QBD

Policy unlawful as failed to allow for 'composite' assessment of need; discretion clause too vague

The applicants were council tenants who applied for a transfer. Their accommodation was overcrowded and otherwise unsatisfactory and several members of their households had medical needs. The council's transfer list was part of its overall allocation scheme, which also contained a category for the homeless and a category for other non-transfer applicants for housing. The scheme was operated on a points-priority system. Fixed points were ascribed to different types and severity of need (medical, overcrowding, etc) but an applicant only got these points for the highest category under which a member of the household qualified, with a lower fixed amount of points being added if more than one need was identified and no points being awarded if more than one member of the household had qualifying needs. There was an overriding discretion to award more points in cases where there was an 'exceptionally serious threat to health, safety or welfare'. The scheme provided that 50% of accommodation would be allocated to the homeless, with the remaining vacancies going to the other two categories. The applicants sought judicial review.

Richards J held that the applicants could not rely on the allocation regime set out in Housing Act 1996 Part VI because it did not apply to allocations to existing tenants. The transfer scheme was to be assessed in accordance with general principles of public law. However, the fact that the council had the same scheme for Part VI applicants helped to illuminate the underlying objectives of the scheme and assist in determining whether the scheme provided a rational way of meeting those objectives. It was clear that in determining priorities the council decided to place considerable weight on the respective housing needs of applicants. However, the scheme was incapable of producing a fair assessment of each applicant's housing needs. It made only limited provision for multiple categories of need and made no allowance for the number of persons in each household who had a need. The scheme could not be 'saved' by the overriding discretion to award additional points as, apart from being unduly restrictive, it was:

> ... too vague and uncertain and results in a disproportionately large element of need being subject to assessment on an undefined and unguided discretionary basis.

The scheme, in not providing for what was phrased a 'composite' assessment of need, was one that no reasonable authority would adopt and was unlawful.

It was contended that the 50% quota for the homeless gave undue priority to the homeless, in contravention of the purpose of the Housing Act 1996. As this submission was dependent on the applicability of Part VI to the claimants, it failed but, in any event, Richards J rejected it. The 50% quota was not set in stone and quotas were not inherently inconsistent with the giving of reasonable preference but could be a lawful and rational means of giving such a preference. There was nothing unlawful about having a quota or, on the material before the court, on the figure adopted.

Note: Transfers on the application of an existing council tenant are now included within Part VI following amendment by Homelessness Act 2002 (see Housing Act 1996 s159(5)).

S3.2   *R v Lambeth LBC ex p Ashley*
(1997) 29 HLR 385, QBD

Scheme unduly restricted circumstances in which physical conditions would be considered and did not take account of differing levels of overcrowding

The applicant lived in a two-bedroom council house with her four children. The children, two boys and two girls whose ages ranged from seven to 14, all slept in one bedroom. The applicant applied for a transfer. The council's transfer scheme provided that (1) no priority would be accorded by reference to the physical condition of accommodation except in two limited circumstances (one relating to medical needs and the other disregarding rooms deemed to be uninhabitable), and (2) a maximum of 20 points per household could be awarded for different sex children sharing the same bedroom, without consideration of the number of people affected. The applicant claimed that these two rules inhibited the council from giving the 'reasonable preference' for unsatisfactory housing conditions and overcrowded households that Housing Act 1985 s22 required.

Tucker J quashed the decision. In relation to the first provision he noted that s22 clearly envisaged that the condition of premises should be an important factor in making a decision about the allocation of housing. The council's scheme substantially excluded such considerations being taken into account, save in the two limited situations. The scheme unduly restricted the scope of the council's power in a way which was inconsistent with the criteria contained in s22. The second provision was illogical and irrational. It did not reflect what might be gross differences between different households and took no account, as it ought to, of the number of persons affected. The scheme, in this regard, was rigid and inflexible. It was illogical and irrational in the *Wednesbury* sense.

S3.3   *R v Tower Hamlets LBC ex p Uddin*
(2000) 32 HLR 391, QBD

Policy unlawful as it failed to award greater preference for more severe medical needs

The council's transfer policy gave preference for medical needs but only one medical category could be accorded per household. A household where more than one person had a medical need to move gained no additional priority.

On an application for judicial review brought by three transfer applicants Keene J, following *R v Islington LBC ex p Reilly and Mannix* (S3.1), held that a scheme for allocation of property to transfer applicants may be challenged only on principles of administrative law. 'Any rational transfer scheme' would observe the principle of greater preference to the more severe cases of need. The council's scheme was unlawful because it was irrational not to accord extra priority to households where more than one member was in medical need. Alternatively, it failed to take account of a relevant consideration, namely the medical needs of the whole family. Although there was a discretion within the scheme to improve an applicant's position, there was no evidence to suggest that the discretion was ever exercised to deal with the presence of more than one person in the household with a particular health problem.

S3.4   *R v Westminster CC ex p Al-Khorsan*
(2001) 33 HLR 6; (2000) *Times* 21 January, QBD

Allocation based on date order for all homeless applicants unlawful; quota lawful

The council had over 2,000 homeless households in temporary accommodation awaiting permanent rehousing. It revised its housing allocation scheme so that in 1999/2000 half of the likely available units of accommodation would be allocated to homeless persons. Within that quota, allocation would be in date order by reference to the date that the household's homelessness application under Housing Act 1996 Part VII had been accepted. The applicant household asserted that this scheme prevented the council according any homeless households the additional or other preferences for rehousing to be given under s167(2), ie within the quota no extra preference was given to reflect special medical, social or other needs.

Latham J granted a declaration that the scheme was unlawful. A quota system can form part of a lawful scheme and the quota for homeless applicants provided lawful preference for that category (following *R v Islington LBC ex p Reilly and Mannix* (S3.1)). He rejected the council's submission that the priority given to homeless applicants was so substantial as, in effect, to subsume the other categories:

> The various categories of need identified [in legislation] were not to be treated ... as separate watertight compartments. They identify needs that are capable of being cumulative.

He also rejected an argument that, because homeless applicants were required to be accommodated in suitable accommodation, the needs identified in s167(2) were already dealt with and did not need to be separately catered for within the homeless category. Allocation within the category of homeless applicants based on date only unlawfully excluded consideration of the other reasonable and additional preference categories set out in s167(2)(a)–(f).

Note: Cf *R (V) v Southwark LBC* (S3.6).

S3.5   *R (Cali) v Waltham Forest LBC*
[2006] EWHC 302 (Admin); [2007] HLR 1; 24 February 2006, QBD

Scheme did not provide for composite assessment and bands inadequately defined

The council adopted a 'choice-based' allocation scheme in October 2003. Applicants were placed into one of three bands: additional preference, reasonable preference and no preference. Housing was allocated under a bidding scheme. Only those in the additional preference and reasonable preference bands could bid, with priority going to the former. Within bands, priority was based on waiting time. The criteria for the reasonable preference band were only loosely defined and to move up a band at least one member of the applicant household had to meet the deliberately narrow qualifying conditions for additional preference status.

On a claim for judicial review, Lloyd Jones J held that:

1) Housing Act 1996 requires schemes to provide for a fair and reasonable assessment of the relative needs of applicants, not simply to identify those with the most extreme need.

2) The provision in s167(1A), regarding choice and preference (with the possibility here of bidding for less desirable properties), did not relieve authorities of their obligation to provide for a comparative assessment of housing need.

3) There was no mechanism in the published scheme whereby a household qualifying a number of times over for a reasonable preference could qualify for additional preference. Within the reasonable preference band priority was based merely on waiting time. The problem of the lack of a composite assessment of need was intensified by the fact that the reasonable preference band was very wide. A large number of applicants with needs of widely varying severity were banded together.

4) The scheme could not be saved by the application of an undefined discretion reserved to council officers. This would lead to inconsistency. Any exercise of the discretion which in practice provided for a composite assessment of need would be a departure from the published scheme and unlawful (s167(8)).

5) The terms of admission to the reasonable preference band were inadequately defined by the terms of the published allocation scheme.

An application for a mandatory order (requiring the council to adopt a lawful scheme) was adjourned to be restored after four months if the council had not by then produced such a scheme.

S3.6   *R (V) v Southwark LBC*

[2001] EWHC Admin 546; October 2001 *Legal Action* 14

Scheme failed to take account of composite needs; removal of priority category award unlawful; super priority to homeless applicants not unlawful

The claimant, a housing association tenant, applied for council accommodation. He was awarded 20 medical points on the council's 'general needs register' based on his son's disability. His partner moved into his home with her disabled daughter. Thirty medical points were awarded on account of her disability. Instead of according a total of 50 points, the allocation scheme treated the points for the daughter as superseding and replacing those for the son. The claimant contended in judicial review proceedings that the defendant's scheme was unlawful as it failed to make adequate provision for the composite assessment of housing need. The council conceded that it had to reconsider its medical points.

The council's scheme also contained a 'priority status' category which included 'social services nominations'. A social worker made a nomination on behalf of the claimant, which was accepted. The next day, on being informed that the claimant had taken legal advice, the priority status was cancelled. The council commented that it could not deliver an offer of a property within the target time scale of six months for this category.

Jackson J quashed that decision and restored the priority status. The inability to achieve the 'target' could not justify withdrawing priority and the taking of legal advice 'cannot possibly be a ground for reversing the [earlier] decision'.

The claimant's contention that a 'super priority' status accorded to homeless applicants was unlawful and contrary to the legislative purpose of Part VI was rejected. The homeless generally had a stronger claim that other applicants. A further contention that it was irrational to allocate properties to the homeless in date order, regardless of other need, was rejected. Homeless people were all near the head of the queue and, on the basis of the council's statistics, a complex system of prioritising the homeless would not serve any useful purpose. Furthermore, exceptions were made to the date order rule. (*R v Westminster CC ex p Al-Khorsan* (S3.4) distinguished).

The judge noted that notwithstanding the claimant's success on these points, he remained outside Housing Act 1996 Part VI (Housing Act 1996 s159(5) before amendment by Homelessness Act 2002), could not establish an enforceable duty to accommodate under Children Act 1989 s17 or s20, and would be better off applying as a homeless person under Housing Act 1996 based on s175(3) (not reasonable to continue to occupy accommodation).

CHAPTER T

Homelessness

T1   **Introduction**

The obligations of local authorities to provide assistance to the poor and
destitute had their origins in the Poor Laws of the sixteenth century. The
Poor Laws were repealed and replaced by the National Assistance Act
1948. That Act remains a safety net for some people (see chapter U), but
its principal homelessness provision was replaced by Housing (Homeless Persons) Act 1977. The provisions of that Act, the first of the modern
homelessness statutes, were codified, with only minor amendments into
Housing Act 1985 Part III. Policy changes saw those provisions replaced
by Housing Act 1996 Part VII. This Act has since been amended by the
Homelessness Act 2002. The leading guides on the homelessness legislation are Arden, Hunter and Johnson, *Homelessness and Allocations*, 7th
edn, Legal Action Group, 2006 and Luba and Davies, *Housing Allocation
and Homelessness Law and Practice*, Jordan Ltd, 2006.

T2   **Eligibility**

A person who is not 'eligible for assistance' does not qualify for any of the
final duties under Part VII. However, any person who an authority has
reason to believe *may be* homeless has the right to make an application for
assistance under Part VII (subject to limited exceptions, see section T33)
and to a decision under s184, including a decision on whether or not he or
she is eligible. Furthermore, if an authority has reason to believe that an
applicant *may be* homeless, eligible and in priority need it is under a duty
to accommodate pending a decision (s188(1)). Where a decision is made
that an applicant is not eligible, an authority may, however, be excluded
from exercising its discretion to accommodate pending a review or an appeal (ss188(3), 202(4)) under Nationality Immigration and Asylum Act
2002 Sch 3 (see section U8). This applies only to 'ineligible persons' as
listed in Schedule 3. These provisions are different from the eligibility
provisions in Part VII. British citizens and children are specifically stated
not to be excluded by Schedule 3 and, even where a person is ineligible
under Schedule 3, the exclusions do not apply to the extent necessary to
avoid a breach of a person's ECHR rights or rights under the EC Treaties.

The provisions regarding eligibility have been subject to frequent
change and amendment since their introduction in Housing Act 1996.
The ambit of the legislation and regulations made thereunder bring into
play other substantive areas of law, such as immigration, human rights
and EU law, the provisions of which can be complex and also subject to frequent change, particularly with the enlargement of the EU. The reported
cases mainly concern the interpretation of previous regulations and EU
directives but remain of relevance to the interpretation of the current law.
The following is a basic outline of the provisions. Note that the eligibility
provisions for Part VI (allocation) are identical to those for Part VII (except in the limited circumstances pointed out below in relation to asylum-
seekers, who are never eligible under Part VI, whereas a small, although
diminishing, number remain eligible under Part VII).

Housing Act 1996 s185 provides that 'persons from abroad' are not eligible for assistance under Part VII. There are two categories of persons from abroad:

1) A person 'subject to immigration control' unless within a class prescribed as eligible by regulations (s185(2)). (A person is subject to immigration control if he or she requires leave to enter or remain the UK, whether or not such leave has been given. This requirement applies to all persons except British citizens, Commonwealth citizens with the right of abode and EEA nationals and their family members with a 'right to reside'.)

2) A person not subject to immigration control but within a class prescribed as ineligible by regulations (s185(3)).

Section 185(4) provides that:

> A person from abroad who is not eligible for housing assistance shall be disregarded in determining for the purposes of [Part VII] whether another person –
> (a) is homeless or threatened with homelessness, or
> (b) has a priority need for accommodation.

For other purposes, the fact that a member of an applicant's household is ineligible is not relevant (eg, ineligible members of an applicant's household are to be accommodated with an applicant owed a housing duty). See *R (Morris) v Westminster CC* (T2.6), regarding the incompatbility of this section with ECHR.

The current regulations made under Housing Act 1996 s185 are:

England:

- Allocation of Housing and Homelessness (Eligibility) (England) Regulations 2006 SI No 1294 (the Eligibility Regs 2006): main provisions.
- Allocation of Housing and Homelessness (Eligibility) (England) (Amendment) Regulations 2006 SI No 2007: people fleeing Lebanon.
- Allocation of Housing and Homelessness (Miscellaneous Provisions) (England) Regulations 2006 SI No 2527: substitution of requalifying class D (humanitarian protection); local connection referral provision (s198(4)(b)).
- Allocation of Housing and Homelessness (Eligibility) (England) (Amendment) (No 2) Regulations 2006 SI No 3340: exclusion of Bulgarian and Romanian nationals subject to worker authorisation from the habitual residence exclusion.

Wales:

- Homelessness (Wales) Regulations 2006 SI No 2646 (W227) (the Welsh Regs)

Persons subject to immigration control who requalify as eligible under the Eligibility Regs 2006 reg 5 include:

- A person granted refugee status by the UK.
- Certain persons granted exceptional or indefinite leave to remain or granted humanitarian protection.
- Certain asylum-seekers who applied for asylum prior to 3 April 2000. Note that this class is not eligible under Part VI.

The Welsh Regs have additional classes that requalify certain nationals of states that have ratified the European Convention on Social and Medical Assistance or the European Social Charter and certain persons in receipt of income support or income-based job seeker's allowance.

Persons not subject to immigration control who are nevertheless taken out of eligibility by Eligibility Regs 2006 reg 6 include:

- A person who is not habitually resident in the UK. This exclusion does not apply to certain non-UK EEA nationals such as 'a worker' or a 'self-employed person' and their family members.
- A person whose only right to reside derives from being a jobseeker (or the family member of a jobseeker) or from the initial right to reside of three months.

In relation to EEA nationals and their family members it is necessary to determine whether they have a 'right to reside' and the basis of any such right. The right to reside is set out in the Immigration (European Economic Area) Regulations 2006 SI No 1003 (I(EEA) Regs 2006). Note that these regulations make significant amendments to the previous provisions. (The regulations transpose into UK law the EU Residence Directive – the ambit of the directive and the lawfulness of the regulations are contentious issues.) If an applicant does *not* have a right to reside, he or she is 'subject to immigration control' and is ineligible (unless within a requalifying class, for example, if granted refugee status by the UK). If an applicant does have a right to reside, he or she is not subject to immigration control and is eligible unless excluded by the regulations.

The combined effect of the I(EEA) Regs 2006 and the Eligibility Regs 2006 is that, for example, an EEA 'worker', 'self-employed person' and 'jobseeker' have a right to reside but a jobseeker is not eligible. It is important to note, however, that a person may retain his or her status as a worker despite not being in employment, for example, where temporarily unable to work or involuntarily unemployed (see I(EEA) Regs 2006 reg 6(2)). Furthermore, family members (who need not themselves be EEA nationals) may remain within the definition of a family member even where they do not remain in the same household. The position of accession state nationals requires particular consideration: in the first 12 months of residence in the UK such a person will generally be eligible only when actually in work and registered as such (see Accession (Immigration and Worker Registration) Regulations 2004 SI No 1219 ('A8' countries) and 2006 SI No 3317 (Bulgaria and Romania – where there is an additional requirement relating to authorisation of work)).

Where an applicant is not eligible for assistance, consideration should be given to assistance that may be available under other welfare provisions: see section U10.

Court of Appeal

T2.1   *Abdi v Barnet LBC; Ismail v Barnet LBC*
[2006] EWCA Civ 383; [2007] 1 All ER 922; [2006] HLR 23; [2006] LGR 559; (2007) *Times* 11 July

EEA nationals not in the UK for a qualifying reason have no right to reside and are 'subject to immigration control'

Abdi and Ismail, both Dutch nationals in receipt of income support, applied to Barnet as homeless persons. Barnet decided that they were excluded from being eligible as a result of regulations made under s185(3), which applied to persons not subject to immigration control. The applicants claimed that they were economically inactive and were not exercising any EU Treaty rights in the UK. As such, they were 'subject to immigration control' and fell to be considered under regulations made under s185(2), Class I of which requalified persons receiving income support as eligible (Homelessness (England) Regulations 2000 reg 3).

The Court of Appeal confirmed that the applicants were eligible. The impact of Asylum and Immigration Act 1996 s13(2) was that persons who could not remain in the UK without leave to do so were subject to immigration control. Although EEA nationals did not require leave to enter the UK, under Immigration (EEA) Regulations 2000 reg 14 only a 'qualifying person' was entitled to reside in the UK without leave to remain. The applicants did not satisfy the requirements for status as 'qualifying persons', required leave to remain and were subject to immigration control and eligible as a result of Class I.

Note: See now I(EEA) Regs 2006 and Eligibility Regs 2006 (which do not contain an equivalent of Class I, although the Welsh Regs do).

T2.2   *Couronne and others v Crawley BC and others; Bontemps and others v Secretary of State for Work and Pensions*
[2007] EWHC Civ 1086; 2 November 2007

Application of habitual residence test to Chagos Islanders not discriminatory

The claimants were members of two groups of British citizens who had left Mauritius to settle in the UK. They had their origins in the Chagos Islands, from which they and their families had been unlawfully displaced by the UK government. Their applications for homelessness assistance were refused on the basis that they were not eligible because they were not 'habitually resident' in the Common Travel Area (s185 and Homelessness (England) Regulations 2000 SI No 701 reg 4(1)(a)). Their claims for judicial review were unsuccessful.

The Court of Appeal dismissed their appeals. It held that the fact that their original displacement had been unlawful did not require the government to make special provision for them. They had not been subject to unlawful discrimination on the ground of race because any other British citizen from outside the Common Travel Area would have been treated in the same way. Articles 8 and 14 of the ECHR had not been infringed and article 1 of the First Protocol did not apply.

T2.3   *Kaya v Haringey LBC*
[2001] EWCA Civ 677; [2002] HLR 1; (2001) *Times* 14 June, CA

Asylum-seekers with temporary admission not 'lawfully present' (overruled)

The applicant sought accommodation under Part VII for himself and his pregnant wife. His wife was a post-April 2000 port entry asylum-seeker from Turkey who had been granted temporary admission under Immigration Act 1971 Sch 2 para 5 pending determination of her asylum application. The council decided, applying s185(4), that the applicant had no priority need as his wife was ineligible and to be disregarded. HHJ Hodge dismissed a s204 appeal. The applicant appealed, contending that his wife fulfilled the three criteria of Class E of the Homelessness (England) Regulations 2000 reg 3 in that (1) she was 'lawfully present' in the UK, (2) she was habitually resident here and (3) she was a national of Turkey which had ratified the European Convention on Social and Medical Assistance.

The Court of Appeal dismissed the appeal. Following and applying *R v Home Department ex p Bugdaycay* [1987] AC 514, HL, a person granted temporary admission as an asylum-seeker was not 'lawfully present' in the UK.

Note: In *Szoma v Secretary of State for Work and Pensions* [2005] UKHL 64; [2006] 1 AC 564; [2005] 3 WLR 955; [2006] 1 All ER 1; (2005) *Times* 1 November; 27 October 2005, a case concerning the eligibility for income support of a Polish Roma who applied for asylum in the UK on his arrival in 1998, the House of Lords held that *Kaya* was wrongly decided and that a person granted 'temporary admission' is 'lawfully present' in the UK. However, the Eligibility Regs 2006 do not include an equivalent of old Class E.

T2.4   *R v Westminster CC ex p Castelli and Tristan-Garcia (No 2)*
(1996) 28 HLR 616; (1996) 8 Admin LR 435, CA (see T34.5)

Applications under Part VII must be considered from anyone lawfully in the UK

T2.5   *R (Badu) v Lambeth LBC*
[2005] EWCA Civ 1184; [2006] HLR 8; [2006] UKHRR 165; (2005) *Times* 19 October; 14 October 2005 (see U6.1)

Where assistance was denied as a result of s185(4), which was incompatible with ECHR, an authority could, but was not obliged, to assist under alternative powers

T2.6   *R (Morris) v Westminster CC*
[2005] EWCA Civ 1184; [2006] HLR 8; [2006] LGR 81; [2006] UKHRR 165; (2005) *Times* 19 October

Section 185(4) incompatible with ECHR

Ms Morris became homeless and applied to the council for accommodation under Housing Act 1996 Part VII. She was a British citizen but, at the date of the council's decision, her daughter (aged 3) was thought to be a citizen of Mauritius and subject to immigration control. Usually, an applicant with a dependent child would have a 'priority need' for accommodation (s189(1)(b)) but s185(4)(b) provides that a person from abroad not eligible for housing assistance shall be disregarded in deciding whether an applicant has a priority need. As the daughter was a person subject to immigration control, she was not eligible and did not count in determining her mother's priority. The claimant contended that this provision infringed the prohibition on discrimination contained in ECHR article 14 (read with article 8) because, had her daughter been a British citizen, she would have had a priority need. Keith J allowed an application for judicial review and granted a declaration of incompatibility. The council and the secretary of state appealed.

The Court of Appeal dismissed the appeal. It held:

- The function of the priority need provisions relating to dependent children in Housing Act 1996 Part VII was to keep families together. That brought them within the ambit of ECHR article 8 dealing with the right to respect for 'family life'.

- The provision was discriminatory on the ground of national origin within ECHR article 14 or a combination of the following forms or aspects of article 14 'status': nationality, immigration control, settled residence and social welfare (Jonathan Parker LJ dissenting on this issue).

- Such discrimination could only be justified if there were 'very weighty' or 'solid' grounds for it and no such justification had been demonstrated by evidence or in submissions.

- Striking down the subsection did not involve an intrusion into the area of discretion to be accorded to the executive or legislature. There was no evidence that either had considered the potentially discriminatory effects of the provision and whether its impact was proportionate and necessary.

The making of a declaration would not of itself have required Westminster to reverse its finding of 'no priority need' but it was later confirmed that Ms Morris's daughter had acquired British nationality and Ms Morris's circumstances had changed and she no longer required housing assistance.

T2.7   *Tower Hamlets LBC v Deugi*

[2006] EWCA Civ 159; [2006] HLR 28; 7 March 2006, CA (see T62.7)

Concession made that Indian national married to EU national, from whom she was divorced, eligible as primary carer for 17-year-old son in full-time education (the Baumbast *exception)*

See also: *Abdirahman v Secretary of State for Work and Pensions* [2007] EWCA Civ 657; [2007] 4 All ER 882; 5 July 2007 (meaning of 'right to reside' for the purpose of entitlement to benefits by EU nationals).

High Court

T2.8   *Putans v Tower Hamlets LBC*

[2006] EWHC 1634; [2007] HLR 10, 20 June 2006, ChD

An accession state national not working is prima facie not eligible and council has no power to accommodate pending appeal except on human rights grounds

Mr Putans came to the UK from Latvia, an accession state. After a period of work, he became unemployed owing to illness and applied to Tower Hamlets as a homeless person. On the basis of the amendments to the Immigration (European Economic Area) Regulations 2000 by the Accession (Immigration and Worker Registration) Regulations 2004 (the Accession Regs) (restricting accession state nationals' right to reside in the UK), Tower Hamlets decided that he was not eligible and upheld that decision on review. Mr Putans lodged a county court appeal (s204) and asked for accommodation pending appeal (s204(4)). That was refused on the basis that the authority had no power to accommodate under s204(4) as a result of Nationality Immigration and Asylum Act 2002 Schedule 3. Mr Putans appealed under s204A. Pending that appeal, he obtained a without-notice injunction but a county court judge later discharged it. Mr Putans appealed against the discharge of the injunction. He argued that:

1) As an EEA worker who had become involuntarily unemployed he would ordinarily retain his status as worker and right to reside. The restrictions placed on A8 nationals by the Accession Regs were unlawful and in breach of his EC Treaty rights.

2) The prohibition under Nationality Immigration and Asylum Act 2002 Sch 3 did not apply where the provision of accommodation was necessary to avoid a breach of his EC Treaty rights (paragraph 3).

The High Court judge dismissed that appeal. The test to be applied on the appeal was whether Mr Putans had a strong prima facie case. It was held that while his case was arguable, it was weak:

1) The provisions of the Accession Regs were a derogation from the rights guaranteed under the EC Treaty and amounted to discrimination on the ground of nationality. However, the derogation was considered to be authorised by the Act of Accession and justifiable on the basis of the concern of existing member states to cushion their economies from the economic shock of having a large potential increase in the number of persons entitled to enter their labour markets from accession states, many of which had higher unemployment than the existing member states.

2) The provision of accommodation under Housing Act 1996 s204(4) was not necessary to enable an accession state national to seek work and the exception to the prohibition on the provision of accommodation under Schedule 3 did not apply.

Note: In *Zalewska v Department for Social Development*, Court of Appeal in Northern Ireland, Reference GIRC 5817, 19 May 2007, it was held, in relation to a refusal of income support to a Polish national, that the difference in treatment of A8 accession state nationals was a permitted derogation under the Act of Accession. Leave to appeal to the House of Lords was granted.

T2.9   *R v Westminster CC ex p Jaafer*

(1998) 30 HLR 698, QBD

Minors not exempt from rule that entry obtained by deception is an illegal entry; applicant's child was 'unlawfully present'

The applicant was a British citizen, originally born in Iraq, who lived in the Lebanon with a Lebanese wife. The couple had a child in January 1996. In early 1996 they decided to come to England. The applicant's mother in England made a statutory declaration stating that she would be responsible for providing maintenance and accommodation for the household. The family arrived and moved in with the applicant's mother but after a few days they left, following an argument. The applicant applied as a homeless person. The council determined that the child of the family was unlawfully present in the UK and so, as the priority need of the household depended on the child, they were not in priority need (s185(4)). The council was satisfied that the entry of the household had been obtained by deception. It relied particularly on the fact that, despite the representation that the mother would provide accommodation and maintenance, the family had only lived with the mother for ten days. Also, despite the representation they had made in order to obtain temporary admission, they had in fact been intending to stay in the UK throughout.

The deputy judge found sufficient material on that basis to uphold the council's decision. Minors are not exempt from the ordinary rule that entry obtained by deception is an illegal entry. It was impossible to say that the applicant had not been treated fairly or that the decision was one which had been reached unreasonably or perversely.

T2.10   **R (Antoine) v Reigate and Banstead DC and First Secretary of State**
December 2004 *Legal Action* 18; 1 November 2004 (see T48.6)

In unusual circumstances of the displacement of a Chagos Islander and his claim to be habitually resident in the UK accommodation should be provided pending review

See *Couronne and others v Crawley BC and others* (T2.2).

T2.11   **R (Bangura) v Southwark LBC**
[2007] EWHC 1681 (Admin); 20 June 2007 (see U6.4)

Powers under Children Act 1989 s17, Local Government Act 2000 s2 and Housing Act 1996 s193(2) not elevated to duties where claimant denied assistance as a homeless person as a result of provision incompatible with ECHR (Housing Act 1996 s185(4))

T2.12   **R (Burns) v Southwark LBC**
[2004] EWHC 1901 (Admin), 19 July 2004

Authority entitled to take refusal of resident's permit at face value and decide applicant not eligible without further enquiry

Ms Burns was a Nigerian national. She sought asylum in the United Kingdom. She subsequently married an EEA national, but later separated from him. She was evicted from her accommodation for non-payment of rent and applied to Southwark as a homeless person. It refused to provide her with accommodation on the day of her application and an interim injunction was obtained under s188(1). The council then made a s184 decision that, as Ms Burns was not an EEA national and had been refused a resident's permit, she was not eligible for assistance. It refused to exercise its discretion to accommodate her under s188(3) pending review, considering that there was little merit in the review. Ms Burns argued that the council's decision was irrational and unreasonable and that it had erred by relying on a decision of the Secretary of State for the Home Department to refuse her a resident's permit.

Gage J dismissed her application for judicial review. The council's decision was not *Wednesbury* unreasonable. Local authorities have a duty to make enquiries, but, where the secretary of state has refused a permit, a local authority is entitled to take such a refusal at face value. It is reasonable not to make further enquiries.

T2.13 **R (Conde) v Lambeth LBC**
[2005] EWHC 62 (Admin); [2005] HLR 29; [2005] 2 FLR 98; (2005) 8 CCLR 486; 13 January 2005 (see U8.8)

No discrimination to refuse EEA national assistance under Children Act 1989 s17

T2.14 **R (Kimvono) v Tower Hamlets LBC**
(2001) 33 HLR 78, QBD (see S1.13)

Unlawful to ignore ineligible members of eligible applicant's household in allocating accommodation

T2.15 **R (Mohamed) v Harrow LBC**
[2005] EWHC Admin; [2006] HLR 18; 13 December 2005

EEA national who was not a worker or work seeker and did not otherwise have a right to reside in the UK ineligible under Part VII

The claimant was a Dutch national, who came to the UK and worked until she was made redundant. She was then joined by her two young children. She registered as unemployed and claimed income support. Eighteen months after her employment had ended she applied as a homeless person. Harrow decided that she was not eligible for assistance (s185). The claimant applied for a review and, pending that review, the provision of interim accommodation under Housing Act 1996 s188(3). The council refused to accommodate her and the claimant sought judicial review of that decision.

Jackson J dismissed the claim.

1) Harrow was entitled to find that the claimant was no longer a 'worker' or 'work seeker'. She was unemployed, had not retained the status of worker, did not have a sufficiently close connection with the employment market, had failed to find work for a period substantially longer than six months and, in her circumstances (lack of English and work skills, inability to afford childcare costs), was unlikely to do so. The claimant had not retained the status of worker by operation of the Immigration (European Economic Area) Regulations 2000 SI No 2326.

2) The claimant did not have the resources to be self-sufficient and so did not otherwise have a right to reside in the UK.

3) Accordingly, the failure to provide accommodation to the claimant under s188(3) by virtue of Nationality, Immigration and Asylum Act 2002 Sch 3 did not breach the claimant's EC Treaty rights as she had not been exercising any such rights. She had not been discriminated against contrary to the EC Treaty.

4) Even if the claimant had been a work seeker, the provision of accommodation would not be 'necessary' in order for the claimant to exercise her right to seek work and her EC rights would not be breached by the denial of accommodation under Schedule 3.

5) As the claimant was ineligible to benefit from the exercise of the s188(3) discretion, Harrow was under no duty to consider the factors relevant to the exercise of that discretion.

Note: See the provisions in Immigration (European Economic Area) Regulations 2006 SI No 1003 reg 6(2) regarding retention of worker status.

Under the Eligibility Regs 2006, a jobseeker is not eligible under Part VII.

T2.16   *R (Paul-Coker) v Southwark LBC*
[2006] EWHC 497 (Admin); 3 March 2006 (see T48.9)

Habitual residence; no explanation why over seven months' residence was insufficient to justify the 'appreciable period of time' element of the test

T3   **The meaning of 'homelessness'**

Housing Act 1996 ss175–177 govern the issue of when a person is homeless:

Homelessness and threatened homelessness

175(1) A person is homeless if he has no accommodation available for his occupation, in the United Kingdom or elsewhere, which he –
   (a) is entitled to occupy by virtue of an interest in it or by virtue of an order of a court
   (b) has an express or implied licence to occupy, or
   (c) occupies as a residence by virtue of any enactment or rule of law giving him the right to remain in occupation or restricting the right of another person to recover possession.
  (2) A person is also homeless if he has accommodation but –
   (a) he cannot secure entry to it, or
   (b) it consists of a moveable structure, vehicle or vessel designed or adapted for human habitation and there is no place where he is entitled or permitted both to place it and to reside in it.
  (3) A person shall not to be treated as having accommodation unless it is accommodation which it would be reasonable for him to continue to occupy.
  (4) A person is threatened with homelessness if it is likely that he will become homeless within 28 days.

Section 176 provides for when accommodation is to be regarded as available (see T14) and s177 makes provision relating to the issue of when it is reasonable to continue to occupy accommodation (see T7).

T4   'Accommodation'

House of Lords

T4.1   *R v Brent LBC ex p Awua*
[1996] AC 55; [1995] 3 WLR 215; [1995] 3 All ER 493; (1995) 27 HLR 453, HL (see also T22.2 (for full report) and T51.1)

Occupying temporary or short-term accommodation does not amount to homelessness

Lord Hoffmann, giving the leading speech in this case on intentional homelessness, observed that '"accommodation" means a place that can fairly be described as accommodation ... and which it would be reasonable, having regard to the general housing conditions in the local authority's district, for the person in question to continue to occupy'. He found it hard to imagine a case in which it could be said that it was not reasonable to continue to occupy accommodation simply because it was temporary. However, he went on to comment that:

> On the other hand, the extent to which the accommodation is physically suitable, so that it would be reasonable for a person to continue to occupy it, must be related to the time for which he has been there and is expected to stay. A local housing authority could take the view that a family like the Puhlhofers [see *R v Hillingdon LBC ex p Puhlhofer* (T8.2)], put into a cramped and squalid bedroom, can be expected to make do for a temporary period. On the other hand, there will come a time at which it is no longer reasonable to expect them to continue to occupy such accommodation. At this point they come back within the definition of homelessness in section 58(1) [Housing Act 1985, see now Housing Act 1996 s175(1)]. ([1995] 3 All ER at 498)

High Court

T4.2 *R v Ealing LBC ex p Sidhu*
(1982) 2 HLR 45; (1982) 80 LGR 534, QBD

A person accommodated in a women's refuge is 'homeless'

After being subjected to violence by her husband, Mrs Sidhu left home and went with her children to live in a women's refuge. She was granted interim care and control of her children by a county court judge. She applied to Ealing as a homeless person. It decided that she was not homeless and insisted that she obtain a final order for custody before it would consider her to be in priority need.

Hodgson J quashed the decision. The fact that Mrs Sidhu was accommodated in a refuge could not justify the council in finding that she was not homeless. It was important that refuges were seen as temporary crisis accommodation. Furthermore, it was clear that Mrs Sidhu was in priority need if she had dependent children living with her. The council was not entitled to require her to obtain a final custody order in respect of the children before treating her as being in priority need.

See also *Moran v Manchester CC* (T8.16)

County courts

T4.3 *Khatun v Newham LBC*
November 2000 *Legal Action* 25, Bow County Court

An authority cannot rely on accommodation it arranges pending enquiries in making a 'not homeless' decision

The appellant fled her matrimonial home, alleging domestic violence. The council arranged interim accommodation under s188 pending inquiries. The accommodation was provided by a housing association on an assured shorthold tenancy. On review the council decided that the appellant was no longer homeless as she had accommodation, ie, the assured shorthold tenancy it had secured for her.

HHJ Mitchell quashed the decision. An authority could not, on a true construction of the provisions of Housing Act 1996 Part VII, determine that a person was not homeless by relying on the accommodation it had itself secured pending enquiries.

T5   Rights of occupation: s175(1)

Court of Appeal

T5.1   *Fletcher v Brent LBC*

[2006] EWCA Civ 960; [2007] HLR 12; 7 July 2006 (see also N2.10)

Wife's notice to quit ended the applicant's tenancy; council had to consider whether husband had any other right to occupy

Mr and Mrs Fletcher were joint secure tenants of the council. On the breakdown of their relationship, Mrs Fletcher obtained a court order ousting her husband. She gave the council notice to quit the property and was rehoused. On his application for homelessness assistance under Housing Act 1996 Part VII, Brent decided that Mr Fletcher was not homeless because the notice was ineffective to end the tenancy and the council was willing to provide him with keys to the property. That decision was upheld on review. On appeal to the county court, the judge held that it was uncertain whether the notice to quit had ended the tenancy. She held that, even if the tenancy had been determined, as the council were willing to give Mr Fletcher the keys, he had a licence to occupy the property, the nature of which it was unnecessary for her to determine.

The Court of Appeal allowed a second appeal. The notice to quit was valid and had ended the joint tenancy. The judge was wrong to find it unnecessary to determine the nature of any other interest Mr Fletcher might have. That question had not been addressed in the council's decision-making and was remitted to the council's reviewing officer to consider.

T5.2   *R (Sacupima) v Newham LBC*

[2001] 1 WLR 563; (2001) 33 HLR 18; (2000) *Times* 1 December, CA

Applicants not homeless under s175(1) until warrant for possession executed

Seven applicants, all residents of the London Borough of Newham, challenged the suitability of interim accommodation provided in seaside resorts (see T53.9). Another issue that arose was the question of the date at which the applicants, all assured or assured shorthold tenants, became homeless. The council considered it was not until the date the applicants were evicted by the court bailiffs. Dyson J at first instance held it was the date on which ordered for possession.

The Court of Appeal, following the reasoning of Collins J in *R v Newham LBC ex p Khan and Hussain* (T14.8), allowed the council's appeal on this point. An assured tenant remaining in possession of premises after the date when a possession order became effective, but before the warrant for possession had been executed, was occupying a residence by virtue of an enactment restricting the right of the landlord to recover possession within the meaning of s175(1)(c). A person therefore only became homeless when the warrant was executed.

Note: This case did not consider the issue of whether it was reasonable to continue to remain in occupation in such circumstances (s175(3)). See *R v Croydon LBC ex p Jarvis* (T8.12) on this point.

High Court

T5.3   *R v Hammersmith and Fulham LBC ex p O'Sullivan*
[1991] EGCS 110, QBD

Unprotected licensee homeless when asked to leave by landlord

The applicant was told to leave by her landlord when she became pregnant, because the house was already overcrowded. The landlord was resident on the premises and accommodation was shared. No formal notice was served nor proceedings started. She left. The council decided that she was intentionally homeless.

Hodgson J quashed the decision. The applicant had been an unprotected licensee with no continuing right to remain in the premises. The reasoning contained in the council's decision letter, based on the premise that she could have remained in occupation, was flawed.

T5.4   *R v Kensington and Chelsea RLBC ex p Minton*
(1988) 20 HLR 648, QBD

Applicant homeless despite employer's offer to re-employ and re-accommodate her

The applicant was a live-in housekeeper. Her employment ended after a dispute with her employer. She applied to the council as a homeless person. The council contacted her former employer, who indicated that she would be prepared to re-employ the applicant and again provide accommodation. The council decided that the applicant was not homeless since it was reasonable for her to return and live in her employer's flat.

Macpherson J quashed the decision as erroneous in law. Mrs Minton had no 'accommodation' because her previous licence to occupy had been terminated when her employment terminated. In the absence of an agreement of re-employment between the applicant and her former employer, there was no licence at all, either express or implied, and no accommodation within the meaning of Housing Act 1985 s58(2)(b) (now Housing Act 1996 s175(1)(b)). Since she had no accommodation, no question of reasonableness arose. The council had misapplied s58.

T5.5   *R (B) v Southwark LBC*
[2003] EWHC 1678 (Admin); (2003) *Times* 30 July; 4 July 2003

A prisoner has no right to occupy a prison cell and is homeless

B, who was 17 years old, was sentenced to eight months in a young offender's institution. His final release date was in July 2003 but he became eligible for release with an electronic tag in June 2003 provided that he had suitable accommodation. In May he applied to Southwark as threatened with homelessness and requested that accommodation be provided in June. The council decided that he was not homeless because he was accommodated in prison, which it was reasonable for him to continue to occupy. He sought judicial review.

Owen J allowed B's application. Prison is not accommodation. It does not fall within s175(1)(a), (b) or (c). For accommodation to exist there has to be a right to occupy which is enforceable or defensible in law. A prisoner cannot be said to have a right to occupy a cell. Detention is the antithesis of any such right (*Stewart v Lambeth LBC* (T27.14)). If it were accommodation, a prison cell would not be accommodation which it is reasonable to occupy within the meaning in s175(3) when a prisoner is entitled to release.

Local government ombudsman

T5.6   *Investigation 90/A/1038 (Ealing LBC)*

Maladministration where unprotected licensees required to await a possession order

Tenants were asked to leave by their landlord. They had no defence to possession proceedings because they were sharing living accommodation with the landlord. They applied to Ealing LBC as homeless people but were told to await a possession order. The landlord obtained a possession order, together with an order for costs of £250. The tenants were then rehoused.

The ombudsman found that neither the *Homelessness Code of Guidance* nor the council's own policy had been followed. The applicants had been subjected to the penalty of costs and to considerable distress. The council was invited to pay the £250 costs incurred and a further £100 in respect of its maladministration.

T6   Inability to secure entry to accommodation/no place to keep moveable structure: s175(2)

Court of Appeal

T6.1   *Begum (Nipa) v Tower Hamlets LBC*
[2000] QB 133; [2000] 1 WLR 306; (2000) 32 HLR 445; (1999) *Times* 9 November, CA (see T14.2)

If applicant could not access accommodation because of cost of travelling to it, s175(2)(a) did not apply; rather the accommodation was not 'available'

T6.2   *Higgs v Brighton and Hove CC*
[2003] EWCA Civ 895; [2003] 3 All ER 753; [2003] 1 WLR 2241; [2004] HLR 2; (2003) *Times* 11 July; 30 June 2003 (see T18.1)

Applicant who had no place where he was entitled to park his caravan was homeless

High Court

T6.3   *R v Chiltern DC ex p Roberts*
(1991) 23 HLR 387, QBD

Travelling showmen without a permanent site were not homeless while they had a series of places they could stay

The applicants, who were travelling showmen, owned their own mobile homes. They were required to leave a permanent site but were setting out on a season of bookings, which would provide sites where their vehicles could be parked. They claimed that they were homeless or threatened with homelessness because they no longer had a place where they were entitled to live with a degree of permanence and continuity.

Pill J held that, at the start of the season, the applicants were neither homeless nor threatened with homelessness. 'Reside' in Housing Act 1985 s58(3)(c) (now Housing Act 1996 s175(2)(b)) means 'live or occupy' and there was no requirement for the permission to place their mobile homes to have a degree of permanence. The showmen had places where they could live through the summer season and accordingly s58(3)(c) was not satisfied. (The council conceded that the section would be satisfied at the end of the season.)

See T33.3 regarding the other issue that arose in this case concerning the acceptance of an application under Part VII by letter.

T6.4 **R v Hillingdon LBC ex p Bax**
December 1992 *Legal Action* 21, QBD

Houseboat owner without permanent mooring but with licence to cruise not homeless

The applicant owned a houseboat which was destroyed by fire. The council found that he had been homeless throughout his residence in the houseboat because he had not had any permanent place to moor or site it (Housing Act 1985 s58(3)(c), now Housing Act 1996 s175(2)(b)). The council considered his homelessness to have arisen from the loss of his earlier accommodation.

Robert Carnwath QC (sitting as a deputy High Court judge) held that, since the applicant had throughout had a licence to cruise and keep the houseboat on the relevant waterways, he had been within s58(3)(c) and only became homeless when the boat was destroyed.

T7 **Reasonable to continue to occupy: s175(3)**

The question of whether accommodation is, or would have been, reasonable for a person to continue to occupy is relevant to the question of whether a person is homeless (s175(3)) or, if homeless, whether intentionally homeless (s191(1)). Cases that have considered the issue in either context are referred to in this section.

Section 177(1) provides that it is not reasonable for a person to continue to occupy accommodation if it is probable that this will lead to violence against the applicant or a member of their household/potential household. Violence includes threats of violence which are likely to be carried out. (Note that the statutory distinction between domestic violence and other violence is not of relevance to the issue of homelessness and intentional homelessness and only becomes of some significance when considering local connection referrals.)

Section 177(2) provides that:

> In determining whether it would be, or would have been, reasonable for a person to continue to occupy accommodation, regard may be had to the general circumstances prevailing in relation to housing in the district of the local housing authority to whom he has applied for accommodation or for assistance in obtaining accommodation.

By s177(3) the secretary of state may by order specify further matters to be taken into account when considering reasonableness. The Homelessness

(Suitability of Accommodation) Order 1996 SI No 3204 provides that, in considering whether it is reasonable to continue to occupy accommodation or whether it is suitable (for the purposes discharge of duty), its affordability to the applicant shall be taken into account.

Cases in the section on suitability of accommodation provided in discharge of duty may also be relevant to the issue of reasonable to continue to occupy (see T53).

T8   ## General

House of Lords

T8.1   ### R v Brent LBC ex p Awua
[1996] AC 55; [1995] 3 WLR 215; [1995] 3 All ER 493; (1995) 27 HLR 453, HL (see T22.2)

Whether it is reasonable to continue to occupy accommodation that is unsatisfactory may depend on the time that a person is expected to stay in it

T8.2   ### R v Hillingdon LBC ex p Puhlhofer
[1986] AC 484; [1986] 1 All ER 467; [1986] 2 WLR 259; (1986) 18 HLR 158, HL

'Accommodation', as referred to in the definition of homelessness in Housing Act 1985, before amendment, did not have to be appropriate or reasonable

Mr and Mrs Puhlhofer were living with their two young children temporarily in bed and breakfast accommodation in a guest house. They had one single bedroom with no means of washing clothes or cooking. They applied to the local authority for accommodation as homeless persons because the room was inadequate for their needs. The council decided that they were not homeless or threatened with homelessness within the meaning of Housing (Homeless Persons) Act 1977 s1 (subsequently Housing Act 1985 s58, now Housing Act 1996 s175). There was no express statutory requirement that accommodation be reasonable in the definition of homelessness in s1. Mr and Mrs Puhlhofer claimed that 'accommodation' in the Act meant 'appropriate accommodation' and applied for judicial review.

The House of Lords upheld the local authority's decision. In deciding whether or not an applicant was homeless, the local authority did not have to consider whether any existing accommodation was appropriate or reasonable.

Note: Following this decision the definition of homelessness in Housing Act 1985 was amended by Housing and Planning Act 1986 s14(2), which added a new s58(2A) (now Housing Act 1996 s175(3)) and a new s58(2B) (now Housing Act 1996 s177(2)). The decision remains of relevance, however, in relation to Lord Brightman's often quoted comments on the use of judicial review proceedings (see T56.2).

Court of Appeal

T8.3   ### Denton v Southwark LBC
[2007] EWCA Civ 623, 4 July 2007 (see T27.4)

Cause of homelessness was applicant's bad behaviour towards mother; that conduct to be ignored in considering whether reasonable to continue to occupy family home

T8.4   *Kacar v Enfield LBC*

(2001) 33 HLR 64, CA

Applicant could have stayed in isolated accommodation longer while alternative accommodation sought

Mr Kacar, a Kurdish refugee from Turkey, lived among the Turkish speaking community in Enfield for six years. After he became unemployed he took up a job in Aylesbury in March 1997. He moved there with his wife and young child and obtained an assured shorthold tenancy. He lost his job after a few days owing to his poor English and was unable to find other employment. He and his wife became extremely socially isolated in Aylesbury as there was no Turkish community and neither of them had a good command of English. His wife became very depressed. In June 1997 they returned to Enfield and he later applied as a homeless person. The council made an intentionally homeless decision which was upheld on review, primarily on the basis that the appellant could have waited in the Aylesbury accommodation at least until he had made enquiries about finding his own accommodation in Enfield. HHJ Riddell quashed the decision. He held that the council had failed to make adequate enquiries into Mrs Kacar's medical condition and the decision-making process was flawed as the central proposition – that the family could have 'held on' while they looked for their own housing – was never put to the appellant in clear terms.

The council's appeal to the Court of Appeal was granted. The court held that:

a) The council had made sufficient enquiries to enable them to assess the seriousness of Mrs Kacar's depression. She was not receiving any medical treatment and was not taking prescribed drugs. She had not consulted her GP or social services. Mr Kacar's solicitors had made representations for the purposes of the review and had not suggested that further enquiries should be made.

b) The council had adequately put to Mr Kacar that he could have 'stayed on longer' in Aylesbury and he had been given ample opportunity to deal with it.

T8.5   *Noh v Hammersmith and Fulham LBC*

[2001] EWCA Civ 905, [2002] HLR 54

Council entitled to balance general circumstances against applicant's personal circumstances and find her intentionally homeless despite psychiatric evidence

Ms Noh fled Somalia after witnessing the murder of her parents and being subjected to sexual violence. Newham LBC provided her with accommodation but after nine months she left and went to stay with her sister in Hammersmith and Fulham. A few months later she applied to Hammersmith and Fulham as a homeless person but was found intentionally homeless. She requested a review. She said that she felt isolated in Newham and needed the support of her brother and sister, both of whom lived in the council's area. She submitted a report from a consultant psychiatrist who described her as one of the most vulnerable people that he had ever seen and as seriously mentally ill. He considered that it was 'wholly unreasonable' for her to continue to live in Newham. The review was unsuccessful and her appeal to the county court was dismissed.

The Court of Appeal dismissed her second appeal. It was clear that the council had taken account of the medical issues arising from the psychiatric report. However, the issue of reasonableness to continue to occupy was a matter for the council itself to decide and it would have been wrong for it to simply adopt the opinion of the psychiatrist on this point. The approach of the council was to accept the psychiatrist's medical opinion but not to accept his views about the effects of the applicant's medical condition on the question of reasonableness. The council had been entitled to adopt this approach. It had taken into account the individual circumstances of the applicant. The case was not exceptional. There was one medical report based on a single consultation and the applicant had not received any treatment for her condition. It was not irrational for the council to balance the general housing circumstances against the applicant's personal circumstances. The council was entitled to take into account the demands for housing in its area and its capacity to absorb homeless families.

T8.6   *R v Brent LBC ex p Bariise*
(1999) 31 HLR 50, CA

It is for authority to assess general housing circumstances in its area

The applicant gave up her privately rented accommodation in a house in multiple occupation (HMO). She claimed that the two other residents in the house left the common parts dirty, stole her food from the communal kitchen and shouted at her children. The council decided that she was intentionally homeless as it had been reasonable for her to continue to occupy the accommodation and she had left it without making adequate arrangements to secure alternative accommodation. The council observed that her situation was not unusual, it had experience of persons who had other similar complaints and there were bound to be conflicts of lifestyle in multi-occupied homes.

Popplewell J quashed the decision ((1998) 30 HLR 518, QBD) and held that the applicant's specific circumstances needed to be considered before being balanced with general circumstances in the borough (Housing Act 1985 s60(4), now Housing Act 1996 s177(2)).

The Court of Appeal allowed an appeal. The council had made sufficient enquiries and had taken into account all relevant matters. In relation to the applicant's contention that the extent of the theft of her food had not been adequately considered by the council Millet J commented:

> I recognise that it may not be sufficient for the decision-maker merely to state that he has considered all the material put before him. If there is something which is so startling that one would not expect it to pass without individual comment, the Court may be justified in drawing the inference that it has not received any or sufficient consideration. But in this case it is very much a matter of degree. The fact that when told of the extent of the alleged thefts the [council] did not react with astonishment suggests to me that this is may indeed be a not uncommon situation in Brent.

The council had a housing crisis and was in the best position to assess the seriousness of the general conditions in its area and the extent to which the respondent's complaints took her case out of the norm and made it unreasonable for her to remain in occupation of the property, having regard to the general conditions in the borough.

T8.7   *R v Brent LBC ex p McManus*
(1993) 25 HLR 643, CA

'Reasonable to continue to occupy' is a subjective test

The applicant lived in an area in Belfast which was the scene of a lot of sectarian violence. She became very anxious and depressed and was prescribed tranquillisers. She left her home in fear, following the explosion of a petrol bomb nearby. She gave up the accommodation and later came to the UK and applied to Brent as a homeless person. Brent decided that the Belfast accommodation was reasonable for her to continue to occupy and that she was intentionally homeless for leaving it without making arrangements to secure alternative accommodation.

Tuckey J quashed the finding that the applicant was intentionally homeless ((1993) 25 HLR 643, QBD). The test of reasonableness to continue to occupy was a subjective one. Brent should have considered how the applicant's particular situation affected her and her daughter. Brent's generalisations in its decision letter about the situation in Belfast and the difficulties for the residents as a whole suggested that it had adopted an objective approach. Brent's approach to decision-making was flawed. Ms McManus was not given the opportunity to comment on a number of matters which it decided against her and which were significant. It did not carry out sufficient enquiries, particularly about the psychiatric state of the applicant and her daughter. It should have delayed making a decision until Ms McManus had the opportunity of obtaining specialist reports. The council was wrong to consider that it had enough medical evidence before it and to conclude that the applicant's nervous condition could be attributable merely to her homelessness.

The Court of Appeal dismissed Brent's appeal.

T8.8   *R v Broxbourne BC ex p Willmoth*
(1990) 22 HLR 118, CA

Reasonableness not limited to consideration of physical conditions of accommodation

The applicant left her council flat in Hackney because of violence from her ex-partner, which continued even after she excluded him from the flat. She applied to Broxbourne, which decided that she was not homeless, considering it reasonable for her to live in Hackney.

The Court of Appeal quashed the decision on the ground that the council had misdirected itself in law. The applicant was the tenant of premises in Hackney which she had been driven to leave by the violent actions of her former (non-resident) partner. Broxbourne BC argued that she was not homeless because she was still the tenant and that the test of 'reasonable to continue to occupy' under Housing Act 1985 s58(2A) (now Housing Act 1996 s175(3)) was confined to consideration of the physical attributes of the accommodation (eg, overcrowding and disrepair) only. It claimed that to allow s58(2A) to cover acts of violent behaviour would make s58(3)(b) (violence within the home; see now the wider s177(1)) redundant. The Court of Appeal (following and applying *R v Kensington and Chelsea RLBC ex p Hammell* (T58.3)) held that s58(2A) required consideration of all matters related to continued occupation. Sir John Megaw said the reasonableness test is:

> ... not necessarily or solely confined to looking at the actual quality of the accommodation within the four walls of the house or the room or flat which is the accommodation available. It may be the duty of the housing authority to consider also circumstances, matters and factors which may fall outside the limited consideration of the actual quality of physical accommodation itself ... Just as the difficulties created by a staircase or other approach to accommodation, to an applicant with physical infirmities, is relevant to reasonableness, so also are threats of violence, even though those threats come from one who is not resident in the accommodation. (p127)

Note: See now Housing Act 1996 s177(1), as amended by Homelessness Act 2002.

T8.9   *R v Newham LBC ex p Tower Hamlets LBC*
[1991] 1 WLR 1032; [1992] 2 All ER 767; (1991) 23 HLR 62; (1992) LGR 123, CA

An authority considering an applicant who would be referred to another authority is required to consider the general housing conditions in that other authority

Mr Ullah applied as a homeless person to Tower Hamlets. It decided that he was intentionally homeless as a result of leaving accommodation he owned in Bangladesh. He then applied to Newham. In determining whether it would have been reasonable for Mr Ullah to have continued to occupy the accommodation in Bangladesh (Housing Act 1985 s60(1), now Housing Act 1996 s191(1)), Newham had regard to housing conditions in its own area (s60(4), now Housing Act 1996 s177(2)). It compared these conditions with the very unsatisfactory state of the applicant's accommodation in Bangladesh and decided that he was not intentionally homeless. However, since he did not have any local connection with Newham, it referred his application to Tower Hamlets under the local connection provisions.

Nolan J quashed the referral and the Court of Appeal dismissed an appeal. Newham's decision that Mr Ullah was not intentionally homeless was so flawed as to vitiate its decision to refer. It should have considered the housing conditions in Tower Hamlets under s60(4) because Mr Ullah had first applied there and Newham were considering his application on the basis of a referral to Tower Hamlets. Furthermore, Newham had failed to take account of the extent to which the accommodation in Bangladesh conformed to accepted local standards and to the applicant's employment prospects in the UK. It had failed to ascertain and consider the reasons for Tower Hamlets' decision. Even if the decision that Mr Ullah was intentionally homeless had been lawfully made, Newham had a discretion whether to refer. Comity and good administration required Newham to consider whether, in the circumstances, it was in the public interest for the duty to be accepted by it, notwithstanding that the conditions for referral were met.

T8.10 **R (B) v Southwark LBC**

[2003] EWHC 1678 (Admin); (2003) *Times* 30 July; 4 July 2003 (see T5.5)

Not reasonable for prisoner to occupy a prison cell when entitled to release

T8.10A **Waltham Forest LBC v Maloba**

[2007] EWCA Civ 1281, 4 December 2007

Accommodation must be reasonable to continue to occupy regardless of whether it is currently occupied by an applicant

Mr Maloba was born in Uganda and came to the UK in 1989 at the age of 27. He became a British citizen in 1997. On a visit to Uganda in 1999 he met his wife. They had a daughter in 2001 and married in 2002. Mr Maloba's wife and child lived in an annex to a family home in Kampala, also occupied by two of his siblings and their families. In December 2004 his wife and child joined him in the UK and in March 2005 he applied to the council as a homeless person. The council decided that he was not homeless as he and his family could live in the accommodation in Kampala. Mr Maloba's review, based on his wish to remain in Britain where he had settled, failed. On appeal to the county court, Hornby HHJ held the council's decision that it was reasonable for Mr Maloba to continue to occupy the accommodation in Kampala was *Wednesbury* unreasonable and the decision was quashed. The council appealed contending: (1) As Mr Maloba was not already occupying the accommodation in Kampala it was immaterial whether it was reasonable to continue to occupy it, all that mattered was that it was available (following the majority (obiter) view in *Begum (Nipa) v Tower Hamlets LBC* (T14.2)); (2) If it was necessary to consider reasonableness all that needed to be considered was reasonableness in terms of size and facilities, not location, and (3) if it was necessary to consider location it was reasonable to expect Mr Maloba to live in Kampala.

The Court of Appeal dismissed the appeal.

1) Accommodation had to be reasonable, even where an applicant was not already living in it. The words 'reasonable for him to continue to occupy' in s175(3) should be construed as synonymous with 'reasonable for him to occupy for a continuing period' ie, for the future. *Nipa Begum* was disapproved on this point.
2) Reasonableness was not solely to be judged in terms of the quality of accommodation. An applicant's personal circumstances had to be taken into account.
3) The council had adopted an over restrictive approach on review. Nowhere was it considered whether it was reasonable for Mr Maloba to relocate to Uganda.

Note: See also T64.4A regarding the issue of costs that arose in this case.

High Court

T8.11 **R v Brent LBC ex p Yusuf**

(1997) 29 HLR 48, QBD

Pregnant applicant who left accommodation unsuitable for a baby (but not a pregnant woman) was intentionally homeless

The applicant was a single woman from Somalia who had been granted exceptional leave to remain in the UK. She moved into a shared house and had a brief relationship with one of the other occupiers. She became pregnant. The house was dirty, noisy and constantly full of the drunken friends of her former boyfriend. She decided that it would be impossible to bring up her expected baby in such an environment and she left. The council decided that she had become homeless intentionally.

Turner J dismissed an application for judicial review. The authority was correct in assessing the applicant's circumstances at the time when she became homeless. It was not required to have regard to future events. The applicant had left the accommodation four months before the baby was due. In those circumstances, the council had not erred in considering the question of whether it would have been reasonable for her to continue in occupation at that date even if the accommodation may later have been rendered inappropriate by the imminent birth of the child.

T8.12   *R v Croydon LBC ex p Jarvis*
(1994) 26 HLR 194, QBD

Reasonable for applicant with AST to remain until court order

The applicant had an assured shorthold tenancy. The landlord gave the requisite two months' notice requiring possession. Within 28 days of the date when the landlord required possession, the applicant applied to Croydon as a homeless person. It decided that she was not homeless or threatened with homelessness because it was reasonable for her to remain until a court order was obtained. The then current *Code of Guidance* issued under Housing Act 1985 s71 (now Housing Act 1996 s182) recommended, inter alia, at paragraph 10.12, that authorities should not require tenants to fight possession actions where the landlord had a certain prospect of success. Authorities need only be satisfied that proper notice had been served and that the landlord intended to proceed. The applicant applied for judicial review. Before her application could be heard, the landlord obtained an order for possession and costs. The council accepted the applicant as unintentionally homeless. The applicant pressed ahead with her application to seek a declaration that the council had acted unlawfully and for damages.

Andrew Collins QC, sitting as a deputy High Court judge, held that the council had not acted unlawfully since, in reaching its decision, it had considered fully the question of whether it would have been reasonable for the applicant to continue in occupation (Housing Act 1985 s58(2A), now Housing Act 1996 s175(3)). It had expressly considered: (a) the respective positions of the landlord and tenant and the expense of possession proceedings; (b) its own costs of providing temporary accommodation; (c) the general housing circumstances in the area (which effectively had been treated as determinative, but all relevant matters had been considered and it was for the council to decide what weight to attach to any particular matter); and (d) the then current *Homelessness Code of Guidance*, which the council did not follow. The decision was not manifestly perverse. The judge considered that the result would not necessarily be the same if an applicant applied as a homeless person after leaving accommodation without a court order – ignorance of a relevant fact might negate intentionality and the council should adopt a sympathetic approach.

The judge concluded by stating 'I am not saying that in all circumstances a council can say "wait until you are evicted". It is lawful for them to adopt that attitude if they consider all the individual circumstances.' The council had given careful thought to what it was going to do and detailed reasons for its decision.

> But I do not say that the same would necessarily apply in other cases where proper reasons were not given, as they have been here. I am not intending to give carte blanche for a general approach to be adopted and to be upheld that in all cases it is right to insist on deferment.

He indicated that, if he had found the decision unlawful, he would have awarded the amount of costs the applicant had to pay her landlord (£175) and a little bit extra for the trauma, a sum probably not exceeding £250 in all.

Note: See paras 8.30–32 of the current *Code of Guidance* (published July 2006)

T8.13   *R v Kensington and Chelsea RLBC ex p Moncada*
(1997) 29 HLR 289, QBD

Applicant could reasonably be expected to reside with ex-wife

Mr and Mrs Moncada were joint tenants of a four-bedroomed house. They had three children. Their marriage broke down but they both continued to live in the house. A Mr Williams, who had a relationship with Mrs Moncada, then went to live there and Mr Moncada was imprisoned for a drugs related offence. In 1993 Mr Williams assaulted one of the children and, partly as a result of this, they were put on the 'at risk' register. Mr and Mrs Moncada divorced after his release from prison. He obtained custody of their two sons while Mrs Moncada was given custody of their daughter. In 1995 Mr Moncada applied as a homeless person. At that time there had been no further incidents of violence. Mr Williams, if not living with Mrs Moncada, was a frequent visitor. The council decided that Mr Moncada was not homeless because he was still the joint secure tenant of the former matrimonial home. Having regard to the prevailing shortage of housing, it decided that the house was large enough for Mr and Mrs Moncada and their children and that it was reasonable for him to reside there.

Popplewell J dismissed Mr Moncada's application for judicial review. The authority had taken into account all relevant factors. Although it was undesirable for a divorced couple to have to live together, the council had addressed that issue and taken its decision in accordance with the shortage of accommodation in London. Furthermore, there had been no incidence of violence against the sons since 1993.

T8.14   *R v Portsmouth CC ex p Knight*
(1983) 10 HLR 115; (1984) LGR 184, QBD

Not reasonable for a service licensee to remain in occupation as a trespasser

The applicant managed a wine merchants' shop and lived with his family in tied accommodation above the shop. He lost his job and was asked to vacate. He left without waiting for a possession order. The local authority decided that he was intentionally homeless.

Woolf J quashed the decision. The applicant was a service licensee. On termination of his licence he became a trespasser and had no legal right of occupation. Even on the assumption that the Protection from Eviction Act 1977 applied, it did not create rights but placed a fetter on the owner's right to recover possession without a court order. Also, the authority had failed to distinguish between a service licence and a service tenancy. In deciding whether it was reasonable for the applicant to remain, the authority had failed to take account of the difficult position the employers would have been put in where they required the accommodation for another employee and would be put to the expense of obtaining a possession order. It would be a case having some special quality or feature before an authority could conclude that it would be reasonable for a service licensee to remain in occupation as a trespasser.

County courts

T8.15 *Khadija Ali v Bristol CC*

October 2007 *Legal Action* 26; 21 June 2007, Bristol County Court

Overcrowding, affordability and service of s21 notice not adequately addressed when making 'not homeless' decision

Mrs Ali was an assured shorthold tenant of an overcrowded terraced house. There was a £12.50 pw shortfall between her housing benefit and the rent. She lived on income support. She accrued rent arrears and her landlord served a Housing Act 1988 s21 notice. The council declared the premises to be so overcrowded as to constitute a Category 1 B and C hazard (for the purposes of Housing Act 2004 Part 1) and served a prohibition notice. The notice was suspended so long as Mrs Ali remained in occupation. On her application for homelessness assistance, Bristol found her not to be homeless because she had property reasonable to continue to occupy.

Recorder Blunt QC quashed that decision:

1) On overcrowding, the council had not given clear reasons why, despite *Code of Guidance* para 17.15, it was reasonable to occupy the premises after they were declared a Category 1 hazard. Furthermore, the review decision letter stated that the council had taken into account conditions in its area (Housing Act 1996 s177(2)) by reference to over 3,400 households which were at least one bedroom short, whereas the true comparators for Mrs Ali were families lacking three bedrooms.

2) On affordability, the reasons given by the council for concluding that her meeting a £50 pm shortfall would not reduce household income to below benefit levels (*Code* para 17.40) were not full, clear and intelligible.

3) On the s21 notice, the reviewing officer had not explained the departure from the guidance given in the code at para 8.32 or even referred to it.

T8.16 **Moran v Manchester CC**

July 2007 *Legal Action* 3; 16 May 2007, Manchester County Court

Not reasonable to continue to occupy women's refuge

Ms Moran fled domestic violence and was temporarily accommodated by a women's refuge. After a dispute with the refuge staff, she was asked to leave. She then applied to the council under HA 1996 Part VII for homelessness assistance. It decided that she had become homeless intentionally when she lost her place at the refuge.

Recorder Rigby allowed her appeal and quashed that decision. The council had been wrong to treat crisis accommodation in the refuge as accommodation reasonable for an applicant 'to continue to occupy' for the purposes of HA 1996 s190: applying *Code of Guidance* para 8.34 and *R v Ealing LBC ex p Sidhu* (T4.2).

Note: The council has been given leave to appeal.

T9 *Physical conditions/overcrowding*

Court of Appeal

T9.1 **Elrify v Westminster CC**

[2007] EWCA Civ 332; [2007] HLR 36; 23 March 2007

Authority had misapplied the test of overcrowding in Housing Act 1985

The claimant, a home owner, applied for homelessness assistance on the basis that his home was so overcrowded that it was no longer reasonable to continue to occupy: s175(3). He occupied a three-bedroom flat with his wife and seven children aged between 5 and 18. The council decided that, although the premises were statutorily overcrowded, using the 'room' standard (Housing Act 1985 s326 Table I), the excess was only by one person. On review, it upheld a decision that the claimant was not homeless. Taking into account the housing conditions in its area, it was reasonable to occupy a property with only one more person than the statutory permitted maximum. The county court dismissed an appeal.

The Court of Appeal quashed the decision. The 'space' standard for statutory overcrowding (Housing Act 985 s326 Table II) had not been considered by the council. It indicated that the excess was two and a half people. That was a relevant matter because s326(3) directed attention to whichever was the lesser permitted number. The decision would need to be reconsidered.

T9.2 **Harouki v Kensington and Chelsea RLBC**

[2007] EWCA Civ 1000; (2007) *Times* 12 November; 17 October 2007

Statutorily overcrowded property was reasonable to continue to occupy

The applicant and her husband occupied a three-bedroom flat with their five children. It was statutorily overcrowded and the applicant was committing an offence by permitting it to be overcrowded. She applied to the council as a homeless person on the ground that it was not 'reasonable to continue to occupy'. The council decided and confirmed on review that, although the accommodation was statutorily overcrowded, it was reasonable to continue to occupy where overcrowding was a prevailing housing condition within the authority's area. There were many families in the authority's area who were more severely overcrowded than the applicant. Her county court appeal was dismissed.

The Court of Appeal dismissed a second appeal. In assessing whether the flat had been 'reasonable to continue to occupy' the council had been entitled to take account of the fact that there were many families even more severely overcrowded in its area.

T9.3   **Osei v Southwark LBC**

[2007] EWCA Civ 787, 25 July 2007 (see T11.2)

Reasonable to continue to occupy overcrowded accommodation in Spain rather than giving it up for more overcrowded accommodation in UK

T9.4   **R v Kensington and Chelsea RLBC ex p Ben-El-Mabrouk**

(1995) 27 HLR 564, CA

Not homeless despite inadequate fire safety where council taking steps against landlord to do works

The applicants and their very young child occupied a small room at the top of a house in multiple occupation with inadequate fire prevention and escape facilities. An independent environmental health officer classified the property as unfit for human habitation and prejudicial to health. The council served statutory notices on the owner. The applicants applied to the council as homeless persons on the basis that it was unreasonable for them to continue to occupy (Housing Act 1985 s58(2A) – now Housing Act 1996 s175(3)) on account of the fire risk and inadequacy of the premises. The council rejected the application, having regard to housing conditions in its area and the fact that it was already taking steps to enforce housing and fire safety standards. At first instance ((1994) 26 HLR 733, QBD) Roger Henderson QC held that the risk to the family was such that the council's decision was *Wednesbury* unreasonable and should be quashed.

The Court of Appeal reversed his decision. The council had taken account of all relevant matters. The deputy judge had been wrong to find the decision so plainly 'irrational' or 'perverse' as to justify judicial intervention. Sir Thomas Bingham MR indicated that the position might be different if, having served the notices, the council took no or only dilatory steps to enforce them.

High Court

T9.5   **R v Haringey LBC ex p Ulger**

December 1992 *Legal Action* 21, QBD (see T47.4)

Interim accommodation duty where applicant 'may' be homeless due to overcrowding

T9.6   **R v Medina BC ex p Dee**

(1992) 24 HLR 562; (1992) *Times* 30 March, QBD

Accommodation unsafe for newborn baby on medical advice

The applicant occupied a beach chalet which was affected by damp and mould growth. She had a baby. Her doctor advised that the accommodation was inappropriate for a newborn baby. On her application as a homeless person, the council decided that the chalet was fit for human habitation and reasonable to continue to occupy.

Henry J quashed the decision. The council could not have expected the applicant to override the clear medical advice she had received and so could not properly find it reasonable under Housing Act 1985 s58(2A) (now Housing Act 1996 s175(3)) for her to continue to occupy the chalet.

T9.7   *R v Westminster CC ex p Alouat*
(1989) 21 HLR 477, QBD

Non-statutory overcrowding should be considered by authority

A married couple and several children were living in a two-bedroomed maisonette. The council decided that it was reasonable for them to continue to occupy the accommodation because, although it was cramped, it was not statutorily overcrowded.

Schiemann J quashed the decision and held that Housing Act 1985 s58(2A) (now Housing Act 1996 s175(3)) 'reasonableness' is not limited to statutory factors – non-statutory overcrowding, medical need and other matters should also be considered by the council.

County courts

T9.8   *Khadija Ali v Bristol CC*
October 2007 *Legal Action* 26; 21 June 2007, Bristol County Court (see T8.15)

Overcrowding, affordability and service of s21 notice not adequately addressed when making 'not homeless' decision

T9.9   *Sabah Mohamoud v Greenwich LBC*
January 2003 *Legal Action* 20; 20 November 2002, Woolwich County Court

Authority could not rely on general assertions about overcrowding in its district

From 1992 Ms Mohamoud was a council tenant of a four-bedroomed flat. Over the years her family grew until she was living with her husband, nephew and nine children. The flat became so cramped that she considered it no longer reasonable to continue to occupy. She applied for accommodation as a homeless person. On a s202 review, the council decided that to avoid being overcrowded the family would need to be in 8-bedroomed accommodation but concluded that it was reasonable for them to continue to occupy the present flat: s175(3). It considered general housing circumstances locally (s177(2)) and particularly the facts that in its borough (1) overcrowding was not uncommon and (2) there were over 9,000 unfit dwellings.

HHJ Cox quashed the decision. The council had not addressed the particular degree of overcrowding experienced by this applicant. It was not satisfactory for general assertions to be made about the prevalence of overcrowding in the borough without evidence showing that there were others who were experiencing a similar degree of overcrowding. The applicant's degree of overcrowding appeared to be gross and possibly in a class of its own. The figures about unfitness were irrelevant in the absence of information to show how those unfit properties could be compared with the applicant's overcrowding.

T10   Affordability

Court of Appeal

T10.1   **Bernard v Enfield LBC**
[2001] EWCA Civ 1831; [2002] HLR 46 (see T38.2)

Decision letter did not need to contain detailed assessment of applicant's resources

T10.2   **R v Brent LBC ex p Baruwa**
(1997) 29 HLR 915, CA

It is for an authority to decide whether applicant had deliberately failed to pay rent or had been unable to pay after paying for the necessities of life

Ms Baruwa was accepted by Brent for the main housing duty. She was moved into accommodation leased by the council from a private landlord. She fell into arrears and, after breaking a number of agreements to pay, was evicted. She applied again as a homeless person. Enquiries revealed that she had spent her available money on a university course, car maintenance and nursery fees, even when she was not working. The council decided that she was intentionally homeless.

The Court of Appeal held that, although eviction as a result of rent arrears is not intentional if it is the result of spending assets on the necessities of life, the 'necessities of life' may vary from family to family. It is for an authority, not the court, to consider whether a failure to pay rent is deliberate or whether it is due to a tenant having insufficient money to pay for the necessities of life. It is not for the authority to investigate every detail in an applicant's figures of income and expenditure and it is not necessary for it to put to applicants its opinion that certain items are not a necessity. In relation to the duty to give reasons, Schiemann J commented:

> where an authority is required to give reasons for its decision, it is required to give reasons which are proper, adequate and intelligible and enable the person affected to know why they have won or lost. That said, the law gives decision-makers a certain latitude in how they express themselves and will recognise that not all those taking decisions will find it easy to express themselves with judicial exactitude. (p920).

The finding of intentional homelessness was upheld.

T10.3   **R v Brent LBC ex p Grossett**
(1996) 28 HLR 9, CA

It is for an authority to assess 'difficult question' of whether applicant could afford the rent

The applicant was a council tenant whose rent was paid by housing benefit. She accumulated substantial arrears of amenity charge (for water rates, heating and hot water). In 1990 the council obtained a suspended possession order on terms that the applicant paid the amenity charge and £1.85 per week towards the arrears. She failed to do this and in 1993 a warrant was obtained and she was evicted. Brent decided that she had become intentionally homeless and an internal appeal panel upheld that decision. The applicant sought judicial review from the High Court and then the Court of Appeal, arguing that all her benefit income had been committed to necessary essentials and so her non-payment had not been 'deliberate'.

The Court of Appeal dismissed the application. Dillon LJ said that it was for the local authority, not the court, to assess the difficult question of whether the applicant could or could not have afforded the payments. There was no deficiency of enquiries or breach of natural justice.

T10.4   **R v Croydon LBC ex p Graham**
(1994) 26 HLR 286, CA

Applicant had not acted unreasonably in moving, without any prospect of homelessness, to cheaper accommodation

The applicant gave up an expensive assured shorthold tenancy to move to the house of a friend, from whom she rented a room at a substantially lower rent. When she later became pregnant, she was given notice to quit and became homeless. The council found that she was intentionally homeless because (a) she had left accommodation which it would have been reasonable for her to continue to occupy as she could, on her income, have continued to meet the rent and (b) the accommodation to which she moved was not settled, as she had herself confirmed that she did not intend it as her permanent home.

The Court of Appeal (Hoffmann LJ dissenting) quashed the decision. On the first question Sir Thomas Bingham MR said that the council was entitled to find that the applicant could have afforded to stay where she was but the question of reasonableness of leaving or staying was not to be 'judged on a Micawber test as to whether one's income exceeds, or fails to measure up to, the rent one is required to pay'. The applicant had not acted unreasonably in moving to cheaper suitable accommodation, unless by doing so she exposed herself to the threat of finding herself homeless. The crucial consideration was therefore whether, on the facts that appeared to her at the time, the move was one which put her in a precarious and vulnerable position. The applicant's admission that she did not regard the new home as permanent did not indicate that she regarded the new premises as being precarious. It was doubted that any single woman in her mid-twenties would regard rented accommodation as a permanent home. The fact that the new tenancy was a monthly tenancy did not, of itself, convey that the tenancy was precarious – many short tenancies continue for years. Furthermore, the fact that she was required to leave after three months was something the council could not properly rely on as it was viewing the story with hindsight. The council's conclusion that it was unreasonable for the applicant to move because there was no prospect of settled accommodation was not justified on the facts. Its reasoning was flawed and the matter should be remitted to the council for reconsideration.

Note: At times the judgment of Sir Thomas Bingham MR appears to focus on the question of whether the applicant acted reasonably in moving, rather than the test of whether it would have been reasonable for her to remain.

T10.5   *R v Wandsworth LBC ex p Hawthorne*
[1994] 1 WLR 1442; [1995] 2 All ER 331; (1995) 27 HLR 59; (1994) 68 P&CR D11; (1994) 93 LGR 20, CA

Authority had failed to consider why applicant had not paid the rent

The applicant was evicted from her council home for rent arrears of over £3,000. She claimed that she had been unable to afford the rent because her income was so low after her husband left her that she had been driven to chose between maintaining her children and paying the council. She was found intentionally homeless for 'wilfully and persistently' failing to pay her rent. She succeeded in her application for judicial review (see [1994] COD 228) and the council appealed.

The Court of Appeal dismissed the council's appeal. The court rejected the contention that, since the applicant had exercised the positive choice to spend the money on her children rather than the rent, she had 'deliberately' omitted to pay for the purposes of Housing Act 1985 s60(1) (now Housing Act 1996 s191(1)). Nourse LJ stated:

> The purpose of Part III of the 1985 Act [now Housing Act 1996 Part VII] is to house the homeless. Admittedly, it is not part of that purpose to house those whose homelessness has been brought upon them by their own fault. But equally it is no part of it to refuse housing to those whose homelessness has been brought upon them without fault on their part, for example by disability, sickness, poverty or even a simple inability to make ends meet.

The council had not considered the matters which had caused the applicant not to pay her rent. That was a fatal omission. It was no answer to assert that there had been a considered decision not to pay. The true question is 'What caused that decision?'. The relevant paragraph of the then *Homelessness Code of Guidance* (para 7.4(b)) correctly stated the law.

T10.6   **William v Wandsworth LBC; Bellamy v Hounslow LBC**
[2006] EWCA Civ 535; [2006] HLR 42; (2006) *Times* 6 June (see T24.3)

Failure to use money from remortgage to pay mortgage instalments a deliberate act

High Court

T10.7   *R v Hillingdon LBC ex p Tinn*
(1988) 20 HLR 305, QBD

Not reasonable to continue to occupy accommodation where resources so strained as to deprive family of the ordinary necessities of life

Joint secure tenants bought their flat on a long lease with a council mortgage. The break-up of their marriage left Mrs Tinn in the property, unable comfortably to afford the mortgage. She asked the council to repurchase the property and grant her a tenancy. The council refused. An application for judicial review based on duties owed under Housing Act 1985 Part III (now Housing Act 1996 Part VII) was dismissed as too precipitate because Mrs Tinn was neither homeless nor threatened with homelessness. She would have to surrender the lease formally or sell it to a willing purchaser before any issues under homelessness legislation would arise.

Note: This decision is based on Housing Act 1985 s58 before the amendment which inserted s58(2A) (now Housing Act 1996 s175(3)). This extended the definition of homelessness to include those having accommodation which it would not be reasonable for them to continue to occupy. Referring to the new provision, in *Tinn*, Kennedy J said, 'This would in appropriate circumstances include owner-occupiers.' He added:

> ... it cannot be reasonable [within the meaning of s60 of the Act – (now Housing Act 1996 s191)] for a person to continue to occupy accommodation when they can no longer discharge the fiscal obligations ... in relation to that accommodation without so straining their resources as to deprive themselves of the ordinary necessities of life, such as food, clothing, heat, transport and so forth. ((1988) 20 HLR at 308)

Note also The Homelessness (Suitability of Accommodation) Order 1996 SI No 3204.

T10.8 *R v Shrewsbury and Atcham BC ex p Griffiths*
(1993) 25 HLR 613, QBD (see T27.23)

Where payments from income support not paid towards mortgage, council should have considered whether homelessness was a likely result of that non-payment

County courts

T10.9 *Khadija Ali v Bristol CC*
October 2007 *Legal Action* 26; 21 June 2007, Bristol County Court (see T8.15)

Overcrowding, affordability and service of s21 notice not adequately addressed when making 'not homeless' decision

T10.10 *Odunsi v Brent LBC*
[1999] 6 CLD 348, Willesden County Court (see T37.29)

Mandatory obligation to consider whether accommodation affordable whether or not issue raised by applicant

T11 *Accommodation abroad*

Housing Act 1996 provides that an applicant is not homeless if he or she has accommodation in the UK or elsewhere. Previously, an applicant was homeless if he or she had no accommodation in the UK. If an applicant did have accommodation abroad, then the question of whether it was reasonable to continue to occupy that accommodation arose in the context of intentional homelessness.

Court of Appeal

T11.1 *De Falco v Crawley BC*
[1980] QB 460; [1980] 2 WLR 664; [1980] 1 All ER 913; 78 LGR 180, CA (see T58.1)

Authority entitled to conclude reasonable to remain in accommodation in Italy

T11.2   *Osei v Southwark LBC*

[2007] EWCA Civ 787, 25 July 2007

Reasonable to continue to occupy overcrowded accommodation in Spain rather than giving it up for more overcrowded accommodation in UK

The claimant and his family rented a room in a shared flat in Spain. When he lost his job and accrued rent arrears, the claimant came to the UK to find work. He stayed with a friend. When he found a job and had accumulated some funds over several months, he returned to Spain and cleared his arrears, terminated his tenancy and brought his wife and children to the UK. The friend could not accommodate the whole family and asked them to leave. The claimant then applied to Southwark for homelessness assistance. The council decided that he had become homeless intentionally: HA 1996 s191. That decision was upheld on review and on appeal. The claimant pursued a second appeal, contending that the council had failed to have regard to the overcrowding of the flat in Spain that had been occupied by two other households in addition to the claimant's family.

The Court of Appeal dismissed the appeal. The council had proceeded on the basis of assuming (without detailed enquiry) that the flat had been overcrowded. It had been entitled to find that, even if overcrowded, it was reasonable for the claimant to continue to occupy rather than giving it up to bring his family to even more overcrowded accommodation with the friend in London. In making that assessment the council had been entitled to have regard to the circumstances relating to housing in its own area: HA 1996 s177(2).

T11.3   *R v Camden LBC ex p Aranda*

(1998) 30 HLR 76, CA

Not reasonable to remain in accommodation in Colombia due to financial circumstances

In 1994 the applicant and her husband surrendered their London council flat under a scheme involving the receipt of a substantial sum to help them to buy privately. They acquired a bungalow in Colombia and moved there. The move was a 'disaster'. The applicant could not find work, her husband did not try and he then abandoned her without financial support. The applicant's capital was quickly depleted. Her expenditure exceeded her income. There was no social security available in Colombia and she used her remaining resources to bring herself and her child back to the UK. Camden Council's finding of intentional homelessness was quashed ((1996) 28 HLR 672, QBD).

The Court of Appeal dismissed the council's appeal. Any finding that giving up the Colombian home was intentional was impossible – no reasonable authority could have found, given the financial circumstances, that it would have been reasonable to continue in occupation. In relation to the decision to leave the UK accommodation in 1994, the applicant had gone reluctantly in an attempt to keep her family together and in ignorance of her husband's intention to abandon her there. Either that ignorance prevented her actions from being described as deliberate (Housing Act 1985 s60(3), now Housing Act 1996 s191(2)) or the husband's actual abandonment of the family 'broke the chain of causation' running from the initial departure from the UK.

T11.4   *R v Tower Hamlets LBC ex p Monaf*
(1988) 20 HLR 529; (1988) 86 LGR 709, CA

Not sufficient consideration of applicants' pattern of life and reasons for coming to the UK

The applicants were Bangladeshis settled in the UK. They returned to Bangladesh before coming back to the UK with their families. The local authority decided that the applicants did not have settled accommodation in the UK but that they had left settled accommodation which it was reasonable for them to occupy in Bangladesh and were intentionally homeless.

The Court of Appeal held that the authority was entitled to conclude that the accommodation in Bangladesh was settled. However, the decision letter did not show that it had properly carried out the balancing act between housing conditions in Tower Hamlets and the applicants' pattern of life. This would be a factor justifying the applicants' leaving accommodation in Bangladesh which it would otherwise be reasonable to expect them to continue to occupy. The court stated that 'the decision letter does not disclose as it should that the Council has considered the factors necessarily involved in deciding whether or not it is reasonable to expect [the applicant] to continue to occupy the settled accommodation available to him in Bangladesh'. For that reason, the decision was quashed.

T11.4A   *Waltham Forest LBC v Maloba*
[2007] EWCA Civ 1281, 4 December 2007 (see T8.10A)

Location of accommodation relevant to question of whether reasonable to continue to occupy

High Court

T11.5   *R v Hammersmith and Fulham LBC ex p Duro-Rama*
(1983) 9 HLR 71; (1983) 81 LGR 702, QBD

Employment prospects and loss of benefits relevant when considering reasonableness

Mr Duro-Rama was a Spanish national with a right of abode in the UK. He returned to the UK with his family after a period living in Spain as he could not find employment there and, under Spanish law, his entitlement to social security benefit lapsed. He had no other means of support. He was found intentionally homeless for leaving accommodation which the council considered to be reasonable for him to occupy. In deciding this, it limited its consideration of reasonableness to housing issues. It did not consider his lack of employment and loss of benefit as relevant matters.

Woolf J quashed the decision. In considering whether or not it is reasonable to continue to occupy accommodation, authorities are not limited to housing issues and can have regard to factors like employment prospects and loss of benefits in that locality. The matter was remitted to the council for reconsideration.

T11.6   **R v Kensington and Chelsea RLBC ex p Bayani (1990)**

(1990) 22 HLR 406, CA (see T37.8)

Sufficient enquiries made of applicant's financial circumstances in the Philippines

T11.7   **R v Newham LBC ex p Ajayi**

(1996) 28 HLR 25, QBD

Returning citizen needed to be considered in light of social history and national status

The applicant was a British citizen born in London. In May 1990 she left her parents' home in Nigeria and came to stay with her cousin. When her children arrived in December 1990 she was asked to leave and applied as a homeless person. The council found her intentionally homeless for leaving the accommodation in Nigeria.

Deputy Judge Sir Louis Blom-Cooper QC quashed the decision. He found that the council had failed to deal with the applicant fairly. The council's enquiries had treated the applicant as a newly arrived immigrant. There had been no proper consideration of her personal circumstances, her social history or her national status and the burden had, in effect, been cast on the applicant to show, unaided, that she was not intentionally homeless.

T12   *Violence/harassment*

The reference in s177(1) (see T7) to violence other than domestic violence was introduced by Homelessness Act 2002 s10. The impact of *Bond v Leicester CC* (T12.1) and these amendments is that, in cases of violence, the question is whether violence (which includes threats of violence which are likely to be carried out) is probable. If it is probable then it is not reasonable to continue to occupy accommodation. Cases with violence as an issue decided prior to the amendments introduced by Homelessness Act 2002 need to be considered in the light of these changes.

Court of Appeal

T12.1   *Bond v Leicester CC*

[2001] EWCA Civ 1544; [2002] HLR 6; (2001) *Times* 23 November, CA

For the purposes of s177(1) the sole question is whether violence is probable

Ms Bond was forced to leave two properties because of domestic violence from her former partner. She was then rehoused by a housing association. She resumed contact with her former partner but he assaulted her. She then excluded him from her home but he continued to harass her. She found the situation intolerable and fled the property. She later applied to the council as a homeless person. The council decided on review that she was intentionally homeless because she had failed to take any preventive measures, whether legal or practical, to stop the harassment. HHJ O'Rourke dismissed her s204 appeal. She appealed.

The Court of Appeal allowed the appeal. When considering whether it was reasonable to continue to occupy accommodation, the question of reasonableness was not at large in domestic violence cases. Section 177(1)

provided that it was not reasonable to continue to occupy accommodation if is was probable that this would lead to domestic violence. Hale LJ, giving the judgment of the court, held that:

> The only test is what is probable. This in my view is a pure question of fact, devoid of value judgements about what an applicant should or should not do. If there are measures which have been taken or probably will be taken which will probably prove effective in preventing actual or threatened violence, then that may reduce the level of risk below one of probability. But those are questions which the authority must ask themselves, rather than assume that such measures will be taken or will be effective if taken.

The council did not ask the right question and there was no finding that violence was 'not probable'. It followed that the council had erred in law. It was likely that if it had asked the right question it would have reached a different conclusion. The appropriate course was to vary the decision to one that Ms Bond had not become intentionally homeless.

T12.2 *R v Croydon LBC ex p Toth*
(1988) 20 HLR 576, CA

Applicant could reasonably have remained in accommodation by seeking police protection

Mrs Toth left her council property after being threatened by associates of her husband, who had disappeared and was being sought in relation to an armed robbery. She later applied to Croydon. It decided that she was intentionally homeless for leaving her accommodation, which she could reasonably have remained in by seeking police protection.

The Court of Appeal rejected her appeal. The council had applied the right test and the decision was not perverse. In the alternative, the appellant asserted that her former joint tenancy had continued (notwithstanding her departure) because it had not been surrendered. The council had found the flat empty apart from bags of rubbish, had taken possession by changing the locks and had re-let to another tenant. O'Connor LJ held that the facts established a surrender of the tenancy:

> In my judgment the evidence that this tenancy had been surrendered in law was overwhelming. A subsequent assertion by the tenant that she had no intention of leaving permanently is not relevant. One must look at the situation as at the time that the local authority accepted the surrender.

An argument that Mrs Toth acted in good faith in ignorance of a relevant fact – that by going she was losing her secure tenancy – was rejected. It was not a relevant fact but the legal result of the factual departure.

T12.3 *R v Greenwich LBC ex p Patterson*
(1994) 26 HLR 159, CA (see T31.6)

Mandatory duty to enquire into the risk of violence in another area

High Court

T12.4 *R v Newham LBC ex p McIlroy*
(1991) 23 HLR 570, QBD

Applicants could have stayed in accommodation pending an urgent transfer

Auld J upheld a finding of intentional homelessness against a family fleeing sectarian violence in Northern Ireland which had led to one of the
applicants being shot at. On the facts, the council was entitled to conclude that the family could have continued in their home or in temporary
accommodation in Belfast pending an urgent transfer application to the
Northern Ireland Housing Executive.

T12.5   *R (Hammia) v Wandsworth LBC*
[2005] EWHC 1127 (Admin); [2005] HLR 45 (see T40.7)

*Policy that former tenancy, which applicant fled because of violence, had to be
relinquished before she would be accepted as a homeless person unlawful*

T13   Threatened with homelessness: s175(4)

Court of Appeal

T13.1   *Dyson v Kerrier DC*
[1980] 1 WLR 1205; [1980] 3 All ER 313; (1980) 78 LGR 603, CA (see T27.5)

*There is no distinction in principle between the definition of homelessness and
threatened with homelessness, other than the 28-day requirement*

High Court

T13.2   *R v Newham LBC ex p Khan and Hussain*
(2001) 33 HLR 269; (2000) *Times* 9 May, QBD (see T14.8)

*Council could not merely do nothing when applicants were threatened with
homelessness*

T14   'Available' accommodation: s176

Accommodation must be available for occupation (s175(1)). This means
it must be practically and legally accessible as well as available within the
meaning of section 176:

> Accommodation shall be regarded as available for a person's occupation
> only if it is available for occupation by him together with-
> (a) any other person who normally resides with him as a member of his
>   family, or
> (b) any other person who might reasonably be expected to reside with
>   him.
> References in this Part to securing that accommodation is available for a
> person's occupation shall be construed accordingly.

Note that cases concerning the issue of 'dependent children' under
s189(1)(b) (T15–T16) may be relevant in determining whether accommodation is available under s176.

House of Lords

T14.1   *R v Hillingdon LBC ex p Islam*
[1983] 1 AC 688; [1981] 3 All ER 901; (1981) 1 HLR 107, HL (see T22.3)

The applicant's single room was not 'available' for him and his family and he could not be intentionally homeless when he lost it as a result of his family joining him

Court of Appeal

T14.2   *Begum (Nipa) v Tower Hamlets LBC*
[2000] QB 133; [2000] 1 WLR 306; (2000) 32 HLR 445; (1999) *Times* 9 November, CA

Accommodation not 'available' if applicant cannot afford to travel to it

Ms Begum, a British citizen, came to England in 1990 when she was aged 13 or 14. In 1993 she visited Bangladesh and married, but then returned to England without her husband, who was unable to obtain permission to enter the country. She later had a son. In 1997 she returned to Bangladesh with her son to spend time with her husband and stayed in her father-in-law's house. She returned to England when her son became ill and stayed with her brother-in-law until required to leave. She applied to the council as a homeless person. It decided that she was not homeless because her father-in-law's house in Bangladesh was accommodation which was available to her and which it was reasonable for her to occupy. The decision was confirmed on review. She appealed to the county court under s204 on the basis, inter alia, that there was no evidence that she could afford to travel to the accommodation in Bangladesh. HHJ Platt quashed the decision.

The Court of Appeal allowed the council's appeal. The judge at first instance was right in construing the words 'any point of law' which qualify the right of appeal to the county court in s204 as being wide enough to embrace any ground of challenge that would have been available in proceedings for judicial review (eg, procedural error, vires, irrationality or inadequacy of reasons). Such appeals are not limited to matters of legal interpretation. However, it was held that:

1) The judge was wrong to hold that accommodation had to have some degree of permanence before an authority could conclude that it would be reasonable to continue to occupy it under s175(3).
2) The case did not come within s175(2)(a). The condition in that subsection requiring a person to be able to secure entry to accommodation refers to some kind of physical bar to gaining entry at the premises themselves (eg, displacement by unlawful eviction, squatting and the like) and not to some difficulty, for whatever reason, of travelling to them.
3) On a proper construction, section 175(3) is relevant only to a person whose application is made *from* extant accommodation. Only then does the reasonableness of continued occupation arise (per Sedley and Stuart-Smith LJJ). (However, in practice it would be 'unreal' for an authority not to consider whether available accommodation, not occupied, is reasonable to occupy.)
4) The question of accessibility arises as an aspect of availability under s175(1) (whether an applicant has accommodation 'available for his occupation'). Accommodation must be legally and practically accessible (per Sedley and Stuart-Smith LJJ).
5) Ms Begum's financial ability to travel to the accommodation in Bangladesh was a relevant consideration in deciding whether or not the

accommodation was available to her. That question would usually involve the applicant being asked whether he or she could get to the accommodation. On the specific facts, the council had given Ms Begum
an opportunity at interview to put forward any such problems. If the
point about inability to travel was not raised by Ms Begum, the council's duty did not require it to investigate the matter. Similarly Ms
Begum did not raise the issue of her entitlement to return to live in
Bangladesh and the council did not fail to inquire into her entitlement
under the law of Bangladesh to live there.

6) The judge wrongly substituted his own view of whether the council's
decision was rational rather than considering whether, having made
the inquiries which a reasonable council would have made, the council
came to a conclusion which no reasonable council could have come
to. Its decision that she was not homeless was not erroneous on the
material before it.

See *Waltham Forest LBC v Maloba* (T8.10A) where it was held that accommodation, whether extant or not, had to be reasonable to occupy under
s175(3) (cf point 3 above).

T14.3   *R v Westminster CC ex p Bishop*
(1993) 25 HLR 459; (1993) 91 LGR 674, CA

*Council failed to consider whether accommodation 'available' for applicant's
daughter who feared living in the property and stayed with her grandmother*

The applicant fled her council flat following violence and harassment from
a former partner. Her daughter, who had already left the flat, was living
with relatives and was terrified to return because she had been harassed
and molested by drug-dealers and others. The council found the applicant
to be intentionally homeless. Its medical adviser had advised that there
was no reason why the child could not return.

Rose LJ, giving the judgment of the court, quashed the decision. The
council might have been entitled to hold that it was reasonable for the
applicant to continue to occupy the accommodation by securing the protection of an injunction but it had failed to consider properly whether she
had left accommodation 'available' to her daughter (Housing Act 1985 s75,
now Housing Act 1996 s176). The council could not rely solely on the
opinion of a medical adviser who had not seen the child and gave no reasoning for his opinion. Her position had not been properly considered.

Note: See now *Bond v Leicester CC* (T12.1) on injunctions.

High Court

T14.4   *R v Barking and Dagenham LBC ex p Okuneye*
(1996) 28 HLR 174, QBD

Authority entitled to decide not reasonable for applicant to reside with fiancé

The applicant left Nigeria in order to study in the UK. Her fiancé had also
previously left other accommodation in Nigeria to come to the UK. They
later began living together, married and had a child. On the applicant's
subsequent application for housing, the council found her intentionally

homeless for leaving her accommodation in Nigeria. She sought judicial review on the basis that the authority had failed to consider whether the accommodation in Nigeria would have been available for her to occupy together with her then fiancé.

Deputy Judge Sir Louis Blom-Cooper QC dismissed an application for judicial review. The authority was entitled to consider whether the applicants could reasonably be expected to reside together under Housing Act 1985 s75 (Housing Act 1996 s176) at the time of her departure from Nigeria. At that time it was entitled to regard them as single persons and not as an established family with expectations to reside together. The change in the applicant's circumstances (marriage and having a baby) did not break the chain of causation between departure from the settled accommodation and her homelessness. All the ingredients of Housing Act 1985 s60(1) (now Housing Act 1996 s191(1)) were in place to support that finding. There was no requirement to treat a betrothed any differently from any other single person.

T14.5   *R v Hackney LBC ex p Tonnicodi*
(1998) 30 HLR 916, QBD

Wrong test of 'available' applied regarding applicant's friend and companion

The applicant was disabled and lived with a companion. They became homeless. The applicant was accepted for the main housing duty but was only provided with accommodation for a single person. The council had simply asked whether or not the applicant was so disabled as to require a live-in carer.

Gerald Moriarty QC, sitting as a deputy High Court judge, quashed the council's decision because it had applied the wrong test. The correct approach was to ask whether it was reasonable for the applicant's friend to live with him either as a carer or as a faithful companion. Paragraph 5.3 of the then *Homelessness Code of Guidance* referred to both carers and companions as persons who might reasonably be expected to live with an applicant and, therefore, applicants might be owed a housing duty in relation to both themselves and their carers/companions. The council had misdirected itself.

T14.6   *R v Kensington and Chelsea RLBC ex p Kassam*
(1994) 26 HLR 455, QBD (see T38.13)

Authority had to consider whether applicant needed a live in carer and, if so, whether the applicant's current accommodation was available and reasonable

T14.7   *R v Lambeth LBC ex p Ly*
(1987) 19 HLR 51, QBD

It is for an authority to decide who might reasonably be expected to reside with applicant

The applicant, a 74-year-old Vietnamese refugee, lived in Vietnam with her son, daughter-in-law and their eight children. They became separated when fleeing Vietnam in 1978 but became reunited in 1985. At that time the rest of the family were living in temporary accommodation in Lambeth, where they had applied to be rehoused under a mobility scheme. For that purpose they had indicated that they were willing to be split into two units, with the four older children being rehoused separately. The applicant could not live with the family in their temporary accommodation and applied to Lambeth as a homeless person. Her application was accepted and, in discharge of duty, the applicant was offered a four-bedroomed property. The authority envisaged that she would live there with her four eldest grandchildren. The flat was about two miles away from the family's temporary accommodation. She refused the offer and contended that Lambeth were bound to offer accommodation for the whole of the family.

Simon Brown J dismissed her application for judicial review. The question of who was to be regarded as 'a person who might reasonably be expected to reside with' the applicant was a question of fact for the local authority. Many considerations came into play – the true nature and ambit of the family unit, blood relationships, and financial and emotional dependency. When the relationship in question was perhaps at the margin of a family group it may be appropriate to have regard to other matters such as the practicability of providing accommodation for everyone together, the possibility of splitting the family unit into smaller coherent groups, the geographical separation of such groups, their preparedness to be separated in this way and the history of the family in terms of their accommodation and separation over proceeding years. It was impossible to hold that the decision not to rehouse the applicant together with the ten other members of her family was perverse.

Note: Housing Act 1985 s75 contained only the second limb of the test of availability set out in Housing Act 1996. The question was solely whether a person might reasonably to be expected to reside with the applicant.

T14.8 *R v Newham LBC ex p Khan and Hussain*
(2001) 33 HLR 269; (2000) *Times* 9 May, QBD

Unlawful decision to 'split' two sisters who lived together with their families

The applicants were sisters. For many years they lived together with their husbands, children and their disabled mother in her house, which was held on an assured tenancy. The landlord obtained a 28-day possession order. Before it expired, the applicants applied to the council as homeless persons. The council accepted the applications and began enquiries but told the applicants to remain in possession until the bailiffs executed a warrant for possession. The applicants initially completed separate application forms but, before a decision was reached on either application, said that they wished to be rehoused together. The council refused this request and, in subsequently discharging its duties, treated the applicants as two separate households.

Collins J held that the decision to 'split' the family was unlawful. Housing Act 1996 s176 required that accommodation be secured not only for occupation by an applicant but also for 'any other person who normally resides with him as a member of his family'. On the facts, the decision that these applicants were not normally residing together as a family was irrational.

The applicants also challenged the advice to await the bailiffs. The council contended that it was justified in doing so because either: (1) the applicants were not 'homeless' until actually evicted and accordingly no duty to provide alternative accommodation was triggered before then under s188, or (2) they were homeless and were owed the s188 duty but that duty had been discharged by advice and assistance under s206(1)(c) to remain in the property. Collins J held that, until evicted by the bailiffs, the former assured tenant was not 'homeless'. Housing Act 1988 s5 restricted recovery of possession of an assured tenancy other than by court order and by CCR Ord 26 r17 an order for possession was only enforceable by warrant to be executed by bailiffs. The former assured tenant therefore occupied the accommodation by virtue of an enactment 'restricting the right of another person to recover possession' (Housing Act 1996 s175(1)(c)). The first instance decision in *R (Sacupima) v Newham LBC* (2000) QBD (subsequently varied on appeal, see T5.2) to contrary effect was per incuriam.

Until actual eviction, the applicants were 'threatened with homelessness' and not 'homeless'. Faced with an application based on threatened homelessness, the council had to take immediate steps under s184 to determine whether the applicant was eligible for assistance and what duty was owed. Where satisfied that the applicant was threatened with homelessness, eligible for assistance and in priority need, the duty to take steps to ensure that accommodation did not cease to be available arose under s195(2). The council could not remain inactive. Newham could not discharge the duty it thought it had owed by telling them to 'stay put' because s206(1)(c) could not be relied on where the advice being given was that the homeless applicants should remain homeless.

T14.9   *R v Peterborough CC ex p Carr*
(1990) 22 HLR 206, QBD

Accommodation not 'available' if applicant's partner could reasonably be expected to reside with her

The applicant was a young pregnant unmarried woman who became homeless on leaving her sister's house. Her departure was caused by the refusal of the sister to allow the applicant's partner (the prospective father) to move in.

The local authority's finding of intentional homelessness was quashed by Hutchison J. He said that the applicant could be intentionally homeless only if she had left accommodation 'available for her occupation' (Housing Act 1985 s60(1), now Housing Act 1996 s191(1)). This phrase was defined by s75 (now Housing Act 1996 s176) to mean accommodation available to both the applicant and any person with whom she might reasonably have been expected to reside. The authority had not addressed itself to this issue at all, having mistakenly thought that the question was whether the applicant and her boyfriend had usually resided together.

T15   **Priority need**

Housing Act 1996 s189 repeats the categories of priority need contained in the previous homelessness legislation:

(1) The following have a priority need for accommodation –
  (a) a pregnant woman or a person with whom she resides or might reasonably be expected to reside;
  (b) a person with whom dependent children reside or might reasonably be expected to reside;
  (c) a person who is vulnerable as a result of old age, mental illness or handicap or physical disability or other special reason, or with whom such a person resides or might reasonable be expected to reside;
  (d) a person who is homeless or threatened with homelessness as a result of an emergency such as flood, fire or other disaster.'

The categories of priority need were significantly extended by the Homelessness (Priority Need for Accommodation) (England) Order 2002 SI No 2051 to include:

- A child aged 16 or 17 (who is not a 'relevant child' nor owed a duty under Children Act 1989 s20);
- A person under 21 who at any time after reaching the age of 16, but while still under 18, was 'looked after, accommodated or fostered';
- A person aged 21 or over who is vulnerable as a result of having been 'looked after, accommodated or fostered'.
- A person who is vulnerable as a result of having been a member of Her Majesty's regular naval, military or air forces.
- A person who is vulnerable as a result of having served a custodial sentence or having been otherwise detained.
- A person who is vulnerable as a result of ceasing to occupy accommodation by reason of violence from another person or threats of violence which are likely to be carried out.

See also the Homeless Persons (Priority Need) (Wales) Order 2001 SI No 607 (W30) which is in similar, but not identical, terms.

Apart from the first two categories of the Order an applicant must be 'vulnerable' as a result of the specified reason, as for the categories in s189(1)(c). Note that the Order only confers priority need on the applicant and not on a person with whom he or she resides, as for s189(1)(a),(b) and (c). Therefore, it is that person who is required to make an application on behalf of a household if reliance is to be placed on his or her priority need.

T16   Dependent children

The Act does not contain a definition of 'dependent children'. The *Homelessness Code of Guidance* for England (published July 2006) suggests that an authority should treat as dependent 'all children under 16, and all children aged 16–18 who are in, or are about to begin, full-time education or training or who for other reasons are unable to support themselves and who live at home' (para 10.7).

House of Lords

T16.1   *R v Hillingdon LBC ex p Islam*
[1983] 1 AC 688; [1981] 3 All ER 901; (1981) 1 HLR 107, HL (see T22.3)

If children do reside with an applicant then the question of whether they can reasonably be expected to do so does not arise

T16.2   *R v Oldham MBC ex p Garlick*
[1993] AC 509, [1993] 2 WLR 609, [1993] 2 All ER 65; (1993) 25 HLR 319; (1993) 91 LGR 287, HL (also known as *R v Oldham MBC ex p G; R v Bexley LB ex p B*, see T34.1)

Dependent children do not qualify as being in priority need in their own right

Court of Appeal

T16.3   *Hackney LBC v Ekinci*
[2001] EWCA Civ 776; [2002] HLR 2; (2001) *Times* 24 July, CA

Applicant's 17-year-old wife was not a child dependent on him

Mr Ekinci applied to the council as a homeless person. His wife was 17 years old, in full-time education and dependent on him. He claimed priority need on the basis that she was a dependent child. HHJ Graham QC referred to the then current *Code of Guidance* (December 1996), which stated that dependent children need not necessarily be the applicant's own children and that children under 19 in full-time education may be treated as dependent. He held that the applicant's wife was a 'dependent child' within the meaning of s189(1)(b).

The Court of Appeal allowed the council's appeal. In the context of the Act as a whole, the priority created in s189(1)(b) was that based on the parent/child relationship. Mr Ekinci's wife was capable of being a dependent child in relation to her parents or someone in a quasi-parental position but could not be a dependent child in relation to her husband. Their relationship was outside the category of persons contemplated by s189(1)(b). Furthermore, there was no breach of ECHR article 8(1) in parliament enacting a scheme of priorities whereby applications for accommodation by homeless persons were to be determined by local housing authorities whose resources would inevitably be limited. In assessing priorities, parliament was entitled to take into account considerations such as vulnerability, which might or might not have an impact on family life, as well as those that inevitably did. Article 8(1) did not require applicants with child spouses to be given priority over applicants with adult spouses or over other categories of applicant.

Note: 16/17-year-olds are now in priority need by virtue of their age (see T15).

T16.4   *Holmes-Moorhouse v Richmond upon Thames LBC*
[2007] EWCA Civ 970; (2007) *Times* 19 November; 10 October 2007

Impact of shared residence orders on the determination of dependent children

The claimant lived with his partner and their children in her council house. In family court proceedings it was ordered, by consent, that he should leave that home and thereafter have shared residence with the three younger children. The children were to spend alternate weeks and half their school holidays with him. On his application as a homeless person, Richmond decided that the requirements of s189(1)(b) ('a person with whom dependent children reside or might reasonably be expected to reside') were not met and that the appellant did not have a priority need. That decision was upheld on review and HHJ Oppenheimer dismissed an appeal.

The Court of Appeal allowed a second appeal. It held that:

1) Because a residence order made in *contested* family proceedings may be determinative of a housing authority's obligations, the authority should (where appropriate) have notice of those proceedings.

2) A residence order made *by consent* in such proceedings did not bind the housing authority on the s189(1)(b) question but the fact that the child's parents had agreed arrangements would be a factor to be taken into account. If the authority decided that it was not reasonable to expect the child to live with the applicant, that applicant could return to the family court for a reconsideration of the consent order.

3) The authority could not have regard to the scarcity of its housing resources in determining whether it would be reasonable to expect a child to live with an applicant for s189(1)(b) purposes.

4) The size of accommodation secured may reflect the length of expected residence 'Cramped quarters may be suitable where residence is limited' [51].

5) Although the reviewing officer had taken account of the consent order and the *Code of Guidance*, there had been an error in eliding the concept of the child merely 'staying' with the appellant and 'shared residence'. Once a residence order had been made, even by consent, the child was 'residing' not simply 'staying'.

The review decision was quashed.

T16.5   *R v Kensington and Chelsea RLBC ex p Amarfio*
(1995) 27 HLR 543; (1995) 94 LGR 99, CA

Son on YTS not a dependent child; YTS course gainful employment

The applicant claimed to be in priority need by virtue of his 16-year-old son living with him. His son was on a two-year Youth Training Scheme (YTS) course. The council decided that he was not a 'dependent' child and that the applicant was consequently not in priority need. Sir Louis Blom-Cooper QC ((1994) 26 HLR 721, QBD) upheld the council's decision.

The Court of Appeal dismissed an appeal by the applicant. After considering the nature of a YTS course, it was held that this amounted to gainful employment and not full-time education or training. Whilst at first instance dependency was held to be limited to financial dependency this was doubted. There may be circumstances where 16- or 17-year-olds, although not financially dependent on their parents, may be sufficiently dependent on them in other ways to bring them within s59(1)(b). However, once a child had gone into full-time employment or the equivalent, he or she was not dependent on his parents.

Note: The son would now be in priority need by virtue of his age (see T15). See note to T34.1 regarding an application by the son.

T16.6   *R v Lambeth LBC ex p Vaglivello*
(1990) 22 HLR 392, CA

Child need not wholly and exclusively depend on and reside with applicant

Mr Vaglivello and the mother of his son were not married. They did not live together and led separate lives, but shared the care of their son equally. He spent three and a half days a week living with each parent. The mother claimed child benefit and other social security benefits in relation to their son. This arrangement had lasted for four years. Mr Vaglivello became homeless and applied to Lambeth as a homeless person. It informed Mr Vaglivello that he was not in priority need as 'your child has to be in your full time custody and [residing] with you permanently'.

The Court of Appeal found that the council had applied too stringent a test under Housing Act 1985 s59(1)(b) (now Housing Act 1996 s189(1)(b)). This required two matters to be established for priority need – the child must be dependent on and must reside with the applicant. The test does not require that a child be 'wholly and exclusively dependent' or 'wholly or exclusively residing only with one parent'. The decision was quashed.

T16.7   *R v Port Talbot BC ex p MacCarthy*
(1991) 23 HLR 207, CA

Council held to have implicitly considered the second limb of the dependent child test

The applicant and his ex-wife had joint custody of their children, with an order for care and control to the mother and reasonable access to him. They agreed that this would mean the children living with the applicant for three days each week and with the mother for four days, if the applicant had suitable accommodation. The applicant applied as a homeless person as he had no accommodation available for him and his children. The council decided that the children could not reasonably be expected to reside with the applicant and that one would usually expect the children to reside with the parent having care and control, in this case the mother. The applicant appealed, contending that the council had failed to consider the second limb of Housing Act 1985 s59(1)(b) (now Housing Act 1996 s189(1)(b)) – whether his children could reasonably be expected to reside with him.

The Court of Appeal, dismissing a renewed application for leave, held that, although the decision was not felicitously worded, the council had implicitly indicated that it had considered the second limb. Furthermore, the council was

> ... not obliged to assume that children should reside with two parents as a normal arrangement. They would be entitled to take into account that the children reside with one parent and visit the other parent. There may be exceptional circumstances where children might reside with both parents, but it would certainly be unlikely to be the normal arrangement. (Butler-Sloss LJ at p210)

High Court

T16.8   *R v Brent LBC ex p Sadiq*
(2001) 33 HLR 525; (2000) *Times* 27 July, QBD (see T41.4)

After deciding that applicant was in priority need, authority could not change its decision when applicant's child was ordered to live with his mother

T16.9   *R v Ealing LBC ex p Sidhu*
(1982) 2 HLR 45; (1982) 80 LGR 534, QBD (see T4.2)

Applicant whose children lived with her was in priority need despite not having a final custody order

T16.10 *R v Kingswood BC ex p Smith-Morse*
[1995] 2 FLR 137; (1994) *Times* 8 December, QBD

'Main' residence not the correct test; both limbs of s189(1)(b) test needed to be considered

Mr Smith-Morse and his wife were separated. They had a son who was living with both of them. Mr Smith-Morse applied to the council as a homeless person. In its decision letter the council stated that he did not have priority need as his son's 'main' residence was with his mother. The letter failed to deal with the second limb of the test – whether the child might reasonably be expected to reside with the applicant in future.

Deputy Judge Sir Louis Blom-Cooper QC quashed the council's decision on the grounds that (a) the reference to 'main' residence represented a misdirection of law: the question for the authority was whether his son resided with the applicant, not whether he mainly resided with the applicant and (b) if the first question was answered adversely to the applicant and his son was found not to reside with him, it was incumbent on the council to consider whether his son would in future reside with him. It was for the council and not the applicant to raise and consider the possible relevance of the second limb.

T16.11 *R v Oxford CC ex p Doyle*
(1998) 30 HLR 506, QBD

Applicant's children could not reasonably be expected to reside with him despite joint residence order

In proceedings between the applicant and his ex-partner, a joint residence order was made by consent. Under the terms of the order their four children, aged between 7 and 13, would reside with their mother from after school on Monday until after school on Thursday and with the applicant for the rest of the week (ie, three nights with the mother and four nights with the applicant). The applicant applied to the council as a homeless person but was found not to be in priority need.

His application for judicial review was dismissed. Although parts of a council report suggested that a wrong test had been considered (whether it was reasonable for the children to reside with the applicant), when considering the report as a whole the council had applied the right test in making its decision (whether the children could reasonably be expected to reside with the applicant, 'reasonably' qualifying the expectation rather than the residence). In reaching its decision the council had not overlooked the joint residence order and had not been unduly influenced by the housing stock crisis in its area.

T16.12 *R v Westminster CC ex p Bishop*
(1997) 29 HLR 546, QBD

Applicant's children were dependent on their mother and not the applicant

The applicant was the father of two children who lived with their mother. They arranged to have some shared care of the children. The council decided that his children were not dependent on him and gave as reasons that: they were adequately housed with their mother; they were not dependent on the applicant because of this and because the mother received income support and child benefit for them; the applicant did not have adequate financial means of supporting them as he was in receipt of income support as a single person.

Deputy Judge Robin Purchas QC dismissed an application for judicial review. He held that for the purposes of Housing Act 1985 s59(1)(b) (now Housing Act 1996 s189(1)(b)) the children needed, at least in some part, to be dependent on the applicant. The authority was entitled to take into account the matters stated in its reasons. It was not necessary for the homelessness officer to have put the reasons to the applicant for comment before making the decision. The existence of adequate housing with the mother and dependency on the mother were relevant to the question of whether the children resided with, or could reasonably be expected to reside with the applicant, rather than merely stay with him. The authority's conclusion that they were not resident was not perverse.

T17   ## Vulnerable

The Act does not contain a definition of vulnerability. The guidance given in *R v Camden LBC ex p Pereira* (T17.6), commonly referred to as the *Pereira* test, is: 'whether [an applicant] is, when homeless, less able to fend for himself than an ordinary homeless person so that injury or detriment to him will result when a less vulnerable man would be able to cope without harmful effects'. See also *Osmani v Camden LBC* (T17.5).

Court of Appeal

T17.1   ### *Aman v Camden LBC*

[2006] EWCA Civ 750; 11 May 2006

Applicant's competency relevant to the Pereira test which had been applied correctly

Mr Aman applied to Camden as a homeless person. It decided that he had no priority need as he was not vulnerable. It also decided that he was intentionally homeless. Both the decisions were confirmed on review. HHJ Ryland QC dismissed an appeal on the priority need point and allowed the appeal on the intentionality point. Mr Aman contended on a second appeal that the council had applied a narrower 'functional' test (considering matters other than his medical problems, such as his intelligence, literacy and ability to communicate) rather than the correct approach to vulnerability set out in *R v Camden LBC ex p Pereira* (T17.6).

The Court of Appeal dismissed a second appeal. Although Mr Aman's GP had expressed the opinion that homelessness would have a deleterious effect on each of his medical problems (chronic low back and shoulder pain, irritable bowel syndrome and depression), the question of whether he was vulnerable was for the council to answer. Both its initial and review decisions had set out the *Pereira* test correctly. The council had been entitled to take account of Mr Aman's eyesight, hearing, intelligence, literacy, ability to communicate and capacity to work, which were factors relevant to the composite question of whether he would be able to fend for himself if made homeless. That did not amount to the application of a test different from the *Pereira* test.

T17.2   *Bellouti v Wandsworth LBC*

[2005] EWCA Civ 602; [2005] HLR 46; 20 May 2005

Any doubt about the correct legal test to apply on vulnerability after Pereira *had been removed by* Osmani

The claimant was an Algerian national who had sought asylum in the UK. He applied to Wandsworth as a homeless person. On a medical form he identified his conditions as including: chronic backache, cramps, rheumatism, hand injury, reduced eyesight and depression. The council received written reports from his GP and a chartered psychologist and referred them to its own medical adviser (who did not examine the claimant or his medical records). It decided that the claimant did not have a priority need for accommodation. That decision was upheld on review. HHJ Zucker dismissed an appeal.

The Court of Appeal dismissed the claimant's second appeal. If, after the decisions in *R v Waveney DC ex p Bowers* (T17.8) or *R v Camden LBC ex p Pereira* (T17.6), there remained any doubt about the correct legal test to apply in deciding whether an applicant was 'vulnerable' within the meaning of Housing Act 1996 s189(1)(c), then Auld LJ's judgment in *Osmani v Camden LBC* (T17.5) had removed it. In the instant case the council had not misstated or misapplied the *Pereira* test. It did not matter whether a reviewing officer expressed his decision in terms of the applicant being at 'no greater risk of injury or detriment than the ordinary homeless person', or in terms of the applicant being no less able to fend for himself than the ordinary homeless person. These were simply two ways of saying the same thing. The use of the words 'peers' rather than 'the ordinary homeless person' did not indicate a misdirection. 'Peers' had been used in *Osmani*. In any event, in the context of the review decision letter as a whole it is plain that the reviewing officer was referring to the ordinary homeless person.

The council had not failed to make adequate enquiries. It was for the applicant to put forward the material on which he intended to rely in support of his assertion of priority need.

There was no procedural unfairness in not disclosing the medical adviser's final report to the claimant. There was no rule that an applicant should always have 'the last word' in respect of medical advice. Whether or not it is unfair will depend on the facts of the case. The council here had not taken into account factual material obtained from a third party, it merely referred material on which the applicant relied to its medical adviser for his comments. The to-ing and fro-ing between the council and the applicant's medical advisers had to stop somewhere.

T17.3   *Crossley v Westminster CC*

[2006] EWCA Civ 140; [2006] HLR 26; 23 Febuary 2006

Authority obliged to evaluate all facts that arguably gave rise to vulnerability; vulnerability and drug addiction

The claimant, a single man aged 36, spent his childhood in care and from the age of 17 lived 'on the streets', except when in prison or in short-term hostels. He had been addicted to hard drugs since the age of 13 and had a history of treatment and relapse. On one occasion, he overdosed and was saved by emergency hospitalization. He suffered with chronic depression, asthma and hepatitis C. He survived by begging, as he was unable to sustain a claim for welfare benefits owing to his difficulty in dealing with authorities. A drug outreach agency took him to Westminster's offices and helped him to make an application as a homeless person. The council provided interim accommodation and his engagement with drug treatment improved. Westminster then received medical advice that his physical condition did not make him less vulnerable than others on medical grounds and that he was not mentally ill. It decided that he was not vulnerable. The council withdrew interim accommodation, declined to provide accommodation pending review and upheld its decision on review. HHJ Collins CBE allowed an appeal under s204 and quashed the decision.

The Court of Appeal dismissed Westminster's appeal. The reviewing officer had had to consider not only vulnerability by reason of physical or mental illness or disability but also vulnerability resulting from 'any other special reason' (s189(1)(c)) and/or as a result of having been in care (Homelessness (Priority Need for Accommodation) (England) Order 2002 SI No 2051 article 5(1)). His decision letter failed to take into account and evaluate material facts, inter alia, those relating to the overdose incident and the claimant's inability to manage his affairs without assistance. The fact that the issue of vulnerability lay in a 'grey area' for the exercise of local authority judgment, so that a decision might quite properly go either way, made it all the more important that decisions were made 'with especially careful regard for the statutory criteria and purposes and conscientious attention to the evidence' (para [14]).

Sedley LJ, who gave the judgment of the court, went on to comment that there was an issue about whether the applicant's introduction at the age of 13 to hard drugs had to do with his period in care and, if so, whether his present state was in part a consquence of this. While drug addiction, by itself, cannot amount to a special reason for vulnerability, authorities should consider carefully whether there are other factors which make a drug addict vulnerable for a special reason. A special reason could be an applicant's vulnerability to relapse into drug use if street homeless. Another factor that could render an applicant vulnerable might be that he had spent a significant amount of time in care. When assessing whether an applicant is vulnerable as a result of more than one prescribed cause (here arguably having been in care and some other special reason) that produces a single set of effects, the effects should not be artificailly distributed between the causes in arriving at a decision on vulnerability.

T17.4   *Griffin v Westminster CC*

[2004] EWCA Civ 108; 28 January 2004

Reference to likelihood of harm in old Code of Guidance wrong

Mr Griffin applied to Westminster as a homeless person. He had alcohol problems and suffered from reactive depression. The council decided that he was not vulnerable and he requested a review. The reviewing officer stated that in assessing vulnerability he had to ask himself whether Mr Griffin, 'when homeless, would be less able to fend for [himself] than an ordinary homeless person so that injury or detriment to [him] would have resulted when a less vulnerable person would be able to cope without harmful effect'. After referring to *R v Camden LBC ex p Pereira* (T17.6), the reviewing officer found that Mr Griffin's medical condition was not sufficiently serious to conclude that he was vulnerable and he gave reasons for this decision.

Mr Griffin appealed on the ground that the *Code of Guidance* had not been applied correctly. Paragraph 8.13 of the code (published July 2002) referred to whether a person 'would be likely to suffer injury or detriment' whereas the test to be applied was whether 'injury or detriment to [him] would have resulted'. The words 'likely to' had been omitted from the reviewing officer's definition of vulnerability and he had asked a question which applied a higher hurdle for the applicant: *would* injury or detriment result. It was further contended that the code was correct in light of the judgment in *Pereira*. The appeal was allowed and Westminster appealed.

The Court of Appeal allowed the appeal. The reviewing officer had applied the right test as set out in *Pereira*. He knew that there would always be an element of uncertainty, but he had to reach his own assessment about what would happen. 'Would the claimant, when homeless, because of his reactive depression, be less well able to fend for himself than an ordinary homeless person so that he would suffer injury of detriment?' Detriment might include a significantly increased risk of suicide or of developing some serious ailment. That would have to be measured in percentage terms. The court should do nothing to add to the guidance already given by the statute and by *Pereira*.

Note: The *Code of Guidance* published in July 2006 omits the reference to 'likely' in the definition of vulnerability (paragraph 10.13).

T17.5   *Osmani v Camden LBC*

[2004] EWCA Civ 1706; [2005] HLR 22; 16 December 2004

Principles given for applying Pereira test of vulnerability; vulnerability must be considered on the assumption that the applicant is homeless

The claimant had mental health problems arising from his experiences in Kosovo. He applied to Camden as a homeless person. The council provided temporary accommodation and received medical reports about his condition. It decided, and confirmed on review, that he was not vulnerable. The decision letter stated that the reviewing officer had considered 'how your depression and post-traumatic stress disorder, back pain and limited English has affected you'. The claimant appealed, contending that the reviewing officer had misdirected herself by wrongly considering how his condition *presently* affected his abilities (ie, while in the temporary accommodation) rather than addressing how he would cope with homelessness (ie, if required to leave the temporary accommodation). HHJ Crawford Lindsay QC dismissed a s204 appeal.

The Court of Appeal dismissed an appeal. The reviewing officer went on, after the passage relied on by the applicant, clearly to indicate that she had considered the future risk of vulnerability *if* the applicant were to become homeless. There had been no misdirection. The decision reached was not perverse. In any event, the 'courts should indeed tread warily before they intervene' in such cases. The reasons given by the council were sufficient to sustain its decision. Auld LJ set out a number of principles to apply when assessing vulnerability:

1) The test for vulnerability set out in *Pereira* is a judicial guide to the interpretation and application of s189(1)(c) and should not be applied as if it were a statutory formulation.

2) It should be applied in its broad and immediate context: determining 'priority' between homeless persons and applying a scheme of social welfare conferring benefits at pubic expense on those identified as in such priority.

3) The scheme of the section is not to establish whether applicants are homeless but whether they have a priority need. It does this by defining a number of circumstances, one of which is vulnerability, by which a person may have a priority need.

4) The application of the *Pereira* test is an imprecise exercise and decisions on vulnerability are likely to be highly judgmental. Authorities are usually best placed to make such judgments.

5) The test does not impose a requirement that an applicant should be less able than a normal homeless person to fend for himself in finding accommodation.

6) The test is a single one of a homeless person's less than normal ability to fend for himself such that he will suffer more harm than would a normal homeless person – it requires a 'composite' assessment.

7) Vulnerability must be assessed on an assumption that a person is or will become street homeless, not on his ability to fend for himself while still housed. In this respect, regard should be had to the particular debilitating effects of depressive disorders and the fragility of those suffering from them if suddenly deprived of the prop of their own home (see *R v Newham LBC ex p Lumley* (T48.3)) .

8) Although authorities should look for and pay close regard to medical evidence, it is for an authority to determine whether an applicant is vulnerable.

9) Reasons should be given for decisions. The reasons should be sufficient to enable an applicant to form a view on whether to challenge it on a point of law. However, decision letters should not be treated as if they were statutes and subjected to 'pedantic exegesis'. When looking for the reasoning in a letter it should be read as a whole to get its full sense.

Auld LJ also observed that '... the main focus of attention on a second appeal ... should be on the decision of the Council rather than of the County Court Judge on appeal from it'. [34]

A petition seeking leave to appeal to the House of Lords was dismissed.

T17.6   ## *R v Camden LBC ex p Pereira*
(1999) 31 HLR 317, CA

Guidance on the meaning of 'vulnerability'

The applicant was 42 and had a long history of drug use and criminal offending. By the time he applied to Camden as a homeless person, he had been drug-free for 18 months. He claimed to be vulnerable on the basis that he was psychiatrically impaired and, as a former drug addict, was liable to relapse if living in the company of drug users and needed suitable accommodation to prevent this. He sought judicial review of the council's decision that he was not vulnerable. Tucker J rejected his application.

The Court of Appeal allowed his appeal. Camden's decision had relied heavily on its assessment that Mr Pereira was able to find accommodation as well as any other person. It had applied the test of vulnerability in *R v Westminster CC ex p Ortiz* (1995) 27 HLR 364, CA, which required an applicant to surmount two hurdles: first, to show that to some material extent he was less able to obtain suitable accommodation than the ordinary person and second, that if he failed to obtain accommodation he would suffer more than most. The requirement for an applicant to be less able to obtain accommodation was incorrect. The correct approach was for the council to ask itself 'whether [an applicant] is, when homeless, less able to fend for himself than an ordinary homeless person so that injury or detriment to him will result when a less vulnerable man would be able to cope without harmful effects'.

A particular inability of a person to obtain accommodation can be an aspect of his inability as a homeless person to fend for himself. However, it is still necessary to assess whether in all the circumstances the applicant's inability to cope comes within s59(1)(c). It must appear that their inability to fend for themselves whilst homeless will result in injury or detriment which would not be suffered by an ordinary homeless person who was able to cope. The assessment is a composite one but there must be the risk of injury or detriment for a person to be vulnerable. (The dicta in *R v Lambeth LBC ex p Carroll* (T17.12) which might be thought to suggest a different approach, should not be followed.)

T17.7   *R v Kensington and Chelsea RLBC ex p Kihara*
(1997) 29 HLR 147, CA

'Other special reason' a free standing category; destitute asylum-seekers vulnerable

The four separate applicants arrived in the UK in February and March 1996. They all claimed asylum 'in country' rather than at their port of entry to the UK. As a result of changes in regulations they were unable to claim benefits. All were destitute, had no support in the UK and were prohibited from taking employment. Most were unable to speak English. They applied for accommodation as homeless people. Although at that time they were eligible for assistance, the various councils decided that they were not in priority need. At first instance, Popplewell J held that all the applicants were plainly 'vulnerable' but that, as a matter of construction of the statute, the councils were entitled to be satisfied that destitution was not within the category 'other special reason' in Housing Act 1985 s59(1)(c) (now Housing Act 1996 s189(1)(c)). The words 'other special reason' had to be construed ejusdem generis with the words that went before – old age, mental illness or physical disability – and needed to be of the same genus.

The Court of Appeal allowed the applicants' appeals, holding that the words 'vulnerable as a result of ... other special reason' introduced a free-standing category which is not restricted by the other specified categories of vulnerability. Although the word 'reason' is in the singular a combination of circumstances could be looked at. The word 'special' indicates that the difficulties faced must be of 'an unusual degree of gravity, and are such to differentiate the applicant from other homeless persons'.

The words 'other special reason' permitted an examination of all the personal circumstances of the applicants. While financial impecuniosity *by itself* is not a 'special' reason, these applicants – who were literally homeless and had no income, no capital, no family or friends, no opportunity to work and, in some cases, no English – were plainly vulnerable for an 'other special reason'.

T17.8   *R v Waveney DC ex p Bowers*

[1982] 3 WLR 661; [1983] QB 238; [1982] 3 All ER 727; (1982) 4 HLR 118; (1982) 80 LGR 721, CA

Alcoholic applicant's brain injury an important factor in his vulnerability rendering him in priority need for a prescribed reason

Mr Bowers was a 59-year-old man who had been staying in a night shelter in Lowestoft, on a night by night basis. He suffered from alcoholism and later had a serious head injury which left him in a disorientated and confused state at times. He applied to the council as a homeless person. The evidence referred to 'a serious head injury with some persistent disability made worse by his drinking habits' and the need for support or sheltered accommodation. The council decided that he was not homeless and not in priority need. The homeless decision was overturned at first instance but not the priority need decision.

The Court of Appeal held that 'vulnerable' means 'less able to fend for oneself so that injury or detriment will result when a less vulnerable man would be able to cope without harmful effects'. The correct approach is first to ask whether there is vulnerability and, if so, to ask whether the vulnerability arises from those matters which are set out within the prescribed categories. Vulnerability may not arise from any single one category but may arise from a combination of them. Whether the brain injury is described as mental handicap or 'other special reason' is immaterial. It was important to draw a distinction between those cases caused solely by problems of drink, where the case will not usually come within priority need, and the applicant's case, where an accident causing brain injury to a man of 59 has become an important factor. The decision was varied to one of priority need.

T17.9   *Shala v Birmingham CC*

[2007] EWCA Civ 624; 27 June 2007

Guidelines on use of medical advisers by an authority

The claimants were Kosovan refugees. They had lost contact with three of their daughters in Kosovo, but reached the UK with their adult children. On the withdrawal of their NASS accommodation, they applied to Birmingham as homeless persons. The council decided that they did not have a priority need by virtue of Mrs Shala's mental illness. The claimants requested a review and supplied medical evidence of her depression. Her consultant psychiatrist diagnosed post-traumatic stress disorder. Her

GP reported that she was on high dose anti-depressants, was mentally unstable, had nightmares, flashbacks and was self-neglecting. The council commissioned medical advice from the organisation NowMedical that was provided by Dr John Keen. He did not examine Mrs Shala nor speak with her doctor or specialists. A decision that she was not 'vulnerable' was upheld on review and on appeal by HHJ McKenna.

The Court of Appeal allowed a second appeal. The reviewing officer had wrongly failed to take account of one medical report and had been plainly wrong to consider that another added nothing. The decision was quashed. The court went on to provide the guidance on the use of medical advisers.

1) Although an authority may take specialist advice about medical evidence, care has to be taken not to appear to be using professional medical advisers simply to provide or shore up reasons for a negative decision.

2) Where an authority's medical adviser is not a qualified psychiatrist, an authority weighing his or her comments against that of a qualified psychiatrist must not fall into the trap of thinking that it is comparing like with like.

3) The authority's adviser has the function of enabling it to understand the medical issues and to evaluate for itself the expert evidence. In the absence of an examination of the patient, the authority's medical adviser's advice cannot itself constitute expert evidence of an applicant's condition. The authority needs to take any absence of an examination of the applicant into account.

4) Where an authority's medical adviser does not examine an applicant he or she may speak to the applicant's medical adviser about matters which need discussion. It might be thought that Dr Keen would have been helped by discussing with the applicant's doctors just how depressed she was (the applicant's doctor's epithet 'quite' depressed had a sizeable range of meaning) and whether the anti-depressant dosage prescribed for her reflected only moderate depression or was conditioned by factors such as her being concomitantly on other medication or a disinclination of the practitioner to over-prescribe. The discussion should be informal and only an agreed minute of it should become part of the case materials.

T17.10 **Tetteh v Kingston upon Thames RLBC**
[2004] EWCA Civ 1775; [2005] HLR 21; 15 December 2004

Authority not required to set out the characteristics of the ordinary homeless person comparator

The claimant applied as a homeless person while serving custodial sentences for drug offences. His application indicated that he had no medical problems but that, although he had overcome his drug habit while in prison, he was at risk of relapsing into drug abuse if homeless on release. The council confirmed on review its decision that he was not vulnerable. His appeal to the county court was dismissed.

The Court of Appeal dismissed a second appeal. The authority had correctly stated and applied the 'test' for vulnerability as set out in *R v Camden LBC ex p Pereira* (T17.6). It was not required to set out the characteristics of the 'ordinary homeless person' whom it had used as a comparator as it had wide experience of such persons; nor was it required to identify what (if any) specific risk of injury or detriment to the applicant it had identified. Failure to mention in terms any possible injury or detriment which the applicant might suffer did not mean that those matters had not been properly considered. Although the council had not interviewed the applicant before notifying him of the negative decision, the statute did not require an interview to be conducted in all cases; nor did it require an authority to notify an applicant, in advance, of its likely decision or the grounds on which it was likely to be based.

High Court

T17.11   *Khelassi v Brent LBC*
[2006] EWCA Civ 1825; 7 December 2006,

Authority had not properly dealt with the conflicting medical evidence

The applicant applied to Brent as a homeless person. It decided that he was not vulnerable and not otherwise in priority need. He requested a review. The council had a report from his GP stating that he was suffering from anxiety, depression and that his homelessness was aggravating his psychological condition. The applicant also had reports from psychiatrists, including a consultant psychiatrist, Dr Steadman, who found that there was a serious suicide risk, that the applicant had symptoms of post-traumatic stress disorder and that there was a substantial risk of his psychological condition worsening if he were homeless. The council obtained a report from Dr Keen who examined the applicant. Dr Keen was not a psychiatrist. He considered that the applicant was suffering from reactive depression and that his condition was not substantial. He remarked that his assessment broadly concurred with that of Dr Steadman. The council confirmed its decision that the applicant was not vulnerable on review. The claimant successfully appealed to the county court. The judge held:

> It is, in my judgment, really inconceivable that the local authority would have preferred the opinion of a non-specialist, non-treating doctor to [the applicant's] body of evidence. It would have been wholly irrational to do so ... On the central question of vulnerability and suicide risk it is, in my judgment, clear that the sharp difference of opinion between Dr Keen and Dr Steadman still existed ... The decision letter does not ... grapple properly with this important difference. There is no adequate consideration of the substantial body of psychiatric evidence which had been obtained ... in my judgment, a decision to proceed on the basis of Dr Keen's report, setting effectively aside the existing psychiatric evidence without making any further enquiry of treating psychiatrists, was out with the standard of any reasonable decision maker.

The Court of Appeal refused the council's application for permission to bring a second appeal as it raised no important point of principle or practice. The judge had not suggested that there was a general principle that in every case of mental illness an authority had to commission a psychiatric report rather than rely on a general medical adviser. All he had said was that a more authoritative opinion had been required in this particular case.

T17.12 **R v Lambeth LBC ex p Carroll**
(1988) 20 HLR 142, QBD

An authority should not merely adopt a medical officer's opinion on the issue of vulnerability

Mr Carroll was a single man in his late forties. The local authority referred the question of whether or not he was vulnerable to the council's medical officer. This was in accordance with the council's then procedure, which was to refer questions of vulnerability to a doctor who, without seeing the applicant, would make a recommendation which the authority would automatically accept. The medical officer did not see Mr Carroll but made enquiries of his GP, who had not seen the applicant for eight months, and decided that he was not vulnerable. After the applicant's legal advisers had obtained a medical report, there were two further assessments by another medical officer, but she refused to alter the earlier decision and the council accepted her decision.

Webster J held that 'vulnerable' means less able to fend for oneself when homeless or in finding and keeping accommodation. Although it is proper for a local authority to consider medical opinion, the question of whether or not someone is vulnerable for 'some other special reason' is to be answered by the authority itself, not by the medical adviser. The council is therefore obliged to consider any other available evidence and make whatever appropriate enquiries are necessary beyond obtaining its own officer's opinion. The decision was quashed.

Note: In *R v Camden LBC ex p Pereira* (T17.6) the Court of Appeal adopted a different test of vulnerability and held that to that extent that *Carroll* was wrong.

T17.13 **R (Ghandali) v Ealing LBC**
[2006] EWHC 1859 (Admin); 11 July 2006
Council's medical adviser's decision irrational

T17.14 **R (Maali) v Lambeth LBC**
[2003] EWHC 2231 (Admin); [2004] HLR 12 (see S1.14)
Medical assessment of need irrational

County courts

T17.15 **Benson v Lewisham LBC**
October 2007 *Legal Action* 26; 2 July 2007, Central London County Court
Inadequate enquiries made regarding single man with health problems

Mr Benson applied for homelessness assistance while street homeless. He was aged 53 with a history of asthma, arthritis, gout, depression, alcohol dependency and high blood pressure. In addition to completing the council's medical form, he supplied letters and records from his GP, his hospital and his psychiatrist (the latter expressly stating that his street homelessness had resulted in him becoming increasingly vulnerable). The council's in-house medical adviser (IMA) met Mr Benson, reviewed his medical evidence, and advised that, whether taken separately or together, none of his problems '... impede his reasonable function ...'. On review, the council upheld a decision that Mr Benson did not have priority need by virtue of vulnerability.

HHJ Ryland allowed an appeal and varied the decision to one that Mr Benson did have priority need. He held that:-

1) the original decision taker had failed to make adequate enquiries of the GP, hospital or psychiatrist and had failed to provide a reasoned explanation for preferring the IMA's opinion;
2) the IMA had failed to provide adequate reasons for departing in her advice from the body of medical evidence before her;
3) the initial decision and review decision could fairly be described as simply 'rubber stamping' the IMA's opinion;
4) the reviewing officer ought to have appreciated that the 'minded-to' procedure in reg 8(2) of the Review Procedures regulations had been triggered by the inadequacy of the original decision;
5) the reviewing officer had himself failed to make adequate enquiries;
6) the IMA had considered discretely each of Mr Benson's conditions without making the composite assessment required by *Crossley v Westminster CC* (T17.3)
7) on the available material the only rational conclusion was that there was a priority need.

Scottish courts

T17.16 **Kelly v Monklands DC**
1985 SLT 165, Court of Session (Outer House)

Decision that 16-year-old not vulnerable perverse

A 16-year-old made an application to the local authority as a homeless person. She said that she had left home as a result of assaults by her father and that she had no capital. The local authority decided that she was not vulnerable.

Lord Ross held that, to demonstrate that an individual was 'vulnerable', it was enough to show that she was less able to fend for herself, giving rise to a risk of harm and sexual or financial exploitation. It is not necessary to demonstrate actual exploitation. The decision that she was not vulnerable was one which no reasonable local authority could have reached.

T17.17 **Wilson v Nithsdale DC**
[1992] SLT 1131, Court of Session (Outer House)

Compared with normal homeless person applicant vulnerable for some other special reason

Since being excluded from her parental home the applicant, who was 18, had been in transient accommodation and had been sexually assaulted. She was anxious and unable to cope on the streets and at risk of further sexual exploitation. The council decided that she was not in priority need, but failed to give reasons for their decision. The applicant asserted that she was vulnerable for some 'other special reason'.

Having considered *R v Waveney DC ex p Bowers* (T17.8), Lord Prosser held that vulnerability was to be measured by comparing the position of the applicant with others:

The comparison must, in my view, be with some assumed average or normal or run-of-the-mill homeless person ... if there is a lesser ability to fend for oneself, against that comparison, in a housing context, so that injury or detriment would result when such an ordinary homeless person would be able to cope without harmful effects, then in my opinion vulnerability for special reason is established for the purposes of the Act, and nothing more special (far less anything odd or exceptional) is required. (1992 SLT at p1134)

The council had failed to make the enquiries necessary to apply that test properly and, together with the failure to provide reasons, these were grounds for quashing the decision.

Note: This decision was cited with apparent approval by Neil LJ in *R v Kensington and Chelsea RLBC ex p Kihara* (T17.7).

T18   ## Homeless as a result of an emergency

Court of Appeal

T18.1   *Higgs v Brighton and Hove CC*
[2003] EWCA Civ 895; [2003] 3 All ER 753; [2003] 1 WLR 2241; [2004] HLR 2; (2003) *Times* 11 July; 30 June 2003

Disappearance of caravan in which applicant lived 'an emergency' and 'a disaster'

Mr Higgs lived in a caravan. He parked it without legal authority in Hove Park. The council served a notice directing him to move it but he did not do so. The council then issued magistrates' court proceedings against him under Criminal Justice and Public Order Act 1994. A few days before the hearing Mr Higgs returned to find that the caravan and all his possessions inside it had disappeared. He applied to the council as a homeless person. It decided that he was homeless but that he did not have a priority need and confirmed this decision on review. Mr Higgs appealed contending that he had priority because he was 'homeless ... as a result of an emergency such as a flood, fire or other disaster' (Housing Act 1996 s189(1)(d)). His appeal was dismissed on the basis that although the disappearance of the caravan was a 'disaster', it was not an emergency which caused homelessness for the purposes of s189(1)(d) (*R v Bristol CC ex p Bradic* (T18.3).

The Court of Appeal held that the loss of Mr Higgs' home was a disaster – he did not have to show that he had lost his home through some physical disaster. The loss of his caravan was also an emergency under s189(1)(d). The phrase 'emergency such as a flood, fire or other disaster' involved the sudden and wholly unexpected loss of the home in circumstances outside his control. However, the court held that he was not homeless as a result of the loss of his caravan, as required by s189(1)(d), because he was already homeless under Housing Act 1996 s175(2)(b) as he had no place he was entitled to place his caravan. His homelessness was caused by whatever circumstances led him to be living in a caravan which he had no right to park anywhere. The supervening event of the loss of the caravan did not change his status as a homeless person.

T18.2 *Noble v South Herefordshire DC*
(1985) 17 HLR 80, CA

The words 'or other disaster' denote disasters similar to flood or fire; demolition order not a qualifying emergency

Sometime before 1983 a demolition order was made. The applicants became weekly tenants of the property in 1984. Later the local authority took steps to enforce the demolition order. As a result, the applicants applied to the council as homeless persons. The council decided that they were not in priority need because a demolition order was not 'an emergency such as a flood, fire or any other disaster'. The applicants sought judicial review.

Their renewed application for leave was dismissed. The Court of Appeal held that the words 'or other disaster' denote disasters similar to flood or fire. A demolition order is not a qualifying emergency.

T18.3 *R v Bristol CC ex p Bradic*
(1995) 27 HLR 584; (1995) 94 LGR 257, CA

Person unlawfully evicted not homeless 'as a result of an emergency'

The applicant, a healthy single man, returned to his privately rented flat to find that he had been unlawfully evicted, the locks changed and his possessions placed outside. On his application as a homeless person, the council decided that his homelessness was not an 'emergency' within Housing Act 1985 s59(1)(d) (now Housing Act 1996 s189(1)(d)) because an illegal eviction was not a 'disaster'. In judicial review proceedings the council asserted that the provision covered only the forms of emergency similar to fire, flood or other natural disaster, ie, those which were 'communal' in nature in that they were experienced by more than one household.

Reversing the decision of Sir Louis Blom-Cooper QC (see (1995) 27 HLR 398, QBD), the Court of Appeal held that a person made homeless by an unlawful eviction is not homeless 'as a result of an emergency' within s59(1)(d). The word 'emergency' is qualified by the phrase 'such as flood, fire or other disaster'. However, emergencies giving rise to priority need are not limited to those with 'natural' causes. Fires or floods caused by humans can give rise to priority need, but there must be physical damage which causes the accommodation to be uninhabitable.

High Court

T18.4 *R v Hillingdon LBC ex p Bax*
December 1992 *Legal Action* 21, QBD (see T6.4)

Houseboat owner without permanent mooring not homeless before boat destroyed

T19 **16/17-year-olds**

Court of Appeal

T19.1 *R (M) v Hammersmith and Fulham LBC*
[2006] EWCA Civ 917; [2007] HLR 6; (2006) 9 CCLR 418; [2007] 1 FLR 256; [2007] LGR 127; 5 July 2006

Authority correctly accepted application from 17-year-old under Part VII; no error in failing to recognise Children Act s20 duty made out

M was a young woman with an unsettled childhood. By 15 she was excluded from school for a year. At 16 she was arrested for robbery and threats to kill. In April 2006 M's mother felt unable to cope with her behaviour and excluded her from the family home. She had nowhere else to live and approached the council, a unitary authority, for assistance. An application was taken under Housing Act 1996 Part VII and she was placed in interim accommodation under s188 while the council made enquiries into her application. M failed to co-operate with the enquiries and some months later was detained in custody by a criminal court. She was not due for release until after she was 18. By this time she was pregnant. Before her release she sought judicial review of the council's prior decision to take an application from her under Part VII, contending that, as a social services authority, the council should have recognised that she was a child in need to whom it owed a duty to accommodate under Children Act 1989 s20. (This would have had the advantage that she would then be regarded as a 'former relevant child' and be entitled to assistance under Children Act 1989 s23C.)

The Court of Appeal dismissed her appeal. It held that:

1) M had not been provided with accommodation in the exercise of any functions under the Children Act 1989, and thus could not be a 'former relevant child'.

2) Whether a child is a 'child in need' is a mixed question of fact and law. M had approached the council seeking accommodation. She had not been in care and was not unwell or disabled. It was entitled to treat her under Housing Act 1996 and was not required to treat her as a 'child in need' under Children Act 1989 s17 or to accommodate her under s20.

3) Under Housing Act 1996 s188 the council had a duty to arrange accommodation for M if it had reason to believe she might be homeless, eligible and in priority need. The council plainly had reason to believe that M was a person with an apparent priority need under the Homelessness (Priority Need for Accommodation) England Order 2002 article 3. The s188 duty must be performed at once. The council was then under a duty to investigate M's circumstances in order to ascertain whether it had a longer-term duty to house her.

4) Every homeless 16- or 17-year-old who approaches the council's housing department should, except where the child is known to have been in care already, be accommodated under s188 pending enquiries. They should not be turned away from a housing authority to seek assistance from social services.

5) If during the course of its enquiries the council identifies factors which indicate that the child is a 'child in need' it must refer him or her to social services to determine whether a duty is owed under the Children Act 1989.

T19.2   *R (S) v Sutton LBC*

[2007] EWCA Civ 790; 26 July 2007 (see U4.5)

Social services owed girl duty under Children Act 1989 s20 on her release from
prison and should not have advised her to make Part VII application

T19.3 **Robinson v Hammersmith and Fulham LBC**
[2006] EWCA Civ 1122; [2006] 1 WLR. 3295;[2007] HLR 7; [2006] LGR 822; (2006)
Times 5 September; 28 July 2006

Not lawful to postpone making decision until after an applicant turned 18;
mediation is independent of the enquiry process and not a reason to delay a
decision

On 17 February 2005 the applicant's mother excluded her from her home.
She was aged 17 and due to turn 18 on 11 March 2005. She applied to the
council as a homeless person. She was told that there was no point making an application because it would take 28 days for enquiries to be made
and by that time she would no longer have a priority need. She returned
the next day, having sought assistance from a law centre, and was placed
in interim accommodation. The council phoned her mother who said that
she could not return home but that she was prepared to engage in mediation. However, she later refused to do so. On 10 March 2005 the council
informed the applicant by telephone that she did not have a priority need
and that was confirmed in a written decision with reasons given on 11
March 2005. On 10 May 2005 the council upheld its decision on review.
An appeal to the county court was dismissed on the basis that, although
the applicant was 17 at the time of the decision, *Mohamed v Hammersmith*
and Fulham LBC (T31.2) required the reviewing officer to consider the
circumstances at the time of the review, by which time the applicant was
18.

The Court of Appeal allowed a second appeal. It held:

1) A decision was not necessarily made at the same time as notification
   of reasons. The council's decision had been made on 10 March 2005
   when the applicant was 17.
2) The decision was unlawful because, on that date, the applicant was 17
   (even if only one day short of 18) and was therefore in priority need
   under the Homelessness (Priority Need for Accommodation) (England) Order 2002 SI No 2051 article 3.
3) *Mohamed* did not apply where an unlawful original decision was made
   which denied rights to an applicant. On review, the original decision
   should have been recognised as unlawful and a decision made to restore to the applicant the rights she would have been entitled to if it had
   been lawful.
4) Where an application is taken from someone who is under 18 and who
   turns 18 before reasonable enquiries are completed and a decision
   made, the decision can take account of the fact that the applicant is
   then 18. It is, however, unlawful to postpone decision-making on the
   basis that by doing so the applicant will turn 18.
5) Mediation is independent of the enquiry process. An authority has
   no power to defer making enquiries on the ground that mediation is
   pending if that would deny the applicant any rights they would otherwise have. In such situations the authority must accept a duty and may
   use mediation to fulfil that duty.

Local government ombudsman

T19.4 *Complaint against South Tyneside Council*
Investigation Report No 04/C/18995, 12 December 2005

Maladministration where council delayed taking application from 17-year-old

The complainant, when aged 17, attended the council's offices to apply for accommodation. The council accepted that he had stated that he had been 'thrown out of' his parental home. He was given a form to complete to join the council's housing allocation scheme but was not given a homelessness application form or provided with any interim accommodation. No enquiry was made into his circumstances and his application for allocation was not even logged on the council's computer for two months. He slept at friends' houses. As he had heard nothing, he returned to the council's offices but was told that because he had by then turned 18 he no longer had a priority need.

The local government ombudsman found maladministration causing injustice. The council agreed to pay £2,000 in compensation and to review its housing services for young people.

T20   Looked after, accommodated or fostered

Court of Appeal

T20.1 *R (S) v Sutton LBC*
[2007] EWCA Civ 790; 26 July 2007 (see U4.5)

Social services owed claimant a duty under s20 on her release from prison

T20.2 *Southwark LBC v D*
[2007] EWCA Civ 182; (2007) 10 CCLR 280; 7 March 2007 (see U4.6)

Fostering arrangement was made under Children Act s23; as soon as duty to accommodate under s20 arose girl 'looked after' despite being accommodated with family friend

High Court

T20.3 *H, Barhanu, B v Wandsworth LBC, Hackney LBC, Islington LBC*
[2007] EWHC 1082 (Admin); (2007) 10 CCLR 439; [2007] 2 FCR 378; 23 April 2007 (see U4.7)

Council had provided services to children under s20 despite labelling it as under s17 and the children had been 'looked after'

T20.4 *R (Behre and Others) v Hillingdon LBC*
[2003] EWHC 2075 (Admin); (2003) 6 CCLR 471; (2003) *Times* 22 September; 29 August 2003 (see U4.12)

Unaccompanied asylum-seekers had been 'looked after' when provided with accommodation by social services and when they turned 18 were in priority need

T20.5 *R (L) v Nottinghamshire CC*
[2007] EWHC (Admin); 26 September 2007 (see U4.15)

Child accommodated under s20 despite social services' assertion it was under s17

T21 **Intentional homelessness**

Section 191 defines intentional homelessness:

(1) A person becomes homeless intentionally if he deliberately does or fails to do anything in consequence of which he ceases to occupy accommodation which is available for his occupation and which it would have been reasonable for him to continue to occupy.

(2) For the purposes of subsection (1) an act or omission in good faith on the part of a person who was unaware of any relevant fact shall not be treated as deliberate.

Subsection 191(3) deals with collusive arrangements to become homeless. It has little, if any, practical effect over and above s191(1). Section 196 defines becoming threatened with homelessness intentionally.

The combined effect of s191(1)–(2) is that a person is intentionally homeless if he or she has:

1) deliberately done/failed to do something, other than in good faith in ignorance of a relevant fact,
2) which caused the loss of accommodation
3) which the applicant ceased to occupy, and
4) which was available, and
5) which it would have been reasonable to continue to occupy.

Where the relevant acts relied on are not the direct acts of the applicant, the issue of whether he or she nevertheless acquiesced in those acts needs to be considered (see T26).

Until *R v Brent LBC ex p Awua* (T22.2) case-law had developed the principle, which was reflected in the *Code of Guidance*, that the accommodation lost had to have been 'settled' accommodation. This is no longer the case – any accommodation, properly so called, can result in intentionality when lost. Settled accommodation, however, remains relevant to the question of whether an act is causative of homelessness – the 'chain of causation' being broken by an applicant obtaining settled accommodation. In dealing with the question of intentional homelessness, a local authority is entitled to look back to the applicant's last 'settled' accommodation (see *Din v Wandsworth LBC* (T22.1)

Since Housing Act 1996 a person is not homeless if they have accommodation in the UK or elsewhere. Therefore issues arising from an applicant having left accommodation which is available abroad will now generally be dealt with under the question of whether an applicant is homeless (T3).

T22 **General**

House of Lords

T22.1 *Din v Wandsworth LBC*
[1983] 1 AC 657; [1981] 3 WLR 918; [1981] 3 All ER 881; (1982) 1 HLR 73, HL

Material date for determining intentional homlessness is date accommodation is left; when considerig intentionality an authority must look back to last period of settled accommodation

Mr and Mrs Din rented a flat. They fell into arrears with their rent and rates and so sought advice from Wandsworth. They were informed that the council could not assist them until a possession order had been made. Mr and Mrs Din then received a distress warrant for rates and, alarmed by this, moved out into temporary accommodation with relatives. When they were forced to leave that overcrowded accommodation, they applied to Wandsworth for housing.

The House of Lords, by a majority, found that the material date for determining whether a person had become homeless intentionally or un-intentionally was the date on which they left the accommodation. What might have happened afterwards was irrelevant. Mr and Mrs Din's home-lessness was a direct result of them leaving the flat in Wandsworth before being required to do so. The local authority was, accordingly, entitled to conclude that they had become intentionally homeless.

A disqualification by reason of intentional surrender is not displaced by obtaining temporary accommodation. As pointed out by Ackner LJ in the Court of Appeal it can be displaced by obtaining settled accommodation.

Note: In the Court of Appeal Ackner LJ, holding that intentional homeless was not displaced by obtaining temporary accommodation, said:

> To remove his self-imposed disqualification, he must therefore have achieved what can be loosely described as a 'settled residence' as opposed to what from the outset is known ... to be only temporary accommoda-tion. What amounts to a 'settled residence' is a question of fact and degree depending upon the circumstances of each individual case.

T22.2   *R v Brent LBC ex p Awua*

[1996] AC 55; [1995] 3 WLR 215; [1995] 3 All ER 493; (1995) 27 HLR 453, HL (see also T4.1 and T51.1)

An applicant can be intentionally homeless from accommodation even if that accommodation is not settled

Miss Awua applied to Tower Hamlets as a homeless person. She was placed in temporary accommodation and was accepted for the full housing duty. In discharge of its duty Tower Hamlets offered Miss Awua a housing asso-ciation tenancy but she rejected it. Tower Hamlets accordingly evicted her from her temporary accommodation. Miss Awua then applied to Brent, with which she also had a local connection. Brent decided that she was in-tentionally homeless from the temporary accommodation as her eviction had resulted from her decision not to accept the housing association ten-ancy. Miss Awua applied for judicial review of Brent's decision. At first instance the decision was quashed. It was held that (1) ceasing to occupy the temporary accommodation could not result in intentional homeless-ness as the accommodation referred to in Housing Act 1985 s60(1) (now Housing Act 1996 s191(1)) must be 'settled', and (2) Miss Awua could not be held to have ceased to occupy the housing association accommodation as she had never moved into it (see *R v Westminster CC ex p Chambers* (T35.6)). The Court of Appeal agreed with the second point but in rela-tion to the first point held that Brent was entitled to regard the temporary accommodation as settled and therefore that Miss Awua was intentionally homeless. Miss Awua appealed. (Brent did not cross-appeal the finding on the second point.)

The House of Lords upheld Brent's decision. There was no reference to 'settled' accommodation in Housing Act 1985 s60(1) (now Housing Act 1996 s191(1)) and there was no warrant in the language of the statute or the decision of the House of Lords in *R v Hillingdon LBC ex p Puhlhofer* (T8.2) for implying such a concept. Lord Hoffmann, who gave the leading speech, held that 'accommodation' in the context of both homelessness and intentional homelessness 'means a place that can fairly be described as accommodation ... and which it would be reasonable, having regard to the general housing conditions in the local authority's district, for the person in question to continue to occupy'.

What Miss Awua had lost was plainly 'accommodation'. It did not matter whether that accommodation was temporary or otherwise. What mattered was whether, by Miss Awua's act or omission, she had lost it. On the facts, her failure to take up an offer of suitable permanent accommodation from Tower Hamlets had caused the loss of the temporary accommodation and she was intentionally homeless.

Lord Hoffmann indicated that nothing in the judgment disturbed the long-established rule that there must be a causal link between past intentionality and present homelessness which could be broken by securing 'settled accommodation'. However, simply obtaining accommodation sufficient to render an intentionally homeless applicant no longer homeless did not suffice: 'what persists until the causal link is broken is the intentionality not the homelessness'. Lord Hoffman expressly left open the possibility that there may be methods of breaking the causal link between past intentionality and present homelessness other than by obtaining a 'settled residence'.

T22.3   *R v Hillingdon LBC ex p Islam*
[1983] 1 AC 688; [1981] 3 All ER 901; (1981) 1 HLR 107, HL

Applicant was not intentionally homeless by bringing his family over from Bangladesh to join him without having accommodation for them

Mr Islam, a Bangladeshi, was settled in the UK and had indefinite leave to remain. He lived in a shared room in Hillingdon. He visited Bangladesh from time to time and in 1968 married. His wife remained in Bangladesh and they had four children. In 1980 his wife received entry clearance and came to the UK with their children. They lived together for about four months in Mr Islam's accommodation until they were evicted as a result of the whole family living there. Mr Islam applied to Hillingdon as a homeless person. Hillingdon decided that he was not in priority need because 'his dependent children might not reasonably be expected to reside with him having lived apart for the last seven years'. It further decided that, even if he were in priority need, he was intentionally homeless because he deliberately arranged for his wife and children to leave accommodation in Bangladesh which it would have been reasonable for them to continue to occupy.

Glidewell J at first instance found that Mr Islam was in priority need. On the facts he had dependent children who were residing with him. He held that the words 'who might reasonably be expected to reside with him' (Housing (Homeless Persons) Act 1977 s2(1)(a), now Housing Act 1996 s189(1)(b)) applied only in a case where children were *not* already residing with the applicant. The council did not appeal this finding. However, Glidewell J found Mr Islam intentionally homeless and this decision was confirmed by a majority of the Court of Appeal. Mr Islam petitioned the House of Lords.

The House of Lords allowed his appeal. Mr Islam could not be intentionally homeless from the accommodation in Bangladesh because he had not been occupying that accommodation. Accordingly, he had not ceased to occupy it. The room which he occupied in the UK and from which he was evicted was not accommodation which was 'available' for him and his family (Housing (Homeless Persons) Act 1977 s16 (now Housing Act 1996 s176) nor would it have been reasonable for them to occupy it. The argument in the Court of Appeal that Mr Islam had made himself intentionally homeless by rendering his accommodation unavailable by bringing his family over was rejected as circular. It was the very lack of such accommodation that s16 of the Act was designed to relieve.

Court of Appeal

T22.4   *R v Slough BC ex p Ealing LBC*
[1981] QB 801; [1981] 2 WLR 399; [1981] 1 All ER 601; (1980) 79 LGR 335, CA (see T36.2)

Where an applicant was found intentionally homeless and applied to a second authority, it was for the second authority to form its own view about the application

T23   Deliberate act/omission

The test of intentionality requires that an applicant 'deliberately does or fails to do' something which results in his or her homelessness. Section 191(2) provides that 'an act or omission in good faith on the part of a person who was unaware of any relevant fact shall not be treated as deliberate'.

The issue of intentionality arising from non-payment of rent or mortgage instalments is sometimes analysed in the context of a deliberate act or omission – with non-payment not being a 'deliberate' omission where an applicant cannot afford to make the payments. At other times, the issue is considered in the context of whether it is reasonable to continue to occupy property – with it not being reasonable if it is not affordable to an applicant. The loss of such accommodation cannot give rise to a finding of intentional homelessness. For ease of reference all cases regarding affordability, whether in the context of homelessness or intentional homelessness, are considered together at T10. Other issues relating to the loss of accommodation as a result of rent/mortgage arrears are considered below (eg, capability of managing affairs, fraudulent taking out of mortgage).

T24   *General*

Court of Appeal

T24.1   *Devenport v Salford CC*
(1983) 8 HLR 54, CA

No requirement of a deliberate intention to become homeless

Mr and Mrs Devenport were council tenants. The council received a petition signed by 237 other tenants calling for them to be removed from their estate as a result of vandalism, assaults and violent misconduct by their children. A possession order was made. Mr and Mrs Devenport then applied to the council as homeless persons. The council decided that they were intentionally homeless. On an application for judicial review, the council's decision was quashed because it had not considered whether Mr and Mrs Devenport had deliberately decided not to try to control their children.

The local authority's appeal was allowed. It was not necessary for the authority to show that the Devonports had deliberately done or failed to do something with the intention of being evicted and becoming homeless. The words 'deliberately' in Housing (Homeless Persons) Act 1977 s17 (now Housing Act 1996 s191) govern only the act or omission. There was ample evidence on which the authority could conclude that the Devonports had failed to take any steps to control their children and that that conduct resulted in the making of a possession order. The authority was not limited to the findings in the county court possession claim. Its task was to review all the facts as it knew them, including the decision of the county court, and reach a conclusion accordingly.

Cf: *Griffiths v St Helens MBC* (T24.5).

T24.2   *Hijazi v Kensington and Chelsea RLBC*
[2003] EWCA Civ 692; [2003] HLR 72

Medical evidence that applicant incapable of managing affairs did not relate to relevant period

Mr Hijazi was an assured shorthold tenant. In May 2001 he was evicted for non-payment of rent. The council decided that he was intentionally homeless. On a review he relied on a doctor's report to support his contention that he suffered from psychological problems which meant that he would have been incapable of deciding to make himself intentionally homeless. The reviewing officer confirmed the decision, stating that Mr Hijazi was in a position to know how to manage his affairs and pay his rent at the date of his eviction. Mr Hijazi appealed that decision on the ground that the reviewing officer failed to take into account the medical report from his doctor. HHJ Knowles allowed in further evidence that the reviewing officer had taken the doctor's report into account but had found that it did not take matters further because it did not deal with Mr Hijazi's medical condition at the time of the eviction.

The Court of Appeal dismissed Mr Hijazi's further appeal:

1) While further evidence ought not to be considered where it added to, or supplemented, the reasons given in a review decision (see *R v*

Westminster CC ex p Ermakov (T38.10)), the statement in this case simply elucidated the reasons already given. It had been properly adduced in evidence.

2) It was unfortunate that the decision letter did not specifically refer to the doctor's report, but the judge was entitled to find that the principles set out in *Ermakov* were not infringed.

3) The reviewing officer was entitled to conclude that the medical evidence did not refer to Mr Hijazi's medical condition when he was evicted and to conclude that there was nothing in the evidence to suggest that he should have sought clarification in order to justify his conclusions.

The judge was entitled to uphold the decision of intentional homelessness.

T24.3　*William v Wandsworth LBC; Bellamy v Hounslow LBC*
[2006] EWCA Civ 535; [2006] HLR 42; (2006) *Times* 6 June

Failure to use money from remortgage to pay mortgage instalments a deliberate act; sale of jointly owned home a deliberate act

Mr William became homeless as a result of repossession by a mortgage lender. Ms Bellamy sold the home jointly owned by herself and her mother, in which she had lived. In both cases, county court judges quashed findings of intentional homelessness made by reviewing officers. In Mr William's case the judge found that the reviewing officer had failed clearly to decide whether the 'deliberate act' had been the taking-out of an unaffordable mortgage or the subsequent failure to make repayments. In Ms Bellamy's case, the judge held that she had been a simple bare trustee of her mother and had had no alternative but to comply with her mother's instruction to sell. He varied the decision to one of 'not' intentionally homeless.

The Court of Appeal allowed both appeals by the local authorities. Neither review decision had contained any error of law and the jurisdiction under s204 had not justified the judges interfering with either of them. In the *William* case, the deliberate act identified in the decision was the failure to use the monies available to Mr William from the remortgage to pay the mortgage instalments, and that had been stated in unequivocal terms. In the *Bellamy* case, it was impossible to support the judge's conclusion that, as a matter of law, if one joint owner wished to sell the property, the other joint owner was compelled to comply with that wish. On an application for an order that trustees of land concurred in a sale, the court could make such order as it thought fit. It was not inevitable that a court would have ordered a sale. It was open to the authority to take the view that it would have been reasonable for Ms Bellamy to remain in the property and contest any application for sale.

High Court

T24.4　*R v Wirral MBC ex p Bell*
(1995) 27 HLR 234, QBD

Applicant can be both vulnerable and capable of managing his own affairs

The applicant was evicted from accommodation for behaviour which was a nuisance and annoyance. The council found him to have a priority need as a result of vulnerability caused by mental illness (Housing Act 1985 s59(1)(c), now Housing Act 1996 s189(1)(c)). However, it also decided that his homelessness was intentional.

Harrison J dismissed an application for judicial review. The council had been entitled to find both that the applicant was presently 'vulnerable' in the housing context and that at the time of the loss of his last accommodation he had been capable of managing his own affairs.

County courts

T24.5   *Griffiths v St Helens MBC*

[2004] 142 Housing Aid Update 3; 28 July 2004, St Helens County Court

Applicant who had tried to stop her children causing nuisance had not been guilty of a deliberate act/omission nor had she acquiesced in their actions

The applicant was an assured tenant of Helena Housing, a stock-transfer registered social landlord. Helena obtained an outright possession order based on the anti-social behaviour of the applicant's two sons who lived with her. The district judge trying the possession claim decided that it would be reasonable to make a possession order even though the applicant had not herself been guilty of any misconduct and had tried (unsuccessfully) to control her sons' behaviour. After eviction, the applicant applied to St Helens council as a homeless person. The council decided that she had become homeless intentionally and confirmed that decision on review.

HHJ Mackay allowed her appeal. He held that the definition of 'intentional homelessness' required a 'deliberate act or failure to act' which causes loss of accommodation. In this case the applicant had tried to stop her children's misconduct and had been commended for her efforts. She had not been guilty of any nuisance herself and had not 'acquiesced' in any nuisance by anyone else (distinguishing her case from *Devenport v Salford CC* (T24.1) and *R v Southampton CC ex p Ward* (1984) 14 HLR 114). There had been no deliberate act or omission on her part capable of satisfying the s191 definition. The judge varied the council's finding to a decision that the applicant was not intentionally homeless.

T25   *Good faith/ignorance of material fact*

Court of Appeal

T25.1   *Aw-Aden v Birmingham CC*

[2005] EWCA Civ 1834; 7 December 2005

Belief in prospect of finding work in UK based 'on a wing and a prayer' and not a 'relevant fact'

Mr Aw-Aden lived in Belgium. He came to the UK to look for work after his employment there ended. He was later joined by his wife and child. He applied as a homeless person after staying with friends in Birmingham for almost a year. The council decided that he had become homeless intentionally from his last settled home in Belgium. That decision was upheld on review and an appeal to the county court was dismissed. On a second appeal, Mr Aw-Aden contended that he had been unaware of a relevant fact – the true prospect of being able to find work in Birmingham sufficient to provide the means for him to pay for his own accommodation

– and that the council had failed to consider whether that ignorance had been in 'good faith' for the purposes of Housing Act 1996 s191(2). That subsection had not been referred to in the original decision or review decision (or in his solicitors' correspondence).

The Court of Appeal dismissed the appeal. The correct legal approach to facts such as these was stated by Carnwath J in *R v Westminster CC ex p Obeid* (T25.16), ie, that ignorance of the true prospect for future employment *could* constitute a relevant fact provided it was 'sufficiently specific (that is related to specific employment ...)' and 'based on some genuine investigation and not mere "aspiration"'. Mr Aw-Aden's prospects when leaving Belgium did not meet that threshold and 'rested on little more than a wing and a prayer'. Accordingly, there had been no error by the council in not addressing the 'good faith' issue in s191(2).

Brooke LJ noted that early in the course of the council's review, Mr Aw-Aden's solicitors had requested a copy of the documents on the homelessness file (and the interview notes) so that they could make effective representations in the review. Those had not been provided. Brooke LJ said:

> ... if the law entitles an appellant to make representations and if solicitors acting for an appellant make a reasonable request for documentary material before they can make their representations, then the review decision should certainly not be made without complying with that request. [para 22]

T25.2   *F v Birmingham CC*

[2006] EWCA Civ 1427; [2007] HLR 18; 2 November 2006

Section 191(2) not relevant where applicant did not know whether or not HB would pay rent

In 2002, the claimant, then a young single parent, gave up her council tenancy to move into a privately rented house. She failed to secure full housing benefit (HB) to pay the rent and was evicted in 2003. On her subsequent homelessness application, the council found that she had become homeless intentionally on giving up her flat and had found no subsequent 'settled' accommodation. That decision was upheld on review and in the county court on appeal. A second appeal was pursued on the basis that the council had not dealt with the claimant's contention that she had thought (in ignorance of the true position) that HB would pay the full rent on her new home.

The Court of Appeal dismissed the appeal. The council had expressly rejected the suggestion that the claimant had been told that the full rent would be covered by HB or that she genuinely thought it would be. The facts showed that the claimant moved home at best without knowing whether HB would be paid or being bothered about the rent. After analysis of s191(2) and the authorities it was held that, as the applicant had proceeded on a 'wing and a prayer', no need had arisen for the council to consider ignorance, in good faith, of a material fact.

T25.3   *Hobbs v Sutton LBC*

(1994) 26 HLR 132, CA

Bad faith – putting adverse material to applicant

The applicants were private tenants, who were evicted following rent arrears. They contended that there had been confusion about payment of the rent, the whereabouts of their landlord and of their entitlement to, and subsequent claim for, housing benefit. The council took into account various findings resulting from its enquiries and concluded that the applicants had not conducted themselves reasonably and were intentionally homeless. In the course of proceedings for judicial review, the council's officer swore a second affidavit indicating that the council was not considering the 'reasonableness' of the applicants' belief, but whether they had acted in good faith. It was suggested that the shift of emphasis was caused by the decision in *R v Tower Hamlets LBC ex p Rouf* (T25.9). If the council had genuinely been considering 'good faith' it would or should have re-interviewed the applicant.

By a majority the Court of Appeal dismissed the applicant's appeal. The reasonableness or otherwise of the applicants' conduct had been properly regarded as relevant to the consideration of good faith. The council had applied the right test of good faith and the second affidavit had explained why this was so. In the interests of fairness, an applicant must be given the opportunity to explain matters that an authority was minded to take against them (*R v Gravesend BC ex p Winchester* (T37.17)). However, this did not mean that, having come to the conclusion that the applicant had not been telling the truth on essential matters or had not been acting bona fide, the authority must recall him for a further interview and put those matters to him again and seek his reaction. Nor did the court in *Rouf* rule that in every case where bad faith arises the matter must specifically be put to the applicant. It was not a requirement that the applicant be heard by the actual decision-maker whenever credibility was in issue. Appropriate enquiries had been made and the substance of the case had been put to the applicants.

T25.4 **O'Connor v Kensington and Chelsea RLBC**
[2004] EWCA Civ 394; [2004] HLR 37

Requirement to consider whether omission deliberate, despite issue not being raised

Mr and Mrs O'Connor left their housing association property in London to travel to Ireland to visit Mr O'Connor's father who was very ill. He died shortly after their arrival in November 2000. Mr O'Connor, who already suffered with depression, was particularly affected by his father's death. The family stayed on temporarily in Ireland and arranged for a family friend to occupy their home and pay their rent. In May 2002 Mrs O'Connor returned to find that: (a) the rent had not been paid; (b) the friend had not forwarded the post which contained a possession claim; (c) a suspended possession order had been made; and (d) the friend would not move out. When she excluded the friend and changed the locks, he broke back in. She reduced the arrears from almost £2,000 to £83 but her application to stay a warrant was refused and the possession order executed. Mr and Mrs O'Connor applied as homeless persons but the council confirmed on review that they were intentionally homeless. They appealed but by the date of the appeal had obtained an assured shorthold tenancy elsewhere in London. HHJ Behar dismissed the appeal but held that, even if the review decision had been defective, he would have refused any remedy because the couple were not homeless.

The Court of Appeal allowed a second appeal. It held:

1) Although an erroneous decision would ordinarily be quashed or varied, in a rare case it would be open to the court to refuse relief on the basis that it was an abuse of process for a pointless appeal to be pursued. Here the appeal was not pointless as the applicants might need to make a further application as homeless persons.

2) The application for the review (and the solicitors' representations in support of it) had asserted that no act or omission by the couple had caused their homelessness. Unsurprisingly, the thrust of the review concentrated on that submission. The 'omission' relied on by the reviewer was the couple's failure during their 16 month absence to protect their tenancy.

3) Even though it had not been raised, the reviewer was obliged to have considered whether that omission was 'deliberate' or whether it could not be treated as such because the couple had, in good faith, been in ignorance of a relevant fact: Housing Act 1996 s191(2). On the facts, the couple had not known of their friend's default, the mounting arrears or the possession proceedings. The action they took in mid 2002 demonstrated what they would have done had they known. There is no requirement that ignorance 'of any relevant fact' must be reasonable, although wilful ignorance must fail the good faith test.

T25.5   *R v Barnet LBC ex p Rughooputh*
(1993) 25 HLR 607, CA

Where mortgage taken out fraudulently s191(2) did not apply

The applicant was made homeless following mortgage possession proceedings. The deliberate act which caused the loss of the home was the applicant taking out a mortgage in 1987 beyond her means – she was unemployed, but had claimed to have an earned income of £18,000.

The council's finding of intentional homelessness was upheld on appeal. Taking out the mortgage was the act that caused the homelessness. It had been induced by fraudulent misrepresentation and so Housing Act 1985 s60(3) (now Housing Act 1996 s191(2)) could not apply to prevent the act from being 'deliberate'.

T25.6   *R v Camden LBC ex p Aranda*
(1998) 30 HLR 76, CA (see T11.3)

Not deliberate act where applicant went to Colombia with husband to keep family together and in ignorance of husband's plans to desert her

T25.7   *R v Croydon LBC ex p Toth*
(1988) 20 HLR 576, CA (see T12.2)

Ignorance that in abandoning accommodation applicant would lose her tenancy not ignorance of a fact but of the legal consequences of a fact

T25.8   *R v Exeter CC ex p Tranckle*
(1994) 26 HLR 244, CA

Prospects of business venture a relevant fact

The applicants became homeless as a result of default on a business loan secured on their home. The council decided that the question of whether the business was or was not originally a sound investment was not relevant and decided that the applicants were intentionally homeless.

The Court of Appeal held that the decision should be quashed, approving the decision in *R v Hammersmith and Fulham LBC ex p Lusi* (T25.13). What the applicants knew or ought to have known of the prospects of the business venture were matters relevant to the question of intentional homelessness and should have been investigated.

T25.9   *R v Tower Hamlets LBC ex p Rouf*
(1991) 23 HLR 460, CA

Ignorance of a relevant fact; question is whether applicant acted in good faith, not whether acted reasonably

The applicant went to Bangladesh with his family. During his absence he arranged for a friend to occupy his council flat and pay the rent. The friend did not pay the rent and the flat was repossessed. Over three years later the applicant returned to the UK and found his flat boarded up. He applied to the authority as a homeless person. It decided that he was intentionally homeless as a result of ceasing to occupy his accommodation in Bangladesh. In its decision letter the authority stated that it had taken into account 'that the length of your absence in Bangladesh was over three years and that it was not therefore reasonable for you to suppose that the [council flat] would still be available for you'.

The Court of Appeal quashed the decision. By Housing Act 1985 s60(3) (now Housing Act 1996 s191(2)), an act or omission in good faith is not to be treated as deliberate if an applicant is unaware of a relevant fact. The question of whether an applicant was unaware of a relevant fact is a straightforward question of fact for the authority. Where an applicant was unaware of a relevant fact the question is simply whether the applicant acted in good faith, not whether he or she acted reasonably. The authority had not enquired into whether the applicant's actions were in good faith. The matter was remitted for reconsideration by the authority. Dillon and Stoker LJJ both considered that if the authority concluded that the applicant was acting in bad faith then this should be put to him for his comment.

Note: see *Hobbs v Sutton* (T25.3) on the latter point.

T25.10   *R v Wandsworth LBC ex p Onwudiwe*
(1994) 26 HLR 302, CA

Business mortgage default; knowledge of risk relevant to good faith

The applicant lost his home as a result of default on a mortgage taken out to finance a business venture. The council found him intentionally homeless because he took the mortgage at a time when his business plan was not finalised and he had obtained the loan by misrepresenting his earnings. The decision letter expressly referred to the housing pressures in Wandsworth as a factor in reaching the decision.

Laws J dismissed the application for judicial review (see [1994] COD 229). He held that (a) the council had misdirected itself and should not have had regard to housing conditions in the borough as these were only relevant to the issue of whether it would have been reasonable to continue to occupy the former home (Housing Act 1985 s60(4), now Housing Act 1996 s177(1)); but (b) the error was not material, as the authority was entitled to find on the information before it, canvassed over six interviews with the applicant, that he had misled the mortgagees and had realised he was putting his home at serious risk.

The Court of Appeal dismissed an application for leave to appeal as 'not even arguable'. In a business mortgage default case 'it is not enough simply to find that he was a hopeless businessman or that the venture was ill advised, but it is necessary to look at all the circumstances to decide whether on the one hand, he honestly believed he was acting sensibly, or on the other, he knew perfectly well the risk he was taking, namely that his house might be repossessed' [305]. Only in the latter category would the defaulter be intentionally homeless. Here, the facts of the case took it beyond the stage of honest incompetence to a stage where the applicant could be said to be deliberately putting his house at risk.

T25.11 *R v Winchester CC ex p Ashton*
(1992) 24 HLR 520, CA

Applicant who moved to take up employment, initially with accommodation to go to, was not intentionally homeless

Mrs Ashton rented accommodation in Tunbridge Wells which was not satisfactory. It was in a state of disrepair and she had been harassed by her landlord. She moved to Winchester because she had been offered permanent employment there. However, 16 months later she lost her job and was evicted from the temporary accommodation she had been living in. She applied to Winchester Council for accommodation. It contacted the police in Tunbridge Wells, who had no record of any complaint of harassment, and her former landlord, who was critical of her as a tenant. It decided that she was intentionally homeless for giving up the rented accommodation in Tunbridge Wells which she 'could have reasonably been expected to continue to occupy'.

The decision was quashed at first instance. Kennedy J found that it was 'nonsense to say that a middle-aged woman in poor health, who left her home in Tunbridge Wells in October 1987 to take up in Winchester the only job she had been offered for six years despite continuing searches, with accommodation to go to and with hopes of improving her status that year, should be held to have become intentionally homeless in March 1989 because her hopes in relation to employment and accommodation were not realised'. However, Kennedy J rejected her contention that her accommodation in Winchester (initially bed and breakfast accommodation and then just over a year in temporary council accommodation which did not enjoy security of tenure) was settled accommodation. The council's appeal to the Court of Appeal was dismissed.

High Court

T25.12 *R v Eastleigh BC ex p Beattie (No 2)*
(1985) 17 HLR 168, QBD (see T26.4)

Ignorance of legal consequences of non-payment of mortgage was not ignorance of a relevant fact

T25.13 *R v Hammersmith and Fulham LBC ex p Lusi and Lusi*
(1991) 23 HLR 260, QBD

Good faith; distinction between honest blundering/carelessness and dishonesty

Mr Lusi lived and worked in England but then sold his home and went with his wife and child to take up a business opportunity in Turkey. They stayed with his parents, intending to find a new home in Turkey, but the business opportunity failed. They left his parents' home and returned to Britain and applied as homeless persons. The council based a decision of intentional homelessness on either (a) the deliberate giving up of accommodation in Britain to go to Turkey or (b) the deliberate giving up of accommodation in Turkey to return to Britain.

Roch J quashed the decision. The accommodation in England had been left in the belief that the applicant was going to a sound business opportunity in Turkey. The business had not been as described and so the applicant had been in ignorance of a relevant fact. The authority had failed to consider whether that ignorance had been 'in good faith' (Housing Act 1985 s60(3), now Housing Act 1996 s191(2)). Roch J held that, when considering that question:

> ... there is a distinction between honest blundering and carelessness on the one hand, where a person can still act in good faith, and dishonesty on the other, where there can be no question of the person acting in good faith.

As regards the departure from accommodation in Turkey, the council had failed to consider properly whether the accommodation with relatives had been 'settled' accommodation. In deciding that question:

> ... the intention of the occupants and of the person who allows them to occupy will be important but not decisive factors ... accommodation may be settled and not temporary although the occupants may from the first intend to move on to better accommodation as soon as that becomes practical.

Note: This decision was approved in *R v Exeter CC ex p Tranckle* (T25.8). Note that after *R v Brent LBC ex p Awua* (T22.2) departure from non-settled accommodation can result in intentionality.

T25.14 *R v Mole Valley DC ex p Burton*
(1988) 20 HLR 479, QBD

Inaccurate assurance by husband of prospects of rehousing a relevant fact

The applicant's partner resigned from his employment and so lost the family home, which was tied accommodation. The applicant applied in her own right for housing, asserting that, although she had known of her partner's intentions, she had relied on his assurance that the family would qualify for rehousing under a special council allocation policy. The council found her to be intentionally homeless because her partner's application had already been rejected.

This decision was quashed for failure to take into account relevant considerations. The council was required on reconsideration to have regard in particular to Housing Act 1985 s60(3) (now Housing Act 1996 s191(2)), ie, that an act or omission done in good faith in ignorance of a material fact should not be treated as deliberate.

T25.15 *R v Wandsworth LBC ex p Rose*
(1983) 11 HLR 105, QBD

Ignorance of lack of satisfactory accommodation with father in England relevant fact

Ms Rose had been born in England but lived with her mother in Jamaica. Her father, who lived in England, paid the air fares for her two brothers and sister to come to England, where they had lived with him at different times. Later her father wrote to say that, although he could not pay her air fare, she could come to England. She understood this to mean that he had adequate accommodation where she and her daughter could stay indefinitely. She stayed with her father for a week but he only had a one-bedroom flat and he asked her to leave and started to make her stay difficult. Wandsworth Council decided that she was intentionally homeless.

Glidewell J quashed this decision because the authority had not taken into account the fact that the applicant had been unaware of the lack of satisfactory accommodation with her father. The council was not entitled to assume, without making proper enquiries, that, simply because she had failed to ask her father about accommodation, she had acted other than in good faith in ignorance of a relevant fact.

T25.16 *R v Westminster CC ex p Obeid*
(1997) 29 HLR 389, QBD

Applicant's belief that housing benefit would cover rent needed consideration

The applicant was accepted for the main housing duty by Wandsworth LBC. She was offered and reluctantly accepted council accommodation provided in discharge of duty. She then found a preferable private flat to rent in Westminster. She made enquiries of friends in the area and satisfied herself that that the rent would be met by housing benefit. She took the tenancy. The rent was £210 but housing benefit was limited to £180 per week. The applicant was unable to make up the shortfall and applied to Westminster as a homeless person. She was found to be intentionally homeless from her previous accommodation.

Carnwath J quashed the decision. The effect of the Court of Appeal's decisions in *R v Exeter ex p Trankle* (T25.8) and *R v Ealing LBC ex p Sukhija* (1994) 26 HLR 726 was that an applicant's appreciation of the prospects of future housing or future employment can be treated as 'awareness of a relevant fact' provided it is sufficiently specific (that is, related to specific employment or specific housing opportunities) and provided it is based on some genuine investigation and not mere 'aspiration'. The test under Housing Act 1985 s60(3) (now Housing Act 1996 s191(2)) is not the reasonableness of an applicant's actions, but whether they are taken in ignorance of relevant facts. It was a 'relevant fact' that the applicant had believed that her entitlement to housing benefit would cover the full rent. If the authority thought that she had made no genuine investigation of the matter it might have dismissed her stated belief as mere aspiration. The issue was one for the authority to decide but they had not considered the correct question.

Note: Approved by CA in *Aw-Aden v Birmingham CC* (T25.1)

Scottish courts

T25.17   *Wincentzen v Monklands DC*
1988 SC 329; 1988 SLT 847; [1988] CLY 4365, Court of Session (Outer House)

Ignorance of father's intention not to allow applicant to return if she left was relevant fact

The applicant was a single homeless teenager who suffered from epilepsy. Until the age of 16 she lived with her father but she decided to move to stay with her mother temporarily while at college. Her father warned that, if she went, he would not allow her to return, but she did not believe him. She was unaware that her father was sincerely expressing his true intentions and genuinely thought that he was bluffing. When she returned, he refused to have her back. The authority accepted that her belief was genuine but that this was irrelevant in the light of her father's clear warning and so found her intentionally homeless.

In the Outer House, Lord Clyde, quashing the decision, held that the council had misdirected itself. The father's state of mind had been a relevant fact and the daughter's action taken in genuine ignorance of her father's true intent could not be classed as deliberate (Housing Act 1985 s60(3), (now Housing Act 1996 s191(2)). This decision was upheld on appeal by the Court of Session First Division.

T26   *Acquiescence*

The case of *R v North Devon DC ex p Lewis* (T26.5) established the principle that an authority is required to give individual consideration to each member of a household applying as a homeless person. However, an authority is entitled to consider whether an applicant acquiesced in the behaviour of another when considering whether they are intentionally homeless.

Court of Appeal

T26.1   *Devenport v Salford CC*
(1983) 8 HLR 54, CA (see T24.1)

Failure to take any steps to control children whose conduct resulted in a possession order resulted in intentional homelessness

T26.2   *R v Nottingham CC ex p Caine*
(1996) 28 HLR 374, CA

Council entitled to infer that applicant was aware that partner was withholding rent

The applicant's partner decided to withhold rent, for which housing benefit was being paid, because of the landlord's failure to repair the couple's home. As a result, they were evicted. They applied as homeless people. Her partner was found to have become homeless intentionally. The applicant denied knowing about the withholding of rent and there was no direct evidence that she was aware of this. However, the council decided that it was likely that she did have knowledge of the withholding of rent. She was found to have acquiesced in the non-payment and to be intentionally homeless. Her application for judicial review was dismissed.

The Court of Appeal dismissed her appeal. It found that the council had undertaken careful enquiries and given the applicant ample opportunity to make representations. The council had a great deal of background information about the nature of the family unit and was entitled to look at the family as a whole. The family received housing benefit of £238.33 for eight months continuously, which was not paid to the landlord. It was open to the council to conclude that the family had used that money with the applicant's knowledge and consent for the benefit of the family and not for the purpose of paying the rent. It was considered unlikely, if not inconceivable, that the applicant was unaware of her partner's dissatisfaction with the state of disrepair and lack of hot water and of the landlord's alleged failure to rectify the defects. The council was entitled to infer that the couple would have discussed the matter including the withholding of the rent.

T26.3   *R v Tower Hamlets LBC ex p Khatun (Asma)*
(1995) 27 HLR 344, CA

Wife content to leave decisions to husband acquiesced in his decisions

The applicant was from Bangladesh and came to the UK in 1987 after marrying her husband. In 1991 she was pregnant and living with her husband and two children in her husband's brother's house in a single room with shared use of the kitchen and bathroom. As a result of the overcrowding and tensions in the house, the applicants left. The husband applied as a homeless person but was held to be intentionally homeless as a result of leaving his brother's house. His application for judicial review was dismissed. His wife (the applicant) then applied to the council and said that her husband had, without warning or discussion, told her that they were leaving the brother's accommodation and that if she wanted them to stay together she had to follow him. She too was held to be intentionally homeless. That decision was challenged on the basis that the applicant had not agreed with or acquiesced in her husband's decision.

The Court of Appeal dismissed a renewed application for leave. Ralph Gibson LJ said that 'If a wife is content in a marriage to leave decisions as to where the family will live to the husband, then a decision to move, in which the wife co-operates and plays her part may properly be regarded as a decision in which the wife has joined unless there is some reason for holding that she did not.' The fact that Ms Khatun, after the issue of proceedings, said that she did not agree with her husband's decision did not oblige the authority to accept what she said. It was entitled to conclude that she made her own decision to go and, although she did not like it, nevertheless joined in the decision to leave the accommodation instead of remaining in the accommodation herself with the children.

High Court

T26.4   *R v Eastleigh BC ex p Beattie (No 2)*
(1985) 17 HLR 168, QBD

In absence of explanation for rejecting wife's evidence council could not conclude acquiescence

Following their earlier application for judicial review (see *R v Eastleigh BC ex p Beattie (No 1)* (1983) 10 HLR 134, QBD) Mr and Mrs Beattie, who were evicted as a result of mortgage arrears, made separate applications to the council. Mr Beattie relied on the property not being reasonable to continue to occupy on the basis of overcrowding and on the failure to pay the mortgage as not being 'deliberate' because it was based on inaccurate legal advice (confirmed in writing by his solicitors) that he would be rehoused if he did not make the payments. Mrs Beattie claimed that she had not been a party to her husband's decision not to pay the mortgage and that she had done all that she could to persuade him to maintain the payments.

Webster J found that:

1) The decision not to pay the mortgage was based on an error of law rather than an error of fact and so was not saved from being deliberate by Housing (Homeless Persons) Act 1977, s17(3) (now Housing Act 1996 s191(2)). In any event, it was unlikely that the 'good faith' limb of s17(3) would have been satisfied.

2) The authority had been entitled to conclude that it would have been reasonable for the family to remain in the house despite the overcrowding.

3) Mrs Beattie had sworn an affidavit in the earlier proceedings that she had protested with her husband about his non-payment of the mortgage. In those circumstances, if the council wished to reject her evidence, it had to put before the court evidence explaining why it had done so. As there was no such evidence, the decision was varied to one of not homeless intentionally.

T26.5 **R v North Devon DC ex p Lewis**
[1981] 1 WLR 328; [1981] 1 All ER 27; (1980) 79 LGR 289, QBD

Application by partner of intentionally homeless applicant must be considered in its own right

Ms Lewis lived with her partner in tied accommodation. He gave up his job, with the result that the family were forced to leave their home. He applied as a homeless person and included Ms Lewis in his application. He was found intentionally homeless. Ms Lewis then made an application in her own name, including her partner in her application. The council decided that Ms Lewis had acquiesced in her partner's decision to give up his job and was intentionally homeless. It contended that it was to the family unit as a whole that it had to look and that, where one member of a family became homeless intentionally, the whole family was to be treated as intentionally homeless.

Woolf J held that a woman who lives with a man who becomes intentionally homeless is not necessarily barred from relief by his conduct or by the fact that he may benefit undeservingly. The council had to consider an application from Ms Lewis and consider whether, by her conduct (rather than that of her partner), she was intentionally homeless:

> ... it would be readily understandable if parliament had provided expressly that the application should be made by the family unit and the question should be whether or not the family should be regarded as having become homeless intentionally. However ... there are no express words which provide that where a man and a woman are living together, if one of the couple becomes homeless intentionally, the other should be treated as becoming

homeless intentionally. The Act does not place any express limitation on who can make an application or as to how many applications can be made. [[1981] 1 WLR 328 at 333B]

However, he considered that '

... the fact that the Act requires consideration of the family unit as a whole indicates that it would be perfectly proper in the ordinary case for the housing authority to look at the family as a whole and assume, in the absence of material which indicates to the contrary, where the conduct of one member of the family was such that he should be regarded as having become homeless intentionally, that was conduct to which the other members of the family were a party ... If, however, at the end of the day because of material put before the housing authority by the wife, the housing authority are not satisfied that she was a party to the decision, they would have to regard her as not having become homeless intentionally. [at 333G–H]

There was ample material before the council to support its decision that Ms Lewis had acquiesced in her partner's conduct and her application was dismissed.

T26.6   *R v Penwith DC ex p Trevena*
(1985) 17 HLR 526, QBD

Where wife left her husband, terminated the tenancy but later reconciled with him, he was not intentionally homeless

Mrs Trevena was a council tenant. She took her children and left her husband to live with another man. She surrendered the tenancy. Mr Trevena unsuccessfully applied to have the tenancy transferred into his name. When he refused to leave, the authority obtained a possession order. Later, Mr and Mrs Trevena became reconciled and lived in a series of premises on short lettings. They applied jointly to the council for accommodation; it determined that they were intentionally homeless. Mr Trevena applied for judicial review.

McNeill J quashed the decision. There was no material on which the authority could conclude that Mr Trevena had been a party to the surrender or that it was a joint surrender or abandonment.

T26.7   *R v Swansea CC ex p John*
(1983) 9 HLR 56, QBD

Failure to remove partner who was a nuisance could amount to acquiescence

Ms John was a 67-year-old council tenant. Her partner was an alcoholic and, when drunk, was a nuisance and annoyance to neighbours. This only occurred when Ms John was away from the flat. He was larger and younger than she was and she was unable to control his behaviour. The council brought possession proceedings and Ms John was evicted. She applied to the council, which determined that she was intentionally homeless on the basis that she had acquiesced in her partner's behaviour in not asking him to leave.

Her application for judicial review was dismissed by Woolf J. It was open to the council to find that by failing to take action to terminate her partner's right to remain she had acquiesced in his conduct.

See also *R v Swansea CC ex p Thomas* (1983) 9 HLR 64, QBD.

T26.8   *R v West Dorset DC ex p Phillips*
(1985) 17 HLR 336, QBD

Council failed to make further enquiries in light of evidence of non-acquiescence

An application was made by Mrs Phillips as a homeless person. She and her husband attended an interview with the council. The family had financial problems as a result of Mr Phillips' drinking. Arrangements had been made for Mr Phillips to pay arrears of rent on his tenancy by instalments but, unbeknown to Mrs Phillips, he failed to keep up with the payments. When the interviewing officer referred to the arrears of rent, Mrs Phillips attacked her husband, knocking him off his chair and shouting that she had always said that his drinking would lead to trouble. The interviewing officer considered that no further enquiries were necessary and found Mrs Phillips intentionally homeless.

Hodgson J found it 'astonishing' that the council had concluded that no further enquiries were necessary. It appeared that the authority had wrongly come to the conclusion that there was a burden of proof on Mrs Phillips and that it had failed to appreciate that the application was made by Mrs Phillips and not her husband. Enquiries should have been made of the social services department, which had had contact with the family. Mrs Phillips' conduct during the interview 'could hardly have been construed as acquiescence by the most hard-hearted of officers'. The council had failed to make its enquiries 'in a caring and sympathetic way' as required by the then *Homelessness Code of Guidance*. A declaration was made that Mrs Phillips was owed the full housing duty.

T27   Causation and settled accommodation

For homelessness to be intentional the loss of accommodation must have been 'in consequence' of an applicant's deliberate act or omission. This raises questions of cause and effect and whether an applicant's current homelessness is attributable to his or her past act or omission.

The causal link between deliberate acts and homelessness is broken by obtaining intervening settled accommodation and an authority cannot look back beyond the cause of the loss of the applicant's last settled accommodation. In *R v Brent LBC ex p Awua* (T22.2) Lord Hoffman indicated that this rule was undisturbed by the judgment. He expressly left open the possibility that there may be methods of breaking the causal link other than by obtaining settled accommodation. What constitutes settled accommodation is a 'question of fact and degree depending upon the circumstances of each individual case' per Ackner LJ in *Din v Wansworth LBC* (T22.1) in the Court of Appeal.

House of Lords

T27.1   *Din v Wandsworth LBC*
[1983] 1 AC 657; [1981] 3 WLR 918; [1981] 3 All ER 881; (1982) 1 HLR 73, HL (see T22.1)

When considering intentionality an authority must look back to the last period of settled accommodation

T27.2   *R v Harrow LBC ex p Fahia*

[1998] 1 WLR 1396; [1998] 4 All ER 137; (1998) 30 HLR 1124, HL (see T35.1)

The chain of causation can be broken by events other than settled accommodation

Court of Appeal

T27.3   *Bratton v Croydon LBC*

[2002] EWCA Civ 1494; 26 July 2002

Where a landlord's reason for evicting an applicant was rent arrears, that was the cause of homelessness, regardless of the basis on which possession was obtained

Ms Bratton had an assured shorthold tenancy. Her landlord served a Housing Act 1988 s21 notice requiring possession after she failed to meet the full rent. The arrears, which were less than a single month's total rent, were not reduced. Her landlord took accelerated possession proceedings and obtained an order for possession. Ms Bratton applied as a homeless person. She was found intentionally homeless as a result of her failure to pay the rent in full. Enquiries had revealed that the landlord's decision to evict her was as a result of the arrears and that she could afford the rent. That decision was upheld on review and her appeal to the county court was dismissed. Ms Bratton appealed. It was submitted that, following *R v Hounslow LBC ex p R* (T27.20), one had to look to see whether the loss of the home was the reasonable result of her deliberate conduct. In circumstances where a tenant was in arrears but not to such an extent that the provisions for possession relating to arrears of rent would take effect, the loss of the home should not be regarded as resulting from the non-payment of rent. It was submitted that no judge would be likely to order outright possession based on the level of Ms Bratton's arrears.

This approach was rejected by the Court of Appeal. The reason the landlord took possession was the non-payment of rent. Even applying the 'reasonable likelihood' approach in *ex p R*, the reasonably likely consequence of Ms Bratton's behaviour was that the landlord would seek possession. Kay LJ observed that if, after service of a s21 notice, Ms Bratton had made good the rent arrears but the landlord had decided nevertheless to seek possession '... then it might have been very difficult to conclude that his true reason for seeking possession against her was her conduct in failing to pay the rent regularly' [25]. In the circumstances of the case and on a correct interpretation of s191, however, it was inevitable that the council concluded that Ms Bratton was intentionally homeless.

T27.4   *Denton v Southwark LBC*

[2007] EWCA Civ 623; 4 July 2007

Cause of homelessness was applicant's bad behaviour towards mother; that conduct to be ignored in considering whether reasonable to continue to occupy family home

The claimant was aged 20 and lived in his mother's home. After warnings about his bad behaviour, his mother excluded him because of his rudeness and his use of drugs in her home, which he admitted. On his application for homelessness assistance under HA 1996 Part VII, Southwark found on review that he had become homeless intentionally. HHJ Cotran allowed his appeal.

The Court of Appeal allowed a further appeal. To determine whether a person is within the statutory definition of intentional homelessness, all the circumstances of the case must be considered. One of those circumstances is the fact that the previous home was a family home. There are significant differences between the family home and rented accommodation. Nonetheless, people living together must show each other appropriate respect and this necessarily involves complying with any reasonable requests which one person makes to another. In this case, the applicant's mother reasonably expected him to behave so as not to cause a nuisance to her or others and he did not do so. The cause of his being asked to leave was his bad behaviour. In determining whether it is reasonable for a person to have continued to occupy his previous home, the court must disregard the deliberate conduct or course of conduct that led him to leave that home. It is for the authority to decide what inquiries to make and the court will not intervene unless the decision of the local authority not to make further inquiries is perverse. It could not be said that Southwark's approach in this case failed to comply with public law principles

T27.5 **Dyson v Kerrier DC**
[1980] 1 WLR 1205; [1980] 3 All ER 313; (1980) 78 LGR 603, CA

In considering causation, authority could consider the reason for the loss of accommodation before that most recently occupied
Ms Dyson surrendered the tenancy of a council flat in Cambridgeshire and went to Cornwall where she had relatives and had arranged an unprotected winter let of a holiday cottage. Not long before the holiday let was due to expire, she applied to the council as a homeless person. It decided that her impending homelessness had been caused intentionally because she had given up the Cambridgeshire flat knowing that after the expiry of the winter let she would have nowhere to live. Ms Dyson argued that in applying the equivalent of s191 (intentional homelessness), the only concern was with the accommodation occupied at the time an applicant became homeless. At first instance Brightman LJ described this as a formidable argument on the literal wording of the section and quashed the council's decision.

The Court of Appeal held that such a construction would enable people to jump the housing queues by making themselves intentionally homeless at one remove. The council was entitled to take into account the fact that, if Ms Dyson had not surrendered the Cambridgeshire tenancy, she would not have become homeless and that there was a causal link between her deliberate action and her impending homelessness. (It was accepted that there was no reason to draw any distinction in principle between the definition of homelessness and threatened with homelessness, other than the 28-day requirement).

T27.6 **Gilby v Westminster CC**
[2007] EWCA Civ 604; 27 June 2007 (see T44.2)

Occupying a council flat for three years, whether as unlawful subtenant or as bare licensee, did not constitute settled accommodation

T27.7   *Knight v Vale Royal BC*

[2003] EWCA Civ 1258; [2004] HLR 9; (2003) *Times* 4 September

Question of fact and degree whether an AST was settled accommodation

Ms Knight applied to the council as a homeless person. It decided that she had become homeless intentionally. She then obtained an assured shorthold tenancy of a flat in the private sector. The landlord served a Housing Act 1988 s21 notice expiring six months after the start of the tenancy. He indicated that if she did not leave he would take proceedings for possession. Ms Knight left and again applied to the council as a homeless person. The council decided and confirmed on review that the private sector tenancy did not constitute 'settled' accommodation as Ms Knight had known from the outset that the landlord intended to recover possession after six months. Accordingly, she was still intentionally homeless. HHJ Hughes dismissed an appeal brought under s204. On a second appeal, Ms Knight contended that, because the assured shorthold tenancy was the default form of tenure in the private rented sector and the most common form of letting, it should always be treated as 'settled' accommodation.

The Court of Appeal agreed that occupation under an assured shorthold tenancy was 'likely to be settled rather than temporary' and that it was not right to assume that occupation for a period of as little as six months was not settled. However, it did not follow that occupation under an assured shorthold tenancy always constituted settled accommodation. That remained a question of fact and degree 'although the existence of an assured shorthold tenancy will normally be a significant pointer to the accommodation being settled'. On the specific facts of the instant case, the council had not erred in finding that Ms Knight had had no settled accommodation. It had been entitled to recognise that the claimant's occupation of accommodation under the assured shorthold tenancy had been temporary, rather than settled, and so the causal link to her intentional homelessness had not been broken.

T27.8   *Minchin v Sheffield CC*

(2000) *Times* 26 April, CA

Loss of accommodation caused by deliberate acts done before the start of a tenancy

Ms Minchin committed offences of theft and handling stolen goods between 1995 and 1997. At that time she was a council tenant but she was evicted for unrelated nuisance. In February 1998 she obtained an assured shorthold tenancy (AST) in the private sector. In March 1998 she was convicted of the offences committed in 1995–1997 and was sentenced to 15 months' imprisonment. She was unable to pay the rent and lost her AST. On release from prison she applied as a homeless person. The council decided that she became intentionally homeless from her last settled accommodation, the AST. Both an application for a review and an appeal to the county court were unsuccessful. Ms Minchin appealed, contending that on a true construction of s191 the loss of her accommodation could not be 'in consequence of' deliberate acts done while she was occupying other premises.

The Court of Appeal dismissed a further appeal. Henry LJ held that the criteria for determining whether or not someone was intentionally homeless under s191 were not ambiguous. There was no practical or policy reason why a woman who had been sent to prison for theft should not be regarded as having made herself intentionally homeless, even though she had moved house between the commission of the offence and the start of her sentence.

T27.9 **Mohamed v Westminster CC**
[2005] EWCA Civ 796; [2005] HLR 47; 15 June 2005

Accommodation unaffordable and overcrowded from the outset not settled

The applicant (a Dutch national) and her children left their accommodation in Holland and arrived in the UK. Westminster decided that she had become homeless intentionally. She then secured an assured shorthold tenancy in the private sector at a rent of £245 pw. Her housing benefit was capped at £200. The shortfall led to arrears of rent and an order for possesion. She applied again to Westminster for accommodation. The council decided that she had not had 'settled' accommodation since her last application because the private sector accommodation had been unaffordable and overcrowded from the outset and the loss of it had been inevitable. That decision was upheld on review and by a county court judge on appeal.

The Court of Appeal dismissed a second appeal. The council had been entitled, in determining whether the accommodation was 'settled', to have regard to:

1) the unsuitability by virtue of overcrowding;
2) the inability to pay the rent from the outset; and
3) its assessment that the flat had been taken with a view to the making of a further homelessness application.

There had been no error of law.

T27.10 **R v Camden LBC ex p Aranda**
(1998) 30 HLR 76, CA (see T11.3)

Husband's abandonment of family after move to Colombia broke the chain of causation

T27.11 **R v Croydon LBC ex p Graham**
(1994) 26 HLR 286, CA (see T10.4)

Accommodation not regarded as a permanent home could nevertheless be settled

T27.12 **R v Gloucester CC ex p Miles**
(1985) 17 HLR 292; (1985) 83 LGR 607; [1985] Fam Law 259, CA

Homelessness caused by vandalism to property, not prior departure from it

Mrs Miles and her husband were joint tenants. After her husband left her, Mrs Miles went to stay with friends. While she was away her husband vandalised the home, making it uninhabitable. When the council heard about this, it changed the locks. Mrs Miles applied for accommodation as a homeless person. The council decided that she was intentionally homeless.

The Court of Appeal quashed the decision. Mrs Miles did not become homeless until the property was vandalised. The vandalisation caused her homelessness. She was not a party to the vandalisation and so could not be intentionally homeless. The Court of Appeal also stated that the reasons given were inadequate. Notifications of intentional homelessness ought to state: (a) that the authority is satisfied that the applicant became homeless intentionally; (b) when he or she is considered to have become homeless; (c) why he or she was said to be at that time (ie, what is the deliberate act or omission in consequence of which it is concluded that at the time he or she ceased to occupy accommodation which was available for his or her occupation); and (d) that it would have been reasonable to continue to occupy the particular property.

T27.13   *Steward v Kingston upon Thames RLBC*

[2007] EWCA Civ 565; [2007] HLR 42; 22 May 2007

Occupation of caravan on unauthorised site not settled accommodation

Ms Steward gave up conventional rented accommodation to live in a caravan as a traveller. She was never able to obtain an authorised site for the caravan and was repeatedly evicted from unauthorised sites. On her subsequent application under Part VII for homelessness assistance, she was found to have become intentionally homeless under s190 for having left the rented accommodation. That decision was upheld on review and on appeal to the county court.

The Court of Appeal dismissed a second appeal. The council had been entitled to decide that occupation of a caravan on an unauthorised did not give rise to settled accommodation. The protection afforded to gypsies could not assist Ms Steward in arguing that her accommodation was settled. In any event she was not a gypsy.

T27.14   *Stewart v Lambeth LBC*

[2002] EWCA Civ 753; [2002] HLR 40; (2002) *Times* 28 May

Real cause of applicant's homelessness was his criminal acts; prison not settled accommodation; ineffectual arrangement to maintain a tenancy while in prison did not break causal link nor did the service of a prison sentence

The council obtained a possession order against Mr Stewart, a long-standing secure tenant, suspended on terms requiring payment of current rent and instalments towards the arrears. In June 1998 Mr Stewart was arrested for supplying heroin and was remanded in custody. He arranged with his sister and a housing officer that his sister would take care of his home and make payments due. While he remained entitled to housing benefit, those payments were to be the amount of the water rates and the instalments of arrears. Unknown to Mr Stewart, his sister did not make the payments. The council applied for a warrant which bailiffs executed in February 1999. Mr Stewart was subsequently convicted and sentenced to five years' imprisonment. On his release on licence in December 2000 he applied to the council for assistance as a homeless person. The council decided on review that he had become homeless intentionally as the result of his criminal offending. HHJ Cox dismissed his appeal under s204. Kay LJ granted permission to appeal on the issue of general importance (rehabilitation of prisoners).

The Court of Appeal dismissed the appeal. It held that:

1) The causal connection between the offending and the homelessness had not been broken by the arrangement with the sister and her failure to perform it.

2) The chain of events which led to the applicant losing his home was his deliberate act of supplying heroin. His imprisonment and eviction for non-payment of rent would reasonably have been regarded as the likely consequence of his conduct. The fact that arrangements were made to avoid the eviction did not mean that the authority had to consider such arrangements and decide, if they failed, whether or not that failure was deliberate. The ineffectual arrangement could not break the chain of causation. If the arrangement had worked out initially and subsequently broken down different considerations might apply.

3) The applicant had had no 'settled accommodation' since the loss of his flat because prison could not be treated as a settled home. He had been detained against his will and so it was 'incarceration' rather than a 'home'.

4) Although the causal connection between earlier intentional homelessness and the present homelessness could be broken by events other than the acquisition of settled accommodation, the service of a prison sentence was not such an event.

T27.15 **Watchman v Ipswich BC**
[2007] EWCA Civ 348; [2007] HLR 33; 8 February 2007

Cause of homelessness was taking out of mortgage rather than loss of job

Mrs Watchman was a council tenant. Despite a history of rent arrears and other debts she exercised the right to buy. The instalments under her mortgage were significantly higher than the rent had been. The rate of repayments gradually increased under the mortgage, causing financial difficulties. When her husband lost his job, Mrs Watchman fell into arrears and she was evicted by the mortgage lender. On her application for assistance as a homeless person, the council decided and confirmed on review that she had become intentionally homeless. Given her financial history, it was considered inevitable that, from the outset of the mortgage, she would get into arrears and lose the home. The loss of her husband's job was not an intervening act sufficient to break the chain of causation. On appeal to the county court, Mrs Watchman asserted that the material date for determining the issue of homelessness was the date the accommodation had been left and that the reviewing officer had therefore erred in law in having regard to the financial history of the couple at the time when the mortgage was taken out. That appeal was dismissed.

The Court of Appeal dismissed a further appeal. All the facts had to be considered in cases where there may be multiple causes of homelessness. Although the reviewing officer was obliged to consider the circumstances at the date on which Mrs Watchman left the accommodation, he was also entitled to have regard to matters before that event, including what would have happened if Mrs Watchman's husband had not lost his job and their financial position at the time the mortgage was taken out. The council had been entitled to find that it was the taking-out of the mortgage rather than the loss of the job that had caused the homelessness.

The House of Lords refused permission to appeal.

High Court

T27.16   *R v Basingstoke and Deane BC ex p Bassett*
(1983) 10 HLR 125; [1984] Fam Law 90; (1983) *Times* 18 July, QBD

Homelessness caused by breakdown of marriage not leaving settled accommodation

Mr and Mrs Bassett gave up their council home to emigrate to Canada. However, after a few months they were deported and returned to the UK. They stayed with relatives but, when the marriage broke down, Mrs Bassett applied to the council as a homeless person. It found her intentionally homeless because she had given up their council home. She contended that she was not homeless as a result of leaving that accommodation, but rather as a result of the breakdown in the marriage and, in particular, her husband's conduct, which made it unreasonable for her to live with him.

Taylor J, quashing the decision, found that the homelessness was due to the breakdown of the marriage and not the unsettled nature of the accommodation on the return to the UK. Despite the unsettled nature of the accommodation, there was no unbroken chain of causation between the family giving up their council home to go to Canada and their homelessness when applying to the local authority.

Note: Approved by the Court of Appeal in *R v Harrow LBC ex p Fahia* (T35.1).

T27.17   *R v Croydon LBC ex p Easom*
(1993) 25 HLR 262, QBD

Accommodation occupied while unlawfully in Australia not settled

A couple gave up their secure council accommodation in the UK to go to Australia. They had earlier been refused permission to emigrate and so entered under visitors' visas and then unlawfully overstayed, hoping that they could live and work without being detected by the immigration authorities and that ultimately they would benefit from an amnesty for illegal entrants. They took successive tenancies of privately rented houses under protected tenancies. After about six years they were detected and deported. They applied as homeless persons on the day of their return to the UK. The council decided that their last settled accommodation was the council flat in the UK. The couple asserted that their last settled accommodation had been their home in Australia.

Andrew Collins QC, sitting as a deputy High Court judge, held that the concept of settled accommodation could be taken beyond the terms of occupancy. In the usual case the fact that someone has been in accommodation for a substantial period of time would lead to the almost inevitable inference that the accommodation was settled. There was no magic time before which it is not settled and after which it is settled; it is a question of fact and degree depending on the circumstances. However, the applicants' case was different – as they were in Australia unlawfully they were liable to be removed at any time and that fact made their accommodation precarious. The application for judicial review was dismissed.

T27.18 *R v Hackney LBC ex p Ajayi*
(1998) 30 HLR 473; QBD

Pregnancy resulting in loss of unsettled accommodation did not break chain of causation

The applicant left accommodation in Nigeria in 1994 and came to the UK. She initially stayed with family friends, which she said she regarded as for an indefinite period. She left that accommodation 20 months later and went to live with another family friend in January 1996. She then discovered that she was pregnant. The friend said that she could stay until she found her own accommodation or until the birth of the baby, whichever was the earliest. When the applicant was required to leave in August 1996, she applied as a homeless person to Hackney. Hackney decided that she was intentionally homeless as she had not had settled accommodation since leaving Nigeria. Her pregnancy was 'merely the trigger which caused [her] already unsettled accommodation arrangements to be terminated' and the real cause of her homelessness was her leaving accommodation in Nigeria.

Dyson J dismissed her claim:

1) The settled accommodation issue: Hackney was entitled to conclude, on the facts, that although at the outset the duration of the accommodation was uncertain or indefinite, it was nevertheless precarious or temporary and not settled. The question of settled accommodation was one of fact and degree. Hackney had taken into account relevant facts such as the duration of the accommodation and the fact that it was not with family members or close friends of the applicant.

2) The causation issue: The fundamental question was whether there was a continuous chain of causation between the loss of the last settled accommodation and the present state of homelessness. Questions of causation are notoriously difficult and the court should be slow to intervene in the decisions of administrative bodies on such questions and should do so only in clear cases. The right question to ask is: what is the real or effective cause of homelessness? The authority should answer the question in a practical commonsense way, having regard to all relevant circumstances.

T27.19 *R v Hammersmith and Fulham LBC ex p P*
(1990) 22 HLR 21; (1990) 88 LGR 119, QBD

Applicants' anti-social behaviour, resulting in death threats from IRA, caused homelessness

The applicants, members of six households who were related, lived in Belfast. People in all the households, except for one, were guilty of criminal or anti-social behaviour. They fled their homes after receiving death threats from the IRA. The council decided that the applicants were intentionally homeless on the basis that it was entitled to consider the activities which led to the death threats. Their misbehaviour was something 'in consequence of which' the applicants ceased to occupy their accommodation.

Schiemann J upheld the findings of intentional homelessness in respect of five of the applicants. He found that it was their anti-social and criminal behaviour which led them to lose their homes. However, he quashed the decision in relation to the sixth household, which had not been engaged in anti-social behaviour.

T27.20 *R v Hounslow LBC ex p R*
(1997) 29 HLR 939, QBD

Test is would the loss of accommodation 'reasonably have been regarded at the time as the likely consequence of the deliberate conduct'

In 1991 the applicant committed serious crimes, resulting in a lengthy sentence of imprisonment. His housing benefit lapsed after one year and, as he could not pay his rent, he surrendered his tenancy. On his release in 1995, his application for housing was met with a finding of intentional homelessness. The council asserted that since, as a matter of fact, the crimes had been deliberate and had ultimately caused his homelessness, Housing Act 1985 s60 (now Housing Act 1996 s191) was satisfied.

Deputy Judge Stephen Richards held that the section was to be read as containing some qualification or limitation disabling an authority from tracing back a chain of linked events indefinitely. After reviewing the conflicting authorities, he held that the true question was objectively whether the loss of accommodation 'would reasonably have been regarded at the time as the likely consequence of the deliberate conduct'. There were no reasons of public policy for applying the test of causation in a special way for ex-prisoners. The council had applied the correct test of reasonable likelihood. The conclusion that the applicant's homelessness was caused by the commission of the offences was not irrational and was one which it was entitled to reach.

T27.21 *R v Merton LBC ex p Ruffle*
(1989) 21 HLR 361, QBD

Accommodation is either settled or temporary

The applicants were found intentionally homeless. They then found a council tenant willing to share his two-bedroomed council flat with them rent free, in return for cooking and cleaning services. The arrangement was meant to be permanent but broke down after four and a half months as a result of the tenant's drinking problem. They left the flat and applied again as homeless persons. The local authority decided that the original intentional homelessness finding still stood, as 'the intervening period has not been one of settled occupation'. The applicants applied for judicial review. They contended that the authority had asked the wrong question and should have asked not whether the intervening accommodation was settled but whether it was more than 'only temporary accommodation'. There was a spectrum of accommodation between 'settled' and 'only temporary' and anything other than the latter broke the chain of causation with previous intentionality. As the intervening accommodation was 'more than temporary' and would count as accommodation for the purposes of Housing Act 1985 s58 (now Housing Act 1996 s175), it broke the link with the earlier period of homelessness.

Simon Brown J upheld the authority's decision. Asking whether there has been an intervening period of settled occupation involves asking the same question as whether the accommodation was only temporary. Those questions are opposite sides of the same coin. One or other of the terms encompasses all states of accommodation. Given the difficulty for intentionally homeless families in finding settled accommodation, his judgment ended with a call for authorities to adopt a 'benevolent' approach to the question of whether or not accommodation can be treated as settled, and for parliamentary consideration of a time limit for the 'length of disqualification' which might arise from an intentional homelessness decision.

T27.22 *R v Newham LBC ex p Campbell*
(1994) 26 HLR 183, QBD

Although a possession order had been made on the basis of the applicant's arrears, the cause of her homeless was violence

In 1989 the council obtained an order for possession of the applicant's flat, suspended on terms about payment of current rent and arrears. By February 1990 the terms had been broken. The council applied to the court for a warrant, which was then suspended on terms. In August 1990 the applicant fled the premises as a result of sexual harassment and violence. As the terms of the suspended warrant had been broken, the council applied again for a warrant and in December 1990 bailiffs took possession. In judicial review proceedings brought to challenge, among other things, a subsequent finding of intentional homelessness, the council argued (following *Thompson v Elmbridge BC* (12.16) that the tenancy had ended in early 1990 on the first breach of the suspended possession order. From that time, the applicant had been homeless and therefore the subsequent abandonment of the premises and reason for that were not directly relevant to whether she was intentionally homeless.

Sir Louis Blom-Cooper QC held that the council had misdirected itself in law. In considering causation for the purpose of intentional homelessness, the council had to look not only at the background of arrears and default but at the true reason which caused the applicant to cease to occupy the accommodation – in this case the harassment and violence.

T27.23 *R v Shrewsbury and Atcham BC ex p Griffiths*
(1993) 25 HLR 613, QBD

Where payments from income support not paid towards mortgage, council should have considered whether homlessness was a likely result of that non-payment

The applicants were home-owners in default with mortgage repayments. Shortly after the mortgage was obtained they both lost their employment. They claimed assistance with the mortgage as part of their income support but were not awarded enough to meet each repayment. They also failed to pay over all of the money they received from the DSS – using it for other living expenses. The lender brought possession proceedings and the applicants applied to the council on the basis that they were threatened with homelessness. The council found that the applicants had deliberately failed to make over all DSS payments received and so their threatened homelessness was intentional.

Anthony Lester QC quashed the decision. The decision letter failed to indicate that the council had considered the essential question of whether the 'likely result' of that failure was homelessness. If it had been considered, the decision was bad for failure to give reasons. The council knew that, irrespective of the failure to pay over the full benefit, the applicants were unable to keep up the mortgage. The council's evidence failed to disclose any consideration of the *Homelessness Code of Guidance* (especially the then current para 2.15) and so indicated failure to comply with Housing Act 1985 s71 (now Housing Act 1996 s182) (duty to have regard to the code).

T27.24   *R v Westminster CC ex p Reid*
(1994) 26 HLR 690, QBD

Question was whether homelessess was 'reasonable result' of slapping child

The applicant became homeless when he was excluded by his ex-wife for slapping one of their children. Leave to move for judicial review of a finding of intentional homelessness was granted by the Court of Appeal. The council failed to appear at the full hearing of the application.

Deputy Judge Robert Carnwath QC held that the council had failed to direct itself on whether the 'reasonable result' of the slapping was homelessness and that, accordingly, the decision should be quashed.

Scottish courts

T27.25   *R v Kyle and Carrick DC ex p Robson*
1993 GWD 1065, Court of Session (Outer House)

Applicant's intentions relevant to question of settled accommodation

The applicant lived with her mother until 1988. In 1989 she was offered her own council tenancy and moved into that accommodation. In October 1990 she gave it up to return to live with her mother. She was rendered homeless when, following disagreements, her mother asked her to leave. The council declared her to be intentionally homeless.

Lord Marnoch quashed the decision. The inference drawn by the council that the accommodation with the mother was tenuous was patently unsound. What were relevant were the applicant's intentions and expectations when she moved back to her mother. The only reasonable inference from her giving up a council tenancy to move to her mother's home was that she anticipated a secure and settled life with her mother.

T28   ## Cease to occupy accommodation

One element of the intentional homelessness test is that an applicant must 'cease to occupy' accommodation. *R v Westminster CC ex p Chambers* (T35.6) established that an applicant could not 'cease to occupy' accommodation that had never been occupied and so the refusal of an offer of accommodation did not result in being intentionally homeless from that accommodation. (However, note that *R v Brent LBC ex p Awua* (T22.2) held that if an applicant lost temporary accommodation as a result of the refusal of other accommodation he or she could be intentionally homeless from the temporary accommodation.)

Court of Appeal

T28.1 *Lee-Lawrence v Penwith DC*

[2006] EWCA Civ 1672; 9 May 2006

Applicant occupied property despite claiming never to have moved into it

Mr Lee-Lawrence's home was rendered uninhabitable by an arson attack. He later accepted a tenancy of a housing association property and claimed housing benefit to pay the rent. He later terminated the tenancy and applied to Penwith as a homeless person. He claimed that he had never occupied the housing association property. The council rejected this and decided that he was intentionally homeless as a result of ceasing to occupy the property. That decision was upheld on review and a county court judge dismissed an appeal.

The Court of Appeal dismissed a second appeal. The fact that a person had a legal right to possession of, or held the keys to, premises was not, of itself, sufficient to establish occupation of the premises. But those factors, combined with the benefit claim, which involved a representation that he was in occupation, and other representations made by the applicant that he had been resident in the premises, were sufficient to ground a finding of occupancy.

T28.2 *R v Wandsworth LBC ex p Oteng*

(1994) 26 HLR 413, CA

Applicant ceasing to occupy property before selling it not intentionally homeless

The applicant and her mother exercised the right to buy the family home, held on a secure tenancy, and so became a joint owners of it. In May 1988 she left home and in August 1990 the applicant applied to the council as a homeless person. She was told that she was not homeless because of her legal interest in the family home (Housing Act 1985 s58(2)(a), now Housing Act 1996 s175(1)(a)) and that if she gave up the interest she would be found intentionally homeless. Later in 1990 she assigned her interest in the property to her mother and in May 1991 was declared intentionally homeless.

The Court of Appeal quashed the decision. The applicant had ceased to occupy the accommodation long before her deliberate act in disposing of it occurred. Her act had not caused her to cease to occupy the property and she could not be intentionally homeless as a result.

High Court

T28.3 *R v Westminster CC ex p Chambers*

(1982) 6 HLR 24; (1982) 81 LGR 401, QBD (see T35.6)

Applicant who refused an offer of accommodation did not 'cease to occupy' it

T28.4 *R v Westminster CC ex p De Souza*

(1997) 29 HLR 649, QBD

Applicant not intentionally homeless in disposing of an interest in a property she had never occupied

The applicant and her husband lost their tied accommodation and separated. On her application as a homeless person the council accepted that it owed her the full housing duty and provided temporary accommodation pending discharge of its duty. It then discovered that she and her husband jointly owned a house which, although it had been tenanted, was available for occupation. The applicant and her husband then sold the house. After it had been sold, the council reopened its enquiries and declared the applicant to be intentionally homeless.

Popplewell J quashed the decision. The applicant had not become homeless after having 'ceased to occupy' the house, as required by the definition of 'intentional homelessness'. Although she had rights in the jointly owned property, she had never lived there. One cannot cease to occupy that which has not been occupied. He declined to follow *R v Westminster CC ex p Khan* (T28.5), preferring dicta in *R v Wandsworth LBC ex p Oteng* (T28.2).

T28.5 *R v Westminster CC ex p Khan*
(1991) 23 HLR 230, QBD

Applicant ceased to occupy accommodation she had never lived in

The applicant and his wife sold a property which they had intended to occupy and had told the immigration authorities that they were going to occupy. Even though the female applicant had at no time been in occupation of the property, the court held that there was sufficient material, on the special facts, for the local authority to conclude that they had both 'ceased to occupy' the property and were intentionally homeless.

T29 Available

The accommodation lost must have been 'available' for the applicant's household to occupy – see section T14.

T30 Reasonable to continue to occupy

The accommodation lost must have been reasonable for the applicant's household to continue to occupy. This is considered in the section dealing with whether an applicant is homeless – see section T7.

T31 Local connection and referral

Housing Act 1996 ss198–200
Where the main housing duty (s193(2)) would arise, but the conditions for referral set out in s198 are satisfied, an authority may refer an applicant to another authority to perform the s193 duty. The decision to refer is discretionary. The conditions for referral are based on an applicant's local connections, defined in s199.

Section 198(2)–(2A) provides that the conditions for referral are met if neither the applicant, nor any person who might reasonably be expected to reside with him or her

a) does not have a local connection with the authority applied to,
b) has a local connection with another authority, and
c) does not run the risk of violence in that other authority (s198(2A) applies a slightly more restrictive test in relation to non-domestic violence).

Section 199(1) provides that a person has a local connection with another authority if he or she has a connection with it because of –

a) present or past normal residence of choice
b) employment,
c) family associations, or
d) special circumstances.

Section 199 goes on to prescribe special provisions relating to those formerly in the armed forces, in detention or seeking asylum.

Section 198(5) provides that the question of whether the conditions for referral are satisfied shall be decided by agreement between the authorities. Local authorities have agreed guidelines, commonly referred to as the Referral Guidelines or the Local Authority Agreement (reproduced in Annex 18 of the *Code of Guidance* and Annex 20 of the *Welsh Code*), on the criteria to be applied when assessing local connection and for procedures on referrals. The Homelessness (Decisions on Referrals) Order 1998 SI No 1578 sets out arrangements for determining disputes where agreement is not reached.

Section 200 sets out the duties owed to an applicant whose case is considered for referral.

House of Lords

T31.1   *Al-Ameri v Kensington and Chelsea RLBC; Osmani v Harrow LBC*
[2004] UKHL 4; [2004] 2 AC 159; [2004] 2 WLR 354; [2004] 1 All ER 1104; [2004] HLR 20; [2004] LGR 161; (2004) *Times* 6 February; 5 February 2004

Residence in NASS accommodation was 'normal residence' but was not 'of choice'

The two applicants were destitute asylum-seekers and were accommodated in Glasgow by the National Asylum Support Service (NASS) under its dispersal scheme (Immigration and Asylum Act 1999 s95). On the determination of their asylum claims they became eligible for assistance under Housing Act 1996 Part VII. They travelled to London and applied as homeless persons. The London local authorities considered that the applicants were owed the main housing duty under s193, but that the conditions were met for referring them to Glasgow City Council because they had a local connection through residence there. It was asserted that this had been their normal residence of choice (s199(1)(a)). The decisions were confirmed on review and appeals to the county court under s204 were dismissed. The Court of Appeal, by a majority, allowed their appeals ([2003] EWCA Civ 235; [2003] 1 WLR 1289). The local authorities appealed to the House of Lords.

The House of Lords dismissed the appeals. The applicants were 'normally resident' in Glasgow pending determination of their claims for asylum (see *Mohamed v Hammersmith and Fulham* LBC (T31.2)). However, the residence was not 'of choice'. It is a cardinal feature of the NASS scheme that destitute asylum-seekers should go where they are sent pending the determination of their asylum claims. They should not be able to pick and choose where they are accommodated. That choice is made by NASS. Indeed Immigration and Asylum Act 1999 s97(2)(a) expressly prevents the secretary of state from having regard to any preference that the asylum-seeker or his or her dependants might have about the locality in which accommodation is to be provided. It followed that it could never be said, however contented asylum-seekers might be to remain there, that 'that residence' was of 'their own' choice for the purposes of s199(1)(a). The categories listed in s199(3), where accommodation is deemed not to be 'of choice', were not exhaustive.

Note: The effect of this decision was reversed by Housing Act 1996 s199(6) and (7), inserted by Asylum and Immigration (Treatment of Claimants, etc) Act 2004 s11, which provides that such accommodation gives rise to a local connection..

T31.2   *Mohamed v Hammersmith and Fulham LBC*
[2001] UKHL 57; [2002] 1 AC 547; [2001] 3 WLR 1339; [2002] 1 All ER 176; [2002] HLR 7; (2001) *Times* 2 November

The time to determine local connection is the date of decision/review; interim accommodation pending decision/review led to normal residence

Mr Mohamed's wife, Mrs Farah, came to the United Kingdom in 1994 and lived in Ealing. Mr Mohamed came to the United Kingdom on 31 January 1998 and lived with a friend in Hammersmith. On 16 April 1998 they made a joint application to Hammersmith as homeless persons. Pending enquiries, Hammersmith placed them in interim accommodation within its own district. In July 1998 it informed them that, although they were owed the full housing duty (s193), they had no local connection with Hammersmith and by reason of Mrs Farah's previous residence in Ealing they were to be referred there under s198. In September 1998 a review was carried out upholding the original decision. The reviewing officer considered that Mr Mohammed's residence in Hammersmith between January and April 1998 (ie, up to the date of their application) was insufficient to give rise to a local connection. Mr Mohammed appealed. He contended that the time he resided in Hammersmith between the initial decision and the review should have been taken into account when determining local connection on the review. Hammersmith argued that occupation of interim accommodation could not amount to 'normal residence'. Furthermore, it was the local connection that existed at the date of the initial decision that was material, even on review. The Court of Appeal (*Ealing LBC v Surdonja; Mohamed v Hammersmith and Fulham* LBC [2001] QB 97; [2000] 3 WLR 481; [2000] 2 All ER 597; (2000) 32 HLR 481; (2000) *Times* 11 February, CA)) allowed an appeal.

The House of Lords dismissed an appeal by Hammersmith. Lord Slynn, giving the judgment of the court, held as follows:

1) *Interim accommodation could count as normal residence of choice*: '... the prima facie meaning of normal residence is a place where at the relevant time a person in fact resides ... So long as that place where he eats and sleeps is voluntarily accepted by him, the reason why he is there rather than somewhere else does not prevent that place from being his normal residence. He may not like it, he may prefer some other place, but that place is for the relevant time the place where he normally resides ... Where he is given interim accommodation by a local housing authority even more clearly is that a place where for the time being he is normally resident. The fact that it is provided subject to a statutory duty does not ... prevent it from being such.' [18] Section 199 did not exclude such accommodation from being treated as 'of choice', as it could have done.

2) *The date of the local connection*: '... since the question is whether an applicant "has a local connection" that must mean such a connection at the date of decision or review, whether in the meantime the applicant had acquired or lost, by moving away, his local connection.' [23]

3) *The material to be looked at on review*: 'I find nothing in the statutory language which requires the review to be confined to the date of the original application or determination ... the process is an administrative one at [the review] stage and there can be no justification for the final administrative decision of the reviewing officer to be limited to the circumstances existing at the date of the initial decision. The decision of the reviewing officer is at large both as to the facts (ie as to whether the three conditions in section 198(2) of the Act are satisfied) and as to the exercise of the discretion to refer. He is not simply considering whether the initial decision was right on the material before it at the date it was made. He may have regard to information relevant to the period before the first decision but only obtained thereafter and to matters occurring after the initial decision.' ([25]–[26])

Note: See *Sahardid v Camden LBC* (T43.12) where it was held that the same principles applied under the Allocation of Housing and Homelessness (Review Procedure) Regulations 1999 (*Mohamed* had been decided under previous regulations) and was not limited to issues of local connection.

T31.3 ## Re Betts

[1983] 2 AC 613; [1983] 3 WLR 397; [1983] 2 All ER 1111; (1983) 10 HLR 97, HL

Legitimate to have regard to guidelines in the Local Authority Agreement

In August 1980 Mr Betts left his home in Blaby DC and went to live in the district of Eastleigh BC, where he had found work. He obtained a tenancy and his family joined him. He later lost his job, fell into arrears of rent and was evicted. He applied as a homeless person to Eastleigh in February 1981. It decided that he was owed the main housing duty but had no local connection with Eastleigh as he had lived there for fewer than six months. It made a referral to Blaby. An application for judicial review of that decision was dismissed but the Court of Appeal allowed an appeal ([1983] 1 WLR 774; (1983) 8 HLR 28), holding that the decision to refer had been reached by a rigid application of the Local Authority Agreement. Normal residence was where a person intended to settle, not necessarily permanently or indefinitely. The concept of normal residence required a consideration of many features of residence and nor merely the application of an arbitrary six-month period.

The House of Lords allowed Eastleigh's appeal. The Court of Appeal's approach was misconceived. The fundamental question was not of 'normal residence' but of the existence of a 'local connection'. In appropriate circumstances a single day's residence may be enough to establish normal residence in an area but local connection meant far more than that. The onus of establishing a local connection rests on the applicant. Applicants must show that they have built up a local connection based on a period of residence, employment, family associations or other special circumstances. Where residence was relevant, the question was whether an applicant's normal residence in an area had been of such duration as to establish a local connection. To answer that question and to avoid disputes, or to settle them quickly and cheaply if they arose, local authorities had agreed guidelines. Lord Brightman held that:

> Although 'an opinion' formed by a housing authority ... must be concluded by reference to the facts of each individual case, there is no objection to the authority operating a policy or establishing guidelines, for reasons which the authority may legitimately entertain, and then applying such policy or guidelines generally to all the applications which come before them, provided that the authority do not close their mind to the particular facts of the individual case. There is ample authority that a body which is charged with an administrative discretion is entitled to promulgate a policy or guidelines as an indication of a norm which is intended to be followed: see, for example, the speech of Lord Reid in *British Oxygen Co Ltd v Board of Trade* [1971] AC 610. [627F–628B]

Eastleigh had not misdirected itself in deciding that no local connection existed.

Court of Appeal

T31.4   *Kensington and Chelsea RLBC v Danesh*
[2006] EWCA Civ 1404; [2007] 1WLR 69; [2007] HLR 17; October 2006

'Violence' did not include words, actions or gestures which caused a person to fear physical attack

Mr Danesh came to the UK as an asylum-seeker and was accommodated by NASS in Swansea. In November 2004, after being granted indefinite leave to remain, he travelled to London and applied to Kensington and Chelsea RLBC as a homeless person. In January 2005 the council accepted that he was owed the main housing duty but informed him that it would refer him to Swansea under the local connection provisions. Mr Danesh requested a review of that decision, which failed. On being informed that the referral had been accepted and that he had a renewed right of review under s200 Mr Danesh sought a further review. He asserted that he had suffered violence in Swansea (s198(2A)(a)) and that it was probable that if he were to return to Swansea he would be subjected to further violence of a similar kind (s198(2A)(b)). He relied on a number of incidents of harassment and racial abuse in Swansea and on two specific incidents, one where he had been pushed to the ground and injured and another where he was mugged. He considered that he was targeted as an asylum-seeker and that there would be a recurrence of attacks if he returned. Kensington confirmed its decision on review: the harassment and racial abuse could occur anywhere and did not amount to threats of violence; the two actual incidents of violence were random acts that were not racially motivated and it was not likely that Mr Danesh would be subjected to further violence of a similar kind if he were to return to Swansea. Mr Danesh's appeal to the county court was successful.

The Court of Appeal allowed a second appeal. Mr Danesh's contention that violence included words, actions or gestures which caused him to fear physical attack was rejected. 'Violence' for the purposes of s198(2A) is defined as violence or threats of violence which are likely to be carried out (s198(2A)(3)). It was limited to actual or threatened physical violence. The question of the likelihood of violence occurring is to be assessed objectively. The council had properly understood the meaning of violence and had carried out a proper assessment of the likelihood of violence occurring and made a lawful decision.

T31.5   *Ozbek v Ipswich BC*
[2006] EWCA Civ 534; [2006] HLR 41; [2006] LGR 853; (2006) *Times* 7 June

Applicant's family associations too tenuous to found a local connection

Mr Ozbek sought asylum in the UK and was accommodated by the National Asylum Support Service (NASS) in Portsmouth. He was granted indefinite leave to remain and, while still in the NASS accommodation, applied to Portsmouth as a homeless person. It accepted him for the main housing duty and offered him accommodation in discharge of its duty. That accommodation was refused. Mr Ozbek left the NASS accommodation and applied to Ipswich as a homeless person. He claimed a 'local connection' with Ipswich as he had brothers and cousins in the area which provided him with an entire support system. Ipswich decided that he did not have a connection with it and to refer him to Portsmouth, where he did have a local connection (s199(6)). (Portsmouth accepted the referral but relied on its discharge of duty not to provide further assistance.) Ipswich confirmed its decision on review. It referred to the Referral Guidelines, which recognise parents, adult children and brothers/sisters living in an area for five years as normally constituting a family association. Although Mr Ozbek's cousins had lived in Ipswich for over five years, his brothers, who had also sought asylum, had only been resident in the area for 18 months. A county court judge allowed an appeal.

The Court of Appeal allowed a second appeal by Ipswich. In light of the guidance in the Referral Guidelines, the decision that Mr Ozbek's brothers did not give rise to a local connection was lawful. Family associations capable of giving rise to a local connection do not have to be based on the presence of 'near relatives', in the sense recognised in the guidance. The presence of a cousin could give rise to a local connection. The relevant question was whether, in the particular circumstances of the case, the bond between Mr Ozbek and his extended family was of such a nature that they could be described as near relatives. The reviewing officer had addressed that question and was entitled to reach the conclusion he made. It was irrelevant that the welfare of the family might be better served by the help and support of the extended family, rather than voluntary and statutory agencies. Furthermore, the decision by Portsmouth that it had discharged its duty was irrelevant to the decision to refer.

T31.6   *R v Greenwich LBC ex p Patterson*
(1994) 26 HLR 159, CA

Mandatory duty to enquire into the risk of violence in another area

Ms Patterson lost accommodation in Birmingham and went to live with her mother in Greenwich. When her mother asked her to leave she applied as a homeless person to Greenwich. She did not have a local connection with Greenwich. In interview she was told that it was likely that any responsibility for housing would fall on Birmingham. She was not asked whether there was a risk of violence in Birmingham and, although she had been subjected to violent assaults from her ex-partner when living there, she did not mention this. The council accepted her for the main housing duty and made a referral to Birmingham.

The Court of Appeal held that, before a council could be satisfied that there was no risk of violence (Housing Act 1985 s67(2)(c), now Housing Act 1996 s198(2)(c) and (2A)), it had to make enquiries to establish that fact. Greenwich was not entitled to rely on the fact that nothing was said by the applicant to alert it to the possibility that a risk existed.

T31.7   *R v Hammersmith and Fulham LBC ex p Avdic*
(1998) 30 HLR 1, CA

No local connection based on presence of cousin nearby and medical treatment

Ms Avdic was a refugee from Bosnia. Soon after her arrival in the United Kingdom she was housed in Kirklees where she lived with her two children for two years. When that accommodation ended she went to London where she had a first cousin once removed living in Kensington and Chelsea. She applied as a homeless person to the neighbouring borough of Hammersmith and Fulham. She submitted medical evidence relating to her serious anxiety and depression. She considered that her depression was due to her isolation and lack of social support in Kirklees. Hammersmith took the view that she had no local connection with its area and made a referral to Kirklees. Her application for judicial review of that decision was dismissed and she appealed.

The Court of Appeal held that there were no grounds on which Hammersmith's decision could be impugned. It had approached the question of local connection flexibly but found no local connection through family associations or other special reasons. It had exercised its residual discretion in making the decision to refer. It was not at fault in relying on its medical adviser's opinion without the adviser examining the applicant or her records. There were two medical issues: the significance to Ms Advic of her cousin's presence in London and any advantages London had to offer in terms of treatment. There was no root medical dispute that could have been illuminated by a physical examination. Ms Advic's medical report was largely dependent on what she had herself expressed. The issue of whether medical treatment could be as well provided in Kirklees as in London did not require any examination of the applicant or her records.

T31.8 *R v Hillingdon LBC ex p Streeting*

[1980] 1 WLR 1425; [1980] 3 All ER 413; (1980) 79 LGR 167, CA (see T34.4)

Where an applicant has no local connection, the main housing duty falls on the authority to whom the applicant applies

T31.9 *R v Newham LBC ex p Tower Hamlets LBC*

[1991] 1 WLR 1032; [1992] 2 All ER 767; (1991) 23 HLR 62; (1992) LGR 123, CA (see T8.9)

An authority, considering an applicant who would be referred to another authority, was required to consider the general housing conditions in that other authority; exercise of discretion to refer

T31.10 *R v Slough BC ex p Ealing LBC*

[1981] QB 801; [1981] 2 WLR 399; [1981] 1 All ER 601; (1980) 79 LGR 335, CA (see T36.2)

Where applicant applied to a second authority, second authority to form its own view on application; arbitrator could only decide questions of local connection

T31.11 *R v Tower Hamlets LBC ex p Ali and Bibi*

(1993) 25 HLR 158, CA (see T51.8)

A referral under the local connection provisions does not amount to a discharge of duty entitling notifying authority to refuse to entertain a subsequent reapplication

T31.12 *Sareen v Hackney LBC*

[2003] EWCA Civ 351; [2003] HLR 54; (2003) *Times* 9 April (see T43.13)

No right of review of a decision not to refer under local connection provisions

High Court

T31.13 *R v Ealing LBC ex p Fox*

(1998) *Times* 9 March, QBD

'Employment' included unpaid work

The applicant lived in the West Midlands for many years but from 1995 visited London frequently and worked as a volunteer in Ealing. He applied to Ealing as a homeless person. It decided that he was owed the main housing duty but did not have a local connection with Ealing and made a referral to the West Midlands. The applicant was told that he was unable to establish a local connection because he did not have paid employment.

Gerald Moriarty QC, sitting as a deputy judge, said that the word 'employed' in Housing Act 1985 s61(1)(b) (now Housing Act 1996 s199(1)(b)) was to be given its ordinary meaning. It referred to both paid and unpaid employment. The council had misdirected itself by deciding that voluntary employment did not come within s61(1)(b). However, as the applicant had not actually been engaged in even unpaid work at the date of application or decision, the application for judicial review on that ground was dismissed. Referring to Tucker J's comments at first instance in *R v Hammersmith and Fulham LBC ex p Avdic* (T31.7) that cousins of any description could not amount to a family association, he held that the applicant's deceased uncle did not qualify, nor could the matters relied on amount to special circumstances. However, there were errors of fact and procedure in making the referral and the council's decision to refer was quashed.

Note: In *Ozbek v Ipswich BC* (T31.5) it was held that family associations could be established by relatives such as uncles and cousins.

T31.14 **R v East Devon DC ex p Robb**
(1998) 30 HLR 922, QBD

Council had a residual discretion not to make a referral

Mrs Robb suffered from a medical condition which seriously affected her blood circulation in cold weather. On medical advice from her GP and consultant specialist to move to a warmer area, she gave up accommodation in Aberdeenshire and moved to Devon. Three months later she applied to East Devon as a homeless person. The council was satisfied that she was not intentionally homeless and that the main housing duty was owed but decided that she had no local connection with its area and her application would be referred back to Aberdeenshire.

Deputy Judge Gerald Moriarty QC quashed the decision. He held that:

1) The council had not taken into account its discretion not to refer back even if the applicant had no connection with it (Housing Act 1985 s67(1), now Housing Act 1996 s198(1)).
2) The council had relied on its own medical advice, which was based on unsubstantiated propositions about comparative climate, a lack of research into the medical condition and no personal knowledge of the applicant. Furthermore, the medical officer's view was inconsistent with the council's view that the applicant was not intentionally homeless for leaving the accommodation in Aberdeen.
3) The applicant had never been informed that her own medical evidence, which had not previously been doubted, was being questioned.

T31.15 **R v Hammersmith and Fulham LBC ex p O'Brian**
(1985) 17 HLR 471; (1985) 84 LGR 202, QBD (see T36.3)

Where an applicant was referred to an authority which had previously discharged its duty to the applicant, that authority could refuse assistance

T31.16 **R v Islington LBC ex p Adigun**
(1988) 20 HLR 600, QBD

Authority not in error in deciding applicant did not run the risk of domestic violence

The applicant rented a flat in Liverpool with her husband. As a result of domestic violence she left and went with her children to stay with a friend in London. When, within a month, she was asked to leave, she applied as a homeless person to Islington. It made enquiries of Liverpool and was told that the applicant's husband had moved out of the flat, taking his furniture with him. It had been re-let and it was believed that the husband had returned to Nigeria. Islington accepted the applicant was owed the main housing duty but referred her to Liverpool. The applicant sought judicial review of this decision.

Mann J upheld the council's decision. Even if the applicant had become 'normally resident' in Islington, that alone was insufficient to establish a local connection (applying *Re Betts* (T31.3)), even if coupled with a desire to remain there and not return to Liverpool. The decision to refer to Liverpool was criticised as breaching the prohibition (in Housing Act 1985 s67(2)(c), now Housing Act 1996 s198(2)(c)) against referring to an area where the applicant 'will run the risk of domestic violence'. Mann J found that the task of determining whether or not there is a risk of domestic violence is a task for the local authority. He was satisfied that, by obtaining the information it had from Liverpool, Islington had conducted sufficient enquiries to satisfy itself that the applicant would not be at risk of violence in returning to that area. The application was dismissed.

T31.17 *R v Tower Hamlets LBC ex p Camden LBC*
(1989) 21 HLR 197, QBD (see T36.4)

Guidance on the responsibilities of authorities considering applications by applicants who had previously applied to another local authority

T31.18 *R (Bantamagbari) v Westminster CC and Southwark LBC*
[2003] EWHC 1350 (Admin); 13 May 2003

Unlawful refusal of referral where authority had delayed in challenging referring authority's decision

The applicant applied to Southwark. It decided that he was owed the main housing duty but made a referral to Westminster because he had a connection with that area and no connection with Southwark (s198). Although the referral was notified to Westminster in January 2002 it did nothing until May 2002 when it rejected the referral because it thought Southwark had been wrong in deciding the applicant was not intentionally homeless.

In August 2002 Mr Bantamgbari made a claim for judicial review of Westminster's decision not to accept the referral. In March 2003 Westminster joined Southwark as a second defendant. Wilson J decided that Westminster had acted unlawfully. It was seeking to cause the court to judicially review Southwark's decision in January 2002. However, its delay precluded an extension of time for bringing proceedings. Even if judicial review proceedings could be brought, the court would refuse to declare Southwark's decision unlawful.

T31.19 *R (W) v Sheffield CC*
[2005] EWHC 720 (Admin); 14 April 2005 (see T53.26)

In exceptional circumstances notified authority ordered to accommodate applicant in notifying authority's area pending appeal against decision to refer

Local government ombudsman

T31.20 *Investigation 91/A/2400-01 (Tower Hamlets LBC)*

Council wrongly deciding that applicant did not have a local connection with it

A homeless person applied to Tower Hamlets Council for accommodation. The council found that the conditions for a referral under Housing Act 1985 s67 (now Housing Act 1996 s198) were satisfied and in February 1989 exercised its discretion to refer the applicant to Epsom and Ewell BC. The referral was not accepted and the dispute between the two boroughs was referred to a referee to determine. The process of arbitration took over two years. In October 1991 the referee decided that the s67 conditions were not fulfilled and that the duty to house lay with Tower Hamlets Council. That council then spent three months considering whether to apply for a judicial review of the referee's decision until in January 1992 it decided to house the applicant. In the following month Tower Hamlets Council offered accommodation. Meanwhile, the applicant had been in poor quality bed and breakfast accommodation for over three years.

The local ombudsman found from the information held by the council, or which should have been acquired, that there was a clear local connection with Tower Hamlets and the referral should never have been made. He recommended a payment of £3,000 compensation for the three unnecessary years in bed and breakfast accommodation and further recommended that the secretary of state should introduce a timetable for the speedy resolution of local connection disputes.

T31.21 *Investigation Nos 97/C/3627 and 3771 (Harrogate BC and Leominster BC)*

Maladministration resulting from actions of homeless officer who had no training

The complainant was a housing association tenant living with his family in Leominster. In July 1997 he was advised by police to leave home following threats of violence made from prison by his brother-in-law. The complainant thought he would move to Harrogate as he had a sister-in-law in that area. He approached his local council, Leominster DC, for assistance as a homeless person. The officer concerned failed to recognise that a local connection referral could not be made (as the complainant had a local connection with Leominster – see Housing Act 1996 s198(2)(a)) and wrongly considered that Harrogate had a duty to provide temporary accommodation as soon as the referral was made (ie, prior to its acceptance) contrary to s200(1). The family travelled to Harrogate but, as no accommodation had been secured for them, had to sleep overnight on the floor in a police station. The ombudsman said

> I am very concerned that the Leominster District Council had an officer who had no formal training in homelessness legislation in a position where he was making decisions on homelessness under the provisions of the Housing Act. That officer was not sufficiently familiar with the legislation and existing agreement to be able to deal with [the complainants] situation properly. His understanding of the legislation was clearly wrong.

The successor authority paid £500 compensation.

Arbitration decisions

T31.22 *Kensington and Chelsea RLBC v City of Westminster*
June 1989 *Legal Action* 23

Referee had jurisdiction to decide afresh whether and with whom an applicant might reasonably be expected to reside (s176)

Kensington and Chelsea Council referred the applicant (a single pregnant woman) to Westminster Council under the local connection referral provisions in Housing Act 1985 s67 (now Housing Act 1996 s198). Westminster Council asserted in response that the acknowledged father with whom the mother wished to live was a 'person who might reasonably be expected to reside with' the applicant. As he had a local connection with Kensington and Chelsea, referral was not possible (s67(2)(a), now s198(2)(a)). Kensington and Chelsea argued that the issue of who might reasonably be expected to reside with the applicant was one over which it had exclusive jurisdiction and, in its view, the putative father was not within that group.

The referee held that he had jurisdiction to determine the s67(2)(a) issue afresh and that, on the particular facts, it was reasonable to expect the father to reside with the mother and child. The notification was therefore not appropriate.

Cf *R v Slough BC ex p Ealing LBC* (T36.2)

T32 # Applications by homeless people

When someone applies to an authority for accommodation, or for assistance in obtaining accommodation, and the authority has reason to believe that he or she is, or may be, homeless or threatened with homelessness it is required to make inquiries into what duty, if any, it owes the applicant (ss184–185).

Although there is no statutory restriction placed on who can make an application nor a limit placed on the number of applications that can be made, restrictions have been applied by the courts.

T33 ## General

Court of Appeal

T33.1 *R v Northavon DC ex p Palmer*
(1995) 27 HLR 576, CA

No private law right to damages arises until council accepted that a duty had arisen

The applicants applied for housing on the council's ordinary housing application form. No enquiries were undertaken for over a year. The council denied that it owed any duty to enquire because (a) the applicant had not applied as 'homeless' and/or (b) there was no material in the applications on which the council ought to have been satisfied that there was homelessness. In judicial review proceedings, the applicant sought a declaration that the council was in breach of its statutory duty and that damages were payable. Roger Toulson QC dismissed the application ((1994) 26 HLR 572).

The Court of Appeal dismissed the applicant's subsequent appeal. Sir Thomas Bingham MR held that the questions: (a) whether a Housing Act 1985 Part III (now Housing Act 1996 Part VII) homelessness application had been made; (b) whether there was reason to believe the applicant might be homeless; and (c) whether the duty to enquire arose, were all for the local authority to determine before any statutory duty could arise. A council's inaction could only be raised in public law proceedings for judicial review and mandamus. No private law right to damages could arise until a council itself accepted (by decision or concession) that a duty had arisen and had not been discharged.

Note: The applicant also made a complaint of maladministration to the local government ombudsman and the complaint was settled without any finding but on the council paying £4,250 plus legal costs of £756. (*Investigation 95/B/1601* (Northavon BC))

High Court

T33.2   *R v Camden LBC ex p Gillan*
(1989) 21 HLR 114, QBD

Councils must have appropriate arrangements to accept homeless applications

Camden's Homeless Persons Unit could only be contacted for three hours each weekday and then only by telephone.

May LJ held that the Act required local authorities to make reasonable arrangements to receive applications, which might entail face-to-face interviews and, in urban areas, a 24-hour service.

T33.3   *R v Chiltern DC ex p Roberts*
(1991) 23 HLR 387; QBD

Applications not required to be in any particular form and can be made by letter

Solicitors wrote to the council on behalf of their clients, who were travelling showmen (T6.3), to apply for assistance under Housing Act 1985 Part III (now Housing Act 1996 Part VII). The names and addresses of the clients were set out in a schedule. The council asserted that no application had been made until the applicants presented themselves personally to the council two months later.

Pill J rejected that submission, stating that 'The Act does not require application to be made in a particular form. The solicitors' letter ... written on behalf of the applicants and giving appropriate particulars in a schedule amounted to applications by them.'

See T6.3 concerning the other issue of whether the showmen were homeless.

T33.4   *R v Islington LBC ex p B*
(1998) 30 HLR 706, QBD

Application for a transfer to be considered under homeless provisions where reason to believe person homeless

The applicant was a secure tenant of Islington for 20 years. She witnessed a murder outside her home and was the prime prosecution witness at a subsequent trial. She was threatened and subjected to abuse and intimidation from neighbours associated with the defendants in the criminal case. She wrote requesting alternative accommodation, without specifying that she was applying under the homelessness legislation. The council treated her application as one for a management transfer. She sought judicial review of the council's failure to treat her application as one made under the provisions of HA1985 Part III (now Housing Act 1996 Part VII)

It was held that the applicant should have been considered under Part III. It was not open to the council to decide to treat the application merely as an application for a transfer if the conditions were satisfied for an application to be considered under Part III (unless the tenant expressly indicated that such consideration should not be given). Those conditions were satisfied where an applicant applied for accommodation, or for assistance in obtaining accommodation, and the authority had reason to believe that he or she might be homeless or threatened with homelessness. The applicant had applied for accommodation and at the very least the authority had reason to believe that she might be threatened with homelessness because it was not reasonable for her to continue to occupy her accommodation. The court distinguished *R v Lambeth LBC ex p Pattinson* (1996) 28 HLR 214, QBD. However, relief was refused because the applicant had not suffered in consequence of the authority's failure to deal with her application under Part III as she had been made three alternative offers of accommodation.

T33.5   *R (Aweys and Others) v Birmingham CC*
[2007] EWHC 52 (Admin); 18 January 2007 (see T51.19)

Threshold under s184(1) a low one and usually satisfied by the making of a homelessness application; duty may be triggered even if no application based specifically on homelessness

Local government ombudsman

T33.6   *Local Government Ombudsman investigation Tower Hamlets LBC*
Investigation 91/A/2474, 18 November 1992

Failure to recognise domestic violence victim as potential homeless applicant

A tenant of Tower Hamlets LBC applied for urgent rehousing after suffering serious domestic violence, but was dealt with as a transfer applicant, rather than under Housing Act 1985 Part III (now Housing Act 1996 Part VII). The local ombudsman concluded:

> Finally, I am very disturbed to note that the Housing Advisory Officer did not believe it was part of his duties to consider whether Ms Ross may have had grounds to apply for assistance as a homeless person. Tenants who seek assistance from a housing officer are entitled to expect to receive full and comprehensive advice on a range of housing matters. The note of interview contains ample evidence that Ms Ross was unwilling to return to her flat because she feared further violence from her former partner. Sufficient information was therefore available to the officer to give him reason to believe Ms Ross might be homeless on the grounds that it was not reasonable

for her to continue to occupy her home. The Council's failure to recognise the approach from Ms Ross as a potential homelessness application, and the failure to refer her to the [homeless persons unit] for a fuller investigation of her circumstances, is also maladministration.

T33.7 *Local Government Ombudsman investigation Thurrock Council*
05/A/9461, 24 October 2006
'Gate-keeping' approach criticised

The complainant fled domestic violence overseas and approached Thurrock for homelessness assistance. The council failed to accept and decide on her homelessness application. The complainant was twice turned away without any written decision. A third application (that was actually taken by the council) was cancelled without her consent or any notice to her. Later, she was told incorrectly that a refusal of an offer of accommodation made by another council could result in her being found intentionally homeless.

The ombudsman recommended that the council apologise to the complainant, pay her £2,250 in compensation and give better training and guidance to front-line staff. [Q33] He said that it was 'vitally important' that the drive to meet targets 'does not lead councils to adopt a gate-keeping approach whereby homeless applicants who are eligible for help are turned away'. [Q34]

T34   Competence to make an application

House of Lords

T34.1 *R v Oldham MBC ex p Garlick; R v Bexley LBC ex p Bentum*
[1993] AC 509, [1993] 2 WLR 609, [1993] 2 All ER 65; (1993) 25 HLR 319; (1993) 91 LGR 287, HL

A dependent child cannot make an application as a homeless person

In two cases, applications were made on behalf of four-year-old children after the adult members of their families had been found intentionally homeless. The councils rejected the applications on the basis that they were not valid.

The House of Lords held that dependent children are not among those classified as in priority need. They depend on their parents to look after them and an offer of accommodation can only sensibly be made to those in charge of them. There will be cases where a child leaves home under the age of 16 and ceases to be dependent on his or her parents and such a child may be vulnerable by virtue of Housing Act 1985 s159(1)(c) (now Housing Act 1996 s189(1)(c)) and in priority need. It cannot be argued that a healthy four-year-old is other than a dependent child. Extreme youth is not a 'special reason' making a child vulnerable under s59(1)(c). 'Old age' is mentioned in s159(c) but not 'young age'. A disabled four-year-old does not acquire an independent priority right to accommodation. If a family has lost its right to accommodation through intentional homelessness, it cannot achieve the same result through the back door by an application in the name of a dependent child. If that was the case the disqualification of intentional homelessness would have no application to families with dependent children.

Note: The judgment places emphasis on the children not being in priority need which, on its own, is not generally accepted as a reason for refusing an application. However, the children in this case were very young and this raised issues of capacity and policy considerations concerning the fact that they depended on their parents. The entitlement of a non-dependent child to make an application remains undisturbed. Furthermore, 16- and 17-year-olds are now prescribed as being in priority need in their own right (see T15). The effect of s176 is that members of their household should be included in their application (see T14) although see *R v Camden LBC ex p Hersi* (T34.3).

T34.2 *R v Tower Hamlets LBC ex p Ferdous Begum*
[1993] AC 509; [1993] 2 WLR 609; [1993] All ER 65; (1993) 25 HLR 319, HL

A person lacking mental capacity cannot make an application as a homeless person

A 23-year-old mentally handicapped adult purported to make an application for accommodation, after other adult members of the family had been found intentionally homeless. The council refused to entertain the application, on the ground that the extent of handicap was such that the applicant could not comprehend what an application for housing was or instruct another to make an application on her behalf.

The House of Lords, reversing the Court of Appeal's decision, held that an adult lacking mental capacity is not owed duties under Housing Act 1985 Part III (now Housing Act 1996 Part VII). It is implicit in the provisions of the Act that the duty to make an offer of accommodation is owed only to those who have a capacity to understand it and, if accepted, to undertake the responsibilities that will be involved. It is for local authorities to determine whether an applicant has sufficient mental capacity (ie, the capacity to understand and deal with the concept of being offered accommodation) and their decisions can only be challenged if they are manifestly perverse or otherwise wrong on *Wednesbury* grounds.

Court of Appeal

T34.3 *R v Camden LBC ex p Hersi*
(2001) 33 HLR 577; (2000) *Times* 11 October, CA

Application cannot be used to circumvent a decision that an authority has discharged duty to family

Mrs Hersi was accepted for the full housing duty (s193), together with her six children. The council offered her Part VI accommodation, which she rejected, and the council treated its duty as discharged (s193(7)). Ms Hersi, the applicant's 19-year-old daughter who lived with her, then applied under Part VII in her own name and sought to include the whole family on her application. The council declined to entertain the application on the basis that it had discharged its duty to the household and there had been no change in the family structure and, therefore, no change of circumstances since her mother's application. Maurice Kay J dismissed an application for judicial review.

The Court of Appeal dismissed an appeal. *R v North Devon DC ex p*

Lewis (T26.5) was of no assistance to the applicant. That case concerned the proper construction of s191 (intentional homelessness). The offer of accommodation to the mother was premised on the basis that it was appropriate for the whole family. The mother could reapply if there was a change of circumstances. However, the daughter had no standing to replace her mother as an applicant for accommodation for the family unit. Her younger siblings were not dependent on her and she had no priority need in her own right. At one stage the council appeared to be saying that if there had been another parent in the family who had no involvement in the decision to refuse the accommodation offered, that other parent could not make an application for rehousing for the family. However, it was accepted on the council's behalf that there would be a duty to enquire into the matter as the children would, prima facie, be seen as dependent on the other parent. The council was entitled not to entertain the daughter's application. Whether she had 'participated' in the decision to refuse the previous offer was immaterial.

Note: As in R v *Oldham MBC ex p Garlick* (T34.1) emphasis is placed on, here, the daughter not being in priority need, which should not prevent an application being taken. (On a straightforward reading of s189(1)(b) the daughter would appear to be someone with whom dependent children reside. The issue was not analysed in any detail but the point was made that the children were not dependent on the daughter. See the later case of *Hackney LBC v Ekinci* (T16.3) for a slightly different but somewhat analogous situation.)

T34.4   *R v Hillingdon LBC ex p Streeting*
[1980] 1 WLR 1425; [1980] 3 All ER 413; (1980) 79 LGR 167, CA

Duty owed to all persons lawfully in the UK regardless of having no local connection

The applicant had been born and brought up in Ethiopia. In 1979 she came to England for the funeral of her English husband. She was unable to return to Ethiopia and was granted refugee status. She applied for assistance under Housing (Homeless Persons) Act 1977 (now Housing Act 1996 Part 7). The local authority accepted that she was unintentionally homeless and in priority need but decided that it owed her no duty as she had no local connection with it or the area of any other authority in the UK.

The Court of Appeal held that duties under the Housing (Homeless Persons) Act 1977 extended to people from abroad who were lawfully in the UK and who otherwise qualified for assistance under the Act. In such circumstances, the duty fell on the local authority to whom the homeless person applied, irrespective of local connection.

T34.5   *R v Westminster CC ex p Castelli and Tristan-Garcia (No 2)*
(1996) 28 HLR 616; (1996) 8 Admin LR 435, CA

Application must be considered from anyone lawfully in the UK

Both applicants were EU nationals who had lawfully entered the UK in exercise of their EU Treaty rights. Neither found employment and both became homeless and dependent on welfare benefits. The council claimed that it owed no duty to them under Housing Act 1985 Part III (now Housing Act 1996 Part VII).

Applications for judicial review were dismissed by Deputy Judge Roger Henderson QC (see (1996) 28 HLR 125) but allowed on appeal to the Court of Appeal. It was held that the applicants had not required leave to enter the UK, had neither overstayed leave nor breached a condition and had not received from the immigration authorities notice of intention to exercise a power to remove them. They were not 'unlawfully' in the country (ie, they were not offenders under Immigration Act 1971 s14) and were not excluded from assistance as homeless persons.

Note: This case preceded the provisions introduced in Housing Act 1996 regarding eligibility, which provide a mechanism whereby an authority can deny assistance to those unlawfully, as well as in some circumstances lawfully, in the UK. It is now likely that those unlawfully in the UK who press their case under Part VII will be dealt with under the elgibility provisions, ie, an application taken and a 'not eligible' decision made (see T2).

T35 Repeat/fresh applications

The homelessness legislation 'does not place any express limitation on who can make an application or as to how many applications can be made' (*R v North Devon DC ex p Le*wis (T26.5)). However, the courts have placed some restriction on the extent to which an authority must entertain an application from a previous applicant. The position was reviewed by the Court of Appeal in *Tower Hamlets LBC v (Rikha) Begum* (T35.5) following the House of Lords decision in *R v Harrow LBC ex p Fahia* (T35.1). An application can only be refused where it is on 'exactly the same facts' as a prior application. Previous case-law which suggested a higher 'material change of facts' test was overruled.

Although Housing Act 1996 s193(9) gives an express right to make a fresh application to those who have ceased to be owed a duty under s193, the application must not be on exactly the same facts (see *Tower Hamlets LBC v (Rikha) Begum*).

For the position regarding applications made to another authority see T36. For out of time reviews see T45.

House of Lords

T35.1 *R v Harrow LBC ex p Fahia*
[1998] 1 WLR 1396; [1998] 4 All ER 137; (1998) 30 HLR 1124, HL

Second application must be accepted where not based on 'exactly the same facts'

The applicant applied as a homeless person to Harrow, which provided her and her six children with temporary accommodation in a guesthouse pending enquiries. It decided that she was intentionally homeless and accommodated her for a further 42 days in the guesthouse. The applicant then made arrangements with the guesthouse to remain in occupation with her rent/licence fee being met by housing benefit. About a year later her housing benefit entitlement was reviewed and was restricted to half the actual rent. She was required to leave the guesthouse and applied again as a homeless person to Harrow. It decided that it did not have a duty to assess another application from her as she had not had any intervening settled accommodation since its decision that she was intentional homelessness. Deputy Judge Roger Toulson QC quashed that decision ((1997) 29 HLR 94, QBD).

The Court of Appeal dismissed the council's appeal ((1997) 29 HLR 974). Intentional homelessness continues until either settled accommodation is obtained, or (even if the applicant remains in unsettled accommodation) a supervening event (such as the break-up of a marriage (see *R v Basingstoke and Deane BC ex p Bassett* (T27.16)) occurs which means that the original intentionality is no longer causative or effective. The council had been wrong to confine its consideration to whether the intervening accommodation had been 'settled'. Unintentional homelessness might result from the loss of non-settled accommodation if the causal link back to the original homelessness was broken. The council had not addressed itself to the issue of whether the sudden reduction in housing benefit and consequent loss of the non-settled accommodation was a new or supervening event causing homelessness and meaning that 'the original intentionality is no longer causative or effective'.

The council appealed to the House of Lords. It conceded that the chain of causation could be broken by events other than by obtaining intervening settled accommodation. The appeal proceeded solely on the question of whether an authority, having discharged its duty to an applicant who then reapplies, is bound to go through the whole statutory enquiry procedure and provide interim accommodation or whether there is a 'threshold test' which a second application must satisfy if it is to be treated as a proper application.

The House of Lords rejected the council's proposition that a person making a second application must demonstrate a change in circumstances which might lead to the second application being successful before the application had to be considered under Housing Act 1985 s62 (now Housing Act 1996 s184). While expressing sympathy with the council's case, Lord Browne-Wilkinson, giving the judgment of the court, was unable to extract from the statutory language a justification for this 'short cut'. While an applicant must have capacity to make an application (*R v Tower Hamlets LBC ex p Ferdous Begum* (T34.2) and cannot reapply on exactly the same facts as an earlier application (*Delahaye v Oswestry BC* (1980) *Times* 28 July, QBD) those were very special cases where it was possible to say that there was no application before the authority and the mandatory duty imposed by s62 had not arisen. In the instant case, the applicant's second application could not be treated as being identical to her earlier application. She was relying on her eviction from the guesthouse which, for a year, she had been occupying as a direct licensee of the guesthouse proprietor, paying the rent for that accommodation, albeit by housing benefit. It was impossible to say there had been no change of circumstances at all. The council had to consider her application in accordance with Housing Act 1985 Part III (now Housing Act 1996 Part VII).

Court of Appeal

T35.2 *R v Ealing LBC ex p McBain*
[1985] 1 WLR 1351; [1986] 1 All ER 13; (1986) 18 HLR 59; (1985) 84 LGR 278, CA

Duty to applicant who refuses offer of accommodation revived in circumstances where offer would no longer be suitable for her

The applicant lived with her sister. In March 1983, when she was pregnant, she applied to Ealing as a homeless person. She was accepted for the full housing duty and, in July 1983, was offered permanent accommodation for her and her soon to be born baby. She refused the offer and continued to live with her sister. In March 1984, when her baby was eight months and she was pregnant with her second child, her sister asked her to leave and she reapplied as a homeless person to Ealing. Ealing claimed that no duty arose because it had discharged its duty by the earlier offer (*R v Westminster CC ex p Chambers* (T35.6)) and there had been no material change in her circumstances since that time. The accommodation with her sister was not settled accommodation and she was therefore in the same period of homelessness as had resulted in the earlier offer. In proceedings for judicial review Glidewell J held that no new duty arose until the applicant had secured settled accommodation.

The Court of Appeal allowed an appeal. The position of a person who had unreasonably refused an offer of accommodation was not the same as someone who was intentionally homeless. It was not incumbent on him or her to establish a period of settled accommodation. An authority's obligation to provide accommodation was revived by a material change in circumstances of the applicant. To establish a material change, the applicant must show that there has been such a change as to make the accommodation previously offered clearly unsuitable. In the present case the previous offer was clearly unsuitable for Miss McBain and her current household.

Note: See comments in *Tower Hamlets LBC v (Rikha) Begum* (T35.5).

T35.3 *R v Southwark LBC ex p Campisi*
(1999) 31 HLR 550, CA

Authority needs to consider whether material change in circumstances

The applicant was accepted for the main housing duty and was offered accommodation in discharge of that duty. The applicant accepted the offer but never moved in. She claimed that her medical condition had materially changed for the worse since the offer was made and that the accommodation was no longer suitable for her. It was common ground that it was suitable for her at the date that it was accepted and that the authority had thereby discharged its duty towards her. The applicant submitted that she was homeless and that the authority once more owed her a duty under Housing Act 1985 s65(2) (now Housing Act 1996 s193(2)). The council stated that it did not owe her any further duty. An application for judicial review was successful.

The Court of Appeal dismissed the council's appeal. Schiemann LJ said:

> The crucial task before the court in this type of situation is to identify the alleged changes and then to consider whether the local authority committed

any error of law in deciding that the changes were not sufficiently significant to give rise to any new duty to provide suitable accommodation ... [W]hat is conspicuous by its absence [in this case] is a reasoned assessment by anyone of whether there has been a material change in circumstances since the original decision.

Note: See comments in *Tower Hamlets LBC v (Rikha) Begum* (T35.5).

T35.4   *R v Tower Hamlets LBC ex p Ali and Bibi*

(1993) 25 HLR 158, CA (see T51.8)

Referral under the local connection provisions not a discharge of duty entitling authority to refuse to entertain a subsequent reapplication

T35.5   *Tower Hamlets LBC v (Rikha) Begum*

[2005] EWCA Civ 340; [2005] 1 WLR 2103; [2005] HLR 34; [2005] LGR 503

Authority had to accept a second application if it was not 'identical' with an earlier one; 'material change of circumstances' test was wrong

In September 2000, the claimant was asked to leave her parents' home because it became overcrowded when her husband and child began to live with her there. She applied to Tower Hamlets, which placed her in temporary accommodation and accepted her for the full housing duty. In June 2001 she had another child. In March 2002 the council offered her permanent accommodation under Housing Act 1996 Part VI, which she rejected. The offer was upheld as suitable on review and an appeal to the county court was dismissed. The council withdrew the temporary accommodation on the basis that its duty had been performed (s193(7)) and in November 2002 the claimant returned to her parents' home. In 2003 the overcrowding problems worsened when two brothers, one of whom was a heroin addict, also returned to live in the parental home. In February 2004 the claimant applied to Tower Hamlets again. It decided that there had been no 'material change in circumstances' and refused to accept an application. The decision letter notified the claimant that she had a right to a review of that decision. The subsequent decision on review notified her that she had the right of appeal to the county court. HHJ Hornby allowed her appeal.

The Court of Appeal dismissed the council's further appeal. Decisions which supported the 'material change of circumstances' test (*R v Westminster CC ex p Chambers* (T35.6), *R v Ealing LBC ex p McBain* (T35.2), *R v Southwark LBC ex p Campisi* (T35.3)) were inconsistent with the House of Lords decision in *R v Harrow LBC ex p Fahia* (T35.1). Applying *Fahia*, the principles in relation to a second application were:

- An authority had to accept and consider a second application if it was not 'identical to', or on 'exactly the same facts' as the earlier one. This test is an easier hurdle for an applicant to satisfy.
- It is for an applicant to identify, in a subsequent application, the facts which are said to render the application different from the earlier application.
- Any new facts raised in the second application (provided not trivial or fanciful) required that it be treated as a fresh application. If no such new facts were revealed the application could be rejected as incompetent.

- The question would be whether the facts as presented were 'new' and comparison was to be made with the facts as they were at the time of the earlier decision or, where appropriate, a review decision, as opposed to the facts at the date of the earlier application (Neuberger LJ at paras 43–44, 46, with whom Keane LJ agreed, Pill LJ at para 93. However, the analysis of the facts of the case by Neuberger LJ at para 54 (see below) made a comparison with the facts known at the date of the offer made in discharge of the earlier application.)
- That question did not involve any 'inquiries' by an authority, nor any investigation as to whether the asserted new facts were accurate (per Neuberger and Keene LJJ). The issue was simply whether, in the purported new application, the applicant had put forward facts that were different and the differences were neither fanciful nor trivial. A safeguard against applicants 'inventing' new facts was the possibility of criminal prosecution (see s214). Pill LJ, however, considered that 'some inquiry' might be necessary to establish (a) what matters were now relied on and (b) whether they were the same matters or new matters.

In the instant case, the birth of the applicant's second child could not be relied on as a different fact as this had occurred before the previous offer of accommodation. However, the fact that the claimant's two brothers had joined the parents' household amounted to 'new' facts, with the result that the council had to investigate the second application and provide temporary accommodation until it was determined.

It was further held that the county court judge had erred in not making a costs order against the council. He had been wrong in relying on speculation about the outcome of the claimant's substantive application under Part VII. In any event, had the council accepted her application, she would have been entitled to the benefit of interim accommodation and it could not be said that she would not derive a benefit from her success in the proceedings.

Note: The council was given leave to appeal to the House of Lords ([2005] 1 WLR 2950).

See also the earlier High Court case of *R (Griffin) v Southwark LBC* (T35.7) which looked at the facts known at the time of the offer in discharge of duty in considering whether the subsequent application was on the same facts.

High Court

T35.6 *R v Westminster CC ex p Chambers*

(1982) 6 HLR 24; (1982) 81 LGR 401, QBD

Council could refuse second applicantion on the basis of an earlier discharge of duty

The council accepted the applicant for the full housing duty and made him an offer of suitable accommodation, which he rejected. He returned to live with his parents. A year later he reapplied, but the council decided that he was intentionally homeless because he had refused the earlier offer.

On his application for judicial review, McCullough J held that the refusal of the earlier offer did not make the applicant intentionally homeless because he had not 'ceased to occupy' that accommodation, as required by (Housing (Homeless Persons) Act 1977 s17(1) (Housing Act 1996 s191(1)). However, it was held that the authority had discharged its duty towards the applicant by the earlier offer of suitable accommodation. One offer of accommodation was sufficient for one incidence of homelessness. As the applicant's homelessness was a continuation of his previous homelessness the council was not under a fresh duty towards him.

Note: See now s193 which codifies the circumstances in which the main housing duty is discharged.

T35.7 *R (Griffin) v Southwark LBC*
[2004] EWHC 2463 (Admin); [2005] HLR 12; (2005) *Times* 3 January; 29 October 2004

Application based on exactly same facts despite applicant's separation from partner

In August 2002, the claimant and her then partner made a joint homelessness application to Southwark. The council accepted that it owed them the full housing duty (s193(2)). It provided temporary accommodation and in December 2002 made a Part VI offer of permanent housing. By the date the offer was made the claimant and her partner had separated. The claimant refused the offer and the council notified her that it considered that its duty had been discharged. That decision was upheld on review. In February 2004 she was evicted from her temporary accommodation. She spent some weeks staying with various friends and relatives and in May 2004 applied again under Part VII. The authority decided that her new application would not be considered as there had been no material change in circumstances since the performance of its earlier duty by the offer of permanent accommodation. On the claimant's application for judicial review, Silber J had to resolve the tension between the different tests for a 'new application' set out in *R v Harrow LBC ex p Fahia* (T35.1) (an application not based on the exact same facts as a previous application) and. *R v Southwark LBC ex p Campisi* (T35.3) (an application based on new material giving reason to believe that the previous decision should be reversed).

Dismissing the application, he held that:

1) The correct test to apply was the *Fahia* test, ie, that a new application would have to be investigated and determined except in those 'very special cases' where the application was based on 'exactly the same facts' as the earlier application.

2) This was a lower threshold than that suggested in Campisi but that case could no longer be followed because *Fahia* was a later and binding decision of the House of Lords.

3) The council had been entitled to find that this was a 'same facts' case.

4) The only factual difference relied on was that the claimant and her partner had separated and that as a result the present application was a sole rather than joint application. However, that separation had occurred *before* the duty arising on the first application had been discharged. There had been no subsequent change of the factual position. It was appropriate to consider the first application at the time of its

determination by the refusal of the accommodation, rather than at the time the application was made.

Note: See the Court of Appeal decision in *Tower Hamlets LBC v (Rikha) Begum* (T35.5) confirming that the test to be applied is that the facts are not exactly the same.

T35.8 **R (Van der Stolk) v Camden LBC**
[2002] EWHC 1261; (Admin) 21 May 2002 (see T57.11)
New information was material; judicial review of failure to reconsider homeless application allowed

County courts

T35.9 **Ali v Camden LBC**
October 1998 *Legal Action* 22, Central London County Court
Award of DLA on basis of need for a carer was a change of circumstances

A disabled woman applied as a homeless person under Housing Act 1985 and was offered, but rejected, single person's accommodation. She contended that she needed accommodation for a carer. A year later she reapplied under Housing Act 1996. In the intervening period, an adjudication officer had awarded her disability living allowance (DLA) on the basis of her need for night-time supervision. The council rejected her reapplication on the basis that (1) she had had no settled accommodation since her last application and (2) she did not in fact have a carer.

HHJ Medawar QC allowed her appeal. He held that (1) the decision of the adjudication officer amounted to a change of circumstances entitling her to apply again (see *R v Harrow LBC ex p Fahia* (T35.1)) and (b) a prospective carer was a 'person with whom the appellant might reasonably be expected to reside' for the purposes of Housing Act 1996 s176 (applying *R v Hackney LBC ex p Tonnicodi* (T14.5)).

T36 Applications to other authorities

Court of Appeal

T36.1 **R v Newham LBC ex p Tower Hamlets LBC**
[1991] 1 WLR 1032; [1992] 2 All ER 767; (1991) 23 HLR 62; (1992) LGR 123, CA (see T8.9)
An authority, considering an application by an applicant who would be referred to another authority, was required to consider the general housing conditions in that other authority

T36.2 **R v Slough BC ex p Ealing LBC**
[1981] QB 801; [1981] 2 WLR 399; [1981] 1 All ER 601; (1980) 79 LGR 335, CA
Where an applicant applied to a second authority, it was for the second authority to form its own view about the application

Two separate families were evicted from their council accommodation in Slough. Slough decided that applicants from both households were intentionally homeless. Each family moved to a different area and later applied as homeless persons to the local authorities in those areas. Those authorities found them unintentionally homeless, but referred them to Slough under the local connection provisions. The cases were referred to an arbitrator under arrangements made pursuant to s5(7) and (8) of the Housing (Homeless Persons) Act 1977 (now Housing Act 1996 s198(5)–(6)). The arbitrator found that the families had local connections with Slough, which was accordingly bound by the duty to secure accommodation for them. Slough, within judicial review proceedings, sought to quash the arbitrator's decision or, alternatively, an order to compel the arbitrator to decide whether the families were intentionally homeless.

The Court of Appeal held that it was for each local authority to whom an application was made to make its own enquiries and to form its own view about whether homelessness was intentional or not, regardless of any decision reached by a different authority. The other authorities had been entitled to find that the applicants were not intentionally homeless and to pass that duty on to Slough. The arbitrator had been correct in deciding that he could only decide questions relating to local connection and did not have jurisdiction to decide whether or not the family were intentionally homeless. Slough was under the main housing duty in relation to both applicants.

High Court

T36.3   *R v Hammersmith and Fulham LBC ex p O'Brian*
(1985) 17 HLR 471; (1985) 84 LGR 202, QBD

Where an applicant was referred to an authority which had previously discharged its duty to the applicant, that authority could refuse assistance

Hammersmith accepted Miss O'Brian for the main housing duty and offered her accommodation in discharge of its duty (under Housing (Homeless Persons) Act 1977 s4(5), subsequently Housing Act 1985 s65(2), now Housing Act 1996 s193(2)). She refused the offer and was evicted from her temporary accommodation. She went to squat in the Bexley Heath area and, when evicted again, applied to Bexley Heath as a homeless person. It decided that she was owed the main housing duty but, since she had no local connection, referred her back to Hammersmith. Hammersmith claimed that it had no obligation to perform the housing duty again as it had previously fulfilled its duty.

Glidewell J dismissed an application for judicial review by Miss O'Brian. Following *R v Westminster CC ex p Chambers* (T35.6), the refusal of an offer of accommodation did not make the applicant intentionally homeless. However, the offer of accommodation made by Hammersmith was a discharge of its duty under s4(5). The duty under s5(3) (subsequently Housing Act 1985 s68(2), now the slightly different provisions of Housing Act 1996 s200(2)/s193(2)) to accommodate following a referral under the local connection provisions was not a separate duty from that imposed by s4(5). It was the same duty but it was imposed on a different authority by s5(3). Hammersmith had discharged its duty. The position was just as if the applicant had remained in the area of Hammersmith throughout. Hammersmith was under no further duty unless and until there was a new set of circumstances and a new incidence of homelessness.

Note: See *R v Tower Hamlets LBC ex p Ali and Bibi* (T51.8) which held that this decision was wrong to the extent that it held that the s4(5)/s65(2) and s5(3)/s68(2) duties were the same. However, due to the slightly different formulation of the duty owed by a notified authority under Housing Act 1996 (see s200(4) and s193(2)) the two duties may now be considered the same thus supporting the outcome in *O'Brian*. Furthermore, following *R v Brent LBC ex p Awua* (T22.2), a refusal of accommodation can result in a finding of intentionality if the refusal causes other accommodation to be lost.

T36.4 *R v Tower Hamlets LBC ex p Camden LBC*
(1989) 21 HLR 197, QBD

Guidance on consideration of applications where applicant has previously applied to another authority; enquiries to be made of other authority

Tower Hamlets sought to refuse to accept a referral of a family whom it had already declared intentionally homeless but who had subsequently been accepted as unintentionally homeless by Camden. Camden sought a judicial review of Tower Hamlets' refusal. Tower Hamlets alleged that Camden's decisions were *Wednesbury* perverse.

Henry J dealt with the responsibility which falls on a second authority to which an applicant subsequently applies:

> They are bound to entertain all applications made to them even when such application is made by someone with no prior connection with the borough. Even when the applicant comes straight from an adverse and legally unchallengeable finding of intentional homelessness made by the borough with which he has the closest connection, the applicant can shop around and, wherever he chooses to shop, that borough must make its own statutory enquiry and reach its own decision wherever he has been before and whatever result on that occasion. ((1989) 21 HLR at 204)

If the second authority decides to accept the applicant and to use the local connection provisions to refer the applicant back to the first authority and if the first authority:

> ... feels that it cannot accept those findings and has a case that might or might not succeed in having the finding set aside in judicial review, it seems to me that comity and good administration, and the avoidance of anarchy, all require the second borough to make a prompt challenge in those circumstances. It is quite unsatisfactory for the first borough simply to ignore a finding by the second borough which it is not prepared to challenge in the courts. (ibid at 210)

However, Henry J dismissed Camden's application because it had not made adequate enquiries to resolve the dispute. The homeless applicant had not been interviewed by Camden and the council had reached its conclusion simply on a statement supplied by the applicant's solicitor. 'Proper', lawful, resolution of the dispute ought 'inevitably' to have involved talking to the applicant and the principal officer in the homeless persons unit in Tower Hamlets.

Enquiries, decisions, reasons and reviews

T37   Enquiries

Housing Act 1996 ss183–184

Once an authority has 'reason to believe' that a person may be homeless or threatened with homelessness, it is under a duty to make enquiries to satisfy itself whether or not the applicant is eligible for assistance and what, if any, duty is owed to him or her (s184(1)).

Inadequate enquiries leave a decision open to challenge for failure to have regard to all relevant considerations.

Court of Appeal

T37.1   *Begum (Nipa) v Tower Hamlets LBC*

[2000] QB 133; [2000] 1 WLR 306; (2000) 32 HLR 445; (1999) *Times* 9 November, CA (see T14.2)

Council not required to enquire whether applicant could afford to travel to accommodation where she was given an opportunity to express any such problems

T37.2   *Bellouti v Wandsworth LBC*

[2005] EWCA Civ 602; [2005] HLR 46; 20 May 2005 (see T17.2)

Applicant not always entitled to 'last word' on medical evidence

T37.3   *Cramp v Hastings LBC; Phillips v Camden LBC*

[2005] EWCA Civ 1005; [2005] 4 All ER 1014; [2005] HLR 48; 29 July 2005, CA (see T43.6)

Further enquiries not necessary where applicants' soliciors had not suggested them

T37.3A   *Green and Coyne v Croydon LBC*

[2007] EWCA Civ 1367; 19 December 2007

Council entitled to rely on fact of possession order based on rent arrears and not obliged to enquire whether order properly made

The claimants had an assured shorthold tenancy. The rent was initially £650 pm. A year after they moved in the landlord informed them that it was to rise to £700 pm. No formal notice of increase was served. The claimants paid the increased sum although from time to time fell into arrears. A few years later, after arrears had built up, the landlord served a Notice of Seeking Possession based on rent arrears (Housing Act 1988 Sch 2 Grounds 8,10 and 11) and subsequently obtained a possession order under Ground 8. In the notice and in the court documents the rent for the period after the first year of the tenancy was variously put as £650 and £700 pm. The court order was apparently made on the basis that the rent was £700 pm. One of the claimants attended the hearing but was not legally represented and appears not to have been effective in mounting any defence to the claim. The claimants applied as homeless persons to the council. It decided that they were intentionally homeless on the basis of their failure to pay the rent. The decision was confirmed on review and the claimants appealed, contending that the council had failed to investigate their assertion that the rent was £650 pm. On this basis there would have been no, or no significant, arrears and a possession order would not have been made. Their appeal was dismissed.

The Court of Appeal dismissed a second appeal. The possession order made by the court was supported by evidence that the tenants had agreed the rent increase. In those circumstances it was impossible to say that any reasonable review officer would have carried out an investigation into the subject in light of the court's decision. Apart from the fact that the evidence supported the inferences to be drawn from the court's decision, it required an impracticable degree of enquiry in the circumstances. The appeal turned on the facts of the case and it was held unnecessary to make a decision on the council's contention that there was never an obligation to go behind a court order. In the usual case a housing authority can rely on what a court decides or seems to have decided.

Note: Housing Act 1988 s13 provides a mechanism for rent to be increased by notice but s13(5) provides that the section does not affect the right of a landlord and tenant to vary the rent by agreement.

T37.4   *Hobbs v Sutton LBC*
(1994) 26 HLR 132, CA (see T25.3)

Putting adverse material to applicant – substance of case had been put to applicant

T37.5   *R v Brent LBC ex p Grossett*
(1996) 28 HLR 9, CA (see T10.3)

For authority to assess 'difficult question' of whether applicant could afford the rent

T37.6   *R v Brent LBC ex p McManus*
(1993) 25 HLR 643, CA (see T8.7)

Applicant not given opportunity to comment on significant matters decided against her; insufficient enquiries made of pyschiatric state of applicant and daughter

T37.7   *R v Greenwich LBC ex p Patterson*
(1994) 26 HLR 159, CA (see T31.6)

Mandatory duty to enquire into the risk of violence in an area to which referral is considered

T37.8   *R v Kensington and Chelsea RLBC ex p Bayani*
(1990) 22 HLR 406, CA

Sufficient enquiries made of applicant's financial circumstances in the Philippines

The applicant was a migrant worker from the Philippines. She spent long periods of time with her family in the Philippines and the rest working in England. Her immigration status was such that her visa would expire if she was not living in the UK in November 1988. Accordingly, after an 11-month stay with her family, she returned to England in order to preserve her migrant worker status. She was unable to obtain employment or accommodation because she was having complications with a pregnancy, and she applied to the council as a homeless person. It declared her intentionally homeless for leaving the family home in the Philippines. Rose J quashed a finding of intentional homelessness because the council had not made sufficient enquiries into the financial circumstances of the family when in the Philippines.

On appeal, the Court of Appeal held (Butler-Sloss LJ dissenting) that, while it would have been more satisfactory if the housing officer had established fully the importance of the applicant's earnings and her prospect of unemployment in the Philippines and while the enquiries were 'clearly less full than they could have been', they were, nevertheless, not so deficient as to undermine a finding of intentional homelessness.

T37.9   *R v Sevenoaks DC ex p Reynolds*
(1990) 22 HLR 250, CA

Interviewing an applicant was usually required but was not always necessary

The applicant lost a private sector protected tenancy as a result of proceedings brought under Rent Act 1977 Sch 15 Cases 3 and 4 (waste and deterioration of furniture). Her counterclaim for disrepair was dismissed. On appeal against dismissal of judicial review proceedings to overturn a subsequent decision of intentional homelessness, the applicant argued that four specific relevant matters had not been put to her, although taken into account by the authority.

Nourse LJ considered that in many cases, perhaps in the great majority, the authority will not properly discharge the duties to make enquiries regarding intentional homelessness if no interview takes place. However, the applicant had been advised throughout by solicitors, she had been offered and rejected both a home visit and an interview, and the authority had sufficient material on which to support a decision of intentional homelessness.

T37.10   *R v Tower Hamlets LBC ex p Khatun (Shafia)*
(1995) 27 HLR 465, CA

While interviews are to be conducted sympathetically, court will only intervene where style of questioning inhibits applicant from stating his/her case

The applicant was found to be intentionally homeless. The council was satisfied from two interviews with her that she had given up settled accommodation in Bangladesh before becoming homeless from unsettled accommodation in England. The interviews were conducted through interpreters. The council gave 11 reasons for finding her intentionally homeless, including the fact that she had returned to the UK for better educational facilities and that, on her departure for the UK, she had no reasonable expectation of finding and maintaining secure accommodation. Sir Louis Blom-Cooper QC found that the flavour of the interviews was one of interrogation and that their conduct had been unsatisfactory or unfair. He quashed the decision.

The Court of Appeal allowed the council's appeal. Neill LJ stated that, although the interview must be conducted sympathetically (then *Home-*

lessness Code of Guidance para 4.4), it was for the council, not the court, to select the interviewer and to determine what questions should be asked. The court should intervene only if the style of questioning had inhibited the applicant from putting forward his or her case or facts which might assist his or her application.

T37.11 *R v Westminster CC ex p Augustin*
[1993] 1 WLR 730; (1993) 25 HLR 281, CA

Council entitled to infer accommodation in St Lucia reasonable without enquiry

The applicant, who lived at her sister's home in St Lucia, and her daughter came to the UK for a six-week holiday, staying temporarily with relatives. She decided not to return to St Lucia because her daughter had not secured entry to the selective education system there and her sister was proposing to move house. She became homeless when relatives could no longer accommodate her. Westminster declared her intentionally homeless. The decision letter did not indicate what factors had been taken into account in determining whether the accommodation in St Lucia was reasonable for her continued occupation.

The Court of Appeal held that the council had been entitled to infer from her only leaving St Lucia temporarily (for a holiday) and not at any time indicating that conditions there were unacceptable, that the accommodation she was giving up was reasonable. Any failure to spell this out in a decision letter was cured by a later letter, responding to representations from the applicant's solicitors, which gave full reasons.

At an earlier hearing, reported at [1993] 1 WLR 730 (see T58.4), the Court of Appeal held that, although it has discretion to grant injunctive relief pending the hearing of an appeal against a decision of a High Court judge dismissing judicial review proceedings, an applicant has to show a strong prima facie case that the appeal will be successful before being granted such relief. In this case it was refused.

T37.12 *R v Westminster CC ex p Bishop*
(1993) 25 HLR 459; (1993) 91 LGR 674, CA (see T14.3)

Council could not rely solely on the opinion of a medical adviser who had not examined applicant's daughter

T37.13 **Robinson v Brent LBC**
(1999) 31 HLR 1015, CA

Failure to give applicant an opportunity to challenge alleged admission

The applicant was a secure tenant. The council obtained a suspended possession order based on arrears of rent. The applicant then went abroad to look after her sick mother. She left her sons in the house to pay the rent. While she was away the rent was not paid. The council obtained and executed a warrant. She returned to the UK almost three years later and applied to the council as a homeless person. At her third interview she seemed to indicate that she had known that the council home had been repossessed before she returned. The council found her intentionally homeless for leaving her accommodation abroad. She applied for a review and made representations that it was not until she returned to the UK that she knew that her home had been repossessed. The crucial issue was accordingly whether she had left the accommodation abroad knowing that her home had been lost (Housing Act 1996 s191(2)). Her application for a review and her appeal to the county court were unsuccessful.

The Court of Appeal allowed her appeal. The council had plainly relied on the alleged admission in the note of the third interview without indicating that it was doing so and notwithstanding her subsequent representations. The view had been unfair because the applicant '... was never given the opportunity to challenge a fact upon which the council were relying and which she would have disputed had she known they were relying on it'.

T37.14 **Williams v Birmingham CC**
[2007] EWCA Civ 691; 14 June 2007

Reviewing officer had not failed to make appropriate enquiries about journey times

Following the death of her parents (who had been joint secure tenants) the claimant was evicted from a council house which had been her family home for over 25 years. On her application for homelessness assistance, Birmingham accepted that it owed her the main housing duty. It offered her accommodation in another area within its district. The claimant sought a review on the basis that her son (then aged 5) did not wish to change schools and that he would have a long and difficult journey on several buses to reach his current school. The reviewing officer upheld the decision. The school was not too far away. Alternatively, a change in a child's school was a common occurrence when a family moved homes and a change of school for this child would not be too detrimental to his educational development. Recorder McNeill QC dismissed an appeal.

On a second appeal, it was asserted that the reviewing officer had failed to make enquiries of the claimant about the difficulties that the journey to the old school would involve. Buxton LJ said that – given the unchallenged finding by the reviewer that this particular child would not suffer on changing schools – the appeal was 'academic'. However, he agreed with the rest of the court that, in any event, the claimant was unable to show that the reviewing officer had failed to make enquiries that any reasonable officer would have made.

High Court

T37.15 **R v Camden LBC ex p Mohammed**
[1997] EWHC Admin 502; (1998) 30 HLR 315, QBD (see T48.1)

Council's decision unfair where it had failed to put to the applicant its concerns about her account or seek her explanation for inconsistencies before finding against her

T37.16 **R v Dacorum BC ex p Brown**
(1989) 21 HLR 405, QBD

10-minute interview without taking notes on an important issue not adequate

The applicant lost accommodation with in-laws, allegedly as a result of unreasonable behaviour, including loud quarrelling. The local authority's enquiries were restricted to a ten-minute interview with the applicant's father to confirm the behaviour, but there had been no investigation of its cause (in particular whether the problems arose from an emotional rather than wilful basis) and no notes of the interview were kept.

Farquharson J quashed a decision of intentional homelessness for failure to make sufficient enquiries.

T37.17 **R v Gravesham BC ex p Winchester**
(1986) 18 HLR 207, QBD

Approach to making of enquiries and court's supervisory jurisdiction

After losing his job on Alderney in the Channel Islands, Mr Winchester left a damp and cramped flat and came to the mainland looking for work. He applied to Gravesham as a homeless person. It decided that he was intentionally homeless because he had acted precipitately in leaving the flat on Alderney.

Simon Brown J dismissed his application for judicial review. He accepted that the burden lies on authorities to make appropriate enquiries in a caring and sympathetic way. Such enquiries should be pursued rigorously and fairly, but there is no duty to conduct 'CID type enquiries'. Applicants should be given an opportunity to explain matters which local authorities consider weigh substantially against them. The burden is on local authorities to satisfy themselves that an applicant has become homeless intentionally. If there is doubt or uncertainty, the issue must be resolved in the applicant's favour. The court's supervisory jurisdiction can only properly be invoked in exceptional cases, for example, where a local authority has misconstrued the Act, abused its powers, or otherwise acted perversely. The court should scrupulously avoid any independent fact-finding or decision-making role. The authority's decision has to be one verging on an absurdity before the *Wednesbury* principle of unreasonableness can be successfully invoked. In this case, the main question for the authority to determine was whether or not it was reasonable for Mr Winchester to remain in the flat. On the evidence, it could not be said that the authority had taken into account irrelevant matters, had asked the wrong question or wrongly placed the burden of proof on the applicant or had reached an unreasonable or perverse decision.

T37.18 **R v Hackney LBC ex p Decordova**
(1995) 27 HLR 108, QBD

Decision quashed where not put to applicant that her account was not believed

The applicant refused accommodation offered in discharge of duty. She told the council that it was just around the corner from where her stepfather and mother lived and that her stepfather had sexually abused her. The council treated that as an internal appeal. An appeals panel considered and rejected her appeal on the papers in October 1992 ('the first decision') on the basis that the account of the abuse, and the assertion that it was the reason for refusal, were untrue. Solicitors then wrote to the council giving full particulars of the history of abuse, the conduct of the stepfather and the relationship of that history to the rejection of the accommodation. The council in July 1993 ('the second decision') decided that the solicitors' letter raised nothing new which required it to reconsider its decision.

Laws J quashed both decisions. The first decision had been taken without giving the applicant an opportunity to deal with the council's concerns that her assertions were untrue. That was a failure in procedural fairness. The second decision was irrational. No council properly directing itself could have decided that the solicitors' letter raised nothing new.

T37.19   *R v Kensington and Chelsea RLBC ex p Silchenstedt*
[1996] EWHC Admin 362; (1997) 29 HLR 728, QBD

In absence of clear evidence on a critical issue, further enquiries required

The applicant, his wife and dependent child were living in hotel accommodation. They were asked to leave because there was a housing benefit shortfall that they could not meet. As they were leaving, the manager suggested they look at accommodation in another hotel, under the same ownership. The applicant was shown round the second hotel by the porter and found, he asserted, that the accommodation comprised a single room, with two single beds, without en suite facilities. The applicant declined the offer and applied to the council for accommodation. The council made enquiries of the hotel owner (not the manager), who indicated that two bedrooms would have been offered. The applicant was found intentionally homeless for having failed to take up the accommodation offered. Solicitors then wrote, stating that only one room had been offered. The authority then spoke on the telephone to (seemingly) the manager, who said that he could not remember but that it might have only been one room that was offered.

Tucker J quashed the decision. No reasonable council would have failed to have made further enquiries at the second hotel to resolve the conflict about whether one or two rooms were offered. If it had been one room, it would have been 'unthinkable' that the council could have considered such a room with two single beds reasonable accommodation for the applicant, his wife and 16-year-old son. (The alternative argument – that the applicant could not be intentionally homeless in respect of accommodation which he had not occupied – was described as 'legalistic, although it may be perfectly proper' and was not pressed.)

Note: The applicant should also have succeeded on the alternative argument – see *R v Westminster CC ex p Chambers* (T35.6) and *R v Kensington and Chelsea RLBC ex p Minton* (T5.4).

T37.20   *R v Lambeth LBC ex p Walters*
(1994) 26 HLR 170, QBD

Council wrong to rely on own medical advice without examining child or obtaining her medical records

The applicant was accepted for the full housing duty. She refused an offer of accommodation made in discharge of duty on the basis that it was not suitable because of her child's medical condition. She lodged an appeal under the council's in-house appeal procedure. The council failed to have the child examined and did not seek or obtain the child's medical records. The notice of rejection of the appeal made no mention of the medical condition and gave no reasons.

Sir Louis Blom-Cooper QC quashed the decision and held (a) it was unfair not to disclose to the applicant the medical advice on which the council relied and (b) it was wrong for the council to have relied on that advice without having the child, or the child's records, examined. The third ground for quashing the decision, namely that the council had failed to give reasons for rejecting the assertion that the accommodation was unsuitable, was subsequently disapproved by the Court of Appeal in *R v Kensington and Chelsea RLBC ex p Grillo* (T38.8).

Note: There is now a statutory duty to give reasons on review (see T38).

T37.21 *R v Newham LBC ex p Lumley*
(2001) 33 HLR 11; 2000 WL 409, QBD (see T48.3)

Failure to make adequate enquiries into medical condition and to put adverse views of council's medical adviser

T37.22 *R v Nottingham CC ex p Costello*
(1989) 21 HLR 301, QBD

Authority could rely on applicant's statements to social workers

The applicant left his home asserting that it was troubled by poltergeists. A decision that he was intentionally homeless was based on records of earlier interviews with social workers in which he blamed his wife for the activities of the poltergeists and said that he believed that they would recur wherever she was. He was seeking to be rehoused with his wife. The council decided that it was reasonable for the applicant to continue to occupy the accommodation as it was impracticable to move the family in view of the applicant's belief that the poltergeists were likely to recur wherever his wife was present. In judicial review proceedings the applicant denied that he had said the poltergeists were linked to his wife.

Schiemann J dismissed an application for judicial review. The council was entitled to act on the hearsay evidence of interviews by social workers and to conclude that the applicant did believe that the visitations were linked to his wife. In a situation involving mental illness and alleged poltergeists the social workers were better able to deal the problem and it was not necessary for the authority to have discussed the matter with the applicant. In relation to the duty to make enquiries Schiemann J stated:

> The duty to make necessary inquiries is not a duty to make all inquiries in fact necessary before the truth is ascertained. A council which makes numerous inquiries can in my judgment only be attacked for failing to [make] one more if it failed to make an inquiry which no reasonable council could have failed to regard as necessary. ((1989) 21 HLR at 309)

T37.23 *R v Poole BC ex p Cooper*
(1995) 27 HLR 605, QBD

Information received in course of enquiries not confidential and should be disclosed

The applicant left privately rented accommodation. The council made enquiries of the landlord, who wrote claiming that the applicant's boyfriend had moved in and caused trouble and that there had been an incident in which he had slashed the tyres on the landlord's car. The council put the substance of the allegations to the applicant but refused to show her the letter and failed to mention the tyre-slashing allegation.

Deputy Judge Sir Louis Blom-Cooper QC heard an application for judicial review of the council's subsequent finding of intentional homelessness. He held that material solicited in the course of Housing Act 1985 s62 (now Housing Act 1996 s184) enquiries was not confidential and so, in fairness, the council should have disclosed the letter so that the applicant had the opportunity to refute the allegations if she could.

T37.24 *R v Sedgemoor DC ex p McCarthy*
(1996) 28 HLR 607, QBD

No requirement to enquire into suitability of accommodation where issue not raised

The applicant occupied privately rented accommodation and applied to the council as a homeless person. The council was told by the applicant's landlord that she would continue to provide the accommodation until her son returned from overseas to occupy the property at some later unspecified date. The council decided that the applicant was neither homeless not threatened with homelessness. The applicant applied for judicial review, contending that Housing Act 1985 s58(2A) (now Housing Act 1996 s175(3)) gave rise to a rebuttable presumption that any accommodation an applicant had was unsuitable.

Deputy Judge Roger Toulson QC dismissed her application. He held that the subsection contained a definition and not a presumption. The duty to make enquiries means enquiries appropriate to the facts known to the authority or of which they ought reasonably to be aware. The council was not to be criticised for not enquiring into suitability in the absence of any suggestion before the decision that the accommodation was unsuitable.

T37.25 *R v West Dorset DC ex p Phillips*
(1985) 17 HLR 336, QBD (see T26.8)

Council failed to make further enquiries in light of evidence of non-acquiescence

T37.26 *R v Westminster CC ex p Iqbal*
(1988) 22 HLR 215, QBD

Failure to make adequate enquiries of applicant's account, including death threats

After being injured in a riot in Pakistan, Mr Iqbal was charged with murder, tortured and imprisoned, before being released in a general amnesty. He then obtained political asylum in France. However, in France he received death threats and his wife was assaulted. His father-in-law, with whom he was living, also received death threats. During the same year Mr Iqbal's father was murdered in Pakistan. Mr Iqbal's father-in-law told him to divorce his daughter or to take her away with him. Accordingly, Mr Iqbal came to England with his pregnant wife and applied for asylum. He also applied to Westminster Council for accommodation. It decided that he was intentionally homeless.

The council's decision was quashed by Simon Brown J. Although the council interviewed Mr Iqbal on three occasions, it had not made adequate enquiries. It should have investigated the matter further and could have made enquiries of the French police, the British Refugee Council and the Home Office. On the limited information which Westminster Council had, it could not be satisfied that the applicant was intentionally homeless.

T37.27 ## *R v Woodspring DC ex p Walters*
(1984) 16 HLR 73, QBD

Burden of making enquiries is on the authority

Mrs Walters lived with her husband, a serving member of the RAF, in Cyprus. When the marriage broke down, she returned to England and lived temporarily with her brother-in-law. She applied to Woodspring for accommodation, but it said she was not homeless because she was living with her brother-in-law. He then gave her a letter requiring her to leave. The housing officer telephoned the armed forces accommodation organisation and was told that the departure of Mrs Walters would probably mean that her husband would lose married quarters accommodation, but that this was not automatic. As a result, the council wrote stating that she was not homeless. A few days later her brother-in-law, who was also her solicitor, wrote to the authority informing them that her husband had in fact lost married quarters accommodation. It made no further enquiries, but required positive evidence from Mrs Walters that the accommodation had been lost.

The decision was quashed by Taylor J. The burden was on the authority to make appropriate enquiries, not on the applicant to prove her case that the accommodation was no longer available.

T37.28 ## *R v Wyre BC ex p Joyce*
(1983) 11 HLR 73, QBD

Failure to enquire into reasons for arrears or give applicant opportunity to explain

Mrs Joyce and her partner lived in their jointly owned home for 17 years. Their relationship broke down in 1979 but they both remained in the accommodation. Mortgage arrears accrued but Mrs Joyce did not know the full extent of the arrears because of her partner withholding information from her and not making the payments. By the time that she became aware, she sought to remedy the situation by offering to pay the arrears by instalments. She did not make these payments and the property was repossessed. She was subsequently found intentionally homeless.

The decision was quashed because the council did not ask why Mrs Joyce had not made the payments nor was she informed of the issue and given an opportunity to explain. From the information available to the council it was clear that she could not afford payments sufficient to avoid repossession.

County courts

T37.29 *Odunsi v Brent LBC*

[1999] 6 CLD 348, Willesden County Court

Mandatory obligation to consider affordability, whether or not issue raised by applicant

Ms Odunsi occupied premises under an assured shorthold tenancy. As a result of leaving employment and losing housing benefit she accrued arrears of over £3,000. Her landlord served an invalid Housing Act 1988 s21 notice. As a result she left. Brent later decided that she was intentionally homeless because she had not waited for the landlord to obtain a possession order. She appealed, claiming that Brent had failed to consider whether the property was affordable. Brent argued that, as she had not raised this issue, it had no obligation to consider that aspect.

Her appeal was allowed. Homelessness (Suitability of Accommodation) Order 1996 SI No 3204 article 2 required the council to consider whether the property was affordable. This is a mandatory obligation. The procedure is inquisitorial, not adversarial. The council had a duty to consider the whole of the applicant's case.

T37.30 *Onyaebor v Newham LBC*

May 2004 *Legal Action* 23; 15 December 2003, Bow County Court (see T49.6)

Unfairness in reaching decision where material taken into account which had not been disclosed to applicant

Complaint to Information Commissioner

T37.31 *London Borough of Lewisham*

Decision Notice FS50092310; 7 August 2006

Complaint under Freedom of Information Act upheld

In February 2005 Lewisham Law Centre asked the council to provide updated information on material originally published as part of the council's Homelessness Review (Homelessness Act 2004 ss1–4). Only part of the requested material was provided. In July 2005 the law centre requested copies of the policies operated by the council's Housing Options Centre (formerly Homeless Persons Unit). The council initially responded that it did not have time to identify all its policies and later said that its relevant guidance (on home visits and provision of temporary accommodation pending review) had not been codified into written policies or procedures. The law centre complained to the Information Commissioner's Office under the Freedom of Information Act (FIA) 2000.

Deputy Commissioner Smith upheld the complaint. The council had given no satisfactory explanation why the material requested in February 2005 had not been disclosed. He rejected the council's argument (in relation to the July 2005 request) that, because it did not have a codified set of procedures, it had no policies to disclose. The delay in dealing with the first request was a breach of FIA 2000 s10. The failure to respond to the second request was a breach of FIA 2000 s1(1). The council was given 35 days to comply with steps relating to disclosure prescribed by the deputy commissioner.

T38   # Reasons

Once an authority has concluded its enquiries, it must inform the applicant of its decision in writing and, if it is adverse to the applicant, give reasons and inform the applicant of his or her right to request a review of the decision (s184(3)). Likewise, an adverse review decision must include reasons (s202(4).

The purpose of the requirement to give reasons is to enable the recipient to see whether they may be challengeable in law.

House of Lords

T38.1   ### South Bucks DC v Porter
[2004] UKHL 33; [2004] 1 WLR 1953; (2004) *Times* 2 July; 1 July 2004

Proper approach to the provision of reasons

Lord Brown gave a broad summary of the authorities governing the proper approach to a reasons challenge in the planning context. He stated:

> The reasons for a decision must be intelligible and they must be adequate. They must enable the reader to understand why the matter was decided as it was and what conclusions were reached on the 'principal important controversial issues', disclosing how any issue of law or fact was resolved. Reasons can be briefly stated, the degree of particularity required depending entirely on the nature of the issues falling for decision. The reasoning must not give rise to a substantial doubt as to whether the decision-maker erred in law, for example by misunderstanding some relevant policy or some other important matter or by failing to reach a rational decision on relevant grounds. But such adverse inference will not readily be drawn. The reasons need refer only to the main issues in the dispute, not to every material consideration. They should enable disappointed developers to assess their prospects of obtaining some alternative development permission, or, as the case may be, their unsuccessful opponents to understand how the policy or approach underlying the grant of permission may impact on future such applications. Decision letters must be read in a straightforward manner, recognising that they are addressed to parties well aware of the issues involved and the arguments advanced. A reasons challenge will only succeed if the party aggrieved can satisfy the court that he has genuinely been substantially prejudiced by the failure to provide an adequately reasoned decision.

Although he specifically referred to a 'planning context', there is no reason why the same principles should not be applied in a housing context, especially in relation to Housing Act 1996 Part VII.

Court of Appeal

T38.2   ### Bernard v Enfield LBC
[2001] EWCA Civ 1831; [2002] HLR 46

Decision letter need not contain detailed assessment of applicant's resources

Mr Bernard and his family were provided with accommodation by Enfield under Part VII. He had to pay £29 per week for charges ineligible for housing benefit. He failed to pay those charges and was evicted. He reapplied to the council as a homeless person. He argued that his income had been insufficient to pay the charges after other expenses had been incurred, including those in caring for his severely disabled wife. The council's decision letter stated that he was intentionally homeless because of his deliberate failure pay the charges. It said that it had considered the family's circumstances, including his wife's disability, but remained satisfied that it was reasonable for him to pay the charges. Its decision was confirmed on review and his s204 appeal was dismissed. He was granted permission to appeal on one ground only – whether the council had complied with its statutory duty to provide adequate reasons for its decision.

The Court of Appeal dismissed the appeal. The reasons given in the review letter satisfied the requirements of the duty to give reasons explained in *R v Westminster CC ex p Ermakov* (T38.10). The review panel had complied with the approach indicated by Nourse LJ in *R v Wandsworth LBC ex p Hawthorne* (T10.5) and had not treated an inability to meet the requisite payments as irrelevant to the issue of whether the failure to pay was deliberate. It was clear that, in deciding that his failure to pay the charges was deliberate, the panel had considered whether the failure was caused by an inadequacy of Mr Bernard's resources to pay the charges and other outgoings. Neither *Hawthorne* nor the Homelessness (Suitability of Accommodation) Order 1999, concerning affordability of accommodation, required the council to set out arithmetical calculations or itemised quantifications of the various expenses of Mr Bernard and his family.

T38.3   **Hijazi v Kensington and Chelsea RLBC**
[2003] EWCA Civ 692; [2003] HLR 72 (see T24.2)

Affidavit evidence allowed in under Ermakov *principles (amplification of reasons)*

T38.4   **Lewis v Havering LBC**
[2006] EWCA Civ 1793; [2007] HLR 20; 23 November 2006 (see T49.3)

Witness statement clarifying what information taken into account on review allowed

T38.5   **R v Brent LBC ex p Baruwa**
(1997) 29 HLR 915, CA (see T10.2)

Decision-makers given a certain latitude in how they express themselves

T38.6   **R v Gloucester CC ex p Miles**
(1985) 17 HLR 292; (1985) 83 LGR 607; [1985] Fam Law 259, CA (see T27.12)

Requirements of reasons to be given in intentionality case set out

T38.7   **R v Islington LBC ex p Hinds**
(1996) 28 HLR 302, CA

A decision letter need not separate all findings of fact from value judgments and then go on to set out conclusions drawn from the findings

The applicant had a secure tenancy. He married a council tenant with a secure tenancy in a neighbouring borough. He moved to her home, allowing his adult son to live in his own flat. In 1991 his marriage broke down and in 'ouster' proceedings arising from his violence he undertook not to return to his wife's home. He moved back to his own flat, from which he was evicted in February 1993. The preliminary issue on consideration of whether his homelessness was intentional was to identify his last 'settled' accommodation. In April 1993 the council issued a four-paragraph Housing Act 1985 s64 (now Housing Act 1996 s184(3)) letter. It later agreed to re-interview the applicant and in September 1993 produced an eight-paragraph letter. It could not be determined from either letter why or for what reasons either address had been treated as the last settled accommodation. At first instance ((1995) 27 HLR 65) Deputy Judge Sir Louis Blom-Cooper QC quashed the decision because the s64 letter mixed up findings of fact, other relevant factual considerations and the conclusions reasonably to be drawn from the facts in such manner as to leave the reader puzzled about the reasoning process.

The Court of Appeal, allowing the council's appeal, rejected this approach. The court held that a decision letter must be examined for adequacy in the context of the actual decision-making process and the findings of fact made. Although the reasons should be 'proper, adequate and intelligible', the decision letter need not separate all findings of fact from value judgments and then go on to set out conclusions drawn from the findings.

T38.8 ### *R v Kensington and Chelsea RLBC ex p Grillo*
(1996) 28 HLR 94; (1996) 94 LGR 144, CA

No general duty to give reasons in homeless cases unless statute required this

The applicant was accepted for the full housing duty. She rejected what the council asserted was suitable accommodation. Her appeal under the council's in-house appeals procedure was dismissed with no reasons. Her application for judicial review was dismissed.

The Court of Appeal rejected her appeal. Neill LJ drew a contrast between Housing Act 1985 s64(4) (now Housing Act 1996 s184(3)), where an express duty to give reasons was imposed by statute, and the situation in relation to decisions on suitability, where no such duty was imposed. He rejected the decision in *R v Lambeth LBC ex p Walters* (T37.20) that there was a general duty to give reasons for decisions in relation to all aspects of the homelessness legislation. However, he stated that reasons might be required where an individual decision was demonstrably out of line with the housing policy of the relevant authority – in such a case the decision may be prima facie 'aberrant' and may require explanation. In other cases an authority may wish to give reasons as part of a sensible and sensitive policy towards homeless applicants. However, the courts should be careful not to impose legal duties on housing authorities where parliament had chosen not to do so, unless the exceptional facts of a particular case justify the interference of the court.

Note: The position under Housing Act 1996 is that s202(1)(f) gives applicants a right to request a review of the suitability of accommodation offered in discharge of duty (although not in relation to s188 interim accommodation) and s203(4) requires reasons to be given for an adverse decision.

T38.9 *R v Tower Hamlets LBC ex p Monaf*
(1988) 20 HLR 529; (1988) 86 LGR 709, CA (see T11.4)

Not sufficient consideration of applicants' reasons for coming to the UK

T38.10 *R v Westminster CC ex p Ermakov*
[1996] 2 All ER 302; (1996) 28 HLR 819; (1996) 95 LGR 119, CA

Applicant entitled to have decision quashed where no reasons or inadequate reasons; save in exceptional circumstances the court will not permit reasons given in notice to be supplemented

The applicant experienced considerable harassment from his brother-in-law and others while living in Greece. He fled that country and applied to Westminster Council as a homeless person. At the council's invitation he provided his own written account of his experiences, which was then translated. On the basis of that account, the council found him intentionally homeless and issued a Housing Act 1985 s64 (now Housing Act 1996 s184(3)) notice, giving as its reason, 'This authority is not satisfied that you and your family experienced harassment.' In proceedings for judicial review, the council sought to rely on late affidavit evidence that it had in fact accepted the applicant's account of the harassment but nevertheless decided that he was intentionally homeless because, on balance, it would have been reasonable for him to have continued in occupation. Deputy Judge Sir Louis Blom-Cooper QC, while acknowledging that Housing Act 1985 s64 imposed a duty to give reasons to the applicant in the decision letter, held that the court would not 'shut out' consideration of the real reason on which the council based its decision as set out in the affidavit (see (1995) 27 HLR 168, QBD).

The Court of Appeal reviewed the authorities on 'reasons' and allowed the applicant's appeal. Hutchison LJ said that:

> Section 64 requires a decision and at the same time reasons and if no reasons, which is the reality of the present case, or wholly deficient reasons are given, the applicant is prima facie entitled to have the decision quashed as unlawful.

He stated that the reasons given must be proper, adequate and intelligible and deal with the substantial points that have been raised.

Note: See also *Bernard v Enfield LBC* (T38.2) where it was held that these comments apply equally to the statutory Housing Act 1996 s203 obligation to give reasons.

High Court

T38.11 *R v Camden LBC ex p Mohammed*
[1997] EWHC Admin 502; (1998) 30 HLR 315, QBD (see T48.1)

Guidance on approach to be taken where inadequate reasons given under s184(3)

T38.12 *R v Islington LBC ex p Okocha*
(1998) 30 HLR 191, QBD

Decision quashed for failure to give reasons why accommodation considered suitable when re-offered to applicant after a non-statutory review

The applicant was accepted for the main housing duty. She rejected an offer of permanent accommodation because of her fears of racial attack – there were racist graffiti and threatening racist notes at the property. The council had a policy of allowing an appeal against the suitability of accommodation and giving an applicant 48 hours after the appeal decision to decide whether to accept the offer. The applicant's appeal was refused without giving reasons. The applicant did not then accept the offer. She applied for judicial review of the council's decision, claiming that the process was merely a cosmetic exercise.

Stephen Richards QC, sitting as a deputy judge, considered affidavit evidence from the council giving their reasons for its refusal of the appeal, including that the area had a good racial mix, was not prone to racial attacks and the council had a pro-active policy of dealing with racial incidents. In the light of this he held that the decision was not *Wednesbury* unreasonable. However, he quashed the decision because of a failure to give reasons. Although there was no general duty to give reasons (*R v Kensington and Chelsea RLBC ex p Grillo* (T38.8)), he held that this was an exceptional case where the decision 'cried out' for an explanation and fairness required the giving of reasons. The applicant had, on the face of it, very good reasons for rejecting the offer of the accommodation. She had been given no reassurance from the council in respect of her legitimate concerns and fairness demanded that she be given the reasons for the rejection of her appeal. Only then could she make a properly informed decision whether or not to accept the accommodation re-offered to her.

T38.13 *R v Kensington and Chelsea RLBC ex p Kassam*
(1994) 26 HLR 455, QBD

Decision letter failed to address material matters and so reasons inadequate

The applicant was the Rent Act protected tenant of a very small flat, comprising one bedroom, a combined kitchen/living room and a very small bathroom. She lived there with her adult son and daughter. The cramped conditions caused the daughter to develop a depressive illness and the daughter was rehoused in 1986. The applicant was in such poor and deteriorating health that her daughter began spending up to 12 hours each day at the flat to care for her. In 1992 the applicant applied for rehousing on the ground that her accommodation was not suitable, since she required a larger flat which her daughter could move into as her full-time carer and have a separate bedroom. The council decided that the applicant was not homeless, even having regard to her wish that the daughter care for her full time, and that it would be reasonable for her to remain in occupation even if the daughter moved back in.

Andrew Collins QC, sitting as a deputy High Court judge, quashed the decision. The council had failed to enquire into and resolve two crucial issues (a) whether there was a 'need', as distinguished from a 'wish', for full-time live-in care and (b) if, as seemed likely on the facts, there was a need for such care and the daughter proposed to meet it, whether being forced to return and deliver that care in the same cramped conditions would cause a repetition of the earlier depressive illness. Neither matter featured in the Housing Act 1985 s64 (now Housing Act 1996 s184(3)) decision letter which, accordingly, gave inadequate reasons. The deputy judge said:

> All too often, in my experience, authorities do not give reasons which are sufficient within section 64, and we have a good example in this case. If they do not give sufficient reasons, it is not surprising that they will face challenges. It may be that, at the end of the day, a challenge turns out to be insubstantial, or, even if successful, not to assist anyone but the lawyers, and only to lead to further delay and further expense. To a large extent, as it seems to me, the remedy lies in the hands of the local authority. ((1994) 26 HLR at 465)

T38.14 *R v Northampton BC ex p Clarkson*
(1992) 24 HLR 529, QBD

Simple assertion that accommodation reasonable to continue to occupy inadequate

The applicant was found intentionally homeless after giving up a council tenancy. On her initial application, the council was aware that the 'nub of the applicant's position was that her brother ... who was temporarily staying with her was pressing his sexual attentions on the applicant'. The decision letter (now s184(3)) simply asserted that it would have been reasonable for her to continue to occupy her home.

Potts J quashed the decision. It failed to reveal that the council had considered the question of alleged sexual abuse and the council's own evidence indicated that it had failed to determine whether or not the allegations were real or true.

T38.15 *R v Wandsworth LBC ex p Dodia*
(1998) 30 HLR 562, QBD

Reason why one account by applicant preferred over another required

The applicant sought judicial review of a finding of intentional homelessness, following her departure from India where she had been deserted by her husband and hounded by his creditors.

Jowitt J quashed the council's decision as a result of three defects in the decision letter: (a) it failed to explain why one of several contradictory accounts given by the applicant had been preferred to others and/or whether it was accepted as the truth; (b) it appeared to reverse the burden of proof on whether it would have been reasonable for the applicant to continue to reside abroad; and (c) it failed to explain the rejection of medical evidence. The judge held that any suggestion that an applicant was not telling the truth should be 'spelt out' in a decision letter. He observed that there could be no objection to decision-makers receiving legal advice on how a decision letter should be drawn to meet the statutory duty to give reasons.

T38.16 *R (Lynch) v Lambeth LBC*
[2006] EWHC 2737 (Admin); [2007] HLR 15; 16 October 2006 (see T43.18)

Inadequate reasons meant decision letter defective but could be remedied on review

T38.17 *R (Paul-Coker) v Southwark LBC*

[2006] EWHC 497 (Admin); 3 March 2006 (see T48.9)

Decision that merely set out criteria and did not apply facts to criteria inadequate

Scottish courts

T38.18 *Hanlin v Nithsdale DC*

1997 Hous LR 6; [1997] CLY 6113, Court of Session (Outer House)

Guidance on reasons to be given in intentional homelessness cases where more than one former address

The applicant fled from home as a result of harassment. The council's subsequent decision that the applicant was intentionally homeless was set aside because the notification letter failed to discharge the obligation to give reasons. Lord Weir gave the following guidance: (a) as each case depended on its own circumstances it was not appropriate for councils to use standard and uninformative wording; (b) a finding on intentional homelessness involving more than one former address must deal with which, if any, was 'settled' accommodation; (c) a finding that it was reasonable to remain at an address in respect of which harassment had been alleged had to be fully explained; and (d) it was not appropriate (in this case) to allow the council to go behind its own notification letter and give evidence of the proper reasons for its decision.

T39 Decisions

Once an authority has concluded its enquiries, it must inform the applicant of its decision in writing and, if it is adverse to the applicant, give reasons and inform the applicant of his or her right to request a review of the decision (s184(3)). Likewise, an adverse review decision must give reasons (s202(4)).

T40 *General principles*

Court of Appeal

T40.1 *R v Brent LBC ex p Bariise*

(1999) 31 HLR 50, CA (see T8.6)

Something 'startling' not commented on may lead to inference it had not been considered.

T40.2 *Robinson v Hammersmith and Fulham LBC*

[2006] EWCA Civ 1122; [2006] 1 WLR. 3295;[2007] HLR 7; (2006) *Times* 5 September; 28 July 2006 (see T19.3)

Decision not necessarily made at the same time as notification of reasons; not lawful to postpone making decision simply to avoid a duty; mediation is independent of the enquiry process and not a reason to delay enquiries or a decision

High Court

T40.3   *R v Beverley BC ex p McPhee*

(1978) *Times* 26 October, DC

'Not homeless' decision after a referral request had been made was flawed

Ms McPhee was living in a hostel with her children and applied to Beverley as a homeless person. In December 1977 Beverley wrote to Hull City Council, stating that it accepted that Ms McPhee was homeless and in priority need, but suggested that she should be rehoused by Hull. However, in August 1978 Beverley Council wrote to Ms McPhee stating that it was not satisfied that she was homeless because she had accommodation.

The court found that that decision was flawed. The authority had obligations to provide accommodation or to refer to another authority from the moment that it was satisfied that Ms McPhee was homeless.

T40.4   *R v Brent LBC ex p Miyanger*

(1997) 29 HLR 628, QBD

Delay in making lawful decision led to order of mandamus

The applicant applied as a homeless person in March 1996. He was provided with temporary accommodation but on 20 May 1996 he was notified that the council owed him no duty because he had entered the country as a sponsored immigrant. A subsequent decision of 18 June 1996 alleged that no duty was owed because the applicant could not have recourse to public funds. Following the grant of leave to challenge those decisions (neither of which could be sustained in law), the council indicated in August 1996 that it did not 'adequately convey the reasons for the decision that [the applicant] is not entitled to assistance' and indicated that a 'fresh decision' would be made. By the date of trial three months later, no new decision had been made but the council invited the dismissal of the proceedings on the ground that the two decisions impugned had each been withdrawn.

Harrison J allowed the application for judicial review with costs and granted an order of mandamus to compel the council to determine the application within 28 days and to notify the decision within three days thereafter. If there were any doubts about the applicant's immigration status, the council had had sufficient time in which to obtain evidence.

T40.5   *R v Lambeth LBC ex p Carroll*

(1988) 20 HLR 142, QBD (see T17.12)

Authority should not merely adopt medical officer's opinion on issue of vulnerability

T40.6   *R (Abdi) v Lambeth LBC*

[2007] EWHC (Admin) 1565, (2007) *Times* 11 July; 26 June 2007 (see T48.4)

Not unfair for s184 decision-maker to make decision under s188(3)

T40.7   *R (Hammia) v Wandsworth LBC*

[2005] EWHC 1127 (Admin); [2005] HLR 45

Policy that tenant had to serve NTQ on tenancy from which she fled before acceptance under s193 unlawful

The claimant and his wife were joint tenants of a council flat. The wife left with the children claiming that she had been the victim of domestic violence. On her application for accommodation, the council accepted that she was homeless, in priority need and not intentionally homeless. The notification of that decision read 'Provided you relinquish your tenancy... the Council accepts that under s193(3) ... it has a duty to secure that accommodation remains available to you.' As required by that proviso, the wife then gave notice to quit the joint tenancy and was accommodated elsewhere. The claimant sought judicial review of the decision to impose the proviso.

Wilkie J held that, once the conditions in s193(1) were met, the duty to accommodate was triggered and it would be unlawful to impose 'any further hurdle or proviso before accepting that the duty arises'. The proviso in the notification letter was not an aberration but a manifestation of council policy requiring the relinquishment of any extant council tenancy before provision of further accommodation. As such it was 'plainly the imposition of a further requirement over and above the statutory requirements'. He granted a declaration that the policy evidenced by the letter was unlawful. He declined to quash the notice to quit, leaving the issue of its validity to be determined in the possession proceedings that the council had initiated and which had been adjourned pending the judicial review.

T41 Reconsidering decisions/reopening enquiries

There is no statutory provision entitling authorities to change a s184 decision, otherwise than on an applicant's request for a review. However, the courts have sanctioned fresh decisions, although only in limited circumstances.

Court of Appeal

T41.1 Crawley BC v B
(2000) 32 HLR 636; (2000) *Times* 28 March, CA

After conceding that decision that applicant not in priority need was wrong, authority can go on to consider whether applicant intentionally homeless

The council decided that the applicant was not in priority need and confirmed that decision on review. She appealed to the county court. Before her appeal was heard the council conceded that she was in priority need. It did not withdraw the review decision (as it could have done – see *Demetri v Westminster CC* (T61.2)). Instead it carried out what it called an 'extra-statutory review' and decided that the applicant had a priority need but had become homeless intentionally (this issue had not been addressed in its previous decisions). The appeal against the original statutory review decision came on for hearing, was dismissed by a district judge but on appeal to a circuit judge was allowed. The judge did not simply quash the decision on priority need but also declared that the council owed the applicant the full housing duty under s193. He considered that the council's duty under s184 when making enquiries was not only to satisfy itself whether or not an applicant was homeless, eligible and in priority need but also to determine whether or not the applicant had become homeless intentionally. He held that the omission of any reference in the decision letter to intentionality meant that the council had to be treated as if it had considered the question and had decided that the applicant had not become homeless intentionally. It could not later reopen its decision and determine against the applicant an issue which, in effect, had been decided in her favour, at least in the absence of fraud or deception.

Allowing the council's appeal, the Court of Appeal held that the declaration could not stand. The council did not have to decide the issue of intentional homelessness if it decided an applicant was not in priority need. It had determined what duty it owed, as required by s184, without having to address that issue. It was not debarred from considering that issue if it later decided that the applicant was in priority need. Decisions under Housing Act 1996 as to whether applicants are in priority need or whether they are intentionally homeless are questions of public law. The application of the jurisprudence of public law to the process of decision-making does not necessarily lead to the conclusion that a decision, once taken, cannot be revisited. To the extent that the decision in *R v Southwark LBC ex p Dagou* (T41.7) may have held otherwise, it was wrong.

Where there is an appeal to a county court, the question for the court is whether the whole of the circumstances justify any relief in public law. A new ground for refusing accommodation should only be ignored if it can be faulted on public law grounds. The extra-statutory review demonstrated that the council was not satisfied of one of the key pre-requisites of the s193 duty – that the applicant was unintentionally homeless. The correct course, after quashing the first review decision, was to leave the applicant to seek a review of the council's subsequent finding of intentional homelessness. The Vice-Chancellor indicated that he would issue a Practice Direction making it clear that s204 appeals should only be listed before circuit judges. (See now CPR PD2B para 9.)

T41.2   *Porteous v West Dorset DC*
[2004] EWCA Civ 244; [2004] HLR 30; [2004] LGR 577

Council entitled to revisit its decision when based on a fundamental mistake of fact

In October 2002 Ms Porteous, a single parent with three children, left her secure tenancy in Hounslow and went to live in Germany. She thought she had 'transferred' the tenancy to her sister but in fact the tenancy remained in her name. In February 2003 she returned to the UK and applied to West Dorset. The council notified her that she was owed the full housing duty (s193(2)). That decision was later purportedly rescinded when West Dorset found out about the accommodation in Hounslow and a 'not homeless' decision made. On 3 September 2003 the council upheld its decision on review on the basis that Ms Porteous still had the tenancy in Hounslow. However, by that date Hounslow had served a notice to quit which had expired. Hounslow had said that it would allow a further period of grace for Ms Porteous to return but that too had expired. A possession order had not been obtained. Ms Porteous appealed to the county court on the grounds that it was not open to the council to revisit its original decision and that, at the date of the review, the property was no longer available to her. HHJ Beashel dismissed an appeal, holding that West Dorset had been entitled to rescind the decision and upholding the review officer's finding that Ms Porteous had not been homeless.

The Court of Appeal dismissed her appeal. The judge had been entitled to find that at the date of the review decision it was open to Ms Porteous to return to the Hounslow property as 'she had at the very least a licence to do so'. Although the review officer had mistakenly thought that she was still a tenant, when at best she then had what 'in all probability was no more than a licence', that was 'nothing to the point'. She was not homeless. Second, the judge was correct to have found that the council was entitled to revisit and rescind its first decision. It would be surprising if a local authority could not revisit and change an earlier decision if that earlier decision resulted from a fundamental mistake of fact. In this case, without there being any suggestion of bad faith on either side, unknown to either party, there was accommodation available at the date of the original decision (see *Crawley BC v B* (T41.1))

T41.3   *R v Hackney LBC ex p K*
(1998) 30 HLR 760, CA

Change in law did not apply retrospectively to applicant already accepted for main housing duty

The applicant, a post-entry asylum-seeker, applied to the council for accommodation. In July 1996 it decided that he was owed the full housing duty under Housing Act 1985 s65(2) (now Housing Act 1996 s193(2)) which was modified by Asylum and Immigration Appeals Act 1993 s4. The effect of s4 was that only temporary accommodation was to be provided until the applicant's asylum claim was finally determined. The applicant was provided with temporary accommodation and his asylum application remained outstanding. After the implementation of the Asylum and Immigration Act 1996 s9 (on 19 August 1996) the council decided that the new Act (placing responsibility for accommodating asylum-seekers with NASS) relieved it of any further duty and it gave notice to quit the temporary accommodation. Dyson J refused leave to move for judicial review, having regard to the decisions in *R v Secretary of State for the Environment ex p Shelter* [1997] COD 49, QBD, *R v Southwark LBC ex p Bediako and R v Westminster CC ex p Zafru* (1997) 30 HLR 22, QBD.

The Court of Appeal allowed a renewed application for leave, granted the motion for judicial review and quashed the council's decisions. Lord Woolf MR stated that (a) the new Act could not apply retrospectively to negate a duty already owed and (b) the coming into force of the Act was not itself a change in circumstances entitling the council to consider whether it still owed a duty (disapproving *ex p Shelter* on this point).

High Court

T41.4   *R v Brent LBC ex p Sadiq*
(2001) 33 HLR 525; (2000) *Times* 27 July, QBD

Decision that applicant was owed main housing duty cannot be revisited on applicant's loss of priority need; Crawley v B distinguished

Mr Sadiq was accepted for the main housing duty under Housing Act 1996 s193(2) on the basis that he was in priority need because his son lived with him. Later, as a result of a court order, his son went to live with his mother. The council reconsidered its decision and informed Mr Sadiq that it was unable to provide him with further assistance because he was no longer in priority need. Mr Sadiq requested a review of that decision but later withdrew that request and sought judicial review of the decision on the basis that the council had no power to make it.

Moses J granted his application. He reviewed the High Court authorities on revisiting decisions under Housing Act 1985. These showed that where a change in circumstances occurred after a lawful decision had been made, the council had no power to reconsider the decision, in the absence of fraud. The specific statutory provisions on when an authority ceases to be under a duty, introduced in Housing Act 1996 s193(6), made the instant case even stronger. Section 193 was a complete code as to the circumstances in which a local housing authority ceases to be under the duty under s193. Loss of priority need was not listed under s193(6) and the council could not revisit its decision.

A contention that *Crawley BC v B* (T41.1) overruled the previous authorities was rejected. The real basis for *Crawley BC v B* was that once the decision that the applicant was not in priority need had gone (the authority having conceded that its s184 and review decisions were wrong) and it was plain that no decision had been made as to intentional homelessness, the authority was entitled and, indeed, required under s184, to make a decision.

Brent also contended that the applicant should have sought a review of its decision under s202, rather than seeking judicial review. Moses J held that the decision was one that came within s202(1)(b) and carried the right of review. However, the applicant had faced the difficulty that the reviewing body and the county court would be bound to consider the facts in existence at the time of the review of the second decision. It was nevertheless appropriate to seek a review. The grounds of the review would be that the original decision stood as valid and that the council had no power to reconsider it. As the matter was not altogether clear and the point was an important one and as the High Court retained residual discretion (see *Begum (Nipa) v Tower Hamlets* (T14.2)) it was appropriate to exercise the discretion to grant relief.

T41.5   *R v Dacorum DC ex p Walsh*
(1992) 24 HLR 401, QBD

Authority could revisit decision made on basis of applicant's fraud

The applicant was accepted for the full housing duty. Subsequently, the council obtained further information from her former landlord and her neighbour, revealing that the application was made on the basis of false or fabricated material. A second decision of intentional homelessness was made.

Macpherson J stated that, if an applicant's circumstances do not change, the authority cannot simply serve a different notice based on the same facts as the former notice. However, just as a local authority may be obliged to review an unfavourable decision in the light of new evidence, it is entitled to reverse an earlier favourable decision if it was obtained fraudulently.

T41.6 *R v Lambeth LBC ex p Miah*
(1995) 27 HLR 21, QBD

After making s184 decision council have no power to reopen inquiries

In February 1992 the applicant was accepted for the full housing duty. Pending an offer of permanent accommodation, the council secured temporary accommodation from a housing association. Subsequent monitoring by the council of the temporary accommodation suggested that the applicant was not living there, had sublet it, and was probably living at the address from which she had originally been accepted as a homeless person. In February 1993 the council issued a new Housing Act 1985 s64 (now Housing Act 1996 s184(3)) notice, containing a decision that the applicant was not homeless.

Latham J granted certiorari to quash the 'new' decision. He held that: (a) the council had purported to be making enquiries pursuant to s62 (now Housing Act 1996 s184) and to have issued a new s64 notice; (b) since the application for rehousing had been resolved by the earlier s64 notice, there was no room for further enquiries into it or the issue of a further decision on it; and, therefore, (c) in conducting such enquiries and issuing a new decision, the council 'was exercising powers that it did not have'. If the authority considered that the applicant was abusing the temporary accommodation, it had rights to recover possession of that property from her.

Note: Housing Act 1996 s193(6)(d) now specifically provides for a discharge of duty in such circumstances.

T41.7 *R v Southwark LBC ex p Dagou*
(1996) 28 HLR 72, QBD

A council cannot rescind its decision in the absence of fraud or deception; decision to refer without reasons given quashed

The council notified the applicant that she was owed the main housing duty but was to be referred to Newham Council under the local connection provisions. It failed to give reasons for the decision to refer. On being given notice of the referral, Newham invited Southwark to reopen its enquiries on intentional homelessness. Southwark agreed and, having reconsidered the matter with the assistance of material provided by Newham, reversed its earlier decision and found the applicant to be intentionally homeless.

Deputy Judge Sir Louis Blom-Cooper QC allowed an application for judicial review. He held that (a) the decision to refer had to be quashed in the absence of any reasons in the May 1994 decision letter and (b) the May 1994 decision on non-intentional homelessness was final because, fraud or deception apart, material coming into the hands of a council post-decision could only influence the manner in which the duties owed were to be discharged, rather than enable a council to rescind a decision that it owed a duty.

T41.8   *R (Slaiman) v Richmond upon Thames LBC*

[2006] EWHC 329 (Admin); [2006] HLR 20; 9 February 2006 (see T45.2)

Where applicant, accepted as homeless and in priority need on basis of domestic violence, returned to matrimonial home, authority could rescind its decision

T42   ## Review

Housing Act 1996 s202, as amended by Homelessness Act 2002, provides a statutory right of review of certain decisions.

202(1) An applicant has a right to request a review of-
    (a) any decision of a local housing authority as to his eligibility for assistance,
    (b) any decision of a local housing authority as to what duty (if any) is owed to him under section 190 to 193 and 195 to 197 (duties to persons found to be homeless or threatened with homelessness),
    [(c)–(e) relate to referrals under the local connection provisions]
    (f) any decision of a local housing authority as to the suitability of accommodation offered to him in discharge of their duty under any of the provisions mentioned in paragraph (d) or (e) or as to the suitability of accommodation offered to him as mentioned in s193(7).
  (2) There is no right to request a review of the decision reached on an earlier review.
  (3) A request for review must be made before the end of the period of 21 days beginning with the day on which he is notified of the authority's decision or such longer period as the authority may in writing allow.
  (4) On a request being duly made to them, the authority ... shall review their decision.

Section 203 provides for the procedure on review. It is to be conducted in accordance with regulations made by the secretary of state and, if the decision is to confirm the original decision against the interests of the applicant, the local housing authority must not only notify the applicant of the decision, but also of the reasons for the decision. In such a case, it must inform him or her of their right of appeal to a county court on a point of law, within the period allowed by s204.

The Allocation of Housing and Homelessness (Review Procedure) Regulations 1999 SI No 71 regs 6(2) and 8(2) provide as follows:

  6(2) Except where a case falls within regulation 7, the authority to whom a request for a review under section 202 has been made shall:
    (a) notify the applicant that he, or someone acting on his behalf, may make representations in writing to the authority in connection with the review; and
    (b) if they have not already done so, notify the applicant of the procedure to be followed in connection with the review.
    ...

  8(2) If the reviewer considers that there is a deficiency or irregularity in the original decision, or in the manner in which it was made, but is minded nonetheless to make a decision which is against the interests of the applicant on one or more issues, the reviewer shall notify the applicant:
    (a) that the reviewer is so minded and the reasons why; and

(b) that the applicant, or someone acting on his behalf, may make representations to the reviewer orally or in writing or both orally and in writing.

T43 General principles

House of Lords

T43.1 **Mohamed v Hammersmith and Fulham LBC**

[2001] UKHL 57; [2002] 1 AC 547; [2001] 3 WLR 1339; [2002] 1 All ER 176; [2002] HLR 7; (2001) *Times* 2 November (see T31.2)

The circumstances existing at the time review conducted should be considered; review officer's role is to consider matter afresh

See *Robinson v Hammersmith and Fulham LBC* (T19.3) for the position where the original decision is unlawful.

Court of Appeal

T43.2 **Abdullah v Westminster CC**

November 2007 *Legal Action* 38; 21 June 2007

Review decision was not to be construed as strictly as a will or statute

The claimant was owed the main housing duty by Westminster under s193. She and her four children were refugees from Yemen and she had been subject to racially motivated attacks in the UK. She was allocated accommodation outside Westminster's area and refused it. She submitted medical and other evidence contending that she needed to be in Westminster where she had a social support network of friends and family. An initial decision by a reviewing officer that the accommodation offered had been 'suitable' had been set aside on appeal. On a second review, the reviewing officer considered the medical evidence and the opinion of the council's social services department that the claimant could be housed 'out of borough' and decided that the accommodation offered had been 'suitable'. An appeal against that decision was dismissed.

The Court of Appeal upheld the judge's dismissal of the appeal. The reviewing officer had sufficiently considered medical evidence that it would be advantageous for the appellant to have the support of family and friends close by. The conclusion that she could cope in another area (where the council had offered accommodation) was not wrong in law on the available material. The social services department could safely be treated as having had the requisite knowledge of the family's circumstances in giving its advice. Although the medical evidence had not been entirely accurately summarised by the reviewing officer, the thrust of it was that although it would be desirable for the family to stay in Westminster they would not be unable to cope elsewhere. A review decision was not to be construed as strictly as a will or statute.

T43.3 **Alghile v Westminster CC**

[2001] EWCA Civ 363; (2001) 33 HLR 627, CA

Prior to amendments introduced by Homelessness Act 2002 an applicant did not have right to accept an offer of accommodation and to seek a review of its suitability

The council accepted that it owed Ms Alghile the main housing duty. It offered her accommodation in Dagenham, East London. It warned her that refusal would result in the duty being discharged (s193(5)). Neither that letter nor a subsequent reminder as to the consequences of refusal mentioned the right to review nor the possibility of both accepting the offer and seeking a review. The offer was refused and the decision that the duty had been discharged was upheld on review. HHJ Brian Knight QC quashed that decision. Applying *R v Kensington and Chelsea RLBC ex p Byfield* (1997) 31 HLR 913, QBD, he held that an offer letter must indicate the possibility of acceptance and review.

The Court of Appeal allowed the council's appeal. Acceptance with a request for a review was a heavily qualified acceptance which was not expressly permitted by the Act. It was not open to an applicant to accept an offer of accommodation under s193(5) and at the same time to challenge the suitability of the accommodation by requesting a review under s202. *Byfield* was wrongly decided.

Note: The effect of *Alghile* is reversed by Housing Act 1996 s202(1A), introduced by Homelessness Act 2002. Section 193(5) was also amended to provide that an authority must inform an applicant of his or her right to request a review.

T43.4   ***Aw-Aden v Birmingham CC***

[2005] EWCA Civ 1834; 7 December 2005 (see T25.1)

Review decision should not be made before complying with request for documents

T43.5   ***Bellouti v Wandsworth LBC***

[2005] EWCA Civ 602; [2005] HLR 46; 20 May 2005 (see T17.2)

It is for applicant to put forward material on which he or she relied for priority need on review

T43.6   ***Cramp v Hastings LBC; Phillips v Camden LBC***

[2005] EWCA Civ 1005; [2005] 4 All ER 1014; [2005] HLR 48; 29 July 2005, CA

Further enquiries not necessary where applicants' solicitors had not suggested them

Hastings and Camden made decisions, upheld on review, that Cramp and Phillips, respectively, had no priority need. Each had asserted that they were 'vulnerable'. On separate appeals by each applicant under Housing Act 1996 s204, the reviewing officer's decisions had been quashed in the county court on the ground that there had been insufficient enquiries made before reaching their decisions. Hastings were granted permission to make a second appeal to the Court of Appeal and Camden sought permission.

The Court of Appeal allowed both appeals. It held that:

1) Parliament had imposed the duty of making the necessary enquiries on a housing officer, and in the event of a review, on a senior housing officer as well. Both Cramp and Phillips had solicitors acting for them and availed themselves of their right to make representations on the

review. In neither case did they suggest that the council should make the enquiries whose absence led to the reviewing officer's decision being quashed as a matter of law. In each case the reviewing officer judged that she could make the decision without making any further enquiries along those lines.

2) It was for the councils to judge what enquiries were necessary, and they were susceptible to a successful challenge on a point of law if and only if a judge in the county court considered that no reasonable council could have failed to regard as necessary the further enquiries suggested by the appellants' advisers.

3) It had not been open to the judge in either case to hold that no reasonable council would not have made the further enquiries.

4) As a matter of law, a quashing order could not be justified on the grounds 'that it would have been helpful' if particular enquiries had been made, or that 'there might well have been additional information' which further enquiries might have produced. Whether to make such inquiries was a matter for the reviewing officer

5) Camden should have permission to make a second appeal because:

these two cases evidence a worrying tendency in judges at [county court] level to overlook the fact that it will never be easy for a judge to say that an experienced senior housing officer on a homelessness review, who has considered all the reports readily available, and all the representations made by the applicant's solicitors, has made an error of law when she considered that it was unnecessary to put in train further detailed inquiries, not suggested by the applicant's solicitors, before she could properly make a decision on the review. The need to correct that tendency raises an important point of practice.

6) The court took the opportunity to give guidance on the procedural aspects of s204 appeals in the county court and said (as to the introduction of evidence in such appeals):

... judges in the county court need to be astute to ensure that evidential material over and above the contents of the housing file and the reviewing officer's decision is limited to that which is necessary to illuminate the points of law that are to be relied on in the appeal, or the issue of what, if any, relief ought to be granted. An undisciplined approach to the admission of new evidence may lead to the danger that the reviewing officer is found guilty of an error of law for not taking into account evidence that was never before her, notwithstanding the applicant's opportunity to make representations about the original decision.

T43.7 *Eren v Haringey LBC*
[2007] EWCA Civ 1796, 24 April 2007
Review officer had considered matter afresh and no error of law in decision

The matrimonial home of the claimant and her husband was a private rented flat. On the breakdown of their marriage in 2004 she made an application to Enfield for homelessness assistance and was found to be not homeless. She applied again, after the tenancy had been surrendered, and was found intentionally homeless. She was provided with temporary accommodation only. A year later she applied to Haringey. She did not disclose in that application information about the former matrimonial home, her applications to Enfield or the accommodation that Enfield had temporarily secured. Haringey obtained the Enfield file. The claimant told Haringey that she had been in fear of her husband and that another woman had impersonated her in giving up the keys. Haringey decided that her account was inconsistent with her earlier account to Enfield and lacked credibility. It decided that had become homeless intentionally. That decision was upheld on review.

HHJ Pearce allowed an appeal on the grounds that the reviewing officer (1) had failed to look at all the facts afresh but had treated himself as simply reviewing the earlier decisions of the two councils and (2) had made an error of fact as to the evidence about who had surrendered the tenancy.

The Court of Appeal allowed Haringey's appeal. The reviewing officer's decision letter had given the factual background, his own findings of fact and reasons for his personal decision. The first error of law identified by the judge had resulted from taking one short passage in a three-page letter out of context. The reviewing officer had given the matter proper and fair consideration. The question of who had actually surrendered the keys of the flat was a subsidiary issue on which the officer had made no error of law.

T43.8   *Feld v Barnet LBC; Pour v Westminster CC*
[2004] EWCA Civ 1307; [2005] HLR 9; [2005] LGR 411; (2004) *Times* 26 October

In circumstances where a second review was conducted there was no unfairness in this being conducted by the same reviewer

Barnet owed Mr Feld the full housing duty (s193). He was offered a one-bedroom flat and sought a review of the suitability of the accommodation on the basis that he needed more than one bedroom. The review officer decided that the accommodation offered was suitable but directed that a further offer of a one-bedroom property be made. Mr Feld rejected the further offer and requested another review. The same review officer (Barnet only had one) upheld the council's decision. Mr Feld appealed under s204 on the basis that the same officer who had conducted the first review (and decided against him) had conducted the second review and that that was unfair.

Ms Pour was owed the s193 duty by Westminster. She sought a review of the suitability of property offered to her. One of the council's three review officers upheld a decision that it was suitable. Ms Pour brought a s204 appeal but that was compromised by the council agreeing to review the matter again. The same review officer then conducted the fresh review and reached the same decision as previously. Miss Pour appealed again under s204 on the ground that a new review officer should have conducted the fresh review.

Mr Feld's appeal was dismissed by HHJ Mayer, but Ms Pour's appeal was allowed by HHJ Crawford Lindsay Q.C. Permission was granted in both cases for second appeals.

The Court of Appeal held that, in the absence of any exceptional circumstances, there was nothing objectionable in the same officer conducting a review and then subsequently a re-review or second review. This was because the reviewing officer was not reviewing his or her own earlier decision but, in what would in any event have to be unusual circumstances (because there is no right to a second review (see s202(2)), would be starting afresh to review a decision made by a more junior officer. There was nothing unfair about that. Furthermore, as the Allocation of Housing and Homelessness (Review Procedures) Regulations 1999 SI No 71 gave no guidance on who was to conduct a review the second time and there was nothing to suggest that it had to be someone who was not involved in the first decision, there was no breach of those regulations.

T43.9 *Goodger v Ealing LBC*
[2002] EWCA Civ 751; [2003] HLR 6

Delay in providing copy of housing file did not render review decision unfair

Mr Goodger was a secure tenant of Hounslow LBC. He was convicted of drug offences committed at the premises and sentenced to six years' imprisonment. Relying on the conviction, Hounslow obtained a possession order. After his release from prison Mr Goodger applied to Ealing as a homeless person. Ealing decided that he had made himself intentionally homeless. He requested a review of that decision and asked for a copy of his housing file. A review date was set but he was not given the file until six working days before the hearing. The review panel upheld the council's decision but Mr Goodger's appeal to the county court was allowed on the basis that there had been a procedural unfairness in the council's delay in providing the housing file. The council appealed.

The Court of Appeal allowed the council's appeal. The judge had been wrong in approaching the failure to provide the housing file as conclusive in itself of unfairness without identifying the issue before the review panel and the respect in which the perceived unfairness undermined the decision on that issue. The only issue before the review panel was whether Mr Goodger had made himself intentionally homeless. That was a factual issue and the file was of no relevance to that issue. The council's delay in providing the housing file earlier did not render its decision on the issue of intentional homelessness unfair.

T43.10 *Osseily v Westminster CC*
[2007] EWCA Civ 1108; 5 October 2007 (see T53.6)

On review, suitability of offer to be judged at time it was refused; withdrawal of offer of accommodation not relevant to issue of suitability on review

T43.11 *Robinson v Hammersmith and Fulham LBC*
[2006] EWCA Civ 1122; [2006] 1 WLR. 3295;[2007] HLR 7; (2006) *Times* 5 September; 28 July 2006 (see T19.3)

Where original decision unlawful, review decision should restore applicant's rights to what they would have been at time of original decision

T43.12 *Sahardid v Camden LBC*
[2004] EWCA Civ 1485; [2005] HLR 11

Review of suitability must take into account facts known at date of review

In November 2000 Camden accepted the applicant and her young child (aged two) for the full housing duty (s193(2)). It provided temporary accommodation and registered the application under its Part VI housing allocation scheme. That scheme stated that homeless applicants living in temporary housing with a single child would be offered one-bedroomed council homes if the child was under five and two bedrooms if the child was five or over. The applicant claimed that she needed two bedrooms for medical reasons. Camden did not accept that and in April 2003 offered her a one-bedroom flat, as her child was by then only four. The applicant accepted the offer but also exercised her right to seek a review on the ground that the flat was unsuitable for medical reasons. The reviewing officer rejected her arguments and on 5 November 2003 notified her of a decision that the accommodation was suitable. Three days earlier the applicant's son had turned five. HHJ Dean QC dismissed her appeal brought under s204.

The Court of Appeal allowed a second appeal. It was held that the reviewer had to consider the facts known at the date of the review: *Mohamed v Hammersmith and Fulham LBC* (T31.2). Although *Mohamed* had been decided under preceding (1996) review regulations (rather than the 1999 regulations) and concerned local connection rather than suitability, the court considered that the principle applied equally. At the time of the review the applicant's son was five. The reviewing officer had overlooked this and had failed to consider the changed position under the council's allocation policy. The policy had to be taken into account when deciding suitability and the failure to do so was an error of law. The council's decision was quashed.

T43.13　*Sareen v Hackney LBC*

[2003] EWCA Civ 351; [2003] HLR 54; (2003) *Times* 9 April

No right to review of decision not to refer under local connection provisions

Mr Sareen applied to Hackney as a homeless person. Hackney decided that it owed him the full housing duty under s193(2). Mr Sareen sought a s202 review of Hackney's decision not to refer his application to Ealing under s198 on the basis that he had no local connection with Hackney but had a connection with Ealing based on relatives and his need to be near a Sikh community. Hackney informed him that there was no right to review a decision not to refer an application to another authority. (Hackney also reconsidered the issue on a non-statutory basis but decided that there was no local connection with Ealing.) Mr Sareen appealed under s204 from that refusal to review. HHJ Cotran held that there was a right to review a decision not to refer and that he had jurisdiction to entertain an appeal under s204. He held that the council's decision was flawed and should be quashed. Hackney appealed.

The Court of Appeal allowed the appeal. There was no statutory right under section 202, or elsewhere in Part VII, to review a decision not to refer an application under s198. Section s202(1)(b) provided a right to review 'any decision ... as to what duty (if any) is owed ... under sections 190 to 193 and 195 to 197'. This expressly limited the ambit of the review procedure to the *duties* owed under those sections and did not extend to decisions in the exercise of the *power* of referral under section 198. Section 202(1)(c) related to a decision to refer, not a decision not to refer. Nor did the other categories in s202(1) apply. Since there was no right of review it followed that there was no right of appeal under s204. It also followed that the judge had no jurisdiction to consider, by way of appeal or otherwise, whether Hackney had a duty to investigate the issue of local connection. (In any event it had no duty to investigate that issue, only a discretion under s184(2) whether to do so.) Any allegation that Hackney had failed to conduct a proper investigation into local connection could only possibly be pursued by judicial review.

T43.14 **Tower Hamlets LBC v Begum (Rahanara)**
[2005] EWCA Civ 116; [2006] HLR 9; [2005] LGR 580; (2005) *Times* 22 February (see T55.8)

Where requirements for discharge of duty not satisfied but council later wrote clearly stating that duty was discharged, then applicant had right of review against that decision

T43.15 **Warsame v Hounslow LBC**
[2000] 1 WLR 696; (2000) 32 HLR 335; (1999) *Times* 21 July

The right in s202 to request a review included a right to request a review of a decision that a duty had been discharged

The applicant sisters were accepted for the full housing duty (s193(2)). In due course they were offered a secure council tenancy under the council's allocation scheme (Housing Act 1996 Part VI). They refused the offer and requested a review of the council's decision that it had discharged its duty to them under s193(7). The decision was upheld on review and the sisters appealed to the county court. HHJ Oppenheimer held that he had no jurisdiction to consider an appeal as no right to review of the decision arose under s202 and that therefore there was no right to appeal (s204(1)).

The Court of Appeal allowed the appeal. The right to request a review arose in respect of any decision of a local authority on what duty, if any, it owed under ss190–193 and 195–197 (s202(1)(b)). These words are wide enough to include a decision that a duty once owed was no longer owed. Accordingly, the phrase 'any decision' in s202(1)(b) extended to decisions on the existence of events or factual situations which, if they had occurred, or had existed, would have the effect that the duty ceased to exist. It followed that the applicants could challenge the findings by the council which had led to the 'no duty' decision (eg, on the 'suitability' and 'acceptability' issues in s193(7) itself).

Note: As a result of amendments to Housing Act 1996, by Homelessness Act 2002, s202 now expressly provides that there is a right to request a review of the suitability of accommodation offered under s193(7) (s202(1)(f)). Section 193(7) was itself amended to include an obligation to inform an applicant of his or her right to request a review.

High Court

T43.16 **R v Camden LBC ex p Mohammed**
[1997] EWHC Admin 502; (1998) 30 HLR 315, QBD (see T48.1)

Guidance on approach to be taken where inadequate reasons given under s184(3) and deficiency such that any attempt to use review mechanism rendered 'unfair'

T43.17   *R (Aguiar) v Newham LBC*
[2002] EWHC 1325 (Admin)

On failure to carry out a review, applicant can seek an order within judicial review proceedings to compel council to make a review decision

The claimant applied under Housing Act 1996 s202 for a review of an adverse decision made on his homelessness application. The council failed to complete the review within the statutory time limit (56 days). That gave the claimant a right to appeal to the county court against the original decision on a point of law (s204(1)(b)). Instead, the claimant applied for judicial review to compel the council to reach a review decision. Before that claim could be heard the council concluded the review.

Jackson J awarded the claimant the costs of the judicial review proceedings which were then discontinued. Applying *R (Boxall) v Waltham Forest LBC* (U12.2) he held that the claimant should have the costs because:

1) the council was unable to explain why it had not conducted the review within the statutory time limit in accordance with its legal duty;
2) an appeal to the county court under s204(1)(b) on a point of law was not a satisfactory alternative to the undertaking of a factual review;
3) the council had only provided the review decision on the afternoon of the last working day before the hearing;
4) if that step had not rendered the proceedings academic, the claimant would have succeeded.

T43.18   *R (Lynch) v Lambeth LBC*
[2006] EWHC 2737 (Admin); [2007] HLR 15; 16 October 2006

Review decision not quashed despite procedural errors

The claimant applied to Lambeth for assistance as a homeless person. She was a tenant of the council and claimed that it was no longer reasonable to continue to occupy her home on medical and disability-related grounds. Her application was made by solicitor's letter supported by medical and other information. The council notified her of a decision that she was not homeless as her tenancy was continuing, and she was not subject to a notice to quit or possession order. The claimant sought judicial review on the ground that the notice gave no or insufficient reasons addressing her application. The council treated the pre-action protocol (judicial review) letter as a request for a review. It failed to complete the review within the statutory 56 days' period, made 'a mess of the procedure', and failed to comply with the duty to notify the claimant of the review procedure that it was following. The reviewing officer did, however, acknowledge that there had been an irregularity in the original decision letter and notified the applicant of this and of his proposed decision that the original decision was nevertheless correct. He invited representations under Allocation of Housing and Homelessness (Review Procedure) Regulations 1999 reg 8(2), but none was made. He upheld the original decision without making any further enquiries. The claimant lodged a county court appeal against the review decision without prejudice to her claim that the initial decision was a nullity. The claim for judicial review and the statutory appeal were heard together.

HHJ Hamilton QC (sitting as a judge of both the High Court and the county court) dismissed the judicial review claim. She held that any irregularity in the original decision could be – and had been – addressed through the alternative route of an internal review and a county court appeal. As to the statutory appeal and a contention that further enquiries should have been made, it was held that no further enquiries were necessary. The authority was not challenging the claimant's medical evidence and no suggestion had been made by her solicitors that further enquiries were necessary. The primary deficiencies alleged in the review process were procedural. There had been no response to a 'minded-to' letter sent by the reviewing officer. In the exercise of discretion, no variation or quashing of the review decision was appropriate, despite the procedural errors, as these had made no difference to the final outcome.

T43.19 **R (Zaher) v Westminster CC**

[2003] EWHC 101 (Admin); 28 January 2003 (see T53.28)

Obligation to provide suitable accommodation a continuing one; where change in circumstances right of review and appeal to county court applied

T44 **Application of reg 8(2)**

Allocation of Housing and Homelessness (Review Procedure) Regulations 1999 SI No 71 reg 8(2) states:

> If the reviewer considers that there is a deficiency or irregularity in the original decision, or in the manner in which it was made, but is minded nonetheless to make a decision which is against the interests of the applicant on one or more issues, the reviewer shall notify the applicant:
>
> (a) that the reviewer is so minded and the reasons why; and
>
> (b) that the applicant, or someone acting on his behalf, may make representations to the reviewer orally or in writing or both orally and in writing.

Court of Appeal

T44.1 **Gentle v Wandsworth LBC**

[2005] EWCA Civ 1377; 3 November 2005 (see T63.4)

Permission for second appeal refused where no obvious injustice to applicant even if failure to apply reg 8(2)

T44.2 **Gilby v Westminster CC**

[2007] EWCA Civ 604; 27 June 2007

Reg 8(2) did not apply as no inconsistency in reasoning of decision of intentionality

The claimant and her husband gave up their privately-rented bungalow and applied as homeless persons. They were found to be intentionally homeless. They then lived for three years in Mrs Gilby's step-sister's council flat, which the sister had vacated, under an informal arrangement. When the council became aware of this, it obtained possession of the flat. The claimants later applied as homeless persons. The council initially decided that they remained intentionally homeless for leaving the bungalow because the council flat did not constitute settled accommodation since the claimants had only been unlawful subtenants of their sister. The claimant requested a review, contending that they had been paying rent for exclusive occupation of the flat and therefore had an assured shorthold tenancy of it. The reviewing officer spoke to the sister, who said that the claimant had occupied the flat as a bare licensee as a temporary arrangement only. The review decision upheld the finding of intentional homelessness but on the different basis that the claimant had been a bare licensee, staying only temporarily in the council flat. HHJ Knight QC dismissed her appeal. On a second appeal, the claimant argued that this shift in reasoning had required the reviewing officer to comply with the 'minded-to' provisions of the Allocation of Housing and Homelessness (Review Procedures) Regulations 1999 reg 8(2) and allow them to be heard.

The Court of Appeal held that there was no inconsistency in the reasoning between the initial and review decisions. The question to be addressed was not the legal character of the claimant's occupation of the council flat but whether it constituted settled accommodation. Both decisions were to the effect that the flat did not constitute settled accommodation. It did not matter whether the occupation was as unlawful subtenant (as the claimant contended) or as a bare licensee (as contended by the sister) if the claimant did not have the required solid grounds of any reasonable expectation of continued occupation for the foreseeable future or a significant period of time. In these circumstances there was no reason for, or purpose in, enquiring into whether as a matter of legal labelling the claimant's occupation was as a lessee or licensee. There was no deficiency or irregularity in the original decision or the manner in which it was made and reg 8(2) was not triggered.

T44.3 *Hall v Wandsworth LBC; Carter v Wandsworth LBC*
[2004] EWCA Civ 1740; [2005] 2 All ER 192; [2005] HLR 23; [2005] LGR 350; [2005] *Times* 7 January

Reg 8(2) applies where an important issue is not addressed adequately

Both claimants applied to Wandsworth as homeless persons. In both cases the council decided that the applicants were not 'vulnerable' and had no other priority need. The decisions were confirmed on review. Appeals brought under s204 were dismissed. The claimants pursued second appeals contending, among other matters, that the initial decision letters were flawed and that the reviewing officers had wrongly failed to comply with the Allocation of Housing and Homelessness (Review Procedures) Regulations 1999 reg 8(2).

Allowing the appeals, Carnwath LJ said (para 30):

> To summarise, the reviewing officer should treat regulation 8(2) as applicable, not merely when he finds some significant legal or procedural error in the decision, but whenever (looking at the matter broadly and untechnically) he considers that an important aspect of the case was either not addressed, or not addressed adequately, by the original decision-maker. In such a case, if he intends to confirm the decision, he must give notice of the grounds on which he intends to do so, and provide an opportunity for written and (if requested) oral representations.

In Hall's case, the initial decision incorrectly expressed the test of vulnerability as relating to ability to secure accommodation instead of relating to risk of harm, or was at least unclear as to what test had been applied. This 'lack of clarity' was a 'deficiency' which should have led to the application of reg 8(2). In Carter's case, the initial decision was sufficiently reasoned and applied the correct legal test. In any event, no prejudice was suffered by her (on the facts) even if reg 8(2) had been triggered. However, her appeal was allowed because the review decision letter and the reviewing officer's witness statement in support of it each failed to explain with substantive reasons why the clear medical opinion of the GP (that the claimant was vulnerable) had been rejected. Both cases were remitted to the council for reconsideration.

T44.4 **Lomotey v Enfield LBC**
[2004] EWCA Civ 627; [2004] HLR 45

Oral review hearing not necessary where matters taken against applicant had been put to her and the original decision was not defective

Ms Lomotey bought a property with her brother. She later surrendered her interest in it to her brother, who served a notice to quit on her. She then applied to Enfield as a homeless person. The housing officer who interviewed her said that Enfield might decide that she had made herself intentionally homeless. Ms Lomotey did not deny that she had colluded with her brother and said that it suited them both for her to be rehoused by the council. Enfield decided that she was intentionally homeless. She requested a review and sought an oral hearing. Enfield refused an oral hearing, but requested further written submissions. The review panel confirmed the earlier decision. Ms Lomotey's appeal to the county court was allowed. Enfield appealed to the Court of Appeal, contending that there was no reason why the review panel should have offered an oral hearing.

The Court of Appeal allowed the appeal. It was accepted that the case did not fall within reg 8(2) of the Homelessness (Review Procedure) Regulations 1999 as there had been no deficiency or irregularity in the original decision making. Ms Lomotey argued that, even under reg 6, the review panel ought to have given her the opportunity to rebut propositions that they used to decide the case against her. It was held that the issue of collusion had been discussed with Ms Lomotey and she had responded accordingly. The judge was wrong to say Enfield had acted in a procedurally unfair manner. The rules of natural justice do not require more than that the substance of a point adverse to an applicant has been put to him or her. While it was considered that the adverse matters had clearly been put to Ms Lomotey, it was noted that caution should be used before holding that a matter had not been put simply because a housing officer's notes do not specifically record the matter.

T44.5 **Rowley v Rugby BC**
[2007] EWCA Civ 483; [2007] HLR 40; 25 April 2007

No deficiency in decision triggering reg 8(2)

The applicant and her partner moved out of their privately rented flat in Kent and applied to Rugby as homeless persons. They said that they had moved out as their landlord had said he was selling the property with vacant possession. They had applied to Rugby as they wanted to be nearer their family, for support. After enquiries of the landlord, the homelessness officer wrote to the couple and invited them to sign and return a tear-off slip to confirm the landlord's account that they had not been given notice of any kind by him, although he had orally said that he was thinking of selling the property. After they returned that slip, a decision was made that they had become homeless intentionally. That decision was upheld on review. The applicant appealed, arguing that the council ought to have invited oral or written representations pursuant to reg 8(2) of the Allocation of Housing and Homelessness (Review Procedures) Regulations 1999, on the basis that its original decision letter was 'deficient' because it failed to explain how their homelessness could be intentional when they felt under an obligation to leave the property, given their landlord's apparent desire to sell. The appeal was dismissed by HHJ Pearce-Higgins QC.

The Court of Appeal dismissed a further appeal. Any implication that they felt obliged to leave was superseded by ratification of the landlord's version of events. There was no factual dispute to resolve and no deficiency in the decision to be considered by the reviewing officer which triggered reg 8(2), even though those terms were to be construed broadly.

T45   *Out of time requests for a review*

A review must be requested within 21 days of an applicant being notified of a decision. Section 202(3) provides that an authority may extend this time limit. This section considers the exercise of this discretion. Where the time limit is missed and an extension is refused, it may be possible to make a further application to the local authority (see T35) or an application to another authority (see T36).

Court of Appeal

T45.1   *R (C) v Lewisham LBC*
[2003] EWCA Civ 927; [2003] 3 All ER 1277; [2004] HLR 4; (2003) *Times* 12 August

Discretion to extend time to request review; reasons for delay and prospects of success relevant

In 2000 Ms C was evicted from her council flat for non-payment of rent. Her case was that she had been incapable of properly managing her finances. In January 2001 the council decided that she had become homeless intentionally. She did not apply for a review within 21 days of the decision. In February 2001 she obtained a letter from a GP, but did not forward it to the council until April 2001. She did not follow it up until she obtained an interview with council officers in July 2001. The council treated her as making a further homelessness application, which it rejected on the ground that there had been no change of circumstances. She consulted solicitors, who wrote on 31 August 2001 asking the council to extend time and entertain a review of the January decision. In the absence of any reply, she began proceedings for judicial review. In autumn 2001 the council provided a decision rejecting, with reasons, the request for an extension of time. The claim for judicial review was amended to attack that decision but permission was refused on the papers. The claimant applied for an oral hearing and, pending that, supplied the council with a report prepared by a consultant psychiatrist and invited it to reconsider. The oral hearing was adjourned to enable the council to consider that report. On 4 March 2002 the council issued a further decision declining to extend time. The claimant then sought to attack that decision and introduce a second report from the consultant. On 12 August 2002 Maurice Kay J dismissed an application for permission to challenge the 4 March 2002 decision and declined to require the council to consider the second report.

The Court of Appeal, on a renewed application for permission to appeal, granted permission to appeal but dismissed the appeal.

1) The discretion to extend time is unfettered and wide, but has to be exercised in a principled way. Where the purpose that the discretion was intended to serve was clear, it could only be validly exercised for reasons relevant to the achievement of that purpose. This required a consideration of the statutory scheme (*R v Tower Hamlets LBC ex p Chetnik Developments Ltd* [1988] 1 AC 858). Reasons for delay and the prospects of success were relevant, but did not always have to be balanced against each other. In this case the principal factors taken into account were: (i) the lack of proper explanation for the failure to seek a review in time and for the late supply of medical evidence; and (ii) the new material was not sufficiently compelling to suggest a good chance of success. When considering whether to extend time the decision maker could properly consider the strength of the new evidence and not just whether it was material. The council was entitled to take the prospects of success into account as a relevant factor. The decision was not irrational or perverse. The judge was entitled to refuse to admit further evidence.

2) On the facts, the council had refused to extend time and Ms C had made a further application for the council to do so. The scheme envisaged only one application for a review or to extend the time for review if the 21-day period had expired. An applicant was not entitled to make repeated applications for extensions of time under s202(3) (*R v Westminster CC ex p Ellioua* (T46.3) and *Demetri v Westminster CC* (T61.2)) although the council had an extra-statutory discretion to allow further requests. Any judicial review challenge to the decision made on such an extra-statutory application was highly unlikely to succeed (applying the test in *R v Brighton and Hove Council ex p Nacion* (T49.4)). The challenge to the further decision did not meet the necessary threshold and the judge had not erred in declining to require the authority to consider the second consultant's report.

High Court

T45.1A *R (Casey) v Restormel BC*

[2007] EWHC Admin 2554, 7 November 2007

Issue of whether a request for a review is out of time arguably a precedent fact for court to determine

The claimant was a young homeless woman. The council decided that she had become homeless intentionally. When the claimant applied for a review the council responded that the application was out of time and that it would not exercise its discretion to extend time (s202). The claimant said that she had not received notice of the original decision until a date within 21 days of her review application so that it was not out of time. The council did not accept that and required the claimant to leave her temporary accommodation. A claim for judicial review was issued and an interim injunction was granted, requiring the council to continue accommodating her pending trial. The council applied to discharge the injunction. The claimant argued that the question of whether she had been notified of the decision, within the meaning of ss184(3) and 202(3), was a 'precedent fact' to the review jurisdiction that fell for determination by the court, not the council. The council argued that the only issue was whether it could rationally have concluded that the claimant's application for a review was out of time (the answer to which was yes). The question was not one of precedent fact but of *Wednesbury* irrationality.

Munby J held that the issue of notification of the decision was arguably a precedent fact to be determined by the court. He refused the application and granted permission. The judgment also gives guidance about the terms in which interim injunctions in homelessness cases should be granted (that is, time limited rather than being made until further order) and on the timetabling of urgent judicial review cases.

T45.2   *R (Slaiman) v Richmond upon Thames LBC*
[2006] EWHC 329 (Admin); [2006] HLR 20; 9 February 2006

Except where decision obviously perverse, authority entitled not to consider merits of challenge to decision when considering whether to allow an out of time review

The applicant was accepted for the full housing duty (s193) on the basis that she had been made homeless from her matrimonial home by domestic violence (this resulted in her homelessness and priority need). In the process of offering her accommodation the council discovered that she had returned to live in the matrimonial home. It then notified the applicant that, in effect, it was rescinding its original decision on the basis that it was not satisfied that she was in fear of her safety. The letter informed her of her right to request a revew within 21 days.

A request for review was made by solicitors three or four weeks after the 21 days had expired. The council re-interviewed the applicant and were satisfied that its decision letter had been translated and read to her (including a passage setting out the 21-day time limit) and that there was no good reason for missing the 21-day time limit. It declined to extend the time for the review request. The applicant appealed contending, among other things, that the council should have taken account of the merits of the proposed review at least where the merits were, on the face of them, very strong.

Hughes J dismissed a claim for judicial review of that decision. On the facts, the council had been entitled to conclude that the applicant knew of the 21-day limit. The power to extend time in s202(3) gives an unfettered discretion. There might be a case where a failure to consider the merits of a review reached the stage of obvious perversity if such a review was, on its face, clearly bound to succeed. Subject to that, the authority is entitled not to have regard to the merits in exercising its discretion whether to extend time. *R (C) v Lewisham LBC* (T45.1) This was not a case where the applicant was bound to suceed on review. The fresh information permitted the council to reconsider its original acceptance of the s193 duty on the basis of a fundamental mistake of fact (see *Porteous v West Dorset DC* (T41.2) and in light of the fresh facts the applicant was not bound to succeed.

County courts

T45.3 **Adams v Southwark LBC**
June 1999 *Legal Action* 24, Lambeth County Court

Request for review made if sent by ordinary post and not returned.

The appellant supported his case for priority need on grounds of vulnerability with a copy of a medical report, which had been produced in relation to his claim for disability living allowance. Although it stated that he had left-side paralysis, was confined to a wheelchair and needed daily assistance with most activities, the council said it would obtain its own report from a specialist. Then, without waiting for that report, it gave notice of its decision that the appellant did not have priority need. The appellant sent a request for review by post. He did not receive a reply and brought an appeal against the original time limit once 56 days had expired (Housing Act 1996 s204(1)(b)). The council contended that the court had no jurisdiction because it had not received the request for review.

HHJ Gibson allowed the appeal. He held: (a) Housing Act 1996 s202(3) refers to a request being 'made' and the review request was made if sent by ordinary post and not returned (see *Lex Service plc v Johns* (1989) 59 P&CR 427); (b) the decision was perverse on the material available to the council and (c), in the alternative, the council had erred in failing to await the further report it had itself commissioned.

T46 *Reconsideration of review decisions*

Court of Appeal

T46.1 **Crawley BC v B**
(2000) 32 HLR 636; (2000) *Times* 28 March, CA (see T41.1)

Authority could reconsider review decision by carrying out an extra statutory review

T46.2 **Demetri v Westminster CC**
[2000] 1 WLR 772; (2000) 32 HLR 470; (1999) Times 4 November, CA (see T61.2)

Unless authority agree to withdraw a review decision time limit for appeal runs from date of review, even if review reconsidered

T46.3 **R v Westminster CC ex p Ellioua**
(1999) 31 HLR 440; EWCA Civ 1142, CA

If authority refuses to reconsider review decision, remedy is appeal to the county court of the original review decision and not judicial review of refusal

The applicant applied as a homeless person to Westminster, which decided that she was intentionally homeless. The decision was upheld on review.

She did not appeal to the county court but her solicitors wrote a lengthy letter, indicating that the review decision was factually inaccurate and asking for the review decision to be reviewed. The council responded by saying that there was no right to request a review of a decision on an earlier review (s202(2)) and that it had considered the information provided but remained of the view that the applicant was intentionally homeless. It refused to carry out a further review. The applicant applied for judicial review. Leave was refused. She renewed her application to the Court of Appeal.

The Court of Appeal held that s202(2) did not preclude an authority from reconsidering a review decision if minded to do so, although there could be no requirement for such reconsideration. The destination for an appeal against a review decision under s202(1) was the county court. In reality the applicant was dissatisfied with the decision on the review. That is why her solicitors sought a further review on her behalf. If the council had agreed to exercise its discretion and reconsider its review decision but nevertheless adhered to it, she would have remained dissatisfied with the decision on the review. If, as here, the authority refused to do so, then her dissatisfaction also stemmed from the decision reached on the earlier review. It was considered that the statutory procedures were plainly intended to cover not only the decision of the authority on the review requested under s202(2), but also any subsequent decision by the housing authority to exercise its discretion to reconsider its decision on the earlier review. As the applicant had not exhausted her statutory remedy, her application for leave was refused.

Discharge of duties

This section concerns the duties under Part VII other than the duties in relation to taking applications, making enquiries and notifying decisions (for which see T32 and T37–42).

Interim accommodation duties and powers

T47   *Duty to accommodate pending decision: s188(1)*

Housing Act 1996 s188(1) states:

> If the local housing authority have reason to believe that an applicant may be homeless, eligible for assistance and have a priority need, they shall secure that accommodation is available for his occupation pending a decision as to the duty (if any) owed to him under the following provisions of this Part.

Where a local connection referral is instigated the s188(1) duty is replaced by a duty under s200(1) pending a decision on whether the conditions for referral are met.

Unlike s193, relating to the main housing duty, s188 does not prescribe any circumstances in which the duty ends, other than by the making of a s184 decision. It is unlikely, however, that the courts would hold that the duty is absolute, by parity of the reasoning in *R v Westminster CC ex p Chambers* (T35.6) and *R v Kensington and Chelsea RLBC ex p Kujtim* (U5.2). Although the s188(1) duty might be held to be discharged, the s184 duty to make a decision remains extant. The loss of any interim accommodation cannot give rise to a finding of intentional homelessness (unlike accommodation lost under s193(2)) as that loss of accommodation did not give rise to the homeless application on which a decision is required to be made.

A challenge to the performance of the duty under s188(1) is by way of judicial review. See section T58 in relation to interim relief within judicial review proceedings.

House of Lords

T47.1 **O'Rourke v Camden LBC**

[1998] AC 188; [1997] 3 WLR 86; [1997] 3 All ER 23; (1997) 29 HLR 793, HL (see T56.1)

To the extent that there was a positive duty to re-accommodate the applicant following his eviction from s188(1), accommodation that duty had been met by advice given and offers of alternative temporary accommodation

Court of Appeal

T47.2 **R v Kensington and Chelsea RLBC ex p Kujtim**

[1999] 4 All ER 161; (1999) 2 CCLR 340; [1999] LGR 761; (2000) 32 HLR 579; (1999) *Times* 5 August, CA (see U5.2)

Council entitled to treat accommodation duty (under National Assistance Act 1948 s21) as discharged if persistent refusal to comply with rules

Note: This case is relevant to the issue of the discharge of a Housing Act 1996 s188 duty which, as with NAA 1948 s21, does not contain a provision whereby the duty is brought to an end.

T47.3 **R (M) v Hammersmith and Fulham LBC**

[2006] EWCA Civ 917; [2007] HLR 6; (2006) 9 CCLR 418; [2007] 1 FLR 256; 5 July 2006 (see T19.1)

Every homeless 16/17-year-old should be accommodated under s188(1), rather than Children Act 1989, unless the child is known to have been in care

High Court

T47.4 **R v Haringey LBC ex p Ulger**

December 1992 *Legal Action* 21, QBD

Section 188(1) duty arises where applicant 'may' be homeless due to over-crowding

The applicant applied to the council as a homeless person on the basis that his existing accommodation was so overcrowded (seven people in a one-bedroomed flat) that it was no longer reasonable for him to continue to occupy it (Housing Act 1985 s58(2A), now Housing Act 1996 s175(3)). The council received the application, visited the premises and made arrangements for the applicant to call at the council's offices a fortnight later to be interviewed about the application. It refused, however, to provide interim accommodation. The council argued that, if a duty to provide interim accommodation arose on such facts, the 'floodgates' would open for the provision of interim accommodation to all those in unsatisfactory housing.

In judicial review proceedings May J held that the arrangement for a further interview clearly showed that (a) the council had not yet determined the application and (b) the council considered that the applicant 'may' be homeless and in priority need. Therefore, Housing Act 1985 s63(1) (now Housing Act 1996 s188(1)) applied and an interim housing duty arose. Leave was granted and an undertaking from the council to provide temporary accommodation was accepted in lieu of an order for interim relief.

T47.5   *R (Carstens) v Basildon DC*

[2007] 122 *Adviser* 122 41; 7 November 2006

Section 188 duty had not ended where applicant had failed to travel to accommodation

The claimant, a disabled man, applied to Basildon for homelessness assistance under Housing Act 1996 Part VII. Pursuant to s188, it booked temporary accommodation for him in Southend. The claimant could not raise the money to travel to Southend until the following day and by the time he got there he found that the council had cancelled the booking. The council refused to offer further accommodation. The council asserted that it had asked the claimant whether he had money to attend Southend and that he had been told that he had to attend the accommodation that day otherwise the duty would be discharged. The claimant asserted that the issue of money had not been discussed. The council relied on *R v Westminster CC ex p Chambers* (T35.6) in asserting that the interim accommodation duty had been discharged. The claimant asserted that the s188 duty remained until the s184 decision was notified. Although not absolute, the council was not entitled to treat the duty as discharged unless an applicant unreasonably refused accommodation or acted in a wholly unreasonable manner for a period of time (*R v Kensington and Chelsea RLBC ex p Kujtim* (U5.2))

In judicial review proceedings, an injunction was granted requiring the council to accommodate pending a Housing Act 1996 s184 decision or a decision on the claimant's application for judicial review. The judge considered that, even if the council's version of facts were true, the claimant had not rejected accommodation in such a way as might have caused the duty to have been brought to an end.

County courts

T47.6   *Khatun v Newham LBC*

November 2000 *Legal Action* 25, Bow County Court (see T4.3)

An authority cannot rely on accommodation it arranges under s188(1) in making a 'not homeless' decision

Local government ombudsman

T47.7   *Complaint against Eastleigh BC*

Investigation No 06/B/07896, 18 September 2007

Failure to accommodate pending decision found where no evidence accommodation offered; delay in decision

The complainants (and their four children) were evicted from their home by bailiffs executing a possession order obtained by their mortgage lender. They complained that, although they had applied to the council for homelessness assistance, they were provided with no accommodation in the seven weeks (spanning Christmas) that it took the council to determine their application. Various friends and relatives allowed the family to sleep on their floors and the father slept in a car for three weeks. The council said it had offered B&B but that had been declined.

The ombudsman rejected the council's account as there was no evidence to support it. Interim accommodation should have been provided and the decision on the application should have been made within the 30 day maximum suggested by the *Code of Guidance*. He recommended £3000 compensation.

T48   *Discretion to accommodate pending review: s188(3)*

Prior to Housing Act 1996, the homelessness legislation did not contain provisions for review and appeal to the county court, nor provisions regarding accommodation pending a challenge to a decision. Applicants could seek an interim injunction requiring an authority to house them within proceedings for judicial review of a substantive decision. Interim relief was usually granted as a concomitant of granting leave, pending a final hearing. Where judicial review remains the appropriate venue for challenge the principles relating to interim relief in the Administrative Court will need to be considered – see section T58.

The s188(1) duty to accommodate pending a s184 decision ceases when the decision is notified to the applicant. Section 188(3) provides that an authority 'may continue to secure that accommodation is available for the applicant's occupation pending a decision on a review'. Note that Nationality Immigration and Asylum Act 2002 s54 and Sch 3 excludes the exercise of this power in relation to relation to non-British citizens, subject to exceptions (see U8).

Section 200(5) provides a similar power where an applicant is notified that the conditions for referral are met.

The principles on which the discretion is to be exercised are set out in *R v Camden LBC ex p Mohammed* (T48.1). A decision under s188(3)/200(5) is not susceptible to the statutory review and appeal process and any challenge is by way of judicial review.

See also cases under section T49: Discretion to accommodate pending appeal.

High Court

T48.1   *R v Camden LBC ex p Mohammed*
[1997] EWHC Admin 502; (1998) 30 HLR 315, QBD
Guidance on exercise of discretion to accommodate pending review

The applicant applied to Camden on the basis that it was not reasonable for her to continue to live in the matrimonial home because of her husband's violence. The council considered that her account contained discrepancies. It did not put these to her for comment. It made a decision that she was not homeless. The decision letter under s184(3) gave as reasons simply, 'there is accommodation available and reasonable for your family to return to'. That statement shed no light on the reasoning which led to the 'not homeless' finding. The applicant applied for a review of the decision and for interim housing pending the review (s188(3)). The council refused to continue to accommodate her, relying on its policy that no interim accommodation was to be provided to an applicant pending a review unless there were 'exceptional reasons'. The applicant sought judicial review.

Latham J allowed the application and quashed the decision not to provide accommodation pending review. He refused to make a declaration that the council's policy was ultra vires. He considered the new statutory provisions in Housing Act 1996 for review and appeal and noted the council's evidence that most reviews were unsuccessful. Given that there was no restriction on the applicant's right to request a review, it could not be the case that the council had to exercise its discretionary power to provide accommodation as a matter of course. The council had a wide discretion in the matter and that use of the phrase 'exceptional reasons' was a rational way of describing the approach to be adopted.

When exercising its discretion the authority had to balance the objective of maintaining fairness between homeless persons in circumstances where it has decided that no duty is owed to them, and a proper consideration of the possibility that an applicant might be right, so that to deprive him or her of accommodation could result in the denial of an entitlement.

In carrying out this balancing exercise there were certain matters that would always require consideration:

> First, the merits of the case itself and the extent to which it can properly be said that the decision was one which was either apparently contrary to the merits of the case or was one which required a very fine balance of judgment which might go either way. Second, it requires consideration of whether there is any new material, information or argument ... which could have a real effect upon the decision under review. Finally, it requires consideration of the personal circumstances of the Applicant and the consequences to him or her of an adverse decision on the exercise of discretion. It may well be that in some cases other considerations may prove to be relevant. (paragraphs 31–33)

In the instant case the original decision had been tainted with unfairness because the council had failed to put to the applicant its concerns about her account or to seek her explanation for inconsistencies before finding against her. When exercising its discretion to accommodate, it had failed to take into account this consideration.

Latham J also set out the approach to be taken, in the context of the new procedures in Housing Act 1996, where the decision letter fails to give adequate reasons, as in the instant case. A failure to give reasons in breach of s184(3) could justify an application to the Administrative Court for relief. Courts should be slow to intervene unless it is clear that the deficiency is such as to render any attempt to use the statutory review mechanism 'unfair'. The purpose of reasons is to enable the applicant to put before the local housing authority a proper case based on a full understanding of the council's decision. Where reasons were defective a 'prompt request for details' should be made so that the deficiency can be rectified by the council.

Note: Approved in *R v Brighton and Hove Council ex p Nacion* (T49.4); in *R v Newham LBC ex p Lumley* (T48.3) Brooke LJ considered that Latham J's use of the expression 'the merits of the case' (see quote above) must be taken to have meant 'the merits of the applicant's case that the council's original decision was flawed' [54].

T48.2 *R v Haringey LBC ex p Erdogan*
August 1998 *Legal Action* 23; 16 June 1998 , QBD

Injunction granted where failure to respond to request for accommodation pending review after 2 days

The council informed Mr Erdogan that it did not consider that he had a priority need. He asked the council to review that decision (s202). By a letter faxed on 17 June 1998 the council was also asked to provide accommodation pending review (s188(3)). On 19 June 1998, without having received a reply, the applicant applied for judicial review.

Dyson J granted leave and an injunction on the basis that, in the circumstances of an urgent application for accommodation pending review, a failure to respond for two days gave rise to an arguable contention that the authority had failed to consider the application at all.

T48.3 *R v Newham LBC ex p Lumley*
(2001) 33 HLR 11; 2000 WL 409, QBD

Where original decision unlawful, justice required authority to accommodate pending review; no duty to consider accommodation pending review until request made

The applicant applied as a homeless person and was placed in interim accommodation. On 1 November 1999 the council notified him of its decision that he did not have a priority need and that his interim accommodation would be withdrawn from 7 November 1999. No reasons were given for this decision. On 2 November the applicant asked for a review of the adverse priority need decision (s202) and requested that accommodation be continued pending the review (s188(3)). On 5 November 1999, in the absence of a reply, the applicant lodged an application for judicial review of the failure to consider the request. On 8 November 1999 the council's appeals officer wrote refusing to extend accommodation pending review. The judicial review application was amended to challenge that decision also. During the course of proceedings the council made two concessions: (1) its decision letter was not a proper decision letter as it gave no substantive explanation for its decision, and (2) it had failed in its duty to carry out enquiries necessary to satisfy itself what duty, if any, it owed (under s184(1)(a)).

Brooke LJ (sitting as a single QBD judge) held:

1) If the council's primary decision on priority need had been correct, there was nothing unlawful in determining the applicant's accommodation at six clear days' notice as he was a young single man (*R v Newham LBC ex p Ojuri (No 5)* (T55.10) distinguished).

2) No duty to consider the discretion to accommodate pending review arose until such accommodation was requested.

3) The original adverse priority need decision was flawed by both a failure to make adequate enquiries into the applicant's medical condition and a failure to put to him the adverse views of the council's medical adviser.

4) Neither of these flaws, which rendered the decision unlawful, was considered by the officer who refused to continue accommodation pending review.

5) Applying *R v Camden ex p Mohammed* (T48.1) justice demanded that the council should have continued accommodating until it reached a lawful decision.

6) Accordingly, the decision to refuse to accommodate was itself unlawful.

Brooke LJ considered that Latham J's use of the expression 'the merits of the case' in *Mohammed* must be taken to have meant 'the merits of the applicant's case that the council's original decision was flawed' (para 54).

T48.4   **R (Abdi) v Lambeth LBC**
[2007] EWHC (Admin) 1565; (2007) *Times* 11 July, 26 June 2007
Not unfair for s184 decision-maker to make decision under s188(3)

The claimant sought a review of an adverse homelessness decision and asked to be accommodated by the council pending the outcome of that review under the discretionary power in Housing Act 1996 s188(3). The decision to refuse that request was taken by the same officer who had made the original adverse s184 decision. The claimant sought judicial review, asserting that fairness required that a different officer not involved in the original adverse decision-making and a more senior officer should take the decision on accommodation pending review or, in default, simply a different officer.

Deputy High Court Judge HHJ Hickinbottom dismissed the claim. The statutory scheme did not restrict the persons who could make a decision relating to interim accommodation under s188(3). The scheme did restrict those who could make a s202 review decision but it did not exclude the s184 decision-maker from being involved further in the case (*Feld v Barnet LBC* (T43.8)). This was not a s202 review. Nor did the general principle of fairness and the need to avoid the appearance of bias require that the decisions should be taken by different officers. A fair-minded and impartial observer would not have considered that there was any real possibility of bias. The s184 decision-maker may be in the best position promptly to determine an application for accommodation pending review. He or she had knowledge and experience of the relevant law and the authority's discretion under s188(3). In this case the decision-maker had conscientiously and objectively considered the claimant's application for accommodation.

T48.6   **R (Antoine) v Reigate and Banstead DC and First Secretary of State**
December 2004 *Legal Action* 18; 1 November 2004
In unusual circumstances of displacement of Chagos Islander and his claim to be habitually resident in the UK, accommodation should be provided pending review

The claimant, and about 30 other British citizens, arrived in the UK from Mauritius. They were Chagosians who had been displaced from what had been the British Indian Ocean territories. They first sought accommodation from West Sussex County Council under the provisions of the National Assistance Act 1948 s21. The county council refused to accommodate them as it was not satisfied that all of them were in need of 'care and attention'. A challenge to that decision failed (*R (Selmour) v West Sussex CC* [2004] EWHC 2413 (Admin)). The claimant then applied to Reigate and Banstead DC for assistance under Housing Act 1996 Part VII. The council provided him with interim accommodation but then notified him of its decision that he was 'ineligible' for Part VII assistance as he was not 'habitually resident'. He applied for a review (s202) and accommodation pending review (s188(3)). The council refused to continue to provide accommodation. The claimant sought judicial review.

On an application for an interim injunction, Moses J held that the review application raised an issue of substance, ie, given the unusual circumstances that had led to the displacement of the claimant, the award of British citizenship and the exercise of the right to enter the UK, the usual approach to determining habitual residence should not be applied. It was appropriate to require the council to accommodate the applicant pending the outcome of that review. He granted the order sought.

See: *Couronne and others v Crawley BC and others* (T2.2).

T48.7 **R (Lawer) v Restormel BC**
[2007] EWHC 2299 (Admin); 12 October 2007 (see T58.5)

Interim injunction obtained without notice relating to judicial review of s188(3) refusal set aside where material non-disclosure and underlying judicial review was without merit

T48.8 **R (Mohamed) v Harrow LBC**
[2005] EWHC Admin; [2006] HLR 18; 13 December 2005 (see T2.15)

Where EEA national not a worker or work-seeker and did not otherwise have a right to reside, decision not to accommodate pending review lawful

T48.9 **R (Paul-Coker) v Southwark LBC**
[2006] EWHC 497 (Admin); 3 March 2006

Mere 'lip service' paid to Mohammed *principles which had not been properly applied*

On 29 December 2005 the claimant, who had given birth a few days earlier, applied to Southwark as a homeless person. The council decided that she was not eligible for assistance because, although she was a British citizen, she had entered the UK from Sierra Leone on 6 May 2005 and was a person from abroad who was not habitually resident in the UK (s185). She requested a review of that decision (s202) and to be accommodated pending the review (s188(3)). Her solicitors emphasized the facts that:

- she had recently given birth to a baby;
- she had lived and been educated in the UK in her formative years;
- she had made extended holiday visits to the UK while living abroad;

- she had travelled to the UK on a single air ticket bringing all her belongings with her;
- her family and friends were in the UK.

The council declined to accommodate her pending the review. Its decision indicated it had had regard to the criteria in *R v Camden LBC ex p Mohammed* (T48.1).

In judicial review proceedings, Forbes J quashed the decision. The decision letter refusing accommodation did little more than identify the relevant criteria and did little or nothing to apply the relevant facts of the case to those criteria and reach an adequately reasoned decision. In particular, no explanation was given of why over seven months' residence was insufficient to justify the 'appreciable period of time' element of the habitual residence test. Nor was the material that had specifically been brought to the council's attention addressed. The 'complete absence of any explanation or reasoning in the decision letter, dealing with these various important aspects of the case, demonstrates that the *ex p Mohammed* balancing exercise has not been fully or properly carried out by the decsion-maker, despite lip service having been paid to it.' [50]

T49   *Discretion to accommodate pending appeal: s204A*

See also section T48: Discretion to accommodate pending review.

Housing Act 1996 s204(4) provides that an authority may secure that accommodation is available to an applicant during the period for appealing to the county court under s204 against an authority's decision and, if an appeal is brought, until the appeal (and any further appeal) is finally determined. Note that Nationality Immigration and Asylum Act 2002 s54 and Sch 3 excludes the exercise of this power in relation to relation to non-British citizens, subject to exceptions (see U8).

Prior to the amendment by Homelessness Act 2002, a decision not to exercise the Housing Act 1996 s204(4) power was only challengeable by judicial review (see *Ali v Westminster CC* (T57.2)). However, s204A introduced a specific statutory right to appeal a s204(4) decision. On such an appeal the court is to apply the same principles applied by the High Court in an application for judicial review (s204A(4)). If the court quashes the decision it may order the authority to exercise the s204(4) power for such period as is specified in the order (s204A(5)). An order may be made only where the court is satisfied that failure to exercise the s204(4) power would substantially prejudice the applicant's ability to pursue the main appeal (s204A(6)). The principles on which the discretion is to be exercised is the same as for s188(3), as set out in *R v Camden LBC ex p Mohammed* (T48.1).

Court of Appeal

T49.1   *Brookes v Croydon LBC*
[2004] EWCA Civ 439; 26 March 2004

A second appeal against a s204A appeal was 'the exception' and refused due to the practicalities involved

Croydon decided in July 2003 that Ms Brookes had become homeless intentionally after being evicted from her previous home for rent arrears. It decided that its duty to her (s190) could be met by a further short period in temporary accommodation. The council agreed to consider a review requested out of time and provided accommodation pending review. The review decision, given on 19 January 2004, confirmed that Ms Brookes had become homeless intentionally. An accompanying letter indicated that her accommodation would be continued until 8 February 2004 and that she could seek assistance at the council's Housing Advice Service. She lodged a county court appeal contending that the intentional homelessness decision was wrong or, if it was right, she had been allowed an inadequate period of accommodation under s190 and that there had been no proper s190(4) assessment. That appeal was scheduled to be heard in April 2004. Ms Brookes asked for accommodation to be provided pending that hearing. The council would agree to extend the accommodation only until 17 February 2004. Ms Brookes brought an appeal against that decision under s204A. On 8 March 2004 HHJ Winstanley dismissed that appeal. Ms Brookes sought permission to bring a second appeal against that decision.

Carnwath LJ refused that application and held that second appeals should be 'the exception'. Even if an appeal raised 'an important point of principle' the grant of permission was discretionary and that discretion would be exercised having regard to the practicalities. Those practicalities included:

- the difficulty of assembling a full Court of Appeal to hear a second s204A appeal before the hearing of the s204 appeal in the county court,
- the difficult questions as to what (if any) interim relief the Court of Appeal had jurisdiction to grant and
- the difficulty for an appellant assisted by solicitors and counsel in the Court of Appeal in demonstrating that she could meet the requirement in s204A(6) to show that her ability to press her s204 appeal was 'substantially prejudiced' by the non-provision of accommodation pending appeal.

Carnwath LJ further noted that authoritative guidance on s204A appeals had been given in *Francis v Kensington and Chelsea RLBC* (T49.2). That guidance remained valid and it was 'difficult to conceive' of further points arising which required Court of Appeal guidance on s204A. In *Brookes* the primary attack on the s204A decision had been on adequacy of reasons, but both the council and the judge had had regard to the *Mohammed* criteria approved in *Francis*. The 'reasons' challenge did not raise an 'important point of principle or practice'. Finally, although the case did raise an interesting point of principle about the timing of the duty to assess needs under s190(4), that point had been raised in the substantive s204 appeal which had yet to be heard.

T49.2 *Francis v Kensington and Chelsea RLBC*
[2003] EWCA Civ 443; [2003] 1 WLR 2248; [2003] 2 All ER 1052; [2003] HLR 50

The effect of s204A was simply to transfer to the county court the limited power of intervention which existed on a judicial review application as set out in Nacion

Mr Francis applied to Kensington and Chelsea as a homeless person and was provided with accommodation pending its decision (s188(1)). The council made a decision that he did not have a priority need and confirmed its decision on review. In November 2002, Mr Francis appealed to the county court under s204. In February 2003, the council terminated the provision of temporary accommodation. Mr Francis appealed against that decision under s204A. HHJ Walker held that he was unable to interfere with the decision as the council had not refused to consider exercising its discretion, and that it was not therefore open to him to address the merits of the case. Mr Francis appealed contending that the new s204A appeal was, in the light of the wording of s204A(4), akin to an application for interim relief, and raised the test of whether an appellant had a strong prima facie case.

The Court of Appeal dismissed his appeal. Section 204A did not give the county court the wide appeal power contended for. It simply transferred to the county court the very limited power of intervention which the Court of Appeal had identified in *R v Brighton and Hove Council ex p Nacion* (T49.4). The county court should follow the approach set out in *ex p Nacion* unless it decides that the local authority did not direct itself in accordance with *R v Camden LBC ex p Mohammed* (T48.1). In that case it should quash the decision and decide whether it should itself exercise the s204A(5) power to order the authority to provide temporary accommodation. There is no question of the county court embarking on an assessment of the merits of the appeal. The court confirmed that a challenge to the exercise of powers under s188 of the Act still has to be brought by way of judicial review.

T49.3   **Lewis v Havering LBC**
[2006] EWCA Civ 1793; [2007] HLR 20; 23 November 2006
Council needs to consider grounds of s204 appeal when making decision under s204A

Mr Lewis applied as a homeless person to Havering. It decided, and confirmed on review, that he was not in priority need. He intended to appeal that decision and asked for accommodation pending appeal under s204(4). The council refused. Mr Lewis then lodged an appeal against both the review decision (s204) and the decision to refuse accommodation pending appeal (s204A).

HHJ Platt allowed the s204A appeal and quashed the council's decision to refuse accommodation pending appeal, on the ground that the decision contained no reasons. The council then reconsidered the position but issued a further decision not to accommodate pending appeal, addressing the criteria in *R v Camden LBC ex p Mohammed* (T48.1) and analysing the evidence. Mr Lewis lodged a further appeal under s204A contending that the council had failed to take into account the grounds of his main s204 appeal. On the second s204A appeal, HHJ Polden allowed the council to put in a witness statement from its officer indicating that he had considered all the documentation, including the grounds of appeal, when making his decision.

The Court of Appeal dismissed a further appeal. It was appropriate in such cases for the grounds of the substantive appeal to be considered when deciding on an application for accommodation pending that appeal. The grounds of appeal would help a local authority assess the merits of a case. This did not mean a local authority had to consider the legal and factual arguments advanced in the same way as a court would do, it merely had to take them into consideration when making its decision. It would often be enough for the authority to make reference to having considered the documents(s). In some cases there may be an important and striking ground that requires specific comment. In the present case, it was fairly to be inferred from the council's decision letter that the officer had not considered those grounds. However, the witness statement showed that this had in fact been done. The judge had not been wrong to admit the evidence, as it had caused no unfairness to the claimant (applying *Hijazi v Kensington and Chelsea RLBC* (T24.2).

T49.4   *R v Brighton and Hove Council ex p Nacion*
(1999) 31 HLR 1095; [1999] 11 Admin LR 472; (1999) *Times* 3 February; 20 June 2006, CA

If Mohammed *principles applied any challenge 'futile'; appropriate to seek expedited hearing of appeal*

The applicant lodged an appeal in the county court against a finding of intentional homelessness, which had been affirmed on review. Pending the hearing, he asked the council to accommodate him in exercise of its discretion under s204(4). It refused and he applied for leave to move for judicial review of that refusal (pre-s204A).

The Court of Appeal dismissed a renewed application for leave. Tuckey LJ indicated that helpful guidance on the approach a local authority should take in exercise of its discretion had been set out in *R v Camden LBC ex p Mohammed* (T48.1). If that guidance was followed, any challenge would be 'futile' and applications for judicial review of council decisions in such cases were to be 'strongly discouraged', with leave being granted only in exceptional cases. Lord Woolf MR agreed, indicating that, since the introduction of s204, it would be 'only in an exceptional case' that the High Court would intervene on judicial review – for example, if a local authority 'refuses even to consider exercising its discretion under s204(4)'. Faced with a refusal to provide accommodation pending an appeal, the appropriate step for an applicant to take was to make an application to expedite the hearing of the substantive appeal by the county court.

High Court

T49.5   *Putans v Tower Hamlets LBC*
[2006] EWHC 1634; [2007] HLR 10, 20 June 2006, ChD (see T2.8)

An accession state national who is not working is prima facie not eligible and there is no power to accommodate pending appeal except on human rights grounds

County courts

T49.6   *Onyaebor v Newham LBC*

May 2004 *Legal Action* 23; 15 December 2003, Bow County Court

Unfairness in reaching decision; Mohammed *principles had not been observed*

The appellant applied to the council for housing assistance after he lost his employment and tied accommodation in London. He told the council that his wife and children lived in Nigeria and he had visited them periodically since coming to the UK in 1963. He gave an address at which he said the family stayed in Lagos. The council instructed enquiry agents who visited the property in Lagos where they found the wife. She told them the appellant owned that property. The council decided that the appellant was not homeless as he had accommodation in Nigeria. Although it indicated that it had an enquiry agent's report, the council did not disclose the information it relied on, either at the initial decision stage or on review. The appellant lodged a s204 appeal and asked the council to accommodate pending the appeal. On its refusal to do so, the appellant appealed that decision under s204A. Shortly before that hearing the enquiry agent's report was disclosed.

HHJ Roberts allowed the s204A appeal. There had been unfairness in reaching decisions against the appellant, most particularly in deciding not to accommodate pending appeal. Relevant material had been taken into account about which he had not had the opportunity to comment. Although the council claimed to have had regard to the principles in *R v Camden LBC ex p Mohammed* (T48.1) in the manner required to reach a proper s204A decision (see *Francis v Kensington and Chelsea RLBC* (T49.2)) it had not observed them. It had drawn adverse inferences from material that it had not allowed the appellant to deal with, before reaching the decision not to accommodate him pending the appeal. That decision was quashed and the council was ordered to accommodate pending the main appeal.

Final housing duties

T50   *The main housing duty: s193*

The most significant duty is that owed to the eligible unintentionally homeless applicant in priority need under s193(2) – often referred to as the 'main' or 'full' housing duty.

Section 193 applies where an authority are satisfied that an applicant is homeless, eligible, has a priority need and is not intentionally homeless.

Subsection 193(2) provides that:

Unless the authority refer the applicant to another local housing authority (see section 198), they shall secure that accommodation is available for occupation by the applicant.

Section 193(3) provides that:

The authority are subject to the duty under this section until it ceases by virtue of this section.

Sub-sections (5)–(8) set out the circumstances in which the duty ceases.

Section 206 specifies how an authority can discharge its housing functions. Section 210 provides the accommodation must be suitable (see T53).

Before the decision of the House of Lords in *R v Brent LBC ex p Awua* (T22.2 and T51.1) it was considered that an authority was obliged to secure what was variously described as indefinite, settled or permanent accommodation for an applicant in order to discharge the main housing duty. This was supported by case-law and the *Code of Guidance*. In practice what was described as 'temporary' or 'staged' accommodation was provided to someone owed the main housing duty while they awaited an offer of permanent accommodation. *Awua* held that there is no requirement for permanent accommodation be offered and cases decided prior to *Awua* must be considered in the light of this significant decision. However, note that Housing Act 1996 s193 now provides a complete code as to when the circumstances in which the s193 is discharged (*R v Brent LBC ex p Sadiq* (T41.4)).

T51   *Discharge of duty*

House of Lords

T51.1   *R v Brent LBC ex p Awua*
[1996] AC 55; [1995] 3 WLR 215; [1995] 3 All ER 493; (1995) 27 HLR 453, HL (see also T22.2 (full report) and T4.1)

There is no requirement that accommodation must be settled to discharge the main housing duty

The House of Lords considered the extent of the duty owed by a council to an applicant under Housing Act 1985 s65(2) (now Housing Act 1996 s193(2)) to 'secure that accommodation is available for occupation by the applicant'. Lord Hoffmann stated that there is no requirement in the legislation that the accommodation secured should be settled or permanent. The courts and the then current edition of the *Homelessness Code of Guidance* were wrong to suggest the contrary. The period for which a council provides accommodation was entirely a matter for the council. The word 'suitable' in Housing Act 1985 s69(1) (now Housing Act 1996 s206(1)) imports no requirement of permanence.

The distinction between the duty owed to the intentionally homeless and that to the unintentionally homeless under s65(2) is simply that in the former case, once the provision of accommodation by the council ceases, it owes no further duty. If accommodation provided under s65(2) ends, the council has a continuing duty to secure accommodation unless 'there is a reason why his consequent homelessness will not give rise to a further duty under section 65(2)'. A council might owe a full housing duty to a couple expecting a first child and discharge it by provision of short-term accommodation to 'wait and see' if the child is actually delivered and stays with the family. If the child is lost or placed for adoption, no further duty will be owed once the temporary accommodation is terminated. Provided that the accommodation is arranged for more than 28 days (so that applicants are not threatened with homelessness), the courts will not interfere with a decision unless it is *Wednesbury* unreasonable.

Note: In *R v Wandsworth LBC ex p Wingrove and Mansoor* (T51.9) the court held that the comments in *Awua* about the discharge of duty were not obiter.

Court of Appeal

T51.2   *Ahmed v Leicester CC*

[2007] EWCA Civ 843, 27 June 2007

Test of whether reasonable for applicant to accept offer objective

A final offer of a four-bedroomed house was made to a single mother of Somali origin in performance of the main homelessness duty. On her first visit to the property she signified an interest in taking the tenancy. On her second visit she found that the windows had been broken and rubbish thrown in the garden. She was told by another Somali woman that there were problems with anti-social behaviour and racial harassment. She was chased away from the house by three teenagers who shouted that if she moved in they would 'burn her out'. She refused the offer. The council decided that the offer had discharged its duty: HA 1996 s193(7). That decision was upheld on review and HHJ Mayor dismissed an appeal.

In the Court of Appeal, the appellant contended that, even if the council had been entitled to find, applying an objective test, that the accommodation was 'suitable', it could only answer the further question 'was it reasonable for the applicant to have accepted it?' (HA 1996 s193(7F)(b)) by reference to what the appellant knew at the time i.e. that a 'subjective' assessment was required (see *Slater v Lewisham LBC* (T51.11)). The court found that the reviewing officer had accepted what the applicant had said about her experience. But the assessment of the reasonableness of her acceptance of the offer was not to be measured by her state of mind alone. *Slater* was not authority for a subjective-only approach. The officer had thoroughly considered the extent of anti-social behaviour and racist incidents on the relevant estate and had applied (correctly) an objective test in determining whether it would have been reasonable for the applicant to have accepted the offer.

T51.3   *Griffiths v St Helens Council*

[2006] EWCA Civ 160; [2006] 1 WLR 2233; [2006] HLR 29; (2006) *Times* 24 April

Refusal of an offer of an AST can discharge s193 duty; offer letter should clearly explain situation.

Mrs Griffiths was accepted for the main housing duty (s193(2)). She was initially accommodated in a hotel but was then offered a six-month assured shorthold tenancy (AST) of accommodation in the private sector. There was the possibilty of renewal of the tennacy and the council agreed to pay the shortfall between the rent and housing benefit for the initial six months and, if necessary, thereafter. She was informed that the property was considered suitable and that if she were to refuse it the council would regard its duty as having been discharged under s193(5). Mrs Griffiths refused the offer and the council decided that its duty to her had ceased. It upheld that decision on review. On appeal she contended that (1) the offer had been 'unsuitable' (on the facts) and (2) the council could not obtain release from the s193 duty by the refusal of an offer of an AST, following amendments to the Housing Act 1996 by Homelessness Act 2002. HHJ Mackay dismissed the appeal.

The Court of Appeal dismissed a further appeal (confined to the second ground). Where a local authority was putting forward an offer of an AST as a qualifying AST (s193(7B)) as a method of relieving itself of the s193 duty, a refusal of that offer could not bring the duty to an end: s193(7C). But where the offer of the AST is made as a method of performing the s193 duty (on the basis it will continue if and when that tenancy ends) a refusal can bring an end to the duty by application of s193(5). Given the importance of that distinction, housing authorities should clearly explain the basis on which the offer is being made. If the authority is relying on s193(5):

> The explanation should include statements to the effect (a) that the authority acknowledges that the accommodation would be temporary if the private landlord lawfully exercises his right to recover possession after the end of the fixed term; and (b) that, if that happens and assuming that the applicant's circumstances have not materially changed, the authority accepts that it would again become obliged to perform its duty under the section to secure that accommodation is available for occupation by the applicant. [42]

T51.4 **Omar v Birmingham CC**
[2007] EWCA Civ 610; [2007] HLR 43; (2007) *Times* 12 June; 7 June 2007

Refusal of offer of accommodation led to discharge under s193(7) and s193(5)

Birmingham owed the claimant the main housing duty (s193). It nominated him to a housing association and he was offered an assured tenancy. The offer letter stated that the council was making a single and final offer of accommodation that it considered suitable and reasonable for the claimant to accept. When that was refused, it said that its homelessness duties had been discharged. That decision was upheld on review. On appeal, the claimant took the point that the offer letter did not expressly include the words required by s193(7A), ie, it did not state that it was a final offer 'for the purposes of subsection (7)'. HHJ Swindells QC dismissed that appeal.

The Court of Appeal held, by a majority, that a literal slavish repetition of the exact words of the subsection was not an immutable statutory requirement. Provided that the offer letter actually conveyed the point that it was a 'final' offer of suitable accommodation and otherwise complied with s193(7) it sufficed. Alternatively, the court held unanimously that the offer could be construed as having been made under s193(5) as it met all the requirements of that subsection. By either route, the failure to accept it had brought the duty to an end. May LJ 'summarily rejected' a submission that only a 'final' offer of Part VI accommodation could bring the s193 duty to an end. Any Part VI offer which satisfied s193(5) could also have that effect.

T51.5 **Orejudos v Kensington and Chelsea RLBC**
[2003] EWCA Civ 1967; [2004] HLR 23 (see T53.5)

Discharge of duty where applicant did not comply with B&B signing-in rules

T51.7   *R v Hackney LBC ex p K*
(1998) 30 HLR 760, CA (see T41.3)

Change in law did not apply retrospectively to applicant already accepted for main housing duty

T51.8   *R v Tower Hamlets LBC ex p Ali and Bibi*
(1993) 25 HLR 158, CA

Referral under the local connection provisions does not amount to discharge of duty

Two separate applicants applied to Tower Hamlets, which decided that they were owed the main housing duty. Neither had a local connection with Tower Hamlets and both were referred to other authorities under the local connection provisions (Housing Act 1985 s67, now Housing Act 1996 s198). The other authorities accepted the applications and made offers of accommodation. Neither applicant took up the accommodation offered and both made their own arrangements to stay in accommodation in Tower Hamlets. About three years later, on subsequently becoming homeless, they applied to Tower Hamlets again. Tower Hamlets rejected both applications on the basis that it had discharged its duties by reason of the earlier referrals. In Ms Bibi's case she then applied to Southwark Council, which decided that the main housing duty was owed but referred her back to Tower Hamlets. It again relied on its earlier discharge of duty. In separate applications for judicial review, the council's decisions were quashed.

The Court of Appeal dismissed the appeals. Glidewell LJ, giving the judgment of the court, held that, in respect of unintentionally homeless people in priority need with no local connection with the council they applied to, the council had two choices: (a) to notify the other authority with whom the applicant has a local connection or (b) to discharge the main housing duty itself (Housing Act 1985 s65(2), now Housing Act 1996 s193(2)). Where an authority chose to notify another authority and the applicant later reapplied, having acquired a local connection, the authority could not say that it had already discharged its duty under s65(2) as no duty under s65(2) had previously arisen. In relation to Ms Bibi's referral from Southwark, Tower Hamlets could not say it had previously discharged its s68(2) duty (see now the slightly different provisions of Housing Act 1996 s200(4)/s193(2)), as it had not previously itself been under, nor discharged, such a duty.

The s65(2) and s68(2) duties were separate and to that extent the decision in *R v Hammersmith and Fulham LBC ex p O'Brian* (T36.3) was wrong.

T51.9   *R v Wandsworth LBC ex p Wingrove and Mansoor*
[1997] QB 953; [1996] 3 WLR 282; [1996] 3 All ER 913; (1997) 29 HLR 801, CA

Comments in Awua on discharge of duty not obiter; authority required to act reasonably in relation to the length of tenure provided

Two applicants were provided with assured shorthold tenancies of accommodation in the private sector in purported discharge of the council's Housing Act 1985 s65(2) (now Housing Act 1996 s193(2)) duty. Their applications for judicial review of the decision that the duty had been discharged were dismissed.

The Court of Appeal upheld that dismissal. The applicants argued that the observation in *R v Brent LBC ex p Awua* (T22.2 and T51.1), that the main accommodation duty could be discharged by the provision of non-settled suitable accommodation, was obiter. The court held that the relevant part of Lord Hoffmann's speech in *Awua* was not obiter but was in any event correct in principle. Furthermore, the court was not persuaded that the House of Lords had overlooked other persuasive case-law or parliamentary material or that its decision was inconsistent with other precedent. Evans LJ, while agreeing that an assured shorthold tenancy may discharge the s65(2) duty, said that the authority is required to act reasonably in relation to the length of tenure to be provided. Its decision on what was 'suitable' tenure was not unfettered but must be proportionate to the circumstances of the case.

T51.10 ## R (Bibi (No 1) and Al-Nashed) v Newham LBC
[2001] EWCA Civ 607; [2002] 1 WLR 237; (2001) 33 HLR 84; (2001) *Times* 10 May, CA

Legitimate expectation resulting from the promise of permanent accommodation needed to be considered when deciding what accommodation was to be made available to the applicants

The council accepted that it owed the applicants the main housing duty (Housing Act 1985 s65(2), now Housing Act 1996 s193(2)). They were repeatedly told that they would be provided with permanent council accommodation but would need to wait in temporary private sector leased accommodation until suitable permanent council accommodation became available. They waited, in a series of units of temporary accommodation, for many years. They then sought judicial review requiring the council to discharge its duty in the promised manner. The council then asserted that, in light of the decision in *R v Brent LBC ex p Awua* (T22.2 and T51,1), the units of temporary accommodation had in fact operated to discharge the s65(2) duty some years earlier. If the applicants were again 'homeless' (on the termination of any particular 'temporary' letting) a new duty might arise (under Housing Act 1996 Part VII).

Turner J allowed the applications. He held that, as a matter of strict law, the earlier temporary accommodation had discharged the s65(2) duty (applying *Awua*). However, the council's representations repeated over many years led to the legitimate expectation that the council would not assert that the duty had been discharged until it had provided permanent accommodation. It was still so bound and the applicants were entitled to declarations to that effect. The council appealed to the Court of Appeal.

The Court of Appeal held that it was clear that the local authority, albeit on the basis of a mistaken view of the law, had lawfully committed itself to providing the applicants with suitable accommodation with security of tenure. As a result the applicants had a legitimate expectation to that effect. The local authority erred in law in regarding itself as free of that commitment (in the light of *Awua*) by simply refusing to acknowledge that the promises made were a relevant consideration in deciding whether they should be honoured. That was an error of law since the law required legitimate expectation properly to be taken into account in the decision-making process. To disregard a legitimate expectation because no concrete detriment could be shown was to place the weakest in society, who were most likely to have no choice other than to trust in what had been promised to them, at a particular disadvantage. Nevertheless, the invidious choice of which of the many people waiting for permanent accommodation should be housed remained one which the local authority was singularly best placed to make. The judge had gone too far in his declaration. It was better simply to declare that the local authority was under a duty to consider the applicants' legitimate expectation when deciding the accommodation to be made available for them. The council's appeal was allowed to that extent.

T51.11   *Slater v Lewisham LBC*

[2006] EWCA Civ 394; (2006) *Times* 3 May

A discharge based on a final offer of accommodation under s193(7) required both limbs of s193(7F) test to be satisfied

Ms Slater was accepted for the main housing duty. She subsequently refused an offer of accommodation under Housing Act 1996 Part VI in the New Cross area of London on the ground that she feared her violent ex-partner was staying in the area and would find her. The council decided on review that the offer had been 'suitable' and that it had discharged its duty under s193(7). Ms Slater succeeded on an appeal to the county court because the reviewing officer had failed to consider not only whether the accommodation offered was 'suitable' for her, but also whether it was 'reasonable for [her] to accept the offer', as required by s193(7F).

The Court of Appeal dismissed the council's appeal. It held that:

a) An offer can discharge the main housing duty under s193(7F) only if the authority is satisfied *both* that the accommodation is suitable and that it would be reasonable for the applicant to accept the offer. The particular needs of the applicant, for example to be protected from domestic violence and to be located near support networks, are relevant when considering suitability but that does not mean that those matters are material only to suitability. The submission that if the premises are suitable it had to follow that it was reasonable to accept them was rejected. There may be subjective factors which make it reasonable to refuse accommodation that is objectively suitable.

b) The decision of the reviewing officer did not address the second limb of that test adequately or at all. Although it was not necessary to use the exact words of the subsection in the decision letter, there must be sufficient material in the document read as a whole to show that both limbs were separately and properly considered.

c) The test required the authority to ask whether 'it was reasonable for *this* applicant to have accepted *this* offer of accommodation' as at the date the offer was rejected. The judge had been entitled to vary the reviewing officer's decision as, on the facts, no reasonable authority could have concluded that it would have been reasonable for this applicant to accept her offer.

T51.12 *Tower Hamlets LBC v Begum (Rahanara)*

[2005] EWCA Civ 116; [2006] HLR 9; [2005] LGR 580; (2005) *Times* 22 February (see T55.8)

Where requirement for discharge of duty under s193(7) not satisfied but council later wrote clearly stating that duty discharged, then duty was discharged

T51.13 *Tower Hamlets LBC v Deugi*

[2006] EWCA Civ 159; [2006] HLR 28; 7 March 2006, CA (see T62.7)

In practice a decision that a duty had been discharged under s193(6)(a) needed to be communicated to an applicant, who would have a right of review and appeal

T51.14 *Warsame v Hounslow LBC*

[2000] 1 WLR 696; (2000) 32 HLR 335; (1999) *Times* 21 July (see T43.15)

Right to request a review in s202 included right to request a review of a decision that a duty had been discharged

High Court

T51.15 *R v Bristol CC ex p Browne*

[1979] 1 WLR 1437; [1979] 3 All ER 344; (1979) 78 LGR 32, QBD

Duty discharged by securing that accommodation provided by someone else

Mrs Browne and her seven children left the matrimonial home in Tralee, Eire, as a result of violence from her husband. She travelled to the UK and applied as a homeless person to Bristol. She had no local connection with Bristol nor any other authority in England, Wales or Scotland. Bristol accepted her for the main housing duty. After receiving an assurance from a community welfare officer in Tralee that he would ensure that she would be housed safely if she returned, Bristol decided to discharge its duty by advising her to return to Tralee and paying for her journey back.

Her application for judicial review was dismissed. Housing (Homeless Persons) Act 1977 s6(1)(c) (now Housing Act 1996 s206(1)(c)) provided that an authority could perform its duty to secure that accommodation became available by giving a person such advice and assistance as would secure that he or she obtained accommodation from some other person. When a council secures that accommodation is made available from some other source, the accommodation does not have to be within the authority's own locality. Although it was not a case of a referral under the local connection provisions and s5(4)(b) (now Housing Act 1996 s198(2)(c)) did not apply, the risk of violence was a matter for Bristol to consider. It had made appropriate enquiries and decided that accommodation could be provided in Tralee without a risk of violence. It was not necessary for the purposes of the Act that the welfare officer in Tralee should specify a particular house there, since it was sufficient for the authority to be satisfied that accommodation would be available.

Cf *Parr v Wyre BC* (1982) 2 HLR 71, where a decision by Wyre BC to provide accommodation in Birmingham, 150 miles away and with which the applicant had no local connection was quashed. See now limits on out of area placements: Housing Act 1996 s208(1).

T51.16 *R v Newham LBC ex p Miah (Askir)*
(1996) 28 HLR 279, QBD

Policy not to move people with rent arrears to permanent accommodation lawful

In 1991 the applicant applied to the council as a homeless person and was provided with temporary accommodation. In 1992 he received a Housing Act 1985 s64 (now Housing Act 1996 s184(3)) notice accepting him for the main housing duty. However, arrears accrued in the temporary accommodation and in 1994 reached £7,000. The council issued a notice to quit and brought possession proceedings. The applicant sought judicial review to challenge the council's policy that it would not move people with arrears of rent from temporary to permanent accommodation, relying on *R v Tower Hamlets LBC ex p Khalique* (T51.17).

Carnwath J dismissed the application. It was lawful for the council to take into account rent arrears in relation to their duty under s65(2). The line of cases including *Khalique* and *R v Westminster CC ex p Mulonso* (March 1995 *Legal Action* 14, CA) had been overtaken by the decision in *R v Brent LBC ex p Awua* (T22.2 and T51.1). Following *Awua* the position was relatively straightforward. The council accepted a duty under s65(2). That duty was to provide suitable accommodation which it did. The accommodation was not precarious in the sense explained by Lord Hoffman in Awua. The provision of the accommodation had itself discharged the council's duties. If and when the applicant was required to leave that accommodation, he would be free to apply again to the council and, if he had lost the accommodation because of rent arrears, he might be found to be intentionally homeless.

Although the council had not published its revised policy on deferring applicants with rent arrears for an allocation of permanent accommodation, the policy was not ineffective:

> It is of the greatest importance that authorities should establish clear policies on these matters and make them known to those who are affected ... However, there is nothing in [Housing Act 1985] section 106 which suggests that failure to comply invalidates the policy itself. As a general principle, a local authority is entitled to adopt policies for the exercise of its various functions. That does not depend on any specific provision in the 1985 Act, and there is nothing in the 1985 Act to take it away.

Although Sedley J tended to a contrary view in *Khalique* he did not need to decide the point and specifically left it open.

Note: Housing Act 1996 s193 sets out the circumstances in which the main housing duty can now be discharged.

T51.17 *R v Tower Hamlets LBC ex p Khalique*
(1994) 26 HLR 517, QBD

Policy to defer allocation of permanent accommodation unlawfully made and rigidly applied

The applicant was owed the main housing duty. Since 1987 he had been in temporary accommodation awaiting an offer of permanent accommodation. No offer had been made because the council applied a policy of deferring permanent rehousing for those in arrears with charges for temporary accommodation. The applicant had fallen into arrears because, among other things, housing benefit had been paid late. He applied for judicial review of the council's failure to perform its duty under Housing Act 1985 s65(2) (now Housing Act 1996 s193(2)).

Sedley J considered that the council was entitled to provide the applicant with temporary accommodation provided that his entitlement to permanent accommodation was not deferred so 'as to frustrate the purpose of the legislation and the rights which it gives to individuals, nor deferred or withheld for some improper or illicit reason' (at p522). He declared the council to be in continuing breach of Housing Act 1985 s65(2) and held that: (a) it was unlawful to make rehousing conditional; (b) the condition had been imposed by officers and councillors acting beyond lawfully delegated authority; and (c) in so far as it was part of the allocation policy, the condition had not been published (Housing Act 1985 s106) and was being operated with unlawful rigidity.

Note: Cf *R v Newham LBC ex p Miah (Askir)* (T51.16)

T51.18 ### *R v Westminster CC ex p Chambers*
(1982) 6 HLR 24; (1982) 81 LGR 401, QBD (see T35.6)

Council could refuse second application on the basis of an earlier discharge of duty

T51.19 ### *R (Aweys and Others) v Birmingham CC*
[2007] EWHC 52 (Admin); [2007] HLR 27; [2007] 1 FLR 2006; (2007) *Times* 21 February; 18 January 2007

Duty to provide suitable accommodate to 'homeless at home' cannot be deferred

Seven separate applicants applied to the council under Housing Act 1996 Part VII. Each of the applicants' households was large and they were all living in statutorily overcrowded accommodation. Their applications met with various responses by the council but they were all eventually accepted for the main housing duty under s193(2) on the basis that it was not reasonable for them to continue to occupy their accommodation. However, the council refused to provide them with alternative accommodation and left them 'homeless at home'. It placed them on its allocation scheme made under Housing Act 1996 Part VI. This provided for applicants to be placed in bands of priority from A to E, with A being the highest. Applicants accepted under s193(2) were placed in band A if they were being provided with accommodation arranged by the council under Part VII but were otherwise placed in band B. The applicants were all placed in band B. They applied for judicial review contending that (1) the allocations policy was irrational and (2) their treatment under Housing Act 1996 Part VII was unlawful.

Collins J allowed the claim.

1) The allocation scheme: The division of homeless applicants between band A and band B could not be justified. It was irrational to give those who had been provided with temporary accommodation by the council, which was by definition suitable, priority over those who were 'homeless

at home', living in what the council had accepted was unsuitable accommodation. In any event, the applicants should have been provided with accommodation by the council under Part VII and placed in band A.

2) Part VII: The council had failed to deal with the applicants in accordance with Part VII. It was held that:

(i) The threshold under s184(1) is a low one which is triggered merely by the council having reason to believe that an applicant may be homeless. In the vast majority of cases, the making of the homelessness application itself will satisfy this requirement.

(ii) The duty is triggered where it is apparent from anything said by the applicant, or from anything in writing, that an applicant may be homeless or threatened with homelessness, even if there is no application based specifically on homelessness.

(iii) There is no power to defer inquiry (*Robinson v Hammersmith and Fulham LBC* (T19.3)). Requiring an applicant to go through a 'home options' interview before accepting a homelessness application amounted to deferment and was unlawful.

(iv) Homelessness Act 2002 s3(1)(b) requires authorities to have a strategy for ensuring that 'sufficient accommodation is and will be available for people in their district who are or may become homeless.' Authorities need to take measures to avoid homelessness.

(v) Sections 188 and 193 placed a duty on the council to provide suitable accommodation. The council's policy of waiting to provide permanent accommodation and not providing other temporary accommodation was unlawful. Suitable accommodation had to be provided immediately or within a reasonably short time. The existing accommodation of the 'homeless at home' can never be regarded as suitable.

(vi) It may be preferable for a homeless person to stay in unsuitable accommodation for a short period of time to prevent the upheaval of a series of short-term moves, but there must be discussion with applicants, leading to agreement, and no compulsion.

(vii) The court has discretion to grant a remedy in judicial review proceedings and will recognise the difficulties faced by local authorities. However, authorities must act quickly to place families in suitable accommodation and must do so within a reasonable amount of time – as a guide, about six weeks. Any longer period will need clear justification such as a certainty of suitable accommodation becoming available in a few weeks.

(viii) Damages can arise from a breach of ECHR article 8. The hurdle is a high one but one which certain of the applicants might be able to satisfy.

An appeal to the Court of Appeal was heard in November 2007. Judgment is expected to be handed down in early 2008.

T52   *Duty to intentionally homeless/those threatened with homelessness: s190/s195*

The only other final accommodation duty is that owed to the eligible intentionally homeless in priority need under s190(2). Such applicants are also owed an advice and assistance duty (s190(2), (4), (5)). The same advice and assistance duty is also owed to other eligible applicants (eg, the non-priority homeless).

If an authority is satisfied that an applicant is eligible, in priority need but intentionally homeless the duty under s190 is to:

> (2) (a) secure that accommodation is available for his occupation for such period as they consider will give him a reasonable opportunity of securing accommodation for his occupation.
>
> (b) provide him with …advice and assistance in any attempts he may make to secure that accommodation becomes available for his occupation
>
> (4) The applicant's housing needs shall be assessed before advice and assistance is provided …
>
> (5) The advice and assistance provided… must include information about the likely availability in the authority's district of types of accommodation appropriate to the applicant's housing needs (including, in particular, the location and sources of such types of accommodation).

Court of Appeal

T52.1   *R (Conville) v Richmond upon Thames LBC*
[2006] EWCA Civ 718; [2006] 1 WLR 2808; [2006] 4 All ER 917; [2006] HLR 45; 8 June 2006

The period for which an intentionally homeless applicant is to be accommodated will depend on their circumstances and an authority should not have regard to its resources when considering this

The claimant applied to Richmond as a homeless person. The council found that she was eligible, homeless, had a priority need (because she had dependent children) but that she had become homeless intentionally. In those circumstances its duty under s190 was to assess her housing needs, to supply advice and assistance and to provide her with accommodation 'for such period as will give [her] a reasonable opportunity' of securing her own housing. The claimant's only realistic opportunity for securing accommodation was to rent in the private sector. She found a suitable property but could not afford the deposit or rent in advance required by the landlord. The council declined to provide a grant or loan to meet those costs and directed itself that in determining the 'reasonable opportunity' it could have regard to its own resources and the other demands made by homeless people on those resources. Goldring J dismissed a claim for judicial review (see [2005] EWHC 1430 (Admin) [2006] HLR 1).

The Court of Appeal allowed her appeal. While it is for an authority to decide what amounts to a 'reasonable opportunity' (challengeable only on public law grounds) it is not permitted, in doing so, to have regard to considerations peculiar to it, such as the extent of its resources and other demands on it. It is what is reasonable from the applicant's standpoint, having regard to his or her circumstances and in the context of the accommodation potentially available. What is reasonable will depend on the particular circumstamces of the applicant. The duty to provide a reasonable opportunity falls short of a duty to provide long-term accoommodation.

A moment will normally be reached when, in spite of reasonable efforts, time willl expire if possibilities have not come to fruition. (Pill LJ at [40]).

Although an authority's reasons for fixing a particular period may be 'stated briefly' the court doubted whether the analysis by the council's officer (essentially listing matters she had taken into account) was 'sufficiently comprehensive in the circumstances' [41].

The House of Lords refused Richmond leave to appeal

Note: The English *Code of Guidance* (published July 2006) no longer refers to a 28 day peiod in reference to the s190 duty. At para 14.28 it advises that authorities must treat each case on its merits and refers to relevant considerations. The Welsh *Code of Guidance* issued April 2003 refers to a 28-day period (see para 16.39).

High Court

T52.2   *R v Newham LBC ex p Khan and Hussain*
(2001) 33 HLR 269; (2000) *Times* 9 May, QBD (see T14.8)

Council cannot fail to take any action when applicants threatened with homelessness

T53   Suitability and out of area placements

All accommodation provided under Part VII must be suitable (s206). In considering whether accommodation is suitable authorities should have regard to Housing Act 1985 Parts IX, X and XI (slum clearance, overcrowding and houses in multiple occupation) and the applicant's financial resources, including various specified forms of income, various specified costs relating to accommodation and other reasonable living expenses (Housing Act 1996 s210; Homelessness (Suitability of Accommodation) Order 1996 SI No 3204). The use of bed and breakfast accommodation for applicants whose households include children or a pregnant women is limited by Homelessness (Suitability of Accommodation) (England) Order 2003 SI 3326 and Homelessness (Suitability of Accommodation) (Wales) Order 2006 SI 650. The Welsh Order also provides that a person's specific health needs and the proximity and accessibility of the support of family and support services must be taken into account.

Section 208 provides that so far as reasonably practicable an authority shall secure accommodation within its own district.

Cases on whether it is reasonable to continue to occupy accommodation may also be relevant to the issue of whether accommodation is suitable (see T7).

Court of Appeal

T53.1   *Abdullah v Westminster CC*
November 2007 *Legal Action* 38; 21 June 2007 (see T43.2)

Out of borough placement suitable despite social support network in borough

T53.2   *Apczynski v Hounslow LBC*
[2006] EWCA Civ 1833; 7 December 2006 (see T55.1)

Where council arranged accommodation in the private sector it was not the applicant's landlord and claim in disrepair against it failed

T53.3 Codona v Mid-Bedfordshire DC

[2004] EWCA Civ 925; [2005] HLR 1; [2005] LGR 241; (2004) *Times* 21 July; 15 July 2004

Offer of temporary B&B accommodation to Gypsy family not unlawful or in breach of human rights

Mrs Codona and members of her extended her family were of traditional Romany Gypsy stock. In 1997 they moved their caravans on to land in Bedfordshire. They were refused planning permission to develop it as a caravan park. They became homeless. The council, in purported discharge of its duties under Housing Act 1996, offered temporary 'bed and breakfast' accommodation until it could make a final offer. Mrs Codona sought a review and then appealed to the county court (s204). There was evidence that she had a 'cultural' aversion to living in 'bricks and mortar' accommodation, but none that it would cause her or any of her family psychiatric harm. HHJ Farnworth dismissed her appeal.

The Court of Appeal dismissed her second appeal. The council had discharged its duty to secure suitable accommodation. The requirement that accommodation be suitable meant suitable for the persons to whom the duty was owed. It encompassed considerations of the range, nature and location of accommodation as well as its standard of condition, and likely duration of the applicant's occupancy. The council had not been able to find an alternative site nor could it provide at short notice long-term conventional housing for the extended family. It had been driven to offer short-term accommodation. Depending on the quality of bed and breakfast accommodation offered, and on the reasonable assumption that the council would see to it that their stay there would only be for a short time, it had so far discharged its statutory duty to secure accommodation without violation of article 8 or article 14.

An appellate committee of the House of Lords subsequently dismissed a petition seeking leave to appeal against the Court of Appeal's decision. On 7 February 2006 Mrs Codona's application to the ECtHR was declared inadmissible by the ECtHR (Fourth Section) sitting as a Chamber. It did not consider that she could be said to have been treated less favourably than a homeless person who lacked her 'cultural aversion' to bricks and mortar accommodation. (Application no 485/05)

T53.4 Khatun, Zeb and Iqbal v Newham LBC and Office of Fair Trading

[2004] EWCA Civ 55; [2005] QB 37; [2004] 3 WLR 417; [2004] HLR 29; [2004] LGR 696

No obligation to give applicants opportunity to view accommodation before accepting it; Unfair Terms in Consumer Contract Regulations apply to tenancies

The three applicants were members of separate households who had all been accepted for the main housing duty by Newham. Initially they were provided with bed and breakfast accommodation. They were then notified by letter that Newham had secured self-contained accommodation for them under a private leasing scheme. No details were provided of the accommodation. In accordance with Newham's policy, none of the applicants was offered the opportunity to see the premises or to consider the offer before being required to accept it. If they did not accept it their bed and breakfast accommodation was to be cancelled immediately and the offer withdrawn. They were informed that the accommodation was considered suitable but that there was a right of review. The property offered to and accepted by Ms Khatun, a Muslim, was a flat above a public house where she was subjected to racist abuse. Newman J granted the claimants' application for judicial review, finding that the policy was unlawful.

The Court of Appeal allowed Newham's appeal. A homeless applicant does not have a right to view, or express an opinion on, accommodation offered before deciding whether to accept it. A policy denying such a right is not unlawful. There is nothing in Housing Act 1996 to the contrary effect and no such right could be inferred from the statutory language. Nor do the common-law's standards of procedural fairness require the court to confer a right to be heard. Laws LJ described the view that no reasonable council would fail to accord an opportunity to view and comment on proposed accommodation as 'entirely unsustainable'. The applicants' subjective views on suitability were not 'a compulsory relevant factor in the authority's process of decision'. In view of applicants' right to seek a review of the accommodation provided after moving into it, the policy was not oppressive, perverse or disproportionate. Furthermore, in so far as the applicants sought to rely on the *Code of Guidance*, it is not a source of law. Although councils must take it into account and give reasons for departing from it, it is not binding on them. The goal of getting families out of bed and breakfast as quickly as possible in accordance with government targets (the reason for departing from the *Code of Guidance*) was a perfectly lawful goal.

Newman J's decision at first instance, that the Unfair Terms in Consumer Contract Regulations 1999 and European Council Directive 93/13/EEC, apply to tenancy agreements and to local authorities such as Newham was confirmed.

T53.5   *Orejudos v Kensington and Chelsea RLBC*
[2003] EWCA Civ 1967; [2004] HLR 23
Signing in requirement at B&B did not breach art 8 rights

The council provided Mr Orejudos with hotel accommodation under its main housing duty (s193). He was required to sign the hotel register each day and sleep there each night unless he provided, in advance, an explanation for his absence. Mr Orejudos was absent on 10 occasions, only three of which he had explained (albeit after the absence). He was given two warnings, including a final warning, that his accommodation would be cancelled if he did not comply with the conditions. After a further unaccounted absence the council decided that it had discharged its duty to Mr Orejudos because he had made himself intentionally homeless (s193(6)). It confirmed this decision on review and his appeal was dismissed. On a second appeal Mr Orejudos contended that the conditions of residence amounted to a violation of respect for his private life (ECHR article 8).

The Court of Appeal held that a homeless person was as much entitled to respect for his private life as anyone else. However, the condition the council had imposed did not prevent him sleeping elsewhere, it simply required that he provide a reasonable explanation for doing so. Having regard to the fact that the accommodation was paid for by the council on a daily basis and that there was an obvious need to control costs, there had been no infringement of article 8. The appeal was dismissed.

T53.6   *Osseily v Westminster CC*

[2007] EWCA Civ 1108; 5 October 2007

On review, suitability of offer to be judged at time it was refused; withdrawal of offer of accommodation not relevant to issue of suitability on review

Westminster owed the claimant the main housing duty under s193. It made him an offer of accommodation that he refused. It decided that the offer was suitable and that the refusal of it brought its duty to an end (s193(5)). The offer was withdrawn. The claimant sought a review. A reviewing officer upheld the decision that the accommodation had been suitable and had discharged the council's duty. The claimant argued that that decision must be wrong in law because by the date of the review decision the once-offered property was not available and therefore could not be suitable at that date. HHJ Collins dismissed an appeal.

The Court of Appeal dismissed a second appeal. The general proposition that the facts of the case must be looked at as they stand at the time of the review was uncontentious (*Mohammed v Hammersmith and Fulham LBC* (T43.1)). However, s193(5) plainly contemplates that where an applicant refuses suitable accommodation the council's duty ends there. There was no conceivable warrant for a construction of that subsection that would effectively postpone that event until the outcome of a review. Suitability and availability are two different things. Where the council has already decided that accommodation offered was suitable and that the duty owed under s193(5) had therefore been discharged, the question the reviewer must address was whether, on the facts as they are known at the date of the review, the accommodation previously offered would now be considered suitable. It was noted that s202(1A) entitled an applicant to accept an offer of accommodation but still seek a review of its suitability.

T53.7   *R v Newham LBC ex p Dada*

[1996] QB 507; [1995] 3 WLR 540; [1995] 2 All ER 522; (1995) 27 HLR 502; (1995) 93 LGR 459, CA

Accommodation offered to pregnant woman must be merely suitable for a pregnant woman, not a woman with a baby.

The applicant was pregnant. She and her husband were offered a one-bedroomed flat on the seventh floor of a tower block in discharge of the council's duty. The accommodation would not have been suitable for a couple with a child, but the issue before the court on the application for judicial review was whether the applicant's foetus was a 'person' for the purposes of having its housing needs taken into account under Housing Act 1985 s75 (now Housing Act 1996 s176). Deputy Judge Sir Louis Blom-Cooper QC quashed the council's decision, holding that the expected child was a person with whom the applicant could reasonably be expected to reside and its housing needs should be taken into account.

The Court of Appeal allowed the council's appeal. The accommodation provided did not have to be suitable for a couple with a child but merely suitable for a pregnant applicant.

T53.8   **R v Wandsworth LBC ex p Wingrove and Mansoor**

[1997] QB 953; [1996] 3 WLR 282; [1996] 3 All ER 913; (1997) 29 HLR 801, CA (see T51.9)

Authority required to act reasonably in relation to length of tenure of accommodation provided under s193

T53.9   **R (Sacupima) v Newham LBC**

[2001] 1 WLR 563; (2001) 33 HLR 2; (2000) *Times* 1 December, CA

Interim accommodation out of borough pursuant to policy which did not include reference to the impact on schooling, employment or medical factors unlawful

See T5.2 regarding the separate issue of whether the applicants were homeless prior to eviction by the bailiffs.

Newham, a London borough, provided seven homeless applicants with interim accommodation (s188) at seaside bed and breakfast hotels on an indefinite booking. In making the placement decisions the council considered that none of the families had a 'serious reason' for not being placed outside the borough because its policy did not include impact on schooling, employment or medical factors (save serious risk to life or health) as 'serious reasons'. At first instance each decision was quashed. Dyson J held that, although an authority could have regard to resources in allocation of interim accommodation, it must always be 'suitable' and there was always a 'bottom line' for the standard of accommodation below which it could not be said to be 'suitable'.

The Court of Appeal dismissed the council's appeal on the issue of suitability. There was no doubt that the question whether or not the accommodation was suitable required an assessment of all the qualities of the accommodation in the light of the needs and requirements of the homeless person and his or her family. That meant that the location of the accommodation might be relevant to an assessment of suitability. The statement of Lord Hoffman in *R v Brent LBC ex p Awua* (T22.2) that suitability was primarily a matter of space and arrangement did not preclude an authority from considering other relevant matters. The purpose of s208 is to ensure that, so far as possible, authorities do not simply decant homeless persons into areas for which other authorities are responsible. Where a housing authority did not consider the effect of the location of accommodation on matters such as the employment of applicants or members of their family or the education of their children, a decision to provide bed and breakfast accommodation outside its area was flawed. Therefore the judge was right to conclude that the council acted unlawfully in apparently failing to have regard to the particular educational and medical requirements of the family which made accommodation in the seaside resorts unsuitable, and to conclude that the council's allocation policy was wrong.

The defendant's petition for leave to appeal to the House of Lords was dismissed ([2001] 1 WLR 1839).

High Court

T53.10 *R v Brent LBC ex p Omar*
(1991) 23 HLR 446, QBD

Accommodation must be suitable for the particular applicant taking account of her personal circumstances

The applicant was a Somali refugee fleeing torture and imprisonment. Brent Council offered a basement flat with high windows on the Chalkhill Estate. The flat was alleged to be filthy and infested with cockroaches. The estate consisted of 30 concrete housing blocks linked by overhead walkways. The corridors reeked of urine. It reminded the applicant of prison and she rejected the offer. She submitted supporting medical and psychiatric reports to the council. The council stated that it had discharged its duty.

Henry J quashed the decision. Brent Council had argued that 'suitability' had to be assessed without regard to any factor personal to the applicant. Henry J stated:

> The question of statutory construction raises the question: suitable for whom or for what? On a reading of the Act, it seems to me this can only mean suitable as accommodation for the person or persons to whom the duty is owed; ... in determining whether the accommodation is suitable the local housing authority must clearly have regard to the circumstances of the applicant and his or her family, in so far as those circumstances are relevant to the suitability of the accommodation, as well as having regard to the matters to which their attention is specifically directed by the statute; that is to say, provisions relating to fitness for habitation, overcrowding and the like. ((1991) 23 HLR at 457)

T53.11 *R v Ealing LBC ex p Parkinson*
(1997) 29 HLR 179, QBD

No damages for breach of public law duty in failing to provide suitable accommodation

Mr Parkinson was a married man with four children. The three youngest all suffered from cerebral palsy and spastic quadriplegia. They had to use electric wheelchairs. In August 1989 he applied to Ealing Council as a homeless person. The council placed him in a three-bedroomed two-storey house as temporary accommodation while it made enquiries. In March 1991 it accepted that it owed the main housing duty. However, Mr Parkinson remained in the temporary accommodation. In October 1994 he was granted leave to apply for judicial review on the basis that the temporary accommodation was totally unsuitable. In August 1995 the authority rehoused him and his family into satisfactory accommodation but Mr Parkinson pursued a claim for damages for breach of statutory duty.

His application was dismissed. The law recognises no right to compensation for breach of duty arising only in public law except when there is misfeasance in public office. He could not recover damages unless it was established that there was breach of a private law duty. The public law duties were not discharged until the authority had completed the process of deciding about the suitable accommodation which it was obliged to provide. The council did not owe a free-standing common-law duty of care.

Note: See, however, cases under ECHR article 1 of the First Protocol: section A5.

T53.12 *R v Haringey LBC ex p Karaman*
(1997) 29 HLR 366, QBD

Offer of accommodation in the Kurdish community, where applicant feared discovery by her husband of whom she was terrified, perverse

The applicant and her daughter were accepted for asylum in the UK. They had serious mental health and medical problems arising from torture and other human rights abuses in Turkey. The applicant was particularly afraid of coming into contact with her husband, from whom she had separated after arrival, and of others in the London Turkish and Kurdish communities. The council made an offer of accommodation which the applicant considered to be insecure, located at the heart of the Turkish and Kurdish communities and on a main bus route from the area in which her husband was known to be living. She was absolutely terrified by the prospect of living there and her state of fear was well documented by her medical and other advisers. The council affirmed the offer as discharging its duty.

Brooke J directed himself that he should be 'slow to interfere' and that there was 'an extremely high hurdle' for an applicant to overcome in 'suitability' cases. Nevertheless, he held that the council's decision was unlawful. The council did not suggest that the applicant's terror was anything other than genuine or real nor dispute the evidence that acceptance of the offer would damage the daughter's mental health. Since it had not made any investigations of its own, it was bound to accept the descriptions of the family's terrified state that it had received. In such circumstances, its affirmation of the offer was perverse. Brooke J noted that this case and *R v Brent LBC ex p Omar* (T53.10) were wholly exceptional.

T53.13 *R v Lewisham LBC ex p Dolan*
(1993) 25 HLR 68; (1993) 91 LGR 224, QBD

Separation of medical and social grounds when determining suitability incorrect

The applicant refused the council's offer of accommodation on the basis that it was not suitable. The council considered the suitability of the offer on both medical and social grounds and determined it to have been suitable.

Sir Louis Blom-Cooper QC quashed the decision. The council had separated the medical and non-medical aspects and delegated them to separate officers. The failure of the council to take an overall or composite view was a fatal procedural irregularity.

T53.14 *R v Newham LBC ex p Begum (Mashuda)*
[2000] 2 All ER 72; (2000) 32 HLR 808; (1999) *Times* 11 October, QBD

Duty to provide suitable accommodation cannot be deferred

The applicant's family included her husband, six children and her husband's half-brother and mother who usually lived with them. In May 1998 the council accepted that it owed her the main housing duty (s193). The family were initially placed in bed and breakfast accommodation and in

November 1998 they were moved to a four-bedroom house on an assured shorthold tenancy. They requested a review of the suitability of that accommodation. In a letter dated January 20 1999 the review was turned down, saying that the property was the most suitable that the council had. On January 30 1999 the husband's mother returned from a visit to Bangladesh where she had broken her hip. As a result she was disabled and had to use a wheelchair. The council accepted that the accommodation was overcrowded and unsuitable for wheelchair access and that the family should be moved. Because the council accepted that the accommodation was not suitable, there was no power of review or appeal to the county court. In May 1999 the applicant applied for judicial review. The council, relying on *R v Southwark LBC ex p Anderson* (2000) 32 HLR 96, QBD and *R v Merton LBC ex p Sembi* (2000) 32 HLR 439, QBD argued that it was not in breach of its s193 duty because it was making reasonable efforts to find suitable accommodation but none was available.

Collins J granted a declaration in favour of the applicants. He held that:

1) The housing duties under ss188, 190, 200 and 193 cannot be deferred and the cases of *Anderson* and *Sembi* were wrong to the extent that they suggested that the s193 duty was qualified and could be construed as a duty to make suitable accommodation available within a reasonable time. The duty is unqualified.

2) Councils unable to secure suitable accommodation immediately are protected to the extent that no court will enforce the housing duty unreasonably. However, as the duty is not qualified, the court must not be too ready to accept that the council is taking all appropriate steps. In this case the council had not done all that it could because it had not considered making accommodation temporarily available from its own housing stock under s207(1) nor had it considered accommodation outside the council's area under s208.

3) Whether or not accommodation is suitable may depend on how long it is to be occupied and what is available. It may be reasonable to expect a family to put up with conditions for a few days which would be clearly unsuitable if they had to be tolerated for a number of weeks. But there is a line to be drawn below which the standard of accommodation cannot fall.

T53.15 *R v Newham LBC ex p C*

(1999) 31 HLR 567, QBD (see U5.10)

Authority misunderstood its powers or fettered its discretion in deciding that it could only provide B&B accommodation and not self-contained accommodation under National Assistance Act 1948 s21

T53.16 *R v Newham LBC ex p Ojuri (No 3)*

(1999) 31 HLR 452; (1998) *Times* 29 August, QBD

Policy of booking all homeless households into B&Bs unlawful; individual needs of applicant need to be considered

The applicant, a single parent with three children, applied as a homeless person under Housing Act 1996 Part VII. The council booked him into a bed and breakfast hotel in Hackney in discharge of its interim duty under s188. The applicant sought judicial review on the grounds that, among other things, the council had not directed itself to the suitability of that type of accommodation for the applicant's household (s206) nor to its duty to place applicants within the council's area (s208). The council's evidence was that (a) bed and breakfast accommodation was all it had available as interim accommodation and (b) most of its homeless households in temporary accommodation were placed in bed and breakfast hotels in other boroughs, and some outside London, owing to lack of alternative accommodation.

Collins J quashed the decision. Although the decision that accommodation in the bed and breakfast hotel was suitable was not perverse, 'suitability' required individual consideration of the particular applicant's circumstances. The council had not done this. The duty could not be met simply by booking all homeless households into bed and breakfast establishments, particularly in the light of the *Homelessness Code of Guidance*'s statement that such accommodation was unsuitable for families (para 20.2 of the *Guidance*).

Note: The use of B&B accommodation is now limited by Homelessness (Suitability of Accommodation) (England) Order 2003 SI No 3326 and Homelessness (Suitability of Accommodation) (Wales) Order 2006 SI No 650.

T53.17   *R v Tower Hamlets LBC ex p Kaur*
(1994) 26 HLR 597, QBD

Where housing benefit shortfall, accommodation not suitable

Several applicants dependent on income support were offered and accepted (in discharge of the main housing duty) assured tenancies granted by private landlords. The local housing benefit authority declined to meet the rents in full, and so, from the start of each tenancy, a substantial shortfall arose each week.

Deputy Judge Robert Carnwath QC quashed the purported discharges of duty. He held that it was clear law that:

> ... accommodation is not suitable unless it is at a rent which the applicant can afford, either from his own resources or with the benefit of such public assistance as is likely to be available to him, [but that in this case] on the evidence, the rents are completely out of reach of those involved and unlikely to be covered by housing benefit.

T53.18   *R (Aweys and Others) v Birmingham CC*
[2007] EWHC 52 (Admin); 18 January 2007 (see T51.19)

Duty to provide suitable accommodate to 'homeless at home' cannot be deferred

T53.19   *R (Calgin) v Enfield LBC*
[2005] EWHC 1716 (Admin); [2006] 1 All ER 112; [2006] HLR 4; [2006] LGR 1; (2005) *Times* 27 September

Policy on out of area placements not unlawful; council entitled to take into account resources

The claimant, his wife and baby daughter arrived in the UK from Turkey in April 2004 and were granted indefinite leave to remain. Having become homeless, they applied to Enfield, which accepted the main housing duty under Housing Act 1996 s193(2). It decided, and confirmed on review, to provide accommodation in Birmingham in discharge of that duty. Mr Calgin's appeal to the county court was stayed pending his judicial review of the council's policy of out of borough placement of homeless households. He contended that a general policy of using cheaper accommodation in the Midlands ran contrary to the statutory requirement to use in-borough accommodation 'so far as reasonably practicable': s208(1).

Elias J dismissed the claim. The evidence showed that Enfield genuinely faced considerable difficulties in finding appropriate accommodation to meet its needs within the borough at a reasonable cost. Although the meaning of 'reasonably practicable' in s208 had to be determined in the light of the particular statutory context, cost was not an irrelevant or improper consideration. The council was entitled to take into account the pressures on accommodation locally and the availability of cheaper accommodation elsewhere. It was for Enfield, at the first stage, to determine whether it was reasonably practicable to obtain accommodation within its area. The court could interfere only if the decision was unlawful on *Wednesbury* grounds. Although the 'suitability' requirement in Housing Act s206 imposed a minimum standard which had to be achieved irrespective of the council's available resources, if that was achieved the only inhibitor on out-borough placement was s208(1). The council's policy was not contrary to that provision and was not *Wednesbury* unreasonable. Furthermore, Homelessness Act 2002 s3(2) did not require that specific objectives or plans should be included within its strategy. It was a matter of discretion whether they were included or not. The out of area policy adopted by Enfield was entirely consistent with the strategy document and did not amount to a modification of the strategy at all.

Cf *R (Yumsack) v Enfield LBC* (T53.27).

T53.20 ### *R (Flash) v Southwark LBC*
[2004] EWHC 717 (Admin); 15 March 2004

Interim accommodation of one-bedroom flat for applicant and grandson suitable and complied with interim order

Ms Flash was aged 74 and in poor health. She usually lived with her grandson. She sought accommodation from Southwark as a homeless person. Southwark accepted that she was a person with an apparent priority need and that it was obliged to provide interim accommodation under s188(1). It also accepted that under s176 accommodation would be regarded as available for her occupation only if it was available for her and her grandson. In December 2003, Ms Flash, in an application for judicial review, obtained an interim order that Southwark provide her with interim accommodation. Southwark offered her a two-bedroom flat, with access via a flight of eight stone steps. Ms Flash was able to ascend the steps, but could not descend them unaided. She refused that accommodation. She was then offered accommodation in a one-bedroom, ground floor flat. Southwark took the view that the grandson could sleep in the living room on a temporary basis. An occupational therapist agreed that those premises were adequate as interim accommodation. The claimant refused that offer. She issued an application to commit on the basis that Southwark had failed to comply with the terms of the interim order.

Owen J dismissed the application. Southwark had fulfilled its obligation under the interim order. The faults with both sets of accommodation were not sufficiently serious to amount to a failure by Southwark to fulfil its obligation under s188. It could not be said that no reasonable authority would not have regarded the accommodation as adequate. The interim order was discharged.

T53.22 *R (Khan) v Newham LBC*
[2001] EWHC Admin 589

Guidance on granting mandatory injunction where authority in breach of duty to secure suitable accommodation

The claimant was owed the main housing duty (s193(2)) by Newham. He lived with his wife and four children aged 10, 7, 5 and 18 months. He sought judicial review of the council's failure to provide suitable accommodation in discharge of the duty. He was accommodated in unsuitable hostel-style accommodation where kitchen and bathroom facilities were shared with another family. There were no facilities for washing clothes. The house was extremely crowded with 10 people sharing one kitchen and two toilets. Furthermore, the children attended primary school in Newham and the accommodation provided was in Ilford, Essex. The journey to primary school involved the children leaving the hostel at 7.45 am and not getting home until after 4.30 pm. On the day of the trial the council conceded that it was in breach of its duty. It put in evidence from its homelessness co-ordinator that the borough was under exceptional pressure in dealing with homeless families. The issue for the court was whether or not to grant mandatory relief.

Scott Baker J held that a local authority may only adequately discharge its s193 duty through the provision of bed and breakfast accommodation for a limited period of time. He said that the following matters were relevant on the exercise of the discretion whether or not to grant a mandatory order. First, the nature of the temporary accommodation occupied. Second, the length of time for which the council had been in breach of the duty. Third, the efforts made by the council to find suitable accommodation. Fourth, the likelihood of accommodation becoming available in the near future. Fifth, any particular factors in relation to the individual case. He rejected the council's contention that lack of available resources was a relevant consideration applying *R v Newham LBC ex p Ojuri* (No 3) (T53.16) endorsed by Latham LJ in *R (Sacupima) v Newham LBC* (T53.9). He held that 'Far too long has now passed without this family having been properly accommodated'. He granted a mandatory order requiring the authority to provide suitable accommodation within two months.

Note: Although not referred to in the judgment, precisely the same result had been achieved in *R v Newham LBC ex p Begum (Mashuda)* (T53.14). The use of B&B accommodation is now limited by Homelessness (Suitability of Accommodation) (England) Order 2003 SI No 3326 and Homelessness (Suitability of Accommodation) (Wales) Order 2006 SI No 650.

T53.23 **R (Maughan) v Leicester CC**

[2004] EWHC 1429 (Admin); 26 May 2004

Traveller's assertion to cultural aversion to conventional housing rejected

The claimant, a traveller, unlawfully moved with his family on to council land in October 2003. In February 2004 the council began possession proceedings. The claimant applied for accommodation as a homeless person. The council accepted the application and, pending inquiries, offered a hostel place as interim accommodation under s188. The claimant rejected the offer on the grounds that he had a cultural aversion to 'bricks and mortar' accommodation and relied on *R (Price) v Carmarthenshire CC* (T53.25).

Richards J dismissed his claim for judicial review. The council's decision letter about the discharge of its s188 duty had specifically referred to *Price*. The council was entitled to reject the claimant's assertion of 'cultural aversion' on the basis that he had held four successive tenancies of conventional council housing, most recently from January to October 2003.

T53.24 **R (Morris) v Newham LBC**

[2002] EWHC 1262 (Admin); 24 May 2002

Claim for damages for failure to provide suitable accommodation based on ECHR art 8 rights dismissed

On 3 November 2001 the council decided that it owed the claimant the main housing duty under Housing Act 1996 s193 but it failed to provide any suitable accommodation. In March 2002 the claimant began proceedings for judicial review to compel performance of the duty. Suitable accommodation was provided from 23 May 2002. The claim for judicial review was pursued to trial to recover damages for the period 3 November 2001 to 23 May 2002. The claim was put on the basis that a right to damages accrued under Human Rights Act 1998 s8 for breach of ECHR article 8.

Jackson J dismissed the application. He held:

- Article 8 did not impose on the state a duty to provide a home and the simple fact of 'homelessness' did not therefore breach art 8. The loss of a previous home had been the starting point for the claimant's homelessness application. The council had not deprived her of that home nor failed to accord respect for any existing home.
- Article 8 could assist if homelessness caused interference with the claimant's family life or private life. On the facts, although the council's breach of duty had caused the claimant to occupy grossly overcrowded and unsuitable accommodation for some 29 weeks, the claimant had not been separated from her children and her health problems had not been so grave as to interfere with her private life.
- As no claim lay for damages in the law of tort for breach of the statutory duties owed to the homeless (*O'Rourke v Camden LBC* (T56.1)) the claimant could not recover recompense for the council's breach in any civil proceedings.

Note: See, however, cases under ECHR article 1 of the First Protocol: section A5.

T53.25 **R (Price) v Carmarthenshire CC**

[2003] EWHC 42 (Admin); 24 January 2003

Council failed to have sufficient respect for Irish traveller's art 8 rights in decid-ing to evict (when accommodation to be provided under Part VII was conven-tional housing)

Ms Price was an Irish traveller. She had no pitch on which to station her caravan and overstayed temporary permission to park in a public open space. On her application for assistance as a homeless person, the council accepted the full housing duty (s193) and in discharge of that duty offered a three-bedroom house until a suitable permanent official caravan pitch became available. Ms Price contended that her aversion to conventional housing made that offer unsuitable and, when the offer was affirmed on review, she appealed to the county court. Meanwhile the council decided to seek her eviction from the open space. She applied for judicial review of that decision.

Newman J reviewed a number of authorities and extracted the follow-ing propositions:

1) Suitability is not an absolute concept. There can be different stand-ards of suitability. However, it must be recognised that there is a min-imum line below which the standard of accommodation cannot fall and remain suitable.
2) If it is clear that a council is doing all that it can, a court will not make an order to force a local authority to do what is impossible.
3) The duty is one which must be fulfilled within a reasonable time, depending on the circumstances in each case and what accommoda-tion the local authority has available.

He allowed the application and quashed the council's decision to claim possession. Although it could not be said that conventional housing would always be unsuitable for a traveller with hostility to conventional housing, the council in this case had failed to accord sufficient 'respect' to the appli-cant's ECHR article 8 rights in deciding to evict her. Respect means more than 'acknowledge' or 'take into account'. It implies some positive obliga-tions on the part of the local authority. It had not put itself in a position to act proportionately for article 8(2) purposes. The decision was remitted.

T53.26 **R (W) v Sheffield CC**

[2005] EWHC 720 (Admin); 14 April 2005

Sheffield ordered to accommodate applicant in London in exceptional circumstances

The claimant lived in Sheffield for three years and in August 2004 moved to Westminster in London. He spent most of his time in Westminster but was also homeless and an in-patient at a psychiatric unit in a different bor-ough. He had serious mental health difficulties, the mental age of a child and was unable to read or write. He found it difficult to accept help from support services but began to react positively to (and co-operate with) The Passage, an organisation for the homeless with a day centre in Westmin-ster. Assisted by The Passage, the claimant applied to Westminster for accommodation. It decided that he was homeless, in priority need and not intentionally homeless. It also decided that he had no connection with Westminster but a local connection with Sheffield. It referred the s193 duty to Sheffield, which accepted the referral. The claimant was suicidal at the prospect of a return to Sheffield. The referral decision was confirmed on review. He lodged an appeal to the county court but Westminster declined to accommodate pending the appeal (s204(4)). The claimant then asked Sheffield to perform the s193 duty by accommodating him in Westminster (at least until the appeal could be heard). It refused and made an offer of accommodation in Sheffield. The claimant sought judicial review of that refusal. Sheffield contended that (a) the correct target for any challenge was Westminster's referral decision and (b) pending the hearing of the appeal relating to that decision, the appropriate course was for the claimant to appeal Westminster's refusal to accommodate pending appeal under s204A (seeking an interim injunction if necessary).

Gibbs J decided that, exceptionally, it would be appropriate to entertain judicial review proceedings 'the claimant having been caught between two stools and faced with an exceptional situation'. He adjourned the substantive claim but ordered Sheffield to continue to accommodate the claimant in Westminster until the determination of the Housing Act 1996 appeal against the Westminster referral decision.

T53.27 *R (Yumsak) v Enfield LBC*
[2002] EWHC 280; [2003] HLR 1

Accommodation provided to London applicant in Birmingham not suitable in view of support needs; breach of ECHR art 8 as it involved disruption in the applicant's children's relationship with their father who lived in London

Ms Yumsak was an asylum-seeker who spoke little English. She had three young children and had lived in Enfield, in accommodation provided by social services, for the eight years since her arrival in the UK. After her application for asylum was granted and she was required to leave the accommodation provided by social services, she applied as a homeless person to Enfield. She was provided with temporary bed and breakfast accommodation in Birmingham. She objected to the placement on the basis that she did not have any family or friends in Birmingham, that she suffered from epilepsy and that her children's schooling would be disrupted by the move. In addition, the children's father, who lived in London, wished to maintain contact with them. Enfield replied that they considered the accommodation suitable. A year or so later a decision had not been made on Ms Yumsak's application and she sought judicial review of the suitability of her accommodation and Enfield's failure to make a decision. Enfield conceded that a mandatory order should be made in relation to its failure to make a decision.

Her appeal was allowed. Maurice Kay J inferred that, although the basis of the placement was temporary, the local authority knew that it would be for a far longer period. There was no evidential assertion that there was no cost-effective temporary accommodation in the borough or that the only way the local authority could meet its statutory obligation under Housing Act 1996 s188 was by sending her to Birmingham. Stepping back and looking at the matter as a whole, it was unreasonable for the local authority to seek to discharge its statutory obligations by providing temporary accommodation in Birmingham. Ms Yumsak should not have been placed in bed-and-breakfast accommodation or in Birmingham. The decision was irrational. It also infringed the claimant's rights under ECHR article 8(1). No evidence had been filed by the council to demonstrate that no other accommodation had been available to it or otherwise to provide a justification under article 8(2).

Cf *R (Calgin) v Enfield LBC* (T53.19).

T53.28   *R (Zaher) v Westminster CC*
[2003] EWHC 101 (Admin); 28 January 2003

Obligation to provide suitable accommodation a continuing one

The applicant lived in Westminster with his family for three and a half years. When his home burnt down he applied to the council as a homeless person. It accepted him for the main housing duty and offered him temporary accommodation in West Drayton, Middlesex. The applicant considered this too far from his children's school and from his friends and family and initially refused it. The council maintained that the property was suitable and wrote informing him that the offer discharged its duty under s193 and that he had a right to request a review under s202. The applicant reluctantly accepted the offer, did not request a review and moved in in October 2001. In May/June 2002, because the accommodation was too far from his children's schools and because his wife was suffering from depression and needed the support of friends and family, he asked to be moved. The council refused and said that any transfer request must be made to Eurolets, who managed the property. The applicant's requests to the council for a review of the suitability of the accommodation were ignored and he made a claim for judicial review.

McCombe J granted the application and quashed the council's decision. The council's submission that the provision of the accommodation had discharged its duty to provide suitable accommodation and that it subsequently had no duty to revisit the question of suitability was rejected. The council's obligation to provide suitable accommodation is a continuing obligation. If there is a change in circumstances, the council is under an obligation to reconsider suitability. In the light of the decision in *Alghile v Westminster CC* (T43.3) the courts would be slow to accept changes in circumstances that were little more than a request for a review of the nature that was considered impermissible in *Alghile* (that is, accepting an offer at the same time as requesting a review). The council could not discharge the duty to reconsider suitability by directing the applicant to a third party, such as Eurolets. The court exercised its discretion to hear the application despite the existence, on the council's failure to conduct a review, of a right to appeal to the county court under s204. A strong factor in reaching this decision was the council's failure to make its position clear and to inform the claimant of the statutory appeal process.

Note: The effect of *Alghile v Westminster CC* was subsequently reversed by Housing Act 1996 s202(1A).

T54   Protection of property

Court of Appeal

T54.1   *Deadman v Southwark LBC*

(2001) 33 HLR 865; (2001) 33 HLR 75; (2000) *Times* 31 August, CA

Council not liable for failing to protect applicant's property

The claimant was a secure tenant. She was harassed by her neighbour and required hospital treatment. She applied to the council as a homeless person. The council accepted a duty to accommodate pending enquiries (Housing Act 1985 s63, now Housing Act 1996 s188). However, no alternative accommodation was provided. The claimant complained that her property was liable to be stolen, but the council took no action to secure the premises, other than to ensure that the flat was locked and visited. After a burglary at her flat she brought proceedings under Housing Act 1985 s70 (now Housing Act 1996 s211) for damages for the loss suffered. HHJ Butter QC held that the council was not under any duty pursuant to s70.

The claimant appealed unsuccessfully. The cause of action depended on the local authority having reason to believe that (a) there was a danger of loss or damage to property as a result of the owner being unable to protect it and (b) no other suitable arrangements being made (see s70(1)(a) and (b)). Taking the meaning of the word 'danger', there had to be a likelihood of harm and not just the possibility of injury. On the facts no duty was owed to Mrs Deadman under s70.

See *Mitchell v Ealing* [1979] QB 1; [1978] 2 WLR 999; [1978] 2 All ER 779; (1978) 76 LGR 703, QBD, for a case concerning theft of goods where the council had agreed to store possessions.

Local government ombudsman

T54.2   *Complaint against Sutton LBC*

03/B/06452, 17 December 2004

Duty to protect property continues until possessions are no longer 'at risk'

Mr Smith applied to the council for assistance as a homeless person under Housing Act 1996 Part VII. He and his daughter were provided with interim accommodation pending a decision (s188) and at the council's direction a contractor moved their possessions into storage (s211). The contractor made a list of the items stored. This included, in addition to specific items, references to 'boxes' 'bags' and a 'crate' of other items. The council accepted the applicant for the main housing duty (s193(2)) and continued to accommodate him. However, following the accrual of rent arrears the council decided that its duty had been brought to an end (s193(6)(b)) and discontinued the temporary accommodation. When contacted by the council by telephone about his belongings in storage Mr Smith said that he could not provide an address as he was still homeless and sleeping in a car. The council gave him 28 days to provide an address. At the end of that period he still had no address and was given a further seven days. When that expired the council instructed the contractor to dispose of the belongings.

The ombudsman found that the council had wrongly treated its duty to secure the belongings as ending at the same time as its housing duty had ended. In law, the duty continues until the possessions are no longer 'at risk' unless stored. The council treated its duty as ended without being properly satisfied that Mr Smith could take care of his own possessions and that was maladministration. The council agreed to (1) pay £6,000, (2) waive the storage charges and (3) review its procedures.

T55   Security of tenure of accommodation provided under Part VII

Various provisions in the Housing Acts of 1985, 1988 and 1996 exempt accommodation provided under Part VII from the normal security of tenure provisions (Housing Act 1985 Sch 1 para 4; Housing Act 1988 Sch 17, Housing Act 1996 s209). If a tenancy/licence falls outside protection of the Housing Acts it may nevertheless attract the basic protection provided by Protection from Eviction Act (PEA) 1977 (s3/s5) unless excluded (s3A).

Court of Appeal

T55.1   *Apczynski v Hounslow LBC*
[2006] EWCA Civ 1833; 7 December 2006

Council not the landlord of accommodation arranged by it in private sector

The claimant applied to Hounslow for homelessness assistance. It acknowledged a duty to secure accommodation for him under Housing Act 1996 Part VII. On 24 May 2005 it wrote to him stating 'You have been booked into the above-named hotel by the London Borough of Hounslow'. He moved into the accommodation which was a house owned by Hounslow Estates Ltd, a private company. He alleged that the premises were in poor condition and brought a claim for damages for disrepair against Hounslow. The council denied that it was his landlord. HHJ Reid QC dismissed the claim. The claimant sought permission to appeal, asserting that it raised an issue of general importance and had prospects of success.

The Court of Appeal refused permission. Neuberger LJ said:

> The problems arising in this case, namely identifying whether or not the applicant has a tenancy, and if so, who is his landlord, may well be frequently encountered, as local housing authorities would frequently house either temporarily or more longer-term applicants in accommodation owned by third parties. However, I am not persuaded that that would be a good reason, if we should otherwise refuse permission, for granting permission to appeal. [7]

There were no reasonable prospects of successfully establishing that the terms of the letter demonstrated that the council rather than the owner was the claimant's landlord. Who was the claimant's landlord was, in every case, a question of fact which was the manner in which the judge had approached it.

T55.2   *Brennan v Lambeth LBC*
(1998) 30 HLR 481, CA (see B2.6)

Provision enabling residents (homeless applicants) to be moved from room to room resulted in licence; accommodation was a 'hostel' within PEA 1977(3A)(8)

T55.3 ## Desnousse v Newham LBC

[2006] EWCA Civ 547; [2006] 1 QB 831; [2006] 3 WLR 349; [2007] 2 All ER 218; [2006] HLR 38; [2007] LGR 368; (2006) *Times* 28 June; 17 May 2006 (see O3.3)

Licence of temporary accommodation provided to intentionally homeless not 'let as a dwelling' and PEA 1977 s3/s5 not applicable; no court order required to evict

T55.4 ## Family Housing Association v Jones

[1990] 1 WLR 779; [1990] 1 All ER 385; (1990) 22 HLR 45; (1990) 60 P&CR 27; [1990] 1 EGLR 82; [1990] 24 EG 118, CA (see B2.11)

Self-contained flat provided to homeless applicant resulted in tenancy despite label as licence

T55.5 ## Hackney LBC v Lambourne

(1993) 25 HLR 172; [1993] COD 231, CA (see L1.5)

Occupant could not raise defence based on non-performance of homelessness duties in possession proceedings

T55.6 ## Mohamed v Manek and Kensington and Chelsea RLBC

(1995) 27 HLR 439; (1995) 94 LGR 211, CA (see O3.5)

B&B accommodation provided under s188 not 'of a dwelling' and PEA 1977 did not apply

T55.7 ## Sheffield CC v Smart

[2002] EWCA Civ 04; [2002] HLR 34; [2002] LGR 467; (2002) *Times* 20 February

County court does not have to consider art 8 when determining possession claim against non-secure tenant housed under s193

The defendant was accepted for the main housing duty (Housing Act 1996 s193). She was granted a non-secure tenancy of accommodation under s193. Later neighbours made complaints of nuisance and as a result her tenancy was terminated and the claimant took proceedings for possession. The judge held that a valid notice to quit had been served and made a possession order. The defendant appealed, contending that it was the judge's duty to determine not merely whether the scheme of the Act struck the necessary and proportionate balance required by ECHR article 8, but also whether on the facts of the particular case a possession order was a necessary and proportionate remedy.

The Court of Appeal dismissed the appeal. If article 8 entitled a tenant in the defendant's position to have a county court judge (or the judicial review court) decide on the particular facts whether eviction was disproportionate to the council's aim of managing its housing stock properly, the effect would be to convert non-secure tenancies enjoyed by homeless persons into a form of secure tenancy. The balance of interests arising under article 8(2) had in all its essentials been struck by the legislature when enacting the current scheme for the housing of homeless persons and their eviction.

T55.8   *Tower Hamlets LBC v Begum (Rahanara)*

[2005] EWCA Civ 116; [2006] HLR 9; [2005] LGR 580; (2005) *Times* 22 February

*No role for county court, within possession proceedings against homeless appli-
cant, to consider challenge under Part VII; court has power to adjourn proceedings pending judicial review of decision to claim possession*

Mrs Begum was accepted for the full housing duty (s193). The council
provided her with a non-secure tenancy of a council flat (Housing Act
1985 Sch 1 para 4). In January 2002 it made her an offer of a secure tenancy of a different flat under Housing Act 1996 Part VI and, at the same
time, gave notice to quit the non-secure tenancy. Mrs Begum refused the
offer. The council considered that it had discharged its duty and in August
2002 began a claim for possession of the flat. Mrs Begum defended the
claim on the basis that the council had not fulfilled its homelessness duty
as it had not complied with a requirement, in the version of s193(7) then
in force, to serve a notice containing certain information on her within 21
days of the refusal of the offer. A district judge dismissed the possession
claim and on appeal, HHJ Hornby held that to grant possession when the
council had not properly performed its duty would amount to an infringement of Mrs Begum's article 8 right to respect for her home.

The Court of Appeal allowed the council's appeal. Although the council
had not complied with the notice requirement in s193(7), a later letter communicated to Mrs Begum, in unambiguous terms, that the council had decided that it owed her no further duty and informed her of a right of appeal
to the county court. That was either a decision in relation to which she had
a right to request a review (applying *Warsame v Hounslow LBC* (T43.15)) or
a review decision that was amendable to appeal. Mrs Begum had until 15
June 2002 to request a review or bring an appeal but she did not do so. There
was no role for the county court on the possession claim other than, in a
suitable case, to adjourn for an application for judicial review of the decision
to bring the possession claim to be pursued in the Administrative Court.

After the Court of Appeal hearing, but before judgment, Mrs Begum
applied for judicial review of the decision to bring the possession proceedings. It was considered (obiter) that she was not entitled to do so as the
review/county court appeal process was the mechanism to challenge the
council's decision that it had discharged its duty. An applicant could not
bring a challenge 'through the back door of a judicial review application'
in the absence of very unusual facts.

High Court

T55.9   *R v Newham LBC ex p Lumley*

(2001) 33 HLR 11; 2000 WL 409, QBD (see T48.3)

*Six days' notice for a young single man to leave interim accommodation not
unlawful, providing the s184 decision lawful*

T55.10   *R v Newham LBC ex p Ojuri (No 5)*

(1999) 31 HLR 631, QBD

*Authority must act reasonably in giving notice to terminate accommodation
even where no duty owed*

The applicant, who had three children of primary school age, applied for a review of a decision that he was intentionally homeless. He was accommodated pending the review (under a court order). The review decision confirmed the intentionality decision and informed the applicant that his temporary accommodation would be cancelled the following morning. The applicant sought judicial review of the decision to cancel the accommodation forthwith on the basis that the council owed him a public law duty to act reasonably and continue his accommodation at least until he could consider making an appeal or apply for further discretionary accommodation pending appeal or arrange other accommodation for himself.

Following a contested application, David Pannick QC, sitting as a deputy High Court judge, gave leave to move for judicial review and granted an injunction requiring the council to accommodate the applicant for a further 28 days. The court expressly adopted the dicta of Carnwath J in *R v Secretary of State for the Environment ex p Shelter* [1997] COD 49, QBD that, even when a council finds it owes no duty to someone it has been accommodating, it must nevertheless act reasonably as a public authority in relation to the further provision of accommodation.

T55.11   *R v Westminster CC ex p Abdulkadir*
August 1999 *Legal Action* 29; 1 February 1999

Seven days' notice to vacate accommodation for single man asserting mental health problems arguably unlawful

The council decided that, although the applicant was homeless, he did not have a priority need. On review it confirmed that decision by letter dated 20 January 1999. On 23 January 1999 it wrote to the applicant requiring him to leave interim accommodation with which he had been provided under s188 by 1 February 1999. The applicant lodged a county court appeal against the review decision and applied for judicial review of the decision not to accommodate him pending appeal.

Jowitt J held that the applicant would only have received the letter requiring him to leave the interim accommodation seven days before it was withdrawn. For a single man asserting vulnerability by reason of mental illness it was arguably *Wednesbury* unreasonable to allow as little as seven days. Accordingly leave to move for judicial review was granted with an injunction requiring the council to accommodate for at least seven further days.

Note: Cf *R v Newham LBC ex p Lumley* (T48.3), where six clear days' notice was held not to be unlawful in relation to an applicant asserting mental health problems.

T55.12   *R (Hammia) v Wandsworth LBC*
[2005] EWHC 1127 (Admin); [2005] HLR 45 (see T40.7)

Policy that tenant had to serve NTQ on tenancy from which she fled unlawful

T55.13   *Rogerson v Wigan MBC*
[2004] EWHC (QB) 1677; [2005] HLR 10; [2005] LGR 549 (see O3.10)

Accommodation no longer referable to temporary duty 'let as a dwelling' and protected by PEA 1977 s3/s5 unless excluded by s3A; accommodation provided a 'hostel' and excluded by s3A(8)

Challenge: appeals and judicial review

T56   General principles

European Court of Human Rights

T56.1   *O'Rourke v UK*

ECtHR Application no 39022/97

Breach of statutory duty under Housing Act 1985 Part III does not give rise to cause of action sounding in damages

The plaintiff applied to the council as a homeless person. The council placed him in temporary accommodation pending a decision on whether he was homeless and in priority need. However, he was evicted from the temporary accommodation before a decision was made. He issued proceedings in the county court for damages for breach of statutory duty and negligence. HHJ Tibber struck out the proceedings. The Court of Appeal allowed his appeal, but the House of Lords reinstated the order striking out the action (*O'Rourke v Camden LBC* [1998] AC 188; [1997] 3 WLR 86; [1997] 3 All ER 23; (1997) 29 HLR 793, HL).

Lord Hoffmann stated that there was no doubt that the Housing Act 1985 created a duty which was enforceable by judicial review, but whether it gave rise to a cause of action sounding in damages was dependent on whether the Act showed a legislative intention to create such a remedy. He accepted the council's submissions that there were contra-indications, namely that (a) the Act was a scheme of social welfare, intended to confer benefits at the public expense on grounds of public policy and (b) the existence of the duty was dependent on a good deal of judgment on the part of the housing authority, which had a wide discretion in deciding how to provide accommodation and what kind of accommodation it would provide. The House of Lords held that it was 'unlikely that Parliament intended errors of judgment to give rise to an obligation to make financial reparation'. The suggestion advanced by Mr O'Rourke that there was a difference between the obligation to provide temporary accommodation and the full housing duty under Housing Act 1985 Part III (now Housing Act 1996 Part VII) was rejected. The breach of statutory duty of which the plaintiff complained did not give rise to any cause of action in private law.

Mr O'Rourke's application to the ECtHR was heard on 26 June 2001. He contended that the failure to re-accommodate him under Housing Act 1985 s63 (now Housing Act 1996 s188), after he had been evicted (for alleged misconduct) from interim accommodation in a hotel constituted interference with his convention rights under ECHR articles 3 and 8. The ECtHR ruled his claim inadmissible ('manifestly ill-founded'). As to article 3 (inhuman or degrading treatment) it held that: (1) the applicant's suffering between his eviction and his rehousing had not attained the requisite level of severity to engage article 3; and (2) if it had, the claimant was largely responsible for that suffering as he had failed to follow advice to go to a night shelter and had refused two further offers of temporary accommodation. As to article 8 (right to respect for a home), it held that: (1) if the hotel room had been his home, he had been lawfully evicted from it in accordance with the hotel proprietor's right to request guests to leave for the protection of staff and other guests; and (2) to the extent that the state had been under any positive duty to re-accommodate following his eviction (see *Mazari v Italy* (A3.9)) that duty had been met by the advice given and the offers of alternative temporary accommodation.

Note: See, however, cases under ECHR article 1 of the First Protocol: section A5.

House of Lords

T56.2 *R v Hillingdon LBC ex p Puhlhofer*
[1986] AC 484; [1986] 1 All ER 467; [1986] 2 WLR 259; (1986) 18 HLR 158, HL
General comment on the use of judicial review in homelessness cases

See T8.2 for the substantive decision that, prior to amendment, the definition of homelessness did not require accommodation to be reasonable. Since amendment, the actual decision has lost some of its importance. However, the following statement made by Lord Brightman remains relevant:

> My Lords, I am troubled at the prolific use of judicial review for the purpose of challenging the performance by local authorities of their function under the 1977 Act. Parliament intended the local authority to be the judge of fact. The Act abounds with the formula when or if, the housing authority is satisfied as to this, or that, or have reason to believe this, or that. Although the action or inaction of a local authority is clearly susceptible to judicial review where they have misconstrued the Act, or abused their powers or otherwise acted perversely, I think that great restraint should be exercised in giving leave to proceed by judicial review. The plight of the homeless is a desperate one and commands the deepest sympathy. But it is not, in my opinion, appropriate that the remedy of judicial review, which is a discretionary remedy, should be made use of to monitor the actions of local authorities under the Act save in the exceptional case. The ground on which the courts will review the exercise of judicial discretion is abuse of power, eg, bad faith, a mistake in construing the limits of the power, a procedural irregularity or unreasonableness in the *Wednesbury* sense ... ie, unreasonableness verging on an absurdity ... Where the existence or non-existence of a fact is left to the judgment and discretion of a public body and that fact involves a broad spectrum ranging from the obvious to the debatable to the just conceivable, it is the duty of the court to leave the decision of that fact to the public body to whom parliament has entrusted the decision-making power save in a case where it is obvious that the public body, consciously or unconsciously, are acting perversely. ([1986] 1 All ER at 474)

T57 ## Which court?

Before the implementation of the Housing Act 1996 the primary method of challenging decisions made by local authorities in relation to applications by homeless persons was by judicial review. Since Housing Act 1996, the main means of challenge has become the statutory method of review (s202) and appeal to the county court (s204). This route of appeal has been extended by amendments introduced by Homelessness Act 2002 to include challenges to refusals to provide accommodation pending the hearing of s204 county court appeals (Housing Act 1996 s204A, reversing the effect of *Ali v Westminster CC* (T57.2)). However, judicial review remains the only method of challenging decisions which do not carry a right of review under s202, such as the failure to provide accommodation pending decision under s188(1) and pending review under s188(3). Furthermore, judicial review proceedings have, in exceptional cases, been allowed where there is a right of appeal to the county court, under the High Court's residual discretion.

House of Lords

T57.1   *Cocks v Thanet DC*
[1983] AC 286; [1982] 3 WLR 1121; [1982] 3 All ER 1135; (1982) 6 HLR 17; (1983) 81 LGR 81, HL

Challenge to homeless decisions (prior to Housing Act 1996) by judicial review

As a general rule, it is contrary to public policy and an abuse of process to allow someone to proceed to challenge a local authority's decision on public law rights by an ordinary action. As a general rule, such a challenge should be bought by judicial review. In homelessness cases, private law rights arise only after councils have made the appropriate public law determination on whether the person is homeless, threatened with homelessness, in priority need and not intentionally homeless. Challenges of such decisions should be brought by judicial review.

Note: See now Housing Act 1996 s204 which provides a right of appeal to the county court against most homelessness decisions.

Court of Appeal

T57.2   *Ali v Westminster CC*
[1999] 1 WLR 384; [1999] 1 All ER 450; (1999) 31 HLR 349; (1998) *Times* 16 September, CA

County court had no power to grant interim injunction to accommodate (pre-s204A)

The Court of Appeal held that the county court does not have power to grant mandatory interim injunctions requiring local authorities to provide accommodation to applicants pending the outcome of appeals to the county court under Housing Act 1996 s204. A refusal to provide accommodation is only challengeable by judicial review.

Note: The effect of this decision has been reversed by Housing Act 1996 s204A. However, judicial review remains the only challenge available if an authority refuses to provide accommodation pending a s202 review.

T57.3   *R v Lambeth LBC ex p Alleyne*
June 1999 *Legal Action* 24, CA

In exceptional circumstances, where an applicant had missed the time limit for an appeal against a review decision, she could seek judicial review of the decision

The Court of Appeal allowed a renewed application by the appellant for permission to move for judicial review of a decision where she had missed the 21-day time limit to appeal in the county court (see Housing Act 1996 s204(2)). Although the jurisdiction of the High Court was to be exercised sparingly in such cases, the appellant had shown an arguable error of law in the review decision and ought to have the opportunity to provide further evidence to show the circumstances were sufficiently 'exceptional' to justify the grant of relief where an alternative remedy had been available.

Note: See now Housing Act 1996 s204(2A) (extension of time limit for appeal) as introduced by Homelessness Act 2002.

T57.4   *R v Westminster CC ex p Ellioua*
(1999) 31 HLR 440; EWCA Civ 1142, CA (see T46.3)

If an authority refuses to reconsider a review decision, remedy is appeal to county court of original review decision not judicial review of the refusal

T57.5   *R (Heather) v Leonard Cheshire Foundation*
[2002] EWCA Civ 366; [2002] 2 All ER 936; [2002] HRLR 30; [2002] UKHRR 883; [2002] HLR 49; (2002) 5 CCLR 317; [2002] ACD 43; (2002) *Times* 8 April; 21 March 2002 (see U2.3)

Appropriate to challenge closure of care home on basis that it breached residents' ECHR rights by way of judicial review where issue whether care home was a 'public authority'

T57.6   *Tower Hamlets LBC v Begum (Rahanara)*
[2005] EWCA Civ 116; [2006] HLR 9; [2005] LGR 580; (2005) *Times* 22 February (see T55.8)

Where the review/county court appeal process was the mechanism to challenge a decision, applicant could not bring a challenge by judicial review in the absence of very unusual facts

High Court

T57.7   *R v Brent LBC ex p Sadiq*
(2001) 33 HLR 525; (2000) *Times* 27 July, QBD (see T41.4)

Despite holding that applicant had right to s202 review appropriate for High Court to exercise its residual discretion and grant relief where the position had been unclear

T57.8   *R v Newham LBC ex p Begum (Mashuda)*
[2000] 2 All ER 72; (2000) 32 HLR 808; (1999) *Times* 11 October, QBD (see T53.14)

Challenge to council's failure to provide suitable accommodation by way of judicial review where council acknowledged accommodation not suitable

T57.9   *R (Aguiar) v Newham LBC*
[2002] EWHC 1325 (Admin) (see T43.17)

Applicant can seek judicial review to compel authority to carry out a review (rather than appeal the original decision)

T57.10   *R (Lynch) v Lambeth LBC*
[2006] EWHC 2737 (Admin); [2007] HLR 15; 16 October 2006 (see T43.18)

Inadequate reasons in decision letter could be remedied on review and no exceptional circumstances justifying application for judicial review

T57.11 *R (Van der Stolk) v Camden LBC*

[2002] EWHC 1261 (Admin); 21 May 2002

Application for judicial review allowed where time limit for appeal had expired

The claimant applied to the council as a homeless person following the loss of tied accommodation. His letter of dismissal mentioned his mental health problems. The council's decision that he had become homeless intentionally was upheld on review and the claimant did not appeal to the county court. Some six weeks after the review decision he submitted a medical report dealing with his mental health problems and asserting that his condition would have disabled him from being fully functional whilst an employee. The council responded that the time limit for appeal to the county court had passed and that there were no exceptional reasons or special circumstances justifying the reopening of the homelessness application.

Goldring J allowed an application for judicial review. He held that although judicial review would not normally lie where the claimant had not availed himself of a county court appeal, this was an unusual case. The claimant's health was poor and deteriorating and the medical report did add materially to what had been known about its effects on the claimant. It would be unfair not to reconsider the matter where the applicant was particularly vulnerable.

Note: Housing Act 1996 s204(2A) now makes provision for an out of time appeal.

T57.12 *R (Zaher) v Westminster CC*

[2003] EWHC 101 (Admin); 28 January 2003 (see T53.28)

Judicial review allowed despite alternative remedy of county court appeal where authority had not made position clear

T58 ## Accommodation pending judicial review of a decision

See also sections T47–T49: Interim accommodation duties and powers, in relation to the provision of accommodation pending a statutory review and appeal.

Court of Appeal

T58.1 *De Falco v Crawley BC*

[1980] QB 460; [1980] 2 WLR 664; [1980] 1 All ER 913; 78 LGR 180, CA

Applicant had to show a strong prima facie case for a mandatory injunction

Mr De Falco, an Italian, who was unemployed, left accommodation in Italy and came to England with his wife and children to look for work. Initially they stayed with relatives but then applied to Crawley as homeless persons. After making enquiries, the local authority decided that Mr De Falco was intentionally homeless. It gave as its reason the fact that he had come to England without ensuring that he had permanent accommodation here. Mr De Falco sought judicial review of the decision and an interim injunction requiring the council to continue to provide accommodation. Chapman J refused the injunctions at first instance.

The Court of Appeal dismissed an appeal. The court would only grant interim mandatory relief if the material before it showed 'a strong prima facie case' that the decision was invalid (per Lord Denning MR, at p478, and Bridge LJ at p481). The court expressly disapproved of the application in such cases of the *American Cyanamid* balance of convenience test, governing the grant of prohibitory injunctions on interlocutory applications (*American Cyanamid Co v Ethicon Ltd* [1975] AC 396, HL). Here, although the decision was bad on its face, the decision was not unlawful. In the light of Mr De Falco's circumstances, the authority was entitled to conclude that he had deliberately left accommodation in Italy which was available to him and which would have been reasonable for him to have continued to occupy, having regard to the housing situation in Crawley. The local authority had not taken into account any irrelevant factors or failed to take into account any relevant factors.

T58.2 *R v Cardiff CC ex p Barry*
(1990) 22 HLR 261, CA

Where permission to apply for judicial review is granted, court will usually grant an injunction requiring applicant to be accommodated

The applicant left accommodation because of alleged harassment and the service of a notice to quit. Cardiff decided she was intentionally homeless. She sought judicial review and, although granted leave, was refused an interlocutory injunction requiring the council to house her pending the final hearing.

The Court of Appeal allowed her renewed application for interim relief and granted an injunction. Giving the judgment of the court Sir John May held that:

> although it cannot be a general rule in every case ... it seems to me that where a court concludes that a local authority's decision under sections 62 or 63 of the Housing Act 1985 [see now Housing Act 1996 s184 and s188] is or may be susceptible of challenge by way of judicial review, the court as a usual concomitant of granting leave to challenge such a decision should preserve the 'ring' as it were, and enable the applicant to stay in any accommodation which he or she may be in pending the ultimate decision in the judicial review proceedings. ((1990) 22 HLR at 263)

T58.3 *R v Kensington and Chelsea RLBC ex p Hammell*
[1989] 1 QB 518; [1989] 2 WLR 90; [1989] 1 All ER 1202; (1988) 20 HLR 666, CA

Judge wrong in holding power to grant interim relief only to be used in 'wholly exceptional' cases

The applicant left her council house in Scotland following harassment from her ex-husband, who lived nearby. After a period staying with her sister she applied to Kensington and Chelsea as a homeless person. It made enquiries which revealed that her former home in Scotland was still available to her and that the local council there were investigating the harassment. Kensington and Chelsea decided that the applicant was not homeless, giving as its reasons that she had accommodation that she was entitled to occupy. A note on its file stated 'no duty – not homeless, violence occurs outside home'. The applicant applied for judicial review of the decision and obtained an interim injunction. On an application by Kensington and Chelsea, Nolan J set aside the injunction on the basis that the case was 'not exceptional'.

The Court of Appeal allowed the applicant's appeal and granted the interim injunction requiring the council to provide accommodation pending the hearing of the application for judicial review. It held that the court always has power to issue interim injunctions once leave to proceed has been given. Applicants for such orders have to show a strong prima facie case. It is not necessary for the case to be exceptional.

In the instant case the applicant had a strong prima facie case. Indeed, since the local authority in this case had issued a notice which was defective on its face for failing to deal with the reasonableness or otherwise of the applicant returning to the accommodation she had left (Housing Act 1985 s58(2A), now Housing Act 1996 s175(3)), it was right that an injunction should issue. The question of violence outside the home, while not relevant to s58(3) (violence within the home; see now the wider s177(1)), was relevant to the question of whether it was reasonable for the occupant to continue to occupy accommodation. The council had made insufficient enquiries in this respect. The applicant's right to accommodation, following the acceptance of an application, could only be removed by a valid decision. The applicant had a public right to have that decision properly taken and, in the meantime, to have her private law right to accommodation protected. The injustice to her if she was not housed, but was right on her application, was immense. If she turned out to be wrong the council would have been obliged to accommodate her temporarily, but there was no question of permanent queue jumping.

T58.4   *R v Westminster CC ex p Augustin*
[1993] 1 WLR 730; (1993) 25 HLR 281, CA

Interim relief, pending hearing of an appeal against dismissal of a claim for judicial review, refused where not strong prima facie case

The applicant appealed to the Court of Appeal against the dismissal of her judicial review of a decision by Westminster that she was intentionally homeless (see T37.11 for report). She applied to the Court of Appeal for interim relief pending the hearing of the appeal. It held that, in considering an application for interim relief at the appellate stage, a very strong case would have to be made out for a successful appeal, in order to justify making a mandatory injunction. In the instant case the applicant had not shown that she did have a strong prima facie case.

High Court

T58.5   *R (Lawer) v Restormel BC*
[2007] EWHC 2299 (Admin); 12 October 2007

Interim injunction obtained without notice set aside where material non-disclosure and underlying judicial review was without merit

The claimant was the secure tenant of accommodation in Newquay which she fled with her children, asserting that she had been the victim of domestic violence. She then gave notice to terminate the tenancy. She applied to Restormel as a homeless person. In a letter dated 23 August 2007 it informed her of its decision that she was intentionally homeless and that it would accommodate her until 21 September. She applied for a review and requested an extension of her accommodation. The council's housing officer, in an undated letter, requested submissions for the review and refused further accommodation, without giving reasons. On 19 September the claimant instructed a solicitor who telephoned the council and requested accommodation pending review (s188(3)). The housing officer refused, stating that on the basis of the evidence there was no merit in the review. The central issue concerned the termination of the tenancy – the claimant asserted that she had been advised to do so by council officers but the housing officer said that the detailed evidence of the council officers was that this assertion was untrue.

On 21 September the claimant and her children were accommodated by her parents until 26 September. Her parents wrote to the council saying that they would not be able to accommodate her after 26 September as their son and daughter-in-law were coming down to stay for a week. The claimant then claimed to be street homeless and sleeping in a car with her children. On Friday 28 September at 1.21 pm the solicitor faxed a Claim for Judicial Review and for Urgent Consideration (N161 and N463) to the council's homelessness department. At 2.12 pm he faxed the full court bundle to the Administrative Court and to the council. The documents came to the attention of the housing officer at 3.20 pm and she informed her legal department. The claimant's solicitor contacted the housing officer at 4.50 pm advising her to place her out of hours service on notice. Attempts were made by the council's legal department to contact the solicitor. A message left for him was not returned and he was not contactable after his office closed at 5 pm. The housing officer's detailed letter in response was e-mailed to the solicitor at 6.22 pm but he had left his office for the weekend.

The claimant's case was that was that in refusing to accommodate pending review the council had not considered the three criteria identified in *R v Camden ex p Mohammed* (T48.1); the council had failed to take account of the claimant's lack of accommodation; the decision was irrational as the claimant had good prospects of success on review and her personal circumstances were exceptional and no or inadequate reasons had been given for its decision.

The claim was not dealt with on the papers on the afternoon of 28th September and counsel for the claimant made an application to the out-of-hours duty judge by telephone early that evening. A mandatory order was made for the council to accommodate the claimant pending review and provided that the defendant could apply to discharge on 24 hours' notice. The council applied to discharge the order. By the time of the hearing the claimant was acting in person and did not attend the hearing.

Munby J discharged the injunction.

1) The claimant's case under s188(3) was 'hopeless' and had no reasonable prospect of success. The council had applied the criteria set out

in *R v Camden ex p Mohammed* – the merits of the review decision had been addressed, no new information or argument had been put forward and it was obvious that the officer was aware and had taken into account the claimant's personal circumstances. The claimant's solicitor had drawn attention to the hardship she would face if not accommodated. The claimant could not show a strong prima facie case to justify an interim mandatory injunction.

2) There had been significant non-disclosure to the out of hours judge. The housing officer had explained and justified her decision to refuse accommodation by reference to the merits of the claimant's case for review. This was confirmed by her note and the solicitor's note of the conversation on 19th September. Counsel had read out to the out of hours judge the officer's initial undated and unreasoned letter refusing accommodation but had not read out the solicitor's attendance note of his later conversation with the officer, or at least not in a way to bring its full significance to the judge's attention, where she gave reasons for refusing accommodation referring to the merits of the case.

Munby J made the following observations:

a) Too often ex parte applications are made which are not urgent or have only become urgent because of unnecessary delay. In the instant case the application had been delayed for nine days.

b) A simple assertion had been made in the N161 that time had not allowed the Pre-Action Protocol to be followed. No explanation was provided as to why the application was delayed for nine days nor why the council had not been given warning, if only informal warning, before 1.30 pm on the Friday afternoon the application was made.

c) The requirement in the protocol for service on the council's legal department was ignored.

d) The solicitor had failed to give the council his out of hours contact details. This information should have proffered without being asked for.

Note: The Pre-Action Protocol for Judicial Review is stated not to be appropriate in urgent cases (para 6). Where possible a pre-action protocol letter should be sent with shortened time limits for response, rather than the recommended 14 days. The claimant was not represented and it is not clear why a pre-action protocol letter or notice of the proposed judicial review was not sent until the day the afternoon the application was made. No submissions for the review appear to have been made in writing and issues regarding whether it was reasonable for the claimant to continue to occupy her previous accommodation are not explored in the judgment.

See also the full report of *R (Casey) v Restormel* BC (T45.1A) regarding interim injunctions and the timetabling of applications to discharge injunctions and the timetabling of judicial review hearings generally.

T59   Appeals

There is a right of appeal from a review decision to the county court on a point of law under Housing Act 1996 s204:

(1) If an applicant who has requested a review under section 202 –
   (a) is dissatisfied with the decision on the review, or
   (b) is not notified of the decision on the review within the time pre-
      scribed under section 203,
   he may appeal to the county court on any point of law arising from the
   decision or, as the case may be, the original decision.
(2) An appeal must be brought within 21 days of his being notified of the
   decision or, as the case may be, of the date on which he should have
   been notified of a decision on review.
(2A) [provision for applying for permission to appeal out of time]
(3) On appeal the court may make such order confirming, quashing or
   varying the decision as it thinks fit.

T60   The nature of an appeal/judicial review and ECHR article 6

European Court of Human Rights

T60.1   *Tsfayo v UK*

Application no 60860/00; [2007] ECHR 656; [2007] LGR 1; (2006) *Times* 23
November; 14 November 2006 (see A2.8)

*Judicial review could not make good lack of independent determination of
factual dispute in relation to housing benefit*

House of Lords

T60.2   *Begum (Runa) v Tower Hamlets LBC*

[2003] UKHL 5; [2003] 2 AC 430; [2003] 2 WLR 388; [2003] 1 All ER 731; [2003] HLR
32; [2003] UKHRR 419; [2003] LGR 205; (2003) *Times* 17 February

Review and appeal on point of law complied with ECHR art 6

Runa Begum applied to Tower Hamlets as a homeless person. The council
accepted that it owed her the main housing duty. It offered her accommodation which she refused because of problems of drugs and racism
in the area. On review, a senior officer not previously involved with her
application, confirmed that the premises offered were suitable. Ms Begum
appealed to the county court. Following *Adan v Newham LBC* (T60.3), HHJ
Roberts allowed her appeal, holding that the procedure for internal review
under Housing Act 1996 s202 did not comply with ECHR article 6.
   The Court of Appeal allowed the council's appeal and the House of
Lords affirmed that decision.

1) The House of Lords assumed, without deciding, that decisions made
   under Housing Act 1996 Part VII do give rise to 'civil rights' for the
   purposes of ECHR article 6. Lord Bingham stated that 'to hold that
   the right enjoyed by Runa Begum is a 'civil right' for the purposes
   of article 6 would ... be to go further than the Strasbourg court has
   yet gone...'. Lord Millett, while considering Strasbourg jurisprudence,
   referred to the three systems of justice in Europe, namely civil and
   criminal (which always come within article 6) and administrative (covering all actions against the state), which, depending on the nature of
   the claim, may or may not come within article 6.
2) The s202 review process does not comply with article 6 because the

reviewing officer is not an 'independent and impartial tribunal' – an employee cannot be independent of the authority.

3) However, an appeal to the county court on a point of law (s204) gives a right of access to a court of 'full jurisdiction' for article 6 purposes. For reasons of good administration, the absence of a full fact-finding jurisdiction in the court or tribunal to which appeal lies from an administrative decision-making body does not disqualify it for the purposes of article 6. '"Full jurisdiction" in this context does not necessarily mean full jurisdiction on fact or law, but ... "jurisdiction to deal with the case as the nature of the decision requires"' (Lord Millett). An authority's factual findings are only 'staging posts on the way to the much broader judgments which the authority has to make' (Lord Bingham). 'I would expect the county court judge to be alert to any indication that an applicant's case might not have been resolved by the authority in a fair, objective and even-handed way' but 'I can see no warrant for applying in this context notions of 'anxious scrutiny' ... or [an] enhanced approach to judicial review ... [or] 'a close and rigorous analysis' if by that is meant an analysis closer or more rigorous than would ordinarily be conducted by a careful and competent judge determining an application for judicial review' (Lord Bingham). Lord Hoffmann considered that the conventional principles of judicial review are sufficient.

The House of Lords declined to follow and apply dicta in *Adan v Newham LBC* (T60.3) that the limited right of appeal under s204 means that the county court is not a court of full jurisdiction and that a local authority may use its contracting-out powers under the Local Authorities (Contracting Out of Allocation of Housing and Homelessness Functions) Order 1996 SI No 3205 to appoint an independent and impartial tribunal to conduct the review in cases where a material dispute of primary fact has to be resolved.

Court of Appeal

T60.3 *Adan v Newham LBC*

[2001] EWCA Civ 1916; [2002] 1 WLR 2120; [2002] 1 All ER 931; [2002] UKHRR 229; [2002] HLR 28; 14 December 2001

Review and appeal on point of law did not comply with ECHR art 6; county court cannot prescribe how a further review is to be conducted

On hearing an appeal under Housing Act 1996 s204, HHJ Laurie quashed Newham's review decision and directed that the statutory review of the decision of Ms Adan's application be remitted for a further review to be conducted by a different reviewing officer whose independence and impartiality complied with ECHR article 6(1). Newham appealed. They did not challenge the first part of the judge's order but contended that he had no jurisdiction under s204 or otherwise to make any direction about who should carry out any further review. It was common ground both that the reviewing officer's decision involved a determination of civil rights within ECHR article 6(1) and that the officer was not an independent and impartial tribunal.

The Court of Appeal allowed Newham's appeal. The judge had no power under s204 or otherwise to direct that the further review be conducted by an independent and impartial tribunal. County Courts Act 1984 s38(3)(a) expressly provides that the county court does not have the power to order mandamus, which was effectively what the judge was doing when he ordered Newham to carry out a public duty in a particular way. In cases where a review under s202 does not require the resolution of any material disputes of primary fact, the county court's supervisory jurisdiction, which is akin to that of judicial review, is sufficient to ensure article 6(1) compliance. However, where there are such disputes, the limited right of appeal under s204 means that the county court is not a court of full jurisdiction and so the procedure taken as a whole does not comply with article 6(1). A local authority may though use its contracting-out powers under the Local Authorities (Contracting Out of Allocation of Housing and Homelessness Functions) Order 1996 SI No 3205 to appoint an independent and impartial tribunal to conduct the review in cases where a material dispute of primary fact has to be resolved.

Note: In *Begum (Runa) v Tower Hamlets LBC* (T60.2) the House of Lords declined to follow *Adan* – see too what was said in the Court of Appeal [2002] EWCA Civ 239, [2002] 2 All ER 668 [2002] UKHRR 1014.

T60.4 **Begum (Nipa) v Tower Hamlets LBC**
[2000] QB 133; [2000] 1 WLR 306; (2000) 32 HLR 445; (1999) *Times* 9 November, CA (see T14.2)

An appeal under s204 is on 'any point of law' which embraces any ground of challenge that would have been available in proceedings for judicial review

T61 # Appeals: time limits, bringing an appeal and fees

Section 204(2) provides that an appeal must be brought within 21 days of an applicant being notified of a review decision or of the date on which he or she should have been notified of the review decision.

Section 204(2A), introduced by Homelessness Act 2002, makes provision for the court to grant permission to appeal out of time where there is good reason for any delay.

Court of Appeal

T61.1 **Aadan v Brent LBC**
(2000) 32 HLR 848, CA

When court closed on day time limit expires, appeal may be filed next working day

Ms Aadan requested a review of Brent's decision on her homeless application. It sent her a letter dated 30 June 1998, confirming its decision, which she received on Saturday 4 July 1998. Accordingly her last day to appeal, as calculated under CCR Ord 3 r6(2), was Saturday 25 July 1998. The court office was closed on that day. She filed her request for entry of an appeal on Monday 27 July 1998. HHJ Simpson dismissed her appeal on the grounds that it was brought out of time.

The Court of Appeal allowed her appeal. It confirmed that the time limit for appealing under s204 started to run from the date an applicant received the s202 decision, and not from the date of the decision itself. CCR Ord 2 r4 required an applicant to file an appeal by 'delivering it to the proper officer for entry by him'. Filing in the county court could only be done when the court office was open and the proper officer was there. In such circumstances, following *Pritam Kaur v S Russell & Sons* [1973] 1 QB 336, the applicant had brought her claim in time by filing the appeal on the next day the court offices were open.

Note: Although decided under the CCR, the same effect is reached under the CPR by virtue of Part 2.8(5).

T61.2   *Demetri v Westminster CC*

[2000] 1 WLR 772; (2000) 32 HLR 470; (1999) *Times* 4 November, CA

Unless authority agrees to withdraw review decision, time limit for an appeal runs from date of notification of original review, even if it is reconsidered

The applicant refused accommodation offered in discharge of the full housing duty and requested a review of its suitability. The authority issued a review decision confirming the suitability of the offer and advising the applicant of her right of appeal to the county court and of the 21-day time limit. Her advisers discovered that certain documents which had been sent to the authority had not been seen by the review officer. The authority agreed to reconsider its review decision on receipt of those missing documents. On reconsidering the matter, it advised the applicant that it had decided not to alter the review decision. An appeal was then lodged in the county court within 21 days of the reconsidered decision, but more than 21 days after the original review decision. The authority successfully applied for the appeal to be struck out as lodged out of time.

The Court of Appeal dismissed the applicant's appeal. An authority could agree to reconsider, or review, a review decision. This was under its extra-statutory discretion – there was no right to reconsideration of a review decision nor a right to a review of a review decision (s202(2)). An applicant only had a right of appeal of an original review decision. An applicant dissatisfied with a review decision should lodge an appeal against the first review decision within 21 days or obtain clear agreement from the authority to reopen its first review decision, treating it as though it had not existed, rather than merely agreeing to reconsider it. If this was not made clear then the applicant or his or her advisers should seek clarification. Where the applicant was not represented, the authority should make it clear to the applicant on what basis the authority were approaching the matter and, particularly if it was merely reconsidering the decision, point out that the time limit was not being extended.

In the instant case, no appeal had been lodged in time, no clear agreement to withdraw the earlier decision had been reached, and the council's agreement to 'reconsider' the review decision did not give rise to a waiver or estoppel or otherwise have the effect of extending the appeal time limit.

T61.3   *Gwynedd CC v Grunshaw*

[2000] 1 WLR 494; (2000) 32 HLR 610; (1999) *Times* 30 August, CA (see P15.2)

Appeal filed when delivered to court, despite court manager's refusal to accept it on basis that appeal should be made in another county court

Note: Although this case relates to Housing Act 1985 s265, similar considerations may apply to the filing of Housing Act 1996 s204 appeals.

T61.4 *Van Aken v Camden LBC*
[2002] EWCA Civ 1724; [2003] 1 WLR 684; [2003] 1 All ER 552; [2003] HLR 33; (2002) *Times* 28 October

Appeal brought in time if delivered to court on final day of time limit even if the court is closed

On the last day of the 21-day time limit for bringing a s204 appeal the claimant's representative arrived at the county court office after it had closed. The appellant's notice was posted through the court office letter box and it was processed the next day. The defendant submitted that the appeal was brought out of time. In the county court a judge accepted that submission. The claimant appealed.

The Court of Appeal allowed the appeal. An appeal is brought by filing the appellant's notice. CPR Part 2.3 provides that '"filing", in relation to a document, means delivering it, by post or otherwise, to the court office'. This was held to mean that there was no need for a person to receive or authenticate the document. Mere delivery of the appellant's notice to the appropriate court office was sufficient to constitute filing on the day that it was so delivered, despite the court office being closed. The position under the CPR was different from that applying under the CCR (see *Aadan v Brent LBC* (T61.1))

High Court

T61.5 *Short v Birmingham CC*
[2004] EWHC 2112 (QB); [2005] HLR 6; 10 September 2004

Permission to file late appeal under s204(2A) – only if good reason for delay

Ms Short lodged an appeal under s204 about three months after the 21-day time limit had expired. She applied for permission to bring a late appeal under s204(2A)(b). She filed a witness statement in which she said that she had been under considerable emotional strain at the time of the decision. She had difficulty finding and obtaining an appointment with a solicitor who was a housing specialist. HHJ Charles Harris QC was not satisfied that the whole delay was explained by 'good reason' and refused to allow the late appeal. Ms Short contended that the judge should have taken account of the 'merits' of her case, the hardship she would suffer if a late appeal were not allowed and CPR r3.9. She sought to appeal that decision but her legal advisers applied to the wrong court. By the time the error was discovered, time for appealing had expired. A new notice of appeal was filed in the Administrative Court for permission to appeal out of time.

Tugendhat J granted permission to appeal to the Administrative Court out of time. The delay was entirely attributable to an unintentional error of law made by Ms Short's legal advisers. That delay had not caused any prejudice to the administration of justice, or to the council. Given the importance of housing to a mother with children, justice required the grant of an extension of time. However, he went on to dismiss the appeal to allow an appeal to the county court out of time. Under s204(2A)(b) permission may be given 'only' if the court is satisfied that there is 'good reason' for the delay. The word 'only' means that there is a threshold which has to be passed before the discretion whether to grant permission or not is exercised. If a judge is not satisfied that there are good reasons it is not possible to go on to consider the merits. It is not open to a judge to have regard to the criteria in CPR r3.9, or any other criteria other than those specified in s204(2A). In this case, the requirements of justice to which the judge could have had regard were limited and, accordingly, the appeal was dismissed.

County courts

T61.6 *Amen v Westminster CC*

June 2002 *Legal Action* 28; 3 April 2002, Central London County Court

Payment of correct court fee not a prerequisite to appeal being 'brought'

The applicant sought to appeal a review decision to the county court under s204. He filed his appellant's notice within the required 21 days, together with a payment of £100 for the fee. The county court office did not enter the appeal until after 21 days had expired because it required a fee of £120. The council applied to strike out the appeal because it was issued out of time.

HHJ Hallgarten QC held that

- The correct fee for a s204 appeal was £100 as specified by Sch 1 para 2.3 of the County Court Fees Order 1999 SI No 689 (rather than the £120 in Sch 1 para 1.3) because that was the fee applicable to all appeals under CPR 52 and clear language would be required to justify a different fee for s204 appeals.
- An appeal was 'brought' when received by the Court (CPR PD 7A 5.1). Nothing in the County Courts Act 1984 or CPR made payment of the correct fee a prerequisite.

Note: The fee was subsequently increased to £120 (see Civil Proceedings Fees Order 2004 SI No 3121 Sch 1 para 2.5(b)).

T62 Appeals: courts' powers

Court of Appeal

T62.1 *Adan v Newham LBC*

[2001] EWCA Civ 1916; [2002] 1 WLR 2120; [2002] 1 All ER 931; [2002] UKHRR 229; [2002] HLR 28; 14 December 2001 (see T60.3)

County court cannot prescribe how a further review is to be conducted

T62.2 *Ali and Nessa v Newham LBC*

[2001] EWCA Civ 73; [2002] HLR 20, CA

Procedural flaws in authority's decision-making process should result in decision being quashed unless the same decision would 'inevitably' be reached

Mr Ali and Ms Nessa were married and had seven children. Mr Ali and their eldest son were disabled. The council accepted that it owed the full housing duty to secure accommodation (s193). The family was on the housing register under Part VI as needing five-bedroom accommodation. Newham offered them a four-bedroom house, which they accepted but sought a review of its suitability under s202. They were having to use the living room of the house as a fifth bedroom for their eldest son because of his special needs. The council decided that the accommodation was not overcrowded and was suitable. The appellants appealed that decision to the county court. Recorder Rylance confirmed the council's decision. He found that the decision was procedurally flawed in that it did not adequately consider the housing needs of the family or their medical and social needs. However, he concluded that, notwithstanding the procedural irregularities, it was unlikely that the medical advisers or social services would have reached the view that the appellants required a living room as well as accommodation with five bedrooms. He therefore dismissed the appeal.

The Court of Appeal allowed the applicant's appeal. Where a decision is found to be procedurally flawed it may be upheld only if the court is satisfied that a properly directed authority would inevitably have reached the same decision. The test of inevitability is a strict test. There was a possibility that a proper assessment would have concluded that the living room was not appropriate to be used as a bedroom. That was a possibility left open by the facts in this case and acknowledged by the recorder. Accordingly, he did not apply the test that it was inevitable or virtually certain that the council would have reached the same conclusion (see *Barthy-King v Ministry of Defence* [1979] 2 All ER 80 and *R v Secretary of State for Education and Science ex p Lewisham LBC* (1990) COD 319). Accordingly, however small the possibility of a different conclusion being reached, the recorder was wrong to have confirmed the council's assessment of the accommodation.

T62.3 **Crawley BC v B**
(2000) 32 HLR 636; (2000) *Times* 28 March, CA (see T41.1)

Judge wrong when quashing decision on priority need to declare that full duty owed when intentionality was an issue

T62.4 **Ekwuru v Westminster CC**
[2003] EWCA Civ 1293; [2004] HLR 14

Decision varied where three defective review decisions and no realistic prospect of finding of intentionality

In August 1998 the appellant applied to the council as a homeless person. In May 2000 the council notified him of a decision that he was intentionally homeless. That was upheld on review and an appeal to the county court was dismissed. The council conceded in the Court of Appeal that the review had been defective and accordingly the appeals in the county court and Court of Appeal were allowed and the review decision quashed (see [2001] EWCA Civ 1497). A second review decision was issued in November 2001. The appellant appealed to the county court. The council conceded that the review decision was defective and withdrew it. The appeal was discontinued and the council was ordered to pay the costs. A third review decision was issued in February 2002. On the appellant's appeal, the council indicated that it was prepared to withdraw that decision and conduct a fourth review. The appellant rejected that offer and asked the county court to vary the third review decision to one of 'not' intentionally homeless in exercise of the power in s204(3). Recorder Davies QC held that it was for the authority to make the factual decisions. She quashed the third review decision and accepted an undertaking from the council to conduct a fourth review. The appellant contended that the power to vary ought to have been exercised in the circumstances.

The Court of Appeal allowed his appeal. There was nothing to gain from further enquiries or a further review because there was no realistic prospect of any further material becoming available on which the council could base a finding of intentional homelessness. In those circumstances the third review decision would be varied to a decision that the appellant was 'not' intentionally homeless.

T62.5   *Kruja v Enfield LBC*
[2004] EWCA Civ 1769; [2005] HLR 13; 5 November 2004
Judge wrongly usurped authority's fact-finding role

The applicant applied as a homeless person, asserting that he had priority need because his adult son was mentally ill and vulnerable. The council considered the medical evidence, decided the son was neither mentally ill nor vulnerable and notified the applicant that he was not in priority need. This decision was confirmed on review. On appeal the judge found that the evidence had been 'all one way' on mental illness and that it was perverse for the council to decide that the son was not vulnerable. He quashed the council's decision.

The Court of Appeal allowed a second appeal by the council. The judge had not been entitled to categorise the local authority's decision as perverse. The evidence had not all favoured a finding of mental illness and there had been material going the other way. The judge had usurped the authority's fact-finding role, instead of adopting a statutory review of the decision. He had failed to direct himself properly as to vulnerability. In contrast, the authority had directed itself in accordance with *R v Camden LBC ex p Pereira* (T17.6) and had not reached an unreasonable decision on the material before it.

T62.6   *O'Connor v Kensington and Chelsea RLBC*
[2004] EWCA Civ 394; [2004] HLR 37 (see T25.4)
Erroneous decision ordinarily to be quashed; in rare cases relief could be refused where appeal was an abuse of process

T62.7   *Tower Hamlets LBC v Deugi*
[2006] EWCA Civ 159; [2006] HLR 28; 7 March 2006, CA
Judge entitled to entertain appeal against purported withdrawn review decision where an order in the applicant's favour would be of enduring benefit to her

Mrs Deugi, an Indian national, left her husband, a Portuguese national, alleging domestic violence. She later applied to Tower Hamlets as a homeless person. On 20 January 2004 Tower Hamlets decided that she was not 'eligible' for assistance on the grounds of her immigration status. She asked for a review on the basis that the child of an EU national working in the UK had the right to live in the UK to attend full-time education. Mrs Deugi asserted that, as the primary carer of her 17-year-old son who was in full-time education, she had a derived right of residence to enable her son to exercise his right, which existed despite her having obtained a divorce and regardless of whether her ex husband was still employed in the UK (see *Baumbast v Secretary of State for Home Department* [2003] INLR 1). The council upheld its decision on review but the review decision was quashed in March 2004 on appeal under s204(1)(a).

Tower Hamlets was therefore required to undertake the review again. It did not complete that review within 56 days or within a number of extended periods agreed with Mrs Deugi. In September 2004 she appealed again, this time against the original (January 2004) decision, under s204(1)(b). In October 2004 Mrs Deugi's son left school and turned 18. Before the appeal was heard the council conceded that the January 2004 decision had been wrong and purported to withdraw it. It issued a new decision in March 2005 that Mrs Deugi was no longer eligible because her son was no longer in full-time education (ie, the *Baumbast* exception no longer applied). She requested a review of that decision but maintained her appeal against the January 2004 decision. On the hearing of that appeal, HHJ Roberts varied the decision of January 2004 to one that Mrs Deugi was owed the main housing duty.

The Court of Appeal allowed Tower Hamlets' appeal. It held that the judge had not been wrong to entertain the appeal against the purportedly withdrawn decision. Tower Hamlets could not prevent Mrs Deugi continuing with her appeal if to do so would deprive her of some enduring benefit or advanatage to which she would have been entitled if their original decision had been taken in accordance with the law. The judge was entitled to quash the decision or to vary it, by substituting a decision that Mrs Deugi was eligible and in priority need. He had gone too far, however, on the facts, in varying the decision to one that the main duty was owed.

May LJ, giving the judgment of the court, reviewed the authorities on the circumstances in which the court's power to vary a decision could be exercised. He held that 'the question for the judge was whether there was any real prospect that Tower Hamlets, acting rationally and with the benefit of further enquiry, might have been satisfied that Mrs Deugi was intentionally homeless' [36]. (This test was said to be an amalgam of the tests in *Crawley BC v B* (T41.1) '... the only decision ... that the Council, acting rationally could reach' and *Ekwuru v Westminster CC* (T62.4) 'there is no real prospect of the Authority turning up further material which would entitle it to reach the conclusion that ...'.) After considering the evidence of the circumstances in which Mrs Deugi became homeless, it was held that the council was entitled to an opportunity to enquire into whether Mrs Deugi had become homeless intentionally or not. The decision was varied to one that, as at 20 January 2004, Mrs Deugi was eligible for assistance and in priority need.

Note: It would appear, from references to an order being of enduring benefit, that the court's decisions that the applicant was eligible and in priority need were not ones that the authority could revisit in the context of any subsequent decision. This issue is dealt with more explicitly in *Robinson v Hammersmith and Fulham LBC* (T19.3). The problem that Mrs Deugi would face is that, even if she were subsequently accepted for the main housing duty under s193 (despite, at the date of the decision, not being eligible or in priority need but having the benefit of the court order), that duty ends on ceasing to be eligible (s193(6)(a)). The statutory provisions about decisions on discharge of duty under s193 are unclear. May LJ considered that, in practice, an authority would need to communicate a decision under s193(6)(a) and an applicant would have a right of review and appeal [33].

See also *Ibrahim v Harrow LBC* January 2008 *Legal Action* 37 regarding the *Baumbast* exception.

T63   Second appeals: appeals to the Court of Appeal

Court of Appeal

T63.1   *Azimi v Newham LBC*
(2001) 33 HLR 569, CA

Appeal from s204 appeal a second appeal and restrictive test for permission applied

Mr Azimi lived in a two-bedroomed flat with his brother. They were later joined by Mr Azimi's wife and four children (three boys aged between 15 and 6, and a girl aged 11), who had arrived from Afghanistan. Mr Azimi applied to the council as a homeless person. The council decided that he was not homeless as the flat was reasonable for him and his family to continue to occupy. After a s202 review, Mr Azimi appealed to the county court under s204. His appeal was allowed on the basis that the council had failed specifically to address the fact that Mr Azimi's daughter was required to share a room with her brothers. The council sought permission to appeal.

The Court of Appeal dismissed the application and held that:

1) An appeal to the county court under s204 was an appeal for the purposes of the Access to Justice Act 1999 (Destination of Appeals) Order 2000 SI No 1071 and therefore an appeal from the county court lay to the Court of Appeal.
2) CPR 52.13 (Second appeals to the Court) applied. Permission can only be obtained from the Court of Appeal and permission will only be granted where:
   (a) the appeal would raise an important point of principle or practice; or
   (b) there is some other compelling reason for the Court of Appeal to hear it.

The court was satisfied that the significance of the county court decision was limited to the particular facts of the case, and the restrictive test for permission was not satisfied.

Note: In *Uphill v BRB (Residuary) Ltd* [2005] EWCA Civ 60, which was not a housing case, the Court of Appeal gave guidance of general relevance to second appeals holding that: (a) the first limb of CPR 52.13 cannot be satisfied if the principle or practice in question has already been decided by the Court of Appeal; and (b) in the second limb, 'compelling' requires something truly exceptional to be present in the appeal.

T63.2   **Brookes v Croydon LBC**

[2004] EWCA Civ 439; 26 March 2004 (see T49.1)

Grant of permission for a second appeal was discretionary and could take account of the practicalities involved

T63.3   **Cramp v Hastings LBC; Phillips v Camden LBC**

[2005] EWCA Civ 1005; [2005] 4 All ER 1014; [2005] HLR 48; 29 July 2005, CA (see T43.6)

Guidance on procedural aspects of s204 appeal; limiting new evidence

T63.4   **Gentle v Wandsworth LBC**

[2005] EWCA Civ 1377; 3 November 2005

Permission to appeal refused where there was no 'obvious injustice' to applicant

The appellant was a young woman who had previously harmed herself. She then had four episodes of surgery for a fractured femur. The council had a report from her consultant orthopaedic surgeon and from its own medical adviser, Dr Keen. It decided that she was not vulnerable but the decision letter referred to neither report. On review, the reviewing officer considered both reports and mentioned them in a decision letter rejecting the review. The appellant appealed, contending that there had been a failure by the reviewing officer to comply with reg 8(2) of the 1999 review regulations. HHJ Knowles found that both the original and review decisions were adequately reasoned and that the requirements of the regulations had not been infringed.

Chadwick LJ refused a renewed application for permission to bring a second appeal. He said that, even if the original decision had been deficient for failing to refer in terms to the two medical reports and reg 8(2) ought to have been applied, there was 'no reason at all' to think that the appellant had suffered any injustice. The proposed appeal raised no important point of principle or practice. While permission could be granted for 'some other compelling reason', which included the need to remedy obvious injustice, that was a high test:

> An obvious injustice is one which might be expected to be so striking that it would be impossible to conceive that any member of this court would fail to recognise it. It is important to keep in mind that this court does not interfere by way of a second appeal simply because it may feel that the judge has gone wrong. What is needed is for the court to be persuaded that there is something so wrong with the decision below, and so likely to result in serious injustice, that something has to be done about it. (para 6)

T63.5   **Osmani v Camden LBC**

[2004] EWCA Civ 1706; [2005] HLR 22; 16 December 2004 (see T17.5)

The main focus of attention on second appeal should be on decision of council rather than decision of county court

T64   Costs: appeals/judicial review

Court of Appeal

T64.1   *Holden v Sutton LBC*

[2004] EWCA Civ 1835; 3 December 2004

Claimant entitled to costs where council withdrew review decision after appeal made

Mr Holden applied to the council on the basis that he was homeless because it was no longer reasonable for him to continue to occupy his home (held on a joint tenancy with his wife from whom he was separating). The council decided that he was not homeless and upheld that decision on review. Mr Holden lodged an appeal to the county court. Three weeks later the council indicated that it would treat its review decision as quashed and deal afresh with a new application. That rendered the appeal academic but the parties could not agree an order as to costs. HHJ William Barnett QC heard argument and awarded Mr Holden his costs. Applying the principles in *R (Boxall) v Waltham Forest LBC* (U12.2), he had directed himself that, but for the concession by the council, the appeal would have succeeded.

A renewed application by the council, for permission to bring a second appeal, was dismissed. Neuberger LJ held that the judge's conclusion that the initial appeal had been bound to succeed (on the basis that the reviewing officer had failed (1) to deal with a matter plainly raised in the evidence and (2) to give reasons) was a conclusion which he was fully entitled to reach. Furthermore, the prospective second appeal raised no issue of principle.

T64.2   *R v Lambeth LBC ex p Wilson*

(1998) 30 HLR 64; (1997) 95 LGR 783, CA

Wasted costs order against council inappropriate in the absence of fraud

The applicant challenged a decision of the council that accommodation offered to her in discharge of duty was suitable. The council failed to reply to correspondence, including a letter before action and delivery of the draft application for leave. It failed to attend at the oral application for leave on notice. After being served with notice of motion, following the grant of leave, it failed to put in any respondent's evidence. The trial was fixed for Monday 5 February 1996. At 4.55 pm on Friday 2 February 1996 the council 'woke up' to the litigation and sought a compromise based on withdrawal of the impugned decision, a further offer of accommodation and payment of costs. It failed to attend the trial.

Deputy Judge Sir Louis Blom-Cooper QC allowed the application for judicial review, quashed the decision, issued mandamus requiring a further offer of accommodation and stood over the question of costs. He gave directions for the council to show why the responsible officers should not pay the wasted costs personally. After an inter partes hearing on 27 February 1996, orders were made for wasted costs to be paid personally by two named officers of the council's housing department who had been responsible for the homeless persons unit at the time ((1997) 29 HLR 104, QBD).

The Court of Appeal allowed an appeal by the officers. In the absence of fraud, it was difficult to think of circumstances where it would be right to make such an order where the local authority was itself a party to the proceedings.

T64.3 **R (Kuzeva) v Southwark LBC**
[2002] EWCA Civ 781; 30 May 2002 (see U12.1)

No order as to costs where no good reason to make other order; legal aid irrelevant

T64.4 **Tower Hamlets LBC v (Rikha) Begum**
[2005] EWCA Civ 340; [2005] 1 WLR 2103; [2005] HLR 34; [2005] LGR 503 (see T35.5)

Judge erred in not making costs order in reliance on speculation of outcome of claimant's substantive application under Part VII

T64.4A **Waltham Forest LBC v Maloba**
[2007] EWCA Civ 1281, 4 December 2007 (see T8.10A)

Not appropriate to stay costs order on s204 appeal pending any fresh appeal

Mr Maloba appealed under Housing Act 1996 s204 against a review decision that he was not homeless (see T8.10A). On quashing the council's decision and remitting the matter for re-determination, Hornby HHJ ordered the council to pay two-thirds of Mr Maloba's costs. Mr Maloba was legally aided. The council applied for the order to be stayed until after the determination of any fresh appeal Mr Maloba might make in relation to the fresh review decision the council was now required to make, so that any costs award in its favour in subsequent proceedings could be set off against Mr Maloba's costs. The application was refused and the council appealed. The Law Society was joined as an interested party. It submitted that, due to the higher rates recoverable by solicitors from another party as opposed to those recoverable from the Legal Services Commission, any practice to stay costs as proposed would reduce the already diminishing number of firms willing to undertake publicly funded work and so impact on access to justice.

The Court of Appeal dismissed the appeal. Previous cases in which there had been a set-off of costs were distinguishable. While the court's discretion was wide enough to grant the council's application, if it considered it just to do so, there should be no practice that a stay should be granted in all cases unless there was good reason for doing so.

High Court

T64.5 **R v Kensington and Chelsea RLBC ex p Ghebregiogis**
(1995) 27 HLR 602, QBD

Council ordered to pay costs of judicial review where concession prior to grant of leave and clear case

The applicant was a refugee who arrived in the UK in August 1993 with his two children to join his wife who had preceded him. The council did not provide accommodation which was large enough for the applicant and all the members of his family (Housing Act 1985 s75, now Housing Act 1996 s176). A law centre instructed by the applicant wrote a clear letter before action, setting out the facts and its propositions of law but the council still refused to provide accommodation as requested. The law centre issued an application for leave to move for judicial review. Before that could be considered by the court, the council conceded the applicant's claim and housed the whole family but refused to pay the legal costs incurred.

Brooke J held that the power to award costs in respect of an application satisfied before grant of leave should only be exercised in 'very clear' cases. Here, the issue and the law centre's letter were clear, the application well-founded and the point a simple one. The council was ordered to pay the costs.

T64.6   *R (Aguiar) v Newham LBC*

[2002] EWHC 1325 (Admin) (see T43.17)

Where applicant sought judicial review of council's failure to carry out a review and review carried out before the hearing, applicant entitled to costs

T64.7   *R (Boxall) v Waltham Forest LBC*

(2001) 4 CCLR 258, QBD (Admin Court); 21 December 2001 (see U12.2)

Council ordered to pay costs where substantive issued resolved before hearing of judicial review

T64.8   *R (H) v Kingston upon Thames RLBC*

[2002] EWHC 3158 (Admin); (2002) 6 CCLR 240 (see U7.9)

Costs awarded where case became academic prior to final hearing and council's case unsustainable; judicial review rather than complaint justified

Housing outside the Housing Act: community care, Children Act and asylum support

U1   Introduction

This chapter considers the main duties and powers that public bodies have for accommodating people outside the mainstream provisions in Housing Act 1996 Parts 6 (Allocation) and 7 (Homelessness).

'Community care' refers to the provision of services, generally by social services authorities, to address a person's need for care under various statutory provisions. This includes services under National Assistance Act 1948 Part III, s21 of which gives rise to a duty to accommodate adults 'in need of care and attention that is not otherwise available to them'.

The Children Act 1989 Part III concerns the provision of services to children and their families by social services, which can include accommodation or assistance in obtaining accommodation.

Local Government Act 2000 s2 is a general provision that has been sought to be relied on by those excluded from mainstream assistance. Section 2(1) empowers local authorities to do anything it considers likely to improve social well-being in its area and this can include providing financial assistance and accommodation to a person resident or present in it (s2(2), (4)(b)). Section 3(1) provides that this power does not enable a local authority to do anything which they are unable to do by virtue of any prohibition, restriction or limitation on their powers which is contained in any enactment.

Immigration and Asylum Act 1999 Part VI set up a scheme for the accommodation and support of adult asylum-seekers and their families, administered initially by the National Asylum Support Service (NASS) and now by the New Asylum Model.

For a comprehensive analysis of the law see Clements and Thompson, *Community Care and the Law*, LAG, 4th edition. For a detailed consideration of the particular issues facing persons from abroad see Willman, Knafler and Pierce, *Support for Asylum-seekers*, LAG, 2nd edition. Owing to frequent changes in the law in this area it is also of particular importance to refer to Sue Willman's bi-annual (January and June) 'Support for asylum-seekers and other migrants update' in *Legal Action*.

U2   What is a public authority?

'Judicial review is only available against public bodies, that is bodies performing a duty or exercising a power which involves a "public element"' (per Sir John Donaldson in *R v Panel on Takeover and Mergers ex p Datafin* [1987] QB 815 at 838E). Furthermore, Human Rights Act 1998 only applies to the actions of public authorities, which includes a body whose functions are functions of a public nature (s6).

House of Lords

U2.1   *YL v Birmingham CC and Others*
[2007] UKHL 27; [2007] 3 WLR 112; [2007] 3 All ER 957; (2007) 10 CCLR 505; [2007] HLR 44; (2007) *Times* 21 June; 20 June 2007

Private sector care home not a 'public authority' under HRA 1998

YL was 83 and suffered from Alzheimer's disease. She was placed in a privately owned care home by the council under its community care functions and National Assistance Act (NAA) 1948 s21 duty. The home required her to leave because of the behaviour of her husband and daughter. In a claim for possession by the care home, YL sought to rely on article 8 of the ECHR on the basis that the care home was a 'public authority' within the meaning Human Rights Act 1998 (HRA) s6.

The House of Lords dismissed the appeal (Lord Bingham and Baroness Hale dissenting) holding that the care home was not a 'public authority'. A distinction has to be made between the function of a local authority making arrangements under NAA 1948 s21 and that of a private company in providing such care and accommodation under contract. Accordingly, YL did not have ECHR rights against the care home. The majority judgments give guidance on the meaning of 'public authority' under the HRA. Baroness Hale and Lord Mance both criticised the reasoning in *Poplar HARCA v Donoghue* (K2.1). They said that the Court of Appeal had relied too heavily on the historical links between the local authority and the RSL, rather than on the nature of the function itself, which was the provision of social housing.

Court of Appeal

U2.2 *Poplar Housing and Regeneration Community Association Ltd v Donoghue*

[2001] EWCA Civ 595; [2002] QB 48; [2001] 3 WLR 183; [2001] 4 All ER 606; (2001) 33 HLR 823; [2001] UKHRR 693; [2001] LGR 489; (2001) *Times* 21 June, CA (see K2.1)

Housing association was acting as a 'functional public authority' within the meaning of the HRA 1998; the mandatory nature of possession for an AST did not conflict with a tenant's right to family life

U2.3 *R (Heather) v Leonard Cheshire Foundation*

[2002] EWCA Civ 366; [2002] 2 All ER 936; [2002] HRLR 30; [2002] UKHRR 883; [2002] HLR 49; (2002) 5 CCLR 317; (2002) *Times* 8 April; 21 March 2002

Charitable care home not a public authority and closure not challengeable under ECHR

The defendant was a charity established to provide care and support for disabled people. It operated residential care homes. The claimants were placed in one of its homes by a local authority in exercise of its powers under National Assistance Act 1948 s26. In 2000 the defendant decided to close the home. The claimants sought to challenge that decision. They argued that, in providing accommodation to publicly funded residents, the defendant was exercising a public function within Human Rights Act 1998 s6. Stanley Burnton J dismissed their application. A body is only a public authority for the purposes of the Human Rights Act if it is exercising a public function. The word 'public' in s6 presupposes some connection with government (see *R (Goldsmith) v Servite Homes* (U2.4)). The defendant was not a public authority. The decision to close the home was not susceptible to judicial review or challenge under the Human Rights Act. *Poplar HARCA v Donoghue* (K2.1) was distinguished because in that case the housing association had been set up by Tower Hamlets

LBC and was closely assimilated into the role and functions of the local authority.

The Court of Appeal dismissed the applicant's appeal. The defendant did not perform a public function within the meaning of Human Rights Act 1998 s6. Its decision to close a care home did not engage the residents' rights under ECHR article 8. The relevant local authorities remained under an obligation under National Assistance Act 1948 s21 and retained their obligations to the claimants under ECHR article 8, even though they had used their powers under National Assistance Act 1948 s26 to use the defendant as a voluntary sector provider. Furthermore, the claimants were protected by their contractual rights against the defendant. It was held that CPR Part 54 was intended to avoid the old demarcation disputes over when judicial review was appropriate under RSC Ord 53. Even though it had failed, the claimants' argument was an appropriate issue to bring before the court by way of judicial review.

High Court

U2.4   *R (Goldsmith) v Servite Homes*
(2000) 3 CCLR 325; (2001) 33 HLR 35; [2001] LGR 55

Private care home not a public body and not amenable to judicial review

The applicants, aged 91 and 79, were residents of Mary Court, a residential care home owned by Servite. They moved to the home in the mid-1990s in accordance with written placement arrangements between Servite and Wandsworth LBC, whose power to make the placements was contained in National Assistance Act 1948 s26. Servite made a decision to close Mary Court in 1999 following an investigation that revealed a financial deficit. The applicants claimed that Servite had promised that Mary Court would be their permanent home for life unless their medical condition required care that Mary Court could no longer provide. They said that they had entered Mary Court as residents in reliance on that promise. They further contended that the decision to terminate the provision of residential accommodation constituted a breach of the public law obligations of Servite and the council. Servite submitted that it was a private body that had a private contract with the council and the only remedy available to the applicants, if any, was in private law. The applicants sought judicial review.

Moses J dismissed the application.

1) Public law standards could not be imposed on a body whose source of power was purely contractual. A body that performed a public duty was amenable to judicial review but where the source of power lay only in contract the court had no public law jurisdiction (*R v Panel on Takeovers and Mergers ex p Datafin plc* [1987] QB 815).

2) Section 26 did not provide sufficient statutory underpinning to enable Servite's functions to be identified as 'public functions'. It was a private body and did not owe its existence to s26. Its power to enter into a contract with the council did not depend on s26. That section merely permitted the council to make arrangements for residential accommodation. Just because legislation permitted a public authority to enter

into arrangements with a private body did not mean that the functions of the private body were to be regarded as public functions.

3) The council was not in breach of any public law obligation. It had fulfilled its public law obligation by making arrangements pursuant to s26. By moving the applicants, there would be no breach of the council's public law obligations. Its obligations were limited to an obligation to reassess the applicant's needs in the light of Servite's lawful termination of the provision of accommodation.

U3   Assessments and care plans

National Health Service and Community Care Act (NHSCCA) 1990 s47(1)(a) provides that where it appears to an authority that a person for whom they may provide any community care services may be in need of such services, it must carry out an assessment of his or her needs for those services and, having regard to the results of that assessment, decide whether the needs call for the provision of services. 'Community care services' includes services which an authority may provide under National Assistance Act 1948 s21 (NHSCCA 1990 s46(3)). There is no equivalent express statutory provision relating to an assessment under Children Act 1989 but there is nevertheless an obligation to assess under the Act (see *R (G) v Barnet LBC* (U4.2).

Court of Appeal

U3.1   *R v Ealing LBC ex p C*
(2000) 3 CCLR 122, CA

Assessment flawed; no proper reasoning process regarding child's accommodation needs

C was a 9-year-old boy. From birth he suffered from profound problems. He was partially sighted, suffered from dyspraxia, dyslexia and severe asthma and was incontinent. It was common ground that he was a child in need for the purposes of Children Act 1989. He lived with his mother and an elder brother in a two-bedroomed maisonette, where he had to share a bed with his mother in a bedroom measuring 13 feet by 9 feet. His mother was unable to leave him unattended. She sought assistance from Ealing. Although the social services department carried out assessments of C's needs, it did not deal with the adequacy or otherwise of his accommodation. Although the family were on the housing department's transfer list, they were assessed as having no points. In March 1999, on an application for judicial review, the council was ordered to draw up a care plan. That plan stated that C's needs could be met by the 'provision of aids and adaptations to the family home' but that no expenditure on adaptations should be carried out while the family remained on the transfer list. However, no one responsible for making the assessment on behalf of the council went upstairs to see the bedrooms. In a further application for judicial review, Scott-Baker J dismissed an application relating to C's accommodation.

The Court of Appeal allowed C's appeal. The decision and the decision-making process were flawed. There was no proper reasoning process.

The decision was *Wednesbury* unreasonable because the right question or questions were not asked and no reasonable steps were taken by the council to enable the question to be answered correctly. Important practical questions, such as how a mother and 9-year-old boy could continue to share a room, let alone a bed, were simply not addressed.

U3.2   *R v Lambeth LBC ex p A*

[2001] EWCA Civ 1624; [2000] 32 HLR 13 (see U4.2)

Where suitable alternative accommodation being sought relief refused; no purpose in assessments under Children Act 1989 and provision under Chronically Sick and Disabled Persons Act 1970 until alternative accommodation identified

U3.3   *R (Ireneschild) v Lambeth LBC*

[2007] EWCA Civ 234; (2007) 10 CCLR 243; [2007] HLR 34; [2007] LGR 619; 16 March 2007

Assessment had followed FACS guidance and was lawful; urgent housing needs did not require community care assessment of needs as 'substantial'

A climbing accident left Ms Ireneschild permanently disabled and unable to walk or stand unaided. Outside the house she was wheelchair bound. She lived in a council flat with her two adult sons, who cared for her. The flat was on the first and second floor of a converted house and had internal and external stairs. She had great difficulty moving around and in and out of the flat and relied on her sons to lift her. She was concerned about injury to herself and her sons and wanted to be transferred to the ground floor flat, which had been vacant for several years. Various assessments and reports were prepared, the latest being a community care assessment in August 2006 which concluded, in relation to Ms Ireneschild's housing needs, that although ideally she would be housed in ground floor accommodation, her needs could be dealt with in accordance with the local authority's normal housing allocation policy under which she had been awarded the maximum number of medical points. In judicial review proceedings Lloyd Jones J held that the council's assessment was unlawful on a number of grounds ([2006] EWHC 2354 (Admin); (2006) 9 CCLR 686).

The Court of Appeal allowed the council's appeal. Ms Ireneschild had not discharged the burden of establishing that the assessment was unlawful. There was no failure to take into account relevant material; despite no express acknowledgement that an occupational therapist's report had been considered, the evidence led to the conclusion that it had been. The council's assessment followed the Fair Access to Care Services (FACS) guidance and adequately addressed the issue of independence, the risk to Ms Ireneschild and her sons and other essential questions. Although, in housing terms, the case was urgent, it did not necessarily follow that Ms Ireneschild's community care needs had to be assessed as substantial. The assessment of housing needs and of community care needs are not necessarily the same and it was for the assessor to form her own view from a community care perspective. She was not bound to follow any previous assessment. There was no procedural unfairness which required the council to invite Ms Ireneschild's comments on any adverse findings. An assessment is part of an ongoing process which by its very nature is capable of further review. The process specifically allows for representations to be made after an assessment is completed. The council had conceded that, if it had been common ground that Ms Ireneschild had had a history of falls and there was a significant risk of her falling in the future, it would have been unfair to depart from that common ground without giving her an opportunity to make representations about it. There was no such common ground.

U3.4   *R (Lloyd) v Barking and Dagenham LBC*
(2001) 4 CCLR 27; (2001) *Times* 11 June, CA

Challenge to community care plan normally to be pursued through complaints procedure

The claimant, a severely disabled woman, lived for many years in a residential home. The council decided that the home needed to be demolished and rebuilt.

In an application for permission to appeal against Keene J's dismissal of her application for judicial review, the Court of Appeal found that it was arguable that the council's care plan was deficient in that it did not cater for the needs of the claimant, either in temporary accommodation or in the reconstituted residential home. Although the matter was not fully argued before it, the Court of Appeal indicated that a challenge to the content of a community care plan made for an individual by a social services authority, ought not to be brought by way of judicial review. The matter should usually be raised with the council, pursued through the complaints procedure, and then (if necessary) raised with the Secretary of State for Health. Judicial review should be confined to cases of alleged illegality. The parties in this case should engage in mediation with a view to compromising all outstanding issues or at least reducing the differences between them, so as to limit the eventual appeal to essential areas of dispute.

U3.5   *R (S) v Wandsworth LBC*
[2005] EWCA Civ 302; 18 March 2005

Council could consider parents' resources when considering whether service necessary under CSDPA s2

The claimants were severely disabled children. They lived at home with their parents, who cared for them. Their home needed adaptations, which the council was requested to provide and pay for under Chronically Sick and Disabled Persons Act 1970 s2. The council decided that it was unnecessary to do so as the parents' financial resources were such that they could pay for the adaptations. The claimants' application for judicial review was dismissed.

The Court of Appeal dismissed the appeal. CSDPA s2 required (1) that the disabled person must have needs of the type listed in s2 and (2) that it was necessary for an authority to make arrangements in order to meet those needs. In relation to the latter part of this test, the council was entitled to look at the possibility of the needs being met by the children's parents (applying *R v Gloucestershire CC ex p Barry* [1997] AC 584). As a general proposition, the council could reasonably expect that parents with sufficient means would undertake the adaptations. It was therefore entitled to have regard to the parents' resources and could refuse to provide the adaptations unless it was satisfied that it was not reasonable to expect the parents to pay for them.

High Court

U3.6   *R v Tower Hamlets LBC ex p Bradford*
(1998) 1 CCLR 294; (1997) 29 HLR 756, QBD

Child entitled to proper assessment of housing needs under s17; needs not addressed by consideration of family circumstances as a whole

The applicant was an 11-year-old boy with special educational needs. One of his parents was severely disabled. They applied for a transfer from their council home where the whole household had been subject to a campaign of harassment, culminating in attempted arson. They were given priority points but the accommodation offered under the allocation scheme did not meet the parents' requirements (which may have been unreasonably restrictive). The son sought judicial review of the council's failure to address his housing needs as part of an assessment under Children Act 1989 s17.

Kay J found that: (a) the applicant was entitled to a proper assessment of his needs for the purposes of s17; (b) such an assessment must include his housing needs as, on the facts, housing circumstances might be hampering his development (as defined by s17(11)) and (c) such needs were not addressed by consideration of the family circumstances as a whole – it was necessary to consider the effect on the child of remaining in the present home, even if he continued living there only because of the unreasonable attitude of his parents. Since no assessment along these lines had been conducted, the council would need to undertake one.

U3.7   *R (Bodimeade) v Camden LBC*
[2001] EWHC Admin 271; (2001) 4 CCLR 246

Decision by council to close care home unlawful

The council operated an old people's home under a needs-led strategy of community care provision for the elderly. The handbook issued to residents stated that it was the council's 'aim to provide you with a home for life' (subject to changed care needs). In pursuit of a new 'best value' strategy for provision of services, the council decided to decant all the residents to alternative units.

In proceedings for judicial review, Turner J quashed the council's decision. He held that the decision to close had failed to have regard to two relevant considerations: (1) the individual needs of each resident and (2) the substantive legitimate expectation that each would be able to remain in the home for life (applying *R v North East Devon HA ex p Coughlan* [2000] 2 WLR 622; [2001] QB 213, CA).

U3.8   *R (Gangera) v Hounslow LBC*
[2003] EWHC 794 Admin; [2003] HLR 68 (see L1.10)

Not unlawful for council to institute possession proceedings without further assessment of claimant's needs; contention that claimant entitled to accommodation pursuant to NAA 1948 s21 premature

U3.9   *R (J) v Newham LBC*

[2001] EWHC Admin 992; (2002) 5 CCLR 302, 22 October 2001

Duty to assess could not be deferred until family permanently rehoused

The claimant was an autistic 7-year-old boy requiring 24-hour one-to-one care and supervision. He was being accommodated with his mother and sister in temporary accommodation provided by Newham. He sought social services assessments by Newham of his needs pursuant to Carers and Disabled Children Act 2000 s6 and Children Act 1989 s17. The council preferred to defer the assessment process until the family was permanently rehoused but there was no indication of when such housing might become available. In a claim for judicial review, Newham failed to lodge an acknowledgement of service and failed to file any evidence.

Scott Baker J allowed the claim and granted a mandatory injunction requiring the completion of assessments within 35 days. He held that if there had been evidence that permanent housing was to be available in a month or two, assessments might have been postponed but in the absence of such evidence it was not acceptable to leave matters 'open-ended'.

County courts

U3.10   *Haringey LBC v Williams*

October 2004 142 *Housing Aid Update* 4; 18 May 2004, Clerkenwell County Court

Possession proceedings stayed pending community care assessment of tenant's needs

Mr Williams was a secure tenant of Haringey LBC. He had significant mental health difficulties and had spent periods in a psychiatric hospital. Haringey decided that he had spent time living away from his home and sought to recover overpaid housing benefit by deductions from current housing benefit payments. When Mr Williams fell into rent arrears, it sought possession. At the possession hearing, it was clear that Mr Williams had no realistic prospect of resolving the housing benefit difficulties without assistance. It was argued on his behalf that the council was in breach of its duty to assess his community care needs under National Health Service and Community Care Act 1990.

District Judge Stary stayed the possession claim and directed that the stay should not be lifted until a statement was filed confirming that an assessment had been undertaken and setting out the steps taken to meet Mr Williams's needs.

U4   # Children Act 1989

Children Act 1989 s17 provides:

> (1) It shall be the general duty of every local authority ... –
> > (a) to safeguard and promote the welfare of children within their area who are in need; and

(b) so far as is consistent with that duty, to promote the upbringing of such children by their families

by providing a range and level of services appropriate to those children's needs.

An authority has the specific duties and powers set out in Sch 2 Part I for this purpose. Any service may be provided for the family of a child, if it is provided with a view to safeguarding and promoting the child's welfare (s17(3)). A child in need is defined by s17(10).

Children Act 1989 s20 concerns specific provision for the accommodation of children on their own:

(1) Every local authority shall provide accommodation for any child in need within their area who appears to them to require accommodation as a result of –

(a) there being no person who has parental responsibility for him ...

(b) his being lost of having been abandoned; or

(c) the person who has been caring for him being prevented (whether permanently, and for whatever reason) from providing him with suitable accommodation or care.

House of Lords

U4.1 **R v Northavon DC ex p Smith**

[1994] 2 AC 402

Homeless persons unit's refusal to assist social services following request under Children Act 1989 s27 in relation to intentionally homeless family lawful

U4.2 **R (G) v Barnet LBC; R (W) v Lambeth LBC; R (A) v Lambeth LBC**

[2003] UKHL 57; [2004] 2 AC 208; [2003] 3 WLR 1194; [2004] 1 All ER 97; (2003) 6 CCLR 500; [2003] LGR 569; [2004] HLR 10; (2003) *Times* 24 October; 23 October 2003

Council has power but not duty under s17 to accommodate children with their families

G was a Dutch national of Somali origin. She came to the UK with her baby. Her applications for income support and accommodation as a homeless person were refused because she failed the habitual residence test. Accommodation and subsistence were provided by social services pending an assessment under Children Act 1989 s17. The council decided that the child's needs were best served by returning to Holland with G and offered G financial assistance to return. If she refused support it intended to place the child in foster care. G did refuse and her support was terminated. Her application for judicial review was granted but the council's appeal to the Court of Appeal was allowed ([2001] EWCA Civ 540; [2001] LGR 34).

A and her three children occupied a two-bedroom council flat with no outdoor play area. It had been in a dangerous state of disrepair since 1994. Two of the children were autistic with severe learning difficulties and required constant supervision. In 1998, on A's application for a transfer, the council granted 'overriding priority' for a transfer to a four-bedroom flat with a garden or other play area. By June 2000 no offer had been made and the council was unable to say when an offer might be made but it would be likely to be 'a long time'. In May 2000 a Children Act assessment by social services found that the children were living in overcrowded, damp, unhygienic and dangerous conditions and that they needed to be rehoused in appropriate accommodation with a garden. The social services and housing departments liaised but neither offered the necessary accommodation. The claimant sought judicial review, contending that the council had failed to comply with Children Act 1989 s17 in that it had not met the children's assessed needs. Scott Baker J dismissed the application ([2001] LGR 513). The Court of Appeal dismissed A's appeal ([2001] EWCA Civ 1624; [2000] 32 HLR 13.). It held that the council did not have power under Children Act 1989 s17 to provide accommodation or money to pay for accommodation, even if a child was in need.

W was evicted from her home for non-payment of rent. She had two children, was unemployed and dependent on income support. Lambeth decided that she had become intentionally homeless under Housing Act 1996 Part VII. W needed £2,000 for a deposit and rent in advance to obtain accommodation privately. Social services assessed the children's needs and accepted that they needed accommodation. However, it decided that, following the Court of Appeal decision in *R (A) v Lambeth LBC* (see above), they were unable to assist. Later, the council reassessed the children's needs on the disputed basis that it did have power to provide assistance under Children Act 1989 s17 and Carers and Disabled Children Act 2000 s2. It decided that there was nothing exceptional in W's case justifying the provision of housing assistance. Should the need arise, provision would be made to accommodate the children under Children Act 1989 s20. W sought judicial review of the council's later decision. The Court of Appeal refused her application ([2002] EWCA Civ 613; [2002] 2 All ER 901; [2002] HLR 41). It held that an authority did have the power to assist with accommodation under s17 and that the Court of Appeal's decision to the contrary in *R(A) v Lambeth* was per incuriam. However, the council were entitled to reserve the exercise of the power to extreme cases, of which W was not one.

The House of Lords heard the appeals in all three cases together. By a majority (3:2) it rejected the claims that Children Act s17 gave rise to an enforceable duty to accommodate the children with their families. Social services departments are not statutorily required to arrange or provide accommodation for families with children who are not entitled to be housed through the usual channels, although they can do so. The majority held that s17(1) is an overriding duty, a statement of general principle. It provides the broad aims which local authorities are to bear in mind when performing other duties set out in the Act and the specific duties for facilitating the discharge of those general duties were set out in Part I of Sch 2 of the Act. A child in need within the meaning of s17(10) is eligible for the provision of those services, but has no absolute right to them. Section 17(1) sets out duties of a general character which are intended to be for the benefit of children in need in the local social services authority's area in general. The other duties and the specific duties which follow have to be performed in each individual case by reference to the general duties which s17(1) sets out. Section 17 refers to a range and level of services appropriate to the children's needs. It is broadly expressed, with a view to giving the greatest possible scope to the local social services authority as to what it chooses to do in the provision of those services. Although the services which the authority provide may include the provision of accommodation (see s17(6)), the provision of residential accommodation to house a child in need so that he or she can live with the family is not the principal or primary purpose of the legislation. Housing is the function of the local housing authority. Detailed provisions for the acquisition and management of housing stock are contained in the Housing Acts. Provisions of that kind are entirely absent from the Children Act. The expenditure of limited resources on the provision of residential accommodation for housing children with their families would be bound to mean that there was less available for expenditure on other services designed for the performance of the general duty which s17(1) identified. It would also sit uneasily with the legislation in the Housing Acts.

Lord Scott considered that there was nothing wrong with a general policy of making accommodation available for children, but not for their parents. Lord Hope, who gave the main majority judgment, stated that 'the question whether decisions taken under [Children Act 1989 s17] are compatible with the child's article 8 Convention rights must, of course, depend on the facts of each case'.

Lord Nicholls, in the minority and with whom Lord Steyn agreed, considered that the duty to promote the welfare and upbringing of children made little sense unless it was a duty in respect of the welfare and upbringing of each such child. He considered that where a child would suffer adverse consequences by being accommodated apart from his or her parent 'it must follow ... that a local authority should not, expressly or tacitly, threaten a parent that the most it would do is to accommodate the child alone' as this would place an improper pressure on the parent.

Note: The issue of whether the provision of accommodation for a child without their parent would amount to a breach of ECHR article 8 did not receive much consideration and the arguments in *R (J) v Enfield LBC* (U6.5) were not addressed. Children Act 1989 s17(6) was amended by Adoption and Children Act 2002 to clarify that accommodation could be provided as a service under s17.

Court of Appeal

U4.3   *R v Ealing LBC ex p C*
(2000) 3 CCLR 122, CA (see U3.1)

Assessment flawed: no proper reasoning process regarding child's accommodation needs

U4.4   *R (M) v Hammersmith and Fulham LBC*
[2006] EWCA Civ 917; [2007] HLR 6; (2006) 9 CCLR 418; [2007] 1 FLR 256; 5 July 2006 (see T19.1)

Authority correctly accepted application from 17-year-old under Housing Act 1996 Part VII; no error in failing to recognise Children Act s20 duty made out

U4.5   *R (S) v Sutton LBC*
[2007] EWCA Civ 790; 26 July 2007

Social services owed claimant a duty under s20 on her release from prison

For the period August 2005 to end of January 2006 S, a young girl, was on bail in relation to an assault on her mother and a robbery. She could no longer stay with her mother and initially resided with her father but that placement failed after only two days. She went to live with W, a family friend. She was then sentenced and detained until 24 November 2006 when she was released, subject to an electronic curfew and supervision. She was 17. She had no accommodation and had applied to social services for assistance while in prison. It had assessed her but initially decided that she did not meet the conditions for the provision of accommodation under Children Act 1989 s20. On release she was taken to a hostel (Wayside) run by a charity for young homeless women. When evicted from that, she was provided with other hostel accommodation by a district council under the homelessness provisions of Housing Act 1996 Part VII. In judicial review proceedings S claimed that she was owed duties by the defendant social services under Children Act 1989 s20 and s23B. Stanley Burnton J dismissed the claim ([2007] EWHC 1196 (Admin)).

The Court of Appeal allowed an appeal. The provisions relating to a 'relevant child' (s23) and the duty under s20 were considered. It was held that in the period prior to sentence S had not been 'looked after' by the defendant for the requisite period to engage s23B. S had been accommodated by W and did not 'require' accommodation under s20. The defendant had not taken the kind of central role, set out in *Southwark LBC v D* (U4.6), to categorise the period she lived with W as being 'looked after' by the defendant. However, the defendant owed the s20 duty immediately prior to S's release. She did require accommodation and s20(1)(c) was satisfied. The defendant had unlawfully sought '... to "side step" its duties under section 20(1) by having the appellant declare herself homeless and thus (hopefully) obtain state benefits with which she could "buy" accommodation, in the first instance from a charity.' [50] The defendant was quite wrong to tell her to apply, on release, for accommodation under the homelessness provisions. It owed her the s20 duty and ought to have performed it: *H v Wandsworth LBC* (U4.7) approved and applied. The accommodation at Wayside would be treated as having been provided pursuant to the s20 duty.

U4.6   ### *Southwark LBC v D*

[2007] EWCA Civ 182; (2007) 10 CCLR 280; 7 March 2007

Fostering arrangement was made under Children Act s23; as soon as duty to accommodate under s20 arose, girl 'looked after' despite being accommodated with family friend

S, a 13-year-old girl whose mother lived overseas, told her teacher that her father, with whom she was living, had been violent to her. The council held an urgent case conference later that day and the father agreed to have no further contact with S. A social worker telephoned D, with whom S had previously stayed, and D agreed to take S in. The council then contended that it had facilitated a private fostering arrangement and that it was under no duty to support D financially. It argued that it had never owed S an accommodation duty under Children Act 1989 s20 because S had not required accommodation as D had agreed to take her. D's claim for judicial review was allowed and the council appealed.

The Court of Appeal dismissed the appeal. The council owed a crystallised duty to accommodate S (under s20(1)(c)) and she became a looked-after child as soon as that duty arose. The council itself was under a duty to provide accommodation for S and the arrangement it made with D was in pursuance of that duty:

> ... in some circumstances, a private fostering arrangement might become available in such a way as to permit a local authority, which is on the verge of having to provide accommodation for a child to 'side-step' that duty by helping to make a private fostering arrangement. However, it will be a question of fact as to whether that happens in any particular case ... Where a local authority takes a major role in making arrangements for a child to be fostered, it is more likely to be concluded that, in doing so, it is exercising its powers and duties as a public authority pursuant to sections 20 and 23.[49]

If an authority was facilitating a private foster arrangement it should make clear to the foster carer that he or she would have to look to the parents for financial support. The only inference that could reasonably be drawn in the instant case was that the council had asked D to accommodate S at its expense under s23(2).

See also *R (S) v Sutton LBC* (U4.5).

High Court

U4.7 *H, Barhanu, B v Wandsworth LBC, Hackney LBC, Islington LBC*
[2007] EWHC 1082 (Admin), (2007) 10 CCLR 439; [2007] 2 FCR 378; 23 April 2007

Council had provided services to children under s20 despite labelling it as under s17 and the children had been 'looked after'

The claimants were teenagers who arrived in the UK as unaccompanied minors and sought asylum. The councils from whom they then sought assistance decided that they were 'children in need' and provided services under Children Act 1989 s.17. The claimants contended that they had in fact been in need of accommodation (which had been provided by the councils) and had been owed duties not under s17 but under s20. That difference has implications for their ongoing service provision by the local authority (under Children (Leaving Care) Act 2000) and, in one case, by the National Asylum Support Service.

In judicial review proceedings, Holman J held that despite the councils' labelling their services as having been provided under s17 '... if a local authority do provide accommodation for a child in need, and if on the facts a duty to do so did arise under section 20, then the local authority must be regarded as providing that accommodation under section 20 and not under section 17.' [57] The judge did not accept that the Department of Health *Guidance on accommodating children in need and their families* (LAC(2003)13) was unlawful, although it had the potential to mislead. An authority should decide whether a child requires to be provided with accommodation or merely needs help with accommodation, without regard to the implications of him or her being, or not being, a 'looked after' child. One of the claims was dismissed on its facts (the claimant had found accommodation and all the council had done was fund a deposit under s17), but the other claims were allowed as the conditions triggering a s20 duty had been made out.

U4.8 **MB v KB**

[2007] EWHC 789 (Fam); 7 March 2007

Jurisdiction under Children Act 1989 Sch 1 not ousted by settlement in ancillary relief proceedings; court could make order against father for benefit of children

On a divorce, ancillary relief proceedings were compromised on the basis that the wife and children would live in a two-bedroomed flat let by the husband's father and shared with another household. The tenancy would last at least until the children of the family reached 18. The agreement, approved by the court, also provided for periodical payments and other financial adjustments. On the basis of the agreement, the wife's claims for secured provision, a lump sum, property adjustment order and pension provision were dismissed. The effect of the compromise was to prevent the wife from seeking any further property adjustment order. As years passed, the flat became increasingly unsatisfactory. It was overcrowded, in poor repair, had inadequate facilities, was in a poor area and was served by unsatisfactory schools. The mother issued an application under the Children Act 1989 Sch 1 seeking an order that the father make (by periodic payments, a lump sum or by property adjustment) provision for the growing children's housing needs. The father applied to strike out the application on the basis that the doctrines of 'issue estoppel' or 'res judicata' prevented a reopening of the agreement about how the children's housing needs would be met.

Baron J rejected the father's application holding:

1) In relation to issue estoppel:

> The requirements of children, as they grow, require the court to preserve its jurisdiction for the protection of the child. No adult compromise can oust that jurisdiction. In the case of *Re B* [1997] 1 FLR Hale J, as she then was, said: 'It seems to me that the weight of Court of Appeal authority is against the existence of any strict rule of issue estoppel which is binding on any of the parties in children's cases.' I agree with that simple maxim. Clearly, no mother or father can seek to oust the court's jurisdiction when it relates to their child. [25–26]

2) In relation to 'res judicata':

> ... I do not accept that A's housing needs are governed by some notion of res judicata in any formal or informal sense. The settlement is part of the background of this case which would inform a judge dealing with the final merits of any application, but that does not mean that the application itself is thereby invalid or should be struck out ... Housing needs, so far as a child is concerned, can be dealt with, if appropriate, to take account of the changing conditions that occur as a child grows... In this case long-term housing has not been definitively decided and there has been a change in circumstances, in the sense that, as time has gone by A's needs have changed. [34–35]

Directions were given for the consideration of the Children Act application on its merits.

U4.8A **R v Hammersmith and Fulham LBC ex p Quigley**

(2000) 32 HLR 379; (1999) *Independent* 24 May, QBD (see L1.9)

Decision to institute possession proceedings quashed where tenant had aban-doned property but partner could apply for transfer of tenancy under Children Act s15

U4.8B **R v Hillingdon LBC ex p McDonagh**

[1999] LGR 459; (1999) 31 HLR 531; (1998) *Times* 9 November, QBD (see L3.16)

Authority seeking possession against trespassers not obliged to carry out Child-ren Act or homeless person assessments

U4.9 **R v Tower Hamlets LBC ex p Bradford**

(1998) 1 CCLR 294; (1997) 29 HLR 756, QBD (see U3.6)

Child entitled to proper assessment of housing needs under s17; needs not addressed by consideration of family circumstances as a whole

U4.10 **R (B) v Merton LBC**

[2003] EWHC 1689 (Admin); [2003] 4 All ER 280; [2003] 2 FLR 888; (2003) 6 CCLR 457; (2003) *Times* 18 July; 14 July 2003

Guidance on the assessment of age

B claimed that he was 17 years old, that both his parents were dead and that he had entered the United Kingdom from Senegal in February 2003 via an unknown airport. National Asylum Support Service decided that he was an adult and refused to provide accommodation on the basis that it was not satisfied that he had made his application as soon as reasonably prac-ticable after his arrival in the UK (Nationality Immigration and Asylum Act 2002 s55). He sought accommodation from Merton which owed him a duty under Children Act 1989 s20 if he was under 18. He did not speak English and was interviewed by the decision-maker using an interpreter on the other end of a phone line. Merton decided that he was at least 18 years old and it did not, therefore, have a duty to provide him with accommoda-tion under s20. B sought judicial review of that decision and both parties sought the court's guidance on how a local authority should assess the age of an unaccompanied asylum-seeking child who claims to be under 18 but cannot substantiate his or her claim with reliable documentary evidence.

Stanley Burnton J stated that there is no statutory procedure or guid-ance to local authorities on how to conduct an assessment of a person claiming to be under 18. Nor is there any reliable medical or scientific test available. However, local authorities are entitled to determine the age of individuals in the absence of documentary evidence on the basis of appear-ance, personal history and behaviour, provided that minimum standards of enquiry and fairness are adhered to. Such matters are difficult but not complex and judicialisation of the process should be avoided. The court should not impose unrealistic and unnecessary burdens on those required to make such decisions. It is not helpful to apply concepts of the burden of proof to such an assessment. Local authorities should not simply adopt decisions already made by the Home Office, but should conduct their own assessment. Interpreters should be present at any interview if required. It is useful for notes to be taken, although they are not essential as a matter of law. Applicants should be given adequate opportunity to answer points held against them. Reasons for any decision should be given, although they do not need to be long or elaborate. In this case the local authority had made its own assessment, but as the applicant had not been given the opportunity to deal with points held against him, and, in the absence of evidence of a suitable alternative procedure for B to challenge the decision, it should be set aside.

See also: *R (T) v Enfield LBC* [2004] EWHC 2297 (Admin) (guidance on age assessments, hostile manner of assessment, mental health of T, paediatrician report); *R (C) v Merton LBC* [2005] EWHC 1753 (Admin) (failure to give reasons for rejecting medical report); *R (A) v Liverpool CC* [2007] EWHC 1477 (Admin) (unfairness in reaching decision without disclosing dental report to claimant).

U4.11 **R (Bangura) v Southwark LBC**
[2007] EWHC 1681 (Admin); 20 June 2007 (see U6.4)

It is for child rather than parent to challenge Children Act 1989 s17 assessment

U4.12 **R (Behre and Others) v Hillingdon LBC**
[2003] EWHC 2075 (Admin); (2003) 6 CCLR 471; (2003) *Times* 22 September; 29 August 2003

Unaccompanied asylum-seekers were 'looked after' when provided with accommodation by social services

All four claimants arrived at Heathrow Airport in 2000 as unaccompanied asylum-seeking children. None had family in the UK. All were destitute. The immigration authorities referred them to Hillingdon social services department, which was responsible for them under the Children Act 1989. The four claimants received assistance from social services, but this ceased when they became adults. The claimants argued that the council owed them duties under the Children (Leaving Care) Act 2000 on the basis that they had been 'looked after' as they had 'accommodated' under Children Act 1989 s17 or s20. The council asserted that it had not accommodated them but had 'supported [them] in housing provision in the community' and thus they had not been 'looked after'.

Sullivan J held that the provision by a local authority of housing assistance to an unaccompanied asylum-seeking child amounted to the provision of accommodation. The claimants had been 'looked after'. Hillingdon's attempt to differentiate between providing 'housing' for children who required somewhere to live as a result of their circumstances and providing 'accommodation' was mere sophistry and a distinction without a difference. Furthermore, there was no basis for requiring the prescribed period in Children Act 1989 s19B(2)(b) or Sch 2 Part II para 19B(2)(a) to begin before a child turned 16. All that was required was that the prescribed period ended when the child was 16 or 17. The claimants had been looked after for the requisite period, were now former relevant children and were owed duties under the 2000 Act. They were also in priority need for the purposes of Housing Act 1996 by virtue of Homelessness (Priority Need for Accommodation) (England) Order 2002 article 4.

See also *R (W) v Essex CC* [2003] EWHC 3175, 19 December 2003

Note: Adoption and Children Act 2002 amended Children Act 1989 s22 to exclude a child accommodated under s17 from the definition of a 'looked after' child. See *H, Barhanu, B v Wandsworth LBC, Hackney LBC, Islington LBC* (U4.7) for a case decided after this amendment.

U4.13   *R (Conde) v Lambeth LBC*
[2005] EWHC 62 (Admin); [2005] HLR 29; [2005] 2 FLR 98; (2005) 8 CCLR 486; 13 January 2005 (see U8.8)

No discrimination to refuse EEA national assistance under Children Act 1989 s17

U4.14   *R (Deeming) v Birmingham CC*
[2006] EWHC 3719 (Admin); 2 November 2006

Pathway plan did not have proper contingency plan if claimant lost his accommodation

Mr Deeming had been in local authority care and the council owed him duties under the Children Act 1989 ss23D and 23E in respect of provision of a personal adviser and a pathway plan into adulthood. Children (Leaving Care) England Regulations 2001 reg 8 and Sch 1 para 9 require that the pathway plan contain 'contingency plans for action to be taken by the responsible authority should the pathway plan for any reason cease to be effective'. Mr Deeming sought judicial review of the adequacy of the pathway plan contending, inter alia, that it contained no proper contingency plan if he lost his current accommodation. It simply provided that a local housing authority could assist under homelessness provisions.

Elias J, allowing the application in part, considered that the reference to the claimant presenting himself to the local housing office for alternative accommodation was not an adequate contingency plan. It simply left the burden on him to cope with the particular problem. What was required was an identification of who within the council would take responsibility for seeking to ensure that steps could be taken in those circumstances to obtain accommodation. The changes need not be very significant but it would require a particular responsibility on somebody within the council who would then know that it was their task to deal with this particular difficulty if and when it arose.

U4.15   *R (L) v Nottinghamshire CC*
[2007] EWHC (Admin); 26 September 2007

Child accommodated under s20 despite social services' assertion it was under s17

The claimant, a teenage girl, was ejected from her mother's home and sought the assistance of her local social services authority. Her mother told the council that she would not have her daughter back as the daughter had assaulted her. The council provided bed and breakfast accommodation, recording that it was exercising its powers under Children Act 1989 s17. The claimant asserted that she had been accommodated under Children Act 1989 s20(1)(c), triggering an entitlement to further assistance as a care-leaver.

In judicial review proceedings, Burton J held that, despite the label which the council had put on the arrangement and the fact that it had not conducted a full assessment, the claimant had actually met the conditions under s20 and was to be treated as having been provided with accommodation under that provision.

U4.16 **R (M) v Barking and Dagenham LBC and Westminster CC**

[2002] EWHC 2663 (Admin); (2003) 6 CCLR 87; 27 November 2002

Children within council's area if physically present in area

The claimant applied to Westminster for accommodation for herself and her children under Housing Act 1996 Part VII (homelessness). Westminster provided interim accommodation in Barking and Dagenham's area. It later decided that the claimant had become intentionally homeless and withdrew the temporary accommodation. The claimant's children then faced the prospect of actual homelessness and the question arose as to which council was obliged to conduct a 'child in need assessment' under Children Act 1989 s17.

Crane J held, in proceedings for judicial review, that the key determinant was actual physical presence and on that basis the duty fell on Barking and Dagenham. However, authorities should not seek to pass on responsibilities for families with children to other authorities and the proper approach should be one of co-operation between the councils involved.

U4.17 **R (Stewart) v Hammersmith and Fulham, Wandsworth and Lambeth LBCs**

[2001] EWHC Admin 709; (2001) 4 CCLR 466; [2002] 1 FLR 469; (2001) *Times* 15 November

Council's duty to children 'within their area' meant to those physically present in area

In June 2000 the claimant applied to Hammersmith and Fulham for assistance as a homeless person. The council secured hostel accommodation in Lambeth for her under Housing Act 1996 s188. She placed her children in schools in Wandsworth. In October 2000 Hammersmith and Fulham notified her of a decision that she had become intentionally homeless and that its duty to her would be discharged by provision of a short period of further accommodation in the hostel. The claimant then sought an assessment of her children's needs under Children Act 1989 s17. The councils could not agree on which of them was required to undertake the assessment and the claimant brought judicial review proceedings against all three.

Deputy Judge Jack Beatson QC held that (1) s17 imposed the duty on an authority in respect of children 'within their area' and (2) that phrase was satisfied by the 'physical presence' of the children. On the facts, the children were physically present in both Lambeth (where they lived) and Wandsworth (where they went to school) but not in Hammersmith and Fulham. Accordingly, the former two authorities were in breach of their mandatory duties to make an assessment of the children's needs.

National Assistance Act 1948 s21(1)

Section 21(1) provides:

> Subject to and in accordance with the provisions of this Part of this Act, a local authority may with the approval of the secretary of state, and to such extent as he may direct shall, make arrangements for providing:
>
> (a) residential accommodation for persons aged eighteen or over who by reason of age, illness, disability or any other circumstances are in need of care and attention which is not otherwise available to them, and
>
> (aa) residential accommodation for expectant and nursing mothers who are in need of care and attention which is not otherwise available to them.

The approvals and directions made under s21 (Local Authority Circular LAC (93)(10) Appendix 1) place a duty on a local authority, where the conditions in s21 are satisfied, to provide residential accommodation to a person ordinarily resident in its area and to other persons who are in urgent need.

Much of the jurisprudence under s21(1) has developed in relation to cases involving claimants who are asylum-seekers or otherwise not entitled to mainstream support. The introduction of s21(1A) and Nationality Immigration and Asylum Act 2002 Sch 3 restricted the ability of people subject to immigration control to rely on s21(1). While the principles of cases decided in relation to such people before the introduction of these provisions still remain relevant to the ambit of s21(1), it must be borne in mind that the outcome on the facts might now be different in the light of s21(1A)/Sch 3. This section concerns the general extent of the duty under s21(1). Sections U7 and U8 concern the restrictions placed on the duty by s21(1A) and Sch 3 respectively.

Court of Appeal

U5.1 *R v Hammersmith and Fulham LBC ex p M*

(also known as *R v Westminster ex p M, P, A and X*, see U5.4)

U5.2 *R v Kensington and Chelsea RLBC ex p Kujtim (also spelt Kutjim)*

[1999] 4 All ER 161; (1999) 2 CCLR 340; [1999] LGR 761; (2000) 32 HLR 579; (1999) *Times* 5 August, CA

Council entitled to treat s21 duty as discharged if persistent refusal to comply with rules

An Albanian asylum-seeker was evicted from two lodgings because of violent behaviour towards staff, threats to kill the management and a failure to abide by the rules and regulations of the house. Scott Baker J held that in those circumstances the council was under no mandatory obligation to meet his continuing need for accommodation under National Assistance Act 1948 s21(1).

The Court of Appeal dismissed his appeal. Where a person's needs satisfy the criteria contained in National Assistance Act 1948 s21(1)(a), the authority has a continuing duty to provide accommodation while the person's needs remain the same. However, an authority is entitled to treat its duty as discharged and to refuse to provide further accommodation if the person refuses accommodation offered or, following its provision, manifests by his or her conduct a persistent and unequivocal refusal to observe the authority's reasonable requirements in relation to occupation of such accommodation. Before concluding that there has been such a refusal it is desirable that the authority write a final warning letter. Any decision by the authority to treat its duty as discharged by conduct requires a reassessment both of current need and careful consideration of the nature of that conduct, including any medical condition or infirmity known to the authority. By the time of the hearing Mr Kujtim had left the UK of his own accord. The authority agreed to reassess the situation in the light of a psychiatric report that had been prepared on him, should he return.

See also *R (Patrick) v Newham LBC* (U5.18); *R (Khana and Karim) v Southwark LBC* (U5.6).

U5.3   **R v Sefton MBC ex p Help the Aged**
(1997) 1 CCLR 57; (1997) *Times* 23 August, CA
Lack of funds did not excuse council from performing s21 duty

Sefton adopted a policy of taking into account its own resources when deciding whether to offer assistance under National Assistance Act 1948 s21(1)(a).

The Court of Appeal granted Help the Aged's appeal against a dismissal of its application for judicial review. Where a local authority is satisfied that a person is in need of care and attention which is not otherwise available to him or her, the s21 duty is owed and lack of funds does not excuse the authority from performing its duty to make appropriate arrangements.

U5.4   **R v Westminster CC ex p M, P, A and X**
(1997) 1 CCLR 85; (1998) 30 HLR 10; 17 February 2007, CA (also known as *R v Hammersmith and Fulham LBC ex p M*)
Characteristics of destitute asylum-seekers such that they are in need of care and attention by reason of 'any other circumstance'

The applicants were asylum-seekers. They had failed to claim asylum at the port of entry and, as a result of the enactment of Asylum and Immigration Act 1996, they were not eligible for homelessness assistance or social security benefits. They applied for assistance under National Assistance Act 1948 s21(1), which provided that local authorities should make available residential accommodation if 'by reason of age, illness, disability or any other circumstances [applicants] are in need of care and attention which is not otherwise available to them'. At first instance Collins J held that if asylum-seekers had no other means of support, the local authorities owed them duties under National Assistance Act 1948 s21(1).

The Court of Appeal rejected an appeal by the local authorities. The words 'any other circumstances' should be given a wide meaning. They are not limited by the words 'age, illness, disability'. Lord Woolf, giving the judgment of the court, said

> Asylum-seekers are not entitled merely because they lack money and accommodation to claim they automatically qualify under s21(1)(a). What they are entitled to claim (and this is a result of the [Asylum and Immigration Act 1996]) is that they can as a result of their predicament after they arrive in this country reach a state where they qualify under the

subsection because of the effect upon them of the problems under which they are labouring. In addition to lack of food and accommodation is to be added their inability to speak the language, their ignorance of this country and the fact that they had been subject to the stress of coming to this country in circumstances which at least involve their contending to be refugees. Inevitably the combined effect of these factors with the passage of time will produce one or more of the conditions specifically referred to in s21(1)(a). It is for the authority to decide whether they qualify. In making their decision ... the authorities can anticipate the deterioration which would otherwise take place in the asylum-seekers' condition by providing assistance under the section. They do not have to wait until the health of the asylum-seeker has been damaged. ([1997] 1CCLR 85 at p95)

Note: See now National Assistance Act s21(1A) (section U7), introduced by Immigration and Asylum Act 1999 in response to this decision.

U5.5   *R (Ireneschild) v Lambeth LBC*

[2007] EWCA Civ 234; (2007) 10 CCLR 243, 16 March 2007 (see U3.3)

Assessment had followed FACS guidance and was lawful; urgent housing needs did not require community care assessment of needs as 'substantial'

U5.6   *R (Khana and Karim) v Southwark LBC*

[2001] EWCA Civ 999; (2001) 4 CCLR 267; [2002] HLR 31; (2001) *Times* 15 September, CA

Section 21 duty is to meet needs, not satisfy preferences

The applicants, an elderly couple, sought judicial review of the council's decision to meet their care needs by provision of places in a residential care home. The applicants wanted, for personal and cultural reasons, to live in the community independently in a home of their own, with the support of their relatives and the statutory services. Hallet J dismissed the application. The council had carefully considered all relevant matters and the central government guidance. That consideration included weight being given to the wishes of the couple but the council concluded that their needs could only be met in a residential setting. If the couple refused 'point blank' to take the residential care unit, even after the judgment had been explained to them, that refusal would be 'unreasonable' for the purpose of relieving the council of a continuing duty (subject to review) – applying *R v Kensington and Chelsea RLBC ex p Kujtim* [1999] 4 All ER 161, QBD (see now the Court of Appeal decision (U5.2)).

The Court of Appeal dismissed the applicants' appeal. A local authority's duty is to assess and meet applicants' needs, not to satisfy their preferences. Where a local authority concludes that the only way to meet needs is to offer space in a full-time residential home and where that conclusion and the reasonableness of the offer cannot be challenged, the local authority has satisfied its duty under the legislation.

Cf: *R v Richmond upon Thames LBC ex p T* (U5.13).

U5.7   *R (Mani) v Lambeth LBC*

[2003] EWCA Civ 836; [2004] HLR 5; [2004] LGR 35; (2002) *Times* 23 July; 9 July 2003 (see U7.7)

Section 21 not limited to those whose need for care and attention is accommodation related

U5.8   *R (Wahid) v Tower Hamlets LBC*

[2002] EWCA Civ 287; (2002) 5 CCLR 239; [2003] HLR 2; [2002] LGR 545

Section 21 is a safety net provision; duty premised on an unmet need; over-crowding did not trigger duty

The claimant, aged 53, lived with his wife and their eight children in a two-bedroomed council flat. From November 2000 to January 2001 he was in hospital receiving treatment for schizophrenia, from which he had been suffering since 1972. On his discharge he sought an assessment under National Health Service and Community Care Act 1990 s47. The council concluded that for the purposes of National Assistance Act 1948 s21 the claimant was not 'in need of care and attention' that was not otherwise available to him. It considered that support was being provided under Mental Health Act s117(2) by social services to address his mental health problems and that the risk of a breakdown being caused by overcrowding was relatively small. It accepted that his accommodation was overcrowded and unsuitable and assisted him in obtaining a medical priority under the allocation scheme. Offers of accommodation were made to him and his adult sons but turned down on the basis that they were unsuitable. Stanley Burnton J dismissed his application for judicial review, holding that s21 was a safety net provision of last resort and that neither overcrowding nor any other risk to health arising from housing conditions triggered the s21 duty.

The Court of Appeal dismissed Mr Wahid's appeal. Although ordinary housing could be provided under s21, it did not follow that because the claimant needed ordinary housing a duty arose to provide it to him. The duty to provide accommodation under s21 is premised on an unmet need for 'care and attention' (a 'condition precedent'). The fact that a person was in need of accommodation did not make him in need of care and attention. It was for the local authority to determine whether the applicant was in need of care and attention. The council had considered the medical evidence and medical opinion on any future risk to the health of the claimant if he were not rehoused and its conclusion that there was no unmet need for care and attention was one which it was entitled to reach and was not irrational. The case was distinguishable from *R v Islington LBC ex p Batantu* (U5.9) because the authority had in that case accepted that there was an unmet need for care and attention.

High Court

U5.9   *R v Islington LBC ex p Batantu*

(2001) 4 CCLR 445; (2001) 33 HLR 871, QBD Admin Ct

Once the need for particular accommodation was assessed a duty arose to meet that need

The claimant suffered from severe mental health problems. He lived with his wife and four children in a two-bedroom flat on the 12th floor of a block of flats. Pain in his knees meant that he had difficulty negotiating stairs. The lift in the block frequently broke down. Following a request from the claimant's solicitor, the council, as the social services authority, carried out an assessment of the claimant's community care needs under

National Health Service and Community Care Act 1990 s47(1)(a). In the assessment the council concluded that the claimant needed a ground floor property, with enough space to house him and his family. A care plan stated that he needed safe, secure, larger and easily accessible accommodation in which to live. However, social services merely referred the matter to the housing department. Under the housing register it would take years, not months, to rehouse the claimant. He issued judicial review proceedings to compel the council to provide him with accommodation, so as to meet his identified needs. He was then reassessed under the housing register and was placed 19th on the four-bedroom register. About 40 such properties became available each year.

Henriques J held that, once a local authority has carried out an assessment pursuant to s47(1)(a) and has identified a need for care and attention that is not otherwise available to an applicant, it is under a duty to provide the applicant with accommodation to meet that need under National Assistance Act 1948 s21. The duty lay with the social services and not the housing department. Accommodation appropriate to the claimant's needs should have been provided. The council was not entitled to rely on its lack of resources as an excuse for failing to meet the need (although it was entitled to have regard to its resources in deciding how to meet it). The council's duty was a continuing one. The claimant's single refusal in principle to contemplate private rented accommodation did not absolve the council of that duty. Nine months had passed since the assessment and it was not an overstatement to say that the present case was an emergency. It was therefore necessary to make a mandatory order.

U5.10 *R v Newham LBC ex p C*
(1999) 31 HLR 567, QBD

Authority misunderstood its powers or fettered its discretion in deciding that it could only provide B&B accommodation and not self-contained accommodation under s21

In 1994 Ms C came from Zambia to the United Kingdom to study banking. Her studies were funded by her employer. In 1996 she was diagnosed as HIV positive. She was unable to continue her studies and her employer withdrew funding. She had no other source of income. She became very ill and suffered from bouts of debilitating diarrhoea. The council accepted that it owed her a duty under the National Assistance Act 1948 s21. It provided her with bed and breakfast accommodation, with shared use of bathroom and cooking facilities, as part of a care plan. Her doctor prepared a report stating that bed and breakfast accommodation was unsuitable because she needed to use the lavatory frequently as a result of severe bouts of diarrhoea and because she needed to be able to control standards of hygiene in the kitchen to reduce the risk of infection. The authority produced a comprehensive assessment of her needs, proposing a care plan which included the continuation of bed and breakfast. In the course of her application for judicial review the authority stated that the social services department did not have any housing stock other than bed and breakfast accommodation and residential homes.

Sullivan J granted Ms C's application for judicial review. The council had confined its consideration to bed and breakfast accommodation. If the particular needs of an applicant mean that bed and breakfast accommodation is not suitable, and self-contained accommodation is needed, there is nothing to prevent the authority from renting a self-contained flat. The authority had either misapprehended the breadth of its powers under s21 or had unlawfully fettered its discretion.

U5.11 *R v Newham LBC ex p Medical Foundation for the Care of Victims of Torture*
(1998) 1 CCLR 227; (1998) 30 HLR 955, QBD

'Residential accommodation' not limited to institutional accommodation

Newham had a policy of offering asylum-seekers who sought assistance under s21 hotel accommodation in Eastbourne. That policy was based on legal advice that it was only permitted to offer accommodation in which it could provide food, laundry and facilities to maintain personal hygiene. That kind of accommodation was not available in Newham. The applicants were destitute asylum-seekers who wanted to remain in Newham where they could receive support and comfort from the local community. They sought judicial review.

Moses J held that the phrase 'residential accommodation' means no more than where a person lives. It does not mean 'accommodation with an institutional quality'. An authority under a duty to provide accommodation under s21 does not have a duty to provide board or other services with it. There was no need for local authorities to cease providing s21 assistance via bed and breakfast accommodation or private lettings. Other services may be provided from outside the accommodation. The applicants did not have to be accommodated in the hotel in Eastbourne.

U5.12 *R v Newham LBC ex p Plastin*
(1998) 1 CCLR 304; (1997) 30 HLR 261, QBD

Able-bodied man entitled to work not in urgent need of care and attention despite lack of English and ineligibility for benefits

P was a 51-year-old British citizen who had lived in Russia and did not speak English. He came to the UK on 23 December 1996. He stayed at a night shelter until it closed in April 1997. He was refused social security benefits as he failed the habitual residence test. He sought assistance under s21. The authority concluded that, although he was homeless and ineligible for benefits, it did not owe him a duty as he had no mental or physical disability and had worked as a cook in the past. It considered that he was not in urgent need of care and attention. P applied for judicial review.

Keene J refused permission. Section 21 is not a safety net on which any person short of money can rely (following *R v Westminster CC ex p M, P, A and X* (U5.4)). The proper test is to consider whether a person is 'in need of care and attention' for one of the reasons set out in s21(1)(a). If a need is identified then, where a person had no settled residence, a duty only arises where the need is urgent (under LAC (93)(10)). P was an able-bodied man of working age who might obtain work, despite his lack of English, because of his experience as a cook. The judge took the view that he was eligible for assistance under Housing Act 1996. The authority had taken into account P's circumstances and it could not be said that the authority's decision was *Wednesbury* unreasonable.

Note: P, a British citizen , would not be excluded from assistance under s21 by s21(1A).

U5.13   *R v Richmond upon Thames LBC ex p T*
January 2001 *Legal Action* 27; 20 July 2000, QBD

Where description of accommodation not mere preference but part of needs, duty was to provide that accommodation

Mr T had a history of mental health problems. He was assessed as ready to return from supported hostel accommodation to ordinary housing in the community. His doctor wrote 'He is requesting to get accommodation in a street house in a residential area which I believe is entirely justified considering his mental health needs.' The council initially offered tower block accommodation (in error) and then flats in smaller blocks of flats.

Newman J held that the council had failed to meet its duties owed to Mr T under National Assistance Act 1948 s21. He held that the description of the accommodation put forward was not mere preference but part of the individual applicant's needs. (See *R v Avon CC ex p M* (1993) 2 CCLR 185, QBD.) He granted an order of mandamus, that the council 'provide the applicant with accommodation in accordance with his lawfully assessed needs, including his psychological needs' within three months.

U5.14   *R v Southwark LBC ex p Hong Cui*
(1999) 2 CCLR 86; (1999) 31 HLR 639; 11 September 1998, QBD

Applicant could be in need of care and attention because of destitution despite being entitled to work where unable to find work

The applicant was a Chinese citizen and an asylum-seeker who was awaiting the outcome of her appeal to the special adjudicator. She worked in Chinese restaurants but became unable to find work when she started to suffer from psoriasis. She applied to the respondent authority for assistance under National Assistance Act 1948 s21(1)(a). It claimed that she was not in need of care and attention because she had accommodation, the cost of which was met by housing benefit. They provided her with a list of soup kitchens. She applied for judicial review.

David Pannick QC granted permission. He held:

1) Applicants must show that they are in desperate need of care and attention and that otherwise there is a risk that there would be damage to their health or for some other reason assistance was urgently required. It is not enough to be destitute.
2) Authorities must consider the circumstances of each individual case.
3) It was at least arguable that the authority had failed to focus on whether or not, given the efforts that the applicant had made to find work and the time that she would have to spend walking to soup kitchens to find food, there was any realistic possibility of her actually finding work.

Note: See now National Assistance Act 1948 s 21(1A).

U5.15   ## R (AA) v Lambeth LBC

[2001] EWHC Admin 741; (2002) 5 CCLR 36; 19 September 2001

Social services have power to provide accommodation pending assessment

The claimant was an asylum-seeker. He suffered from hepatitis B. He was destitute and sought assistance from the defendant council, a social services authority. It failed to assess his needs under National Health Service and Community Care Act 1990 s47. The claimant sought judicial review (for which permission was granted) and an interim order requiring the provision of accommodation. The council contended that until the s47 assessment was completed, there could be no duty (or power) to accommodate pursuant to National Assistance Act s21 and that, accordingly, the provision of interim accommodation would be ultra vires.

Forbes J held that, as enacted, s21 gave a local authority a power (and thus the vires) to accommodate a person in the claimant's circumstances. Even if that were wrong, the court itself had power in appropriate cases (of which this was one) to order the council to secure accommodation on an interim basis.

U5.16   ## R (Greenwich LBC) v Secretary of State

[2006] EWHC 2576 (Admin); (2007) 10 CCLR 60; 13 July 2006

'Ordinary residence' for purposes of responsibility under s21

An elderly woman lived all her life in Bexley where she owned her own home. She went into residential care in Bexley in May 2001 and sold her home to meet the care costs. In 2002 she required alternative care arrangements and Bexley LBC found a place for her in a care home in Greenwich. Shortly afterwards she became eligible for social services assistance with care costs.

Charles J dismissed an application for judicial review of the secretary of state's decision that she was 'ordinarily resident' in Greenwich and that Greenwich, rather that Bexley, was liable to meet the costs of providing assistance.

U5.17   ## R (Mooney) v Southwark LBC

[2006] EWHC 1912 (Admin); (2006) 9 CCLR 670; 6 July 2006

Where need is for 'housing' but not 'care and attention', no s21 duty owed; alternatively need being met by priority for transfer

The claimant was the single parent of three children. She had a disability rendering her incapable of using stairs. She had a room on the ground floor of a maisonette. Her two nine-year-old twins, who had emotional and behavioural problems and required constant supervision, had their bedroom upstairs, as did her 17-year-old son. After carrying out assessments, social services nominated her for a priority transfer under the council's allocation scheme. The claimant sought judicial review of the council's failure to accommodate her under National Assistance Act 1948 s21.

Jackson J dismissed the claim. The first question to ask was whether the council was in breach of duty under s21. The council's assessments undoubtedly identified a need for more suitable accommodation, both for the claimant and for her children. However, identifying a need for housing was not the same as identifying a need under s21(1) (applying *R (Wahid) v Tower Hamlets* (U5.8)). The needs of the children could not trigger a duty under s21. On analysis, there was no acceptance by the council of a need that triggered s21(1) – the various assessments did not suggest that the claimant was in need of care and attention by reason of her disability and that such care and attention was not available to her otherwise than by the provision of accommodation under s21. On the contrary, the assessments were to the effect that additional social services support would be provided and a priority nomination made under the allocation scheme. That brought into play s21(8) which prevented s21(1) from imposing an obligation in the circumstances. The second question was whether the council acted lawfully in deciding that the claimant did not have a need triggering s21. There was nothing irrational or otherwise unlawful in the council's decision that the need for better accommodation could be met by means of a priority nomination. (*R v Wigan MBC ex p Tammadge* (1997–98) 1 CCLR 581 and *R v Islington LBC ex p Batantu* (U5.9) distinguished.)

U5.18   *R (Patrick) v Newham LBC*
(2001) 4 CCLR 48, QBD

Council's reliance on applicant's refusal of hostel did not discharge s21 duty

The claimant was evicted from accommodation provided under Housing Act 1996 s190 (short-term duty to intentionally homeless). Within a fortnight she began sleeping rough. Later the same month she came to the attention of the council again and it offered her a hostel place in south London at a charitable centre for those with mental health problems. She refused it. Ten days later a certificate of mental incapacity was granted. Solicitors instructed by the Official Solicitor asked the council to arrange accommodation. It refused. On her application for judicial review, the council contended that the offer of the hostel place had discharged any duty under National Assistance Act 1948 s21.

Henriques J granted judicial review. He held that the council had failed to carry out any assessment of her needs under the National Health Service and Community Care Act 1990 s47. The council's reliance on the refusal of the hostel place was vitiated by its failure, at the time of its offer, to ensure that it had explained the offer and the consequences of refusal to the point of comprehension. He made an order that the council conduct a s47 assessment and provide accommodation forthwith.

Exclusion from assistance

U6   Persons from abroad – miscellaneous

Court of Appeal

U6.1   *R (Badu) v Lambeth LBC*
[2005] EWCA Civ 1184; [2006] HLR 8; [2006] UKHRR 165; (2005) *Times* 19 October; 14 October 2005

Where assistance was denied as a result of HA 1996 s185(4), which was incompatible with ECHR, an authority could, but was not obliged, to assist under alternative powers

Mr Badu was a Ghanaian national with indefinite leave to remain in the UK. As such he was eligible for assistance under Housing Act 1996 Part VII. His dependent son was not a UK national or otherwise eligible. Lambeth decided that Mr Badu was not in priority need by virtue of s185(4). Mr Badu acknowledged that, even though declared incompatible (see *R (Morris) v Westminster CC* (T2.6)), s185(4) still operated to debar the council from according him priority need. He asserted that the council should instead assist him under: (1) Local Government Act 2000 s2 (power 'to do anything' for the benefit of any persons 'resident or present' in a local authority area which promotes the social well-being of that area), (2) Children Act 1989 s17 (general duty to safeguard and promote the welfare of children in need and to promote the upbringing of children by their families) or (3) Housing Act 1996 s192(3) (power to secure accommodation for non-priority unintentionally homeless). The council refused to accommodate him.

Elias J granted permission and the Court of Appeal constituted itself as an Administrative Court to try the claim. The council submitted that to accord assistance would directly subvert parliament's intention in enacting s185(4), which remained the law. Mr Badu argued that, as s185(4) was incompatible with ECHR, the council's powers under the various Acts effectively became duties where their exercise was necessary to avoid a breach of ECHR article 8.

The Court held that:

- the council was not obliged to use its alternative powers in every case caught by s185(4);
- it would be permitted to use the powers where the individual circumstances of the applicant justified that use; but
- the powers could not be used with the object of circumventing the restriction imposed by s185(4). Accordingly, a council could not resolve to use the powers every time an applicant was caught by s185(4).

Once in the 'space' formed by this triangle of rules, the taking of a particular decision in exercise of discretionary powers would be subject to the familiar public law considerations. The court remitted the decision on what to do in Mr Badu's case for further consideration by the council.

See also *R (Bangura) v Southwark LBC* (U6.4)

High Court

U6.2   *R v Brent LBC ex p D*
(1999) 31 HLR 10; (1998) 1 CCLR 234, QBD

Applicant unlawfully in UK but who could not travel had right to claim under s21

The applicant was a Brazilian national who was HIV positive. He entered the UK on a six months visitor's visa but remained in the country unlawfully. He became seriously ill and was admitted to hospital. After being discharged he slept in a garage. He was exceptionally weak and underweight and his consultant advised that he was not fit to travel. He applied to Brent for assistance under National Assistance Act 1948 s21. It refused his application on the ground that he was in the UK unlawfully.

Moses J granted his application for judicial review. Public policy prohibited an applicant for benefits from relying on his own wrongdoing. 'Illegal immigrants' and overstayers cannot apply for assistance under s21 because in doing so they are compelled to rely on their own wrongdoing. They have a choice, whether to stay or leave. However, the applicant's right to life and a minimum state of health overrode that principle. An illegal entrant or overstayer has a right to make a claim under s21 where he cannot undertake the journey out of the UK without risk to life or serious injury to health.

Note: In *R v Wandsworth LBC ex p O* (U7.3) it was held that Moses J was wrong to hold that the public policy exclusion applies to persons other than those unable to travel. See now National Assistance Act 1948 s21(1A) and Nationality Immigration and Asylum Act 2002 Sch 3.

U6.3   *R v Lambeth LBC ex p Sarhangi*
(1999) 2 CCLR 145; [1999] LGR 641; (1999) 31 HLR 1022, QBD

Applicant unlawfully in UK but who could not be removed eligible under s21(1)

Mr Sarhangi, an Iranian, was granted asylum in Sweden. He came to the UK and was imprisoned for drugs offences. He was ordered to be deported to Sweden, but the Swedish authorities would not accept him because of his convictions. On his release from prison he was not allowed to work. He applied for assistance under National Assistance Act 1948 s21(1). The council refused his request on the grounds that he was not lawfully present and had not applied for asylum in the UK and was fit to travel.

Kay J granted his application for judicial review. Although as a matter of public policy an illegal entrant or overstayer is not entitled to benefit from his own wrong doing (*R v Brent LBC ex p D* (U6.2)) that policy applies only where the person is exercising a choice to remain illegally. Mr Sarhangi had no choice. It was difficult to say that he was unlawfully in the UK in the light of his imprisonment and the inability to remove him under the deportation order. He was fully co-operating with the authorities to effect his removal, but was prevented by factors outside his control. Public policy did not require that he should be denied the protection afforded by s21(1).

See now National Assistance Act 1948 s21(1A) and Nationality Immigration and Asylum Act 2002 Sch 3.

U6.4   *R (Bangura) v Southwark LBC*
[2007] EWHC 1681 (Admin); 20 June 2007

Powers under Children Act 1989 s17, Local Government Act 2000 s2 and HA 1996 s193(2) not elevated to duties where claimant denied assistance as a homeless person as a result of provision incompatible with ECHR (HA 1996 s185(4))

The claimant was homeless. His two-year-old son lived with him. The son was not a British citizen and was subject to immigration control. In consequence, the claimant could not rely on his dependent child to secure priority need as a homeless person: Housing Act 1996 s185(4). However, that provision had been declared incompatible with convention rights: *R (Morris) v Westminster CC* (T2.5). When the council declined to accommodate, the claimant sought judicial review, contending that the council – in order to avoid a breach of his ECHR rights – had a duty to accommodate him under Housing Act 1996 s192(3) or under the Local Government Act (LGA) 2000 s2 or under the Children Act 1989.

Hodge J dismissed the claim. The discretion to accommodate the homeless (who are not in priority need) available to a council under HA 1996 s192(3) was not elevated into a duty by the fact that the claimant had been deprived of priority need by a provision not compatible with the ECHR. The discretion itself had been exercised (adversely) in his case. Although the council had been wrong to contend that it did not have to give reasons for not accommodating under that discretion, it had given sufficient explanation of its refusal. The discretion under LGA 2000 s2 had been exercised by making available a deposit-guarantee scheme to help those in the claimant's circumstances to access private sector accommodation. The council had completed a Children Act 1989 assessment of the child's needs and if the outcome of that was unsatisfactory it was for the child rather than the claimant to challenge it.

See also *R (Badu) v Lambeth LBC* (U6.1).

U6.5   **R (J) v Enfield LBC and Secretary of State for Health (Intervener)**
[2002] EWHC 432 (Admin); (2002) 5 CCLR 434; [2002] HLR 38; [2002] LGR 390; [2002] 2 FLR 1; (2002) *Times* 18 April

LGA 2000 s2 could be used to prevent infringement of art 8 rights

The claimant came to the UK from Ghana in 1995. She overstayed the period permitted on her visa. Her daughter was born in February 2000 and during her ante-natal care the claimant was diagnosed as being HIV positive. In July 2001 she was threatened with homelessness and applied to the council for accommodation for herself and her daughter. She had applied for leave to remain in the UK in July 2000, but that application was not determined. As an overstayer she was ineligible for assistance under Housing Act 1996 Parts 6 or 7, but the council carried out a community care assessment. It decided that the claimant was at low risk and required minimal care and support notwithstanding that it accepted she would lose her accommodation. In subsequent judicial review proceedings the claimant put in 'fresh and powerful medical evidence' but the council refused to provide accommodation under National Assistance Act 1948 s21 on the basis that her need for care and attention resulted solely from her destitution (s21(1A)).

Elias J held that the new medical evidence had been insufficiently considered. He declined to order the council to accommodate under s21 because it needed an opportunity to obtain its own medical evidence and investigate further its concerns about the claimant's means. However, even if accommodation were provided under s21, that would not assist the claimant's child. The judge held that he was bound by the Court of Appeal decision in *R (A) v Lambeth LBC* (later held to have been decided per incuriam by the Court of Appeal in *R (W) v Lambeth LBC* [2002] EWCA

613 (see U4.2 for the House of Lords decision)) to hold that neither accommodation nor money to pay for accommodation could be provided under Children Act 1989 s17 even if the council accepted that the child was in need. In those circumstances, he held that ECHR article 8 would be engaged because the family faced separation by the reception of the child into care. The council conceded that the claimant's accommodation problems could not justify the child being taken into care and that the conditions in article 8(2) could not be satisfied. In those circumstances, the statutory safety net would fail the claimant and her convention rights would be infringed. However, the Secretary of State for Health contended that the council had a wide-ranging power under Local Government Act 2000 s2(1) to 'do anything' to promote or improve the 'social well-being' of their area. By s2(4)(b) that included a power to 'give financial assistance to any person'. The limit placed on the exercise of the s2 power by s3 was not invoked by the restrictions on eligibility for support under Housing Act 1996 or Children Act 1989. The power could be used to provide financial assistance to the claimant to secure accommodation for herself and her child. Accordingly, the statutory framework was capable of preventing an infringement of the claimant's convention rights.

Cf *R (PB) v Haringey LBC* (U8.10), *R (Khan) v Oxfordshire CC* (U7.5) regarding LGA 2000 s2.

See *R (M) v Slough BC* (U7.6) regarding s21(1A) and HIV positive applicants. See also Nationality Immigration and Asylum Act 2002 Sch 3.

U6.6   *R (P) v Camden LBC*

[2004] EWHC 55 (Admin), 14 January 2004

Reasonable to consider wife would accommodate applicant who could alternatively return to USA

Mr P was an American national who lived in the UK. He was married to a British national who had a tenancy of a flat. He was subject to immigration control, the terms of which included a condition that he could not have recourse to public funds. He suffered from mental health problems. At times he had received support from relatives in the USA. Although both he and his wife wanted their marriage to succeed, she said that she was unable to live with Mr P when he was ill. In October 2003, he was admitted to a psychiatric unit. On his discharge, his wife felt unable to live with him and he applied to Camden for assistance under National Assistance Act 1948 s21. Following an assessment, Camden concluded that it was not under a duty to provide assistance since accommodation was otherwise available to him. He could reasonably live with his wife and, failing that, he could return to the United States and obtain assistance there. Camden's assessment was that it was not breaching his rights under ECHR article 8. Mr P sought judicial review of the assessment, claiming that Camden's assessment was irrational.

   Richards J dismissed the application. It was reasonably open to Camden to conclude that P's wife would not leave the claimant without accommodation. In any case, it had been reasonable for the authority to conclude that the claimant would be able to obtain assistance in the United States.

There was no basis on which it could be said that the Mr P's rights under ECHR article 8 had been infringed.

U6.7 *R (Salih) v Secretary of State for the Home Department*
[2003] EWHC 2273 (Admin); (2003) *Times* 13 October; 8 October 2003
Policy of not informing failed asylum-seekers of hard cases support unlawful

Mr Salih was a Kurd from Northern Iraq. In October 2002 he was notified that his claim for asylum had failed and informed that his support under Immigration and Asylum Act 1999 s95 would end 21 days later. He was not informed of the possibility of 'hard cases' support under Asylum and Immigration Act 1999 s4. The Home Secretary's policy was to restrict such support to persons who cannot travel because of physical impediment or whose cases are otherwise exceptional, provided that they fulfil stringent conditions relating to their need for support. In 2001 that policy was extended to Iraqis unable to return to Northern Iraq owing to the lack of a safe route and to people who have applied for judicial review of the decision to reject their asylum claim. Mr Salih became aware of, and applied for, hard cases support on obtaining specialist advice. He sought judicial review of the Home Secretary's failure to notify him and others of the availability of hard cases support and an eight-week delay between making the application and support being provided. The Home Secretary's justification for the policy of not informing failed asylum-seekers of hard cases support was to see if they could find an avenue of support other than public funds.

Stanley Burnton J held that the policy of the secretary of state not to inform failed asylum-seekers of the availability of the discretionary statutory scheme for the provision of accommodation was unlawful. It was not consistent with the constitutional imperative that statute law be made known for the government to withhold information about its policy relating to the exercise of a statutory power. On principle, the hard cases support policy should be made known to those who might need to avail themselves of it. The judge accepted the criticisms made of the delay in providing support but considered that each case must be considered on its merits and refused to give guidelines.

See also *R (Matembera) v Secretary of State for Home Department* [2007] EWHC 2334 (Admin); December 2007 *Legal Action* 19 regarding delays in decisions under s4.

U7 ## National Assistance Act 1948 s21(1A)

National Assistance Act 1948 s21(1A), introduced by Immigration and Asylum Act 1999 s116, excludes some people from assistance under s21 (see U6) where their need for care arises solely from their destitution. It provides:

> A person to whom section 115 of the Immigration and Asylum Act 1999 (exclusion from benefits) applies may not be provided with residential accommodation under section (1)(a) if his need for care and attention has arisen solely –
> (a) because he is destitute; or

 (b) because of the physical effects, or anticipated physical effects, of being
   destitute.

Immigration and Asylum Act 1999 s115 broadly applies to a non-EEA
national who (a) requires leave to enter and remain in the UK but does not
have it, or (b) has such leave but subject to a condition that he or she does
not have recourse to public funds, or (c) was granted such leave as a result
of a maintenance undertaking.

 A person who would be excluded from assistance on the basis of his or
her immigration status but who satisfies the more restrictive needs test in
s21(1A) is commonly referred to as 'destitute plus'.

House of Lords

U7.1 *R (Westminster CC) v National Asylum Support Service*
[2002] UKHL 38; [2002] 1 WLR 2956; [2002] 4 All ER 654; [2002] HLR 58; (2002) 5
CCLR 511; [2003] LGR 23; (2002) *Times* 18 October; 17 October 2002 (also known as
R (Westminster CC) v Secretary of State for the Home Department)

*Infirm destitute asylum-seekers are the responsibility of local authorities, not
NASS*

Mrs Y-Ahmad came to the UK with her daughter and sought asylum. She
was not only destitute but also suffered from spinal cancer and required
special facilities as a result of that condition. Westminster argued that
the burden to support and accommodate destitute asylum-seekers was
removed in its entirety from local government to central government under
the Immigration and Asylum Act 1999 (Part VI of which made provision
for support of destitute asylum-seekers and s116 of which amended National Assistance Act 1948 by introducing s21(1A)). It contended that Mrs
Y-Ahmad and her daughter were entitled to support provided by NASS
under Immigration and Asylum Act 1999 s95. NASS claimed that the burden was moved to central government only in relation to asylum-seekers
whose need arose solely from their destitution rather than because they
were also sick, elderly or disabled and that Westminster was obliged to
provide accommodation under s21. NASS conceded that, if Westminster
was not obliged to accommodate and support Mrs Y-Ahmad, it would do
so under Immigration and Asylum Act 1999 s95. Westminster's judicial
review and appeal to the Court of Appeal were dismissed and it appealed
to the House of Lords.

 The House of Lords dismissed Westminster's appeal. Local authorities
are obliged to provide accommodation for destitute asylum-seekers who
are in need of care and attention and whose need does not arise solely
from destitution but also arises from infirmity. Lord Hoffman said:

> The use of the word 'solely' [in s21(1A)] makes it clear that only the able
> bodied destitute are excluded from the powers and duties of s21(1)(a). The
> infirm destitute remain within. Their need for care and attention arises be-
> cause they are infirm as well as destitute. They would need care and atten
> tion even if they were wealthy. They would not, of course, need accommo-
> dation, but that is not where section 21(1A) draws the line.

As support was available to infirm asylum-seekers under National Assistance Act 1948 s21 they could not be deemed destitute for the purposes of

Immigration and Asylum Act 1999 s95(1) and were excluded from such support.

See *R (O) v Haringey LBC* (U7.8) for the position where an infirm destitute applicant has non-infirm destitute children.

Court of Appeal

U7.2 *Croydon LBC; Hackney LBC v R (AW, A and Y)*
[2007] EWCA Civ 266 (Admin); (2007) 9 CCLR 225; [2007] LGR 417; (2007) *Times* 11 May; 4 April 2007

Local authorities are responsible under s21 for 'destitute plus' failed asylum-seekers who make purported fresh claims for asylum, not NASS under hard cases support

The claimants were asylum-seekers who were held not to have made their claims for asylum as soon as reasonably practicable after entering the UK. As such they were in the UK unlawfully by virtue of Nationality, Immigration and Asylum Act 2002 (NIAA 2002) s11. After their asylum claims failed they purported to make fresh claims for asylum. (Such claims are only accepted and recorded as a claim for asylum in limited circumstances and, unless and until accepted and recorded, a claimant does not regain the status of an asylum-seeker.) Y's claim was not accepted and the Secretary of State for the Home Department (SSHD) had not made a decision whether or not to accept those made by AW and A. Removal directions had not been issued against them. The claimants claimed to be 'destitute plus' and applied to the authorities for assistance under National Assistance Act 1948 s21. Their applications were refused. Within judicial review proceedings (*R (AW) v Croydon LBC* [2005] EWHC 2950 (Admin); 16 December 2005) in which the SSHD was an interested party, the parties sought a preliminary ruling on three distinct matters:

1) Is a failed asylum-seeker who is in the UK in breach of the immigration laws excluded from assistance under s21 by NIAA 2002 Sch 3 para 7?
   Held: Yes, unless provision is necessary in order to avoid a breach of ECHR rights. (Sch 3 para 6(1) excludes from assistance failed asylum-seekers who fail to co-operate with removal directions. Although the claimants were not excluded by that provision, they were caught by para 7 which provides that a person unlawfully in the UK, except an asylum-seeker, is excluded. Failed asylum-seekers unlawfully in the UK were excluded by para 7.)

2) If a failed asylum-seeker satisfies the criteria under s21(1) and (1A) and the provision of support is necessary to avoid a breach of Convention rights, is the support to be provided by a local authority under s21 or the secretary of state under Immigration and Asylum Act 1999 s4 ('hard cases' support)?
   Held: Provision is to be made by the local authority under s21.

3) If article 3 of the Convention threshold is engaged does the making of a purported fresh claim for asylum always make it necessary for support to be provided pending a decision by the secretary of state whether to accept and record the claim?

Held: No, the public body could have regard to all the relevant circumstances. However, 'in many cases – possibly the great majority – it may well be inappropriate for the public body to embark on any consideration of the purported fresh claim' and it should provide support.

The local authorities appealed against the second finding.

The Court of Appeal dismissed the appeal. Following what was described as a 'paper chase' through the relevant provisions it was held that, as regards the division of responsibilities between local authorities and the secretary of state, the position of failed asylum-seekers was no different to that of asylum-seekers as determined in *R (Westminster CC) v NASS* (U7.1). The destitute plus were the responsibility of local authorities under s21 and the secretary of state was prohibited from providing hard cases support.

See also: *R (Binomugisha) v Southwark LBC* (U8.6).

U7.3   *R v Wandsworth LBC ex p O; R v Leicester CC ex p Bhikha*
[2000] 1 WLR 2539; [2000] 4 All ER 590; (2000) 3 CCLR 237; [2000] LGR 591; (2001) 33 HLR 419; 22 June 2000, CA

Sction 21(1A) applies where an applicant's need for care and attention is to any material extent made more acute by circumstances other than destitution; s21 concerned with need – unlawful presence irrelevant

The claimants were subject to immigration control and 'overstayers'. One had severe psychiatric problems and the other had recurring cancer of the duodenum which required continuous medical treatment. Both were destitute. They applied to the Secretary of State for the Home Department for exceptional leave to remain (ELR) in the United Kingdom, on the ground that there was credible medical evidence that return to their countries of nationality would result in substantial damage to their physical or psychological health. Both appellants were ineligible for benefits and became destitute. They applied to their local authorities for accommodation and support under National Assistance Act 1948 s21. In reliance on *R v Brent LBC ex p D* (U6.2) the authorities refused assistance to the appellants on the ground that, although they might suffer serious injury as the result of having to go back to live in their countries of origin, they were nonetheless able to travel and leave the United Kingdom without risking life or serious injury. Accordingly, it was contended, the principle that no one may take advantage of their own wrongdoing applied to them and they could not be assisted under s21 if they remained unlawfully in the UK.

The Court of Appeal held that this principle did not apply in the context of National Assistance Act 1948 s21. Section 21 was concerned exclusively with questions of need. Unlawful conduct – including unlawful presence in the United Kingdom – did not preclude eligibility for assistance. *R v Brent LBC ex p D* was wrong to hold that a public policy exclusion applies to persons other than those unable to travel. Simon Brown LJ said:

> ... s21(1) affords the very last possibility of relief, the final hope of keeping the needy off the streets. Not even illegality should to my mind bar an applicant who otherwise qualifies for support ... the local authority has no business with the applicant's immigration status save only for the purpose of learning why the care and attention 'is not otherwise available to

them' as s21(1) requires – and indeed ... for reporting such applications to the immigration authorities if they conclude that the Home Office is unaware of their presence here. In my judgment, however, it should be for the Home Office to decide (and ideally decide speedily) any claim for ELR and to ensure that those unlawfully here are promptly removed, rather than for local authorities to, so to speak, starve immigrants out of the country by withholding last resort assistance from those who today will by definition be not merely destitute but for other reasons too in urgent need of care and attention ... this particular benefit is of such a nature that, where otherwise claimable, it should not be withheld on the public policy ground of illegality.

The Court of Appeal also considered the meaning and effect of the new s21(1A), inserted by Immigration and Asylum Act 1999 s116. On this Simon Brown LJ said:

The appellants ... submit that if an applicant's need for care and attention is to any material extent made more acute by some circumstances other than the mere lack of accommodation and funds, then, despite being subject to immigration control, he qualifies for assistance. Other relevant circumstances include, of course, age, illness and disability, all of which are expressly mentioned in s21(1) itself. If, for example, an immigrant, as well as being destitute, is old, ill or disabled, he is likely to be yet more vulnerable and less well able to survive than if he were merely destitute ... I have not the slightest hesitation in preferring [this approach]. The word 'solely' in the new section is a strong one and its purpose there seems to me evident. Assistance under the 1948 Act is, it need hardly be emphasised, the last refuge for the destitute. If there are to be immigrant beggars on our streets, then let them at least not be old, ill or disabled.

Note: Lord Hoffman in *R (Westminster CC) v NASS* (U7.1) at para [50] expressly left open the correctness of this test. However, in *R (Mani) v Lambeth LBC* (U7.7) and *R (M) v Slough BC* (U7.6) the Court of Appeal has treated itself as bound by the interpretation adopted in *ex p O*. The claimants would now also have to contend with the provisions in Nationality Immigration and Asylum Act 2002 Sch 3 (see U8).

U7.4　*R (A) v National Asylum Support Service and Waltham Forest LBC*
[2003] EWCA Civ 1473; [2004] 1 WLR 752; [2004] 1 All ER 15; (2003) 6 CCLR 538; [2004] LGR 1; [2004] HLR 24; [2004] 1 FLR 704; (2003) *Times* 31 October; 23 October 2003 (see U10.1)

Children cannot rely on s21; disabled children of asylum-seekers only able to rely on asylum support

U7.5　*R (Khan) v Oxfordshire CC*
[2004] EWCA Civ 309; [2004] LGR 257; [2004] HLR 41; (2004) *Times* 24 March

Domestic violence did not render applicant's needs more acute and s21(1A) applied; assistance under LGA 2000 prohibited

Ms Khan, a Pakistani national, was granted leave to enter the UK on the basis of her marriage. Her marriage broke down as a result of her husband's violence. After being kidnapped twice, she escaped and found a place in a women's refuge. She was not eligible for assistance under Housing Act 1996 Part VII or for state benefits. She applied to the council for financial assistance. It carried out an assessment of her needs under

National Health Service and Community Care Act 1990 s47, and stated that her needs were for safe and secure accommodation. On 20 June 2002, the council wrote to her stating that it had decided that she did not qualify for support under National Assistance Act 1948 s21 because she had 'no significant needs either mentally or physically'. In a later statement, the council indicated that Ms Khan did not suffer from a physical or learning disability, could take steps through the police to prevent violence from her husband and did not suffer physical or mental deterioration and that there were no circumstances, other than lack of accommodation or funds, that made her needs more acute. Any other need for care and attention would arise from destitution caused by lack of funds and meeting such a need was debarred by National Assistance Act s21(1A). Moses J granted her application for judicial review ([2002] EWHC 2211 Admin; [2003] HLR 23).

The Court of Appeal allowed the council's appeal. The correct test in considering an application under s21(1A) is that, if an applicant's need for care and attention is to any material extent made more acute by some circumstances other than mere lack of accommodation and funds, then, despite being subject to immigration control, he or she qualifies for assistance. In this case, the judge had been in error in holding that the defendant had considered that domestic violence could not have made the need for care and attention more acute. In the circumstances, the defendant had acknowledged that domestic violence could, in certain circumstances, make the need for care and attention more acute, but had concluded that it had not done so in this case. That was a conclusion to which it had been entitled to come. Second, Moses J had been entitled to find that s21(1A) prevented the defendant from providing the claimant with accommodation under Local Government Act 2000 s2. The effect of s3(1) is to prohibit the doing of 'anything' which a local authority is unable to do by virtue of any prohibition on its powers contained in any enactment. In this case, the 'thing' which was under consideration was the provision of residential accommodation to persons who, but for the prohibition in s 21(1A), would be entitled to accommodation. The very reason why s3(1) had been enacted was to prevent s2 from being used to do that which was prohibited by another statute. It followed that accommodation could not be provided under s2(4)(f), and the making of payments for accommodation under s2(4)(b) could not be provided under s 21(1A).

Cf *R (J) v Enfield LBC* (U6.5) regarding LGA 2000 s2.

U7.6   ***R (M) v Slough BC***
[2006] EWCA Civ 655; (2006) 9 CCLR 438; [2007] LGR 225; (2006) *Times* 13 June; 25 May 2006

'Care and attention' could extend to provision of shelter, warmth, food and other basic necessities

M came to the UK from Zimbabwe on a visitor's visa. He was later diagnosed as being HIV positive and as possibly having AIDS. He was provided with retroviral medication to manage his condition. He overstayed his visa and later sought leave to remain under ECHR article 3, stating that if he was returned to Zimbabwe he would be unable to receive effective medical treatment and would die within a year of returning. As a result of this application he came within the definition of an asylum-seeker (Nationality Immigration and Asylum Act 2002 s18(3)). He was staying with a cousin but that accommodation was due to end. He required accommodation which would include provision for refrigeration of his medication. He applied to Slough BC for assistance under National Assistance Act 1948 s21. Following an assessment and a series of reviews Slough concluded that M did not qualify for accommodation under s21 as he was able-bodied and could care for himself. He was not in need of 'care and attention'. If he were to become homeless, any physical effects of this would solely result from his destitution and accordingly s21(1A) debarred him from assistance that might otherwise have been provided under s21. M applied for judicial review. The issue was whether housing should be provided by NASS (on the basis that the claimant had no need of care and attention) or by Slough.

In judicial review proceedings, Collins J ([2004] EWHC 1109 (Admin), 27 April 2004) held that responsibility lay on Slough. Slough appealed. By the time the appeal was heard, M's claim under article 3 had been refused but he had successfully appealed against removal directions. The secretary of state had applied for a statutory review of that decision which was ous-tanding.

The Court of Appeal dismissed Slough's appeal. Maurice Kay LJ gave the judgment of the court.

1) Did the case come within s21(1)(a)?

It was implicit in the decision of *R v Westminster CC ex p M, P, A and X* (U5.4) that '... "care and attention" was not to be interpreted in the narrow way for which [Slough] contends but could extend to the provision of shelter, warmth, food and other basic necessities' [para 15]. The court was bound by that authority.

2) Did s21(1A) apply?

R v Wandsworth LBC ex p O (U7.3) set out the test. The judge had been right to direct himself that it could not be said, on the facts of this case, that the claimant's need for such assistance would derive 'solely' from his destitution as s21(1A) requires.

3) Was M still eligible for assistance?

After considering the legislation relating to the definition of asylum-seekers it was held that M was no longer an asylum-seeker. As an over-stayer he was in the UK in breach of the immigration laws and was caught by Nationality Immigration and Asylum Act 2002 Sch 3 para 7. This denied him assistance under s21 unless this was necessary in order to avoid a breach of his ECHR rights.

4) The ECHR safeguard

It was noted that in *R (AW) v Croydon LBC and others* ([2005] EWHC 2950 (Admin); see U7.2 for Court of Appeal decision) it was held that if an applicant was 'destitute plus' and provision of support was necessary to prevent a breach of ECHR, that provison was to be made by the local authority under s21 rather than by the secretary of state under Immigration and Asylum Act 1999 s4 ('hard cases' support). The local authority now needed to consider whether M had any further entitlement based on his ECHR rights as an exception to his exclusion from assistance under Sch 3.

See also: *R (N) v Lambeth LBC* [2006] EWHC 3427 (Admin), 20 December 2006 (application of council's general eligibility criteria formulated under FACS guidance not sufficient to address s21(1A) test in relation to applicant with AIDS). An appeal to the Court of Appeal became academic and the merits of the case were therefore not fully considered (see *R(N) v Lambeth LBC* [2007] EWCA Civ 862; 25 July 2007).

U7.7   R (Mani) v Lambeth LBC

[2003] EWCA Civ 836; [2004] HLR 5; [2004] LGR 35; (2002) *Times* 23 July; 9 July 2003

Destitute plus test in R v Wandsworth ex p O *applied equally to asylum-seekers and non-asylum-seekers; s21 not limited to those whose need for care and attention is accommodation related*

Mr Mani was a destitute asylum-seeker. He suffered from a congenital abnormality of his right leg, which was half the length of his left leg. His mobility was impaired and he experienced pain when walking with crutches or when using a prosthesis. On days when he was in pain he could not undertake basic tasks such as bed-making, vacuuming and carrying heavy shopping. He was also vulnerable to psychotic illness which led to a reduced capacity to cope in times of stress. Lambeth considered that it was not obliged to assist him under National Assistance Act 1948 s21 as his need was not an accommodation-related need. He was therefore the responsibility of NASS. Mr Mani sought judicial review. Wilson J allowed the claim ([2002] EWHC 735 (Admin)).

The Court of Appeal dismissed Lambeth's appeal. Simon Brown LJ, giving the judgment of the court, reviewed the development of the relevant jurisprudence from the exclusion of asylum-seekers from mainstream benefits (*R v Westminster CC ex p M, P, A and X* (U5.4)) through to the introduction of s21(1A) (*R v Wandsworth LBC ex p O* (U7.3) and *R (Westminster CC) v NASS* (U7.1)). Lambeth's contention that s21(1)(a) applied, not to all those who had a need for care and attention, but solely and exclusively to those who had a need care and attention calling for the provision of accommodation – an 'accommodation-related need' – was rejected as 'an impossible one in light of the authorities'. Subsection 21(1A) could not alter the meaning of s21(1)(a) and suddenly confine its scope to accommodating those who have 'an accommodation related need'. None of the claimants in the previous cases, all of whom were more disabled than Mr Mani, would have required s21 accommodation had they been British citizens, yet they were all held to qualify for s21 accommodation. Had they been British citizens they would have been housed as homeless persons and their accommodation needs would have been met under that legislation rather than under s21.

The test laid down in *R v Wandsworth LBC ex p O* applies equally to asylum-seekers and to non-asylum-seekers and must remain so unless the House of Lords decides otherwise or parliament adjusts the responsibility between NASS and local authorities. Mr Mani had a need for care and attention which did not arise solely because he was destitute and he was entitled to assistance under s21. Asylum Support Regulations 2000 SI No 704 require local authorities to ignore any asylum support that is, or might be, provided. Lambeth could not avoid its responsibility under s21 by reference to Immigration and Asylum Act 1999 s95 and NASS's willingness to provide Mr Mani with accommodation.

The House of Lords refused Lambeth's petition for leave to appeal.

U7.8 **R (O) v Haringey LBC**
[2004] EWCA Civ 535; [2004] FLR 476; (2004) 7 CCLR 310; [2004] LGR 672; [2004] HLR 44; (2004) *Times* 27 May

Where applicant infirm and destitute but children merely destitute, local authority responsible for applicant and NASS responsible for children

Mrs O, a Ugandan citizen, married a man lawfully in the UK. After eight years she left the matrimonial home, with the couple's children, because of the husband's violence. She applied to Haringey and it provided her and the children with accommodation and subsistence. Mrs O applied for exceptional leave to remain in the UK on human rights grounds. That had the legal effect of making her an 'asylum-seeker'. Haringey decided that as she was HIV positive it owed her a continuing accommodation duty as an 'infirm destitute' under the National Assistance Act 1948 s21. However, the council decided it could not be responsible for the children (who continued to live with her) under the 1948 Act or the Children Act 1989. It said they had become the responsibility of the National Asylum Support Service (NASS). In proceedings for judicial review of that decision, Mrs O and NASS claimed that the whole family was the council's responsibility. Ouseley J dismissed the claim and Mrs O and NASS appealed.

The Court of Appeal held that: (1) Mrs O was a destitute person in need of care and attention and that the council was right to find it owed her a s21 duty; (2) that duty did not extend to accommodating her children; (3) responsibility for the children fell on NASS rather than on the local authority and they were to be treated as 'destitute' even though actually sheltered with their mother; and (4) the appropriate practical solution was for the council to accommodate the whole family with NASS meeting the cost of accommodating the children.

U7.9 **R (Pajaziti and Pajaziti) v Lewisham LBC**
[2007] EWCA Civ 1351; 18 December 2007

Council had not addressed whether need for accommodation made more acute by depressive illness

Mr and Mrs Pajaziti came to the UK from Kosovo as asylum-seekers. Mr Pajaziti had been living in London for almost 10 years when NASS sought to disperse him and his family to accommodation outside London. They then applied to the council for assistance under National Assistance Act 1948 s21 claiming that they were 'destitute plus' and overcame the restriction to s21 support contained in s21(1A). They relied on a consultant psychiatrist's report that indicated that they were both suffering from major depressive episodes associated with periods in detention and also contributed to by their current concerns including their destitution. The psychiatrist indicated that they were able to receive treatment through the

NHS but that the most powerful intervention would be to offer them accommodation in London. Lewisham posed the question of whether any of their needs for care and attention had been made materially more acute by circumstances other than a need for accommodation and funds. It considered that there was no unmet need for care and attention because the needs could be met by primary healthcare. It refused them assistance. The Pajazitis' application for judicial review was refused.

The Court of Appeal allowed an appeal. Although the council had asked itself the right question, the inference was that it either misunderstood its true sense or in fact answered a different question. Its decision letter proceeded on the erroneous basis that at all stages the Pajazitis' care and attention needs were *solely* for medical services, including NHS services in respect of their psychiatric disorders. However, they also had an additional need for accommodation. Were they not ill, s21(1A) would exclude them from the right to s21 assistance in order to meet their need. But they were ill and the crucial question was whether their need for accommodation was made more acute by their depressive disorders and the fact that, absent any s21 assistance, they would have to cope with that disorder on the streets, albeit with the benefit of NHS counselling. The council had not answered that question and its decision was quashed and remitted for reconsideration. It was observed that arguably only a decision in the Pajazitis' favour was lawfully possible on the available material.

High Court

U7.10   *R (H) v Kingston upon Thames RLBC*
[2002] EWHC 3158 (Admin); (2002) 6 CCLR 240

No justification to differentiate community care from health needs under s21; costs

The claimant sought assistance with accommodation from the council for herself and for her daughter under National Assistance Act 1948 s21. They were homeless asylum-seekers and had advanced HIV. The council assessed them as being in need of stable accommodation and counselling. It contended that there were no care needs of the type normally provided by social services and that such needs had to exist before a duty under s21 would arise in the light of s21(1A). The claimant sought judicial review and an interim order. Permission was granted and the council agreed to provide accommodation pending trial. Shortly before trial, when the claimant was diagnosed with breast cancer, the council agreed to accommodate her. The council resisted an application for costs on the grounds that: (1) there was a genuine dispute as to the scope of the statutory provisions and (2) the claimant had not used the complaints procedure.

Elias J awarded the claimant her costs. The council's argument regarding s21 was unsustainable in the light of *R v Wandsworth ex p O* (U7.3). There was no justification to differentiate between those who are in need of the kind of services provided by social services (community care needs) and those who have a health need. The claimant had been justified in proceeding by way of judicial review rather than the complaints procedure as she had an urgent need for an order for accommodation. The council had not suggested that the complaints procedure might provide a solution to the issue (for example, by agreeing to provide accommodation itself pending the outcome of the complaint) until the substantive matter was resolved, shortly before the final hearing.

U8 Nationality Immigration and Asylum Act 2002 Sch 3

Nationality Immigration and Asylum Act 2002 introduced wide-ranging exclusions to assistance under a range of 'safety net' welfare provisions. Section 54 merely provides that Sch 3 shall have effect. Schedule 3 denies 'ineligible persons' assistance under specified statutory provisions unless this would breach a person's ECHR rights or rights under EC Treaties (para 3). British citizens or children are never ineligible under Sch 3 (para 2).

The support or assistance denied, listed in paragraph 1, includes that under:

a) National Assistance Act 1948 s21
b) Children Act 1989 s17, s23C, s24A or s24B
c) Housing Act 1996 s188(3), s204(4) (accommodation pending review or appeal)
d) Local Government Act 2000 s2 (promotion of well being – see below)
e) a provision of Immigration and Asylum Act 1999
f) a provision of Nationality Immigration and Asylum Act 2002.

The classes of ineligible persons are:

1) A person with refugee status abroad (para 4)
2) An EEA national (para 5)
3) A failed asylum-seeker who fails to cooperate with removal directions (para 6)
4) A person in the UK unlawfully (who is not an asylum-seeker) (para 7)
5) A person treated as an asylum-seeker for the purposes of asylum support by virtue of having dependent children and who is certified as not having taken reasonable steps to leave the UK (para 7A). (Introduced by Asylum (Treatment of Claimants Act) 2004 s9. This provision was introduced on a pilot basis which has ended. It appears likely that it will not now be implemented.)

The dependants of such persons, except those within group 4, are also ineligible.

The Withholding and Withdrawal of Support (Travel Assistance and Temporary Accommodation) Regulations 2002 SI No 3078 (the Withholding Regs) were made under Sch 3 paras 8–10. A local authority is empowered to make travel arrangements for the return of EEA refugees and nationals and to make arrangements to accommodate such persons with dependent children pending travel. An authority does not have the power under the Withholding Regs to make travel arrangements for persons in other ineligible groups but does have the power to accommodate such persons with dependent children who have not failed to co-operate with removal directions.

Court of Appeal

U8.1   *Croydon LBC; Hackney LBC v R (AW, A and Y)*
[2007] EWCA Civ 266 (Admin); (2007) 9 CCLR 225; (2007) *Times* 11 May; 4 April 2007 (see U7.2)

A failed asylum-seeker who is unlawfully in the UK is ineligible under Sch 3; in most cases support necessary to avoid ECHR breach where fresh claim for asylum made

U8.2   *R (Grant) v Lambeth LBC*
[2004] EWCA Civ 1711; [2005] 1 WLR 1781; [2005] HLR 27; [2005] LGR 81; (2005) *Times* 5 January; 16 December 2004

Claimant's ECHR rights could be met by returning her and children to home country

The claimant, a Jamaican national, came to the UK in 1992 on a visitor's visa which she overstayed. In 1995 she married a British national. In 1998 her two children from a previous relationship joined her. In 2000 she had a child by her husband. In 2002 they separated. The claimant made various applications to remain in the UK, all of which were unsuccessful. She was unlawfully present in the UK but had not been made subject to removal directions. In 1993 she became homeless and applied to Lambeth for assistance. She was ineligible under Housing Act 1996 Parts 6 and 7 and was not entitled to welfare benefits. As a result of Nationality, Immigration and Asylum Act 2002 Sch 3 she was ineligible for assistance under various provisions including Children Act 1989 s17, National Assistance Act 1948 s21 and Local Government Act 2000 (LGA 2000) s2 except to the extent necessary to avoid a breach of her ECHR rights.

Lambeth carried out an assessment of the children's needs under the Children Act 1989 and concluded that it would be in the best interests of the claimant and her children to return to Jamaica. Under the Withholding and Withdrawal of Support (Travel Assistance and Temporary Accommodation) Regulations 2002 SI No 3078 (the Withholding Regs) Lambeth had a discretion to accommodate a person unlawfully in the UK, who had a dependent child and who had not failed to co-operate with removal directions. Lambeth decided that it would exercise that power and provide temporary accommodation to the claimant pending her return to Jamaica, which it proposed to fund using its powers under LGA 2000 s2. Its evidence was that the decision had taken account of the need to preserve the council's scarce resources. Mitting J allowed an application for judicial review and the council appealed. The claimant asserted that Lambeth had no power to meet the travel and associated costs of an overstayer under Local Government Act 2000 s2 and that it could only avoid a breach of ECHR article 8 by continuing to accommodate her pending any removal directions.

The Court of Appeal allowed Lambeth's appeal. It was entitled to make arrangements for the claimant's return to Jamaica, and was required to support her under the Withholding Regs only until such time as she could return. The effect of Nationality, Immigration and Asylum Act 2002 Sch 3 was that the power conferred by LGA 2000 s2 could be used, to the extent that it was necessary to avoid a breach of ECHR rights, to fund the return of persons unlawfully present in the UK. In the instant case the council's decision had been that the ECHR rights of the claimant could be met by the funding arrangement it proposed. That decision was not unlawful.

U8.3   **R (K) v Lambeth LBC**

[2003] EWCA Civ 1150; [2004] 1 WLR 272; (2003) 6 CCLR 484; [2004] HLR 15; [2003] FLR 1217; (2003) *Times* 6 August; 31 July 2003 (commonly referred to as *R (Kimani) v Lambeth*)

Sch 3 applied where no impediment to claimant returning to home country

Ms Kimani was a Kenyan national who arrived in the UK in March 1998 with her 4-year-old son. She claimed asylum and was granted temporary admission. Her asylum claim and appeal were rejected. In May 2000 she married an Irish national with a right of residence in the UK. She applied for permission to reside in the UK as his spouse under Immigration (European Economic Area) Regulations 2000 SI No 232 para 12 which conferred the right of residence on a spouse of an EEA citizen. This was refused on the basis that the marriage was a marriage of convenience. She appealed against this decision and that appeal was outstanding. She retained the right of temporary admission pending the appeal. Ms Kimani also remained an asylum-seeker for the purposes of Immigration and Asylum Act 1999 Part VI as, although her claim for asylum had failed, she had a dependent child. She was initially supported by Lambeth under Part VI. (This was at a time prior to NASS taking over all such responsibility.) When Nationality Immigration and Asylum Act 2002 Sch 3 came into force, Lambeth refused to continue support contending that, as the dependant of a non-British EEA national, she was excluded from assistance (Sch 3 para 5). Ms Kimani contended that she was not to be treated as the spouse nor, therefore, the dependant of an EEA national where it was asserted that her marriage was a marriage of convenience. Furthermore, to deny her assistance would breach her ECHR rights.

The Court of Appeal held that Ms Kimani was a spouse and was within Sch 3 para 5. The removal of support did not breach her ECHR rights. There was no impediment to her return to Kenya. She had not contended that it was not viable for her to return to Kenya, although she had asserted that she would not return 'come what may'. She and her husband were already separated and therefore article 8 did not require that she should remain in the UK pending her appeal. A foreign national who, pending the determination of a residence appeal, was entitled to remain in the UK had no right to support out of public funds if there was no impediment to her returning to her home country. Furthermore, it had been open to the judge at first instance to find that she would be able to support herself and her son without the local authority's assistance as she had achieved this in the past.

U8.4   **R (M) v Islington LBC and Secretary of State for the Home Department (interested party)**

[2004] EWCA Civ 235; [2005] 1 WLR 884; [2004] 4 All ER 709; [2004] 2 FLR 867; [2004] LGR 815; (2004) *Times* 22 April; 2 April 2004

Council's power under the Withholding Regs to provide accommodation not time limited; child with British citizenship

The claimant came to the UK from Guyana in 1998 on a visitor's visa, which she overstayed. In 1999 she married an Antiguan with indefinite leave to remain in the UK and in October 2001 she had a daughter who was a British citizen. In August 2002 her husband left her, although he maintained contact with their daughter. In November 2002 M applied for the grant of exceptional leave to remain in the UK on compassionate grounds relating, in particular, to her daughter's connections with the UK and her alleged inability to provide for her in Guyana. That application was pending (it was later refused but an appeal pursued). She was ineligible for support as a result of Nationality, Immigration and Asylum Act 2002 Sch 3 para 7 unless an exception applied. The council assessed the child's needs under Children Act 1989 s17 and decided that it was not prepared to support M and her child in the UK but would fund the purchase of one-way tickets to Guyana for them under s17, on the basis that the return to Guyana would best safeguard and promote the child's welfare. The council agreed to provide accommodation while the travel arrangements were made, under the Withholding and Withdrawal of Support (Travel Assistance and Temporary Accommodation) Regulations 2002 SI No 3078 (the Withholding Regs) reg 3(3). Guidance issued under the Witholding Regs stated that it was preferable for accommodation not to be provided for more than 10 days to persons returning to non-EEA countries. M sought judicial review. Wilson J held that the council was required to do no more than provide short-term temporary accommodation.

The Court of Appeal allowed M's appeal by a majority. A local authority's power was limited under Sch 3 and the Withholding Regs para 3 to the provision of accommodation to a person unlawfully in the UK who has a dependent child, so long as there is no breach of removal directions. The law does not impose a time limit on accommodation provided under the Withholding Regs. It was open to the council to provide accommodation for longer than 10 days and it could be provided until removal directions were made. There is no requirement to accommodate in such circumstances, although in exercising this power, councils must be aware of their obligations under ECHR article 8. The council had to take account of the fact that M had an outstanding application for leave to remain and that her child was a British citizen with whom her father maintained contact. That might leave the council little choice but to offer accommodation.

High Court

U8.5   *Putans v Tower Hamlets LBC*
[2006] EWHC 1634; [2007] HLR 10, 20 June 2006, ChD (see T2.8)

An accession state national not working is prima facie not eligible under Housing Act 1996 Part VII and council has no power to accommodate pending appeal except on human rights grounds

U8.6   *R (Binomugisha) v Southwark LBC*
[2006] EWHC 2254 (Admin); (2007) UKHRR 1200; [2007] 1 FLR 916; 18 September 2006

Decision that return to Uganda would not infringe applicant's ECHR rights was a question for Home Office; question for authority was whether his claim to remain in UK was manifestly ill-founded

The claimant arrived from Uganda as an unaccompanied minor and made an 'in country' claim for asylum. He was accommodated by Southwark under Children Act 1989 s20. His application for asylum failed but he was not to be removed from the UK until he turned 18. The council referred him for counselling because of concerns about his mental health. When he was 18 he applied to the Home Office to remain in the UK on the basis that his removal would so adversely affect his health as to amount to a breach of his right to respect for his private life (article 8). For a time the council supported him as a former relevant child under Children Act 1989 s23. It then decided that it was prevented from providing him with support as a result of Nationality Immigration and Asylum Act 2002 Sch 3. He was assessed by the council as having mild to moderate depression for which, it contended, he could be adequately treated in Uganda. The council considered that Sch 3 para 3 did not apply as the claimant's outstanding article 8 application would not be successful and he could return to Uganda without his ECHR rights being infringed. The claimant contended that the council should assist him under National Assistance Act 1948 s21 and/or Children Act 1989 s23C or 24A. He applied for judicial review.

Deputy Judge Andrew Nicol QC allowed his claim. The council had attempted to ask and answer the same question that awaited determination by the Home Office. The proper question for the authority was whether the claim made to the Home Office was manifestly ill-founded. Where there is an outstanding application with the Home Office on the basis that an applicant's return to his or her home country would violate their article 8 rights, it is only in the clearest of cases that a local authority should make a decision to refuse assistance on the basis that that application was bound to fail [72]. The decision was quashed because it was not inevitable that, on the facts, the council must find the claim manifestly ill-founded. If the council did consider the article 8 application was not manifestly ill founded it would have to go on to consider whether there would be a breach of the claimant's article 3 rights if he was not provided with support. Only if that were the case could support be withdrawn. The claimant was, in any event, entitled to a personal adviser and reviews of his pathway plan under Children Act 1989 as these were a form of advice and not 'support and assistance' caught by Sch 3.

U8.7 ## R (Blackburn-Smith) v Lambeth LBC

[2007] EWHC 767 (Admin); (2007) 10 CCLR 352; 4 April 2007

Claimant could return to Jamaica taking her children with her to avoid art 8 breach

The claimant was a Jamaican national with two young British children. She separated from her British husband who did not maintain contact with the children after their separation. She applied to Lambeth as a homeless person under Housing Act 1996 Part VII. It provided interim accommodation before determining that she was not eligible for assistance under Part VII by virtue of her immigration status. The council's social services department then provided accommodation pending community care and Children Act assessments. Those assessments concluded that the claimant and her husband could themselves make adequate arrangements for the children in the UK or, alternatively, the claimant could return to Jamaica, where she could work, taking the children with her. In the latter case, the council would help with air fares and expenses. As a fall back, the council indicated that it would receive the children into care under Children Act (CA) 1989 s20, if requested. It terminated the claimant's accommodation and financial support. Dobbs J dismissed an application for judicial review. The claimant appealed.

The Court of Appeal dismissed her appeal. It was common ground that the children had been children in 'need' for the purposes of CA 1989 s17 when evicted from the social services accommodation. However, s17 imposed no absolute duty to accommodate either mother or children: R (G) v Barnet LBC (U4.2). In the circumstances of the case the council was entitled to be confident that the children's needs would be met if the claimant returned to Jamaica. Alternatively, it had offered to accommodate the children under a s20 duty but that had been declined. As to the discretion to accommodate the family together under s17 (read with ECHR article 8), there had been no flaw in the council's assessment or conclusions that the children's needs could be met without assistance from the council either in the UK or in Jamaica because:

a) the defendant had considered and acted upon its duty under Section 20 by offering accommodation to the children;
b) it was the claimant who declined the offer;
c) the defendant sought the engagement and assistance of the father and the relatives but was unable to progress these options due to the lack of co-operation of the parties including the claimant;
d) the defendant considered the 'need' of the children under the option of the claimant's returning to Jamaica;
e) the defendant had considered the article 8 rights of the claimant, her children and their father with regard to return to Jamaica and found that they would not be breached;
f) the defendant had to consider the priority needs of others (such as disabled children, children at risk of abuse, children that act as carers, looked after children, children and adults with mental health needs, those with special needs and the elderly) in the light of their finite resources;
g) the defendant's powers were never intended to enable it to act as an alternative welfare agency in circumstances where parliament had determined that the claimant should be excluded from mainstream benefits; and
h) the defendant, when deciding how to exercise its powers, is entitled to have regard to the state's entitlement to control the entry of non-nationals into its territory and to determine to what benefits they are entitled, as evidenced from schedule 3 of [Nationality Immigration and Asylum Act 2002]. [36]

The defendant was entitled to take the view that the claimant could return to Jamaica with the children. If the option to return to Jamaica was not available the council would be required to consider whether the claimant would need to be accommodated with her children in order to avoid a breach of article 8. Separation of mother and child is not automatically an infringement of article 8. Even if it were, there may be justification. Each case needs to be judged on its own particular facts. It was considered that, on the particular facts of the case, such separation might be justified. [37]

U8.8   **R (Conde) v Lambeth LBC**

[2005] EWHC 62 (Admin); [2005] HLR 29; [2005] 2 FLR 98; (2005) 8 CCLR 486; 13 January 2005

No discrimination to refuse EEA national assistance under Children Act 1989 s17

Ms Conde, a Spanish national, came to the United Kingdom with her two children to look for work. Although she initially had accommodation, she became homeless and applied to Lambeth under Part VII. Lambeth refused assistance on the ground that she was not habitually resident in the UK. She then applied for housing assistance under Children Act 1989 s17. That application was refused on the ground that she could house herself and her children in Spain. She claimed that as she was an EEA work-seeker, the refusal to provide her with housing assistance discriminated against her.

Collins J dismissed her application for judicial review. As an EEA national, she was excluded by the Nationality, Immigration and Asylum Act 2002 Sch 3 from the provision of housing assistance under Children Act 1989 s17. As the provision of housing assistance under s17 is not related to the act of seeking work, a refusal to provide housing assistance does not violate rights under the EC Treaty (Nice) article 39. Furthermore, UK nationals in a similar position to Ms Conde would not be housed under s17 so there was no discrimination against her (*R (G) v Barnet LBC* (U4.2)).

U8.9   **R (Mohamed) v Harrow LBC**

[2005] EWHC Admin; [2006] HLR 18; 13 December 2005 (see T2.15)

Provision of accommodation not necessary in order to avoid breach of an EEA national's EC Treaty right to seek work

U8.10   **R (PB) v Haringey LBC**

[2006] EWHC 2255 (Admin); [2007] HLR 13; 18 September 2006

Council needed to address whether applicant's art 8 rights would be contravened by her return to Jamaica while her children remained in the UK

The claimant was a Jamaican national and an 'overstayer', having remained in the UK without leave since 1999. She suffered from moderate depression. She had five children, four of whom were born in the UK. One child, with whom she had regular contact, was living with his father and the other four were subject to care proceedings. The claimant applied to regularise her position in the UK under the Home Office family policy, as she had been living in the UK for over seven years. Her application had not been determined and accordingly she was a person subject to immigration control and was not eligible for assistance under Housing Act 1996 Parts 6 or 7. When she became homeless she applied to Haringey LBC for support under Housing Act 1985 s21 (general powers of management) and National Assistance Act 1948 s21. She argued that, if the council was prevented from exercising its powers under the above Acts, it should exercise its general power of promoting well-being under Local Government Act 2000 s2. Haringey refused to provide assistance. It decided that if PB did have a need for care or attention this arose solely from her destitution and therefore did not entitle her to assistance under National Assistance Act 1948 s21 because of s21(1A). Furthermore, as a person unlawfully in the UK she was excluded from assistance under s21 and the various other provisions set out in Nationality Immigration and Asylum Act 2002 Sch 3. She could avoid what might otherwise be a breach of her article 3 rights by returning to Jamaica. PB sought judicial review.

Deputy Judge Andrew Nicol QC held that:

1) Haringey did not have power to provide accommodation for the claimant under Housing Act 1985 s21. She was not eligible under Housing Act 1996 Part VII and any remaining power to pick and choose tenants under Housing Act 1985 s21 had to be exercised in conformity with Part VII.

2) Haringey's decision that the claimant was not entitled to assistance under National Assistance Act 1948 s21 was legally flawed:
   a) In relation to the s21(1A) issue it decided that her depression stemmed from her destitution but did not ask itself whether this was *solely* as a result of her destitution and the anticipated effects of destitution. Although there was evidence of her financial and housing problems contributing to her depression, there were also repeated references to her anxieties about her children being a further cause.
   b) In relation to the Schedule 3 issue, on the information before the court, the council was not entitled to rely on the claimant being able to avoid destitution and degradation by returning to Jamaica. The council had failed to consider whether the claimant's right to respect for family life under ECHR article 8 would be breached if she was effectively forced to leave the UK while care proceedings were pending. There were also impediments to her returning to Jamaica and pursuing her immigration application from there.

3) Local Government Act 2000 s2 gives local authorities a wide power to assist people but the limit to that power contained in s3 applied, as Haringey was prohibited from providing accommodation under Housing Acts 1996 and 1985.

A quashing order would have been made in relation to the decision under s21 but the claimant in the meantime had been sentenced to 12 months' imprisonment

Cf *R (J) v Enfield LBC* (U6.5) regarding LGA 2000 s2.

U9   Asylum support: Nationality Immigration and Asylum Act 2002 s55

Nationality Immigration and Asylum Act 2002 s55 provides that an asylum-seeker who fails to claim asylum 'as soon as reasonably practicable' after arrival in the UK cannot be provided with support under Immigration and Asylum Act 1999 ss4, 98 or 95. This exclusion does not apply to asylum-seekers with dependent children. Furthermore, it does not prevent support to the extent necessary to avoid breach of an applicant's ECHR rights (s55(5)).

Following a large number of claims issued in the Administrative Court and successful challenges to the implementation of s55, culminating in the House of Lords decision in *R (Limbuela, Tesema and Adam) v Secretary of State for the Home Department* (U9.1) concerning ECHR article 3, the use of s55 has been very limited. Refusals of support generally relate to asylum-seekers staying with friends or relatives and seeking 'subsistence only' support. NASS's position is generally that the article 3 threshold is not met as such applicants will have access to sanitary facilities and food, as well as shelter. Cases concerning s55 remain of importance outside of their immediate statutory context in that they consider the ambit of ECHR article 3 and the fairness of decision-making processes.

House of Lords

U9.1 *R (Limbuela, Tesema and Adam) v Secretary of State for the Home Department*

[2005] UKHL 66; [2006] 1AC 396; [2005] 3 WLR 1014; [2007] 1 All ER 951; (2006) 9 CCLR 30; [2006] HLR 10; (2005) *Times* 4 November; 3 November 2005

Refusal of asylum support to destitute asylum-seekers breached ECHR art 3

The claimants were all destitute asylum-seekers who were refused asylum support as a result of Nationality Immigration and Asylum Act 2002 s55 on the basis that they had not applied for asylum as soon as reasonably practicable and that the denial of support would not breach their ECHR rights.

Mr Limbuela, a 23-year-old Angolan national, spent two nights sleeping on the street, outside a police station. He begged for food without success. He was then provided with accommodation and food in a night shelter for four nights. He suffered from stomach pains and had also been to his GP concerning other complaints including constipation, a cough and pain in his testicles. When he was no longer able to stay in the night shelter he applied for judicial review and obtained interim relief.

Mr Tesema, a 26-year-old Ethiopian national, obtained interim relief before having to spend any time without accommodation or food. A psychiatrist then prepared a report which recounted Mr Tesema's maltreatment in Ethiopia and set out various physical ailments of which Mr Tesema complained (some loss of hearing and intermittent pain). The psychiatrist diagnosed him as suffering from some anxiety.

Mr Adam, a 27-year-old Sudanese national, spent nearly a month sleeping on the streets outside the Refugee Council's offices in Brixton, where he obtained a meal and had access to washing facilities during the day. He obtained medical evidence indicating that he suffered from haemorrhoids, back pain and gastritis and was psychologically depressed.

All three claimants applied for judicial review and their claims were allowed at first instance. The secretary of state's appeals were heard together. Shelter was joined as an interested party and submitted evidence that charities in London were unable to accommodate destitute asylum-seekers and that the availability of food and washing facilities was limited. The Court of Appeal, by a majority, dismissed the appeals and the secretary of state appealed to the House of Lords.

The House of Lords dismissed the appeal.

1) ECHR article 3 imposes an absolute obligation on a state to refrain from acts or omissions which result in inhuman or degrading treatment.

The test of what amounts to such treatment is no more exacting where the treatment is the result of a legitimate government policy.

2) In the context of the regime applied to asylum-seekers, including the general prohibition on work, the refusal of support by virtue of s55 amounted to 'treatment' for the purposes of ECHR article 3.

3) The article 3 threshold is a high one and it is not possible to imply a general public duty to house the homeless or provide for the destitute. The secretary of state's power under s55(5)(a) to avoid a breach of article 3 arises when it appears on a fair and objective assessment of all relevant facts and circumstances that an individual applicant faces an imminent prospect of serious suffering caused or materially aggravated by the denial of shelter, food or the most basic necessities of life. Many factors may affect that judgment, including age, gender, mental and physical health and condition, any facilities or sources available, the weather and time of year and the period for which the applicant has already suffered or is likely to continue to suffer privation. It is not possible to formulate any simple test applicable in all cases. However, the threshold is, in the ordinary way, crossed if there is persuasive evidence than an applicant is obliged to sleep in the street, except perhaps for a short and foreseeably finite period, or is seriously hungry, or unable to satisfy the most basic requirements of hygiene. The first instance judge had not been shown to have erred.

Court of Appeal

U9.2   *R (Q and Others) v Secretary of State for the Home Department*
[2003] EWCA Civ 364; [2004] 1 QB 36; [2003] 3 WLR 365; [2003] 2 All ER 905; [2003] HLR 57; (2003) 6 CCLR 136; (2003) *Times* 19 March; 18 March 2003

Meaning of application 'as soon as reasonably practicable' considered; NASS decision-making procedure unfair; ECHR art 6 breached

A number of asylum-seekers sought judicial review of decisions to refuse support under Nationality, Immigration and Asylum Act 2002 s55 on the basis that they did not claim asylum as soon as reasonably practicable after their arrival in the United Kingdom.

Collins J granted the applications. The Court of Appeal dismissed the secretary of state's appeal.

- The test whether an asylum-seeker had claimed asylum 'as soon as reasonably practicable' under s55(1) may be framed as: 'On the premise that the purpose of coming to this country was to claim asylum and having regard both to the practical opportunity of claiming asylum and to the asylum-seeker's personal circumstances, could the asylum-seeker reasonably have been expected to claim asylum earlier than he or she did?' [119]

- The burden of satisfying the secretary of state that asylum had been claimed as soon as reasonably practicable was on the asylum-seeker.

- If the secretary of state was not so satisfied, the applicant could claim support on the basis that it was necessary for the purpose of avoiding a breach of his rights under ECHR article 3 (prohibition on inhuman or degrading treatment) or 8 (right to private life).

- The regime imposed on asylum-seekers who were denied support by reason of s55(1) constituted 'treatment' within article 3 because the prohibition on asylum-seekers from working and receiving support when they were destitute amounted to action directed against them and not to mere inaction.
- The burden of proving that support was necessary to avoid subjecting the applicant to inhuman or degrading treatment in breach of article 3 was on the asylum-seeker. The threshold was a high one (*Pretty v United Kingdom* (2002) 35 EHRR 1).
- The judge was wrong to hold that the fact that there was a 'real risk' that an asylum-seeker would be reduced to this state of degradation of itself engaged article 3.
- Article 8 was capable of being engaged but added little to article 3.
- In deciding whether the applicant had discharged the burden of proof the secretary of state had to act fairly. He must lay down a fair system and operate it fairly.
- The system was not fair or fairly operated: (a) the purpose of the interview was not explained to the applicant in clear terms; (b) the case-workers were not properly directed as to the relevant test, with regard either to 'reasonably practicable' or article 3; (c) the secretary of state should have had regard to the applicant's state of mind on arrival; (d) fairness required the interviewer to try to ascertain the precise reason that the applicant did not claim asylum on arrival, which called for interviewing skills and a more flexible approach than simply completing a standard form questionnaire. The questions to ask would vary from case to case and be a matter for the interviewer; (e) since it was likely that the credibility of the individual applicant would or might be important, it was desirable that the interviewer and the decision-maker should be the same person. This should happen in future; and (f) where the decision-maker concluded that the applicant was not telling the truth the applicant should be given the opportunity of rebutting the suggestion of incredibility and of explaining himself if he could.
- The judge was right to hold that in each of the individual cases the applicant had been treated unfairly initially.
- Article 6 (right to a fair hearing) was not satisfied by the right to apply for judicial review given the system that was operated by the secretary of state. If the secretary of state remedied the deficiencies in procedure the combination of his decision-making process and judicial review of the decision reached by that process would satisfy the requirements of article 6. Accordingly the provisions of s55(10) were not incompatible with article 6.

See now *R (Limbuela, Tesema and Adam) v Secretary of State for the Home Department* (U9.1) on the article 3 point.

U9.3   **R (T) v Secretary of State for the Home Department**
[2003] EWCA Civ 1285; [2004] HLR 17; (2004) 7CCLR 53; [2003] UKHRR 1321; (2003) *Times* 9 October

No breach of art 3 to deny support to asylum-seeker with some money and shelter

S, D and T were refused asylum support under Nationality, Immigration and Asylum Act 2002 s55. Maurice Kay J ([2003] EWHC 1941 (Admin); (2004) 7 CCLR 32) gave detailed consideration to the circumstances that would result in a breach of article 3 and held that the refusal of support to S, D and T amounted to such a breach. The secretary of state did not appeal the decisions to grant judicial review in the cases of S and D, but did appeal in relation to T.

The Court of Appeal allowed the secretary of state's appeal in respect of T. *Pretty v United Kingdom* (2002) 35 EHRR 1 considered what will amount to inhuman or degrading treatment. There is no simple test, however, to determine whether a refusal by the secretary of state to provide support to an asylum-seeker is contrary to ECHR article 3. Each case has to be judged in relation to all the relevant circumstances. Loss of dignity may be relevant, but is not determinative. Emotional distress, by itself, is also not enough, although it is a factor. The judge's decision in the case of T did not follow the facts that he had found. T had shelter, access to sanitary facilities and some money to buy food. Even though he was not entirely well physically, it was impossible to find that his treatment had reached or is verging on the inhuman or the degrading. The article 3 threshold fell somewhere between the cases of S and T. S had been sleeping rough and had resorted to begging. He had lost weight almost to the point of malnutrition, his neck had swelled and he had a GP's report indicating that he was psychologically disturbed.

Note: The correctness of this decision was questioned by Lord Brown in *R (Limbuela, Tesema and Adam) v Secretary of State for the Home Department* (U9.1) [at 102] as street homelessness was imminent for T.

High Court

U9.4   *R (Zardasht) v Secretary of State for the Home Department*
[2004] EWHC 91 (Admin), 23 January 2004

Where no evidence presented of lack of charitable support, court could infer that applicant had sufficient food and art 3 not breached

Mr Zardasht, an Iraqi asylum-seeker, was refused asylum support. He gave evidence that he had spent four nights sleeping in a park and two nights in a church and had only intermittent access to food as he had no money. There was no evidence of health problems. He had no relations or friends in the United Kingdom and said that neither he nor his solicitors were aware of any charities that could assist him. NASS decided that there was no obligation to provide support under Nationality, Immigration and Asylum Act 2002 s55(5). It produced a detailed witness statement about day centres and voluntary organisations which it claimed could offer food and other assistance to asylum-seekers.

Newman J dismissed Mr Zardasht's application for judicial review. The evidence put forward on his behalf was insufficient to show that the lack of support involved inhuman or degrading treatment within ECHR article 3. There had recently been too many cases before the courts where lawyers and their clients had provided insufficient detail of evidence about the condition of the claimants. Proof was required that a claimant had no charitable support and could not fend for himself. To say that a claimant was destitute did not begin to move into the area of detailed fact that the legislation required. Furthermore, being destitute for a week did not necessarily verge on the condition described in *Pretty v United Kingdom* (2002) 35 EHRR 1. A majority of asylum-seekers have no home, no income, few or no possessions, little or no money, are strangers to the United Kingdom, have little or no English, are lonely, disconcerted, anxious about their welfare and vulnerable. Merely because some or all of those factors exist should not, in the normal run of things, be sufficient to justify support. The purpose of the legislation is to deny asylum-seekers the prior benevolence conferred by the previous legislation. Where a claimant suffers from bad health, a disability, is aged or has a mental condition or disorder, those particular circumstances may justify a different conclusion. If so, such matters should be clearly stated in the evidence and supported by independent evidence. That evidence should also state whether charitable assistance is available and the result of any enquiries in that regard. To launch an application without such evidence involves a failure to discharge lawyers' duties to their clients and the court. In this case, it was clear that the evidence was not such that the high threshold in *Pretty* had been crossed. In particular, there was an absence of detailed information about the quality and quantity of food provided to Mr Zardasht. The court could infer that he had had sufficient food to prevent debilitation by starvation. In those circumstances, the secretary of state had not misdirected himself in law.

In *R (Limbuela, Tesema and Adam) v Secretary of State for the Home Department* (U9.1) evidence was submitted in response to the NASS evidence and indicating that the support available to asylum-seekers generally was limited.

U10 Asylum support: adequate accommodation

Before 1996, asylum-seekers were eligible for benefits and homelessness assistance in much the same way as British citizens. These rights were taken away from them by various provisions from 1996 onwards, which resulted in the focus on destitute asylum-seekers seeking assistance under National Assistance Act 1948 s21. The Immigration and Asylum Act 1999 Part VI introduced a new scheme for the support of asylum-seekers and introduced s21(1A) into National Assistance Act 1948 to deny assistance under s21 to all but the 'destitute plus' asylum-seekers (see U7). Provision under the asylum support scheme was administered by the National Asylum Support Service (NASS). The New Asylum Model is now to administer the scheme.

Where not eligible for assistance under s21 an asylum-seeker who is eligible for asylum support should be provided with 'adequate' accommodation and their essential living needs. It is expressly provided that, in providing accommodation, an asylum-seeker's preference as to the type and location of his or her accommodation must not be taken into account but that his or her individual circumstances must be taken into account (s97).

Accommodation is generally provided in 'dispersal' areas where there is a ready supply of accommodation.

There are detailed provisions regarding eligibility and service provision. Anyone advising in this area should refer to Willman, Knafler and Pierce, *Support for Asylum-seekers*, LAG, 2nd edition, and Sue Willman's bi-annual (January and June) 'Support for asylum-seekers and other migrants update' in *Legal Action*.

Court of Appeal

U10.1 **R (A) v National Asylum Support Service and Waltham Forest LBC**
[2003] EWCA Civ 1473; [2004] 1 WLR 752; [2004] 1 All ER 15; (2003) 6 CCLR 538; [2004] LGR 1; [2004] HLR 24; [2004] 1 FLR 704; (2003) *Times* 31 October; 23 October 2003

Adequacy of accommodation has to be tested in context – that it is intended to be temporary and to prevent destitution

A arrived in the UK with her two sons on 31 May 2001 and claimed asylum. A local authority placed them in accommodation in Waltham Forest and assisted A in applying to NASS. The children were severely disabled as a result of a progressively degenerative neurological condition. One son could not easily use the stairs in the accommodation and could not access the bathroom at night. NASS decided to disperse the family out of London. The children were by then in a special education needs school and A requested that they be allowed to stay in London. NASS said that they could remain in London and that more suitable accommodation would be sought, although this might not be found quickly in London. A remained in the accommodation and after the passage of time and the deterioration of the children's condition she wrote to NASS insisting on alternative suitable accommodation. NASS liaised with Waltham Forest and requested it to find suitable accommodation, but none could be found. A did not follow a recommendation that the children's beds be moved downstairs. A issued judicial review proceedings against NASS and Waltham Forest for an alleged failure to discharge its statutory duties. Keith J dismissed her application. She appealed.

The Court of Appeal dismissed her appeal.

1) As National Assistance Act 1948 s21 only applies to those aged over 18 and as the corresponding provision for disabled children (Children Act 1989 s17) is expressly excluded by Immigration and Asylum Act 1999 s95, there is no provision other than s95 under which a disabled child of an asylum-seeker may be provided with accommodation. That duty lies with NASS, not local authorities.

2) The local authority's duty was to assist NASS in finding accommodation.

3) Immigration and Asylum Act 1999 ss95 and 122(3) provides that the accommodation be adequate. This should be equated with the suitability of accommodation under National Assistance Act 1948 s21. There is no justification for providing a different standard of accommodation for disabled children under s95 compared with disabled adults under s21. To do so would be discriminatory under ECHR article 14.

4) The difference lay in the context. The context of asylum support was

that the accommodation is intended to be temporary and to prevent destitution.

5) When considering the adequacy of accommodation a balancing exercise had to be carried out. The question at the forefront is whether the accommodation is adequate for the needs of the disabled children in the circumstances which persist at that moment in time. Accommodation that may be adequate in the short term might become inadequate over the longer term. Where accommodation had been accepted as adequate, an applicant could later challenge its adequacy where there was a change of circumstances such as a protracted asylum appeal process.

6) The assessment of adequacy in this case could take account of the difficulty in finding adequate accommodation in London, particularly as A had requested to stay in London.

7) Neither NASS or the local authority were in breach of their duty at the time the application was heard, having regard to the efforts that they had made to find accommodation and A's failure to use the accommodation in a way that would mitigate the difficulties for the family. Although moving the children downstairs was contrary to an assessment adequacy must be tested in the context of avoiding destitution.

U10.2 **R (Gezer) v Secretary of State for the Home Department**
[2004] EWCA Civ 1730; [2005] HLR 16; 17 December 2004

No breach of ECHR in treatment of claimant who suffered racial attack in dispersed accommodation

Mr Gezer was a Turkish national of Kurdish origin who came to the UK with his family and sought asylum. He was diagnosed as suffering from psychotic depression as a result of having been tortured in Turkey. He claimed asylum support and NASS dispersed him and his family to accommodation on the Toryglen estate in Glasgow, a NASS dispersal area. From their arrival on the estate, the family were subjected to serious ongoing racial abuse and harassment as a result of which Mr Gezer's health deteriorated. After their 'deck access' flat was attacked by a group of men who threatened Mr Gezer's son with a knife, the police placed the family in emergency accommodation. The incident was treated as a racist attack by the police who issued advice that deck access accommodation was no longer suitable for asylum-seekers because of the lack of security. The family returned to London, where they stayed in overcrowded conditions with relatives. NASS offered the family alternative accommodation in Glasgow which they refused, as a result of which they received subsistence-only support. Mr Gezer applied for judicial review of both the decision to send him and his family to Glasgow and the decision to return them there. He claimed that this infringed their rights under ECHR articles 3 and 8. He argued that, as someone with a frail mental state, NASS should have made enquiries to ensure that he would not be exposed to the ill treatment that he and his family suffered. Following receipt of a further medical report NASS withdrew its decision that the family should return to Glasgow. Mr Gezer pursued a claim for damages. Moses J dismissed the application but indicated that if Mr Gezer had been entitled to damages for the alleged exacerbation of his psychological injuries, the sum of £5,000 would have been awarded.

The Court of Appeal dismissed his appeal. Where there is a real risk of ill treatment as the hands of non-state agents and the treatment would, in the absence of any protection afforded by the state, involve a breach of article 3, the state must provide reasonable protection. This was a positive obligation. It was accepted that the treatment of the family was grave enough to fall within article 3. The question was whether NASS was in breach of its positive obligation. This, in turn, depended on whether NASS owed any duty of enquiry to obtain information regarding conditions on the estate (it was accepted that NASS was not aware of the problems). It was held that article 3 did not impose such a requirement on NASS. It was only after the knife attack that the police took the view that it was no longer viable for the family to remain on the estate. Before that, NASS was entitled to regard the ordinary measures of police protection as adequate. Once NASS became aware of the problems on the estate, it did not require the family to return to the estate. There was nothing exceptional in Mr Gezer's health problems that would have led NASS to treat him in a different way from other applicants. In considering whether the ill treatment violated article 3, it was considered relevant that Mr Gezer and his family had a choice of whether or not to accept the offer of housing on the estate, despite the fact that financial support would have been withdrawn if they had declined (Elias.J, dissenting, considered there was no element of real choice). The state, through NASS, had not imposed a compulsory result on the individual.

High Court

U10.3   *R (Agolli) v Secretary of State for the Home Department*
[2002] EWHC 1250 (Admin)

Policy of not dispersing asylum-seekers where children in school for one year did not apply to claimant who sought to 'manipulate' policy by reapplying for support after his children had been in school for over a year

U10.4   *R (Altun) v Secretary of State for Home Department*
[2001] EWHC Admin 296; 28 February 2001

Asylum-seekers must, within reason, accept accommodation in dispersal area

The claimant was a Turkish national of Kurdish origin. He arrived in the UK in January 1993 and claimed asylum. His claim was refused and he exhausted the appeal process. He then made further representations and had an outstanding claim based on his ECHR rights. In August 2000 his wife and three youngest children arrived in the UK. The wife claimed asylum and applied for asylum support for the family. NASS accepted her application and decided to disperse the family to Nottingham. The claimant, who had been living in London for seven and a half years, sought judicial review of the decision.

Scott Baker J dismissed his application. NASS had taken into account and given proper weight to the claimant's circumstances when making its decision. The decision did not depart from the principle, expounded by the secretary of state, that there should be no interference with a settled life without good reason. There was good reason in the present case. There was a great deal of pressure on space for asylum-seekers in London. The decision involved not just the claimant but also his family who had only recently arrived in the UK. Asylum-seekers do not have an unfettered right to choose where they live. They must, within reason, accept what is on offer if they wish to receive such support as they are entitled to.

U10.5 *R (Blackwood) v Secretary of State for the Home Department*
[2003] EWHC 98 Admin; [2003] HLR 44; 21 January 2003

In exceptional circumstances NASS should support claimant in her council flat

The claimant, a 22-year-old Jamaican national, was brought to the UK in 1991 when aged 10. She was raised and educated in London. She obtained a council flat, a NI number and worked. She had a baby, but did not maintain contact with its father. She had a small network of friends and was seeking to re-establish her relationship with her mother, who lived in London. When she applied for a civil service post, immigration checks revealed that her status in the UK had never been regularised. She then applied for indefinite leave to remain in the UK on the basis that her rights under ECHR articles 3 and 8 would be infringed if she were to be returned to Jamaica. She was, accordingly, treated as an asylum-seeker and provided with NASS support. However, NASS refused to pay the rent on her council flat and said that it would accommodate her outside London in accordance with its dispersal policy. NASS Policy Bulletin 31 provided for dispersal except in exceptional circumstances. NASS considered there were insufficient compelling or compassionate reasons why the claimant should not be dispersed. The claimant applied for judicial review. She obtained a psychologist's report which stated that her mental health would suffer if she were dispersed. NASS maintained that she should be dispersed.

Collins J held that this was plainly an unusual and exceptional case. On ordinary common-law principles it was difficult to see how anyone could rationally reach the conclusion that the factual matrix did not constitute exceptional circumstances. ECHR article 8 was clearly engaged because of the adverse effect a dispersal might have on the claimant's 'psychological well being'. NASS had failed to recognise that this was a case where dispersal was likely to breach article 8 and accordingly the decision had to be quashed and the matter reconsidered.

U10.6 *R (Hetoja) v Secretary of State for the Home Department*
[2002] EWHC 2146 (Admin); (2002) *Times* 11 November; 24 October 2002

Accommodation in hostel separate from claimant's son's fiancée and her children not in breach of ECHR art 8; art 6 not breached

NASS took over responsibility for accommodating Mrs Hetoja, her husband and two sons. The eldest son, Petrit, was engaged to Carly, a British citizen . They had two children ('the grandchildren'). The extended family were all living together in the same accommodation provided by the local authority in Leicester. NASS then allocated accommodation in a hostel in Leicester to Mrs Hetoja and her immediate family, rescinding an earlier decision to disperse them to Bradford. Carly and the grandchildren were due to move into a council house (where Petrit could alternatively stay) located two miles away from the hostel. Mrs Hetoja claimed that the decision was damaging to the family, particularly the grandchildren, as she was the primary carer for them (because of difficulties that Carly had). She claimed that the arrangements at the hostel, the distance to the grandchildren and her very limited income would make it difficult for her to carry on in this role. She argued that Immigration and Asylum Act 1999 s97(2)(a) and Asylum Support Regulations 2000 SI No 704 reg 13(a) precluded NASS from considering factors (eg, preference about locality) that were critical for its decision to comply with the ECHR. She contended that the decision breached ECHR articles 6 and 8 and was irrational, unreasonable and disproportionate. NASS argued that she could continue to care for the children and that it would cost NASS more to keep the family where they were, rather than transfer them to the hostel which it had procured for the accommodation of asylum-seekers.

Lightman J dismissed her application for judicial review. When deciding what was adequate accommodation, NASS was not required to go further than giving Ms Hetoja the opportunity to state her circumstances, including her personal needs and her family ties. Article 8 did not require NASS to take account of her accommodation preferences. It could not be said that NASS's decision to accommodate her in the hostel, free of charge, breached article 8. On the contrary, the decision enhanced her private life by providing accommodation where otherwise there would be none. Alternatively, even if there was an interference under article 8(1) it would be justified under article 8(2). With regards to article 6, the challenge did not raise primary issues of fact. The issue was whether NASS had made an error of law when exercising its discretion. The Administrative Court had full jurisdiction to determine the issues raised. As a result, the provisions of article 6 were fully met. The common-law challenge to NASS's decision was hopeless. NASS had taken account of the relevant factors and had reached a decision that was open to it.

U10.7   *R (M) v Secretary of State for the Home Department*
[2002] EWHC Admin 1924; November 2002 *Legal Action* 25

Dispersal to Middlesborough unlawful as no evidence that services could be provided in such a way as to compensate for problems arising from the disruption to services provided in London to applicant's son, who had suffered from trauma

U10.8   *R (Thiab) v National Asylum and Support Service*
[2002] EWHC 905 (Admin); 18 April 200

Refusal to transfer claimant after racial violence and harassment not unlawful

Mr Thiab, a Palestinian asylum-seeker, and his family were provided with accommodation by NASS on the Sighthill Estate in Glasgow in May 2000 under Immigration and Asylum Act 1999 Part VI. He and his family, along with other asylum-seekers on the estate, complained of racial violence and harassment. He was diagnosed as suffering from depression and requested relocation on medical grounds, which was refused. At about that time there were some serious violent attacks on asylum-seekers in the Sighthill area, including a brutal assault on two Palestinian brothers and the stabbing to death of a Kurdish asylum-seeker in the next block to Mr Thiab. Four families, including the Thiabs, then fled to London. The Thiabs were housed in emergency accommodation for about two weeks and then returned to the Sighthill accommodation, as they had no alternative accommodation. Mr Thiab applied for judicial review, claiming that NASS had failed properly or at all to apply the provisions of paragraph 2.4 of its own Policy Bulletin 18 entitled 'Dealing with Allegations of Racial Harassment, General Harassment and Domestic Violence.'

Harrison J dismissed his application. NASS's policy bulletin was not relevant since Mr Thiab sought permanent relocation of his accommodation and the bulletin dealt solely with the provision of emergency accommodation, which Mr Thiab had eventually been provided with. In any event, by the time that Mr Thiab's application was heard in April 2002 there had been a significant improvement to the situation on the Sighthill estate, with no reports of any further incidents of racial harassment affecting Mr Thiab and his family. In view of this, the application was purely historical and nothing more than an academic exercise.

U10.9 *R (Wanjugu) v Secretary of State for the Home Department*
[2003] EWHC 3116 (Admin)

Policy of not dispersing asylum-seekers receiving counselling from the Medical Foundation did not apply where analogous treatment provided by other organisation

U11 **Damages**

Court of Appeal

U11.1 *Anufrijeva v Southwark LBC*
[2003] EWCA Civ 1406; [2004] QB 1124; [2004] 2 WLR 603; [2004] 1 All ER 833; [2004] 1 FLR 8; [2004] UKHRR 1; [2004] HLR 22; [2004] LGR 184; (2003) 6 CCLR 415; (2003) *Times* 17 October; 16 October 2003

Delay and maladministration do not infringe art 8 unless consequences serious; isolated acts unlikely to suffice

The Anufrijevas were asylum-seekers. They brought proceedings for damages under the Human Rights Act 1998 for breach of ECHR article 8. They claimed that the council had failed to discharge its duty under National Assistance Act 1948 s21 because a property in which they had been housed was unsuitable. The stairs were too steep for the family's grandmother, who was isolated on the top floor. They claimed that as a result of the defendant local authority's failure to rehouse them, her quality of life was so poor that prompt action ought to have been taken and that failure by the defendant to act contributed to her physical and mental decline. It was not alleged that the defendant's action infringed article 8, but that there was a failure to take positive action that was necessary to ensure that the family's article 8 rights were respected. Newman J dismissed the claim.

The Court of Appeal dismissed their appeal. There is a stage at which the dictates of humanity require the state to intervene to prevent any person within its territory suffering dire consequences as a result of deprivation of sustenance. If support is necessary to prevent a person in this country reaching the point of article 3 degradation, then that support should be provided. If such a basic standard exists, it must require intervention by the state, whether the claimant is an asylum-seeker who has not sought asylum promptly on entry or is a citizen entitled to all the benefits of our system. Article 8 is capable of imposing on a state a positive obligation to provide support (*R (Bernard) v Enfield LBC* (U11.2)). Those obligations are not, however, absolute. There must be some ground for criticising the failure to act – an element of culpability and knowledge that the claimant's private and family life are at risk. If there is delay, there is no infringement of article 8 unless substantial prejudice has been caused to the applicant. Maladministration does not infringe article 8 unless the consequences are serious. Isolated acts of even significant carelessness are unlikely to suffice. At first instance courts dealing with claims for maladministration should adopt a broad brush approach, without a close examination of authorities or a prolonged examination of the facts. Remedies have to be just and appropriate and necessary to afford just satisfaction. Levels of damages awarded in tort, by the CICB and local government ombudsmen might all provide some rough guidance. Courts should look critically at any attempt to recover damages for maladministration under the Human Rights Act 1998 other than in the Administrative Court. Before giving permission to apply for judicial review, the Administrative Court should require the claimant to explain why it is not more appropriate to use any internal complaints procedure. In this case the local authority had made reasonable efforts to meet the requirements of the family. The accommodation provided fell far short of placing the family in the type of conditions that would impose a positive obligation under article 8 to install them in superior accommodation.

The House of Lords subsequently refused a petition for leave to appeal ([2005] 1 WLR 2809).

High Court

U11.2 *R (Bernard) v Enfield LBC*
[2002] EWHC 2282 (Admin); [2003] UKHRR 148; (2002) 5 CCLR 577; [2003] HLR 27; [2003] LGR 423 Admin; (2002) *Times* 8 November; 25 October 2002

Art 8 breached where council's failure to provide suitable accommodation under s21 made it virtually impossible for meaningful private and family life; just satisfaction required damages owing to council's failure to apologise

Mr Bernard was the carer of his wife, who was severely disabled. She had limited mobility and was dependent on an electronic wheelchair. She was doubly incontinent and suffered from diabetes. He also looked after the couple's six children. After accruing mortgage arrears, the family was forced to move from its fully-adapted house and took a tenancy in an unadapted property. When the tenancy expired, they applied to the defendant local authority as homeless persons. The council provided accommodation for the family in October 1998. In June 2000 the authority found them intentionally homeless (that decision was confirmed on review and Mr Bernard's appeals to the county court and subsequently the Court of Appeal were finally dismissed in December 2001, see T38.2).

In the meantime they remained in the property. In September 2000, the social services department undertook a number of assessments of Mrs Bernard's needs, which indicated that the property was unsuitable since it was not adapted to her needs: she could not use her wheelchair, she could not access the toilet, she spent much of the day in a shower chair in the lounge where she slept, together with Mr Bernard and their two youngest children. The care plan stated that she needed assistance to move to a suitably adapted property. The council accepted that it was under a duty to make arrangements for the provision of suitably adapted accommodation under National Assistance Act 1948 s21(1)(a), but provided no explanation for the failure to comply with that duty or to act on the social services' recommendation.

Judicial review was granted on 27 March 2002 and the council was ordered to provide the claimants with suitable and adapted accommodation within six months. A claim for damages under Human Rights Act 1998 s8 was adjourned. The order was not complied with until 14 October 2002 when the claimants threatened to apply for an order requiring the council to show cause why its director should not be committed to prison for contempt of court. The council gave no explanation for the delay or failure to respond to correspondence.

Sullivan J held that, although some would describe the conditions in which the claimants were forced to live as degrading, particularly in light of Mrs Bernard's incontinence, there was no breach of ECHR article 3 (prohibition of inhuman or degrading treatment). The minimum level of severity threshold had not been crossed. Although not conclusive, the fact that there was no intention to humiliate or debase the claimants was an important consideration. Cases concerned with prisoner's rights should be treated with caution outside the prison gates because a prisoner was in a uniquely vulnerable position. However, following the assessments in September 2000, the council was under an obligation to take positive steps to enable the claimants and their children to lead as normal a family life as possible (under ECHR article 8). The failure to act showed a singular lack of respect for the claimants' private and family life. It condemned them to living conditions which made it virtually impossible for them to have any meaningful private and family life. If a public body took steps once a problem had been drawn to its attention, it might be the case that nothing more would be required in order to afford just satisfaction. That was not the case here. Furthermore, the council had not acknowledged its error, provided an explanation or apology for its failure nor indicated that its procedures had been improved. The housing department had threatened to evict the claimant and the council had delayed in complying with the court order. An award of damages was necessary. It was difficult to see why awards should not be comparable to tortious awards. Furthermore, the awards recommended by the local government ombudsman were of great assistance. The award set should not be minimal because that would diminish respect for the policy underlying Human Rights Act 1998. Sullivan J awarded £8,000 to Mrs Bernard and £2,000 to Mr Bernard.

Note: See now damages cases under ECHR article 1 of the First Protocol, section A.

U12   **Costs**

See also section T64 for costs in judicial review proceedings.

Court of Appeal

U12.1   *R (Kuzeva) v Southwark LBC*
[2002] EWCA Civ 781; 30 May 2002

No order on costs where no good reason to make other order; legal aid irrelevant

The claimants sought asylum in the UK. The claim was initially rejected but the family remained, pending a final determination on compassionate grounds. They sought accommodation from the defendant authority. The authority failed to provide appropriate accommodation and the claimants applied for judicial review. Permission to apply for judicial review was granted on paper. Without opposition the claimants obtained an interim injunction requiring the defendant to use its best endeavours to find the claimants suitable accommodation. Accommodation was offered by the defendant but rejected by the claimants as unsuitable. After two adjourned hearings, the judge made an order requiring the defendant to use its best endeavours to find the claimants suitable accommodation as soon as possible and in any event within eight weeks. The judge further held that, since public funds were involved on both sides, there should be no order on costs, including the costs of previous hearings which had been reserved. The claimants appealed.

The appeal was dismissed. The judge was wrong if he took into account the claimants' legally aided status since that was not a relevant consideration by virtue of the Access to Justice Act 1999 s22. The Court of Appeal could, and in the circumstances of this case should, consider what costs order to make. The principles to be applied were those set out by Scott Baker J in *R (Boxall) v Waltham Forest LBC* (U12.2). In the absence of a good reason to make any other order the fall-back was to make no order on costs. This was one of those cases where there was no good reason to make an order for costs against either party. Exercising the discretion afresh the court came to the same conclusion as the judge.

High Court

U12.2   *R (Boxall) v Waltham Forest LBC*
(2001) 4 CCLR 258, QBD (Admin Court); 21 December 2001

Council ordered to pay costs where substantive issued resolved before hearing of judicial review

On 20 August 1998 the claimants brought proceedings for judicial review against the defendant local authority, alleging that it had failed to assess their accommodation, community care and welfare needs under various enactments and that it was not providing suitable accommodation for them. Permission to apply for judicial review was granted on 10 November 1999 by Keene J. On 23 December 1998 the defendant produced a care plan. In March 2000 the defendant offered the claimants new accommodation and so brought the judicial review proceedings to an end as the claimants had obtained what they had set out to achieve. The claimants sought the costs of the claim up until 23 December 1999.

Scott Baker J, the presiding judge in the Administrative Court, reviewed the authorities on the award of costs pre- and post-permission in the light of the CPR rules on costs. He identified six principles as follows:

1) The court has power to make a costs order when the substantive proceedings have been resolved without a trial but the parties have not agreed about costs.

2) It will ordinarily be irrelevant that the claimant is legally aided.

3) The overriding objective is to do justice between the parties without incurring unnecessary court time and consequently additional cost.

4) At each end of the spectrum there will be cases where it is obvious which side would have won had the substantive issues been fought to a conclusion. In between, the position will, in differing degrees, be less clear. How far the court will be prepared to look into the previously unresolved substantive issues will depend on the circumstances of the particular case, not least the amount of costs at stake and the conduct of the parties.

5) In the absence of a good reason to make any other order the fall-back is to make no order on costs.

6) The court should take care to ensure that it does not discourage parties from settling judicial review proceedings, for example by a local authority making a concession at an early stage.

Applying them to the facts of the case, the just order was that the council should pay the costs.

U12.3   *R (H) v Kingston upon Thames RLBC*

[2002] EWHC 3158 (Admin); (2002) 6 CCLR 240 (see U7.9)

Costs awarded where case became academic prior to final hearing and council's case unsustainable; judicial review, rather than complaint, justified

Index

LegalAction

The only independent magazine to cover areas of interest to legal aid practitioners, advisers and local authority staff.

Each month Legal Action includes:

editorial
Legal Action's editorials are renowned and respected for their challenging and thought-provoking approach to recent events.

news and features
The news and features pages give the latest information and critical opinion on a broad range of subjects.

noticeboard
Legal Action also gives you access to information on courses, meetings, conferences, seminars, and training contracts.

law and practice
Legal Action's authoritative law and practice pages are written by a team of expert solicitors, barristers and advisers. These pages will keep you up to date with the law, practice and procedure that affect your area of work.

ISSN 0306 7963

For more information on subscription rates visit:
www.lag.org.uk/magazine

lag.org.uk

- Read sample chapters of our titles.

- Access the *Legal Action* editorial archive.

- Read the news stories from the latest issue of *Legal Action*.

- Register your interests to receive free e-mail bulletins on relevant LAG products and policy.

- Find out more details on our full range of training courses.

- Use the new simplified ordering process for secure online purchases of our products.

- Find out more about the LAG membership scheme and donate money to help fund our campaigns.

- Get access to our full policy archives: discussion papers, press releases, consultation responses and parliamentary briefings.

Legal Action Group | working with lawyers and advisers to promote equal access to justice